中国统计年鉴

CHINA STATISTICAL YEARBOOK

2024

（总第43期 No.43）

国家统计局　编

Compiled by

National Bureau of Statistics of China

图书在版编目 (CIP) 数据

图书在版编目（CIP）数据
中国统计年鉴 . 2024 = China Statistical Yearbook 2024 ：汉、英 / 国家统计局编 .-- 北京 ：中国统计出版社，2024. 9. --ISBN 978-7-5230-0486-9
Ⅰ . C832-54
中国国家版本馆 CIP 数据核字第 2024GV6941 号

中国统计年鉴 2024

作　　者／ 国家统计局
责任编辑／ 张　怡
封面设计／ 李雪燕
出版发行／ 中国统计出版社有限公司
地　　址／ 北京市丰台区西三环南路甲 6 号
邮政编码／ 100073
Address: Jia 6, Xisanhuan Nanlu, Fengtai District, Beijing 100073, P. R. China
E-mail: yearbook@stats.gov.cn
电　　话／ (010)63376898、63376907、68783173（发行部）、63376861（编辑部）
网　　址／ www.zgtjcbs.com
印　　刷／ 河北鑫兆源印刷有限公司
经　　销／ 新华书店
开　　本／ 890 毫米 ×1240 毫米　1/16
字　　数／ 1960 千字
印　　张／ 60.75
版　　别／ 2024 年 9 月第 1 版
版　　次／ 2024 年 9 月第 1 次印刷
定　　价／ 588.00 元　　Price: 588.00 yuan (RMB)

如有印装差错，请与发行部联系退换。本书附 CD-ROM 一张，如有差异，以图书内容为准。

《中国统计年鉴 2024》

编委会和编辑出版人员

China Statistical Yearbook 2024
EDITORIAL BOARD AND EDITORIAL STAFF

编 者 说 明

一、《中国统计年鉴2024》系统收录了全国和各省、自治区、直辖市2023年经济、社会各方面，以及多个重要历史年份和近年全国主要统计数据，是一部全面反映中华人民共和国经济和社会发展情况的资料性年刊。

二、本年鉴正文内容分为28个篇章，即：1.综合；2.人口；3.国民经济核算；4.就业和工资；5.价格；6.人民生活；7.财政；8.资源和环境；9.能源；10.固定资产投资；11.对外经济贸易；12.农业；13.工业；14.建筑业；15.批发和零售业；16.运输、邮电和软件业；17.住宿、餐饮业和旅游；18.金融业；19.房地产；20.科学技术；21.教育；22.卫生和社会服务；23.文化和体育；24.公共管理、社会保障和社会组织；25.城市、农村和区域发展；26.香港特别行政区主要社会经济指标；27.澳门特别行政区主要社会经济指标；28.台湾省主要社会经济指标；以及附录部分，国际主要社会经济指标。

为方便读者使用，各篇章前设有简要说明，对本篇章的主要内容、资料来源、统计范围、统计方法以及历史变动情况予以简要概述。篇末附有主要统计指标解释。

三、本年鉴所涉及的全国性统计数据，除行政区划、森林资源及特殊注明外，均未包括香港、澳门特别行政区和台湾省数据。根据中华人民共和国“香港特别行政区基本法”和“澳门特别行政区基本法”的有关原则，香港、澳门与内地是相对独立的统计区域，依据各自不同的统计制度和法律规定，独立进行统计工作，本年鉴中有关统计资料分别由香港特别行政区政府统计处、澳门特别行政区政府统计暨普查局提供，国家统计局进行编辑。

四、本年鉴所涉及东部、中部、西部和东北地区的具体划分为：

东部地区：有10个省（直辖市），包括北京、天津、河北、上海、江苏、浙江、福建、山东、广东和海南。

中部地区：有6个省，包括山西、安徽、江西、河南、湖北和湖南。

西部地区：有12个省（自治区、直辖市），包括内蒙古、广西、重庆、四川、贵州、云南、西藏、陕西、甘肃、青海、宁夏和新疆。

东北地区：有3个省，包括辽宁、吉林和黑龙江。

五、本年鉴所使用的度量衡单位均采用国际统一标准计量单位，并统一使用最新颁布实施的产品目录。

六、本年鉴中涉及的历史数据，均以最新出版的本年鉴数据为准；本年鉴中部分数据合计数或相对数由于单位取舍不同而产生的计算误差，均未作机械调整。

七、符号使用说明：年鉴各表中的“空格”表示该项统计指标数据不详或无该项数据；“#”表示其中的主要项；“*”或“①”表示本表下有注解。香港及澳门部分的符号使用方法具体见其篇章说明。

八、与《中国统计年鉴2023》相比较，本年鉴根据现行统计调查制度和统计工作开展情况，主要作如下修订：

为了满足统计调查划分经济类型需要，国家统计局会同市场监管总局对《关于划分企业登记注册类型的规定》（国统字〔2011〕86号）（以下简称“原标准”）进行修订，联合印发《关于市场主体统计分类的划分规定》（国统字〔2023〕14号）（以下简称“新标准”），本年鉴对相关分组按“新标准”作出相应调整。

1.修订工作背景

原标准是由国家统计局和原国家工商总局于1998年共同制定印发，并于2011年进行修订。实施以来，该标准为开展统计调查、统计分析和市场监管等工作提供了重要支撑。近年来，《中华人民共和国外商投资法》《中华人民共和国市场主体登记管理条例》等新法律法规陆续出台实施，原《中华人民共和国公司登记管理条例》《中华人民共和国企业法人登记管理条例》《中华人民共和国私营企业暂行条例》等法规已被废止，原标准所依据相关法律法规发生重大变化。为适应市场监管部门登记注册管理范围从“企业”扩大为“市场主体”的新变化，确保依法依规开展统计工作，国家统计局会同市场监管总局于2022年起开展该项标准修订工作，在广泛征求各专业各地方和相关部门意见建议的基础上，于2023年1月联合印发《关于市场主体统计分类的划分规定》（“新标准”）。

2.修订主要内容

（1）拓展适用范围

为了更全面覆盖统计调查对象，新标准按照市场主体登记注册管理实际对分类范围作相应调整，从“企业”扩大至所有“市场主体”，增加了“农民专业合作社（联合社）”和“个体工商户”等类别。

（2）取消相关类别

由于《中华人民共和国私营企业暂行条例》已被废止，根据《中华人民共和国公司法》《中华人民共和国个人独资企业法》《中华人民共和国合作企业法》，将相关“私营有限责任公司”“私营股份有限公司”分别列入“有限责任公司”“股份有限公司”类别范围，“私营独资企业”调整为“个人独资企业”，“私营合伙企业”调整为“合伙企业”。

（3）调整分类结构

一是关于“内资企业”。根据《中华人民共和国市场主体登记管理条例》规定，将原内资企业分类“国有企业”“集体企业”“股份合作企业”“联营企业”“有限责任公司”“股份有限公司”“私营企业”“其他企业”等8个类别调整为“有限责任公司”“股份有限公司”“非公司企业法人”“个人独资企业”“合伙企业”“其他内资企业”等6个类别。其中，原“国有企业”“集体企业”“股份合作企业”“联营企业”纳入新类别“非公司企业法人”下；原“私营企业”类别取消（上段已述）。二是关于“外商投资企业”和“港澳台投资企业”。根据《中华人民共和国外商投资法》规定，将原外商投资企业分类“中外合资经营企业”“中外合作经营企业”“外资企业”“外商投资股份有限公司”“其他外商投资企业”等5个类别调整为“外商投资有限责任公司”“外商投资股份有限公司”“外商投资合伙企业”“其他外商投资企业”等4个类别。港澳台投资企业参照外商投资企业分类方法调整。

（4）规范类别名称

根据市场监管部门对登记注册管理的规范名称，分别将原“国有企业”“集体企业”更名为“全民所有制企业（国有企业）”“集体所有制企业（集体企业）”。

（5）统一内资范围

根据《中华人民共和国外商投资法》和相关部门规定，将登记注册为内资公司的有限责任公司（外商投资企业投资）、登记注册为内资公司的股份有限公司(上市、外商投资企业投资)等市场主体，即外商投资企业市场主体在中国境内的再投资市场主体，由原标准中的“外商投资企业”调整为新标准中的“内资企业”相关类别。

此外，在“资源和环境”部分，增加“倒塌房屋间数”。在“农业”部分，增加“大豆”“花生”“油菜籽”“芝麻”“甘蔗”“甜菜”“烤烟”播种面积和“农林牧渔专业及辅助性活动”产值和指数。在“工业”部分，增加“智能手机”产量。在“卫生和社会服务”部分，增加“分地区儿童健康情况”和“分地区孕产妇健康情况”2张表。在“文化和体育”部分，增加公共图书馆“少儿文献数”和国有博物馆“未成年人参观人次”情况。在“城市、农村和区域发展”部分，增加“乡村办水电站”“农村水电装机容量”“农村水电年发电量”情况。

Editor's Notes

I. *China Statistical Yearbook 2024* is an annual statistical publication, which reflects comprehensively the economic and social development of China. It covers data for 2023and key statistical data in recent years and some historically important years at the national level and the local levels of province, autonomous region and municipality directly under the Central Government.

II. The *Yearbook* contains twenty-eight chapters: 1. General Survey; 2. Population; 3. National Accounts; 4. Employment and Wages; 5. Prices; 6. People's Livelihoods; 7. Government Finance; 8. Resources and Environment; 9. Energy; 10. Investment in Fixed Assets; 11. International Trade and Economic Cooperation; 12. Agriculture; 13. Industry; 14. Construction; 15. Wholesale and Retail Trades; 16. Transport, Postal and Telecommunication Services, and Software Industry; 17. Hotels, Catering Services and Tourism; 18. Financial Intermediation; 19. Real Estate; 20. Science and Technology; 21. Education; 22. Public Health and Social Services; 23. Culture and Sports; 24. Public Management, Social Security and Social Organizations; 25. Urban, Rural and Regional Development; 26. Main Social and Economic Indicators of Hong Kong Special Administrative Region; 27. Main Social and Economic Indicators of Macao Special Administrative Region; 28. Main Social and Economic Indicators of Taiwan Province. One chapter listed as Appendix is Main Social and Economic Indicators of Other Countries/Regions.

To facilitate readers, the Brief Introduction at the beginning of each chapter provides a summary of the main contents of the chapter, data sources, statistical coverage, statistical methods and historical changes. At the end of each chapter, Explanatory Notes on Main Statistical Indicators are included.

III. The national data in this book do not include those of the Hong Kong Special Administrative Region, the Macao Special Administrative Region and Taiwan Province, except for the divisions of administrative areas, forest resources and otherwise specified. In accordance with the principles set down in the *Basic Law of Hong Kong Special Administrative Region*, and the *Basic Law of Macao Special Administrative Region*, statistically Hong Kong, Macao and the mainland of China are three mutually independent regions, each following its own and different statistical systems and legal provisions in conducting statistical operation independently. Statistics on the Hong Kong Special Administrative Region and the Macao Special Administrative Region as included in this yearbook are provided by the Census and Statistics Department of the Government of Hong Kong Special Administrative Region and the Statistics and Census Service of the Government of Macao Special Administrative Region respectively; and are edited by the National Bureau of Statistics.

IV. Eastern region, central region, western region and northeastern region in the *Yearbook* are divided as following:

Eastern region with 10 provinces (municipalities) includes: Beijing, Tianjin, Hebei, Shanghai, Jiangsu, Zhejiang, Fujian, Shandong, Guangdong and Hainan;

Central region with 6 provinces includes: Shanxi, Anhui, Jiangxi, Henan, Hubei and Hunan;

Western region with 12 provinces (autonomous regions and municipalities) includes: Inner Mongolia, Guangxi, Chongqing, Sichuan, Guizhou, Yunnan, Xizang, Shaanxi, Gansu, Qinghai, Ningxia and Xinjiang;

Northeastern region with 3 provinces includes: Liaoning, Jilin and Heilongjiang.

V. The units of measurement used in the *Yearbook* are international standard measurement units, and newly published and implemented *Product Categories* are uniformly used.

VI. For updated historical data, please refer to the newly published version of the *Yearbook*. Statistical discrepancies on totals and relative figures due to rounding are not adjusted in the *Yearbook*.

VII. Notations used in the *Yearbook*: (blank space) indicates that the data are unknown, or are not available; " # " indicates a major breakdown of the total; and " * " or " ① " indicates footnotes at the end of the table. For notations in the chapters of data on Hong Kong SAR and Macao SAR, please refer to the brief introduction or explanation in the relevant chapters.

VIII. In comparison with *China Statistical Yearbook 2023*, following revisions have been made in this new version in terms of the current statistical survey system and the progress of statistical work.

In order to meet the needs of economic classification in statistical surveys, the National Bureau of Statistics together with the State Administration for Market Regulation revised the Regulations on the Classification of Enterprises by Registration Status (Guotongzi [2011] No. 86) (hereinafter referred to as the original standard) and then jointly issued the Regulations on the Classification of Market Entity Statistics (Guotongzi [2023] No. 14) (hereinafter referred to as the new standard). The yearbook has made corresponding adjustments to the relevant groups according to the "new standard".

1. Revision work background

The original standard was jointly formulated and issued by the National Bureau of Statistics and the former State Administration for Industry and Commerce in 1998, and revised in 2011. Since its implementation, this standard has provided important support for conducting statistical surveys, statistical analysis, and market supervision. In recent years, new laws and regulations such as the Foreign Investment Law of the People's Republic of China and the Regulations on the Administration of Market Entity Registration of the People's Republic of China have been successively introduced and implemented. The original Regulations on the Administration of Company Registration of the People's Republic of China, the Regulations on the Administration of Enterprise Legal Person Registration of the People's Republic of China, and the Interim Regulations on Private Enterprises of the People's Republic of China have been abolished, and significant changes have occurred in the relevant laws and regulations on which the original standards were based. In order to adapt to the new changes in the registration and management scope of the market supervision department from "enterprises" to "market entities", and to ensure that statistical work is carried out in accordance with laws and regulations, the National Bureau of Statistics, together with the State Administration for Market Regulation, will carry out the revision of this standard from 2022. Based on extensive solicitation of opinions and suggestions from various professions, localities, and relevant departments, the Regulations on the Classification of Market Entity Statistics (the new standard) will be jointly issued in January 2023.

2. Revision of the main contents

(1) Expand the scope of application

In order to comprehensively cover the statistical survey objects, the new standard adjusts the classification scope according to the actual registration and management of market entities, expanding from enterprises to all market entities, and adding categories such as professional farmers cooperatives and individual businesses and other categories.

(2) Cancel related categories

Due to the abolition of the Provisional Regulations of the People's Republic of China on Private Enterprises, according to the Company Law of the People's Republic of China, the Law of the People's Republic of China on Sole Proprietorship Enterprises, and the Law of the People's Republic of China on Cooperative Enterprises, the private limited liability corporations and private share-holding limited corporations are respectively included in the categories of limited liability corporations and share-holding limited corporations. The private sole-proprietorship enterprises are adjusted to the sole proprietorship enterprises and the private partnership enterprises are adjusted to partnership enterprises.

(3) Adjust the classification structure

The first is about domestic invested enterprises. According to the Regulations on the Administration of Market Entity Registration of the People's Republic of China, the original classification of domestic invested enterprises, including "state-owned enterprises", "collective-owned enterprises", "share-holding cooperative enterprises", "joint ownership enterprises", "limited liability corporations", " share-holding limited corporations", "private enterprises" and "other enterprises" have been adjusted to six categories, including "limited liability corporations", "share-holding limited corporations", "non corporate legal entity", "sole proprietorship enterprises", "partnership enterprises" and "other domestic invested enterprises" with which the original "state-owned enterprises", "collective-owned enterprises", "share-holding cooperative enterprises," and "joint ownership enterprises" are included in the new category of "non corporate legal entity"; The original category of "private enterprises" has been cancelled (as mentioned in the previous paragraph). The second is about foreign invested enterprises and enterprises with investment from Hong Kong, Macao, and Taiwan. According to the Foreign Investment Law of the People's Republic of China, the original classification of foreign invested enterprises, including "Sino foreign joint ventures", "Sino foreign cooperative enterprises", "foreign funded enterprises", "foreign invested share-holding companies", and "other foreign-invested enterprises" are adjusted to four categories: "foreign invested limited liability corporations", "foreign-invested share-holding corporations", "foreign invested partnership enterprises", and "other foreign invested enterprises". Enterprises with investment from Hong Kong, Macao, and Taiwan are adjusted according to the classification method for foreign invested enterprises.

(4) Standardize names of categories

According to the standardized names for registration management by the market supervision department, the original "state-owned enterprises" and "collective-owned enterprises" will be renamed as "state-owned enterprises" and "collective-owned enterprises" respectively.

(5) Unify domestic invested scope

According to the Foreign Investment Law of the People's Republic of China and relevant departmental regulations, market entities such as limited liability companies registered as domestic invested companies (foreign-invested enterprises investment) and share-holding limited companies registered as domestic companies (listed and foreign-invested enterprises investment), namely the reinvestment market entities of foreign-invested enterprises in China, have been adjusted from the original category of "foreign-invested enterprises" to the relevant category of "domestic enterprises" in the new standard.

In addition, in the chapter on "Resources and Environment", the data of "collapsed houses" have been added. In the chapter on "Agriculture", the data of the planting area of "soybean", "peanut", "rapeseed", "sesame", "sugarcane", "sugar beet", "flue-cured tobacco" and the output value and index of "agricultural, forestry, animal husbandry and fishery professional and auxiliary activities" have been added. In the chapter on "Industry", the output of "smartphone" have been added. In the chapter on "Public Health and Social Services", the tables which named "Health Status of Children by Region" and "Health status of Maternity Female by Region" have been added. In the chapter on "Culture and Sports", the number of "children's literature" on public libraries and number of "underage visitors" to state-owned museums have been added. In the chapter on "Urban, Rural and Regional Development", the data of "rural hydropower stations", "rural hydropower installed capacity" and "rural hydropower annual electricity generation" have been added.

目　　录

CONTENTS

一、综　合
General Survey

二、人　口
Population

三、国民经济核算
National Accounts

四、就业和工资
Employment and Wages

五、价 格
Prices

六、人民生活
People's Livelihoods

七、财　政
Government Finance

八、资源和环境
Resources and Environment

九、能 源
Energy

十、固定资产投资
Investment in Fixed Assets

十一、对外经济贸易
International Trade and Economic Cooperation

十二、农　业
Agriculture

十三、工 业
Industry

十四、建筑业
Construction

十五、批发和零售业
Wholesale and Retail Trades

十六、运输、邮电和软件业
Transport, Postal and Telecommunication Services, and Software Industry

十七、住宿、餐饮业和旅游
Hotels, Catering Services and Tourism

十八、金融业
Financial Intermediation

十九、房地产
Real Estate

二十、科学技术
Science and Technology

二十一、教 育
Education

二十二、卫生和社会服务
Public Health and Social Services

二十三、文化和体育
Culture and Sports

二十四、公共管理、社会保障和社会组织
Public Management, Social Security and Social Organizations

二十五、城市、农村和区域发展
Urban, Rural and Regional Development

二十六、香港特别行政区主要社会经济指标
Main Social and Economic Indicators of Hong Kong Special Administrative Region

二十七、澳门特别行政区主要社会经济指标
Main Social and Economic Indicators of Macao Special Administrative Region

二十八、台湾省主要社会经济指标
Main Social and Economic Indicators of Taiwan Province

附录、国际主要社会经济指标
APPENDIX. Main Social and Economic Indicators of Other Countries/Regions

1

综　合

General Survey

简 要 说 明

本篇主要内容和资料来源

一、综合资料主要包括我国行政区划、国民经济和社会发展综合资料。由民政部和国家统计局编辑整理。

二、全国行政区划资料由民政部根据国务院批准的、截止到上一年末全国行政区划变更情况汇总整理并提供。

三、国民经济和社会发展综合表集中反映中国国民经济和社会发展的总量、速度、结构、比例和效益状况及变化。

四、基本单位统计资料填报范围为所有法人单位和产业活动单位，来源是各部门的单位审批登记资料和经常性统计调查中查到的新增、变更和注销单位情况。

Brief Introduction

Main Contents and Sources of Data

I. This chapter consists divisions of administrative areas, and summary data on the national economic and social development, which are compiled by the Ministry of Civil Affairs and National Bureau of Statistics respectively.

II. Data on divisions of administrative areas in China are prepared and provided by the Ministry of Civil Affairs on the basis of the changes in the divisions of administrative areas as approved by the State Council at the end of the previous year.

III. The summary data on the national economy reflect the overall situation of and changes in economic and social development in terms of total size, growth, structure, ratio, and efficiency.

IV. Statistical coverage of basic units include all corporate units and establishments. Data come from administrative records on unit examination and registration by various departments, and information on increase, changes and cancellation of units obtained in regular statistical survey.

1-1 全国行政区划（2023年底）
Divisions of Administrative Areas in China (End of 2023)

单位：个 (unit)

省级区划名称 Provinces, Autonomous Regions and Municipalities	地级区划数 Number of Divisions at Prefecture Level	#地级市 Cities at Pre-fecture Level	县级区划数 Number of Divisions at County Level	#市辖区 Districts under the Jurisdiction of Cities	#县级市 Cities at County Level	#县 Counties	#自治县 Auto-nomous Counties	乡级区划数 Number of Divisions at Township Level	#镇 Towns	#乡 Town-ships	#街道 Sub-districts
全　　国 National Total	**333**	**293**	**2844**	**977**	**397**	**1299**	**117**	**38658**	**21421**	**8190**	**9045**
北　京　市 Beijing			16	16				343	143	35	165
天　津　市 Tianjin			16	16				252	125	3	124
河　北　省 Hebei	11	11	167	49	21	91	6	2254	1332	611	310
山　西　省 Shanxi	11	11	117	26	11	80		1280	631	430	219
内蒙古自治区 Inner Mongolia	12	9	103	23	11	17		1025	509	270	246
辽　宁　省 Liaoning	14	14	100	59	16	17	8	1354	640	201	513
吉　林　省 Jilin	9	8	60	21	20	16	3	970	426	181	363
黑 龙 江 省 Heilongjiang	13	12	121	54	21	45	1	1315	574	334	407
上　海　市 Shanghai			16	16				215	106	2	107
江　苏　省 Jiangsu	13	13	95	55	21	19		1237	701	17	519
浙　江　省 Zhejiang	11	11	90	37	20	32	1	1364	618	258	488
安　徽　省 Anhui	16	16	104	45	9	50		1522	1011	224	287
福　建　省 Fujian	9	9	84	31	11	42		1108	653	252	203
江　西　省 Jiangxi	11	11	100	27	12	61		1581	832	560	189
山　东　省 Shandong	16	16	136	58	26	52		1825	1072	57	696
河　南　省 Henan	17	17	157	54	21	82		2459	1192	567	700
湖　北　省 Hubei	13	12	103	39	26	35	2	1260	761	161	338
湖　南　省 Hunan	14	13	122	36	19	60	7	1946	1134	388	424
广　东　省 Guangdong	21	21	122	65	20	34	3	1613	1112	11	490
广西壮族自治区 Guangxi	14	14	111	41	10	48	12	1256	806	312	138
海　南　省 Hainan	4	4	25	10	5	4	6	218	175	21	22
重　庆　市 Chongqing			38	26		8	4	1031	625	161	245
四　川　省 Sichuan	21	18	183	55	19	105	4	3101	2016	626	459
贵　州　省 Guizhou	9	6	88	16	10	50	11	1510	831	314	365
云　南　省 Yunnan	16	8	129	17	18	65	29	1426	666	537	223
西藏自治区 Xizang	7	6	74	8	2	64		711	142	534	35
陕　西　省 Shaanxi	10	10	107	31	7	69		1317	973	17	327
甘　肃　省 Gansu	14	12	86	17	5	57	7	1356	892	337	127
青　海　省 Qinghai	8	2	44	7	5	25	7	404	140	222	42
宁夏回族自治区 Ningxia	5	5	22	9	2	11		243	103	90	50
新疆维吾尔自治区 Xinjiang	14	4	108	13	29	60	6	1162	480	457	224
香港特别行政区 Hong Kong Special Administrative Region											
澳门特别行政区 Macao Special Administrative Region											
台　湾　省 Taiwan											

注：乡级区划总数包含河北省、新疆维吾尔自治区的各一个区公所。

a) Number of divisions at township level includes one district public office of Hebei and of Xinjiang separately.

1-2 国民经济和社会发展总量与速度指标

指 标	Item	1978
人口 (万人)	**Population (10 000 persons)**	
总人口(年末)	Total Population (year-end)	96259
城镇人口	Urban Population	17245
乡村人口	Rural Population	79014
就业 (万人)	**Employment (10 000 persons)**	
就业人员	Number of Employed Persons	40152
第一产业	Primary Industry	28318
第二产业	Secondary Industry	6945
第三产业	Tertiary Industry	4890
城镇登记失业人员	Number of Registered Unemployed Persons in Urban Areas	530
国民经济核算	**National Accounts**	
国民总收入 (亿元)	Gross National Income (GNI) (100 million yuan)	3678.7
国内生产总值 (亿元)	Gross Domestic Product (GDP) (100 million yuan)	3678.7
第一产业	Primary Industry	1018.5
第二产业	Secondary Industry	1755.1
第三产业	Tertiary Industry	905.1
人均国民总收入 (元)	Per Capita GNI (yuan)	385
人均国内生产总值 (元)	Per Capita GDP (yuan)	385
人民生活 (元)	**People's Livelihoods (yuan)**	
全国居民人均可支配收入	Per Capita Disposable Income of Households	171
城镇居民人均可支配收入	Per Capita Disposable Income of Urban Households	343
农村居民人均可支配收入	Per Capita Disposable Income of Rural Households	134
财政 (亿元)	**Government Finance (100 million yuan)**	
一般公共预算收入	General Public Budget Revenue	1132.3
一般公共预算支出	General Public Budget Expenditure	1122.1
能源	**Energy**	
一次能源生产总量(万吨标准煤)	Total Primary Energy Production (10 000 tce)	62770
能源消费总量 (万吨标准煤)	Total Energy Consumption (10 000 tce)	57144
主要能源产品产量	Output of Main Energy Product	
原 煤 (亿吨)	Raw Coal (100 million tons)	6.2
天然气 (亿立方米)	Natural Gas (100 million cu.m)	137.3
发电量 (亿千瓦时)	Electricity (100 million kW·h)	2565.5
固定资产投资	**Investment in Fixed Assets**	
全社会固定资产投资 (亿元)	Total Investment in Fixed Assets (100 million yuan)	
#房地产开发	Real Estate Development	

注：2023年能源数据为初步核算数(以下相关表同)。

Aggregate Indicators on National Economic and Social Development and Growth Rates

总量指标 Aggregate Indicator			指数(%) Index (%) (2023为以下各年) (2023 as Percentage of the Following Years)			平均增长速度(%) Average Annual Growth Rate (%)	
2000	2022	2023	1978	2000	2022	1979–2023	2001–2023
126743	141175	140967	146.4	111.2	99.9	0.9	0.5
45906	92071	93267	540.8	203.2	101.3	3.8	3.1
80837	49104	47700	60.4	59.0	97.1	-1.1	-2.3
72085	73351	74041	184.4	102.7	100.9	1.4	0.1
36043	17663	16882	59.6	46.8	95.6	-1.1	-3.2
16219	21105	21520	309.9	132.7	102.0	2.5	1.2
19823	34583	35639	728.8	179.8	103.1	4.5	2.6
595	1203	1074	202.6	180.5	89.3	1.6	2.6
99066.1	1194401.4	1249990.6	4673.9	622.4	105.3	8.9	8.3
100280.1	1204724.0	1260582.1	4713.5	620.0	105.2	8.9	8.3
14717.4	88207.0	89755.2	686.1	249.1	104.1	4.4	4.0
45663.7	473789.9	482588.5	7010.3	653.6	104.7	9.9	8.5
39899.1	642727.1	688238.4	6859.6	715.6	105.8	9.9	8.9
7846	84579	88607	3167.9	557.0	105.4	8.0	7.8
7942	85310	89358	3194.8	555.0	105.4	8.0	7.7
3721	36883	39218	3232.2	645.6	106.1	8.0	8.4
6256	49283	51821	1976.4	517.0	104.8	6.9	7.4
2282	20133	21691	2638.2	538.9	107.6	7.5	7.6
13395.2	203649.3	216795.4	18482.6	1562.9	106.5	12.3	12.7
15886.5	260552.1	274622.9	23641.8	1675.1	105.4	12.9	13.0
138570	463808	483000	769.9	348.8	104.2	4.6	5.6
146964	540956	572000	1000.6	389.1	105.7	5.3	6.1
13.8	45.6	47.2	764.2	341.2	103.6	4.6	5.5
272.0	2201.1	2324.3	1692.9	854.5	105.6	6.5	9.8
13556.0	88487.1	94564.4	3686.0	697.6	106.9	8.3	8.8
32917.7	495966.4	509707.9		1548.4	102.8		15.0
4984.1	123847.8	112142.3		2250.0	90.5		18.5

a) Energy data of 2023 are preliminary accounting figures. The same applies to the following tables.

1–2 续表 1

指　　标	Item	1978
对外贸易和外商直接投资	**International Trade and Foreign Direct Investment**	
货物进出口总额 (亿元)	Total Value of Imports and Exports (100 million yuan)	355.0
出口总额	Exports	167.7
进口总额	Imports	187.4
实际使用外资金额 (亿美元)	Total Amount of Foreign Investment Actually Utilized (100 million USD)	
农业	**Agriculture**	
农林牧渔业总产值 (亿元)	Gross Output Value of Agriculture, Forestry, Animal Husbandry and Fishery (100 million yuan)	1397.0
主要农产品产量 (万吨)	Output of Major Farm Products (10 000 tons)	
谷　物	Cereals	
棉　花	Cotton	216.7
油　料	Oil-bearing Crops	521.8
肉　类	Meat	943.0
水产品	Aquatic Products	465.4
工业	**Industry**	
主要工业产品产量	Output of Main Industrial Products	
水　泥 (万吨)	Cement (10 000 tons)	6524.0
粗　钢 (万吨)	Crude Steel (10 000 tons)	3178.0
钢　材 (万吨)	Rolled Steel (10 000 tons)	2208.0
金属切削机床 (万台)	Metal-cutting Machine Tools (10 000 units)	18.3
汽　车 (万辆)	Motor Vehicles (10 000 units)	14.9
发电机组 (万千瓦)	Power Generation Equipment (10 000 kW)	483.8
规模以上工业企业主要指标 (亿元)	Principal Indicators of Industrial Enterprises above Designated Size (100 million yuan)	
资产总计	Total Assets	4525
营业收入	Business Revenue	
利润总额	Total Profits	599
建筑业	**Construction**	
建筑业总产值 (亿元)	Gross Output Value of Construction (100 million yuan)	
房地产业	**Real Estate**	
房地产企业房屋施工面积 (万平方米)	Floor Space of Buildings under Construction (10 000 sq.m)	
房地产企业房屋竣工面积 (万平方米)	Floor Space of Buildings Completed (10 000 sq.m)	
房地产企业新建商品房销售面积(万平方米)	Floor Space of Newly-built Commercial Buildings Sold (10 000 sq.m)	
#住宅	Residential Buildings	
房地产企业新建商品房销售额 (亿元)	Value of Sale of Newly-built Commercial Buildings (100 million yuan)	
#住宅	Residential Buildings	

注：主要工业产品产量2023年数据统计范围为规模以上工业企业，即年主营业务收入2000万元及以上的工业企业。

continued

总量指标 Aggregate Indicator			指数(%) Index (%) (2023为以下各年) (2023 as Percentage of the Following Years)			平均增长速度(%) Average Annual Growth Rate (%)	
2000	2022	2023	1978	2000	2022	1979–2023	2001–2023
39273.3	416727.8	417510.1	117608.5	1063.1	100.2	17.0	10.8
20634.4	236336.8	237656.4	141715.2	1151.7	100.6	17.5	11.2
18638.8	180391.0	179853.7	95973.2	964.9	99.7	16.5	10.4
407.1	1891.3	1632.5		401.0	86.3		6.2
24915.8	156065.9	158507.2	1097.5	280.3	104.2	5.5	4.6
40522.4	63324.3	64143.0		158.3	101.3		2.0
441.7	598.0	561.8	259.2	127.2	93.9	2.1	1.1
2954.8	3654.2	3863.7	740.5	130.8	105.7	4.5	1.2
6013.9	9328.4	9748.2	1033.7	162.1	104.5	5.3	2.1
3706.2	6865.9	7116.2	1528.9	192.0	103.6	6.2	2.9
59700.0	212927.2	201940.2	3095.3	338.3	94.8	7.9	5.4
12850.0	101795.9	102886.0	3237.4	800.7	101.1	8.0	9.5
13146.0	134033.5	138378.7	6267.2	1052.6	103.2	9.6	10.8
17.7	57.3	69.1	377.6	390.4	120.6	3.0	6.1
207.0	2713.6	3009.9	20200.7	1454.1	110.9	12.5	12.3
1249.0	18371.1	26815.8	5542.7	2147.0	146.0	9.3	14.3
126211	1601926	1720756					
84152	1333214	1360317					
4393	84162	82897					
12498	298675	314394		2515.6	105.3		15.1
65897	904500	840157		1275.0	92.9		11.7
25105	85358	101999		406.3	119.5		6.3
18637	122154	111762		599.7	91.5		8.1
16570	103306	94819		572.2	91.8		7.9
3935	124720	116661		2964.4	93.5		15.9
3229	109583	103013		3190.6	94.0		16.2

a) The statistical scope of the main industrial product output in 2023 includes industrial enterprises above designated size, which have an annual main business income of 20 million yuan or more.

1–2 续表 2

指 标		Item		1978
批发、零售和旅游业		**Wholesale, Retail Sales and Tourism**		
社会消费品零售总额	(亿元)	Total Retail Sales of Consumer Goods	(100 million yuan)	1558.6
入境旅客	(万人次)	Number of Inbound Tourists	(10 000 person-times)	180.9
#外国人	(万人次)	Foreigners	(10 000 person-times)	23.0
国内旅客	(百万人次)	Number of Domestic Tourists	(million person-times)	
国内游客出游总花费	(亿元)	Total Travel Expenses of Domestic Tourists	(100 million yuan)	
交通运输业		**Transport**		
客运量	(万人)	Passenger Traffic	(10 000 persons)	253993.0
铁 路		Railways		81491.0
公 路		Highways		149229.0
水 路		Waterways		23042.0
民 航		Civil Aviation		231.0
货运量	(万吨)	Freight Traffic	(10 000 tons)	319431.4
铁 路		Railways		110119.0
公 路		Highways		151602.0
水 路		Waterways		47357.0
民 航		Civil Aviation		6.4
管 道		Pipelines		10347.0
沿海规模以上港口货物吞吐量	(万吨)	Volume of Freight Handled at Coastal Ports above Designated Size	(10 000 tons)	
民用汽车拥有量	(万辆)	Possession of Civil Motor Vehicles	(10 000 sets)	135.8
#私人汽车		Private Vehicles		
电信和信息软件业		**Telecommunication & Information Services**		
电信业务总量	(亿元)	Business Volume of Telecommunication Services	(100 million yuan)	19.2
移动电话年末用户	(万户)	Number of Mobile Phone Subscribers at Year-end	(10 000 subscribers)	
固定电话年末用户	(万户)	Number of Fixed Telephone Subscribers at Year-end	(10 000 subscribers)	192.5
互联网宽带接入用户	(万户)	Broadband Subscribers of Internet	(10 000 subscribers)	
软件业务收入	(亿元)	Revenue from Software Service	(100 million yuan)	
金融业		**Financial Intermediation**		
社会融资规模存量	(万亿元)	Aggregate Financing to the Real Economy (Stock)	(trillion yuan)	
货币和准货币(M_2)	(万亿元)	Money and Quasi-money (M_2)	(trillion yuan)	
货币(M_1)	(万亿元)	Money (M_1)	(trillion yuan)	
流通中现金(M_0)	(万亿元)	Currency in Circulation (M_0)	(trillion yuan)	
金融机构人民币各项存款余额	(万亿元)	Deposits of Financial Institutions	(trillion yuan)	0.1
金融机构人民币各项贷款余额	(万亿元)	Loans of Financial Institutions	(trillion yuan)	0.2
境内股票发行金额	(亿元)	Proceeds Raised in Domestic Stock Market	(100 million yuan)	
保险公司保费金额	(亿元)	Insurance Premium of Insurance Companies	(100 million yuan)	
保险公司赔款及给付金额	(亿元)	Claim and Payment of Insurance Companies	(100 million yuan)	

注：1.2023年起，公路客运量口径发生变化，包括班车包车客运量、公共汽电车城际城乡客运量、出租汽车(含巡游出租汽车、网络预约出租汽车)城际城乡客运量，与以前年份数据不可比(以下相关表同)。
2.自2023年起，移动电话用户将中国广电数据纳入行业汇总数据(以下相关表同)。

continued

总量指标	Aggregate Indicator		指数(%) Index (%) (2023为以下各年) (2023 as Percentage of the Following Years)			平均增长速度(%) Average Annual Growth Rate (%)	
2000	2022	2023	1978	2000	2022	1979—2023	2001—2023
38447.1	439732.5	471495.2	30251.2	1226.3	107.2	13.5	11.5
8344.4		8202.5	4533.7	98.3		8.8	-0.1
1016.0		1378.4	6002.2	135.7		9.5	1.3
744.0	2530.0	4891.0		657.4	193.3		8.5
3175.5	20444.0	49133.1		1547.2	240.3		12.6
1478572.5	558737.6	1574330.8					
105072.5	167296.3	385449.6	473.0	366.8	230.4	3.5	5.8
1347392.0	354642.8	1101152.9					
19386.0	11627.5	25770.7	111.8	132.9	221.6	0.2	1.2
6721.7	25171.0	61957.6	26821.5	921.8	246.1	13.2	10.1
1358681.7	5152571.1	5570636.1	1743.9	410.0	108.1	6.6	6.3
178581.0	498423.7	503534.6	457.3	282.0	101.0	3.4	4.6
1038813.0	3711927.9	4033681.2	2660.7	388.3	108.7	7.6	6.1
122391.0	855351.5	936746.2	1978.1	765.4	109.5	6.9	9.3
196.7	607.6	735.4	11490.3	373.8	121.0	11.1	5.9
18700.0	86260.4	95938.8	927.2	513.0	111.2	5.1	7.4
125603.0	1013101.5	1083471.0		862.6	106.9		9.8
1608.9	31184.4	32911.6	24228.2	2045.6	105.5	13.0	14.0
625.3	27792.1	29356.9		4694.6	105.6		18.2
4559.9	17501.1	18359.3					
8453.3	168344.3	174358.1		2062.6	103.6		14.1
14482.9	17941.4	17332.6	9001.9	119.7	96.6	10.5	0.8
	58964.8	63630.6			107.9		
	107790.1	123642.7			114.7		
	344.2	378.1			109.5		
13.5	266.4	292.3		2073.2	109.7		14.1
5.3	67.2	68.1		1258.3	101.3		11.6
1.5	10.5	11.3		774.4	108.3		9.3
12.4	258.5	284.3	232608.2	2182.5	110.0	18.8	14.3
9.9	214.0	237.6	154627.3	2558.4	110.6	17.7	15.1
1515.8	14342.4	10056.4		663.4	70.1		8.6
1598.0	46957.2	51246.7			109.1		
526.0	15485.1	18883.0			121.9		

a) Since 2023, the coverage of highway passenger traffic has changed, which includes passenger traffic volume of shuttle buses and charter passenger transportation, intercity urban and rural passenger traffic volume of public buses and trams and intercity urban and rural passenger traffic volume of taxis (including cruising taxis and online reservation taxis). The data are not comparable to previous years. The same applies to the relevant following tables.

b) Since 2023, mobile phone subscribers have include China Broadcast Network data in industry summary data. The same applies to the relevant following tables.

1–2　续表 3

指　　标		Item		1978
科学技术		**Science and Technology**		
R&D经费支出	(亿元)	Expenditure on R&D	(100 million yuan)	
发明专利授权数	(件)	Number of Invention Patent Grants	(pieces)	
技术市场成交额	(亿元)	Transaction Value in Technical Markets	(100 million yuan)	
教育		**Education**		
专任教师数	(万人)	Full-time Teachers	(10 000 persons)	
#普通、职业高等学校		Regular and Vocational Higher Education Institutions		20.6
普通高中		Regular Senior Secondary Schools		74.1
初中阶段		Junior Secondary Schools		244.1
小学阶段		Primary Education		522.6
在校生数	(万人)	Total Enrollment	(10 000 persons)	
#普通、职业本专科		Regular and Vocational Higher Education Institutions		85.6
普通高中		Regular Senior Secondary Schools		1553.1
初中阶段		Junior Secondary Schools		4995.2
小学阶段		Primary Education		14624.0
教育经费支出	(亿元)	Government Expenditure on Education	(100 million yuan)	
卫生		**Public Health**		
医院	(个)	Hospitals	(unit)	9293
执业(助理)医师	(万人)	Licensed (Assistant) Physicians	(10 000 persons)	97.8
医院床位数	(万张)	Number of Hospital Beds	(10 000 units)	110.0
卫生总费用	(亿元)	Total Health Expenditure	(100 million yuan)	110.2
文化		**Culture**		
图书出版总印数	(亿册、亿张)	Number of Books Published	(100 million copies)	37.7
电视节目制作时间	(万小时)	Time for TV Programs Production	(10 000 hours)	
故事影片产量	(部)	Production of Feature Films	(film)	46
社会保险		**Social Insurance**		
社会保险基金收入	(亿元)	Revenue of Social Insurance Fund	(100 million yuan)	
社会保险基金支出	(亿元)	Expenses of Social Insurance Fund	(100 million yuan)	
参加基本养老保险人数	(万人)	Participants in Basic Endowment Insurance	(10 000 persons)	
参加失业保险人数	(万人)	Participants in Unemployment Insurance	(10 000 persons)	
参加基本医疗保险人数	(万人)	Participants in Basic Medical Insurance	(10 000 persons)	

注：本表速度指标中，国民总收入、国内生产总值及三次产业增加值、城乡居民收入、财政收支、货币供应量、金融机构人民币各项存贷款余额、保险公司保费金额、保险公司赔款及给付金额等指标均按可比价格计算；固定资产投资类指标平均增长速度按累计法计算；其他指标按绝对数计算。

continued

总量指标 Aggregate Indicator			指数(%) Index (%) (2023为以下各年) (2023 as Percentage of the Following Years)			平均增长速度(%) Average Annual Growth Rate (%)	
2000	2022	2023	1978	2000	2022	1979-2023	2001-2023
895.7	30782.9	33357.1		3724.1	108.4		17.0
12683	798347	920797		7260.1	115.3		20.5
650.8	47791.0	61475.7		9446.2	128.6		21.9
46.3	196.3	206.1	1000.4	445.1	105.0	5.3	6.7
75.7	213.3	221.5	298.9	292.6	103.8	2.5	4.8
328.7	402.5	408.3	167.3	124.2	101.4	1.1	0.9
586.0	662.9	665.6	127.4	113.6	100.4	0.5	0.6
556.1	3659.4	3775.0	4410.1	678.8	103.2	8.8	8.7
1201.3	2713.9	2803.6	180.5	233.4	103.3	1.3	3.8
6256.3	5120.6	5243.7	105.0	83.8	102.4	0.1	-0.8
13013.3	10732.1	10836.0	74.1	83.3	101.0	-0.7	-0.8
3849.1	61329.1						
16318	36976	38355	412.7	235.0	103.7	3.2	3.8
207.6	443.5	478.2	488.9	230.4	107.8	3.6	3.7
216.7	766.3	800.5	727.7	369.4	104.5	4.5	5.8
4586.6	85327.5	90575.8	82184.7	1974.8	106.2	16.1	13.8
62.7	114.0	125.0	331.5	199.3	109.6	2.7	3.0
58.5	285.2	260.0		444.5	91.2		6.7
91	380	792	1721.7	870.3	208.4	6.5	9.9
2644.9	102504.8	113214.9		4280.5	110.4		17.7
2385.6	90719.1	99301.8		4162.6	109.5		17.6
13617.4	105307.3	106643.3		783.1	101.3		9.4
10408.4	23806.6	24372.7		234.2	102.4		3.8
3786.9	134592.5	133389.0		3522.3	99.1		16.7

a)Indices and growth rates of the follow indicators are calculated at comparable prices: gross national income, gross domestic product, value added of the primary, secondary and tertiary industries, income of urban and rural residents. These are calculated at comparable caliber: government finance, aggregate financing to the real economy, money supply, the balance of RMB deposits and loans of financial institutions. The average annual growth rate of total investment in fixed assets is calculated at the accumulate method.Growth rates of other indicators are calculated with their values.

1-3 国民经济和社会发展结构指标
Composition Indicators on National Economic and Social Development

单位：% (%)

指 标	Item	1978	2000	2022	2023
人口	**Population**				
性别	Gender Composition				
男	Male	51.5	51.6	51.1	51.1
女	Female	48.5	48.4	48.9	48.9
年龄	Age				
0-14岁	Aged 0-14		22.9	16.9	16.3
15-64岁	Aged 15-64		70.1	68.2	68.3
65岁及以上	Aged 65 and Over		7.0	14.9	15.4
城乡	Urban and Rural Composition				
城镇	Urban Areas	17.9	36.2	65.2	66.2
乡村	Rural Area	82.1	63.8	34.8	33.8
国民经济核算	**National Accounts**				
国内生产总值(生产法)	Gross Domestic Product (Production Approach)				
第一产业	Primary Industry	27.7	14.7	7.3	7.1
第二产业	Secondary Industry	47.7	45.5	39.3	38.3
第三产业	Tertiary Industry	24.6	39.8	53.4	54.6
国内生产总值(支出法)	Gross Domestic Product (Expenditure Approach)				
最终消费支出	Final Consumption Expenditure	61.9	63.9	53.5	55.7
资本形成总额	Gross Capital Formation	38.4	33.7	43.2	42.1
货物和服务净出口	Net Exports of Goods and Services	-0.3	2.4	3.2	2.1
就业	**Employment**				
第一产业	Primary Industry	70.5	50.0	24.1	22.8
第二产业	Secondary Industry	17.3	22.5	28.8	29.1
第三产业	Tertiary Industry	12.2	27.5	47.1	48.1
人民生活	**People's Livelihoods**				
城镇居民人均消费支出	Per Capita Consumption Expenditure of Urban Households				
食品烟酒	Food, Tobacco and Alcohol		38.6	29.5	28.8
衣 着	Clothing and Footwear		9.7	5.7	5.7
居 住	Housing		13.5	25.2	23.7
生活用品及服务	Household Equipments, Furnishings and Services		7.4	5.9	5.8
交通通信	Transport and Communications		8.2	12.9	13.6
教育文化娱乐	Education, Culture and Recreation		12.9	10.0	10.9
医疗保健	Health Care and Medical Services		6.4	8.2	8.6
其他用品及服务	Miscellaneous Goods and Services		3.2	2.7	2.9
农村居民人均消费支出	Per Capita Consumption Expenditure of Rural Households				
食品烟酒	Food, Tobacco and Alcohol		48.3	33.0	32.4
衣 着	Clothing and Footwear		5.7	5.2	5.1
居 住	Housing		15.8	21.1	20.3
生活用品及服务	Household Facilities, Articles and Services		4.5	5.6	5.5
交通通信	Transport and Communications		5.6	13.4	13.6
教育文化娱乐	Education, Culture and Recreation		11.9	10.1	10.7
医疗保健	Health Care and Medical Services		5.2	9.8	10.5
其他用品及服务	Miscellaneous Goods and Services		3.0	1.8	1.9

1-3 续表 1 continued

单位：% (%)

指 标	Item	1978	2000	2022	2023
财政	**Government Finance**				
一般公共预算收入	General Public Budget Revenue				
中央	Central Government	15.5	52.2	46.6	45.9
地方	Local Governments	84.5	47.8	53.4	54.1
一般公共预算支出	General Public Budget Expenditure				
中央	Central Government	47.4	34.7	13.7	13.9
地方	Local Governments	52.6	65.3	86.3	86.1
一般公共预算收入中	Of General Public Budget Revenue				
税收收入	Tax Revenue	45.9	93.9	81.8	83.6
#国内增值税	Domestic Value-added Tax		34.0	23.9	32.0
国内消费税	Domestic Consumption Tax		6.4	8.2	7.4
企业所得税	Corporate Income Tax		7.5	21.5	19.0
个人所得税	Individual Income Tax		4.9	7.3	6.8
关税	Tariffs	2.5	5.6	1.4	1.2
能源	**Energy**				
能源生产	Energy Production				
原煤	Raw Coal	70.3	72.9	67.2	66.6
原油	Crude Oil	23.7	16.8	6.3	6.2
天然气	Natural Gas	2.9	2.6	5.9	6.0
一次电力及其他能源	Primary Electricity and Other Energy	3.1	7.7	20.6	21.2
能源消费	Energy Consumption				
煤炭	Coal	70.7	68.5	56.0	55.3
石油	Petroleum	22.7	22.0	18.0	18.3
天然气	Natural Gas	3.2	2.2	8.4	8.5
一次电力及其他能源	Primary Electricity and Other Energy	3.4	7.3	17.6	17.9
货物进出口	**Imports and Exports of Goods**				
出口	Exports				
初级产品	Primary Goods		10.2	4.8	4.9
工业制品	Manufactured Goods		89.8	95.2	95.1
进口	Imports				
初级产品	Primary Goods		20.8	40.2	42.5
工业制品	Manufactured Goods		79.2	59.8	57.5
农业	**Agriculture**				
农林牧渔业总产值	Gross Output Value of Agriculture, Forestry, Animal Husbandry and Fishery				
农业	Farming	80.0	55.7	54.1	54.9
林业	Forestry	3.4	3.8	4.4	4.4
牧业	Animal Husbandry	15.0	29.7	26.0	24.6
渔业	Fishery	1.6	10.9	9.9	10.2
农林牧渔专业及辅助性活动	Professional and Support Activities for Agriculture, Forestry, Animal Husbandry and Fishery			5.6	5.9
工业(规模以上)	**Industry (above designated size)**				
工业企业资产	Assets of Industrial Enterprises				
采矿业	Mining			8.1	8.1
制造业	Manufacturing			75.5	75.2
电力、热力、燃气及水生产和供应业	Production and Supply of Electricity, Heat, Gas and Water			16.4	16.7

1-3 续表 2 continued

单位：% (%)

指　　标	Item	1978	2000	2022	2023
工业企业资产	Assets of Industrial Enterprises				
大型企业	Large Enterprises		56.3	45.6	45.9
中型企业	Medium-sized Enterprises		12.9	21.5	21.4
小型企业	Small Enterprises		30.8	32.8	32.7
交通运输业	**Transport**				
货运量	Freight Traffic				
铁　路	Railways	34.5	13.1	9.7	9.0
公　路	Highways	47.5	76.5	72.0	72.4
水　路	Waterways	14.8	9.0	16.6	16.8
民　航	Civil Aviation	0.002	0.014	0.012	0.013
管　道	Pipelines	3.2	1.4	1.7	1.7
科技	**Science and Technology**				
R&D经费支出	Expenditure on R&D				
#基础研究	Basic Research		5.2	6.6	6.8
应用研究	Applied Research		17.0	11.3	11.0
试验发展	Experimental Development		77.8	82.1	82.3
#政府资金	Government Funds			17.8	17.1
企业资金	Enterprises Funds			79.0	79.3
教育	**Education**				
教育经费	Education Funds				
国家财政性教育经费	Government Appropriation for Education		66.6	79.0	
#一般公共预算教育经费	General Public Budget Expenditure on Education		56.9	64.0	
卫生	**Public Health**				
卫生技术人员	Health Technical Personnel				
#执业(助理)医师	Licensed (Assistant) Physicians	39.7	46.2	38.0	38.3
注册护士	Registered Nurses	16.4	28.2	44.8	45.1
药师(士)	Pharmacists	10.8	9.2	4.6	4.6
卫生总费用	Total Health Expenditure				
政府卫生支出	Government Health Expenditure	32.2	15.5	28.2	26.7
社会卫生支出	Social Health Expenditure	47.4	25.6	44.9	46.0
个人卫生支出	Personal Health Expenditure	20.4	59.0	26.9	27.3
社会保障	**Social Security**				
社会保险基金收入	Revenue of Social Insurance Fund				
基本养老保险	Basic Endowment Insurance		86.1	67.2	67.7
失业保险	Unemployment Insurance		6.1	1.6	1.6
基本医疗保险	Basic Medical Insurance		6.4	30.2	29.6
工伤保险	Work-Related Injury Insurance		0.9	1.0	1.1
生育保险	Birth Insurance		0.4		
社会保险基金支出	Expenses of Social Insurance Fund				
基本养老保险	Basic Endowment Insurance		88.7	69.5	68.9
失业保险	Unemployment Insurance		5.2	2.2	1.5
基本医疗保险	Basic Medical Insurance		5.2	27.1	28.4
工伤保险	Work-Related Injury Insurance		0.6	1.1	1.2
生育保险	Birth Insurance		0.3		

注：1.从2017年起，"公共财政教育经费"改为"一般公共预算教育经费"。"一般公共预算教育经费"数据1992-2011年包括教育事业费基本建设经费、教育费附加、科研经费和其他经费，2012年起仅包括教育事业费、基本建设经费和教育费附加，2015年起教育事业费包含地方教育附加和土地出让收益计提的教育资金。

2.2007年及以后基本医疗保险基金中包括职工基本医疗保险和城乡居民基本医疗保险。

3.2010年及以后基本养老保险基金中包括城镇职工基本养老保险和城乡居民基本养老保险。

4.2019年起，基本医疗保险基金包含生育保险基金。

a) Since 2017, the "public expenditure on education" has been changed to "general public budget expenditure on education". From 1992 to 2011, the "general public budget expenditure on education" included the appropriated funds for education, capital construction, education surcharges, scientific research, and other funds. Since 2012, it only includes the appropriated funds for education, capital construction, and education surcharges. Since 2015, the "appropriated funds for education" includes the education funds accrued from local education surcharges and land transfer income.

b) Data of basic medical insurance include the basic medical insurance for workers and the basic medical insurance for urban and rural residents from 2007.

c) Data of basic endowment insurance for 2010 and following years include the basic endowment insurance for urban workers and basic endowment insurance for urban and rural residents.

d) Since 2019, the data of basic medical care insurance fund includes the data of birth insurance fund.

1—4　国民经济和社会发展比例和效益指标
Proportion and Efficiency Indicators on National Economic and Social Development

指　　标	Item	1978	2000	2022	2023
人口与就业	**Population and Employment**				
出生率 (‰)	Birth Rate (‰)	18.25	14.03	6.77	6.39
死亡率 (‰)	Death Rate (‰)	6.25	6.45	7.37	7.87
自然增长率 (‰)	Natural Growth Rate (‰)	12.00	7.58	-0.60	-1.48
总抚养比 (%)	Gross Dependency Ratio (%)		42.6	46.6	46.5
少儿抚养比 (%)	Children Dependency Ratio (%)		32.6	24.8	24.0
老年抚养比 (%)	Elderly Dependency Ratio (%)		9.9	21.8	22.5
城镇调查失业率 (%)	Surveyed Unemployment Rate in Urban Areas (%)			5.6	5.2
国民经济核算	**National Accounts**				
人均国民总收入 (元)	Per Capita GNI (yuan)	385	7846	84579	88607
人均国内生产总值 (元)	Per Capita GDP (yuan)	385	7942	85310	89358
人民生活	**People's Livelihoods**				
城乡收入比(农村居民收入为1)	Urban and Rural Income Ratio(Rural Income as 1)	2.57	2.74	2.45	2.39
基尼系数	Gini Coefficient			0.467	0.465
农村贫困发生率(2010年标准) (%)	Rural Poverty(2010's standard) (%)	97.5	49.8		
财政	**Government Finance**				
一般公共预算收入与国内生产总值之比(%)	Proportion of Government Revenue to GDP (%)	30.8	13.4	16.9	17.2
一般公共预算支出与国内生产总值之比(%)	Proportion of Government Expenditure to GDP (%)	30.5	15.8	21.6	21.8
外债	Foreign Debts				
偿债率 (%)	Debt Servicing Ratio (%)		9.2	10.5	7.6
负债率 (%)	Liability Ratio (%)		12.0	13.6	13.7
债务率 (%)	Debt Ratio (%)		52.1	66.0	69.7
能源	**Energy**				
能源生产弹性系数	Elasticity Ratio of Energy Production		0.59	2.87	0.81
电力生产弹性系数	Elasticity Ratio of Electricity Production		1.11	1.23	1.33
能源消费弹性系数	Elasticity Ratio of Energy Consumption		0.53	0.97	1.10
电力消费弹性系数	Elasticity Ratio of Electricity Consumption		1.12	1.23	1.29
万元国内生产总值能源消费量 (吨标准煤/万元)	Energy Consumption per 10000 yuan of GDP (tce/10 000 yuan)		1.47	0.48	0.48
能源加工转换总效率 (%)	Total Efficiency of Energy Transformation (%)		69.4	73.2	
对外贸易	**International Trade**				
进出口总额与国内生产总值之比 (按人民币计算) (%)	Proportion of Total Value of Imports & Exports to GDP (calculated by RMB) (%)	9.7	39.2	34.6	33.1

注：1.2020年，我国现行农村贫困标准下的农村贫困人口全部脱贫。
2.2023年电力消费数据来源于中国电力企业联合会。
3.计算万元国内生产总值能源消费量的国内生产总值，2000年按2000年可比价计算，2022年、2023年按2020年可比价计算。
4.城镇调查失业率为每年1—12月平均值。

a) China has eliminated absolute poverty by 2020.
b) The electricity consumption data of 2023 are from China Electricity Council.
c) The national energy consumption per 10000 yuan of GDP are calculated at 2000 constant prices in 2000, and at 2020 constant prices in 2022 and 2023.
d) The surveyed unemployment rate in urban areas is the annual average.

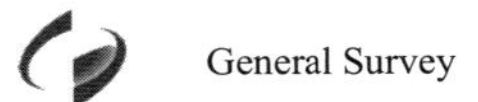

1-4 续表 continued

指 标	Item	1978	2000	2022	2023
农业	**Agriculture**				
每公顷播种面积农产品产量（公斤）	Output of Farm Crops per Hectare of Sown Area (kg)				
谷物	Cereals		4753	6379	6419
棉花	Cotton	445	1093	1993	2015
工业	**Industry**				
资产负债率 (%)	Assets-Liability Ratio (%)		60.81	57.43	57.35
流动资产周转次数 （次／年）	Turnover of Current Assets (times/year)		1.62	1.60	1.54
成本费用利润率 (%)	Ratio of Profits to Cost (%)		5.56	6.82	6.56
交通运输业	**Transport**				
铁路网密度 （公里／万平方公里）	Railway Density (km/10 000 sq.km)	53.9	71.5	161.1	165.4
公路网密度 （公里／万平方公里）	Highway Density (km/10 000 sq.km)	927.3	1749.8	5578.0	5663.4
邮电通信业	**Postal and Telecommunication Services**				
电话普及率(含移动电话)(部/百人)	Popularization Rate of Telephones (Include Mobile Phones) (set/100 persons)	0.4	19.1	132.0	136.0
#移动电话普及率 （部/百人）	Popularization Rate of Mobile Phones (set/100 persons)		6.7	119.2	123.7
金融业	**Financial Intermediation**				
货币和准货币(M_2)与国内生产总值之比 (%)	Proportion of Money and Quasi-money(M_2) to GDP (%)		134.2	221.2	231.9
金融机构存款与国内生产总值之比 (%)	Proportion of Deposits of Financial Institutions to GDP (%)	31.4	123.5	214.6	225.5
金融机构贷款与国内生产总值之比 (%)	Proportion of Loans of Financial Institutions to GDP (%)	51.4	99.1	177.6	188.5
科技	**Science and Technology**				
R&D经费支出与国内生产总值之比 (%)	Proportion of R&D Expenditure to GDP (%)		0.89	2.56	2.65
教育	**Education**				
九年义务教育巩固率 (%)	Consolidation Rate of 9-year Compulsory Education (%)			95.5	95.7
高中阶段毛入学率 (%)	Gross Enrollment Rate of High School Education (%)		42.8	91.6	91.8
高等教育毛入学率 (%)	Gross Enrollment Rate of Higher Education (%)		12.5	59.6	60.2
卫生	**Public Health**				
每万人口执业(助理)医师数 （人）	Number of Licensed Physicians & Physician Assistants per 10 000 Population (person)	10.8	16.8	31.5	34.0
每万人口医疗卫生机构床位数(张)	Number of Beds at Health Institutions per 10 000 Population (bed)			69.2	72.3
医院病床使用率 (%)	Utilization Rate of Beds at Health Institutions (%)		60.8	71.0	79.4
城市市政建设	**Urban Municipal Development**				
供水普及率 (%)	Coverage Rate of Urban Population with Access to Tap Water(%)		63.9	99.4	99.4
燃气普及率 (%)	Coverage Rate of Urban Population with Access to Gas (%)		45.4	98.1	98.3
人均公园绿地面积 （平方米）	Public Recreational Green Space Per Capita (sq.m)		3.7	15.3	15.6

注：1.城市市政建设中，计算人均和普及率指标所使用的人口数2006年以前为城市人口，2006年起为城区人口与城区暂住人口之和，以公安部门的户籍统计和暂住人口统计为准。
2.2006年以前“人均公园绿地面积”为“人均公共绿地面积”。

a) In urban municipal development, per capita data and coverage rate are calculated on the basis of city population before 2006. Since 2006, they are calculated on the basis of the sum of urban area population and temporary residing population from the household registration by the Ministry of Public Security.

b) Since 2006, Public Green Space Per Capita is changed to be Public Recreational Green Space Per Capita.

1-5 按主要行业分法人单位数

Number of Corporate Units by Sector

单位：个 (unit)

年份 地区	Year Region	合计 Total	农、林、牧、渔业 Agriculture, Forestry, Animal Husbandry and Fishery	采矿业 Mining	制造业 Manufacturing	电力、热力、燃气及水生产和供应业 Production and Supply of Electricity, Heating, Gas and Water	建筑业 Construction	批发和零售业 Wholesale and Retail Trades
	2005	5647823	68800	89430	1451556	43148	149471	994953
	2006	6068912	78205	93967	1579406	45922	170180	1122489
	2007	6495064	98546	97678	1702455	49052	190517	1246042
	2008	7214683	117941	97315	1818370	57923	226768	1403141
	2009	8003868	184764	103403	1959254	62038	261694	1670315
	2010	8754588	242429	104065	2098370	64151	302232	1965118
	2011	9593729	321086	105490	2240315	66652	346026	2276295
	2012	10616530	440853	107596	2380759	69947	391392	2630690
	2013	11258282	594495	89112	2252225	70409	347519	2810531
	2014	13701440	951045	101673	2616671	79679	464975	3513338
	2015	15729199	1204724	103426	2801143	87486	574128	4199026
	2016	18191382	1481473	104074	3019269	99469	754512	5041698
	2017	22009092	1926771	108900	3483617	120736	1045232	6252424
	2018	23481046	1926591	70191	3269606	110714	1218463	6499161
	2019	25280211	1879887	70983	3463346	113649	1458539	7155907
	2020	29389255	2090924	80683	3846747	123729	1901819	8415106
	2021	32866972	2189201	82830	4167767	133875	2367010	9575504
	2022	37169634	2495358	88033	4529585	153266	2901293	10881533
北京	Beijing	1409824	7815	78	26482	2186	62635	341260
天津	Tianjin	454320	11470	77	48214	1321	35445	119079
河北	Hebei	1843390	127507	5452	310895	7352	171485	517926
山西	Shanxi	918982	114798	6164	48278	7207	85348	275470
内蒙古	Inner Mongolia	540833	72051	5569	34049	4254	45894	147316
辽宁	Liaoning	822961	59907	3871	107050	4166	55977	234520
吉林	Jilin	343503	42186	1201	32419	2250	23546	94609
黑龙江	Heilongjiang	470714	69960	2710	39224	3695	29973	116509
上海	Shanghai	600897	6361	8	58167	288	25167	189122
江苏	Jiangsu	3296990	55571	492	641215	7484	327980	955561
浙江	Zhejiang	2690588	53653	980	564339	7760	118054	907259
安徽	Anhui	1454974	124583	1632	171586	6685	156889	382064
福建	Fujian	1547266	72500	1826	192832	7576	78975	594100
江西	Jiangxi	1213076	109191	4866	131457	9921	102325	354064
山东	Shandong	3546922	186582	2817	473971	10700	337300	1168922
河南	Henan	2100519	220588	3789	205705	7118	180153	645383
湖北	Hubei	1546917	119182	3190	137732	6853	162582	423006
湖南	Hunan	1250273	140324	3924	101083	9307	109020	311644
广东	Guangdong	3838391	53402	2832	708572	11300	175201	1201165
广西	Guangxi	923514	95980	4303	64915	4614	54445	250762
海南	Hainan	215496	13914	265	6274	793	18248	53469
重庆	Chongqing	782091	94654	1393	68144	2611	34016	232551
四川	Sichuan	1595275	148381	4763	97886	7755	136965	392191
贵州	Guizhou	753217	134015	6007	67048	3149	55342	191704
云南	Yunnan	823861	115316	5475	47602	3973	71358	224315
西藏	Xizang	56279	3615	346	4592	325	9646	8241
陕西	Shaanxi	951841	75521	5973	64222	4515	142129	250288
甘肃	Gansu	422728	82186	2024	22363	2525	39381	99167
青海	Qinghai	137903	21692	649	6663	1010	11411	28594
宁夏	Ningxia	163985	21978	789	11211	1026	13640	44572
新疆	Xinjiang	452104	40475	4568	35395	3547	30763	126700

注：2008年、2013年、2018年主要行业法人单位数为经济普查数据，根据相关统计资料对以上年份的农、林、牧、渔业法人单位数及合计数进行了修正。2013年法人单位数不包括金融业、铁路运输业和无分组标识的部分数据。2018年法人单位数不包括无分组标识的数据。

a) Number of legal entities by major industries in 2008, 2013 and 2018 is the economic census data. According to the relevant statistical data, the number and total number of legal entities in agriculture, forestry, animal husbandry and fishery in the above years have been revised. Number of legal entities in 2013 refers to those excluding financial intermediation, railway transportation and some no divided identifier.Number of legal entities in 2018 refers to those excluding financial intermediation, railway transportation and some no divided identifier.

1-5 续表 1 continued

单位：个 (unit)

年 份 地 区	Year Region	交通运输、仓储和邮政业 Transport, Storage and Post	住宿和餐饮业 Hotels and Catering Services	信息传输、软件和信息技术服务业 Information Transmission, Software and Information Technology	金 融 业 Financial Intermediation	房地产业 Real Estate	租赁和商务服 务 业 Leasing and Business Services	科学研究和技术服务业 Scientific Research and Technical Services
	2005	91565	101853	85499	26828	148059	291498	153076
	2006	104635	109892	100614	29201	165865	331904	166240
	2007	117228	118173	115101	31815	187444	368763	176677
	2008	157589	145297	153290	28668	214391	427001	201689
	2009	175914	154895	176326	36907	244043	511666	233221
	2010	195829	164762	191182	45512	284726	590478	256865
	2011	219630	172070	208867	55513	323985	687575	283777
	2012	249832	186837	245669	67554	356717	813851	324932
	2013	262048	199592	226107		343924	916953	455778
	2014	323044	235337	289162	91583	419618	1161947	544309
	2015	378705	274283	387842	109711	466100	1440572	661022
	2016	443325	317619	507674	122516	533557	1768005	813251
	2017	540994	378974	719150	135068	642893	2242096	1035170
	2018	577233	431323	919879	137934	744924	2551306	1275579
	2019	629631	449277	1047408	131744	811663	2825375	1390741
	2020	748046	514980	1285534	142488	933969	3394995	1738335
	2021	858447	583028	1488072	149813	1038260	3876456	2053759
	2022	973096	669628	1747117	159901	1115183	4432416	2439143
北 京	Beijing	23086	38689	77669	8119	35163	256127	318636
天 津	Tianjin	19996	7107	20039	5291	16362	61141	60246
河 北	Hebei	48300	23326	67885	4379	60318	158945	110660
山 西	Shanxi	27209	16659	44387	2870	27746	93675	46139
内蒙古	Inner Mongolia	18028	6375	15040	1764	18634	55142	30190
辽 宁	Liaoning	30509	11527	36057	3916	30160	85869	46009
吉 林	Jilin	10241	4244	12418	1630	11442	32418	16363
黑龙江	Heilongjiang	16017	4385	19527	2108	15953	43979	31308
上 海	Shanghai	23971	20626	33365	9567	25226	97004	45725
江 苏	Jiangsu	101561	46499	156201	8342	86864	344553	277407
浙 江	Zhejiang	58524	41276	147366	16133	67589	286215	133915
安 徽	Anhui	39777	27441	63669	3913	41233	186060	83221
福 建	Fujian	29961	22796	92964	4392	33487	158089	84579
江 西	Jiangxi	36514	17278	63116	2826	29574	156650	52257
山 东	Shandong	101311	54539	146362	13055	87970	391014	214342
河 南	Henan	41178	32528	84395	3259	64024	208580	125182
湖 北	Hubei	46250	29522	94654	4368	45288	195365	88216
湖 南	Hunan	26378	25451	59489	2774	34898	145306	85457
广 东	Guangdong	96391	70299	192060	32283	147384	572160	236298
广 西	Guangxi	26349	17372	36590	4046	33303	127280	48979
海 南	Hainan	5355	5614	15175	2134	16955	35754	11328
重 庆	Chongqing	18325	28535	38830	2273	23373	98099	34579
四 川	Sichuan	36222	32083	97501	5304	48671	234871	99577
贵 州	Guizhou	15248	24445	19420	2091	20776	77322	20735
云 南	Yunnan	21609	19862	31377	3482	25830	91028	37529
西 藏	Xizang	834	1307	1099	347	765	6253	1558
陕 西	Shaanxi	19878	18701	47653	3187	30314	106686	46084
甘 肃	Gansu	8390	8809	7755	1740	11303	36073	14002
青 海	Qinghai	2738	3148	3763	456	3993	19746	6265
宁 夏	Ningxia	5726	2846	5979	757	4472	18198	7624
新 疆	Xinjiang	17220	6339	15312	3095	16113	52814	24733

1-5 续表 2 continued

单位：个 (unit)

年 份 Year 地 区 Region	水利、环境和公共设施管理业 Management of Water Conservancy, Environment and Public Facilities	居民服务、修理和其他服务业 Service to Households, Repair and Other Services	教育 Education	卫生和社会工作 Health and Social Service	文化、体育和娱乐业 Culture, Sports and Entertainment	公共管理、社会保障和社会组织 Public Management, Social Security and Social Organization
2005	46847	93947	305446	183760	69490	1252597
2006	48811	102228	308760	185014	72873	1252706
2007	50953	110525	312339	187376	76430	1257950
2008	57553	120467	335065	206480	81878	1363857
2009	61740	141936	342003	209016	90891	1383842
2010	64794	158152	342408	205778	95633	1382104
2011	69186	175813	346390	205173	102775	1387111
2012	75981	196880	355072	206885	121126	1393957
2013	84803	190692	413908	249567	230544	1520075
2014	97522	242251	444038	265537	263384	1596327
2015	108069	298958	461451	271571	297274	1603708
2016	122367	359932	486026	275554	341182	1599879
2017	146295	420667	517739	286858	414973	1590535
2018	148860	497292	665883	272504	566593	1597010
2019	172856	522903	698893	279155	585224	1593030
2020	216714	598808	769578	299142	686805	1600853
2021	250799	667130	793247	296031	766821	1528922
2022	286257	758665	816766	320513	861807	1540074
北 京 Beijing	8939	41370	20850	9748	111767	19205
天 津 Tianjin	2425	10706	8627	3947	11193	11634
河 北 Hebei	14969	31340	39761	15706	36844	90340
山 西 Shanxi	7271	20480	17926	8915	20674	47766
内蒙古 Inner Mongolia	5647	10646	14186	5846	10954	39248
辽 宁 Liaoning	5047	16713	23993	12829	16319	38522
吉 林 Jilin	2768	6967	10332	5294	5864	27311
黑龙江 Heilongjiang	4127	7228	14877	6718	9861	32555
上 海 Shanghai	2825	17928	9905	5937	14793	14912
江 苏 Jiangsu	23013	59909	43458	31061	57846	71973
浙 江 Zhejiang	15204	52717	54115	21468	63849	80172
安 徽 Anhui	13526	29293	29132	12769	27812	53689
福 建 Fujian	9596	27262	24392	10214	42593	59132
江 西 Jiangxi	9348	19066	26448	9665	23553	54957
山 东 Shandong	29965	58525	68579	23184	58476	119308
河 南 Henan	21821	32645	65631	17819	41117	99604
湖 北 Hubei	15716	28909	30907	12258	32443	70476
湖 南 Hunan	11606	26133	36430	12970	39562	68517
广 东 Guangdong	16521	74396	77691	19072	71134	80230
广 西 Guangxi	8144	32826	35054	7115	17474	53963
海 南 Hainan	1908	4998	6443	2315	6611	7943
重 庆 Chongqing	7815	20329	18750	7704	20373	29737
四 川 Sichuan	11333	36497	41901	22867	46780	93727
贵 州 Guizhou	6554	25188	21094	7331	13522	42226
云 南 Yunnan	8032	19835	20046	7313	17295	52584
西 藏 Xizang	311	712	1109	629	1021	13569
陕 西 Shaanxi	10854	23124	23631	8481	20461	50139
甘 肃 Gansu	2837	8497	13835	4113	8264	49464
青 海 Qinghai	1878	2619	2561	1613	2639	16465
宁 夏 Ningxia	1492	3324	4286	1145	3094	11826
新 疆 Xinjiang	4765	8483	10816	4467	7619	38880

1−6 分地区按三次产业和机构类型分法人单位数(2022年)
Number of Corporate Units by Three Strata of Industry and Type of Institutions and Region (2022)

单位：个 (unit)

地区	Region	法人单位数 Number of Corporate Units	按三次产业分 Grouped by Three Strata of Industry			按机构类型分 By Type of Institutions				
			第一产业 Primary Industry	第二产业 Secondary Industry	第三产业 Tertiary Industry	企业法人 Enterprises	事业法人 Institution Units	机关法人 Government Units	社会团体 Social Organization	其他 Others
全国	**National Total**	**37169634**	**2184048**	**7612180**	**27373406**	**32828734**	**744326**	**225072**	**350596**	**3020906**
北京	Beijing	1409824	7351	90015	1312458	1361791	11093	1842	6394	28704
天津	Tianjin	454320	10707	83636	359977	425393	5661	1848	2452	18966
河北	Hebei	1843390	115706	492570	1235114	1630410	32333	11190	14234	155223
山西	Shanxi	918982	105387	144693	668902	776575	19061	7494	9204	106648
内蒙古	Inner Mongolia	540833	63144	88503	389186	422887	18549	7702	9482	82213
辽宁	Liaoning	822961	48977	168778	605206	715559	18887	7625	6422	74468
吉林	Jilin	343503	32824	58830	251849	270241	16482	4925	3228	48627
黑龙江	Heilongjiang	470714	62309	74501	333904	358180	18949	8342	5017	80226
上海	Shanghai	600897	6009	82289	512599	561659	7703	1825	3929	25781
江苏	Jiangsu	3296990	44551	970547	2281892	3120366	35593	8228	28094	104709
浙江	Zhejiang	2690588	48829	687571	1954188	2501809	26954	8158	25619	128048
安徽	Anhui	1454974	103129	334746	1017099	1289469	20326	8276	16708	120195
福建	Fujian	1547266	65574	279652	1202040	1419816	24402	6698	21103	75247
江西	Jiangxi	1213076	98597	247388	867091	1058341	27551	7714	11554	107916
山东	Shandong	3546922	150581	818299	2578042	3202958	40425	11087	16478	275974
河南	Henan	2100519	180056	394518	1525945	1761349	64635	12164	11529	250842
湖北	Hubei	1546917	99852	308551	1138514	1333259	37797	9118	15288	151455
湖南	Hunan	1250273	113262	222108	914903	1046672	36452	9168	16234	141747
广东	Guangdong	3838391	45057	892014	2901320	3531927	43856	12467	27571	222570
广西	Guangxi	923514	86986	127202	709326	760559	42419	8276	11299	100961
海南	Hainan	215496	12455	25292	177749	193121	4184	1604	1888	14699
重庆	Chongqing	782091	88054	105081	588956	705066	16393	3449	7372	49811
四川	Sichuan	1595275	138252	245472	1211551	1341701	54210	15162	17881	166321
贵州	Guizhou	753217	130141	130888	492188	638787	21884	7548	7420	77578
云南	Yunnan	823861	107710	127682	588469	682662	28107	10230	12521	90341
西藏	Xizang	56279	3123	14815	38341	33092	2790	5714	692	13991
陕西	Shaanxi	951841	66540	212187	673114	810083	24502	7752	14218	95286
甘肃	Gansu	422728	76857	65578	280293	288360	16715	6586	14316	96751
青海	Qinghai	137903	20901	19592	97410	99784	4709	2867	5264	25279
宁夏	Ningxia	163985	20199	26335	117451	136425	3357	1694	1911	20598
新疆	Xinjiang	452104	30928	72847	348329	350433	18347	8319	5274	69731

1-7 按地区和控股情况分企业法人单位数(2022年)
Numbers of Corporate Enterprises by Region and the Status of Holdings (2022)

单位：个　　　　(unit)

地 区	Region	企业单位数 Number of Enterprises	国有控股 State-holding	集体控股 Collective-holding	私人控股 Private-holding	港、澳、台商控股 Holding by Investors from Hong Kong, Macao and Taiwan	外商控股 Holding by Foreign Investors	其 他 Others
全 国	**National Total**	**32828734**	**361996**	**195375**	**31491401**	**141236**	**115304**	**523422**
北 京	Beijing	1361791	17280	16495	1291592	7491	10701	18232
天 津	Tianjin	425393	8002	2451	409282	2113	3359	186
河 北	Hebei	1630410	17888	8183	1579658	997	1446	22238
山 西	Shanxi	776575	10812	5472	759624	284	304	79
内蒙古	Inner Mongolia	422887	6838	2019	413409	239	382	
辽 宁	Liaoning	715559	12208	8619	667210	1575	3455	22492
吉 林	Jilin	270241	5241	1808	256402	219	533	6038
黑龙江	Heilongjiang	358180	8636	3401	324887	343	427	20486
上 海	Shanghai	561659	13709	7126	491949	13376	19097	16402
江 苏	Jiangsu	3120366	22052	11296	3028144	13490	16215	29169
浙 江	Zhejiang	2501809	16541	13860	2441212	8015	14641	7540
安 徽	Anhui	1289469	13208	7278	1249692	1217	1169	16905
福 建	Fujian	1419816	11183	4923	1385002	11106	5194	2408
江 西	Jiangxi	1058341	12906	4374	1022737	2182	852	15290
山 东	Shandong	3202958	21243	10054	3125563	4625	8717	32756
河 南	Henan	1761349	15464	8003	1723499	1018	969	12396
湖 北	Hubei	1333259	11603	6448	1301768	1598	2037	9805
湖 南	Hunan	1046672	9925	5142	1005828	1057	721	23999
广 东	Guangdong	3531927	27363	22056	3239884	62999	17719	161906
广 西	Guangxi	760559	9070	5778	741437	1527	1327	1420
海 南	Hainan	193121	3126	1642	163628	783	402	23540
重 庆	Chongqing	705066	6912	2212	693574	1132	1229	7
四 川	Sichuan	1341701	20185	12230	1300930	1687	1701	4968
贵 州	Guizhou	638787	13361	4894	619753	348	277	154
云 南	Yunnan	682662	9794	8370	661002	692	838	1966
西 藏	Xizang	33092	1507	810	27875	26	19	2855
陕 西	Shaanxi	810083	12090	5044	767882	631	1118	23318
甘 肃	Gansu	288360	7031	2223	260726	120	85	18175
青 海	Qinghai	99784	2222	828	96187	63	65	419
宁 夏	Ningxia	136425	1579	409	133511	76	78	772
新 疆	Xinjiang	350433	13017	1927	307554	207	227	27501

主要统计指标解释

行政区划 指国家对行政区域的划分。根据有关法规规定，我国的行政区域划分如下：(1)全国分为省、自治区、直辖市；(2)省、自治区分为自治州、县、自治县、市；(3)自治州分为县、自治县、市；(4)县、自治县分为乡、民族乡、镇；(5)直辖市和较大的市分为区、县；(6)国家在必要时设立的特别行政区。

平均增长速度 平均增长速度表明社会经济现象在一个较长的时期内逐期平均增长变化的程度，它不能根据各个环比增长速度直接求得，但与平均发展速度之间存在着一定的数量关系：平均增长速度＝平均发展速度－1。

平均发展速度是一种根据环比发展速度计算的序时平均数，由于各时期对比的基础不同，所以计算平均发展速度不能采用一般的序时平均数的计算方法，计算方法分为水平法和累计法。水平法，又称几何平均法，即将环比发展速度按连乘法用几何平均数公式计算。累计法，也称方程法，根据一段时期内各年发展水平总和与基期水平的关系，列出方程式计算平均发展速度。水平法着重考虑最后一年所达到的发展水平；累计法着重考虑整个时期累计发展水平的总量。

本《年鉴》内所列的平均增长速度，除固定资产投资用“累计法”计算外，其余均用“水平法”计算。从某年到某年平均增长速度的年份，均不包括基期年在内。如建国四十三年以来的平均增长速度是以 1949 年为基期计算的，则写为 1950-1992 年平均增长速度，其余类推。

国民经济行业分类 自 2017 年年报和 2018 年定期报表开始使用新的《国民经济行业分类》(GB/T4754-2017)。该分类是由国家统计局组织修订，原国家质量监督检验检疫总局和中国国家标准化管理委员会于 2017 年 6 月 30 日发布。这次修订是在 2011 年分类标准的基础上，结合我国经济活动特点，参照联合国《全部经济活动的国际标准产业分类》（ISIC/Rev.4）进行的。修订后的《国民经济行业分类》（GB/T4754-2017）共有门类 20 个，大类 97 个，中类 473 个，小类 1382 个。

Explanatory Notes on Main Statistical Indicators

Divisions of Administrative Areas refer to the division of administrative areas by the State. The relative laws define the administrative division as follows: 1) the whole country is divided into provinces, autonomous regions and municipalities directly under the Central Government; 2) provinces and autonomous regions are further divided into autonomous prefectures, counties, autonomous counties and cities; 3) autonomous prefectures are further divided into counties, autonomous counties and cities; 4) counties and autonomous counties are further divided into townships, ethnic townships and towns; 5) municipalities directly under the Central Government and large cities are divided into districts and counties, 6) the State shall, when necessary, establish special administrative regions.

Average Annual Growth Rate shows the average growth rate of social and economic development during a longer period. It can not be directly calculated by chain based growth rate. The relation is:

Average growth rate = average speed of development – 1

Average speed of development is the time series average of speed which is obtained through chain-based calculation. Because the reference bases during the different periods are different, average speed of development can not be calculated by the general method. Level approach and accumulative approach for calculating average speed of development rate are applied. The "level approach", or geometric average approach, is derived by the formula of geometric average of the chain-based speeds of development by continuous multiplication. The other is called the "accumulative approach" or the "equation" method, which is derived by the summation of the actual figure of each year in the interval divided by the figure in the base year. The level approach focuses on the level of the last year, while the accumulative approach emphasizes the aggregate development for the entire duration.

The average annual growth rates listed in the *Yearbook* are calculated by the level approach except for the growth rate of investment in fixed assets. The base year is not listed in the duration for which average annual growth rates are computed. For instance, the average annual growth rate of the 43 years since 1949 is shown as the average annual growth rate of 1950-1992 without showing the base year 1949.

Industrial Classification of the National Economy The new *Industrial Classification of the National Economy* (GB/T 4754-2017) is introduced starting from the compilation of 2017 annual statistics and 2018 monthly or quarterly statistics. The revision, based on the 2011 classification, was organized by the National Bureau of Statistics taking into consideration of the characteristics of economic activities in China and the *International Standards of the Industrial Classification of All Economic Activities* (ISIC/Rev.4) of the United Nations. The new *Classification* was promulgated by the former National Administration of Quality Supervision, Inspection and Quarantine and the Standardization Administration of the People's Republic of China on June 30, 2017. The revised version of the *Industrial Classification of the National Economy* (GB/T 4754-2017) is composed of 20 sections, 97 divisions, 473 groups and 1382 classes.

2

人　口

Population

简 要 说 明

一、本篇资料的主要内容

本篇资料反映我国 2023 年及历年人口方面的基本情况，包括全国及 31 个省、自治区、直辖市的主要人口统计数据，如：全国历年人口数、城镇人口、乡村人口、出生率、死亡率、自然增长率；2023 年各地区人口数、人口负担系数、家庭户规模、人口受教育程度等。

二、本篇的资料来源

本篇资料由国家统计局人口和就业统计司整理。其中表 2−1 至 2−6 中，1981 年及以前数据为户籍统计数；1982、1990、2000、2010、2020 年数据为当年普查数据推算数；其余年份数据为年度人口抽样调查推算数据，部分年份数据根据人口普查数据进行了修订。表 2−7 为 2023 年全国人口变动情况抽样调查推算数据，表 2−8 至 2−15 为 2023 年全国人口变动情况抽样调查样本数据。

本篇各表如不做特殊说明，均未包括香港特别行政区、澳门特别行政区和台湾地区的人口数据。

三、本篇的统计调查方法

目前由国家统计局人口和就业统计司实施的人口统计调查有：

在逢“0”的年份进行全国人口普查；在逢“5”的年份进行全国 1%人口抽样调查；其余年份进行全国人口变动情况抽样调查，其样本量约占全国总人口的 1‰左右。人口抽样调查是以全国为总体，省级单位为次总体，采用分层、多阶段、整群概率比例抽样方法抽取样本。

Brief Introduction

I. Main Contents

Data in this chapter show the basic condition of the population in 2023 as well as in previous years for the whole nation and 31 provinces, autonomous regions and municipalities directly under the Central Government. They include the sizes of the national population, urban population, rural population, birth rates, death rates and natural growth rates over the years; as well as size, population dependency coefficient, average family household size and education attainments of the population by the end of 2023.

II. Sources of Data

Data in this chapter are prepared by the Department of Population and Employment Statistics of the National Bureau of Statistics. In tables 2-1 to 2-6, figures for 1981 and before are from household registrations; data for the year 1982, 1990, 2000, 2010 and 2020 are the census year estimates; the rest of the data covered in those tables are estimates from the annual national sample survey on population changes and data for selected years have been revised according to the census results. In table 2-7, data are estimates from the 2023 National Sample Survey on Population Changes. In tables 2-8 to 2-15, data are the sample data from the 2023 National Sample Survey on Population Changes.

Data in all the tables of this chapter do not include that from Hong Kong SAR, Macao SAR and Taiwan unless otherwise stated.

III. Statistical Survey Methods

The statistical surveys on population which are conducted by Department of Population and Employment Statistics of NBS are as follows:

The national population census is conducted in the year ending with 0; the national 1 percent population sample survey is conducted in the year ending with 5; sample surveys on population changes are conducted in the rest of the years which cover about 1 per thousand of the total population of the country. The sample survey on population change takes the whole nation as the population and each province, autonomous region or municipality as sub-populations, and the stratified multi-stage systematic PPS cluster sampling scheme is used.

2-1 人口数及构成
Population and Its Composition

单位：万人 (10 000 persons)

年 份 Year	总人口(年末) Total Population (year-end)	按性别分 By Gender				按城乡分 By Residence			
		男 Male		女 Female		城 镇 Urban		乡 村 Rural	
		人口数 Population	比重(%) Proportion	人口数 Population	比重(%) Proportion	人口数 Population	比重(%) Proportion	人口数 Population	比重(%) Proportion
1949	54167	28145	51.96	26022	48.04	5765	10.64	48402	89.36
1950	55196	28669	51.94	26527	48.06	6169	11.18	49027	88.82
1951	56300	29231	51.92	27069	48.08	6632	11.78	49668	88.22
1955	61465	31809	51.75	29656	48.25	8285	13.48	53180	86.52
1960	66207	34283	51.78	31924	48.22	13073	19.75	53134	80.25
1965	72538	37128	51.18	35410	48.82	13045	17.98	59493	82.02
1970	82992	42686	51.43	40306	48.57	14424	17.38	68568	82.62
1971	85229	43819	51.41	41410	48.59	14711	17.26	70518	82.74
1972	87177	44813	51.40	42364	48.60	14935	17.13	72242	82.87
1973	89211	45876	51.42	43335	48.58	15345	17.20	73866	82.80
1974	90859	46727	51.43	44132	48.57	15595	17.16	75264	82.84
1975	92420	47564	51.47	44856	48.53	16030	17.34	76390	82.66
1976	93717	48257	51.49	45460	48.51	16341	17.44	77376	82.56
1977	94974	48908	51.50	46066	48.50	16669	17.55	78305	82.45
1978	96259	49567	51.49	46692	48.51	17245	17.92	79014	82.08
1979	97542	50192	51.46	47350	48.54	18495	18.96	79047	81.04
1980	98705	50785	51.45	47920	48.55	19140	19.39	79565	80.61
1981	100072	51519	51.48	48553	48.52	20171	20.16	79901	79.84
1982	101654	52352	51.50	49302	48.50	21480	21.13	80174	78.87
1983	103008	53152	51.60	49856	48.40	22274	21.62	80734	78.38
1984	104357	53848	51.60	50509	48.40	24017	23.01	80340	76.99
1985	105851	54725	51.70	51126	48.30	25094	23.71	80757	76.29
1986	107507	55581	51.70	51926	48.30	26366	24.52	81141	75.48
1987	109300	56290	51.50	53010	48.50	27674	25.32	81626	74.68
1988	111026	57201	51.52	53825	48.48	28661	25.81	82365	74.19
1989	112704	58099	51.55	54605	48.45	29540	26.21	83164	73.79
1990	114333	58904	51.52	55429	48.48	30195	26.41	84138	73.59
1991	115823	59466	51.34	56357	48.66	31203	26.94	84620	73.06
1992	117171	59811	51.05	57360	48.95	32175	27.46	84996	72.54
1993	118517	60472	51.02	58045	48.98	33173	27.99	85344	72.01
1994	119850	61246	51.10	58604	48.90	34169	28.51	85681	71.49
1995	121121	61808	51.03	59313	48.97	35174	29.04	85947	70.96
1996	122389	62200	50.82	60189	49.18	37304	30.48	85085	69.52
1997	123626	63131	51.07	60495	48.93	39449	31.91	84177	68.09
1998	124761	63940	51.25	60821	48.75	41608	33.35	83153	66.65
1999	125786	64692	51.43	61094	48.57	43748	34.78	82038	65.22
2000	126743	65437	51.63	61306	48.37	45906	36.22	80837	63.78
2001	127627	65672	51.46	61955	48.54	48064	37.66	79563	62.34
2002	128453	66115	51.47	62338	48.53	50212	39.09	78241	60.91
2003	129227	66556	51.50	62671	48.50	52376	40.53	76851	59.47
2004	129988	66976	51.52	63012	48.48	54283	41.76	75705	58.24
2005	130756	67375	51.53	63381	48.47	56212	42.99	74544	57.01
2006	131448	67728	51.52	63720	48.48	58288	44.34	73160	55.66
2007	132129	68048	51.50	64081	48.50	60633	45.89	71496	54.11
2008	132802	68357	51.47	64445	48.53	62403	46.99	70399	53.01
2009	133450	68647	51.44	64803	48.56	64512	48.34	68938	51.66
2010	134091	68748	51.27	65343	48.73	66978	49.95	67113	50.05
2011	134916	69161	51.26	65755	48.74	69927	51.83	64989	48.17
2012	135922	69660	51.25	66262	48.75	72175	53.10	63747	46.90
2013	136726	70063	51.24	66663	48.76	74502	54.49	62224	45.51
2014	137646	70522	51.23	67124	48.77	76738	55.75	60908	44.25
2015	138326	70857	51.22	67469	48.78	79302	57.33	59024	42.67
2016	139232	71307	51.21	67925	48.79	81924	58.84	57308	41.16
2017	140011	71650	51.17	68361	48.83	84343	60.24	55668	39.76
2018	140541	71864	51.13	68677	48.87	86433	61.50	54108	38.50
2019	141008	72039	51.09	68969	48.91	88426	62.71	52582	37.29
2020	141212	72357	51.24	68855	48.76	90220	63.89	50992	36.11
2021	141260	72311	51.19	68949	48.81	91425	64.72	49835	35.28
2022	141175	72206	51.15	68969	48.85	92071	65.22	49104	34.78
2023	140967	72032	51.10	68935	48.90	93267	66.16	47700	33.84

注：1.1981年及以前数据为户籍统计数；1982、1990、2000、2010、2020年数据为当年人口普查数据推算数；其余年份数据为年度人口抽样调查推算数据(以下相关表同)。

2.总人口和按性别分人口中包括现役军人，按城乡分人口中现役军人计入城镇人口。

a) Figures before and of 1981 are from household registrations; for years of 1982,1990,2000, 2010 and 2020 are the census year estimates;and figures for the rest of years are estimated on the basis of the annual national sample survey of population. The same applies to the relevant following tables.

b) Total population and population by gender include the servicemen of the Chinese People's Liberation Army, who are classified as urban population in population by residence.

2-2 人口出生率、死亡率和自然增长率
Birth Rate, Death Rate and Natural Growth Rate of Population

单位：‰ (‰)

年 份 Year	出生率 Birth Rate	死亡率 Death Rate	自然增长率 Natural Growth Rate
1978	18.25	6.25	12.00
1979	17.82	6.21	11.61
1980	18.21	6.34	11.87
1981	20.91	6.36	14.55
1982	22.28	6.60	15.68
1983	20.19	6.90	13.29
1984	19.90	6.82	13.08
1985	21.04	6.78	14.26
1986	22.43	6.86	15.57
1987	23.33	6.72	16.61
1988	22.37	6.64	15.73
1989	21.58	6.54	15.04
1990	21.06	6.67	14.39
1991	19.68	6.70	12.98
1992	18.24	6.64	11.60
1993	18.09	6.64	11.45
1994	17.70	6.49	11.21
1995	17.12	6.57	10.55
1996	16.98	6.56	10.42
1997	16.57	6.51	10.06
1998	15.64	6.50	9.14
1999	14.64	6.46	8.18
2000	14.03	6.45	7.58
2001	13.38	6.43	6.95
2002	12.86	6.41	6.45
2003	12.41	6.40	6.01
2004	12.29	6.42	5.87
2005	12.40	6.51	5.89
2006	12.09	6.81	5.28
2007	12.10	6.93	5.17
2008	12.14	7.06	5.08
2009	11.95	7.08	4.87
2010	11.90	7.11	4.79
2011	13.27	7.14	6.13
2012	14.57	7.13	7.43
2013	13.03	7.13	5.90
2014	13.83	7.12	6.71
2015	11.99	7.07	4.93
2016	13.57	7.04	6.53
2017	12.64	7.06	5.58
2018	10.86	7.08	3.78
2019	10.41	7.09	3.32
2020	8.52	7.07	1.45
2021	7.52	7.18	0.34
2022	6.77	7.37	-0.60
2023	6.39	7.87	-1.48

2-3 平均预期寿命
Life Expectancy at Birth

单位：岁 (year)

年份 Year	合计 Total	男 Male	女 Female
1981	67.77	66.28	69.27
1990	68.55	66.84	70.47
1996	70.80		
2000	71.40	69.63	73.33
2005	72.95	70.83	75.25
2010	74.83	72.38	77.37
2015	76.34	73.64	79.43
2020	77.93	75.37	80.88

2-4 人口年龄结构和抚养比
Age Composition and Dependency Ratio of Population

单位：万人 (10 000 persons)

年份 Year	总人口(年末) Total Population (year-end)	按年龄组分 By Age						总抚养比 (%) Gross Dependency Ratio(%)	少儿抚养比 (%) Children Dependency Ratio(%)	老年抚养比 (%) Elderly Dependency Ratio(%)
		0-14岁 Aged 0-14		15-64岁 Aged 15-64		65岁及以上 Aged 65 and Over				
		人口数 Population	比重(%) Proportion	人口数 Population	比重(%) Proportion	人口数 Population	比重(%) Proportion			
1982	101654	34146	33.6	62517	61.5	4991	4.9	62.6	54.6	8.0
1987	109300	31347	28.7	71985	65.9	5968	5.4	51.8	43.5	8.3
1990	114333	31659	27.7	76306	66.7	6368	5.6	49.8	41.5	8.3
1991	115823	32095	27.7	76791	66.3	6938	6.0	50.8	41.8	9.0
1992	117171	32339	27.6	77614	66.2	7218	6.2	51.0	41.7	9.3
1993	118517	32177	27.2	79051	66.7	7289	6.2	49.9	40.7	9.2
1994	119850	32360	27.0	79868	66.6	7622	6.4	50.1	40.5	9.5
1995	121121	32218	26.6	81393	67.2	7510	6.2	48.8	39.6	9.2
1996	122389	32311	26.4	82245	67.2	7833	6.4	48.8	39.3	9.5
1997	123626	32093	26.0	83448	67.5	8085	6.5	48.1	38.5	9.7
1998	124761	32064	25.7	84338	67.6	8359	6.7	47.9	38.0	9.9
1999	125786	31950	25.4	85157	67.7	8679	6.9	47.7	37.5	10.2
2000	126743	29012	22.9	88910	70.1	8821	7.0	42.6	32.6	9.9
2001	127627	28716	22.5	89849	70.4	9062	7.1	42.0	32.0	10.1
2002	128453	28774	22.4	90302	70.3	9377	7.3	42.2	31.9	10.4
2003	129227	28559	22.1	90976	70.4	9692	7.5	42.0	31.4	10.7
2004	129988	27947	21.5	92184	70.9	9857	7.6	41.0	30.3	10.7
2005	130756	26504	20.3	94197	72.0	10055	7.7	38.8	28.1	10.7
2006	131448	25961	19.8	95068	72.3	10419	7.9	38.3	27.3	11.0
2007	132129	25660	19.4	95833	72.5	10636	8.1	37.9	26.8	11.1
2008	132802	25166	19.0	96680	72.7	10956	8.3	37.4	26.0	11.3
2009	133450	24659	18.5	97484	73.0	11307	8.5	36.9	25.3	11.6
2010	134091	22259	16.6	99938	74.5	11894	8.9	34.2	22.3	11.9
2011	134916	22261	16.5	100378	74.4	12277	9.1	34.4	22.1	12.3
2012	135922	22427	16.5	100718	74.1	12777	9.4	34.9	22.2	12.7
2013	136726	22423	16.4	101041	73.9	13262	9.7	35.3	22.2	13.1
2014	137646	22712	16.5	101032	73.4	13902	10.1	36.2	22.5	13.7
2015	138326	22824	16.5	100978	73.0	14524	10.5	37.0	22.6	14.3
2016	139232	23252	16.7	100943	72.5	15037	10.8	37.9	22.9	15.0
2017	140011	23522	16.8	100528	71.8	15961	11.4	39.3	23.4	15.9
2018	140541	23751	16.9	100065	71.2	16724	11.9	40.4	23.7	16.8
2019	141008	23689	16.8	99552	70.6	17767	12.6	41.5	23.8	17.8
2020	141212	25277	17.9	96871	68.6	19064	13.5	45.9	26.2	19.7
2021	141260	24678	17.5	96526	68.3	20056	14.2	46.3	25.6	20.8
2022	141175	23908	16.9	96289	68.2	20978	14.9	46.6	24.8	21.8
2023	140967	23063	16.3	96228	68.3	21676	15.4	46.5	24.0	22.5

2-5 分地区年末人口数
Population at Year-end by Region

单位：万人 (10 000 persons)

地 区	Region	2014	2015	2016	2017	2018	2019	2020	2021	2022	2023
全 国	**National Total**	**137646**	**138326**	**139232**	**140011**	**140541**	**141008**	**141212**	**141260**	**141175**	**140967**
北 京	Beijing	2171	2188	2195	2194	2192	2190	2189	2189	2184	2186
天 津	Tianjin	1429	1439	1443	1410	1383	1385	1387	1373	1363	1364
河 北	Hebei	7323	7345	7375	7409	7426	7447	7464	7448	7420	7393
山 西	Shanxi	3528	3519	3514	3510	3502	3497	3490	3480	3481	3466
内蒙古	Inner Mongolia	2449	2440	2436	2433	2422	2415	2403	2400	2401	2396
辽 宁	Liaoning	4358	4338	4327	4312	4291	4277	4255	4229	4197	4182
吉 林	Jilin	2642	2613	2567	2526	2484	2448	2399	2375	2348	2339
黑龙江	Heilongjiang	3608	3529	3463	3399	3327	3255	3171	3125	3099	3062
上 海	Shanghai	2467	2458	2467	2466	2475	2481	2488	2489	2475	2487
江 苏	Jiangsu	8281	8315	8381	8423	8446	8469	8477	8505	8515	8526
浙 江	Zhejiang	5890	5985	6072	6170	6273	6375	6468	6540	6577	6627
安 徽	Anhui	5997	6011	6033	6057	6076	6092	6105	6113	6127	6121
福 建	Fujian	3945	3984	4016	4065	4104	4137	4161	4187	4188	4183
江 西	Jiangxi	4480	4485	4496	4511	4513	4516	4519	4517	4528	4515
山 东	Shandong	9808	9866	9973	10033	10077	10106	10165	10170	10163	10123
河 南	Henan	9645	9701	9778	9829	9864	9901	9941	9883	9872	9815
湖 北	Hubei	5816	5850	5885	5904	5917	5927	5745	5830	5844	5838
湖 南	Hunan	6611	6615	6625	6633	6635	6640	6645	6622	6604	6568
广 东	Guangdong	11489	11678	11908	12141	12348	12489	12624	12684	12657	12706
广 西	Guangxi	4770	4811	4857	4907	4947	4982	5019	5037	5047	5027
海 南	Hainan	936	945	957	972	982	995	1012	1020	1027	1043
重 庆	Chongqing	3043	3070	3110	3144	3163	3188	3209	3212	3213	3191
四 川	Sichuan	8139	8196	8251	8289	8321	8351	8371	8372	8374	8368
贵 州	Guizhou	3677	3708	3758	3803	3822	3848	3858	3852	3856	3865
云 南	Yunnan	4653	4663	4677	4693	4703	4714	4722	4690	4693	4673
西 藏	Xizang	325	330	340	349	354	361	366	366	364	365
陕 西	Shaanxi	3827	3846	3874	3904	3931	3944	3955	3954	3956	3952
甘 肃	Gansu	2531	2523	2520	2522	2515	2509	2501	2490	2492	2465
青 海	Qinghai	576	577	582	586	587	590	593	594	595	594
宁 夏	Ningxia	678	684	695	705	710	717	721	725	728	729
新 疆	Xinjiang	2325	2385	2428	2480	2520	2559	2590	2589	2587	2598

2–6 分地区年末城镇人口比重
Proportion of Urban Population at Year-end by Region

单位：% (%)

地 区	Region	2014	2015	2016	2017	2018	2019	2020	2021	2022	2023
全 国	**National Total**	**55.75**	**57.33**	**58.84**	**60.24**	**61.50**	**62.71**	**63.89**	**64.72**	**65.22**	**66.16**
北 京	Beijing	86.50	86.71	86.76	86.93	87.09	87.35	87.55	87.50	87.57	87.83
天 津	Tianjin	82.55	82.88	83.27	83.57	83.95	84.31	84.70	84.88	85.11	85.49
河 北	Hebei	49.36	51.67	53.87	55.74	57.33	58.77	60.07	61.14	61.65	62.77
山 西	Shanxi	54.30	55.87	57.27	58.59	59.85	61.29	62.53	63.42	63.96	64.97
内蒙古	Inner Mongolia	60.97	62.09	63.40	64.60	65.51	66.46	67.48	68.21	68.60	69.58
辽 宁	Liaoning	67.05	68.05	68.87	69.49	70.26	71.21	72.14	72.81	73.00	73.51
吉 林	Jilin	56.81	57.64	58.75	59.71	60.85	61.63	62.64	63.36	63.72	64.73
黑龙江	Heilongjiang	59.22	60.47	61.09	61.90	63.46	64.62	65.61	65.69	66.21	67.11
上 海	Shanghai	89.30	88.53	89.00	89.10	89.13	89.22	89.30	89.30	89.33	89.46
江 苏	Jiangsu	65.70	67.49	68.93	70.18	71.19	72.47	73.44	73.94	74.42	75.04
浙 江	Zhejiang	64.96	66.32	67.72	68.91	70.02	71.58	72.17	72.66	73.38	74.23
安 徽	Anhui	49.31	50.97	52.62	54.29	55.65	57.02	58.33	59.39	60.15	61.51
福 建	Fujian	61.99	63.22	64.39	65.78	66.98	67.87	68.75	69.70	70.11	71.04
江 西	Jiangxi	50.55	52.30	53.99	55.70	57.34	59.07	60.44	61.46	62.07	63.13
山 东	Shandong	54.77	56.97	59.13	60.79	61.46	61.86	63.05	63.94	64.54	65.53
河 南	Henan	45.05	47.02	48.78	50.56	52.24	54.01	55.43	56.45	57.07	58.08
湖 北	Hubei	55.73	57.18	58.57	59.88	61.00	61.83	62.89	64.09	64.67	65.47
湖 南	Hunan	48.98	50.79	52.70	54.62	56.09	57.45	58.76	59.71	60.31	61.16
广 东	Guangdong	68.62	69.51	70.15	70.74	71.81	72.65	74.15	74.63	74.79	75.42
广 西	Guangxi	46.54	47.99	49.24	50.59	51.82	52.98	54.20	55.08	55.65	56.78
海 南	Hainan	53.30	54.91	56.70	58.04	59.13	59.37	60.27	60.97	61.49	62.46
重 庆	Chongqing	59.74	61.47	63.33	65.00	66.61	68.24	69.46	70.32	70.96	71.67
四 川	Sichuan	46.51	48.27	50.00	51.78	53.50	55.36	56.73	57.82	58.35	59.49
贵 州	Guizhou	40.24	42.96	45.56	47.76	49.54	51.48	53.15	54.33	54.81	55.94
云 南	Yunnan	41.21	42.93	44.64	46.29	47.44	48.67	50.05	51.05	51.72	52.92
西 藏	Xizang	26.23	28.87	31.57	33.38	33.80	34.51	35.73	36.61	37.39	38.88
陕 西	Shaanxi	53.01	54.74	56.39	58.07	59.65	61.28	62.66	63.63	64.02	65.16
甘 肃	Gansu	42.28	44.24	46.07	48.12	49.69	50.70	52.23	53.33	54.19	55.49
青 海	Qinghai	50.84	51.67	53.55	55.45	57.27	58.78	60.08	61.02	61.43	62.80
宁 夏	Ningxia	54.82	56.98	58.74	60.95	62.15	63.63	64.96	66.04	66.34	67.31
新 疆	Xinjiang	46.79	48.78	50.42	51.90	54.01	55.51	56.53	57.26	57.89	59.24

2-7 分地区人口的城乡构成和出生率、死亡率、自然增长率（2023年）
Total Population by Urban and Rural Residence, Birth Rate, Death Rate, Natural Growth Rate and by Region (2023)

地 区	Region	总人口(年末)(万人) Total Population (year-end) (10 000 persons)	城镇人口 Urban Population		乡村人口 Rural Population		出生率(‰) Birth Rate (‰)	死亡率(‰) Death Rate (‰)	自然增长率(‰) Natural Growth Rate (‰)
			人口数 Population	比重（%） Proportion	人口数 Population	比重（%） Proportion			
全 国	**National Total**	**140967**	**93267**	**66.16**	**47700**	**33.84**	**6.39**	**7.87**	**-1.48**
北 京	Beijing	2186	1920	87.83	266	12.17	5.63	6.13	-0.50
天 津	Tianjin	1364	1166	85.49	198	14.51	4.47	7.04	-2.57
河 北	Hebei	7393	4641	62.77	2752	37.23	5.54	8.33	-2.79
山 西	Shanxi	3466	2252	64.97	1214	35.03	6.13	8.38	-2.25
内蒙古	Inner Mongolia	2396	1667	69.58	729	30.42	5.00	8.42	-3.42
辽 宁	Liaoning	4182	3074	73.51	1108	26.49	4.06	9.69	-5.63
吉 林	Jilin	2339	1514	64.73	825	35.27	3.76	9.17	-5.41
黑龙江	Heilongjiang	3062	2055	67.11	1007	32.89	2.92	9.84	-6.92
上 海	Shanghai	2487	2225	89.46	262	10.54	3.95	6.37	-2.42
江 苏	Jiangsu	8526	6398	75.04	2128	24.96	4.81	7.55	-2.74
浙 江	Zhejiang	6627	4919	74.23	1708	25.77	5.80	6.66	-0.86
安 徽	Anhui	6121	3765	61.51	2356	38.49	6.45	8.56	-2.11
福 建	Fujian	4183	2972	71.04	1211	28.96	6.81	6.95	-0.14
江 西	Jiangxi	4515	2850	63.13	1665	36.87	6.52	7.36	-0.84
山 东	Shandong	10123	6634	65.53	3489	34.47	6.01	8.19	-2.18
河 南	Henan	9815	5701	58.08	4114	41.92	7.06	8.00	-0.94
湖 北	Hubei	5838	3822	65.47	2016	34.53	5.48	8.63	-3.15
湖 南	Hunan	6568	4017	61.16	2551	38.84	6.00	9.08	-3.08
广 东	Guangdong	12706	9583	75.42	3123	24.58	8.12	5.36	2.76
广 西	Guangxi	5027	2854	56.78	2173	43.22	8.04	7.62	0.42
海 南	Hainan	1043	651	62.46	392	37.54	9.28	6.47	2.81
重 庆	Chongqing	3191	2287	71.67	904	28.33	5.58	8.90	-3.32
四 川	Sichuan	8368	4978	59.49	3390	40.51	6.32	9.44	-3.12
贵 州	Guizhou	3865	2162	55.94	1703	44.06	10.65	7.77	2.88
云 南	Yunnan	4673	2473	52.92	2200	47.08	8.22	8.61	-0.39
西 藏	Xizang	365	142	38.88	223	61.12	13.72	5.76	7.96
陕 西	Shaanxi	3952	2575	65.16	1377	34.84	6.83	8.14	-1.31
甘 肃	Gansu	2465	1368	55.49	1097	44.51	7.71	9.04	-1.33
青 海	Qinghai	594	373	62.80	221	37.20	9.25	7.57	1.68
宁 夏	Ningxia	729	491	67.31	238	32.69	10.02	6.59	3.43
新 疆	Xinjiang	2598	1539	59.24	1059	40.76	7.10	6.17	0.93

注：1.本表数据根据2023年全国人口变动情况抽样调查数据推算。
2.全国总人口包括现役军人数，分地区数据中未包括。

a) Data in the table are estimates from the 2023 National Sample Survey on Population Changes.
b) The military personnel were included in the national total population, but were not included in the population by region.

2–8 按年龄和性别分人口数（2023年）
Population by Age and Gender (2023)

本表是2023年全国人口变动情况抽样调查样本数据，抽样比为1.051‰。
Data in this table are obtained from the 2023 National Sample Survey on Population Changes. The sampling fraction is 1.051‰.

年龄	Age	人口数（人） Population (person)	男 Male	女 Female	占总人口比重（%） Percentage to Total Population (%)	男 Male	女 Female	性别比 (女=100) Sex Ratio (Female=100)
总计	**Total**	**1482230**	**756458**	**725772**	**100.00**	**51.04**	**48.96**	**104.23**
0–4岁	0-4 years	57537	30045	27492	3.88	2.03	1.85	109.28
5–9岁	5-9 years	90498	47754	42744	6.11	3.22	2.88	111.72
10–14岁	10-14 years	94775	50567	44208	6.39	3.41	2.98	114.39
15–19岁	15-19 years	85813	45956	39858	5.79	3.10	2.69	115.30
20–24岁	20-24 years	73696	39213	34483	4.97	2.65	2.33	113.72
25–29岁	25-29 years	84358	44602	39756	5.69	3.01	2.68	112.19
30–34岁	30-34 years	113258	58895	54362	7.64	3.97	3.67	108.34
35–39岁	35-39 years	118381	60757	57624	7.99	4.10	3.89	105.44
40–44岁	40-44 years	101291	51953	49338	6.83	3.51	3.33	105.30
45–49岁	45-49 years	102401	52120	50281	6.91	3.52	3.39	103.66
50–54岁	50-54 years	126579	63944	62634	8.54	4.31	4.23	102.09
55–59岁	55-59 years	120926	60470	60456	8.16	4.08	4.08	100.02
60–64岁	60-64 years	84465	41879	42585	5.70	2.83	2.87	98.34
65–69岁	65-69 years	81497	40202	41295	5.50	2.71	2.79	97.35
70–74岁	70-74 years	64545	31014	33532	4.35	2.09	2.26	92.49
75–79岁	75-79 years	39405	18568	20837	2.66	1.25	1.41	89.11
80–84岁	80-84 years	23524	10616	12907	1.59	0.72	0.87	82.25
85–89岁	85-89 years	13443	5662	7781	0.91	0.38	0.52	72.77
90–94岁	90-94 years	4885	1904	2981	0.33	0.13	0.20	63.86
95岁及以上	95 years and over	953	334	619	0.06	0.02	0.04	53.92

注：由于各地区数据采用加权汇总的方法，全国(部分省区)人口变动情况抽样调查样本数据合计与各分项或分组相加略有误差(以下相关表同)。

a) Data by region are calculated by the method of weighted sum, total data of the National (some Provinces and Autonomous Regions) Sample Survey on Population Changes is not equal to the sum of each item or group. The following related tables are the same.

2–9 分地区户数、人口数、性别比和户规模（2023年）
Household, Population, Sex Ratio and Household Size by Region (2023)

本表是2023年全国人口变动情况抽样调查样本数据，抽样比为1.051‰。
Data in this table are obtained from the 2023 National Sample Survey on Population Changes. The sampling fraction is 1.051‰.

地 区	Region	户数（户） Number of Households (household)	家庭户 Family Households	集体户 Collective Households	人口数（人） Population (person)	男 Male	女 Female	性别比（女=100） Sex Ratio (Female=100)
全 国	**National Total**	**522152**	**507031**	**15121**	**1482230**	**756458**	**725772**	**104.23**
北 京	Beijing	9158	8759	399	23018	11718	11299	103.71
天 津	Tianjin	5668	5381	288	14362	7343	7019	104.62
河 北	Hebei	26612	26078	534	77846	38660	39186	98.66
山 西	Shanxi	13257	12941	316	36496	18634	17862	104.33
内蒙古	Inner Mongolia	9985	9801	184	25229	12921	12308	104.97
辽 宁	Liaoning	18189	17857	332	44035	21693	22342	97.09
吉 林	Jilin	9964	9685	279	24629	12287	12342	99.55
黑龙江	Heilongjiang	13956	13781	176	32242	16111	16131	99.87
上 海	Shanghai	10373	9895	479	26187	13555	12632	107.31
江 苏	Jiangsu	31513	30466	1047	89776	45505	44271	102.79
浙 江	Zhejiang	26431	25309	1121	69780	36423	33358	109.19
安 徽	Anhui	22919	22175	743	64452	32922	31530	104.41
福 建	Fujian	15006	14500	505	44046	22785	21261	107.17
江 西	Jiangxi	15115	14744	371	47541	24563	22978	106.90
山 东	Shandong	39287	38718	570	106592	53864	52727	102.16
河 南	Henan	34058	33314	745	103349	51822	51527	100.57
湖 北	Hubei	21204	20686	518	61472	31477	29996	104.94
湖 南	Hunan	23935	23318	618	69159	35420	33739	104.98
广 东	Guangdong	45338	43317	2021	133790	70433	63357	111.17
广 西	Guangxi	16686	16094	592	52933	27367	25566	107.05
海 南	Hainan	3180	3099	80	10982	5831	5152	113.18
重 庆	Chongqing	12534	12288	246	33600	16928	16673	101.53
四 川	Sichuan	31420	30629	790	88112	44450	43662	101.81
贵 州	Guizhou	12615	12115	501	40697	20820	19877	104.75
云 南	Yunnan	15412	14887	525	49205	25289	23916	105.74
西 藏	Xizang	1100	1053	47	3843	2023	1820	111.14
陕 西	Shaanxi	15304	14844	460	41613	21234	20379	104.19
甘 肃	Gansu	8431	8187	244	25956	13175	12780	103.09
青 海	Qinghai	2051	1984	68	6255	3145	3110	101.13
宁 夏	Ningxia	2557	2461	97	7676	3903	3773	103.43
新 疆	Xinjiang	8893	8668	225	27356	14157	13199	107.26

2-9 续表 continued

地 区	Region	家庭户人口数(人) Family Household Population (person)	男 Male	女 Female	集体户人口数(人) Collective Household Population (person)	男 Male	女 Female	平均家庭户规模(人/户) Average Family Size (person/household)
全 国	**National Total**	**1421022**	**722294**	**698728**	**61208**	**34163**	**27044**	**2.80**
北 京	Beijing	21540	10826	10714	1478	893	585	2.46
天 津	Tianjin	13501	6871	6630	862	472	389	2.51
河 北	Hebei	75508	37407	38102	2337	1253	1084	2.90
山 西	Shanxi	35186	17935	17251	1310	700	610	2.72
内蒙古	Inner Mongolia	24349	12476	11873	881	445	435	2.48
辽 宁	Liaoning	42746	21014	21732	1289	679	611	2.39
吉 林	Jilin	23760	11878	11882	869	408	460	2.45
黑龙江	Heilongjiang	31447	15587	15859	795	523	272	2.28
上 海	Shanghai	24264	12324	11939	1923	1231	693	2.45
江 苏	Jiangsu	85280	42646	42634	4496	2860	1637	2.80
浙 江	Zhejiang	66113	34100	32013	3667	2323	1344	2.61
安 徽	Anhui	61692	31333	30359	2760	1589	1171	2.78
福 建	Fujian	41857	21567	20291	2188	1218	970	2.89
江 西	Jiangxi	45775	23782	21993	1767	782	985	3.10
山 东	Shandong	104181	52821	51360	2410	1043	1367	2.69
河 南	Henan	99975	49877	50098	3373	1944	1429	3.00
湖 北	Hubei	59071	30121	28950	2401	1356	1045	2.86
湖 南	Hunan	66390	34058	32332	2769	1362	1407	2.85
广 东	Guangdong	126395	65907	60488	7395	4526	2869	2.92
广 西	Guangxi	50214	25978	24236	2719	1389	1330	3.12
海 南	Hainan	10704	5699	5005	279	132	147	3.45
重 庆	Chongqing	32302	16100	16202	1299	828	470	2.63
四 川	Sichuan	84818	42804	42014	3294	1646	1648	2.77
贵 州	Guizhou	38880	19820	19059	1817	1000	817	3.21
云 南	Yunnan	46936	24190	22746	2270	1099	1170	3.15
西 藏	Xizang	3671	1932	1739	172	91	81	3.49
陕 西	Shaanxi	39917	20368	19549	1696	866	830	2.69
甘 肃	Gansu	24841	12556	12284	1115	619	496	3.03
青 海	Qinghai	6003	3008	2995	252	137	115	3.03
宁 夏	Ningxia	7308	3702	3606	368	201	168	2.97
新 疆	Xinjiang	26401	13608	12792	955	549	406	3.05

2-10 分地区分性别、户口登记状况的人口(2023年)
Population by Gender, Household Registration Status and Region (2023)

本表是2023年全国人口变动情况抽样调查样本数据，抽样比为1.051‰。
Data in this table are obtained from the 2023 National Sample Survey on Population Changes. The sampling fraction is 1.051‰.

单位：人 (person)

地区	Region	人口数 Population			住本乡、镇、街道，户口在本乡、镇、街道 Residing in the Townships, Towns and Street Communities with Permanent Household Registration There		
		合计 Total	男 Male	女 Female	小计 Sub-total	男 Male	女 Female
全国	**National Total**	**1482230**	**756458**	**725772**	**1065913**	**543654**	**522259**
北京	Beijing	23018	11718	11299	10356	5211	5146
天津	Tianjin	14362	7343	7019	9390	4815	4575
河北	Hebei	77846	38660	39186	62331	31360	30971
山西	Shanxi	36496	18634	17862	26234	13423	12811
内蒙古	Inner Mongolia	25229	12921	12308	15672	8086	7586
辽宁	Liaoning	44035	21693	22342	31296	15572	15724
吉林	Jilin	24629	12287	12342	16102	8188	7914
黑龙江	Heilongjiang	32242	16111	16131	25922	12927	12995
上海	Shanghai	26187	13555	12632	12005	6040	5965
江苏	Jiangsu	89776	45505	44271	64047	32202	31844
浙江	Zhejiang	69780	36423	33358	41645	20983	20661
安徽	Anhui	64452	32922	31530	46884	24150	22734
福建	Fujian	44046	22785	21261	27872	14091	13781
江西	Jiangxi	47541	24563	22978	36504	19064	17440
山东	Shandong	106592	53864	52727	82984	42095	40889
河南	Henan	103349	51822	51527	85136	42706	42430
湖北	Hubei	61472	31477	29996	45140	23382	21758
湖南	Hunan	69159	35420	33739	53576	27796	25780
广东	Guangdong	133790	70433	63357	82766	42225	40540
广西	Guangxi	52933	27367	25566	41308	21557	19751
海南	Hainan	10982	5831	5152	8495	4596	3899
重庆	Chongqing	33600	16928	16673	21271	10800	10471
四川	Sichuan	88112	44450	43662	63780	32475	31305
贵州	Guizhou	40697	20820	19877	31321	16192	15130
云南	Yunnan	49205	25289	23916	38786	20197	18589
西藏	Xizang	3843	2023	1820	3159	1643	1516
陕西	Shaanxi	41613	21234	20379	31364	16116	15248
甘肃	Gansu	25956	13175	12780	20191	10234	9957
青海	Qinghai	6255	3145	3110	4651	2341	2310
宁夏	Ningxia	7676	3903	3773	4787	2409	2378
新疆	Xinjiang	27356	14157	13199	20939	10779	10160

2-10 续表 continued

单位：人 (person)

地 区	Region	住本乡、镇、街道，户口在外乡、镇、街道，离开户口登记地半年以上 Residing in Townships, Towns and Street Communities, with Permanent Household Registration Elsewhere and Away from Registration Place For More Than 6 Months			住本乡、镇、街道，户口待定 Residing in Townships, Towns and Street Communities, with Place of Permanent Household Registration Unsettled			居住在港澳台或国外，户口在本乡、镇、街道 Residing in Hong Kong SAR, Macao SAR and Taiwan or abroad, with Permanent Household Registration in Townships,Towns and Street Communities		
		小 计 Sub-total	男 Male	女 Female	小 计 Sub-total	男 Male	女 Female	小 计 Sub-total	男 Male	女 Female
全 国	**National Total**	**410308**	**209593**	**200716**	**2823**	**1378**	**1445**	**3185**	**1833**	**1352**
北 京	Beijing	12527	6448	6079	37	18	19	97	41	55
天 津	Tianjin	4929	2510	2418	13	6	8	31	13	18
河 北	Hebei	15414	7242	8172	54	23	31	47	34	13
山 西	Shanxi	10185	5163	5022	36	23	13	41	25	16
内蒙古	Inner Mongolia	9516	4811	4705	21	13	9	20	11	9
辽 宁	Liaoning	12502	6008	6494	76	31	45	161	82	80
吉 林	Jilin	8406	4021	4385	11	6	5	110	71	39
黑龙江	Heilongjiang	6186	3125	3061	61	28	33	72	30	42
上 海	Shanghai	13947	7411	6536	45	16	29	191	88	103
江 苏	Jiangsu	25474	13172	12301	95	38	57	160	92	68
浙 江	Zhejiang	27609	15155	12453	199	115	85	328	170	158
安 徽	Anhui	17409	8693	8716	93	39	54	65	40	25
福 建	Fujian	15241	8156	7085	141	79	62	792	459	333
江 西	Jiangxi	10950	5462	5488	68	28	40	19	9	9
山 东	Shandong	23186	11520	11666	233	127	106	188	123	66
河 南	Henan	17989	8977	9013	100	39	61	123	100	23
湖 北	Hubei	16209	8027	8182	66	36	30	57	31	26
湖 南	Hunan	15383	7504	7879	125	63	62	75	57	18
广 东	Guangdong	50261	27778	22483	535	313	222	228	117	111
广 西	Guangxi	11462	5729	5733	120	57	63	43	24	19
海 南	Hainan	2448	1219	1229	31	13	18	9	3	6
重 庆	Chongqing	12255	6094	6161	29	11	17	46	23	23
四 川	Sichuan	24129	11853	12276	101	49	52	102	73	29
贵 州	Guizhou	9236	4569	4667	113	45	68	27	15	11
云 南	Yunnan	10300	5031	5269	56	23	33	63	38	25
西 藏	Xizang	673	374	299	11	6	5			
陕 西	Shaanxi	10041	5014	5027	165	71	94	42	32	10
甘 肃	Gansu	5646	2912	2734	107	22	85	11	7	4
青 海	Qinghai	1584	794	790	16	8	9	3	2	1
宁 夏	Ningxia	2880	1488	1392	6	4	3	3	3	1
新 疆	Xinjiang	6331	3331	3000	54	27	27	32	20	12

2–11 分地区人口年龄构成和抚养比（2023年）
Age Composition and Dependency Ratio of Population by Region (2023)

本表是2023年全国人口变动情况抽样调查样本数据，抽样比为1.051‰。
Data in this table are obtained from the 2023 National Sample Survey on Population Changes. The sampling fraction is 1.051‰.

地区	Region	人口数（人） Population (person)	0–14岁 Aged 0-14	15–64岁 Aged 15-64	65岁及以上 Aged 65 and Over	总抚养比（%） Gross Dependency Ratio (%)	少年儿童抚养比 Children Dependency Ratio	老年人口抚养比 Elderly Dependency Ratio
全　国	**National Total**	**1482230**	**242810**	**1011168**	**228252**	**46.59**	**24.01**	**22.57**
北　京	Beijing	23018	2764	16603	3650	38.63	16.65	21.98
天　津	Tianjin	14362	1800	9990	2572	43.76	18.02	25.75
河　北	Hebei	77846	13865	51341	12640	51.63	27.01	24.62
山　西	Shanxi	36496	5449	25498	5549	43.13	21.37	21.76
内蒙古	Inner Mongolia	25229	3249	18081	3899	39.53	17.97	21.56
辽　宁	Liaoning	44035	4456	30307	9273	45.30	14.70	30.60
吉　林	Jilin	24629	2538	17497	4594	40.76	14.51	26.26
黑龙江	Heilongjiang	32242	2843	23333	6065	38.18	12.19	25.99
上　海	Shanghai	26187	2509	18555	5123	41.13	13.52	27.61
江　苏	Jiangsu	89776	12186	61022	16569	47.12	19.97	27.15
浙　江	Zhejiang	69780	8794	50231	10756	38.92	17.51	21.41
安　徽	Anhui	64452	11183	43041	10228	49.75	25.98	23.76
福　建	Fujian	44046	7849	30636	5561	43.77	25.62	18.15
江　西	Jiangxi	47541	8959	32171	6411	47.78	27.85	19.93
山　东	Shandong	106592	18426	69589	18577	53.17	26.48	26.70
河　南	Henan	103349	21014	66946	15389	54.38	31.39	22.99
湖　北	Hubei	61472	9135	41920	10418	46.64	21.79	24.85
湖　南	Hunan	69159	12040	45733	11386	51.22	26.33	24.90
广　东	Guangdong	133790	24052	96407	13330	38.78	24.95	13.83
广　西	Guangxi	52933	11349	34274	7310	54.44	33.11	21.33
海　南	Hainan	10982	2007	7691	1284	42.79	26.09	16.70
重　庆	Chongqing	33600	4697	22550	6353	49.00	20.83	28.17
四　川	Sichuan	88112	12775	59069	16268	49.17	21.63	27.54
贵　州	Guizhou	40697	9155	26326	5216	54.59	34.77	19.81
云　南	Yunnan	49205	9011	34314	5880	43.40	26.26	17.14
西　藏	Xizang	3843	937	2672	234	43.85	35.08	8.77
陕　西	Shaanxi	41613	6826	28450	6338	46.27	23.99	22.28
甘　肃	Gansu	25956	4779	17634	3542	47.19	27.10	20.09
青　海	Qinghai	6255	1239	4362	654	43.40	28.41	14.99
宁　夏	Ningxia	7676	1474	5395	806	42.27	27.33	14.94
新　疆	Xinjiang	27356	5451	19529	2376	40.08	27.91	12.17

2-12 分地区按性别和婚姻状况分的人口(2023年)
Population by Gender, Marital Status and Region (2023)

本表是2023年全国人口变动情况抽样调查样本数据，抽样比为1.051‰。
Data in this table are obtained from the 2023 National Sample Survey on Population Changes. The sampling fraction is 1.051‰.

单位：人 (person)

地区	Region	15岁及以上人口 Population Aged 15 and Over	男 Male	女 Female	未婚 Never Married	男 Male	女 Female	有配偶 Married	男 Male	女 Female
全国	**National Total**	**1239420**	**628091**	**611328**	**246566**	**147640**	**98926**	**881848**	**441212**	**440635**
北京	Beijing	20253	10284	9970	4125	2233	1892	14581	7582	6999
天津	Tianjin	12563	6403	6160	2386	1345	1041	9002	4658	4344
河北	Hebei	63981	31375	32606	10995	6253	4742	47665	23143	24522
山西	Shanxi	31047	15832	15215	5705	3300	2404	22850	11680	11170
内蒙古	Inner Mongolia	21980	11236	10744	3470	2088	1382	16368	8390	7978
辽宁	Liaoning	39579	19393	20187	6235	3632	2604	28589	14087	14502
吉林	Jilin	22091	10974	11116	3528	2018	1509	15840	7966	7875
黑龙江	Heilongjiang	29399	14645	14753	4771	2789	1982	21104	10559	10545
上海	Shanghai	23678	12246	11432	4404	2520	1884	17422	9176	8245
江苏	Jiangsu	77590	39063	38528	12819	7563	5256	58345	29294	29051
浙江	Zhejiang	60987	31775	29211	10989	6815	4174	45381	23459	21922
安徽	Anhui	53269	26936	26333	9708	5975	3733	38854	19135	19718
福建	Fujian	36196	18529	17667	7310	4437	2874	25999	13173	12826
江西	Jiangxi	38582	19695	18887	9029	5449	3580	26423	13172	13250
山东	Shandong	88166	43978	44189	14978	8702	6276	66149	32934	33215
河南	Henan	82335	40737	41598	18708	10845	7863	57029	27454	29576
湖北	Hubei	52338	26564	25773	9628	6007	3621	37768	18696	19073
湖南	Hunan	57119	29007	28112	12109	7323	4786	39219	19625	19594
广东	Guangdong	109738	57563	52174	28659	17719	10940	73801	37480	36321
广西	Guangxi	41584	21318	20265	10603	6561	4042	26938	13427	13511
海南	Hainan	8976	4736	4240	2343	1492	851	6005	3049	2956
重庆	Chongqing	28903	14487	14416	5961	3548	2413	19771	9793	9978
四川	Sichuan	75337	37832	37505	14501	8721	5780	52536	26087	26449
贵州	Guizhou	31542	15949	15593	6232	3791	2441	21870	10746	11124
云南	Yunnan	40194	20614	19580	8661	5311	3350	27617	13832	13784
西藏	Xizang	2906	1545	1361	920	527	393	1754	946	807
陕西	Shaanxi	34788	17676	17112	6716	4097	2619	24920	12387	12532
甘肃	Gansu	21177	10693	10484	4040	2430	1610	15139	7516	7623
青海	Qinghai	5016	2510	2506	1171	666	505	3319	1658	1661
宁夏	Ningxia	6202	3141	3061	1180	693	487	4553	2285	2267
新疆	Xinjiang	21906	11355	10550	4680	2789	1891	15037	7822	7215

2–12 续表 continued

单位：人 (person)

地 区	Region	离 婚 Divorced	男 Male	女 Female	丧 偶 Widowed	男 Male	女 Female
全 国	**National Total**	**33101**	**18667**	**14434**	**77905**	**20571**	**57333**
北 京	Beijing	586	247	339	961	222	740
天 津	Tianjin	454	208	246	721	192	528
河 北	Hebei	1236	763	473	4084	1215	2869
山 西	Shanxi	605	370	235	1887	482	1406
内蒙古	Inner Mongolia	712	395	317	1431	363	1068
辽 宁	Liaoning	1770	921	849	2984	753	2232
吉 林	Jilin	985	529	456	1738	461	1277
黑龙江	Heilongjiang	1400	727	673	2124	570	1554
上 海	Shanghai	737	314	423	1116	237	879
江 苏	Jiangsu	1638	920	719	4787	1286	3502
浙 江	Zhejiang	1608	835	773	3008	666	2342
安 徽	Anhui	1304	807	497	3403	1019	2385
福 建	Fujian	919	521	398	1968	398	1570
江 西	Jiangxi	840	529	312	2290	545	1745
山 东	Shandong	1449	813	636	5590	1528	4062
河 南	Henan	1401	852	548	5197	1586	3611
湖 北	Hubei	1413	855	558	3528	1007	2522
湖 南	Hunan	1586	950	636	4205	1110	3095
广 东	Guangdong	2377	1269	1108	4901	1095	3806
广 西	Guangxi	1017	608	409	3025	721	2304
海 南	Hainan	173	101	71	455	93	361
重 庆	Chongqing	1103	600	503	2068	546	1522
四 川	Sichuan	2593	1464	1129	5707	1560	4147
贵 州	Guizhou	1173	776	397	2268	637	1631
云 南	Yunnan	1308	771	537	2608	699	1909
西 藏	Xizang	73	28	46	159	44	115
陕 西	Shaanxi	830	516	314	2322	676	1647
甘 肃	Gansu	504	309	195	1494	438	1056
青 海	Qinghai	219	106	113	306	80	226
宁 夏	Ningxia	178	89	89	291	74	217
新 疆	Xinjiang	911	475	436	1277	270	1008

2-13 分地区按性别、受教育程度分的6岁及以上人口(2023年)
Population Aged 6 and Over by Gender, Educational Attainment and Region (2023)

本表是2023年全国人口变动情况抽样调查样本数据，抽样比为1.051‰。
Data in this table are obtained from the 2023 National Sample Survey on Population Changes. The sampling fraction is 1.051‰.

单位：人 (person)

地 区	Region	6岁及以上人口 Population Aged 6 and Over			未上过学 No Schooling			小学 Primary Schools		
		合计 Total	男 Male	女 Female	小计 Subtotal	男 Male	女 Female	小计 Subtotal	男 Male	女 Female
全 国	**National Total**	**1409041**	**718135**	**690906**	**55292**	**15954**	**39338**	**350424**	**164256**	**186168**
北 京	Beijing	22048	11216	10832	290	81	209	2342	1090	1251
天 津	Tianjin	13817	7061	6756	272	84	187	2101	967	1134
河 北	Hebei	74209	36807	37403	1990	585	1406	17414	8154	9260
山 西	Shanxi	34767	17747	17020	669	220	449	6205	2859	3346
内蒙古	Inner Mongolia	24211	12402	11808	1008	293	716	5566	2541	3025
辽 宁	Liaoning	42642	20989	21653	661	224	435	7930	3608	4321
吉 林	Jilin	23897	11907	11990	471	159	314	5302	2416	2886
黑龙江	Heilongjiang	31486	15720	15767	982	326	656	6622	3058	3564
上 海	Shanghai	25370	13140	12230	473	123	350	2984	1357	1627
江 苏	Jiangsu	86335	43750	42585	2275	631	1644	19235	8420	10816
浙 江	Zhejiang	66775	34847	31927	3111	861	2249	16994	8111	8883
安 徽	Anhui	61057	31105	29952	3866	959	2907	16810	7842	8968
福 建	Fujian	41687	21531	20157	1588	353	1236	11965	5454	6512
江 西	Jiangxi	45017	23179	21838	1611	415	1196	12389	5600	6789
山 东	Shandong	100932	50880	50052	4343	1116	3227	24025	10885	13140
河 南	Henan	97747	48948	48799	3599	1142	2457	23129	11015	12114
湖 北	Hubei	58740	30018	28723	2221	558	1663	14696	6888	7807
湖 南	Hunan	65784	33644	32140	1853	560	1293	15943	7539	8404
广 东	Guangdong	125895	66149	59747	3527	1025	2503	28693	13116	15576
广 西	Guangxi	49612	25595	24016	1719	531	1188	13625	6433	7191
海 南	Hainan	10310	5466	4844	331	111	221	2072	991	1081
重 庆	Chongqing	32163	16190	15974	897	270	627	9271	4289	4982
四 川	Sichuan	84187	42408	41780	4629	1312	3317	26338	12504	13834
贵 州	Guizhou	37627	19207	18420	3203	792	2410	12761	6460	6302
云 南	Yunnan	46186	23771	22415	2922	879	2043	16675	8380	8295
西 藏	Xizang	3509	1853	1656	930	404	526	1298	713	585
陕 西	Shaanxi	39440	20112	19328	1645	508	1138	8854	4252	4602
甘 肃	Gansu	24383	12356	12027	2304	729	1576	7645	3700	3945
青 海	Qinghai	5839	2934	2906	630	226	405	2024	997	1027
宁 夏	Ningxia	7151	3631	3520	489	150	339	1965	920	1045
新 疆	Xinjiang	26216	13574	12642	781	326	455	7551	3696	3855

2-13 续表 1 continued

单位：人 (person)

地 区	Region	初中 Junior Secondary Schools 小计 Subtotal	男 Male	女 Female	高中 Senior Secondary Schools 小计 Subtotal	男 Male	女 Female
全 国	**National Total**	**511117**	**275849**	**235269**	**221678**	**124611**	**97067**
北 京	Beijing	4494	2495	1999	3868	1978	1891
天 津	Tianjin	4254	2281	1973	2446	1276	1170
河 北	Hebei	31264	16278	14985	11430	6091	5339
山 西	Shanxi	14239	7519	6721	6120	3346	2774
内蒙古	Inner Mongolia	8692	4835	3857	3683	2027	1656
辽 宁	Liaoning	18728	9602	9126	6323	3221	3102
吉 林	Jilin	9372	4914	4458	3719	1940	1779
黑龙江	Heilongjiang	13217	6840	6377	4954	2564	2389
上 海	Shanghai	7224	3953	3271	4938	2703	2235
江 苏	Jiangsu	30357	16008	14349	14137	8247	5891
浙 江	Zhejiang	22351	12724	9627	10299	5964	4335
安 徽	Anhui	22236	12037	10200	8660	5091	3569
福 建	Fujian	14913	8526	6387	6045	3583	2462
江 西	Jiangxi	17207	9488	7719	6971	4138	2833
山 东	Shandong	38145	20392	17753	16078	9218	6861
河 南	Henan	38913	19877	19036	17361	9377	7984
湖 北	Hubei	20754	11132	9622	10306	5930	4376
湖 南	Hunan	24154	12660	11495	12382	7041	5341
广 东	Guangdong	45599	25277	20322	22706	13389	9317
广 西	Guangxi	19526	10909	8617	7092	4006	3087
海 南	Hainan	4404	2417	1987	1633	955	679
重 庆	Chongqing	10235	5429	4805	5485	2980	2505
四 川	Sichuan	28003	15316	12687	11360	6372	4988
贵 州	Guizhou	12769	7219	5550	3703	2077	1626
云 南	Yunnan	15170	8768	6402	4795	2645	2150
西 藏	Xizang	596	362	234	223	132	91
陕 西	Shaanxi	14058	7473	6586	6335	3580	2755
甘 肃	Gansu	7426	4021	3405	3175	1792	1382
青 海	Qinghai	1518	858	660	610	327	283
宁 夏	Ningxia	2257	1287	970	988	541	447
新 疆	Xinjiang	9041	4953	4088	3853	2083	1771

2-13 续表 2 continued

单位：人 (person)

地 区	Region	大学专科 College Students			大学本科 Undergraduates			研究生 Postgraduates		
		小计 Subtotal	男 Male	女 Female	小计 Subtotal	男 Male	女 Female	小计 Subtotal	男 Male	女 Female
全 国	**National Total**	**136312**	**70443**	**65869**	**120776**	**60283**	**60493**	**13441**	**6739**	**6702**
北 京	Beijing	3441	1776	1664	5692	2827	2865	1922	969	953
天 津	Tianjin	1948	1041	908	2437	1228	1209	359	185	174
河 北	Hebei	6698	3236	3462	4921	2222	2700	492	240	250
山 西	Shanxi	3996	2143	1852	3296	1552	1743	243	109	134
内蒙古	Inner Mongolia	2618	1443	1176	2433	1186	1248	210	78	132
辽 宁	Liaoning	4235	2081	2154	4388	2094	2294	379	158	221
吉 林	Jilin	1967	1053	915	2803	1331	1472	263	96	167
黑龙江	Heilongjiang	2517	1238	1279	2853	1521	1332	342	171	170
上 海	Shanghai	3345	1779	1566	5190	2571	2619	1216	654	562
江 苏	Jiangsu	10105	5206	4898	9233	4710	4523	994	529	465
浙 江	Zhejiang	6704	3548	3155	6712	3298	3414	605	341	264
安 徽	Anhui	5073	2696	2377	4087	2302	1785	326	178	147
福 建	Fujian	3794	1884	1910	3108	1573	1535	273	159	115
江 西	Jiangxi	4136	2202	1934	2462	1248	1213	242	88	154
山 东	Shandong	9755	5066	4689	7788	3831	3957	797	372	425
河 南	Henan	8084	4180	3904	6148	3087	3061	512	270	242
湖 北	Hubei	5359	2808	2551	4825	2387	2438	581	316	265
湖 南	Hunan	6753	3535	3218	4274	2075	2199	425	233	191
广 东	Guangdong	13031	6795	6235	11247	5947	5300	1091	598	493
广 西	Guangxi	4065	2119	1945	3306	1524	1783	280	74	205
海 南	Hainan	973	518	455	841	438	404	55	37	17
重 庆	Chongqing	3306	1745	1561	2729	1344	1386	239	132	107
四 川	Sichuan	7572	3807	3765	5698	2811	2887	588	284	303
贵 州	Guizhou	2471	1289	1182	2584	1325	1258	135	45	90
云 南	Yunnan	3947	1866	2081	2545	1186	1360	132	48	84
西 藏	Xizang	186	100	86	266	138	128	10	5	5
陕 西	Shaanxi	4247	2101	2146	3891	2004	1887	410	195	214
甘 肃	Gansu	1974	1102	873	1701	917	784	157	94	63
青 海	Qinghai	516	281	236	512	235	277	29	11	18
宁 夏	Ningxia	676	358	318	737	357	380	40	18	21
新 疆	Xinjiang	2820	1447	1373	2069	1018	1051	100	51	49

2-14 分地区按性别分的15岁及以上文盲人口（2023年）
Illiterate Population Aged 15 and Over by Gender and Region (2023)

本表是2023年全国人口变动情况抽样调查样本数据，抽样比为1.051‰。
Data in this table are obtained from the 2023 National Sample Survey on Population Changes. The sampling fraction is 1.051‰.

地区	Region	15岁及以上人口(人) Population Aged 15 and Over (person)	男 Male	女 Female	文盲人口(人) Illiterate Population (person)	男 Male	女 Female	文盲人口占15岁及以上人口的比重(%) Percentage of Illiterate Population to Total Aged 15 and Over(%)	男 Male	女 Female
全国	**National Total**	**1239420**	**628091**	**611328**	**42460**	**10427**	**32033**	**3.43**	**1.66**	**5.24**
北京	Beijing	20253	10284	9970	191	37	154	0.94	0.36	1.55
天津	Tianjin	12563	6403	6160	173	39	134	1.38	0.61	2.18
河北	Hebei	63981	31375	32606	1427	323	1104	2.23	1.03	3.39
山西	Shanxi	31047	15832	15215	492	128	364	1.58	0.81	2.39
内蒙古	Inner Mongolia	21980	11236	10744	862	220	641	3.92	1.96	5.97
辽宁	Liaoning	39579	19393	20187	465	128	338	1.18	0.66	1.67
吉林	Jilin	22091	10974	11116	302	94	208	1.37	0.86	1.87
黑龙江	Heilongjiang	29399	14645	14753	787	237	550	2.68	1.62	3.73
上海	Shanghai	23678	12246	11432	373	74	299	1.58	0.61	2.62
江苏	Jiangsu	77590	39063	38528	1274	290	984	1.64	0.74	2.55
浙江	Zhejiang	60987	31775	29211	2561	636	1924	4.2	2	6.59
安徽	Anhui	53269	26936	26333	3216	699	2517	6.04	2.59	9.56
福建	Fujian	36196	18529	17667	1008	174	834	2.78	0.94	4.72
江西	Jiangxi	38582	19695	18887	1257	276	982	3.26	1.40	5.20
山东	Shandong	88166	43978	44189	3168	624	2544	3.59	1.42	5.76
河南	Henan	82335	40737	41598	2752	748	2004	3.34	1.84	4.82
湖北	Hubei	52338	26564	25773	1676	371	1305	3.20	1.40	5.06
湖南	Hunan	57119	29007	28112	1395	338	1057	2.44	1.17	3.76
广东	Guangdong	109738	57563	52174	2439	517	1922	2.22	0.9	3.68
广西	Guangxi	41584	21318	20265	1150	237	913	2.77	1.11	4.50
海南	Hainan	8976	4736	4240	264	76	189	2.95	1.60	4.45
重庆	Chongqing	28903	14487	14416	534	124	411	1.85	0.85	2.85
四川	Sichuan	75337	37832	37505	3677	928	2749	4.88	2.45	7.33
贵州	Guizhou	31542	15949	15593	2817	617	2200	8.93	3.87	14.11
云南	Yunnan	40194	20614	19580	2468	677	1791	6.14	3.28	9.15
西藏	Xizang	2906	1545	1361	842	356	486	28.98	23.06	35.71
陕西	Shaanxi	34788	17676	17112	1330	356	974	3.82	2.01	5.69
甘肃	Gansu	21177	10693	10484	2079	611	1468	9.82	5.71	14.00
青海	Qinghai	5016	2510	2506	507	167	340	10.11	6.64	13.59
宁夏	Ningxia	6202	3141	3061	423	120	303	6.82	3.83	9.88
新疆	Xinjiang	21906	11355	10550	550	205	345	2.51	1.80	3.27

注：本表“文盲人口”指15岁及以上不识字及识字很少的人口。
a) The "illiterate population" in this table refers to the population aged 15 and above who are illiterate or have little literacy.

2-15 分地区按家庭户规模分的户数（2023年）
Family Households by Size and Region (2023)

本表是2023年全国人口变动情况抽样调查样本数据，抽样比为1.051‰。
Data in this table are obtained from the 2023 National Sample Survey on Population Changes. The sampling fraction is 1.051‰.

单位：户 (household)

地 区	Region	家庭户户 数 Number of Family Households	一人户 One Person	二人户 Two Persons	三人户 Three Persons	四人户 Four Persons	五人户 Five Persons	六人户 Six Persons	七人户 Seven Persons	八人户 Eight Persons	九人户 Nine Persons	十人及以上户 Ten Persons and Over
全 国	**National Total**	**507031**	**90456**	**118852**	**106790**	**93323**	**48937**	**30083**	**11045**	**4042**	**1732**	**1771**
北 京	Beijing	8759	2210	2541	2049	1046	549	247	60	33	17	7
天 津	Tianjin	5381	1132	1709	1414	706	280	99	28	8	3	1
河 北	Hebei	26078	3955	6730	5296	5543	2313	1451	501	183	52	54
山 西	Shanxi	12941	2068	3391	3058	2717	991	509	132	46	17	12
内蒙古	Inner Mongolia	9801	1658	3154	2752	1480	459	215	53	19	9	2
辽 宁	Liaoning	17857	3509	5359	4953	2355	1050	481	119	26	3	2
吉 林	Jilin	9685	1752	2912	2590	1350	635	297	106	30	8	5
黑龙江	Heilongjiang	13781	2947	5114	3515	1363	575	192	54	14	3	3
上 海	Shanghai	9895	2209	2882	2521	1218	719	247	58	25	7	8
江 苏	Jiangsu	30466	5130	7496	6757	5168	3209	1741	621	199	81	65
浙 江	Zhejiang	25309	5702	6494	5363	3888	2105	1263	319	103	41	30
安 徽	Anhui	22175	3394	4973	4519	4490	2278	1635	547	200	79	59
福 建	Fujian	14500	2708	2813	2727	2799	1571	1084	426	169	92	112
江 西	Jiangxi	14744	2186	2719	2547	3199	1785	1390	571	185	97	64
山 东	Shandong	38718	6459	10680	8831	8106	2713	1379	376	106	39	29
河 南	Henan	33314	5016	7160	6082	7231	3572	2708	1093	296	103	53
湖 北	Hubei	20686	2999	4655	5046	3988	2121	1255	395	134	54	40
湖 南	Hunan	23318	3680	4796	4787	4887	2599	1697	561	188	69	53
广 东	Guangdong	43317	11007	8061	6639	7122	4524	2858	1474	726	357	549
广 西	Guangxi	16094	2524	2376	2894	3397	2180	1400	693	299	134	196
海 南	Hainan	3099	492	463	517	711	382	250	128	62	37	57
重 庆	Chongqing	12288	2244	2962	2708	2116	1258	690	197	56	34	23
四 川	Sichuan	30629	5276	7070	6556	5253	3480	2015	623	223	87	47
贵 州	Guizhou	12115	1459	1885	2101	2602	1748	1253	580	253	117	116
云 南	Yunnan	14887	2295	2391	2712	3337	1952	1352	533	185	72	56
西 藏	Xizang	1053	303	162	147	139	100	66	45	32	19	39
陕 西	Shaanxi	14844	2719	3493	3311	2828	1420	819	187	42	9	14
甘 肃	Gansu	8187	1282	1510	1581	1609	947	788	287	104	41	38
青 海	Qinghai	1984	398	419	377	345	198	144	58	21	13	10
宁 夏	Ningxia	2461	377	591	539	509	243	119	52	17	8	5
新 疆	Xinjiang	8668	1368	1891	1900	1820	981	436	164	58	28	21

主要统计指标解释

人口数 指一定时点、一定地区范围内有生命的个人总和。

年度统计的年末人口数指每年 12 月 31 日 24 时的人口数。年度统计的全国人口总数内未包括香港、澳门特别行政区和台湾地区以及海外华侨人数。

城镇人口和乡村人口 城镇人口是指居住在城镇范围内的全部常住人口；乡村人口是除上述人口以外的全部人口。

出生率(又称粗出生率) 指在一定时期内(通常为一年)一定地区的出生人数与同期内平均人数(或期中人数)之比，用千分率表示。本资料中的出生率指年出生率，其计算公式为：

$$出生率=\frac{年出生人数}{年平均人数}\times 1000‰$$

式中：出生人数指活产婴儿，即胎儿脱离母体时(不管怀孕月数)，有过呼吸或其他生命现象。年平均人数指年初、年底人口数的平均数，也可用年中人口数代替。

死亡率(又称粗死亡率) 指在一定时期内(通常为一年)一定地区的死亡人数与同期内平均人数(或期中人数)之比，用千分率表示。本资料中的死亡率指年死亡率，其计算公式为：

$$死亡率=\frac{年死亡人数}{年平均人数}\times 1000‰$$

人口自然增长率 指在一定时期内(通常为一年)人口自然增加数(出生人数减死亡人数)与该时期内平均人数(或期中人数)之比，用千分率表示。计算公式为：

$$人口自然增长率=\frac{本年出生人数-本年死亡人数}{年平均人数}\times 1000‰$$

$$=人口出生率-人口死亡率$$

总抚养比 也称总负担系数。指人口总体中非劳动年龄人口数与劳动年龄人口数之比。通常用百分比表示。说明每 100 名劳动年龄人口大致要负担多少名非劳动年龄人口。计算公式为：

$$GDR=\frac{P_{0\sim14}+P_{65^+}}{P_{15\sim64}}\times 100\%$$

其中：GDR 为总抚养比；

$P_{0\sim14}$ 为 0～14 岁少年儿童人口数；

P_{65^+} 为 65 岁及 65 岁以上的老年人口数；

$P_{15\sim64}$ 为 15～64 岁劳动年龄人口数。

老年人口抚养比 也称老年人口抚养系数。指某一人口中老年人口数与劳动年龄人口数之比。通常用百分比表示。用以表明每 100 名劳动年龄人口要负担多少名老年人。计算公式为：

$$EDR=\frac{P_{65^+}}{P_{15-64}}\times 100\%$$

其中：EDR 为老年人口抚养比；

P_{65^+} 为 65 岁及 65 岁以上的老年人口数；

$P_{15\sim64}$ 为 15～64 岁的劳动年龄人口数。

少年儿童抚养比 也称少年儿童抚养系数。指某一人口中少年儿童人口数与劳动年龄人口数之比。通常用百分比表示。以反映每 100 名劳动年龄人口要负担多少名少年儿童。计算公式为：

$$CDR=\frac{P_{0\sim14}}{P_{15\sim64}}\times 100\%$$

其中：CDR 为少年儿童抚养比；

$P_{0\sim14}$ 为 0～14 岁少年儿童人口数；

$P_{15\sim64}$ 为 15～64 岁劳动年龄人口数。

人户分离人口 是指居住地与户口登记地所在的乡镇街道不一致且离开户口登记地半年以上的人口。

流动人口 是指人户分离人口中扣除市辖区内人户分离的人口。市辖区内人户分离的人口是指一个直辖市或地级市所辖区内和区与区之间，居住地和户口登记地不在同一乡镇街道的人口。

Explanatory Notes on Main Statistical Indicators

Total Population refers to the total number of people alive at a certain point of time within a given area.

The annual statistics on total population is taken at midnight, the 31st of December, not including residents in Hong Kong SAR, Macao SAR and Taiwan and Chinese national residing abroad.

Urban Population and Rural Population Urban population refers to all people residing in cities and towns, while rural population refers to population other than urban population.

Birth Rate (or Crude Birth Rate) refers to the ratio of the number of births to the average population (or mid-year population) during a certain period of time (usually a year), expressed in ‰. Birth rate in the chapter refers to annual birth rate. The following formula is used:

$$\text{Birth rate} = \frac{\text{Number of births}}{\text{Annual average population}} \times 1000‰$$

Number of births in the formula refers to live births, i.e. when a baby has breathed or showed any vital phenomena regardless of the length of pregnancy.

Annual average population is the average of the number of population at the beginning of the year and that at the end of the year. Sometimes it is substituted by the mid-year population.

Death Rate (or Crude Death Rate) refers to the ratio of the number of deaths to the average population (or mid-year population) during a certain period of time (usually a year), expressed in ‰. Death rate in the chapter refers to annual death rate. The following formula is used:

$$\text{Death rate} = \frac{\text{Number of deaths}}{\text{Annual average population}} \times 1000‰$$

Natural Growth Rate of Population refers to the ratio of natural increase in population (number of births minus number of deaths) in a certain period of time (usually a year) to the average population (or mid-year population) of the same period, expressed in ‰. The following formula is applied:

$$\text{Natural growth rate of population} = \frac{\text{Number of births - number of deaths}}{\text{Annual average population}} \times 1000‰$$

Natural growth rate of population = Birth rate-death rate

Gross Dependency Ratio also called gross dependency coefficient, refers to the ratio of non-working-age population to the working-age population, express in %. Describing in general the number of non-working-age population that every 100 people at working ages will take care of. The gross dependency ratio is calculated with the following formula:

$$GDR = \frac{P_{0\sim14} + P_{65^+}}{P_{15\sim64}} \times 100\%$$

Where: GDR is the gross dependency ratio,

$P_{0\text{-}14}$ is the population of children aged 0-14,

P_{65+} is the elderly population aged 65 and over, and

$P_{15\text{-}64}$ is the working-age population aged 15-64.

Elderly Dependency Ratio also called elderly dependency coefficient, refers to the ratio of the elderly population to the working-age population, express in %. It describes the number of the elderly population that every 100 people at working ages will take care of. Elderly dependency ratio is one of the indicators reflecting the social implication of population aging from the economic perspective. The elderly dependency ratio is calculated with the following formula:

$$EDR = \frac{P_{65^+}}{P_{15\sim64}} \times 100\%$$

Where: EDR is the elderly dependency ratio,

P_{65+} is the elderly population aged 65 and over, and

$P_{15\text{-}64}$ is the working-age population aged 15-64.

Children Dependency Ratio also called children dependency coefficient, refers to the ratio of the children population to the working-age population, express in %. It describes the number of children population that every 100 people at working ages will take care of. The children dependency ratio is calculated with the following formula:

$$CDR = \frac{P_{0\sim14}}{P_{15\sim64}} \times 100\%$$

Where: CDR is the children dependency ratio,

$P_{0\text{-}14}$ is the children population aged 0-14, and

$P_{15\text{-}64}$ is the working-age population aged 15-64.

Population of Residence-registration Inconsistency refer to those who have been residing in places other than the registered streets or towns and been away from their registration areas for over half a year.

Migrant Population refer to the population of residence-registration inconsistency excluding those intra-city ones. Population of intra-city residence-registration inconsistency refer to those whose residing streets or towns and registered ones are inconsistent but still in the same municipality or prefecture city either the two are in the same district or different ones.

3

国民经济核算

National Accounts

简 要 说 明

本篇章的主要内容和资料来源

国民经济核算资料主要包括国内生产总值、投入产出表、资金流量表和国际收支平衡表四个部分。

一、国内生产总值

国内生产总值数据是由国家统计局国民经济核算司根据不同产业部门、不同支出构成的特点和资料来源情况采用不同方法计算的。国民总收入是在国内生产总值的基础上加上来自国外的初次分配收入净额求得的。

本年鉴公布的国内生产总值以及与之有关的指标数据，最后一年数据不是最终数，还会在获得更多的财务和行政记录等资料后发生变动。如果遇到普查或者重大核算方法改革，在能够获得更详细的基础资料的情况下，国内生产总值的历史数据还会发生变动。

国内生产总值是一个价值量指标，其价值的变化受价格变化和物量变化两大因素影响。不变价国内生产总值是把按当期价格计算的国内生产总值换算成按某个固定期（基期）价格计算的价值，从而使两个不同时期的价值进行比较时，能够剔除价格变化的影响，以反映物量变化，反映生产活动成果的实际变动。国内生产总值指数就是根据两个时期不变价国内生产总值计算得到的。随着经济的不断发展，行业的价格结构也会不断发生变化，为了更好地反映这种变化对于经济的影响，计算不变价国内生产总值需要每隔若干年调整一次基期。我国自开始核算国内生产总值以来，共有1952年、1957年、1970年、1980年、1990年、2000年、2005年、2010年、2015年、2020年10个不变价基期，目前的基期是2020年。也就是说，2021年以来的不变价国内生产总值是按照2020年价格计算的。由于计算不变价国内生产总值采用按不同基期分段计算，因此本年鉴中的不变价国内生产总值数据也按分段方式公布。

该指标在地区层面被称为地区生产总值。本年鉴所列地区生产总值数据由国家统计局与各省、自治区、直辖市统计局统一核算得到。由于部分活动仅核算在全国不核算在地区，各地区数据相加之和略小于全国。

二、投入产出表

投入产出表分为竞争型投入产出表和非竞争型投入产出表。国家统计局国民经济核算司利用 2017 年投入产出调查和 2020 年有关统计资料，编制了 2020 年投入产出表（竞争型）。同时，还利用 2020 年进口货物使用去向调查及进出口资料，编制了 2020 年非竞争型投入产出表。本年鉴中的投入产出表和非竞争型投入产出表数据为 17×17 产品部门表。

三、资金流量表

我国资金流量表表式与国际上通用的表式相似，是机构部门与交易项目的矩阵表式。主栏为交易项目，主要反映分配方式和融资工具；宾栏按机构部门分类。机构部门分类是根据机构单位具有的基本特征所进行的部门分类。资金流量表把参与资金活动的主体分为非金融企业、金融机构、广义政府、住户和国外五个部门。每一部门下设资金来源与资金运用两栏。现行的资金流量表分为两大部分，上半部分为非金融交易部分，由国家统计局国民经济核算司编制；下半部分为金融交易部分，由中国人民银行调查统计司编制。

2018年第四次全国经济普查后，国家统计局根据国民经济核算国际标准的变化以及《中国国民经济核算体系（2016）》，利用第四次全国经济普查资料和相关部门资料，改进和完善资金流量表编制方法，编制了2018年资金流量表（非金融交易部分），并修订了1992年以来的资金流量表（非金融交易部分）历史数据。本年鉴中的数据是修订后的数据。

四、国际收支平衡表

国际收支平衡表由国家外汇管理局国际收支司依据国际货币基金组织编写的《国际收支统计手册》第六版编制。

Brief Introduction

Statistics on national accounts include mainly four parts, namely, gross domestic product, input-output tables,flow of funds table and balance of payments table.

I. Gross Domestic Product

Data on gross domestic product (GDP) are computed by the Department of National Accounts of the National Bureau of Statistics (NBS) based on different approaches in the light of the different features of various sectors, various expenditure structures and different data sources. Data on Gross National Income (GNI) are calculated on the basis of GDP, which is equal to GDP plus the net primary distribution income from the rest of the world.

Data on GDP and related indicators of the most recent year published in the Yearbook are not final and are subject to revision when more information from financial data and administrative records become available. Where a census has been conducted, or significant accounting methods reform implemented, historical GDP data will also be revised.

Gross Domestic Product (GDP) is a measurement of value which changes depending on changes of price and volume. GDP at constant prices converts the gross domestic product based on the current price into a value based on the price of certain base period. After price effects are removed, the values of two different periods can be compared to reflect the volume changes, i.e., the real changes of production activity results. GDP index is derived from the constant-price GDP. As the economy grows, changes will take place in the price structures of various industries, and the base period for the measurement of constant-price GDP thus needs to be adjusted every few years in order to better reflect the impact of price change in the economy. Since China started GDP calculation, ten constant-price base periods have been used, i.e., 1952, 1957, 1970, 1980, 1990, 2000, 2005, 2010, 2015 and 2020, and the current base period is 2020. That is to say, the GDP at constant prices since 2021 is calculated on the basis of the 2020 prices. As the calculation of constant-price GDP is based on different base periods, the constant-price GDP data in this yearbook are also published on the basis of different base periods.

This indicator is called Gross Regional Product (GRP) at the regional level. GRP data in this yearbook are jointly compiled by the National Bureau of Statistics and the statistics bureaus of the provinces, autonomous regions and municipalities. As some activities are only calculated at the national level but not at regional level, the sum of the GRP is slightly smaller than GDP.

II. Input-output Tables

The input-output table is divided into competitive input-output table and non competitive input-output table. The national economic accounting division of the National Bureau of statistics compiled the input-output table for 2020 (competitive type) by using the input-output survey in 2017 and relevant statistical data for 2020. At the same time, the non competitive input-output table of 2020 is also prepared by using the investigation on the use of imported goods in 2020 and the import and export data. The input-output table and non competitive input-output table data in this yearbook are 17 × 17 product department table.

III. Flow of Funds Table

Similar to internationally accepted approaches, the Flow of Funds table of China constitutes a matrix of institutional sectors by transaction items. Items of transactions are expressed as row headings representing forms of distribution and methods of financing. Institutional sectors are shown as column headings, grouped by the characteristics of the transactor. There are 5 groups of institutional sectors in the flow of funds table, namely, non-financial corporations, financial institutions, general governments, households, and the rest of the world. Under each sector there are 2 headings: sources of funds and uses of funds. The current flow of funds table is composed of two parts: the first part, comprising the non-financial transactions, is compiled by the Department of National Accounts of the National Bureau of Statistics; and the second part, comprising financial transactions, is compiled by the Research and Statistics Department of the People's Bank of China.

After the fourth national economic census in 2018, according to the change of international standard of national accounting and the new standard of China, Chinese System of National Accounts (2016), based on the economic census data and related administrative records, the National Bureau of Statistics of China improved the compilation methods of Flow of Funds Table, compiled the Flow of Funds Table (non-financial transaction) of 2018, and revised the historical Flow of Funds Table (non-transaction) since 1992. Data in this Yearbook are revised data.

IV . Balance of Payments Table

The Balance of Payments Table is compiled by the Balance of Payments Department of the State Administration of Foreign Exchanges in accordance with the 6th edition of the Manual on Balance of Payments prepared by the International Monetary Fund.

3–1 国内生产总值
Gross Domestic Product

本表按当年价格计算。
Data in this table are calculated at current prices.

单位：亿元 (100 million yuan)

年 份 Year	国 民 总收入 Gross National Income	国内生产 总 值 Gross Domestic Product	第一产业 Primary Industry	第二产业 Secondary Industry	第三产业 Tertiary Industry	农林牧渔业 Agriculture, Forestry, Animal Husbandry and Fishery	工业 Industry
1978	3678.7	3678.7	1018.5	1755.1	905.1	1027.5	1621.4
1979	4100.5	4100.5	1259.0	1925.3	916.1	1270.2	1786.5
1980	4586.1	4587.6	1359.5	2204.7	1023.4	1371.6	2014.8
1981	4933.7	4935.8	1545.7	2269.0	1121.1	1559.4	2067.7
1982	5380.5	5373.4	1761.7	2397.6	1214.0	1777.3	2183.0
1983	6043.8	6020.9	1960.9	2663.0	1397.1	1978.3	2399.0
1984	7314.2	7278.5	2295.6	3124.7	1858.2	2316.0	2815.8
1985	9123.6	9098.9	2541.7	3886.4	2670.8	2564.3	3478.2
1986	10375.4	10376.2	2764.1	4515.1	3097.0	2788.6	4000.7
1987	12166.6	12174.6	3204.5	5273.8	3696.3	3232.9	4621.1
1988	15174.4	15180.4	3831.2	6607.2	4742.0	3865.2	5814.0
1989	17188.4	17179.7	4228.2	7300.7	5650.8	4265.8	6525.5
1990	18923.3	18872.9	5017.2	7744.1	6111.6	5061.8	6904.5
1991	22050.3	22005.6	5288.8	9129.6	7587.2	5341.9	8137.9
1992	27208.2	27194.5	5800.3	11725.0	9669.2	5866.2	10340.2
1993	35599.2	35673.2	6887.6	16472.7	12313.0	6963.3	14248.4
1994	48548.2	48637.5	9471.8	22452.5	16713.1	9572.1	19546.3
1995	60356.6	61339.9	12020.5	28676.7	20642.7	12135.1	25023.2
1996	70779.6	71813.6	13878.3	33827.3	24108.0	14014.7	29528.9
1997	78802.9	79715.0	14265.2	37545.0	27904.8	14440.8	33022.6
1998	83817.6	85195.5	14618.7	39017.5	31559.3	14816.4	34133.9
1999	89366.5	90564.4	14549.0	41079.9	34935.5	14768.7	36014.4
2000	99066.1	100280.1	14717.4	45663.7	39899.1	14943.6	40258.5
2001	109276.2	110863.1	15502.5	49659.4	45701.2	15780.0	43854.3
2002	120480.4	121717.4	16190.2	54104.1	51423.1	16535.7	47774.9
2003	136576.3	137422.0	16970.2	62695.8	57756.0	17380.6	55362.2
2004	161415.4	161840.2	20904.3	74285.0	66650.9	21410.7	65774.9
2005	185998.9	187318.9	21806.7	88082.2	77430.0	22416.2	77958.3
2006	219028.5	219438.5	23317.0	104359.2	91762.2	24036.4	92235.8
2007	270704.0	270092.3	27674.1	126630.5	115787.7	28483.7	111690.8
2008	321229.5	319244.6	32464.1	149952.9	136827.5	33428.1	131724.0
2009	347934.9	348517.7	33583.8	160168.8	154765.1	34659.7	138092.6
2010	410354.1	412119.3	38430.8	191626.5	182061.9	39619.0	165123.1
2011	483392.8	487940.2	44781.5	227035.1	216123.6	46122.6	195139.1
2012	537329.0	538580.0	49084.6	244639.1	244856.2	50581.2	208901.4
2013	588141.2	592963.2	53028.1	261951.6	277983.5	54692.4	222333.2
2014	644380.2	643563.1	55626.3	277282.8	310654.0	57472.2	233197.4
2015	685571.2	688858.2	57774.6	281338.9	349744.7	59852.6	234968.9
2016	742694.1	746395.1	60139.2	295427.8	390828.1	62451.0	245406.4
2017	830945.7	832035.9	62099.5	331580.5	438355.9	64660.0	275119.3
2018	915243.5	919281.1	64745.2	364835.2	489700.8	67558.7	301089.3
2019	983751.2	986515.2	70473.6	380670.6	535371.0	73576.9	311858.7
2020	1005451.3	1013567.0	78030.9	383562.4	551973.7	81396.5	312902.9
2021	1141230.8	1149237.0	83216.5	451544.1	614476.4	86994.8	374545.6
2022	1194401.4	1204724.0	88207.0	473789.9	642727.1	92576.8	395043.7
2023	1249990.6	1260582.1	89755.2	482588.5	688238.4	94462.6	399103.1

注：1980年以后国民总收入(原称国民生产总值)与国内生产总值的差额为来自国外的初次分配收入净额。

a) Since 1980, the difference between the Gross Domestic Product and the Gross National Income (formerly, the Gross National Product) is the net income of primary distribution from the rest of the world.

3-1 续表 continued

单位：亿元 (100 million yuan)

年 份 Year	建筑业 Construction	批发和零售业 Wholesale and Retail Trades	交通运输、仓储和邮政业 Transport, Storage and Post	住宿和餐饮业 Hotels and Catering Services	金融业 Financial Intermediation	房地产业 Real Estate	其他 Others	人均国民总收入(元) Per Capita GNI (yuan)	人均国内生产总值(元) Per Capita GDP (yuan)
1978	138.9	242.4	182.0	44.6	76.5	79.7	265.6	385	385
1979	144.6	200.9	193.7	44.0	75.9	86.2	298.5	423	423
1980	196.3	193.8	213.4	47.4	85.8	96.2	368.2	467	468
1981	208.0	231.2	220.8	54.1	91.7	99.8	403.3	496	497
1982	221.6	171.5	246.9	62.3	130.6	110.6	469.5	533	533
1983	271.7	198.7	275.0	72.5	168.9	121.6	535.2	591	588
1984	317.9	363.6	338.6	96.8	230.6	162.0	637.3	705	702
1985	419.3	802.5	421.8	138.3	293.9	214.8	765.8	868	866
1986	527.3	852.7	499.0	163.2	401.2	297.5	846.1	973	973
1987	667.5	1059.7	568.5	187.1	506.2	381.9	949.8	1122	1123
1988	811.8	1483.6	685.9	241.4	658.9	472.8	1146.8	1377	1378
1989	796.1	1536.4	812.9	277.4	1079.9	565.1	1320.7	1537	1536
1990	861.7	1269.2	1167.2	301.9	1144.1	660.9	1501.7	1667	1663
1991	1017.7	1834.8	1420.5	442.3	1195.2	762.2	1853.1	1916	1912
1992	1417.9	2405.4	1689.2	584.6	1482.1	1099.1	2309.8	2336	2334
1993	2269.9	2817.0	2174.3	712.1	1903.5	1376.9	3207.8	3021	3027
1994	2968.8	3774.0	2788.2	1008.5	2557.9	1905.6	4516.1	4073	4081
1995	3733.7	4779.4	3244.7	1200.1	3211.5	2349.4	5662.8	5009	5091
1996	4393.0	5600.5	3782.6	1336.8	3700.7	2611.9	6844.5	5813	5898
1997	4628.3	6328.4	4149.1	1561.3	4179.2	2914.5	8490.9	6406	6481
1998	4993.0	6914.3	4661.5	1786.9	4318.2	3427.7	10143.7	6749	6860
1999	5180.9	7492.2	5175.9	1941.2	4489.7	3674.5	11827.0	7134	7229
2000	5534.0	8159.8	6161.9	2146.3	4842.2	4140.9	14092.9	7846	7942
2001	5945.5	9120.8	6871.3	2400.1	5202.8	4705.8	16982.6	8592	8717
2002	6482.1	9996.8	7494.3	2724.8	5555.8	5334.5	19818.6	9410	9506
2003	7510.8	11171.2	7914.8	3126.1	6045.7	6157.0	22753.8	10600	10666
2004	8720.5	12455.8	9306.5	3664.8	6600.2	7152.1	26754.6	12454	12487
2005	10400.5	13968.5	10668.8	4195.7	7486.0	8482.7	31742.1	14267	14368
2006	12450.1	16533.4	12186.3	4792.6	9972.3	10320.9	36910.8	16707	16738
2007	15348.0	20941.1	14605.1	5548.1	15200.0	13714.0	44561.5	20541	20494
2008	18807.6	26186.2	16367.6	6616.1	18345.6	14600.3	53169.3	24250	24100
2009	22681.5	29004.6	16522.4	6957.0	21836.8	18760.5	60002.6	26136	26180
2010	27259.3	35907.9	18783.6	7712.0	25733.1	23326.6	68654.7	30676	30808
2011	32926.5	43734.5	21842.0	8565.4	30747.2	27780.7	81082.2	35939	36277
2012	36896.1	49835.5	23763.2	9536.9	35272.2	30751.9	93041.6	39679	39771
2013	40896.8	56288.9	26042.7	10228.3	41293.4	35340.4	105847.3	43143	43497
2014	45401.7	63170.4	28534.4	11228.7	46853.4	38086.4	119618.5	46971	46912
2015	47761.3	67719.6	30519.5	12306.1	56299.8	42573.8	136856.5	49684	49922
2016	51498.9	73724.5	33028.7	13607.8	59964.0	49969.4	156744.3	53516	53783
2017	57905.6	81156.6	37121.9	15056.0	64844.3	57086.0	179086.3	59514	59592
2018	65493.0	88903.7	40337.2	16520.6	70610.3	64623.0	204145.2	65246	65534
2019	70648.1	95650.9	42466.3	17903.1	76250.6	70444.8	227715.8	69881	70078
2020	72444.7	96086.1	40582.9	15285.4	83617.7	73425.3	237825.3	71253	71828
2021	78741.2	110147.0	48423.9	18026.9	90308.7	77215.9	264833.0	80803	81370
2022	80766.0	116294.1	51076.9	17755.0	93285.3	73766.1	284160.2	84579	85310
2023	85691.1	123072.4	57819.8	21023.6	100676.6	73722.7	305010.2	88607	89358

3-2 国内生产总值构成
Composition of Gross Domestic Product

本表按当年价格计算。
Data in this table are calculated at current prices.
单位：% (%)

年 份 Year	国内生产总值 Gross Domestic Product	第一产业 Primary Industry	第二产业 Secondary Industry	第三产业 Tertiary Industry	农林牧渔业 Agriculture, Forestry, Animal Husbandry and Fishery	工业 Industry
1978	100.0	27.7	47.7	24.6	27.9	44.1
1979	100.0	30.7	47.0	22.3	31.0	43.6
1980	100.0	29.6	48.1	22.3	29.9	43.9
1981	100.0	31.3	46.0	22.7	31.6	41.9
1982	100.0	32.8	44.6	22.6	33.1	40.6
1983	100.0	32.6	44.2	23.2	32.9	39.8
1984	100.0	31.5	42.9	25.5	31.8	38.7
1985	100.0	27.9	42.7	29.4	28.2	38.2
1986	100.0	26.6	43.5	29.8	26.9	38.6
1987	100.0	26.3	43.3	30.4	26.6	38.0
1988	100.0	25.2	43.5	31.2	25.5	38.3
1989	100.0	24.6	42.5	32.9	24.8	38.0
1990	100.0	26.6	41.0	32.4	26.8	36.6
1991	100.0	24.0	41.5	34.5	24.3	37.0
1992	100.0	21.3	43.1	35.6	21.6	38.0
1993	100.0	19.3	46.2	34.5	19.5	39.9
1994	100.0	19.5	46.2	34.4	19.7	40.2
1995	100.0	19.6	46.8	33.7	19.8	40.8
1996	100.0	19.3	47.1	33.6	19.5	41.1
1997	100.0	17.9	47.1	35.0	18.1	41.4
1998	100.0	17.2	45.8	37.0	17.4	40.1
1999	100.0	16.1	45.4	38.6	16.3	39.8
2000	100.0	14.7	45.5	39.8	14.9	40.1
2001	100.0	14.0	44.8	41.2	14.2	39.6
2002	100.0	13.3	44.5	42.2	13.6	39.3
2003	100.0	12.3	45.6	42.0	12.6	40.3
2004	100.0	12.9	45.9	41.2	13.2	40.6
2005	100.0	11.6	47.0	41.3	12.0	41.6
2006	100.0	10.6	47.6	41.8	11.0	42.0
2007	100.0	10.2	46.9	42.9	10.5	41.4
2008	100.0	10.2	47.0	42.9	10.5	41.3
2009	100.0	9.6	46.0	44.4	9.9	39.6
2010	100.0	9.3	46.5	44.2	9.6	40.1
2011	100.0	9.2	46.5	44.3	9.5	40.0
2012	100.0	9.1	45.4	45.5	9.4	38.8
2013	100.0	8.9	44.2	46.9	9.2	37.5
2014	100.0	8.6	43.1	48.3	8.9	36.2
2015	100.0	8.4	40.8	50.8	8.7	34.1
2016	100.0	8.1	39.6	52.4	8.4	32.9
2017	100.0	7.5	39.9	52.7	7.8	33.1
2018	100.0	7.0	39.7	53.3	7.3	32.8
2019	100.0	7.1	38.6	54.3	7.5	31.6
2020	100.0	7.7	37.8	54.5	8.0	30.9
2021	100.0	7.2	39.3	53.5	7.6	32.6
2022	100.0	7.3	39.3	53.4	7.7	32.8
2023	100.0	7.1	38.3	54.6	7.5	31.7

3-2 续表 continued

单位：% (%)

年 份 Year	建筑业 Construction	批发和零售业 Wholesale and Retail Trades	交通运输、仓储和邮政业 Transport, Storage and Post	住宿和餐饮业 Hotels and Catering Services	金融业 Financial Intermediation	房地产业 Real Estate	其他 Others
1978	3.8	6.6	4.9	1.2	2.1	2.2	7.2
1979	3.5	4.9	4.7	1.1	1.9	2.1	7.3
1980	4.3	4.2	4.7	1.0	1.9	2.1	8.0
1981	4.2	4.7	4.5	1.1	1.9	2.0	8.2
1982	4.1	3.2	4.6	1.2	2.4	2.1	8.7
1983	4.5	3.3	4.6	1.2	2.8	2.0	8.9
1984	4.4	5.0	4.7	1.3	3.2	2.2	8.8
1985	4.6	8.8	4.6	1.5	3.2	2.4	8.4
1986	5.1	8.2	4.8	1.6	3.9	2.9	8.2
1987	5.5	8.7	4.7	1.5	4.2	3.1	7.8
1988	5.3	9.8	4.5	1.6	4.3	3.1	7.6
1989	4.6	8.9	4.7	1.6	6.3	3.3	7.7
1990	4.6	6.7	6.2	1.6	6.1	3.5	8.0
1991	4.6	8.3	6.5	2.0	5.4	3.5	8.4
1992	5.2	8.8	6.2	2.1	5.5	4.0	8.5
1993	6.4	7.9	6.1	2.0	5.3	3.9	9.0
1994	6.1	7.8	5.7	2.1	5.3	3.9	9.3
1995	6.1	7.8	5.3	2.0	5.2	3.8	9.2
1996	6.1	7.8	5.3	1.9	5.2	3.6	9.5
1997	5.8	7.9	5.2	2.0	5.2	3.7	10.7
1998	5.9	8.1	5.5	2.1	5.1	4.0	11.9
1999	5.7	8.3	5.7	2.1	5.0	4.1	13.1
2000	5.5	8.1	6.1	2.1	4.8	4.1	14.1
2001	5.4	8.2	6.2	2.2	4.7	4.2	15.3
2002	5.3	8.2	6.2	2.2	4.6	4.4	16.3
2003	5.5	8.1	5.8	2.3	4.4	4.5	16.6
2004	5.4	7.7	5.8	2.3	4.1	4.4	16.5
2005	5.6	7.5	5.7	2.2	4.0	4.5	16.9
2006	5.7	7.5	5.6	2.2	4.5	4.7	16.8
2007	5.7	7.8	5.4	2.1	5.6	5.1	16.5
2008	5.9	8.2	5.1	2.1	5.7	4.6	16.7
2009	6.5	8.3	4.7	2.0	6.3	5.4	17.2
2010	6.6	8.7	4.6	1.9	6.2	5.7	16.7
2011	6.7	9.0	4.5	1.8	6.3	5.7	16.6
2012	6.9	9.3	4.4	1.8	6.5	5.7	17.3
2013	6.9	9.5	4.4	1.7	7.0	6.0	17.9
2014	7.1	9.8	4.4	1.7	7.3	5.9	18.6
2015	6.9	9.8	4.4	1.8	8.2	6.2	19.9
2016	6.9	9.9	4.4	1.8	8.0	6.7	21.0
2017	7.0	9.8	4.5	1.8	7.8	6.9	21.5
2018	7.1	9.7	4.4	1.8	7.7	7.0	22.2
2019	7.2	9.7	4.3	1.8	7.7	7.1	23.1
2020	7.1	9.5	4.0	1.5	8.2	7.2	23.5
2021	6.9	9.6	4.2	1.6	7.9	6.7	23.0
2022	6.7	9.7	4.2	1.5	7.7	6.1	23.6
2023	6.8	9.8	4.6	1.7	8.0	5.8	24.2

3-3 不变价国内生产总值
Gross Domestic Product at Constant Prices

单位：亿元 (100 million yuan)

年 份 Year	国内生产总 值 Gross Domestic Product	第一产业 Primary Industry	第二产业 Secondary Industry	第三产业 Tertiary Industry	农林牧渔业 Agriculture, Forestry, Animal Husbandry and Fishery	工业 Industry
			按1970年价格计算	Price Base Year=1970		
1978	3593.0	927.8	1776.4	888.8	936.0	1659.5
1979	3865.8	984.7	1922.5	958.5	993.4	1803.6
1980	4168.6	970.1	2181.9	1016.6	978.7	2030.5
			按1980年价格计算	Price Base Year=1980		
1980	4587.6	1359.5	2204.7	1023.4	1371.6	2014.8
1981	4822.1	1454.4	2246.2	1121.5	1467.3	2050.0
1982	5257.0	1622.1	2371.4	1263.4	1636.5	2168.6
1983	5823.1	1757.1	2617.7	1448.3	1772.7	2379.8
1984	6707.8	1983.5	2995.3	1729.0	2001.1	2731.8
1985	7608.7	2020.0	3546.4	2042.2	2038.0	3224.4
1986	8289.6	2087.1	3908.8	2293.8	2105.6	3535.1
1987	9256.0	2185.3	4440.2	2630.6	2204.7	3999.4
1988	10294.7	2240.8	5076.9	2977.0	2260.8	4603.1
1989	10727.8	2309.8	5267.2	3150.8	2330.3	4835.4
1990	11148.3	2479.0	5434.4	3234.9	2501.0	4997.8
			按1990年价格计算	Price Base Year=1990		
1990	18872.9	5017.2	7744.1	6111.6	5061.8	6904.5
1991	20621.0	5135.3	8811.6	6674.1	5183.2	7892.0
1992	23554.3	5374.1	10665.1	7515.0	5426.9	9552.4
1993	26824.5	5624.0	12770.9	8429.6	5682.0	11458.9
1994	30321.5	5845.9	15087.7	9387.9	5909.3	13611.4
1995	33642.9	6134.8	17173.6	10334.5	6204.7	15515.4
1996	36981.2	6444.0	19250.3	11286.9	6521.2	17453.4
1997	40397.0	6665.5	21267.3	12464.2	6749.4	19429.3
1998	43566.6	6894.3	23160.8	13511.5	6985.5	21157.0
1999	46904.5	7082.6	25060.7	14761.2	7181.1	22969.1
2000	50886.7	7247.5	27434.9	16204.3	7353.5	25233.3
			按2000年价格计算	Price Base Year=2000		
2000	100280.1	14717.4	45663.7	39899.1	14943.6	40258.5
2001	108639.2	15105.6	49541.1	43992.5	15362.0	43768.0
2002	118561.9	15513.5	54443.1	48605.4	15807.4	48163.1
2003	130463.2	15881.4	61339.5	53242.3	16202.5	54304.5
2004	143657.8	16851.0	68176.3	58630.4	17223.2	60578.7
2005	160027.0	17706.0	76445.0	65875.9	18124.5	67633.9
			按2005年价格计算	Price Base Year=2005		
2005	187318.9	21806.7	88082.2	77430.0	22416.2	77958.3
2006	211147.7	22843.7	99929.8	88374.1	23537.2	88037.2
2007	241195.8	23648.6	114970.0	102577.2	24418.7	101196.3
2008	264472.8	24867.9	126281.9	113323.0	25732.2	111288.0
2009	289329.9	25863.3	139279.8	124186.8	26809.9	121401.5
2010	320102.6	26962.7	156945.5	136194.4	27954.2	136671.7
			按2010年价格计算	Price Base Year=2010		
2010	412119.3	38430.8	191626.5	182061.9	39619.0	165123.1
2011	451480.1	40035.1	212108.9	199336.2	41303.3	183193.8
2012	486983.3	41823.2	229848.9	215311.2	43181.0	198078.1
2013	524803.1	43415.5	248207.4	233180.2	44891.2	213397.7
2014	563773.8	45174.1	265968.0	252631.7	46773.7	227776.8
2015	603470.9	46935.2	281731.3	274804.4	48667.5	240736.1
			按2015年价格计算	Price Base Year=2015		
2015	688858.2	57774.6	281338.9	349744.7	59852.6	234968.9
2016	736036.5	59668.4	298307.8	378060.3	61918.9	248317.4
2017	787170.4	62032.0	315813.4	409325.0	64459.4	263770.4
2018	840302.6	64192.5	334106.6	442003.5	66811.6	279848.2
2019	890304.8	66167.6	350393.0	473744.2	68982.9	293252.3
2020	910235.6	68239.4	359027.6	482968.6	71265.6	300215.5
			按2020年价格计算	Price Base Year=2020		
2020	1013567.0	78030.9	383562.4	551973.7	81396.5	312902.9
2021	1099197.9	83550.6	416833.7	598813.5	87163.1	345370.3
2022	1131631.6	87062.7	427827.5	616741.4	90996.6	354528.1
2023	1191037.3	90590.6	447953.3	652493.3	94802.5	369482.7

注：1.更换基期的年份有两个不变价数据，一个按上一基期价格计算，一个按新基期价格计算。
2.有关不变价国内生产总值的解释见简要说明。

a) There are two figures for the base switching years, one at the former base year prices and the other at the new base year prices.
b) Please refer to the brief introduction for the definition of gross domestic product at constant prices.

3-3 续表 continued

单位：亿元 (100 million yuan)

年份 Year	建筑业 Construction	批发和零售业 Wholesale and Retail Trades	交通运输、仓储和邮政业 Transport, Storage and Post	住宿和餐饮业 Hotels and Catering Services	金融业 Financial Intermediation	房地产业 Real Estate	其他 Others
			按1970年价格计算 Price Base Year=1970				
1978	122.0	253.4	179.7	44.8	77.0	64.8	255.7
1979	124.5	275.5	194.6	49.8	75.5	67.5	281.4
1980	157.7	270.4	202.9	51.7	81.0	72.8	322.9
			按1980年价格计算 Price Base Year=1980				
1980	196.3	193.8	213.4	47.4	85.8	96.2	368.2
1981	202.6	251.0	217.4	55.7	89.8	92.8	395.4
1982	209.5	249.2	242.1	73.3	128.5	101.3	447.9
1983	245.2	302.1	265.1	87.5	162.7	106.5	501.5
1984	271.8	376.8	304.6	94.6	212.7	136.0	578.4
1985	331.9	503.1	346.6	100.6	249.1	170.0	645.0
1986	384.6	550.6	394.6	116.3	324.4	214.0	664.4
1987	453.1	631.7	432.6	127.5	397.6	276.7	732.7
1988	489.2	706.0	486.7	159.5	477.9	311.7	799.7
1989	448.0	630.4	507.2	175.4	601.3	361.4	838.4
1990	453.4	597.2	549.5	181.5	614.3	384.0	869.6
			按1990年价格计算 Price Base Year=1990				
1990	861.7	1269.2	1167.2	301.9	1144.1	660.9	1501.7
1991	944.0	1334.9	1290.4	326.5	1176.5	739.9	1733.6
1992	1142.1	1475.2	1420.2	414.7	1252.6	936.9	1933.3
1993	1347.3	1601.8	1598.2	448.9	1393.9	1037.7	2255.8
1994	1531.2	1733.1	1734.4	570.7	1529.6	1161.8	2540.1
1995	1720.8	1875.7	1924.8	629.1	1664.6	1306.4	2801.4
1996	1867.2	2018.9	2137.3	672.1	1796.3	1358.9	3155.8
1997	1916.4	2195.9	2333.9	745.7	1958.6	1414.9	3652.9
1998	2089.1	2338.9	2581.0	828.2	2058.9	1523.9	4003.9
1999	2179.1	2542.6	2895.2	892.1	2169.3	1614.4	4461.5
2000	2303.4	2782.1	3143.7	975.4	2320.6	1729.1	5045.7
			按2000年价格计算 Price Base Year=2000				
2000	5534.0	8159.8	6161.9	2146.3	4842.2	4140.9	14092.9
2001	5910.3	8901.9	6704.6	2310.4	5182.0	4596.0	15904.0
2002	6431.0	9686.2	7182.5	2590.9	5572.0	5050.2	18078.6
2003	7208.2	10648.9	7622.6	2911.0	5986.5	5543.5	20035.5
2004	7795.6	11348.3	8726.1	3270.2	6267.2	5867.4	22581.1
2005	9043.2	12826.5	9703.9	3671.2	7152.7	6578.9	25292.2
			按2005年价格计算 Price Base Year=2005				
2005	10400.5	13968.5	10668.8	4195.7	7486.0	8482.7	31742.1
2006	12192.3	16687.2	11732.4	4723.0	9262.6	9786.1	35189.6
2007	14166.5	20060.5	13117.2	5177.3	11652.1	12137.8	39269.5
2008	15514.3	23240.1	14078.2	5674.3	13060.6	12212.1	43673.1
2009	18453.8	26005.6	14552.9	5887.4	15195.1	13610.4	47413.2
2010	21005.1	29801.8	15930.6	6371.4	16555.6	14585.8	51226.4
			按2010年价格计算 Price Base Year=2010				
2010	27259.3	35907.9	18783.6	7712.0	25733.1	23326.6	68654.7
2011	29910.4	40383.5	20598.3	8106.2	27710.1	24975.0	75299.4
2012	32827.7	44542.3	21852.4	8629.3	30329.6	26060.7	81482.2
2013	36004.7	49225.9	23294.2	8966.1	33534.6	27844.8	87643.7
2014	39476.5	54275.6	24907.1	9521.6	37059.8	28434.0	95548.8
2015	42372.3	57925.7	26014.1	10146.8	43263.1	29528.0	104817.2
			按2015年价格计算 Price Base Year=2015				
2015	47761.3	67719.6	30519.5	12306.1	56299.8	42573.8	136856.5
2016	51442.4	72916.2	32620.3	13256.1	59007.1	46313.9	150244.2
2017	53463.7	78615.8	35737.5	14338.1	61815.6	49534.8	165435.2
2018	56041.8	83869.1	38691.8	15296.5	64771.8	51254.3	183717.5
2019	58979.8	88572.0	41205.0	16136.3	69077.2	52576.4	201523.0
2020	60586.6	87783.9	41545.2	13423.0	73150.0	53246.0	209019.8
			按2020年价格计算 Price Base Year=2020				
2020	72444.7	96086.1	40582.9	15285.4	83617.7	73425.3	237825.3
2021	73211.6	106624.8	46723.2	17664.3	86926.2	76004.4	259509.7
2022	75370.1	109265.2	47053.9	17161.4	89587.5	73057.7	274611.1
2023	80690.0	116043.3	50800.0	19656.3	95640.1	72091.1	291831.2

3-4 国内生产总值指数
Indices of Gross Domestic Product

本表按不变价格计算。
Data in this table are calculated at constant prices.

(上年=100) (preceding year=100)

年份 Year	国民总收入 Gross National Income	国内生产总值 Gross Domestic Product	第一产业 Primary Industry	第二产业 Secondary Industry	第三产业 Tertiary Industry	农林牧渔业 Agriculture, Forestry, Animal Husbandry and Fishery	工业 Industry
1978	111.7	111.7	104.1	115.0	113.6	104.1	116.4
1979	107.6	107.6	106.1	108.2	107.8	106.1	108.7
1980	107.8	107.8	98.5	113.5	106.1	98.5	112.6
1981	105.1	105.1	107.0	101.9	109.6	107.0	101.7
1982	109.2	109.0	111.5	105.6	112.7	111.5	105.8
1983	111.0	110.8	108.3	110.4	114.6	108.3	109.7
1984	115.3	115.2	112.9	114.4	119.4	112.9	114.8
1985	113.2	113.4	101.8	118.4	118.1	101.8	118.0
1986	108.6	108.9	103.3	110.2	112.3	103.3	109.6
1987	111.6	111.7	104.7	113.6	114.7	104.7	113.1
1988	111.3	111.2	102.5	114.3	113.2	102.5	115.1
1989	104.3	104.2	103.1	103.7	105.8	103.1	105.0
1990	104.1	103.9	107.3	103.2	102.7	107.3	103.4
1991	109.2	109.3	102.4	113.8	109.2	102.4	114.3
1992	114.1	114.2	104.7	121.0	112.6	104.7	121.0
1993	113.6	113.9	104.6	119.7	112.2	104.7	120.0
1994	113.1	113.0	103.9	118.1	111.4	104.0	118.8
1995	109.4	111.0	104.9	113.8	110.1	105.0	114.0
1996	110.1	109.9	105.0	112.1	109.2	105.1	112.5
1997	109.6	109.2	103.4	110.5	110.4	103.5	111.3
1998	107.3	107.8	103.4	108.9	108.4	103.5	108.9
1999	108.0	107.7	102.7	108.2	109.2	102.8	108.6
2000	108.6	108.5	102.3	109.5	109.8	102.4	109.9
2001	108.1	108.3	102.6	108.5	110.3	102.8	108.7
2002	109.6	109.1	102.7	109.9	110.5	102.9	110.0
2003	110.5	110.0	102.4	112.7	109.5	102.5	112.8
2004	110.5	110.1	106.1	111.1	110.1	106.3	111.6
2005	110.9	111.4	105.1	112.1	112.4	105.2	111.6
2006	113.3	112.7	104.8	113.5	114.1	105.0	112.9
2007	114.7	114.2	103.5	115.1	116.1	103.7	114.9
2008	110.1	109.7	105.2	109.8	110.5	105.4	110.0
2009	108.5	109.4	104.0	110.3	109.6	104.2	109.1
2010	110.3	110.6	104.3	112.7	109.7	104.3	112.6
2011	109.0	109.6	104.2	110.7	109.5	104.3	110.9
2012	108.6	107.9	104.5	108.4	108.0	104.5	108.1
2013	107.1	107.8	103.8	108.0	108.3	104.0	107.7
2014	108.4	107.4	104.1	107.2	108.3	104.2	106.7
2015	106.4	107.0	103.9	105.9	108.8	104.0	105.7
2016	106.8	106.8	103.3	106.0	108.1	103.5	105.7
2017	107.3	106.9	104.0	105.9	108.3	104.1	106.2
2018	106.4	106.7	103.5	105.8	108.0	103.6	106.1
2019	106.1	106.0	103.1	104.9	107.2	103.2	104.8
2020	101.7	102.2	103.1	102.5	101.9	103.3	102.4
2021	108.6	108.4	107.1	108.7	108.5	107.1	110.4
2022	102.8	103.0	104.2	102.6	103.0	104.4	102.7
2023	105.3	105.2	104.1	104.7	105.8	104.2	104.2

3-4 续表 continued

(上年＝100) (preceding year=100)

年份 Year	建筑业 Construction	批发和零售业 Wholesale and Retail Trades	交通运输、仓储和邮政业 Transport, Storage and Post	住宿和餐饮业 Hotels and Catering Services	金融业 Financial Intermediation	房地产业 Real Estate	其他 Others	人均国民总收入 Per Capita GNI	人均国内生产总值 Per Capita GDP
1978	99.5	123.1	108.9	118.1	110.1	105.7	111.2	110.2	110.2
1979	102.0	108.7	108.3	111.1	98.0	104.1	110.1	106.2	106.2
1980	126.6	98.1	104.3	103.9	107.3	107.9	114.8	106.5	106.5
1981	103.2	129.5	101.9	117.5	104.7	96.5	107.4	103.8	103.8
1982	103.4	99.3	111.4	131.6	143.1	109.1	113.3	107.6	107.4
1983	117.0	121.2	109.5	119.4	126.5	105.2	112.0	109.5	109.2
1984	110.8	124.7	114.9	108.1	130.7	127.7	115.3	113.8	113.7
1985	122.1	133.5	113.8	106.3	117.1	125.0	111.5	111.7	111.9
1986	115.8	109.4	113.9	115.6	130.2	125.9	103.0	107.0	107.3
1987	117.8	114.7	109.6	109.7	122.6	129.3	110.3	109.8	109.9
1988	108.0	111.8	112.5	125.1	120.2	112.7	109.1	109.5	109.4
1989	91.6	89.3	104.2	109.9	125.8	115.9	104.8	102.7	102.6
1990	101.2	94.7	108.3	103.5	102.2	106.2	103.7	102.6	102.4
1991	109.6	105.2	110.6	108.2	102.8	112.0	115.4	107.7	107.8
1992	121.0	110.5	110.1	127.0	106.5	126.6	111.5	112.7	112.8
1993	118.0	108.6	112.5	108.2	111.3	110.8	116.7	112.3	112.6
1994	113.6	108.2	108.5	127.1	109.7	112.0	112.6	111.8	111.8
1995	112.4	108.2	111.0	110.2	108.8	112.4	110.3	108.2	109.8
1996	108.5	107.6	111.0	106.8	107.9	104.0	112.7	109.0	108.8
1997	102.6	108.8	109.2	110.9	109.0	104.1	115.8	108.4	108.1
1998	109.0	106.5	110.6	111.1	105.1	107.7	109.6	106.3	106.8
1999	104.3	108.7	112.2	107.7	105.4	105.9	111.4	107.1	106.7
2000	105.7	109.4	108.6	109.3	107.0	107.1	113.1	107.8	107.6
2001	106.8	109.1	108.8	107.6	107.0	111.0	112.9	107.3	107.6
2002	108.8	108.8	107.1	112.1	107.5	109.9	113.7	108.9	108.4
2003	112.1	109.9	106.1	112.4	107.4	109.8	110.8	109.8	109.4
2004	108.2	106.6	114.5	112.3	104.7	105.8	112.7	109.9	109.5
2005	116.0	113.0	111.2	112.3	114.1	112.1	112.0	110.3	110.7
2006	117.2	119.5	110.0	112.6	123.7	115.4	110.9	112.7	112.1
2007	116.2	120.2	111.8	109.6	125.8	124.0	111.6	114.1	113.6
2008	109.5	115.9	107.3	109.6	112.1	100.6	111.2	109.5	109.1
2009	118.9	111.9	103.4	103.8	116.3	111.5	108.6	108.0	108.9
2010	113.8	114.6	109.5	108.2	109.0	107.2	108.0	109.8	110.1
2011	109.7	112.5	109.7	105.1	107.7	107.1	109.7	108.4	109.0
2012	109.8	110.3	106.1	106.5	109.5	104.3	108.2	107.9	107.1
2013	109.7	110.5	106.6	103.9	110.6	106.8	107.6	106.4	107.1
2014	109.6	110.3	106.9	106.2	110.5	102.1	109.0	107.8	106.8
2015	107.3	106.7	104.4	106.6	116.7	103.8	109.7	105.8	106.4
2016	107.7	107.7	106.9	107.7	104.8	108.8	109.8	106.2	106.2
2017	103.9	107.8	109.6	108.2	104.8	107.0	110.1	106.7	106.3
2018	104.8	106.7	108.3	106.7	104.8	103.5	111.1	105.9	106.3
2019	105.2	105.6	106.5	105.5	106.6	102.6	109.7	105.7	105.6
2020	102.7	99.1	100.8	83.2	105.9	101.3	103.7	101.5	102.0
2021	101.1	111.0	115.1	115.6	104.0	103.5	109.1	108.5	108.4
2022	102.9	102.5	100.7	97.2	103.1	96.1	105.8	102.8	103.0
2023	107.1	106.2	108.0	114.5	106.8	98.7	106.3	105.4	105.4

3–5 国内生产总值指数
Indices of Gross Domestic Product

本表按不变价格计算。
Data in this table are calculated at constant prices.

(1978年=100) (year of 1978=100)

年份 Year	国民总收入 Gross National Income	国内生产总值 Gross Domestic Product	第一产业 Primary Industry	第二产业 Secondary Industry	第三产业 Tertiary Industry	农林牧渔业 Agriculture, Forestry, Animal Husbandry and Fishery	工业 Industry
1978	100.0	100.0	100.0	100.0	100.0	100.0	100.0
1979	107.6	107.6	106.1	108.2	107.8	106.1	108.7
1980	116.0	116.0	104.6	122.8	114.4	104.6	122.4
1981	121.9	122.0	111.9	125.1	125.3	111.9	124.5
1982	133.1	132.9	124.8	132.1	141.2	124.8	131.7
1983	147.8	147.3	135.1	145.8	161.9	135.1	144.5
1984	170.5	169.6	152.6	166.9	193.2	152.6	165.9
1985	192.9	192.4	155.4	197.6	228.3	155.4	195.8
1986	209.6	209.6	160.5	217.8	256.4	160.5	214.7
1987	233.9	234.1	168.1	247.4	294.0	168.1	242.9
1988	260.3	260.4	172.3	282.8	332.7	172.3	279.5
1989	271.4	271.3	177.6	293.4	352.2	177.6	293.6
1990	282.7	281.9	190.7	302.8	361.6	190.7	303.5
1991	308.7	308.1	195.2	344.5	394.8	195.2	346.9
1992	352.1	351.9	204.2	416.9	444.6	204.4	419.9
1993	399.9	400.7	213.7	499.3	498.7	214.0	503.7
1994	452.1	453.0	222.2	589.8	555.4	222.6	598.3
1995	494.5	502.6	233.1	671.4	611.4	233.7	682.0
1996	544.5	552.5	244.9	752.6	667.7	245.6	767.2
1997	596.6	603.5	253.3	831.4	737.4	254.2	854.1
1998	640.3	650.8	262.0	905.5	799.3	263.1	930.0
1999	691.4	700.7	269.2	979.7	873.3	270.5	1009.7
2000	751.0	760.2	275.4	1072.6	958.6	277.0	1109.2
2001	811.8	823.6	282.7	1163.6	1057.0	284.7	1205.9
2002	889.7	898.8	290.3	1278.8	1167.8	293.0	1327.0
2003	982.9	989.0	297.2	1440.8	1279.2	300.3	1496.2
2004	1086.2	1089.0	315.4	1601.3	1408.7	319.2	1669.1
2005	1204.6	1213.1	331.4	1795.6	1582.8	336.0	1863.5
2006	1364.9	1367.4	347.1	2037.1	1806.5	352.8	2104.4
2007	1565.6	1562.0	359.3	2343.7	2096.8	366.0	2418.9
2008	1723.4	1712.8	377.9	2574.3	2316.5	385.6	2660.1
2009	1870.6	1873.8	393.0	2839.2	2538.5	401.8	2901.9
2010	2064.2	2073.1	409.7	3199.3	2784.0	418.9	3266.9
2011	2249.9	2271.1	426.8	3541.3	3048.1	436.8	3624.4
2012	2444.0	2449.6	445.9	3837.5	3292.4	456.6	3918.9
2013	2618.4	2639.9	462.8	4144.0	3565.7	474.7	4222.0
2014	2839.5	2835.9	481.6	4440.5	3863.1	494.6	4506.5
2015	3021.1	3035.6	500.4	4703.7	4202.2	514.6	4762.9
2016	3227.4	3243.5	516.8	4987.4	4542.4	532.4	5033.4
2017	3464.3	3468.8	537.2	5280.1	4918.0	554.2	5346.7
2018	3686.7	3703.0	555.9	5585.9	5310.7	574.5	5672.6
2019	3912.3	3923.3	573.1	5858.2	5692.0	593.1	5944.3
2020	3979.0	4011.2	591.0	6002.6	5802.9	612.8	6085.4
2021	4319.7	4350.0	632.8	6523.2	6295.3	656.2	6716.8
2022	4440.0	4478.4	659.4	6695.3	6483.7	685.0	6894.9
2023	4673.9	4713.5	686.1	7010.3	6859.6	713.7	7185.8

3-5 续表 continued

(1978年＝100) (year of 1978=100)

年份 Year	建筑业 Construction	批发和零售业 Wholesale and Retail Trades	交通运输、仓储和邮政业 Transport, Storage and Post	住宿和餐饮业 Hotels and Catering Services	金融业 Financial Intermediation	房地产业 Real Estate	其他 Others	人均国民总收入 Per Capita GNI	人均国内生产总值 Per Capita GDP
1978	100.0	100.0	100.0	100.0	100.0	100.0	100.0	100.0	100.0
1979	102.0	108.7	108.3	111.1	98.0	104.1	110.1	106.2	106.2
1980	129.2	106.7	112.9	115.5	105.2	112.3	126.3	113.0	113.1
1981	133.3	138.2	115.0	135.6	110.2	108.4	135.6	117.3	117.3
1982	137.9	137.2	128.1	178.5	157.7	118.2	153.6	126.2	126.0
1983	161.3	166.3	140.2	213.1	199.5	124.3	172.0	138.1	137.6
1984	178.8	207.4	161.1	230.3	260.8	158.7	198.4	157.2	156.4
1985	218.4	277.0	183.3	244.8	305.5	198.4	221.2	175.5	175.1
1986	253.0	303.1	208.8	283.1	397.9	249.7	227.9	187.9	187.9
1987	298.1	347.7	228.8	310.5	487.8	322.9	251.3	206.3	206.5
1988	321.8	388.7	257.5	388.5	586.2	363.8	274.3	225.9	226.0
1989	294.8	347.1	268.3	426.9	737.6	421.8	287.6	232.0	231.9
1990	298.3	328.8	290.7	441.8	753.5	448.2	298.3	238.1	237.5
1991	326.8	345.8	321.4	477.9	774.9	501.7	344.3	256.5	256.0
1992	395.4	382.2	353.7	607.0	825.0	635.3	384.0	289.0	288.8
1993	466.4	415.0	398.0	657.0	918.1	703.6	448.1	324.5	325.1
1994	530.0	449.0	432.0	835.3	1007.5	787.8	504.5	362.7	363.4
1995	595.7	485.9	479.4	920.8	1096.4	885.8	556.4	392.5	398.9
1996	646.4	523.0	532.3	983.8	1183.2	921.4	626.8	427.6	433.9
1997	663.4	568.9	581.3	1091.4	1290.1	959.4	725.5	463.7	469.1
1998	723.2	605.9	642.8	1212.2	1356.1	1033.3	795.3	493.0	501.1
1999	754.3	658.7	721.1	1305.7	1428.8	1094.7	886.1	527.7	534.8
2000	797.3	720.7	782.9	1427.7	1528.4	1172.5	1002.2	568.7	575.7
2001	851.5	786.3	851.9	1536.8	1635.7	1301.4	1131.0	610.3	619.1
2002	926.6	855.5	912.6	1723.4	1758.8	1430.0	1285.6	664.4	671.2
2003	1038.5	940.6	968.5	1936.4	1889.6	1569.7	1424.8	729.5	734.0
2004	1123.2	1002.3	1108.8	2175.3	1978.2	1661.4	1605.8	801.3	803.4
2005	1302.9	1132.9	1233.0	2442.0	2257.7	1862.8	1798.6	883.5	889.7
2006	1527.4	1353.4	1355.9	2748.9	2793.5	2149.1	1993.9	995.5	997.3
2007	1774.7	1627.0	1516.0	3013.3	3514.2	2665.5	2225.1	1135.9	1133.3
2008	1943.5	1884.9	1627.0	3302.6	3939.0	2681.8	2474.6	1244.0	1236.3
2009	2311.8	2109.2	1681.9	3426.6	4582.7	2988.9	2686.5	1343.6	1345.8
2010	2631.4	2417.0	1841.1	3708.3	4993.1	3203.1	2902.6	1475.4	1481.8
2011	2887.3	2718.3	2019.0	3897.9	5376.7	3429.4	3183.5	1599.4	1614.5
2012	3168.9	2998.2	2141.9	4149.4	5884.9	3578.5	3444.9	1725.6	1729.6
2013	3475.6	3313.5	2283.2	4311.4	6506.8	3823.5	3705.4	1836.5	1851.6
2014	3810.8	3653.4	2441.3	4578.5	7190.8	3904.4	4039.6	1979.1	1976.6
2015	4090.3	3899.1	2549.8	4879.1	8394.5	4054.6	4431.5	2093.5	2103.5
2016	4405.6	4198.3	2725.3	5255.8	8798.1	4410.8	4864.9	2223.6	2234.7
2017	4578.7	4526.5	2985.7	5684.8	9216.9	4717.6	5356.8	2372.4	2375.6
2018	4799.5	4829.0	3232.6	6064.8	9657.6	4881.3	5948.8	2513.0	2524.1
2019	5051.1	5099.7	3442.5	6397.7	10299.6	5007.2	6525.4	2657.3	2664.8
2020	5188.7	5054.4	3471.0	5322.0	10906.8	5071.0	6768.1	2696.2	2718.0
2021	5243.6	5608.7	3996.1	6150.2	11338.4	5249.1	7385.2	2924.5	2945.0
2022	5398.2	5747.6	4024.4	5975.1	11685.5	5045.6	7815.0	3006.3	3032.3
2023	5779.2	6104.2	4344.8	6843.8	12475.0	4978.9	8305.0	3167.9	3194.8

3–6 分行业增加值
Value-added by Sector

本表按当年价格计算。
Data in this table are calculated at current prices.

单位：亿元 (100 million yuan)

行　　业	Sector	2019	2020	2021	2022
国内生产总值	**Gross Domestic Product**	**986515.2**	**1013567.0**	**1149237.0**	**1204724.0**
农林牧渔业	Agriculture, Forestry, Animal Husbandry and Fishery	73576.9	81396.5	86994.8	92576.8
采矿业	Mining	23695.5	22011.5	34566.1	42273.9
制造业	Manufacturing	264136.7	266417.8	316581.5	326077.0
电力、热力、燃气及水生产和供应业	Production and Supply of Electricity, Heating, Gas and Water	24026.4	24473.6	23397.9	26692.7
建筑业	Construction	70648.1	72444.7	78741.2	80766.0
批发和零售业	Wholesale and Retail Trades	95650.9	96086.1	110147.0	116294.1
交通运输、仓储和邮政业	Transport, Storage and Post	42466.3	40582.9	48423.9	51076.9
住宿和餐饮业	Hotels and Catering Services	17903.1	15285.4	18026.9	17755.0
信息传输、软件和信息技术服务业	Information Transmission, Software and Information Technology	33391.8	38244.1	44510.4	49470.0
金融业	Financial Intermediation	76250.6	83617.7	90308.7	93285.3
房地产业	Real Estate	70444.8	73425.3	77215.9	73766.1
租赁和商务服务业	Leasing and Business Services	32638.0	32467.6	37484.2	39764.4
科学研究和技术服务业	Scientific Research and Technical Services	22624.3	24166.2	28164.0	29735.4
水利、环境和公共设施管理业	Management of Water Conservancy, Environment and Public Facilities	5861.3	5863.1	6053.1	6320.2
居民服务、修理和其他服务业	Service to Households, Repair and Other Services	16983.4	16353.2	18455.3	19218.7
教育	Education	37934.1	40091.9	43885.3	46738.9
卫生和社会工作	Health and Social Service	22354.6	24396.1	27514.6	30818.5
文化、体育和娱乐业	Culture, Sports and Entertainment	8137.8	6981.2	8495.4	8578.2
公共管理、社会保障和社会组织	Public Management, Social Security and Social Organization	47790.5	49261.9	50270.7	53515.6

3-7 三次产业和主要行业贡献率

Share of the Contributions of the Three Strata of Industry and Main Sectors to the Increase of the GDP

本表按不变价格计算。

Data in this table are calculated at constant prices.

单位：%　　(%)

年份 Year	国内生产总值 Gross Domestic Product	第一产业 Primary Industry	第二产业 Secondary Industry	第三产业 Tertiary Industry	#工业 Industry	#批发和零售业 Wholesale and Retail Trades	#金融业 Financial Intermediation
1978	100.0	9.8	61.8	28.4	62.2	12.7	1.9
1979	100.0	20.9	53.6	25.6	52.8	8.1	-0.6
1980	100.0	-4.8	85.6	19.2	74.9	-1.7	1.8
1981	100.0	40.5	17.7	41.8	15.0	24.4	1.7
1982	100.0	38.6	28.8	32.6	27.3	-0.4	8.9
1983	100.0	23.9	43.5	32.7	37.3	9.3	6.0
1984	100.0	25.6	42.7	31.7	39.8	8.4	5.6
1985	100.0	4.1	61.2	34.8	54.7	14.0	4.0
1986	100.0	9.8	53.2	36.9	45.6	7.0	11.1
1987	100.0	10.2	55.0	34.8	48.0	8.4	7.6
1988	100.0	5.4	61.3	33.4	58.1	7.2	7.7
1989	100.0	15.9	44.0	40.1	53.6	-17.5	28.5
1990	100.0	40.2	39.8	20.0	38.6	-7.9	3.1
1991	100.0	6.8	61.1	32.2	56.5	3.8	1.9
1992	100.0	8.1	63.2	28.7	56.6	4.8	2.6
1993	100.0	7.6	64.4	28.0	58.3	3.9	4.3
1994	100.0	6.3	66.3	27.4	61.6	3.8	3.9
1995	100.0	8.7	62.8	28.5	57.3	4.3	4.1
1996	100.0	9.3	62.2	28.5	58.1	4.3	3.9
1997	100.0	6.5	59.0	34.5	57.8	5.2	4.8
1998	100.0	7.2	59.7	33.0	54.5	4.5	3.2
1999	100.0	5.6	56.9	37.4	54.3	6.1	3.3
2000	100.0	4.1	59.6	36.2	56.9	6.0	3.8
2001	100.0	4.6	46.4	49.0	42.0	8.9	4.1
2002	100.0	4.1	49.4	46.5	44.3	7.9	3.9
2003	100.0	3.1	57.9	39.0	51.6	8.1	3.5
2004	100.0	7.3	51.8	40.8	47.6	5.3	2.1
2005	100.0	5.2	50.5	44.3	43.1	9.0	5.4
2006	100.0	4.4	49.7	45.9	42.3	11.4	7.5
2007	100.0	2.7	50.1	47.3	43.8	11.2	8.0
2008	100.0	5.2	48.6	46.2	43.4	13.7	6.1
2009	100.0	4.0	52.3	43.7	40.7	11.1	8.6
2010	100.0	3.6	57.4	39.0	49.6	12.3	4.4
2011	100.0	4.1	52.0	43.9	45.9	11.4	5.0
2012	100.0	5.0	50.0	45.0	41.9	11.7	7.4
2013	100.0	4.2	48.5	47.2	40.5	12.4	8.5
2014	100.0	4.5	45.6	49.9	36.9	13.0	9.0
2015	100.0	4.4	39.7	55.9	32.6	9.2	15.6
2016	100.0	4.0	36.0	60.0	28.3	11.0	5.7
2017	100.0	4.6	34.2	61.1	30.2	11.1	5.5
2018	100.0	4.1	34.4	61.5	30.3	9.9	5.6
2019	100.0	3.9	32.6	63.5	26.8	9.4	8.6
2020	100.0	10.4	43.3	46.3	34.9	-4.0	20.4
2021	100.0	6.4	38.9	54.7	37.9	12.3	3.9
2022	100.0	10.8	33.9	55.3	28.2	8.1	8.2
2023	100.0	5.9	33.9	60.2	25.2	11.4	10.2

注：贡献率指三次产业或主要行业增加值增量与GDP增量之比。

a) Share of the contributions of the three strata of industry or main sectors to the increase of the GDP refers to the proportion of the increment of the value-added of each industry or sector to the increment of GDP.

3-8 三次产业和主要行业对国内生产总值增长的拉动
Contribution of the Three Strata of Industry and Main Sectors to GDP Growth

本表按不变价格计算。

Data in this table are calculated at constant prices.

单位：百分点 (percentage points)

年 份 Year	国内生产总值 Gross Domestic Product	第一产业 Primary Industry	第二产业 Secondary Industry	第三产业 Tertiary Industry	#工业 Industry	#批发和零售业 Wholesale and Retail Trades	#金融业 Financial Intermediation
1978	11.7	1.1	7.2	3.3	7.3	1.5	0.2
1979	7.6	1.6	4.1	1.9	4.0	0.6	0.0
1980	7.8	-0.4	6.7	1.5	5.9	-0.1	0.1
1981	5.1	2.1	0.9	2.1	0.8	1.2	0.1
1982	9.0	3.5	2.6	2.9	2.5	0.0	0.8
1983	10.8	2.6	4.7	3.5	4.0	1.0	0.6
1984	15.2	3.9	6.5	4.8	6.0	1.3	0.9
1985	13.4	0.5	8.2	4.7	7.3	1.9	0.5
1986	8.9	0.9	4.8	3.3	4.1	0.6	1.0
1987	11.7	1.2	6.4	4.1	5.6	1.0	0.9
1988	11.2	0.6	6.9	3.7	6.5	0.8	0.9
1989	4.2	0.7	1.8	1.7	2.3	-0.7	1.2
1990	3.9	1.6	1.6	0.8	1.5	-0.3	0.1
1991	9.3	0.6	5.7	3.0	5.2	0.3	0.2
1992	14.2	1.2	9.0	4.1	8.1	0.7	0.4
1993	13.9	1.1	8.9	3.9	8.1	0.5	0.6
1994	13.0	0.8	8.6	3.6	8.0	0.5	0.5
1995	11.0	1.0	6.9	3.1	6.3	0.5	0.4
1996	9.9	0.9	6.2	2.8	5.8	0.4	0.4
1997	9.2	0.6	5.5	3.2	5.3	0.5	0.4
1998	7.8	0.6	4.7	2.6	4.3	0.4	0.2
1999	7.7	0.4	4.4	2.9	4.2	0.5	0.3
2000	8.5	0.4	5.1	3.1	4.8	0.5	0.3
2001	8.3	0.4	3.9	4.1	3.5	0.7	0.3
2002	9.1	0.4	4.5	4.2	4.0	0.7	0.4
2003	10.0	0.3	5.8	3.9	5.2	0.8	0.3
2004	10.1	0.7	5.2	4.1	4.8	0.5	0.2
2005	11.4	0.6	5.8	5.0	4.9	1.0	0.6
2006	12.7	0.6	6.3	5.8	5.4	1.5	0.9
2007	14.2	0.4	7.1	6.7	6.2	1.6	1.1
2008	9.7	0.5	4.7	4.5	4.2	1.3	0.6
2009	9.4	0.4	4.9	4.1	3.8	1.0	0.8
2010	10.6	0.4	6.1	4.2	5.3	1.3	0.5
2011	9.6	0.4	5.0	4.2	4.4	1.1	0.5
2012	7.9	0.4	3.9	3.5	3.3	0.9	0.6
2013	7.8	0.3	3.8	3.7	3.1	1.0	0.7
2014	7.4	0.3	3.4	3.7	2.7	1.0	0.7
2015	7.0	0.3	2.8	3.9	2.3	0.6	1.1
2016	6.8	0.3	2.5	4.1	1.9	0.8	0.4
2017	6.9	0.3	2.4	4.2	2.1	0.8	0.4
2018	6.7	0.3	2.3	4.2	2.0	0.7	0.4
2019	6.0	0.2	1.9	3.8	1.6	0.6	0.5
2020	2.2	0.2	1.0	1.0	0.8	-0.1	0.5
2021	8.4	0.5	3.3	4.6	3.2	1.0	0.3
2022	3.0	0.3	1.0	1.6	0.8	0.2	0.2
2023	5.2	0.3	1.8	3.2	1.3	0.6	0.5

注：拉动指GDP增长速度与三次产业或主要行业贡献率之乘积。

a) Contribution of the three strata of industry or main sectors to GDP growth refers to the growth rate of GDP multiplied by the contribution share of every industry or sector.

3–9 地区生产总值（2023年）
Gross Regional Product (2023)

本表绝对数按当年价格计算，指数按不变价格计算。
Data on value in this table are calculated at current prices, while indices are calculated at constant prices.

单位：亿元 (100 million yuan)

地 区	Region	地区生产总值 Gross Regional Product	三次产业增加值 Value-Added by Three Strata of Industry			分行业增加值 Value-Added by Sector		
			第一产业 Primary Industry	第二产业 Secondary Industry	第三产业 Tertiary Industry	农林牧渔业 Agriculture, Forestry, Animal Husbandry and Fishery	工 业 Industry	建筑业 Construction
北 京	Beijing	43760.7	105.5	6525.6	37129.6	106.9	5008.5	1603.4
天 津	Tianjin	16737.3	268.5	5982.6	10486.2	279.4	5359.0	769.6
河 北	Hebei	43944.1	4466.2	16435.3	23042.6	4783.7	13968.7	2507.1
山 西	Shanxi	25698.2	1388.9	13329.7	10979.6	1468.8	12263.3	1080.1
内蒙古	Inner Mongolia	24627.0	2737.3	11703.6	10186.1	2804.8	9889.8	1813.8
辽 宁	Liaoning	30209.4	2651.0	11734.5	15823.9	2743.5	10220.2	1648.0
吉 林	Jilin	13531.2	1644.8	4585.0	7301.4	1700.6	3705.0	913.7
黑龙江	Heilongjiang	15883.9	3518.3	4291.3	8074.3	3626.9	3963.6	438.0
上 海	Shanghai	47218.7	96.1	11613.0	35509.6	102.7	10846.2	882.3
江 苏	Jiangsu	128222.2	5075.8	56909.7	66236.7	5529.9	49244.6	7765.7
浙 江	Zhejiang	82553.2	2332.0	33952.7	46268.6	2404.1	29412.1	4623.5
安 徽	Anhui	47050.6	3496.6	18871.8	24682.2	3727.2	14021.1	4881.2
福 建	Fujian	54355.1	3217.7	23966.4	27171.0	3340.2	18548.3	5498.0
江 西	Jiangxi	32200.1	2450.4	13706.5	16043.2	2591.9	11180.7	2531.7
山 东	Shandong	92068.7	6506.2	35987.9	49574.6	7026.9	29191.2	6961.1
河 南	Henan	59132.4	5360.1	22175.3	31597.0	5825.1	16915.0	5322.2
湖 北	Hubei	55803.6	5073.4	20215.5	30514.7	5447.9	16357.0	3916.1
湖 南	Hunan	50012.9	4621.3	18822.8	26568.8	4920.4	14567.1	4277.1
广 东	Guangdong	135673.2	5540.7	54437.3	75695.2	5753.6	48712.9	5892.5
广 西	Guangxi	27202.4	4468.2	8924.1	13810.1	4613.1	6918.3	2028.4
海 南	Hainan	7551.2	1507.4	1448.5	4595.3	1568.5	861.4	592.7
重 庆	Chongqing	30145.8	2074.7	11699.1	16372.0	2126.4	8333.4	3365.8
四 川	Sichuan	60132.9	6056.6	21306.7	32769.5	6236.2	16705.2	4846.5
贵 州	Guizhou	20913.3	2894.3	7311.4	10707.5	3055.9	5682.8	1636.6
云 南	Yunnan	30021.1	4206.6	10256.3	15558.2	4289.1	7202.8	3064.6
西 藏	Xizang	2392.7	215.0	883.0	1294.7	220.2	252.3	630.6
陕 西	Shaanxi	33786.1	2649.8	16068.9	15067.4	2796.5	13258.7	2955.0
甘 肃	Gansu	11863.8	1641.3	4080.8	6141.8	1690.7	3389.6	707.7
青 海	Qinghai	3799.1	387.0	1612.8	1799.2	391.9	1272.4	340.4
宁 夏	Ningxia	5315.0	428.1	2487.2	2399.6	450.6	2130.1	359.9
新 疆	Xinjiang	19125.9	2742.2	7710.3	8673.4	2905.5	6434.7	1428.0

注：表中数据为初步核算数。
a) Data in this table are preliminary data.

3–9 续表 1 continued

单位：亿元 (100 million yuan)

地 区	Region	批发和零售业 Wholesale and Retail Trades	交通运输、仓储和邮政业 Transport, Storage and Post	住宿和餐饮业 Hotels and Catering Services	金融业 Financial Intermediation	房地产业 Real Estate	其 他 Others	人均地区生产总值(元) Per Capita Gross Regional Product (yuan)
北 京	Beijing	3073.1	1065.3	453.1	8663.1	2612.0	21175.3	200278
天 津	Tianjin	1412.2	1157.3	154.8	2249.8	1057.6	4297.6	122752
河 北	Hebei	3742.3	3420.9	415.1	3015.8	2343.0	9747.5	59332
山 西	Shanxi	1663.3	1335.9	252.0	1390.2	1163.8	5080.9	73984
内蒙古	Inner Mongolia	1647.6	1512.5	368.2	1081.0	884.7	4624.5	102677
辽 宁	Liaoning	2378.8	1566.2	364.5	2174.7	1571.4	7542.1	72107
吉 林	Jilin	869.1	679.2	191.7	1077.4	700.1	3694.4	57739
黑龙江	Heilongjiang	1362.2	648.0	248.1	1146.0	684.3	3766.9	51563
上 海	Shanghai	5094.5	2331.5	408.7	8646.9	3555.2	15350.8	190321
江 苏	Jiangsu	14225.6	4224.5	1793.1	10230.8	7783.7	27424.3	150487
浙 江	Zhejiang	10296.3	2808.5	1515.0	7293.9	5192.4	19007.4	125043
安 徽	Anhui	4750.5	2469.2	976.5	3035.6	2839.5	10349.8	76830
福 建	Fujian	6825.8	2238.4	851.6	4355.9	2552.4	10144.5	129865
江 西	Jiangxi	3080.9	1495.1	651.2	2170.2	1955.4	6542.9	71216
山 东	Shandong	12868.3	5190.2	1518.2	5500.7	4581.5	19230.8	90771
河 南	Henan	4745.6	4246.8	1091.4	3252.9	3631.6	14101.7	60073
湖 北	Hubei	4025.9	2950.8	1356.6	3645.2	3687.3	14416.8	95538
湖 南	Hunan	5126.6	1984.3	1098.0	2598.2	2876.9	12564.3	75938
广 东	Guangdong	13174.5	4847.7	2073.8	12418.8	10545.7	32253.5	106985
广 西	Guangxi	2316.9	1260.1	453.5	1940.6	1874.3	5797.1	54005
海 南	Hainan	1070.3	502.2	266.0	453.3	670.7	1566.2	72958
重 庆	Chongqing	3073.8	1191.1	635.1	2590.9	1605.5	7224.0	94147
四 川	Sichuan	5684.0	2004.6	1344.3	3997.4	3644.2	15670.5	71835
贵 州	Guizhou	1690.0	927.3	498.4	1226.9	877.1	5318.2	54172
云 南	Yunnan	3248.5	1686.2	827.1	1602.6	1570.8	6529.3	64107
西 藏	Xizang	118.8	53.3	32.2	233.6	103.1	748.5	65642
陕 西	Shaanxi	2190.5	1416.9	468.0	2212.7	1642.6	6845.2	85448
甘 肃	Gansu	848.1	691.4	190.6	955.9	568.7	2821.1	47867
青 海	Qinghai	167.7	208.3	42.6	280.2	156.2	939.4	63903
宁 夏	Ningxia	228.9	251.7	61.7	385.4	198.7	1247.9	72957
新 疆	Xinjiang	875.1	1039.7	171.1	1249.4	613.0	4409.5	73774

3-9 续表 2 continued

地 区	Region	构 成（地区生产总值=100） Composition (GRP=100)			指 数 （上年=100） Indices (preceding year=100)				
		第一产业 Primary Industry	第二产业 Secondary Industry	第三产业 Tertiary Industry	地区生产总值 Gross Regional Product	第一产业 Primary Industry	第二产业 Secondary Industry	第三产业 Tertiary Industry	人均地区生产总值 Per Capita Gross Regional Product
北 京	Beijing	0.2	14.9	84.8	105.2	95.4	100.4	106.1	105.2
天 津	Tianjin	1.6	35.7	62.7	104.3	101.2	103.2	104.9	104.6
河 北	Hebei	10.2	37.4	52.4	105.5	102.6	106.2	105.5	105.8
山 西	Shanxi	5.4	51.9	42.7	105.0	104.0	105.1	105.0	105.2
内蒙古	Inner Mongolia	11.1	47.5	41.4	107.3	105.5	108.1	107.0	107.4
辽 宁	Liaoning	8.8	38.8	52.4	105.3	104.7	105.0	105.5	105.9
吉 林	Jilin	12.2	33.9	54.0	106.3	105.0	105.9	106.9	107.1
黑龙江	Heilongjiang	22.2	27.0	50.8	102.6	102.6	97.7	105.0	103.6
上 海	Shanghai	0.2	24.6	75.2	105.0	98.5	101.9	106.0	105.0
江 苏	Jiangsu	4.0	44.4	51.7	105.8	103.5	106.7	105.1	105.6
浙 江	Zhejiang	2.8	41.1	56.0	106.0	104.2	105.0	106.7	105.3
安 徽	Anhui	7.4	40.1	52.5	105.8	103.9	106.1	105.8	105.7
福 建	Fujian	5.9	44.1	50.0	104.5	104.2	103.7	105.2	104.5
江 西	Jiangxi	7.6	42.6	49.8	104.1	104.0	104.6	103.6	104.1
山 东	Shandong	7.1	39.1	53.8	106.0	104.5	106.5	105.8	106.2
河 南	Henan	9.1	37.5	53.4	104.1	101.8	104.7	104.0	104.4
湖 北	Hubei	9.1	36.2	54.7	106.0	104.1	104.9	107.0	105.9
湖 南	Hunan	9.2	37.6	53.1	104.6	103.5	104.6	104.8	105.0
广 东	Guangdong	4.1	40.1	55.8	104.8	104.8	104.8	104.7	104.7
广 西	Guangxi	16.4	32.8	50.8	104.1	104.7	103.2	104.4	104.2
海 南	Hainan	20.0	19.2	60.9	109.2	104.6	110.6	110.3	108.0
重 庆	Chongqing	6.9	38.8	54.3	106.1	104.6	106.5	105.9	106.4
四 川	Sichuan	10.1	35.4	54.5	106.0	104.0	105.0	107.1	106.0
贵 州	Guizhou	13.8	35.0	51.2	104.9	103.9	104.4	105.5	104.7
云 南	Yunnan	14.0	34.2	51.8	104.4	104.2	102.4	105.7	104.6
西 藏	Xizang	9.0	36.9	54.1	109.5	114.9	107.7	109.9	109.7
陕 西	Shaanxi	7.8	47.6	44.6	104.3	104.0	104.5	104.1	104.3
甘 肃	Gansu	13.8	34.4	51.8	106.4	105.9	106.5	106.4	106.9
青 海	Qinghai	10.2	42.5	47.4	105.3	104.7	104.1	106.5	105.3
宁 夏	Ningxia	8.1	46.8	45.1	106.6	107.7	108.5	104.7	106.3
新 疆	Xinjiang	14.3	40.3	45.3	106.8	106.3	107.2	106.6	106.6

3-10 支出法国内生产总值
Gross Domestic Product by Expenditure Approach

本表按当年价格计算。
Data in this table are calculated at current prices.

年 份 Year	支出法国内生产总值(亿元) Gross Domestic Product by Expenditure Approach (100 million yuan)	最终消费支出 Final Consumption Expenditure	资本形成总额 Gross Capital Formation	货物和服务净出口 Net Exports of Goods and Services	最终消费率(消费率)(%) Final Consumption Rate (%)	资本形成率(投资率)(%) Capital Formation Rate (%)
1978	3606	2234	1383	-11	61.9	38.4
1979	4047	2579	1488	-20	63.7	36.8
1980	4541	2968	1588	-15	65.4	35.0
1981	4922	3278	1626	17	66.6	33.0
1982	5386	3577	1718	91	66.4	31.9
1983	6034	4061	1922	51	67.3	31.9
1984	7290	4787	2502	1	65.7	34.3
1985	9108	5921	3554	-367	65.0	39.0
1986	10390	6731	3915	-255	64.8	37.7
1987	12198	7644	4544	11	62.7	37.2
1988	15210	9429	5932	-151	62.0	39.0
1989	17250	11044	6392	-186	64.0	37.1
1990	18969	12012	6447	510	63.3	34.0
1991	21997	13626	7754	618	61.9	35.2
1992	27140	16239	10625	276	59.8	39.1
1993	35576	20815	15440	-679	58.5	43.4
1994	48410	28297	19479	634	58.5	40.2
1995	61050	36229	23823	999	59.3	39.0
1996	71541	43122	26960	1459	60.3	37.7
1997	79416	47549	28317	3550	59.9	35.7
1998	84791	51502	29660	3629	60.7	35.0
1999	90095	56667	30891	2537	62.9	34.3
2000	99799	63749	33667	2383	63.9	33.7
2001	110388	68661	39403	2325	62.2	35.7
2002	121327	74227	44005	3094	61.2	36.3
2003	137147	79735	54447	2965	58.1	39.7
2004	161356	89394	67726	4236	55.4	42.0
2005	187658	101873	75576	10209	54.3	40.3
2006	219598	115364	87579	16655	52.5	39.9
2007	270499	137737	109339	23423	50.9	40.4
2008	318068	158899	134942	24227	50.0	42.4
2009	347650	174539	158075	15037	50.2	45.5
2010	408505	201581	191867	15057	49.3	47.0
2011	484109	244747	227673	11688	50.6	47.0
2012	539040	275444	248960	14636	51.1	46.2
2013	596344	306664	275129	14552	51.4	46.1
2014	646548	338031	294906	13611	52.3	45.6
2015	692094	371921	297827	22346	53.7	43.0
2016	745981	410806	318198	16976	55.1	42.7
2017	828983	456518	357886	14578	55.1	43.2
2018	915774	506135	402585	7054	55.3	44.0
2019	990708	552632	426679	11398	55.8	43.1
2020	1025628	560811	439550	25267	54.7	42.9
2021	1145283	619688	495784	29810	54.1	43.3
2022	1202471	643828	519793	38850	53.5	43.2
2023	1258647	701361	530440	26847	55.7	42.1

注：最终消费率指最终消费支出占支出法国内生产总值的比重；资本形成率指资本形成总额占支出法国内生产总值的比重。

a) Final consumption rate refers to the share of final consumption expenditure in GDP by expenditure approach, capital formation rate refers to the share of gross capital formation in GDP by expenditure approach.

3-11 支出法国内生产总值及构成
Components of Gross Domestic Product by Expenditure Approach

本表按当年价格计算。
Data in this table are calculated at current prices.

年份 Year	最终消费支出(亿元) Final Consumption Expenditure (100 million yuan)				资本形成总额(亿元) Gross Capital Formation (100 million yuan)		货物和服务净出口(亿元) Net Exports of Goods and Services (100 million yuan)	
	居民消费支出 Household Consumption Expenditure	城镇居民 Urban Households	农村居民 Rural Households	政府消费支出 Government Consumption Expenditure	固定资本形成总额 Gross Fixed Capital Formation	存货变动 Changes in Inventories	出口 Exports	进口 Imports
1978	1759	667	1092	475	1079	304		
1979	2014	759	1255	565	1163	326		
1980	2337	922	1415	631	1310	277		
1981	2628	1017	1610	651	1345	281		
1982	2867	1050	1817	710	1517	201		
1983	3221	1197	2024	840	1697	226		
1984	3690	1438	2251	1097	2134	368		
1985	4627	1841	2787	1293	2769	786		
1986	5294	2180	3113	1437	3212	702		
1987	6048	2576	3472	1596	3720	823		
1988	7532	3381	4152	1897	4714	1218		
1989	8778	3913	4865	2266	4399	1993		
1990	9435	4194	5241	2577	4527	1919		
1991	10544	4971	5573	3081	5656	2098		
1992	12312	6366	5947	3927	8253	2373		
1993	15695	8694	7001	5120	13232	2209		
1994	21443	12271	9172	6854	16751	2728		
1995	28066	16528	11538	8163	19838	3985		
1996	33644	19489	14155	9478	22723	4237		
1997	36586	21625	14961	10963	24714	3603		
1998	38768	23894	14875	12733	28014	1645		
1999	41846	27035	14811	14821	29467	1424		
2000	46863	31251	15612	16886	32669	998		
2001	50465	34167	16297	18196	37088	2315		
2002	54667	37650	17017	19561	42672	1333		
2003	58690	40915	17775	21045	52574	1872		
2004	65725	46492	19233	23670	63975	3751		
2005	74154	53242	20912	27719	73852	1724		
2006	82842	60203	22640	32522	84979	2600		
2007	98231	72643	25589	39506	102345	6995		
2008	112655	84414	28241	46245	124701	10241		
2009	123122	93198	29924	51417	152691	5383		
2010	141465	108938	32527	60116	181041	10826		
2011	170391	131555	38836	74357	214017	13656		
2012	190585	148273	42312	84859	238321	10639		
2013	212477	165890	46588	94186	263980	11149		
2014	236238	184739	51500	101793	282242	12664		
2015	260202	203780	56423	111718	289970	7856		
2016	288668	226960	61708	122138	310145	8054	146177	129201
2017	320690	252083	68606	135829	348300	9586	163847	149268
2018	354124	277365	76759	152011	393848	8737	175694	168640
2019	387188	305131	82057	165444	422451	4227	182470	171072
2020	387186	304086	83099	173625	430625	8925	187926	162659
2021	438015	345085	92931	181673	482119	13665	229166	199355
2022	450468	353906	96562	193360	504835	14959	250235	211385
2023	493247	389677	103570	208113	521112	9327	247946	221099

3-11 续表 continued

年份 Year	最终消费支出=100 Final Consumption Expenditure=100		居民消费支出=100 Household Consumption Expenditure=100		资本形成总额=100 Gross Capital Formation=100		货物和服务净出口=100 Net Exports of Goods and Services=100	
	居民消费支出 Household Consumption Expenditure	政府消费支出 Government Consumption Expenditure	城镇居民 Urban Households	农村居民 Rural Households	固定资本形成总额 Gross Fixed Capital Formation	存货变动 Changes in Inventories	出口 Exports	进口 Imports
1978	78.8	21.2	37.9	62.1	78.0	22.0		
1979	78.1	21.9	37.7	62.3	78.1	21.9		
1980	78.7	21.3	39.5	60.5	82.5	17.5		
1981	80.2	19.8	38.7	61.3	82.7	17.3		
1982	80.2	19.8	36.6	63.4	88.3	11.7		
1983	79.3	20.7	37.1	62.9	88.3	11.7		
1984	77.1	22.9	39.0	61.0	85.3	14.7		
1985	78.2	21.8	39.8	60.2	77.9	22.1		
1986	78.6	21.4	41.2	58.8	82.1	17.9		
1987	79.1	20.9	42.6	57.4	81.9	18.1		
1988	79.9	20.1	44.9	55.1	79.5	20.5		
1989	79.5	20.5	44.6	55.4	68.8	31.2		
1990	78.5	21.5	44.5	55.5	70.2	29.8		
1991	77.4	22.6	47.1	52.9	72.9	27.1		
1992	75.8	24.2	51.7	48.3	77.7	22.3		
1993	75.4	24.6	55.4	44.6	85.7	14.3		
1994	75.8	24.2	57.2	42.8	86.0	14.0		
1995	77.5	22.5	58.9	41.1	83.3	16.7		
1996	78.0	22.0	57.9	42.1	84.3	15.7		
1997	76.9	23.1	59.1	40.9	87.3	12.7		
1998	75.3	24.7	61.6	38.4	94.5	5.5		
1999	73.8	26.2	64.6	35.4	95.4	4.6		
2000	73.5	26.5	66.7	33.3	97.0	3.0		
2001	73.5	26.5	67.7	32.3	94.1	5.9		
2002	73.6	26.4	68.9	31.1	97.0	3.0		
2003	73.6	26.4	69.7	30.3	96.6	3.4		
2004	73.5	26.5	70.7	29.3	94.5	5.5		
2005	72.8	27.2	71.8	28.2	97.7	2.3		
2006	71.8	28.2	72.7	27.3	97.0	3.0		
2007	71.3	28.7	74.0	26.0	93.6	6.4		
2008	70.9	29.1	74.9	25.1	92.4	7.6		
2009	70.5	29.5	75.7	24.3	96.6	3.4		
2010	70.2	29.8	77.0	23.0	94.4	5.6		
2011	69.6	30.4	77.2	22.8	94.0	6.0		
2012	69.2	30.8	77.8	22.2	95.7	4.3		
2013	69.3	30.7	78.1	21.9	95.9	4.1		
2014	69.9	30.1	78.2	21.8	95.7	4.3		
2015	70.0	30.0	78.3	21.7	97.4	2.6		
2016	70.3	29.7	78.6	21.4	97.5	2.5		
2017	70.2	29.8	78.6	21.4	97.3	2.7		
2018	70.0	30.0	78.3	21.7	97.8	2.2		
2019	70.1	29.9	78.8	21.2	99.0	1.0		
2020	69.0	31.0	78.5	21.5	98.0	2.0		
2021	70.7	29.3	78.8	21.2	97.2	2.8		
2022	70.0	30.0	78.6	21.4	97.1	2.9		
2023	70.3	29.7	79.0	21.0	98.2	1.8		

3-12 实际最终消费及构成
Actual Final Consumption and Its Composition

本表按当年价格计算。
Data in this table are calculated at current price.

年份	实际最终消费 Actual Final Consumption (亿元) (100 million yuan)		构成 Composition (实际最终消费=100) (Actual Final Consumption=100)	
Year	居民实际最终消费 Households Actual Final Consumption	政府实际最终消费 Government Actual Final Consumption	居民实际最终消费 Household Actual Final Consumption	政府实际最终消费 Government Actual Final Consumption
1978	1878	355	84.1	15.9
1979	2154	425	83.5	16.5
1980	2497	470	84.2	15.8
1981	2803	475	85.5	14.5
1982	3066	511	85.7	14.3
1983	3446	615	84.9	15.1
1984	3952	835	82.6	17.4
1985	4944	977	83.5	16.5
1986	5672	1059	84.3	15.7
1987	6448	1195	84.4	15.6
1988	8013	1417	85.0	15.0
1989	9327	1717	84.5	15.5
1990	10047	1965	83.6	16.4
1991	11250	2376	82.6	17.4
1992	13095	3145	80.6	19.4
1993	16635	4180	79.9	20.1
1994	22694	5603	80.2	19.8
1995	29506	6722	81.4	18.6
1996	35313	7810	81.9	18.1
1997	38449	9100	80.9	19.1
1998	40886	10616	79.4	20.6
1999	44202	12465	78.0	22.0
2000	49549	14200	77.7	22.3
2001	53768	14894	78.3	21.7
2002	58627	15600	79.0	21.0
2003	63241	16494	79.3	20.7
2004	70915	18480	79.3	20.7
2005	80354	21518	78.9	21.1
2006	90417	24947	78.4	21.6
2007	107731	30006	78.2	21.8
2008	125340	33559	78.9	21.1
2009	138331	36207	79.3	20.7
2010	159745	41836	79.2	20.8
2011	193613	51134	79.1	20.9
2012	219686	55758	79.8	20.2
2013	244570	62094	79.8	20.2
2014	271512	66519	80.3	19.7
2015	302130	69791	81.2	18.8
2016	334763	76043	81.5	18.5
2017	371343	85175	81.3	18.7
2018	409743	96392	81.0	19.0
2019	449646	102986	81.4	18.6
2020	455205	105606	81.2	18.8
2021	511336	108352	82.5	17.5
2022	530352	113476	82.4	17.6

3-13 居民消费水平
Household Consumption Expenditure

本表绝对数按当年价格计算，指数按不变价格计算。
Data on value in this table are calculated at current prices, while indices are calculated at constant prices.

年 份 Year	绝对数(元) Value (yuan)			城乡消费水平对比(农村居民=1) Urban/Rural Consumption Ratio (Rural Household=1)	指数（上年=100) Index (Preceding Year=100)			指数(1978年=100) Index (year of 1978=100)		
	全体居民 All Households	城镇居民 Urban Households	农村居民 Rural Households		全体居民 All Households	城镇居民 Urban Households	农村居民 Rural Households	全体居民 All Households	城镇居民 Urban Households	农村居民 Rural Households
1978	184	393	139	2.8	104.1	102.9	104.4	100.0	100.0	100.0
1980	238	490	178	2.7	109.1	107.3	108.6	116.8	113.8	115.0
1985	440	750	346	2.2	112.7	107.4	114.4	181.3	141.6	191.3
1990	831	1404	627	2.2	102.8	101.4	103.4	227.5	168.6	238.8
1995	2329	4767	1344	3.5	108.3	109.5	105.0	339.7	294.2	286.9
2000	3712	6972	1917	3.6	110.5	109.6	106.6	491.9	393.0	375.2
2001	3968	7272	2032	3.6	105.9	103.4	104.6	520.7	406.5	392.7
2002	4270	7662	2157	3.6	108.1	105.9	106.6	563.1	430.6	418.5
2003	4555	7977	2292	3.5	105.4	103.0	104.6	593.4	443.4	437.7
2004	5071	8718	2521	3.5	106.6	105.2	103.9	632.7	466.6	454.9
2005	5688	9637	2784	3.5	109.5	108.3	106.8	693.0	505.4	485.8
2006	6319	10516	3066	3.4	108.0	105.9	107.3	748.3	535.4	521.4
2007	7454	12217	3538	3.5	112.4	111.2	108.7	841.4	595.5	566.8
2008	8504	13722	3981	3.4	107.5	106.2	104.8	904.2	632.2	593.8
2009	9249	14687	4295	3.4	110.5	108.6	110.1	999.4	686.6	654.0
2010	10575	16570	4782	3.5	107.5	105.9	105.4	1074.7	726.9	689.2
2011	12668	19218	5880	3.3	109.8	106.8	110.8	1179.7	776.3	764.0
2012	14074	20869	6573	3.2	109.1	107.1	108.1	1286.9	831.0	826.1
2013	15586	22620	7397	3.1	107.9	105.7	109.4	1388.9	878.2	903.9
2014	17220	24430	8365	2.9	108.4	105.9	110.9	1505.1	930.3	1002.3
2015	18857	26119	9409	2.8	109.5	106.9	112.7	1648.4	994.3	1129.1
2016	20801	28154	10609	2.7	108.2	105.6	110.8	1783.2	1050.4	1251.4
2017	22968	30323	12145	2.5	106.6	104.0	110.8	1901.7	1092.0	1386.6
2018	25245	32483	13985	2.3	107.4	104.7	112.4	2041.9	1143.0	1558.8
2019	27504	34900	15382	2.3	106.1	104.6	107.0	2166.0	1195.9	1668.2
2020	27439	34043	16046	2.1	97.5	95.4	101.8	2111.9	1140.7	1697.9
2021	31013	37995	18434	2.1	111.4	109.9	113.5	2352.8	1254.0	1927.1
2022	31899	38574	19520	2.0	100.9	99.6	103.9	2374.1	1248.9	2002.1
2023	34964	42050	21398	2.0	108.9	108.4	109.0	2586.5	1353.3	2181.6

注：1.城乡消费水平对比没有剔除城乡价格不可比的因素(以下相关表同)。
2.居民消费水平指按年中常住人口计算的人均居民消费支出(以下相关表同)。

a) The effect of price differentials between urban and rural areas has not been removed in the calculation of the urban/rural consumption ratio. The same applies to the relevant tables.

b) Household consumption level refers to per capita household consumption expenditure on the basis of mid-year resident population. The same applies to the relevant tables.

3-14 三大需求对国内生产总值增长的贡献率和拉动
Contribution Share and Contribution of the Three Components of GDP to the Growth of GDP

本表按不变价格计算。
Data in this table are calculated at constant prices.

年 份 Year	最终消费支出 Final Consumption Expenditure		资本形成总额 Gross Capital Formation		货物和服务净出口 Net Exports of Goods and Services	
	贡献率 (%) Contribution Share (%)	拉 动 (百分点) Contribution (percentage points)	贡献率 (%) Contribution Share (%)	拉 动 (百分点) Contribution (percentage points)	贡献率 (%) Contribution Share (%)	拉 动 (百分点) Contribution (percentage points)
1978	38.7	4.5	66.7	7.8	-5.4	-0.6
1980	78.1	6.1	20.1	1.6	1.8	0.1
1985	71.9	9.7	79.6	10.7	-51.5	-6.9
1990	89.0	3.5	-69.4	-2.7	80.5	3.2
1995	46.7	5.1	46.1	5.0	7.2	0.8
2000	78.8	6.7	21.7	1.8	-0.5	0.0
2001	50.0	4.2	63.5	5.3	-13.5	-1.1
2002	58.1	5.3	40.0	3.7	1.9	0.2
2003	36.1	3.6	68.8	6.9	-4.9	-0.5
2004	42.9	4.3	62.0	6.3	-4.9	-0.5
2005	56.8	6.5	33.1	3.8	10.1	1.1
2006	43.2	5.5	42.5	5.4	14.3	1.8
2007	47.9	6.8	44.2	6.3	7.8	1.1
2008	44.0	4.2	53.3	5.1	2.7	0.3
2009	57.6	5.4	85.3	8.0	-42.8	-4.0
2010	47.4	5.0	63.4	6.7	-10.8	-1.1
2011	65.7	6.3	41.1	3.9	-6.8	-0.6
2012	55.4	4.4	42.1	3.3	2.5	0.2
2013	50.2	3.9	53.1	4.1	-3.3	-0.3
2014	56.3	4.2	45.0	3.3	-1.3	-0.1
2015	69.0	4.9	22.6	1.6	8.4	0.6
2016	66.0	4.5	45.7	3.1	-11.7	-0.8
2017	55.9	3.9	39.5	2.7	4.7	0.3
2018	64.0	4.3	43.2	2.9	-7.2	-0.5
2019	58.6	3.5	28.9	1.7	12.6	0.7
2020	-6.8	-0.2	81.5	1.8	25.3	0.6
2021	58.3	4.9	19.8	1.7	21.9	1.9
2022	39.4	1.2	46.8	1.4	13.8	0.4
2023	82.5	4.3	28.9	1.5	-11.4	-0.6

注：1.三大需求指支出法国内生产总值的三大构成项目，即最终消费支出、资本形成总额、货物和服务净出口。
2.贡献率指三大需求增量与支出法国内生产总值增量之比。
3.拉动指国内生产总值增长速度与三大需求贡献率的乘积。

a) Three components of GDP by expenditure approach are final consumption expenditure,gross capital formation and net exports of goods and services
b) Contribution share of the three components to the increase of the GDP refers to the proportion of the increment of the each component of GDP by expenditure approach to the increment of GDP.
c) Contribution of the three components to GDP growth refers to the growth rate of GDP multiplied by the contribution share of the three components.

3-15 资金流量表(非金融交易，2022年)
Flow of Funds Accounts (Non-financial Transaction, 2022)

单位：亿元 (100 million yuan)

机构部门	Sectors	非金融企业部门 Non-financial Enterprises		金融机构部门 Financial Institutions		广义政府部门 General Government	
交易项目	Items	运用 Uses	来源 Resources	运用 Uses	来源 Resources	运用 Uses	来源 Resources
一、净出口	**Net Exports**						
二、增加值	**Value Added**		**762031.6**		**93285.3**		**121378.7**
三、劳动者报酬	**Compensation of Employees**	**343518.0**		**24562.4**		**107395.5**	
四、生产税净额	**Taxes on Production, Net**	**93601.2**		**9997.9**		**329.7**	**103532.8**
五、财产收入	**Property Income**	**93200.1**	**35659.4**	**96044.3**	**87484.5**	**14592.6**	**31387.7**
(一)利息	Interest	42314.3	22521.4	84897.2	83701.1	12434.8	8176.7
(二)红利	Distributed Income of Corporations	35853.7	12931.4	5325.5	3783.4		7892.7
(三)地租	Rent	15005.6					15009.8
(四)其他	Others	26.4	206.6	5821.6		2157.8	308.5
六、初次分配总收入	**Gross Primary Income**		**267371.8**		**50165.2**		**133981.4**
七、经常转移	**Current Transfers**	**41423.2**	**3113.9**	**17065.1**	**8011.2**	**82849.2**	**147910.3**
(一)所得税、财产税等经常税	Current Taxes on Income, Wealth, etc.	34387.2		9308.2			58627.3
(二)社会保险缴款	Social Insurance Contributions						79504.4
(三)社会保险福利	Social Insurance Benefits					65947.0	
(四)社会补助	Social Assistance	774.0				16640.2	
(五)其他	Others	6262.0	3113.9	7756.9	8011.2	262.0	9778.5
八、可支配总收入	**Gross Disposable Income**		**229062.5**		**41111.2**		**199042.5**
九、实物社会转移	**Social Transfers in Kind**					**79883.5**	
十、调整后可支配总收入	**Adjusted Gross Disposable Income**		**229062.5**		**41111.2**		**119158.9**
十一、实际最终消费	**Actual Final Consumption**					**113476.2**	
(一)居民实际最终消费	Households Actual Final Consumption						
(二)政府实际最终消费	Government Actual Final Consumption					113476.2	
十二、总储蓄	**Gross Saving**		**229062.5**		**41111.2**		**5682.7**
十三、资本转移	**Capital Transfers**		**10299.4**			**10335.5**	**16.0**
(一)投资性补助	Investment Grants		10299.4			10299.4	
(二)其他	Others					36.1	16.0
十四、资本形成总额	**Gross Capital Formation**	**338229.0**		**2552.4**		**63517.5**	
(一)固定资本形成总额	Gross Fixed Capital Formation	325102.9		2552.4		63499.3	
(二)存货变动	Changes in Inventories	13126.1				18.2	
十五、其他非金融资产获得减处置	**Acquisitions Less Disposals of Other Non-financial Assets**	**56966.0**				**-32891.3**	
十六、净金融投资	**Net Financial Investment**	**-155833.0**		**38558.8**		**-35263.0**	

3-15 续表 continued

单位：亿元 (100 million yuan)

机构部门 交易项目	Sectors Items	住户部门 Households 运用 Uses	住户部门 Households 来源 Resources	国内合计 Total of Domestic Sectors 运用 Uses	国内合计 Total of Domestic Sectors 来源 Resources	国外 The Rest of the World 运用 Uses	国外 The Rest of the World 来源 Resources	合计 Total 运用 Uses	合计 Total 来源 Resources
一、净出口	**Net Exports**						**-38930.5**		**-38930.5**
二、增加值	**Value Added**		**228028.3**		**1204724.0**				**1204724.0**
三、劳动者报酬	**Compensation of Employees**	**158614.9**	**634272.7**	**634090.9**	**634272.7**	**1383.8**	**1202.0**	**635474.7**	**635474.7**
四、生产税净额	**Taxes on Production, Net**	**-396.1**		**103532.8**	**103532.8**			**103532.8**	**103532.8**
五、财产收入	**Property Income**	**17609.0**	**56409.9**	**221445.9**	**210941.5**	**16878.8**	**27383.2**	**238324.7**	**238324.7**
(一)利息	Interest	17604.8	42959.9	157251.0	157359.1	3665.4	3557.3	160916.4	160916.4
(二)红利	Distributed Income of Corporations		5735.4	41179.3	30342.9	12931.4	23767.7	54110.7	54110.7
(三)地租	Rent	4.2		15009.8	15009.8			15009.8	15009.8
(四)其他	Others		7714.6	8005.8	8229.7	282.0	58.2	8287.8	8287.8
六、初次分配总收入	**Gross Primary Income**		**742883.0**		**1194401.4**				**1194401.4**
七、经常转移	**Current Transfers**	**107322.4**	**90980.5**	**248660.0**	**250015.9**	**2984.9**	**1629.0**	**251644.9**	**251644.9**
(一)所得税、财产税等经常税	Current Taxes on Income, Wealth, etc.	14932.0		58627.3	58627.3			58627.3	58627.3
(二)社会保险缴款	Social Insurance Contritutions	79504.4		79504.4	79504.4			79504.4	79504.4
(三)社会保险福利	Social Insurance Benefits		65947.0	65947.0	65947.0			65947.0	65947.0
(四)社会补助	Social Assistance		17414.2	17414.2	17414.2			17414.2	17414.2
(五)其他	Others	12886.1	7619.3	27167.0	28522.9	2984.9	1629.0	30151.9	30151.9
八、可支配总收入	**Gross Disposable Income**		**726541.1**		**1195757.3**				**1195757.3**
九、实物社会转移	**Social Transfers in Kind**		**79883.5**	**79883.5**	**79883.5**			**79883.5**	**79883.5**
十、调整后可支配总收入	**Adjusted Gross Disposable Income**		**806424.6**		**1195757.3**				**1195757.3**
十一、实际最终消费	**Actual Final Consumption**	**530351.6**		**643827.8**				**643827.8**	
(一)居民实际最终消费	Households Actual Final Consumption	530351.6		530351.6				530351.6	
(二)政府实际最终消费	Government Actual Final Consumption			113476.2				113476.2	
十二、总储蓄	**Gross Saving**		**276073.0**		**551929.5**		**-29963.8**		**521965.7**
十三、资本转移	**Capital Transfers**			**10335.5**	**10315.4**	**16.0**	**36.1**	**10351.6**	**10351.6**
(一)投资性补助	Investment Grants			10299.4	10299.4			10299.4	10299.4
(二)其他	Others			36.1	16.0	16.0	36.1	52.2	52.2
十四、资本形成总额	**Gross Capital Formation**	**115494.3**		**519793.2**				**519793.2**	
(一)固定资本形成总额	Gross Fixed Capital Formation	113680.0		504834.6				504834.6	
(二)存货变动	Changes in Inventories	1814.2		14958.6				14958.6	
十五、其他非金融资产获得减处置	**Acquisitions Less Disposals of Other Non-financial Assets**	**-24074.6**							
十六、净金融投资	**Net Financial Investment**	**184653.4**		**32116.2**		**-29943.8**		**2172.4**	

3-16 资金流量表(金融交易，2022年)
Flow of Funds Accounts (Financial Transaction, 2022)

单位：亿元 (100 million yuan)

机构部门	Sectors	非金融企业部门 Non-financial Enterprises		金融机构部门 Financial Institutions		广义政府部门 General Government	
交易项目	Items	运 用 Uses	来 源 Resources	运 用 Uses	来 源 Resources	运 用 Uses	来 源 Resources
净金融投资	Net Financial Investment	-99320		21619		-83706	
资金运用合计	Total Funds Uses	70805		387537		12504	
资金来源合计	Total Funds Sources		170125		365918		96210
通货	Currency	1237			13745	275	
存款	Deposits	51633	-4	11792	260776	11481	
活期存款	Demand Deposits	707			36913	-4880	
定期存款	Time Deposits	50379			211006	16710	
财政存款	Fiscal Deposits				-586	-586	
外汇存款	Foreign Exchange Deposits	-168	-4	-108	-4089	-93	
其他存款	Other Deposits	715		11900	17533	330	
证券公司客户保证金	Customer Margin of Securities Companies	16		8	42	1	
贷款	Loans		148723	211923	868		16336
短期贷款与票据融资	Short-term Loans & Bills Financing		55964	72573			
中长期贷款	Medium-term and Long-term Loans		98681	129247			
外汇贷款	Foreign Exchange Loans		-4583	-7015	-42		220
委托贷款	Entrusted Loans		137	3509	-39		176
其他贷款	Other Loans		-1475	13609	948		15939
未贴现的银行承兑汇票	Undiscounted Bankers' Acceptance Bills	-3411	-3411	-3411	-3411		
保险准备金	Insurance Technical Reserves	1566			21267		11972
金融机构往来	Inter-financial Institutions Accounts			9573	13467		
存款准备金	Required and Excessive Reserves			14529	15106		
债券	Bonds	-30	11552	129767	33696	-628	71860
政府债券	Government Bonds	10		72643		-106	71860
金融债券	Financial Bonds	-100		44100	33696	-168	
中央银行债券	Central Bank Bonds			28			
企业债券	Corporate Bonds	60	11552	12996		-354	
股票	Shares	8260	12301	2321	1845	273	
证券投资基金份额	Securities Investment Fund Shares	7676		3765	19348	579	
库存现金	Cash in Vault			68	-33		
中央银行贷款	Central Bank Loans			5606	5606		
其他（净）	Miscellaneous (net)	-3232	-4360	-10547	-13470	524	223
直接投资	Foreign Direct Investment	8143	11899	2452	857		
其他对外债权债务	Other Foreign Assets and Debts	-1054	-2579	2969	-3790		-4180
国际储备资产	International Reserve Assets			6723			
国际收支错误与遗漏	Errors and Omissions in the Balance of Payments		-3996				

3-16 续表 continued

单位：亿元 (100 million yuan)

机构部门 交易项目	Sectors Items	住户部门 Households 运用 Uses	住户部门 Households 来源 Resources	国内合计 Total of Domestic Sectors 运用 Uses	国内合计 Total of Domestic Sectors 来源 Resources	国外 The Rest of the World 运用 Uses	国外 The Rest of the World 来源 Resources	合计 Total 运用 Uses	合计 Total 来源 Resources
净金融投资	Net Financial Investment	189221		27814		-27814		0	
资金运用合计	Financial Uses	237608		708455		-5065		703390	
资金来源合计	Financial Sources		48387		680641		22749		703390
通货	Currency	12232		13744	13745	1		13745	13745
存款	Deposits	188871		263776	260772	-2558	446	261218	261218
活期存款	Demand Deposits	41086		36913	36913			36913	36913
定期存款	Time Deposits	143917		211006	211006			211006	211006
财政存款	Fiscal Deposits			-586	-586			-586	-586
外汇存款	Foreign Exchange Deposits	617		248	-4093	-3895	446	-3647	-3647
其他存款	Other Deposits	3251		16196	17533	1337		17533	17533
证券公司客户保证金	Customer Margin of Securities Companies	13		39	42	3		42	42
贷款	Loans		48638	211923	214564	-1299	-3941	210623	210623
短期贷款与票据融资	Short-term Loans & Bills Financing		16609	72573	72573			72573	72573
中长期贷款	Medium-term and Long-term Loans		30566	129247	129247			129247	129247
外汇贷款	Foreign Exchange Loans		16	-7015	-4388	-1299	-3927	-8314	-8314
委托贷款	Designated Loans		3229	3509	3503		6	3509	3509
其他贷款	Other Loans		-1783	13609	13629		-20	13609	13609
未贴现的银行承兑汇票	Undiscounted Bankers' Acceptance Bills			-6822	-6822			-6822	-6822
保险准备金	Insurance Technical Reserves	31673		33239	33239			33239	33239
金融机构往来	Inter-financial Institutions Accounts			9573	13467	-2157	-6051	7416	7416
存款准备金	Required and Excessive Reserves			14529	15106	577		15106	15106
债券	Bonds	-930		128180	117109	-1315	9756	126865	126865
政府债券	Government and Public Bonds	-1171		71376	71860	3222	2738	74598	74598
金融债券	Financial Bonds	24		43856	33696	-3959	6201	39897	39897
中央银行债券	Central Bank Bonds			28			28	28	28
企业债券	Corporate Bonds	216		12919	11552	-578	789	12341	12341
股票	Shares	4192		15045	14146	2309	3208	17354	17354
证券投资基金份额	Securities Investment Fund Shares	6099		18119	19348	1229		19348	19348
库存现金	Cash in Vault			68	-33		101	68	68
中央银行贷款	Central Bank Loans			5606	5606			5606	5606
其他（净）	Miscellaneous (net)	-4543	-251	-17798	-17858	-63	-3	-17861	-17861
直接投资	Foreign Direct Investment			10595	12756	12756	10595	23352	23352
其他对外债权债务	Other Foreign Assets and Debts			1915	-10550	-10550	1915	-8634	-8634
国际储备资产	International Reserve Assets			6723			6723	6723	6723
国际收支错误与遗漏	Errors and Omissions in the Balance of Payments				-3996	-3996		-3996	-3996

3–17 企业、广义政府与住户部门初次分配总收入及比重
Gross Primary Income of Enterprises, General Government and Households Sector

年份 Year	企业部门 Enterprises Sector		广义政府部门 General Government Sector		住户部门 Households Sector	
	初次分配总收入(亿元) Gross Primary Income (100 million yuan)	占比(%) Share (%)	初次分配总收入(亿元) Gross Primary Income (100 million yuan)	占比(%) Share (%)	初次分配总收入(亿元) Gross Primary Income (100 million yuan)	占比(%) Share (%)
1992	6411.3	23.6	2983.3	11.0	17813.6	65.5
1993	9495.0	26.7	4037.0	11.3	22067.3	62.0
1994	12229.1	25.2	5111.4	10.5	31207.7	64.3
1995	15634.3	25.9	6006.5	10.0	38715.8	64.1
1996	15403.9	21.8	8054.2	11.4	47321.5	66.9
1997	18192.2	23.1	9209.3	11.7	51401.3	65.2
1998	18472.0	22.0	10180.7	12.1	55164.9	65.8
1999	19912.0	22.3	11242.4	12.6	58212.0	65.1
2000	22050.0	22.3	12679.1	12.8	64337.0	64.9
2001	25636.6	23.5	14212.8	13.0	69426.7	63.5
2002	28450.6	23.6	17198.5	14.3	74831.3	62.1
2003	34837.1	25.5	18794.6	13.8	82944.6	60.7
2004	44249.4	27.4	22726.9	14.1	94439.2	58.5
2005	51570.5	27.7	26516.7	14.3	107911.7	58.0
2006	61195.1	27.9	31704.6	14.5	126128.7	57.6
2007	76064.4	28.1	39105.7	14.4	155533.9	57.5
2008	92899.9	28.9	45254.9	14.1	183074.8	57.0
2009	97564.7	28.0	49222.7	14.1	201147.4	57.8
2010	114853.3	28.0	61074.7	14.9	234426.2	57.1
2011	128324.5	26.5	74461.1	15.4	280607.2	58.0
2012	136413.1	25.4	85003.2	15.8	315912.6	58.8
2013	148284.0	25.2	89261.7	15.2	350595.6	59.6
2014	162643.7	25.2	97949.6	15.2	383786.8	59.6
2015	168223.5	24.5	100962.7	14.7	416385.0	60.7
2016	185687.7	25.0	104442.7	14.1	452563.7	60.9
2017	212823.1	25.6	111450.7	13.4	506672.0	61.0
2018	238899.0	26.1	116898.0	12.8	559446.5	61.1
2019	254877.5	25.9	124632.1	12.7	604241.6	61.4
2020	270314.9	26.9	111398.3	11.1	623738.1	62.0
2021	321960.3	28.2	122685.7	10.8	696584.9	61.0
2022	317537.0	26.6	133981.4	11.2	742883.0	62.2

注：1.第四次全国经济普查后，1992—2017年资金流量表(非金融交易部分)进行了修订，表中历史数据为修订后的数据(以下相关表同)。
2.企业部门包括非金融企业部门和金融机构部门。

a) After the Fourth National Economic Census(2018), the Flow of Funds Accounts (Non-financial Transaction) for 1992-2017 have been revised. The historical data in this table are revised data. The same applies to the following related tables.

b) Enterprises Sector includes non-financial and financial enterprises sector.

3-18 企业、广义政府与住户部门可支配总收入及比重
Gross Disposable Income of Enterprises, General Government and Households Sector

年份 Year	企业部门 Enterprises Sector		广义政府部门 General Government Sector		住户部门 Households Sector	
	可支配总收入 (亿元) Gross Disposable Income (100 million yuan)	占比 (%) Share (%)	可支配总收入 (亿元) Gross Disposable Income (100 million yuan)	占比 (%) Share (%)	可支配总收入 (亿元) Gross Disposable Income (100 million yuan)	占比 (%) Share (%)
1992	5187.6	19.0	3515.2	12.9	18569.2	68.1
1993	8142.9	22.8	4607.9	12.9	22916.0	64.3
1994	10687.7	22.0	5755.3	11.8	32220.4	66.2
1995	13525.7	22.4	7087.0	11.7	39863.7	65.9
1996	12904.8	18.2	9401.3	13.2	48650.5	68.6
1997	15033.8	19.0	10784.0	13.6	53411.4	67.4
1998	15994.6	19.0	11448.8	13.6	56728.5	67.4
1999	18597.1	20.7	12409.9	13.8	58768.6	65.5
2000	20396.0	20.5	14428.1	14.5	64764.5	65.0
2001	23096.0	21.0	17191.7	15.6	69691.3	63.4
2002	25997.6	21.4	20541.9	16.9	75015.7	61.7
2003	31966.0	23.2	23042.2	16.7	83012.3	60.1
2004	40520.5	24.8	28244.5	17.3	94545.6	57.9
2005	46632.7	24.8	34104.2	18.1	107217.0	57.0
2006	54769.3	24.8	41379.1	18.7	125117.6	56.5
2007	67207.1	24.6	54052.9	19.8	152265.3	55.7
2008	81371.3	25.1	62975.1	19.4	179880.3	55.5
2009	85972.0	24.6	66637.2	19.0	197488.3	56.4
2010	102163.3	24.7	80976.7	19.6	229965.4	55.7
2011	110295.3	22.7	99761.9	20.6	274930.2	56.7
2012	114300.6	21.3	114900.4	21.4	308344.8	57.4
2013	122765.5	20.9	123086.2	20.9	341749.7	58.2
2014	135796.0	21.1	135045.9	21.0	373626.5	58.0
2015	138237.9	20.2	141642.1	20.7	404897.5	59.1
2016	154123.5	20.8	146768.3	19.8	441165.5	59.5
2017	178105.8	21.5	162859.5	19.6	489176.9	58.9
2018	200543.6	21.9	171265.6	18.7	543300.9	59.4
2019	215373.1	21.9	175371.8	17.8	593712.7	60.3
2020	230656.4	22.9	149567.5	14.9	625798.5	62.2
2021	275673.4	24.1	184973.4	16.2	681605.8	59.7
2022	270173.8	22.6	199042.5	16.6	726541.1	60.8

注：企业部门包括非金融企业部门和金融机构部门。
a) Enterprises Sector includes non-financial and financial enterprises sector.

3-19 企业、广义政府与住户部门调整后可支配总收入及比重
Adjusted Gross Disposable Income of Enterprises, General Government and Households Sector

年份 Year	企业部门 Enterprises Sector 调整后可支配总收入(亿元) Adjusted Gross Disposable Income (100 million yuan)	占比(%) Share (%)	广义政府部门 General Government Sector 调整后可支配总收入(亿元) Adjusted Gross Disposable Income (100 million yuan)	占比(%) Share (%)	住户部门 Households Sector 调整后可支配总收入(亿元) Adjusted Gross Disposable Income (100 million yuan)	占比(%) Share (%)
1992	5187.6	19.0	2732.9	10.0	19351.5	71.0
1993	8142.9	22.8	3667.3	10.3	23856.6	66.9
1994	10687.7	22.0	4504.7	9.3	33471.0	68.8
1995	13525.7	22.4	5646.2	9.3	41304.5	68.3
1996	12904.8	18.2	7732.8	10.9	50319.0	70.9
1997	15033.8	19.0	8921.1	11.3	55274.4	69.8
1998	15994.6	19.0	9331.4	11.1	58845.8	69.9
1999	18597.1	20.7	10053.3	11.2	61125.3	68.1
2000	20396.0	20.5	11742.2	11.8	67450.4	67.7
2001	23096.0	21.0	13888.8	12.6	72994.2	66.4
2002	25997.6	21.4	16581.8	13.6	78975.8	65.0
2003	31966.0	23.2	18491.5	13.4	87563.0	63.4
2004	40520.5	24.8	23054.6	14.1	99735.6	61.1
2005	46632.7	24.8	27903.5	14.8	113417.7	60.3
2006	54769.3	24.8	33804.2	15.3	132692.4	60.0
2007	67207.1	24.6	44553.6	16.3	161764.6	59.1
2008	81371.3	25.1	50289.7	15.5	192565.8	59.4
2009	85972.0	24.6	51427.6	14.7	212697.8	60.8
2010	102163.3	24.7	62697.2	15.2	248244.9	60.1
2011	110295.3	22.7	76539.5	15.8	298152.6	61.5
2012	114300.6	21.3	85799.4	16.0	337445.8	62.8
2013	122765.5	20.9	90993.6	15.5	373842.3	63.6
2014	135796.0	21.1	99772.3	15.5	408900.1	63.4
2015	138237.9	20.2	99714.8	14.6	446824.8	65.3
2016	154123.5	20.8	100673.0	13.6	487260.8	65.7
2017	178105.8	21.5	112205.6	13.5	539830.8	65.0
2018	200543.6	21.9	115646.7	12.6	598919.8	65.4
2019	215373.1	21.9	112914.2	11.5	656170.3	66.7
2020	230656.4	22.9	81548.4	8.1	693817.6	69.0
2021	275673.4	24.1	111652.4	9.8	754926.8	66.1
2022	270173.8	22.6	119158.9	10.0	806424.6	67.4

注：企业部门包括非金融企业部门和金融机构部门。
a) Enterprises Sector includes non-financial and financial enterprises sector.

3-20 国际收支平衡表(2023年)
Balance of Payments (2023)

单位：万美元 (USD 10 000)

项　目	Type of Transaction	2023
1. 经常账户	**1.Current Account**	**25298727**
贷方	Credit	378872538
借方	Debit	-353573810
1.A 货物和服务	**1.A Goods and Services**	**38606315**
贷方	Credit	351124775
借方	Debit	-312518460
1.A.a 货物	**1.A.a Goods**	**59389647**
贷方	Credit	317919296
借方	Debit	-258529649
1.A.b 服务	**1.A.b Services**	**-20783332**
贷方	Credit	33205479
借方	Debit	-53988811
1.A.b.1 加工服务	1.A.b.1 Manufacturing Services on Physical Inputs Owned by Others	1203865
贷方	Credit	1299951
借方	Debit	-96086
1.A.b.2 维护和维修服务	1.A.b.2 Maintenance and Repair Services n.i.e	407394
贷方	Credit	998788
借方	Debit	-591394
1.A.b.3 运输	1.A.b.3 Transport	-7307206
贷方	Credit	8704108
借方	Debit	-16011314
1.A.b.4 旅行	1.A.b.4 Travel	-17166891
贷方	Credit	2479843
借方	Debit	-19646734
1.A.b.5 建设	1.A.b.5 Construction	793874
贷方	Credit	1575421
借方	Debit	-781548
1.A.b.6 保险和养老金服务	1.A.b.6 Insurance and Pension Services	-924453
贷方	Credit	694038
借方	Debit	-1618491
1.A.b.7 金融服务	1.A.b.7 Financial Service	65469
贷方	Credit	435789
借方	Debit	-370320

注：1.根据《国际收支和国际投资头寸手册》(第六版)编制，资本和金融账户中包含储备资产。
2.“贷方”按正值列示，“借方”按负值列示，差额等于“贷方”加上“借方”。本表除标注“贷方”和“借方”的项目外，其他项目均指差额。
3.金融账户下，对外金融资产的净增加用负值列示，净减少用正值列示。对外负债的净增加用正值列示，净减少用负值列示。
4.本表计数采用四舍五入原则。

a) By Manual on Balance of Payments and International Investment Position (the 6th edition), Capital and Finance Account includes Reserve Assets.
b) Credit is listed on positive, debit is on negative, the balance equals to Credit plus Debit. Except the item noted as credit and debit, other items all refer to the balance.
c) In the financial account, a positive value for assets represents a net decrease while a negative value represents a net increase. A positive value for liabilites represents a net increase while a negative value represents a net decrease.
d) Data in this table are rounded.

3-20 续表 1 continued

单位：万美元 (USD 10 000)

项　　目	Type of Transaction	2023
1.A.b.8 知识产权使用费	1.A.b.8 Charges for the Use of Intellectual Property	-3174642
贷方	Credit	1097728
借方	Debit	-4272369
1.A.b.9 电信、计算机和信息服务	1.A.b.9 Telecommunications, Computer, and Information Service	1926258
贷方	Credit	5809644
借方	Debit	-3883386
1.A.b.10 其他商业服务	1.A.b.10 Other Business Services	3803529
贷方	Credit	9821432
借方	Debit	-6017903
1.A.b.11 个人、文化和娱乐服务	1.A.b.11 Personal, Cultural, and Recreational Services	-262668
贷方	Credit	138925
借方	Debit	-401593
1.A.b.12 别处未提及的政府服务	1.A.B.12 Government Goods and Services n.i.e	-147862
贷方	Credit	149812
借方	Debit	-297673
1.B 初次收入	**1.B Primary Income**	**-14824165**
贷方	Credit	23998864
借方	Debit	-38823029
1.B.1 雇员报酬	**1.B.1 Compensation of Employees**	**721041**
贷方	Credit	2264129
借方	Debit	-1543088
1.B.2 投资收益	**1.B.2 Investment Income**	**-15895892**
贷方	Credit	21282907
借方	Debit	-37178799
1.B.3 其他初次收入	**1.B.3 Other Primary Income**	**350687**
贷方	Credit	451828
借方	Debit	-101141
1.C 二次收入	**1.C Secondary Income**	**1516577**
贷方	Credit	3748898
借方	Debit	-2232321
2. 资本和金融账户	**2.Capital and Finance Account**	**-21506142**
2.1 资本账户	**2.1 Capital Account**	**-29793**
贷方	Credit	18955
借方	Debit	-48748
2.2 金融账户	**2.2 Financial Account**	**-21476349**
资产	Assets	-22819243
负债	Liabilities	1342894
2.2.1 非储备性质的金融账户	**2.2.1 Financial Account Excluding Reserve Assets**	**-20993732**
资产	Financial Assets Excluding Reserve Assets	-22336626
负债	Liabilities	1342894
2.2.1.1 直接投资	2.2.1.1 Direct Investments	-14257377

3-20 续表 2 continued

单位：万美元 (USD 10 000)

项　　目	Type of Transaction	2023
2.2.1.1.1 资产	2.2.1.1.1 Assets	-18530145
2.2.1.1.1.1 股权	2.2.1.1.1.1 Equity and Investment Fund Shares	-11086657
2.2.1.1.1.2 关联企业债务	2.2.1.1.1.2 Debt Instruments	-7443488
2.2.1.1.2 负债	2.2.1.1.2 Liabilities	4272768
2.2.1.1.2.1 股权	2.2.1.1.2.1 Equity and Investment Fund Shares	7166026
2.2.1.1.2.2 关联企业债务	2.2.1.1.2.2 Debt Instruments	-2893258
2.2.1.2 证券投资	2.2.1.2 Portfolio Investment	-6324411
2.2.1.2.1 资产	2.2.1.2.1 Assets	-7730095
2.2.1.2.1.1 股权	2.2.1.2.1.1 Equity and Investment Fund Shares	-5519412
2.2.1.2.1.2 债券	2.2.1.2.1.2 Debt Instruments	-2210683
2.2.1.2.2 负债	2.2.1.2.2 Liabilities	1405684
2.2.1.2.2.1 股权	2.2.1.2.2.1 Equity and Investment Fund Shares	744611
2.2.1.2.2.2 债券	2.2.1.2.2.2 Debt Instruments	661073
2.2.1.3 金融衍生工具	2.2.1.3 Financial Derivatives(other than reserves) and Employee Stock Options	-753546
2.2.1.3.1 资产	2.2.1.3.1 Assets	-486951
2.2.1.3.2 负债	2.2.1.3.2 Liabilities	-266595
2.2.1.4 其他投资	2.2.1.4 Other Investment	341602
2.2.1.4.1 资产	2.2.1.4.1 Assets	4410565
2.2.1.4.1.1 其他股权	2.2.1.4.1.1 Other Equity	-20138
2.2.1.4.1.2 货币和存款	2.2.1.4.1.2 Currency and Deposits	2488558
2.2.1.4.1.3 贷款	2.2.1.4.1.3 Loans	3729739
2.2.1.4.1.4 保险和养老金	2.2.1.4.1.4 Insurance, Pension, and Standardized Guarantee Schemes	-261267
2.2.1.4.1.5 贸易信贷	2.2.1.4.1.5 Trade Credit and Advances	-1064990
2.2.1.4.1.6 其他	2.2.1.4.1.6 Other Accounts Receivable	-461336
2.2.1.4.2 负债	2.2.1.4.2 Liabilities	-4068963
2.2.1.4.2.1 其他股权	2.2.1.4.2.1 Other Equity	
2.2.1.4.2.2 货币和存款	2.2.1.4.2.2 Currency and Deposits	-1777050
2.2.1.4.2.3 贷款	2.2.1.4.2.3 Loans	-2922455
2.2.1.4.2.4 保险和养老金	2.2.1.4.2.4 Insurance, Pension, and Standardized Guarantee Schemes	3181
2.2.1.4.2.5 贸易信贷	2.2.1.4.2.5 Trade Credit and Advances	-2364307
2.2.1.4.2.6 其他	2.2.1.4.2.6 Other Accounts Receivable	2991668
2.2.1.4.2.7 特别提款权	2.2.1.4.2.7 Special Drawing Rights	
2.2.2 储备资产	**2.2.2 Reserve Assets**	**-482617**
2.2.2.1 货币黄金	2.2.2.1 Monetary Gold	
2.2.2.2 特别提款权	2.2.2.2 Special Drawing Rights	-243700
2.2.2.3 在国际货币基金组织的储备头寸	2.2.2.3 Reserve Position in the IMF	109200
2.2.2.4 外汇储备	2.2.2.4 Foreign Exchange Reserves	-348117
2.2.2.5 其他储备资产	2.2.2.5 Other Reserve Assets	
3. 净误差与遗漏	**3.Net Errors and Omissions**	**-3792585**

3–21 2020年投入产出基本流量表(中间使用部分)

按当年生产者价格计算。

单位：亿元

产出 Output / 投入 Input	农林牧渔产品和服务 Agriculture, Forestry, Animal Husbandry & Fishery Products and Services	采掘产品 Mining	食品和烟草 Foods and Tobacco	纺织、服装、鞋及皮革羽绒制品 Textile, Wearing Apparel, Shoes and Leather Products
农林牧渔产品和服务 Agriculture, Forestry, Animal Husbandry & Fishery Products and Services	18313.4	23.6	46758.7	8200.6
采掘产品 Mining	60.4	7042.1	269.6	183.0
食品和烟草 Foods and Tobacco	10818.5	145.0	24937.2	1412.9
纺织、服装、鞋及皮革羽绒制品 Textile, Wearing Apparel, Shoes and Leather Products	25.5	244.0	369.7	31484.6
木材加工、家具、造纸印刷和文教工美用品 Wood Processing, Furniture, Paper Making, Printing, and Educational & Artistic Products	136.2	435.1	1406.0	451.8
炼油、炼焦和化学产品 Oil Refining, Coking and Chemical Products	9567.0	2975.2	1874.1	6678.2
非金属矿物制品 Nonmetallic Mineral Products	52.8	298.8	488.8	57.1
金属冶炼、加工及制品 Metal Manufacture & Processing and Metal Products	106.4	2122.5	390.5	276.8
机械设备、交通运输设备、电子电气及其他设备 Machinery and Equipment, Transport Equipment, Electronic and Electrical & Other Facilities	1382.0	2611.3	366.5	427.9
其他各类制造产品 Other Manufactured Products	16.5	88.5	65.1	136.6
电力、热力、燃气和水的生产和供应 Production and Supply of Electric Power, Heat Power, Gas and Water	1083.3	2774.9	995.7	974.0
建筑 Construction	76.8	21.1	21.5	22.7
批发零售、运输仓储邮政 Wholesale and Retail Trades, Transport, Storage and Post	5794.8	2205.6	11525.6	8007.3
信息传输、软件和信息技术服务 Information Transmission, Software & Information Technology Services	238.0	116.4	298.5	279.5
金融和房地产 Finance and Real Estate	1578.7	2056.6	680.6	653.9
科学研究和技术服务 Research & Development and Technical Services	818.4	487.6	167.6	147.2
其他服务 Other Services	925.1	1948.0	3819.1	1897.1
中间投入合计 Total Intermediate Inputs	**50993.6**	**25596.3**	**94434.9**	**61291.1**
劳动者报酬 Compensation of Employees	82110.9	10305.9	9228.8	7807.0
生产税净额 Net Taxes on Production	-4552.8	8045.4	8292.8	105.5
固定资产折旧 Depreciation of Fixed Assets	2304.9	5071.9	3061.6	1716.0
营业盈余 Operating Surplus	2311.8	6633.9	10118.2	4819.1
增加值合计 Total Value Added	**82174.7**	**30057.1**	**30701.4**	**14447.6**
总投入 Total Inputs	**133168.3**	**55653.4**	**125136.3**	**75738.7**

Intermediate Use Part of 2020 Input-Output Table

Data are calculated at producers' prices in 2020.

(100 million yuan)

木材加工、家具、造纸印刷和文教工美用品 Wood Processing, Furniture, Paper Making, Printing, and Educational & Artistic Products	炼油、炼焦和化学产品 Oil Refining, Coking and Chemical Products	非金属矿物制品 Nonmetallic Mineral Products	金属冶炼、加工及制品 Metal Manufacture & Processing and Metal Products	机械设备、交通运输设备、电子电气及其他设备 Machinery and Equipment, Transport Equipment, Electronic and Electrical & Other Facilities
5373.6	6403.2	21.9	13.4	21.6
467.6	26471.1	8662.3	24423.6	363.0
301.6	3668.2	176.6	1084.1	2208.4
2114.1	1201.8	405.0	312.0	1700.2
19525.7	1342.1	1087.3	737.0	2691.9
7251.1	66975.4	5839.4	8264.9	15907.4
283.1	1123.1	13914.4	2213.5	5551.2
3422.6	2315.4	3809.4	56702.6	48404.2
1078.6	2124.8	1957.1	3959.4	158212.4
1340.4	570.1	363.0	7561.9	564.8
1354.8	6517.9	3728.5	8843.2	4493.9
23.8	54.6	16.3	28.7	147.0
7257.1	15378.1	6243.6	10188.7	31475.2
287.1	610.2	188.0	318.5	3910.7
922.8	2999.4	1460.6	4307.3	5327.0
229.7	1071.1	280.6	563.8	2959.9
2031.8	6353.2	2091.2	2936.6	11713.8
53265.5	**145179.8**	**50245.2**	**132459.2**	**295652.5**
7060.8	12685.8	7496.0	13202.4	29992.1
1173.6	10790.1	2347.3	4813.3	7565.2
2347.7	6992.6	3625.2	6944.0	9931.5
5533.0	16619.6	9589.5	15347.2	23750.9
16115.1	**47088.0**	**23058.0**	**40307.0**	**71239.7**
69380.6	**192267.8**	**73303.2**	**172766.2**	**366892.2**

3-21 续表

单位：亿元

产出 Output / 投入 Input	其他各类制造产品 Other Manufactured Products	电力、热力、燃气和水的生产和供应 Production and Supply of Electric Power, Heat Power, Gas and Water	建筑 Construction	批发零售、运输仓储邮政 Wholesale and Retail Trades, Transport, Storage and Post
农林牧渔产品和服务 Agriculture, Forestry, Animal Husbandry & Fishery Products and Services	345.1	10.3	1883.4	16.8
采掘产品 Mining	23.5	13705.9	2495.7	41.4
食品和烟草 Foods and Tobacco	61.8	597.7	574.3	995.3
纺织、服装、鞋及皮革羽绒制品 Textile, Wearing Apparel, Shoes and Leather Products	418.7	160.0	454.1	833.4
木材加工、家具、造纸印刷和文教工美用品 Wood Processing, Furniture, Paper Making, Printing, and Educational & Artistic Products	210.3	70.1	6256.0	1447.6
炼油、炼焦和化学产品 Oil Refining, Coking and Chemical Products	928.0	1576.3	14923.7	11495.5
非金属矿物制品 Nonmetallic Mineral Products	48.6	202.2	45462.8	70.3
金属冶炼、加工及制品 Metal Manufacture & Processing and Metal Products	910.5	168.8	42158.0	413.1
机械设备、交通运输设备、电子电气及其他设备 Machinery and Equipment, Transport Equipment, Electronic and Electrical & Other Facilities	977.9	6379.8	14816.2	13440.3
其他各类制造产品 Other Manufactured Products	1318.5	391.0	388.3	154.2
电力、热力、燃气和水的生产和供应 Production and Supply of Electric Power, Heat Power, Gas and Water	262.8	23028.2	4472.4	5003.1
建筑 Construction	9.0	278.4	10277.8	350.2
批发零售、运输仓储邮政 Wholesale and Retail Trades, Transport, Storage and Post	645.0	3330.7	22053.8	31091.1
信息传输、软件和信息技术服务 Information Transmission, Software & Information Technology Services	29.0	545.7	3943.1	4762.8
金融和房地产 Finance and Real Estate	218.0	3625.5	10521.8	30392.2
科学研究和技术服务 Research & Development and Technical Services	22.9	370.6	24091.5	1508.4
其他服务 Other Services	307.8	1861.9	9248.4	26715.0
中间投入合计 Total Intermediate Inputs	**6737.5**	**56303.2**	**214021.2**	**128730.8**
劳动者报酬 Compensation of Employees	2554.2	7728.4	46964.5	75031.6
生产税净额 Net Taxes on Production	1343.2	2356.9	9811.6	10389.7
固定资产折旧 Depreciation of Fixed Assets	672.2	11014.8	2771.4	31868.9
营业盈余 Operating Surplus	5111.0	4741.8	12461.7	23747.6
增加值合计 Total Value Added	**9680.7**	**25842.0**	**72009.3**	**141037.8**
总投入 Total Inputs	**16418.2**	**82145.2**	**286030.5**	**269768.6**

continued

(100 million yuan)

信息传输、软件和信息技术服务 Information Transmission, Software & Information Technology Services	金融和房地产 Finance and Real Estate	科学研究和技术服务 Research & Development and Technical Services	其他服务 Other Services	中间使用合计 Total Intermediate Use
51.0	40.4	538.0	7470.4	95485.5
0.0	8.2	74.5	212.6	84504.5
559.5	753.0	807.3	18865.4	67966.9
99.9	681.4	413.1	6382.7	47300.5
2844.3	2640.5	857.1	11959.0	54098.0
407.2	645.1	5501.3	24467.2	185276.9
9.1	5.6	246.7	300.8	70328.7
60.6	128.5	1981.2	3226.8	166598.0
6800.3	402.3	8664.7	14195.8	237797.3
46.3	135.9	722.5	1379.7	15243.1
983.7	1185.1	661.1	3902.4	70265.0
95.4	1668.4	93.9	1813.8	14999.3
2965.3	2686.8	4935.7	27627.2	193411.5
19410.5	5021.0	1445.4	9469.6	50874.1
8250.2	32762.6	3512.3	27946.6	137216.0
328.1	172.8	8727.9	265.2	42213.4
8811.4	20078.8	7844.7	40443.5	149027.1
51722.8	**69016.5**	**47027.3**	**199928.5**	**1682605.8**
20697.4	40801.5	18126.0	137772.1	529565.5
1309.3	20616.1	1330.4	3842.5	89580.2
12669.4	10648.2	6815.2	32126.5	150582.0
10125.4	88518.1	1835.3	5430.3	246694.3
44801.4	**160583.9**	**28107.0**	**179171.4**	**1016422.0**
96524.3	**229600.4**	**75134.2**	**379099.9**	**2699027.8**

3–22 2020年投入产出基本流量表(最终使用部分)

按当年生产者价格计算。

单位：亿元

产出 Output / 投入 Input	最终使用 Final Use				
	最终消费支出 Final Consumption Expenditure				
	居民消费支出 Household Consumption Expenditure			政府消费支出 Government Consumption Expenditure	合计 Total Final Consumption Expenditure
	农村居民 Rural Household	城镇居民 Urban Household	小计 Subtotal		
农林牧渔产品和服务 Agriculture, Forestry, Animal Husbandry & Fishery Products and Services	10974.5	22105.5	33080.0	1964.0	35044.0
采掘产品 Mining	75.3	46.9	122.2		122.2
食品和烟草 Foods and Tobacco	15618.8	45232.7	60851.5		60851.5
纺织、服装、鞋及皮革羽绒制品 Textile, Wearing Apparel, Shoes and Leather Products	2301.4	10819.4	13120.8		13120.8
木材加工、家具、造纸印刷和文教工美用品 Wood Processing, Furniture, Paper Making, Printing, and Educational & Artistic Products	1112.8	4699.3	5812.2		5812.2
炼油、炼焦和化学产品 Oil Refining, Coking and Chemical Products	2640.4	10048.3	12688.7		12688.7
非金属矿物制品 Nonmetallic Mineral Products	156.1	392.6	548.7		548.7
金属冶炼、加工及制品 Metal Manufacture & Processing and Metal Products	66.5	421.5	488.0		488.0
机械设备、交通运输设备、电子电气及其他设备 Machinery and Equipment, Transport Equipment, Electronic and Electrical & Other Facilities	5424.3	22188.1	27612.4		27612.4
其他各类制造产品 Other Manufactured Products	118.8	336.7	455.5		455.5
电力、热力、燃气和水的生产和供应 Production and Supply of Electric Power, Heat Power, Gas and Water	1611.1	9998.4	11609.5		11609.5
建筑 Construction					
批发零售、运输仓储邮政 Wholesale and Retail Trades, Transport, Storage and Post	8206.5	27390.1	35596.6	4278.8	39875.4
信息传输、软件和信息技术服务 Information Transmission, Software & Information Technology Services	2773.0	9699.2	12472.2		12472.2
金融和房地产 Finance and Real Estate	14912.3	70032.6	84944.9	4510.2	89455.2
科学研究和技术服务 Research & Development and Technical Services	84.6	355.4	440.0	14632.0	15072.0
其他服务 Other Services	15587.8	68577.3	84165.1	148240.4	232405.5
中间投入合计 Total Intermediate Inputs	**81664.3**	**302344.0**	**384008.3**	**173625.4**	**557633.7**

Final Use Part of 2020 Input-Output Table

Data are calculated at producers' prices in 2020.

(100 million yuan)

最终使用 Final Use					进口 Imports	总产出 Gross Output
资本形成总额 Gross Capital Formation			出口 Exports	最终使用合计 Total Final Use		
固定资本形成总额 Gross Fixed Capital Formation	存货变动 Changes in Inventories	合计 Total Gross Capital Formation				
1757.7	5490.2	7247.9	1817.2	44109.1	6426.2	133168.3
	46.2	46.2	467.9	636.4	29487.5	55653.4
	852.6	852.6	3583.3	65287.4	8118.1	125136.3
	-357.1	-357.1	18680.1	31443.8	3005.5	75738.7
2587.7	-636.5	1951.2	11084.0	18847.3	3564.8	69380.6
	-2560.5	-2560.5	16224.1	26352.3	19361.4	192267.8
	214.1	214.1	3455.4	4218.2	1243.7	73303.2
2516.3	1295.7	3812.0	10808.2	15108.3	8940.1	172766.2
78322.3	3724.9	82047.2	82232.4	191892.0	62797.1	366892.2
194.6	-210.4	-15.8	1662.7	2102.4	927.4	16418.2
	178.5	178.5	104.5	11892.5	12.3	82145.2
270717.6		270717.6	868.1	271585.7	554.5	286030.5
11930.2	1113.4	13043.6	27370.3	80289.3	3932.2	269768.6
32868.7		32868.7	3074.5	48415.4	2765.2	96524.3
3296.0		3296.0	689.5	93440.7	1056.3	229600.4
19655.9		19655.9	967.8	35695.6	2774.8	75134.2
523.5		523.5	4835.9	237764.9	7692.1	379099.9
424370.4	**9151.0**	**433521.4**	**187926.1**	**1179081.2**	**162659.2**	**2699027.8**

3–23　2020年非竞争型投入产出表(17×17产品部门)

单位：亿元

产　出 Output / 投　入 Input	农林牧渔产品和服务 Agriculture, Forestry, Animal Husbandry & Fishery Products and Services	采掘产品 Mining	食品和烟草 Foods and Tobacco	纺织、服装、鞋及皮革羽绒制品 Textile, Wearing Apparel, Shoes and Leather Products	木材加工、家具、造纸印刷和文教工美用品 Wood Processing, Furniture, Paper Making, Printing, and Educational & Artistic Products
国产品 Domestic Products					
农林牧渔产品和服务 Agriculture, Forestry, Animal Husbandry & Fishery Products and Services	17917.0	23.6	43506.5	7837.1	4816.8
采掘产品 Mining	60.3	5860.4	269.4	182.7	393.6
食品和烟草 Foods and Tobacco	10776.3	144.8	22690.4	1348.7	301.2
纺织、服装、鞋及皮革羽绒制品 Textile, Wearing Apparel, Shoes and Leather Products	25.4	243.7	369.2	30715.1	2056.8
木材加工、家具、造纸印刷和文教工美用品 Wood Processing, Furniture, Paper Making, Printing, and Educational & Artistic Products	135.5	433.7	1375.0	434.1	17453.7
炼油、炼焦和化学产品 Oil Refining, Coking and Chemical Products	9463.1	2824.3	1752.4	6303.9	6911.1
非金属矿物制品 Nonmetallic Mineral Products	52.7	288.4	486.1	55.9	254.6
金属冶炼、加工及制品 Metal Manufacture & Processing and Metal Products	106.1	2060.9	388.3	270.0	3086.3
机械设备、交通运输设备、电子电气及其他设备 Machinery and Equipment, Transport Equipment, Electronic and Electrical & Other Facilities	1370.1	2558.2	351.4	410.3	833.4
其他各类制造产品 Other Manufactured Products	15.4	88.2	63.7	128.9	1197.0
电力、热力、燃气和水的生产和供应 Production and Supply of Electric Power, Heat Power, Gas and Water	1083.3	2774.9	995.7	974.0	1354.8
建筑 Construction	76.8	21.1	21.5	22.7	23.8
批发零售、运输仓储邮政 Wholesale and Retail Trades, Transport, Storage and Post	5756.9	2199.9	11507.2	7982.0	7240.8
信息传输、软件和信息技术服务 Information Transmission, Software & Information Technology Services	237.9	116.3	296.9	277.9	285.5
金融和房地产 Finance and Real Estate	1572.6	2049.3	676.8	650.1	917.4
科学研究和技术服务 Research & Development and Technical Services	818.4	487.6	167.6	147.2	229.7
其他服务 Other Services	904.7	1924.9	3592.0	1791.0	1923.7
国产品中间投入合计 Total Intermediate Inputs of Domestic Products	**50372.4**	**24100.0**	**88510.3**	**59531.6**	**49280.1**

Non Competitive Input-Output Table of 2020 (17 × 17 Product Department)

(100 million yuan)

炼油、炼焦和化学产品 Oil Refining, Coking and Chemical Products	非金属矿物制品 Nonmetallic Mineral Products	金属冶炼、加工及制品 Metal Manufacture & Processing and Metal Products	机械设备、交通运输设备、电子电气及其他设备 Machinery and Equipment, Transport Equipment, Electronic and Electrical & Other Facilities	其他各类制造产品 Other Manufactured Products	电力、热力、燃气和水的生产和供应 Production and Supply of Electric Power, Heat Power, Gas and Water	建 筑 Construction
6212.9	21.9	13.4	21.1	344.8	10.3	1853.5
14684.6	8279.4	12792.7	297.5	21.8	10321.2	2344.0
3585.5	176.4	1083.7	2207.3	61.7	597.4	573.3
1191.9	404.8	311.2	1658.4	414.0	160.0	454.1
1282.3	1068.7	732.1	2589.2	207.3	70.0	6190.3
56116.9	5629.1	7889.5	13836.6	845.6	1482.1	14715.7
1070.8	13497.8	2168.9	5105.7	45.1	198.7	45331.1
2173.6	3750.6	52376.7	45693.7	865.1	160.0	41952.9
2030.0	1917.0	3852.5	116438.9	890.1	5987.9	14503.7
547.8	344.3	7194.6	538.2	1236.9	390.0	387.4
6517.9	3728.5	8843.2	4493.9	262.8	23021.9	4472.4
54.6	16.3	28.7	147.0	9.0	278.4	10277.8
15318.7	6226.7	10166.4	31341.9	642.2	3308.9	21952.2
607.0	187.5	317.1	3882.6	29.0	545.6	3943.0
2981.1	1451.7	4279.8	5295.1	216.9	3614.1	10470.5
1071.1	280.6	563.8	2959.9	22.9	370.6	24091.5
5996.2	1983.8	2774.6	11098.3	294.9	1823.7	9132.5
121443.0	**48965.0**	**115389.1**	**247605.3**	**6409.9**	**52340.8**	**212645.9**

3-23 续表 1

单位：亿元

投入 Input \ 产出 Output	农林牧渔产品和服务 Agriculture, Forestry, Animal Husbandry & Fishery Products and Services	采掘产品 Mining	食品和烟草 Foods and Tobacco	纺织、服装、鞋及皮革羽绒制品 Textile, Wearing Apparel, Shoes and Leather Products	木材加工、家具、造纸印刷和文教工美用品 Wood Processing, Furniture, Paper Making, Printing, and Educational & Artistic Products
进口品 Imported Products					
农林牧渔产品和服务 Agriculture, Forestry, Animal Husbandry & Fishery Products and Services	396.4	0.0	3252.2	363.5	556.8
采掘产品 Mining	0.1	1181.8	0.2	0.4	74.0
食品和烟草 Foods and Tobacco	42.2	0.2	2246.8	64.1	0.4
纺织、服装、鞋及皮革羽绒制品 Textile, Wearing Apparel, Shoes and Leather Products	0.1	0.3	0.4	769.5	57.4
木材加工、家具、造纸印刷和文教工美用品 Wood Processing, Furniture, Paper Making, Printing, and Educational & Artistic Products	0.7	1.4	31.0	17.7	2072.0
炼油、炼焦和化学产品 Oil Refining, Coking and Chemical Products	103.9	150.9	121.7	374.3	340.1
非金属矿物制品 Nonmetallic Mineral Products	0.1	10.4	2.7	1.2	28.5
金属冶炼、加工及制品 Metal Manufacture & Processing and Metal Products	0.3	61.7	2.3	6.7	336.3
机械设备、交通运输设备、电子电气及其他设备 Machinery and Equipment, Transport Equipment, Electronic and Electrical & Other Facilities	12.0	53.1	15.0	17.6	245.1
其他各类制造产品 Other Manufactured Products	1.0	0.3	1.4	7.7	143.4
电力、热力、燃气和水的生产和供应 Production and Supply of Electric Power, Heat Power, Gas and Water					
建筑 Construction					
批发零售、运输仓储邮政 Wholesale and Retail Trades, Transport, Storage and Post	37.9	5.7	18.4	25.2	16.3
信息传输、软件和信息技术服务 Information Transmission, Software & Information Technology Services	0.1	0.1	1.6	1.6	1.6
金融和房地产 Finance and Real Estate	6.1	7.3	3.8	3.8	5.4
科学研究和技术服务 Research & Development and Technical Services	0.0	0.0	0.0	0.0	0.0
其他服务 Other Services	20.3	23.2	227.1	106.1	108.1
进口品中间投入合计 Total Intermediate Inputs of Imported Products	**621.2**	**1496.2**	**5924.6**	**1759.5**	**3985.4**
劳动者报酬 Compensation of Employees	82110.9	10305.9	9228.8	7807.0	7060.8
生产税净额 Net Taxes on Production	-4552.8	8045.4	8292.8	105.5	1173.6
固定资产折旧 Depreciation of Fixed Assets	2304.9	5071.9	3061.6	1716.0	2347.7
营业盈余 Operating Surplus	2311.8	6633.9	10118.2	4819.1	5533.0
增加值合计 Total Value Added	**82174.7**	**30057.1**	**30701.4**	**14447.6**	**16115.1**
总投入 Total Inputs	**133168.3**	**55653.4**	**125136.3**	**75738.7**	**69380.6**

continued

(100 million yuan)

炼油、炼焦和化学产品 Oil Refining, Coking and Chemical Products	非金属矿物制品 Nonmetallic Mineral Products	金属冶炼、加工及制品 Metal Manufacture & Processing and Metal Products	机械设备、交通运输设备、电子电气及其他设备 Machinery and Equipment, Transport Equipment, Electronic and Electrical & Other Facilities	其他各类制造产品 Other Manufactured Products	电力、热力、燃气和水的生产和供应 Production and Supply of Electric Power, Heat Power, Gas and Water	建　筑 Construction
190.3	0.0	0.0	0.6	0.3	0.0	29.9
11786.5	382.9	11630.8	65.4	1.6	3384.7	151.7
82.7	0.3	0.4	1.1	0.2	0.3	1.0
9.9	0.3	0.8	41.9	4.8	0.0	0.0
59.8	18.6	4.8	102.6	3.1	0.1	65.7
10858.5	210.3	375.4	2070.8	82.4	94.2	208.0
52.3	416.5	44.5	445.4	3.5	3.4	131.6
141.8	58.8	4325.9	2710.5	45.4	8.8	205.0
94.8	40.1	107.0	41773.5	87.8	391.9	312.5
22.4	18.7	367.2	26.6	81.6	1.0	0.8
					6.2	
59.4	16.9	22.2	133.3	2.8	21.8	101.5
3.2	0.4	1.3	28.1	0.1	0.1	0.1
18.3	8.9	27.5	31.9	1.1	11.5	51.4
0.0	0.0	0.0	0.0	0.0	0.0	0.0
357.0	107.3	162.0	615.5	13.0	38.2	115.9
23736.8	**1280.2**	**17070.1**	**48047.2**	**327.6**	**3962.4**	**1375.3**
12685.8	7496.0	13202.4	29992.1	2554.2	7728.4	46964.5
10790.1	2347.3	4813.3	7565.2	1343.2	2356.9	9811.6
6992.6	3625.2	6944.0	9931.5	672.2	11014.8	2771.4
16619.6	9589.5	15347.2	23750.9	5111.0	4741.8	12461.7
47088.0	**23058.0**	**40307.0**	**71239.7**	**9680.7**	**25842.0**	**72009.3**
192267.8	**73303.2**	**172766.2**	**366892.2**	**16418.2**	**82145.2**	**286030.5**

3-23 续表 2

单位：亿元

产出 Output / 投入 Input	批发零售、运输仓储邮政 Wholesale and Retail Trades, Transport, Storage and Post	信息传输、软件和信息技术服务 Information Transmission, Software & Information Technology Services	金融和房地产 Finance and Real Estate	科学研究和技术服务 Research & Development and Technical Services	其他服务 Other Services
国产品 Domestic Products					
农林牧渔产品和服务 Agriculture, Forestry, Animal Husbandry & Fishery Products and Services	16.8	50.9	40.4	537.7	7465.3
采掘产品 Mining	37.1		8.2	66.5	210.2
食品和烟草 Foods and Tobacco	994.2	559.1	752.1	805.7	18779.4
纺织、服装、鞋及皮革羽绒制品 Textile, Wearing Apparel, Shoes and Leather Products	831.4	99.8	681.4	412.0	6372.6
木材加工、家具、造纸印刷和文教工美用品 Wood Processing, Furniture, Paper Making, Printing, and Educational & Artistic Products	1442.2	2828.5	2627.5	847.9	11834.2
炼油、炼焦和化学产品 Oil Refining, Coking and Chemical Products	11466.9	404.5	643.2	5306.2	24070.9
非金属矿物制品 Nonmetallic Mineral Products	63.9	9.1	5.6	242.3	297.9
金属冶炼、加工及制品 Metal Manufacture & Processing and Metal Products	405.9	60.5	128.3	1977.7	3217.7
机械设备、交通运输设备、电子电气及其他设备 Machinery and Equipment, Transport Equipment, Electronic and Electrical & Other Facilities	13238.1	6602.4	364.0	7858.5	13473.2
其他各类制造产品 Other Manufactured Products	96.3	43.0	135.2	717.1	1372.7
电力、热力、燃气和水的生产和供应 Production and Supply of Electric Power, Heat Power, Gas and Water	5003.1	983.7	1185.1	661.1	3902.4
建筑 Construction	350.2	95.4	1668.4	93.9	1813.8
批发零售、运输仓储邮政 Wholesale and Retail Trades, Transport, Storage and Post	30636.3	2781.0	2562.3	4688.8	25900.1
信息传输、软件和信息技术服务 Information Transmission, Software & Information Technology Services	4740.0	19102.7	5010.1	1438.0	9435.4
金融和房地产 Finance and Real Estate	30327.5	8243.2	32261.4	3502.9	27878.6
科学研究和技术服务 Research & Development and Technical Services	1508.4	328.1	172.8	8727.9	265.2
其他服务 Other Services	25975.6	8558.2	19694.4	7547.3	38368.6
国产品中间投入合计 Total Intermediate Inputs of Domestic Products	**127134.1**	**50750.0**	**67940.5**	**45431.8**	**194658.1**

continued

(100 million yuan)

中间使用合计 Total Intermediate Use	最终使用 Final Use					进口 Imports	国内产出 Domestic Output
	消费支出合计 Total Gross Consumption Expenditure	固定资本形成总额 Gross Fixed Capital Formation	存货变动 Changes in Inventories	出口 Exports	最终使用合计 Total Final Use		
90690.1	33755.3	1716.0	5190.6	1816.5	42478.3		133168.3
55829.6	122.2		-567.4	269.0	-176.2		55653.4
65437.2	55560.9		562.8	3575.4	59699.1		125136.3
46401.7	11017.7		-360.8	18680.1	29337.0		75738.7
51552.3	4943.3	2524.8	-676.0	11036.3	17828.3		69380.6
169662.0	9389.0		-2737.8	15954.6	22605.8		192267.8
69174.6	494.0		213.2	3421.4	4128.6		73303.2
158674.3	436.0	2400.4	614.2	10641.3	14091.9		172766.2
192679.7	24836.0	66629.3	3411.5	79335.7	174212.5		366892.2
14496.8	417.6	66.8	-225.8	1662.7	1921.4		16418.2
70258.8	11603.4		178.5	104.5	11886.5		82145.2
14999.3		270163.1		868.1	271031.2		286030.5
190212.6	39142.1	11930.2	1113.4	27370.3	79556.0		269768.6
50452.6	12420.9	30576.3		3074.5	46071.7		96524.3
136389.0	89225.9	3296.0		689.5	93211.4		229600.4
42213.4	15072.0	16881.1		967.8	32920.9		75134.2
143384.5	230389.1	490.5		4835.9	235715.4		379099.9
1562508.0	**538825.4**	**406674.4**	**6716.4**	**184303.6**	**1136519.8**		**2699027.8**

3-23 续表 3

单位：亿元

产出 Output / 投入 Input	批发零售、运输仓储邮政 Wholesale and Retail Trades, Transport, Storage and Post	信息传输、软件和信息技术服务 Information Transmission, Software & Information Technology Services	金融和房地产 Finance and Real Estate	科学研究和技术服务 Research & Development and Technical Services	其他服务 Other Services
进口品 Imported Products					
农林牧渔产品和服务 Agriculture, Forestry, Animal Husbandry & Fishery Products and Services	0.0	0.0	0.0	0.3	5.1
采掘产品 Mining	4.3	0.0	0.0	7.9	2.4
食品和烟草 Foods and Tobacco	1.1	0.4	0.9	1.6	86.0
纺织、服装、鞋及皮革羽绒制品 Textile, Wearing Apparel, Shoes and Leather Products	2.1	0.1	0.1	1.1	10.1
木材加工、家具、造纸印刷和文教工美用品 Wood Processing, Furniture, Paper Making, Printing, and Educational & Artistic Products	5.4	15.8	13.0	9.1	124.8
炼油、炼焦和化学产品 Oil Refining, Coking and Chemical Products	28.5	2.7	1.8	195.0	396.3
非金属矿物制品 Nonmetallic Mineral Products	6.4	0.0	0.0	4.4	2.9
金属冶炼、加工及制品 Metal Manufacture & Processing and Metal Products	7.3	0.1	0.2	3.5	9.1
机械设备、交通运输设备、电子电气及其他设备 Machinery and Equipment, Transport Equipment, Electronic and Electrical & Other Facilities	202.2	197.9	38.4	806.2	722.6
其他各类制造产品 Other Manufactured Products	57.8	3.3	0.7	5.4	7.0
电力、热力、燃气和水的生产和供应 Production and Supply of Electric Power, Heat Power, Gas and Water					
建筑 Construction					
批发零售、运输仓储邮政 Wholesale and Retail Trades, Transport, Storage and Post	454.7	184.3	124.5	246.9	1727.1
信息传输、软件和信息技术服务 Information Transmission, Software & Information Technology Services	22.8	307.8	10.9	7.3	34.2
金融和房地产 Finance and Real Estate	64.7	7.0	501.1	9.4	68.0
科学研究和技术服务 Research & Development and Technical Services	0.0	0.0	0.0	0.0	0.0
其他服务 Other Services	739.4	253.2	384.3	297.3	2074.8
进口品中间投入合计 Total Intermediate Inputs of Imported Products	**1596.7**	**972.8**	**1076.0**	**1595.5**	**5270.4**
劳动者报酬 Compensation of Employees	75031.6	20697.4	40801.5	18126.0	137772.1
生产税净额 Net Taxes on Production	10389.7	1309.3	20616.1	1330.4	3842.5
固定资产折旧 Depreciation of Fixed Assets	31868.9	12669.4	10648.2	6815.2	32126.5
营业盈余 Operating Surplus	23747.6	10125.4	88518.1	1835.3	5430.3
增加值合计 Total Value Added	**141037.8**	**44801.4**	**160583.9**	**28107.0**	**179171.4**
总投入 Total Inputs	**269768.6**	**96524.3**	**229600.4**	**75134.2**	**379099.9**

continued

(100 million yuan)

中间使用合计 Total Intermediate Use	最终使用 Final Use					进 口 Imports	国内产出 Domestic Output
	消费支出合计 Total Gross Consumption Expenditure	固定资本形成总额 Gross Fixed Capital Formation	存货变动 Changes in Inventories	出 口 Exports	最终使用合计 Total Final Use		
4795.4	1288.8	41.8	299.6	0.7	1630.8	6426.2	
28674.9			613.6	198.9	812.6	29487.5	
2529.7	5290.6		289.8	7.9	5588.3	8118.1	
898.8	2103.1		3.6		2106.7	3005.5	
2545.7	868.8	62.9	39.5	47.7	1019.0	3564.8	
15615.0	3299.7		177.3	269.5	3746.5	19361.4	
1154.1	54.6		0.9	34.1	89.6	1243.7	
7923.8	52.1	115.9	681.5	166.9	1016.4	8940.1	
45117.6	2776.4	11693.0	313.4	2896.7	17679.5	62797.1	
746.4	37.9	127.8	15.4		181.0	927.4	
6.2	6.1				6.1	12.3	
		554.5			554.5	554.5	
3199.0	733.3				733.3	3932.2	
421.5	51.3	2292.4			2343.6	2765.2	
827.0	229.3				229.3	1056.3	
0.0		2774.8			2774.8	2774.8	
5642.6	2016.4	33.0			2049.4	7692.1	
120097.8	**18808.2**	**17696.0**	**2434.6**	**3622.5**	**42561.3**	**162659.2**	
529565.5							
89580.2							
150582.0							
246694.3							
1016422.0							
2699027.8							

主要统计指标解释

国内生产总值(GDP) 指一个国家所有常住单位在一定时期内生产活动的最终成果。国内生产总值有三种表现形态，即价值形态、收入形态和产品形态。从价值形态看，它是所有常住单位在一定时期内生产的全部货物和服务价值与同期投入的全部非固定资产货物和服务价值的差额，即所有常住单位的增加值之和；从收入形态看，它是所有常住单位在一定时期内创造的各项收入之和，包括劳动者报酬、生产税净额、固定资产折旧和营业盈余；从产品形态看，它是所有常住单位在一定时期内最终使用的货物和服务价值与货物和服务净出口价值之和。在实际核算中，国内生产总值有三种计算方法，即生产法、收入法和支出法。三种方法分别从不同的方面反映国内生产总值及其构成。

对于一个地区来说，称为地区生产总值或地区 GDP。

国民总收入（GNI） 原称国民生产总值（GNP），指一个国家所有常住单位在一定时期内收入初次分配的最终结果。一国常住单位从事生产活动所创造的增加值在初次分配中主要分配给该国的常住单位，但也有一部分以生产税（扣除生产补贴）、劳动者报酬和财产收入等形式分配给非常住单位；同时，国外生产所创造的增加值也有一部分以生产税(扣除生产补贴)、劳动者报酬和财产收入等形式分配给该国的常住单位，从而产生了国民总收入的概念。它等于国内生产总值加上来自国外的初次分配收入净额。与国内生产总值不同，国民总收入是个收入概念，而国内生产总值是个生产概念。

三次产业 三次产业的划分是世界上较为常用的产业结构分类，但各国的划分不尽一致。根据《国民经济行业分类》（GB/T 4754—2017）和《三次产业划分规定》，我国的三次产业划分是：

第一产业是指农、林、牧、渔业（不含农、林、牧、渔专业及辅助性活动)。

第二产业是指采矿业（不含开采专业及辅助性活动)，制造业（不含金属制品、机械和设备修理业），电力、热力、燃气及水生产和供应业，建筑业。

第三产业即服务业，是指除第一产业、第二产业以外的其他行业。

劳动者报酬 指劳动者从事生产活动应获得的全部报酬，既包括货币形式的报酬，也包括实物形式的报酬。主要包括工资、奖金、津贴和补贴，单位为其员工交纳的社会保险费、补充社会保险费和住房公积金、行政事业单位职工的离退休金、单位为其员工提供的其他各种形式的福利和报酬等。

生产税净额 指生产税减生产补贴后的差额。其中，生产税指政府对生产单位从事生产、销售和经营活动，以及因从事生产活动使用某些生产要素（如固定资产和土地等）所征收的各种税收、附加费和其他规费。生产税分为产品税和其他生产税，产品税主要有：增值税、消费税、进口关税、出口税等；其他生产税主要有：房产税、车船使用税、城镇土地使用税等。生产补贴则相反，它是政府为影响生产单位的生产、销售及定价等生产活动而对其提供的无偿支付，包括农业生产补贴、政策亏损补贴、进口补贴等。生产补贴作为负生产税处理。

固定资产折旧 指由于自然退化、正常淘汰或损耗而导致的固定资产价值下降，用以代表固定资产通过生产过程被转移到其产出中的价值。原则上，固定资产折旧应按照固定资产的重置价值计算。

营业盈余 指常住单位创造的增加值扣除劳动者报酬、生产税净额和固定资产折旧后的余额。

支出法国内生产总值 是从最终使用的角度反映一个国家(或地区)一定时期内生产活动最终成果的一种方法，包括最终消费支出、资本形成总额及货物和服务净出口三部分。计算公式为：

支出法国内生产总值=最终消费支出+资本形成总额+货物和服务净出口

最终消费支出 指常住单位为满足物质、文化和精神生活的需要，从本国经济领土和国外购买的货物和服务的支出。它不包括非常住单位在本国经济领土内的消费支出。最终消费支出分为居民消费支出和政府消费支出。

居民消费支出 指常住住户在一定时期内对于货物和服务的全部最终消费支出。居民消费支出除了直接以货币形式购买的货物和服务的消费支出外，还包括以其他方式获得的货物和服务的消费支出，例如，单位以实物报酬形式提供给劳动者的货物和服务；住户生产用于自身消费的货物（如自产自用的农产品），以及纳入生产核算范围并用于自身消费的服务（如住户的自有住房服务）；银行和保险机构提供的间接计算的金融服务。

政府消费支出 指广义政府部门为全社会提供的公共服务的消费支出和免费或以较低的价格向居民住户提供的货物和服务的净支出，前者等于政府服务的产出价值减去政府单位所获得的经营收入的价值，后者等于广义政府部门免费或以较低价格向居民住户提供的货物和服务的市场价值减去向住户收取的价值。

实际最终消费 指核算期内常住单位实际获得的用于满足他们个人或公共需要或需求而使用的货物和服务。分为居民实际最终消费和政府实际最终消费。实际最终消费在数值上等于最终消费支出。

实物社会转移 指广义政府部门免费或以没有显著经

济意义的价格向居民提供消费性货物和服务的支出。

居民实际最终消费 指常住住户获得的用于消费的货物和服务价值，它等于居民自身承担的消费性货物和服务支出加上广义政府部门以实物社会转移形式向居民提供的消费性货物和服务支出。

政府实际最终消费 指广义政府部门向全社会提供的公共服务的价值，它等于政府最终消费支出减去以实物转移形式向居民提供的消费性货物和服务支出。

资本形成总额 指常住单位在一定时期内获得减去处置的固定资产和存货的净额，包括固定资本形成总额和存货变动两部分。

固定资本形成总额 指常住单位在一定时期内获得的固定资产减处置的固定资产的价值总额。固定资产是通过生产活动生产出来的，且其使用年限在一年以上、单位价值在规定标准以上的资产，不包括自然资产、耐用消费品、小型工器具。固定资本形成总额包括住宅、其他建筑和构筑物、机器和设备、培育性生物资源、知识产权产品的价值获得减处置。

存货变动 指常住单位在一定时期内存货实物量变动的市场价值，即期末价值减期初价值的差额，再扣除当期由于价格变动而产生的持有收益。存货变动可以是正值，也可以是负值，正值表示存货上升，负值表示存货下降。存货包括生产单位购进的原材料、燃料和储备物资等存货，以及生产单位生产的产成品、在制品和半成品等存货。

货物和服务净出口 指货物和服务出口减货物和服务进口的差额。出口包括常住单位向非常住单位出售或无偿转让的各种货物和服务的价值；进口包括常住单位从非常住单位购买或无偿得到的各种货物和服务的价值。货物的出口和进口都按离岸价格计算。

机构单位 指能够以自己的名义拥有资产和承担负债，能够独立地从事经济活动并与其他主体进行交易的经济主体。

机构部门 将相同性质的机构单位归并在一起，就形成机构部门。资金流量核算将常住机构单位划分为以下四个机构部门：非金融企业部门、金融机构部门、广义政府部门、住户部门。与常住单位发生交易的非常住单位称为国外，在资金流量核算中也视同机构部门。

非金融企业与非金融企业部门 非金融企业指主要从事市场性货物生产或提供非金融市场性服务的常住企业，它主要包括从事上述活动的各类法人企业。所有非金融企业组成非金融企业部门。

金融机构与金融机构部门 金融机构指主要从事金融媒介及与金融媒介密切相关的辅助金融活动的常住机构单位，包括从事货币金融服务、资本市场服务、保险服务、其他金融服务等活动的法人单位。所有金融机构组成金融机构部门。

广义政府机构与广义政府部门 广义政府机构指在设定区域内对其他机构单位拥有立法、司法或行政权的法律实体及其附属单位。广义政府机构的主要职能是利用征税和其他方式获得的资金向社会和公众提供货物和服务；通过转移支付，对社会收入和财产进行再分配；从事非市场性生产。它主要包括各级党政机关、群众团体、事业单位、基层群众性自治组织等。所有广义政府机构组成广义政府部门。

住户与住户部门 住户指共享同一生活设施，共同使用部分或全部收入和财产，共同消费住房、食品和其他消费品与服务的常住个人或个人群体。所有住户组成住户部门。

非常住单位与国外 所有不具有常住性的机构单位都是非常住单位。与我国常住单位发生交易的所有非常住单位称为国外。

初次分配总收入 收入初次分配是生产活动创造的价值在参与生产活动的生产要素所有者及政府之间的分配。生产活动的最终成果是增加值。生产要素主要包括劳动力、资本、自然资源。劳动力所有者因提供劳动而获得劳动者报酬；资本的所有者因提供资本而获得不同形式的收入，如借贷资本所有者获得利息收入；股权所有者获得红利或参与利润分配；自然资源所有者因出让自然资源使用权而获得地租；政府因国家管理需要对生产活动或生产要素征收生产税，同时也因扶持有关生产活动而支付生产补贴。初次分配的结果形成各个机构部门的初次分配总收入。各部门的初次分配总收入之和就等于国民总收入。

经常转移 转移是一个机构单位向另一个机构单位提供货物、服务或资产，但又不从后者获取任何直接对应回报的一种交易。经常转移指交易的一方或双方都不涉及获得或处置资产（除存货和现金外）的转移。其形式有所得税、财产税等经常税、社会保险缴款、社会保险福利、社会补助和其他经常转移。

可支配总收入 在初次分配总收入的基础上，通过经常转移的形式对初次分配总收入进行再次分配。再分配的结果形成各个机构部门的可支配总收入。各部门的可支配总收入之和称为国民可支配总收入。

调整后可支配总收入 在各机构部门可支配总收入的基础上，加上该部门应得的实物社会转移，减去该部门应付的实物社会转移，形成调整后可支配总收入，反映各部门获得的对应于实际最终消费的收入总和。

总储蓄 指可支配总收入用于最终消费后的余额。各部门的总储蓄之和称为国民总储蓄。

资本转移 指交易的一方或双方涉及获得或处置资产（除存货和现金外）的转移。资本转移包括资本税、投资性补助和其他资本转移。

净金融投资 它反映各机构部门或经济总体非金融投资过程中资金富余或短缺的状况。从非金融交易角度看，它是指总储蓄加资本转移收入减资本转移支出减非金融投资后的差额。从金融交易角度看，它是金融资产的增加额减金融负债的增加额之后的差额。

通货 指以现金形式存在于市场流通领域中的货币，包括辅币和纸币。

存款 指以各种形式存在存款类金融机构的存款，包括活期存款、定期存款、财政存款、外汇存款和其他存款等。

贷款 指金融机构发放的各类贷款，包括短期贷款、票据融资、中长期贷款、外汇贷款、委托贷款和其他贷款等。

债券 指机构单位为筹措资金而发行，并且承诺按约定条件偿还的有价证券，包括政府债券、金融债券、中央银行债券、企业债券等。

股票 指股份有限公司根据公司法的规定，为筹集公司资本所发行的、用于证明股东身份和权益并据以获得股息和红利的凭证。

保险准备金 指社会保险和商业保险基金的净权益、保险费预付款和未结索赔准备金。

金融机构往来 指金融机构部门子部门之间发生的同业存放、同业拆借和债券回购等。

存款准备金 指各金融机构在中央银行的存款及缴存中央银行的法定准备金。

中央银行贷款 指中央银行向各金融机构的贷款。

国际储备资产 指我国中央银行拥有的对外资产，包括外汇、货币黄金、特别提款权、在国际货币基金组织的储备头寸等。

经常账户 包括货物和服务、初次收入和二次收入。

货物 指经济所有权在我国居民与非居民之间发生转移的货物交易。

服务 包括加工服务，维护和维修服务，运输，旅行，建设，保险和养老金服务，金融服务，知识产权使用费，电信、计算机和信息服务，其他商业服务，个人、文化和娱乐服务以及别处未提及的政府服务。

初次收入 指由于提供劳务、金融资产和出租自然资源而获得的回报，包括雇员报酬、投资收益和其他初次收入三部分。

二次收入 指居民与非居民之间的经常转移，包括现金和实物。

资本账户 指居民与非居民之间的资本转移，以及居民与非居民之间非生产非金融资产的取得和处置。

金融账户 指发生在居民与非居民之间、涉及金融资产与负债的各类交易。金融账户细分为非储备性质的金融账户和国际储备资产。

直接投资 以投资者寻求在本国以外运行企业获取有效发言权为目的的投资，包括直接投资资产和直接投资负债两部分。相关投资工具可划分为股权和关联企业债务。股权包括股权和投资基金份额，以及再投资收益。关联企业债务包括关联企业间可流通和不可流通的债权和债务。

证券投资 包括证券投资资产和证券投资负债，相关投资工具可划分为股权和债券。股权包括股权和投资基金份额，记录在证券投资项下的股权和投资基金份额均应可流通（可交易）。股权通常以股份、股票、参股、存托凭证或类似单据作为凭证。投资基金份额指投资者持有的共同基金等集合投资产品的份额。债券指可流通的债务工具，是证明其持有人（债权人）有权在未来某个（些）时点向其发行人（债务人）收回本金或收取利息的凭证，包括可转让存单、商业票据、公司债券、有资产担保的证券、货币市场工具以及通常在金融市场上交易的类似工具。

金融衍生工具 又称金融衍生工具和雇员认股权，用于记录我国居民与非居民金融衍生工具和雇员认股权交易情况。

其他投资 除直接投资、证券投资、金融衍生工具和储备资产外，居民与非居民之间的其他金融交易。包括其他股权、货币和存款、贷款、保险和养老金、贸易信贷和其他。

净误差与遗漏 国际收支平衡表采用复式记账法，由于统计资料来源和时点不同等原因，会形成经常账户与资本和金融账户不平衡，形成统计残差项，称为净误差与遗漏。

Explanatory Notes on Main Statistical Indicators

Gross Domestic Product (GDP) refers to the final products produced by all resident units in a country during a certain period of time. Gross domestic product is expressed in three different perspectives, namely value, income, and products respectively. GDP in its value perspective refers to the balance of total value of all goods and services produced by all resident units during a certain period of time, minus the total value of input of goods and services of the nature of non-fixed assets; in other words, it is the sum of the value-added of all resident units. GDP from the perspective of income refers to the sum of all kinds of revenue, including compensation of employees, net taxes on production, depreciation of fixed assets, and operating surplus. GDP from the perspective of products refers to the value of all goods and services for final demand by all resident units plus the net exports of goods and services during a given period of time. In the practice of national accounting, gross domestic product is calculated by three approaches, namely production approach, income approach and expenditure approach, which reflect gross domestic product and its composition from different angles.

For a region, it is called as gross regional product(GRP) or regional GDP.

Gross National Income (GNI) originally known as gross national product(GNP), refers to the final result of the primary distribution of the income created by all resident units of a country during a certain period of time. The value-added created by the resident units of a country engaged in production activities is distributed, during the primary distribution, mainly to the resident units of that country, while part of it is distributed to the non-resident units in the form of production tax (minus subsidies to production), compensation of employees and property income. In the meantime, a part of the value-added created abroad is distributed to the resident units of the country in the form of production tax (minus subsidies to production), compensation of employees and property income. The concept of gross national income is thus developed, which equals to gross domestic product plus the net income from primary distribution from abroad. Unlike GDP which is a concept of production, GNI is a concept of income.

Three Strata of Industry Classification of economic activities into three strata of industries is a common practice in the world, although the grouping varies to some extent from country to country. In China, according to *Industrial Classification for National Economic Activities* (GB/T 4754—2017) and *Rules on Division of Three Strata of Industries*, economic activities are categorized into the following three strata of industries:

Primary industry refers to agriculture, forestry, animal husbandry and fishery industries (not including services in support of agriculture, forestry, animal husbandry and fishery industries).

Secondary industry refers to mining and quarrying (not including support activities for mining), manufacturing (not including repair service of metal products, machinery and equipment), production and supply of electricity, heat, gas and water, and construction.

Tertiary industry refers to all other economic activities not included in the primary or secondary industries.

Compensation of Employees refers to the total payment of various forms to employees for the productive activities they are engaged in. It includes the compensation earned by employees in cash or in kind. It mainly includes: wages, bonuses and allowances, subsidies, social insurance paid by company or employer for its staff, supplementary social insurance, housing fund, the pension for the employees of the administrative institution, other forms of welfare and remuneration provided by the employers for its employees.

Net Taxes on Production refers to taxes on production less subsidies on production. The taxes on production refers to the various taxes, extra charges and fees levied on the production units on their production, sale and business activities as well as on the use of some factors of production, such as fixed assets, land etc. in the production activities they are engaged in. Taxes on production are divided into product tax and other kinds of taxes on production, where product tax mainly includes: value-added tax, consumption tax, import duty, export duty; and other taxes on production mainly include: house property tax, tax on vehicles and boat operation, urban land use tax, etc. In contrast to taxes on production, subsidies on production refer to the payment by the government for free to the production units to influence production units's activities such as production, sales and pricing. Subsidies on production include agricultural production subsidies, subsidies for policy losses, import subsidies, etc., and are treated as negative taxes on production.

Depreciation of Fixed Assets refers to the decline of the value of fixed assets due to natural deterioration, normal elimination or loss, and it reflects the value of the fixed assets transferred into the output through production. In principle, the depreciation of fixed assets should be calculated on the basis of the re-purchased value of the fixed assets.

Operating Surplus refers to the balance of the value added created by the resident units after deducting the compensation of employees, net taxes on production and the depreciation of fixed assets.

GDP by Expenditure Approach refers to the method of measuring the final results of production activities of a country (region) during a given period from the perspective of final uses. It includes final consumption expenditure, gross capital formation and net export of goods and services. The formula for computation is:

GDP by expenditure approach = final consumption expenditure + gross capital formation + net export of goods and services

Final Consumption Expenditure refers to the total expenditure of resident units for purchases of goods and services from both the domestic economic territory and abroad to meet the needs of material, cultural and spiritual life. It does not include the expenditure of non-resident units on consumption in the economic territory of the country. The final consumption expenditure is broken down into household consumption expenditure and government consumption expenditure.

Household Consumption Expenditure refers to the total expenditure of resident households on the final consumption of goods and services. In addition to the consumption of goods and services bought by the households directly with money, the household consumption expenditure also includes expenditure on goods and services obtained by the households in other ways. For example, (a) the goods and services provided to households by employers in the form of payment in kind; (b) goods and services produced and consumed by the households themselves (such as self-producing-and-self-consuming agricultural products) and services included in the scope of production accounting and used for personal consumption (such as self -owned housing services for households); (c) financial intermediate services provided by banking and insurance institutions.

Government Consumption Expenditure refers to the consumption expenditure spent for the provision of public services provided by the government to the whole country and the net expenditure on the goods and services provided by the government to households free of charge or at low prices. The former equals to the output value of the government services minus the value of operating income obtained by the government departments. The latter equals to the market value of the goods and services provided by the government free of charge or at low prices to the households minus the value received by the government from the households.

Actual Final Consumption refers to all goods and services acquired and used by resident units, for the satisfaction of their individual or collective needs or wants. It is broken down into household actual final consumption and government actual final consumption. From the numerical point of view, actual final consumption is equal to final consumption expenditure.

Social Transfer in Kind refers to the expenditure on goods and services provided by government, free of charge or at economically insignificant prices, to households for consumption purpose.

Household Actual Final Consumption refers to the value of goods and services for consumption, acquired by resident households, which is equal to the expenditure of households on goods and services for consumption plus the expenditure on goods and services for consumption provided by government to households in the form of social transfer in kind.

Government Actual Final Consumption refers to the value of the collective consumption services provided by government to the whole society, which is equal to the government final consumption expenditure minus the expenditure on goods and services for consumption provided by government to households in the form of social transfer in kind.

Gross Capital Formation refers to resident units' acquisitions less disposals of fixed assets and inventory during a given period, including gross fixed capital formation and changes in inventories.

Gross Fixed Capital Formation refers to the value of acquisitions less disposals of fixed assets during a given period. Fixed assets are the assets produced through production activities with unit value above a specified amount and which could be used for over one year. Natural assets, consumer durables, small instruments are not included. Gross fixed capital formation includes the value of housing, other buildings and structure, equipment and machinery, breeding biological resources, intellectual property right product minus the disposal of them.

Changes in Inventories refer to the market value of the change in the physical volume of inventory of resident units during a given period, i.e. the difference between the values at the beginning and at the end of the period minus the gains due to the change in prices. The changes in inventories can have a positive or a negative value. A positive value indicates an increase in inventory while a negative value indicates a decrease in inventory. The inventory includes raw materials, fuels and reserve materials purchased by the production units as well as the inventory of finished products, semi-finished products and work-in-progress.

Net Export of Goods and Services refers to the exports of goods and services subtracting the imports of goods and services. Exports include the value of various goods and services sold or gratuitously transferred by resident units to non-resident units. Imports include the value of various goods and services purchased or gratuitously acquired by resident units from non-resident units. The exports and imports of goods are calculated at FOB.

Institutional Units refer to economic entities that are capable, in its own rights, of owning assets, incurring liabilities and engaging independently in economic activities and in transactions with other entities.

Institutional Sectors refer to groups of institutional units that are homogenous in nature and grouped together. The following 4 institutional sectors are identified in the flow of funds accounts: non-financial corporations, financial institutions, government and households. Also treated as an institutional sector is the rest of the world, which is composed of non-resident units that have transactions with resident units.

Non-Financial Corporations and the Sector of Non-Financial Corporations Non-financial corporations refer to resident corporations that are engaged in the production of goods and the provision of non-financial services in the market, mainly covering corporate enterprises of various types engaging in the above-mentioned activities. All non-financial corporations make up the sector of non-financial corporations.

Financial Institutions and the Sector of Financial Institutions Financial institutions refer to resident institutions that are engaged in the financial intermediary services or auxiliary financial activities that are closely related with financial intermediary services, mainly covering legal entities engaging in activities of monetary services, capital market services, insurance services, and other financial services. All financial institutions make up the sector of financial institutions.

General Government and the Sector of General Governments General government refer to legal entities and their auxiliary units that are established through the political process and are empowered with legislative, administrative or judicial rights over other institutional within specific regions. The main function of general government is to acquire funds through taxation or other means in order to provide goods and services to society and households; and to conduct redistribution of income and properties of society through transfer payment; and to engage in non-market production. General government cover mainly: party and government organizations at all levels, mass organizations, public institutions, grass roots self-governing organizations, etc. All general governments make up the sector of general governments.

Households and the Sector of Households Households refer to resident individuals or groups of resident individuals who share common living facilities, jointly use entire or part of their income and properties, and share their housing, food and other consumer goods and services. All households make up the sector of households.

Non-resident Units and the Rest of the World All units that are not resident units are non-resident units. All non-resident units that have transactions with resident units make up the rest of the world.

Gross Primary Income Primary income refers to the distribution of the value created from production activities among the owners of factors of production and the governments. The final result from production activities is the value-added. Factors of production mainly include labour force, capital, natural resources. Owners of labour force gain compensation of employees by providing labour. Owners of capitals gain income of various forms by providing capital: owners of loan capital receive income from interests; share holders receive dividends or participate in profit distribution; owners of natural resources receive rents for assign the use right of natural resources. Government levies production tax on production activities or factors of production for state administration needs and pay production subsidies for supporting related production activities. Results of primary distribution generate the gross primary income of each sector, and the sum of the gross primary income of all sectors make up the gross national income, or the gross national product.

Current Transfers Transfer refers to the transaction in the form of provision of goods, services or assets by an institutional unit to another institutional unit without receiving any direct corresponding return from the recipient. Current transfers are transfers that don't involve obtaining or disposing property (except inventory and cash) of one side or both sides. They include regular tax such as income tax and property tax, social insurance contributions, social insurance benefits, social assistance and other current transfers.

Gross Disposable Income Gross income from primary distribution is re-distributed through current transfer, resulting in the gross disposable income of various institutional sectors. The sum of gross disposable income of all institutional sectors is the gross national disposable income.

Adjusted Gross Disposable Income The adjusted gross disposal income of each institutional sector, is equal to gross disposal income plus social transfer in kind receivable minus social transfer in kind payable of the institutional sector. It reflects the total income responding to the actual final consumption of each institutional sector.

Gross Savings refer to gross disposable income subtracting final consumption. The sum of gross savings of all sectors is the gross national savings.

Capital Transfer refers to the transfers that involve obtaining or disposing of property (except inventory and cash) of one side or both sides. Capital transfer includes: capital tax, investment grants and other capital transfers.

Net Financial Investment reflects the surplus or shortage of capitals of institutional sectors or of the economy in general in the process of non-financial investment. It is equal to gross savings plus net capital transfer minus non-financial investment. From the point of view of financial transaction, it is the difference between the increase of financial assets minus the increase of the financial liabilities.

Currency refers to currency that is in circulation in the market, including paper money and coin.

Deposits refer to deposits in depository financial institutions in various forms, which mainly include demand deposit, time deposit, fiscal deposit, foreign exchange deposit and other deposit, etc.

Loans refer to various types of loans granted by financial institutions, which mainly include short-term loan and bill financing, medium- and long-term loan, foreign exchange loan, entrusted loans and other loans.

Bonds refer to securities issued by institutional units to raise funds and promised to be repaid on agreed terms. They include government bonds, financial bonds, central bank bonds, and corporation bonds, etc.

Stock is certificate issued by limited liability company in accordance with the provisions of the company law, to raise capital, to justify the shareholder rights and interests and accordingly obtain the dividend and bonus.

Insurance Technical Reserves consists of net equity of social insurance fund and commercial insurance fund, prepayments of insurance premiums, and reserves for outstanding claims, and bond repurchase.

Inter- financial Institutions Accounts refer to flow of capital between financial institutions, consisting of nostro & vostro accounts, inter-bank lending.

Required and Excessive Reserves refer to financial institutions' deposits and required reserves in the People's Bank of China.

Central Bank Loans refer to lending to financial institutions by the People's Bank of China

International Reserve Assets refers to the foreign assets owned by the central bank, including foreign exchange, monetary gold, SDRs, and reserve position in the International Monetary Fund and other creditor's rights.

Current Account includes goods, services, primary income, and secondary income.

Goods refer to transactions of goods where economic ownership is transferred between residents and non-residents.

Services include processing services, maintenance and repair services, transportation, travel, construction, insurance and pension services, financial services, intellectual property rights royalties, telecommunications, computer and information services, other business services, personal, cultural and entertainment services and government services not mentioned elsewhere.

Primary Income refers to the returns received for the provision of services, financial assets, and leasing of natural resources, which includes three parts: employee compensation, investment income, and other primary income.

Secondary Income refers to the current transfers between resident units and non-resident units, including cash and transfers in kind.

Capital Account reflects the capital transfers between resident units and non-resident units, and the acquisition and disposal of non-productive non-financial assets between residents and non-residents.

Financial Account refers to the transaction of financial assets and liabilities between resident units and non-resident units, including non-reserve financial accounts and international reserves.

Direct Investment is an investment aimed at investors seeking effective voice for enterprises operating outside their own country. It includes two parts: direct investment assets and direct investment liabilities. Related investment instruments can be divided into equity and related enterprise debt. Equity includes equity and investment fund shares, as well as reinvestment returns. The liabilities of affiliated enterprises include negotiable and non-negotiable creditor's rights and liabilities among affiliated enterprises.

Security Investment includes securities investment assets and securities investment liabilities, and related investment instruments can be divided into equity and bonds. Equity rights include share rights and investment fund shares. Shares recorded under securities investment and investment fund shares should be negotiable (tradable). Equity rights are usually evidenced by shares, stocks, shares, depository receipts or similar documents. Investment fund share refers to the share of collective investment products such as mutual funds held by investors. A bond is a negotiable debt instrument, which is a certificate proving that its holder (creditor) has the right to recover principal or interest from its issuer (debtor) at some point in the future, including negotiable deposits, commercial instruments, corporate bonds, asset-backed securities, money market instruments, and a similar tool for usually trading on the financial market.

Financial Derivatives also known as financial derivatives and employee stock options, are used to record the transactions of financial derivatives and employee stock options between resident units and non-resident units.

Other Investments refer to financial transactions between residents and non-residents other than direct investment, securities investment, financial derivatives and reserve assets. They include other equity, currency and deposits, loans, insurance and pensions, trade credit and others.

Net Errors and Omissions Balance of payments statement adopts double-entry accounting method. Because of the differences in source data and recording time, it will cause imbalance between current account and capital and financial account, and result in statistical residual, which is called net errors and omissions.

4

就业和工资

Employment and Wages

简 要 说 明

一、本篇资料的主要内容

本篇资料反映我国劳动经济方面的基本情况，包括全国及 31 个省、自治区、直辖市的主要劳动统计数据。如：劳动力，就业人员，城镇调查失业率，单位就业人员，工资总额，平均工资及指数变化情况等。

二、本篇资料的统计范围

《劳动工资统计报表制度》的调查范围为全部法人单位；《劳动力调查制度》的调查范围为我国大陆地区的城镇和乡村地域。

三、本篇的资料来源

1.就业基本情况及分组资料、工资总额等资料，是国家统计局人口和就业统计司根据《劳动工资统计报表制度》和《劳动力调查制度》搜集资料，加工整理。1990 年及以后的劳动力、就业人员总量及结构数据根据劳动力调查、全国人口普查推算；其中 1991—2019 年非普查年份数据已根据历次人口普查修订。

2.城镇登记失业人员数据，是人力资源和社会保障部根据其《人力资源和社会保障统计调查制度》整理提供。

四、本篇的统计调查方法

劳动工资统计采用全面调查和抽样调查相结合的方法；劳动力调查采用抽样调查方法。

Brief Introduction

I. Main Contents

Data in this chapter show the basic conditions of China's labour economy, including main labour statistics on the whole country and 31 provinces, autonomous regions and municipalities directly under the Central Government, such as the number of labour force, number of employed persons, surveyed unemployment rate in urban areas, persons employed in various units, total wage bills and average wages of employed persons as well as changes in related indices.

II. Scope of Statistics

The Reporting Form System on Labour and Wage Statistics covers all corporate units. *The Labour Force Survey* covers all population in urban and rural areas in China.

III. Sources of Data

(1) Data on basic conditions of employment and their breakdowns, total wage bills of staff and workers are collected and compiled through *The Reporting Form System on Labour and Wage Statistics* and *The Labour Force Survey* by the Department of Population and Employment Statistics, NBS. From 1990, the total and structural data of labour force and employed persons were estimated according to Labour Force Survey and Population Census. The data for non-census years from 1991 to 2019 has been revised based on previous population censuses.

(2) Data on the number of registered unemployed persons in urban areas are collected through *The Human Resources and Social Security Statistical Survey System,* which are provided by the Ministry of Human Resources and Social Security.

IV. Methodology of Survey

The method of overall survey and sampling survey is used in the labour wage statistics. The Labour Force Survey is conducted by using sampling methods.

4-1 就业基本情况
Employment

项　目	Item	2019	2020	2021	2022	2023
劳动力 （万人）	**Labour Force (10 000 persons)**	**78985**	**78392**	**78024**	**76863**	**77216**
就业人员 （万人）	**Number of Employed Persons (10 000 persons)**	**75447**	**75064**	**74652**	**73351**	**74041**
第一产业	Primary Industry	18652	17715	17072	17663	16882
第二产业	Secondary Industry	21234	21543	21712	21105	21520
第三产业	Tertiary Industry	35561	35806	35868	34583	35639
按城乡分就业人员 （万人）	**Number of Employed Persons by Urban and Rural Areas (10 000 persons)**					
城镇就业人员	Urban Employed Persons	45249	46271	46773	45931	47032
乡村就业人员	Rural Employed Persons	30198	28793	27879	27420	27009
按登记注册统计类别分城镇非私营单位就业人员 （万人）	**Number of Employed Persons in Urban Non-private Units by Status of Registered Statistical Categories (10 000 persons)**	**17162**	**17039**	**17015**	**16701**	**16368**
内资单位	Domestic Invested Units	14801	14665	14619	14423	14287
#国有单位	State-owned Units	5473	5563	5633	5612	5400
港澳台投资单位	Units with Funds from Hong Kong, Macao and Taiwan	1157	1159	1175	1114	1093
外商投资单位	Foreign Funded Units	1203	1216	1220	1164	988
城镇登记失业人员 （万人）	**Number of Registered Unemployed Persons in Urban Areas (10 000 persons)**	**945**	**1160**	**1040**	**1203**	**1074**
城镇调查失业率(1-12月均值)(%)	**Surveyed Unemployment Rate in Urban Areas (Annual Average) (%)**	**5.2**	**5.6**	**5.1**	**5.6**	**5.2**
城镇调查失业率(12月) (%)	**Surveyed Unemployment Rate in Urban Areas (Year-end) (%)**	**5.2**	**5.2**	**5.1**	**5.5**	**5.1**

注：1.1990年及以后的劳动力、就业人员数据根据劳动力调查、全国人口普查推算，其中1991-2019年非普查年份数据已根据历次人口普查修订(以下相关表同)。
2.本表登记注册统计类别按《关于市场主体统计分类的划分规定》(国统字〔2023〕14号)执行。
3.表中国有单位包括机关事业单位和全民所有制企业(国有企业)。

a) From 1990, the total number of labour force and employed persons were estimated according to Labour Force Survey and Population Census. The data for non-census years from 1991 to 2019 has been revised based on previous population censuses. The same applies to the relevant following tables.
b) The registered statistical categories of this table is implemented in accordance with the Regulations on the Classification of Market Entity Statistics (Guotongzi [2023] No. 14).
c) The state-owned enterprises in the tables include government agencies and all state-owned enterprises.

4–2 按三次产业分就业人员数（年底数）
Number of Employed Persons at Year-end by Three Strata of Industry

年份 Year	就业人员（万人）Employed Persons (10 000 persons)				构成（合计=100）Composition in Percentage		
		第一产业 Primary Industry	第二产业 Secondary Industry	第三产业 Tertiary Industry	第一产业 Primary Industry	第二产业 Secondary Industry	第三产业 Tertiary Industry
1952	20729	17317	1531	1881	83.5	7.4	9.1
1957	23771	19309	2142	2320	81.2	9.0	9.8
1962	25910	21276	2059	2575	82.1	8.0	9.9
1965	28670	23396	2408	2866	81.6	8.4	10.0
1970	34432	27811	3518	3103	80.8	10.2	9.0
1975	38168	29456	5152	3560	77.2	13.5	9.3
1978	40152	28318	6945	4890	70.5	17.3	12.2
1979	41024	28634	7214	5177	69.8	17.6	12.6
1980	42361	29122	7707	5532	68.7	18.2	13.1
1981	43725	29777	8003	5945	68.1	18.3	13.6
1982	45295	30859	8346	6090	68.1	18.4	13.5
1983	46436	31151	8679	6606	67.1	18.7	14.2
1984	48197	30868	9590	7739	64.0	19.9	16.1
1985	49873	31130	10384	8359	62.4	20.8	16.8
1986	51282	31254	11216	8811	60.9	21.9	17.2
1987	52783	31663	11726	9395	60.0	22.2	17.8
1988	54334	32249	12152	9933	59.3	22.4	18.3
1989	55329	33225	11976	10129	60.1	21.6	18.3
1990	64749	38914	13856	11979	60.1	21.4	18.5
1991	65491	39098	14015	12378	59.7	21.4	18.9
1992	66152	38699	14355	13098	58.5	21.7	19.8
1993	66808	37680	14965	14163	56.4	22.4	21.2
1994	67455	36628	15312	15515	54.3	22.7	23.0
1995	68065	35530	15655	16880	52.2	23.0	24.8
1996	68950	34820	16203	17927	50.5	23.5	26.0
1997	69820	34840	16547	18432	49.9	23.7	26.4
1998	70637	35177	16600	18860	49.8	23.5	26.7
1999	71394	35768	16421	19205	50.1	23.0	26.9
2000	72085	36043	16219	19823	50.0	22.5	27.5
2001	72797	36399	16234	20165	50.0	22.3	27.7
2002	73280	36640	15682	20958	50.0	21.4	28.6
2003	73736	36204	15927	21605	49.1	21.6	29.3
2004	74264	34830	16709	22725	46.9	22.5	30.6
2005	74647	33442	17766	23439	44.8	23.8	31.4
2006	74978	31941	18894	24143	42.6	25.2	32.2
2007	75321	30731	20186	24404	40.8	26.8	32.4
2008	75564	29923	20553	25087	39.6	27.2	33.2
2009	75828	28890	21080	25857	38.1	27.8	34.1
2010	76105	27931	21842	26332	36.7	28.7	34.6
2011	76196	26472	22539	27185	34.7	29.6	35.7
2012	76254	25535	23226	27493	33.5	30.4	36.1
2013	76301	23838	23142	29321	31.3	30.3	38.4
2014	76349	22372	23057	30920	29.3	30.2	40.5
2015	76320	21418	22644	32258	28.0	29.7	42.3
2016	76245	20908	22295	33042	27.4	29.3	43.3
2017	76058	20295	21762	34001	26.7	28.6	44.7
2018	75782	19515	21356	34911	25.7	28.2	46.1
2019	75447	18652	21234	35561	24.7	28.2	47.1
2020	75064	17715	21543	35806	23.6	28.7	47.7
2021	74652	17072	21712	35868	22.9	29.1	48.0
2022	73351	17663	21105	34583	24.1	28.8	47.1
2023	74041	16882	21520	35639	22.8	29.1	48.1

4-3 分地区就业人员数(2023年底数)
Number of Employed Persons by Region (End of 2023)

单位：万人 (10 000 persons)

地 区	Region	就业人员 Employed Persons	按城乡分 By Urban and Rural Areas		按三次产业分 By Three Industries		
			城镇 Urban	乡村 Rural	第一产业 Primary Industry	第二产业 Secondary Industry	第三产业 Tertiary Industry
全 国	**National Total**	**74041**	**47032**	**27009**	**16882**	**21520**	**35639**
北 京	Beijing	1129	989	140	24	183	922
天 津	Tianjin	635	535	100	32	218	385
河 北	Hebei	3623	2151	1472	789	1147	1687
山 西	Shanxi	1704	1023	681	399	434	871
内蒙古	Inner Mongolia	1211	784	427	416	214	581
辽 宁	Liaoning	2091	1431	660	589	466	1036
吉 林	Jilin	1170	689	481	451	176	543
黑龙江	Heilongjiang	1319	854	465	472	207	640
上 海	Shanghai	1345	1178	167	20	436	889
江 苏	Jiangsu	4840	3554	1286	620	1959	2261
浙 江	Zhejiang	3921	2861	1060	197	1744	1980
安 徽	Anhui	3191	1827	1364	768	1025	1398
福 建	Fujian	2192	1527	665	289	731	1172
江 西	Jiangxi	2231	1352	879	391	777	1063
山 东	Shandong	5370	3352	2018	1267	1818	2285
河 南	Henan	4828	2638	2190	1224	1411	2193
湖 北	Hubei	3254	1930	1324	874	871	1509
湖 南	Hunan	3238	1916	1322	773	887	1578
广 东	Guangdong	7057	5573	1484	688	2584	3785
广 西	Guangxi	2529	1361	1168	829	655	1045
海 南	Hainan	552	338	214	168	62	322
重 庆	Chongqing	1662	1109	553	361	425	876
四 川	Sichuan	4722	2545	2177	1535	1100	2087
贵 州	Guizhou	1884	1005	879	649	461	774
云 南	Yunnan	2748	1316	1432	1184	493	1071
西 藏	Xizang	194	79	115	67	30	97
陕 西	Shaanxi	2085	1268	817	619	437	1029
甘 肃	Gansu	1316	635	681	587	231	498
青 海	Qinghai	271	176	95	70	59	142
宁 夏	Ningxia	341	227	114	84	81	176
新 疆	Xinjiang	1388	809	579	446	198	744

4-4 按登记注册统计类别分城镇非私营单位就业人员数(年底数)
Number of Employed Persons in Urban Non-Private Units at Year-end by Registered Statistical Categories

单位：万人 (10 000 persons)

年 份 Year	单位就业人员 Persons Employed in Various Units	内资单位 Domestic Invested Units	#国有单位 State-owned Units	港澳台投资单位 Units with Funds from Hong Kong, Macao and Taiwan	外商投资单位 Foreign Funded Units
1971	6787	6787	5318		
1975	8198	8198	6426		
1980	10444	10444	8019		
1981	10940	10940	8372		
1982	11281	11281	8630		
1983	11515	11515	8771		
1984	11890	11890	8637		
1985	12358	12358	8990		
1986	12809	12809	9333		
1987	13214	13214	9654		
1988	13608	13608	9984		
1989	13742	13742	10108		
1990	14059	13993	10346	4	62
1991	14508	14343	10664	69	96
1992	14792	14571	10889	83	138
1993	14849	14561	10920	155	133
1994	14849	14443	10890	211	195
1995	15301	14788	11261	272	241
1996	15221	14681	11244	265	275
1997	15036	14455	11044	281	300
1998	12696	12109	9058	294	293
1999	12130	11518	8572	306	306
2000	11612	10970	8102	310	332
2001	11166	10495	7640	326	345
2002	10985	10227	7163	367	391
2003	10970	10107	6876	409	454
2004	11099	10066	6710	470	563
2005	11404	10159	6488	557	688
2006	11713	10306	6430	611	796
2007	12024	10441	6424	680	903
2008	12193	10571	6447	679	943
2009	12573	10874	6420	721	978
2010	13052	11229	6516	770	1053
2011	14413	12264	6704	932	1217
2012	15236	13021	6839	969	1246
2013	18108	15145	6365	1397	1566
2014	18278	15323	6312	1393	1562
2015	18062	15273	6208	1344	1446
2016	17888	15222	6170	1305	1361
2017	17644	15062	6064	1290	1291
2018	17258	14893	5740	1153	1212
2019	17162	14801	5473	1157	1203
2020	17039	14665	5563	1159	1216
2021	17015	14619	5633	1175	1220
2022	16701	14423	5612	1114	1164
2023	16368	14287	5400	1093	988

注：1.1994年及以前为职工数(以下相关表同)。
2.1998年及以后城镇单位就业人员、工资总额、平均工资等指标中不再包括离开本单位仍保留劳动关系的职工及其生活费。
3.2013年部分经济类型单位、部分行业就业人员数、工资总额变动较大，系将原属于乡镇企业的规模以上法人单位纳入劳动工资统计范围所致。
4.本表登记注册统计类别按《关于市场主体统计分类的划分规定》(国统字〔2023〕14号)执行。
5.表中国有单位包括机关事业单位和全民所有制企业(国有企业)。

a) Data before 1994 are figures for staff and workers. The same applies to the following tables.
b) The scope of statistics on employed person in urban units, total wage bills, average wages do not include the persons who had left their working units and while keeping their labour contract/employment relation unchanged since 1998.
c) In 2013, there is fairly big change in figures on employment and total wage bill for some units by status of registration and for some industries, because some corporate units above designated size originally classified as township enterprises are taken into statistics of labour wages.
d) The registered statistical categories of this table is implemented in accordance with the Regulations on the Classification of Market Entity Statistics (Guotongzi [2023] No. 14).
e) The state-owned enterprises in the tables include government agencies and all state-owned enterprises.

4-5 按登记注册统计类别和行业分城镇非私营单位就业人员数（2023年底数）
Number of Employed Persons in Urban Non-Private Units by Registered Statistical Categories and Sector (End of 2023)

单位：万人 (10 000 persons)

项　　目	Item	单位就业人员 Persons Employed in Various Units	内资单位 Domestic Invested Units	#国有单位 State-owned Units	港澳台投资单位 Units with Funds from Hong Kong, Macao and Taiwan	外商投资单位 Foreign Funded Units
全国总计	**National Total**	**16368.3**	**14287.4**	**5399.6**	**1092.8**	**988.1**
农、林、牧、渔业	Agriculture, Forestry, Animal Husbandry and Fishery	69.3	67.8	26.5	0.9	0.6
采矿业	Mining	329.3	319.2	21.4	6.3	3.9
制造业	Manufacturing	3577.8	2252.8	22.5	674.3	650.7
电力、热力、燃气及水生产和供应业	Production and Supply of Electricity, Heat, Gas and Water	361.0	336.1	23.6	16.9	8.0
建筑业	Construction	1638.1	1621.6	35.6	8.9	7.7
批发和零售业	Wholesale and Retail Trades	782.4	592.8	30.1	94.4	95.3
交通运输、仓储和邮政业	Transport, Storage and Post	767.9	721.9	46.7	32.3	13.7
住宿和餐饮业	Hotels and Catering Services	288.4	190.7	9.2	52.1	45.6
信息传输、软件和信息技术服务业	Information Transmission, Software and Information Technology	529.5	390.7	17.1	83.0	55.8
金融业	Financial Intermediation	692.4	647.3	57.7	11.9	33.2
房地产业	Real Estate	509.4	461.2	9.1	35.7	12.5
租赁和商务服务业	Leasing and Business Services	827.8	757.4	60.7	39.0	31.4
科学研究和技术服务业	Scientific Research and Technical Services	451.7	412.0	128.1	19.2	20.5
水利、环境和公共设施管理业	Management of Water Conservancy, Environment and Public Facilities	257.9	254.0	110.0	3.3	0.6
居民服务、修理和其他服务业	Services to Households, Repair and Other Services	85.2	74.7	11.4	8.6	1.9
教育	Education	1940.5	1938.7	1731.7	0.9	0.9
卫生和社会工作	Health and Social Service	1126.9	1122.7	996.2	2.4	1.8
文化、体育和娱乐业	Culture, Sports and Entertainment	147.0	140.0	80.5	3.0	4.0
公共管理、社会保障和社会组织	Public Management, Social Security and Social Organization	1985.8	1985.8	1981.4		

注：1.本表登记注册统计类别按《关于市场主体统计分类的划分规定》(国统字〔2023〕14号)执行。
2.表中国有单位包括机关事业单位和全民所有制企业(国有企业)。

a) The registered statistical categories of this table is implemented in accordance with the Regulations on the Classification of Market Entity Statistics (Guotongzi [2023] No. 14).

b) The state-owned enterprises in the tables include government agencies and all state-owned enterprises.

4–6 按行业分城镇非私营单位就业人员数(年底数)
Number of Employed Persons in Urban Non-Private Units at Year-end by Sector

单位：万人 (10 000 persons)

年份 地区	Year Region	单位就业人员 Persons Employed in Various Units	农、林、牧、渔业 Agriculture, Forestry, Animal Husbandry and Fishery	采矿业 Mining	制造业 Manufacturing	电力、热力、燃气及水生产和供应业 Production and Supply of Electricity, Heat, Gas and Water	建筑业 Construction	批发和零售业 Wholesale and Retail Trades
	2005	11404.0	446.3	509.2	3210.9	299.9	926.6	544.0
	2010	13051.5	375.7	562.0	3637.2	310.5	1267.5	535.1
	2011	14413.3	359.5	611.6	4088.3	334.7	1724.8	647.5
	2012	15236.4	338.9	631.0	4262.2	344.6	2010.3	711.8
	2013	18108.4	294.8	636.5	5257.9	404.5	2921.9	890.8
	2014	18277.8	284.6	596.5	5243.1	403.7	2921.2	888.6
	2015	18062.5	270.0	545.8	5068.7	396.0	2796.0	883.3
	2016	17888.1	263.2	490.9	4893.8	387.6	2724.7	875.0
	2017	17643.8	255.4	455.4	4635.5	377.0	2643.2	842.8
	2018	17258.2	192.6	414.4	4178.3	369.2	2710.9	823.3
	2019	17161.8	134.1	367.7	3832.0	373.1	2270.5	830.0
	2020	17039.1	85.7	352.1	3805.5	379.7	2153.3	786.9
	2021	17014.5	86.8	344.8	3828.0	382.0	1971.9	797.5
	2022	16700.7	78.9	340.9	3738.4	375.3	1835.2	785.3
	2023	16368.3	69.3	329.3	3577.8	361.0	1638.1	782.4
北京	Beijing	755.6	1.5	2.4	55.7	9.4	41.3	53.7
天津	Tianjin	219.0	0.1	5.0	53.5	3.9	15.9	13.5
河北	Hebei	554.7	1.5	16.0	93.0	18.3	29.9	21.8
山西	Shanxi	434.8	1.5	86.0	52.1	15.7	22.6	15.3
内蒙古	Inner Mongolia	268.7	4.4	11.9	38.7	14.1	7.1	8.3
辽宁	Liaoning	424.5	6.1	15.3	83.8	13.6	21.0	15.8
吉林	Jilin	233.9	5.3	5.0	40.9	8.8	11.7	7.7
黑龙江	Heilongjiang	274.6	15.3	21.7	22.8	12.6	9.2	9.5
上海	Shanghai	647.6	0.6	0.2	116.6	3.4	22.8	89.7
江苏	Jiangsu	1311.4	2.1	5.9	439.5	15.1	224.4	53.7
浙江	Zhejiang	1064.8	0.9	0.5	336.4	13.7	143.5	47.4
安徽	Anhui	591.3	1.9	12.8	152.9	9.2	84.3	23.5
福建	Fujian	548.6	1.0	0.9	130.4	10.8	103.6	24.3
江西	Jiangxi	419.4	1.4	2.6	96.1	9.5	55.9	16.5
山东	Shandong	1077.0	1.3	23.9	261.6	27.0	111.1	48.9
河南	Henan	786.9	1.2	22.9	132.6	23.0	90.0	31.7
湖北	Hubei	626.0	1.7	2.7	121.3	10.5	89.8	32.2
湖南	Hunan	585.3	1.4	4.2	102.4	15.9	96.4	24.1
广东	Guangdong	1990.0	1.4	1.7	750.6	25.8	124.4	102.3
广西	Guangxi	390.8	2.9	0.9	53.5	10.4	30.0	13.6
海南	Hainan	102.1	3.2	0.5	7.9	2.3	1.9	7.0
重庆	Chongqing	337.4	0.4	0.6	61.2	7.1	57.9	14.7
四川	Sichuan	883.6	1.6	8.5	144.2	21.4	106.8	37.5
贵州	Guizhou	310.8	1.3	14.9	34.4	8.4	23.9	11.8
云南	Yunnan	345.0	2.4	5.2	37.6	9.8	24.2	13.9
西藏	Xizang	40.8	0.1	0.7	1.2	1.5	1.3	1.8
陕西	Shaanxi	456.4	1.4	28.0	74.9	14.3	43.1	19.9
甘肃	Gansu	234.1	1.6	7.2	25.4	9.5	18.3	8.0
青海	Qinghai	65.9	0.7	2.3	9.9	2.4	2.9	2.1
宁夏	Ningxia	74.2	0.9	6.1	13.0	3.8	2.3	2.7
新疆	Xinjiang	313.4	1.9	13.1	34.1	10.0	20.7	9.5

4–6 续表 1 continued

单位：万人 (10 000 persons)

年 份 / 地 区	Year / Region	交通运输、仓储和邮政业 Transport, Storage and Post	住宿和餐饮业 Hotels and Catering Services	信息传输、软件和信息技术服务业 Information Transmission, Software and Information Technology	金 融 业 Financial Intermediation	房地产业 Real Estate	租赁和商务服务业 Leasing and Business Services
	2005	613.9	181.2	130.1	359.3	146.5	218.5
	2010	631.1	209.2	185.8	470.1	211.6	310.1
	2011	662.8	242.7	212.8	505.3	248.6	286.6
	2012	667.5	265.1	222.8	527.8	273.7	292.3
	2013	846.2	304.4	327.3	537.9	373.7	421.9
	2014	861.4	289.3	336.3	566.3	402.2	449.4
	2015	854.4	276.1	349.9	606.8	417.3	474.0
	2016	849.5	269.7	364.1	665.2	431.7	488.4
	2017	843.9	265.9	395.4	688.8	444.8	522.6
	2018	819.0	269.8	424.3	699.3	466.0	529.5
	2019	815.5	265.2	455.3	826.1	510.3	660.4
	2020	812.2	256.6	487.1	859.0	525.4	643.6
	2021	798.1	265.3	519.2	818.5	529.3	680.3
	2022	776.2	255.0	529.2	739.6	511.5	738.3
	2023	767.9	288.4	529.5	692.4	509.4	827.8
北 京	Beijing	47.6	32.1	100.0	58.9	44.3	77.2
天 津	Tianjin	14.2	5.0	4.7	12.1	7.2	11.9
河 北	Hebei	27.6	4.6	13.1	29.7	10.8	16.3
山 西	Shanxi	23.0	4.6	4.9	21.0	7.4	13.5
内蒙古	Inner Mongolia	19.8	2.7	4.4	15.4	6.8	7.1
辽 宁	Liaoning	28.3	7.2	14.5	22.8	9.7	14.2
吉 林	Jilin	13.8	1.8	4.6	15.1	4.3	4.5
黑龙江	Heilongjiang	21.7	1.6	5.7	14.4	4.1	8.5
上 海	Shanghai	43.4	26.7	52.8	36.5	30.8	78.0
江 苏	Jiangsu	47.8	22.6	37.3	41.3	31.9	56.9
浙 江	Zhejiang	37.9	16.9	34.7	43.3	33.1	81.2
安 徽	Anhui	26.7	6.8	13.6	18.2	15.0	34.8
福 建	Fujian	20.3	10.5	10.7	20.4	15.2	38.6
江 西	Jiangxi	16.2	4.9	6.3	12.7	9.4	9.7
山 东	Shandong	43.9	14.6	19.9	50.7	31.9	41.6
河 南	Henan	35.9	7.5	18.7	23.3	21.8	24.3
湖 北	Hubei	29.6	10.3	16.8	21.1	20.8	33.5
湖 南	Hunan	23.1	6.9	9.6	23.9	13.6	15.8
广 东	Guangdong	74.0	45.0	81.6	71.2	89.7	126.0
广 西	Guangxi	17.8	5.1	6.9	15.9	7.7	18.3
海 南	Hainan	7.0	4.4	2.0	4.4	7.8	3.9
重 庆	Chongqing	19.8	3.5	6.3	17.5	13.5	16.3
四 川	Sichuan	35.9	19.6	27.6	33.1	29.9	41.5
贵 州	Guizhou	11.7	3.3	4.2	11.5	6.7	8.8
云 南	Yunnan	15.8	5.0	5.3	11.4	8.0	12.7
西 藏	Xizang	2.3	0.5	0.8	1.8	0.6	1.3
陕 西	Shaanxi	24.1	8.3	13.4	17.1	13.1	12.9
甘 肃	Gansu	12.2	2.4	3.1	11.0	5.2	4.8
青 海	Qinghai	5.0	0.5	0.9	2.8	1.5	1.7
宁 夏	Ningxia	3.9	0.4	0.9	3.6	1.5	1.7
新 疆	Xinjiang	17.6	3.0	4.2	10.1	6.0	10.3

4–6 续表 2 continued

单位：万人 (10 000 persons)

年份 地区	Year Region	科学研究和技术服务业 Scientific Research and Technical Services	水利、环境和公共设施管理业 Management of Water Conservancy, Environment and Public Facilities	居民服务、修理和其他服务业 Services to Households, Repair and Other Services	教育 Education	卫生和社会工作 Health and Social Service	文化、体育和娱乐业 Culture, Sports and Entertainment	公共管理、社会保障和社会组织 Public Management, Social Security and Social Organization
	2005	227.7	180.4	53.9	1483.2	508.9	122.5	1240.8
	2010	292.3	218.9	60.2	1581.8	632.5	131.4	1428.5
	2011	298.5	230.3	59.9	1617.8	679.1	135.0	1467.6
	2012	330.7	243.8	62.1	1653.4	719.3	137.7	1541.5
	2013	387.8	259.2	72.3	1687.2	770.0	147.0	1567.0
	2014	408.0	269.1	75.4	1727.3	810.4	145.5	1599.3
	2015	410.6	273.3	75.2	1736.5	841.6	149.1	1637.8
	2016	419.6	269.6	75.4	1729.2	867.0	150.8	1672.6
	2017	420.4	268.5	78.2	1730.4	897.9	152.2	1725.6
	2018	411.5	260.6	77.4	1735.6	912.4	146.6	1817.5
	2019	434.3	244.5	86.3	1909.3	1006.2	151.2	1989.8
	2020	431.2	245.6	82.8	1958.9	1051.9	149.5	1972.2
	2021	450.1	252.6	85.9	1971.9	1094.7	151.7	1985.8
	2022	455.8	253.6	90.1	1950.6	1114.5	146.5	1985.8
	2023	451.7	257.9	85.2	1940.5	1126.9	147.0	1985.8
北 京	Beijing	64.0	11.6	6.4	50.8	36.8	19.4	42.5
天 津	Tianjin	10.5	2.2	4.8	21.2	12.3	1.4	19.7
河 北	Hebei	14.7	10.6	2.8	84.4	48.8	5.2	105.7
山 西	Shanxi	8.0	7.9	1.2	53.8	27.8	4.2	64.3
内蒙古	Inner Mongolia	5.6	6.5	0.5	36.6	20.5	3.0	55.3
辽 宁	Liaoning	8.9	8.0	1.5	52.2	35.0	3.9	62.7
吉 林	Jilin	5.9	6.0	1.1	34.6	21.2	3.0	38.8
黑龙江	Heilongjiang	5.1	6.6	1.3	37.7	25.1	2.5	49.0
上 海	Shanghai	38.0	9.9	6.3	38.8	28.5	5.6	18.8
江 苏	Jiangsu	29.7	13.3	6.0	116.3	68.0	9.0	90.5
浙 江	Zhejiang	24.7	11.3	4.8	89.7	58.6	7.2	78.9
安 徽	Anhui	11.0	9.7	2.4	67.8	38.5	3.5	58.7
福 建	Fujian	7.9	7.1	3.9	61.1	27.6	3.7	50.9
江 西	Jiangxi	7.1	8.7	1.4	64.9	30.5	3.3	62.5
山 东	Shandong	24.6	17.0	3.5	129.1	79.2	8.0	139.3
河 南	Henan	16.9	15.2	4.5	119.5	69.4	6.6	121.7
湖 北	Hubei	16.4	9.1	3.6	74.8	49.0	5.9	77.1
湖 南	Hunan	12.7	10.3	2.7	81.5	47.5	5.9	87.3
广 东	Guangdong	48.2	21.3	13.6	155.1	95.1	12.1	150.9
广 西	Guangxi	9.1	6.3	1.3	85.8	41.4	3.5	60.4
海 南	Hainan	2.8	5.2	0.5	16.9	8.3	1.7	14.4
重 庆	Chongqing	7.7	5.9	0.7	43.1	22.1	2.6	36.4
四 川	Sichuan	28.0	12.2	4.5	123.8	74.5	7.3	125.7
贵 州	Guizhou	4.8	5.1	2.0	59.2	30.0	2.0	66.7
云 南	Yunnan	8.4	6.9	1.4	64.4	34.8	3.4	74.4
西 藏	Xizang	1.2	0.6	0.1	5.8	2.6	0.7	15.8
陕 西	Shaanxi	13.6	9.4	1.5	60.9	35.7	5.2	59.5
甘 肃	Gansu	6.4	5.6	0.2	39.3	21.1	2.7	50.0
青 海	Qinghai	1.9	1.0	0.1	8.9	5.8	0.9	14.8
宁 夏	Ningxia	1.3	1.7	0.1	11.2	6.0	0.8	12.2
新 疆	Xinjiang	6.3	5.5	0.7	51.3	25.1	3.0	81.1

4-7 城镇非私营单位就业人员工资总额和指数
Total Wage Bill of Employed Persons in Urban Non-Private Units and Indices

年份 地区	Year Region	工资总额(亿元) Total Wage Bill (100 million yuan)	内资单位 Domestic Invested Units	#国有单位 State-owned Units	港澳台投资单位 Units with Funds from Hong Kong, Macao and Taiwan	外商投资单位 Foreign Funded Units	指数(上年=100) Indices (preceding year=100)	内资单位 Domestic Invested Units	#国有单位 State-owned Units	港澳台投资单位 Units with Funds from Hong Kong, Macao and Taiwan	外商投资单位 Foreign Funded Units
	1995	8055.8	7647.1	6172.6	205.6	203.1	119.0	117.4	117.4	152.9	152.9
	2000	10954.7	10070.6	7744.9	376.6	507.5	107.9	107.4	106.2	109.1	117.7
	2005	20627.1	18098.5	12291.7	968.6	1560.0	117.1	115.6	111.4	130.6	128.8
	2010	47269.9	40504.0	24886.4	2431.5	4334.4	117.3	116.7	113.8	121.2	121.2
	2015	112007.8	92346.7	40387.9	8446.5	11214.6	108.9	109.8	111.9	108.4	102.5
	2016	120074.8	99898.7	44462.9	8878.4	11297.8	107.2	108.2	110.1	105.1	100.7
	2017	129889.1	108890.5	48884.1	9377.8	11620.7	108.2	109.0	109.9	105.6	102.9
	2018	141480.0	119787.1	51126.6	9572.1	12120.7	108.9	110.0	104.6	102.1	104.3
	2019	154296.1	130600.8	53743.7	10771.3	12924.0	109.1	109.0	105.1	112.5	106.6
	2020	164126.9	138875.8	59628.1	11594.3	13656.7	106.4	106.3	110.9	107.6	105.7
	2021	180817.5	151991.1	64547.9	13488.4	15337.9	110.2	109.4	108.3	116.3	112.3
	2022	190820.2	160077.7	69000.2	14444.0	16298.6	105.5	105.3	106.9	107.1	106.3
	2023	197416.7	167698.2	68673.0	14756.7	14961.8	103.5	104.8	99.5	102.2	91.8
北京	Beijing	16629.8	12654.4	3478.0	2034.6	1940.8	104.9	107.0	106.1	101.9	95.5
天津	Tianjin	3047.1	2367.0	907.2	251.2	428.9	94.9	95.1	95.0	88.0	97.7
河北	Hebei	5308.7	5005.9	2438.5	162.5	140.3	103.6	104.7	99.6	104.2	75.9
山西	Shanxi	4146.3	4046.7	1381.4	58.4	41.1	103.7	104.9	100.9	73.6	69.4
内蒙古	Inner Mongolia	2932.8	2868.6	1306.2	22.9	41.3	108.6	108.9	103.9	146.3	83.3
辽宁	Liaoning	4171.0	3648.3	1678.3	128.0	394.7	100.6	100.1	93.7	109.3	102.3
吉林	Jilin	2239.7	2096.8	1064.3	21.0	122.0	104.7	105.3	105.0	123.8	94.1
黑龙江	Heilongjiang	2659.5	2600.4	1297.2	30.3	28.8	100.2	100.3	96.3	111.9	84.1
上海	Shanghai	14983.7	8234.8	2285.8	2842.8	3906.1	104.5	105.8	98.4	105.7	100.9
江苏	Jiangsu	16203.8	12540.7	4789.6	1402.9	2260.2	104.2	106.8	101.3	98.7	94.4
浙江	Zhejiang	14042.1	11856.6	4128.0	1234.4	951.1	105.2	108.5	100.9	104.9	76.2
安徽	Anhui	6061.8	5691.5	2112.6	184.9	185.3	107.4	107.2	96.4	121.9	99.0
福建	Fujian	5826.5	4954.3	2006.7	525.1	347.0	101.0	105.9	102.0	89.1	69.3
江西	Jiangxi	3874.7	3667.0	1868.1	99.4	108.3	102.0	101.8	102.2	97.9	110.8
山东	Shandong	11574.2	10556.9	4651.9	448.9	568.4	104.8	105.2	98.6	107.2	96.7
河南	Henan	6668.3	6383.1	2817.8	170.4	114.8	98.8	99.6	95.5	91.5	74.0
湖北	Hubei	6782.1	6347.6	2659.6	181.5	252.9	105.4	106.4	95.8	109.6	83.3
湖南	Hunan	5688.4	5388.9	2518.6	210.4	89.0	105.9	106.6	96.7	104.4	77.8
广东	Guangdong	26266.9	19879.8	7010.2	4089.4	2297.7	100.3	101.0	96.4	102.3	91.4
广西	Guangxi	3745.4	3589.2	2017.7	58.9	97.3	103.6	104.8	107.6	114.6	70.5
海南	Hainan	1165.6	1097.3	486.1	40.8	27.4	101.3	101.4	103.5	85.1	133.6
重庆	Chongqing	3825.9	3532.3	1549.1	146.0	147.7	102.8	104.2	100.8	106.9	75.0
四川	Sichuan	9625.1	9129.0	4130.8	234.2	261.9	107.7	109.3	107.6	90.6	81.0
贵州	Guizhou	3149.5	3108.3	1628.7	26.8	14.5	101.3	101.9	97.0	114.0	43.5
云南	Yunnan	3686.8	3621.9	2111.0	37.5	27.4	100.8	101.0	93.8	120.0	68.6
西藏	Xizang	670.1	664.4	467.2	4.4	1.3	101.9	102.3	99.3	113.2	30.2
陕西	Shaanxi	4842.1	4671.8	1716.4	55.8	114.5	104.7	106.4	93.9	119.4	60.8
甘肃	Gansu	2320.1	2291.0	1341.7	8.7	20.4	99.0	99.0	96.4	124.7	91.0
青海	Qinghai	804.1	796.0	424.9	3.9	4.1	105.3	105.5	95.7	113.9	72.7
宁夏	Ningxia	873.4	842.6	372.6	22.1	8.7	107.2	108.0	87.2	95.7	80.2
新疆	Xinjiang	3601.2	3564.9	2026.3	18.6	17.7	108.0	108.2	108.2	120.6	71.6

注：1.1995—2008年的城镇非私营单位就业人员工资总额即为原来的城镇单位就业人员劳动报酬总额(以下相关表同)。
2.本表登记注册统计类别按《关于市场主体统计分类的划分规定》(国统字〔2023〕14号)执行。
3.表中国有单位包括机关事业单位和全民所有制企业(国有企业)。

a) Total wage bill of employed persons in urban non-private units from 1995 to 2008 refers to total earning of employed persons in urban non-private units. The same applies to the related following tables.

b) The registered statistical categories of this table is implemented in accordance with the Regulations on the Classification of Market Entity Statistics (Guotongzi [2023] No. 14).

c) The state-owned enterprises in the tables include government agencies and all state-owned enterprises.

4-8 按行业分城镇非私营单位就业人员工资总额
Total Wage Bill of Employed Persons in Urban Non-Private Units by Sector

单位：亿元 (100 million yuan)

年份 地区	Year Region	工资总额 Total Wage Bill	农、林、牧、渔业 Agriculture, Forestry, Animal Husbandry and Fishery	采矿业 Mining	制造业 Manufacturing	电力、热力、燃气及水生产和供应业 Production and Supply of Electricity, Heat, Gas and Water	建筑业 Construction	批发和零售业 Wholesale and Retail Trades
	2005	20627.1	368.7	1031.2	5056.6	741.8	1324.7	832.0
	2010	47269.9	627.1	2458.8	11140.8	1468.3	3471.5	1783.0
	2011	59954.7	697.7	3174.2	15031.4	1755.7	5596.4	2594.8
	2012	70914.2	760.8	3600.7	17668.1	1999.6	7392.7	3271.3
	2013	93064.3	758.0	3833.2	24566.6	2715.3	12315.1	4451.9
	2014	102817.2	808.9	3728.2	27011.4	2965.8	13389.4	4931.4
	2015	112007.8	862.6	3318.2	28341.6	3137.4	13619.3	5324.6
	2016	120074.8	882.1	3038.1	29088.9	3235.7	13969.2	5681.2
	2017	129889.1	949.9	3208.6	29740.5	3406.6	14283.9	5980.1
	2018	141480.0	716.1	3413.4	30385.0	3704.0	15949.5	6628.5
	2019	154296.1	535.1	3388.2	30197.5	4030.1	14431.7	7402.2
	2020	164126.9	410.6	3428.8	31352.9	4420.0	14376.2	7623.4
	2021	180817.5	471.4	3742.3	35232.8	4784.4	14515.0	8560.6
	2022	190820.2	463.7	4162.8	36978.4	4994.9	14015.9	9184.1
	2023	197416.7	438.5	4488.5	37480.3	5205.3	13681.9	9815.0
北京	Beijing	16629.8	11.5	47.9	1064.9	205.9	676.4	1084.7
天津	Tianjin	3047.1	1.4	99.8	649.9	78.2	204.1	172.9
河北	Hebei	5308.7	10.3	175.4	829.6	258.2	262.5	162.2
山西	Shanxi	4146.3	9.4	1069.2	434.6	180.1	193.7	134.2
内蒙古	Inner Mongolia	2932.8	36.3	233.6	431.7	195.5	62.5	79.5
辽宁	Liaoning	4171.0	16.2	173.5	807.1	142.5	174.4	135.4
吉林	Jilin	2239.7	33.5	53.3	421.4	104.7	94.6	63.7
黑龙江	Heilongjiang	2659.5	84.9	267.6	214.4	133.2	74.1	84.3
上海	Shanghai	14983.7	6.5	6.4	2093.8	92.0	369.6	2194.6
江苏	Jiangsu	16203.8	14.4	89.2	5001.9	260.2	1744.4	653.2
浙江	Zhejiang	14042.1	8.9	4.8	3637.8	244.3	1086.6	669.2
安徽	Anhui	6061.8	12.5	193.6	1440.2	136.1	670.2	222.1
福建	Fujian	5826.5	7.6	8.1	1223.1	160.7	720.9	267.9
江西	Jiangxi	3874.7	8.2	22.4	758.0	94.7	382.0	139.6
山东	Shandong	11574.2	8.8	350.1	2500.2	373.9	967.1	424.6
河南	Henan	6668.3	6.6	248.4	1050.7	285.0	613.3	241.9
湖北	Hubei	6782.1	10.6	37.2	1155.9	168.7	779.9	281.1
湖南	Hunan	5688.4	9.0	31.7	941.1	197.0	736.9	196.7
广东	Guangdong	26266.9	11.5	38.2	7945.4	485.1	1103.8	1225.3
广西	Guangxi	3745.4	23.4	7.1	420.4	142.7	229.2	121.7
海南	Hainan	1165.6	20.2	8.9	79.1	33.3	15.3	86.5
重庆	Chongqing	3825.9	3.3	6.1	631.6	91.0	461.8	147.0
四川	Sichuan	9625.1	14.1	136.4	1428.3	293.9	817.1	358.0
贵州	Guizhou	3149.5	8.6	144.4	364.5	120.7	199.4	122.1
云南	Yunnan	3686.8	14.4	53.0	375.8	152.9	199.4	147.6
西藏	Xizang	670.1	1.1	9.3	12.3	21.3	12.9	25.8
陕西	Shaanxi	4842.1	10.4	445.8	753.8	200.1	374.7	172.7
甘肃	Gansu	2320.1	12.3	100.0	246.5	106.1	137.2	65.4
青海	Qinghai	804.1	3.8	43.5	101.9	34.1	35.2	19.3
宁夏	Ningxia	873.4	6.2	125.9	124.7	60.9	26.5	21.6
新疆	Xinjiang	3601.2	12.5	258.0	339.7	152.2	256.4	94.3

4-8 续表 1 continued

单位：亿元 (100 million yuan)

年份 地区	Year Region	交通运输、仓储和邮政业 Transport, Storage and Post	住宿和餐饮业 Hotels and Catering Services	信息传输、软件和信息技术服务业 Information Transmission, Software and Information Technology	金融业 Financial Intermediation	房地产业 Real Estate	租赁和商务服务业 Leasing and Business Services
	2005	1279.5	249.8	491.8	1047.7	293.0	449.8
	2010	2541.9	484.6	1171.7	3219.0	745.6	1198.5
	2011	3074.1	655.2	1475.6	4007.0	1052.5	1325.3
	2012	3531.5	824.4	1769.4	4669.0	1271.3	1531.2
	2013	4834.6	1038.3	2957.7	5269.0	1882.3	2629.4
	2014	5435.4	1079.1	3375.8	6017.4	2220.5	2985.9
	2015	5898.0	1130.0	3912.7	6730.1	2493.0	3399.9
	2016	6238.7	1167.9	4431.8	7557.3	2802.1	3704.3
	2017	6754.1	1211.9	5198.4	8295.0	3059.3	4176.0
	2018	7273.3	1293.0	6204.1	8907.3	3507.8	4453.3
	2019	7913.9	1330.5	7281.1	10711.3	4057.4	5727.2
	2020	8171.8	1228.0	8444.5	11619.0	4401.7	5890.2
	2021	8793.4	1414.1	10289.0	13063.7	4852.7	6923.3
	2022	9014.6	1408.0	11769.5	13260.2	4713.6	7817.5
	2023	9488.2	1645.8	12417.6	13851.0	4761.1	8905.2
北京	Beijing	761.9	221.5	3363.1	2105.0	564.2	1393.4
天津	Tianjin	185.0	22.0	92.0	243.5	73.2	119.0
河北	Hebei	300.6	24.1	179.5	382.3	80.2	127.0
山西	Shanxi	256.1	20.9	57.3	235.8	44.4	93.2
内蒙古	Inner Mongolia	228.5	13.6	59.1	202.9	38.4	53.9
辽宁	Liaoning	299.2	24.8	216.2	287.0	73.7	98.5
吉林	Jilin	139.1	7.9	50.9	178.6	27.8	31.3
黑龙江	Heilongjiang	231.5	7.5	59.8	157.1	23.0	83.9
上海	Shanghai	779.3	181.8	1962.3	1603.4	423.1	1782.3
江苏	Jiangsu	593.0	136.7	741.1	888.2	314.4	529.8
浙江	Zhejiang	492.3	108.6	1055.8	945.5	347.2	723.8
安徽	Anhui	289.1	36.2	181.6	280.0	117.9	218.3
福建	Fujian	251.4	56.6	180.0	362.4	141.4	321.8
江西	Jiangxi	173.2	23.3	71.9	175.1	71.9	72.2
山东	Shandong	506.9	82.4	290.2	689.8	248.0	347.3
河南	Henan	363.6	37.0	197.3	349.2	154.2	154.0
湖北	Hubei	343.0	52.1	266.2	321.6	176.0	283.9
湖南	Hunan	246.0	35.9	140.1	339.1	108.0	121.6
广东	Guangdong	1030.0	256.5	2007.2	1931.1	914.2	1339.6
广西	Guangxi	196.9	23.9	97.1	232.6	63.5	128.6
海南	Hainan	98.4	29.0	48.1	75.1	67.5	56.4
重庆	Chongqing	213.1	19.9	108.6	300.2	112.4	121.9
四川	Sichuan	423.7	102.2	438.6	512.0	253.7	321.1
贵州	Guizhou	127.7	16.9	62.9	198.0	54.4	61.1
云南	Yunnan	184.0	25.4	70.4	177.9	66.3	80.5
西藏	Xizang	32.3	4.1	17.8	48.7	5.3	16.7
陕西	Shaanxi	275.4	41.9	277.7	251.4	106.7	91.4
甘肃	Gansu	134.2	12.1	36.7	118.6	30.8	31.7
青海	Qinghai	63.5	2.7	14.7	44.4	8.3	11.6
宁夏	Ningxia	42.9	2.1	14.8	50.4	11.4	11.9
新疆	Xinjiang	226.4	16.3	58.7	163.8	39.4	77.6

4-8 续表 2 continued

单位：亿元 (100 million yuan)

年份 Year 地区 Region		科学研究和技术服务业 Scientific Research and Technical Services	水利、环境和公共设施管理业 Management of Water Conservancy, Environment and Public Facilities	居民服务、修理和其他服务业 Services to Households, Repair and Other Services	教育 Education	卫生和社会工作 Health and Social Service	文化、体育和娱乐业 Culture, Sports and Entertainment	公共管理、社会保障和社会组织 Public Management, Social Security and Social Organization
	2005	614.0	257.3	85.1	2690.8	1047.8	275.8	2489.6
	2010	1619.3	555.9	168.4	6136.5	2506.4	543.7	5428.8
	2011	1879.6	659.8	197.9	6938.8	3078.6	642.1	6118.1
	2012	2259.4	784.6	217.1	7851.0	3718.5	735.4	7058.3
	2013	2940.3	933.7	277.2	8721.1	4397.8	867.8	7675.0
	2014	3339.7	1049.9	312.9	9722.5	5057.8	936.8	8448.6
	2015	3665.8	1177.7	336.1	11492.1	5941.3	1086.0	10141.4
	2016	4037.3	1278.2	357.8	12787.1	6825.6	1204.4	11787.2
	2017	4491.5	1394.3	390.2	14324.4	7930.8	1339.9	13753.5
	2018	5045.1	1456.5	423.8	15928.1	8857.8	1450.7	15882.8
	2019	5740.5	1491.2	520.1	18445.3	10812.9	1628.7	18651.1
	2020	5960.0	1576.1	498.7	20565.8	11966.8	1670.0	20522.3
	2021	6770.6	1668.8	555.3	21754.3	13673.0	1778.1	21974.8
	2022	7424.2	1747.4	590.3	23320.2	14903.7	1797.6	23253.8
	2023	7773.9	1795.9	588.1	23875.8	16058.5	1879.4	23266.8
北京	Beijing	1535.4	150.9	55.3	1178.0	912.1	460.3	837.8
天津	Tianjin	228.4	23.6	26.3	313.7	215.3	18.4	280.3
河北	Hebei	174.7	52.1	17.0	839.0	500.1	43.8	890.1
山西	Shanxi	79.7	35.5	6.4	496.4	261.0	30.9	507.5
内蒙古	Inner Mongolia	63.4	35.9	2.7	400.9	224.6	29.0	540.6
辽宁	Liaoning	119.8	42.1	8.7	552.8	372.6	34.7	592.0
吉林	Jilin	70.8	27.9	4.9	347.3	229.9	23.8	328.1
黑龙江	Heilongjiang	58.3	32.5	5.6	402.3	273.2	19.5	446.8
上海	Shanghai	1084.1	108.4	65.6	904.1	717.7	115.2	493.6
江苏	Jiangsu	516.8	122.9	54.8	1806.4	1122.7	116.5	1497.3
浙江	Zhejiang	452.4	105.9	34.4	1470.6	1146.3	109.1	1398.6
安徽	Anhui	147.5	45.3	15.7	803.5	523.4	34.7	693.8
福建	Fujian	115.1	51.9	31.3	781.9	448.9	42.8	652.7
江西	Jiangxi	83.6	39.6	6.6	669.5	376.9	30.8	675.3
山东	Shandong	315.1	102.5	19.6	1595.2	1043.3	88.0	1621.4
河南	Henan	166.7	65.0	18.8	984.1	695.8	51.5	985.2
湖北	Hubei	265.8	71.2	19.7	860.8	683.8	64.0	940.6
湖南	Hunan	156.6	70.7	23.1	801.3	603.7	68.4	861.4
广东	Guangdong	887.9	181.4	96.3	2362.9	1861.9	165.7	2422.8
广西	Guangxi	103.3	41.2	7.2	777.6	492.3	31.3	605.4
海南	Hainan	40.6	29.9	2.7	190.3	108.5	16.3	159.6
重庆	Chongqing	120.1	46.1	5.2	589.3	347.5	28.6	472.3
四川	Sichuan	405.3	89.2	27.5	1424.0	1021.1	77.7	1481.2
贵州	Guizhou	57.3	28.0	9.9	578.9	354.3	17.8	622.5
云南	Yunnan	109.5	42.6	6.9	746.0	413.4	34.4	786.5
西藏	Xizang	17.6	4.7	0.6	106.7	40.8	10.4	281.7
陕西	Shaanxi	192.4	56.9	7.8	620.1	372.2	42.7	548.0
甘肃	Gansu	79.7	35.5	1.5	426.2	212.6	24.4	508.7
青海	Qinghai	25.6	7.6	0.8	116.1	73.4	8.5	188.9
宁夏	Ningxia	15.9	11.1	0.5	123.9	80.4	8.0	134.1
新疆	Xinjiang	84.6	37.9	4.5	605.9	329.0	32.0	811.9

4–9 按登记注册统计类别分城镇非私营单位就业人员平均工资
Average Wage of Employed Persons in Urban Non-Private Units by Registered Statistical Categories

年 份 地 区	Year Region	平均工资(元) Average Wage (yuan)	#在岗职工 Staff and Workers	内资单位 Domestic Invested Units	#国有单位 State-owned Units	港澳台投资单位 Units with Funds from Hong Kong, Macao and Taiwan	外商投资单位 Foreign Funded Units
	1995	5348	5500	5250	5553	7711	8812
	2000	9333	9371	9068	9441	12210	15692
	2005	18200	18364	17866	18978	17833	23625
	2010	36539	37147	36366	38359	31983	41739
	2015	62029	63241	60652	65296	62017	76302
	2016	67569	68993	66190	72538	67506	82902
	2017	74318	76121	73067	81114	73016	90064
	2018	82413	84744	81044	89474	82027	99367
	2019	90501	93383	89105	98899	91304	106604
	2020	97379	100512	95919	108132	100155	112089
	2021	106837	110221	104644	115583	114034	126019
	2022	114029	117177	111247	123623	124841	137199
	2023	120698	123734	117783	127672	132342	149130
北 京	Beijing	218312	224562	205812	231908	281474	260128
天 津	Tianjin	138007	141769	141296	158688	111621	139398
河 北	Hebei	94818	96958	94397	94528	109566	95124
山 西	Shanxi	95025	97315	95306	87760	77817	97377
内蒙古	Inner Mongolia	108856	111602	108742	104454	102868	121706
辽 宁	Liaoning	97330	99733	96488	100722	97653	105756
吉 林	Jilin	94937	97562	93755	96372	82630	125278
黑龙江	Heilongjiang	95750	99046	96010	97153	80481	91612
上 海	Shanghai	229337	235520	216282	263880	235593	257083
江 苏	Jiangsu	125102	127620	126522	164986	112727	125839
浙 江	Zhejiang	133045	135653	131778	184226	153616	126240
安 徽	Anhui	103688	106769	103295	125346	102586	118837
福 建	Fujian	108520	111401	111923	136249	88755	98920
江 西	Jiangxi	92794	94742	94119	109315	66089	83932
山 东	Shandong	107131	109805	107675	126459	104960	99426
河 南	Henan	84156	85583	84449	87026	69603	95353
湖 北	Hubei	109227	112255	109642	125884	90588	115298
湖 南	Hunan	97015	99480	97774	108029	83432	89392
广 东	Guangdong	131418	133452	138838	172245	107949	122197
广 西	Guangxi	96184	98809	96670	102304	68817	101838
海 南	Hainan	114572	116686	113237	120111	149842	130414
重 庆	Chongqing	113653	117446	114521	140595	103582	104746
四 川	Sichuan	110160	113223	110282	124016	103341	112473
贵 州	Guizhou	102010	104802	102068	102376	98715	96178
云 南	Yunnan	106769	112908	107381	114200	76626	87906
西 藏	Xizang	165004	172077	165035	178527	175839	126960
陕 西	Shaanxi	106969	109908	106559	101948	86495	147016
甘 肃	Gansu	99124	102934	98911	105486	82643	147414
青 海	Qinghai	121457	125114	121461	127891	140063	107208
宁 夏	Ningxia	117681	121648	117819	116884	116379	108468
新 疆	Xinjiang	112305	115093	112311	113739	111912	111561

注：1.1995–2008年的城镇非私营单位就业人员平均工资即为原来的城镇单位就业人员平均劳动报酬(以下相关表同)。
2.本表登记注册统计类别按《关于市场主体统计分类的划分规定》(国统字〔2023〕14号)执行。
3.表中国有单位包括机关事业单位和全民所有制企业(国有企业)。

a)Average wage of employed persons in urban non-private units from 1995 to 2008 refers to average earning of employed persons in urban non-private units. The same applies to the related following tables.

b) The registered statistical categories of this table is implemented in accordance with the Regulations on the Classification of Market Entity Statistics (Guotongzi [2023] No. 14).

c) The state-owned enterprises in the tables include government agencies and all state-owned enterprises.

4-10 按登记注册统计类别分城镇非私营单位就业人员平均工资指数
Average Wage Indices of Employed Persons in Urban Non-Private Units by Registered Statistical Categories

年份 地区	Year Region	平均名义工资指数(上年=100) Indices of Average Nominal Wage (preceding year=100)	#在岗职工 Staff and Workers	内资单位 Domestic Invested Units	#国有单位 State-owned Units	港澳台投资单位 Units with Funds from Hong Kong, Macao and Taiwan	外商投资单位 Foreign Funded Units
	1995	118.9	121.2	117.0	117.3	120.9	134.9
	2000	112.2	112.3	112.2	111.8	107.6	109.3
	2005	114.3	114.6	114.8	115.4	109.8	106.2
	2010	113.3	113.5	113.3	112.4	113.9	112.5
	2015	110.1	110.3	110.2	114.0	110.9	109.3
	2016	108.9	109.1	109.1	111.1	108.9	108.6
	2017	110.0	110.3	110.4	111.8	108.2	108.6
	2018	110.9	111.3	110.9	110.3	112.3	110.3
	2019	109.8	110.2	109.9	110.5	111.3	107.3
	2020	107.6	107.6	107.6	109.3	109.7	105.1
	2021	109.7	109.7	109.1	106.9	113.9	112.4
	2022	106.7	106.3	106.3	107.0	109.5	108.9
	2023	105.8	105.6	105.9	103.3	106.0	108.7
北京	Beijing	104.5	104.4	105.7	106.0	102.2	101.0
天津	Tianjin	106.6	106.0	107.4	105.8	95.8	109.1
河北	Hebei	104.5	103.8	104.2	99.4	106.8	109.6
山西	Shanxi	105.0	104.8	105.2	101.8	90.4	107.1
内蒙古	Inner Mongolia	107.8	107.5	107.8	105.7	104.2	114.7
辽宁	Liaoning	105.1	105.1	105.1	100.9	110.4	104.0
吉林	Jilin	108.8	108.3	109.1	109.3	105.0	108.0
黑龙江	Heilongjiang	108.5	107.4	108.4	111.7	106.9	121.2
上海	Shanghai	107.9	108.4	108.6	108.5	106.6	108.1
江苏	Jiangsu	102.8	102.8	101.9	101.4	105.1	105.1
浙江	Zhejiang	103.3	102.8	103.0	102.4	108.8	100.0
安徽	Anhui	105.1	104.7	104.7	101.5	107.4	119.1
福建	Fujian	104.5	104.1	103.9	101.2	104.6	102.4
江西	Jiangxi	105.5	104.8	105.2	102.7	104.5	115.0
山东	Shandong	104.8	104.3	104.5	101.0	105.7	108.3
河南	Henan	108.4	108.5	108.3	100.9	109.3	114.8
湖北	Hubei	107.7	107.6	107.7	104.0	105.3	111.4
湖南	Hunan	106.1	105.2	106.0	101.7	109.3	100.5
广东	Guangdong	105.2	105.1	104.7	102.8	105.5	108.0
广西	Guangxi	104.5	104.3	104.2	102.0	108.6	114.2
海南	Hainan	109.3	108.2	109.9	106.1	92.4	115.5
重庆	Chongqing	106.2	105.4	105.9	104.5	107.7	108.3
四川	Sichuan	108.2	107.8	108.7	104.0	102.0	99.4
贵州	Guizhou	106.9	105.2	106.9	104.2	112.9	98.9
云南	Yunnan	103.5	103.8	103.5	98.7	115.7	91.4
西藏	Xizang	106.5	106.3	106.5	99.9	122.8	73.8
陕西	Shaanxi	108.2	107.7	108.4	104.3	97.5	125.5
甘肃	Gansu	109.1	109.2	109.1	105.7	91.8	126.2
青海	Qinghai	104.8	105.3	104.6	103.0	118.7	111.9
宁夏	Ningxia	102.7	102.6	102.8	97.2	98.6	98.6
新疆	Xinjiang	110.4	109.8	110.4	112.0	105.7	103.4

注：1.本表登记注册统计类别按《关于市场主体统计分类的划分规定》(国统字〔2023〕14号)执行。
2.表中国有单位包括机关事业单位和全民所有制企业(国有企业)。

a) The registered statistical categories of this table is implemented in accordance with the Regulations on the Classification of Market Entity Statistics (Guotongzi [2023] No. 14).

b) The state-owned enterprises in the tables include government agencies and all state-owned enterprises.

4-10 续表 continued

年份 地区	Year Region	平均实际工资指数(上年=100) Indices of Average Real Wage (preceding year=100)	#在岗职工 Staff and Workers	内资单位 Domestic Invested Units	#国有单位 State-owned Units	港澳台投资单位 Units with Funds from Hong Kong, Macao and Taiwan	外商投资单位 Foreign Funded Units
	1995	101.8	103.8	101.2	100.4	100.5	105.6
	2000	111.3	111.4	111.3	110.9	106.7	108.5
	2005	112.5	112.8	113.0	113.6	108.1	104.5
	2010	109.8	110.0	109.8	108.9	110.3	109.0
	2015	108.5	108.6	108.6	112.3	109.2	107.7
	2016	106.7	106.9	106.9	108.8	106.6	106.4
	2017	108.2	108.5	108.5	110.0	106.4	106.8
	2018	108.6	109.0	108.6	108.0	110.0	108.1
	2019	106.8	107.2	107.0	107.5	108.3	104.4
	2020	105.2	105.2	105.2	106.9	107.2	102.8
	2021	108.6	108.6	108.0	105.8	112.7	111.3
	2022	104.6	104.2	104.2	104.9	107.3	106.7
	2023	105.5	105.3	105.6	103.0	105.7	108.4
北京	Beijing	104.1	104.0	105.3	105.6	101.7	100.6
天津	Tianjin	106.1	105.6	107.0	105.4	95.4	108.6
河北	Hebei	103.8	103.1	103.5	98.7	106.0	108.8
山西	Shanxi	105.1	104.9	105.3	101.9	90.5	107.2
内蒙古	Inner Mongolia	107.1	106.9	107.1	105.1	103.6	114.1
辽宁	Liaoning	104.9	104.9	104.8	100.7	110.2	103.8
吉林	Jilin	108.8	108.3	109.1	109.3	105.0	108.0
黑龙江	Heilongjiang	107.8	106.7	107.6	110.9	106.1	120.4
上海	Shanghai	107.6	108.0	108.2	108.1	106.3	107.7
江苏	Jiangsu	102.3	102.3	101.4	100.9	104.6	104.5
浙江	Zhejiang	103.0	102.5	102.7	102.1	108.5	99.7
安徽	Anhui	105.0	104.6	104.5	101.4	107.3	119.0
福建	Fujian	104.4	104.0	103.8	101.1	104.5	102.3
江西	Jiangxi	105.1	104.4	104.8	102.3	104.1	114.5
山东	Shandong	104.6	104.1	104.3	100.8	105.5	108.0
河南	Henan	108.8	108.9	108.7	101.3	109.8	115.3
湖北	Hubei	107.5	107.4	107.5	103.8	105.0	111.2
湖南	Hunan	105.8	104.9	105.7	101.4	109.0	100.2
广东	Guangdong	104.6	104.5	104.1	102.2	104.9	107.3
广西	Guangxi	104.8	104.6	104.5	102.3	109.0	114.5
海南	Hainan	109.0	107.9	109.6	105.8	92.2	115.1
重庆	Chongqing	106.5	105.7	106.2	104.8	108.0	108.6
四川	Sichuan	108.1	107.7	108.6	103.9	101.9	99.3
贵州	Guizhou	107.2	105.5	107.2	104.5	113.3	99.2
云南	Yunnan	103.0	103.3	103.0	98.2	115.1	90.9
西藏	Xizang	106.3	106.1	106.3	99.7	122.6	73.6
陕西	Shaanxi	108.1	107.6	108.3	104.2	97.4	125.4
甘肃	Gansu	108.5	108.7	108.5	105.2	91.3	125.6
青海	Qinghai	104.3	104.9	104.2	102.6	118.3	111.5
宁夏	Ningxia	102.1	102.0	102.3	96.7	98.1	98.1
新疆	Xinjiang	110.4	109.8	110.4	112.0	105.7	103.4

4-11 按登记注册统计类别和行业分城镇非私营单位就业人员平均工资（2023年）

Average Wage of Employed Persons in Urban Non-Private Units by Registered Statistical Categories and Sector (2023)

单位：元 (yuan)

项目	Item	平均工资 Average Wage	内资单位 Domestic Invested Units	#国有单位 State-owned Units	港澳台投资单位 Units with Funds from Hong Kong, Macao and Taiwan	外商投资单位 Foreign Funded Units
全国	**National Average**	**120698**	**117783**	**127672**	**132342**	**149130**
农、林、牧、渔业	Agriculture, Forestry, Animal Husbandry and Fishery	62952	62645	61632	76313	77198
采矿业	Mining	135025	133979	161579	152269	193796
制造业	Manufacturing	103932	102299	109987	95654	118118
电力、热力、燃气及水生产和供应业	Production and Supply of Electricity, Heat, Gas and Water	143594	143664	128200	145042	137584
建筑业	Construction	85804	85543	76286	103278	120542
批发和零售业	Wholesale and Retail Trades	124362	105610	171019	155189	209518
交通运输、仓储和邮政业	Transport, Storage and Post	122705	120033	106261	172240	145964
住宿和餐饮业	Hotels and Catering Services	58094	62511	68414	50581	47956
信息传输、软件和信息技术服务业	Information Transmission, Software and Information Technology	231810	195706	135157	356461	296256
金融业	Financial Intermediation	197663	193299	190029	319278	239729
房地产业	Real Estate	91932	88894	91375	118733	125366
租赁和商务服务业	Leasing and Business Services	109264	93735	103524	224224	326196
科学研究和技术服务业	Scientific Research and Technical Services	171447	162210	160202	250926	281384
水利、环境和公共设施管理业	Management of Water Conservancy, Environment and Public Facilities	68656	68484	79254	76444	97498
居民服务、修理和其他服务业	Services to Households, Repair and Other Services	68919	68183	98139	66158	109553
教育	Education	124067	123981	128805	189559	239856
卫生和社会工作	Health and Social Service	143818	143702	149661	179602	168517
文化、体育和娱乐业	Culture, Sports and Entertainment	127334	127787	131735	117317	119204
公共管理、社会保障和社会组织	Public Management, Social Security and Social Organization	117108	117108	117133		

注：1.本表登记注册统计类别按《关于市场主体统计分类的划分规定》(国统字〔2023〕14号)执行。
2.表中国有单位包括机关事业单位和全民所有制企业(国有企业)。

a) The registered statistical categories of this table is implemented in accordance with the Regulations on the Classification of Market Entity Statistics (Guotongzi [2023] No. 14).

b) The state-owned units in the table include government agencies and state-owned enterprises.

4-12 按行业分城镇非私营单位就业人员平均工资
Average Wage of Employed Persons in Urban Non-Private Units by Sector

单位：元 (yuan)

年份 地区	Year Region	平均工资 Average Wage	农、林、牧、渔业 Agriculture, Forestry, Animal Husbandry and Fishery	采矿业 Mining	制造业 Manufacturing	电力、热力、燃气及水生产和供应业 Production and Supply of Electricity, Heat, Gas and Water	建筑业 Construction	批发和零售业 Wholesale and Retail Trades
	2005	18200	8207	20449	15934	24750	14112	15256
	2010	36539	16717	44196	30916	47309	27529	33635
	2011	41799	19469	52230	36665	52723	32103	40654
	2012	46769	22687	56946	41650	58202	36483	46340
	2013	51483	25820	60138	46431	67085	42072	50308
	2014	56360	28356	61677	51369	73339	45804	55838
	2015	62029	31947	59404	55324	78886	48886	60328
	2016	67569	33612	60544	59470	83863	52082	65061
	2017	74318	36504	69500	64452	90348	55568	71201
	2018	82413	36466	81429	72088	100162	60501	80551
	2019	90501	39340	91068	78147	107733	65580	89047
	2020	97379	48540	96674	82783	116728	69986	96521
	2021	106837	53819	108467	92459	125332	75762	107735
	2022	114029	58976	121522	97528	132964	78295	115408
	2023	120698	62952	135025	103932	143594	85804	124362
北京	Beijing	218312	76654	197469	188602	220232	161172	199716
天津	Tianjin	138007	96097	193887	119879	196345	127402	125704
河北	Hebei	94818	69655	106884	88100	140598	86269	74339
山西	Shanxi	95025	59581	124277	80540	115131	86540	85568
内蒙古	Inner Mongolia	108856	82918	196182	110819	137753	78573	95212
辽宁	Liaoning	97330	26105	109027	93900	103915	80285	83730
吉林	Jilin	94937	63165	104620	103288	116867	71403	82046
黑龙江	Heilongjiang	95750	54853	122568	92129	104694	74524	87211
上海	Shanghai	229337	107870	360794	175688	272347	162683	241787
江苏	Jiangsu	125102	67261	150448	113582	171988	84491	119615
浙江	Zhejiang	133045	95044	107327	108026	178209	79719	139543
安徽	Anhui	103688	65541	149675	95640	148159	80764	92812
福建	Fujian	108520	79383	89918	93196	149565	75673	110445
江西	Jiangxi	92794	58563	87296	78999	99422	69509	83764
山东	Shandong	107131	69137	143460	94524	137881	87232	86752
河南	Henan	84156	53599	107431	75178	122306	69071	75662
湖北	Hubei	109227	63351	137350	95738	160295	89175	87446
湖南	Hunan	97015	62461	76366	91588	123361	77149	82358
广东	Guangdong	131418	83936	213297	104424	187410	92727	117872
广西	Guangxi	96184	80331	77217	79309	135205	75788	88327
海南	Hainan	114572	67172	172817	100756	149434	86162	122405
重庆	Chongqing	113653	76405	118449	101745	127438	80678	99036
四川	Sichuan	110160	85299	159113	99675	135500	80698	96458
贵州	Guizhou	102010	63124	94589	107315	142977	88303	103104
云南	Yunnan	106769	58351	101160	100645	156234	81528	104887
西藏	Xizang	165004	82426	132431	102972	143982	95576	140531
陕西	Shaanxi	106969	72573	158775	101092	140130	91351	86731
甘肃	Gansu	99124	76382	140388	97020	112778	72672	81888
青海	Qinghai	121457	51608	186666	100763	144765	115039	90714
宁夏	Ningxia	117681	61550	206495	97399	161003	100198	80115
新疆	Xinjiang	112305	66231	195631	99565	152921	98395	100700

4-12 续表 1 continued

单位：元 (yuan)

年 份 地 区	Year Region	交通运输、仓储和邮政业 Transport, Storage and Post	住宿和餐饮业 Hotels and Catering Services	信息传输、软件和信息技术服务业 Information Transmission, Software and Information Technology	金融业 Financial Intermediation	房地产业 Real Estate	租赁和商务服务业 Leasing and Business Services
	2005	20911	13876	38799	29229	20253	21233
	2010	40466	23382	64436	70146	35870	39566
	2011	47078	27486	70918	81109	42837	46976
	2012	53391	31267	80510	89743	46764	53162
	2013	57993	34044	90915	99653	51048	62538
	2014	63416	37264	100845	108273	55568	67131
	2015	68822	40806	112042	114777	60244	72489
	2016	73650	43382	122478	117418	65497	76782
	2017	80225	45751	133150	122851	69277	81393
	2018	88508	48260	147678	129837	75281	85147
	2019	97050	50346	161352	131405	80157	88190
	2020	100642	48833	177544	133390	83807	92924
	2021	109851	53631	201506	150843	91143	102537
	2022	115345	53995	220418	174341	90346	106500
	2023	122705	58094	231810	197663	91932	109264
北 京	Beijing	159018	69455	330135	357192	124451	179496
天 津	Tianjin	128026	45783	183684	201690	99338	99351
河 北	Hebei	108463	52765	137412	125780	72311	68219
山 西	Shanxi	110202	46909	114701	111392	59693	69421
内蒙古	Inner Mongolia	117244	52797	131580	129609	56585	76518
辽 宁	Liaoning	104293	42311	145153	122661	74356	70437
吉 林	Jilin	99700	46303	109923	115172	66233	69695
黑龙江	Heilongjiang	105335	45627	103841	105062	55230	89125
上 海	Shanghai	177369	67565	363745	442860	135170	227968
江 苏	Jiangsu	120293	61114	196104	216999	97457	93365
浙 江	Zhejiang	130065	65371	296276	219310	101291	91790
安 徽	Anhui	104417	54836	133985	152955	78689	69358
福 建	Fujian	121439	55675	165488	178790	90760	93004
江 西	Jiangxi	107129	48404	114977	136854	76055	74020
山 东	Shandong	115462	57295	144716	131105	77248	84510
河 南	Henan	101760	49171	107987	147227	69956	62903
湖 北	Hubei	117358	50705	157175	151817	81826	89680
湖 南	Hunan	104658	51869	146253	138760	79190	73778
广 东	Guangdong	137150	57881	243832	267444	99128	107547
广 西	Guangxi	109881	46888	141988	145943	79985	71223
海 南	Hainan	141500	65790	231021	169637	84992	143495
重 庆	Chongqing	106411	56821	170118	166984	83919	78125
四 川	Sichuan	118242	55068	160257	149098	85844	79693
贵 州	Guizhou	108204	50173	147771	170227	79532	70991
云 南	Yunnan	116549	51946	133597	153189	80681	65903
西 藏	Xizang	143691	75472	213532	271731	85934	129220
陕 西	Shaanxi	115305	50844	207975	144563	80012	74447
甘 肃	Gansu	110187	49936	116925	106770	57901	66435
青 海	Qinghai	129914	52794	157986	159142	58372	70146
宁 夏	Ningxia	110800	53792	156124	139473	73686	68079
新 疆	Xinjiang	130662	54516	134907	159968	64878	76654

4-12 续表 2 continued

单位：元 (yuan)

年份 地区	Year Region	科学研究和技术服务业 Scientific Research and Technical Services	水利、环境和公共设施管理业 Management of Water Conservancy, Environment and Public Facilities	居民服务、修理和其他服务业 Services to Households, Repair and Other Services	教育 Education	卫生和社会工作 Health and Social Service	文化、体育和娱乐业 Culture, Sports and Entertainment	公共管理、社会保障和社会组织 Public Management, Social Security and Social Organization
	2005	27155	14322	15747	18259	20808	22670	20234
	2010	56376	25544	28206	38968	40232	41428	38242
	2011	64252	28868	33169	43194	46206	47878	42062
	2012	69254	32343	35135	47734	52564	53558	46074
	2013	76602	36123	38429	51950	57979	59336	49259
	2014	82259	39198	41882	56580	63267	64375	53110
	2015	89410	43528	44802	66592	71624	72764	62323
	2016	96638	47750	47577	74498	80026	79875	70959
	2017	107815	52229	50552	83412	89648	87803	80372
	2018	123343	56670	55343	92383	98118	98621	87932
	2019	133459	61158	60232	97681	108903	107708	94369
	2020	139851	63914	60722	106474	115449	112081	104487
	2021	151776	65802	65193	111392	126828	117329	111361
	2022	163486	68256	65478	120422	135222	121151	117440
	2023	171447	68656	68919	124067	143818	127334	117108
北京	Beijing	236855	125387	87629	230965	251981	236493	197846
天津	Tianjin	217952	105617	54548	149140	176468	133261	142373
河北	Hebei	121616	46857	59602	99772	103504	85770	84034
山西	Shanxi	99828	44188	57276	93047	94660	73147	79235
内蒙古	Inner Mongolia	111981	53989	54045	110236	110565	96222	98103
辽宁	Liaoning	133070	50966	57449	105994	106856	87979	94852
吉林	Jilin	120708	46350	43770	100625	108891	80903	84872
黑龙江	Heilongjiang	113566	48986	45028	106987	109095	77725	91624
上海	Shanghai	281661	108043	99399	235503	254760	206752	262453
江苏	Jiangsu	171206	90941	93628	156922	167041	127246	166014
浙江	Zhejiang	186407	91039	75730	166068	198037	150143	177400
安徽	Anhui	136621	47549	65079	119779	136840	97730	117886
福建	Fujian	146922	73153	76832	129492	164846	112808	128140
江西	Jiangxi	118645	45208	48474	104152	124536	92763	108489
山东	Shandong	127863	58618	57472	124519	132962	111057	116560
河南	Henan	97744	42470	40068	83020	101133	78775	81089
湖北	Hubei	161074	78680	54535	116242	140527	108294	122004
湖南	Hunan	123027	66987	85200	98761	127551	116331	98212
广东	Guangdong	181616	83890	70693	153345	197354	136749	161104
广西	Guangxi	112992	62400	56347	91957	120491	90062	100442
海南	Hainan	141814	56463	60523	114177	131695	98467	110893
重庆	Chongqing	156008	79576	71359	139334	158423	106083	129911
四川	Sichuan	146232	72529	61230	116527	138142	105808	117329
贵州	Guizhou	118820	56098	50941	98825	119350	87443	93321
云南	Yunnan	126509	60138	51862	116750	119497	99493	104940
西藏	Xizang	141995	78683	83668	185945	160758	147543	179437
陕西	Shaanxi	142532	60116	52535	102288	105843	82433	92113
甘肃	Gansu	123998	63820	60859	109294	101666	89269	102066
青海	Qinghai	130796	70213	63365	132767	128265	97365	127938
宁夏	Ningxia	120829	65895	79474	111737	135092	95864	110765
新疆	Xinjiang	133384	68159	62465	118364	132404	107619	97415

4-13 按行业分城镇私营单位就业人员平均工资
Average Wage of Employed Persons in Urban Private Units by Sector

单位：元 (yuan)

年份 地区	Year Region	平均工资 Average Wage	农、林、牧、渔业 Agriculture, Forestry, Animal Husbandry and Fishery	采矿业 Mining	制造业 Manufacturing	电力、热力、燃气及水生产和供应业 Production and Supply of Electricity, Heat, Gas and Water	建筑业 Construction	批发和零售业 Wholesale and Retail Trades
	2010	20759	16370	20981	20090	18834	22228	19928
	2011	24556	19223	25519	24138	22091	26108	22791
	2012	28752	21973	29684	28215	25478	30911	27233
	2013	32706	24645	33081	32035	29597	34882	30604
	2014	36390	26862	35819	35653	33184	38838	33894
	2015	39589	28869	38192	38948	34631	41710	36635
	2016	42833	31301	39600	42115	38605	44803	39589
	2017	45761	34272	41236	44991	41510	46944	42359
	2018	49575	36375	44096	49275	44239	50879	45177
	2019	53604	37760	49675	52858	49633	54167	48722
	2020	57727	38956	54563	57910	54268	57309	53018
	2021	62884	41442	62665	63946	59271	60430	58071
	2022	65237	42605	68509	67352	61870	60918	60630
	2023	68340	44465	75648	71762	64826	63857	63701
北京	Beijing	105931	60271	114034	124232	79639	78728	93562
天津	Tianjin	72966	66696	90809	75751	81092	61068	74029
河北	Hebei	51281	38690	56709	56629	58621	48970	45947
山西	Shanxi	50452	37531	69054	54895	50809	55420	45541
内蒙古	Inner Mongolia	57410	56484	93909	67337	66352	58362	54452
辽宁	Liaoning	53333	45380	55954	57216	57405	51813	51876
吉林	Jilin	51214	41637	59128	53107	46608	52815	56846
黑龙江	Heilongjiang	47281	41566	61020	52962	46345	41604	46251
上海	Shanghai	111347	60719		103648	105503	78737	110377
江苏	Jiangsu	75088	51430	116212	82190	91903	70027	68861
浙江	Zhejiang	74325	55858	83705	72552	75593	67684	77868
安徽	Anhui	59498	44674	82536	64099	62059	62237	53816
福建	Fujian	67651	54909	62601	72590	63595	65705	61886
江西	Jiangxi	55201	42841	61633	59379	56318	54339	50582
山东	Shandong	61046	49616	73029	65406	71632	63703	56167
河南	Henan	48841	38384	55337	52265	52356	51896	44738
湖北	Hubei	60583	49898	64785	66617	62313	60913	56801
湖南	Hunan	60277	45102	67960	65933	57431	59871	53415
广东	Guangdong	80685	66331	67865	79930	80876	70782	77468
广西	Guangxi	51527	51699	58960	55691	59396	53185	48145
海南	Hainan	66059	50373	69184	63070	46874	60725	70463
重庆	Chongqing	63941	39595	70487	71752	66959	61248	58192
四川	Sichuan	62105	40910	75176	67789	64031	62996	55906
贵州	Guizhou	54156	37723	83715	51284	58223	53928	53538
云南	Yunnan	53944	39198	78060	54746	54905	56474	51568
西藏	Xizang	70084	58409	111459	62443	115215	59197	83751
陕西	Shaanxi	58022	37824	88465	64901	65336	52737	52776
甘肃	Gansu	51380	41836	78675	57544	55947	51295	49044
青海	Qinghai	56424	38955	79176	67651	76294	59760	55597
宁夏	Ningxia	61567	49749	73222	72403	89738	62756	54674
新疆	Xinjiang	62220	48880	96275	61861	88030	65579	58810

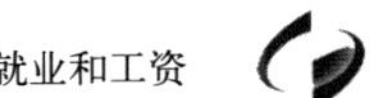

4-13 续表 1 continued

单位：元 (yuan)

年份 地区	Year Region	交通运输、仓储和邮政业 Transport, Storage and Post	住宿和餐饮业 Hotels and Catering Services	信息传输、软件和信息技术服务业 Information Transmission, Software and Information Technology	金融业 Financial Intermediation	房地产业 Real Estate	租赁和商务服务业 Leasing and Business Services
	2010	21989	17531	31226	30513	23228	23879
	2011	25949	20882	35562	28664	27017	27115
	2012	28159	23933	39518	32696	30778	31796
	2013	33141	27352	44060	37253	35038	36243
	2014	38891	29483	51044	41553	37826	39414
	2015	40495	31889	57719	44898	41767	43770
	2016	42705	34712	63578	50366	46063	47836
	2017	45852	36886	70415	52289	48025	51394
	2018	50547	39632	76326	62943	51393	53382
	2019	54006	42424	85301	76107	54416	57248
	2020	57313	42258	101281	82930	55759	58155
	2021	62411	46817	114618	95416	58288	64490
	2022	66059	47547	123894	110304	56435	65731
	2023	68051	51583	129215	124812	56119	67107
北京	Beijing	75589	65442	186287	208248	67392	95668
天津	Tianjin	77437	53104	115906	139156	62000	73728
河北	Hebei	55131	42263	55648	85957	47716	49618
山西	Shanxi	51807	40203	57865	75866	39841	46140
内蒙古	Inner Mongolia	60605	47591	59407	95985	43634	61925
辽宁	Liaoning	54769	43589	77318	39859	40452	51206
吉林	Jilin	49360	45092	67828	32550	41537	44269
黑龙江	Heilongjiang	46450	39645	57598	40018	35857	50053
上海	Shanghai	97327	69958	233366	257487	77221	95715
江苏	Jiangsu	72026	56832	110384	137648	59445	68754
浙江	Zhejiang	81616	59364	139598	150798	65709	76313
安徽	Anhui	61553	49600	79893	90820	46382	55905
福建	Fujian	69698	52524	111298	117648	64284	64158
江西	Jiangxi	57001	46124	65704	62234	54936	52227
山东	Shandong	62328	48607	70363	75085	49574	57358
河南	Henan	52896	40731	55206	90391	44332	47910
湖北	Hubei	58694	52273	82400	91759	52716	54594
湖南	Hunan	58263	47938	81564	84575	52949	57170
广东	Guangdong	81880	56142	154699	166307	70333	79808
广西	Guangxi	51552	42735	73410	75998	46359	52302
海南	Hainan	71298	47274	126355	106678	60321	74571
重庆	Chongqing	65408	48034	92470	137434	59989	61458
四川	Sichuan	57971	47994	108470	77469	51238	55682
贵州	Guizhou	53003	42805	108518	110202	52657	53347
云南	Yunnan	52022	43540	68329	105039	54580	50555
西藏	Xizang	72074	63320	115710	104063	74713	76712
陕西	Shaanxi	68781	44606	98989	54492	51903	53102
甘肃	Gansu	54810	43703	69405	67415	45897	52561
青海	Qinghai	62252	47494	62640	106482	44966	55327
宁夏	Ningxia	65701	45670	68994	71985	47748	56690
新疆	Xinjiang	69200	49482	66734	100848	53505	65767

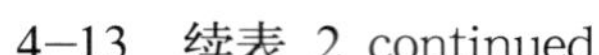

4−13 续表 2 continued

单位：元 (yuan)

年 份 Year / 地 区 Region		科学研究和技术服务业 Scientific Research and Technical Services	水利、环境和公共设施管理业 Management of Water Conservancy, Environment and Public Facilities	居民服务、修理和其他服务业 Services to Households, Repair and Other Services	教育 Education	卫生和社会工作 Health and Social Service	文化、体育和娱乐业 Culture, Sports and Entertainment
	2010	28886	19607	18350	21862	21571	20012
	2011	31320	22958	20543	23636	25590	22666
	2012	36598	26402	24068	26625	29173	26177
	2013	42854	31241	27483	31521	33862	30402
	2014	47462	33847	30580	33678	37205	32024
	2015	50441	37222	33203	37040	40558	34974
	2016	54764	40099	35824	39508	43993	38228
	2017	58102	41061	38417	43263	47296	41201
	2018	61876	42409	41058	46228	52343	44592
	2019	67642	44444	43926	50761	57140	49289
	2020	72233	43287	44536	48443	60689	51300
	2021	77708	43366	47193	52579	67750	56171
	2022	81569	44714	47760	52771	71060	56769
	2023	82277	47504	49907	55775	74462	59407
北 京	Beijing	124695	70823	55047	121367	107905	105909
天 津	Tianjin	91555	42973	49612	67696	70123	67582
河 北	Hebei	52692	27422	37868	49086	55045	44277
山 西	Shanxi	51211	33761	34873	43680	49044	36199
内蒙古	Inner Mongolia	59700	41476	44927	40973	62370	41053
辽 宁	Liaoning	63852	41410	39793	43199	61251	39051
吉 林	Jilin	58742	37110	39018	51851	55884	46408
黑龙江	Heilongjiang	51272	31682	36177	40442	58886	42801
上 海	Shanghai	151504	61592	61832	117585	115435	106607
江 苏	Jiangsu	83585	53575	53639	72553	88258	68351
浙 江	Zhejiang	99659	55431	57737	81628	96616	64870
安 徽	Anhui	61954	34779	46476	51329	66030	49652
福 建	Fujian	67241	47652	50580	53128	77549	55552
江 西	Jiangxi	57084	32088	47795	48907	65383	49234
山 东	Shandong	68248	40115	45403	54524	64410	54024
河 南	Henan	51748	34248	40613	45005	51966	41272
湖 北	Hubei	66804	46267	48320	51599	73316	52743
湖 南	Hunan	64326	51795	51411	52470	71262	54607
广 东	Guangdong	97020	58095	52829	66390	100227	70158
广 西	Guangxi	56980	46932	38695	38528	61552	43287
海 南	Hainan	69522	50360	47273	41791	66206	98840
重 庆	Chongqing	72991	48559	46276	61093	84043	52515
四 川	Sichuan	70868	49155	48642	54692	72523	51585
贵 州	Guizhou	61781	39193	42321	49609	58707	44512
云 南	Yunnan	65074	41957	46226	47205	63944	46326
西 藏	Xizang	97251	66552	81711	66926	121380	67925
陕 西	Shaanxi	67804	45786	42651	48996	63357	46817
甘 肃	Gansu	56273	35603	45271	40540	50015	41060
青 海	Qinghai	71259	49169	44328	38183	54905	46054
宁 夏	Ningxia	65899	36830	47819	43335	57311	49635
新 疆	Xinjiang	69420	45981	47177	47824	59003	52099

4-14 分地区城镇登记失业人员
Registered Unemployed Persons in Urban Area by Region

单位：万人 (10 000 persons)

地 区	Region	1990	2005	2010	2015	2020	2022	2023
北 京	Beijing	1.7	10.6	7.7	7.8	29.0	36.4	35.5
天 津	Tianjin	8.1	11.7	16.1	25.1	27.0	25.4	42.8
河 北	Hebei	7.7	27.8	35.1	39.4	38.5	20.5	9.3
山 西	Shanxi	5.5	14.3	20.4	25.6	27.7	19.9	26.4
内蒙古	Inner Mongolia	15.2	17.7	20.8	25.9	30.0	29.0	26.2
辽 宁	Liaoning	23.7	60.4	38.9	46.2	50.7	48.5	55.9
吉 林	Jilin	10.5	27.6	22.7	23.9	20.6	19.6	24.2
黑龙江	Heilongjiang	20.4	31.3	36.2	41.0	31.0	20.2	15.1
上 海	Shanghai	7.7	27.5	27.6	24.8	19.7	14.6	76.3
江 苏	Jiangsu	22.5	41.6	40.6	36.0	36.7	62.9	64.7
浙 江	Zhejiang	11.2	29.0	31.1	33.7	42.1	37.2	47.2
安 徽	Anhui	15.2	27.8	26.9	30.9	30.0	17.9	16.6
福 建	Fujian	9.0	14.9	14.5	15.4	35.7	28.3	25.1
江 西	Jiangxi	10.3	22.8	26.3	29.9	29.9	28.5	36.5
山 东	Shandong	26.2	42.9	44.5	43.7	46.7	20.4	33.1
河 南	Henan	25.1	33.0	38.2	42.5	62.2	54.6	65.8
湖 北	Hubei	12.7	52.6	55.7	33.4	55.3	51.2	42.7
湖 南	Hunan	15.9	41.9	43.2	45.1	31.4	25.3	18.2
广 东	Guangdong	19.2	34.5	39.3	37.0	73.9	53.9	114.6
广 西	Guangxi	13.9	18.5	19.1	18.1	22.9	22.8	21.0
海 南	Hainan	3.5	5.1	4.8	4.8	7.9	10.9	11.2
重 庆	Chongqing		16.9	13.0	14.3	29.6	21.9	34.9
四 川	Sichuan	38.0	34.3	34.6	54.6	54.4	51.6	83.1
贵 州	Guizhou	10.7	12.1	12.2	14.5	19.5	32.9	26.5
云 南	Yunnan	7.8	13.0	15.7	19.5	31.9	32.5	38.6
西 藏	Xizang			2.1	1.8	2.1	1.8	0.7
陕 西	Shaanxi	11.2	21.5	21.4	22.3	24.5	23.8	19.5
甘 肃	Gansu	12.5	9.3	10.7	9.5	12.2	13.4	20.5
青 海	Qinghai	4.2	3.6	4.2	4.4	3.1	2.1	2.7
宁 夏	Ningxia	4.0	4.4	4.8	4.9	5.6	10.9	16.9
新 疆	Xinjiang	9.6	11.1	11.0	10.3	9.4	8.8	18.3

注：1.新疆数据不包括新疆生产建设兵团。
2.2020年起，登记失业统计口径有所调整，与历史数据不可比。

a) The data of Xinjiang does not include Xinjiang Production and Construction Corps.
b) Since 2020, the statistical caliber of registered unemployment has been adjusted, which is not comparable with historical data.

主要统计指标解释

劳动力 指年满16周岁，有劳动能力，参加或要求参加社会经济活动的人口。包括就业人员和失业人员。

就业人员 指年满16周岁，为取得报酬或经营利润，在调查参考周内从事了1小时(含1小时)以上劳动的人员；或由于在职学习、休假、临时停工等原因在调查参考周内暂时未工作的人员。

单位就业人员 指报告期末最后一日在本单位工作，并取得工资或其他形式劳动报酬的人员数。该指标为时点指标，不包括最后一日当天及以前已经与单位解除劳动合同关系的人员，是在岗职工、劳务派遣人员及其他就业人员之和。就业人员不包括：

(1)离开本单位仍保留劳动关系，并定期领取生活费的人员；

(2)在本单位实习的各类在校学生。

在岗职工 指在本单位工作且与本单位签订劳动合同，并由单位支付各项工资和社会保险、住房公积金的人员，以及上述人员中由于学习、病伤、产假等原因暂未工作仍由单位支付工资的人员。在岗职工还包括：

(1)应订立劳动合同而未订立劳动合同人员；

(2)处于试用期人员；

(3)编制外招用的人员，如临时人员；

(4)派往外单位工作，但工资仍由本单位发放的人员(如挂职锻炼、外派工作等情况)。

工资总额 指根据《关于工资总额组成的规定》(1990年1月1日国家统计局发布的一号令)进行修订，本单位在报告期内(季度或年度)直接支付给本单位全部就业人员的劳动报酬总额。包括计时工资、计件工资、奖金、津贴和补贴、加班加点工资、特殊情况下支付的工资。

工资总额是税前工资，包括单位从个人工资中直接为其代扣或代缴的个人所得税、社会保险基金和住房公积金等个人缴纳部分以及房费、水电费等。

工资总额不论是计入成本的还是不计入成本的，不论是以货币形式支付的还是以实物形式支付的，均应列入工资总额的计算范围。

平均工资 指单位就业人员在一定时期内平均每人所得的工资额。计算公式为：

$$\text{平均工资}=\frac{\text{报告期就业人员工资总额}}{\text{报告期就业人员平均人数}}$$

平均名义工资指数 指报告期就业人员平均工资与基期就业人员平均工资的比率，是反映不同时期就业人员名义工资水平变动情况的相对数。计算公式为：

$$\text{平均名义工资指数}=\frac{\text{报告期就业人员平均工资}}{\text{基期就业人员平均工资}}\times100\%$$

平均实际工资指数 就业人员平均实际工资指扣除物价变动因素后的就业人员平均工资。就业人员平均实际工资指数是反映实际工资变动情况的相对数，表明就业人员实际工资水平提高或降低的程度。计算公式为:

$$\text{平均实际工资指数}=\frac{\text{报告期就业人员平均工资指数}}{\text{报告期城市居民消费价格指数}}\times100\%$$

城镇登记失业人员 劳动年龄（年满16周岁（含）至依法享受基本养老保险待遇）内，有劳动能力，有就业要求，处于无业状态，并在公共就业和人才服务机构进行失业登记的城镇常住人员。

城镇调查失业率 指城镇失业人口占城镇就业人口与失业人口之和的百分比，根据劳动力调查数据计算。

Explanatory Notes on Main Statistical Indicators

Labour Force refers to the population aged 16 and over who are capable of working, are participating in or willing to participate in economic activities, including employed persons and unemployed persons.

Employed Persons refer to persons, aged 16 and over, who performed some work for compensation or business gains for one hour or more during the reference period; or persons who do not work for the reasons of study or on holiday; or persons who are temporarily absent from a job for disorganization or suspension of work, etc.

Persons Employed in Various Units refer to the total number of employees who work at his unit on the last day and obtain wages or other forms of payment at the end of the reporting period. This indicator is a kind of time point index and it equals to the sum of the number of employed staff and workers, labor dispatch personnel and other employed persons, excluding those who have terminated labor contracts with working unit on or before the last day of the reporting period. Employed persons do not include:

1)persons who have left their working units while keeping their labour contract (employment relation) unchanged and receiving regular alimony;

2)all kinds of enrolled students who do internship in various units.

Employed Staff and Workers refer to persons who signed labor contracts with working units and working units would pay wages, social insurance and housing funds for them. Persons who have their work posts but are temporarily absent from work for reasons of study or on sick, injury or maternal leave and still receive wages from their working units are also included. Employed staff and workers also include:

1)Persons who should have signed the labor contracts but not;

2)Employees on probation;

3)Employees beyond the staffing quota, for example, temporary employees;

4)Employees who are sent to other working units but still obtain wages from their original units (situations like on-the-job placement, expatriated assignment, etc.)

Total Wage Bill It is revised according to the "Provision of Composition of Total Wages" (Order No.1 by National Bureau of Statistics on January, 1st, ,1990), total wage bill refers to the total remuneration payment to all employed persons in various units during the reporting period (by quarter or by year), including hourly-paid wages, piece-rate wages, bonuses, allowance and subsidies, overtime wages and wages paid under special circumstances.

Total wage bill is pre-tax wages, including the room charges, utility bills, housing funds and social insurance paid or withheld by employee's units.

Total wage bill, whether or not included in cost, whether or not paid in money or in kind, shall be included in the calculation of total wage.

Average Wage refers to the average per capita wage during a certain period of time for employed persons. It is calculated as follows:

$$\text{Average Wage} = \frac{\text{Total wage bill of employed persons at reference time}}{\text{Average number of persons employed at reference time}}$$

Average Nominal Wage Indices refers to the ratio of average wage of employed persons at the reporting period to that at the base period, which reflects the change of money wage of employed persons at the different period. It is calculated as follows:

$$\text{Average Nominal wage indices} = \frac{\text{Average wage of employed persons at reference time}}{\text{Average wage of persons employeds at base period}} \times 100\%$$

Average Real Wage Indices average real wage of employed persons refers to the average wage of employed persons after removing the effects of the price changes and average real wage indices of employed persons refers to the change of real wage, which reflects the relative increasing or decreasing level of real wage of employed persons ,which is calculated as follows:

$$\text{Average real wage indices} = \frac{\text{Average wage indices of employed persons at the reference time}}{\text{City consumer price indices at reference time}} \times 100\%$$

Registered Unemployed Persons in Urban Areas refer to the persons residing in urban areas at certain working ages (16 years old to the age of enjoying primary endowment insurance benefits according to the law), who are capable of working, unemployed and willing to work, and have been registered at the public employment and talent service agencies to apply for a job.

Surveyed Unemployment Rate in Urban Areas refers to the ratio of the number of the unemployed persons in urban areas to the sum of the number of the employed persons and the unemployed persons in urban areas, calculated on the basis of the Labour Force Survey.

5

价　格

Prices

简要说明

一、本篇资料的主要内容

本篇价格指数资料，反映生产、流通、消费等环节的价格变动趋势和变动幅度。主要包括居民消费价格指数、农产品生产者价格指数、工业生产者出厂价格指数、工业生产者购进价格指数、进出口商品价格指数等。

二、本篇的资料来源

除进出口商品价格指数以外的价格指数编制由国家统计局城市社会经济调查司和农村社会经济调查司组织实施。由各省、自治区、直辖市及抽选出的市、县调查队依据国家统计局统一制定的价格统计调查制度从基层采集原始数据汇总后上报。进出口商品价格指数统计资料由海关总署提供。

三、居民消费价格指数

编制居民消费价格指数的资料采用抽样调查的方法取得，即在全国选择不同经济区域和分布合理的地区，以及有代表性的商品（服务）作为样本，对其市场价格进行定期调查，以样本推断总体。目前，参加国家级数据汇总的调查市、县近500个。编制过程按下列几个步骤进行：

1.选择调查地区和调查点。调查地区按照经济区域和地区分布合理等原则，选出具有代表性的大、中、小城市和县作为国家的调查地区，在此基础上选定经营规模大、商品种类多的商场(店)、超市、农贸市场、服务网点和互联网电商等作为调查点。

2.选择代表规格品。代表规格品是选择那些消费量大、价格变动有代表性的商品（服务）；代表规格品的确定是根据城乡居民的消费支出记账资料，按照有关规定筛选的。筛选原则：(1)与社会生产和人民生活关系密切；(2)消费(销售)数量(金额)大；(3)市场供应稳定；(4)价格变动趋势有代表性；(5)所选的代表规格品之间性质差异大，价格变动特征的相关性低。

目前，居民消费价格调查按用途划分为8个大类，268个基本分类。

3.价格调查方式。通过手持数据采集器，采用定人、定点、定时的方法直接调查，选中的调查对象应协助做好价格数据填报工作。在保证价格准确的前提下，经国家统计局审定，各地可通过相关政府部门发布的通知、公告等文件，以及部分企业、单位公开发布的收费信息资料和被调查单位的电子数据进行采价，也可从互联网采集特定商品和服务价格。

4.权数的确定。居民消费价格指数的权数主要根据城乡居民家庭消费支出构成确定。

四、工业生产者出厂价格指数

工业生产者出厂价格是工业品第一次出售时的出厂价格。该项调查采用重点调查与典型调查相结合的调查方法。重点调查对象为年主营业务收入2000万元及以上的工业法人企业；典型调查对象为年主营业务收入2000万元以下的工业法人企业。

1.选择代表企业的原则：(1)按工业行业选择调查企业；(2)大型企业应尽量都选上(或占相当大比重)；(3)选择生产正常、稳定的企业作为调查对象。

2.选择代表产品的原则：(1)按工业行业选择代表产品；(2)选择对国计民生影响大的产品；(3)选择生产较为稳定的产品；(4)选择有发展前景的产品；(5)选择具有地方特色的产品。

目前《工业生产者出厂价格调查目录》包括20000多种产品，并将其划分为1300多个基本分类。

3.价格调查方式。每月4万多家工业企业通过联网直报上报数据资料。

4.权数的确定。工业生产者出厂价格统计中，工业小类及小类以上的权数资料来源于工业统计中分行业工业销售产值数据资料；基本分类的权数资料来源于独立的工业企业产品权数调查。

五、农产品生产者价格指数

农产品生产者价格是农产品生产者直接出售其产品时实际获得的单位产品价格。农产品生产者价格调查采用抽样调查和重点调查相结合的方法。内容包括被调查单位生产并出售的主要农产品。农产品代表产品的选择涵盖农、林、牧、渔四大类、各中类以及90%以上的小类，共180种代表品。一般是生产量和销售量大的对国计民生影响大、稳定性强的产品，具有发展前景的新产品和具有地方特色的产品。代表品一般稳定五年。调查周期为季度。农产品生产者价格指数的权数主要来源于农村住户和农场的农产品出售金额资料，也可结合农产品产值、产量等资料进行推算。

六、进出口商品价格指数

进出口商品价格指数是反映一定时期内进出口商品价格变动趋势及幅度的统计指标。采用“单位价值法”编制，计算指数的资料全部来自中国海关的进出口货物贸易统计。计量单位按人民币计价，进口价格指数的计算按到岸价格（CIF）计算，出口价格指数的计算按离岸价格（FOB）计算。

Brief Introduction

I. Main Contents

Data on price indices in this chapter show the trends and rates of changes in the prices of production, distribution and consumption, including mainly consumer price indices, producer price indices for farm products, producer price indices for industrial products, purchasing price indices for industrial producers and price indices for imports and exports.

II. Sources of Data

Compilation of statistics on price indices is organized by the Department of Urban Social and Economic Surveys and the Department of Rural Social and Economic Surveys of NBS. The social and economic survey organizations of provinces, autonomous regions and municipalities directly under the Central Government and of the selected cities and counties collect data from the grassroots units in accordance with the scheme of price survey system stipulated by the NBS, tabulate them and report them to agencies at higher levels. Statistics on price for imports and exports are provided by the General Administration of Customs.

III. Consumer Price Indices and Retail Price Indices

Data for compilation of the consumer price indices in China are collected through sample surveys. Areas distributed in different economic regions are selected as the sample areas and representative goods or services are selected as the sample commodities. Regular surveys are conducted to collect data on their market prices. Price statistics are estimated on the basis of the results from the samples. At present, nearly 500 cities and counties have been selected for this purpose. Following are major steps in the process of calculation of the price indices:

(1) The selection of areas and outlets: Based on such principles as regional economic features and reasonable geographic distribution, representative sample areas for the national survey are selected which include large, medium and small cities and counties. When the sample areas have been selected, shopping malls (stores), supermarkets, farmers' markets, service outlets and Internet e-commerce with large operation scale and various commodity types are selected as outlets for the survey.

(2) The selection of representative commodities and their specifications or varieties: The representative specifications are to choose those goods or services that have large consumption and representative price changes. The representative specifications or varieties are determined based on the consumption expenditure account data of urban and rural residents. The principles for selection are: (a) The commodities are closely related to social production and people's living conditions; (b) They are consumes (or sold) in large quantities (or large values); (c) The market supply is stable; (d) The changes of their prices are representative in trend; (e) There is great heterogeneity among the specifications or varieties selected, and the correlation of price changes is low.

At present, data are collected under 268 basic headings in 8 categories in the consumer price surveys.

(3) Method of data collection: Through hand-held data capturing device, direct investigation is conducted by the method of fixed data collector, fixed outlet and fixed timing, the selected respondents should assist in filling in the price data. On the premise of ensuring accurate prices and with the approval by the NBS, local governments can collect prices of specific goods and services from the Internet through announcements and other documents issued by relevant government departments, as well as publicly published fee-collecting information of some enterprises and units, and electronic data of the units under investigation.

(4) Determination of the weights: The weights of the consumer price indices are determined according to the composition of the consumption expenditures of urban and rural households.

IV. Producer Price Indices for Industrial Products

Producer price for industrial products refer to the ex-factory price of manufactured goods when they are first sold. The survey covers both key industrial enterprises with annual revenue from the primary activities at and above 20 million yuan, and typical industrial enterprises with annual revenue from the primary activities below 20 million yuan.

(1) Principles for selecting the representative enterprises: (a) Enterprises to be covered in the survey are selected by industrial sectors; (b) All (or a majority of) large-scaled enterprises should be selected; (c) Enterprises selected should be those with normal and stable production.

(2) Principle for the selection of representative products:

(a) Products are selected by industrial sectors; (b) The selected products should have great impact on the national economy and people's living conditions; (c) The production of the products selected are relatively more stable; (d) The prospects of the products selected are promising; (e) The products selected are representative to the localities.

The *Survey Catalog of Producer Price for Industrial*

Products includes over 20,000 products under more than 1300 basic headings.

(3) Method of data collection: There are more than 40,000 industrial enterprises reporting their data through online direct reporting.

(4) Determination of the weights: In statistics of producer price indices for industrial products, the weights of small groups and above of industrial classification come from the output value of industrial sales by sector in industrial statistics; the weights of basic headings come from independent weights surveys of industrial products.

V. Producer Prices Indices for Agricultural Products

Producer prices indices for agricultural products refer to the actual price per unit through directly selling their products by producers of farm products. The survey program of producer prices indices for agricultural products is a combined use of sampling survey and survey of typical units'. It covers main farm products produced and sold by the units surveyed. Representative farm products covered about 90% of small groups of all major groups in 4 branches of agriculture, forestry, animal husbandry and fishery, with a total of 180 representative products. The products are generally with large production and sales, having great impact on the national economy and people's living conditions, with strong stability, with promising to new products and with local characters. Representative products are in the sample for 5 years. The survey is conducted quarterly. The weight of producer prices indices for agricultural products mainly comes from the information on the sales amount of agricultural products by rural households and farms, and can also be calculated based on information such as agricultural product output value and yield.

VI. Price Indices for Imports and Exports

Price indices for imports and exports reflect trend and degree of price changes in import and export of commodity over a given period of time. They are compiled with the unit value method on the basis of statistics of imports and exports of goods of the China Customs. With Renminbi as the unit of measurements, import price index is computed at CIF prices and export price index is computed at FOB prices.

5-1 各种价格指数
Price Indices

(上年=100) (preceding year=100)

年 份 Year	居民消费价格指数 Consumer Price Index	城市居民消费价格指数 Urban	农村居民消费价格指数 Rural	农产品生产者价格指数 Producer Price Index for Agriculture Products	工业生产者出厂价格指数 Producer Price Index for Industrial Products	工业生产者购进价格指数 Purchasing Price Index for Industrial Producers
1978	100.7	100.7		103.9	100.1	
1980	107.5	107.5		107.1	100.5	
1985	109.3	111.9	107.6	108.6	108.7	
1990	103.1	101.3	104.5	97.4	104.1	105.6
1995	117.1	116.8	117.5	119.9	114.9	115.3
1996	108.3	108.8	107.9	104.2	102.9	103.9
1997	102.8	103.1	102.5	95.5	99.7	101.3
1998	99.2	99.4	99.0	92.0	95.9	95.8
1999	98.6	98.7	98.5	87.8	97.6	96.7
2000	100.4	100.8	99.9	96.4	102.8	105.1
2001	100.7	100.7	100.8	103.1	98.7	99.8
2002	99.2	99.0	99.6	99.7	97.8	97.7
2003	101.2	100.9	101.6	104.4	102.3	104.8
2004	103.9	103.3	104.8	113.1	106.1	111.4
2005	101.8	101.6	102.2	101.4	104.9	108.3
2006	101.5	101.5	101.5	101.2	103.0	106.0
2007	104.8	104.5	105.4	118.5	103.1	104.4
2008	105.9	105.6	106.5	114.1	106.9	110.5
2009	99.3	99.1	99.7	97.6	94.6	92.1
2010	103.3	103.2	103.6	110.9	105.5	109.6
2011	105.4	105.3	105.8	116.5	106.0	109.1
2012	102.6	102.7	102.5	102.7	98.3	98.2
2013	102.6	102.6	102.8	103.2	98.1	98.0
2014	102.0	102.1	101.8	99.8	98.1	97.8
2015	101.4	101.5	101.3	101.7	94.8	93.9
2016	102.0	102.1	101.9	103.4	98.6	98.0
2017	101.6	101.7	101.3	96.5	106.3	108.1
2018	102.1	102.1	102.1	99.1	103.5	104.1
2019	102.9	102.8	103.2	114.5	99.7	99.3
2020	102.5	102.3	103.0	115.0	98.2	97.7
2021	100.9	101.0	100.7	97.8	108.1	111.0
2022	102.0	102.0	102.0	100.4	104.1	106.1
2023	100.2	100.3	100.1	97.7	97.0	96.4

注：从2011年起工业品出厂价格指数改为工业生产者出厂价格指数，原材料、燃料、动力购进价格指数改为工业生产者购进价格指数(以下相关表同)。

a) Since 2011, the producer price index for manufactured good has been replaced by the producer price index for industrial products, and the purchasing price index for raw materials, fuel and power has been replaced by the purchasing price index for industrial producers. The same applies to the relevant following tables.

5-2 各种价格定基指数
Fixed-base Price Indices

年 份 Year	居民消费价格指数 Consumer Price Index (1978年=100) (year of 1978=100)	城市居民消费价格指数 Urban (1978年=100) (year of 1978=100)	农村居民消费价格指数 Rural (1985年=100) (year of 1985=100)	农产品生产者价格指数 Producer Price Index for Agriculture Products (1978年=100) (year of 1978=100)	工业生产者出厂价格指数 Producer Price Index for Industrial Products (1985年=100) (year of 1985=100)	工业生产者购进价格指数 Purchasing Price Index for Industrial Producers (1990年=100) (year of 1990=100)
1978	100.0	100.0		100.0		
1980	109.5	109.5		130.8		
1985	131.1	134.2	100.0	166.9	100.0	
1990	216.4	222.0	165.1	274.0	159.0	100.0
1995	396.9	429.6	291.4	528.1	307.1	222.9
1996	429.9	467.4	314.4	550.3	316.0	231.6
1997	441.9	481.9	322.3	525.5	315.0	234.6
1998	438.4	479.0	319.1	483.5	302.1	224.7
1999	432.2	472.8	314.3	424.5	294.8	217.3
2000	434.0	476.6	314.0	409.2	303.1	228.4
2001	437.0	479.9	316.5	421.9	299.2	227.9
2002	433.5	475.1	315.2	420.6	292.6	222.7
2003	438.7	479.4	320.2	439.0	299.3	233.4
2004	455.8	495.2	335.6	496.5	317.6	260.0
2005	464.0	503.1	343.0	503.4	333.2	281.6
2006	471.0	510.6	348.1	509.4	343.2	298.5
2007	493.6	533.6	366.9	603.6	353.8	311.6
2008	522.7	563.5	390.7	688.5	378.2	344.3
2009	519.0	558.4	389.5	672.0	357.8	317.2
2010	536.1	576.3	403.5	745.5	377.5	347.7
2011	565.0	606.8	426.9	868.2	400.2	379.3
2012	579.7	623.2	437.6	892.0	393.4	372.5
2013	594.8	639.4	449.9	920.7	385.9	365.1
2014	606.7	652.8	458.0	919.2	378.6	357.1
2015	615.2	662.6	464.0	934.5	358.9	335.3
2016	627.5	676.5	472.8	966.4	353.9	328.6
2017	637.5	688.0	478.9	932.3	376.2	355.2
2018	650.9	702.4	489.0	923.6	389.4	369.8
2019	669.8	722.1	504.6	1057.6	388.2	367.2
2020	686.5	738.7	519.7	1216.4	381.2	358.8
2021	692.7	746.1	523.3	1189.6	412.1	398.3
2022	706.6	761.0	533.8	1193.8	429.0	422.6
2023	708.0	763.3	534.3	1166.5	416.1	407.4

5-3 居民消费价格分类指数(2023年)
Consumer Price Indices by Category (2023)

(上年=100) (preceding year=100)

项目名称	Item	全国 National Indices	城市 Urban Indices	农村 Rural Indices
居民消费价格总指数	**Consumer Price Index**	**100.2**	**100.3**	**100.1**
食品烟酒	**Food, Tobacco and Alcohol**	**100.3**	**100.4**	**100.1**
食品	Food	99.7	99.7	99.6
粮食	Grain	101.0	101.0	101.1
薯类	Tubers	105.5	105.0	106.9
豆类	Beans	101.1	101.1	101.1
食用油	Edible Oil and Fats	100.7	100.8	100.4
菜及食用菌	Vegetables and Edible Mushrooms	98.0	97.8	98.4
#鲜菜	Fresh Vegetables	97.4	97.3	97.9
畜肉类	Meat of Livestock	92.7	93.0	91.8
禽肉类	Meat of Poultry	103.1	103.1	103.3
水产品	Aquatic Products	100.0	99.8	100.6
蛋类	Eggs	100.3	100.1	101.0
奶类	Milk and Other Dairy Products	100.4	100.4	100.3
干鲜瓜果类	Fruits and Nuts	104.5	104.4	104.8
#鲜果	Fresh Fruits	104.9	104.8	105.4
糖果糕点类	Candy and Cake	101.8	101.9	101.5
调味品	Flavoring	101.3	101.2	101.3
其他食品类	Other Foods	101.4	101.5	101.2
茶及饮料	Tea and Beverages	101.3	101.4	101.1
烟酒	Tobacco and Alcohol	101.0	101.0	101.0
在外餐饮	Dining Out	101.8	101.8	101.6
衣着	**Clothing and Footwear**	**101.0**	**101.1**	**100.6**
服装	Garments	101.0	101.1	100.7
鞋类	Footwear	100.7	100.8	100.3
居住	**Housing**	**100.0**	**100.0**	**100.0**
租赁房房租	Rent of Rental Housing	99.8	99.8	99.7
住房保养维修及管理	Housing Maintenance and Management	100.5	100.5	100.6
水电燃料	Water, Electricity and Fuels	100.2	100.3	100.1

5–3 续表 continued

(上年=100) (preceding year=100)

项目名称	Item	全国 National Indices	城市 Urban Indices	农村 Rural Indices
生活用品及服务	**Household Equipments, Furnishings and Services**	**100.1**	**100.1**	**99.9**
家具及室内装饰品	Furniture and Interior Decorations	100.2	100.2	100.1
家用器具	Home Appliances	98.9	98.9	98.8
家用纺织品	Home Textiles	99.7	99.7	99.6
家庭日用杂品	Household Articles for Daily Use	100.2	100.2	100.0
个人护理用品	Personal-care Supplies	100.7	100.7	100.7
家庭服务	Household Services	101.7	101.8	101.5
交通通信	**Transport and Communications**	**97.7**	**97.7**	**97.6**
交通	Transport	97.3	97.4	97.1
交通工具	Transport Facility	96.0	95.8	96.5
交通工具用燃料	Fuels for Transport Facility	94.6	94.6	94.5
交通工具使用和维修	Use and Maintenance of Transport Facility	100.7	100.7	100.9
交通费	Traffic Fee	104.0	104.3	102.6
通信	Communications	99.1	99.0	99.2
教育文化娱乐	**Education, Culture and Recreation**	**102.0**	**102.1**	**101.5**
教育	Education	101.4	101.3	101.6
教育用品	Education Articles	101.7	101.7	101.8
教育服务	Education Services	101.4	101.3	101.6
文化娱乐	Culture and Recreation	103.0	103.2	101.5
文娱耐用消费品	Durable Consumer Goods for Culture and Recreation	98.1	98.1	98.2
其他文娱用品	Other Articles of Culture and Recreation	100.3	100.3	100.4
文化娱乐服务	Cultural and Recreational Services	101.0	101.0	100.8
旅游	Touring	109.0	109.1	108.0
医疗保健	**Health Care and Medical Services**	**101.1**	**101.1**	**101.3**
药品及医疗器具	Medicine and Medical Instruments	101.3	101.2	101.7
医疗服务	Medical Services	101.1	101.0	101.1
其他用品及服务	**Other Articles and Services**	**103.2**	**103.4**	**102.5**
其他用品	Other Articles	104.6	104.8	103.6
其他服务	Other Services	101.9	102.1	101.1

5–4 居民消费价格指数
Consumer Price Indices

(上年=100) (preceding year=100)

年 份 Year / 地 区 Region	总指数 General	城 市 Urban	农 村 Rural
1994	124.1	125.0	123.4
1995	117.1	116.8	117.5
2000	100.4	100.8	99.9
2005	101.8	101.6	102.2
2006	101.5	101.5	101.5
2007	104.8	104.5	105.4
2008	105.9	105.6	106.5
2009	99.3	99.1	99.7
2010	103.3	103.2	103.6
2011	105.4	105.3	105.8
2012	102.6	102.7	102.5
2013	102.6	102.6	102.8
2014	102.0	102.1	101.8
2015	101.4	101.5	101.3
2016	102.0	102.1	101.9
2017	101.6	101.7	101.3
2018	102.1	102.1	102.1
2019	102.9	102.8	103.2
2020	102.5	102.3	103.0
2021	100.9	101.0	100.7
2022	102.0	102.0	102.0
2023	100.2	100.3	100.1
北 京 Beijing	100.4	100.4	
天 津 Tianjin	100.4	100.4	
河 北 Hebei	100.6	100.7	100.4
山 西 Shanxi	99.9	99.9	99.9
内蒙古 Inner Mongolia	100.6	100.6	100.6
辽 宁 Liaoning	100.1	100.2	99.8
吉 林 Jilin	99.9	100.0	99.5
黑龙江 Heilongjiang	100.6	100.7	100.5
上 海 Shanghai	100.3	100.3	
江 苏 Jiangsu	100.4	100.5	100.3
浙 江 Zhejiang	100.3	100.3	100.3
安 徽 Anhui	100.2	100.1	100.5
福 建 Fujian	100.0	100.1	100.0
江 西 Jiangxi	100.3	100.4	100.2
山 东 Shandong	100.1	100.2	99.8
河 南 Henan	99.8	99.6	100.2
湖 北 Hubei	100.1	100.2	99.9
湖 南 Hunan	100.2	100.3	99.9
广 东 Guangdong	100.4	100.6	99.6
广 西 Guangxi	99.8	99.7	100.0
海 南 Hainan	100.3	100.3	100.4
重 庆 Chongqing	99.7	99.7	
四 川 Sichuan	100.0	100.1	99.9
贵 州 Guizhou	99.7	99.7	99.6
云 南 Yunnan	100.3	100.5	99.9
西 藏 Xizang	99.9	100.2	99.5
陕 西 Shaanxi	100.1	100.1	100.2
甘 肃 Gansu	100.5	100.5	100.5
青 海 Qinghai	100.5	100.4	100.7
宁 夏 Ningxia	100.4	100.5	100.1
新 疆 Xinjiang	100.0	100.0	99.8

5-5 分地区居民消费价格分类指数(2023年)
Consumer Price Indices by Category and by Region (2023)

(上年=100) (preceding year=100)

地 区	Region	总指数 General Index	食品烟酒 Food, Tobacco and Alcohol	食品 Food	粮食 Grain	薯类 Tubers	豆类 Beans	食用油 Edible Oil and Fats	菜及食用菌 Vegetables and Edible Fungi	#鲜菜 Fresh Vegetables
全 国	**National Average**	**100.2**	**100.3**	**99.7**	**101.0**	**105.5**	**101.1**	**100.7**	**98.0**	**97.4**
北 京	Beijing	100.4	100.1	99.0	99.6	99.9	100.2	101.3	94.0	93.1
天 津	Tianjin	100.4	100.5	99.8	100.1	111.6	102.1	101.5	97.4	96.9
河 北	Hebei	100.6	100.5	100.1	101.4	105.3	101.7	100.6	97.3	96.4
山 西	Shanxi	99.9	99.8	99.2	100.0	104.0	102.2	100.2	95.2	94.5
内蒙古	Inner Mongolia	100.6	100.6	100.1	102.2	107.8	100.1	101.4	97.0	96.5
辽 宁	Liaoning	100.1	100.1	99.6	100.8	102.8	101.1	100.7	94.3	92.7
吉 林	Jilin	99.9	99.3	98.7	100.4	101.5	100.3	98.2	93.7	92.3
黑龙江	Heilongjiang	100.6	100.6	100.4	102.0	104.7	101.5	99.8	97.0	96.1
上 海	Shanghai	100.3	98.8	97.0	98.5	101.2	100.0	102.7	94.6	94.0
江 苏	Jiangsu	100.4	101.0	100.5	101.8	99.5	102.0	102.1	99.5	99.2
浙 江	Zhejiang	100.3	100.6	100.3	101.2	103.9	101.7	101.0	99.1	98.8
安 徽	Anhui	100.2	100.5	99.4	100.7	106.2	101.3	101.1	96.6	95.8
福 建	Fujian	100.0	100.9	100.9	100.9	103.8	101.4	99.7	100.5	100.0
江 西	Jiangxi	100.3	100.4	99.9	101.4	109.7	101.0	100.9	99.6	99.3
山 东	Shandong	100.1	100.3	99.6	101.7	103.6	100.8	99.1	97.2	96.8
河 南	Henan	99.8	99.6	99.0	101.2	107.3	101.5	100.7	96.7	95.8
湖 北	Hubei	100.1	99.9	99.1	101.2	107.2	100.6	102.9	97.9	97.4
湖 南	Hunan	100.2	99.4	98.7	100.5	107.1	101.5	101.0	97.9	97.3
广 东	Guangdong	100.4	101.4	100.7	100.3	105.3	99.8	100.9	99.8	99.6
广 西	Guangxi	99.8	100.0	99.3	100.6	105.7	99.9	99.9	98.7	98.2
海 南	Hainan	100.3	101.3	101.0	100.6	105.4	102.1	101.3	101.6	101.5
重 庆	Chongqing	99.7	98.6	97.5	101.1	101.1	99.3	98.9	95.0	94.0
四 川	Sichuan	100.0	99.8	99.1	100.7	109.6	101.1	101.0	99.4	98.9
贵 州	Guizhou	99.7	99.8	99.4	100.8	106.5	99.5	99.9	101.1	100.6
云 南	Yunnan	100.3	100.9	100.4	100.9	110.5	101.5	98.2	103.2	103.5
西 藏	Xizang	99.9	99.9	99.4	101.1	104.0	99.5	101.1	95.8	95.7
陕 西	Shaanxi	100.1	99.8	99.1	100.9	102.9	100.9	100.6	96.5	95.8
甘 肃	Gansu	100.5	100.3	100.1	102.6	110.0	102.1	101.6	96.7	96.3
青 海	Qinghai	100.5	99.4	98.0	101.9	101.8	101.9	102.2	94.6	94.1
宁 夏	Ningxia	100.4	100.3	100.0	101.1	107.3	99.4	99.5	98.4	98.3
新 疆	Xinjiang	100.0	99.6	98.7	104.0	101.6	102.2	100.5	96.7	96.0

5-5 续表 1 continued

(上年=100) (preceding year=100)

地区	Region	畜肉类 Meat of Livestock	禽肉类 Meat of Poultry	水产品 Aquatic Products	蛋类 Eggs	奶类 Milk and Other Dairy Products	干鲜瓜果类 Fruits and Nuts	#鲜果 Fresh Fruits	糖果糕点类 Candy and Cake	调味品 Flavoring	其他食品类 Other Foods
全国	**National Average**	**92.7**	**103.1**	**100.0**	**100.3**	**100.4**	**104.5**	**104.9**	**101.8**	**101.3**	**101.4**
北京	Beijing	93.5	101.4	100.6	99.8	98.3	104.1	104.0	103.4	101.2	100.5
天津	Tianjin	93.3	101.8	102.5	99.7	98.6	103.6	104.3	101.7	101.7	101.0
河北	Hebei	93.0	102.8	99.4	100.6	100.3	105.6	105.8	101.2	100.8	102.2
山西	Shanxi	94.4	104.1	97.8	99.3	99.6	102.4	102.3	101.5	101.6	102.0
内蒙古	Inner Mongolia	94.1	103.2	100.3	99.4	101.0	105.7	106.3	102.0	102.0	102.7
辽宁	Liaoning	93.3	101.7	100.9	99.4	100.2	105.8	106.5	100.9	100.7	101.4
吉林	Jilin	90.2	100.2	100.2	98.0	101.3	105.4	105.4	102.4	101.3	104.3
黑龙江	Heilongjiang	92.7	102.2	103.2	100.4	99.1	107.7	108.5	101.8	99.8	101.3
上海	Shanghai	91.6	104.3	96.2	93.7	97.5	98.4	97.5	101.6	101.2	98.5
江苏	Jiangsu	94.8	104.1	100.2	100.7	101.0	105.1	105.6	102.6	102.7	103.3
浙江	Zhejiang	93.8	104.9	100.5	102.0	101.6	103.5	103.6	101.4	102.4	101.5
安徽	Anhui	92.4	104.6	98.0	99.6	99.7	105.6	106.2	101.7	102.1	100.9
福建	Fujian	94.0	105.0	101.8	100.3	101.9	105.7	106.8	102.6	102.3	101.4
江西	Jiangxi	90.8	106.0	98.4	103.0	100.9	107.6	108.8	99.1	101.3	100.8
山东	Shandong	93.2	101.9	101.6	100.4	100.7	103.1	103.6	102.3	100.8	100.9
河南	Henan	89.9	102.2	98.3	97.7	99.1	106.1	106.6	102.4	99.9	101.3
湖北	Hubei	90.9	103.7	97.1	102.9	101.1	103.8	104.1	101.1	102.2	101.4
湖南	Hunan	90.5	103.0	97.2	101.7	100.2	104.1	104.6	101.6	102.8	101.3
广东	Guangdong	94.7	102.7	101.4	103.0	103.0	105.0	105.7	101.5	101.2	100.8
广西	Guangxi	91.6	102.0	100.9	101.6	97.9	103.0	103.2	101.4	101.1	99.6
海南	Hainan	92.1	102.7	106.1	105.4	100.9	103.5	103.9	101.7	100.2	102.8
重庆	Chongqing	90.0	103.7	95.8	96.7	101.1	101.7	101.4	100.7	100.6	101.2
四川	Sichuan	91.3	102.8	97.8	102.2	100.1	103.1	103.2	101.8	100.5	101.0
贵州	Guizhou	92.5	102.1	98.0	102.7	99.6	102.7	103.0	101.4	100.8	100.3
云南	Yunnan	94.2	102.4	99.5	100.6	99.0	103.7	103.8	102.1	101.4	101.7
西藏	Xizang	98.0	99.7	100.2	110.7	101.1	100.6	101.3	101.4	102.1	101.1
陕西	Shaanxi	92.4	100.2	93.4	98.0	99.1	104.7	105.7	102.9	100.2	101.6
甘肃	Gansu	92.4	102.3	96.0	99.4	99.6	106.7	107.7	102.9	101.6	101.8
青海	Qinghai	91.3	100.1	95.7	99.1	100.5	103.6	104.1	102.8	101.1	100.8
宁夏	Ningxia	93.4	101.6	98.3	104.9	99.3	107.5	109.3	100.8	100.1	100.3
新疆	Xinjiang	92.1	98.9	95.7	99.1	99.0	105.7	107.5	101.8	101.4	101.5

5-5 续表 2 continued

(上年=100) (preceding year=100)

地区	Region	茶及饮料 Tea and Beverages	烟酒 Tobacco and Alcohol	在外餐饮 Dining Out	衣着 Clothing and Footwear	服装 Garments	鞋类 Footwear
全国	**National Average**	**101.3**	**101.0**	**101.8**	**101.0**	**101.0**	**100.7**
北京	Beijing	102.3	102.3	101.7	100.6	100.8	100.0
天津	Tianjin	99.6	100.8	101.9	101.0	100.8	101.4
河北	Hebei	101.2	101.1	101.5	102.3	102.4	102.0
山西	Shanxi	101.2	101.1	101.1	100.3	100.0	101.8
内蒙古	Inner Mongolia	101.7	101.6	101.7	101.2	101.3	100.7
辽宁	Liaoning	99.4	101.2	101.6	100.5	100.6	100.4
吉林	Jilin	103.0	101.1	100.5	100.1	100.4	99.1
黑龙江	Heilongjiang	102.1	100.5	101.2	101.7	101.5	102.6
上海	Shanghai	102.3	101.7	102.2	102.0	102.3	100.9
江苏	Jiangsu	102.0	102.3	101.5	101.4	101.3	101.8
浙江	Zhejiang	101.5	100.5	101.5	101.0	100.9	101.3
安徽	Anhui	106.0	101.3	103.0	101.6	101.8	100.8
福建	Fujian	101.2	100.5	101.2	100.0	100.2	98.8
江西	Jiangxi	100.1	100.9	101.7	101.9	102.0	101.0
山东	Shandong	101.2	101.4	101.7	100.6	100.8	99.9
河南	Henan	100.0	101.1	101.0	99.8	100.0	99.1
湖北	Hubei	100.0	100.3	102.0	101.3	101.2	101.8
湖南	Hunan	100.6	100.9	100.8	101.0	101.0	100.9
广东	Guangdong	100.7	100.8	102.8	101.8	101.9	101.0
广西	Guangxi	100.9	100.5	101.4	102.1	102.2	101.3
海南	Hainan	101.0	100.8	102.1	99.8	99.9	99.5
重庆	Chongqing	102.2	101.1	100.1	101.0	100.9	101.4
四川	Sichuan	102.9	100.0	101.4	99.0	99.1	98.7
贵州	Guizhou	99.9	100.1	100.7	102.0	101.8	102.8
云南	Yunnan	100.3	101.8	101.9	100.5	100.5	100.2
西藏	Xizang	99.9	100.2	102.3	100.1	100.4	99.5
陕西	Shaanxi	100.9	100.7	101.0	100.4	100.6	99.3
甘肃	Gansu	102.3	101.0	100.4	100.2	100.6	98.6
青海	Qinghai	100.7	100.8	102.8	100.5	100.4	101.1
宁夏	Ningxia	101.7	101.1	100.8	100.5	100.5	100.5
新疆	Xinjiang	102.2	100.8	101.9	102.5	102.6	102.0

5-5 续表 3 continued

(上年=100) (preceding year=100)

地 区	Region	居住 Housing	租赁房房租 Rent of Rental Housing	住房保养维修及管理 Housing Maintenance and Management	水电燃料 Water, Electricity and Fuels	生活用品及服务 Household Equipments, Furnishings and Services	家具及室内装饰品 Furniture and Interior Decorations	家用器具 Home Appliances	家用纺织品 Home Textiles
全 国	**National Average**	**100.0**	**99.8**	**100.5**	**100.2**	**100.1**	**100.2**	**98.9**	**99.7**
北 京	Beijing	100.3	100.3	101.1	100.0	100.3	99.8	99.9	100.3
天 津	Tianjin	100.5	101.4	99.8	100.3	100.0	99.1	99.0	98.9
河 北	Hebei	100.3	99.3	101.5	101.4	100.6	100.8	99.7	100.0
山 西	Shanxi	100.0	99.6	100.2	100.1	100.3	100.8	98.9	100.5
内蒙古	Inner Mongolia	100.1	100.5	100.2	100.3	100.5	102.1	98.9	99.7
辽 宁	Liaoning	100.4	100.5	100.6	99.9	100.2	99.9	98.5	99.6
吉 林	Jilin	100.0	100.6	99.5	99.9	100.2	100.3	99.0	100.1
黑龙江	Heilongjiang	100.1	100.2	100.2	100.2	100.3	99.8	98.9	100.3
上 海	Shanghai	100.2	100.2	101.2	99.6	100.4	101.4	99.2	101.7
江 苏	Jiangsu	100.0	99.8	100.7	100.1	100.6	102.0	98.9	100.1
浙 江	Zhejiang	99.6	99.4	100.3	100.1	100.4	100.1	99.7	100.0
安 徽	Anhui	99.7	99.4	100.2	99.7	100.1	99.8	99.6	99.8
福 建	Fujian	99.8	99.8	100.1	100.0	99.9	99.4	98.9	99.5
江 西	Jiangxi	100.1	100.0	101.3	99.3	99.8	99.9	98.8	100.2
山 东	Shandong	100.1	100.1	100.7	100.1	100.0	100.0	99.2	99.8
河 南	Henan	99.6	99.1	99.9	100.2	99.6	99.6	98.4	99.1
湖 北	Hubei	100.4	100.5	100.3	99.9	100.2	100.0	98.9	100.2
湖 南	Hunan	100.4	100.7	100.1	100.5	100.1	100.4	99.1	99.8
广 东	Guangdong	99.5	99.4	101.2	99.6	99.9	100.3	98.3	97.9
广 西	Guangxi	99.1	99.3	99.5	99.2	99.0	98.4	98.1	98.4
海 南	Hainan	99.4	99.7	100.5	98.6	100.2	98.8	100.4	97.3
重 庆	Chongqing	100.2	99.1	99.7	101.7	99.8	99.5	98.3	100.4
四 川	Sichuan	100.4	100.3	101.0	102.9	100.0	100.1	98.4	98.8
贵 州	Guizhou	99.8	99.0	99.7	101.0	100.0	100.6	98.7	100.0
云 南	Yunnan	100.3	100.6	100.1	101.0	100.2	100.1	98.7	100.6
西 藏	Xizang	100.2	100.0	101.9	100.3	100.0	100.5	98.6	99.5
陕 西	Shaanxi	100.4	100.5	99.9	101.0	99.7	100.6	98.2	99.8
甘 肃	Gansu	99.6	98.5	100.0	101.0	100.0	99.9	99.0	100.0
青 海	Qinghai	100.1	99.9	100.1	100.8	100.1	100.0	98.5	100.1
宁 夏	Ningxia	100.6	101.8	100.2	101.5	99.8	100.4	97.5	99.8
新 疆	Xinjiang	100.0	100.4	101.2	100.7	99.4	97.7	98.5	99.8

5-5 续表 4 continued

(上年=100) (preceding year=100)

地 区	Region	家庭日用杂品 Household Articles for Daily Use	个人护理用品 Personal-care Supplies	家庭服务 Household Services	交通通信 Transport and Communications	交通 Transport	交通工具 Transport Facility	交通工具用燃料 Fuels for Transport Facility	交通工具使用和维修 Use and Maintenance of Transport Facility	交通费 Traffic Fee	通信 Communications
全 国	**National Average**	**100.2**	**100.7**	**101.7**	**97.7**	**97.3**	**96.0**	**94.6**	**100.7**	**104.0**	**99.1**
北 京	Beijing	100.1	100.2	102.2	98.3	97.9	94.8	94.5	100.9	104.8	99.6
天 津	Tianjin	100.1	100.7	102.2	97.2	96.6	94.8	94.4	103.1	102.2	99.6
河 北	Hebei	100.4	101.5	102.1	97.6	97.0	96.2	94.4	101.4	103.8	99.2
山 西	Shanxi	100.2	101.3	100.5	98.0	97.8	98.2	94.5	98.7	104.3	98.6
内蒙古	Inner Mongolia	100.0	100.7	103.3	98.0	97.6	97.9	94.5	99.1	105.4	99.0
辽 宁	Liaoning	100.2	100.5	104.9	98.1	97.7	95.6	94.7	100.7	103.7	99.4
吉 林	Jilin	99.9	101.1	101.9	97.8	97.4	96.2	94.6	100.6	101.8	98.9
黑龙江	Heilongjiang	100.3	100.8	102.9	98.1	97.6	95.5	94.5	100.1	103.1	99.5
上 海	Shanghai	100.4	100.6	100.6	99.1	99.3	95.5	94.7	102.3	109.8	98.3
江 苏	Jiangsu	100.6	100.7	103.3	96.7	96.2	93.8	94.5	102.0	103.3	98.4
浙 江	Zhejiang	100.7	101.4	100.8	97.9	97.5	97.1	94.5	100.4	104.2	99.1
安 徽	Anhui	99.6	100.5	102.8	97.5	97.0	95.8	94.6	99.8	105.6	98.7
福 建	Fujian	100.0	101.0	102.0	96.7	95.8	94.1	94.5	100.2	100.0	99.2
江 西	Jiangxi	99.9	100.0	102.2	97.5	96.8	96.3	94.4	101.1	103.6	99.7
山 东	Shandong	99.7	101.0	101.4	97.7	97.2	97.0	94.2	100.3	103.6	99.3
河 南	Henan	99.6	100.8	101.5	97.9	97.2	96.9	94.5	101.3	103.1	99.6
湖 北	Hubei	100.9	100.4	103.0	97.5	97.1	96.0	94.5	100.8	104.1	99.0
湖 南	Hunan	100.2	101.0	100.6	98.0	97.6	97.7	94.5	100.9	104.4	99.5
广 东	Guangdong	100.2	100.1	101.5	97.7	97.3	95.7	94.8	100.0	103.9	99.3
广 西	Guangxi	99.4	99.8	100.6	96.9	96.9	95.0	94.5	100.2	104.4	97.0
海 南	Hainan	100.8	100.4	102.1	98.5	98.2	98.9	95.1	101.0	101.1	99.4
重 庆	Chongqing	100.9	100.2	101.4	98.8	98.9	96.7	94.6	103.6	104.8	98.4
四 川	Sichuan	100.9	101.1	101.8	97.9	97.6	95.4	94.7	100.2	106.7	98.6
贵 州	Guizhou	100.3	100.4	100.7	97.3	96.9	96.6	94.8	99.6	99.9	98.7
云 南	Yunnan	100.3	101.1	100.5	97.2	96.7	94.6	94.6	101.7	104.9	99.1
西 藏	Xizang	99.7	100.8	100.4	98.1	97.4	99.2	94.8	99.8	99.6	99.4
陕 西	Shaanxi	99.1	100.5	100.8	97.9	97.4	94.5	95.2	100.4	103.3	99.3
甘 肃	Gansu	100.1	100.9	100.6	99.2	99.0	98.8	94.5	100.1	104.9	99.5
青 海	Qinghai	100.2	100.4	102.6	99.2	99.1	94.5	96.0	100.5	111.5	99.6
宁 夏	Ningxia	99.8	101.0	100.9	98.5	98.3	97.1	95.2	99.9	105.4	98.9
新 疆	Xinjiang	99.2	100.7	101.3	98.0	97.5	97.6	95.5	100.8	98.2	100.0

5-5 续表 5 continued

(上年=100) (preceding year=100)

地 区	Region	教育文化娱乐 Education, Culture and Recreation	教育 Education	教育用品 Education Articles	教育服务 Education Services	文化娱乐 Culture and Recreation	文娱耐用消费品 Durable Consumer Goods for Culture and Recreation	其他文娱用品 Other Articles of Culture and Recreation
全 国	**National Average**	**102.0**	**101.4**	**101.7**	**101.4**	**103.0**	**98.1**	**100.3**
北 京	Beijing	102.8	100.6	100.0	100.7	104.8	98.0	100.2
天 津	Tianjin	103.1	102.3	103.4	102.3	104.1	98.3	100.2
河 北	Hebei	101.5	101.5	100.2	101.5	101.6	99.1	100.4
山 西	Shanxi	100.4	99.6	103.0	99.4	101.9	98.7	100.4
内蒙古	Inner Mongolia	101.5	101.5	102.1	101.4	101.4	99.4	100.8
辽 宁	Liaoning	101.0	100.7	100.6	100.7	101.6	97.9	100.3
吉 林	Jilin	101.4	101.1	100.2	101.1	101.9	97.9	100.4
黑龙江	Heilongjiang	101.6	101.2	102.1	101.1	102.3	99.9	100.1
上 海	Shanghai	103.6	102.2	95.2	102.5	105.0	96.6	97.9
江 苏	Jiangsu	101.8	101.4	103.9	101.3	102.3	97.6	101.3
浙 江	Zhejiang	102.8	101.8	101.0	101.8	104.6	99.5	101.0
安 徽	Anhui	102.0	101.9	101.6	101.9	102.0	97.8	99.6
福 建	Fujian	101.6	101.5	103.0	101.4	101.8	99.1	100.5
江 西	Jiangxi	102.3	101.6	100.3	101.6	103.9	99.5	101.2
山 东	Shandong	102.0	101.4	100.9	101.4	103.3	99.1	100.3
河 南	Henan	101.4	101.3	102.0	101.3	101.7	97.2	100.0
湖 北	Hubei	101.8	101.3	104.6	101.2	102.8	98.6	100.7
湖 南	Hunan	101.6	100.5	100.5	100.5	103.9	99.6	100.1
广 东	Guangdong	102.7	101.9	103.8	101.8	104.2	97.7	100.6
广 西	Guangxi	101.8	102.5	100.6	102.7	100.3	95.8	100.2
海 南	Hainan	101.8	101.4	103.7	101.3	102.7	98.6	101.4
重 庆	Chongqing	101.3	101.7	105.3	101.3	100.9	98.4	99.2
四 川	Sichuan	102.5	101.5	104.5	101.3	103.8	97.0	100.5
贵 州	Guizhou	100.4	100.8	100.5	100.8	99.8	97.6	100.6
云 南	Yunnan	102.2	100.9	100.4	100.9	104.6	98.2	100.8
西 藏	Xizang	100.6	100.4	102.4	100.0	100.9	100.0	100.3
陕 西	Shaanxi	101.0	100.8	101.7	100.6	101.7	96.8	99.0
甘 肃	Gansu	101.6	101.6	101.3	101.7	101.4	99.7	100.2
青 海	Qinghai	104.2	105.9	103.4	106.0	101.2	96.9	101.1
宁 夏	Ningxia	101.7	101.5	101.2	101.6	102.0	95.0	101.3
新 疆	Xinjiang	101.0	101.0	101.6	101.0	101.0	97.8	100.7

5-5 续表 6 continued

(上年=100) (preceding year=100)

地 区	Region	文化娱乐服务 Cultural and Recreational Services	旅游 Touring	医疗保健 Health Care and Medical Services	药品及医疗器具 Medicine and Medical Instruments	医疗服务 Medical Services	其他用品及服务 Other Articles and Services	其他用品 Other Articles	其他服务 Other Services
全 国	**National Average**	**101.0**	**109.0**	**101.1**	**101.3**	**101.1**	**103.2**	**104.6**	**101.9**
北 京	Beijing	102.7	110.2	100.2	100.5	100.0	104.2	106.1	102.5
天 津	Tianjin	100.5	111.2	100.4	100.4	100.3	103.6	106.3	101.3
河 北	Hebei	101.2	104.7	103.2	101.6	104.0	103.2	104.7	101.8
山 西	Shanxi	99.1	108.0	100.9	102.3	100.2	102.4	102.8	102.0
内蒙古	Inner Mongolia	100.5	104.0	103.3	103.3	103.4	103.5	105.0	101.9
辽 宁	Liaoning	100.4	105.2	100.1	100.4	100.0	103.1	104.6	101.8
吉 林	Jilin	100.0	105.9	100.7	102.4	99.9	103.4	105.1	101.8
黑龙江	Heilongjiang	101.0	107.1	102.5	101.1	103.2	102.8	104.4	101.2
上 海	Shanghai	102.7	116.3	100.2	100.6	99.9	104.8	106.3	103.3
江 苏	Jiangsu	100.7	106.4	103.2	100.8	103.9	103.9	104.9	102.7
浙 江	Zhejiang	101.2	110.9	101.0	100.9	101.0	103.6	105.6	101.7
安 徽	Anhui	101.3	106.4	100.7	100.8	100.6	103.2	104.8	101.0
福 建	Fujian	100.6	104.7	100.7	101.8	100.2	103.1	104.4	101.6
江 西	Jiangxi	101.4	110.7	100.7	101.4	100.4	103.3	103.8	102.5
山 东	Shandong	100.8	111.7	100.2	100.9	99.8	103.7	105.2	102.0
河 南	Henan	101.6	109.6	100.9	101.5	100.7	103.2	104.7	101.7
湖 北	Hubei	101.5	108.2	100.5	102.1	100.0	102.9	104.6	101.2
湖 南	Hunan	100.2	110.9	102.0	101.7	102.1	103.0	104.7	101.2
广 东	Guangdong	101.5	111.9	100.4	101.8	100.0	102.3	103.0	101.8
广 西	Guangxi	100.1	104.7	101.5	101.8	101.3	102.1	102.3	101.9
海 南	Hainan	101.3	107.1	99.8	98.3	100.6	102.0	103.7	100.5
重 庆	Chongqing	103.6	101.4	100.2	100.5	100.0	102.4	104.4	101.2
四 川	Sichuan	101.3	110.6	100.6	100.9	100.5	102.6	103.4	102.1
贵 州	Guizhou	98.7	101.9	100.0	100.5	99.8	101.9	103.4	100.6
云 南	Yunnan	100.1	113.4	100.7	101.2	100.5	103.0	103.3	102.6
西 藏	Xizang	101.0	104.3	101.0	100.7	101.1	103.7	106.1	101.5
陕 西	Shaanxi	101.0	106.9	101.4	102.3	101.0	103.8	104.7	103.1
甘 肃	Gansu	99.7	106.2	103.5	102.3	104.1	103.2	104.4	102.1
青 海	Qinghai	100.4	105.6	102.1	103.0	101.7	103.5	104.6	102.2
宁 夏	Ningxia	101.4	109.1	100.8	101.0	100.7	104.6	105.7	103.2
新 疆	Xinjiang	100.2	104.0	100.3	100.4	100.3	104.4	105.6	102.9

5–6 农产品生产者价格指数
Producer Price Indices for Agriculture Products

(上年＝100) (preceding year=100)

指 标	Item	2019	2020	2021	2022	2023
农产品生产者价格指数	**Producer Price Index for Agriculture Products**	**114.5**	**115.0**	**97.8**	**100.4**	**97.7**
农业产品	**Agriculture Products**	**100.8**	**102.8**	**110.6**	**102.9**	**99.2**
谷物	Cereals	100.3	104.1	113.8	104.3	100.6
#小麦	Wheat	100.1	100.5	106.6	112.8	97.3
稻谷	Rice	96.5	100.8	101.9	99.7	101.7
玉米	Corn	102.0	107.6	125.5	102.7	101.6
大豆	Soybeans	100.1	105.5	112.8	105.3	98.1
油料	Oil-bearing Crops	105.2	107.9	107.2	105.0	104.4
棉花	Cotton	97.8	98.5	117.3	102.9	101.0
糖料	Sugar Crops	97.7	103.1	100.9	104.5	103.5
蔬菜	Vegetables	101.2	105.2	105.6	101.4	95.9
水果	Fruits	103.6	95.3	99.7	106.6	102.3
林业产品	**Forestry Products**	**100.1**	**100.7**	**102.4**	**98.4**	**97.3**
饲养动物及其产品	**Raised Animals and Related Products**	**133.5**	**132.4**	**82.1**	**95.7**	**91.7**
生猪	Live Pigs	150.5	155.7	64.9	90.2	86.0
活牛	Live Cattle and Buffaloes	112.5	110.5	106.1	98.1	92.2
活羊	Live Sheep and Goats	114.3	110.4	102.3	93.3	95.1
活家禽	Live Poultry	107.8	92.9	104.7	103.8	100.1
禽蛋	Poultry Eggs	102.1	85.9	115.5	107.3	99.4
生奶	Raw Milk	105.6	101.5	107.8	100.0	94.9
渔业产品	**Fishery Products**	**99.4**	**100.2**	**108.8**	**100.4**	**99.4**
海水养殖产品	Seawater Cultured Products	97.2	96.3	105.6	101.1	99.6
海水捕捞产品	Seawater Fishing Products	100.6	99.6	103.0	102.3	102.6
淡水养殖产品	Freshwater Cultured Products	99.8	102.0	112.4	99.3	97.6

5-7 分地区农产品生产者价格指数
Producer Price Indices for Agriculture Products by Region

(上年=100) (preceding year=100)

地 区	Region	2022					2023				
		总指数 General Index	农业产品 Agriculture Products	林业产品 Forestry Products	饲养动物及其产品 Raised Animals and Related Products	渔业产品 Fishery Products	总指数 General Index	农业产品 Agriculture Products	林业产品 Forestry Products	饲养动物及其产品 Raised Animals and Related Products	渔业产品 Fishery Products
全 国	**National Average**	**100.4**	**102.9**	**98.4**	**95.7**	**100.4**	**97.7**	**99.2**	**97.3**	**91.7**	**99.4**
北 京	Beijing	102.7	103.3		102.0	99.3	99.7	102.1		94.6	103.9
天 津	Tianjin	98.4	102.3		98.7	87.2	98.1	98.5		90.8	93.3
河 北	Hebei	103.5	106.0	102.9	100.7	84.9	95.5	96.6	99.6	92.6	106.6
山 西	Shanxi	104.0	105.3	100.0	101.9	101.2	101.6	104.9	100.5	95.6	100.3
内蒙古	Inner Mongolia	100.8	107.3	85.4	95.4	101.0	97.8	100.1	111.2	93.7	100.7
辽 宁	Liaoning	103.6	103.6	111.3	103.6	101.5	98.8	99.5	86.1	98.0	103.5
吉 林	Jilin	100.7	102.1	98.6	96.6	105.2	95.8	98.1	93.9	88.9	96.5
黑龙江	Heilongjiang	102.5	103.6		96.7	99.2	100.6	103.1	84.9	87.9	112.4
上 海	Shanghai	102.6	103.4	108.1	93.5	107.0	98.4	95.9	95.5	93.3	110.8
江 苏	Jiangsu	100.1	102.9	99.0	95.3	100.9	98.3	101.4	100.5	92.7	99.3
浙 江	Zhejiang	101.5	102.3	99.5	96.2	103.1	101.2	100.8	97.1	90.2	107.0
安 徽	Anhui	102.8	105.3	100.4	97.8	102.2	96.7	97.3	98.8	90.6	99.8
福 建	Fujian	100.8	103.2	98.3	95.8	104.8	99.8	102.1	102.8	95.1	99.1
江 西	Jiangxi	97.5	100.7	97.4	93.2	95.3	95.3	100.4	86.7	89.1	96.1
山 东	Shandong	100.6	101.4	95.3	98.3	102.8	101.0	106.2	94.0	91.2	103.8
河 南	Henan	97.2	103.9	99.5	91.9	100.8	91.4	100.0	99.7	84.9	90.1
湖 北	Hubei	100.6	104.1	102.3	94.9	96.3	97.1	101.6	102.5	87.1	97.6
湖 南	Hunan	103.6	108.7	100.5	96.4	105.0	97.6	99.7	105.0	94.4	95.9
广 东	Guangdong	100.1	102.8	99.8	92.0	101.6	98.0	97.4	98.7	93.6	100.1
广 西	Guangxi	100.8	103.5	100.2	94.3	100.3	97.1	100.1	95.9	90.1	96.8
海 南	Hainan	106.8	111.7	104.1	100.1	105.1	98.2	102.0	90.9	89.0	103.5
重 庆	Chongqing	98.7	103.2	98.5	92.5	95.6	97.5	100.4	99.1	92.5	100.7
四 川	Sichuan	99.1	104.6	99.0	94.7	100.0	95.6	100.1	100.9	90.9	99.0
贵 州	Guizhou	95.9	103.1	103.5	90.0	105.7	95.1	98.8	101.0	92.1	99.2
云 南	Yunnan	96.7	101.5	96.2	88.2	106.0	98.8	104.7	93.2	89.8	99.5
西 藏	Xizang										
陕 西	Shaanxi	104.4	109.3	64.7	94.1	98.4	101.3	105.6	104.2	89.5	95.4
甘 肃	Gansu	100.2	104.7		92.3		103.3	106.7		97.3	
青 海	Qinghai	98.4	110.7		86.7		97.4	102.2		93.8	
宁 夏	Ningxia	98.3	103.1		94.4	81.6	96.6	103.6		89.5	93.7
新 疆	Xinjiang	99.6	104.6	106.2	94.9	94.2	102.4	106.2	105.0	91.7	97.6

5-8 按工业行业分工业生产者出厂价格指数
Producer Price Indices for Industrial Products by Sector

(上年＝100) (preceding year=100)

行 业	Sector	2020	2021	2022	2023
总指数	**General Index**	**98.2**	**108.1**	**104.1**	**97.0**
煤炭开采和洗选业	Mining and Washing of Coal	94.6	145.1	117.0	88.1
石油和天然气开采业	Extraction of Petroleum and Natural Gas	72.6	138.7	135.9	89.8
黑色金属矿采选业	Mining and Processing of Ferrous Metal Ores	107.0	131.0	84.6	98.1
有色金属矿采选业	Mining and Processing of Non-Ferrous Metal Ores	104.8	113.1	108.3	106.0
非金属矿采选业	Mining and Processing of Non-metal Ores	101.5	103.1	105.9	100.2
开采专业及辅助性活动	Professional and Support Activities for Mining	99.1	98.4	99.0	100.5
其他采矿业	Mining of Other Ores				
农副食品加工业	Processing of Food from Agricultural Products	104.8	103.9	104.7	99.4
食品制造业	Manufacture of Foods	100.6	101.8	103.7	99.4
酒、饮料和精制茶制造业	Manufacture of Alcohol, Beverages and Refined Tea	100.7	101.6	101.0	101.2
烟草制品业	Manufacture of Tobacco	101.4	100.6	100.6	100.9
纺织业	Manufacture of Textiles	95.3	104.1	103.6	96.8
纺织服装、服饰业	Manufacture of Textile Wearing Apparel and Accessories	98.8	99.9	101.3	100.8
皮革、毛皮、羽毛及其制品和制鞋业	Manufacture of Leather, Fur, Feather and Related Products and Footware	99.3	99.7	101.8	101.9
木材加工和木、竹、藤、棕、草制品业	Processing of Timber, Manufacture of Wood, Bamboo, Rattan, Palm and Straw Products	99.3	101.4	101.8	98.6
家具制造业	Manufacture of Furniture	100.0	100.2	101.7	100.6
造纸和纸制品业	Manufacture of Paper and Paper Products	97.2	104.9	100.6	94.7
印刷和记录媒介复制业	Printing and Reproduction of Recorded Media	98.7	100.5	101.0	99.4
文教、工美、体育和娱乐用品制造业	Manufacture of Articles for Culture, Education, Arts and Crafts, Sport and Entertainment Activities	103.3	101.7	103.2	104.8
石油、 煤炭及其他燃料加工业	Processing of Petroleum, Coal and Other Fuels	85.7	128.2	123.6	91.7
化学原料和化学制品制造业	Manufacture of Raw Chemical Materials and Chemical Products	94.1	119.1	107.7	91.0
医药制造业	Manufacture of Medicines	100.6	99.6	100.3	100.3
化学纤维制造业	Manufacture of Chemical Fibres	86.5	116.1	104.1	97.3
橡胶和塑料制品业	Manufacture of Rubber and Plastic Products	98.1	103.2	101.3	96.5
非金属矿物制品业	Manufacture of Non-metallic Mineral Products	98.4	103.7	101.2	93.3
黑色金属冶炼和压延加工业	Smelting and Pressing of Ferrous Metals	97.9	128.5	94.2	90.4
有色金属冶炼和压延加工业	Smelting and Pressing of Non-ferrous Metals	100.8	122.7	105.4	97.0
金属制品业	Manufacture of Metal Products	99.9	106.7	102.2	96.9
通用设备制造业	Manufacture of General Purpose Machinery	99.7	101.4	101.1	99.7
专用设备制造业	Manufacture of Special Purpose Machinery	100.0	100.4	100.7	99.7
汽车制造业	Manufacture of Automobiles	99.6	99.6	100.2	98.8
铁路、船舶、航空航天和其他运输设备制造业	Manufacture of Railway, Ship, Aerospace and Other Transport Equipment	100.4	100.6	101.5	100.2
电气机械和器材制造业	Manufacture of Electrical Machinery and Apparatus	97.4	104.4	104.6	98.5
计算机、通信和其他电子设备制造业	Manufacture of Computers, Communication and Other Electronic Equipment	98.5	99.9	100.7	98.3
仪器仪表制造业	Manufacture of Measuring Instruments and Machinery	100.2	99.7	101.5	100.8
其他制造业	Other Manufacturing	100.3	100.6	102.2	99.6
废弃资源综合利用业	Utilization of Waste Resources	100.2	117.5	103.2	91.9
金属制品、机械和设备修理业	Repair Service of Metal Products, Machinery and Equipment	103.6	99.7	102.1	102.9
电力、热力生产和供应业	Production and Supply of Electric Power and Heat Power	98.1	100.2	108.6	101.2
燃气生产和供应业	Production and Supply of Gas	95.7	105.1	115.9	101.1
水的生产和供应业	Production and Supply of Water	100.1	101.1	101.3	100.6

5-9 分地区工业生产者出厂价格指数
Producer Price Indices for Industrial Products by Region

(上年=100) (preceding year=100)

地 区	Region	2016	2017	2018	2019	2020	2021	2022	2023
全 国	**National Average**	**98.6**	**106.3**	**103.5**	**99.7**	**98.2**	**108.1**	**104.1**	**97.0**
北 京	Beijing	98.1	100.7	100.0	99.6	99.1	101.1	102.3	99.2
天 津	Tianjin	97.9	108.4	105.4	99.3	97.1	110.9	105.8	96.4
河 北	Hebei	99.9	115.0	106.2	100.2	98.5	116.4	100.5	94.7
山 西	Shanxi	96.8	119.4	106.7	99.7	96.7	130.2	111.4	91.3
内蒙古	Inner Mongolia	98.9	110.6	103.2	102.1	99.7	128.5	108.6	92.1
辽 宁	Liaoning	98.8	108.1	104.8	99.5	97.0	113.6	107.9	96.6
吉 林	Jilin	98.4	103.1	102.8	98.9	98.6	105.1	101.9	98.1
黑龙江	Heilongjiang	95.1	109.3	109.0	98.2	93.4	112.3	110.9	95.7
上 海	Shanghai	98.8	103.5	101.7	98.8	98.3	102.1	102.6	99.7
江 苏	Jiangsu	98.1	104.8	102.8	98.9	97.8	106.3	103.2	96.7
浙 江	Zhejiang	98.3	104.8	103.4	98.9	96.9	106.3	104.0	97.3
安 徽	Anhui	98.5	108.0	103.0	100.3	99.1	107.7	103.2	96.6
福 建	Fujian	99.1	104.1	102.8	100.6	98.4	104.9	102.9	98.2
江 西	Jiangxi	98.6	107.9	104.2	98.9	98.3	110.5	103.5	96.6
山 东	Shandong	98.5	105.5	103.7	99.7	98.1	110.3	105.1	96.5
河 南	Henan	99.0	106.8	103.6	100.2	99.2	107.8	105.0	97.4
湖 北	Hubei	99.0	105.6	104.2	100.2	99.1	104.1	103.4	97.4
湖 南	Hunan	98.9	105.8	103.2	99.6	99.0	105.9	102.0	98.5
广 东	Guangdong	99.4	103.3	101.8	100.2	99.0	103.4	103.0	98.5
广 西	Guangxi	99.1	107.6	103.2	99.3	99.4	108.9	102.5	97.0
海 南	Hainan	96.0	108.8	108.2	97.4	93.8	113.5	115.0	97.3
重 庆	Chongqing	98.6	104.1	102.1	99.8	99.1	103.2	102.3	97.8
四 川	Sichuan	98.9	106.5	103.6	100.4	98.8	105.9	102.8	97.6
贵 州	Guizhou	97.9	107.2	101.8	99.8	98.3	106.5	105.7	98.1
云 南	Yunnan	97.6	105.2	102.4	100.0	98.6	110.0	105.4	96.7
西 藏	Xizang	102.9	110.0	100.1	98.9	99.4	101.5	104.1	101.1
陕 西	Shaanxi	97.6	110.8	105.4	100.8	95.1	116.9	107.3	94.9
甘 肃	Gansu	94.9	114.5	109.5	98.3	93.9	116.4	110.9	95.9
青 海	Qinghai	98.5	116.7	104.8	98.5	96.6	114.5	112.2	96.3
宁 夏	Ningxia	99.1	112.1	107.3	99.4	96.9	119.9	111.1	92.7
新 疆	Xinjiang	94.5	113.7	111.2	98.5	91.6	119.4	112.3	93.5

5-10 工业生产者出厂价格分类指数
Producer Price Indices for Industrial Products by Category

(上年=100) (preceding year=100)

类 别	Item	2016	2017	2018	2019	2020	2021	2022	2023
总指数	**General Index**	**98.6**	**106.3**	**103.5**	**99.7**	**98.2**	**108.1**	**104.1**	**97.0**
生产资料	**Means of Production**	**98.2**	**108.3**	**104.6**	**99.2**	**97.3**	**110.7**	**104.9**	**96.1**
采掘工业	Mining & Quarrying Industry	95.4	120.7	108.8	102.4	94.8	134.4	116.5	92.3
原材料工业	Raw Materials Industry	96.7	111.5	106.3	97.4	94.4	115.8	110.3	95.6
加工工业	Processing Industry	99.0	106.1	103.5	99.7	98.7	106.6	101.5	96.7
生活资料	**Consumer Goods**	**100.0**	**100.7**	**100.5**	**100.9**	**100.5**	**100.4**	**101.5**	**99.9**
食品类	Food	100.6	100.6	100.5	102.7	102.9	101.4	102.7	100.2
衣着类	Clothing	100.9	101.2	100.8	101.1	99.0	99.8	101.8	101.1
一般日用品	Articles for Daily Use	100.0	101.3	101.0	100.4	99.7	100.5	101.6	100.5
耐用消费品	Durable Consumer Goods	98.5	99.9	99.8	98.8	98.2	99.4	100.1	98.9

5-11 工业生产者购进价格指数
Purchasing Price Indices for Industrial Producers

(上年=100) (preceding year=100)

年 份 Year	总指数 General Index	燃料、动力类 Fuel and Power	黑色金属材料类 Ferrous Metals	有色金属材料及电线类 Non-ferrous Metals and Cables	化工原料类 Raw Chemical Materials	木材及纸浆类 Timber and Paper Pulp	建筑材料及非金属类 Building Materials and Non-metals	农副产品类 Agricultural Products	纺织原料类 Textile Materials
1989	126.4	124.7	130.3	127.6	124.4	111.4	122.7	128.9	128.5
1990	105.6	110.7	103.9	97.2	95.6	99.4	115.2	107.8	107.4
1991	109.1	112.9	112.5	101.2	99.8	105.6	101.2	106.8	108.9
1992	111.0	116.4	114.5	112.4	102.6	102.0	118.8	103.4	100.5
1993	135.1	136.7	174.1	115.8	114.3	128.6	140.9	112.2	107.1
1994	118.2	118.0	103.8	110.7	111.7	115.1	114.3	148.3	139.6
1995	115.3	108.7	98.2	128.3	127.2	115.8	102.6	143.1	123.6
1996	103.9	110.2	99.3	92.4	98.0	101.9	102.5	114.7	94.5
1997	101.3	109.3	97.4	96.2	97.1	100.9	99.7	102.0	94.7
1998	95.8	99.1	95.1	88.3	93.6	96.7	98.6	94.5	94.3
1999	96.7	100.9	94.7	98.9	97.6	100.4	98.8	89.8	96.8
2000	105.1	115.4	100.9	110.3	105.6	99.8	101.5	99.9	102.4
2001	99.8	100.2	100.5	95.6	98.4	100.4	98.6	101.2	99.7
2002	97.7	100.1	98.2	96.5	97.5	98.7	98.2	95.7	97.1
2003	104.8	107.4	107.9	105.3	102.9	100.3	99.7	106.7	101.4
2004	111.4	109.7	120.4	120.1	108.9	102.8	105.1	114.2	104.7
2005	108.3	115.0	107.5	114.0	108.3	103.5	103.1	101.7	102.4
2006	106.0	111.9	98.3	130.8	102.1	102.6	101.9	104.3	102.9
2007	104.4	104.3	105.4	111.6	103.6	102.7	103.0	106.1	101.4
2008	110.5	120.6	118.4	98.6	105.2	105.2	109.5	107.5	103.1
2009	92.1	89.2	86.3	81.1	91.3	95.8	101.1	97.0	98.8
2010	109.6	116.3	106.6	122.2	107.0	103.0	103.8	110.4	106.7
2011	109.1	110.8	109.4	112.1	110.4	104.6	108.4	115.6	112.7
2012	98.2	100.9	92.9	94.5	96.1	100.1	99.7	100.2	99.1
2013	98.0	96.6	95.7	95.4	97.3	99.6	98.7	101.6	99.9
2014	97.8	97.1	94.6	96.1	98.3	99.4	99.8	99.4	98.9
2015	93.9	88.7	88.4	92.7	93.7	99.3	95.9	97.7	97.8
2016	98.0	95.6	97.7	97.9	97.6	99.7	97.6	100.1	99.7
2017	108.1	113.0	115.9	115.3	108.4	106.2	108.6	101.5	104.0
2018	104.1	107.1	106.1	103.9	104.6	105.4	110.5	99.6	102.2
2019	99.3	98.2	102.3	97.6	94.8	97.5	104.2	102.8	99.3
2020	97.7	91.6	100.5	99.8	92.7	98.1	100.5	105.4	96.8
2021	111.0	120.5	120.3	120.9	115.1	105.6	105.5	104.4	105.0
2022	106.1	120.9	96.4	105.4	106.5	104.5	103.1	105.1	105.0
2023	96.4	94.7	93.8	99.3	91.7	96.9	94.1	97.8	97.0

5-12 进出口商品价格指数
Price Indices of Imports and Exports of Commodity

(上年=100) (preceding year=100)

年份 Year	出口 Exports	进口 Imports	年份 Year	出口 Exports	进口 Imports
1983	91.6	91.5	2004	106.6	113.3
1984	102.3	98.2	2005	103.0	103.5
1985	97.0	98.0	2006	102.5	103.2
1986	85.3	106.4	2007	105.5	106.6
1987	103.4	100.6	2008	108.6	115.8
1988	105.1	114.9	2009	93.8	87.3
1989	106.6	108.3	2010	102.9	113.6
1990	103.3	96.7	2011	110.0	113.9
1991	97.6	94.3	2012	102.0	99.3
1992	99.3	103.3	2013	99.2	97.6
1993	96.0	101.5	2014	99.3	96.6
1994	105.3	104.6	2015	99.0	88.4
1995	110.7	112.1	2016	98.0	97.6
1996	102.9	102.2	2017	103.9	109.4
1997	101.5	103.2	2018	103.3	106.1
1998	95.3	99.4	2019	103.5	101.9
1999	95.6	104.4	2020	101.6	96.2
2000	100.8	110.1	2021	103.8	112.8
2001	98.4	100.1	2022	112.5	111.9
2002	97.5	102.3	2023	97.5	96.9
2003	103.0	109.2			

注：本表数据2013年及以前用美元值计算，2014年起，改用人民币值计算。
a) Data in this table are calculated in USD for 2013 and before, and in Renminbi since 2014.

5-13 分行业进出口商品价格指数
Price Indices of Imports and Exports of Commodity by Industry

(上年=100)　　(preceding year=100)

行　业	Industry	出口 Exports		进口 Imports	
		2022	2023	2022	2023
农、林、牧、渔业	Agriculture, Forestry, Animal Husbandry and Fishery	100.4	101.5	114.2	96.2
农业	Farming	100.0	102.3	118.9	96.6
林业	Forestry	106.8	95.1	102.8	91.1
畜牧业	Animal Husbandry	92.4	95.6	102.0	93.3
渔业	Fishery	109.7	99.0	113.5	101.7
采矿业	Mining	119.1	98.2	118.2	92.1
煤炭开采和洗选业	Mining and Washing of Coal	160.9	88.1	132.3	76.8
石油和天然气开采业	Extraction of Petroleum and Natural Gas	154.3	100.0	148.0	87.7
黑色金属矿采选业	Mining and Processing of Ferrous Metal Ores	88.2	91.1	75.2	104.6
有色金属矿采选业	Mining and Processing of Non-Ferrous Metal Ores	123.4	100.5	100.4	100.9
非金属矿采选业	Mining and Processing of Non-metal Ores	118.4	103.6	113.3	106.5
制造业	Manufacturing	112.4	97.3	110.2	100.2
农副食品加工业	Processing of Food from Agricultural Products	109.2	97.6	117.0	93.6
食品制造业	Manufacture of Foods	114.6	99.3	116.8	109.6
酒、饮料和精制茶制造业	Manufacture of Alcohol, Beverages and Refined Tea	103.5	108.1	108.1	113.9
烟草制品业	Manufacture of Tobacco	99.7	85.3	108.9	120.5
纺织业	Manufacture of Textiles	108.7	98.2	109.6	102.5
纺织服装、服饰业	Manufacture of Textile, Wearing Apparel and Accessories	108.0	98.4	126.2	109.9
皮革、毛皮、羽毛及其制品和制鞋业	Manufacture of Leather, Fur, Feather and Related Products and Footwear	113.0	97.2	106.6	109.5
木材加工和木、竹、藤、棕、草制品业	Processing of Timber, Manufacture of Wood, Bamboo, Rattan, Palm and Straw Products	109.7	96.4	114.6	95.2
家具制造业	Manufacture of Furniture	113.3	96.5	125.0	116.5
造纸和纸制品业	Manufacture of Paper and Paper Products	108.2	90.7	116.5	89.6
印刷和记录媒介复制业	Printing, Reproduction of Recorded Media	112.7	97.8	139.0	82.9
文教、工美、体育和娱乐用品制造业	Manufacture of Articles for Culture, Education, Arts and Crafts, Sport and Entertainment Activities	108.7	96.0	102.3	105.4
石油、煤炭及其他燃料加工业	Processing of Petroleum, Coal and Other Fuels	164.8	87.6	129.5	86.7
化学原料和化学制品制造业	Manufacture of Raw Chemical Materials and Chemical Products	120.0	83.4	110.5	92.9
医药制造业	Manufacture of Medicines	108.2	90.9	99.9	97.8
化学纤维制造业	Manufacture of Chemical Fibres	107.5	93.2	112.8	99.0
橡胶和塑料制品业	Manufacture of Rubber and Plastics Products	109.8	96.0	106.5	106.9
非金属矿物制品业	Manufacture of Non-metallic Mineral Products	116.1	89.6	116.5	100.8
黑色金属冶炼和压延加工业	Smelting and Pressing of Ferrous Metals	116.2	80.0	111.0	88.3
有色金属冶炼和压延加工业	Smelting and Pressing of Non-ferrous Metals	112.6	93.3	104.0	104.5
金属制品业	Manufacture of Metal Products	113.7	94.4	102.8	108.7
通用设备制造业	Manufacture of General Purpose Machinery	112.8	102.6	100.5	113.0
专用设备制造业	Manufacture of Special Purpose Machinery	109.0	102.8	99.5	113.6
汽车制造业	Manufacture of Automobiles	111.3	106.9	103.8	102.8
铁路、船舶、航空航天和其他运输设备制造业	Manufacture of Railway, Ship, Aerospace and Other Transport Equipments	110.2	99.8	107.7	106.2
电气机械和器材制造业	Manufacture of Electrical Machinery and Apparatus	115.5	103.5	109.5	109.0
计算机、通信和其他电子设备制造业	Manufacture of Computers, Communication and Other Electronic Equipment	110.5	98.4	113.2	98.3
仪器仪表制造业	Manufacture of Measuring Instruments and Machinery	110.2	105.8	116.5	112.6
其他制造业	Other Manufacturing	100.2	97.4	104.9	105.3
废弃资源综合利用业	Utilization of Waste Resources	110.6	76.4	107.2	98.8
电力、热力、燃气及水生产和供应业	Production and Supply of Electricity, Heat, Gas and Water	107.3	104.0	100.8	101.4
文化、体育和娱乐业	Culture, Sports and Entertainment	110.6	101.8	103.0	120.5

注：本表行业类别按照《国民经济行业分类》(GB/T 4754-2017)划分。
a) Industries in this table are classified by Industrial Classification for National Economy Activities (GB/T 4754-2017).

主要统计指标解释

居民消费价格指数 是反映一定时期内城乡居民所购买的生活消费品和服务项目价格变动趋势和程度的相对数。

农产品生产者价格指数 是反映一定时期内，农产品生产者出售农产品价格水平变动趋势及幅度的相对数。该指数可以客观反映全国农产品生产者价格水平和结构变动情况，满足农业与国民经济核算需要。其中某代表品生产者价格指数是通过对全部有出售该产品行为的调查单位的个体指数进行几何平均求得的，类价格指数是通过对其所属的类（或代表品）的价格指数进行加权平均求得的。季度累计价格指数的计算方法与分季指数的计算方法相同。

工业生产者出厂价格指数 是反映一定时期内全部工业产品第一次出售时的出厂价格总水平的变动趋势和变动幅度的相对数。

工业生产者购进价格指数 是反映作为中间投入的原材料、燃料、动力购进价格总水平的变动趋势和变动幅度的相对数。

Explanatory Notes on Main Statistical Indicators

Consumer Price Indices are relative figures reflecting the trend and degree of changes in prices of consumer goods and services purchased by urban and rural households during a given period.

Producer Prices Indices for Agricultural Products are relative figures reflecting the trend and degree of changes in producers' prices received by farmers when they sell agricultural products during a given period. These indices depict the change in the level and structure of producer prices for agricultural products of the country and meet the needs of agricultural statistics and national accounts statistics. The producer price index for a given product is calculated as the geometrical mean of individual indices for all surveyed units which sell such products, and the indices for a product category is obtained as the weighted mean of price indices for all products in the category. Method for calculating accumulative quarterly indices is the same as for calculating the distinctive quarterly indices.

Producer Price Indices for Industrial Products are relative figures reflecting the trend and degree of changes in general ex-factory prices of all manufactured goods for first sale during a given period.

Purchasing Price Indices for Industrial Producers are relative figures reflecting the trend and degree of changes in the purchasing prices of intermediate inputs such as raw materials, fuels and power.

6

人民生活

People's Livelihoods

简 要 说 明

一、本篇资料的主要内容

本篇资料反映我国人民生活现状及变化情况，主要包括居民家庭基本情况及生活状况、收入及支出、住房等。

二、数据来源及调查方法

2013 年及以后数据，来源于国家统计局的住户收支与生活状况调查。1978—2012 年的数据，根据国家统计局的城镇住户调查和农村住户调查历史数据，按照住户收支与生活状况调查可比口径推算得到。

（一）住户收支与生活状况调查的调查方法

国家统计局住户调查司从 2012 年四季度起对分别进行的城乡住户调查实施了一体化改革，开始实施住户收支与生活状况抽样调查。主要内容包括：居民收入和消费情况，同时收集反映居民就业、社会保障参与、住房状况、家庭经营和生产投资以及收入分配影响因素等调查内容。

住户收支与生活状况调查是以省为总体，综合采用分层、多阶段、与人口规模大小成比例和随机等距抽样相结合的方法抽选村级单位、确定调查小区、抽选样本住户。

全国共抽选出 1800 个县(市、区)的 1.6 万个调查小区，对抽中小区中的 160 多万个住户进行全面摸底调查，在此基础上随机等距抽选出约 16 万住户参加记账调查。定期对调查小区和调查住宅进行轮换。

住户收支与生活状况调查是在 95%的置信度下，全国居民人均可支配收入的抽样误差小于 1%。主要是采用调查户记日记账的方式采集居民收支数据，同时辅之以统一的调查问卷，收集与收入支出有关的其他调查内容。所有调查工作由国家统计局派驻各地的调查队独立完成。由市县级调查队使用统一的方法和数据处理程序对原始调查资料进行编码、审核、录入，然后将分户基础数据直接传输至国家统计局进行统一汇总计算。

2013 年起，按照住户收支与生活状况调查制度，国家统计局每年收集 16 万调查户 12 个月的记账数据，在此基础上汇总计算出各年的全国居民可支配收入、城镇居民可支配收入、农村居民可支配收入等收支数据。

（二）城镇住户调查的调查方法

2012 年及以前，国家统计局城市司组织开展城镇住户调查。调查内容主要包括家庭人口及其构成、家庭现金收支、主要商品购买数量及支出金额、劳动就业状况、居住状况和耐用消费品的拥有量等。

调查对象在 2001 年以前为全国非农业住户，2002 至 2012 年改为全国城市市区和县城关镇区住户。

城镇住户调查采用分层随机抽样的方法确定，首先，按照城镇规模将全国所有省（自治区、直辖市）的城镇划分为三层：大中城市（地级和地级以上的城市）、县级市和县城（镇）。第二，按各层人口占全省（自治区、直辖市）人口的比例来分配每层的样本量。第三，按城镇就业者年人均工资从高到低排队，依次计算各城镇人口累计数，然后根据样本量的大小随机起点等距抽取所需数量的调查城镇。

城镇调查户的抽选工作分两步进行。第一步进行一次性的大样本调查；第二步从大样本调查中抽出一个小样本，作为经常性调查户，开展记账工作。

大样本调查每三年进行一次，其目的主要是为经常性调查提供抽样框和为经常性调查数据评估提供基础资料。在大样本调查中，各调查市、县采取分层、二（多）阶段、与大小成比例（PPS 方法）的随机等距方法选取调查样本。即先按区分层，在层内按照 PPS 方法随机等距抽选调查社区/居委会，在抽中社区/居委会内随机等距抽选调查住宅。部分大城市根据需要可以采用三阶段抽样，即先抽选社区/居委会，再抽选调查小区，最后抽选调查住宅。对选出的大样本或小样本开展调查，取得调查户家庭人口、就业人口、收入等辅助资料，然后，根据这些资料进行分组，从中按比例抽出一个小样本也称二相样本，作为经常性调查户，开展日记账工作。每年轮换三分之一的经常性调查户。

截至 2012 年底，参加国家汇总的调查样本量为 6.6 万户。

（三）农村住户调查的调查方法

2012 年及以前，国家统计局农村司组织开展农村住户调查。主要内容包括农村居民家庭基本情况、住房情况、收入、生活消费支出、主要食品消费量、耐用消费品拥有量等。

农村住户调查是以各省(自治区、直辖市)为总体，直接抽选调查村，在抽中村中抽选调查户。综合运用多种抽样方法确定住户调查网点。农村住户调查网点分布在全国 7000 多个村，共抽取了 7.4 万个样本户。

农村住户调查在 95%的概率把握程度下要求抽样误差不得超过 ± 3%。为保证农村住户调查资料的准确性，国家统计局农村司为调查户设置了现金和实物两本账，并聘请了近万名辅助调查员帮助做好记账工作，及时核实、汇总住户调查资料。

为解决调查户的厌烦情绪及样本老化问题，增强抽样调查网点的代表性，更加准确、及时地反映农村社会经济情况，对农村住户调查网点实行样本轮换制度，每五年为一个周期。

Brief Introduction

I. Main Contents

Data in this chapter show the people's living conditions and their changes in China, mainly including basic conditions, living status, income and expenditure, and housing of households.

II. Sources of Data and Methodology on Survey

Data of 2013 and after come from Household Survey on Income and Expenditure and Living Conditions. Data from 1978 to 2012 are estimated based on the historical data of Urban Household Survey and Rural Household Survey according to the comparable definition and coverage of main income and consumption indicators of Household Survey on Income and Expenditure and Living Conditions.

1. Methodology of Household Survey on Income and Expenditures and Living Conditions

In the fourth quarter of 2012, NBS launched reform on the household survey programme, to develop an integrated survey, instead of the two separate urban and rural household surveys. Main contents of the survey include: income and expenditure of households, employment, social security participation, housing, family operation, production, investment, and factors affecting the income distribution.

The survey is conducted by randomly selecting village-level units, small enumeration area and surveyed households, adopting the sampling method of combining stratification, multi-stage, probability proportional to population size and systematic sampling,with all households in a province as the population. More than 1.6 million households in 16,000 communities of 1,800 counties in the country are selected, and surveyed for pre-investigation. On this large sample, about 160,000 households are selected by systematic sampling for diary-keeping. Selected communities and households are rotated regularly.

Survey on Income and Expenditures and Living Conditions is so designed that the sampling error should not exceed ±1%, with a confidence probability of 95%. Income and expenditure data are collected with household diaries as the main source, assisted by questionnaires to collect other relevant data. All field work is conducted independently by local survey offices under NBS. Coding, checking, data entering are conducted by survey offices at city level with the unified methods and data processing program, and then household basic data are transferred to NBS for final tabulation.

Starting from 2013, NBS collected diary accounts of 160,000 households for 12 months, and tabulated national disposable income of all residents, urban residents and rural residents, with this system of Household Survey on Income and Expenditures and Living Conditions.

2. Methodology of Urban Household Survey

Urban Household Survey was conducted by the Office of Urban Household Surveys of the NBS prior to 2012. The main contents of the survey included persons in the household and the household composition; cash income and expenditure of the household; quantity of major commodities purchased and expenditure; the employment of household members; the housing condition; and the possession of durable consumer goods.

The survey covered only non-agricultural households prior to 2001. From 2002 to 2012, the survey covered the households in district areas of all city and county towns.

Sample cities and towns in urban areas were selected by using stratified random sampling method. Firstly, all the urban areas and towns of all provinces (autonomous regions and municipalities directly under the Central Government) were stratified into three strata according to population size: large and medium-sized cities (at and above prefecture level), county-level cities and county towns. Secondly, the sample size was decided by proportion of population in selected stratus to the provincial total. Thirdly, cities and towns were arranged in ranking the annual average wages of the employed persons, then with the accumulative population in each city and town sample cities and towns were selected by systematic sampling scheme according to the size of the samples.

The selection of sample households in urban areas was done by two steps: the first step was to conduct an ad hoc large sample survey; the second step was to select a small sample from the large sample, to be used as regular sample households for diary-keeping.

The ad hoc survey with large sample was conducted every three years; with the objective of providing sample frame for regular surveys and basic information for data evaluation of regular surveys. In the large sample survey, samples in sampled cities and towns were selected with stratified two (multi)-stage and probability proportional to size (PPS) method. Namely, stratification was done at district level, and then PPS sampling method was used to select sample communities/resident's committees, and finally the systematic sampling method was used to select dwellings from the selected communities/resident's committees. In some large cities, three-stage sampling method was used. Firstly, the communities/resident's committees were selected. Secondly, small enumeration areas were selected. Thirdly, sample dwellings were selected. A survey would be conducted to the large samples or the first phase samples to collect relevant information on population, persons employed, income and so on of the households. Then grouping is made based on the information collected, small samples or the second phase samples were selected according to proportions which were regular sample households to keep diary.

The national sample included 66,000 households at the end of 2012.

3. Methodology of Rural Household Survey

Rural Household Survey was organized by the Office of Rural Household Survey of the NBS prior to 2012. The main contents of the survey included basic condition of rural households, housing conditions, income, consumption expenditure, consumption of major consumer goods and the quantity of durable consumer goods owned.

Sample survey on rural households was conducted by first selecting sampled villages and then selecting households in the selected villages in each province, with all rural households in the province as the population. A combination of various sampling approaches is used to identify a sample of 74,000 households selected from 7,000 villages throughout the whole country.

The survey was so designed that the sampling error should not exceed ±3%, with a confidence probability of 95%. In order to ensure the accuracy of the survey data on the rural households, two accounts were designed for the respondent households by the Office of Household Survey of the NBS: the cash account and the account on goods in kind. Nearly 10 thousand assistant interviewers were recruited to help the households keep good accounts and to check on a timely basis, and to check and tabulate data from the survey.

In order to overcome the tedium of respondent households and to ensure that the sample was accurately representative over time and reflected the changing rural social and economic situation, a 5-year sample rotation scheme was implemented.

6-1 全国居民人均收支情况
Nationwide Per Capita Income and Consumption Expenditure

单位：元 (yuan)

指标	Item	2017	2018	2019	2020	2021	2022	2023
全国居民人均收入	**Nationwide Per Capita Income**							
可支配收入	Disposable Income	25974	28228	30733	32189	35128	36883	39218
1.工资性收入	1.Income of Wages and Salaries	14620	15829	17186	17917	19629	20590	22053
2.经营净收入	2.Net Business Income	4502	4852	5247	5307	5893	6175	6542
3.财产净收入	3.Net Income from Property	2107	2379	2619	2791	3076	3227	3362
4.转移净收入	4.Net Income from Transfer	4744	5168	5680	6173	6531	6892	7261
现金可支配收入	Disposable Income in Cash	24202	26291	28612	29919	32383	34180	36850
1.工资性收入	1.Income of Wages and Salaries	14538	15746	17097	17818	19493	20449	21884
2.经营净收入	2.Net Business Income	4424	4880	5270	5307	5665	6045	6816
3.财产净收入	3.Net Income from Property	812	878	1001	1068	1247	1334	1498
4.转移净收入	4.Net Income from Transfer	4429	4787	5244	5726	5979	6351	6651
全国居民人均支出	**Nationwide Per Capita Expenditure**							
消费支出	Consumption Expenditure	18322	19853	21559	21210	24100	24538	26796
#服务性消费	Consumption Expenditure on Services	7803	8781	9886	9037	10645	10590	12114
1.食品烟酒	1.Food,Tobacco and Alcohol	5374	5631	6084	6397	7178	7481	7983
2.衣着	2.Clothing and Footwear	1238	1289	1338	1238	1419	1365	1479
3.居住	3.Housing	4107	4647	5055	5215	5641	5882	6095
4.生活用品及服务	4.Household Equipments, Furnishings and Services	1121	1223	1281	1260	1423	1432	1526
5.交通通信	5.Transport and Communications	2499	2675	2862	2762	3156	3195	3652
6.教育文化娱乐	6.Education, Culture and Recreation	2086	2226	2513	2032	2599	2469	2904
7.医疗保健	7.Health Care and Medical Services	1451	1685	1902	1843	2115	2120	2460
8.其他用品及服务	8.Miscellaneous Goods and Services	447	477	524	462	569	595	697
现金消费支出	Consumption Expenditure in Cash	15122	16175	17526	16995	19411	19784	21944
1.食品烟酒	1.Food, Tobacco and Alcohol	5073	5366	5798	6068	6783	7098	7610
2.衣着	2.Clothing and Footwear	1237	1288	1338	1238	1418	1364	1478
3.居住	3.Housing	1519	1615	1756	1774	1900	2034	2241
4.生活用品及服务	4.Household Equipments, Furnishings and Services	1111	1211	1267	1246	1411	1421	1519
5.交通通信	5.Transport and Communications	2495	2669	2857	2758	3150	3191	3647
6.教育文化娱乐	6.Education, Culture and Recreation	2085	2224	2512	2031	2598	2468	2902
7.医疗保健	7.Health Care and Medical Services	1161	1333	1482	1426	1597	1635	1858
8.其他用品及服务	8.Miscellaneous Goods and Services	441	468	516	453	554	572	689

6-2 全国居民按收入五等份分组的人均可支配收入
Nationwide Per Capita Disposable Income of Households by Income Quintile

单位：元 (yuan)

组 别	Group	2017	2018	2019	2020	2021	2022	2023
20%低收入组家庭人均可支配收入	Lowest 20% Households	5958	6440	7380	7869	8333	8601	9215
20%中间偏下收入组家庭人均可支配收入	Second 20% Households	13843	14361	15777	16443	18445	19303	20442
20%中间收入组家庭人均可支配收入	Third 20% Households	22495	23189	25035	26249	29053	30598	32195
20%中间偏上收入组家庭人均可支配收入	Fourth 20% Households	34547	36471	39230	41172	44949	47397	50220
20%高收入组家庭人均可支配收入	Highest 20% Households	64934	70640	76401	80294	85836	90116	95055

注：全国居民按收入五等份分组是指将所有调查户按人均可支配收入水平从低到高顺序排列，平均分为五个等份，处于最低20%的收入群体为低收入组，依此类推依次为中间偏下收入组、中间收入组、中间偏上收入组、高收入组。本表数据为不同分组家庭的人均可支配收入。6-7和6-12表与此相同。

a) The income quintile refers to the five equal partitions of all surveyed households, who are ranked from low to high based on per capita disposable income level. The 20 percent with lowest income are classified as low-income group (Lowest 20%), and the other four levels are lower-middle-income group (Second 20%), middle-income group (Third 20%), higher-middle-income group (Fourth 20%) and high-income group (Highest 20%). The figures in table 6-2 are the per capita disposable income of the households in the different income groups.The same applies to Table 6-7 and Table 6-12.

6-3 全国居民按东、中、西部及东北地区分组的人均可支配收入
Nationwide Per Capita Disposable Income of Households in Eastern, Central, Western and Northeastern Regions

单位：元 (yuan)

组 别	Group	2017	2018	2019	2020	2021	2022	2023
东部地区	Eastern Region	33414	36298	39439	41240	44980	47027	49822
中部地区	Central Region	21834	23798	26025	27152	29650	31434	33328
西部地区	Western Region	20130	21936	23986	25416	27798	29267	31100
东北地区	Northeastern Region	23900	25543	27371	28266	30518	31405	33207

6–4 全国居民人均主要食品消费量
Nationwide Per Capita Consumption of Major Foods

单位：千克 (kg)

指　标	Item	2017	2018	2019	2020	2021	2022	2023
粮食(原粮)	Grain (Unprocessed)	130.1	127.2	130.1	141.2	144.6	136.8	134.4
谷物	Cereals	119.6	116.3	117.9	128.1	131.4	123.7	120.6
薯类	Tuber	2.5	2.6	2.9	3.1	2.9	2.7	2.8
豆类	Beans and Products	8.0	8.3	9.3	10.0	10.3	10.3	10.9
食用油	Edible Oil and Fats	10.4	9.6	9.5	10.4	10.8	10.0	10.0
#食用植物油	Edible Vegetable Oil	9.8	8.9	8.9	9.8	10.1	9.4	9.4
蔬菜及食用菌	Vegetable and Edible Fungi	99.2	96.1	98.6	103.7	109.8	108.2	113.6
#鲜菜	Fresh Vegetables	96.1	93.0	95.2	100.2	106.2	104.8	109.9
肉类	Meat and Products	26.7	29.5	26.9	24.8	32.9	34.6	39.8
#猪肉	Pork	20.1	22.8	20.3	18.2	25.2	26.9	30.5
牛肉	Beef	1.9	2.0	2.2	2.3	2.5	2.5	3.1
羊肉	Mutton	1.3	1.3	1.2	1.2	1.4	1.4	1.7
禽类	Poultry	8.9	9.0	10.8	12.7	12.3	11.7	12.4
水产品	Aquatic Products	11.5	11.4	13.6	13.9	14.2	13.9	15.2
蛋类	Eggs	10.0	9.7	10.7	12.8	13.2	13.5	15.0
奶类	Milk and Dairy Products	12.1	12.2	12.5	13.0	14.4	12.4	13.2
干鲜瓜果类	Fruits and Nuts	50.1	52.1	56.4	56.3	61.0		
#鲜瓜果	Fresh Melons and Fruits	45.6	47.4	51.4	51.3	55.5	54.7	60.8
坚果类	Nuts and Processed Products	3.5	3.5	3.8	3.7	4.1		
食糖	Sugar	1.3	1.3	1.3	1.3	1.3	1.2	1.2

注：1.居民人均主要食品消费量仅包括居民日常购买或自产自食的食品消费数量，不包括居民在外饮食服务中消费的食品数量。表6–9和6–14与此相同。

2.根据《住户收支与生活状况调查方案》，薯类食品在计算原粮消费量时，按照5:1的比例对鲜薯进行了折算。表6–9和6–14与此相同。

3.根据2021年11月新修订的《住户收支与生活状况调查方案》，2022年起不再发布"干鲜瓜果类"指标数据，改为发布"居民人均鲜瓜果消费量"。表6–9和6–14与此相同。

a) The per capita consumption quantity of major foods only include the quantity of food purchased or self-produced and self-comsumed by households on a daily basis,and do not include the food quantity consumed by households in catering services outside.The same applies to tables 6-9 and 6-14.

b) According to the scheme of Household Survey on Income and Expenditure ang Living Conditions , the consumption of tubers are converted with the ratio of 5:1, i.e. 5 kilograms of fresh tubers are equivalent to 1 kilogram of grain.The same applies to tables 6-9 and 6-14.

c) According to the newly revised scheme of Household Survey on Income and Expenditure ang Living Conditions in November 2021, the data of Dried and Fresh Melons and Fruits will no longer be released from 2022, but Per Captia Consumption on Fresh Melons and Fruits will be released instead. The same applies to tables 6-9 and 6-14.

6–5 全国居民平均每百户年末主要耐用消费品拥有量
Main Durable Goods Owned Per 100 Households Nationwide

指　标	Item	2017	2018	2019	2020	2021	2022	2023
家用汽车 (辆)	Automobile (unit)	29.7	33.0	35.3	37.1	41.8	43.5	49.7
摩托车 (辆)	Motorcycle (unit)	39.3	35.7	34.2	33.1	31.5	30.8	24.5
电动助力车 (辆)	Electric Bicycle (unit)	56.5	59.2	63.9	66.7	73.8	75.5	74.0
洗衣机 (台)	Washing Machine (set)	91.7	93.8	96.0	96.7	98.7	99.0	98.2
电冰箱(柜) (台)	Refrigerator (set)	95.3	98.8	100.9	101.8	103.9	104.2	103.4
彩色电视机 (台)	Color TV Set (set)	122.2	119.3	120.6	120.8	118.7	118.9	107.8
空调 (台)	Air Conditioner (set)	96.1	109.3	115.6	117.7	131.2	133.9	145.9
热水器 (台)	Water Heater (set)	78.6	85.0	86.9	90.4	89.6	89.9	89.8
排油烟机 (台)	Kitchen Ventilator (set)	51.0	56.4	59.3	60.9	63.1	64.6	68.9
移动电话 (部)	Mobile Phone (set)	240.0	249.1	253.2	253.8	259.1	259.4	251.9
计算机 (台)	Computer (set)	58.7	53.4	53.2	54.2	47.0	47.5	44.5

6–6 城镇居民人均收支情况
Per Capita Income and Consumption Expenditure of Urban Households

单位：元 (yuan)

指 标	Item	2017	2018	2019	2020	2021	2022	2023
城镇居民人均收入	**Per Capita Income of Urban Households**							
可支配收入	Disposable Income	36396	39251	42359	43834	47412	49283	51821
1.工资性收入	1.Income of Wages and Salaries	22201	23792	25565	26381	28481	29578	31321
2.经营净收入	2.Net Business Income	4065	4443	4840	4711	5382	5584	5903
3.财产净收入	3.Net Income from Property	3607	4028	4391	4627	5052	5238	5392
4.转移净收入	4.Net Income from Transfer	6524	6988	7563	8116	8497	8882	9205
现金可支配收入	Disposable Income in Cash	33757	36316	39148	40378	43596	45354	48277
1.工资性收入	1.Income of Wages and Salaries	22073	23671	25439	26240	28299	29393	31090
2.经营净收入	2.Net Business Income	4322	4808	5181	4987	5631	5784	6515
3.财产净收入	3.Net Income from Property	1234	1312	1495	1569	1836	1945	2188
4.转移净收入	4.Net Income from Transfer	6129	6526	7033	7581	7831	8232	8485
城镇居民人均支出	**Per Capita Expenditure of Urban Households**							
消费支出	Consumption Expenditure	24445	26112	28063	27007	30307	30391	32994
#服务性消费	Consumption Expenditure on Services	10854	12130	13518	12013	14058	13723	15673
1.食品烟酒	1.Food, Tobacco and Alcohol	7001	7239	7733	7881	8678	8958	9495
2.衣着	2.Clothing and Footwear	1758	1808	1832	1645	1843	1735	1880
3.居住	3.Housing	5564	6255	6780	6958	7405	7644	7822
4.生活用品及服务	4.Household Equipments, Furnishings and Services	1525	1629	1689	1640	1820	1800	1910
5.交通通信	5.Transport and Communications	3322	3473	3671	3474	3932	3909	4495
6.教育文化娱乐	6.Education, Culture and Recreation	2847	2974	3328	2592	3322	3050	3589
7.医疗保健	7.Health Care and Medical Services	1777	2046	2283	2172	2521	2481	2850
8.其他用品及服务	8.Miscellaneous Goods and Services	652	687	747	646	786	814	953
现金消费支出	Consumption Expenditure in Cash	20329	21287	22798	21556	24380	24375	26863
1.食品烟酒	1.Food, Tobacco and Alcohol	6861	7099	7584	7710	8444	8716	9255
2.衣着	2.Clothing and Footwear	1757	1807	1831	1644	1842	1734	1879
3.居住	3.Housing	1987	2045	2223	2222	2393	2503	2681
4.生活用品及服务	4.Household Equipments, Furnishings and Services	1515	1618	1676	1627	1807	1789	1902
5.交通通信	5.Transport and Communications	3316	3466	3665	3469	3925	3903	4488
6.教育文化娱乐	6.Education, Culture and Recreation	2845	2972	3326	2591	3320	3049	3587
7.医疗保健	7.Health Care and Medical Services	1404	1604	1755	1658	1881	1895	2130
8.其他用品及服务	8.Miscellaneous Goods and Services	645	675	738	635	769	785	942

6–7 城镇居民按收入五等份分组的人均可支配收入
Per Capita Disposable Income of Urban Households by Income Quintile

单位：元 (yuan)

组 别	Group	2017	2018	2019	2020	2021	2022	2023
20%低收入组家庭人均可支配收入	Lowest 20% Households	13723	14387	15549	15598	16746	16971	17478
20%中间偏下收入组家庭人均可支配收入	Second 20% Households	24550	24857	26784	27501	30133	31180	32202
20%中间收入组家庭人均可支配收入	Third 20% Households	33781	35196	37876	39278	42498	44283	46276
20%中间偏上收入组家庭人均可支配收入	Fourth 20% Households	45163	49174	52907	54910	59005	61724	65430
20%高收入组家庭人均可支配收入	Highest 20% Households	77097	84907	91683	96062	102596	107224	110639

6–8 城镇居民按东、中、西部及东北地区分组的人均可支配收入
Per Capita Disposable Income of Urban Households in Eastern, Central, Western and Northeastern Regions

单位：元 (yuan)

组 别	Group	2017	2018	2019	2020	2021	2022	2023
东部地区	Eastern Region	42990	46433	50145	52027	56378	58460	61472
中部地区	Central Region	31294	33803	36607	37658	40707	42733	44706
西部地区	Western Region	30987	33389	36041	37548	40583	42173	44136
东北地区	Northeastern Region	30960	32994	35130	35700	38225	39098	41009

6–9 城镇居民人均主要食品消费量
Per Capita Consumption of Major Foods of Urban Households

单位：千克 (kg)

指 标	Item	2017	2018	2019	2020	2021	2022	2023
粮食(原粮)	Grain (Unprocessed)	109.7	110.0	110.6	120.2	124.8	116.2	115.6
谷物	Cereals	98.6	98.8	98.5	107.3	112.0	103.6	102.5
薯类	Tuber	2.3	2.4	2.6	2.8	2.7	2.6	2.6
豆类	Beans and Products	8.8	8.8	9.5	10.0	10.1	10.0	10.5
食用油	Edible Oil and Fats	10.7	9.4	9.2	9.9	10.1	9.4	9.3
#食用植物油	Edible Vegetable Oil	10.3	8.9	8.7	9.5	9.6	9.0	8.9
蔬菜及食用菌	Vegetable and Edible Mushroom	106.7	103.1	105.8	109.8	112.0	110.9	114.0
#鲜菜	Fresh Vegetables	102.5	99.0	101.5	105.4	107.7	106.9	109.8
肉类	Meat and Products	29.2	31.2	28.7	27.4	34.4	35.2	39.6
#猪肉	Pork	20.6	22.7	20.3	19.0	25.1	26.0	28.7
牛肉	Beef	2.6	2.7	2.9	3.1	3.2	3.2	3.9
羊肉	Mutton	1.6	1.5	1.4	1.4	1.6	1.5	1.8
禽类	Poultry	9.7	9.8	11.4	13.0	12.3	11.9	12.6
水产品	Aquatic Products	14.8	14.3	16.7	16.6	16.7	16.2	17.4
蛋类	Eggs	10.9	10.8	11.5	13.5	13.4	13.8	14.6
奶类	Milk and Dairy Products	16.5	16.5	16.7	17.3	18.2	15.4	16.3
干鲜瓜果类	Dried and Fresh Melons and Fruits	59.9	62.0	66.8	65.9	67.7		
#鲜瓜果	Fresh Melons and Fruits	54.3	56.4	60.9	60.1	61.6	60.5	67.6
坚果类	Nuts and Processed Products	4.3	4.1	4.3	4.2	4.4		
食糖	Sugar	1.3	1.3	1.2	1.2	1.1	1.0	1.0

6–10 城镇居民平均每百户年末主要耐用消费品拥有量
Main Durable Goods Owned Per 100 Urban Households

指 标	Item	2017	2018	2019	2020	2021	2022	2023
家用汽车 (辆)	Automobile (unit)	37.5	41.0	43.2	44.9	50.1	51.4	55.9
摩托车 (辆)	Motorcycle (unit)	20.8	19.5	18.7	18.2	18.2	17.9	13.7
电动助力车 (辆)	Electric Bicycle (unit)	53.1	55.0	59.4	62.0	68.8	70.5	67.1
洗衣机 (台)	Washing Machine (set)	95.7	97.7	99.2	99.7	100.5	100.6	98.5
电冰箱(柜) (台)	Refrigerator (set)	98.0	100.9	102.5	103.1	104.2	104.4	101.9
彩色电视机 (台)	Color TV Set (set)	123.8	121.3	122.8	123.0	120.3	120.6	107.2
空调 (台)	Air Conditioner (set)	128.6	142.2	148.3	149.6	161.7	163.5	171.7
热水器 (台)	Water Heater (set)	90.7	97.2	98.2	100.7	98.1	98.2	97.2
排油烟机 (台)	Kitchen Ventilator (set)	73.7	79.1	81.7	82.6	82.3	83.2	84.6
移动电话 (部)	Mobile Phone (set)	235.4	243.1	247.4	248.7	253.6	254.0	239.5
计算机 (台)	Computer (set)	80.8	73.1	72.2	72.9	63.2	63.4	58.2

6-11 农村居民人均收支情况
Per Capita Income and Consumption Expenditure of Rural Households

单位：元 (yuan)

指　标	Item	2017	2018	2019	2020	2021	2022	2023
农村居民人均收入	**Per Capita Income of Rural Households**							
可支配收入	Disposable Income	13432	14617	16021	17131	18931	20133	21691
1.工资性收入	1.Income of Wages and Salaries	5498	5996	6583	6974	7958	8449	9163
2.经营净收入	2.Net Business Income	5028	5358	5762	6077	6566	6972	7431
3.财产净收入	3.Net Income from Property	303	342	377	419	469	509	540
4.转移净收入	4.Net Income from Transfer	2603	2920	3298	3661	3937	4203	4557
现金可支配收入	Disposable Income in Cash	12704	13913	15280	16395	17596	19084	20958
1.工资性收入	1.Income of Wages and Salaries	5471	5961	6540	6927	7882	8368	9080
2.经营净收入	2.Net Business Income	4547	4969	5382	5720	5709	6397	7236
3.财产净收入	3.Net Income from Property	303	342	377	419	469	509	540
4.转移净收入	4.Net Income from Transfer	2383	2640	2980	3329	3536	3810	4102
农村居民人均支出	**Per Capita Expenditure of Rural Households**							
消费支出	Consumption Expenditure	10955	12124	13328	13713	15916	16632	18175
#服务性消费	Consumption Expenditure on Services	4130	4645	5290	5190	6143	6358	7164
1.食品烟酒	1.Food,Tobacco and Alcohol	3415	3646	3998	4479	5200	5485	5880
2.衣着	2.Clothing and Footwear	612	648	713	713	859	864	921
3.居住	3.Housing	2354	2661	2871	2962	3315	3503	3694
4.生活用品及服务	4.Household Equipments, Furnishings and Services	634	720	764	768	900	934	992
5.交通通信	5.Transport and Communications	1509	1690	1837	1841	2132	2230	2480
6.教育文化娱乐	6.Education, Culture and Recreation	1171	1302	1482	1309	1645	1683	1951
7.医疗保健	7.Health Care and Medical Services	1059	1240	1421	1418	1580	1632	1916
8.其他用品及服务	8.Miscellaneous Goods and Services	201	218	241	224	284	300	341
现金消费支出	Consumption Expenditure in Cash	8856	9862	10854	11097	12858	13581	15103
1.食品烟酒	1.Food, Tobacco and Alcohol	2921	3226	3538	3945	4594	4912	5324
2.衣着	2.Clothing and Footwear	611	647	713	712	859	864	920
3.居住	3.Housing	956	1084	1164	1195	1250	1400	1629
4.生活用品及服务	4.Household Equipments, Furnishings and Services	625	709	749	753	887	924	986
5.交通通信	5.Transport and Communications	1508	1685	1835	1839	2129	2229	2478
6.教育文化娱乐	6.Education, Culture and Recreation	1171	1301	1481	1308	1645	1683	1950
7.医疗保健	7.Health Care and Medical Services	868	997	1138	1125	1224	1284	1481
8.其他用品及服务	8.Miscellaneous Goods and Services	196	213	236	218	270	286	336

6-12 农村居民按收入五等份分组的人均可支配收入
Per Capita Disposable Income of Rural Households by Income Quintile

单位：元 (yuan)

组 别	Group	2017	2018	2019	2020	2021	2022	2023
20%低收入组家庭人均可支配收入	Lowest 20% Households	3302	3666	4263	4681	4856	5025	5264
20%中间偏下收入组家庭人均可支配收入	Second 20% Households	8349	8508	9754	10392	11586	11965	12864
20%中间收入组家庭人均可支配收入	Third 20% Households	11978	12530	13984	14712	16546	17451	18479
20%中间偏上收入组家庭人均可支配收入	Fourth 20% Households	16944	18051	19732	20884	23167	24646	25981
20%高收入组家庭人均可支配收入	Highest 20% Households	31299	34043	36049	38520	43082	46075	50136

6-13 农村居民按东、中、西部及东北地区分组的人均可支配收入
Per Capita Disposable Income of Rural Households in Eastern, Central, Western and Northeastern Regions

单位：元 (yuan)

组 别	Group	2017	2018	2019	2020	2021	2022	2023
东部地区	Eastern Region	16822	18286	19989	21286	23556	25037	26907
中部地区	Central Region	12806	13954	15290	16213	17858	19080	20518
西部地区	Western Region	10829	11831	13035	14111	15608	16632	17911
东北地区	Northeastern Region	13116	14080	15357	16582	18280	18919	20300

6-14 农村居民人均主要食品消费量
Per Capita Consumption of Major Foods of Rural Households

单位：千克 (kg)

指 标	Item	2017	2018	2019	2020	2021	2022	2023
粮食(原粮)	Grain (Unprocessed)	154.6	148.5	154.8	168.4	170.8	164.6	159.8
谷物	Cereals	144.8	137.9	142.6	155.0	156.9	150.8	145.2
薯类	Tuber	2.8	3.0	3.2	3.5	3.3	3.0	3.2
豆类	Beans and Products	7.1	7.7	9.1	9.9	10.6	10.8	11.5
食用油	Edible Oil and Fats	10.1	9.9	9.8	11.0	11.7	10.8	10.9
#食用植物油	Edible Vegetable Oil	9.2	9.0	9.0	10.2	10.8	10.0	10.2
蔬菜及食用菌	Vegetable and Edible Fungi	90.2	87.5	89.5	95.8	107.0	104.6	113.0
#鲜菜	Fresh Vegetables	88.5	85.6	87.2	93.5	104.3	102.0	110.0
肉类	Meat and Products	23.6	27.5	24.7	21.4	30.9	33.7	40.1
#猪肉	Pork	19.5	23.0	20.2	17.1	25.4	28.1	32.9
牛肉	Beef	0.9	1.1	1.2	1.3	1.5	1.6	2.2
羊肉	Mutton	1.0	1.0	1.0	1.0	1.2	1.3	1.6
禽类	Poultry	7.9	8.0	10.0	12.4	12.4	11.4	12.0
水产品	Aquatic Products	7.4	7.8	9.6	10.3	10.9	10.7	12.2
蛋类	Eggs	8.9	8.4	9.6	11.8	13.0	13.1	15.4
奶类	Milk and Dairy Products	6.9	6.9	7.3	7.4	9.3	8.4	8.9
干鲜瓜果类	Fruits and Nuts	38.4	39.9	43.3	43.8	52.4		
#鲜瓜果	Fresh Melons and Fruits	35.1	36.3	39.3	39.9	47.5	46.7	51.7
坚果类	Nuts and Processed Products	2.6	2.8	3.1	3.1	3.8		
食糖	Sugar	1.4	1.3	1.4	1.4	1.5	1.5	1.4

6-15 农村居民平均每百户年末主要耐用消费品拥有量
Main Durable Goods Owned Per 100 Rural Households

指 标		Item		2017	2018	2019	2020	2021	2022	2023
家用汽车	(辆)	Automobile	(unit)	19.3	22.3	24.7	26.4	30.2	32.4	40.0
摩托车	(辆)	Motorcycle	(unit)	64.1	57.4	55.1	53.6	49.9	49.0	41.4
电动助力车	(辆)	Electric Bicycle	(unit)	61.1	64.9	70.1	73.1	80.7	82.5	84.9
洗衣机	(台)	Washing Machine	(set)	86.3	88.5	91.6	92.6	96.1	96.8	97.6
电冰箱(柜)	(台)	Refrigerator	(set)	91.7	95.9	98.6	100.1	103.5	103.9	105.7
彩色电视机	(台)	Color TV Set	(set)	120.0	116.6	117.6	117.8	116.3	116.5	108.8
空调	(台)	Air Conditioner	(set)	52.6	65.2	71.3	73.8	89.0	92.2	105.7
热水器	(台)	Water Heater	(set)	62.5	68.7	71.7	76.2	77.9	78.1	78.1
排油烟机	(台)	Kitchen Ventilator	(set)	20.4	26.0	29.0	30.9	36.6	38.5	44.3
移动电话	(部)	Mobile Phone	(set)	246.1	257.0	261.2	260.9	266.6	266.9	271.2
计算机	(台)	Computer	(set)	29.2	26.9	27.5	28.3	24.6	25.0	23.1

6-16 居民人均可支配收入和指数
Per Capita Disposable Income of Households and Indices

年份 Year	全国居民人均可支配收入 Nationwide Per Capita Disposable Income of Households		城镇居民人均可支配收入 Per Capita Disposable Income of Urban Households		农村居民人均可支配收入 Per Capita Disposable Income of Rural Households	
	绝对数（元） Value(yuan)	指数（1978年=100） Index(year of 1978=100)	绝对数（元） Value(yuan)	指数（1978年=100） Index(year of 1978=100)	绝对数（元） Value(yuan)	指数（1978年=100） Index(year of 1978=100)
1978	171	100.0	343	100.0	134	100.0
1980	247	131.6	478	127.0	191	139.0
1985	479	213.2	739	160.4	398	268.9
1990	904	243.8	1510	198.1	686	311.2
1995	2363	347.6	4283	290.3	1578	383.6
2000	3721	500.7	6256	382.3	2282	489.6
2001	4070	543.8	6824	414.1	2407	512.3
2002	4532	610.4	7652	469.1	2529	539.2
2003	5007	666.3	8406	510.6	2690	564.9
2004	5661	725.1	9335	549.0	3027	606.1
2005	6385	803.4	10382	600.9	3370	646.6
2006	7229	896.2	11620	662.5	3731	697.6
2007	8584	1015.4	13603	742.2	4327	767.7
2008	9957	1112.2	15549	803.5	4999	833.1
2009	10977	1234.8	16901	881.0	5435	908.3
2010	12520	1363.3	18779	948.5	6272	1012.1
2011	14551	1503.3	21427	1028.1	7394	1127.4
2012	16510	1662.5	24127	1126.8	8389	1248.1
2013	18311	1797.1	26467	1205.4	9430	1364.5
2014	20167	1940.5	28844	1287.1	10489	1490.5
2015	21966	2084.4	31195	1371.5	11422	1602.3
2016	23821	2216.1	33616	1448.0	12363	1702.1
2017	25974	2378.4	36396	1541.6	13432	1825.5
2018	28228	2532.1	39251	1627.6	14617	1945.3
2019	30733	2679.7	42359	1708.4	16021	2066.0
2020	32189	2737.3	43834	1728.4	17131	2144.2
2021	35128	2959.7	47412	1851.6	18931	2352.9
2022	36883	3046.8	49283	1886.1	20133	2452.1
2023	39218	3232.2	51821	1976.4	21691	2638.2

注：1.本表2013年及以后人均可支配收入来源于住户收支与生活状况调查，1978—2012年数据是根据历史数据按住户收支与生活状况调查可比口径推算获得。可支配收入绝对数按当年价计算，指数按可比价计算。

2.全国居民人均收入是根据全国十几万户抽样调查基础数据，依据每个样本户所代表的户数加权汇总而成。由于受城镇化和人口迁移等因素影响，各时期的分城乡、分地区人口构成发生变化，有时会导致全国居民收入增速超出分城乡居民收入增速区间的现象发生。全国居民收入增速快于分城乡居民收入增速的原因主要是在城镇化过程中，一部分在农村收入较高的人口进入城镇地区，但在城镇属于较低收入人群，他们的迁移对城乡居民收入均有拉低作用；但无论在城镇还是农村，其收入增长效应都会体现在全体居民收入增长中。

a) The per capita disposable income in this table in 2013 and later comes from the household income and expenditure and living conditions survey. The data from 1978 to 2012 are calculated based on historical data and the comparable caliber of household income and expenditure and living conditions survey. The absolute amount of disposable income is calculated at the current price, and the index is calculated at the comparable price.

b) The nationwide per capita disposable income of households is based on the sample survey of more than 100,000 households and is aggregated according to the weight of each household in the sample. Due to the factors such as urbanization and migration, the population composition of different cities and regions has changed in different periods, the growth rate of household income nationwide sometimes outpaces the growth rate in urban and rural areas. The reason of this phenomenon is that, in urbanization process, some population with higher income in rural areas move to cities and fall into lower income group in urban areas. Their migration brings down the income of both urban and rural households. However, the effect of income growth, whether in urban or rural areas, is reflected in the national income growth.

6–17 居民人均消费支出和指数
Per Capita Consumption Expenditure of Households and Indices

年份 Year	全国居民人均消费支出 Nationwide Per Capita Consumption Expenditure of Households		城镇居民人均消费支出 Per Capita Consumption Expenditure of Urban Households		农村居民人均消费支出 Per Capita Consumption Expenditure of Rural Households	
	绝对数(元) Value(yuan)	指数（1978年=100） Index(year of 1978=100)	绝对数(元) Value(yuan)	指数（1978年=100） Index(year of 1978=100)	绝对数(元) Value(yuan)	指数（1978年=100） Index(year of 1978=100)
1978	151	100.0	311	100.0	116	100.0
1980	211	127.4	412	121.0	162	131.2
1985	402	203.0	673	161.2	317	220.6
1990	768	234.9	1279	185.1	585	246.3
1995	1957	326.4	3538	264.6	1310	312.8
2000	2914	444.6	5027	338.9	1714	380.0
2001	3139	475.5	5350	358.3	1803	396.4
2002	3548	541.8	6089	411.8	1917	423.2
2003	3889	586.8	6587	441.5	2050	445.5
2004	4395	638.4	7280	472.4	2326	482.6
2005	5035	718.4	8068	515.5	2749	543.6
2006	5634	792.0	8851	557.3	3072	598.7
2007	6592	884.1	10196	614.3	3536	653.6
2008	7548	955.9	11489	655.6	4054	703.6
2009	8377	1068.4	12558	723.2	4464	777.1
2010	9378	1158.0	13821	771.0	4945	830.7
2011	10820	1267.5	15554	823.4	5892	935.4
2012	12054	1376.3	17107	881.9	6667	1032.7
2013	13220	1471.2	18488	928.9	7485	1127.8
2014	14491	1581.0	19968	982.7	8383	1240.7
2015	15712	1690.6	21392	1037.2	9223	1347.5
2016	17111	1804.9	23079	1096.0	10130	1452.5
2017	18322	1902.3	24445	1141.4	10955	1550.6
2018	19853	2019.7	26112	1194.0	12124	1681.2
2019	21559	2131.6	28063	1248.6	13328	1790.4
2020	21210	2046.3	27007	1174.1	13713	1788.6
2021	24100	2303.8	30307	1304.3	15916	2062.1
2022	24538	2299.3	30391	1282.6	16632	2112.7
2023	26796	2505.8	32994	1388.7	18175	2306.9

注：本表2013年及以后人均消费支出来源于住户收支与生活状况调查，1978–2012年数据是根据历史数据按住户收支与生活状况调查可比口径推算获得。消费支出绝对数按当年价计算，指数按可比价计算。

a) The per capita consumption expenditure in this table in 2013 and later is derived from the household income and expenditure and living conditions survey. The data from 1978 to 2012 are calculated based on historical data and the comparable caliber of the household income and expenditure and living conditions survey. The absolute amount of consumption expenditure is calculated at the current year's price, and the index is calculated at the comparable price.

6-18 分地区居民人均可支配收入
Per Capita Disposable Income of Households by Region

单位：元 (yuan)

地 区	Region	2017	2018	2019	2020	2021	2022	2023
全 国	**National Average**	**25974**	**28228**	**30733**	**32189**	**35128**	**36883**	**39218**
北 京	Beijing	57230	62361	67756	69434	75002	77415	81752
天 津	Tianjin	37022	39506	42404	43854	47449	48976	51271
河 北	Hebei	21484	23446	25665	27136	29383	30867	32903
山 西	Shanxi	20420	21990	23828	25214	27426	29178	30924
内蒙古	Inner Mongolia	26212	28376	30555	31497	34108	35921	38130
辽 宁	Liaoning	27835	29701	31820	32738	35112	36089	37992
吉 林	Jilin	21368	22798	24563	25751	27770	27975	29797
黑龙江	Heilongjiang	21206	22726	24254	24902	27159	28346	29694
上 海	Shanghai	58988	64183	69442	72232	78027	79610	84834
江 苏	Jiangsu	35024	38096	41400	43390	47498	49862	52674
浙 江	Zhejiang	42046	45840	49899	52397	57541	60302	63830
安 徽	Anhui	21863	23984	26415	28103	30904	32745	34893
福 建	Fujian	30048	32644	35616	37202	40659	43118	45426
江 西	Jiangxi	22031	24080	26262	28017	30610	32419	34242
山 东	Shandong	26930	29205	31597	32886	35705	37560	39890
河 南	Henan	20170	21964	23903	24810	26811	28222	29933
湖 北	Hubei	23757	25815	28319	27881	30829	32914	35146
湖 南	Hunan	23103	25241	27680	29380	31993	34036	35895
广 东	Guangdong	33003	35810	39014	41029	44993	47065	49327
广 西	Guangxi	19905	21485	23328	24562	26727	27981	29514
海 南	Hainan	22553	24579	26679	27904	30457	30957	33192
重 庆	Chongqing	24153	26386	28920	30824	33803	35666	37595
四 川	Sichuan	20580	22461	24703	26522	29080	30679	32514
贵 州	Guizhou	16704	18430	20397	21795	23996	25508	27098
云 南	Yunnan	18348	20084	22082	23295	25666	26937	28421
西 藏	Xizang	15457	17286	19501	21744	24950	26675	28983
陕 西	Shaanxi	20635	22528	24666	26226	28568	30116	32128
甘 肃	Gansu	16011	17488	19139	20335	22066	23273	25011
青 海	Qinghai	19001	20757	22618	24037	25919	27000	28587
宁 夏	Ningxia	20562	22400	24412	25735	27904	29599	31604
新 疆	Xinjiang	19975	21500	23103	23845	26075	27063	28947

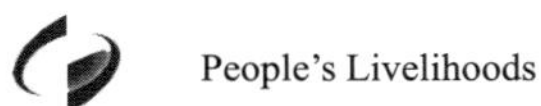

6–19 分地区居民人均可支配收入来源（2023年）
Per Capita Disposable Income of Households by Source and Region (2023)

单位：元 (yuan)

地 区	Region	可支配收入 Disposable Income	工资性收入 Income from Wages and Salaries	经营净收入 Net Business Income	财产净收入 Net Income from Property	转移净收入 Net Income from Transfer
全 国	**National Average**	**39218**	**22053**	**6542**	**3362**	**7261**
北 京	Beijing	81752	51632	1026	12280	16814
天 津	Tianjin	51271	32361	3458	4577	10875
河 北	Hebei	32903	19723	5300	2457	5423
山 西	Shanxi	30924	16630	4278	1832	8184
内蒙古	Inner Mongolia	38130	19896	10171	1847	6216
辽 宁	Liaoning	37992	20724	6040	1580	9648
吉 林	Jilin	29797	15252	7287	1277	5982
黑龙江	Heilongjiang	29694	13987	5894	1276	8538
上 海	Shanghai	84834	53260	1592	10764	19219
江 苏	Jiangsu	52674	30054	6645	5417	10557
浙 江	Zhejiang	63830	35769	10664	7783	9615
安 徽	Anhui	34893	18435	7619	2329	6510
福 建	Fujian	45426	26659	8365	4978	5425
江 西	Jiangxi	34242	19089	5408	2669	7077
山 东	Shandong	39890	22908	8374	2676	5932
河 南	Henan	29933	15166	6037	1889	6841
湖 北	Hubei	35146	17626	7146	2449	7924
湖 南	Hunan	35895	17811	7541	2701	7842
广 东	Guangdong	49327	33663	6328	6412	2924
广 西	Guangxi	29514	14020	7426	2329	5739
海 南	Hainan	33192	18385	6743	2634	5431
重 庆	Chongqing	37595	20175	5873	2312	9235
四 川	Sichuan	32514	16154	6433	2049	7878
贵 州	Guizhou	27098	13912	6031	1579	5577
云 南	Yunnan	28421	14806	6394	2445	4776
西 藏	Xizang	28983	15832	6531	1801	4820
陕 西	Shaanxi	32128	17302	4127	1978	8720
甘 肃	Gansu	25011	14236	4382	1435	4958
青 海	Qinghai	28587	16534	4349	1072	6632
宁 夏	Ningxia	31604	19003	5670	841	6089
新 疆	Xinjiang	28947	15211	5871	1177	6687

6-20 分地区居民人均消费支出
Per Capita Consumption Expenditure of Households by Region

单位：元 (yuan)

地 区	Region	2017	2018	2019	2020	2021	2022	2023
全 国	**National Average**	**18322**	**19853**	**21559**	**21210**	**24100**	**24538**	**26796**
北 京	Beijing	37425	39843	43038	38903	43640	42683	47586
天 津	Tianjin	27841	29903	31854	28461	33188	31324	34914
河 北	Hebei	15437	16722	17987	18037	19954	20890	22920
山 西	Shanxi	13664	14810	15863	15733	17191	17537	19756
内蒙古	Inner Mongolia	18946	19665	20743	19794	22658	22298	27025
辽 宁	Liaoning	20463	21398	22203	20672	23831	22604	24865
吉 林	Jilin	15632	17200	18075	17318	19605	17898	21411
黑龙江	Heilongjiang	15577	16994	18111	17056	20636	20412	22052
上 海	Shanghai	39792	43351	45605	42536	48879	46045	52508
江 苏	Jiangsu	23469	25007	26697	26225	31451	32848	35491
浙 江	Zhejiang	27079	29471	32026	31295	36668	38971	42194
安 徽	Anhui	15752	17045	19137	18877	21911	22542	23607
福 建	Fujian	21249	22996	25314	25126	28440	30042	31869
江 西	Jiangxi	14459	15792	17650	17955	20290	21708	23379
山 东	Shandong	17281	18780	20427	20940	22821	22640	24293
河 南	Henan	13730	15169	16332	16143	18391	19019	21011
湖 北	Hubei	16938	19538	21567	19246	23846	24828	27106
湖 南	Hunan	17160	18808	20479	20998	22798	24083	25462
广 东	Guangdong	24820	26054	28995	28492	31589	32169	34331
广 西	Guangxi	13424	14935	16418	16357	18088	18343	19749
海 南	Hainan	15403	17528	19555	18972	22242	21500	23752
重 庆	Chongqing	17898	19248	20774	21678	24598	25371	26515
四 川	Sichuan	16180	17664	19338	19783	21518	22302	23550
贵 州	Guizhou	12970	13798	14780	14874	17957	17939	20161
云 南	Yunnan	12658	14250	15780	16792	18851	18951	20995
西 藏	Xizang	10320	11520	13029	13225	15343	15886	17220
陕 西	Shaanxi	14900	16160	17465	17418	19347	19848	22012
甘 肃	Gansu	13120	14624	15879	16175	17456	17489	19013
青 海	Qinghai	15503	16557	17545	18284	19020	17261	20327
宁 夏	Ningxia	15350	16715	18297	17506	20024	19136	21629
新 疆	Xinjiang	15087	16189	17397	16512	18961	17927	19715

6-21 分地区居民人均消费支出构成（2023年）

Per Capita Consumption Expenditure of Households by Composition and Region (2023)

单位：元 (yuan)

地区	Region	消费支出 Consumption Expenditure	食品烟酒 Food, Tobacco and Alcohol	衣着 Clothing and Footwear	居住 Housing	生活用品及服务 Household Equipments, Furnishings and Services	交通通信 Transport and Communi-cations	教育文化娱乐 Education, Culture and Recreation	医疗保健 Health Care and Medical Services	其他用品及服务 Miscellaneous Goods and Services
全国	**National Average**	**26796**	**7983**	**1479**	**6095**	**1526**	**3652**	**2904**	**2460**	**697**
北京	Beijing	47586	10142	2053	18668	2352	4858	3799	4276	1438
天津	Tianjin	34914	9815	1796	7772	1927	4698	3673	3937	1296
河北	Hebei	22920	6739	1534	4964	1459	3129	2309	2174	613
山西	Shanxi	19756	5258	1372	4316	1217	2621	2291	2138	543
内蒙古	Inner Mongolia	27025	7446	1862	5058	1500	4717	2656	2935	851
辽宁	Liaoning	24865	7346	1491	4995	1264	3358	2701	2899	812
吉林	Jilin	21411	5863	1351	3957	1014	3153	2569	2816	688
黑龙江	Heilongjiang	22052	6648	1441	4092	1013	2993	2386	2903	577
上海	Shanghai	52508	13214	1996	17944	2270	5728	4976	4650	1730
江苏	Jiangsu	35491	9926	1891	9169	2030	5075	3334	2916	1151
浙江	Zhejiang	42194	11757	2254	10458	2472	6484	4458	2939	1371
安徽	Anhui	23607	7919	1543	4902	1451	2665	2619	1962	546
福建	Fujian	31869	10183	1546	8646	1727	3706	3169	2125	765
江西	Jiangxi	23379	7460	1145	5061	1221	2815	2967	2231	479
山东	Shandong	24293	6791	1549	4726	1762	3795	2915	2247	509
河南	Henan	21011	6275	1509	4334	1267	2570	2461	2116	479
湖北	Hubei	27106	8069	1480	5815	1514	3449	3142	2984	652
湖南	Hunan	25462	7415	1426	5193	1547	3367	3533	2486	496
广东	Guangdong	34331	11137	1290	8849	1693	4865	3538	2120	840
广西	Guangxi	19749	6255	736	4098	1009	2668	2630	2021	334
海南	Hainan	23752	9315	791	5417	1031	2830	2379	1566	423
重庆	Chongqing	26515	8644	1696	4920	1707	3337	2873	2646	691
四川	Sichuan	23550	7846	1355	4157	1450	3300	2418	2435	589
贵州	Guizhou	20161	5858	1129	3512	1198	3446	2611	1895	511
云南	Yunnan	20995	6816	1057	4197	1142	2949	2261	2110	463
西藏	Xizang	17220	6406	1445	3543	1188	2460	913	838	427
陕西	Shaanxi	22012	6212	1331	4759	1341	2897	2293	2704	475
甘肃	Gansu	19013	5687	1222	4065	1057	2604	2071	1893	414
青海	Qinghai	20327	6361	1458	3631	1072	3504	1551	2174	576
宁夏	Ningxia	21629	6150	1366	3941	1397	3301	2469	2455	549
新疆	Xinjiang	19715	6261	1432	3585	1106	2753	1725	2173	679

6-22 分地区居民家庭人均主要食品消费量(2023年)
Per Capita Consumption of Major Foods of Households by Region (2023)

单位：千克 (kg)

地 区	Region	粮食 (原粮) Grain (Unprocessed)	#谷物 Cereals	食用油 Edible Oil and Fats	#食用植物油 Edible Vegetable Oil	蔬菜及食用菌 Vegetable and Edible Mushroom	肉类 Meat and Products	#猪肉 Pork
全 国	**National Average**	**134.4**	**120.6**	**10.0**	**9.4**	**113.6**	**39.8**	**30.5**
北 京	Beijing	91.5	79.2	6.3	6.2	112.0	31.1	18.2
天 津	Tianjin	98.1	88.1	7.4	7.3	109.3	29.1	18.3
河 北	Hebei	171.4	152.4	9.1	8.9	139.7	36.1	24.5
山 西	Shanxi	113.6	97.7	8.2	8.1	88.6	20.2	14.3
内蒙古	Inner Mongolia	168.6	151.7	7.4	7.1	122.4	44.1	27.4
辽 宁	Liaoning	145.7	128.0	10.1	9.9	129.5	42.0	30.7
吉 林	Jilin	140.7	124.2	11.7	11.6	102.0	32.5	24.7
黑龙江	Heilongjiang	144.1	129.7	15.1	15.0	115.1	36.6	27.0
上 海	Shanghai	99.1	88.0	8.9	8.8	101.7	35.1	24.1
江 苏	Jiangsu	136.7	118.0	8.5	8.2	128.3	42.9	30.9
浙 江	Zhejiang	133.8	117.8	9.8	9.3	106.3	41.8	31.9
安 徽	Anhui	147.1	129.8	9.3	8.7	123.5	40.7	31.1
福 建	Fujian	129.0	118.7	11.0	10.1	104.7	43.8	35.7
江 西	Jiangxi	158.4	141.4	13.7	13.2	129.6	47.8	39.4
山 东	Shandong	127.7	115.4	7.9	7.9	107.2	35.8	25.6
河 南	Henan	151.0	135.6	8.3	8.1	117.3	33.3	24.8
湖 北	Hubei	116.7	102.5	13.9	13.5	128.1	38.5	30.6
湖 南	Hunan	143.9	133.5	12.2	9.8	117.1	46.4	39.8
广 东	Guangdong	114.3	105.2	9.5	9.1	107.0	50.9	40.7
广 西	Guangxi	122.1	115.3	9.0	8.0	90.2	40.0	34.9
海 南	Hainan	100.0	94.3	9.8	8.6	109.9	45.6	38.7
重 庆	Chongqing	149.7	132.4	14.9	13.6	146.4	57.9	48.5
四 川	Sichuan	126.1	114.4	11.5	10.4	119.6	49.5	42.5
贵 州	Guizhou	122.2	108.7	8.0	7.1	83.7	33.8	30.3
云 南	Yunnan	125.8	110.5	6.8	5.8	108.8	41.1	35.4
西 藏	Xizang	168.7	166.0	17.1	9.0	64.1	41.6	7.1
陕 西	Shaanxi	145.8	129.0	11.7	11.6	106.4	24.6	18.6
甘 肃	Gansu	138.0	125.9	10.1	10.0	87.3	25.0	17.9
青 海	Qinghai	106.5	100.1	9.0	7.8	65.6	31.1	12.6
宁 夏	Ningxia	109.4	101.7	9.2	9.2	86.9	21.4	7.9
新 疆	Xinjiang	133.5	129.4	12.9	12.7	92.9	29.8	4.1

6-22 续表 continued

单位：千克 (kg)

地 区	Region	#牛肉 Beef	#羊肉 Mutton	禽类 Poultry	水产品 Aquatic Products	蛋类 Eggs	奶类 Milk and Dairy Products	鲜瓜果 Fresh Melons and Fruits	食糖 Sugar
全 国	**National Average**	**3.1**	**1.7**	**12.4**	**15.2**	**15.0**	**13.2**	**60.8**	**1.2**
北 京	Beijing	3.8	3.4	7.3	10.2	17.4	20.7	70.6	0.9
天 津	Tianjin	2.9	3.1	6.6	16.7	19.9	15.2	79.7	0.9
河 北	Hebei	2.0	2.3	9.1	10.2	23.4	17.8	81.0	1.5
山 西	Shanxi	1.0	1.4	4.0	3.6	15.0	16.3	59.4	0.9
内蒙古	Inner Mongolia	4.3	7.4	8.3	8.0	16.5	25.4	77.6	1.4
辽 宁	Liaoning	3.9	1.9	7.5	18.1	19.4	15.6	74.6	1.1
吉 林	Jilin	3.2	1.1	6.0	10.1	15.1	8.4	57.7	1.2
黑龙江	Heilongjiang	2.9	2.0	6.9	11.8	16.5	10.5	67.9	1.6
上 海	Shanghai	4.9	1.3	12.7	24.5	15.0	21.9	54.1	1.2
江 苏	Jiangsu	4.0	1.4	15.9	25.5	17.4	16.8	59.8	1.3
浙 江	Zhejiang	4.7	1.1	13.2	29.6	13.2	14.3	68.3	1.4
安 徽	Anhui	3.2	1.4	17.1	16.0	17.1	13.3	67.6	0.9
福 建	Fujian	3.5	0.9	14.6	31.5	14.0	13.0	55.0	1.4
江 西	Jiangxi	4.1	0.7	14.6	19.6	13.1	11.6	59.2	1.1
山 东	Shandong	1.9	1.9	9.5	15.1	25.1	15.8	83.5	0.8
河 南	Henan	2.1	1.6	10.6	7.7	24.3	13.4	73.8	1.1
湖 北	Hubei	2.9	1.0	9.6	17.6	10.8	9.2	49.6	1.1
湖 南	Hunan	3.1	0.8	13.1	14.6	12.3	7.9	58.9	1.1
广 东	Guangdong	4.2	0.9	24.9	27.7	10.0	9.6	47.7	1.0
广 西	Guangxi	2.3	0.6	21.7	12.4	6.7	6.4	41.1	1.0
海 南	Hainan	3.5	1.1	25.8	33.5	6.0	5.8	35.7	0.7
重 庆	Chongqing	3.3	1.0	14.1	15.6	15.3	17.4	60.0	2.2
四 川	Sichuan	2.6	0.5	12.4	10.1	11.4	12.8	46.6	1.5
贵 州	Guizhou	1.2	0.3	7.0	3.7	5.2	6.7	39.3	1.0
云 南	Yunnan	2.3	0.5	11.2	6.3	7.8	8.0	45.7	1.3
西 藏	Xizang	25.8	6.7	1.2	0.6	3.0	7.6	13.1	2.3
陕 西	Shaanxi	1.4	1.4	4.5	3.7	12.8	13.7	55.3	1.0
甘 肃	Gansu	2.0	2.4	5.2	3.0	9.5	11.6	56.5	1.3
青 海	Qinghai	10.3	6.6	3.9	2.4	6.6	17.8	34.8	1.5
宁 夏	Ningxia	6.5	5.5	8.3	3.2	7.6	14.5	74.3	1.3
新 疆	Xinjiang	6.9	16.6	5.2	2.9	8.6	19.6	59.4	1.3

6-23 分地区居民平均每百户年末主要耐用消费品拥有量(2023年)
Main Durable Goods Owned Per 100 Households at Year-end by Region (2023)

地 区	Region	家用汽车(辆) Automobile (unit)	摩托车(辆) Motorcycle (unit)	电动助力车(辆) Electric Bicycle (unit)	洗衣机(台) Washing Machine (set)	电冰箱(柜)(台) Refrigerator (set)	彩色电视机(台) Color TV Set (set)
全 国	**National Average**	**49.7**	**24.5**	**74.0**	**98.2**	**103.4**	**107.8**
北 京	Beijing	51.2	4.4	26.8	98.8	102.2	105.4
天 津	Tianjin	67.3	2.2	49.6	99.9	104.1	104.1
河 北	Hebei	63.5	14.0	119.3	102.6	103.3	105.7
山 西	Shanxi	48.6	17.3	74.8	100.0	97.8	98.4
内蒙古	Inner Mongolia	58.2	17.5	66.4	98.5	116.5	98.4
辽 宁	Liaoning	39.7	13.6	28.7	95.7	99.7	99.9
吉 林	Jilin	39.9	15.6	23.5	95.8	98.7	95.8
黑龙江	Heilongjiang	35.4	13.4	28.7	96.0	99.2	95.9
上 海	Shanghai	46.5	2.2	75.6	95.7	103.0	143.1
江 苏	Jiangsu	59.0	7.2	128.0	102.7	109.4	148.2
浙 江	Zhejiang	64.7	8.4	79.8	95.8	105.9	151.3
安 徽	Anhui	43.1	12.9	110.8	97.1	105.0	112.5
福 建	Fujian	35.6	36.7	75.0	94.4	101.8	101.1
江 西	Jiangxi	45.9	35.8	90.9	91.7	101.3	115.7
山 东	Shandong	63.5	14.4	106.5	99.8	103.3	101.2
河 南	Henan	55.1	15.1	137.6	103.4	102.0	108.2
湖 北	Hubei	42.6	45.8	51.8	99.1	110.2	108.6
湖 南	Hunan	43.8	46.3	34.2	99.6	107.1	105.8
广 东	Guangdong	52.1	41.3	59.4	91.3	96.0	85.1
广 西	Guangxi	42.0	48.0	106.1	96.9	102.6	99.0
海 南	Hainan	38.7	28.8	129.1	82.9	96.3	89.7
重 庆	Chongqing	42.2	23.4	16.3	98.0	103.8	110.2
四 川	Sichuan	39.3	31.0	45.1	100.7	111.1	113.6
贵 州	Guizhou	38.6	39.9	25.1	98.7	99.9	95.7
云 南	Yunnan	54.1	58.7	44.5	99.5	104.1	102.6
西 藏	Xizang	61.8	58.7	25.2	117.3	114.3	108.5
陕 西	Shaanxi	45.2	29.0	56.4	98.6	97.7	99.8
甘 肃	Gansu	42.4	25.5	46.6	99.5	96.3	98.3
青 海	Qinghai	68.1	29.2	21.4	101.7	111.9	96.6
宁 夏	Ningxia	51.2	18.8	79.9	102.2	102.2	98.7
新 疆	Xinjiang	41.2	14.9	68.5	99.7	106.0	98.4

6–23 续表 continued

地 区	Region	空 调 (台) Air Conditioner (set)	热水器 (台) Water Heater (set)	排油烟机 (台) Kitchen Ventilator (set)	移动电话 (部) Mobile Phone (set)	计算机 (台) Computer (set)
全 国	**National Average**	**145.9**	**89.8**	**68.9**	**251.9**	**44.5**
北 京	Beijing	189.5	98.7	91.9	217.3	74.3
天 津	Tianjin	186.3	97.7	94.0	233.9	60.1
河 北	Hebei	142.9	81.5	76.6	259.5	39.2
山 西	Shanxi	55.6	72.1	69.5	246.5	35.8
内蒙古	Inner Mongolia	18.5	67.1	62.4	229.7	36.2
辽 宁	Liaoning	65.6	76.0	73.6	204.5	32.2
吉 林	Jilin	21.5	57.1	57.8	225.9	23.1
黑龙江	Heilongjiang	15.6	56.9	63.8	220.5	26.4
上 海	Shanghai	203.6	98.2	83.8	218.8	81.0
江 苏	Jiangsu	237.3	96.9	83.3	249.5	61.5
浙 江	Zhejiang	220.2	104.3	84.7	242.8	63.0
安 徽	Anhui	179.3	90.0	68.2	251.5	39.5
福 建	Fujian	181.7	111.6	64.6	238.8	52.5
江 西	Jiangxi	154.9	96.9	70.0	279.8	40.0
山 东	Shandong	160.2	96.1	81.2	228.1	50.2
河 南	Henan	193.4	87.5	65.5	273.6	39.9
湖 北	Hubei	163.6	96.3	74.0	267.2	44.0
湖 南	Hunan	167.7	95.9	67.7	278.1	42.7
广 东	Guangdong	206.2	99.7	65.7	246.3	63.2
广 西	Guangxi	153.3	99.1	56.3	276.4	36.5
海 南	Hainan	158.9	93.8	49.6	266.4	38.4
重 庆	Chongqing	208.5	96.2	69.0	262.0	41.6
四 川	Sichuan	151.2	92.2	54.6	270.5	34.0
贵 州	Guizhou	28.0	88.3	43.1	296.6	29.0
云 南	Yunnan	17.9	81.0	49.5	292.5	36.4
西 藏	Xizang	14.1	42.3	28.6	242.2	26.6
陕 西	Shaanxi	113.9	76.8	58.8	253.4	32.8
甘 肃	Gansu	12.9	62.9	51.5	283.2	36.2
青 海	Qinghai	4.2	67.1	64.4	279.2	34.4
宁 夏	Ningxia	20.3	96.7	72.0	259.9	41.6
新 疆	Xinjiang	29.1	85.3	63.6	229.3	25.6

6-24 分地区城镇居民人均可支配收入
Per Capita Disposable Income of Urban Households by Region

单位：元 (yuan)

地 区	Region	2017	2018	2019	2020	2021	2022	2023
全 国	**National Average**	**36396**	**39251**	**42359**	**43834**	**47412**	**49283**	**51821**
北 京	Beijing	62406	67990	73849	75602	81518	84023	88650
天 津	Tianjin	40278	42976	46119	47659	51486	53003	55355
河 北	Hebei	30548	32977	35738	37286	39791	41278	43631
山 西	Shanxi	29132	31035	33262	34793	37433	39532	41327
内蒙古	Inner Mongolia	35670	38305	40782	41353	44377	46295	48676
辽 宁	Liaoning	34993	37342	39777	40376	43051	44003	45896
吉 林	Jilin	28319	30172	32299	33396	35646	35471	37503
黑龙江	Heilongjiang	27446	29191	30945	31115	33646	35042	36492
上 海	Shanghai	62596	68034	73615	76437	82429	84034	89477
江 苏	Jiangsu	43622	47200	51056	53102	57743	60178	63211
浙 江	Zhejiang	51261	55574	60182	62699	68487	71268	74997
安 徽	Anhui	31640	34393	37540	39442	43009	45133	47446
福 建	Fujian	39001	42121	45620	47160	51140	53817	56153
江 西	Jiangxi	31198	33819	36546	38556	41684	43697	45554
山 东	Shandong	36789	39549	42329	43726	47066	49050	51571
河 南	Henan	29558	31874	34201	34750	37095	38484	40234
湖 北	Hubei	31889	34455	37601	36706	40278	42626	44990
湖 南	Hunan	33948	36698	39842	41698	44866	47301	49243
广 东	Guangdong	40975	44341	48118	50257	54854	56905	59307
广 西	Guangxi	30502	32436	34745	35859	38530	39703	41287
海 南	Hainan	30817	33349	36017	37097	40213	40118	42661
重 庆	Chongqing	32193	34889	37939	40006	43502	45509	47435
四 川	Sichuan	30727	33216	36154	38253	41444	43233	45227
贵 州	Guizhou	29080	31592	34404	36096	39211	41086	42772
云 南	Yunnan	30996	33488	36238	37500	40905	42168	43563
西 藏	Xizang	30671	33797	37410	41156	46503	48753	51900
陕 西	Shaanxi	30810	33319	36098	37868	40713	42431	44713
甘 肃	Gansu	27763	29957	32323	33822	36187	37572	39833
青 海	Qinghai	29169	31515	33830	35506	37745	38736	40408
宁 夏	Ningxia	29472	31895	34328	35720	38291	40194	42395
新 疆	Xinjiang	30775	32764	34664	34838	37642	38410	40578

6-25 分地区城镇居民人均可支配收入来源（2023年）
Per Capita Disposable Income of Urban Households by Source and Region (2023)

单位：元 (yuan)

地 区	Region	可支配收入 Disposable Income	工资性收入 Income from Wages and Salaries	经营净收入 Net Business Income	财产净收入 Net Income from Property	转移净收入 Net Income from Transfer
全 国	**National Average**	**51821**	**31321**	**5903**	**5392**	**9205**
北 京	Beijing	88650	55487	861	13617	18686
天 津	Tianjin	55355	35451	2678	5234	11992
河 北	Hebei	43631	27371	4028	4224	8008
山 西	Shanxi	41327	23505	3964	3070	10788
内蒙古	Inner Mongolia	48676	29756	9276	2637	7006
辽 宁	Liaoning	45896	26839	4344	2104	12610
吉 林	Jilin	37503	23371	4072	1830	8231
黑龙江	Heilongjiang	36492	21006	3169	1163	11153
上 海	Shanghai	89477	56171	1521	11809	19976
江 苏	Jiangsu	63211	37332	6049	7522	12308
浙 江	Zhejiang	74997	41439	10833	10880	11844
安 徽	Anhui	47446	28466	7306	4038	7636
福 建	Fujian	56153	35054	7509	7505	6085
江 西	Jiangxi	45554	27314	4406	4648	9186
山 东	Shandong	51571	30908	8565	4230	7868
河 南	Henan	40234	23114	5674	3567	7879
湖 北	Hubei	44990	25232	5961	3984	9813
湖 南	Hunan	49243	26398	7604	4842	10399
广 东	Guangdong	59307	41580	6422	8665	2639
广 西	Guangxi	41287	22333	7526	4387	7040
海 南	Hainan	42661	25834	5656	4332	6840
重 庆	Chongqing	47435	27656	5350	3364	11065
四 川	Sichuan	45227	26228	5250	3508	10240
贵 州	Guizhou	42772	24107	7811	3438	7417
云 南	Yunnan	43563	26055	5430	5200	6877
西 藏	Xizang	51900	38400	1871	4178	7452
陕 西	Shaanxi	44713	25805	3390	3388	12130
甘 肃	Gansu	39833	27141	2810	3001	6880
青 海	Qinghai	40408	26641	3272	1638	8858
宁 夏	Ningxia	42395	28642	4364	1338	8052
新 疆	Xinjiang	40578	24963	4006	1844	9765

6-26 分地区城镇居民人均消费支出
Per Capita Consumption Expenditure of Urban Households by Region

单位：元 (yuan)

地 区	Region	2017	2018	2019	2020	2021	2022	2023
全 国	**National Average**	**24445**	**26112**	**28063**	**27007**	**30307**	**30391**	**32994**
北 京	Beijing	40346	42926	46358	41726	46776	45617	50897
天 津	Tianjin	30284	32655	34811	30895	36067	33824	37586
河 北	Hebei	20600	22127	23483	23167	24192	25071	27906
山 西	Shanxi	18404	19790	21159	20332	21965	21923	24524
内蒙古	Inner Mongolia	23638	24437	25383	23888	27194	26667	32249
辽 宁	Liaoning	25379	26448	27355	24849	28438	26652	29091
吉 林	Jilin	20051	22394	23394	21623	24421	21835	26677
黑龙江	Heilongjiang	19270	21035	22165	20397	24422	24011	25882
上 海	Shanghai	42304	46015	48272	44839	51295	48111	54919
江 苏	Jiangsu	27726	29462	31329	30882	36558	37796	40461
浙 江	Zhejiang	31924	34598	37508	36197	42193	44511	47762
安 徽	Anhui	20740	21523	23782	22683	26495	26832	27900
福 建	Fujian	25980	28145	30946	30487	33942	35692	37674
江 西	Jiangxi	19244	20760	22714	22134	24587	25976	27733
山 东	Shandong	23072	24798	26731	27291	29314	28555	30251
河 南	Henan	19422	20989	21972	20645	23178	23539	25570
湖 北	Hubei	21276	23996	26422	22885	28506	29121	31500
湖 南	Hunan	23163	25064	26924	26796	28294	29580	31035
广 东	Guangdong	30198	30924	34424	33511	36621	36936	39333
广 西	Guangxi	18349	20159	21591	20907	22555	22438	24427
海 南	Hainan	20372	22971	25317	23560	27565	26418	28930
重 庆	Chongqing	22759	24154	25785	26464	29850	30574	31531
四 川	Sichuan	21991	23484	25367	25133	26971	27637	29280
贵 州	Guizhou	20348	20788	21402	20587	25333	24230	27693
云 南	Yunnan	19560	21626	23455	24569	27441	26240	28338
西 藏	Xizang	21088	23029	25637	24927	28159	28265	28858
陕 西	Shaanxi	20388	21966	23514	22866	24784	24766	27303
甘 肃	Gansu	20659	22606	24454	24615	25757	25207	27044
青 海	Qinghai	21473	22998	23799	24315	24513	21700	25373
宁 夏	Ningxia	20219	21977	24161	22379	25386	24213	27076
新 疆	Xinjiang	22797	24191	25594	22952	25724	24142	26134

6-27 分地区城镇居民人均消费支出构成(2023年)
Per Capita Consumption Expenditure of Urban Households by Composition and Region (2023)

单位：元 (yuan)

地区	Region	消费支出 Consumption Expenditure	食品烟酒 Food, Tobacco and Alcohol	衣着 Clothing and Footwear	居住 Housing	生活用品及服务 Household Equipments, Furnishings and Services	交通通信 Transport and Communi-cations	教育文化娱乐 Education, Culture and Recreation	医疗保健 Health Care and Medical Services	其他用品及服务 Miscellaneous Goods and Services
全国	**National Average**	**32994**	**9495**	**1880**	**7822**	**1910**	**4495**	**3589**	**2850**	**953**
北京	Beijing	50897	10584	2180	20261	2454	5072	4151	4609	1587
天津	Tianjin	37586	10384	1933	8411	2054	5036	4108	4205	1454
河北	Hebei	27906	7755	1923	6617	1846	3691	2704	2538	831
山西	Shanxi	24524	6216	1755	5317	1556	3336	2975	2633	737
内蒙古	Inner Mongolia	32249	8707	2414	6243	1875	5543	3270	3069	1127
辽宁	Liaoning	29091	8530	1780	5992	1524	3865	3168	3192	1039
吉林	Jilin	26677	6967	1825	5304	1348	3942	3249	3076	966
黑龙江	Heilongjiang	25882	7608	1790	5207	1286	3333	2804	3104	751
上海	Shanghai	54919	13568	2077	19100	2357	5895	5339	4733	1849
江苏	Jiangsu	40461	10746	2174	10971	2268	5822	3898	3185	1397
浙江	Zhejiang	47762	12909	2623	11550	2848	7558	5298	3248	1728
安徽	Anhui	27900	9164	1925	5968	1695	3170	3109	2131	737
福建	Fujian	37674	11730	1847	10664	2053	4379	3795	2283	921
江西	Jiangxi	27733	8628	1455	6017	1535	3569	3456	2400	672
山东	Shandong	30251	8275	2050	6058	2327	4510	3742	2592	697
河南	Henan	25570	7436	1836	5487	1575	3099	2934	2506	698
湖北	Hubei	31500	9247	1805	6795	1677	3877	3809	3453	837
湖南	Hunan	31035	8835	1962	6167	1990	4336	4311	2739	695
广东	Guangdong	39333	12290	1559	10329	2011	5661	4115	2350	1018
广西	Guangxi	24427	7758	1036	5041	1320	3276	3142	2382	473
海南	Hainan	28930	10775	1029	6985	1325	3529	2866	1857	565
重庆	Chongqing	31531	10033	2137	5926	2038	4031	3460	3003	903
四川	Sichuan	29280	9614	1852	5370	1870	4106	3017	2683	769
贵州	Guizhou	27693	7709	1727	4361	1688	5289	3559	2537	823
云南	Yunnan	28338	8843	1601	5769	1658	3744	3002	2966	756
西藏	Xizang	28858	10005	2893	5763	2260	3875	1628	1551	884
陕西	Shaanxi	27303	7562	1752	5969	1722	3594	2886	3148	670
甘肃	Gansu	27044	7793	1871	6039	1583	3740	2937	2407	674
青海	Qinghai	25373	7490	1846	5005	1327	4359	2012	2547	787
宁夏	Ningxia	27076	7558	1780	4944	1768	4187	3160	2960	719
新疆	Xinjiang	26134	8296	1852	4667	1520	3519	2248	2986	1045

6-28 分地区城镇居民家庭人均主要食品消费量(2023年)
Per Capita Consumption of Major Foods of Urban Households by Region (2023)

单位：千克 (kg)

地区	Region	粮食 (原粮) Grain (Unprocessed)	#谷物 Cereals	食用油 Edible Oil and Fats	#食用植物油 Edible Vegetable Oil	蔬菜及食用菌 Vegetable and Edible Mushroom	肉类 Meat and Products	#猪肉 Pork
全　国	**National Average**	**115.6**	**102.5**	**9.3**	**8.9**	**114.0**	**39.6**	**28.7**
北　京	Beijing	86.3	74.3	6.0	5.9	110.2	30.1	17.1
天　津	Tianjin	92.1	82.4	6.7	6.6	107.8	28.5	17.2
河　北	Hebei	163.5	144.2	8.9	8.8	145.8	37.9	24.3
山　西	Shanxi	101.1	86.3	7.3	7.3	94.9	21.9	14.5
内蒙古	Inner Mongolia	148.9	132.0	7.5	7.3	129.6	44.1	25.6
辽　宁	Liaoning	128.6	112.2	9.4	9.3	133.3	41.1	28.0
吉　林	Jilin	113.8	101.3	10.4	10.3	94.9	31.7	21.9
黑龙江	Heilongjiang	117.9	105.7	12.5	12.4	106.7	35.5	24.0
上　海	Shanghai	92.2	81.3	8.3	8.2	99.6	34.1	22.8
江　苏	Jiangsu	123.2	106.6	8.0	7.7	125.5	41.9	29.2
浙　江	Zhejiang	115.4	101.5	8.8	8.5	98.0	39.1	28.7
安　徽	Anhui	125.7	108.9	8.3	7.8	125.0	41.3	30.3
福　建	Fujian	108.2	98.7	11.1	10.4	101.5	45.0	35.0
江　西	Jiangxi	137.1	120.9	12.9	12.4	126.6	48.9	38.9
山　东	Shandong	115.7	103.8	7.2	7.2	113.0	37.0	25.1
河　南	Henan	132.4	117.6	8.0	7.9	118.6	33.0	22.8
湖　北	Hubei	98.3	85.0	11.9	11.5	120.8	37.9	28.6
湖　南	Hunan	115.3	105.1	11.8	9.8	128.9	44.1	35.8
广　东	Guangdong	102.0	93.0	8.7	8.3	102.1	48.1	37.4
广　西	Guangxi	90.2	83.2	8.3	7.7	90.8	40.5	33.3
海　南	Hainan	85.2	79.3	9.3	8.6	107.7	43.7	35.3
重　庆	Chongqing	131.8	114.8	14.9	13.7	153.2	59.1	47.1
四　川	Sichuan	98.2	86.9	11.1	10.3	118.2	48.3	38.8
贵　州	Guizhou	103.7	90.4	8.7	7.8	82.7	35.9	30.5
云　南	Yunnan	107.3	92.1	7.4	6.3	105.5	36.3	28.4
西　藏	Xizang	131.6	128.8	9.2	8.8	97.2	52.9	16.1
陕　西	Shaanxi	125.4	109.3	10.2	10.0	108.9	25.8	18.1
甘　肃	Gansu	112.7	100.6	9.8	9.8	98.3	28.5	18.2
青　海	Qinghai	89.0	82.9	7.8	7.6	72.9	27.7	12.5
宁　夏	Ningxia	93.9	86.0	8.3	8.2	88.5	21.1	8.2
新　疆	Xinjiang	123.8	117.9	11.6	11.5	97.3	31.0	7.0

6–28 续表 continued

单位：千克 (kg)

地 区	Region	#牛肉 Beef	#羊肉 Mutton	禽类 Poultry	水产品 Aquatic Products	蛋类 Eggs	奶类 Milk and Dairy Products	鲜瓜果 Fresh Melons and Fruits	食糖 Sugar
全 国	**National Average**	**3.9**	**1.8**	**12.6**	**17.4**	**14.6**	**16.3**	**67.6**	**1.0**
北 京	Beijing	3.9	3.3	7.4	10.3	17.0	21.6	70.5	0.9
天 津	Tianjin	3.2	3.1	6.7	17.0	19.7	16.4	79.2	0.8
河 北	Hebei	2.8	2.8	10.1	12.5	24.2	22.1	87.7	1.3
山 西	Shanxi	1.4	1.7	4.7	4.5	14.9	19.0	66.7	0.7
内蒙古	Inner Mongolia	5.0	7.3	8.8	9.4	16.7	30.0	88.9	1.1
辽 宁	Liaoning	4.7	2.2	8.4	21.3	19.6	19.7	84.1	0.9
吉 林	Jilin	4.2	1.3	6.4	11.3	14.8	10.9	66.5	0.8
黑龙江	Heilongjiang	3.5	2.2	7.0	12.9	15.8	13.6	74.5	1.2
上 海	Shanghai	5.1	1.3	12.2	24.2	14.7	22.6	54.3	1.1
江 苏	Jiangsu	4.5	1.4	16.4	25.4	16.3	18.5	63.1	1.1
浙 江	Zhejiang	5.0	1.2	13.1	29.8	12.5	15.8	69.7	1.2
安 徽	Anhui	3.9	1.5	17.1	17.9	15.7	15.1	70.9	0.8
福 建	Fujian	4.6	1.1	14.5	32.0	13.8	15.6	60.5	1.1
江 西	Jiangxi	4.9	0.9	14.7	21.3	11.5	14.2	68.4	1.0
山 东	Shandong	2.6	2.3	9.7	18.8	24.9	18.8	88.5	0.7
河 南	Henan	2.7	2.1	10.7	8.5	22.9	16.2	78.8	0.8
湖 北	Hubei	3.5	0.9	9.2	18.9	9.7	11.7	56.0	0.8
湖 南	Hunan	3.8	0.9	13.1	16.7	10.0	10.1	66.4	0.9
广 东	Guangdong	4.6	0.9	22.7	26.8	10.0	11.5	53.6	0.9
广 西	Guangxi	3.3	0.8	21.2	15.2	7.1	9.0	49.7	1.0
海 南	Hainan	4.3	1.3	23.7	33.1	6.4	8.6	44.9	0.8
重 庆	Chongqing	4.5	1.1	15.4	17.3	14.3	21.6	69.7	1.8
四 川	Sichuan	3.4	0.6	12.9	12.0	10.4	16.5	56.8	1.1
贵 州	Guizhou	1.8	0.3	8.6	5.3	6.1	10.5	49.8	0.9
云 南	Yunnan	3.1	0.5	10.8	7.7	6.0	12.0	57.7	1.2
西 藏	Xizang	28.9	3.0	2.6	2.2	5.8	19.5	27.1	1.3
陕 西	Shaanxi	2.0	1.6	5.3	5.1	13.6	17.3	66.0	0.8
甘 肃	Gansu	3.2	3.2	5.7	5.0	11.2	18.1	72.7	1.0
青 海	Qinghai	7.8	5.0	4.7	3.8	8.5	23.0	45.0	1.0
宁 夏	Ningxia	5.8	5.1	7.6	4.5	8.8	18.5	77.9	1.1
新 疆	Xinjiang	7.6	13.5	6.5	4.9	10.6	28.9	66.6	1.0

6-29 分地区城镇居民平均每百户年末主要耐用消费品拥有量(2023年)
Main Durable Goods Owned Per 100 Urban Households at Year-end by Region (2023)

地 区	Region	家用汽车(辆) Automobile (unit)	摩托车(辆) Motorcycle (unit)	电动助力车(辆) Electric Bicycle (unit)	洗衣机(台) Washing Machine (set)	电冰箱(柜)(台) Refrigerator (set)	彩色电视机(台) Color TV Set (set)
全 国	**National Average**	**55.9**	**13.7**	**67.1**	**98.5**	**101.9**	**107.2**
北 京	Beijing	51.1	4.0	21.4	98.2	101.2	104.0
天 津	Tianjin	69.5	1.2	35.8	99.2	103.4	102.7
河 北	Hebei	67.6	7.4	108.0	101.8	103.1	105.6
山 西	Shanxi	54.3	9.9	63.8	100.1	98.7	97.4
内蒙古	Inner Mongolia	66.2	5.9	52.3	99.3	112.9	97.5
辽 宁	Liaoning	42.1	3.9	16.7	97.0	99.5	99.1
吉 林	Jilin	47.0	4.8	13.1	97.6	99.1	95.3
黑龙江	Heilongjiang	38.7	4.8	15.7	96.9	99.3	96.1
上 海	Shanghai	47.8	2.2	70.1	96.7	103.1	144.6
江 苏	Jiangsu	67.4	4.5	116.6	103.0	107.7	151.1
浙 江	Zhejiang	72.2	6.8	74.6	98.0	103.7	150.0
安 徽	Anhui	49.7	8.5	101.9	98.8	102.6	112.1
福 建	Fujian	40.1	27.1	75.7	93.0	99.5	94.8
江 西	Jiangxi	54.5	22.2	94.4	97.3	100.8	116.8
山 东	Shandong	71.3	6.2	93.9	100.2	102.7	99.9
河 南	Henan	58.0	7.5	129.3	102.3	101.0	106.3
湖 北	Hubei	48.8	28.2	53.7	100.3	107.4	107.7
湖 南	Hunan	52.5	32.3	36.3	102.2	105.8	105.0
广 东	Guangdong	58.1	36.9	55.8	96.6	100.1	90.0
广 西	Guangxi	53.3	24.8	114.2	101.6	102.3	100.6
海 南	Hainan	51.0	12.6	124.3	90.4	97.7	89.4
重 庆	Chongqing	46.0	13.4	12.8	98.4	100.3	110.8
四 川	Sichuan	49.0	17.5	44.1	101.1	106.2	114.2
贵 州	Guizhou	53.9	25.2	22.5	101.8	101.8	100.0
云 南	Yunnan	64.8	33.3	58.4	103.3	104.2	103.0
西 藏	Xizang	61.1	16.4	21.4	105.2	106.9	106.4
陕 西	Shaanxi	50.6	17.4	50.8	98.8	98.0	98.7
甘 肃	Gansu	47.2	10.4	35.6	101.0	98.8	98.7
青 海	Qinghai	62.4	8.4	10.3	101.1	108.4	95.5
宁 夏	Ningxia	56.9	7.0	73.4	101.0	100.6	97.4
新 疆	Xinjiang	52.8	5.9	35.8	98.2	104.5	97.9

6–29 续表 continued

地区	Region	空调 (台) Air Conditioner (set)	热水器 (台) Water Heater (set)	排油烟机 (台) Kitchen Ventilator (set)	移动电话 (部) Mobile Phone (set)	计算机 (台) Computer (set)
全国	**National Average**	**171.7**	**97.2**	**84.6**	**239.5**	**58.2**
北京	Beijing	188.0	97.8	92.2	216.1	78.7
天津	Tianjin	188.8	100.6	96.6	231.8	65.6
河北	Hebei	160.4	91.5	89.5	246.9	49.2
山西	Shanxi	65.8	90.7	86.8	232.9	45.1
内蒙古	Inner Mongolia	25.8	88.6	87.3	223.8	48.2
辽宁	Liaoning	79.9	92.4	89.6	198.2	39.5
吉林	Jilin	33.6	85.2	86.2	216.6	32.5
黑龙江	Heilongjiang	24.0	82.9	90.3	215.1	33.7
上海	Shanghai	208.0	98.9	87.4	222.1	88.1
江苏	Jiangsu	254.5	101.2	93.2	246.5	74.5
浙江	Zhejiang	238.5	105.5	89.8	242.4	75.4
安徽	Anhui	209.2	96.1	84.8	238.9	54.2
福建	Fujian	208.6	111.1	71.5	235.0	65.1
江西	Jiangxi	188.3	100.9	83.3	262.9	51.6
山东	Shandong	179.8	100.4	92.8	226.6	62.7
河南	Henan	220.4	94.4	85.4	252.2	52.7
湖北	Hubei	196.4	100.3	86.9	254.5	56.7
湖南	Hunan	222.0	102.0	85.7	266.3	57.0
广东	Guangdong	232.2	103.4	75.0	252.0	76.0
广西	Guangxi	206.7	104.5	80.3	264.5	57.7
海南	Hainan	187.9	99.2	70.3	256.2	54.6
重庆	Chongqing	256.7	101.1	88.1	252.7	53.2
四川	Sichuan	197.1	97.9	81.7	262.0	50.0
贵州	Guizhou	50.5	99.9	73.6	275.8	50.2
云南	Yunnan	27.3	88.1	81.2	264.1	60.9
西藏	Xizang	28.1	68.6	59.0	188.5	44.5
陕西	Shaanxi	148.5	90.2	83.4	241.0	47.8
甘肃	Gansu	20.9	81.9	86.4	248.2	55.7
青海	Qinghai	1.5	86.1	88.7	246.8	45.7
宁夏	Ningxia	28.9	97.3	92.6	239.3	53.0
新疆	Xinjiang	44.3	89.2	88.4	217.4	40.0

6-30 分地区农村居民人均可支配收入
Per Capita Disposable Income of Rural Households by Region

单位：元 (yuan)

地 区	Region	2017	2018	2019	2020	2021	2022	2023
全 国	**National Average**	**13432**	**14617**	**16021**	**17131**	**18931**	**20133**	**21691**
北 京	Beijing	24240	26490	28928	30126	33303	34754	37358
天 津	Tianjin	21754	23065	24804	25691	27955	29018	30851
河 北	Hebei	12881	14031	15373	16467	18179	19364	20688
山 西	Shanxi	10788	11750	12902	13878	15308	16323	17677
内蒙古	Inner Mongolia	12584	13803	15283	16567	18337	19641	21221
辽 宁	Liaoning	13747	14656	16108	17450	19217	19908	21483
吉 林	Jilin	12950	13748	14936	16067	17642	18134	19472
黑龙江	Heilongjiang	12665	13804	14982	16168	17889	18577	19756
上 海	Shanghai	27825	30375	33195	34911	38521	39729	42988
江 苏	Jiangsu	19158	20845	22675	24198	26791	28486	30488
浙 江	Zhejiang	24956	27302	29876	31930	35247	37565	40311
安 徽	Anhui	12758	13996	15416	16620	18372	19575	21144
福 建	Fujian	16335	17821	19568	20880	23229	24987	26722
江 西	Jiangxi	13242	14460	15796	16981	18684	19936	21358
山 东	Shandong	15118	16297	17775	18753	20794	22110	23776
河 南	Henan	12719	13831	15164	16108	17533	18697	20053
湖 北	Hubei	13812	14978	16391	16306	18259	19709	21293
湖 南	Hunan	12936	14093	15395	16585	18295	19546	20921
广 东	Guangdong	15780	17168	18818	20143	22306	23598	25142
广 西	Guangxi	11325	12435	13676	14815	16363	17433	18656
海 南	Hainan	12902	13989	15113	16279	18076	19117	20708
重 庆	Chongqing	12638	13781	15133	16361	18100	19313	20820
四 川	Sichuan	12227	13331	14670	15929	17575	18672	19978
贵 州	Guizhou	8869	9716	10756	11642	12856	13707	14817
云 南	Yunnan	9862	10768	11902	12842	14197	15147	16361
西 藏	Xizang	10330	11450	12951	14598	16932	18209	19924
陕 西	Shaanxi	10265	11213	12326	13316	14745	15704	16992
甘 肃	Gansu	8076	8804	9629	10344	11433	12165	13131
青 海	Qinghai	9462	10393	11499	12342	13604	14456	15614
宁 夏	Ningxia	10738	11708	12858	13889	15337	16430	17772
新 疆	Xinjiang	11045	11975	13122	14056	15575	16550	17948

6–31 分地区农村居民人均可支配收入来源（2023年）
Per Capita Disposable Income of Rural Households by Source and Region (2023)

单位：元 (yuan)

地 区	Region	可支配收 入 Disposable Income	工资性收入 Income from Wages and Salaries	经营净收入 Net Business Income	财产净收入 Net Income from Properties	转移净收入 Net Income from Transfers
全 国	**National Average**	**21691**	**9163**	**7431**	**540**	**4557**
北 京	Beijing	37358	26819	2090	3682	4768
天 津	Tianjin	30851	16912	7356	1293	5290
河 北	Hebei	20688	11015	6749	446	2479
山 西	Shanxi	17677	7875	4676	256	4869
内蒙古	Inner Mongolia	21221	4086	11607	580	4948
辽 宁	Liaoning	21483	7952	9585	487	3459
吉 林	Jilin	19472	4373	11595	535	2969
黑龙江	Heilongjiang	19756	3724	9877	1442	4713
上 海	Shanghai	42988	27019	2233	1345	12392
江 苏	Jiangsu	30488	14733	7901	986	6869
浙 江	Zhejiang	40311	23825	10307	1259	4920
安 徽	Anhui	21144	7449	7962	456	5276
福 建	Fujian	26722	12020	9857	570	4274
江 西	Jiangxi	21358	9720	6549	415	4674
山 东	Shandong	23776	11872	8110	532	3262
河 南	Henan	20053	7544	6385	279	5844
湖 北	Hubei	21293	6923	8814	290	5267
湖 南	Hunan	20921	8179	7470	299	4973
广 东	Guangdong	25142	14474	6101	952	3615
广 西	Guangxi	18656	6353	7333	431	4538
海 南	Hainan	20708	8565	8176	395	3573
重 庆	Chongqing	20820	7421	6766	518	6115
四 川	Sichuan	19978	6220	7599	609	5548
贵 州	Guizhou	14817	5924	4636	122	4135
云 南	Yunnan	16361	5846	7161	251	3103
西 藏	Xizang	19924	6910	8373	861	3779
陕 西	Shaanxi	16992	7077	5013	283	4619
甘 肃	Gansu	13131	3893	5642	180	3417
青 海	Qinghai	15614	5443	5530	452	4189
宁 夏	Ningxia	17772	6649	7345	204	3574
新 疆	Xinjiang	17948	5989	7636	546	3777

6-32 分地区农村居民人均消费支出
Per Capita Consumption Expenditure of Rural Households by Region

单位：元 (yuan)

地 区	Region	2017	2018	2019	2020	2021	2022	2023
全 国	**National Average**	**10955**	**12124**	**13328**	**13713**	**15916**	**16632**	**18175**
北 京	Beijing	18810	20195	21881	20913	23574	23745	26277
天 津	Tianjin	16386	16863	17843	16844	19285	18934	21553
河 北	Hebei	10536	11383	12372	12644	15391	16271	17244
山 西	Shanxi	8424	9172	9728	10290	11410	12091	13684
内蒙古	Inner Mongolia	12184	12661	13816	13594	15691	15444	18650
辽 宁	Liaoning	10787	11455	12030	12311	14606	14326	16040
吉 林	Jilin	10279	10826	11457	11864	13411	12729	14354
黑龙江	Heilongjiang	10524	11417	12495	12360	15225	15162	16453
上 海	Shanghai	18090	19965	22449	22095	27205	27430	30782
江 苏	Jiangsu	15612	16567	17716	17022	21130	22597	25029
浙 江	Zhejiang	18093	19707	21352	21555	25415	27483	30468
安 徽	Anhui	11106	12748	14546	15024	17163	17980	18905
福 建	Fujian	14003	14943	16281	16339	19290	20467	21746
江 西	Jiangxi	9870	10885	12497	13579	15663	16984	18421
山 东	Shandong	10342	11270	12309	12660	14299	14687	16075
河 南	Henan	9212	10392	11546	12201	14073	14824	16638
湖 北	Hubei	11633	13946	15328	14472	17647	18991	20922
湖 南	Hunan	11534	12721	13969	14974	16951	18078	19210
广 东	Guangdong	13200	15411	16949	17132	20012	20800	22209
广 西	Guangxi	9437	10617	12045	12431	14165	14658	15435
海 南	Hainan	9599	10956	12418	13169	15487	15145	16924
重 庆	Chongqing	10936	11977	13112	14140	16096	16727	17964
四 川	Sichuan	11397	12723	14056	14953	16444	17199	17901
贵 州	Guizhou	8299	9170	10222	10818	12557	13172	14260
云 南	Yunnan	8027	9123	10260	11069	12386	13309	15147
西 藏	Xizang	6691	7452	8418	8917	10577	11139	12619
陕 西	Shaanxi	9306	10071	10935	11376	13158	14094	15647
甘 肃	Gansu	8030	9065	9694	9923	11206	11494	12575
青 海	Qinghai	9903	10352	11343	12134	13300	12516	14790
宁 夏	Ningxia	9982	10790	11465	11724	13536	12825	14649
新 疆	Xinjiang	8713	9421	10318	10778	12821	12169	13645

6–33　分地区农村居民人均消费支出构成（2023年）
Per Capita Consumption Expenditure of Rural Households by Composition and Region (2023)

单位：元　　　　(yuan)

地　区	Region	消费支出 Consumption Expenditure	食品烟酒 Food, Tobacco and Alcohol	衣　着 Clothing and Footwear	居　住 Housing	生活用品及服务 Household Equipments, Furnishings and Services	交通通信 Transport and Communi-cations	教育文化娱乐 Education, Culture and Recreation	医疗保健 Health Care and Medical Services	其他用品及服务 Miscellaneous Goods and Services
全　国	**National Average**	**18175**	**5880**	**921**	**3694**	**992**	**2480**	**1951**	**1916**	**341**
北　京	Beijing	26277	7301	1241	8411	1692	3487	1534	2132	479
天　津	Tianjin	21553	6967	1113	4576	1289	3010	1498	2596	505
河　北	Hebei	17244	5582	1091	3081	1018	2489	1858	1760	364
山　西	Shanxi	13684	4038	884	3040	786	1711	1421	1509	295
内蒙古	Inner Mongolia	18650	5423	978	3157	897	3394	1672	2720	408
辽　宁	Liaoning	16040	4874	887	2911	720	2297	1726	2288	337
吉　林	Jilin	14354	4383	715	2153	567	2096	1658	2467	316
黑龙江	Heilongjiang	16453	5245	930	2462	614	2496	1774	2609	322
上　海	Shanghai	30782	10025	1262	7517	1483	4231	1708	3904	652
江　苏	Jiangsu	25029	8199	1294	5377	1529	3501	2147	2348	634
浙　江	Zhejiang	30468	9331	1476	8158	1682	4223	2689	2289	620
安　徽	Anhui	18905	6555	1125	3734	1183	2111	2083	1777	336
福　建	Fujian	21746	7486	1021	5125	1160	2533	2077	1849	493
江　西	Jiangxi	18421	6129	791	3973	864	1956	2411	2038	259
山　东	Shandong	16075	4743	858	2888	984	2808	1774	1772	248
河　南	Henan	16638	5162	1195	3228	972	2063	2008	1742	269
湖　北	Hubei	20922	6410	1023	4436	1285	2846	2205	2324	393
湖　南	Hunan	19210	5822	824	4100	1050	2281	2659	2202	272
广　东	Guangdong	22209	8342	639	5263	922	2934	2141	1561	407
广　西	Guangxi	15435	4869	459	3227	722	2107	2158	1687	205
海　南	Hainan	16924	7389	478	3349	644	1908	1737	1182	237
重　庆	Chongqing	17964	6278	946	3203	1144	2154	1872	2037	329
四　川	Sichuan	17901	6103	865	2961	1036	2505	1828	2190	412
贵　州	Guizhou	14260	4408	660	2847	814	2003	1869	1393	267
云　南	Yunnan	15147	5202	623	2945	731	2317	1672	1429	230
西　藏	Xizang	12619	4984	873	2666	764	1900	631	557	246
陕　西	Shaanxi	15647	4589	825	3303	883	2059	1580	2169	240
甘　肃	Gansu	12575	3999	702	2482	635	1694	1376	1481	205
青　海	Qinghai	14790	5122	1031	2124	792	2566	1045	1765	345
宁　夏	Ningxia	14649	4345	835	2656	922	2166	1585	1808	331
新　疆	Xinjiang	13645	4336	1035	2561	715	2028	1231	1404	333

6-34 分地区农村居民家庭人均主要食品消费量(2023年)
Per Capita Consumption of Major Foods of Rural Households by Region (2023)

单位：千克 (kg)

地区	Region	粮食(原粮) Grain (Unprocessed)	#谷物 Cereals	食用油 Edible Oil and Fats	#食用植物油 Edible Vegetable Oil	蔬菜及食用菌 Vegetable and Edible Mushroom	肉类 Meat and Products	#猪肉 Pork
全国	**National Average**	**159.8**	**145.2**	**10.9**	**10.2**	**113.0**	**40.1**	**32.9**
北京	Beijing	122.4	108.0	8.1	7.9	122.4	36.7	24.9
天津	Tianjin	127.9	116.3	11.0	10.7	116.6	32.5	23.6
河北	Hebei	180.3	161.8	9.2	9.0	132.7	34.1	24.7
山西	Shanxi	129.3	112.1	9.2	9.1	80.8	18.2	14.0
内蒙古	Inner Mongolia	200.2	183.0	7.3	6.8	110.8	44.2	30.4
辽宁	Liaoning	180.7	160.2	11.6	11.3	121.6	43.7	36.1
吉林	Jilin	176.7	154.8	13.4	13.2	111.4	33.6	28.3
黑龙江	Heilongjiang	181.3	163.9	18.9	18.8	127.0	38.1	31.3
上海	Shanghai	158.7	146.0	14.0	13.8	119.1	44.3	34.9
江苏	Jiangsu	164.9	141.8	9.7	9.4	134.2	45.0	34.6
浙江	Zhejiang	171.2	150.8	11.6	11.0	123.1	47.1	38.6
安徽	Anhui	169.8	152.0	10.4	9.7	121.9	40.0	31.9
福建	Fujian	164.6	152.8	10.8	9.4	110.3	41.8	36.9
江西	Jiangxi	182.5	164.6	14.7	14.1	133.1	46.6	40.0
山东	Shandong	143.0	130.1	8.8	8.7	99.7	34.3	26.2
河南	Henan	168.5	152.6	8.5	8.3	116.0	33.6	26.7
湖北	Hubei	142.4	126.8	16.6	16.2	138.2	39.3	33.3
湖南	Hunan	175.7	165.1	12.6	9.9	104.0	49.0	44.4
广东	Guangdong	143.5	134.1	11.5	10.8	118.7	57.4	48.6
广西	Guangxi	150.1	143.4	9.7	8.3	89.6	39.6	36.2
海南	Hainan	118.6	113.1	10.4	8.6	112.5	48.1	43.0
重庆	Chongqing	179.1	161.3	14.8	13.4	135.3	55.9	50.9
四川	Sichuan	153.6	141.5	11.9	10.5	121.1	50.7	46.1
贵州	Guizhou	136.6	122.9	7.5	6.5	84.5	32.2	30.1
云南	Yunnan	140.5	125.2	6.3	5.3	111.4	44.9	41.0
西藏	Xizang	183.3	180.7	20.2	9.0	51.0	37.2	3.5
陕西	Shaanxi	169.8	152.2	13.6	13.3	103.5	23.2	19.2
甘肃	Gansu	158.3	146.2	10.3	10.2	78.4	22.2	17.7
青海	Qinghai	124.0	117.3	10.1	8.0	58.3	34.5	12.6
宁夏	Ningxia	128.8	121.5	10.5	10.4	84.8	21.8	7.5
新疆	Xinjiang	142.7	140.3	14.1	13.8	88.8	28.7	1.3

6-34 续表 continued

单位：千克 (kg)

地 区	Region	#牛肉 Beef	#羊肉 Mutton	禽类 Poultry	水产品 Aquatic Products	蛋类 Eggs	奶类 Milk and Dairy Products	鲜瓜果 Fresh Melons and Fruits	食糖 Sugar
全 国	**National Average**	**2.2**	**1.6**	**12.0**	**12.2**	**15.4**	**8.9**	**51.7**	**1.4**
北 京	Beijing	2.8	3.8	7.0	9.6	19.4	15.1	70.8	1.2
天 津	Tianjin	1.5	3.1	6.0	15.4	20.7	9.4	81.9	1.2
河 北	Hebei	1.1	1.8	7.9	7.7	22.6	13.0	73.3	1.7
山 西	Shanxi	0.5	1.2	3.3	2.4	15.1	12.8	50.4	1.0
内蒙古	Inner Mongolia	3.1	7.6	7.5	5.7	16.2	18.0	59.6	1.9
辽 宁	Liaoning	2.3	1.2	5.5	11.5	18.9	7.4	55.3	1.3
吉 林	Jilin	1.9	0.8	5.4	8.5	15.6	4.9	45.8	1.6
黑龙江	Heilongjiang	2.0	1.6	6.9	10.3	17.4	6.1	58.6	2.1
上 海	Shanghai	3.3	1.3	16.6	27.5	17.2	16.0	53.0	1.9
江 苏	Jiangsu	3.0	1.4	14.7	25.8	19.6	13.5	52.8	1.6
浙 江	Zhejiang	4.1	1.0	13.5	29.0	14.6	11.3	65.4	1.9
安 徽	Anhui	2.5	1.3	17.0	14.0	18.6	11.4	64.1	1.1
福 建	Fujian	1.8	0.5	14.6	30.6	14.5	8.5	45.8	1.9
江 西	Jiangxi	3.2	0.5	14.6	17.7	14.9	8.6	48.9	1.2
山 东	Shandong	1.1	1.5	9.2	10.4	25.5	12.0	77.1	0.8
河 南	Henan	1.5	1.1	10.5	6.9	25.7	10.7	69.2	1.3
湖 北	Hubei	2.1	1.1	10.1	15.7	12.3	5.7	40.8	1.4
湖 南	Hunan	2.2	0.6	13.2	12.3	14.9	5.4	50.7	1.2
广 东	Guangdong	3.2	0.7	30.1	29.9	9.9	5.1	33.6	1.1
广 西	Guangxi	1.3	0.4	22.2	10.0	6.3	4.1	33.5	1.0
海 南	Hainan	2.6	0.8	28.4	34.0	5.4	2.4	24.2	0.7
重 庆	Chongqing	1.3	0.7	12.1	12.8	16.9	10.6	44.0	2.8
四 川	Sichuan	1.8	0.4	11.9	8.3	12.3	9.2	36.6	1.9
贵 州	Guizhou	0.8	0.2	5.8	2.5	4.5	3.9	31.1	1.1
云 南	Yunnan	1.7	0.5	11.6	5.2	9.2	4.8	36.1	1.4
西 藏	Xizang	24.6	8.2	0.6	0.0	1.8	2.9	7.5	2.7
陕 西	Shaanxi	0.7	1.2	3.5	2.2	12.0	9.4	42.7	1.1
甘 肃	Gansu	1.1	1.7	4.9	1.5	8.1	6.5	43.5	1.6
青 海	Qinghai	12.8	8.1	3.1	1.1	4.8	12.6	24.7	2.1
宁 夏	Ningxia	7.4	6.0	9.2	1.5	6.1	9.6	69.7	1.4
新 疆	Xinjiang	6.2	19.5	4.1	0.9	6.7	10.9	52.7	1.6

6-35 分地区农村居民平均每百户年末主要耐用消费品拥有量(2023年)
Main Durable Goods Owned Per 100 Rural Households at Year-end by Region (2023)

地区	Region	家用汽车(辆) Automobile (unit)	摩托车(辆) Motorcycle (unit)	电动助力车(辆) Electric Bicycle (unit)	洗衣机(台) Washing Machine (set)	电冰箱(柜)(台) Refrigerator (set)	彩色电视机(台) Color TV Set (set)
全　国	**National Average**	**40.0**	**41.4**	**84.9**	**97.6**	**105.7**	**108.8**
北　京	Beijing	51.8	7.5	64.7	103.2	109.1	115.2
天　津	Tianjin	55.2	8.0	123.9	103.4	108.3	111.6
河　北	Hebei	58.1	22.5	133.9	103.6	103.6	105.7
山　西	Shanxi	40.9	27.3	89.7	99.9	96.7	99.7
内蒙古	Inner Mongolia	45.2	36.4	89.3	97.3	122.4	99.8
辽　宁	Liaoning	34.1	35.6	56.4	92.8	100.1	101.9
吉　林	Jilin	29.6	31.5	38.7	93.1	98.1	96.6
黑龙江	Heilongjiang	30.3	26.9	49.3	94.7	98.9	95.4
上　海	Shanghai	36.4	2.1	119.0	87.1	101.8	131.7
江　苏	Jiangsu	40.9	12.9	152.5	102.0	113.2	141.9
浙　江	Zhejiang	48.8	11.9	90.9	91.0	110.6	153.4
安　徽	Anhui	35.1	18.3	121.5	95.0	107.8	113.0
福　建	Fujian	26.8	55.4	73.4	97.1	106.2	113.5
江　西	Jiangxi	35.1	52.7	86.5	84.6	101.9	114.3
山　东	Shandong	52.4	25.9	124.3	99.3	104.3	102.9
河　南	Henan	52.1	23.0	146.3	104.6	103.2	110.1
湖　北	Hubei	33.6	71.3	49.0	97.3	114.2	110.0
湖　南	Hunan	33.3	63.1	31.7	96.4	108.7	106.7
广　东	Guangdong	44.2	93.2	70.9	98.6	104.1	109.6
广　西	Guangxi	31.1	70.3	98.2	92.3	102.9	97.5
海　南	Hainan	20.4	52.9	136.4	71.7	94.2	90.1
重　庆	Chongqing	35.7	41.0	22.4	97.3	110.1	109.2
四　川	Sichuan	28.9	45.4	46.2	100.3	116.3	113.0
贵　州	Guizhou	25.9	52.0	27.3	96.2	98.4	92.2
云　南	Yunnan	44.2	82.4	31.6	95.9	104.1	102.3
西　藏	Xizang	62.3	91.0	28.1	126.5	120.0	110.2
陕　西	Shaanxi	38.3	43.7	63.5	98.4	97.3	101.3
甘　肃	Gansu	38.0	39.3	56.8	98.1	94.1	98.0
青　海	Qinghai	76.7	60.5	38.2	102.7	117.0	98.3
宁　夏	Ningxia	41.8	38.2	90.5	104.1	104.8	100.7
新　疆	Xinjiang	26.4	26.5	110.4	101.7	108.0	99.2

6-35 续表 continued

地 区	Region	空 调 (台) Air Conditioner (set)	热水器 (台) Water Heater (set)	排油烟机 (台) Kitchen Ventilator (set)	移动电话 (部) Mobile Phone (set)	计算机 (台) Computer (set)
全 国	**National Average**	**105.7**	**78.1**	**44.3**	**271.2**	**23.1**
北 京	Beijing	200.5	104.5	89.7	225.9	43.5
天 津	Tianjin	172.7	81.9	80.2	245.1	30.6
河 北	Hebei	120.2	68.4	60.0	275.9	26.1
山 西	Shanxi	41.9	47.0	46.1	264.8	23.3
内蒙古	Inner Mongolia	6.8	32.1	21.9	239.4	16.6
辽 宁	Liaoning	32.9	38.4	37.2	218.8	15.5
吉 林	Jilin	3.8	16.0	16.2	239.4	9.4
黑龙江	Heilongjiang	2.3	15.9	22.1	229.2	15.0
上 海	Shanghai	169.1	92.4	54.7	192.4	25.4
江 苏	Jiangsu	200.3	87.6	62.0	255.9	33.6
浙 江	Zhejiang	181.8	101.9	73.9	243.4	37.0
安 徽	Anhui	143.2	82.8	48.2	266.7	21.8
福 建	Fujian	129.2	112.7	51.2	246.2	28.0
江 西	Jiangxi	112.9	91.8	53.2	301.1	25.6
山 东	Shandong	132.4	90.1	64.9	230.2	32.6
河 南	Henan	165.3	80.3	44.8	295.8	26.7
湖 北	Hubei	116.2	90.4	55.2	285.6	25.7
湖 南	Hunan	102.3	88.6	46.1	292.3	25.4
广 东	Guangdong	185.3	103.8	61.5	289.3	32.2
广 西	Guangxi	101.8	93.9	33.1	287.8	16.1
海 南	Hainan	115.6	85.9	18.8	281.6	14.4
重 庆	Chongqing	123.4	87.4	35.3	278.3	21.2
四 川	Sichuan	102.4	86.1	25.8	279.6	17.0
贵 州	Guizhou	9.5	78.8	18.0	313.8	11.5
云 南	Yunnan	9.1	74.3	19.9	319.1	13.5
西 藏	Xizang	3.3	22.2	5.4	283.3	12.9
陕 西	Shaanxi	70.2	59.8	27.8	269.1	13.7
甘 肃	Gansu	5.6	45.4	19.5	315.3	18.4
青 海	Qinghai	8.4	38.3	27.7	328.1	17.5
宁 夏	Ningxia	6.1	95.7	38.2	293.6	23.1
新 疆	Xinjiang	9.6	80.3	31.7	244.4	7.2

6-36 中西部22省(区、市)脱贫县农村居民人均可支配收入

Per Capita Disposable Income of Rural Households in Poverty Relief Counties in 22 Provinces and Equivalent Administrative Units in Central and Western China

地 区	Region	2022	2023	
		绝对数(元) Absolute Figures(yuan)	绝对数(元) Absolute Figures(yuan)	比上年增长(%) Growth Rate over Preceding Year(%)
脱贫地区	**Poverty Relief Regions Average**	**15111**	**16396**	**8.5**
河 北	Hebei	15425	16700	8.3
山 西	Shanxi	12724	13937	9.5
内蒙古	Inner Mongolia	16223	17751	9.4
吉 林	Jilin	13667	14990	9.7
黑龙江	Heilongjiang	14393	15583	8.3
安 徽	Anhui	17781	19232	8.2
江 西	Jiangxi	15741	17210	9.3
河 南	Henan	16880	18221	7.9
湖 北	Hubei	16188	17612	8.8
湖 南	Hunan	14714	16036	9.0
广 西	Guangxi	15796	17066	8.0
海 南	Hainan	16935	18516	9.3
重 庆	Chongqing	17875	19299	8.0
四 川	Sichuan	15949	17196	7.8
贵 州	Guizhou	13569	14688	8.2
云 南	Yunnan	14027	15218	8.5
西 藏	Xizang	18209	19924	9.4
陕 西	Shaanxi	14838	16074	8.3
甘 肃	Gansu	11190	12107	8.2
青 海	Qinghai	14456	15614	8.0
宁 夏	Ningxia	14151	15339	8.4
新 疆	Xinjiang	15417	16881	9.5

注：1.脱贫县包括原832个国家扶贫开发工作重点县和集中连片特困地区县，以及新疆阿克苏地区7个市县。

2.2020年我国现行农村贫困标准下的农村贫困人口全部脱贫，国家统计局不再发布农村贫困人口和贫困发生率数据，如需要查询相关历史数据和国家脱贫攻坚普查主要结果数据，可查阅《中国统计年鉴2021》。

a) Poverty relief counties include the original 832 key counties of the national poverty alleviation and development work and counties in contiguous poverty-stricken areas, as well as 7 cities and counties in Aksu Prefecture, Xinjiang.

b) China has eliminated absolute poverty by 2020. The National Bureau of Statistics of China will no longer release the data on rural poverty population and poverty headcount ratio. Related historical data and main results of National Poverty Relief Census could be found in China Statistical Yearbook 2021 if needed.

主要统计指标解释

从2012年四季度起，国家统计局对分别进行的城乡住户调查实施了一体化改革，规范了城乡划分范围，统一了城乡居民收入指标名称、分类和统计标准，建立了城乡统一的一体化住户调查，并据此采集全国居民有关数据。1978—2012年的数据，根据国家统计局城镇住户调查和农村住户调查的历史数据，按照住户收支与生活状况调查可比口径推算得到。

一、居民可支配收入

居民可支配收入指居民可用于最终消费支出和储蓄的总和，即居民可用于自由支配的收入。既包括现金收入，也包括实物收入。按照收入的来源，可支配收入包含四项，分别为：工资性收入、经营净收入、财产净收入和转移净收入。

工资性收入 指就业人员通过各种途径得到的全部劳动报酬和各种福利，包括受雇于单位或个人、从事各种自由职业、兼职和零星劳动得到的全部劳动报酬和福利。

经营净收入 指住户或住户成员从事生产经营活动所获得的净收入，是全部经营收入中扣除经营费用、生产性固定资产折旧和生产税之后得到的净收入。计算公式为：

经营净收入=经营收入－经营费用－生产性固定资产折旧－生产税

财产净收入 指住户或住户成员将其所拥有的金融资产、住房等非金融资产和自然资源交由其他机构单位、住户或个人支配而获得的回报并扣除相关的费用之后得到的净收入。财产净收入包括利息净收入、红利收入、储蓄性保险净收益、转让承包土地经营权租金净收入、出租房屋净收入、出租其他资产净收入和自有住房折算净租金等。财产净收入不包括转让资产所有权的溢价所得。

转移净收入 计算公式为：转移净收入=转移性收入－转移性支出

转移性收入 指国家、单位、社会团体对住户的各种经常性转移支付和住户之间的经常性收入转移。包括养老金或退休金、社会救济和补助、政策性生产补贴、政策性生活补贴、经常性捐赠和赔偿、报销医疗费、住户之间的赡养收入，本住户非常住成员寄回带回的收入等。转移性收入不包括住户之间的实物馈赠。

转移性支出 指调查户对国家、单位、住户或个人的经常性或义务性转移支付。包括缴纳的税款、各项社会保障支出、赡养支出、经常性捐赠和赔偿支出以及其他经常转移支出等。

根据住户收支与生活状况调查，分城镇和农村的居民人均可支配收入等数据的覆盖人群主要变化：一是计算城镇居民人均可支配收入时分母包括了在城镇地区常住的农民工，计算农村居民人均可支配收入时分母不包括在城镇地区常住的农民工；二是由本户供养的在外大学生视为常住人口。

二、居民消费支出

居民消费支出是指居民用于满足家庭日常生活消费需要的全部支出，既包括现金消费支出，也包括实物消费支出。消费支出可划分为食品烟酒、衣着、居住、生活用品及服务、交通通信、教育文化娱乐、医疗保健以及其他用品及服务八大类。

食品烟酒 指用于各种食品和烟草、酒类的支出。

衣着 指与居民穿着有关的支出，包括服装、服装材料、鞋类、其他衣类及配件、衣着相关加工服务的支出。

居住 指与居住有关的支出，包括房租、水、电、燃料、物业管理等方面的支出，也包括自有住房折算租金。

生活用品及服务 指家庭及个人的各类生活品及家庭服务。包括家具及室内装饰品、家用器具、家用纺织品、家庭日用杂品、个人用品和家庭服务。

交通通信 指用于交通和通信工具及相关的各种服务费、维修费和车辆保险等支出。

教育文化娱乐 指用于教育、文化和娱乐方面的支出。

医疗保健 指用于医疗和保健的药品、用品和服务的总费用。包括医疗器具及药品，以及医疗服务。

其他用品及服务 指无法直接归入上述各类支出的其他用品与服务支出。

服务性消费 指住户用于各种生活服务的消费支出，包括餐饮服务、衣着鞋类加工服务、居住服务、家庭服务、交通通信服务、教育文化娱乐服务、医疗服务和其他服务等。

Explanatory Notes on Main Statistical Indicators

In the fourth quarter of 2012, the NBS launched its reform on the household survey programme, to develop an integrated survey, instead of two separate urban and rural household surveys. The reform aims at regulating the division of urban and rural areas, integrating the concepts, classifications and standards, implementing the integrated household survey, and collecting household data in the whole country thereafter. Data from 1978 to 2012 are estimated based on the historical data of Urban Household Survey and Rural Household Survey according to the comparable definition and coverage of main income and consumption indicators of Household Survey on Income and Expenditure and Living Conditions.

I. Disposable Income of Residents

Disposable Income of Residents refers to the income of residents for purpose of final expenditure and savings. It includes income both in cash and in kind. By sources of income, disposable income includes four categories: income from wages and salaries, net business income, net income from properties and net income from transfer.

Income from Wages and Salaries refers to remuneration and benefits of all kinds of employed persons, including those employed by other units or individuals, freelance workers, part-time jobs, and sporadic workers.

Net Business Income refers to net income earned by households and their members engaged in production and business activities. It refers to the net income of operating revenue minus operating costs, depreciation of productive fixed assets, and production tax. The formula is:

Net business income = operating revenue-operating costs -depreciation of productive fixed assets-production tax

Net Income from Properties refers to the net income received as returns by households or members through lending of their financial assets, non-financial assets such as housing, to other institutions, households or individuals, minus relevant costs. Net income from properties includes net income of interest, bonus income, net income of saving insurance, net income from transferring management right of contract land, income from lending of housing, income from lending other assets, net converted rents of self-owned housing. Net income from properties do not include premium of transferring ownership of assets.

Net Income from Transfer The formula is:

Net income from transfer = income from transfer - expenditure from transfer

Income from Transfer refers to the regular transfer received from governments, institutions, social organizations to households and between households. It includes old-age and retirement pension, regular donation and compensation, reimbursement of medical fees, supporting income between households, income from non-resident members of households, etc. Income from transfer do not include gifts in kinds between households.

Expenditure from Transfer refers to regular or obligatory transfer paid to government, institutions, households or individuals. It includes tax payment, expenditure on all kinds of social security, supporting expenditure, regular donation, compensation payment and other regular transfer expenditure.

According to Household Survey on Income and Expenditure and Living Conditions, main changes of population coverage of per capita disposable income of urban and rural residents includes: migrant workers residing in urban areas are included in the denominator when calculating per capita disposable income of urban residents, and not included in denominator when calculating per capita disposable income of rural residents; students studying in universities or colleges in other places who are supported by the households are regarded as permanent residents of the households.

II. Consumption Expenditure of Residents

Consumption Expenditure of Residents refers to all expenditure of residents for living expenditure to satisfy family daily living. It includes expenditure in cash and in kind. It includes eight categories: food, tobacco and liquor; clothing and footwear; housing; household equipments, furnishings and services; transport and communications; education, culture and recreation; health care and medical services, and miscellaneous goods and services.

Food, Tobacco and Liquor refers to expenditure for food, tobacco and liquor of all kinds.

Clothing and Footwear refers to expenditure related to clothing, including clothes, clothing materials, footwear, other clothing and accessories, processing services related to clothing.

Housing refers to expenditure related to housing, including rents, water, electricity, fuel, property management, as well as imputed rent on owner-occupied dwellings.

Household Equipments, Furnishings and Services refers to expenditure of households and individuals on equipments, furnishings and articles for living purpose and on household services. It includes furniture and interior decoration, home appliances, home textiles, household miscellaneous daily articles, personal articles, and household services.

Transport and Communications refers to expenditure on transport and communication and related services, maintenance and repairs, and vehicle insurance.

Education, Culture and Recreation refers to expenditure on educational, cultural and recreational activities.

Health Care and Medical Services refers to expenditure on drugs, supplies and services of medical and health care. It includes medical appliances and drugs, and medical services.

Miscellaneous Goods and Services refers to expenditure on all other articles and services that can not classified into the above categories.

Service Consumption refers to consumption expenditure of households for various living services, including catering services, clothing and footwear processing services, housing services, household services, transportation and communication services, education, culture and entertainment services, medical services and other services.

7

财　政

Government Finance

简 要 说 明

本篇反映国家财政收支状况，包括全国一般公共预算收支、全国政府性基金收支和全国国有资本经营收支三个方面。资料来源于财政部，基础资料为国家财政决算有关报表。

一般公共预算是指对以税收为主体的财政收入，安排用于保障和改善民生、推动经济社会发展、维护国家安全、维持国家机构正常运转等方面的收支预算。政府性基金预算是指对依照法律、行政法规的规定在一定期限内向特定对象征收、收取或者以其他方式筹集的资金，专项用于特定公共事业发展的收支预算。国有资本经营预算是指对国有资本收益作出支出安排的收支预算。

财政决算包括财政总决算和部门决算。财政总决算是指各级政府依照法律规定和法定程序编制，经同级人民代表大会常务委员会（乡级为人民代表大会）批准的全面反映各级政府年度预算收支执行结果的综合报表，是政府收支预算执行的最终结果。部门决算是指各部门依据国家有关法律法规规定及其履行职能情况编制，反映部门所有预算收支和结余执行结果及绩效等情况的综合性年度报告，是改进部门预算执行以及编制后续年度部门预算的参考和依据。各部门决算由部门本级决算及所属单位决算组成。全国财政决算由中央本级财政决算和地方财政决算组成。省（自治区、直辖市）本级财政决算及其所属市（州）、县（区）财政决算汇总组成省（自治区、直辖市）财政决算；各省（自治区、直辖市）财政决算汇总成地方财政决算。

为保持决算口径一致，财政部每年要制定和颁发各省(自治区、直辖市)财政总决算报表格式和部门决算报表格式。各级财政部门和中央主管部门也要结合本地区、本部门的具体情况下达有关决算表格。决算表数据根据财政或单位的会计账簿填报。

Brief Introduction

The data in this chapter present the government revenue and expenditure situation, including three categories of revenue and expenditures: state general public budget revenue and expenditure, government funds, and operation of state-owned assets. The data are based on final State accounts from the Ministry of Finance.

The State General Public Budget refers to the budget of revenues and expenditures that the revenue mainly in a form of taxes are arranged to assure and improve the people’s life, to promote economic and social development and safeguard national security, to maintain the regular operation of the government. The government budget funds refer to the budget revenue and expenditure that the funds are collected, charged or in other form to specific objects in accordance with laws and administrative regulations within a certain period, that are earmarked for the specific public development. The state-owned capital management budget refers to the budget for the expenditure of state-owned capital.

The final financial accounts include the final financial budget and the final accounts of department. Final fiscal accounts refers to the consolidated statements that are budgeted by all levels of government in accordance with the provisions of law and legal procedures, approved by the Standing Committee of the people's Congress (Township People's Congress), reflecting the annual budget execution results at all levels of government, it is the final result of government budget execution. Department final accounts refer to the comprehensive annual reports prepared by each department according to relevant national laws and regulations and their functions, reflecting the implementation results and performance of all budget revenues and expenditures and balances of the department, and are the reference and basis for improving department budget implementation and preparing department budgets for subsequent years. The final accounts of each department consist of the final accounts of the department at its own level and those of its subordinate units.The national financial accounts are composed of the central financial budget at the corresponding level and the final accounts of the local governments. financial accounts of provinces (autonomous regions and municipalities) level, and subordinate prefectures and counties (cities) aggregated into financial accounts of provinces (autonomous regions and municipalities); financial accounts of provinces (autonomous regions and municipalities) aggregated into local financial accounts.

In order to ensure the consistency in the coverage of the final accounts, the Ministry of Finance works out and issues the forms for the financial final account for the provinces, autonomous regions and municipalities directly under the Central Government and the forms for the final accounts for the departments at the central level. The financial departments at various regions and levels and the Central Government departments would also work out and issue the forms for the final accounts in the light of the specific departmental conditions to the departments or units at the lower level. The data for the final accounts are filled out in accordance with the data in the account books of the financial departments of governments at various levels, departments and units.

7-1 一般公共预算收支总额及增长速度
General Public Budget Revenue and Expenditure and Their Growth Rates

年 份 Year	一般公共预算收入(亿元) General Public Budget Revenue (100 million yuan)	中央 Central Government	地方 Local Governments	一般公共预算支出(亿元) General Public Budget Expenditure (100 million yuan)	中央 Central Government	地方 Local Governments	增长速度 (%) Growth Rates (%) 一般公共预算收入 General Public Budget Revenue	增长速度 (%) Growth Rates (%) 一般公共预算支出 General Public Budget Expenditure
1978	1132.26	175.77	956.49	1122.09	532.12	589.97	29.5	33.0
1979	1146.38	231.34	915.04	1281.79	655.08	626.71	1.2	14.2
1980	1159.93	284.45	875.48	1228.83	666.81	562.02	1.2	-4.1
1981	1175.79	311.07	864.72	1138.41	625.65	512.76	1.4	-7.5
1982	1212.33	346.84	865.49	1229.98	651.81	578.17	3.1	8.0
1983	1366.95	490.01	876.94	1409.52	759.60	649.92	12.8	14.6
1984	1642.86	665.47	977.39	1701.02	893.33	807.69	20.2	20.7
1985	2004.82	769.63	1235.19	2004.25	795.25	1209.00	22.0	17.8
1986	2122.01	778.42	1343.59	2204.91	836.36	1368.55	5.8	10.0
1987	2199.35	736.29	1463.06	2262.18	845.63	1416.55	3.6	2.6
1988	2357.24	774.76	1582.48	2491.21	845.04	1646.17	7.2	10.1
1989	2664.90	822.52	1842.38	2823.78	888.77	1935.01	13.1	13.3
1990	2937.10	992.42	1944.68	3083.59	1004.47	2079.12	10.2	9.2
1991	3149.48	938.25	2211.23	3386.62	1090.81	2295.81	7.2	9.8
1992	3483.37	979.51	2503.86	3742.20	1170.44	2571.76	10.6	10.5
1993	4348.95	957.51	3391.44	4642.30	1312.06	3330.24	24.8	24.1
1994	5218.10	2906.50	2311.60	5792.62	1754.43	4038.19	20.0	24.8
1995	6242.20	3256.62	2985.58	6823.72	1995.39	4828.33	19.6	17.8
1996	7407.99	3661.07	3746.92	7937.55	2151.27	5786.28	18.7	16.3
1997	8651.14	4226.92	4424.22	9233.56	2532.50	6701.06	16.8	16.3
1998	9875.95	4892.00	4983.95	10798.18	3125.60	7672.58	14.2	16.9
1999	11444.08	5849.21	5594.87	13187.67	4152.33	9035.34	15.9	22.1
2000	13395.23	6989.17	6406.06	15886.50	5519.85	10366.65	17.0	20.5
2001	16386.04	8582.74	7803.30	18902.58	5768.02	13134.56	22.3	19.0
2002	18903.64	10388.64	8515.00	22053.15	6771.70	15281.45	15.4	16.7
2003	21715.25	11865.27	9849.98	24649.95	7420.10	17229.85	14.9	11.8
2004	26396.47	14503.10	11893.37	28486.89	7894.08	20592.81	21.6	15.6
2005	31649.29	16548.53	15100.76	33930.28	8775.97	25154.31	19.9	19.1
2006	38760.20	20456.62	18303.58	40422.73	9991.40	30431.33	22.5	19.1
2007	51321.78	27749.16	23572.62	49781.35	11442.06	38339.29	32.4	23.2
2008	61330.35	32680.56	28649.79	62592.66	13344.17	49248.49	19.5	25.7
2009	68518.30	35915.71	32602.59	76299.93	15255.79	61044.14	11.7	21.9
2010	83101.51	42488.47	40613.04	89874.16	15989.73	73884.43	21.3	17.8
2011	103874.43	51327.32	52547.11	109247.79	16514.11	92733.68	25.0	21.6
2012	117253.52	56175.23	61078.29	125952.97	18764.63	107188.34	12.9	15.3
2013	129209.64	60198.48	69011.16	140212.10	20471.76	119740.34	10.2	11.3
2014	140370.03	64493.45	75876.58	151785.56	22570.07	129215.49	8.6	8.3
2015	152269.23	69267.19	83002.04	175877.77	25542.15	150335.62	5.8	13.2
2016	159604.97	72365.62	87239.35	187755.21	27403.85	160351.36	4.5	6.3
2017	172592.77	81123.36	91469.41	203085.49	29857.15	173228.34	7.4	7.6
2018	183359.84	85456.46	97903.38	220904.13	32707.81	188196.32	6.2	8.7
2019	190390.08	89309.47	101080.61	238858.37	35115.15	203743.22	3.8	8.1
2020	182913.88	82770.72	100143.16	245679.03	35095.57	210583.46	-3.9	2.9
2021	202554.64	91470.41	111084.23	245673.00	35049.96	210623.04	10.7	0.0
2022	203649.29	94887.14	108762.15	260552.12	35570.83	224981.29	0.5	6.1
2023	216795.43	99566.70	117228.73	274622.94	38219.48	236403.46	6.5	5.4

注：1.在一般公共预算收支中，价格补贴1985年以前冲减财政收入，1986年以后列为财政支出。为了可比，本表将1985年以前冲减财政收入的价格补贴改列在财政支出中。
2.一般公共预算收入中不包括国内外债务收入。
3.从2000年起，一般公共预算支出中包括国内外债务付息支出。

a) For the general public budget revenue and expenditure, the government price subsidies were listed as negative revenue items prior to 1985, but they have been listed as expenditure items in government accounts since 1986. For comparison purpose, budgetary price subsidies before 1985 were adjusted and listed as expenditure items.

b) General public budget revenue does not include the receipts of domestic and foreign debts.

c) General public budget expenditure include the interest payment on domestic and foreign debts since 2000.

7–2 中央和地方一般公共预算主要收入项目（2023年）
Main Items of General Public Budget Revenue of the Central and Local Governments (2023)

单位：亿元 (100 million yuan)

项目	Item	一般公共预算收入 General Public Budget Revenue	中央 Central Government	地方 Local Governments
合计	**Total**	**216795.43**	**99566.70**	**117228.73**
税收收入	**Tax Revenue**	**181136.25**	**95834.07**	**85302.18**
国内增值税	Domestic Value-added Tax	69334.28	34588.05	34746.23
国内消费税	Domestic Consumption Tax	16117.81	16117.81	
进口货物增值税	VAT from Imports	18385.88	18385.88	
进口消费品消费税	Consumption Tax from Imports	1098.94	1098.94	
出口业务退增值税	VAT Rebate for Export Business	-17068.87	-17068.87	
出口消费品退消费税	Consumption Tax Rebate for Exports	-53.05	-53.05	
企业所得税	Corporate Income Tax	41102.09	26409.22	14692.87
个人所得税	Individual Income Tax	14775.30	8865.28	5910.02
资源税	Resource Tax	3070.42	92.67	2977.75
城市维护建设税	City Maintenance and Construction Tax	5222.96	253.82	4969.14
房产税	House Property Tax	3994.19		3994.19
印花税	Stamp Tax	3784.19	1800.60	1983.59
其中：证券交易印花税	Stamp Tax on Security Exchange	1800.60	1800.60	
城镇土地使用税	Urban Land Use Tax	2212.71		2212.71
土地增值税	Land Appreciation Tax	5294.00		5294.00
车船税	Tax on Vehicles and Boat Operation	1114.03		1114.03
船舶吨税	Tax on Ship Tonnage	57.59	57.59	
车辆购置税	Vehicle Purchase Tax	2681.00	2681.00	
关税	Tariffs	2590.88	2590.88	
耕地占用税	Farm Land Occupation Tax	1126.52		1126.52
契税	Deed Tax	5910.43		5910.43
烟叶税	Tobacco Leaf Tax	151.37		151.37
环境保护税	Environmental Protection Tax	205.05		205.05
其他税收收入	Other Tax Revenue	28.53	14.25	14.28
非税收入	**Non-Tax Revenue**	**35659.18**	**3732.63**	**31926.55**
专项收入	Special Program Receipts	8077.88	226.08	7851.80
行政事业性收费收入	Charge of Administrative and Institutional Units	4067.88	619.15	3448.73
罚没收入	Penalty Receipts	3936.88	307.00	3629.88
国有资本经营收入	Operating Income from Government Capital	1658.94	664.49	994.45
国有资源(资产)有偿使用收入	Income from Use of State-owned Resources (Assets)	15053.94	1674.17	13379.77
其他收入	Other Revenue	2863.66	241.74	2621.92

7-3 中央和地方一般公共预算主要支出项目（2023年）
Main Items of General Public Budget Expenditure of the Central and Local Governments (2023)

单位：亿元 (100 million yuan)

项 目	Item	一般公共预算支出 General Public Budget Expenditure	中央 Central Government	地方 Local Governments
合计	**Total**	**274622.94**	**38219.48**	**236403.46**
一般公共服务支出	Expenditure for General Public Services	21242.45	1516.94	19725.51
外交支出	Expenditure for Foreign Affairs	572.08	570.31	1.77
国防支出	Expenditure for National Defense	15805.08	15536.78	268.30
公共安全支出	Expenditure for Public Security	14870.12	2245.58	12624.54
教育支出	Expenditure for Education	41248.29	1570.81	39677.48
科学技术支出	Expenditure for Science and Technology	10885.84	3371.19	7514.65
文化旅游体育与传媒支出	Expenditure for Culture, Tourism, Sport and Media	3965.36	172.69	3792.67
社会保障和就业支出	Expenditure for Social Security and Employment	39881.65	1053.41	38828.24
卫生健康支出	Expenditure for Health Care	22396.01	296.72	22099.29
节能环保支出	Expenditure for Energy Conservation and Environment Protection	5636.78	195.53	5441.25
城乡社区支出	Expenditure for Urban and Rural Community Affairs	20535.76	3.36	20532.40
农林水支出	Expenditure for Agriculture, Forestry and Water Conservancy	23989.85	256.98	23732.87
交通运输支出	Expenditure for Transportation	12222.11	773.04	11449.07
资源勘探工业信息等支出	Expenditure for Resource Exploration and Industrial Information	8245.86	403.48	7842.38
商业服务业等支出	Expenditure for Commerce and Services	1971.87	30.34	1941.53
金融支出	Expenditure for Financial Affairs	1970.66	524.54	1446.12
援助其他地区支出	Expenditure for Assistance to Other Regions	437.17		437.17
自然资源海洋气象等支出	Expenditure for Nature Resources, Ocean and Weather	2646.28	286.37	2359.91
住房保障支出	Expenditure for Housing Security	8213.56	621.47	7592.09
粮油物资储备支出	Expenditure for Reserve of Grain, Oil and Other Materials	2017.35	1300.96	716.39
灾害防治及应急管理支出	Expenditure for Prevention of Disasters and Emergency Management	2436.99	422.53	2014.46
债务付息支出	Expenditure for Interest Payments on Debts	11832.84	6945.96	4886.88
债务发行费用支出	Expenditure for Issuing Debts	83.90	54.10	29.80
其他支出	Other Expenditure	1515.08	66.39	1448.69

7–4 各项税收
Taxes

单位：亿元 (100 million yuan)

年 份 Year	合 计 Total	#国内增值税 Domestic Value-added Tax	#国内消费税 Domestic Consumption Tax	#营业税 Business Tax	#企业所得税 Corporate Income Tax	#个人所得税 Individual Income Tax	#关 税 Tariffs
1978	519.28						28.76
1979	537.82						26.00
1980	571.70						33.53
1981	629.89						54.04
1982	700.02						47.46
1983	775.59						53.88
1984	947.35						103.07
1985	2040.79	147.70		211.07	696.06		205.21
1986	2090.73	232.19		261.07	692.40		151.62
1987	2140.36	254.20		302.00	664.71		142.67
1988	2390.47	384.37		397.92	676.04		155.02
1989	2727.40	430.83		487.30	700.43		181.54
1990	2821.86	400.00		515.75	716.00		159.01
1991	2990.17	406.36		564.00	731.13		187.28
1992	3296.91	705.93		658.67	720.78		212.75
1993	4255.30	1081.48		966.09	678.60		256.47
1994	5126.88	2308.34	487.40	670.02	708.49		272.68
1995	6038.04	2602.33	541.48	865.56	878.44		291.83
1996	6909.82	2962.81	620.23	1052.57	968.48		301.84
1997	8234.04	3283.92	678.70	1324.27	963.18		319.49
1998	9262.80	3628.46	814.93	1575.08	925.54		313.04
1999	10682.58	3881.87	820.66	1668.56	811.41	413.66	562.23
2000	12581.51	4553.17	858.29	1868.78	999.63	659.64	750.48
2001	15301.38	5357.13	929.99	2064.09	2630.87	995.26	840.52
2002	17636.45	6178.39	1046.32	2450.33	3082.79	1211.78	704.27
2003	20017.31	7236.54	1182.26	2844.45	2919.51	1418.03	923.13
2004	24165.68	9017.94	1501.90	3581.97	3957.33	1737.06	1043.77
2005	28778.54	10792.11	1633.81	4232.46	5343.92	2094.91	1066.17
2006	34804.35	12784.81	1885.69	5128.71	7039.60	2453.71	1141.78
2007	45621.97	15470.23	2206.83	6582.17	8779.25	3185.58	1432.57
2008	54223.79	17996.94	2568.27	7626.39	11175.63	3722.31	1769.95
2009	59521.59	18481.22	4761.22	9013.98	11536.84	3949.35	1483.81
2010	73210.79	21093.48	6071.55	11157.91	12843.54	4837.27	2027.83
2011	89738.39	24266.63	6936.21	13679.00	16769.64	6054.11	2559.12
2012	100614.28	26415.51	7875.58	15747.64	19654.53	5820.28	2783.93
2013	110530.70	28810.13	8231.32	17233.02	22427.20	6531.53	2630.61
2014	119175.31	30855.36	8907.12	17781.73	24642.19	7376.61	2843.41
2015	124922.20	31109.47	10542.16	19312.84	27133.87	8617.27	2560.84
2016	130360.73	40712.08	10217.23	11501.88	28851.36	10088.98	2603.75
2017	144369.87	56378.18	10225.09		32117.29	11966.37	2997.85
2018	156402.86	61530.77	10631.75		35323.71	13871.97	2847.78
2019	158000.46	62347.36	12564.44		37303.77	10388.53	2889.13
2020	154312.29	56791.24	12028.10		36425.81	11568.26	2564.25
2021	172735.67	63519.59	13880.70		42042.38	13992.68	2806.14
2022	166620.10	48717.71	16698.81		43695.38	14922.85	2860.29
2023	181136.25	69334.28	16117.81		41102.09	14775.30	2590.88

注：1.企业所得税2001年以前只包括国有及集体企业所得税，从2001年起，企业所得税还包括除国有企业和集体企业外的其他所有制企业所得税。

2.国内增值税不包括进口货物增值税；国内消费税不包括进口消费品消费税。

3.自2016年5月1日起，在全国范围内全面推开营业税改征增值税试点，全部营业税纳税人由缴纳营业税改为缴纳增值税。

a) Before 2001, the corporate income tax only included that of state-owned and collective-owned enterprises. Since 2001, the corporate income tax also includes the income tax levied on enterprises of other forms of ownership except for state-owned and collective-owned enterprises.

b) Domestic value-added tax does not include VAT from imports; Domestic consumption tax does not include consumption tax from imports.

c) Since May 1,2016, the replacement of business tax with VAT has been extended to all industries. All business tax payers pay VAT instead of business tax.

7-5 分地区一般公共预算收入（2023年）
General Public Budget Revenue by Region (2023)

单位：亿元 (100 million yuan)

地 区	Region	地方一般公共预算收入 General Public Budget Revenue	税收收入 Tax Revenue	国内增值税 Domestic Value-added Tax	企业所得税 Corporate Income Tax	个人所得税 Individual Income Tax	资源税 Resource Tax	城市维护建设税 City Maintenance and Construction Tax	房产税 House Property Tax
地方合计	**Total of All Regions**	**117228.73**	**85302.18**	**34746.23**	**14692.87**	**5910.02**	**2977.75**	**4969.14**	**3994.19**
北 京	Beijing	6181.10	5357.09	1877.13	1434.81	772.81	33.34	232.99	368.50
天 津	Tianjin	2027.51	1579.13	719.27	289.53	113.80	12.59	100.53	92.51
河 北	Hebei	4286.60	2578.11	1056.24	311.35	82.90	70.47	145.55	107.30
山 西	Shanxi	3479.37	2557.05	904.82	500.69	66.09	619.02	118.08	60.72
内蒙古	Inner Mongolia	3083.64	2331.22	691.18	345.57	72.88	672.03	91.13	65.96
辽 宁	Liaoning	2755.29	1871.05	776.58	275.05	77.36	48.89	131.11	110.71
吉 林	Jilin	1074.84	699.57	305.79	103.78	35.81	14.39	58.54	40.62
黑龙江	Heilongjiang	1396.15	859.65	345.31	97.79	34.80	80.40	55.73	46.24
上 海	Shanghai	8312.50	7109.14	2669.80	1716.42	952.93		347.24	333.07
江 苏	Jiangsu	9930.18	7976.99	3665.17	1408.71	505.39	9.30	486.24	405.80
浙 江	Zhejiang	8600.51	7124.55	3011.53	1311.79	582.55	13.42	405.02	348.54
安 徽	Anhui	3939.16	2593.10	1233.05	379.54	107.37	45.68	171.89	103.51
福 建	Fujian	3592.04	2341.94	1017.41	429.65	137.58	9.59	131.80	113.98
江 西	Jiangxi	3059.59	2021.80	1029.71	255.71	96.59	29.07	126.75	69.39
山 东	Shandong	7464.78	5229.66	2027.15	724.94	260.17	160.60	319.84	229.61
河 南	Henan	4518.10	2855.48	1220.21	344.36	99.68	104.78	166.04	103.70
湖 北	Hubei	3692.79	2673.15	1105.98	374.44	124.71	26.30	177.17	129.02
湖 南	Hunan	3360.51	2208.51	824.18	225.90	91.30	14.33	149.67	140.79
广 东	Guangdong	13850.78	10244.77	4291.82	1784.12	946.13	13.96	598.22	470.67
广 西	Guangxi	1783.80	1081.99	483.71	129.71	47.51	20.74	76.99	59.12
海 南	Hainan	900.71	667.37	221.78	115.38	49.74	3.59	29.27	23.79
重 庆	Chongqing	2440.77	1476.09	598.21	216.02	80.53	15.37	94.09	104.50
四 川	Sichuan	5529.09	3700.90	1404.46	629.78	185.56	92.32	213.23	165.40
贵 州	Guizhou	2078.37	1221.87	489.05	255.95	44.28	47.82	97.66	43.49
云 南	Yunnan	2149.44	1387.76	562.35	213.07	55.46	40.84	133.58	35.58
西 藏	Xizang	236.62	156.51	91.94	14.57	13.47	8.31	10.99	
陕 西	Shaanxi	3437.60	2693.85	999.31	412.46	143.80	509.87	139.17	100.46
甘 肃	Gansu	1003.58	698.65	322.47	82.40	24.84	41.45	50.93	34.03
青 海	Qinghai	381.34	282.97	113.33	49.73	11.25	35.17	15.50	11.56
宁 夏	Ningxia	502.31	353.20	142.99	48.31	15.58	31.07	20.62	16.52
新 疆	Xinjiang	2179.69	1369.08	544.32	211.34	77.17	153.04	73.56	59.09

注：由于体制调整，2022年起新疆数据包含新疆生产建设兵团。

a) Due to institutional adjustments, since 2022, the data of Xinjiang includes the data of Xinjiang Production and Construction Corps.

7-5 续表 1 continued

单位：亿元 (100 million yuan)

地 区	Region	印花税 Stamp Tax	城镇土地使用税 Urban Land Use Tax	土地增值税 Land Appreciation Tax	车船税 Tax on Vehicles and Boat Operation	耕地占用税 Farm Land Occupation Tax	契 税 Deed Tax	烟叶税 Tobacco Leaf Tax	环境保护税 Environment Protection Tax
地方合计	**Total of All Regions**	**1983.59**	**2212.71**	**5294.00**	**1114.03**	**1126.52**	**5910.43**	**151.37**	**205.05**
北 京	Beijing	120.60	19.45	223.15	33.41	5.81	225.17		9.85
天 津	Tianjin	53.40	14.44	77.31	15.34	2.26	84.64		2.67
河 北	Hebei	78.42	155.04	173.22	64.76	76.96	241.17	0.19	14.30
山 西	Shanxi	46.94	37.37	44.10	31.06	27.61	89.64	0.38	10.08
内蒙古	Inner Mongolia	30.63	98.71	35.28	29.21	110.63	64.77	0.16	21.31
辽 宁	Liaoning	40.76	147.12	66.10	50.72	11.03	127.22	0.53	7.49
吉 林	Jilin	15.42	25.43	19.92	24.35	8.30	45.08	0.42	1.36
黑龙江	Heilongjiang	16.89	72.29	15.22	28.51	11.83	50.30	1.33	2.36
上 海	Shanghai	144.82	20.62	566.43	21.42	4.30	330.06		1.97
江 苏	Jiangsu	196.54	158.73	303.15	68.82	61.41	668.44		39.08
浙 江	Zhejiang	191.90	130.44	404.42	68.92	41.60	609.13	0.02	4.02
安 徽	Anhui	54.75	104.25	99.24	32.23	39.07	217.88	1.36	2.63
福 建	Fujian	72.11	36.28	142.85	30.56	10.94	196.00	10.22	2.64
江 西	Jiangxi	44.66	53.12	99.10	25.75	26.91	159.95	2.00	2.94
山 东	Shandong	138.98	315.09	431.42	101.57	75.59	424.57	3.26	16.25
河 南	Henan	62.29	141.54	157.25	65.90	119.17	251.01	7.41	11.84
湖 北	Hubei	61.18	68.31	252.38	41.42	77.64	221.92	5.59	6.18
湖 南	Hunan	47.66	85.96	265.98	36.63	52.66	254.47	14.27	4.53
广 东	Guangdong	223.82	85.38	1033.79	97.58	67.01	621.88	1.86	7.33
广 西	Guangxi	32.92	22.81	56.57	29.15	27.32	89.60	1.37	4.36
海 南	Hainan	18.95	18.16	116.14	6.40	4.09	58.72	0.11	0.87
重 庆	Chongqing	39.62	91.79	77.93	19.51	28.16	103.18	3.20	2.87
四 川	Sichuan	81.21	99.48	343.93	46.99	97.09	322.92	11.62	5.58
贵 州	Guizhou	22.96	29.46	45.19	20.17	11.54	91.72	17.47	5.17
云 南	Yunnan	32.90	22.90	82.95	29.92	23.53	82.97	66.18	5.39
西 藏	Xizang	3.40	0.38	4.32	2.31	3.91	2.72		0.20
陕 西	Shaanxi	51.53	56.06	77.06	33.02	26.58	139.55	2.26	2.62
甘 肃	Gansu	15.87	28.75	22.36	19.90	8.79	44.06	0.15	2.50
青 海	Qinghai	5.27	4.83	4.61	5.16	15.14	10.51		0.80
宁 夏	Ningxia	8.57	12.29	11.28	6.92	13.09	24.56	0.02	1.37
新 疆	Xinjiang	28.63	56.25	41.35	26.42	36.55	56.62		4.46

7–5 续表 2 continued

单位：亿元 (100 million yuan)

地 区	Region	其他税收收入 Other Tax Revenue	非税收入 Non-Tax Revenue	专项收入 Special Program Receipts	行政事业性收费收入 Charge of Administrative and Institutional Units	罚没收入 Penalty Receipts	国有资本经营收入 Operating Income from Government Capital	国有资源(资产)有偿使用收入 Income from Use of State-owned Resources (Assets)	其他收入 Other Revenue
地方合计	**Total of All Regions**	**14.28**	**31926.55**	**7851.80**	**3448.73**	**3629.88**	**994.45**	**13379.77**	**2621.92**
北 京	Beijing	0.08	824.01	366.89	65.91	73.96	0.83	202.86	113.56
天 津	Tianjin	0.85	448.38	123.41	34.30	47.77	0.78	184.73	57.39
河 北	Hebei	0.23	1708.50	366.72	114.41	137.37	52.29	916.82	120.89
山 西	Shanxi	0.48	922.32	204.48	99.45	118.37	114.00	328.40	57.61
内蒙古	Inner Mongolia	1.75	752.42	143.01	126.94	89.85	6.48	352.95	33.19
辽 宁	Liaoning	0.40	884.24	167.70	97.77	194.38	4.83	371.31	48.24
吉 林	Jilin	0.36	375.27	74.08	51.30	47.04	5.24	170.55	27.06
黑龙江	Heilongjiang	0.64	536.50	66.05	58.07	81.87	6.32	285.23	38.97
上 海	Shanghai	0.04	1203.37	617.26	75.72	53.48	2.60	408.63	45.67
江 苏	Jiangsu	0.21	1953.20	487.88	275.42	241.02	84.09	700.52	164.26
浙 江	Zhejiang	1.25	1475.96	546.22	177.19	166.75	-35.86	557.51	64.16
安 徽	Anhui	0.67	1346.05	332.44	111.54	108.03	35.54	665.74	92.76
福 建	Fujian	0.33	1250.11	343.97	89.86	114.91	35.76	608.64	56.97
江 西	Jiangxi	0.15	1037.79	157.55	116.14	197.96	8.20	494.50	63.44
山 东	Shandong	0.62	2235.11	438.29	295.72	312.77	43.79	1027.08	117.47
河 南	Henan	0.30	1662.62	398.64	218.37	201.97	119.72	560.06	163.85
湖 北	Hubei	0.91	1019.65	258.83	138.51	116.41	3.41	423.25	79.24
湖 南	Hunan	0.18	1151.99	260.41	118.91	183.18	11.00	417.90	160.58
广 东	Guangdong	1.19	3606.00	1086.09	297.21	338.45	132.44	1277.18	474.64
广 西	Guangxi	0.11	701.81	107.17	91.61	138.01	12.57	307.89	44.57
海 南	Hainan	0.37	233.34	98.61	30.23	30.38	-0.16	61.00	13.28
重 庆	Chongqing	1.11	964.68	146.36	74.42	57.53		618.15	68.23
四 川	Sichuan	1.33	1828.19	259.62	184.25	183.30	66.57	947.32	187.12
贵 州	Guizhou	-0.03	856.49	117.60	76.29	83.36	258.52	271.16	49.57
云 南	Yunnan	0.14	761.68	196.46	111.05	97.52	-0.62	279.02	78.26
西 藏	Xizang	0.00	80.11	20.67	17.99	13.97	0.86	18.20	8.42
陕 西	Shaanxi	0.08	743.75	215.13	111.19	78.14	4.48	288.27	46.54
甘 肃	Gansu	0.16	304.94	78.87	48.65	38.87	6.40	100.51	31.63
青 海	Qinghai	0.12	98.37	18.52	14.00	11.62		42.51	11.72
宁 夏	Ningxia	-0.01	149.11	43.99	20.79	12.60	1.38	54.17	16.18
新 疆	Xinjiang	0.28	810.60	108.90	105.54	59.06	12.97	437.70	86.45

7–6 分地区一般公共预算支出（2023年）
General Public Budget Expenditure by Region (2023)

单位：亿元 (100 million yuan)

地 区	Region	地方一般公共预算支出 General Public Budget Expenditure	一般公共服务支出 Expenditure for General Public Services	外交支出 Expenditure for Foreign Affairs	国防支出 Expenditure for National Defense	公共安全支出 Expenditure for Public Security	教育支出 Expenditure for Education	科学技术支出 Expenditure for Science and Technology	文化旅游体育与传媒支出 Expenditure for Culture, Tourism, Sport and Media
地方合计	**Total of All Regions**	**236403.46**	**19725.51**	**1.77**	**268.30**	**12624.54**	**39677.48**	**7514.65**	**3792.67**
北 京	Beijing	7971.25	545.81		7.71	501.66	1227.90	521.91	215.87
天 津	Tianjin	3280.42	244.25		3.84	215.46	491.79	77.03	30.63
河 北	Hebei	9606.21	871.59		9.10	455.70	1807.51	131.04	130.39
山 西	Shanxi	6345.61	547.77		5.19	285.91	910.55	84.14	117.16
内蒙古	Inner Mongolia	6836.24	543.65		8.62	294.75	774.62	74.97	130.20
辽 宁	Liaoning	6574.78	494.67		5.81	398.88	737.49	78.93	88.12
吉 林	Jilin	4406.85	363.33		5.03	228.57	535.13	38.54	55.09
黑龙江	Heilongjiang	5776.44	399.89		6.35	290.83	608.69	49.41	67.67
上 海	Shanghai	9638.51	426.95		12.26	473.55	1206.14	528.05	152.70
江 苏	Jiangsu	15242.28	1315.40		17.24	903.66	2709.98	761.46	229.93
浙 江	Zhejiang	12353.09	1169.86		13.52	763.08	2365.17	787.48	291.44
安 徽	Anhui	8643.57	594.53		7.38	360.08	1516.66	535.34	82.66
福 建	Fujian	5859.39	477.19		5.76	350.34	1257.68	146.92	106.83
江 西	Jiangxi	7492.88	639.82		11.94	346.52	1376.21	244.15	121.16
山 东	Shandong	12581.74	1193.50		12.91	647.18	2713.74	322.70	157.42
河 南	Henan	11052.54	1162.92		8.10	492.03	1993.35	470.10	125.99
湖 北	Hubei	9299.07	822.09		7.94	438.59	1357.80	397.84	133.80
湖 南	Hunan	9581.12	812.14		12.20	440.92	1579.39	314.12	142.49
广 东	Guangdong	18527.03	1718.76	0.01	19.53	1374.67	4004.45	980.46	360.52
广 西	Guangxi	6101.37	502.76		10.75	312.66	1187.14	107.31	82.77
海 南	Hainan	2248.96	183.47	1.15	6.33	110.42	361.96	69.54	42.75
重 庆	Chongqing	5304.56	352.23	0.19	5.99	269.74	855.97	102.54	66.19
四 川	Sichuan	12732.79	1118.66		22.87	600.22	1949.20	244.12	213.25
贵 州	Guizhou	6203.70	483.23		4.33	280.72	1202.79	80.06	95.52
云 南	Yunnan	6730.08	500.82		10.50	383.23	1173.93	61.33	97.50
西 藏	Xizang	2809.02	344.25	0.11	3.54	154.22	335.32	8.71	52.93
陕 西	Shaanxi	7175.08	625.13		5.88	329.09	1089.44	133.68	136.51
甘 肃	Gansu	4521.82	385.02		2.44	210.79	715.57	58.60	83.98
青 海	Qinghai	2188.72	149.84		1.59	98.62	234.05	11.86	43.59
宁 夏	Ningxia	1751.38	100.10		0.98	68.67	223.69	28.06	25.76
新 疆	Xinjiang	7566.98	635.92	0.32	12.68	543.79	1174.15	64.27	111.83

注：由于体制调整，2022年起新疆数据包含新疆生产建设兵团。
a) Due to institutional adjustments, since 2022, the data of Xinjiang includes the data of Xinjiang Production and Construction Corps.

7–6 续表 1 continued

单位：亿元 (100 million yuan)

地 区 Region	社会保障和就业支出 Expenditure for Social Security and Employment	卫生健康支出 Expenditure for Health Care	节能环保支出 Expenditure for Energy Conservation and Environment Protection	城乡社区支出 Expenditure for Urban and Rural Community Affairs	农林水支出 Expenditure for Agriculture, Forestry and Water Conservancy	交通运输支出 Expenditure for Transportation	资源勘探工业信息等支出 Expenditure for Resource Exploration and Industrial Information	商业服务业等支出 Expenditure for Commerce and Services
地方合计 Total of All Regions	**38828.24**	**22099.29**	**5441.25**	**20532.40**	**23732.87**	**11449.07**	**7842.38**	**1941.53**
北 京 Beijing	1145.82	704.86	220.67	929.61	515.53	373.10	272.53	26.60
天 津 Tianjin	667.29	211.48	33.79	432.42	126.95	104.49	315.72	57.53
河 北 Hebei	1691.14	929.84	320.60	969.64	928.51	355.43	168.20	35.67
山 西 Shanxi	1103.45	516.56	241.65	675.96	660.99	337.65	207.08	33.36
内蒙古 Inner Mongolia	1131.90	473.25	178.06	710.64	982.68	408.28	300.33	27.37
辽 宁 Liaoning	1970.58	425.97	87.06	571.17	490.96	233.06	202.85	39.59
吉 林 Jilin	982.22	361.89	152.38	327.58	618.30	238.83	65.41	18.12
黑龙江 Heilongjiang	1504.70	442.26	153.82	300.56	1087.15	291.62	91.69	42.04
上 海 Shanghai	1187.63	881.74	254.97	1346.56	399.14	538.84	1303.08	215.63
江 苏 Jiangsu	2048.33	1384.06	247.22	1749.13	1187.82	600.00	453.93	111.18
浙 江 Zhejiang	1497.70	1148.02	187.98	1094.06	910.65	547.19	395.55	300.78
安 徽 Anhui	1503.62	813.92	193.59	755.74	1049.29	320.86	140.97	85.84
福 建 Fujian	767.10	620.40	120.49	441.47	415.14	261.09	251.00	124.40
江 西 Jiangxi	1104.93	718.51	249.37	637.07	802.43	265.58	332.62	41.82
山 东 Shandong	2181.75	1253.98	209.31	1200.13	1051.73	302.92	281.07	82.49
河 南 Henan	1932.18	1140.93	178.61	978.56	1059.78	347.81	135.58	42.48
湖 北 Hubei	1734.13	827.24	188.34	862.25	953.45	520.09	280.87	56.63
湖 南 Hunan	1556.24	869.10	170.41	1216.86	1068.21	410.71	127.07	47.56
广 东 Guangdong	2265.67	2021.59	444.65	1367.66	1076.77	614.73	600.85	158.87
广 西 Guangxi	1076.52	714.99	70.43	290.16	729.94	313.42	155.98	33.36
海 南 Hainan	352.23	247.92	44.52	168.88	271.84	79.24	48.92	9.37
重 庆 Chongqing	1093.78	493.44	184.85	499.01	415.66	296.71	187.49	32.42
四 川 Sichuan	2440.04	1231.90	253.90	775.06	1455.20	708.83	449.81	114.27
贵 州 Guizhou	824.50	632.26	128.85	244.20	775.88	467.16	329.53	22.12
云 南 Yunnan	1174.25	772.45	154.00	244.84	903.93	461.39	127.20	34.64
西 藏 Xizang	234.18	188.68	62.21	149.00	414.87	568.99	77.12	8.00
陕 西 Shaanxi	1185.94	679.03	245.01	578.91	754.49	328.07	206.88	61.92
甘 肃 Gansu	724.52	443.28	146.34	193.84	762.61	227.59	63.25	11.70
青 海 Qinghai	344.35	197.72	109.13	185.06	271.36	241.63	63.08	7.50
宁 夏 Ningxia	292.48	146.46	76.33	141.73	274.52	153.75	45.49	8.40
新 疆 Xinjiang	1109.06	605.57	132.72	494.66	1317.08	529.99	161.22	49.88

7-6 续表 2 continued

单位：亿元 (100 million yuan)

地区 Region	金融支出 Expenditure for Financial Affairs	援助其他地区支出 Expenditure for Assistance to Other Regions	自然资源海洋气象等支出 Expenditure for Nature Resources, Ocean and Weather	住房保障支出 Expenditure for Housing Security	粮油物资储备支出 Expenditure for Reserve of Grain, Oil and Other Materials	灾害防治及应急管理支出 Expenditure for Prevention of Disasters and Emergency Management	债务付息支出 Expenditure for Interest Payments on Debts	债务发行费用支出 Expenditure for Issuing Debts	其他支出 Other Expenditure
地方合计 Total of All Regions	**1446.12**	**437.17**	**2359.91**	**7592.09**	**716.39**	**2014.46**	**4886.88**	**29.80**	**1448.69**
北京 Beijing	23.63	58.46	34.53	186.01	10.45	207.00	77.86	0.33	163.41
天津 Tianjin	4.39	27.09	35.50	86.93	8.42	25.68	65.46	0.99	13.28
河北 Hebei	19.04	9.06	149.11	249.56	19.52	88.67	227.00	1.17	38.73
山西 Shanxi	83.90	3.19	98.50	199.09	18.81	69.11	99.64	0.49	45.45
内蒙古 Inner Mongolia	70.94	0.00	106.43	203.83	21.38	42.64	217.32	1.56	132.82
辽宁 Liaoning	101.39	13.11	65.76	221.11	19.07	40.87	226.57	1.66	60.11
吉林 Jilin	6.47	3.19	28.77	143.28	34.96	33.83	131.41	1.01	33.52
黑龙江 Heilongjiang	32.34	3.68	36.30	186.08	18.10	42.85	114.55	0.80	5.05
上海 Shanghai	96.41	84.22	28.45	314.24	13.87	43.18	112.31	0.50	18.07
江苏 Jiangsu	23.62	65.58	131.88	850.72	34.95	89.80	255.87	1.21	69.29
浙江 Zhejiang	27.27	34.15	161.94	281.54	33.68	74.05	257.16	1.04	9.78
安徽 Anhui	97.19	5.65	61.79	280.63	31.39	41.92	151.08	0.88	12.55
福建 Fujian	20.12	5.94	89.89	150.43	27.03	46.50	123.49	0.60	49.57
江西 Jiangxi	63.05	3.23	64.40	221.45	20.72	65.18	143.00	0.58	19.16
山东 Shandong	78.46	32.07	131.99	325.62	28.90	89.75	253.80	1.35	28.96
河南 Henan	107.02	5.83	104.43	325.65	37.92	93.40	193.86	0.83	115.20
湖北 Hubei	42.09	8.79	84.78	239.67	40.23	65.32	182.14	0.96	54.04
湖南 Hunan	10.06	5.93	113.28	263.99	32.96	75.36	252.74	1.42	57.97
广东 Guangdong	147.65	59.56	144.97	660.69	73.47	158.80	237.41	1.15	34.14
广西 Guangxi	51.88		70.78	156.57	16.17	41.76	165.52	1.53	8.97
海南 Hainan	24.72		34.01	61.22	5.76	15.69	58.02	0.28	50.71
重庆 Chongqing	7.96	1.36	48.21	218.59	16.95	42.04	104.87	0.87	7.52
四川 Sichuan	38.59	6.70	116.60	431.49	41.88	153.63	257.90	1.20	107.45
贵州 Guizhou	19.93		73.41	207.17	23.62	51.52	229.22	2.10	25.59
云南 Yunnan	5.35		75.26	244.98	17.22	59.72	193.64	2.19	31.70
西藏 Xizang	18.85		30.90	74.78	6.96	21.53	12.64	0.07	41.17
陕西 Shaanxi	199.48	0.07	82.38	243.20	19.91	81.75	160.38	0.89	27.06
甘肃 Gansu	17.28		58.73	181.30	13.36	81.37	85.45	0.65	54.17
青海 Qinghai	1.27	0.32	30.66	79.20	3.58	27.50	79.88	0.49	6.43
宁夏 Ningxia	2.64		21.65	64.60	4.74	11.81	53.04	0.30	6.19
新疆 Xinjiang	3.12		44.61	238.45	20.40	32.22	163.68	0.71	120.65

7-7 中央财政债务余额情况
Outstanding of Debts of Central Government

单位：亿元 (100 million yuan)

年份 Year	合计 Total	国内债务 Domestic Debts	国外债务 External Debts
2006	35015.26	34380.24	635.02
2007	52074.65	51467.39	607.26
2008	53271.54	52799.32	472.22
2009	60237.68	59736.95	500.73
2010	67548.11	66987.97	560.14
2011	72044.51	71410.80	633.71
2012	77565.70	76747.91	817.79
2013	86746.91	85836.05	910.86
2014	95655.45	94676.31	979.14
2015	106599.59	105467.48	1132.11
2016	120066.75	118811.24	1255.51
2017	134770.15	133447.43	1322.72
2018	149607.41	148208.62	1398.79
2019	168038.04	166032.13	2005.91
2020	208905.87	206290.31	2615.56
2021	232697.29	229643.71	3053.58
2022	258692.76	255591.55	3101.21
2023	300325.50	296979.22	3346.28

注：自2006年起，国债发行实行余额管理。

a)Since 2006, balance management has been implemented in the issuance of domestic debts.

7-8 按部门划分的外债总额头寸
Gross External Debt Position by Sector

单位：亿美元 (USD 100 million)

债务类型	Type of Debts	2022末 End of 2022	2023末 End of 2023
广义政府	**General Government**	**4363**	**4345**
短期	Short-term	355	405
货币与存款	Currency and Deposits		
债务证券	Debt Securities	355	405
贷款	Loans		
贸易信贷与预付款	Trade Credit and Advances		
其他债务负债	Other Debt Liabilities		
长期	Long-term	4008	3940
货币与存款	Currency and Deposits		
债务证券	Debt Securities	3471	3400
贷款	Loans	537	540
贸易信贷与预付款	Trade Credit and Advances		
其他债务负债	Other Debt Liabilities		
中央银行	**Central Bank**	**815**	**1072**
短期	Short-term	293	302
货币与存款	Currency and Deposits	189	147
债务证券	Debt Securities	105	155
贷款	Loans		
贸易信贷与预付款	Trade Credit and Advances		
其他债务负债	Other Debt Liabilities		
长期	Long-term	521	770
SDR分配	Special Drawing Rights	482	486
货币与存款	Currency and Deposits		
债务证券	Debt Securities		
贷款	Loans		
贸易信贷与预付款	Trade Credit and Advances		
其他债务负债	Other Debt Liabilities	39	284
其他接受存款公司	**Other Depository Corporations**	**10104**	**10093**
短期	Short-term	7736	7853
货币与存款	Currency and Deposits	4916	4714
债务证券	Debt Securities	656	863
贷款	Loans	2104	2214
贸易信贷与预付款	Trade Credit and Advances		
其他债务负债	Other Debt Liabilities	61	62
长期	Long-term	2367	2241
货币与存款	Currency and Deposits		
债务证券	Debt Securities	1799	1820
贷款	Loans	557	408
贸易信贷与预付款	Trade Credit and Advances		
其他债务负债	Other Debt Liabilities	11	13
其他部门	**Other Sectors**	**6161**	**6007**
短期	Short-term	4268	4314
货币与存款	Currency and Deposits	2	3
债务证券	Debt Securities	16	21
贷款	Loans	258	167
贸易信贷与预付款	Trade Credit and Advances	3759	3843
其他债务负债	Other Debt Liabilities	232	281
长期	Long-term	1893	1693
货币与存款	Currency and Deposits		
债务证券	Debt Securities	913	830
贷款	Loans	520	407
贸易信贷与预付款	Trade Credit and Advances	67	68
其他债务负债	Other Debt Liabilities	393	387
直接投资：公司间贷款	**Direct Investment: Intercompany Lending**	**3086**	**2958**
直接投资企业对直接投资者的债务负债	Debt Liabilities of Direct Investment Enterprises to Direct Investors	1705	1658
直接投资者对直接投资企业的债务负债	Debt Liabilities of Direct Investors to Direct Investment Enterprises	185	187
对关联企业的债务负债	Debt Liabilities to Affiliated Enterprises	1195	1113
外债总额头寸	**Gross External Debt Position**	**24528**	**24475**

注：1.本表按照签约期限划分长期、短期外债。
2.本表统计采用四舍五入法。

a) The short-term and long-term herein are broken down by contractual (original) maturity.
b) The data in this table are rounded.

7–9 外债风险指标
Risk Indicators on External Debt

单位：% (%)

年 份 Year	偿 债 率 Debt Servicing Ratio	负 债 率 Liability Ratio	债 务 率 Debt Ratio
1985	2.7	5.1	56.0
1986	15.4	7.1	72.1
1987	9.0	9.2	77.1
1988	6.5	9.8	87.1
1989	8.3	9.1	86.4
1990	8.7	13.3	91.6
1991	8.5	14.6	91.9
1992	7.1	14.1	87.9
1993	10.2	13.5	96.5
1994	9.1	16.4	78.0
1995	7.6	14.5	72.4
1996	6.0	13.5	67.7
1997	7.3	13.6	63.2
1998	10.9	14.2	70.4
1999	11.2	13.9	68.7
2000	9.2	12.0	52.1
2001	7.5	15.2	67.9
2002	7.9	13.8	55.5
2003	6.9	13.2	45.2
2004	3.2	13.4	40.2
2005	3.1	13.0	35.4
2006	2.1	12.3	31.9
2007	2.0	11.0	29.0
2008	1.8	8.5	24.7
2009	2.9	8.4	32.2
2010	1.6	9.0	29.2
2011	1.7	9.2	33.3
2012	1.6	8.6	32.8
2013	1.6	9.0	35.6
2014	2.6	17.0	69.9
2015	5.0	12.5	58.6
2016	6.1	12.6	64.4
2017	5.5	14.3	72.6
2018	5.5	14.3	74.8
2019	6.7	14.5	78.3
2020	6.5	16.3	87.9
2021	5.9	15.4	77.3
2022	10.5	13.6	66.0
2023	7.6	13.7	69.7

注：1.2015年，我国按照国际货币基金组织数据公布特殊标准(SDDS)调整了外债统计口径并对外公布全口径外债数据，将人民币外债纳入统计，并按照签约期限划分中长期和短期外债。为保证数据的可比性，将2014年末外债数据相应调整为全口径外债数据，之前年份未做调整。表内数据根据最新国际收支平衡表数据及GDP数据进行调整。

2.负债率是指年末外债余额与当年国内生产总值的比率；债务率是指年末外债余额与当年国际收支统计口径的货物与服务贸易出口收入的比率；偿债率是指当年外债还本付息额(中长期外债还本付息额加上短期外债付息额)与当年国际收支统计口径的货物与服务贸易出口收入的比率。

a) In accordance with the Special Data Dissemination Standard (SDDS) of the IMF, China adjusted the statistical coverage of external debt and disseminated the full-scale data on China's external debt in 2015, including RMB-denominated external debt, which was classified into medium-and long-term external debt and short-term external debt by contractual maturity. Outstanding external debt at the end of 2014 was adjusted to the full-scale data on the base of comparable coverage. No adjustments were made for previous years. Figures in the table were adjusted according to the latest BOP and GDP data.

b) Liability ratio is defined as the outstanding external debt at the end of the year divided by annual GDP for that year. Debt ratio is defined as the outstanding external debt at the end of the year divided by income from exports of goods and services according to the statistical coverage of the BOP for that year. Debt servicing ratio is defined as the repayment of principal and payment of interest on medium-and long-term external debt, plus payment of interest on short-term external debt, divided by income from exports of goods and services according to the statistical coverage of the BOP for that year.

7-10 全国政府性基金收入决算表(2023年)
Final Accounts for Revenue of Government Funds (2023)

单位：亿元 (100 million yuan)

项 目	Item	预算数 Budget	决算数 Final Accounts	决算数为预算数的% Final as % of Budget	决算数为上年决算数的% Final as % of Previous Year
一、农网还贷资金收入	1. Credit Repayment for Rural Power Grid	275.91	278.25	100.8	106.0
二、铁路建设基金收入	2. Railway Construction Fund	601.00	606.25	100.9	100.3
三、民航发展基金收入	3. Civil Aviation Development Fund	340.00	333.33	98.0	216.2
四、海南省高等级公路车辆通行附加费收入	4. Hainan Province Highway Traffic Surcharge	25.25	26.30	104.2	108.1
五、旅游发展基金收入	5.Tourism Development Fund	0.96	5.22	543.8	
六、国家电影事业发展专项资金收入	6. National Special Fund for Film Development	16.65	9.97	59.9	69.8
七、国有土地使用权出让金收入	7. Transfer of Use Rights of State Land	65341.49	56633.68	86.7	86.7
八、国有土地收益基金收入	8. State Land Income Fund	1414.19	1290.33	91.2	90.4
九、农业土地开发资金收入	9. Agricultural Land Development Funds	98.39	69.82	71.0	70.4
十、中央水库移民扶持基金收入	10. Central Fund for Support to Reservoir Resettlement	350.51	353.99	101.0	102.4
十一、中央特别国债经营基金财务收入	11. Special National Debt Management Fund	452.29	452.64	100.1	71.6
十二、彩票公益金收入	12. Public Welfare Fund from Lottery	1051.00	1519.17	144.5	139.6
十三、城市基础设施配套费收入	13. Urban Infrastructure Support Fee	1822.69	1691.16	92.8	92.8
十四、地方水库移民扶持基金收入	14. Local Fund for Support to Reservoir Resettlement	68.09	57.77	84.8	87.7
十五、国家重大水利工程建设基金收入	15. Fund for National Key Projects on Water Conservancy	168.75	170.52	101.0	103.1
十六、车辆通行费收入	16. Vehicle Toll	858.33	630.27	73.4	79.5
十七、核电站乏燃料处理处置基金收入	17. Fund for Disposal of Spent Fuel of Nuclear Power Plants	63.65	64.85	101.9	114.7
十八、可再生能源电价附加收入	18. Electricity Surcharge Due to Renewable Energy	1113.60	1113.76	100.0	102.8
十九、船舶油污损害赔偿基金收入	19. Vessel-Induced Oil Pollution Compensation Fund	1.80	2.00	111.1	117.6
二十、废弃电器电子产品处理基金收入	20. Fund for Disposal of Waste Electrical and Electronic Equipment	28.50	27.36	96.0	99.0
廿一、彩票发行和销售机构业务费收入	21.Business of Lottery Issuance and Sales Agency	153.50	227.20	148.0	133.1
廿二、污水处理费收入	22.Sewage Treatment	843.00	771.19	91.5	107.7
廿三、抗疫特别国债财务基金收入	23.Fund for Fighting the Epidemic Special Treasury Bond	272.35	272.35	100.0	100.0
廿四、其他政府性基金收入	24. Other Government Funds	1376.00	1846.89	134.2	138.2
廿五、专项债务对应项目专项收入	25.Special Program Receipts of Projects Corresponding to Special Debt	1432.00	2252.66	157.3	160.2
全国政府性基金收入	**Total Revenue of Government Funds**	**78169.90**	**70706.93**	**90.5**	**90.8**

7-11 全国政府性基金支出决算表(2023年)
Final Accounts for Expenditure of Government Funds (2023)

单位：亿元 (100 million yuan)

项　目	Item	预算数 Budget	决算数 Final Accounts	决算数为预算数的% Final as % of Budget	决算数为上年决算数的% Final as % of Previous Year
一、农网还贷资金支出	1. Credit Repayment for Rural Power Grid	289.68	292.55	101.0	109.1
二、铁路建设基金支出	2. Railway Construction Fund	642.88	642.88	100.0	86.4
三、民航发展基金支出	3. Civil Aviation Development Fund	345.43	287.71	83.3	171.9
四、海南省高等级公路车辆通行附加费安排的支出	4. Hainan Province Highway Traffic Surcharge	111.45	85.38	76.6	74.8
五、旅游发展基金支出	5. Tourism Development Fund	1.04	1.63	156.7	236.2
六、国家电影事业发展专项资金支出	6. National Special Fund for Film Development	17.11	10.91	63.8	74.0
七、国有土地使用权出让金收入安排的支出	7. Transfer of Use Rights of State Land	71503.49	54748.60	76.6	87.1
八、国有土地收益基金安排的支出	8. State Land Income Fund	1414.19	831.99	58.8	89.8
九、农业土地开发资金安排的支出	9. Agricultural Land Development Funds	98.39	28.75	29.2	56.5
十、中央水库移民扶持基金支出	10. Central Fund for Support to Reservoir Resettlement	365.70	335.73	91.8	120.8
十一、中央特别国债经营基金财务支出	11. Special National Debt Management Fund	454.47	454.47	100.0	71.8
十二、彩票公益金安排的支出	12 Public Welfare Fund from Lottery	1109.10	979.63	88.3	100.2
十三、城市基础设施配套费安排的支出	13. Urban Infrastructure Support Fee	1875.65	1174.74	62.6	81.7
十四、地方水库移民扶持基金支出	14. Local Fund for Support to Reservoir Resettlement	68.25	34.74	50.9	138.7
十五、国家重大水利工程建设基金安排的支出	15. Fund for National Key Projects on Water Conservancy	177.84	138.32	77.8	92.5
十六、车辆通行费安排的支出	16. Vehicle Toll	2119.65	1908.16	90.0	87.1
十七、核电站乏燃料处理处置基金支出	17. Fund for Disposal of Spent Fuel of Nuclear Power Plants	125.45	9.38	7.5	131.9
十八、可再生能源电价附加收入安排的支出	18. Electricity Surcharge Due to Renewable Energy	2684.62	2688.58	100.1	87.1
十九、船舶油污损害赔偿基金支出	19. Vessel-Induced Oil Pollution Compensation Fund	2.30	0.07	3.0	41.2
二十、废弃电器电子产品处理基金支出	20. Fund for Disposal of Waste Electrical and Electronic Equipment	29.08	27.23	93.6	96.2
廿一、彩票发行和销售机构业务费安排的支出	21.Business of Lottery Issuance and Sales Agency	168.69	158.49	94.0	110.1
廿二、污水处理费安排的支出	22.Sewage Treatment	999.50	760.66	76.1	99.7
廿三、抗疫特别国债财务基金支出	23.Fund for Fighting the Epidemic Special Treasury Bond	272.35	272.35	100.0	100.0
廿四、其他政府性基金支出	24. Other Government Funds	33086.68	35404.89	107.0	99.9
全国政府性基金支出	**Total Expenditure of Government Funds**	**117962.99**	**101277.84**	**85.9**	**91.6**

7-12 全国国有资本经营收入决算表(2023年)
Final Accounts for Operating Revenue of State-owned Capital (2023)

单位：亿元 (100 million yuan)

项目	Item	预算数 Budget	决算数 Final Accounts	决算数为预算数的% Final as % of Budget	决算数为上年决算数的% Final as % of Previous Year
一、利润收入	I. Revenue from Profits	3589.15	4460.11	124.3	120.0
烟草企业利润收入	Tobacco Enterprises	540.00	584.90	108.3	110.8
石油石化企业利润收入	Petroleum and Petrochemical Enterprises	423.64	561.93	132.6	181.0
电力企业利润收入	Power Enterprises	196.69	271.01	137.8	134.3
电信企业利润收入	Telecommunication Enterprises	190.05	193.55	101.8	108.6
煤炭企业利润收入	Coal Enterprises	336.21	245.32	73.0	103.0
有色冶金采掘企业利润收入	Non-Ferrous Metal Enterprises	13.36	18.30	137.0	233.7
钢铁企业利润收入	Iron and Steel Enterprises	41.01	46.12	112.5	86.0
化工企业利润收入	Chemical Enterprises	12.95	16.87	130.3	115.9
运输企业利润收入	Transportation Enterprises	73.90	102.45	138.6	106.0
电子企业利润收入	Electronics Enterprises	1.63	6.17	378.5	135.0
机械企业利润收入	Machinery Enterprises	106.75	87.73	82.2	83.6
投资服务企业利润收入	Investment Services Enterprises	327.59	383.01	116.9	99.3
纺织轻工企业利润收入	Textile and Light Industry Enterprises	37.51	129.97	346.5	105.5
贸易企业利润收入	Trade Enterprises	87.15	51.48	59.1	93.8
建筑施工企业利润收入	Construction Enterprises	135.11	143.29	106.1	108.7
房地产企业利润收入	Real Estate Enterprises	37.43	36.32	97.0	85.4
建材企业利润收入	Building Material Enterprises	8.19	6.96	85.0	78.2
境外企业利润收入	Overseas Enterprises	112.13	110.80	98.8	115.6
对外合作企业利润收入	Enterprises of Economic Cooperation with Foreign Countries	1.14	2.10	184.2	124.3
医药企业利润收入	Medicine Enterprises	1.52	2.81	184.9	111.5
农林牧渔企业利润收入	Agriculture, Forestry, Animal Husbandry and Fishery Enterprises	23.35	25.33	108.5	132.6
邮政企业利润收入	Post Enterprises	23.00	14.29	62.1	98.8
转制科研院所利润收入	Transformed Scientific Research Institutes	5.06	5.39	106.5	107.2
地质勘查企业利润收入	Geological Prospecting Enterprises	3.26	2.63	80.7	97.8
卫生体育福利企业利润收入	Public Health, Sports and Welfare Enterprises	0.18	0.14	77.8	66.7
教育文化广播企业利润收入	Education, Culture and Broadcasting Enterprises	33.21	48.88	147.2	139.9
科学研究企业利润收入	Scientific Research Enterprises	0.17	0.50	294.1	250.0
机关社团所属企业利润收入	Enterprise under Government Agencies and Social Organizations	7.85	18.98	241.8	193.5
金融企业利润收入	Financial Enterprises	55.86	74.36	133.1	141.1
其他国有资本经营预算企业利润收入	Other Enterprises with State-owned Capital	753.25	1268.52	168.4	128.0
二、股利、股息收入	II. Revenue from Stock Dividends	925.21	448.25	48.4	44.2
国有控股公司股利、股息收入	State Controlling Companies	232.58	228.07	98.1	73.5
国有参股公司股利、股息收入	State Holding Companies	71.46	68.03	95.2	85.0
金融企业股利、股息收入	Financial Enterprises	537.94	94.04	17.5	17.6
其他国有资本经营预算企业股利、股息收入	Other Enterprises with State-owned Capital	83.23	58.11	69.8	63.8
三、产权转让收入	III. Revenue from Property Right Transfer	410.76	877.79	213.7	192.3
国有股减持收入	Revenue from Reduction of State-owned Shares		0.06		
国有股权、股份转让收入	From Shares Transfer	165.66	407.62	246.1	235.0
国有独资企业产权转让收入	From Property Rights Transfer from Entirely SOEs	27.71	111.10	400.9	268.6
其他国有资本经营预算企业产权转让收入	Other Property Rights Transfers	217.39	359.01	165.1	149.0
四、清算收入	IV. Revenue from Clearing	9.00	9.81	109.0	90.1
国有股权、股份清算收入	State-owned Shares	2.00	3.65	182.5	131.8
国有独资企业清算收入	Entirely SOEs	3.00	2.98	99.3	89.5
其他国有资本经营预算清算收入	Other State-owned Capital	4.00	3.18	79.5	66.4
五、其他国有资本经营预算收入	V. Revenue from Other Activities of Operation of State-owned Capital	424.28	945.88	222.9	190.1
全国国有资本经营收入	**Operating Revenue of State-owned Capital**	**5358.40**	**6741.84**	**125.8**	**118.4**

7-13 全国国有资本经营支出决算表(2023年)
Final Accounts for Operating Expenditure of State-owned Capital (2023)

单位：亿元 (100 million yuan)

项 目	Item	预算数 Budget	决算数 Final Accounts	决算数为预算数的% Final as % of Budget	决算数为上年决算数的% Final as % of Previous Year
一、解决历史遗留问题及改革成本支出	I. Solving Historical Issues and Reforming Cost	236.55	191.35	80.9	78.7
其中：厂办大集体改革支出	Reforming Collectively Owned Factories	0.58	0.46	79.3	
“三供一业”移交补助支出	"Three Supplies and Property Management" Transferring Subsidy	0.70	11.83		32.6
国有企业办职教幼教补助支出	Subsidy of Vocational and Preschool Education Run by State-owned Enterprises	4.00	3.55	88.8	80.1
国有企业办公共服务机构移交补助支出	Subsidy of Transferring Public Service Organization Run by State-owned Enterprises	10.76	14.18	131.8	295.4
国有企业退休人员社会化管理补助支出	Subsidy of Socialized Management of Retirees of State-owned Enterprises	33.63	27.54	81.9	97.2
国有企业棚户区改造支出	Slum Upgrading of State-owned Enterprises	0.30	-1.42		
国有企业改革成本支出	Reforming Cost of State-owned Enterprises	20.00	14.26	71.3	60.7
离休干部医药费补助支出	Medical Expenses Subsidy for Retired Cadres	1.72	1.79	104.1	89.9
金融企业改革性支出	Reforming Expenditure of Financial Enterprises	70.00	62.11	88.7	89.4
其他解决历史遗留问题及改革成本支出	Other Expenditure Related to Solving Historical Issues and Reforming Cost	94.86	57.05	60.1	79.8
二、国有企业资本金注入	II. Capital Injection into State-owned Enterprises	1966.50	2008.56	102.1	101.1
其中：国有经济结构调整支出	Structural Adjustment of State Owned Economy	789.50	725.26	91.9	101.8
公益性设施投资支出	Investment in Public Welfare Facilities	77.00	105.90	137.5	150.6
前瞻性战略性产业发展支出	Development of Forward Looking Strategic Industries	274.00	248.53	90.7	59.2
生态环境保护支出	Ecological Environmental Protection	16.00	19.80	123.8	78.0
支持科技进步支出	Support for Scientific and Technological Progress	72.00	47.39	65.8	71.0
保障国家经济安全支出	Guaranteeing National Economic Security	18.00	17.58	97.7	66.2
金融企业资本性支出	Capital Expenditure of Financial Enterprises	230.00	88.71	38.6	71.8
其他国有企业资本金注入	Other Capital Injection into State-owned Enterprises	490.00	755.39	154.2	139.3
三、国有企业政策性补贴	III. Policy Subsidy to State-owned Enterprises	827.79	802.49	96.9	113.6
四、其他国有资本经营预算支出	IV.Other State-owned Capital Operating Budget Expenditure	437.97	344.03	78.6	95.8
全国国有资本经营支出	**State-owned Capital Operating Expenditure**	**3468.81**	**3346.43**	**96.5**	**98.6**

主要统计指标解释

一般公共预算收入 指国家财政参与社会产品分配所取得的收入，是实现国家职能的财力保证。主要包括：(1)各项税收：包括国内增值税、国内消费税、进口货物增值税、进口消费品消费税、出口货物退增值税、出口消费品退消费税、企业所得税、个人所得税、资源税、城市维护建设税、房产税、印花税、城镇土地使用税、土地增值税、车船税、船舶吨税、车辆购置税、关税、耕地占用税、契税、烟叶税、环境保护税等。(2) 非税收入：包括专项收入、行政事业性收费收入、罚没收入、国有资本经营收入、国有资源（资产）有偿使用收入和其他收入。财政收入按现行分税制财政体制划分为中央本级收入和地方本级收入。

一般公共预算支出 指国家财政将筹集起来的资金进行分配使用，以满足经济建设和各项事业的需要。主要包括：一般公共服务、外交、国防、公共安全、教育、科学技术、文化旅游体育与传媒、社会保障和就业、卫生健康、节能环保、城乡社区、农林水、交通运输、资源勘探工业信息等、商业服务业等、金融、援助其他地区、自然资源海洋气象等、住房保障、粮油物资储备、灾害防治及应急管理、债务付息、债务发行费用等方面的支出。财政支出根据政府在经济和社会活动中的不同职权，划分为中央财政支出和地方财政支出。

中央一般公共预算收入和地方一般公共预算收入 属于中央一般公共预算的收入包括关税，进口货物增值税和消费税，出口货物退增值税和消费税，国内消费税，铁道部门、各银行总行、各保险公司总公司等集中缴纳的城市维护建设税，增值税 50%部分，纳入共享范围的企业所得税 60%部分，未纳入共享范围的中央企业所得税、中央企业上交的利润，个人所得税 60%部分，车辆购置税，船舶吨税，证券交易印花税，海洋石油资源税，中央非税收入等。属于地方一般公共预算的收入包括城市维护建设税（不含铁道部门、各银行总行、各保险公司总公司集中缴纳的部分），房产税，城镇土地使用税，土地增值税，车船税，耕地占用税，契税，烟叶税，印花税（不含证券交易印花税），增值税 50%部分，纳入共享范围的企业所得税 40%部分，个人所得税 40%部分，海洋石油资源税以外的其他资源税，地方非税收入等。

中央一般公共预算支出和地方一般公共预算支出 指根据政府在经济和社会活动中的不同职责，划分中央和地方政府的责权，按照政府的责权划分确定的支出。中央一般公共预算支出包括一般公共服务，外交支出，国防支出，公共安全支出，以及中央政府调整国民经济结构、协调地区发展、实施宏观调控的支出等。地方一般公共预算支出包括一般公共服务，公共安全支出，地方统筹的各项社会事业支出等。

Explanatory Notes on Main Statistical Indicators

General Public Budget Revenue refers to income for the government finance through participating in the distribution of social products. It is the financial guarantee to ensure government functioning. The government revenue includes the following main items: (1) Various tax revenues including domestic value added tax (VAT), domestic consumption tax, VAT from imports, consumption tax from imports, VAT rebate for exports, consumption tax rebate for exports, corporate income tax, individual income tax, resource tax, city maintenance and construction tax, house property tax, stamp tax, urban land use tax, land appreciation tax, tax on vehicles and boat operation, ship tonnage tax, vehicle purchase tax, tariffs, farm land occupation tax, deed tax, and tobacco tax, environment protection tax, etc. (2) Non-tax revenue, including special program receipts, charge income of administrative and institutional units, penalty receipts, operating income from government capital, income from use of state-owned resources (assets) and others non-tax receipts.

General Public Budget Expenditure refers to the distribution and use of the funds which the government finance has raised, so as to meet the needs of economic construction and various undertakings. It includes the following main items: expenditure for general public services, expenditure for foreign affairs, expenditure for national defence expenditure for public security, expenditure for education, expenditure for science and technology, expenditure for culture, tourism, sport and media, expenditure for social safety net and employment effort, expenditure for health care, expenditure for energy conservation and environment protection, expenditure for urban and rural community affairs, expenditure for agriculture, forestry and water conservancy, expenditure for transportation, expenditure for resource exploration and industrial information, expenditure for affairs of commerce and services, expenditure for finance, aid to other regions, expenditure for nature resources, ocean and weather, expenditure for housing security, expenditure for grain & oil reserves, expenditure for prevention of disasters and emergency management, interest payment for public debts, expenditure for issuing debts. General public budget expenditure is divided into general public budget expenditure of central government and general public budget expenditure of local government according to the different functions of the governments played in economic and social activities.

General Public Budget Revenue of the Central Government and the Local Governments The general public budget revenue of the Central Government includes tariff, VAT and consumption tax from imports, VAT and consumption tax rebate for exports, domestic consumption tax, city maintenance and construct tax from the Ministry of Railways, head offices of banks, head offices of insurance company, which are handed over to the government in a centralized way, 50% of the value added tax, 60% the share part of the corporate income tax, unshared part of corporate income tax of the central enterprises, profit handed in by the central enterprises, 60% of individual income tax, vehicle purchase tax, ship tonnage tax, stamp tax on securities transactions, resource tax on the offshore petroleum resources. The general public budget revenue of the local governments includes city maintenance and construct tax (excluding the part of the Ministry of Railways, head offices of banks, head offices of insurance company, which are handed over to the government in a centralized way), house property tax, urban land use tax, land appreciation tax, tax on vehicles and boat operation, farm land occupation tax, deed tax, and tobacco leaf tax, stamp tax (not including stamp tax on security exchange), 50% of the value added tax, 40% the share part of the corporate income tax, 40% of individual income tax, resource tax other than the tax on offshore petroleum resources, local non-tax revenue, etc.

General Public Budget Expenditure of the Central Government and Local Governments according to the different functions of the Central Government and local governments in economic and social activities, the rights of administration are demarcated between those of the Central Government and those of local governments; and the classification of the expenditure between the Central Government and local governments are made on the basis of the classification of the rights administration between them. The general public budget expenditure of the Central Government includes the expenditure for general public services, expenditure for foreign affairs, expenditure for public security, and the general public budget expenditure of the Central Government for adjusting the national economic structure; coordinating the development among different regions; and exercising macroeconomic regulation. The general public budget expenditure of the local governments includes mainly the expenditure for general public services, expenditure for public security, and expenditures for social development which are planed by local governments, etc.

8

资源和环境

Resources and Environment

简 要 说 明

一、本篇资料的主要内容

本篇主要反映我国自然资源状况和生态环境保护事业发展情况。

自然资源包括土地状况、水资源、森林资源、矿产资源和气象等资料。

生态环境保护事业发展情况主要包括供水用水情况；废水和废气中主要污染物排放情况；固体废物处理利用情况；城市空气质量情况；城市生活垃圾清运及处理情况；城市道路交通和区域环境噪声监测情况；造林、草原建设及自然保护基本情况；地质、地震、海洋、森林灾害及突发环境事件情况；环境污染治理投资情况等。

二、本篇的资料来源

土地状况、河流、矿产资源、海洋灾害、水资源、气象、城市生活垃圾清运及处理、森林资源和造林、草原建设利用、自然保护区、自然灾害损失、地震灾害等情况分别由自然资源部、水利部、中国气象局、住房和城乡建设部、国家林业和草原局、应急管理部提供。

环境污染与治理、空气质量、噪声、工业污染治理投资等情况由生态环境部提供。

Brief Introduction

I. Main Contents

This chapter provides information that reflects natural resource conditions and the progress of ecological of ecological environment protection in China.

Data on natural resources cover land conditions water resources, forest resources, mineral resources and meteorological conditions.

The progress of ecological environment protection mainly include water supply and water use, discharge of main pollutant contents in wastewater and waste gas; treatment and reuse of solid wastes; urban air quality; collection, transportation and disposal of municipal waste; monitoring of urban road traffic noise and environmental noise in major cities; afforestation, grassland construction and natural reserve protection; incidences of geological disasters, earthquake, marine disasters and forest disasters, environmental emergency events; investment in environment pollution treatment, etc.

II. Sources of Data

Data on land conditions, rivers, mineral resources, marine disasters, water resources, meteorological conditions, collection and disposal of municipal wastes, forest resources and afforestation, grassland construction, natural reserve, losses of natural disasters and extreme events, earthquake, etc. are provided respectively by Ministry of Natural Resources, Ministry of Water Resources, China Meteorological Administration, Ministry of Housing and Urban-Rural Development, State Forestry and Grassland Administration, Ministry of Agriculture and Rural Affairs, Ministry of Emergency Management.

Data on environmental pollution and treatment, air quality, noise and investment in the treatment of industrial pollution are provided by the Ministry of Ecology and Environment.

8-1 土地状况(2023年)
Land Use (2023)

项　目	Item	面　积 (万平方公里) Area (10 000 sq.km)
耕地	Cultivated Land	128.6
园地	Garden Land	19.6
林地	Forest Land	283.7
草地	Grassland	263.2
湿地	Wetland	23.5
城镇村及工矿用地	Land Used for Urban, Rural, Industrial and Mining Activities	36.1
交通运输用地	Land Used for Transport	10.4
水域及水利设施用地	Land Used for Water and Water Conservancy Facilities	36.3

8-2 主要河流基本情况
Major Rivers

名　称	River	流域面积 (平方公里) Drainage Area (sq.km)	河　长 (公里) Length (km)	年径流量 (亿立方米) Annual Volume of Runoff (100 million cu.m)
长　江	Changjiang River (Yangtze River)	1782715	6300	9857
黄　河	Huanghe River (Yellow River)	752773	5464	592
松花江	Songhuajiang River	561222	2308	818
辽　河	Liaohe River	221097	1390	137
珠　江	Zhujiang River (Pearl River)	442527	2214	3381
海　河	Haihe River	265511	1090	163
淮　河	Huaihe River	268957	1000	595

注：本表数据由水利部提供，为2002年至2005年进行的第二次水资源评价数据。
a) Figures in this table are provided by the Ministry of Water Resources, and are from the Second Water Resources Assessment between 2002 and 2005.

8-3 河流流域面积
Drainage Area of Rivers

流域名称	River	流域面积（平方公里） Drainage Area (sq.km)	占外流河、内陆河流域面积合计 Percentage to Total (%)
合计	**Total**	**9506678**	**100.00**
外流河	**Out-flowing Rivers**	**6150927**	**64.70**
黑龙江及绥芬河	Heilongjiang River and Suifenhe River	934802	9.83
辽河、鸭绿江及沿海诸河	Liaohe, Yalujiang and Related Coastal Rivers	314146	3.30
海滦河	Haihe River and Luanhe River	320041	3.37
黄河	Huanghe River (Yellow River)	752773	7.92
淮河及山东沿海诸河	Huaihe and Related Coastal Rivers in Shandong Province	330009	3.47
长江	Changjiang River (Yangtze River)	1782715	18.75
浙闽台诸河	Rivers in Zhejiang, Fujian and Taiwan Provinces	244574	2.57
珠江及沿海诸河	Zhujiang River (Pearl River) and Related Coastal Rivers	578974	6.09
元江及澜仓江	Yuanjiang River and Lancang River	240389	2.53
怒江及滇西诸河	Nujiang River and West Yunnan Rivers	157392	1.66
雅鲁藏布江及藏南诸河	Yarlung Zangbo River and Southern Xizang Rivers	387550	4.08
藏西诸河	Western Xizang Rivers	58783	0.62
额尔齐斯河	Ertix River	48779	0.51
内陆河	**Inland Rivers**	**3355751**	**35.30**
内蒙内陆河	Rivers in Inner Mongolia	311378	3.28
河西内陆河	Rivers in Huanghe Upper Reach Area	469843	4.94
准噶尔内陆河	Rivers in Junggar Basin	323621	3.40
中亚细亚内陆河	Rivers in Central Asia	77757	0.82
塔里木内陆河	Rivers in Tarim Basin	1079643	11.36
青海内陆河	Rivers in Qinghai Province	321161	3.38
羌塘内陆河	Rivers in Qiangtang	730077	7.68
松花江、黄河、藏南闭流区	Blind Drainage Areas of Songhua River, Huanghe River and Southern Xizang	42271	0.44

注：本表数据由水利部提供，为2002年至2005年进行的第二次水资源评价数据。

a) Figures in this table are provided by the Ministry of Water Resources, and are from the Second Water Resources Assessment between 2002 and 2005.

8-4 主要矿产储量(年底数)
Reserves of Major Minerals (Year-end Figure)

矿产		Item		2022	2023
煤炭	(亿吨)	Coal	(100 million tons)	2070.12	2185.70
石油	(亿吨)	Petroleum	(100 million tons)	38.06	38.51
天然气	(亿立方米)	Natural Gas	(100 million cu.m)	65690.12	67424.52
铁矿矿石	(亿吨)	Iron Ore	(100 million tons)	162.46	169.17
锰矿矿石	(万吨)	Manganese Ore	(10 000 tons)	27561.45	26129.79
钒矿V_2O_5	(万吨)	Vanadium Ore V_2O_5	(10 000 tons)	734.39	1029.82
铜矿金属	(万吨)	Copper Ore Metals	(10 000 tons)	4077.18	4064.79
铅矿金属	(万吨)	Lead Ore Metals	(10 000 tons)	2186.50	2487.45
锌矿金属	(万吨)	Zinc Ore Metals	(10 000 tons)	4607.86	5992.71
铝土矿矿石	(万吨)	Bauxite Ore	(10 000 tons)	67552.60	70752.22
钨矿WO_3	(万吨)	Tungsten Ore WO_3	(10 000 tons)	299.56	285.11
锡矿金属	(万吨)	Tin Ore Metals	(10 000 tons)	100.49	117.44
钼矿金属	(万吨)	Molybdenum Ore Metals	(10 000 tons)	590.05	780.56
锑矿金属	(万吨)	Antimony Ore Metals	(10 000 tons)	66.69	82.74
金矿金属	(吨)	Gold Ore Metals	(ton)	3127.46	3203.77
银矿金属	(吨)	Silver Ore Metals	(ton)	70344.21	66866.44
菱镁矿矿石	(万吨)	Magnesite Ore	(10 000 tons)	68011.87	69521.05
普通萤石矿物	(万吨)	Fluorite Minerals	(10 000 tons)	8592.06	10690.01
硫铁矿矿石	(万吨)	Pyrite Ore	(10 000 tons)	114785.58	104666.05
磷矿矿石	(亿吨)	Phosphate Ore	(100 million tons)	36.90	34.41
钾盐KCl	(万吨)	Potassium KCl	(10 000 tons)	28788.70	33200.80
盐矿NaCl	(亿吨)	Salt Minerals NaCl	(100 million tons)	142.90	155.35
芒硝Na_2SO_4	(亿吨)	Glauber's Salt Na_2SO_4	(100 million tons)	12.26	9.21
重晶石矿石	(万吨)	Barite Ore	(10 000 tons)	10735.58	12068.88
高岭土矿石	(万吨)	Kaolin Ore	(10 000 tons)	69345.14	72147.37
晶质石墨矿物	(万吨)	Crystalline Graphite Minerals	(10 000 tons)	8100.80	10040.01
滑石矿石	(万吨)	Talc Ore	(10 000 tons)	6045.66	4843.89

注：1.矿产资源储量标准依据2020年5月1日起实施的《固体矿产资源储量分类》(GB/T 17766—2020)和《油气矿产资源储量分类》(GB/T 19492—2020)。

2.石油、天然气为剩余探明技术可采储量。

a) Data are referred to The Classification of Solid Mineral Reserves (GB/T17766-2020) and The Classification of Oil and Gas Reservers (GB/T 19492-2020), which were implemented since May 1,2020.

b) Data on oil and gas mineral reserves (petroleum, natural gas, coal seam gas, shale gas) are the remaining recoverable reserves.

8-5 主要城市平均气温(2023年)

Monthly Average Temperature by Major City (2023)

单位：摄氏度 (℃)

城 市	City	1月 Jan.	2月 Feb.	3月 Mar.	4月 Apr.	5月 May	6月 June	7月 July	8月 Aug.	9月 Sept.	10月 Oct.	11月 Nov.	12月 Dec.	年平均 Annual Average
北 京	Beijing	-2.5	1.6	10.7	15.2	21.9	28.4	29.0	27.3	22.7	15.6	4.8	-3.5	14.3
天 津	Tianjin	-2.4	2.0	10.7	15.1	21.5	27.9	28.5	26.8	22.9	15.9	5.1	-3.6	14.2
石家庄	Shijiazhuang	0.4	3.7	13.1	15.6	21.4	29.1	30.2	27.3	23.3	17.3	6.5	-1.3	15.6
太 原	Taiyuan	-4.3	0.2	8.9	12.1	18.2	23.2	25.7	24.0	19.5	11.7	3.3	-5.7	11.4
呼和浩特	Hohhot	-10.7	-3.5	3.2	8.3	16.2	22.2	23.4	21.8	17.7	9.8	-2.8	-10.7	7.9
沈 阳	Shenyang	-9.0	-3.3	5.4	11.0	18.4	23.2	25.7	24.4	19.8	12.2	-0.9	-9.2	9.8
大 连	Dalian	-1.8	0.8	6.8	12.1	17.9	22.0	25.4	25.8	23.0	17.1	5.9	-1.9	12.8
长 春	Changchun	-12.1	-6.7	3.5	9.5	17.2	22.4	24.0	22.7	18.7	10.3	-4.8	-11.7	7.8
哈尔滨	Harbin	-17.7	-10.5	1.5	8.1	16.3	22.0	23.2	22.2	17.8	9.1	-7.5	-15.9	5.7
上 海	Shanghai	5.5	7.1	12.4	17.1	21.6	25.5	29.7	28.8	25.8	20.1	14.0	6.7	17.9
南 京	Nanjing	4.8	6.0	12.7	17.2	21.5	25.7	28.6	28.0	24.4	18.9	12.2	4.8	17.1
杭 州	Hangzhou	6.8	8.2	13.4	18.3	22.6	26.5	30.3	28.9	26.7	20.5	14.7	7.4	18.7
合 肥	Hefei	3.4	5.6	12.4	17.1	21.3	25.7	28.7	28.1	23.8	17.9	11.1	3.6	16.6
福 州	Fuzhou	11.9	12.6	16.1	19.8	24.1	27.9	30.5	29.1	28.1	23.0	19.1	14.1	21.4
南 昌	Nanchang	8.0	9.3	14.6	19.2	24.2	27.3	30.6	29.6	27.2	21.2	15.4	8.2	19.6
济 南	Jinan	1.7	5.1	13.9	16.0	21.9	28.2	29.1	26.9	23.7	19.1	8.9	0.7	16.3
青 岛	Qingdao	1.7	3.1	8.8	12.9	18.2	22.3	26.3	26.4	23.6	19.3	9.8	2.0	14.5
郑 州	Zhengzhou	2.8	5.6	14.0	17.0	21.9	27.8	30.1	28.2	24.1	18.2	9.9	2.2	16.8
武 汉	Wuhan	4.9	7.3	13.5	18.5	22.6	26.4	29.9	29.6	25.4	19.0	12.2	5.4	17.9
长 沙	Changsha	7.3	7.6	13.4	18.4	22.7	26.0	29.9	28.5	24.7	19.3	14.2	7.4	18.3
广 州	Guangzhou	14.0	17.2	19.3	22.6	26.1	28.2	29.7	28.5	27.3	23.9	20.0	15.2	22.7
南 宁	Nanning	13.8	16.1	19.7	22.9	25.9	28.2	29.7	27.5	26.9	24.1	20.3	15.4	22.5
桂 林	Guilin	10.8	11.5	16.2	20.3	24.4	27.8	30.9	28.7	27.8	23.1	17.7	11.3	20.9
海 口	Haikou	17.0	21.1	23.0	26.2	28.7	29.2	29.7	29.0	27.7	26.2	24.0	20.3	25.2
重庆(沙坪坝)	Chongqing(Shapingba)	8.5	12.2	15.9	21.1	24.0	25.6	29.3	30.3	27.0	20.0	16.5	10.8	20.1
成都(温江)	Chengdu(Wenjiang)	5.7	9.6	13.5	18.4	21.4	24.4	26.9	25.8	23.1	17.8	13.3	7.5	17.3
贵 阳	Guiyang	5.4	6.6	11.6	17.4	20.4	22.0	24.2	23.3	22.6	17.0	13.3	8.0	16.0
昆 明	Kunming	9.0	13.1	15.6	19.8	21.6	21.7	21.7	20.9	20.3	17.2	13.7	11.3	17.2
拉 萨	Lhasa	2.3	4.4	5.7	9.7	13.0	17.1	17.2	17.3	16.4	10.9	4.9	1.3	10.0
西安(泾河)	Xi'an(Jinghe)	1.8	5.5	13.0	15.9	20.0	25.3	28.1	27.1	22.6	15.8	8.7	2.1	15.5
兰州(皋兰)	Lanzhou(Gaolan)	-9.7	-3.0	5.2	9.1	15.9	20.2	22.8	21.8	17.1	8.7	0.2	-7.0	8.4
西 宁	Xining	-6.8	-2.5	3.6	7.3	11.1	15.0	18.1	17.1	13.2	7.1	1.9	-3.6	6.8
银 川	Yinchuan	-5.8	-0.2	8.2	11.4	18.1	23.9	25.8	24.3	19.3	11.7	1.9	-4.0	11.2
乌鲁木齐	Urumqi	-12.0	-6.4	4.4	9.6	15.4	24.1	26.1	24.3	16.7	12.6	2.0	-8.7	9.0

注：从2004年1月份开始成都站被温江站替代、兰州站被皋兰站替代；从2006年1月份开始重庆站被沙坪坝站替代、西安站被泾河站替代（以下相关表同）。

a) Since January 2004, Chengdu station was substituted by Wenjiang station, Lanzhou station by Gaolan station; Since January 2006, Chongqing station was substituted by Shapingba station, Xi'an station by Jinghe station, same as the following tables.

8-6 主要城市平均相对湿度（2023年）
Monthly Average Relative Humidity by Major City (2023)

单位：% (%)

城 市	City	1月 Jan.	2月 Feb.	3月 Mar.	4月 Apr.	5月 May	6月 June	7月 July	8月 Aug.	9月 Sept.	10月 Oct.	11月 Nov.	12月 Dec.	年平均 Annual Average
北 京	Beijing	37	46	35	42	50	42	60	73	70	62	45	55	51
天 津	Tianjin	45	52	40	48	56	48	69	77	72	66	52	60	57
石家庄	Shijiazhuang	40	56	39	55	60	41	56	76	72	58	53	60	56
太 原	Taiyuan	43	61	38	56	59	53	62	76	76	65	47	58	58
呼和浩特	Hohhot	53	53	23	42	39	33	52	59	53	42	42	62	46
沈 阳	Shenyang	56	48	44	44	51	63	78	77	73	63	67	63	61
大 连	Dalian	54	54	53	48	60	71	82	77	70	61	62	63	63
长 春	Changchun	59	57	41	37	44	59	79	79	66	54	74	59	59
哈尔滨	Harbin	66	65	51	46	45	66	89	88	72	58	74	67	66
上 海	Shanghai	67	72	65	66	70	79	80	79	83	74	68	72	73
南 京	Nanjing	60	70	58	62	69	74	84	79	83	71	65	65	70
杭 州	Hangzhou	69	74	68	67	68	75	73	75	78	70	62	63	70
合 肥	Hefei	72	76	68	71	77	77	83	81	85	81	73	76	77
福 州	Fuzhou	71	73	69	77	72	79	72	80	76	74	67	71	73
南 昌	Nanchang	66	73	70	78	72	77	72	74	75	72	70	70	72
济 南	Jinan	41	43	33	52	53	46	66	73	69	50	47	57	52
青 岛	Qingdao	59	64	61	62	71	80	87	83	78	58	61	62	69
郑 州	Zhengzhou	46	58	45	56	62	54	64	71	72	67	55	56	59
武 汉	Wuhan	71	75	72	72	76	78	77	73	79	81	75	72	75
长 沙	Changsha	66	79	78	77	79	81	76	80	86	80	75	71	77
广 州	Guangzhou	71	77	78	80	80	83	77	84	86	82	78	74	79
南 宁	Nanning	64	76	77	82	81	84	78	87	84	77	76	71	78
桂 林	Guilin	56	69	70	75	75	77	66	75	72	67	69	66	70
海 口	Haikou	84	81	79	80	79	81	78	80	86	84	80	83	81
重庆(沙坪坝)	Chongqing(Shapingba)	77	72	75	68	71	76	73	67	71	84	80	78	74
成都(温江)	Chengdu(Wenjiang)	76	81	80	74	77	75	77	84	84	86	83	79	79
贵 阳	Guiyang	72	86	81	73	76	78	76	81	73	78	79	77	77
昆 明	Kunming	66	59	54	45	54	69	72	79	74	78	73	73	66
拉 萨	Lhasa	15	21	35	34	34	42	57	59	44	37	28	29	36
西安(泾河)	Xi'an(Jinghe)	45	62	48	60	68	62	64	70	75	76	56	53	62
兰州(皋兰)	Lanzhou(Gaolan)	39	59	36	40	41	47	49	50	63	79	57	52	51
西 宁	Xining	36	51	40	43	56	60	56	64	68	63	42	40	52
银 川	Yinchuan	42	53	28	44	47	43	51	60	64	65	49	55	50
乌鲁木齐	Urumqi	70	74	60	38	39	32	35	41	53	49	68	77	53

8-7 主要城市降水量（2023年）
Monthly Precipitation by Major City (2023)

单位：毫米 (milimeter)

城 市	City	1月 Jan.	2月 Feb.	3月 Mar.	4月 Apr.	5月 May	6月 June	7月 July	8月 Aug.	9月 Sept.	10月 Oct.	11月 Nov.	12月 Dec.	全年 Annual Total
北 京	Beijing	1.2	6.4	0.3	21.0	14.3	15.7	337.3	89.0	119.8	3.7	8.0	14.1	630.8
天 津	Tianjin	1.5	2.3	0.9	44.2	40.7	65.6	384.5	145.2	27.3	5.9	13.8	13.3	745.2
石家庄	Shijiazhuang	5.8	21.8	1.1	76.0	51.6	34.9	332.7	193.2	18.9	4.8	9.0	20.6	770.4
太 原	Taiyuan	4.0	16.5	0.0	97.3	64.3	38.5	48.5	76.7	16.2	7.3	13.6	14.9	397.8
呼和浩特	Hohhot	0.4	6.8	0.0	37.1	29.7	27.3	58.5	72.8	22.6	4.2	0.2	6.3	265.9
沈 阳	Shenyang	8.0	3.0	4.7	58.8	32.2	77.4	199.3	155.0	82.6	14.8	94.9	16.7	747.4
大 连	Dalian	7.3	1.4	0.3	69.5	91.4	119.1	172.5	134.2	23.6	15.0	62.4	27.9	724.6
长 春	Changchun	2.6	2.9	3.0	38.3	11.6	48.5	218.5	107.9	30.0	5.4	61.9	6.7	537.3
哈尔滨	Harbin	1.5	3.3	11.8	22.3	59.7	35.9	355.5	184.0	38.0	4.3	55.9	4.2	776.4
上 海	Shanghai	62.5	74.7	63.0	36.7	146.6	381.7	254.6	152.9	196.3	37.9	29.6	36.0	1472.5
南 京	Nanjing	27.1	64.7	49.9	46.2	57.7	250.6	240.7	330.8	104.1	27.3	22.9	54.9	1276.9
杭 州	Hangzhou	57.7	88.3	73.8	56.4	129.1	199.8	176.1	183.4	77.4	11.3	67.3	46.9	1167.5
合 肥	Hefei	18.8	40.3	41.5	94.3	86.2	157.7	125.9	48.5	117.0	38.1	29.9	44.9	843.1
福 州	Fuzhou	69.3	69.7	140.8	107.7	92.8	297.4	473.8	301.9	499.6	26.7	9.2	26.6	2115.5
南 昌	Nanchang	90.3	106.6	181.4	317.3	152.1	390.3	178.4	172.6	105.4	32.1	89.4	14.4	1830.3
济 南	Jinan	4.7	7.9	0.5	56.6	31.5	40.3	303.7	178.5	83.9	0.0	42.2	24.6	774.4
青 岛	Qingdao	3.7	6.3	11.1	61.0	35.8	85.1	107.1	185.5	52.5	0.0	9.8	14.9	572.8
郑 州	Zhengzhou	10.8	20.5	21.0	99.9	124.8	35.1	141.8	223.5	98.7	8.3	35.4	35.1	854.9
武 汉	Wuhan	28.4	41.7	72.2	269.3	243.8	125.3	131.0	71.5	70.5	43.4	63.6	59.7	1220.4
长 沙	Changsha	14.3	74.6	126.0	197.6	132.7	194.7	124.7	107.2	70.4	62.4	95.9	9.4	1209.9
广 州	Guangzhou	35.1	44.5	163.4	77.5	222.3	421.5	192.6	223.4	428.1	63.1	21.2	7.9	1900.6
南 宁	Nanning	30.8	55.4	20.3	75.4	84.9	231.7	105.3	226.8	137.6	99.9	15.4	17.7	1101.2
桂 林	Guilin	11.4	77.6	124.8	277.3	349.5	391.7	44.9	110.8	39.8	15.4	74.0	8.7	1525.9
海 口	Haikou	31.1	8.8	74.5	21.5	179.8	229.5	281.5	236.6	348.6	428.2	94.0	19.8	1953.9
重庆(沙坪坝)	Chongqing(Shapingba)	7.7	15.2	37.5	80.9	103.3	154.5	346.9	66.0	197.9	151.5	66.9	4.6	1232.9
成都(温江)	Chengdu(Wenjiang)	0.8	10.3	42.3	68.3	98.3	70.8	305.1	227.8	148.5	48.8	23.7	0.1	1044.8
贵 阳	Guiyang	14.5	37.1	109.7	88.4	49.2	244.5	149.6	168.2	43.5	91.2	57.0	9.7	1062.6
昆 明	Kunming	1.7	3.2	0.2	2.8	15.2	68.3	149.0	520.7	126.1	60.4	3.2	21.7	972.5
拉 萨	Lhasa	0.0	0.9	7.5	20.2	17.3	115.1	139.8	124.0	2.5	8.8	0.0	3.5	439.6
西安(泾河)	Xi'an(Jinghe)	1.5	14.1	30.0	99.8	122.0	92.1	119.0	113.6	82.3	59.3	13.8	11.6	759.1
兰州(皋兰)	Lanzhou(Gaolan)	0.0	9.7	0.8	10.8	17.5	19.9	33.6	12.2	31.3	44.5	2.3	0.0	182.6
西 宁	Xining	0.0	11.8	4.8	18.5	73.1	36.2	60.1	75.0	75.0	64.1	1.7	0.9	421.2
银 川	Yinchuan	0.9	6.8	0.0	23.6	17.4	6.1	1.2	28.0	13.4	3.1	2.4	1.6	104.5
乌鲁木齐	Urumqi	18.8	1.7	30.2	22.3	16.6	6.3	13.2	21.8	41.0	10.6	13.1	26.4	222.0

8-8 主要城市日照时数（2023年）
Monthly Sunshine Hours by Major City (2023)

单位：小时 (hour)

城市	City	1月 Jan.	2月 Feb.	3月 Mar.	4月 Apr.	5月 May	6月 June	7月 July	8月 Aug.	9月 Sept.	10月 Oct.	11月 Nov.	12月 Dec.	全年 Annual Total
北　京	Beijing	218.3	166.0	237.4	184.1	212.4	313.1	232.8	198.4	189.3	233.9	200.5	177.3	2563.5
天　津	Tianjin	217.7	187.4	254.0	194.3	225.2	337.9	249.2	214.6	214.4	239.3	204.3	195.7	2734.0
石家庄	Shijiazhuang	200.3	149.2	244.7	177.6	190.9	311.2	241.4	230.4	183.0	233.8	216.1	187.0	2565.6
太　原	Taiyuan	190.0	125.8	234.1	160.3	161.4	274.8	240.1	224.2	181.9	209.6	216.2	177.1	2395.5
呼和浩特	Hohhot	220.2	180.1	287.5	192.6	226.1	321.7	241.6	257.8	264.5	242.5	202.3	184.7	2821.6
沈　阳	Shenyang	189.9	181.2	247.1	194.5	270.3	252.5	174.7	190.4	229.0	221.5	168.5	153.8	2473.4
大　连	Dalian	182.7	198.9	248.3	214.8	229.8	290.3	219.9	229.5	230.8	244.3	151.2	162.0	2602.5
长　春	Changchun	165.0	194.9	253.3	193.9	243.6	227.4	127.2	161.5	227.7	260.0	144.2	170.1	2368.8
哈尔滨	Harbin	184.8	205.7	228.9	201.1	274.5	211.8	161.0	175.3	235.1	255.3	142.5	179.1	2455.1
上　海	Shanghai	189.3	109.1	178.4	202.2	196.0	167.9	142.7	186.8	107.0	152.5	190.8	140.2	1962.9
南　京	Nanjing	196.9	105.1	173.3	188.2	167.6	163.2	139.7	234.0	130.6	209.4	214.2	165.1	2087.3
杭　州	Hangzhou	173.6	103.7	140.5	158.8	158.8	147.3	218.1	222.9	184.5	201.3	211.6	180.2	2101.3
合　肥	Hefei	184.0	102.3	183.7	195.0	160.1	152.1	159.8	247.3	116.2	192.7	192.1	155.3	2040.6
福　州	Fuzhou	96.6	120.6	165.9	122.8	141.4	166.0	211.6	173.6	163.4	119.6	154.4	116.2	1752.1
南　昌	Nanchang	131.1	82.4	131.2	133.6	142.0	108.6	179.6	173.1	164.0	149.9	171.1	121.7	1688.3
济　南	Jinan	207.4	186.1	249.9	194.2	199.9	270.5	221.5	249.2	182.6	230.6	194.3	182.1	2568.3
青　岛	Qingdao	176.1	190.0	232.4	193.7	209.6	129.5	155.1	245.6	181.2	226.9	164.1	161.4	2265.6
郑　州	Zhengzhou	143.3	78.8	179.0	170.2	155.6	206.4	157.0	184.1	127.6	177.2	171.0	171.5	1921.7
武　汉	Wuhan	149.0	70.8	109.1	155.0	127.5	119.8	136.8	242.4	127.0	152.8	173.4	149.3	1712.9
长　沙	Changsha	131.6	54.1	89.9	121.4	121.1	100.5	183.1	192.0	116.6	128.0	153.1	130.9	1522.3
广　州	Guangzhou	133.9	148.3	110.4	73.1	119.6	142.8	206.0	137.2	146.9	140.9	188.7	135.6	1683.4
南　宁	Nanning	102.3	76.8	84.0	69.5	147.9	143.9	220.0	104.0	125.4	145.5	152.4	123.8	1495.5
桂　林	Guilin	113.4	75.5	78.1	123.3	143.8	107.5	166.6	119.5	141.8	156.8	112.0	110.1	1448.4
海　口	Haikou	76.7	107.4	183.3	112.2	203.9	177.4	235.2	195.7	119.1	70.2	118.5	81.1	1680.7
重庆(沙坪坝)	Chongqing(Shapingba)	57.7	38.5	92.4	154.9	111.4	93.4	163.2	205.4	158.4	57.8	73.9	36.2	1243.2
成都(温江)	Chengdu(Wenjiang)	109.2	43.7	108.5	148.5	96.9	86.9	166.6	111.8	73.7	43.3	98.7	74.5	1162.3
贵　阳	Guiyang	124.0	60.0	94.2	168.4	152.5	142.1	171.5	207.8	209.4	135.0	128.0	109.5	1702.4
昆　明	Kunming	206.7	182.9	221.7	280.4	261.4	140.7	128.2	86.3	148.9	133.6	183.5	136.0	2110.3
拉　萨	Lhasa	278.2	209.9	232.1	238.8	286.5	276.8	185.9	207.8	272.6	265.5	252.5	248.7	2955.3
西安(泾河)	Xi'an(Jinghe)	155.3	80.4	203.1	179.0	165.3	219.0	227.7	222.9	150.3	152.5	183.6	158.2	2097.3
兰州(皋兰)	Lanzhou(Gaolan)	205.1	133.4	227.9	184.8	185.8	218.0	254.6	224.8	174.6	183.6	216.8	217.8	2427.2
西　宁	Xining	232.8	169.1	227.5	210.6	181.3	196.2	247.0	218.2	183.0	207.9	244.3	233.5	2551.4
银　川	Yinchuan	206.9	182.3	279.3	189.9	218.2	287.3	271.2	246.1	202.8	183.5	209.8	186.4	2663.7
乌鲁木齐	Urumqi	176.6	138.4	228.7	243.4	188.7	308.4	302.7	280.0	227.6	261.3	155.1	120.4	2631.3

8–9 水资源情况
Water Resources

年 份 地 区	Year Region	水资源总量（亿立方米） Total Water Resources (100 million cu.m)	地表水资源量 Surface Water Resources	地下水资源量 Groundwater Resources	地表水与地下水资源重复量 Overlapped Measurement Between Surface Water and Groundwater	人均水资源量（立方米/人） Per Capita Water Resources (cu.m/person)
	2000	27700.8	26561.9	8501.9	7363.0	2193.9
	2005	28053.1	26982.4	8091.1	7020.4	2151.8
	2006	25330.1	24358.1	7642.9	6670.8	1932.1
	2007	25255.2	24242.5	7617.2	6604.5	1916.3
	2008	27434.3	26377.0	8122.0	7064.7	2071.1
	2009	24180.2	23125.2	7267.0	6212.1	1816.3
	2010	30906.4	29797.6	8417.0	7308.2	2310.4
	2011	23256.7	22213.6	7214.5	6171.4	1729.1
	2012	29528.8	28373.3	8296.4	7140.9	2180.5
	2013	27957.9	26839.5	8081.1	6962.7	2050.8
	2014	27266.9	26263.9	7745.0	6742.0	1987.6
	2015	27962.6	26900.8	7797.0	6735.2	2026.5
	2016	32466.4	31273.9	8854.8	7662.3	2339.4
	2017	28761.2	27746.3	8309.6	7294.7	2059.9
	2018	27462.5	26323.2	8246.5	7107.2	1957.7
	2019	29041.0	27993.3	8191.5	7143.8	2062.9
	2020	31605.2	30407.0	8553.5	7355.3	2239.8
	2021	29638.2	28310.5	8195.7	6868.0	2098.5
	2022	27088.1	25984.4	7924.4	6820.7	1918.2
	2023	25782.5	24633.5	7807.1	6658.1	1827.6
北 京	Beijing	41.5	21.9	28.5	8.9	189.9
天 津	Tianjin	17.8	12.2	7.0	1.3	130.5
河 北	Hebei	241.4	121.9	182.8	63.3	325.9
山 西	Shanxi	143.9	102.1	103.3	61.6	414.3
内蒙古	Inner Mongolia	491.9	357.0	215.1	80.2	2050.9
辽 宁	Liaoning	305.5	271.0	109.4	74.9	729.2
吉 林	Jilin	498.8	421.7	164.0	86.9	2128.4
黑龙江	Heilongjiang	1015.0	847.0	346.1	178.1	3294.9
上 海	Shanghai	41.5	34.8	9.8	3.1	167.3
江 苏	Jiangsu	422.1	369.7	122.7	70.4	495.4
浙 江	Zhejiang	730.1	715.5	187.7	173.0	1105.9
安 徽	Anhui	692.8	614.3	187.1	108.6	1131.3
福 建	Fujian	979.4	977.6	259.5	257.7	2340.0
江 西	Jiangxi	1409.5	1389.3	341.4	321.1	3117.3
山 东	Shandong	249.8	157.6	159.7	67.6	246.3
河 南	Henan	472.3	348.9	230.3	106.9	479.8
湖 北	Hubei	1094.2	1071.3	307.0	284.1	1873.3
湖 南	Hunan	1190.1	1183.2	312.8	305.9	1807.0
广 东	Guangdong	1956.0	1946.3	483.0	473.3	1542.4
广 西	Guangxi	1520.2	1517.7	409.5	407.0	3018.1
海 南	Hainan	326.1	319.1	88.7	81.7	3150.7
重 庆	Chongqing	698.4	698.4	117.7	117.7	2181.1
四 川	Sichuan	2166.8	2165.4	540.0	538.6	2588.5
贵 州	Guizhou	647.1	647.1	240.1	240.1	1676.2
云 南	Yunnan	1502.3	1502.3	533.1	533.1	3208.0
西 藏	Xizang	4427.3	4427.3	1001.7	1001.7	121462.3
陕 西	Shaanxi	546.3	508.7	167.2	129.6	1381.6
甘 肃	Gansu	222.6	213.7	107.9	98.9	898.1
青 海	Qinghai	855.4	837.9	361.7	344.2	14388.6
宁 夏	Ningxia	8.1	6.5	14.6	13.0	111.2
新 疆	Xinjiang	868.3	826.2	467.7	425.5	3349.3

8-10 供水用水情况
Water Supply and Water Use

年 份 Year 地 区 Region	供水总量 (亿立方米) Water Supply (100 million cu.m)	地表水 Surface Water	地下水 Ground-water	其 他 Others	用水总量 (亿立方米) Water Use (100 million cu.m)	农 业 Agriculture	工 业 Industry	生 活 Households and Service	人工生态环境补水 Artificial Eco-environment	人均用水量 (立方米/人) Per Capita Water Use (cu.m/person)
2000	5530.7	4440.4	1069.2	21.1	5497.6	3783.5	1139.1	574.9		435.4
2005	5633.0	4572.2	1038.8	22.0	5633.0	3580.0	1285.2	675.1	92.7	432.1
2006	5795.0	4706.7	1065.5	22.7	5795.0	3664.4	1343.8	693.8	93.0	442.0
2007	5818.7	4723.9	1069.1	25.7	5818.7	3599.5	1403.0	710.4	105.7	441.5
2008	5910.0	4796.4	1084.8	28.7	5910.0	3663.5	1397.1	729.3	120.2	446.2
2009	5965.2	4839.5	1094.5	31.2	5965.2	3723.1	1390.9	748.2	103.0	448.1
2010	6022.0	4881.6	1107.3	33.1	6022.0	3689.1	1447.3	765.8	119.8	450.2
2011	6107.2	4953.3	1109.1	44.8	6107.2	3743.6	1461.8	789.9	111.9	454.1
2012	6131.2	4952.8	1133.8	44.6	6131.2	3902.5	1380.7	739.7	108.3	452.8
2013	6183.4	5007.3	1126.2	49.9	6183.4	3921.5	1406.4	750.1	105.4	453.6
2014	6094.9	4920.5	1116.9	57.5	6094.9	3869.0	1356.1	766.6	103.2	444.3
2015	6103.2	4969.5	1069.2	64.5	6103.2	3852.2	1334.8	793.5	122.7	442.3
2016	6040.2	4912.4	1057.0	70.8	6040.2	3768.0	1308.0	821.6	142.6	435.2
2017	6043.4	4945.5	1016.7	81.2	6043.4	3766.4	1277.0	838.1	161.9	432.8
2018	6015.5	4952.7	976.4	86.4	6015.5	3693.1	1261.6	859.9	200.9	428.8
2019	6021.2	4982.5	934.2	104.5	6021.2	3682.3	1217.6	871.7	249.6	427.7
2020	5812.9	4792.3	892.5	128.1	5812.9	3612.4	1030.4	863.1	307.0	411.9
2021	5920.2	4928.1	853.8	138.3	5920.2	3644.3	1049.6	909.4	316.9	419.2
2022	5998.2	4994.2	828.2	175.8	5998.2	3781.3	968.4	905.7	342.8	424.7
2023	5906.5	4874.7	819.5	212.3	5906.5	3672.4	970.2	909.8	354.1	418.7
北 京 Beijing	40.7	15.5	12.4	12.8	40.7	2.5	2.8	19.0	16.4	186.3
天 津 Tianjin	32.7	23.9	2.6	6.2	32.7	9.4	4.6	7.6	11.2	239.8
河 北 Hebei	186.5	94.0	75.0	17.6	186.5	100.7	16.2	28.0	41.6	251.8
山 西 Shanxi	69.7	36.9	26.6	6.2	69.7	37.8	11.6	15.2	5.1	200.7
内蒙古 Inner Mongolia	202.9	86.8	108.2	7.9	202.9	154.1	14.8	11.2	22.8	845.9
辽 宁 Liaoning	126.1	75.7	43.0	7.5	126.1	74.6	14.7	26.4	10.4	301.0
吉 林 Jilin	105.4	71.1	31.0	3.3	105.4	77.4	8.6	13.1	6.2	449.8
黑龙江 Heilongjiang	288.9	186.4	99.5	3.1	288.9	259.4	11.6	14.7	3.2	937.8
上 海 Shanghai	104.8	103.9		0.9	104.8	13.7	66.0	24.2	1.0	422.4
江 苏 Jiangsu	571.4	553.9	2.5	15.0	571.4	240.0	251.9	66.0	13.4	670.6
浙 江 Zhejiang	169.6	163.7	0.1	5.8	169.6	73.1	36.3	53.6	6.7	256.9
安 徽 Anhui	273.7	243.8	22.2	7.8	273.7	148.2	79.9	36.5	9.1	446.9
福 建 Fujian	168.1	159.8	2.3	6.1	168.1	97.6	23.9	30.1	16.5	401.6
江 西 Jiangxi	240.6	234.7	2.6	3.4	240.6	169.2	37.9	29.5	4.0	532.1
山 东 Shandong	223.4	133.8	71.1	18.6	223.4	128.1	33.5	43.7	18.1	220.3
河 南 Henan	208.8	107.5	87.8	13.5	208.8	118.6	20.7	42.1	27.3	212.1
湖 北 Hubei	336.4	325.3	4.3	6.7	336.4	189.7	70.0	52.5	24.2	575.9
湖 南 Hunan	308.9	297.8	6.0	5.1	308.9	197.2	51.1	45.5	15.1	469.0
广 东 Guangdong	400.4	382.0	5.3	13.1	400.4	197.5	73.6	115.9	13.4	315.7
广 西 Guangxi	258.5	249.1	5.5	3.9	258.5	182.5	35.4	35.3	5.3	513.2
海 南 Hainan	45.6	43.7	1.4	0.5	45.6	32.1	1.7	9.7	2.1	440.6
重 庆 Chongqing	70.8	64.1	0.4	6.3	70.8	25.5	21.4	22.3	1.6	221.1
四 川 Sichuan	252.5	239.8	5.7	7.0	252.5	162.0	20.7	59.8	10.1	301.6
贵 州 Guizhou	93.2	90.8	1.0	1.4	93.2	60.3	11.0	20.8	1.2	241.4
云 南 Yunnan	162.3	155.2	3.0	4.1	162.3	113.9	13.1	26.4	8.8	346.6
西 藏 Xizang	32.2	29.7	2.3	0.2	32.2	27.6	1.2	3.0	0.3	883.4
陕 西 Shaanxi	93.6	59.2	27.3	7.1	93.6	55.0	10.5	20.7	7.4	236.7
甘 肃 Gansu	115.8	76.5	35.5	3.8	115.8	91.4	6.4	10.7	7.3	467.2
青 海 Qinghai	24.9	18.9	5.0	1.0	24.9	16.7	3.2	3.1	1.9	418.8
宁 夏 Ningxia	64.8	57.1	5.2	2.4	64.8	53.0	4.9	3.7	3.3	889.5
新 疆 Xinjiang	633.3	494.5	124.8	14.0	633.3	563.6	11.3	19.4	39.1	2442.8

注：2012年起，生活用水量中的牲畜用水量调整至农业用水量中。

a) Since 2012, water use on animal husbandry is moved to agriculture use from households and service use.

8-11 分地区废水中主要污染物排放情况（2023年）
Main Pollutant Contents Discharged in Wastewater by Region (2023)

地区	Region	废水中主要污染物排放量 Main Pollutant Contents Discharged in Wastewater							
		化学需氧量(吨) COD (ton)	氨氮(吨) Ammonia Nitrogen (ton)	总氮(吨) Total Nitrogen (ton)	总磷(吨) Total Phosphorus (ton)	石油类(吨) Petroleum (ton)	挥发酚(千克) Volatile Phenol (kg)	氰化物(千克) Cyanide (kg)	重金属(千克) Heavy Metals (kg)
全　国	**National Total**	**29543680.0**	**1193435.4**	**3427299.8**	**408438.4**	**1514.9**	**48588**	**22600**	**45535**
北　京	Beijing	118717.7	9726.7	24600.4	1241.5	4.4	67	22	35
天　津	Tianjin	176365.3	6010.1	17036.0	1962.4	5.6	8	41	147
河　北	Hebei	1593109.1	48710.6	138689.0	16677.7	110.9	5748	3819	729
山　西	Shanxi	768093.9	24907.4	66079.7	9047.3	20.7	1813	1008	1180
内蒙古	Inner Mongolia	865427.9	20915.9	71295.9	5517.7	14.1	169	54	154
辽　宁	Liaoning	1423857.8	37285.3	119163.1	16656.3	103.9	8584	782	1687
吉　林	Jilin	900175.4	16980.7	65317.6	7517.8	26.9	535	276	377
黑龙江	Heilongjiang	1070997.2	25219.9	93950.5	9585.3	16.8	1256	133	72
上　海	Shanghai	109687.4	7415.8	26797.2	1266.8	25.0	340	216	298
江　苏	Jiangsu	1276830.0	53997.1	171259.0	19795.3	126.8	3008	1645	1018
浙　江	Zhejiang	542991.7	41594.2	117004.4	12706.1	107.0	1145	706	2316
安　徽	Anhui	1491272.3	66283.6	183233.0	23473.8	141.1	778	848	3277
福　建	Fujian	662372.9	53693.3	130707.0	15822.8	35.0	444	1108	2091
江　西	Jiangxi	1126188.0	54065.3	140176.1	18185.2	89.7	8865	1519	4899
山　东	Shandong	1745572.6	69121.0	177698.3	18077.6	109.4	2241	881	3194
河　南	Henan	1867605.4	60373.1	187161.5	22956.4	51.0	184	313	1391
湖　北	Hubei	1785127.5	79041.3	216580.3	28642.8	45.0	1043	1765	801
湖　南	Hunan	1795685.8	73630.0	210344.3	29211.8	63.5	1993	2941	3609
广　东	Guangdong	1880656.6	116262.8	304607.8	36282.5	125.9	1270	1434	5590
广　西	Guangxi	1035344.1	61932.0	206975.0	25354.2	15.1	303	492	1163
海　南	Hainan	195334.5	10080.7	32502.6	4516.4	1.9	317	191	21
重　庆	Chongqing	439427.6	24654.7	64933.4	6599.2	58.0	4124	442	296
四　川	Sichuan	1610365.6	75139.1	207024.7	22597.8	75.3	348	27	900
贵　州	Guizhou	1271621.2	37525.7	113256.2	16772.6	15.9	417	408	853
云　南	Yunnan	802309.1	39306.8	123058.1	12367.7	35.5	279	328	1886
西　藏	Xizang	356296.2	6358.2	20550.3	2856.7	0.0			19
陕　西	Shaanxi	418121.2	19612.8	48448.5	4837.6	31.8	1227	281	707
甘　肃	Gansu	879172.6	13530.7	46411.6	6610.3	21.9	653	155	920
青　海	Qinghai	313971.0	7400.7	19793.6	1797.6	4.7	187	91	5310
宁　夏	Ningxia	260159.0	5357.8	16186.3	2526.6	3.0	214	506	74
新　疆	Xinjiang	760823.3	27302.2	66458.6	6974.8	29.2	1025	167	520

注：1.本表数据为初步数。
　　2. 2023年，生态环境部调整了生活源中城镇生活水污染物排放量核算方法。与历史数据不可比(下表同)。

a) The data in this table is preliminary.
b) In 2023, the Ministry of Ecology and Environment adjusted the accounting method for urban domestic water pollutant emissions in domestic sources. Not comparable to historical data. The same applies to the following tables.

8-12 主要城市废水中主要污染物排放情况（2023年）
Main Pollutant Contents Discharged in Wastewater by Main City (2023)

城市	City	工业化学需氧量排放量（吨）Industrial COD Discharged (ton)	工业氨氮排放量（吨）Industrial Ammonia Nitrogen Discharged (ton)	生活化学需氧量排放量（吨）Municipal COD Discharged (ton)	生活氨氮排放量（吨）Municipal Ammonia Nitrogen Discharged (ton)
北京	Beijing	1360	26	104815	9524
天津	Tianjin	1714	30	50644	4797
石家庄	Shijiazhuang	2048	54	51591	4005
太原	Taiyuan	260	9	14932	1202
呼和浩特	Hohhot	435	12	17848	1544
沈阳	Shenyang	1311	25	82161	7354
长春	Changchun	568	13	64708	4389
哈尔滨	Harbin	550	36	60662	4011
上海	Shanghai	6583	165	92070	6947
南京	Nanjing	1979	42	20944	1324
杭州	Hangzhou	3660	48	75650	6380
合肥	Hefei	1385	29	92498	8075
福州	Fuzhou	1270	21	71375	6685
南昌	Nanchang	2266	92	47299	4208
济南	Jinan	1180	34	46493	3729
郑州	Zhengzhou	635	17	54015	4218
武汉	Wuhan	2297	96	200109	18632
长沙	Changsha	1996	101	61197	5630
广州	Guangzhou	2212	37	56043	4643
南宁	Nanning	2131	64	69341	6509
海口	Haikou	105	7	27220	2651
重庆	Chongqing	6185	235	221080	20599
成都	Chengdu	1381	30	198182	20718
贵阳	Guiyang	578	108	44747	4467
昆明	Kunming	1154	58	33988	3078
拉萨	Lhasa	17	1	12532	1327
西安	Xi'an	903	34	30529	1549
兰州	Lanzhou	609	16	17928	1466
西宁	Xining	252	12	23917	2289
银川	Yinchuan	902	14	14221	1248
乌鲁木齐	Urumqi	401	7	25385	4940

注：1.本表生活化学需氧量排放量和生活氨氮排放量包括城镇和农村。
2.本表数据为初步数。

a) The discharge of COD and Ammonia Nitrogen includes urban and rural areas.
b) The data in this table is preliminary.

8–13 分地区废气中主要污染物排放情况（2023年）
Main Pollutant Contents Emission in Waste Gas by Region (2023)

单位：万吨 (10 000 tons)

地 区	Region	二氧化硫 Sulphur Dioxide	氮氧化物 Nitrogen Oxides	颗粒物 Particulate Matter
全 国	**National Total**	**237.97**	**1207.29**	**510.96**
北 京	Beijing	0.11	10.15	0.55
天 津	Tianjin	0.63	10.88	0.95
河 北	Hebei	14.25	100.29	25.35
山 西	Shanxi	13.20	49.00	25.86
内蒙古	Inner Mongolia	22.02	52.18	110.51
辽 宁	Liaoning	13.10	58.52	24.90
吉 林	Jilin	5.50	31.67	16.23
黑龙江	Heilongjiang	9.53	42.32	32.36
上 海	Shanghai	0.64	12.87	0.91
江 苏	Jiangsu	7.04	52.50	9.65
浙 江	Zhejiang	3.82	41.09	6.64
安 徽	Anhui	7.29	49.14	12.00
福 建	Fujian	5.69	26.84	8.75
江 西	Jiangxi	6.40	32.32	9.89
山 东	Shandong	13.45	125.68	20.96
河 南	Henan	6.04	82.68	9.05
湖 北	Hubei	7.89	40.99	13.36
湖 南	Hunan	6.53	32.84	14.18
广 东	Guangdong	7.98	62.85	12.75
广 西	Guangxi	7.69	31.94	8.12
海 南	Hainan	0.35	6.19	0.91
重 庆	Chongqing	3.58	19.72	4.46
四 川	Sichuan	10.90	46.90	15.30
贵 州	Guizhou	13.44	22.36	8.66
云 南	Yunnan	18.73	28.01	22.71
西 藏	Xizang	0.31	6.09	0.86
陕 西	Shaanxi	6.13	31.37	20.38
甘 肃	Gansu	7.77	23.38	10.52
青 海	Qinghai	3.92	6.96	4.42
宁 夏	Ningxia	5.31	15.84	5.18
新 疆	Xinjiang	8.73	53.75	54.58

注：1.本表数据为初步数。
2.2023年，生态环境部将移动源调查范围由机动车扩展至非道路移动机械、沥青道路铺装、储油库。氮氧化物和颗粒物排放量与历史数据不可比(下表同)。

a) The data in this table is preliminary.

b) In 2023, the Ministry of Ecology and Environment will expand the scope of mobile source investigation from motor vehicles to non road mobile machinery, asphalt road paving, and oil storage tanks. The emissions of nitrogen oxides and particulate matter are not comparable to historical data. The same applies to the following tables.

8-14 主要城市废气中主要污染物排放情况（2023年）
Main Pollutant Contents Emission in Waste Gas by Main City (2023)

单位：吨 (ton)

城市	City	工业二氧化硫排放量 Industrial Sulphur Dioxide Emission	工业氮氧化物排放量 Industrial Nitrogen Oxides Emission	工业颗粒物排放量 Industrial Particulate Matter Emission	生活及其他二氧化硫排放量 Domestic and Other Sulphur Dioxide Emission	生活及其他氮氧化物排放量 Domestic and Other Nitrogen Oxides Emission	生活及其他颗粒物排放量 Domestic and Other Particulate Matter Emission
北京	Beijing	896	9428	1633	162	8236	1537
天津	Tianjin	6151	21156	6080	123	3280	1499
石家庄	Shijiazhuang	7256	14132	10384	1739	3290	8904
太原	Taiyuan	8671	18193	15967	1	2600	238
呼和浩特	Hohhot	11535	17446	7604	962	1146	4867
沈阳	Shenyang	6413	14926	2514	2680	1641	6783
长春	Changchun	9301	20155	6227	8911	5012	35740
哈尔滨	Harbin	7042	17486	6088	27473	15737	137420
上海	Shanghai	6257	22218	7007	95	4865	814
南京	Nanjing	5747	14588	8680	1	1348	124
杭州	Hangzhou	2057	8254	7037	79	391	259
合肥	Hefei	3773	11576	4943	1339	3655	13577
福州	Fuzhou	12248	27008	15064	720	594	1480
南昌	Nanchang	2773	4906	3638	5218	1713	10487
济南	Jinan	8314	19047	9202	1291	1639	3557
郑州	Zhengzhou	5136	11577	7568	52	1623	242
武汉	Wuhan	5687	15660	6084	9429	4388	19068
长沙	Changsha	739	2023	1777	1408	1188	3592
广州	Guangzhou	2230	11301	4052	559	1759	1741
南宁	Nanning	2651	11909	8555	1107	713	2256
海口	Haikou	93	374	64	0	380	35
重庆	Chongqing	31970	57975	34028	3792	6212	4982
成都	Chengdu	2849	10527	3683	913	7249	2049
贵阳	Guiyang	14003	8827	4395	2502	731	2819
昆明	Kunming	20821	23485	17205	5721	1974	9620
拉萨	Lhasa	387	1473	1472	0	66	6
西安	Xi'an	1673	4532	634	1414	5351	4485
兰州	Lanzhou	17660	15310	6614	305	1210	1318
西宁	Xining	26467	10261	7029	231	1165	2386
银川	Yinchuan	7673	12267	2974	268	1222	1435
乌鲁木齐	Urumqi	4175	10184	4385	32	1756	366

注：本表数据为初步数。
a) The data in this table is preliminary.

8-15 分地区固体废物处理利用情况（2023年）
Disposal and Reuse of Industrial Solid Wastes by Region (2023)

单位：万吨 (10 000 tons)

地 区	Region	一般工业固体废物产生量 Common Industrial Solid Wastes Generated	一般工业固体废物综合利用量 Integrated Reuse of Common Industrial Solid Wastes	一般工业固体废物处置量 Common Industrial Solid Wastes Disposed	一般工业固体废物贮存量 Stock of Common Industrial Solid Wastes	一般工业固体废物倾倒丢弃量 Common Industrial Solid Wastes Discharged	危险废物产生量 Hazardous Wastes Generated	危险废物利用处置量 Integrated Reuse and Disposal of Hazardous Wastes	危险废物本年末贮存量 Year-end Stock of Hazardous Wastes
全 国	**National Total**	**427001**	**258123**	**83252**	**93131**	**0.00**	**10546.50**	**10502.93**	**8849.82**
北 京	Beijing	182	174	9	0		27.34	27.38	0.10
天 津	Tianjin	2069	2064	5	1		91.93	91.87	0.41
河 北	Hebei	39496	21744	5926	12403		665.12	665.90	9.50
山 西	Shanxi	49357	20716	23488	5348		417.08	420.86	3.35
内蒙古	Inner Mongolia	43644	20345	13638	10618		693.16	693.93	20.27
辽 宁	Liaoning	23313	13137	4386	6055		229.74	207.23	65.32
吉 林	Jilin	5763	2759	1484	1556		264.90	319.96	733.04
黑龙江	Heilongjiang	10594	3968	795	6316		121.04	127.12	2.48
上 海	Shanghai	2180	2070	110	2		136.24	136.45	0.92
江 苏	Jiangsu	14141	13288	901	77		722.74	722.59	8.37
浙 江	Zhejiang	5848	5829	22	7		606.50	608.17	11.43
安 徽	Anhui	16435	15647	630	484		267.30	265.67	16.03
福 建	Fujian	7312	6444	696	221		202.29	204.17	4.94
江 西	Jiangxi	12960	6896	513	5751		248.57	250.10	18.49
山 东	Shandong	26989	21943	1568	3684		1202.46	1218.45	66.18
河 南	Henan	18281	15042	1516	1919		425.02	417.51	47.48
湖 北	Hubei	10431	8310	762	1823		232.30	237.29	9.18
湖 南	Hunan	4894	3769	486	743		281.52	273.41	28.77
广 东	Guangdong	8737	7589	891	325		614.01	620.88	20.81
广 西	Guangxi	11712	6303	1420	4225		450.68	451.40	40.25
海 南	Hainan	749	549	201	2		31.04	30.69	0.98
重 庆	Chongqing	3100	2388	686	67		128.46	126.38	10.60
四 川	Sichuan	15229	7449	3807	4240		603.39	607.96	34.45
贵 州	Guizhou	12820	8535	2048	2508		95.22	97.07	2.69
云 南	Yunnan	18248	9666	4857	4460		312.56	317.82	23.02
西 藏	Xizang	5187	66	27	5096		0.19	0.20	0.01
陕 西	Shaanxi	14193	7497	5339	1530	0.00	217.54	256.74	281.70
甘 肃	Gansu	7178	3174	1500	3201		203.98	232.89	312.31
青 海	Qinghai	16070	9887	202	6498		375.02	194.58	6991.07
宁 夏	Ningxia	8187	5059	2906	329		138.98	139.54	7.49
新 疆	Xinjiang	11701	5816	2434	3642		540.17	538.73	78.16

注：本表数据为初步数。
a) The data in this table is preliminary.

8-16 主要城市固体废物处理利用情况(2023年)
Disposal and Reuse of Industrial Solid Wastes by Main City (2023)

单位：万吨 (10 000 tons)

城市	City	一般工业固体废物产生量 Common Industrial Solid Wastes Generated	一般工业固体废物综合利用量 Integrated Reuse of Common Industrial Solid Wastes	一般工业固体废物处置量 Common Industrial Solid Wastes Disposed	一般工业固体废物贮存量 Stock of Common Industrial Solid Wastes
北京	Beijing	182	174	9	0
天津	Tianjin	2069	2064	5	1
石家庄	Shijiazhuang	1413	1333	84	2
太原	Taiyuan	3964	1838	2039	88
呼和浩特	Hohhot	1583	923	621	61
沈阳	Shenyang	891	845	119	3
长春	Changchun	654	535	120	0
哈尔滨	Harbin	722	637	63	32
上海	Shanghai	2180	2070	110	2
南京	Nanjing	1791	1686	75	30
杭州	Hangzhou	583	576	7	2
合肥	Hefei	1538	1297	88	154
福州	Fuzhou	1406	1389	4	16
南昌	Nanchang	450	437	13	1
济南	Jinan	2361	2355	34	3
郑州	Zhengzhou	1571	1332	252	2
武汉	Wuhan	1375	1357	21	8
长沙	Changsha	167	131	28	9
广州	Guangzhou	781	762	19	2
南宁	Nanning	208	190	14	4
海口	Haikou	13	8	5	0
重庆	Chongqing	3100	2388	686	67
成都	Chengdu	420	407	14	2
贵阳	Guiyang	2268	1516	788	18
昆明	Kunming	3332	2507	690	674
拉萨	Lhasa	3512	30	24	3458
西安	Xi'an	364	266	98	0
兰州	Lanzhou	545	538	7	0
西宁	Xining	462	477	6	9
银川	Yinchuan	1785	1376	467	7
乌鲁木齐	Urumqi	1028	831	199	0

注：本表数据为初步数。
a) The data in this table is preliminary.

8-17 主要城市空气质量情况（2023年）
Ambient Air Quality by Main City (2023)

城市	City	二氧化硫年平均浓度(μg/m³) Annual Average Concentration of SO_2 (μg/m³)	二氧化氮年平均浓度(μg/m³) Annual Average Concentration of NO_2 (μg/m³)	可吸入颗粒物(PM_{10})年平均浓度(μg/m³) Annual Average Concentration of PM_{10} (μg/m³)	一氧化碳日均值第95百分位浓度(mg/m³) 95th Percentile Daily Average Concentration of CO (mg/m³)	臭氧(O_3)日最大8小时第90百分位浓度(μg/m³) 90th Percentile Daily Maximum 8 Hours Average Concentration of O_3(μg/m³)	细颗粒物($PM_{2.5}$)年平均浓度(μg/m³) Annual Average Concentration of $PM_{2.5}$ (μg/m³)	空气质量达到或好于二级的天数(天) Days of Air Quality Reaching or Better than Level 2 (day)
北京	Beijing	3	26	61	0.9	175	32	271
天津	Tianjin	8	35	74	1.2	190	41	232
石家庄	Shijiazhuang	7	32	78	1.4	184	44	225
太原	Taiyuan	11	40	78	1.5	178	41	235
呼和浩特	Hohhot	11	33	62	1.1	148	29	292
沈阳	Shenyang	14	32	59	1.4	155	33	302
长春	Changchun	9	29	53	0.9	132	32	314
哈尔滨	Harbin	11	29	59	1.0	121	36	304
上海	Shanghai	7	31	48	1.0	158	28	320
南京	Nanjing	6	27	52	0.9	170	29	299
杭州	Hangzhou	6	30	51	0.9	165	31	308
合肥	Hefei	7	31	62	0.9	150	34	314
福州	Fuzhou	4	16	35	0.7	130	19	358
南昌	Nanchang	8	26	57	1.0	142	33	337
济南	Jinan	9	33	73	1.1	193	38	214
郑州	Zhengzhou	7	29	73	1.1	182	43	226
武汉	Wuhan	8	35	58	1.3	161	38	289
长沙	Changsha	6	26	76	1.2	163	55	292
广州	Guangzhou	6	29	41	0.9	159	23	330
南宁	Nanning	8	21	42	1.0	126	25	361
海口	Haikou	6	11	29	0.7	127	16	356
重庆	Chongqing	9	29	54	1.0	142	37	325
成都	Chengdu	3	28	60	1.0	168	39	285
贵阳	Guiyang	7	17	38	0.8	116	24	363
昆明	Kunming	8	19	36	0.9	138	23	356
拉萨	Lhasa	8	16	21	0.8	148	10	355
西安	Xi'an	7	37	81	1.4	172	48	228
兰州	Lanzhou	13	41	71	1.8	156	37	282
西宁	Xining	17	32	53	1.6	133	30	346
银川	Yinchuan	14	33	71	1.4	162	32	281
乌鲁木齐	Urumqi	6	34	74	1.6	138	38	299

8-18 分地区城市生活垃圾清运和处理情况（2023年）
Collection, Transportation and Treatment of Municipal Domestic Garbage by Region (2023)

地 区	Region	生活垃圾清运量（万吨）Volume of Domestic Garbage Collected and Transported (10 000 tons)	无害化处理厂数（座）Number of Plants for Harmless Treatment of Domestic Garbage (number)	卫生填埋 Sanitary Landfill	焚 烧 Incinerate	其 他 Others	无害化处理能力（吨/日）Harmless Treatment Capacity (ton/day)	卫生填埋 Sanitary Landfill	焚 烧 Incinerate	其 他 Others
全 国	**National Total**	**25407.8**	**1423**	**366**	**696**	**361**	**1144391**	**173880**	**861777**	**108734**
北 京	Beijing	758.9	33	4	12	17	28426	1691	19090	7645
天 津	Tianjin	301.9	22		13	9	20200		18200	2000
河 北	Hebei	784.4	40		34	6	36083		34481	1602
山 西	Shanxi	518.5	29	11	16	2	22507	3807	18100	600
内蒙古	Inner Mongolia	356.0	32	23	8	1	15454	7654	7700	100
辽 宁	Liaoning	1033.5	47	18	22	7	38656	11166	25670	1820
吉 林	Jilin	452.6	44	22	19	3	26070	8940	16450	680
黑龙江	Heilongjiang	523.8	45	24	17	4	25301	7073	17228	1000
上 海	Shanghai	974.8	27	1	13	13	42536	5000	23000	14536
江 苏	Jiangsu	2081.7	84	10	46	28	87472	6285	68811	12376
浙 江	Zhejiang	1467.8	82	1	50	31	81452	144	72550	8758
安 徽	Anhui	771.9	55	3	30	22	35993	1270	30720	4003
福 建	Fujian	878.9	38	4	23	11	32895	2250	27435	3210
江 西	Jiangxi	553.3	30		20	10	23791		22450	1341
山 东	Shandong	1804.5	108	21	63	24	79348	10228	63520	5600
河 南	Henan	1121.2	48	10	34	4	49867	4002	44760	1105
湖 北	Hubei	1085.8	69	19	35	15	47636	8044	35956	3636
湖 南	Hunan	904.2	50	25	17	8	40448	15532	21625	3291
广 东	Guangdong	3389.5	181	27	79	75	180294	30628	132382	17283
广 西	Guangxi	615.3	43	18	18	7	31919	8219	21150	2550
海 南	Hainan	317.4	10		8	2	12250		11150	1100
重 庆	Chongqing	643.3	36	13	16	7	29062	5282	19600	4180
四 川	Sichuan	1322.3	52	14	27	11	49754	10300	37534	1920
贵 州	Guizhou	461.9	42	5	22	15	20864	1325	17500	2039
云 南	Yunnan	544.9	36	15	17	4	21273	4537	15011	1725
西 藏	Xizang	70.9	8	7	1		2422	1778	644	
陕 西	Shaanxi	715.9	41	15	11	15	23529	4623	15950	2956
甘 肃	Gansu	282.9	33	17	10	6	12552	3902	7650	1000
青 海	Qinghai	115.0	8	7	1		4515	1515	3000	
宁 夏	Ningxia	122.8	11	4	5	2	5783	1423	3760	600
新 疆	Xinjiang	432.2	39	28	9	2	16040	7262	8700	78

8-18 续表 continued

地 区	Region	无害化处理量(万吨) Volume of Domestic Garbage Harmlessly Treated (10 000 tons)	卫生填埋 Sanitary Landfill	焚 烧 Incinerate	其 他 Others	生活垃圾无害化处理率(%) Rate of Domestic Garbage Harmless Treatment (%)
全 国	**National Total**	**25401.7**	**1892.6**	**20954.4**	**2554.7**	**100.0**
北 京	Beijing	758.8	30.8	545.1	183.0	100.0
天 津	Tianjin	301.9		266.0	36.0	100.0
河 北	Hebei	784.4		730.8	53.5	100.0
山 西	Shanxi	518.5	45.6	458.7	14.2	100.0
内蒙古	Inner Mongolia	356.0	152.5	198.9	4.6	100.0
辽 宁	Liaoning	1029.3	184.1	783.6	61.6	99.6
吉 林	Jilin	452.6	57.5	384.7	10.3	100.0
黑龙江	Heilongjiang	523.8	147.2	360.5	16.1	100.0
上 海	Shanghai	974.8		586.9	388.0	100.0
江 苏	Jiangsu	2081.7	1.7	1783.3	296.7	100.0
浙 江	Zhejiang	1467.8		1246.0	221.8	100.0
安 徽	Anhui	771.9		689.5	82.4	100.0
福 建	Fujian	878.9	12.4	786.2	80.4	100.0
江 西	Jiangxi	553.3		520.8	32.5	100.0
山 东	Shandong	1804.5	6.5	1666.2	131.8	100.0
河 南	Henan	1121.1	58.7	1054.3	8.1	100.0
湖 北	Hubei	1085.8	78.1	921.2	86.6	100.0
湖 南	Hunan	904.0	150.5	698.6	55.0	100.0
广 东	Guangdong	3388.8	210.9	2770.8	407.1	100.0
广 西	Guangxi	615.3	51.7	522.0	41.6	100.0
海 南	Hainan	317.4		299.1	18.3	100.0
重 庆	Chongqing	643.3	18.2	503.9	121.2	100.0
四 川	Sichuan	1321.7	93.9	1173.1	54.7	100.0
贵 州	Guizhou	461.9	11.3	414.5	36.1	100.0
云 南	Yunnan	544.9	85.5	444.4	15.0	100.0
西 藏	Xizang	70.8	47.3	23.5		99.9
陕 西	Shaanxi	715.9	142.1	518.8	55.0	100.0
甘 肃	Gansu	282.9	70.8	188.9	23.2	100.0
青 海	Qinghai	114.8	28.8	85.9		99.8
宁 夏	Ningxia	122.8	9.8	101.6	11.4	100.0
新 疆	Xinjiang	432.1	196.7	226.9	8.5	100.0

8-19 主要城市噪声监测情况（2023年）
Monitoring of Noise by Main City (2023)

城　市	City	道路交通噪声 等效声级 dB(A) Road Traffic Noise Average Noise Level dB(A)	区域环境噪声 等效声级 dB(A) Urban Environment Noise Average Noise Level dB(A)
北　京	Beijing	68.5	53.5
天　津	Tianjin	65.6	53.0
石家庄	Shijiazhuang	65.3	54.8
太　原	Taiyuan	68.0	49.0
呼和浩特	Hohhot	67.8	53.5
沈　阳	Shenyang	69.4	54.4
长　春	Changchun	69.6	57.1
哈尔滨	Harbin	67.1	53.0
上　海	Shanghai	68.5	54.5
南　京	Nanjing	67.4	53.6
杭　州	Hangzhou	66.0	55.5
合　肥	Hefei	69.6	57.2
福　州	Fuzhou	69.9	56.3
南　昌	Nanchang	65.1	55.9
济　南	Jinan	67.2	55.5
郑　州	Zhengzhou	66.7	54.3
武　汉	Wuhan	69.7	57.1
长　沙	Changsha	68.3	53.1
广　州	Guangzhou	69.4	56.0
南　宁	Nanning	67.9	54.9
海　口	Haikou	67.8	58.6
重　庆	Chongqing	67.4	52.8
成　都	Chengdu	67.6	56.0
贵　阳	Guiyang	69.7	54.6
昆　明	Kunming	64.0	52.2
拉　萨	Lhasa	62.1	53.1
西　安	Xi'an	65.8	55.3
兰　州	Lanzhou	66.9	54.3
西　宁	Xining	66.8	50.4
银　川	Yinchuan	64.8	51.9
乌鲁木齐	Urumqi	66.4	53.9

8-20 分地区耕地面积
Area of Cultivated Land by Region

单位：千公顷 (1 000 hectares)

地 区	Region	2015	2016	2017	2019	2020	2021	2022	2023
全 国	**National Total**	**134998.7**	**134920.9**	**134881.2**	**127861.9**	**127436.7**	**127516.8**	**127579.9**	**128608.8**
北 京	Beijing	219.3	216.3	213.7	93.5	93.6	120.0	124.8	130.7
天 津	Tianjin	436.9	436.9	436.8	329.6	328.5	330.3	332.4	336.7
河 北	Hebei	6525.5	6520.5	6518.9	6034.2	6011.4	5968.7	6011.2	6088.4
山 西	Shanxi	4058.8	4056.8	4056.3	3869.5	3861.7	3863.2	3870.5	3893.5
内蒙古	Inner Mongolia	9238.0	9257.9	9270.8	11496.5	11497.7	11559.6	11561.1	11617.4
辽 宁	Liaoning	4977.4	4974.5	4971.6	5182.1	5159.4	5153.6	5156.7	5162.2
吉 林	Jilin	6999.2	6993.4	6986.7	7498.5	7466.8	7449.8	7444.3	7452.6
黑龙江	Heilongjiang	15854.1	15850.1	15845.7	17195.4	17180.2	17165.8	17131.3	17167.7
上 海	Shanghai	189.8	190.7	191.6	162.0	160.6	159.7	161.6	160.9
江 苏	Jiangsu	4574.9	4571.1	4573.3	4089.7	4075.9	4085.8	4091.2	4139.6
浙 江	Zhejiang	1978.6	1974.7	1977.0	1290.5	1281.0	1294.9	1304.8	1320.8
安 徽	Anhui	5872.9	5867.5	5866.8	5546.9	5520.3	5541.8	5550.9	5563.5
福 建	Fujian	1336.3	1336.3	1336.9	932.0	926.6	920.3	920.9	926.3
江 西	Jiangxi	3082.7	3082.2	3086.0	2721.6	2711.8	2711.2	2712.8	2718.3
山 东	Shandong	7611.0	7606.9	7589.8	6461.9	6409.6	6414.9	6456.4	6539.3
河 南	Henan	8105.9	8111.0	8112.3	7514.1	7488.1	7519.4	7534.9	7579.6
湖 北	Hubei	5255.0	5245.3	5235.9	4768.6	4754.1	4741.4	4698.0	4752.0
湖 南	Hunan	4150.2	4148.7	4151.0	3629.2	3621.2	3626.1	3654.2	3666.6
广 东	Guangdong	2615.9	2607.6	2599.7	1901.9	1898.7	1899.7	1906.3	1914.7
广 西	Guangxi	4402.3	4395.1	4387.5	3307.6	3285.9	3260.2	3279.7	3286.7
海 南	Hainan	725.9	722.7	722.4	486.9	486.9	487.5	484.3	494.8
重 庆	Chongqing	2430.5	2382.5	2369.8	1870.2	1866.3	1853.8	1850.3	1869.6
四 川	Sichuan	6731.4	6732.9	6725.2	5227.2	5181.8	5195.3	5209.9	5252.6
贵 州	Guizhou	4537.4	4530.2	4518.8	3472.6	3415.0	3393.3	3366.1	3415.2
云 南	Yunnan	6208.5	6207.8	6213.3	5395.5	5377.9	5383.5	5286.7	5484.5
西 藏	Xizang	443.0	444.6	444.0	442.1	441.0	448.7	441.2	445.3
陕 西	Shaanxi	3995.2	3989.5	3982.9	2934.3	2930.7	2962.6	2989.3	3040.6
甘 肃	Gansu	5374.9	5372.4	5377.0	5209.5	5199.5	5205.6	5195.2	5220.3
青 海	Qinghai	588.4	589.4	590.1	564.2	565.0	565.6	564.4	570.0
宁 夏	Ningxia	1290.1	1288.8	1289.9	1195.4	1198.4	1198.5	1200.9	1207.3
新 疆	Xinjiang	5188.9	5216.5	5239.6	7038.6	7041.2	7035.9	7087.8	7191.3

8-21 分地区土地利用情况（2023年）
Land Use by Region (2023)

单位：千公顷 (1 000 hectares)

地 区	Region	耕 地 Cultivated Land	园 地 Garden Land	林 地 Forest Land	草 地 Grassland	湿 地 Wetland	城镇村及工矿用地 Land for Urban, Rural, Industrial and Mining Activities	交通运输用 地 Land Used for Transport	水域及水利设施用地 Land Used for Water and Water Conservancy Facilities
全 国	**National Total**	**128608.8**	**19610.9**	**283695.7**	**263215.7**	**23519.8**	**36103.7**	**10429.1**	**36264.8**
北 京	Beijing	130.7	105.3	963.2	16.1	3.0	295.8	52.2	63.7
天 津	Tianjin	336.7	34.6	145.5	14.2	32.9	332.9	47.4	234.6
河 北	Hebei	6088.4	955.3	6333.9	1916.6	135.9	2163.8	434.6	590.8
山 西	Shanxi	3893.5	622.9	6099.0	3046.6	49.1	1029.6	297.3	177.9
内蒙古	Inner Mongolia	11617.4	49.2	24355.6	53939.6	3793.0	1556.8	829.8	1097.2
辽 宁	Liaoning	5162.2	525.9	5985.5	475.1	294.0	1347.3	317.0	701.2
吉 林	Jilin	7452.6	88.8	8804.8	619.7	221.4	864.3	277.2	631.6
黑龙江	Heilongjiang	17167.7	74.2	21611.3	1169.5	3474.7	1177.2	558.3	1721.5
上 海	Shanghai	160.9	14.1	88.5	17.8	70.7	285.3	37.0	185.3
江 苏	Jiangsu	4139.6	216.0	792.6	105.4	407.6	2059.9	392.1	2464.8
浙 江	Zhejiang	1320.8	681.8	6079.0	79.8	156.8	1179.4	282.2	685.1
安 徽	Anhui	5563.5	369.3	4047.2	66.1	40.3	1755.5	333.7	1709.1
福 建	Fujian	926.3	922.0	8769.6	76.7	186.3	730.3	235.2	372.3
江 西	Jiangxi	2718.3	586.2	10334.3	102.5	225.5	1133.7	372.0	1089.9
山 东	Shandong	6539.3	1199.4	2443.7	243.7	245.5	2863.1	489.1	1346.1
河 南	Henan	7579.6	385.5	4299.9	250.5	33.5	2470.7	415.0	868.5
湖 北	Hubei	4752.0	474.4	9292.5	98.2	47.0	1428.3	364.4	1949.1
湖 南	Hunan	3666.6	906.2	12612.5	141.5	230.9	1645.2	398.5	1250.2
广 东	Guangdong	1914.7	1282.9	10698.5	244.0	176.3	1849.6	374.3	1322.7
广 西	Guangxi	3286.7	1625.3	16025.4	287.0	125.6	1034.6	416.0	750.7
海 南	Hainan	494.8	1220.6	1142.3	18.3	121.5	253.2	65.2	184.0
重 庆	Chongqing	1869.6	280.2	4671.0	27.5	14.5	640.0	184.6	273.3
四 川	Sichuan	5252.6	1185.4	25387.1	9607.1	1228.4	1872.1	567.0	1080.5
贵 州	Guizhou	3415.2	563.3	11213.6	195.2	7.0	788.1	373.7	264.9
云 南	Yunnan	5484.5	2517.1	24797.6	1311.8	35.0	1116.0	573.8	631.3
西 藏	Xizang	445.3	14.0	17885.0	80038.7	4297.9	176.3	177.7	5941.3
陕 西	Shaanxi	3040.6	1105.4	12436.5	2188.8	45.9	941.7	321.6	283.1
甘 肃	Gansu	5220.3	413.4	8218.9	14039.3	1182.1	887.1	358.3	413.7
青 海	Qinghai	570.0	59.2	4604.0	39432.9	5100.0	384.2	154.3	2455.3
宁 夏	Ningxia	1207.3	89.2	981.3	1980.6	25.4	303.7	101.2	170.7
新 疆	Xinjiang	7191.3	1044.1	12576.0	51465.0	1511.9	1538.0	628.4	5354.3

8-22 分地区森林资源情况
Forest Resources by Region

地 区	Region	林业用地面积 (万公顷) Area of Afforested Land (10 000 hectares)	森林面积 (万公顷) Forest Area (10 000 hectares)	#人工林 Planted Forest	森林覆盖率 (%) Forest Coverage Rate (%)	活立木总蓄积量 (万立方米) Total Stock Volume of Living Trees (10 000 cu.m)	森林蓄积量 (万立方米) Stock Volume of Forest (10 000 cu.m)
全 国	**National Total**	**32368.55**	**22044.62**	**8003.10**	**22.96**	**1900713.20**	**1756022.99**
北 京	Beijing	107.10	71.82	43.48	43.77	3000.81	2437.36
天 津	Tianjin	20.39	13.64	12.98	12.07	620.56	460.27
河 北	Hebei	775.64	502.69	263.54	26.78	15920.34	13737.98
山 西	Shanxi	787.25	321.09	167.63	20.50	14778.65	12923.37
内蒙古	Inner Mongolia	4499.17	2614.85	600.01	22.10	166271.98	152704.12
辽 宁	Liaoning	735.92	571.83	315.32	39.24	30888.53	29749.18
吉 林	Jilin	904.79	784.87	175.94	41.49	105368.45	101295.77
黑龙江	Heilongjiang	2453.77	1990.46	243.26	43.78	199999.41	184704.09
上 海	Shanghai	10.19	8.90	8.90	14.04	664.32	449.59
江 苏	Jiangsu	174.98	155.99	150.83	15.20	9609.62	7044.48
浙 江	Zhejiang	659.77	604.99	244.65	59.43	31384.86	28114.67
安 徽	Anhui	449.33	395.85	232.91	28.65	26145.10	22186.55
福 建	Fujian	924.40	811.58	385.59	66.80	79711.29	72937.63
江 西	Jiangxi	1079.90	1021.02	368.70	61.16	57564.29	50665.83
山 东	Shandong	349.34	266.51	256.11	17.51	13040.49	9161.49
河 南	Henan	520.74	403.18	245.78	24.14	26564.48	20719.12
湖 北	Hubei	876.09	736.27	197.42	39.61	39579.82	36507.91
湖 南	Hunan	1257.59	1052.58	501.51	49.69	46141.03	40715.73
广 东	Guangdong	1080.29	945.98	615.51	53.52	50063.49	46755.09
广 西	Guangxi	1629.50	1429.65	733.53	60.17	74433.24	67752.45
海 南	Hainan	217.50	194.49	140.40	57.36	16347.14	15340.15
重 庆	Chongqing	421.71	354.97	95.93	43.11	24412.17	20678.18
四 川	Sichuan	2454.52	1839.77	502.22	38.03	197201.77	186099.00
贵 州	Guizhou	927.96	771.03	315.45	43.77	44464.57	39182.90
云 南	Yunnan	2599.44	2106.16	507.68	55.04	213244.99	197265.84
西 藏	Xizang	1798.19	1490.99	7.84	12.14	230519.15	228254.42
陕 西	Shaanxi	1236.79	886.84	310.53	43.06	51023.42	47866.70
甘 肃	Gansu	1046.35	509.73	126.56	11.33	28386.88	25188.89
青 海	Qinghai	819.16	419.75	19.10	5.82	5556.86	4864.15
宁 夏	Ningxia	179.52	65.60	43.55	12.63	1111.14	835.18
新 疆	Xinjiang	1371.26	802.23	121.42	4.87	46490.95	39221.50

注：1.本表为第九次全国森林资源清查（2014—2018）资料。
2.除林业用地面积外，其他指标全国总计数包括台湾省和香港、澳门特别行政区数据。

a) Data in the table are results of the Ninth National Forestry Survey (2014-2018).
b) Data of national total include forest resources in Taiwan province and Hong Kong SAR and Macao SAR except Area of Afforested Land.

8-23 造林面积
Area of Afforestation

单位：公顷 (hectare)

年份 Year 地区 Region	造林总面积 Total Area of Afforestation	按造林方式分 By Afforestation Approach				
		人工造林 Manual Planting	飞播造林 Airplane Planting	封山育林 Closed Hillsides for Afforestation	退化林修复 Restoration of Degraded Forest	人工更新 Artificial Regeneration
2000	5105138	4345008	760130			
2005	5403791	3231556	416386	1755849		
2006	3838794	2446122	271803	1120869		
2007	3907711	2738521	118671	1050519		
2008	5354387	3684913	154065	1515409		
2009	6262330	4156293	226337	1879700		
2010	5909919	3872762	195948	1841209		
2011	5996613	4065693	196931	1733989		
2012	5595791	3820704	136409	1638678		
2013	6100057	4209686	154400	1735971		
2014	5549612	4052912	108055	1388645		
2015	7683695	4362589	128390	2152877	739334	300505
2016	7203509	3823656	162322	1953638	991088	272805
2017	7680711	4295890	141220	1657169	1280993	305439
2018	7299473	3677952	135429	1785067	1329166	371859
2019	7390294	3458315	125565	1898314	1537877	370223
2020	6933696	3000060	151496	1774608	1619648	387884
2021	3754373	1085095	172239	1235098	1011349	250593
2022	4202790	930860	166099	1057316	1582935	465579
2023	4636119	1014361	66997	1133101	1795750	625911
北京 Beijing	847	389			459	
天津 Tianjin	5149	66		4760	12	312
河北 Hebei	173678	58828	3333	70392	39578	1546
山西 Shanxi	306235	204068	10000	53613	38553	
内蒙古 Inner Mongolia	314383	127237	10667	21379	152431	2668
辽宁 Liaoning	63901	30766		2001	26321	4813
吉林 Jilin	88263	415		576	72429	14842
黑龙江 Heilongjiang	82981	2765		32103	41915	6198
上海 Shanghai	200	200				
江苏 Jiangsu	2266	1009		67	482	708
浙江 Zhejiang	20074	3135			10683	6256
安徽 Anhui	137922	6541		70396	47728	13257
福建 Fujian	152503	3251		31988	70599	46664
江西 Jiangxi	252818	18089		36805	124555	73369
山东 Shandong	17647	6493			8788	2367
河南 Henan	122113	20916	16361	30352	34480	20005
湖北 Hubei	193950	30596		37358	111265	14732
湖南 Hunan	425039	104337		125411	172653	22637
广东 Guangdong	153001	11021		34287	58201	49492
广西 Guangxi	324309	20634		5106	42064	256506
海南 Hainan	12837	812				12026
重庆 Chongqing	137423	23182		40111	70231	3899
四川 Sichuan	123086	20943		21222	66159	14762
贵州 Guizhou	230473	7250		32191	182809	8223
云南 Yunnan	287370	42185		90488	117575	37122
西藏 Xizang	44942	4176	3660	33981	2839	285
陕西 Shaanxi	352245	62026	22249	154011	108145	5814
甘肃 Gansu	269597	130044	727	64448	74361	17
青海 Qinghai	104677	16301		68207	20169	
宁夏 Ningxia	84271	23999		5339	54933	
新疆 Xinjiang	136538	32688		66509	29946	7394
大兴安岭 Daxinganling	15385				15385	

注：自2015年起造林面积包括人工造林、飞播造林、新封山育林、退化林修复和人工更新。自2019年起新封山育林指标名称改为封山育林。

a) Since 2015, total area of afforestation includes that of manual planting, airplane planting, new closed hillsides for afforestation, restoration of degraded forest, artificial regeneration. Since 2019, New Closed Hillsides for Afforestation is renamed as Closed Hillsides for Afforestation.

8-24 分地区草原建设利用情况(2023年)
Grassland Protection and Use by Region (2023)

单位：千公顷 (1 000 hectares)

地 区	Region	种草改良面积 Grass Planting Improvement Area	草原鼠害 Rat Plague in Grassland		草原虫害 Insect Plague in Grassland		草原火灾受害草原面积(公顷) Grassland Area Affected by Fire (hectare)
			发生面积 Area of Occurrence	防治面积 Area of Prevention and Control	发生面积 Area of Occurrence	防治面积 Area of Prevention and Control	
全 国	**National Total**	**4378.4**	**28471.5**	**5375.2**	**6519.2**	**3430.3**	**143.4**
北 京	Beijing						
天 津	Tianjin						
河 北	Hebei	49.2	115.9	114.1	174.8	167.4	
山 西	Shanxi	76.7	253.5	70.0	302.1	160.0	
内蒙古	Inner Mongolia	586.2	3188.1	1987.4	2299.9	1444.6	143.1
辽 宁	Liaoning	21.9	51.9	23.0	74.0	46.9	
吉 林	Jilin	19.9	27.3	23.7	30.7	30.0	
黑龙江	Heilongjiang	18.4	2.2	2.0	45.6	44.7	
上 海	Shanghai						
江 苏	Jiangsu						
浙 江	Zhejiang						
安 徽	Anhui						
福 建	Fujian						
江 西	Jiangxi						
山 东	Shandong						
河 南	Henan	2.0					
湖 北	Hubei						
湖 南	Hunan	13.8					
广 东	Guangdong						
广 西	Guangxi	0.9					
海 南	Hainan						
重 庆	Chongqing						
四 川	Sichuan	254.2	1548.0	355.3	564.2	130.7	
贵 州	Guizhou	7.9					
云 南	Yunnan	36.7	26.0	24.0	35.2	35.2	
西 藏	Xizang	409.5	16052.1	342.2	572.0	205.9	
陕 西	Shaanxi	22.6	81.4	76.0	41.8	37.1	
甘 肃	Gansu	627.6	2413.3	513.3	655.3	220.0	0.1
青 海	Qinghai	1876.7	4064.8	1640.7	434.0	284.6	
宁 夏	Ningxia	21.4	100.3	37.2	85.3	34.2	
新 疆	Xinjiang	333.0	546.8	166.4	1204.2	589.1	0.1

8-25 分地区自然保护基本情况（2023年）
Basic Conditions of Natural Protection by Region (2023)

地 区	Region	国家级自然保护区个数（个） Number of National Nature Reserves (number)	国家级自然保护区面积（万公顷） Area of National Nature Reserves (10 000 hectares)
全 国	**National Total**	**449**	**9821.3**
北 京	Beijing	2	2.9
天 津	Tianjin	3	3.1
河 北	Hebei	14	27.1
山 西	Shanxi	8	14.1
内蒙古	Inner Mongolia	29	434.9
辽 宁	Liaoning	19	90.5
吉 林	Jilin	22	122.8
黑龙江	Heilongjiang	39	389.4
上 海	Shanghai	2	6.5
江 苏	Jiangsu	3	30.2
浙 江	Zhejiang	11	14.8
安 徽	Anhui	8	14.4
福 建	Fujian	16	22.7
江 西	Jiangxi	15	26.1
山 东	Shandong	7	22.1
河 南	Henan	13	44.2
湖 北	Hubei	22	54.6
湖 南	Hunan	23	60.6
广 东	Guangdong	15	33.9
广 西	Guangxi	23	37.2
海 南	Hainan	5	16.3
重 庆	Chongqing	7	25.5
四 川	Sichuan	22	304.9
贵 州	Guizhou	11	29.0
云 南	Yunnan	21	152.2
西 藏	Xizang	11	3712.3
陕 西	Shaanxi	25	62.8
甘 肃	Gansu	19	671.7
青 海	Qinghai	5	2116.2
宁 夏	Ningxia	9	46.6
新 疆	Xinjiang	15	1232.0
大兴安岭	Daxinganling	8	

注：国家级自然保护区面积为2021年数据。
a)The area of national nature reserves is the data of 2021.

8-26 分地区自然灾害损失情况(2023年)
Losses Caused by Natural Disasters by Region (2023)

地区	Region	农作物受灾面积(千公顷) Total Areas Affected of Farm Crops (1 000 hectares)	旱灾 Drought	洪涝和地质灾害 Flood and Geological Disasters	台风灾害 Typhoon Disasters	风雹灾害 Wind and Hail Disasters	低温冷冻和雪灾 Low-temperature, Freezing and Snow Disasters
全国	**National Total**	**10539.3**	**3803.7**	**4634.6**	**347.6**	**1174.5**	**519.2**
北京	Beijing	15.1		14.5		0.6	
天津	Tianjin	26.3		26.2			0.0
河北	Hebei	643.8	225.1	375.9		35.3	7.5
山西	Shanxi	440.4	175.4	67.0		75.1	122.8
内蒙古	Inner Mongolia	2223.8	1526.9	389.5		302.4	4.8
辽宁	Liaoning	328.4	256.1	32.5		38.3	1.5
吉林	Jilin	260.8		227.8		33.0	0.0
黑龙江	Heilongjiang	410.1		396.1		14.0	
上海	Shanghai	0.4					0.4
江苏	Jiangsu	29.6		23.8		5.8	
浙江	Zhejiang	9.8	0.7	2.9	6.1	0.2	
安徽	Anhui	28.8		27.3	1.5		
福建	Fujian	83.4		18.7	57.7	6.2	0.8
江西	Jiangxi	201.8		176.9	1.9	17.7	5.3
山东	Shandong	17.4		10.7		6.6	0.1
河南	Henan	1987.6		1943.8		16.4	27.5
湖北	Hubei	359.2	38.7	288.3		32.2	
湖南	Hunan	276.0	151.2	103.5		21.3	
广东	Guangdong	217.5		5.6	211.8		0.0
广西	Guangxi	219.8	107.2	40.8	68.3	2.7	0.8
海南	Hainan	1.0		0.8	0.3		
重庆	Chongqing	98.0	12.6	81.1		3.7	0.6
四川	Sichuan	228.0	126.6	97.0		4.4	0.0
贵州	Guizhou	242.7	106.0	39.2		96.8	0.8
云南	Yunnan	672.5	503.0	75.1		75.2	19.2
西藏	Xizang	6.8		4.2		2.5	0.1
陕西	Shaanxi	517.8	310.2	134.4		57.9	15.3
甘肃	Gansu	375.3	211.0	26.2		36.9	85.7
青海	Qinghai	41.0	14.4	3.2		20.7	2.6
宁夏	Ningxia	163.6	37.9			40.7	84.5
新疆	Xinjiang	413.0	0.8	1.7		228.0	139.0

8-26 续表 continued

地 区	Region	受灾人口 (万人次) Population Affected (10 000 person-times)	死亡失踪人口 (人) Deaths and Missing (person)	倒塌房屋间数 (万间) Collapsed Houses (10 000 rooms)	直接经济损失 (亿元) Direct Economic Losses (100 million yuan)
全 国	**National Total**	**9544.4**	**691**	**20.91**	**3454.5**
北 京	Beijing	132.0	61	1.60	637.7
天 津	Tianjin	13.2		0.03	52.3
河 北	Hebei	598.2	51	8.73	994.6
山 西	Shanxi	276.8	12	0.06	68.8
内蒙古	Inner Mongolia	253.5	5		114.3
辽 宁	Liaoning	199.2	1	0.01	33.5
吉 林	Jilin	75.6	23	0.27	77.8
黑龙江	Heilongjiang	74.9	25	1.51	146.5
上 海	Shanghai	0.0			0.2
江 苏	Jiangsu	7.4	16	0.07	6.1
浙 江	Zhejiang	20.2	10		9.1
安 徽	Anhui	35.9	4		4.0
福 建	Fujian	561.2	12	0.58	301.2
江 西	Jiangxi	200.4	4	0.01	22.9
山 东	Shandong	15.3			4.8
河 南	Henan	2464.3	5	0.01	118.5
湖 北	Hubei	386.9	25	0.05	38.0
湖 南	Hunan	341.0	10	0.14	48.1
广 东	Guangdong	448.6	5	0.15	170.2
广 西	Guangxi	441.7	22	0.15	73.1
海 南	Hainan	9.9			0.6
重 庆	Chongqing	169.3	25	0.23	45.7
四 川	Sichuan	741.3	79	0.15	81.1
贵 州	Guizhou	426.3	11	0.03	27.5
云 南	Yunnan	723.2	29	0.02	76.8
西 藏	Xizang	19.7	40	0.05	4.4
陕 西	Shaanxi	388.3	36	0.06	63.2
甘 肃	Gansu	358.4	135	5.88	145.6
青 海	Qinghai	56.5	41	1.12	50.0
宁 夏	Ningxia	50.3			11.8
新 疆	Xinjiang	55.1	4		26.4

8-27 地质灾害及防治情况
Geological Disasters and Prevention

年份 地区	Year Region	发生地质灾害数量(处) Geological Disasters (case)	#滑坡 Landslide	#崩塌 Collapse	#泥石流 Debris Flow	#地面塌陷 Ground Collapse
	2000	19653	13431	2945	1958	347
	2005	17751	9367	7654	566	137
	2006	102804	88523	13160	417	398
	2007	25364	15478	7722	1215	578
	2008	26580	13450	8080	843	454
	2009	10580	6310	2378	1442	326
	2010	30670	22250	5688	1981	478
	2011	15804	11504	2445	1356	386
	2012	14675	11112	2152	952	364
	2013	15374	9832	3288	1547	385
	2014	10937	8149	1860	554	307
	2015	8355	5668	1870	483	292
	2016	10997	8194	1905	652	225
	2017	7521	5524	1356	387	206
	2018	2966	1631	858	339	122
	2019	6181	4220	1238	599	121
	2020	7840	4810	1797	899	183
	2021	4761	2335	1746	374	285
	2022	5659	3919	1366	202	153
	2023	3668	925	2176	374	193
北京	Beijing	1266	22	1099	132	13
天津	Tianjin					
河北	Hebei	251	88	85	70	8
山西	Shanxi	9	4	5		
内蒙古	Inner Mongolia					
辽宁	Liaoning					
吉林	Jilin	22	1	21		
黑龙江	Heilongjiang	3	2		1	
上海	Shanghai					
江苏	Jiangsu					
浙江	Zhejiang	66	45	12	7	2
安徽	Anhui	204	37	157	10	
福建	Fujian	102	41	52	9	
江西	Jiangxi	77	42	19		16
山东	Shandong	1		1		
河南	Henan	18	6	11		1
湖北	Hubei	95	62	28	4	1
湖南	Hunan	212	154	41	2	15
广东	Guangdong	23	6	16		1
广西	Guangxi	496	51	379	1	65
海南	Hainan					
重庆	Chongqing	380	177	125	11	67
四川	Sichuan	145	34	39	71	1
贵州	Guizhou	38	17	17	1	3
云南	Yunnan	103	73	17	13	
西藏	Xizang	44	4	7	33	
陕西	Shaanxi	46	28	16	2	
甘肃	Gansu	7	4	3		
青海	Qinghai	47	23	21	3	
宁夏	Ningxia	4	1	3		
新疆	Xinjiang	9	3	2	4	

8-28 森林火灾情况(2023年)
Forest Fires (2023)

地区	Region	森林火灾次数(次) Forest Fires (case)	一般火灾 Ordinary Fires	较大火灾 Major Fires	重大火灾 Severe Fires	特别重大火灾 Extraordinarily Severe Fires	火场总面积(公顷) Total Area of Fires (hectare)	受害森林面积(公顷) Destructed Forest Area (hectare)	伤亡人数(人) Casualties (person)	其他损失折款(万元) Other Losses (10 000 yuan)
全　国	**National Total**	**328**	**189**	**136**	**3**		**10349**	**4135**	**5**	**4260.5**
北　京	Beijing	7	7				4	3		6.0
天　津	Tianjin									
河　北	Hebei	5	2	3			2239	104	4	
山　西	Shanxi	3	2	1			261	99		687.8
内蒙古	Inner Mongolia	42	10	29	3		2656	2274		149.1
辽　宁	Liaoning	8	2	6			198	93		71.2
吉　林	Jilin	1	1				3	1		1.1
黑龙江	Heilongjiang	35	35				100	15		
上　海	Shanghai									
江　苏	Jiangsu	2	2				2			
浙　江	Zhejiang	13	6	7			222	57		50.8
安　徽	Anhui	4	4				20	1		9.2
福　建	Fujian	7	2	5			47	37		
江　西	Jiangxi	5	2	3			56	22		15.4
山　东	Shandong	7	6	1			49	9		146.0
河　南	Henan	21	13	8			93	66		1.0
湖　北	Hubei	16	13	3			130	52		131.6
湖　南	Hunan	16	13	3			124	23		12.2
广　东	Guangdong	11	3	8			226	110		110.5
广　西	Guangxi	37	18	19			612	216		220.1
海　南	Hainan	11	9	2			23	9		0.8
重　庆	Chongqing	2	2				1	1		1.1
四　川	Sichuan	10	6	4			447	166		2184.8
贵　州	Guizhou	15	5	10			512	75	1	9.9
云　南	Yunnan	34	11	23			2171	699		448.2
西　藏	Xizang	4	3	1			8			
陕　西	Shaanxi	5	5				126	2		3.9
甘　肃	Gansu	2	2				15	1		
青　海	Qinghai									
宁　夏	Ningxia									
新　疆	Xinjiang	5	5				4	1		

8-29 林业有害生物防治情况
Prevention of Forest Harmful Organisms

单位：万公顷 (10 000 hectares)

年份 Year / 地区 Region		合计 Total			森林病害 Forest Diseases	
		发生面积 Area of Occurrence	防治面积 Area of Prevention	防治率(%) Prevention Rate (%)	发生面积 Area of Occurrence	防治面积 Area of Prevention
	2000	851.86	574.19	67.4	93.45	61.95
	2005	961.03	640.75	66.7	101.20	70.62
	2006	1100.67	735.47	66.8	103.87	71.80
	2007	1209.68	801.20	66.2	110.95	85.88
	2008	1141.84	783.96	68.7	116.83	90.48
	2009	1141.97	819.38	71.8	103.12	81.88
	2010	1164.24	812.36	69.8	129.06	89.56
	2011	1168.14	728.50	62.4	119.72	79.23
	2012	1176.90	782.59	66.5	131.16	84.26
	2013	1223.05	766.83	62.7	139.17	89.88
	2014	1206.45	787.43	65.3	137.28	86.71
	2015	1218.35	877.77	72.0	139.05	97.71
	2016	1211.34	833.82	68.8	138.89	95.90
	2017	1253.12	962.17	76.8	133.09	101.71
	2018	1219.52	948.93	77.8	176.87	134.54
	2019	1236.77	1015.31	82.1	229.54	165.18
	2020	1278.45	1009.24	78.9	295.14	237.37
	2021	1255.37	1008.81	80.4	284.74	225.05
	2022	1427.96	1168.29	81.8	262.95	205.07
	2023	1092.30	912.95	83.6	225.04	186.23
北京	Beijing	2.93	2.93	100.0	0.13	0.13
天津	Tianjin	4.86	4.86	100.0	0.43	0.43
河北	Hebei	37.94	36.08	95.1	2.08	1.83
山西	Shanxi	20.71	16.13	77.9	1.35	1.02
内蒙古	Inner Mongolia	102.35	65.27	63.8	21.87	11.78
辽宁	Liaoning	50.21	47.30	94.2	3.59	3.05
吉林	Jilin	24.86	23.42	94.2	1.84	1.81
黑龙江	Heilongjiang	35.30	30.77	87.2	2.70	1.89
上海	Shanghai	0.94	0.93	99.2	0.14	0.14
江苏	Jiangsu	7.51	6.31	84.0	1.14	1.08
浙江	Zhejiang	31.83	27.98	87.9	28.95	25.60
安徽	Anhui	33.37	30.40	91.1	9.75	8.30
福建	Fujian	25.19	24.82	98.5	7.08	7.07
江西	Jiangxi	43.35	43.02	99.2	21.38	21.34
山东	Shandong	45.31	42.15	93.0	10.07	7.80
河南	Henan	35.45	32.64	92.1	5.32	4.99
湖北	Hubei	48.27	43.67	90.5	9.72	9.21
湖南	Hunan	31.29	23.68	75.7	7.18	4.11
广东	Guangdong	36.79	33.58	91.3	24.23	22.69
广西	Guangxi	33.77	12.92	38.3	7.14	4.69
海南	Hainan	2.54	0.74	29.0		
重庆	Chongqing	30.12	30.12	100.0	8.30	8.30
四川	Sichuan	58.67	44.02	75.0	10.36	7.39
贵州	Guizhou	18.33	17.30	94.4	1.90	1.63
云南	Yunnan	35.77	35.50	99.3	5.70	5.65
西藏	Xizang	12.93	2.14	16.6	2.40	0.39
陕西	Shaanxi	35.23	31.56	89.6	7.45	6.68
甘肃	Gansu	36.77	27.82	75.6	6.30	5.02
青海	Qinghai	23.97	18.90	78.9	2.93	2.29
宁夏	Ningxia	24.90	11.84	47.6	0.12	0.08
新疆	Xinjiang	146.78	141.15	96.2	10.50	9.82
大兴安岭	Daxinganling	14.05	3.00	21.3	3.01	0.04

8-29 续表 continued

单位：万公顷 (10 000 hectares)

年份 Year		森林虫害 Forest Pest Plague		森林鼠(兔)害 Forest Rat & Rabbit Plague		有害植物 Harmful Plants	
地区	Region	发生面积 Area of Occurrence	防治面积 Area of Prevention	发生面积 Area of Occurrence	防治面积 Area of Prevention	发生面积 Area of Occurrence	防治面积 Area of Prevention
	2000	669.28	456.59	89.12	55.65		
	2005	726.09	498.51	133.73	71.62		
	2006	829.87	557.20	166.93	106.47		
	2007	887.72	604.53	211.02	110.79		
	2008	843.19	590.23	181.81	103.25		
	2009	850.30	638.14	188.55	99.36		
	2010	852.32	628.70	182.86	94.11		
	2011	845.91	546.58	202.51	102.69		
	2012	846.29	572.93	199.45	125.41		
	2013	847.46	589.56	224.25	82.97	12.16	4.43
	2014	841.28	599.54	211.60	96.03	16.29	5.16
	2015	846.64	620.92	214.82	150.19	17.84	8.94
	2016	857.02	615.03	195.51	112.13	19.92	10.77
	2017	905.97	714.40	194.20	133.24	19.88	12.82
	2018	840.41	665.25	184.40	138.60	17.85	10.54
	2019	811.46	701.32	178.03	138.52	17.74	10.30
	2020	790.62	627.07	174.00	133.09	18.68	11.71
	2021	776.65	639.41	174.67	130.38	19.31	13.98
	2022	729.74	604.01	177.01	138.21	17.38	12.69
	2023	677.70	579.19	171.80	135.56	17.76	11.97
北京	Beijing	2.80	2.80				
天津	Tianjin	4.43	4.43				
河北	Hebei	33.64	32.35	2.22	1.90		
山西	Shanxi	13.84	10.36	5.40	4.74	0.13	0.01
内蒙古	Inner Mongolia	63.84	42.19	16.64	11.30		
辽宁	Liaoning	45.73	43.42	0.90	0.84		
吉林	Jilin	18.59	17.24	4.43	4.37		
黑龙江	Heilongjiang	18.20	15.50	14.39	13.37		
上海	Shanghai	0.80	0.79				
江苏	Jiangsu	6.23	5.09			0.14	0.14
浙江	Zhejiang	2.88	2.38				
安徽	Anhui	23.62	22.10				
福建	Fujian	18.11	17.74				
江西	Jiangxi	21.97	21.68			0.00	0.00
山东	Shandong	35.24	34.35				
河南	Henan	30.14	27.65				
湖北	Hubei	31.13	28.65	0.54	0.52	6.88	5.29
湖南	Hunan	24.12	19.57			0.00	0.00
广东	Guangdong	8.87	7.90			3.69	3.00
广西	Guangxi	23.77	6.85	0.03	0.03	2.83	1.35
海南	Hainan	0.80	0.49			1.74	0.25
重庆	Chongqing	20.47	20.47	1.14	1.14	0.21	0.21
四川	Sichuan	45.28	33.94	3.02	2.69	0.01	0.01
贵州	Guizhou	15.73	15.05	0.32	0.27	0.37	0.35
云南	Yunnan	27.58	27.38	1.22	1.22	1.26	1.25
西藏	Xizang	5.14	0.89	5.36	0.84	0.02	0.02
陕西	Shaanxi	20.21	17.65	7.57	7.22	0.00	0.00
甘肃	Gansu	16.26	11.49	14.21	11.31		
青海	Qinghai	10.48	8.13	10.11	8.41	0.45	0.08
宁夏	Ningxia	7.56	3.83	17.20	7.92	0.02	0.01
新疆	Xinjiang	78.11	76.16	58.17	55.17		
大兴安岭	Daxinganling	2.13	0.67	8.91	2.29		

注：自2019年起，森林鼠害指标改为森林鼠(兔)害。

a) Since 2019, Forest Rat Plague is renamed as Forest Rat & Rabbit Plague.

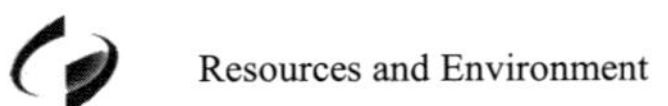

8–30 突发环境事件情况(2023年)
Environmental Emergency Events (2023)

地 区	Region	突发环境事件次数(次) Number of Environmental Emergency Events (case)	特别重大环境事件 Extraordinarily Severe Environmental Emergency Events	重大环境事件 Serious Environmental Emergency Events	较大环境事件 Comparatively Severe Environmental Emergency Events	一般环境事件 Ordinary Environmental Emergency Events
全 国	**National Total**	**130**			**3**	**127**
北 京	Beijing	1				1
天 津	Tianjin					
河 北	Hebei	4				4
山 西	Shanxi	20			1	19
内蒙古	Inner Mongolia	1				1
辽 宁	Liaoning	3				3
吉 林	Jilin					
黑龙江	Heilongjiang					
上 海	Shanghai					
江 苏	Jiangsu	9				9
浙 江	Zhejiang					
安 徽	Anhui	15				15
福 建	Fujian	2				2
江 西	Jiangxi	10				10
山 东	Shandong	5				5
河 南	Henan	6				6
湖 北	Hubei	4				4
湖 南	Hunan	5				5
广 东	Guangdong	9				9
广 西	Guangxi	4				4
海 南	Hainan	1				1
重 庆	Chongqing	3				3
四 川	Sichuan	4				4
贵 州	Guizhou	2			1	1
云 南	Yunnan	2				2
西 藏	Xizang	1				1
陕 西	Shaanxi	6			1	5
甘 肃	Gansu					
青 海	Qinghai	2				2
宁 夏	Ningxia	5				5
新 疆	Xinjiang	6				6

8-31 地震灾害情况
Earthquake Disasters

年份 Year / 地区 Region		5.0级及以上地震次数(次) Number of Earthquakes of Magnitude 5.0 and Above (case)	#5.0-5.9级 5.0-5.9 Richter Scale	#6.0-6.9级 6.0-6.9 Richter Scale	#7.0级以上 Over 7.0 Richter Scale	死亡人数(人) Deaths (person)	直接经济损失(亿元) Direct Economic Losses (100 million yuan)
	2000	10	7	2		10	14.68
	2005	13	9	2		15	26.28
	2006	10	9			25	8.00
	2007	3	1	1		3	20.19
	2008	17	6	4	2	69283	8594.96
	2009	8	5	2		3	27.38
	2010	12	4		1	2705	236.11
	2011	18	11	2	1	32	602.09
	2012	12	8	3		86	82.88
	2013	14	10	3	1	294	995.36
	2014	20	14	4	1	623	332.61
	2015	14	13	1		30	179.19
	2016	16	8	4		1	66.87
	2017	12	4	3	1	38	147.66
	2018	11	7				30.27
	2019	16	9	2		17	91.00
	2020	5	3	2		5	20.54
	2021	19	16	2	1	9	106.52
	2022	27	22	5		122	224.56
	2023	11	9	2		151	153.32
内蒙古	Inner Mongo						0.04
山 东	Shandong	1	1				2.37
广 东	Guangdong						0.01
四 川	Sichuan	1	1				0.78
云 南	Yunnan	2	2				2.93
西 藏	Xizang						1.01
甘 肃	Gansu	3	2	1		117	101.06
青 海	Qinghai					34	45.06
宁 夏	Ningxia						0.02
新 疆	Xinjiang	4	3	1			0.04

8-32 主要海洋灾害情况（2023年）
Major Marine Disasters (2023)

地区	Region	发生次数(次) Occurence of Disasters(case)	因灾死亡人口(人) Death Toll due to Disasters (person)	因灾失踪人口(人) Missing People due to Disasters (person)	受损海堤、护岸 Damaged Seawall and Revetment: 数量(处) Number (case)	长度(千米) Length (km)	直接经济损失(万元) Direct Economic Losses (10000 yuan)
合 计	**Total**	**13**	**4**	**4**	**65**	**7**	**250717.77**
天 津	Tianjin						
河 北	Hebei						
辽 宁	Liaoning	1			2	1	1330.00
上 海	Shanghai						
江 苏	Jiangsu	4			2	1	1700.00
浙 江	Zhejiang	2			3	0	3775.53
福 建	Fujian	5	3	4	45	4	212348.35
山 东	Shandong						
广 东	Guangdong	3	1		5	2	18253.39
广 西	Guangxi	2			8	0	13310.50
海 南	Hainan						

8-33 管辖海域未达到第一类海水水质标准的海域面积(2023年)
Sea Area with Marine Water Quality Not Reaching Standard of Grade 1 (2023)

单位：平方公里 (sq.km)

项　目	Item	第二类水质海域面积 Sea Area with Marine Water Quality at Grade 2	第三类水质海域面积 Sea Area with Marine Water Quality at Grade 3	第四类水质海域面积 Sea Area with Marine Water Quality at Grade 4	劣于第四类水质海域面积 Sea Area with Marine Water Quality Below Grade 4
总　计	**Total**	**30630**	**6980**	**4860**	**21410**
渤　海	Bohai Sea	6660	2360	860	2330
黄　海	Huanghai Sea	4850	470	120	260
东　海	Donghai Sea	16190	3260	2980	16640
南　海	Nanhai Sea	2930	890	900	2180

8-34 城镇环境基础设施建设投资情况(2023年)
Investment in Urban Environmental Infrastructure (2023)

单位：万元 (10 000 yuan)

地　区	Region	城镇环境基础设施建设投资 Investment in Urban Environmental Infrastructure	燃气 Gas Supply	集中供热 Centralized Heating	排水 Drainage Works	园林绿化 Gardening & Greening	市容环境卫生 Environmental Sanitation
全　国	**National Total**	**56680962**	**4393606**	**6701394**	**27439117**	**12979959**	**5166886**
北　京	Beijing	1791031	157952	328336	591053	495723	217967
天　津	Tianjin	294395	20151	11702	203075	48412	11055
河　北	Hebei	3101087	179448	825432	1030689	849699	215819
山　西	Shanxi	923375	52628	289177	348991	116750	115829
内蒙古	Inner Mongolia	1999027	41839	1412881	253406	215519	75382
辽　宁	Liaoning	634085	134655	134420	210800	91193	63017
吉　林	Jilin	382573	55292	118799	162400	38558	7524
黑龙江	Heilongjiang	743145	45920	113633	426106	56423	101063
上　海	Shanghai	1313858	87406		682194	443936	100322
江　苏	Jiangsu	3317561	315462	30520	1761806	931592	278181
浙　江	Zhejiang	2845355	171710	6546	992125	1523194	151780
安　徽	Anhui	3533223	293110	29988	1833606	721809	654710
福　建	Fujian	1265221	95180		631413	349822	188806
江　西	Jiangxi	2724615	172659		1832110	396761	323085
山　东	Shandong	6276314	136492	1317316	3418537	1300061	103908
河　南	Henan	3387906	79068	475608	1213807	1408834	210589
湖　北	Hubei	3318468	352508	79054	1980072	560492	346342
湖　南	Hunan	785170	112110	12000	445585	90279	125196
广　东	Guangdong	2659177	321807		1816119	333817	187434
广　西	Guangxi	816736	72951		472097	125825	145863
海　南	Hainan	227391	6438		156944	58674	5335
重　庆	Chongqing	1380996	145022	7695	617329	563237	47713
四　川	Sichuan	5361743	590550	42120	2908087	1137580	683406
贵　州	Guizhou	550977	94679	4707	309085	51346	91160
云　南	Yunnan	1312817	124399		820258	226315	141845
西　藏	Xizang	115615		65346	35409	923	13937
陕　西	Shaanxi	2646047	251335	329375	1201597	608561	255179
甘　肃	Gansu	1542025	113446	612215	580481	100540	135343
青　海	Qinghai	132525	27295	39404	45545	17098	3183
宁　夏	Ningxia	246043	26419	49959	116277	27572	25816
新　疆	Xinjiang	1052461	115675	365161	342114	89414	140097

8-35 工业污染治理投资完成情况
Investment Completed in the Treatment of Industrial Pollution

单位：万元 (10 000 yuan)

年份 地区	Year Region	工业污染治理完成投资 Investment Completed in the Treatment of Industrial Pollution	治理废水 Treatment of Wastewater	治理废气 Treatment of Waste Gas	治理固体废物 Treatment of Solid Waste	治理噪声 Treatment of Noise Pollution	治理其他 Treatment of Other Pollution
	2000	2347895	1095897	909242	114673	13692	214390
	2005	4581909	1337147	2129571	274181	30613	810396
	2006	4839485	1511165	2332697	182631	30145	782848
	2007	5523909	1960722	2752642	182532	18279	606838
	2008	5426404	1945977	2656987	196851	28383	598206
	2009	4426207	1494606	2324616	218536	14100	374349
	2010	3969768	1295519	1881883	142692	14193	620021
	2011	4443610	1577471	2116811	313875	21623	413831
	2012	5004573	1403448	2577139	247499	11627	764860
	2013	8496647	1248822	6409109	140480	17628	680608
	2014	9976511	1152473	7893935	150504	10950	768649
	2015	7736822	1184138	5218073	161468	27892	1145251
	2016	8190041	1082395	5614702	466733	6236	1019974
	2017	6815345	763760	4462628	127419	12862	1448676
	2018	6212736	640082	3931104	184249	15181	1442119
	2019	6151513	699004	3676995	170729	14168	1590616
	2020	4542586	573852	2423725	173064	7405	1364540
	2021	3352364	361241	2220982	36611	5437	728094
	2022	2857077	377220	1984251	60275	4213	431118
	2023	3624239	809614	2043227	118405	5319	647674
北京	Beijing	11419	716	10165	2		536
天津	Tianjin	141383	11669	100074	113	50	29477
河北	Hebei	228001	38726	131613	1931	54	55677
山西	Shanxi	213171	24367	127285	6886	270	54363
内蒙古	Inner Mongolia	160052	44939	104280	895		9938
辽宁	Liaoning	61548	12910	27882	17911	706	2139
吉林	Jilin	21554	2016	19318	2		218
黑龙江	Heilongjiang	69009	3192	45281	3877		16659
上海	Shanghai	80711	8461	42384	307	85	29474
江苏	Jiangsu	194809	37446	133549	2076	185	21553
浙江	Zhejiang	213561	62056	127607	2178	47	21673
安徽	Anhui	125112	13647	79465	324	50	31627
福建	Fujian	130992	35172	65415	6695	382	23327
江西	Jiangxi	79371	12277	35867	17	60	31151
山东	Shandong	281548	74729	157035	16498	72	33215
河南	Henan	128914	31153	65688	2202		29871
湖北	Hubei	265884	97214	135445	2830	2000	28395
湖南	Hunan	78664	6825	46938	5710		19191
广东	Guangdong	217325	40404	128035	1629	90	47168
广西	Guangxi	70588	44071	26218	261		38
海南	Hainan	1497	60	1411			26
重庆	Chongqing	77503	28542	37786	6	1	11168
四川	Sichuan	144298	38730	84660	4528	46	16335
贵州	Guizhou	48809	8876	16215	19396	610	3712
云南	Yunnan	103109	17992	55682	1744	387	27304
西藏	Xizang	648	648				
陕西	Shaanxi	56083	29152	16801	180	205	9745
甘肃	Gansu	64480	10359	47850	3831		2440
青海	Qinghai	32293	3021	4938			24334
宁夏	Ningxia	107027	41519	54730	9100		1678
新疆	Xinjiang	214876	28727	113608	7280	20	64390

注：本表数据为初步数。
a) The data in this table is preliminary.

8-36 林业草原投资完成情况(2023年)

单位：万元

地 区	Region	本年完成投资 Investment Completed in the Year	造林 Afforestation	森林经营 Forest Management	草原保护修复 Grassland Protection and Restoration	湿地保护修复 Wetland Protection and Restoration
全 国	**National Total**	**35810484**	**7224096**	**5440567**	**941940**	**384308**
北 京	Beijing	1332697	195412	68160		847
天 津	Tianjin	50879	16365	21849		7417
河 北	Hebei	832558	336715	123612	30596	9392
山 西	Shanxi	1020400	462355	46846	29405	1116
内蒙古	Inner Mongolia	1833206	231164	518026	90080	15718
辽 宁	Liaoning	316598	69765	21436	14242	2970
吉 林	Jilin	852892	130364	71208	9204	6891
黑龙江	Heilongjiang	1755268	72958	214388	10630	12125
上 海	Shanghai	131393	34484	66343		8954
江 苏	Jiangsu	290511	126065	41473		12535
浙 江	Zhejiang	777770	249791	50447		19897
安 徽	Anhui	962825	174831	239878	531	17092
福 建	Fujian	713277	233192	106487	450	5177
江 西	Jiangxi	962205	224698	192149		16654
山 东	Shandong	559036	47273	39795		24550
河 南	Henan	714590	366694	68054	1050	19332
湖 北	Hubei	1168791	299985	257394	6444	30228
湖 南	Hunan	1413495	321201	314864	72700	23939
广 东	Guangdong	1191887	235726	111557	6664	12768
广 西	Guangxi	6748287	987100	1566766	20962	14034
海 南	Hainan	196818	5071	2837		20811
重 庆	Chongqing	744977	188936	76902		9460
四 川	Sichuan	2519459	335630	135592	61609	17968
贵 州	Guizhou	2193298	460265	483350	64556	4425
云 南	Yunnan	1574265	280174	273414	71778	9348
西 藏	Xizang	486469	183379	88893	113344	16451
陕 西	Shaanxi	983604	314632	79048	21392	2792
甘 肃	Gansu	1193028	269762	18688	77953	16577
青 海	Qinghai	672188	90844	15385	151746	8547
宁 夏	Ningxia	320912	144132	21088	13994	8522
新 疆	Xinjiang	907040	122224	57197	72609	6588
局直属单位(含大兴安岭)	Units under the Bureau (including Daxinganling)	389862	12909	47442		1184

Investment of Forestry and Grassland Completed (2023)

(10 000 yuan)

荒漠化治理 Desertification Control	林草有害生物防治 Prevention and Control of Forest and Grass Pests	林草防火 Forest and Grass Fire Prevention	自然保护地管理和监测 Nature Reserve Management and Monitoring	生物多样性保护 Biodiversity Conservation	其他 Others
204434	**587362**	**716864**	**613116**	**318412**	**19379385**
509	8823	23377	2133	1925	1031513
	2225	555		963	1506
	12339	26376	8884	4366	280278
446	3584	51134	5969	2804	416742
33626	16336	29096	15125	5628	878406
2119	12205	12527	9394	3965	167975
	3997	24990	3531	7551	595156
1030	4392	45734	10348	3537	1380126
105	2850	208	294	1579	16576
	10024	10152	1408	5015	83838
	103673	18556	21672	14167	299569
	40147	23215	5525	13409	448197
9	29439	7653	11635	20858	298377
	39886	13092	8986	8015	458725
26	38008	45258	2355	9059	352710
	6997	11174	9805	5825	225659
67	35039	19721	27712	28172	464029
4503	27784	31153	11613	21949	583788
220	37985	38991	70535	9382	668060
	25117	15905	105809	32159	3980435
	3770	3341	41549	233	119205
335	35191	37508	12715	8089	375842
22382	19529	70420	52829	11741	1791759
95812	7760	13337	12713	7447	1043634
2554	5483	56250	27404	65742	782117
11099	2552	12019	55207	2060	1464
141	16360	11475	13044	10035	514685
7485	6219	20443	31040	5269	739592
12287	8077	3276	9645	1937	370444
900	2405	4452	9559	1529	114331
8779	17075	18363	11515	4001	588688
	2090	17113	3163		305961

主要统计指标解释

耕地 指利用地表耕作层种植农作物为主，每年种植一季及以上（含以一年一季以上的耕种方式种植多年生作物）的土地，包括熟地，新开发、复垦、整理地，休闲地（含轮歇地、休耕地）；以及间有零星果树、桑树或其他树木的耕地；包括南方宽度＜1.0 米，北方宽度＜2.0 米固定的沟、渠、路和地坎(埂)；包括直接利用地表耕作层种植的温室、大棚、地膜等保温、保湿设施用地。

园地 指种植以采集果、叶、根、茎、枝、汁等为主的集约经营的多年生木本和草本作物，覆盖度大于 50%和每亩株数大于合理株数 70%的土地。包括用于育苗的土地。

林地 指生长乔木、竹类、灌木的土地。不包括生长林木的湿地，城镇、村庄范围内的绿化林木用地，铁路、公路征地范围内的林木，以及河流、沟渠的护堤林用地。

草地 指生长草本植物为主的土地，包括乔木郁闭度＜0.1 的疏林草地、灌木覆盖度＜40%的灌丛草地，不包括生长草本植物的湿地。

湿地 指陆地和水域的交汇处，水位接近或处于地表面，或有浅层积水，且处于自然状态的土地。

城镇村及工矿用地 指城乡居民点、独立居民点以及居民点以外的工矿、国防、名胜古迹等企事业单位用地，包括其内部交通、绿化用地。

交通运输用地 指用于运输通行的地面线路、场站等的土地。包括民用机场、汽车客货运场站、港口、码头、地面运输管道和各种道路以及轨道交通用地。

水域及水利设施用地 指陆地水域、沟渠、水工建筑物等用地。不包括滞洪区。

径流量 指在一定时段内通过河流某一过水断面的水量，用以反映一个国家或地区水资源的丰歉程度。计算公式为：

径流量=降水量-蒸发量

流域 每条河流都有自己的干流和支流，干支流共同组成这条河流的水系。每条河流都有自己的集水区域，这个集水区域就称为该河流的流域。

外流河 指直接或间接流入海洋的河流。供给外流河河水的区域称为外流区域。

内陆河 指在陆地内部干燥地区，河水沿途消失于沙漠或注入内陆湖泊的河流。供给内陆河河水的区域称为内陆区域。

矿产资源 矿产资源指由地质作用形成的，具有利用价值的，呈固态、液态、气态的自然资源。目前我国已发现矿种有 173 种，按其特点和用途，可分为能源矿产(如煤炭、石油、天然气)、金属矿产(如铁矿、锰矿、铜矿、铅矿、铝土矿)、非金属矿产(如磷矿、钾盐、萤石)和水气矿产(如矿泉水、二氧化碳气、氦气)四大类。其中：金属矿产按其物质成分和性质又可分为：黑色金属矿产、有色金属矿产、贵金属矿产、稀有金属矿产、稀土金属矿产、稀散金属矿产六类。

储量 为探明资源量和（或）控制资源量中可经济采出的部分，是经过预可行性研究、可行性研究或与之相当的技术经济评价，充分考虑了可能的矿石损失和贫化，合理使用转换因素后估算的，满足开采的技术可行性和经济合理性。石油、天然气为剩余探明技术可采储量。油气（石油、天然气、煤层气、页岩气）储量参照国家标准《油气矿产资源储量分类》（GB/T 19492—2020），为剩余探明技术可采储量；其他矿产储量参照国家标准《固体矿产资源储量分类》（GB/T 17766—2020），为证实储量与可信储量之和。

平均气温 气温指空气的温度，我国一般以摄氏度为单位表示。气象观测的温度表是放在离地面约 1.5 米处通风良好的百叶箱里测量的，因此，通常说的气温指的是离地面 1.5 米处百叶箱中的温度。计算方法：月平均气温是将全月各日的平均气温相加，除以该月的天数而得。年平均气温是将 12 个月的月平均气温累加后除以 12 而得。

平均相对湿度 指空气中实际水气压与当时气温下的饱和水气压之比。其统计方法与气温相同。

降水量 指从天空降落到地面的液态或固态(经融化后)水，未经蒸发、渗透、流失而在地面上积聚的深度。通常以毫米为单位计量。计算方法：月降水量是将全月各日的降水量累加而得。年降水量是将 12 个月的月降水量累加而得。

日照时数 指太阳实际照射地面的时数，通常以小时为单位表示。其统计方法与降水量相同。

水资源总量 指当地降水形成的地表和地下产水总量，即地表径流量与降水入渗补给地下水量之和。

地表水资源量 指河流、湖泊、冰川等地表水体逐年更新的动态水量，即当地天然河川径流量。

地下水资源量 指地下饱和含水层逐年更新的动态水量，即降水和地表水入渗对地下水的补给量。

地表水与地下水重复计算量 指地表水和地下水相互转化的部分，即天然河川径流量中的地下水排泄量和地下水补给量中来源于地表水的入渗补给量。

供水总量 指各种水源提供的包括输水损失在内的水量之和。

地表水源供水量 指地表水工程的取水量，按蓄水工程、引水工程、提水工程、调水工程四种形式统计。

地下水源供水量 指水井工程的开采量，按浅层淡水、深层承压水和微咸水分别统计。

其他水源供水量 包括再生水厂、集雨工程、海水淡化

设施供水量及矿坑水利用量。

用水总量 指各类河道外用水户取用的包括输水损失在内的毛水量之和。不包括海水直接利用量以及水力发电、航运等河道内用水量。

农业用水 包括耕地和林地、园地、牧草地灌溉，鱼塘补水及牲畜用水。

工业用水 指工矿企业在生产过程中用于制造、加工、冷却、空调、净化、洗涤等方面的用水，按新水取用量计，不包括企业内部的重复利用水量。

生活用水 包括城镇生活用水和农村生活用水。城镇生活用水由城镇居民生活用水和公共用水（含第三产业及建筑业等用水）组成；农村生活用水指农村居民生活用水。

人工生态环境补水 仅包括人为措施供给的城镇环境用水和部分河湖、湿地补水，而不包括降水、径流自然满足的水量。

一般工业固体废物产生量 指当年全年调查对象实际产生的一般工业固体废物的量。一般工业固体废物指企业在工业生产过程中产生且不属于危险废物的工业固体废物。

一般工业固体废物综合利用量 指调查年度企业通过回收、加工、循环、交换等方式，从固体废物中提取或者使其转化为可以利用的资源、能源和其他原材料的固体废物量（包括当年利用的往年工业固体废物累计贮存量）。如用作农业肥料、生产建筑材料、筑路、用作充填回填材料等。综合利用量由原产生固体废物的单位统计。

一般工业固体废物处置量 指调查年度企业将工业固体废物焚烧和用其他改变工业固体废物的物理、化学、生物特性的方法，达到减少或者消除其危险成分的活动，或者将工业固体废物最终置于符合环境保护规定要求的填埋场的活动中，所消纳固体废物的量（包括当年处置的往年工业固体废物贮存量）。

一般工业固体废物贮存量 指调查年度企业以综合利用或处置为目的，将固体废物暂时贮存或堆存在专设的贮存设施或专设的集中堆存场所内的量。专设的固体废物贮存场所或贮存设施必须有防扩散、防流失、防渗漏、防止污染大气、水体的措施。

一般工业固体废物倾倒丢弃量 指调查年度企业将所产生的固体废物倾倒或者丢弃到固体废物污染防治设施、场所以外的量。

危险废物产生量 指调查年度调查对象实际产生的危险废物的量，包括利用处置危险废物过程中二次产生的危险废物的量。危险废物指列入国家危险废物名录或者根据国家规定的危险废物鉴别标准和鉴别方法认定的具有危险特性的废物。按《国家危险废物名录》（2016）填报。

危险废物利用处置量 指调查年度调查对象从危险废物中提取物质作为原材料或者燃料的活动中消纳危险废物的量，以及将危险废物焚烧和用其他改变危险废物物理、化学、生物特性的方法，达到减少或者消除其危险成分的活动，或者将危险废物最终置于符合环境保护规定要求的填埋场的活动中，所消纳危险废物的量。包括本单位自行处置利用的本单位产生和接收外单位危险废物量。

危险废物本年末贮存量 指截至调查年度年末，调查对象将危险废物以一定包装方式暂时存放在专设的贮存设施内的量。专设的贮存设施应符合《危险废物贮存污染控制标准》（GB18597-2001）等相关环保法律法规要求，具有防扩散、防流失、防渗漏、防止污染大气和水体措施的设施。包括本单位自行贮存的本单位产生的和接收外单位的危险废物量。

生活垃圾清运量 指报告期收集和运送到各生活垃圾处理厂(场)和生活垃圾最终消纳点的生活垃圾数量。生活垃圾指城市日常生活或为城市日常生活提供服务的活动中产生的固体废物以及法律行政规定的视为城市生活垃圾的固体废物。包括：居民生活垃圾、商业垃圾、集市贸易市场垃圾、街道清扫垃圾、公共场所垃圾和机关、学校、厂矿等单位的生活垃圾。

生活垃圾无害化处理率 指报告期生活垃圾无害化处理量与生活垃圾产生量的比率。在统计上，由于生活垃圾产生量不易取得，可用清运量代替。计算公式为：

$$\text{生活垃圾无害化处理率}=\frac{\text{生活垃圾无害化处理量}}{\text{生活垃圾产生量}}\times 100\%$$

森林面积 包括郁闭度0.2以上的乔木林地面积和竹林面积，国家特别规定的灌木林地面积，农田林网以及村旁、路旁、水旁、宅旁林木的覆盖面积。

人工林面积 指由人工播种、植苗或扦插造林形成的生长稳定，(一般造林3-5年后或飞机播种5-7年后)每公顷保存株数大于或等于造林设计植树株数80%或郁闭度0.20以上(含0.20)的林分面积。

森林覆盖率 以行政区域为单位的森林面积占区域土地总面积的百分比。计算公式为：

$$\text{森林覆盖率}=\frac{\text{森林面积}}{\text{土地总面积}}\times 100\%$$

活立木总蓄积量 指一定范围土地上全部树木蓄积的总量，包括森林蓄积、疏林蓄积、散生木蓄积和四旁树蓄积。

森林蓄积量 指一定森林面积上存在着的林木树干部分的总材积。

造林面积 指在宜林荒山荒地、宜林沙荒地、无立木林地、疏林地和退耕地等其他宜林地上通过人工措施形成或恢复森林、林木、灌木林的过程。

人工造林 指在宜林荒山荒地、宜林沙荒地、无立木林地、疏林地和退耕地等其他宜林地上通过播种、植苗和分植来提高森林植被覆被率的技术措施。

飞播造林 通过飞机播种，并辅以适当的人工措施，在自然力的作用下使其形成森林或灌草植被，提高森林植被覆被率或提高森林植被质量的技术措施。

封山育林 对宜林地、无立木林地、疏林地或低质低效有林地、灌木林地实施封禁并辅以人工促进手段，使其形成森林或灌草植被或提高林分质量的一项技术措施。包括无林地和疏林地封育、有林地和灌木林地封育、新造林地封育。

退化林修复 为改善林分的活力和结构，有效遏制防护林退化，提高林分质量和恢复森林功能，对结构失调和稳定性降低、功能退化甚至丧失且自然更新能力弱的林分采取的结构调整、树种替换、补植补播、嫁接复壮等森林经营措施。

人工更新造林 指在采伐迹地、火烧迹地、林中空地上通过人工造林重新形成森林的过程。

自然保护区 指保护典型的自然生态系统、珍稀濒危野生动植物种的天然集中分布区、有特殊意义的自然遗迹的区域。具有较大面积，确保主要保护对象安全，维持和恢复珍稀濒危野生动植物种群数量及赖以生存的栖息环境。

滑坡 指斜坡上不稳定的岩土体在重力作用下沿一定软弱面(或滑动带)整体向下滑动的物理地质现象。

崩塌 指陡坡上大块的岩土体在重力作用下突然脱离母体崩落的物理地质现象。

泥石流 指山地突然爆发的饱含大量泥沙、石块的特殊洪流。

地面塌陷 指地表岩、土体在自然或人为因素作用下向下陷落，并在地面形成塌陷坑(洞)的一种动力地质现象。

森林火灾次数 指发生在城市市区外的一切森林、林木和林地的火灾次数。按照受害森林面积和伤亡人数，森林火灾分为一般森林火灾、较大森林火灾、重大森林火灾和特别重大森林火灾：1.一般森林火灾：受害森林面积在 1 公顷以下或者其他林地起火的，或者死亡 1 人以上 3 人以下的，或者重伤 1 人以上 10 人以下的；2.较大森林火灾：受害森林面积在 1 公顷以上 100 公顷以下的，或者死亡 3 人以上 10 人以下的，或者重伤 10 人以上 50 人以下的；3.重大森林火灾：受害森林面积在 100 公顷以上 1000 公顷以下的，或者死亡 10 人以上 30 人以下的，或者重伤 50 人以上 100 人以下的；4.特别重大森林火灾：受害森林面积在 1000 公顷以上的，或者死亡 30 人以上的，或者重伤 100 人以上的。本条所称“以上”包括本数，“以下”不包括本数。

林业有害生物 危害森林、林木、荒漠植被、湿地植被等的病虫鼠兔及有害植物。

突发环境事件 指突然发生，造成或可能造成重大人员伤亡、重大财产损失和对全国或者某一地区的经济社会稳定、政治安定构成重大威胁和损害，有重大社会影响的涉及公共安全的环境事件。

Explanatory Notes on Main Statistical Indicators

Cultivated Land refers to the land that mainly for the regular cultivation of farm crops by using the surface tillage layer, planting more than one harvest a year (including perennial crops cultivated by more than one harvest a year), including cultivated land, newly-developed land, reclaimed land, consolidated land, fallow; It covers the land with some fruit trees, mulberry trees and others; It also covers fixed ditch, canal, road and sill (ridge) with width less than 1 meter in the South and 2 meters in the North; It covers the land for thermal insulation and moisturizing facilities such as greenhouse, greenhouse and plastic film planted directly by surface tillage layer.

Garden Land refers to land for intensive cultivation of perennial woody plants and herbs to collect fruits, leaves, roots, stems, branches and juice, with a coverage rate over 50% and plant number over 70% of rational plant number per mu. Land for nursery is included.

Forest Land refers to land for planting arbor, bamboo, bush shrub. It does not include the wetland where trees grow, the land for greening trees within the scope of towns and villages, the forest within the scope of railway and highway land acquisition, the land for revetment forest of rivers and ditches.

Grassland refers to land mainly for the growth of herbaceous forage crops. It includes sparse forest grassland with tree canopy density less than 0.1, shrub grassland with shrub coverage less than 40%, excluding wetlands with herbaceous plants.

Wetland refers to the land at the intersection of land and water, where the water level is close to or on the ground surface, or there is shallow ponding and is in a natural state.

Land for Urban, Rural, Industrial and Mining Activities refer to urban and rural residential areas, independent residential areas, and the land used by enterprises and institutions such as industrial and mining, national defense and scenic spots outside residential areas, including their internal traffic and greening land.

Land Used for Transport refers to the land for ground lines, stations, etc. used for transportation. It includes civil airport, automobile passenger and freight transport station, port, wharf, ground transportation pipeline, various roads and rail transit land.

Land Used for Water and Water Conservancy Facilities refers to land for water areas, ditches, hydraulic structures, etc. Flood detention area is not included.

Volume of Runoff refers to the total volume of water running through a certain cross section of a river during a certain period of time, reflecting the water resources condition in a country or a region. The formula for calculating volume of runoff is as follows:

River Runoff =Precipitation- Evapotranspiration

Drainage Area Each river has its own main stream and branches to form the water system of the river. Each river has its own catchment's area, which is also called as the drainage area of the river.

Out-flowing Rivers refer to rivers directly or indirectly flowing into the sea. The area providing water to the out-flowing rivers is called as out-flowing area.

Inland Rivers refer to rivers in inland dry areas that die away in desert on the way or infuse into inland lakes. The area providing water to the inland rivers is called as inland area.

Mineral Resources refer to the useful natural resources with solid state, liquid state, gaseity, which is formulated by the geological process, At present, there are 173 kinds of minerals discovered in China, classified into four categories: energy minerals (covering coal, oil and natural gas), metallic minerals (covering iron ore, manganese ore, copper, lead and bauxite), nonmetallic minerals (covering phosphorite, potash and fluorspar), and water/gas related minerals (covering mineral water, carbon dioxide and helium). Metallic minerals can be classified into six sub-categories based on its material composition and properties: ferrous, non-ferrous, noble metal, rare metal, rare earth and dispersed metals.

Reserves are the economically recoverable part of the proved and/or controlled resources, are estimated after pre feasibility study, feasibility study or equivalent technical and economic evaluation, fully considering possible ore loss and dilution, and rational use of conversion factors, which meet the technical feasibility and economic rationality of mining. The data for oil and gas (oil, natural gas, coalbed methane, and shale gas) reserves are remaining proved technically recoverable reserves as per Classifications for Petroleum Resources and Reserves (GB/T 19492-2020) and those of other minerals are the total of proved reserves and probable reserves as per Classifications for Mineral Resources and Mineral Reserves (GB/T 17766-2020).

Average Temperature refers to the average air temperature on a regular basis, generally expressed in centigrade in China. Thermometers used for meteorological observation are placed in well-ventilated shelters about 1.5 meters above the ground. Therefore, the commonly used temperature refers to the temperature in the shelter 1.5 meters above the ground. The calculation method is as follows:

The summation of daily average temperature of one month divided by the actual days of that month represents the monthly average temperature. The summation of monthly average temperature of a year divided by 12 represents the annual average temperature.

Average Relative Humidity refers to the ratio of actual vapour pressure in the air to the saturation water vapour pressure at the current temperature. The calculation method is the same as that of average temperature.

Precipitation refers to the depth of water in liquid state or solid state (thawed), falling from atmosphere onto the ground without being evaporated, percolating or running off. It is usually expressed in millimeters. The calculation method is as follows:

The monthly precipitation is obtained by the sum of daily precipitation of the month, and the annual precipitation is the sum of monthly precipitation of the 12 months of the year.

Sunshine Hours refer to the actual hours of sun irradiating the earth, usually expressed in hours. The calculation method is the same as that of the precipitation.

Total Water Resources refers to total volume of surface water and groundwater which is from the local precipitation and is measured as the summation of run-off for surface water and recharge of groundwater from local precipitation.

Surface Water Resources refers to total volume of yearly renewable water flow which exist in rivers, lakes, glaciers and other surface water, and are measured as the natural run-off of local rivers.

Groundwater Resources refers to total volume of yearly renewable water flow which exist in saturation aquifers of groundwater, and are measured as recharge of groundwater from local precipitation and surface water.

Overlapped Measurement between Surface Water and Groundwater refers to the part of mutual transfer between surface water and groundwater, i.e. which is the run-off of rivers includes some depletion into groundwater while groundwater includes recharge from surface water.

Water Supply refers to gross water supplied by various sources, including losses during distribution.

Surface Water Supply refers to withdrawals through the surface water supply system, which can be divided into four categories: storage, flow, pumping and transfer project.

Groundwater Supply refers to withdrawals from supplying wells, which can be divided into three categories: shallow layer freshwater, deep confided freshwater and slightly brackish water.

Other Water Supply Sources include supplies by water reclamation plants, rainwater collection projects, seawater desalinization facilities and the consumption of mine water.

Water Use refers to gross water used by various off-stream water users, including losses during distribution, while excluding the direct use of seawater and in-stream water use such as hydroelectric generation and shipping.

Water Use for Agriculture includes uses of water for irrigation of cultivated land, forest land, garden land and grass land, replenishment of fishing farms and water used for livestock raising.

Water Use for Industry refers to water use by industrial and mining enterprises in the production process of manufacturing, processing, cooling, air conditioning, cleansing, washing, etc. Only including new withdrawals of water, excluding reuse of water within enterprise.

Water Use for Households and Service includes water use in both urban and rural areas. Urban water use is composed of households use and public use (including tertiary industry and construction). Rural water use refers to households use.

Water Use for Artificial Eco-environment only includes the artificially replenishment of some rivers, lakes and wetlands, and use for urban environment, excluding the natural precipitation and runoff meet.

Common Industrial Solid Wastes Generated refers to the amount of common industrial solid wastes the surveyed units actual generated over the year. The common industrial solid wastes refers to the industrial solid wastes that are generated during the industrial process and are not hazardous wastes.

Common Industrial Solid Wastes Integrated Use refers to amount of solid wastes from which useable materials can be extracted or converted into usable resources, energy or other materials through reclamation, processing, recycling and exchange (including utilizing in the year the stocks of industrial solid wastes of the previous year) generated by surveyed units over the year of the survey, e.g. being used as agricultural fertilizers, building materials, material for paving road or as backfill material. The information should be measured as the unit of generating wastes.

Common Industrial Solid Wastes Disposed refers to the amount of industrial solid wastes disposed, which covers the amount of previous years, through incineration or other methods to change its physical, chemical and biological properties to reduce or eliminate the hazards or land filled in the sites following the requirements for environmental protection by surveyed units over the year of the survey.

Stock of Common Industrial Solid Wastes refers to the amount of solid wastes placed in special facilities or special sites by enterprises for the purposes of integrated use or disposal over the year of the survey. The sites or facilities should take measures against dispersion, loss, seepage, and air and water contamination.

Common Industrial Solid Wastes Discharged refers to the amount of industrial solid wastes dumped or discharged by producing enterprises to disposal facilities or to other sites over the year of the survey.

Hazardous Wastes Generated refers to the amount of actual hazardous wastes generated by surveyed units over the year of the survey, which is covered secondary generation during the process of disposal and reuse of hazardous wastes. Hazardous waste refers to those listed in *the National Hazardous Wastes* catalogue or identified as any one of the hazardous properties in light of the national hazardous wastes identification standards and methods. It should be reported following the *National Catalogue of Hazardous Wastes* (2016 Version).

Hazardous Wastes Reused and Disposed refers to the amount of hazardous wastes that are used to extract materials for raw materials or fuel over the year of the survey, and the amount of hazardous wastes which are incineration or specially disposed using other methods to change its physical, chemical and biological properties and thus to reduce or eliminate the hazards, or placed ultimately in the sites following the requirements for environmental protection over the year of the survey. It includes the hazardous wastes generated by the enterprise itself and received from other enterprises.

Year-end Stock of Hazardous Wastes refers to the amount of hazardous wastes specially packaged and placed in special facilities or special sites by enterprises by the end of the year, which covered stock of surveyed units generated and received from other units. The special stock facilities should meet the requirements set in relevant environment protection laws and regulations such as *"Pollution Control Standards for Hazardous Waste Stock"* (GB18597-2001) and take measures against dispersion, loss, seepage, and air and water contamination.

Domestic Garbage Collected and Transported refers to volume of domestic garbage collected and transported to disposal factories or sites during the reference period. Domestic garbage are solid wastes generated from urban households or from service activities for urban households, and solid wastes regarded as municipal domestic garbage according to the laws and administrative regulations, including those from households, commercial activities, markets, cleaning of streets, public sites, offices, schools, factories, mining units and other sources.

Rate of Domestic Garbage Harmless Treatment refers to the ratio of the volume of domestic garbage harmlessly treated to the volume of domestic garbage produced during the reference period. In practical statistics, as the volume of domestic garbage produced is difficult to obtain, it can be replaced by the volume of collected and transported. It is calculated as:

$$\text{rate of domestic garbage harmless treatment} = \frac{\text{volume of domestic garbage harmless treated}}{\text{volume of domestic garbage collected and transported}} \times 100\%$$

Forest Area refers to the area of trees and bamboo grow with a canopy density above 0.2 degree, the area of shrubby tree according to regulations of the government, area of land under agroforestry and the area of trees planted by the side of villages, farm houses and along roads and rivers.

Area of Planted Forests refer to the area of stable growing forests, planted manually or by airplanes, with a survival rate of 80% or higher of the designed number of trees per hectare, or with a canopy density of 0.20 degree or above (after 3-5 years of manual planting or 5-7 years of airplane planting).

Forest Coverage Rate refers to the ratio of forest area to the total land area within the administrative region. The formula is as follows:

$$\text{forest coverage rate} = \frac{\text{forest area}}{\text{area of total land}} \times 100\%$$

Total Stock Volume of Living Trees refers to the total stock volume of trees accumulated on a certain area of land, including trees in forest, tress in sparse forest, scattered wood and trees planted by the side of villages, farm houses and along roads and rivers.

Stock Volume of Forest refers to total stock volume of timber of tree trunk in a given forest area.

Area of Afforestation refers to the total area of land suitable for afforestation, including barren hills, idle land, sand dunes, non-timber forest land, woodland and "grain for green" land, on which acres of forests, trees and shrubs are planted through manual planting.

Manual Planting refers to technical measures of sowing, planting seedlings and divided transplanting on land suitable for afforestation, including barren hills, idle land, sand dunes, non-timber forest land, woodland and "grain for green" land to increase vegetation coverage rate of forests.

Airplane Planting refers to technical measures of airplane planting with of appropriate artificial help taken under the influence of natural power to restore certain amount of seedlings on land suitable for afforestation, with an aim of increasing vegetation coverage rate of forests or improving forest quality.

Closed Hillsides for Afforestation is a technical measure by isolation with artificial means to form forest or shrub and grass or improve forest quality land, to the suitable area for forest, forest land without stumpage, sparse forest land, or low quality forest, shrub forest.

Restoration of Degraded Forest In order to improve the vitality and structure of forest, effectively control forest degradation, improve forest quality and restore forest function, management measures are taken to the forest of structural imbalance and stability reduction, function reduction or even loss and natural regeneration ability is weak, which include structural adjustment, species replacement, replanting sowing, grafting rejuvenation, etc.

Artificial Regeneration refers to forest reforming process in logging slash, slash burning, the glade through afforestation.

Natural Reserves refer to the area that protect typical natural ecosystems, natural concentrated distribution of rare and endangered wild animal and plant species, and natural relics of special significance. It has a large area to ensure the safety of the main protected objects, and to maintain and restore the quantity of rare and endangered wild animals and plants and their habitats.

Landslides refer to the geological phenomenon of unstable rocks or earth on slopes sliding down along certain soft surface as a result of gravity.

Collapse refers to the geological phenomenon of large mass of rocks or earth suddenly collapsing from the mountain or cliff as a result of gravity.

Debris Flow refers to the sudden rush of flood torrents containing large amount of mud and rocks in mountainous areas.

Ground Collapse refers to the geological phenomenon of surface rocks or earth subsiding into holes or pits as a result of natural or human factors.

Number of Forest Fires refers to the number of wild fires in forests, woods and woodland outside of cities. In light of the area plagued by fires and the number of casualties, forest fires can be categorized into general forest fires, relatively larger fires, serious forest fires and extraordinary serous forest fires: 1). General forest fires: the destructed forest area is less than 1 hectare, or the fire erupts in other woodland, or the number of deaths is no less than 1 but less than 3, or the number of seriously injured persons is no less than 1 but less than 10 persons. 2). Relatively larger forest fires: the destructed forest area is no less than 1 hectare but less than 100 hectares, or the number of deaths is no less than 3 but less than 10, or the number of seriously injured persons is no less than 10 but less than 50 persons. 3). Serious forest fires: the destructed forest area is no less than 100 hectares but less than 1000 hectares, or the number of deaths is no less than 10 but less than 30, or the number of seriously injured persons is no less than 50 but less than 100 persons. 4). Extraordinary serious forest fires: the destructed forest area is no less than 1000 hectares, or the number of deaths is no less than 30, or the number of seriously injured persons is no less than 100 persons.

Forest Harmful Organisms refer to the diseases, pests, rats and harmful plants that plague forests, wood, desert and wetland vegetation.

Abrupt Environmental Accidents refer to environmental emergencies that caused or likely to cause significant causalities, serious property damages and pose a major threat and damage to the economic, social or political stability of the country or a region, or have significant social impact that related to the public safety.

9

能　源

Energy

简 要 说 明

一、本篇资料的主要内容

本篇包括的主要内容有能源生产、消费及品种构成，能源生产和消费弹性系数，综合能源平衡表和主要能源品种的单项平衡表，分行业、分主要能源品种的消费量，能源加工转换效率及居民生活用能源消费量等。从2013年开始，增加全国单位国内生产总值能耗和发电装机容量等指标。

二、本篇资料的统计范围

本篇资料的统计范围为全社会。

三、本篇的资料来源

9—1表数据来自能源产品产量统计，并以此为依据计算；9—14、9—15表数据来自中国电力企业联合会；其他表的数据均来自历年能源平衡表。

四、关于数据口径与计算方法的说明

1.一次能源生产量与能源产品产量统计数字一致。

2.能源生产与消费弹性系数分别以能源生产、消费增长速度与国内生产总值增长速度相比求得。

3.能源平衡表中，进口量和出口量采用海关统计数据。进口量中包括境内飞机和轮船在境外的加油量，出口量中包括境外飞机和轮船在境内的加油量。电力折算标准煤系数按平均发电煤耗计算。

4.能源加工转换效率表中，电力折算标准煤系数采用当量值计算，每千瓦小时折0.1229千克标准煤。

5.GDP按可比价格计算。

Brief Introduction

I. Main Contents

Data in this chapter cover mainly energy production, consumption, and composition; elasticity ratio of energy production and consumption; overall balance sheet of energy and balance sheets by main types of energy; consumption of energy by sector and by main types of energy; efficiency of energy transformation; and the household energy consumption. Since 2013, indicators like energy intensity by GDP and installed capacity of power generation are also included.

II. Scope of Data

The scope of data in this chapter is the whole country.

III. Sources of Data

Data in Table 9-1 are calculated on the basis of statistics on output of energy products; data in Tables 9-14 and 9-15 come from the China Electricity Council; and data in other tables in this chapter are from the energy balance sheets over the years.

IV. Notes on Coverage and Compilation of Data

(1) The data on production of primary energy are the same as the corresponding data on output of energy products.

(2) The elasticity ratio of energy production is calculated as the quotient of the growth rate of energy production divided by the growth rate of GDP; and the elasticity ratio of energy consumption is calculated as the quotient of the growth rate of energy consumption divided by the growth rate of GDP.

(3) In the energy balance sheet, data on imports and exports are from Customs statistics. Data on imports include the domestic airplanes and ships refueling abroad. Data on exports include the oversea airplanes and ships refueling domestically. The coefficient for conversion of electric power into the standard coal equivalent is calculated according to the average consumption of coal for generating electricity.

(4) In the table on the efficiency of energy transformation, the coefficient for the conversion of electric power into the standard coal equivalent is calculated on the basis of the heat value equivalent. One kilowatt is equal to 0.1229 kgce.

(5) Gross domestic product are calculated at constant prices.

9-1 一次能源生产总量及构成
Total Primary Energy Production and Its Composition

年 份 Year	一次能源生产总量 (万吨标准煤) Total Primary Energy Production (10 000 tce)	占一次能源生产总量的比重 (%) Proportion to Total Primary Energy Production (%)			
		原 煤 Raw Coal	原 油 Crude Oil	天然气 Natural Gas	一次电力及其他能源 Primary Electricity and Other Energy
1978	62770	70.3	23.7	2.9	3.1
1980	63735	69.4	23.8	3.0	3.8
1985	85546	72.8	20.9	2.0	4.3
1990	103922	74.2	19.0	2.0	4.8
1991	104844	74.1	19.2	2.0	4.7
1992	107256	74.3	18.9	2.0	4.8
1993	111059	74.0	18.7	2.0	5.3
1994	118729	74.6	17.6	1.9	5.9
1995	129034	75.3	16.6	1.9	6.2
1996	133032	75.0	16.9	2.0	6.1
1997	133460	74.2	17.2	2.1	6.5
1998	129834	73.3	17.7	2.2	6.8
1999	131935	73.9	17.3	2.5	6.3
2000	138570	72.9	16.8	2.6	7.7
2001	147425	72.6	15.9	2.7	8.8
2002	156277	73.1	15.3	2.8	8.8
2003	178299	75.7	13.6	2.6	8.1
2004	206108	76.7	12.2	2.7	8.4
2005	229037	77.4	11.3	2.9	8.4
2006	244763	77.5	10.8	3.2	8.5
2007	264173	77.8	10.1	3.5	8.6
2008	277419	76.8	9.8	3.9	9.5
2009	286092	76.8	9.4	4.0	9.8
2010	312125	76.2	9.3	4.1	10.4
2011	340178	77.8	8.5	4.1	9.6
2012	351041	76.2	8.5	4.1	11.2
2013	358784	75.4	8.4	4.4	11.8
2014	362212	73.5	8.3	4.7	13.5
2015	362193	72.2	8.5	4.8	14.5
2016	345954	69.8	8.3	5.2	16.7
2017	358867	69.6	7.6	5.4	17.4
2018	378859	69.2	7.2	5.4	18.2
2019	397317	68.5	6.9	5.6	19.0
2020	407295	67.5	6.8	6.0	19.7
2021	427115	66.7	6.7	6.0	20.6
2022	463808	67.2	6.3	5.9	20.6
2023	483000	66.6	6.2	6.0	21.2

注：电力折算标准煤的系数根据当年平均发电煤耗计算(以下相关表同)。

a) The coefficient for conversion of electric power into the standard coal equivalent is calculated according to the average consumption of coal for generating electricity in the year. The same applies to the following tables.

9-2 能源消费总量及构成
Total Energy Consumption and Its Composition

年 份 Year	能源消费总量 (万吨标准煤) Total Energy Consumption (10 000 tce)	占能源消费总量的比重 (%) Proportion to Total Energy Consumption (%)			
		煤 炭 Coal	石 油 Petroleum	天然气 Natural Gas	一次电力及其他能源 Primary Electricity and Other Energy
1978	57144	70.7	22.7	3.2	3.4
1980	60275	72.2	20.7	3.1	4.0
1985	76682	75.8	17.1	2.2	4.9
1990	98703	76.2	16.6	2.1	5.1
1991	103783	76.1	17.1	2.0	4.8
1992	109170	75.7	17.5	1.9	4.9
1993	115993	74.7	18.2	1.9	5.2
1994	122737	75.0	17.4	1.9	5.7
1995	131176	74.6	17.5	1.8	6.1
1996	135192	73.5	18.7	1.8	6.0
1997	135909	71.4	20.4	1.8	6.4
1998	136184	70.9	20.8	1.8	6.5
1999	140569	70.6	21.5	2.0	5.9
2000	146964	68.5	22.0	2.2	7.3
2001	155547	68.0	21.2	2.4	8.4
2002	169577	68.5	21.0	2.3	8.2
2003	197083	70.2	20.1	2.3	7.4
2004	230281	70.2	19.9	2.3	7.6
2005	261369	72.4	17.8	2.4	7.4
2006	286467	72.4	17.5	2.7	7.4
2007	311442	72.5	17.0	3.0	7.5
2008	320611	71.5	16.7	3.4	8.4
2009	336126	71.6	16.4	3.5	8.5
2010	360648	69.2	17.4	4.0	9.4
2011	387043	70.2	16.8	4.6	8.4
2012	402138	68.5	17.0	4.8	9.7
2013	416913	67.4	17.1	5.3	10.2
2014	428334	65.8	17.3	5.6	11.3
2015	434113	63.8	18.4	5.8	12.0
2016	441492	62.2	18.7	6.1	13.0
2017	455827	60.6	18.9	6.9	13.6
2018	471925	59.0	18.9	7.6	14.5
2019	487488	57.7	19.0	8.0	15.3
2020	498314	56.9	18.8	8.4	15.9
2021	525896	55.9	18.6	8.8	16.7
2022	540956	56.0	18.0	8.4	17.6
2023	572000	55.3	18.3	8.5	17.9

9–3 综合能源平衡表
Overall Energy Balance Sheet

单位：万吨标准煤 (10 000 tce)

项 目	Item	1990	1995	2000	2005	2010	2015	2020	2021	2022
可供消费的能源总量	**Total Energy Available for Consumption**	**96138**	**129535**	**144234**	**254619**	**365588**	**431636**	**507479**	**533841**	**556234**
一次能源生产总量	Total Primary Energy Production	103922	129034	138570	229037	312125	362193	407295	427115	463808
回收能	Recovery of Energy		2312	3087	7452	8958				
进口量	Imports	1310	5456	14327	26823	57671	77695	124805	124807	120236
出口量(–)	Exports (-)	5875	6776	9327	11257	8803	9785	12838	13122	12197
年初年末库存差额	Stock Changes in the Year	-3219	-491	-2424	2564	-4363	1532	-11784	-4959	-15612
能源消费总量	**Total Energy Consumption**	**98703**	**131176**	**146964**	**261369**	**360648**	**434113**	**498314**	**525896**	**540956**
在总量中：	Consumption by Sector									
农、林、牧、渔业	Agriculture, Forestry, Animal Husbandry and Fishery	4852	5505	4233	6860	7266	8271	9263	9661	10090
工 业	Industry	67578	96191	103014	187914	261377	295953	332625	348551	363782
建筑业	Construction	1213	1335	2207	3486	5533	7545	9320	9608	8371
交通运输、仓储和邮政业	Transport, Storage and Post	4541	5863	11447	19136	27102	38510	41309	43935	40434
批发和零售业、住宿和餐饮业	Wholesale and Retail Trades, Hotels and Catering Services	1247	2018	3251	5917	7847	11447	13171	14898	15342
其 他	Other Sectors	3473	4519	6118	10484	15052	21925	28245	31762	32375
居民生活	Household Consumption	15799	15745	16695	27573	36470	50461	64380	67481	70563
在总量中：	Consumption by Usage									
终端消费	Final Consumption	94289	124252	140476	250877	337469	420110	488156	514744	530867
#工 业	Industry	63239	89473	96871	177775	238652	282291	322677	337621	353950
加工转换损失量	Losses During the Process of Energy Transformation	2264	3634	2472	3882	14294	18770	23020	24311	24800
#炼 焦	Coking	905		526	855	1595	4261	3938	3840	4005
炼油及煤制油	Petroleum Refining and Coal-to-liquids	326		781	1273	1960	2866	6132	6421	5904
回收能(–)	Recovery of Energy (-)						14492	23037	23296	24255
损失量	Other Losses	2150	3289	4016	6610	8885	9724	10175	10138	9543
平衡差额	**Balance**	**-2565**	**-1641**	**-2730**	**-6751**	**4940**	**-2477**	**9165**	**7945**	**15279**

注：进口量包括境内飞机和轮船在境外的加油量；出口量包括境外飞机和轮船在境内的加油量(以下相关表同)。

a) Data on imports include the domestic airplanes and ships refueling abroad. Data on exports include the oversea airplanes and ships refueling domestically. The same applies to the following tables.

9-4 石油平衡表
Petroleum Balance Sheet

单位：万吨 (10 000 tons)

项　目	Item	1990	1995	2000	2005	2010	2015	2020	2021	2022
可供量	**Available for Consumption**	**11435**	**16073**	**22631**	**32539**	**44178**	**55688**	**67554**	**69048**	**69538**
生产量	Production	13831	15004	16300	18135	20301	21456	19477	19888	20472
进口量	Imports	756	3673	9748	17163	29437	39749	61272	58820	58701
出口量(−)	Exports (-)	3110	2455	2172	2888	4079	5128	7551	7617	6704
年初年末库存差额	Stock Changes in the Year	-41	-151	-1245	129	-1481	-388	-5644	-2043	-2931
消费量	**Consumption**	**11486**	**16065**	**22496**	**32547**	**44101**	**55960**	**65369**	**68393**	**68049**
在消费量中：	Consumption by Sector									
农、林、牧、渔业	Agriculture, Forestry, Animal Husbandry and Fishery	1034	1203	789	1452	1383	1733	1773	1981	2024
工　业	Industry	7322	9349	11249	14030	18555	19718	27711	28219	31339
建筑业	Construction	327	243	841	1502	2483	3384	4180	4270	3454
交通运输、仓储和邮政业	Transport, Storage and Post	1683	2864	6399	10928	15079	20663	20481	21988	20006
批发和零售业、住宿和餐饮业	Wholesale and Retail Trades, Hotels and Catering Services	78	334	247	376	481	616	583	641	643
其　他	Other Sectors	758	1390	1636	1974	2578	3683	3470	3791	3532
居民生活	Household Consumption	285	682	1336	2284	3542	6162	7170	7505	7051
在消费量中：	Consumption by Usage									
终端消费	Final Consumption	9305	13676	19950	29496	41243	52946	62085	65630	65926
#工　业	Industry	5180	7096	8860	11108	15858	16740	24428	25457	29217
中间消费(用于加工转换)	Intermediate Consumption (Consumed in Transformation)	1630	2230	2353	2896	2663	2927	3266	2743	2099
火力发电	Thermal Power	1234	1359	1178	1306	385	266	322	324	242
供　热	Heating	356	400	427	429	593	493	678	678	698
制　气	Gas Production	40	52	26	14			29	61	63
炼油损失量	Losses in Petroleum Refining	296	420	722	1146	1685	2168	2233	1681	1096
损失量	Other Losses	255	159	193	155	194	88	18	20	24
平衡差额	**Balance**	**-51**	**8**	**135**	**-8**	**77**	**-272**	**2185**	**655**	**1489**

注：生产量为原油产量。
a) Data on production refer to the crude oil production.

9–5 煤炭平衡表
Coal Balance Sheet

单位：万吨 (10 000 tons)

项 目	Item	1990	1995	2000	2005	2010	2015	2020	2021	2022
可供量	**Available for Consumption**	**102221**	**133462**	**131895**	**235508**	**355578**	**397074**	**414519**	**440618**	**469122**
生产量	Production	107988	136073	138418	236515	342845	374654	390158	412583	455855
进口量	Imports	200	164	218	2622	18307	20406	30361	32327	29370
出口量(−)	Exports (-)	1729	2862	5506	7173	1911	534	319	261	401
年初年末库存差额	Stock Changes in the Year	-4239	87	-1235	3545	-3663	2547	-5680	-4031	-15703
消费量	**Consumption**	**105523**	**137677**	**135690**	**243375**	**349008**	**399834**	**404860**	**429576**	**448246**
在消费量中：	Consumption by Sector									
农、林、牧、渔业	Agriculture, Forestry, Animal Husbandry and Fishery	2095	1857	1051	1802	2147	2625	2254	1790	1722
工 业	Industry	81091	117571	121807	224766	329728	378190	390891	417585	437175
建筑业	Construction	438	440	537	604	731	878	639	444	369
交通运输、仓储和邮政业	Transport, Storage and Post	2161	1315	882	811	639	492	241	120	94
批发和零售业、住宿和餐饮业	Wholesale and Retail Trades, Hotels and Catering Services	1058	977	1461	2627	3192	3864	1981	1489	1331
其 他	Other Sectors	1980	1987	1495	2727	3412	4159	2571	2218	2004
居民生活	Household Consumption	16700	13530	8457	10039	9159	9627	6283	5929	5550
在消费量中：	Consumption by Usage									
终端消费	Final Consumption	60206	66156	50511	86386	114826	112975	72426	68828	71525
#工 业	Industry	35774	46050	36628	67776	95546	91331	58457	56838	60454
中间消费（用于加工转换）	Intermediate Consumption (Consumed in Transformation)	41258	69488	81987	152208	222948	267061	321133	350636	366548
#火力发电	Thermal Power	27204	44440	55811	103663	153742	179568	211635	233487	237813
供 热	Heating	2996	5887	8794	13542	17553	24115	36933	44185	50492
炼 焦	Coking	10698	18396	16496	33446	49950	60874	65968	65334	69449
煤制油	Coal-to-liquids					213	679	3047	3746	4046
制 气	Gas Production	360	764	960	1277	1040	1320	3309	3667	4710
洗选损耗	Losses in Coal Washing and Dressing	4059	2033	3191	4782	11235	19798	11301	10111	10173
平衡差额	**Balance**	**-3302**	**-4215**	**-3795**	**-7868**	**6569**	**-2760**	**9659**	**11043**	**20876**

注：生产量为原煤产量。
a) Data on production refer to the raw coal production.

9–6 电力平衡表
Electricity Balance Sheet

单位：亿千瓦时 (100 million kW·h)

项 目	Item	1990	1995	2000	2005	2010	2015	2020	2021	2022
可供量	**Available for Consumption**	**6230**	**10023**	**13473**	**24941**	**41936**	**58021**	**77620**	**85200**	**88358**
生产量	Production	6212	10077	13556	25003	42072	58146	77791	85343	88487
水 电	Hydropower	1267	1906	2224	3970	7222	11303	13552	13390	13522
火 电	Thermal Power	4945	8043	11142	20473	33319	42842	53303	58059	58888
核 电	Nuclear Power		128	167	531	739	1708	3663	4075	4178
风 电	Wind Power					446	1858	4665	6561	7627
进口量	Imports	19	6	15	50	55	62	48	59	71
出口量(−)	Exports (-)	1	60	99	112	191	187	218	202	201
消费量	**Consumption**	**6230**	**10023**	**13472**	**24940**	**41934**	**58020**	**77620**	**85200**	**88358**
在消费量中：	Consumption by Sector									
农、林、牧、渔业	Agriculture, Forestry, Animal Husbandry and Fishery	427	582	533	776	976	1040	1422	1597	1757
工 业	Industry	4873	7660	10005	18522	30872	41550	52353	56622	57412
建筑业	Construction	65	160	160	234	483	699	1011	1133	1091
交通运输、仓储和邮政业	Transport, Storage and Post	106	182	281	430	735	1126	1751	1993	2041
批发和零售业、住宿和餐饮业	Wholesale and Retail Trades, Hotels and Catering Services	76	200	419	752	1292	2122	3169	3870	4043
其 他	Other Sectors	202	234	623	1341	2452	3919	6517	7707	8077
居民生活	Household Consumption	481	1006	1452	2885	5125	7565	11397	12279	13936
在消费量中：	Consumption by Usage									
终端消费	Final Consumption	5796	9279	12536	23234	39366	55032	74387	81944	85295
#工 业	Industry	4439	6915	9068	16815	28304	38562	49120	53366	54350
输配电损失量	Losses in Transmission	435	745	937	1706	2568	2988	3234	3256	3063

9–7 能源生产弹性系数
Elasticity Ratio of Energy Production

年 份 Year	能源生产比上年增长 (%) Growth Rate of Energy Production over Preceding Year (%)	电力生产比上年增长 (%) Growth Rate of Electricity Production over Preceding Year(%)	国内生产总值比上年增长 (%) Growth Rate of Gross Domestic Product (GDP) over Preceding Year(%)	能源生产弹性系数 Elasticity Ratio of Energy Production	电力生产弹性系数 Elasticity Ratio of Electricity Production
1985	9.9	8.9	13.4	0.74	0.66
1990	2.2	6.2	3.9	0.56	1.59
1991	0.9	9.1	9.3	0.10	0.98
1992	2.3	11.3	14.2	0.16	0.80
1993	3.6	15.3	13.9	0.26	1.10
1994	6.9	10.7	13.0	0.53	0.82
1995	8.7	8.6	11.0	0.79	0.78
1996	3.1	7.2	9.9	0.31	0.73
1997	0.3	5.1	9.2	0.03	0.55
1998	-2.7	2.7	7.8		0.35
1999	1.6	6.3	7.7	0.21	0.82
2000	5.0	9.4	8.5	0.59	1.11
2001	6.4	9.2	8.3	0.77	1.11
2002	6.0	11.7	9.1	0.66	1.29
2003	14.1	15.5	10.0	1.41	1.55
2004	15.6	15.3	10.1	1.54	1.51
2005	11.1	13.5	11.4	0.97	1.18
2006	6.9	14.6	12.7	0.54	1.15
2007	7.9	14.5	14.2	0.56	1.02
2008	5.0	5.6	9.7	0.52	0.58
2009	3.1	7.1	9.4	0.33	0.76
2010	9.1	13.3	10.6	0.86	1.25
2011	9.0	12.0	9.6	0.94	1.25
2012	3.2	5.8	7.9	0.41	0.73
2013	2.2	8.9	7.8	0.28	1.14
2014	1.0	6.7	7.4	0.14	0.91
2015		0.3	7.0		0.04
2016	-4.5	5.5	6.8		0.81
2017	3.7	7.7	6.9	0.54	1.12
2018	5.6	8.5	6.7	0.84	1.27
2019	4.9	4.7	6.0	0.82	0.78
2020	2.5	3.7	2.2	1.14	1.68
2021	4.9	9.7	8.4	0.58	1.15
2022	8.6	3.7	3.0	2.87	1.23
2023	4.2	6.9	5.2	0.81	1.33

注：国内生产总值增长速度按不变价格计算(以下相关表同)。

a) The growth rates of GDP are calculated at constant prices. The same applies to the following tables.

9–8 能源消费弹性系数
Elasticity Ratio of Energy Consumption

年 份 Year	能源消费 比上年增长(%) Growth Rate of Energy Consumption over Preceding Year (%)	电力消费 比上年增长(%) Growth Rate of Electricity Consumption over Preceding Year(%)	国内生产总值 比上年增长(%) Growth Rate of Gross Domestic Product (GDP) over Preceding Year(%)	能源消费 弹性系数 Elasticity Ratio of Energy Consumption	电力消费 弹性系数 Elasticity Ratio of Electricity Consumption
1985	8.1	9.0	13.4	0.60	0.67
1990	1.8	6.2	3.9	0.46	1.59
1991	5.1	9.2	9.3	0.55	0.99
1992	5.2	11.5	14.2	0.37	0.81
1993	6.3	11.0	13.9	0.45	0.79
1994	5.8	9.9	13.0	0.45	0.76
1995	6.9	8.2	11.0	0.63	0.75
1996	3.1	7.4	9.9	0.31	0.75
1997	0.5	4.8	9.2	0.05	0.52
1998	0.2	2.8	7.8	0.03	0.36
1999	3.2	6.1	7.7	0.42	0.79
2000	4.5	9.5	8.5	0.53	1.12
2001	5.8	9.3	8.3	0.70	1.12
2002	9.0	11.8	9.1	0.99	1.30
2003	16.2	15.6	10.0	1.62	1.56
2004	16.8	15.4	10.1	1.66	1.52
2005	13.5	13.5	11.4	1.18	1.18
2006	9.6	14.6	12.7	0.76	1.15
2007	8.7	14.4	14.2	0.61	1.01
2008	2.9	5.6	9.7	0.30	0.58
2009	4.8	7.2	9.4	0.51	0.77
2010	7.3	13.2	10.6	0.69	1.25
2011	7.3	12.1	9.6	0.76	1.26
2012	3.9	5.9	7.9	0.49	0.75
2013	3.7	8.9	7.8	0.47	1.14
2014	2.7	6.7	7.4	0.36	0.91
2015	1.3	0.3	7.0	0.19	0.04
2016	1.7	5.5	6.8	0.25	0.81
2017	3.2	7.7	6.9	0.46	1.12
2018	3.5	8.5	6.7	0.52	1.27
2019	3.3	4.7	6.0	0.55	0.78
2020	2.2	3.7	2.2	1.00	1.68
2021	5.5	9.8	8.4	0.65	1.17
2022	2.9	3.7	3.0	0.97	1.23
2023	5.7	6.7	5.2	1.10	1.29

注：2023年电力消费数据来源于中国电力企业联合会。
a) The electricity consumption data of 2023 are from China Electricity Council.

9–9 按行业分能源消费量（2022年）

行 业	Sector	能源消费总量（万吨标准煤） Total Energy Consumption (10 000 tce)
消 费 总 量	**Total Consumption**	**540956**
农、林、牧、渔业	**Agriculture, Forestry, Animal Husbandry and Fishery**	**10090**
工业	**Industry**	**363782**
采矿业	**Mining**	**18258**
煤炭开采和洗选业	Mining and Washing of Coal	8811
石油和天然气开采业	Extraction of Petroleum and Natural Gas	4461
黑色金属矿采选业	Mining and Processing of Ferrous Metal Ores	1757
有色金属矿采选业	Mining and Processing of Non-ferrous Metal Ores	1114
非金属矿采选业	Mining and Processing of Non-metal Ores	1209
开采专业及辅助性活动	Professional and Support Activities for Mining	406
其他采矿业	Mining of Other Ores	499
制造业	**Manufacturing**	**307086**
农副食品加工业	Processing of Food from Agricultural Products	4296
食品制造业	Manufacture of Foods	2769
酒、饮料和精制茶制造业	Manufacture of Alcohol, Beverages and Refined Tea	1339
烟草制品业	Manufacture of Tobacco	192
纺织业	Manufacture of Textile	7268
纺织服装、服饰业	Manufacture of Textile, Wearing Apparel and Accessories	912
皮革、毛皮、羽毛及其制品和制鞋业	Manufacture of Leather, Fur, Feather and Related Products and Footwear	531
木材加工和木、竹、藤、棕、草制品业	Processing of Timber, Manufacture of Wood, Bamboo, Rattan, Palm and Straw Products	1094
家具制造业	Manufacture of Furniture	439
造纸和纸制品业	Manufacture of Paper and Paper Products	4462
印刷和记录媒介复制业	Printing and Reproduction of Recording Media	550
文教、工美、体育和娱乐用品制造业	Manufacture of Articles for Culture, Education, Arts and Crafts, Sport and Entertainment Activities	460
石油、煤炭及其他燃料加工业	Processing of Petroleum, Coal and Other Fuels	41969
化学原料和化学制品制造业	Manufacture of Raw Chemical Materials and Chemical Products	66327
医药制造业	Manufacture of Medicines	2603
化学纤维制造业	Manufacture of Chemical Fibers	2634
橡胶和塑料制品业	Manufacture of Rubber and Plastics Products	5380
非金属矿物制品业	Manufacture of Non-metallic Mineral Products	37049
黑色金属冶炼和压延加工业	Smelting and Pressing of Ferrous Metals	66011
有色金属冶炼和压延加工业	Smelting and Pressing of Non-ferrous Metals	27663
金属制品业	Manufacture of Metal Products	6451
通用设备制造业	Manufacture of General Purpose Machinery	4199
专用设备制造业	Manufacture of Special Purpose Machinery	1903
汽车制造业	Manufacture of Automobiles	4781
铁路、船舶、航空航天和其他运输设备制造业	Manufacture of Railway, Ship, Aerospace and Other Transport Equipments	975
电气机械和器材制造业	Manufacture of Electrical Machinery and Apparatus	4632
计算机、通信和其他电子设备制造业	Manufacture of Computers, Communication and Other Electronic Equipment	6721
仪器仪表制造业	Manufacture of Measuring Instruments and Machinery	298
其他制造业	Other Manufacture	2334
废弃资源综合利用业	Utilization of Waste Resources	727
金属制品、机械和设备修理业	Repair Service of Metal Products, Machinery and Equipment	115
电力、热力、燃气及水生产和供应业	**Production and Supply of Electricity, Heat, Gas and Water**	**38438**
电力、热力生产和供应业	Production and Supply of Electric Power and Heat Power	34378
燃气生产和供应业	Production and Supply of Gas	1792
水的生产和供应业	Production and Supply of Water	2268
建筑业	**Construction**	**8371**
交通运输、仓储和邮政业	**Transport, Storage and Post**	**40434**
批发和零售业、住宿和餐饮业	**Wholesale and Retail Trades, Hotels and Catering Services**	**15342**
其他	**Others**	**32375**
居民生活	**Household Consumption**	**70563**

注：本表中“空格”表示该项统计指标数据不足本表最小位数、数据不详或无该项数据。

Energy Consumption by Sector (2022)

煤炭 (万吨) Coal (10 000 tons)	焦炭 (万吨) Coke (10 000 tons)	原油 (万吨) Crude Oil (10 000 tons)	汽油 (万吨) Gasoline (10 000 tons)	煤油 (万吨) Kerosene (10 000 tons)	柴油 (万吨) Diesel Oil (10 000 tons)	燃料油 (万吨) Fuel Oil (10 000 tons)	天然气 (亿立方米) Natural Gas (100 million cu.m)	电力 (亿千瓦时) Electricity (100 million kW·h)
448246	**46395**	**70023**	**13277**	**2074**	**15782**	**5471**	**3747**	**88358**
1722	**1**		**278**	**12**	**1724**	**1**	**2**	**1757**
437175	**46392**	**70022**	**307**	**8**	**1645**	**3264**	**2676**	**57412**
16568	**223**	**681**	**12**	**1**	**545**	**2**	**231**	**2697**
15447	8		3		184		25	951
68		680	5	1	42		198	557
270	200		1		54			433
72	4		1		22	1	1	340
655	11		1		81		4	219
39			2		161		4	33
16					0			165
166819	**46033**	**69342**	**275**	**7**	**1015**	**3255**	**1765**	**44220**
1041	12		4		17	2	39	947
2014	11		4		9	1	37	380
512	3		1		4	2	20	202
3					1		2	54
491	5		2		7	5	48	1777
10			2		6	1	11	249
14			1		4	1	3	155
11			1		7		4	310
1			1		4		3	133
3282	2		1		16	8	22	901
23			2		10		6	143
6			1		5		12	94
60013	94	66372	176		219	2367	184	1598
25963	4324	2967	10	1	68	700	544	6612
643	1		2		6	3	22	523
1072	1				2	2	20	502
242	6		5		17	5	20	1609
25438	1027	3	9		365	132	260	4019
29929	39357		1		56	5	147	6861
15354	475		2	1	43	7	77	7782
212	455		7		25	2	73	1649
7	190		9	1	21		28	1213
18			7	1	13	1	16	547
55	14		10		15		35	1420
58			2	1	19	4	32	164
26			7		20	3	25	1410
185			5		15		52	1989
2			2		2		1	92
1					3	1	2	778
149	57				9	1	20	92
45				1	5		1	15
253788	**135**		**20**		**85**	**7**	**680**	**10495**
251356	135		16		80	7	640	9542
2403			2		1		39	193
29			2		3		1	761
369	**2**	**1**	**544**	**25**	**532**	**41**	**4**	**1091**
94			**5846**	**1809**	**10058**	**2149**	**340**	**2041**
1331			**287**	**24**	**226**	**10**	**74**	**4043**
2004			**2249**	**194**	**989**	**5**	**62**	**8077**
5550			**3766**	**2**	**608**		**589**	**13936**

a) The (blank space) indicates that the figure is not large enough to be measured with the smallest unit in the table, or data are unknown or are not available.

9−10 能源加工转换效率
Efficiency of Energy Transformation

单位：%　　　　(%)

年 份 Year	总效率 Total Efficiency	发电及供热 Power Generation and Heating	炼 焦 Coking	炼油及煤制油 Petroleum Refining and Coal-to-liquids
1983	69.9	36.9	91.2	99.2
1984	69.2	37.0	90.1	99.2
1985	68.3	36.9	90.8	99.1
1986	68.3	36.7	90.6	99.0
1987	67.5	36.8	90.5	98.8
1988	66.5	36.3	90.8	98.8
1989	66.5	36.7	90.3	98.6
1990	66.5	37.3	91.3	90.2
1991	65.9	37.6	89.9	98.1
1992	66.0	37.8	92.7	96.8
1993	67.3	39.9	98.1	98.5
1994	65.2	39.4	89.6	97.5
1995	71.1	37.3	92.0	97.7
1996	70.2	36.6	94.1	97.5
1997	69.8	35.9	94.0	97.4
1998	69.3	37.1	95.0	96.4
1999	69.3	37.0	96.1	97.5
2000	69.4	37.8	96.2	97.3
2001	69.7	38.2	96.5	97.6
2002	69.0	38.7	96.6	96.7
2003	69.4	38.5	96.1	96.4
2004	70.6	38.6	97.1	96.5
2005	71.1	39.0	97.1	96.9
2006	70.9	39.1	97.0	96.9
2007	71.2	39.8	97.5	97.2
2008	71.5	40.5	98.5	96.2
2009	72.4	41.2	98.0	96.7
2010	72.5	42.0	96.4	97.0
2011	72.2	42.1	96.3	97.4
2012	72.7	42.8	95.7	97.1
2013	73.0	43.1	95.6	97.7
2014	73.1	43.5	93.7	97.5
2015	73.4	44.2	92.1	96.9
2016	73.5	44.6	92.8	96.4
2017	73.0	45.0	92.8	96.0
2018	72.8	45.5	92.4	95.6
2019	73.3	45.8	92.6	95.3
2020	73.7	46.2	93.1	95.3
2021	73.2	47.1	93.2	95.4
2022	73.2	47.9	93.3	95.5

9−11 平均每天能源消费量
Average Daily Energy Consumption

能源品种	Type of Energy	1990	1995	2000	2005	2010	2015	2020	2021	2022
合计 （万吨标准煤）	**Total (10 000 tce)**	**270.4**	**359.4**	**401.5**	**716.1**	**988.1**	**1189.4**	**1361.5**	**1440.8**	**1482.1**
煤炭 （万吨）	Coal (10 000 tons)	289.1	377.2	370.7	666.8	956.2	1095.4	1106.2	1176.9	1228.1
焦炭 （万吨）	Coke (10 000 tons)	18.9	29.4	29.6	68.8	106.0	120.7	132.0	127.8	127.1
原油 （万吨）	Crude Oil (10 000 tons)	32.2	40.8	58.0	82.4	117.5	150.1	189.8	198.1	191.8
燃料油 （万吨）	Fuel Oil (10 000 tons)	9.2	10.2	10.6	11.6	10.3	12.8	14.7	15.0	15.0
汽油 （万吨）	Gasoline (10 000 tons)	5.2	8.0	9.6	13.3	19.1	31.1	34.9	39.0	36.4
煤油 （万吨）	Kerosene (10 000 tons)	1.0	1.4	2.4	3.0	4.8	7.3	9.2	9.6	5.7
柴油 （万吨）	Diesel Oil (10 000 tons)	7.4	11.8	18.6	30.1	40.3	47.6	39.0	41.6	43.2
天然气 （亿立方米）	Natural Gas (100 million cu.m)	0.4	0.5	0.7	1.3	3.0	5.3	9.1	10.3	10.3
电力 （亿千瓦时）	Electricity (100 million kW·h)	17.1	27.5	36.8	68.3	114.9	159.0	212.1	233.4	242.1

9−12 居民生活能源消费量
Household Energy Consumption

能源品种	Type of Energy	1990	1995	2000	2005	2010	2015	2020	2021	2022
合计 （万吨标准煤）	**Total (10 000 tce)**	**15799**	**15745**	**16695**	**27573**	**36470**	**50461**	**64380**	**67481**	**70563**
煤炭 （万吨）	Coal (10 000 tons)	16700	13530	8457	10039	9159	9627	6283	5929	5550
煤油 （万吨）	Kerosene (10 000 tons)	105	64	72	25	21	29	12	3	2
液化石油气 （万吨）	Liquefied Petroleum Gas (10 000 tons)	159	534	858	1329	1537	2549	2860	2732	2674
天然气 （亿立方米）	Natural Gas (100 million cu.m)	19	19	32	79	227	360	560	592	589
煤气 （亿立方米）	Coal Gas (100 million cu.m)	29	57	126	145	167	80	50	43	37
热力 （万百万千焦）	Heat (10 billion kilo-joule)	8972	12637	23234	52044	67410	93841	141349	158018	165428
电力 （亿千瓦时）	Electricity (100 million kW·h)	481	1006	1452	2885	5125	7565	11396	12279	13936

9-13 人均生活能源消费量
Household Energy Consumption Per Capita

年 份 Year	人均生活能源消费量(千克标准煤) Household Energy Consumption per Capita (kgce)	煤 炭(千克) Coal (kg)	电 力(千瓦时) Electricity (kW·h)	液化石油气(千克) Liquefied Petroleum Gas (kg)	天然气(立方米) Natural Gas (cu.m)	煤 气(立方米) Coal Gas (cu.m)
1983	107	128	13	0.6	0.1	1.5
1984	113	135	15	0.6	0.4	1.6
1985	127	149	21	0.9	0.4	1.3
1986	127	148	23	1.1	0.6	1.3
1987	132	152	26	1.1	0.7	1.6
1988	141	159	31	1.2	1.4	1.6
1989	139	152	35	1.4	1.5	2.4
1990	139	147	42	1.4	1.6	2.5
1991	139	143	47	1.8	1.6	3.2
1992	134	127	55	2.1	1.8	4.4
1993	133	123	63	2.5	1.5	4.6
1994	129	109	73	3.2	1.7	6.3
1995	131	112	83	4.4	1.6	4.7
1996	121	83	88	5.9	1.7	6.4
1997	119	77	99	6.2	1.7	8.9
1998	119	73	104	6.9	1.9	9.7
1999	122	70	109	6.8	2.1	9.3
2000	132	67	115	6.8	2.6	10.0
2001	136	66	127	6.7	3.3	9.4
2002	146	66	138	7.6	3.6	9.8
2003	166	70	160	8.6	4.0	10.1
2004	191	75	184	10.4	5.2	10.7
2005	211	77	221	10.2	6.1	11.1
2006	230	77	256	11.5	7.8	12.7
2007	250	74	308	12.4	10.9	14.1
2008	254	69	332	11.0	12.8	13.9
2009	264	69	366	11.2	13.3	12.5
2010	273	68	383	11.5	17.0	12.5
2011	294	68	418	11.9	19.7	10.9
2012	312	68	459	12.1	21.3	10.1
2013	334	68	513	13.5	23.7	7.9
2014	344	68	523	15.8	25.0	7.1
2015	366	70	548	18.5	26.1	5.8
2016	392	68	607	21.3	27.4	4.5
2017	412	66	650	23.1	30.1	3.7
2018	431	55	717	22.4	33.4	3.4
2019	438	47	756	20.3	35.7	3.3
2020	456	45	808	20.3	39.7	3.5
2021	478	42	869	19.3	41.9	3.1
2022	500	39	987	18.9	41.7	2.6

注：1.计算消费量所使用的人口数为平均人口数。
2.2011—2019年数据根据第七次全国人口普查结果修订。

a) Data in the table are calculated with the data on the annual average population.
b) Data from 2011 to 2019 were revised based on the results of the Seventh National Population Census.

9-14 分地区用电量
Electricity Consumption by Region

单位：亿千瓦时 (100 million kW·h)

地 区	Region	1995	2000	2005	2010	2015	2020	2022	2023
北 京	Beijing	262	384	571	810	953	1140	1281	1358
天 津	Tianjin	179	234	385	646	801	875	991	1051
河 北	Hebei	603	809	1502	2692	3176	3934	4344	4757
山 西	Shanxi	399	502	946	1460	1737	2342	2721	2885
内蒙古	Inner Mongolia	187	254	668	1537	2543	3900	4291	4823
辽 宁	Liaoning	623	749	1111	1715	1985	2423	2551	2663
吉 林	Jilin	268	291	378	577	652	805	852	928
黑龙江	Heilongjiang	409	442	556	748	869	1014	1139	1184
上 海	Shanghai	403	559	922	1296	1406	1576	1746	1849
江 苏	Jiangsu	685	971	2193	3864	5115	6374	7400	7833
浙 江	Zhejiang	440	738	1642	2821	3554	4830	5799	6192
安 徽	Anhui	289	339	582	1078	1640	2428	2993	3214
福 建	Fujian	261	402	757	1315	1852	2483	2900	3090
江 西	Jiangxi	181	208	392	701	1087	1627	1983	2026
山 东	Shandong	741	1001	1912	3298	5117	6940	7559	7966
河 南	Henan	571	719	1353	2354	2880	3392	3908	4090
湖 北	Hubei	415	503	789	1330	1665	2144	2648	2706
湖 南	Hunan	375	406	674	1172	1448	1929	2236	2277
广 东	Guangdong	788	1335	2674	4060	5311	6926	7870	8502
广 西	Guangxi	221	314	510	993	1334	2029	2217	2449
海 南	Hainan	32	38	82	159	272	363	415	482
重 庆	Chongqing		308	348	626	875	1186	1404	1453
四 川	Sichuan	583	521	943	1549	1992	2865	3447	3711
贵 州	Guizhou	204	288	487	835	1174	1586	1743	1783
云 南	Yunnan	224	274	557	1004	1439	2025	2390	2513
西 藏	Xizang				20	41	82	119	135
陕 西	Shaanxi	240	293	516	859	1222	1741	2372	2450
甘 肃	Gansu	241	295	489	804	1099	1376	1501	1645
青 海	Qinghai	69	109	207	465	658	742	922	1018
宁 夏	Ningxia	92	136	303	547	878	1038	1250	1387
新 疆	Xinjiang	120	183	310	662	2160	3099	3487	3821

注：2000年及以后数据来源于中国电力企业联合会，2023年为快报数。
a) Data since 2000 are from China Electricity Council. The data for 2023 are in the form of express reports.

9–15 发电装机容量
Installed Capacity of Power Generation

单位：万千瓦 (10 000 kW)

年份 Year	发电装机容量 Installed Capacity of Power Generation	火电 Thermal Power	水电 Hydropower	核电 Nuclear Power	风电 Wind Power	太阳能发电 Solar Power	其他 Others
2000	31932	23754	7935	210	34		
2001	33849	25301	8301	210	38		
2002	35657	26555	8607	447	47		
2003	39141	28977	9490	619	55		
2004	44239	32948	10524	696	82		
2005	51718	39138	11739	696	106		
2006	62370	48382	13029	696	207		
2007	71822	55607	14823	908	420		
2008	79273	60286	17260	908	839		
2009	87410	65108	19629	908	1760	3	3
2010	96641	70967	21606	1082	2958	26	3
2011	106253	76834	23298	1257	4623	212	19
2012	114676	81968	24947	1257	6142	341	20
2013	125768	87009	28044	1466	7652	1589	8
2014	137887	93232	30486	2008	9657	2486	19
2015	152527	100554	31954	2717	13075	4218	9
2016	165051	106094	33207	3364	14747	7631	7
2017	177708	110495	34359	3582	16325	12942	7
2018	189997	114408	35259	4466	18427	17433	5
2019	200985	118957	35804	4874	20915	20429	5
2020	220504	124960	37028	4989	28165	25356	5
2021	237689	129739	39094	5326	32871	30654	5
2022	256317	133527	41396	5557	36564	39268	5
2023	292224	139099	42237	5691	44144	61048	5

注：数据来源于中国电力企业联合会。
a) The data are from China Electricity Council.

9-16 万元国内生产总值能源消费量
Energy Intensity of GDP

年 份 Year	万元国内生产总值能源消费量(吨标准煤/万元) Total (tce/10 000 yuan)	万元国内生产总值煤炭消费量(吨/万元) Coal (ton/10 000 yuan)	万元国内生产总值焦炭消费量(吨/万元) Coke (ton/10 000 yuan)	万元国内生产总值石油消费量(吨/万元) Petroleum (ton/10 000 yuan)	万元国内生产总值原油消费量(吨/万元) Crude Oil (ton/10 000 yuan)	万元国内生产总值燃料油消费量(吨/万元) Fuel Oil (ton/10 000 yuan)	万元国内生产总值电力消费量(万千瓦时/万元) Electricity (10 000 kW·h/10 000 yuan)
	国内生产总值按1980年可比价格计算 GDP at 1980 constant price						
1980	13.14	13.30	0.94	1.91	2.01	0.67	0.66
1981	12.33	12.56	0.81	1.93	1.81	0.59	0.64
1982	11.81	12.20	0.76	1.56	1.65	0.53	0.62
1983	11.34	11.80	0.71	1.44	1.56	0.49	0.60
1984	10.57	11.18	0.66	1.29	1.37	0.43	0.56
1985	10.08	10.72	0.62	1.21	1.25	0.37	0.54
1986	9.75	10.38	0.63	1.17	1.23	0.36	0.54
1987	9.36	10.03	0.62	1.11	1.15	0.34	0.54
1988	9.03	9.65	0.59	1.08	1.09	0.31	0.53
1989	9.04	9.64	0.59	1.08	1.08	0.32	0.55
1990	8.85	9.47	0.62	1.03	1.06	0.30	0.56
	国内生产总值按1990年可比价格计算 GDP at 1990 constant price						
1990	5.23	5.59	0.37	0.61	0.62	0.18	0.33
1991	5.03	5.36	0.35	0.60	0.60	0.17	0.33
1992	4.63	4.84	0.33	0.57	0.56	0.15	0.32
1993	4.32	4.51	0.33	0.55	0.52	0.14	0.31
1994	4.05	4.24	0.30	0.49	0.46	0.12	0.31
1995	3.90	4.09	0.32	0.48	0.44	0.11	0.30
1996	3.66	3.79	0.32	0.48	0.43	0.10	0.29
1997	3.36	3.41	0.27	0.48	0.43	0.09	0.28
1998	3.13	3.10	0.26	0.45	0.40	0.09	0.27
1999	3.00	2.97	0.23	0.45	0.40	0.08	0.26
2000	2.89	2.67	0.21	0.44	0.42	0.08	0.26
	国内生产总值按2000年可比价格计算 GDP at 2000 constant price						
2000	1.47	1.35	0.11	0.22	0.21	0.04	0.13
2001	1.43	1.32	0.11	0.21	0.20	0.04	0.14
2002	1.43	1.30	0.11	0.21	0.19	0.03	0.14
2003	1.51	1.41	0.12	0.21	0.19	0.03	0.15
2004	1.60	1.48	0.13	0.22	0.20	0.03	0.15
2005	1.63	1.52	0.16	0.20	0.19	0.03	0.16
	国内生产总值按2005年可比价格计算 GDP at 2005 constant price						
2005	1.40	1.30	0.13	0.17	0.16	0.02	0.13
2006	1.36	1.28	0.13	0.17	0.15	0.02	0.14
2007	1.29	1.20	0.13	0.15	0.14	0.02	0.14
2008	1.21	1.14	0.12	0.14	0.13	0.01	0.13
2009	1.16	1.12	0.13	0.13	0.13	0.01	0.13
2010	1.13	1.09	0.12	0.14	0.13	0.01	0.13
	国内生产总值按2010年可比价格计算 GDP at 2010 constant price						
2010	0.88	0.85	0.09	0.11	0.10	0.01	0.10
2011	0.86	0.86	0.09	0.10	0.10	0.01	0.10
2012	0.83	0.85	0.09	0.10	0.10	0.01	0.10
2013	0.79	0.81	0.09	0.10	0.09	0.01	0.10
2014	0.76	0.73	0.08	0.09	0.09	0.01	0.10
2015	0.72	0.66	0.07	0.09	0.09	0.01	0.10
	国内生产总值按2015年可比价格计算 GDP at 2015 constant price						
2015	0.63	0.58	0.06	0.08	0.08	0.01	0.08
2016	0.60	0.53	0.06	0.08	0.08	0.01	0.08
2017	0.58	0.50	0.06	0.08	0.08	0.01	0.08
2018	0.56	0.47	0.05	0.07	0.07	0.01	0.09
2019	0.55	0.45	0.05	0.07	0.08	0.01	0.08
2020	0.55	0.44	0.05	0.07	0.08	0.01	0.09
	国内生产总值按2020年可比价格计算 GDP at 2020 constant price						
2020	0.49	0.40	0.05	0.06	0.07	0.01	0.08
2021	0.48	0.39	0.04	0.06	0.07	0.00	0.08
2022	0.48	0.40	0.04	0.06	0.06	0.00	0.08

9-17 主要能源产品产量
Output of Main Energy Products

产品名称		Item		2022	2023
原煤	(亿吨)	Coal	(100 million tons)	45.59	47.23
原油	(万吨)	Crude Oil	(10 000 tons)	20472.24	20902.61
天然气	(亿立方米)	Natural Gas	(100 million cu.m)	2201.10	2324.30
汽油	(万吨)	Gasoline	(10 000 tons)	14634.55	16253.88
柴油	(万吨)	Diesel Oil	(10 000 tons)	19290.07	21918.26
焦炭	(万吨)	Coke	(10 000 tons)	47343.64	49260.00
发电量	(亿千瓦时)	Electricity Generation	(100 million kW·h)	88487.12	94564.42
#火电	(亿千瓦时)	Thermal Power	(100 million kW·h)	58887.95	62657.40
水电	(亿千瓦时)	Hydropower	(100 million kW·h)	13521.95	12858.48

注：1.原煤包括无烟煤、烟煤、褐煤，不包括石煤。
2.原油包括天然原油和人造原油。
a) Coal includes anthracite, bituminous coal and lignite, but excludes stone coal.
b) Crude oil includes natural and synthetic crude oil.

9-18 人均主要能源产品产量
Per Capita Output of Main Energy Products

年份 Year	原煤 (吨) Coal (ton)	原油 (公斤) Crude Oil (kg)	发电量 (千瓦时) Electricity Generation (kW·h)
1978	0.65	108.82	268.36
1980	0.63	107.97	306.35
1985	0.83	118.83	390.76
1990	0.95	121.84	547.22
1995	1.13	124.53	836.39
1996	1.15	129.22	888.10
1997	1.13	130.68	923.16
1998	1.07	129.64	939.66
1999	1.09	127.72	989.28
2000	1.10	129.09	1073.62
2001	1.16	128.91	1164.29
2002	1.21	130.43	1291.78
2003	1.42	131.64	1482.91
2004	1.64	135.70	1699.99
2005	1.81	139.10	1917.79
2006	1.96	140.93	2185.88
2007	2.09	141.38	2490.01
2008	2.19	143.77	2617.20
2009	2.34	142.34	2790.33
2010	2.56	151.76	3145.06
2011	2.80	150.83	3504.01
2012	2.91	153.21	3683.05
2013	2.92	153.98	3984.36
2014	2.82	154.12	4223.80
2015	2.72	155.49	4213.89
2016	2.46	143.89	4419.37
2017	2.52	137.16	4730.25
2018	2.64	134.97	5108.60
2019	2.73	136.12	5330.10
2020	2.77	138.03	5512.76
2021	2.92	140.81	6042.54
2022	3.23	144.97	6266.02
2023	3.35	148.17	6703.32

注：1.计算消费量所使用的人口数为平均人口数。
2.2011—2019年数据根据第七次全国人口普查结果修订。
a) Data in the table are calculated with the data on the annual average population.
b) Data from 2011 to 2019 were revised based on the results of the Seventh National Population Census.

9-19 分地区主要能源产品产量
Output of Main Energy Products by Region

年 份 Year 地 区 Region		原 煤 (亿吨) Coal (100 million tons)	天然气 (亿立方米) Natural Gas (100 million cu.m)	焦 炭 (万吨) Coke (10 000 tons)	发电量 (亿千瓦时) Electricity Generation (100 million kW·h)	#水 电 Hydropower
	1978	6.18	137.30	4690.00	2565.50	445.88
	1980	6.20	142.70	4343.00	3006.30	582.10
	1985	8.72	129.30	4802.10	4106.90	923.70
	1990	10.80	152.98	7328.30	6212.00	1267.20
	1995	13.61	179.47	13424.49	10077.30	1905.77
	2000	13.84	272.00	12184.02	13556.00	2224.14
	2005	23.65	493.20	26511.70	25002.60	3970.17
	2006	25.70	585.53	30074.36	28657.26	4357.86
	2007	27.60	692.40	33105.28	32815.53	4852.64
	2008	29.03	802.99	32313.94	34668.82	5851.87
	2009	31.15	852.69	35744.05	37146.51	6156.44
	2010	34.28	957.91	38657.83	42071.60	7221.72
	2011	37.64	1053.37	43433.00	47130.19	6989.45
	2012	39.45	1106.08	43831.45	49875.53	8721.07
	2013	39.74	1208.58	48179.38	54316.35	9202.92
	2014	38.74	1301.57	47980.86	57944.57	10728.82
	2015	37.47	1346.10	44822.54	58145.73	11302.70
	2016	34.11	1368.65	44911.48	61331.60	11840.48
	2017	35.24	1480.35	43142.55	66044.47	11978.65
	2018	36.98	1601.59	44834.20	71661.33	12317.87
	2019	38.46	1753.62	47126.16	75034.28	13044.38
	2020	39.02	1924.95	47116.12	77790.60	13552.09
	2021	41.26	2075.84	46445.78	85342.48	13389.99
	2022	45.59	2201.10	47343.64	88487.12	13521.95
	2023	47.23	2324.30	49260.00	94564.42	12858.48
北 京	Beijing		1.22		471.55	8.41
天 津	Tianjin		41.67	169.90	837.45	0.11
河 北	Hebei	0.46	5.88	4315.68	4125.94	58.29
山 西	Shanxi	13.78	145.92	9571.56	4572.79	38.15
内蒙古	Inner Mongolia	12.42	305.66	5069.26	7629.94	44.74
辽 宁	Liaoning	0.29	8.32	2065.47	2362.91	65.24
吉 林	Jilin	0.09	19.27	499.43	1158.73	98.46
黑龙江	Heilongjiang	0.70	59.45	889.34	1327.41	44.61
上 海	Shanghai		36.10	526.69	1006.63	
江 苏	Jiangsu	0.08	0.75	1833.37	6390.53	30.99
浙 江	Zhejiang			220.63	4580.70	210.33
安 徽	Anhui	1.12	2.63	1374.93	3549.45	86.60
福 建	Fujian	0.04		243.00	3302.52	368.51
江 西	Jiangxi	0.02	0.07	705.03	1852.60	159.94
山 东	Shandong	0.87	8.46	3067.68	6508.08	37.89
河 南	Henan	1.03	4.38	2240.68	3534.64	129.50
湖 北	Hubei	0.01	1.73	987.32	3206.02	1312.61
湖 南	Hunan	0.09	0.04	660.73	1797.48	376.28
广 东	Guangdong		123.65	767.45	7010.32	370.16
广 西	Guangxi	0.04	0.36	1300.96	2382.92	400.46
海 南	Hainan		34.96		478.89	21.17
重 庆	Chongqing		95.56	333.82	1120.21	224.36
四 川	Sichuan	0.21	602.00	977.61	5006.49	3863.44
贵 州	Guizhou	1.33	10.50	313.21	2368.80	431.62
云 南	Yunnan	0.75	0.23	1239.94	4151.01	3078.76
西 藏	Xizang				163.02	132.14
陕 西	Shaanxi	7.62	328.48	4565.21	3103.75	126.58
甘 肃	Gansu	0.60	7.52	560.32	2108.97	373.49
青 海	Qinghai	0.08	60.00	18.03	1009.71	398.33
宁 夏	Ningxia	0.99	2.23	1351.91	2314.28	17.05
新 疆	Xinjiang	4.60	417.27	3390.85	5130.66	350.26

主要统计指标解释

一次能源生产总量 指一定时期内，全国一次能源生产量的总和。该指标是观察全国能源生产水平、规模、构成和发展速度的总量指标。包括：原煤、原油、天然气、水电、核能及其他动力能(如风能、地热能等)发电量等，不包括低热值燃料生产量和由一次能源加工转换而成的二次能源产量。

能源消费总量 指一定地域内，国民经济各行业和居民家庭在一定时期内消费的各种能源的总和。包括：原煤、原油、天然气、水能、核能、风能、太阳能、地热能、生物质能等一次能源；一次能源通过加工转换产生的洗煤、焦炭、煤气、电力、热力、成品油等二次能源和同时产生的其他产品；其他化石能源、可再生能源和新能源。其中水能、风能、太阳能、地热能、生物质能等可再生能源，是指人们通过一定技术手段获得的，并作为商品能源使用的部分。在核算过程中，一次能源、二次能源消费不能重复计算。能源消费总量分为终端能源消费量、能源加工转换损失量和能源损失量三部分。

(1)终端能源消费量：指一定时期内，用于消费（而非用于加工转换产出其他能源）的各种能源之和。

(2)能源加工转换损失量：指一定时期内，全国投入加工转换的各种能源数量之和与产出各种能源产品之和的差额。该指标是观察能源在加工转换过程中损失量变化的指标。

(3)能源损失量：指一定时期内，能源在输送、分配、储存过程中发生的损失和由客观原因造成的各种损失量，不包括各种气体能源放空、放散量。

能源生产弹性系数 是研究能源生产增长速度与国民经济增长速度之间关系的指标。计算公式为：

$$能源生产弹性系数=\frac{能源生产量年平均增长速度}{国民经济年平均增长速度}$$

国民经济年平均增长速度，可根据不同的目的或需要，用国民生产总值、国内生产总值等指标来计算，本书是采用国内生产总值指标计算。

电力生产弹性系数 是研究电力生产增长速度与国民经济增长速度之间关系的指标。计算公式为：

$$电力生产弹性系数=\frac{电力生产量年平均增长速度}{国民经济年平均增长速度}$$

能源消费弹性系数 反映能源消费增长速度与国民经济增长速度之间关系的指标。计算公式为：

$$能源消费弹性系数=\frac{能源消费量年平均增长速度}{国民经济年平均增长速度}$$

电力消费弹性系数 反映电力消费增长速度与国民经济增长速度之间关系的指标。计算公式为：

$$电力消费弹性系数=\frac{电力消费量年平均增长速度}{国民经济年平均增长速度}$$

能源加工转换效率 指一定时期内，能源经过加工、转换后，产出的各种能源产品的数量与同期内投入加工转换的各种能源数量的比率。该指标是观察能源加工转换装置和生产工艺先进与落后、管理水平高低等的重要指标。计算公式为：

$$能源加工转换效率=\frac{能源加工转换产出量}{能源加工转换投入量}\times 100\%$$

单位国内生产总值能耗 指一定时期内，一个国家或地区每生产一个单位的国内生产总值所消费的能源。计算公式为：

$$单位国内生产总值能耗=\frac{能源消费总量}{国内生产总值}$$

单位国内生产总值电耗 指一定时期内，一个国家或地区每生产一个单位的国内生产总值所消费的电力。计算公式为：

$$单位国内生产总值电耗=\frac{全社会用电量}{国内生产总值}$$

Explanatory Notes on Main Statistical Indicators

Total Primary Energy Production refers to the total production of primary energy in a given period of time. It is a comprehensive indicator to show the level, scale, composition and growth of energy production of the country. It includes that of coal, crude oil, natural gas, hydropower and electricity generated by nuclear energy and other means such as wind power and geothermal power, etc. However, it does not include the production of fuels of low calorific value and secondary energy converted from primary energy.

Total Energy Consumption refers to the total consumption of energy of various kinds by the production sectors of the economy and the households in a given period of time. It includes primary energy such as coal, crude oil, natural gas, hydropower, nuclear power, wind power, solar power, geothermal power and bio-energy; the secondary energy and their products which are transformed from the primary energy such as washed coal, coke, coal gas, electricity, heating, and petroleum products; and other kinds of fossil energy, renewable energy and new energy. The renewable energy refers to the part of renewable energy that is attained with some given technical means and used for commercial purposes, including hydropower, wind power, solar power, geothermal power and bio-energy. In the process of accounting, there should be no double or multiple counting between and primary and the secondary accounting. Total energy consumption can be divided into three parts: final energy consumption; loss during the process of energy transformation; and other losses.

(1) Final Energy Consumption: It refers to the consumption of various kinds of energy in a given period of time, not involving the energy consumed for transformation.

(2) Losses During the Process of Energy Transformation: It refers to the total input of various kinds of energy for transformation, minus the total output of various kinds of energy products in a given period of time. It is an indicator to show the losses that occurs during the process of energy transformation.

(3) Other Losses: It refers to the total of the losses of energy during the course of energy transport, distribution and storage and the losses caused by any objective reason in a given period of time. The losses of various kinds of gas due to gas discharges and stocktaking is not included.

Elasticity Ratio of Energy Production is an indicator to show the relationship between the growth rate of energy production and the growth rate of the national economy. The formula is:

$$\text{Elasticity ratio of energy production} = \frac{\text{Average annual growth rate of energy production}}{\text{Average annual growth rate of national economy}}$$

The average annual growth rate of the national economy can be measured by indicators such as the gross national product or the gross domestic product, depending on the purposes or needs. The gross domestic product has been used in the calculation of the ratio in the Yearbook.

Elasticity Ratio of Electricity Production is an indicator to show the relationship between the growth rate of electricity production and the growth rate of the national economy. The formula is:

$$\text{Elasticity ratio of electricity production} = \frac{\text{Average annual growth rate of electricity production}}{\text{Average annual growth rate of national economy}}$$

Elasticity Ratio of Energy Consumption is an indicator to show the relationship between the growth rate of energy consumption and the growth rate of the national economy. The formula is:

$$\text{Elasticity ratio of energy consumption} = \frac{\text{Average annual growth Rate of energy consumption}}{\text{Average annual growth rate of national economy}}$$

Elasticity Ratio of Electricity Consumption is an indicator to show the relationship between the growth rate of electricity consumption and the growth rate of the national economy. The formula is:

$$\text{Elasticity ratio of electricity consumption} = \frac{\text{Average annual growth rate of electricity consumption}}{\text{Average annual growth rate of national economy}}$$

Efficiency of Energy Transformation refers to the ratio of the total output of various kinds of energy products after transformation to the total input of various kinds of energy for transformation during a given period. It is an important indicator to show the current conditions of energy transformation equipment, production technique and management. The formula is:

$$\text{Efficiency of energy transformation} = \frac{\text{Output of energy after transformation}}{\text{Input of energy for transformation}} \times 100\%$$

Energy Consumption per Unit of GDP refers to the energy consumption per unit of gross domestic product in a country or in a region during a given period. The formula is:

$$\text{Energy consumption per unit of GDP} = \frac{\text{Total energy consumption}}{\text{Gross domestic product}}$$

Electricity Consumption per Unit of GDP refers to the electricity consumption per unit of gross domestic product in a country or in a region during a given period. The formula is:

$$\text{Electricity consumption per unit of GDP} = \frac{\text{Total electricity consumption}}{\text{Gross domestic product}}$$

10

固定资产投资

Investment in Fixed Assets

简要说明

一、本篇资料的主要内容

本篇资料通过对一定时期全社会建造和购置固定资产活动的数量方面的描述，反映报告期内固定资产投资的规模、速度、结构和比例关系、固定资产投资的资金来源等。

二、本篇资料的统计范围

固定资产投资统计的范围包括：建设项目投资、房地产开发投资及农户投资。

三、本篇的资料来源

跨省（区）项目资料来自国务院有关部门（企业）等；农户固定资产投资资料来自国家统计局住户调查司的住户调查；除此以外的固定资产投资统计资料均来自国家统计局固定资产投资统计司的统计调查。

四、本篇的统计调查方法

除农户固定资产投资统计采用抽样调查方法外，其他均为全面调查。

五、统计口径的变化

自 1997 年起，除房地产开发投资、农村非农户投资、农户投资及城镇和工矿区私人建房投资外，固定资产投资的统计起点由 5 万元提高到 50 万元。

自 2006 年起，农村非农户固定资产投资统计改为按项目统计，调查方法由抽样调查改为全面调查，起点提高到 50 万元。

自 2006 年起，城镇和工矿区私人建房投资改为按项目统计，起点为 50 万元。

自 2011 年起，除房地产开发投资、农户投资外，固定资产投资项目统计起点由计划总投资 50 万元提高到 500 万元。

六、数据使用注意事项

本资料对 2010 年以来全国固定资产投资主要指标总量及增速进行了修订，主要原因是：①加强投资项目审核管理，剔除流动资产、消耗性生物资产等不符合固定资产投资统计范围的项目。②改进和完善数据质量审核管理方法，剔除不应纳入报告期完成投资的前期土地费用以及跨地区、跨行业重复统计数据。③加强统计执法，对统计执法检查中发现的问题数据，按照相关规定进行了改正。

Brief Introduction

I. Main Contents

Statistics in this chapter describe activities on the construction and purchase of fixed assets of the whole country during a given period of time, and reflect the size, growth, structure, ratio, financing of the investment in fixed assets.

II. Scope of Statistics

Statistics on the investment in fixed assets cover investments in capital construction projects in urban and rural areas, investments in real estate development, and rural household investment.

III. Sources of Data

Data on trans-provincial projects are provided by various departments under the State Council. Data on investments in fixed assets by individuals in rural areas are provided by the Department of Rural Social and Economic Survey of the NBS through its rural social and economic survey. Other data on investments in fixed assets are from surveys conducted by the Department of Investment and Construction Statistics of the NBS.

IV. Methodology of Data Collection

All data on investments in fixed assets are collected by the system of reporting form with complete enumeration, except data on individual investments in fixed assets in rural areas, which are collected through sample surveys.

V. Changes in Statistical Scope

Since 1997, the cut-off point of projects covered by statistics of investment in fixed assets are raised from an investment of 50,000 yuan to 500,000 yuan, except investment in real estate development, farm household investment, non-farm household investment and private investment in housing construction in urban areas and industrial and mining areas. For the convenience of comparison, relevant data of 1996 are adjusted accordingly, and figures compiled on the basis of the old standard are enclosed in brackets.

Since 2006, statistics on investments in fixed assets of rural non-farm households are changed to project-based. Survey method is changed from sample survey to the system of reporting form with complete enumeration. The cut-off point has been raised to 500,000 yuan.

Since 2006, statistics on private investment in housing construction in urban areas and industrial and mining areas have become project-based. The cut-off point has been raised to 500,000 yuan.

Since 2011, the cut-off size of fixed assets investment projected rose from a total planned investment above 500 thousand yuan to 5 million yuan.

VI. Revision of Content

This document revises the total amount and growth rate of major indicators of fixed assets investment in China since 2010. The main reasons are that: (1) strengthen the verification and management of investment projects, and eliminate those that do not meet the statistical scope of fixed assets investment such as current assets, consumable biological assets and other projects. (2) improve and enrich data quality audit management methods, eliminate pre investment land costs that should not be included in the reporting period, as well as cross-regional and cross-industry duplicate statistical data. (3) strengthen statistical law enforcement and correct inaccurate data found during statistical law enforcement inspections in accordance with relevant regulations.

10-1 全社会固定资产投资
Total Investment in Fixed Assets in the Whole Country

年份 Year	全社会固定资产投资 Total Investment in Fixed Assets		房地产开发投资 Real Estate Development	
	绝对数(亿元) Value (100 million yuan)	比上年增长(%) Growth Rate over Preceding Year (%)	绝对数(亿元) Value (100 million yuan)	比上年增长(%) Growth Rate over Preceding Year (%)
1981	961	5.5		
1982	1230	28.0		
1983	1430	16.2		
1984	1833	28.2		
1985	2543	38.8		
1986	3121	22.7	101	
1987	3792	21.5	150	48.5
1988	4754	25.4	257	71.6
1989	4410	-7.2	273	6.0
1990	4517	2.4	253	-7.1
1991	5595	23.9	336	32.7
1992	8080	44.4	731	117.5
1993	13072	61.8	1938	165.0
1994	17042	30.4	2554	31.8
1995	20019	17.5	3149	23.3
1996	22974	14.8	3216	2.1
1997	24941	8.8	3178	-1.2
1998	28406	13.9	3614	13.7
1999	29855	5.1	4103	13.5
2000	32918	10.3	4984	21.5
2001	37214	13.0	6344	27.3
2002	43500	16.9	7791	22.8
2003	53841	23.8	10154	30.3
2004	66235	23.0	13158	29.6
2005	80994	22.3	15909	20.9
2006	97583	20.5	19423	22.1
2007	118323	21.3	25289	30.2
2008	144587	22.2	31203	23.4
2009	181760	25.7	36242	16.1
2010	218834	20.4	47562	31.2
2011	205036	20.1	60146	26.5
2012	241746	17.9	69211	15.1
2013	282486	16.9	82198	18.8
2014	320331	13.4	90247	9.8
2015	347827	8.6	90911	0.7
2016	372021	7.0	96900	6.6
2017	394926	6.2	103427	6.7
2018	418215	5.9	112740	9.0
2019	439541	5.1	123610	9.6
2020	451155	2.6	132014	6.8
2021	473003	4.8	137633	4.3
2022	495966	4.9	123848	-10.0
2023	509708	2.8	112142	-9.5
平均每年增长(%) Annual Growth Rate(%)				
1982-2023	17.8			
1991-2023	17.5		24.0	
2001-2023	15.0		18.5	

10-2 全社会固定资产投资实际到位资金比上年增长情况
Growth Rate of Actual Funds Available for Investment in Total Investment in Fixed Assets in the Whole Country over Preceding Year

单位：% (%)

年 份 Year	本年实际到位资金 Actual Funds Available for Investment	国家预算资金 State Budget	国内贷款 Domestic Loans	利用外资 Foreign Investment	自筹资金 Self-raised Funds	其他资金 Other Funds
1996	14.1	1.4	9.0	19.7	5.2	58.9
1997	8.1	11.3	4.6	-2.3	12.6	6.5
1998	13.7	71.9	15.9	-2.5	11.6	17.7
1999	3.6	54.7	3.3	-23.3	4.4	3.5
2000	11.3	13.9	17.5	-15.5	11.5	13.2
2001	14.7	20.7	7.6	2.0	15.9	20.7
2002	18.6	24.1	22.4	20.5	20.6	7.5
2003	30.1	-15.0	36.0	24.7	37.8	21.0
2004	27.2	21.1	14.5	26.4	31.2	31.8
2005	26.9	27.6	18.4	21.1	33.5	16.0
2006	25.8	12.5	20.0	8.9	29.0	28.3
2007	26.8	25.4	17.6	18.4	28.6	31.7
2008	21.3	35.8	14.8	3.5	29.7	-2.8
2009	36.8	59.5	48.6	-13.0	29.5	62.4
2010	24.3	15.7	20.2	7.9	28.4	17.1
2011	21.1	14.1	5.3	7.6	28.3	11.2
2012	18.4	27.7	11.3	-11.7	21.1	12.9
2013	20.0	17.7	15.2	-3.3	20.3	25.3
2014	10.6	19.9	9.7	-6.2	13.6	-5.0
2015	7.5	15.6	-6.4	-29.6	9.2	10.1
2016	5.6	17.1	10.1	-20.5	-0.2	30.7
2017	4.7	7.8	8.7	-3.1	2.2	11.5
2018	3.4	0.1	-5.4	-2.3	3.7	8.7
2019	4.1	-0.9	2.0	33.3	1.4	11.4
2020	7.3	32.8	0.0	-4.4	6.7	7.5
2021	4.3	-3.8	-3.1	-10.9	5.7	7.2
2022	0.5	39.3	-6.0	-19.8	9.0	-19.8
2023	-1.4	9.0	5.1	-17.5	1.1	-13.4

10-3 民间固定资产投资
Non-governmental Investment in Fixed Assets

年 份 Year	民间固定资产投资 (亿元) Non-governmental Investment in Fixed Assets (100 million yuan)	比上年增长 (%) Growth Rate over Preceding Year (%)	占固定资产投资 (不含农户)比重(%) As Percentage of Total Investment (Excluding investment by rural households) (%)
2012	125300		54.0
2013	150542	20.1	55.4
2014	174306	15.8	56.3
2015	189659	8.8	56.2
2016	194952	2.8	53.8
2017	205153	5.2	53.2
2018	223001	8.7	54.6
2019	233482	4.7	54.3
2020	235701	1.0	53.2
2021	252082	7.0	54.3
2022	254451	0.9	52.1
2023	253544	-0.4	50.4

注：10-3至10-18表中数据均为固定资产投资(不含农户)口径。
a) Data in tables 10-3 to 10-18 are fixed asset investment (excluding rural households).

10-4 三次产业固定资产投资
Total Investment in Fixed Assets by Three Strata of Industries

年 份 Year	全部投资 (亿元) Investment in Fixed Assets (100 million yuan)	第一产业 Primary Industry	第二产业 Secondary Industry	第三产业 Tertiary Industry	全部投资比上年增长(%) Growth Rate over Preceding Year (%)	第一产业 Primary Industry	第二产业 Secondary Industry	第三产业 Tertiary Industry
2003	44389	518	16112	27759				
2004	55475	595	21017	33862	25.0	14.8	30.4	22.0
2005	68514	727	27588	40199	23.5	22.1	31.3	18.7
2006	82830	898	33263	48670	20.9	23.6	20.6	21.1
2007	101212	1096	41001	59114	22.2	22.1	23.3	21.5
2008	124434	1588	50365	72481	22.9	44.8	22.8	22.6
2009	156933	2220	61177	93536	26.1	39.9	21.5	29.0
2010	189964	2493	72647	114825	21.0	12.3	18.7	22.8
2011	195947	2542	71626	121780	20.3	16.4	19.7	20.8
2012	231905	3041	81454	147410	18.4	19.6	13.7	21.0
2013	271939	3696	91211	177032	17.3	21.6	12.0	20.1
2014	309575	4527	99583	205465	13.8	22.5	9.2	16.1
2015	337418	5542	105319	226557	9.0	22.4	5.8	10.3
2016	362056	6261	107694	248100	7.3	13.0	2.3	9.5
2017	385372	6716	109853	268803	6.4	7.3	2.0	8.3
2018	408176	7582	116872	283722	5.9	12.9	6.4	5.6
2019	430145	7628	120495	302022	5.4	0.6	3.1	6.5
2020	442791	9115	120787	312889	2.9	19.5	0.2	3.6
2021	464665	10018	134722	319926	4.9	9.9	11.5	2.2
2022	488549	10098	148800	329652	5.1	0.8	10.4	3.0
2023	503036	10085	162136	330815	3.0	-0.1	9.0	0.4

注：2003—2010年为城镇固定资产投资口径，2011—2023年全部投资为固定资产投资(不含农户)口径，增速为可比口径。
a) From 2003 to 2010 is the diameter of urban fixed assets investment, and total investment from 2011 to 2023 is the diameter of fixed assets investment (excluding rural households), and the growth rate is comparable.

10-5 分地区按领域分固定资产投资比上年增长情况(2023年)

Growth Rate of Total Investment in Fixed Assets over Preceding Year by Region and Field (Excluding Rural Households)(2023)

单位：% (%)

地 区	Region	全部投资 Total Investment in Fixed Assets	#基础设施 Infrastructure	制造业 Manufacturing	房地产开发 Real Estate Development
全 国	**National Average**	**3.0**	**5.9**	**6.5**	**-9.5**
北 京	Beijing	4.9	2.2	-1.6	0.6
天 津	Tianjin	-16.4	-16.7	-5.6	-42.1
河 北	Hebei	6.3	26.8	12.6	-12.7
山 西	Shanxi	-6.6	-18.1	-11.7	-0.2
内蒙古	Inner Mongolia	19.8	-7.9	46.4	1.0
辽 宁	Liaoning	4.0	9.4	14.0	-26.2
吉 林	Jilin	0.3	4.0	3.9	-18.9
黑龙江	Heilongjiang	-14.8	-7.1	-34.1	-27.1
上 海	Shanghai	13.8	4.2	6.7	18.2
江 苏	Jiangsu	5.2	6.3	9.1	-4.2
浙 江	Zhejiang	6.1	1.6	14.1	2.0
安 徽	Anhui	4.0	6.3	20.0	-16.4
福 建	Fujian	2.5	3.6	11.6	-12.7
江 西	Jiangxi	-5.9	19.1	-21.1	-6.4
山 东	Shandong	5.2	18.9	11.5	-8.8
河 南	Henan	2.1	4.6	7.4	-8.9
湖 北	Hubei	5.0	6.4	6.7	-3.7
湖 南	Hunan	-3.1	-16.1	4.4	-13.1
广 东	Guangdong	2.5	-0.5	20.7	-9.3
广 西	Guangxi	-15.5	-16.4	-9.6	-31.2
海 南	Hainan	1.1	1.7	-15.6	0.9
重 庆	Chongqing	4.3	6.1	13.5	-13.1
四 川	Sichuan	2.4	8.5	21.6	-23.3
贵 州	Guizhou	-5.7	0.7	1.9	-19.7
云 南	Yunnan	-10.6	-21.5	11.8	-45.6
西 藏	Xizang	35.1	34.8	38.2	30.9
陕 西	Shaanxi	0.2	8.0	9.4	-11.2
甘 肃	Gansu	5.9	0.0	11.0	-14.7
青 海	Qinghai	-7.5	-21.4	26.4	-32.0
宁 夏	Ningxia	5.5	-9.2	5.7	3.9
新 疆	Xinjiang	12.4	-0.7	1.5	6.8

10–6 分地区实际到位资金比上年增长情况(2023年)
Growth Rate of Actual Funds Available for Investment over Preceding Year by Region (2023)

单位：% (%)

地 区	Region	本年实际到位资金 Actual Funds Available for Investment	国家预算资金 State Budget	国内贷款 Domestic Loans	利用外资 Foreign Investment	自筹资金 Self-raised Funds	其他资金 Other Funds
全 国	**National Average**	**-1.4**	**9.0**	**5.1**	**-17.5**	**1.1**	**-13.4**
北 京	Beijing	4.0	3.2	-26.1	-37.8	15.8	7.1
天 津	Tianjin	3.3	-28.6	0.1	3.7	1.8	15.3
河 北	Hebei	-2.9	39.5	16.2	-3.2	-11.4	-6.9
山 西	Shanxi	-9.6	-7.0	-4.1	-80.7	-9.8	-12.7
内蒙古	Inner Mongolia	20.4	-5.5	48.8	55.3	18.2	16.0
辽 宁	Liaoning	6.1	1.4	41.8	64.8	9.3	-12.6
吉 林	Jilin	-7.4	36.9	9.3	84.5	-10.9	-29.2
黑龙江	Heilongjiang	-12.6	-26.0	16.9	-79.3	-16.9	17.5
上 海	Shanghai	1.6	3.7	4.0	142.8	3.6	-5.7
江 苏	Jiangsu	-0.2	53.7	-5.4	-19.4	6.9	-18.1
浙 江	Zhejiang	-6.1	52.3	-14.0	38.2	6.0	-26.8
安 徽	Anhui	-1.5	-1.3	21.9	-63.0	1.8	-14.0
福 建	Fujian	-5.5	14.1	-5.5	-36.2	-2.1	-25.6
江 西	Jiangxi	-10.8	102.7	10.1	-24.2	-17.9	-28.9
山 东	Shandong	-1.2	1.4	9.3	-12.3	5.5	-26.2
河 南	Henan	-3.7	13.2	18.4	-14.9	-6.2	-10.6
湖 北	Hubei	0.5	5.7	0.4	-44.8	10.2	-23.4
湖 南	Hunan	-3.3	51.4	-5.8	-73.0	-2.3	-15.5
广 东	Guangdong	4.6	3.9	9.5	-26.7	4.7	2.1
广 西	Guangxi	-14.5	-29.6	1.1	-50.4	-15.2	-20.3
海 南	Hainan	7.4	5.1	19.1	145.8	0.5	12.3
重 庆	Chongqing	-1.1	16.2	-4.7	-91.4	8.8	-19.8
四 川	Sichuan	3.9	48.9	46.8	84.5	-3.6	-4.3
贵 州	Guizhou	-21.4	7.8	-1.4	-34.2	-28.9	-27.2
云 南	Yunnan	-11.5	-13.6	-17.3	-16.2	-4.3	-20.0
西 藏	Xizang	-3.8	-22.8	38.0		15.0	-25.3
陕 西	Shaanxi	1.3	8.4	39.4	-8.7	-3.4	-4.4
甘 肃	Gansu	4.9	-1.4	10.6	-50.7	8.0	-1.0
青 海	Qinghai	-0.6	6.1	0.5		1.6	-15.0
宁 夏	Ningxia	10.0	-13.6	5.7	-67.4	18.1	6.0
新 疆	Xinjiang	15.1	-7.6	94.8	105.3	16.3	-0.1

10-7 分地区按构成分固定资产投资比上年增长情况(2023年)

Growth Rate of Total Investment in Fixed Assets over Preceding Year by Region and Composition of Investment (2023)

单位：% (%)

地 区	Region	全部投资 Total Investment in Fixed Assets	建筑安装工程 Construction and Installation	设备工器具购置 Purchase of Equipment and Instruments	其他费用 Other Expenses
全 国	**National Average**	**3.0**	**2.1**	**6.6**	**3.1**
北 京	Beijing	4.9	-0.2	24.4	3.7
天 津	Tianjin	-16.4	-4.4	11.9	-42.6
河 北	Hebei	6.3	8.6	11.8	-1.8
山 西	Shanxi	-6.6	-9.3	-3.8	5.2
内蒙古	Inner Mongolia	19.8	14.6	43.0	9.2
辽 宁	Liaoning	4.0	2.1	14.7	1.9
吉 林	Jilin	0.3	-2.5	12.5	6.7
黑龙江	Heilongjiang	-14.8	-14.8	-11.0	-19.2
上 海	Shanghai	13.8	18.9	-0.5	12.6
江 苏	Jiangsu	5.2	7.3	0.8	1.7
浙 江	Zhejiang	6.1	1.9	10.4	11.1
安 徽	Anhui	4.0	2.5	11.1	4.4
福 建	Fujian	2.5	2.6	2.6	2.1
江 西	Jiangxi	-5.9	-5.4	-18.6	8.6
山 东	Shandong	5.2	7.0	-4.1	3.2
河 南	Henan	2.1	4.1	1.5	-12.0
湖 北	Hubei	5.0	6.6	3.6	-1.3
湖 南	Hunan	-3.1	0.4	-16.7	-15.1
广 东	Guangdong	2.5	3.9	10.6	-3.6
广 西	Guangxi	-15.5	-17.8	2.8	-16.9
海 南	Hainan	1.1	1.1	6.9	-1.0
重 庆	Chongqing	4.3	7.2	8.1	-9.2
四 川	Sichuan	2.4	2.8	19.1	-8.0
贵 州	Guizhou	-5.7	-10.0	47.0	-12.2
云 南	Yunnan	-10.6	-12.9	39.1	-21.7
西 藏	Xizang	35.1	35.3	53.7	21.3
陕 西	Shaanxi	0.2	1.2	3.5	-6.6
甘 肃	Gansu	5.9	0.4	25.7	16.2
青 海	Qinghai	-7.5	-13.8	10.3	-6.4
宁 夏	Ningxia	5.5	-0.5	23.7	3.2
新 疆	Xinjiang	12.4	1.4	64.0	25.6

10-8 分地区按建设性质分固定资产投资比上年增长情况(2023年)
Growth Rate of Total Investment in Fixed Assets over Preceding Year by Region and Type of Construction (2023)

单位：% (%)

地区	Region	全部投资 Total Investment in Fixed Assets	#新建 New Construction	扩建 Expansion	改建和技术改造 Reconstruction and Technical Transformation
全国	**National Average**	**3.0**	**7.3**	**9.3**	**2.6**
北京	Beijing	4.9	1.6	0.2	7.8
天津	Tianjin	-16.4	-4.2	-19.4	36.0
河北	Hebei	6.3	15.9	22.6	11.0
山西	Shanxi	-6.6	-9.3	8.4	-13.6
内蒙古	Inner Mongolia	19.8	29.6	-7.0	-0.9
辽宁	Liaoning	4.0	26.3	-8.3	3.6
吉林	Jilin	0.3	8.8	-13.3	-5.8
黑龙江	Heilongjiang	-14.8	-12.7	-14.8	-9.0
上海	Shanghai	13.8	8.8	-2.6	12.9
江苏	Jiangsu	5.2	11.3	6.2	5.4
浙江	Zhejiang	6.1	10.1	6.9	4.3
安徽	Anhui	4.0	11.1	23.0	17.9
福建	Fujian	2.5	10.4	8.5	9.2
江西	Jiangxi	-5.9	0.2	-2.1	-24.2
山东	Shandong	5.2	10.7	6.1	13.1
河南	Henan	2.1	7.0	14.0	3.4
湖北	Hubei	5.0	10.4	3.9	-3.7
湖南	Hunan	-3.1	1.9	2.5	-8.5
广东	Guangdong	2.5	6.8	24.8	14.5
广西	Guangxi	-15.5	-8.0	-18.8	-37.1
海南	Hainan	1.1	3.5	-35.6	7.9
重庆	Chongqing	4.3	14.2	-0.5	0.5
四川	Sichuan	2.4	13.3	6.1	6.7
贵州	Guizhou	-5.7	-1.9	17.9	-4.6
云南	Yunnan	-10.6	-5.4	-7.1	-10.4
西藏	Xizang	35.1	32.4	105.8	68.3
陕西	Shaanxi	0.2	7.2	15.3	-12.6
甘肃	Gansu	5.9	14.1	11.5	-1.5
青海	Qinghai	-7.5	-1.0	-34.3	0.4
宁夏	Ningxia	5.5	5.4	-31.2	16.6
新疆	Xinjiang	12.4	14.8	1.5	13.0

10-9 分地区按隶属关系分固定资产投资比上年增长情况(2023年)
Growth Rate of Total Investment in Fixed Assets over Preceding Year by Region and Jurisdiction of Management (2023)

单位：%　　　　(%)

地区	Region	全部投资 Total Investment in Fixed Assets	中央项目 Central Government Projects	地方项目 Local Projects
全　国	**National Average**	**3.0**	**11.3**	**1.3**
北　京	Beijing	4.9	-16.6	7.1
天　津	Tianjin	-16.4	12.1	-19.9
河　北	Hebei	6.3	-11.4	7.5
山　西	Shanxi	-6.6	-4.6	-6.8
内蒙古	Inner Mongolia	19.8	35.8	17.6
辽　宁	Liaoning	4.0	33.7	-0.3
吉　林	Jilin	0.3	15.5	-1.2
黑龙江	Heilongjiang	-14.8	15.9	-20.8
上　海	Shanghai	13.8	1.5	14.6
江　苏	Jiangsu	5.2	30.0	4.7
浙　江	Zhejiang	6.1	15.8	5.8
安　徽	Anhui	4.0	7.3	3.9
福　建	Fujian	2.5	2.5	2.5
江　西	Jiangxi	-5.9	62.5	-6.9
山　东	Shandong	5.2	16.4	4.8
河　南	Henan	2.1	-7.6	2.4
湖　北	Hubei	5.0	17.6	4.6
湖　南	Hunan	-3.1	-1.1	-3.2
广　东	Guangdong	2.5	5.2	2.3
广　西	Guangxi	-15.5	6.5	-16.8
海　南	Hainan	1.1	20.7	-0.7
重　庆	Chongqing	4.3	13.0	3.8
四　川	Sichuan	2.4	22.1	0.9
贵　州	Guizhou	-5.7	16.8	-7.2
云　南	Yunnan	-10.6	21.6	-12.5
西　藏	Xizang	35.1	38.1	34.3
陕　西	Shaanxi	0.2	22.3	-1.7
甘　肃	Gansu	5.9	41.5	2.9
青　海	Qinghai	-7.5	25.0	-13.9
宁　夏	Ningxia	5.5	43.1	-0.4
新　疆	Xinjiang	12.4	42.7	5.2

10-10 分地区按登记注册统计类别分固定资产投资比上年增长情况(2023年)
Growth Rate of Total Investment in Fixed Assets over Preceding Year by Region and Registered Statistical Categories (2023)

单位：% (%)

地 区	Region	全部投资 Total Investment in Fixed Assets	#内资 Domestic Invested	港澳台投资 Investment from Hong Kong, Macao and Taiwan	外商投资 Foreign Invested
全 国	**National Average**	**3.0**	**3.2**	**-2.7**	**0.6**
北 京	Beijing	4.9	2.8	49.0	-0.2
天 津	Tianjin	-16.4	-19.6	7.5	-9.1
河 北	Hebei	6.3	5.8	35.6	31.2
山 西	Shanxi	-6.6	-6.2	-54.4	-21.8
内蒙古	Inner Mongolia	19.8	20.2	17.2	-48.9
辽 宁	Liaoning	4.0	5.8	-7.0	-20.2
吉 林	Jilin	0.3	-0.3	10.2	34.0
黑龙江	Heilongjiang	-14.8	-13.8	-21.3	-75.1
上 海	Shanghai	13.8	16.2	-5.9	3.5
江 苏	Jiangsu	5.2	6.0	-8.6	8.6
浙 江	Zhejiang	6.1	6.3	-4.3	9.4
安 徽	Anhui	4.0	4.0	13.3	-0.5
福 建	Fujian	2.5	3.0	-21.7	15.2
江 西	Jiangxi	-5.9	-5.8	-14.0	5.7
山 东	Shandong	5.2	5.7	-7.7	-0.4
河 南	Henan	2.1	2.2	-4.0	-0.4
湖 北	Hubei	5.0	5.2	3.2	1.0
湖 南	Hunan	-3.1	-3.2	1.7	6.2
广 东	Guangdong	2.5	3.2	-3.8	-8.0
广 西	Guangxi	-15.5	-15.8	3.4	-19.7
海 南	Hainan	1.1	3.2	-21.1	-6.1
重 庆	Chongqing	4.3	5.1	-12.1	-15.7
四 川	Sichuan	2.4	2.3	23.8	1.0
贵 州	Guizhou	-5.7	-6.0	24.3	6.7
云 南	Yunnan	-10.6	-11.3	41.2	23.7
西 藏	Xizang	35.1	35.1		-6.1
陕 西	Shaanxi	0.2	-0.2	-4.9	18.5
甘 肃	Gansu	5.9	6.8	-47.2	-33.6
青 海	Qinghai	-7.5	-7.5	-27.7	
宁 夏	Ningxia	5.5	8.7	-40.1	-34.7
新 疆	Xinjiang	12.4	12.1	181.2	-11.1

注：本表登记注册统计类别按《关于市场主体统计分类的划分规定》(国统字〔2023〕14号)执行。

a) The registered statistical categories of this table is implemented in accordance with the Regulations on the Classification of Market Entity Statistics (Guotongzi [2023] No. 14).

10-11 分地区按控股情况分固定资产投资比上年增长情况(2023年)
Growth Rate of Total Investment in Fixed Assets over Preceding Year by Region and Holding Type (2023)

单位：% (%)

地 区	Region	全部投资 Total Investment in Fixed Assets	#国有控股 State-holding	集体控股 Collective-holding	私人控股 Private-holding
全 国	**National Average**	**3.0**	**6.4**	**6.0**	**0.1**
北 京	Beijing	4.9	2.6	19.4	-7.9
天 津	Tianjin	-16.4	-15.1	37.6	-21.0
河 北	Hebei	6.3	13.1	-13.5	1.6
山 西	Shanxi	-6.6	-4.0	-11.5	-5.8
内蒙古	Inner Mongolia	19.8	27.4	-59.2	10.9
辽 宁	Liaoning	4.0	33.7	71.8	-11.4
吉 林	Jilin	0.3	14.4	67.6	-20.0
黑龙江	Heilongjiang	-14.8	-5.9	-36.9	-23.8
上 海	Shanghai	13.8	18.9	22.3	15.2
江 苏	Jiangsu	5.2	13.4	-1.1	5.3
浙 江	Zhejiang	6.1	16.3	1.8	2.3
安 徽	Anhui	4.0	10.0	29.9	-0.6
福 建	Fujian	2.5	19.0	19.4	-10.0
江 西	Jiangxi	-5.9	16.7	28.3	-18.3
山 东	Shandong	5.2	9.3	10.0	7.0
河 南	Henan	2.1	11.5	-8.2	-0.8
湖 北	Hubei	5.0	7.7	-3.5	7.4
湖 南	Hunan	-3.1	-10.5	32.7	2.4
广 东	Guangdong	2.5	12.4	-1.9	5.0
广 西	Guangxi	-15.5	-13.5	-53.7	-19.4
海 南	Hainan	1.1	7.5	3.3	5.3
重 庆	Chongqing	4.3	9.8	23.8	2.3
四 川	Sichuan	2.4	13.2	28.6	-10.1
贵 州	Guizhou	-5.7	-4.0	104.1	-6.7
云 南	Yunnan	-10.6	-13.7	-19.0	-4.4
西 藏	Xizang	35.1	39.6	31.6	16.3
陕 西	Shaanxi	0.2	4.3	16.2	-1.3
甘 肃	Gansu	5.9	12.9	37.4	2.0
青 海	Qinghai	-7.5	-4.1	22.4	-15.2
宁 夏	Ningxia	5.5	7.9	-27.7	7.5
新 疆	Xinjiang	12.4	14.3	95.1	14.9

10-12 各行业按构成分固定资产投资比上年增长情况(2023年) Growth Rate of Total Investment in Fixed Assets over Preceding Year by Sector and Composition of Investment (2023)

单位：% (%)

指标	Item	全部投资 Total Investment in Fixed Assets	建筑安装工程投资 Construction and Installations	设备工器具购置 Purchase of Equipment and Instruments	其他费用 Other Expenses
全国	**National Average**	**3.0**	**2.1**	**6.6**	**3.1**
农、林、牧、渔业	**Agriculture, Forestry, Animal Husbandry and Fishery**	**1.2**	**-0.9**	**-6.3**	**18.6**
农业	Farming	9.3	4.9	-4.1	30.9
林业	Forestry	1.5	0.3	19.1	6.1
畜牧业	Animal Husbandry	-18.2	-17.6	-19.9	-24.0
渔业	Fishery	8.7	6.3	18.4	32.2
农、林、牧、渔专业及辅助性活动	Professional and Support Activities for Agriculture, Forestry, Animal Husbandry and Fishery	7.4	8.1	7.4	-6.9
采矿业	**Mining**	**2.1**	**9.8**	**5.9**	**-8.4**
煤炭开采和洗选业	Mining and Washing of Coal	12.1	14.4	13.1	2.8
石油和天然气开采业	Extraction of Petroleum and Natural Gas	15.2	14.7	13.5	28.0
黑色金属矿采选业	Mining and Processing of Ferrous Metal Ores	-6.8	-14.8	-21.0	46.5
有色金属矿采选业	Mining and Processing of Non-Ferrous Metal Ores	42.7	24.3	7.9	183.7
非金属矿采选业	Mining and Processing of Non-metal Ores	16.2	-10.0	-29.9	85.6
开采专业及辅助活动	Professional and Support Activities for Mining	-3.1	-15.7	35.4	-50.6
其他采矿业	Mining of Other Ores	-25.1	5.3	-57.6	-57.9
制造业	**Manufacturing**	**6.5**	**11.5**	**3.0**	**11.5**
农副食品加工业	Processing of Food from Agricultural Products	7.7	10.6	-5.0	0.9
食品制造业	Manufacture of Foods	12.5	15.1	5.9	4.5
酒、饮料和精制茶制造业	Manufacture of Alcohol, Beverages and Refined Tea	7.6	11.8	-10.2	10.3
烟草制品业	Manufacture of Tobacco	46.6	31.4	50.7	165.6
纺织业	Manufacture of Textile	-0.4	4.4	-8.8	-8.6
纺织服装、服饰业	Manufacture of Textile, Wearing Apparel and Accessories	-2.2	-0.2	-10.1	-7.8
皮革、毛皮、羽毛及其制品和制鞋业	Manufacture of Leather, Fur, Feather and Related Products and Footware	-3.0	0.1	-17.8	19.2
木材加工和木、竹、藤、棕、草制品业	Processing of Timber, Manufacture of Wood, Bamboo, Rattan, Palm and Straw Products	2.8	4.7	-2.4	-8.7
家具制造业	Manufacture of Furniture	-7.7	-2.6	-25.2	-31.0
造纸及纸制品业	Manufacture of Paper and Paper Products	10.1	12.0	13.5	-21.9
印刷和记录媒介复制业	Printing and Reproduction of Recording Media	-0.9	7.1	-13.4	-13.3
文教、工美、体育和娱乐用品制造业	Manufacture of Articles for Culture, Education, Arts and Crafts, Sport and Entertainment Activities	0.1	4.3	-23.0	17.5
石油、煤炭及其他燃料加工业	Processing of Petroleum, Coal and Other Fuels	-18.9	-25.4	-7.5	-12.7
化学原料及化学制品制造业	Manufacture of Raw Chemical Materials and Chemical Products	13.4	18.3	5.8	5.8
医药制造业	Manufacture of Medicines	1.8	9.2	-17.4	-2.2
化学纤维制造业	Manufacture of Chemical Fibres	-9.8	0.3	-23.6	11.2
橡胶和塑料制品业	Manufacture of Rubber and Plastics Products	4.6	7.6	-0.6	0.9
非金属矿物制品业	Manufacture of Non-metallic Mineral Products	0.6	1.8	-5.4	11.7
黑色金属冶炼和压延加工业	Smelting and Pressing of Ferrous Metals	0.2	-3.0	1.2	24.6
有色金属冶炼和压延加工业	Smelting and Pressing of Non-ferrous Metals	12.5	12.1	10.7	22.6
金属制品业	Manufacture of Metal Products	3.5	7.6	-10.0	14.9
通用设备制造业	Manufacture of General Purpose Machinery	4.8	8.0	-3.8	4.9
专用设备制造业	Manufacture of Special Purpose Machinery	10.4	16.0	-7.0	8.8
汽车制造业	Manufacture of Automobiles	19.4	19.9	16.2	35.7
铁路、船舶、航空航天和其他运输设备制造业	Manufacture of Railway, Ship, Aerospace and Other Transport Equipments	3.1	4.5	-2.8	8.0
电气机械和器材制造业	Manufacture of Electrical Machinery and Apparatus	32.2	36.8	23.7	38.8
计算机、通信和其他电子设备制造业	Manufacture of Computers, Communication and Other Electronic Equipment	9.3	12.3	6.3	7.0
仪器仪表制造业	Manufacture of Measuring Instruments and Machinery	14.4	21.4	-12.4	29.4
其他制造业	Other Manufacture	-22.0	7.0	-10.3	-25.1
废弃资源综合利用业	Utilization of Waste Resources	6.8	5.8	4.9	26.9
金属制品、机械和设备修理业	Repair Service of Metal Products, Machinery and Equipment	71.4	81.9	72.3	14.5
电力、热力、燃气及水生产和供应业	**Production and Supply of Electricity, Heat, Gas and Water**	**23.0**	**19.2**	**33.2**	**15.3**
电力、热力生产和供应业	Production and Supply of Electric Power and Heat Power	27.3	23.9	35.5	15.8
燃气生产和供应业	Production and Supply of Gas	16.7	17.6	12.9	15.3
水的生产和供应业	Production and Supply of Water	7.6	8.3	-6.8	11.7
建筑业	**Construction**	**22.5**	**39.5**	**-12.6**	**16.5**
房屋建筑业	Construction of Buildings	-6.1	9.4	-57.2	-55.9
土木工程建筑业	Civil Engineering	30.2	45.5	-3.6	56.6
建筑安装业	Building Installation	29.8	20.3	197.4	225.6
建筑装饰、装修和其他建筑业	Building Decoration and Other Constructions	37.4	172.1	-40.2	99.6

10-12 续表 continued

单位：% (%)

指　　标	Item	全部投资 Total Investment in Fixed Assets	建筑安装工程投资 Construction and Installations	设备工器具购置 Purchase of Equipment and Instruments	其他费用 Other Expenses
批发和零售业	**Wholesale and Retail Trades**	**-0.4**	**-0.4**	**-3.5**	**0.6**
批发业	Wholesale Trade	3.6	1.6	-0.3	23.4
零售业	Retail Trade	-3.3	-1.9	-7.1	-8.4
交通运输、仓储和邮政业	**Transport, Storage and Post**	**10.5**	**5.1**	**-18.1**	**23.4**
铁路运输业	Railway Transport	25.2	27.0	-78.2	59.0
道路运输业	Road Transport	-0.7	-0.3	2.7	-3.4
水上运输业	Water Transport	22.0	17.3	9.4	67.5
航空运输业	Air Transport	4.1	27.1	-8.4	-23.6
管道运输业	Transport Via Pipelines	2.0	-3.7	1.7	43.1
多式联运和运输代理业	Multimodal and Forwarding Agencies	-5.6	1.5	-71.4	50.9
装卸搬运和仓储业	Loading, Unloading and Storage	27.5	9.0	3.7	32.6
邮政业	Post	-17.2	-3.8	-33.1	-55.9
住宿和餐饮业	**Hotels and Catering Services**	**8.2**	**9.5**	**39.2**	**-10.6**
住宿业	Hotels	8.5	10.9	20.4	-11.0
餐饮业	Catering Services	5.7	-0.1	75.8	-4.6
信息传输、软件和信息技术服务业	**Information Transmission, Software and Information Technology**	**13.8**	**12.5**	**19.2**	**-16.4**
电信、广播电视和卫星传输服务	Telecommunication, Radio and Television and Satellite Transmission Service	2.8	4.7	7.1	-33.3
互联网和相关服务	Internet and Related Service	13.1	17.9	7.9	9.3
软件和信息技术服务业	Software and Information Technology	14.6	14.6	74.9	-20.6
金融业	**Financial Intermediation**	**-11.9**	**3.7**	**32.4**	**-58.1**
货币金融服务	Monetary and Financial Service	-21.5	-6.5	23.1	-70.5
资本市场服务	Capital Market Service	14.0	10.4	161.1	-32.9
保险业	Insurance	-2.5	12.6	103.4	-58.1
其他金融业	Other Financial Activities	8.0	22.4		-23.0
房地产业	**Real Estate**	**-8.1**	**-9.9**	**-6.7**	**-5.0**
租赁和商务服务业	**Leasing and Business Services**	**9.9**	**13.2**	**15.3**	**-5.3**
租赁业	Leasing	25.0	-31.1	36.8	-1.9
商务服务业	Business Services	9.3	13.5	-22.8	-5.3
科学研究和技术服务业	**Scientific Research and Technical Services**	**18.1**	**19.7**	**10.0**	**16.9**
研究和试验发展	Research and Experimental Development	8.6	15.4	-9.4	-3.8
专业技术服务业	Professional Technical Services	8.5	7.5	30.7	-13.1
科技推广和应用服务业	Science and Technology Popularization and Application Services	31.8	28.3	32.1	51.9
水利、环境和公共设施管理业	**Management of Water Conservancy, Environment and Public Facilities**	**0.1**	**-0.9**	**-17.8**	**8.6**
水利管理业	Management of Water Conservancy	5.2	2.0	-14.8	29.7
生态保护和环境治理业	Ecological Protection and Environmental Treatment	-2.9	1.8	-20.1	-27.0
公共设施管理业	Management of Public Facilities	-0.8	-2.1	-17.7	8.0
土地管理业	Management of Land	47.9	43.3	43.3	125.0
居民服务、修理和其他服务业	**Service to Households, Repair and Other Services**	**15.8**	**14.3**	**-2.1**	**40.5**
居民服务业	Services to Households	17.8	16.4	-12.5	43.6
机动车、电子产品和日用产品修理业	Repair of Motor Vehicles, Electronics and Household Products	-12.3	-14.5	25.9	-11.6
其他服务业	Other Services	34.4	33.6	7.0	97.6
教育	**Education**	**2.8**	**2.3**	**21.8**	**-0.2**
卫生和社会工作	**Health and Social Service**	**-3.8**	**-7.4**	**15.3**	**7.1**
卫生	Health	-4.4	-8.7	16.2	9.0
社会工作	Social Service	0.6	1.5	-22.9	-1.3
文化、体育和娱乐业	**Culture, Sports and Entertainment**	**2.6**	**2.6**	**-23.6**	**13.8**
新闻和出版业	Journalism and Publishing Activities	16.4	14.1	196.1	9.1
广播、电视、电影和影视录音制作业	Radio, Television, Motion Picture and Audio-visual Programme Production Services	-6.1	6.7	-40.4	-37.7
文化艺术业	Cultural and Art Activities	6.1	3.5	0.8	22.8
体育	Sports Activities	-6.6	-10.1	-26.1	21.3
娱乐业	Entertainment	3.7	5.5	-27.1	1.3
公共管理、社会保障和社会组织	**Public Management, Social Security and Social Organization**	**-37.0**	**-39.7**	**-4.6**	**-15.2**
中国共产党机关	Organs of Communist Party of China	4.8	-4.4	-15.9	250.0
国家机构	Government Agencies	-38.7	-41.8	-4.6	-14.9
人民政协、民主党派	People's Political Consultative Conference and Democratic Parties	63.4	60.8		169.6
社会保障	Social Security	6.5	15.8	-21.4	-70.7
群众团体、社会团体和其他成员组织	Mass Organizations, Social Organizations and Other Membership Organizations	2.7	6.1	62.5	-35.4
基层群众自治组织	Grass Roots Self-Governing Organizations	-39.3	-39.0	-12.4	-55.7
国际组织	**International Organizations**				

10-13 各行业按建设性质分固定资产投资比上年增长情况(2023年)
Growth Rate of Total Investment in Fixed Assets over Preceding Year by Sector and Type of Construction (2023)

单位：% (%)

指 标	Item	全部投资 Total Investment in Fixed Assets	#新建 New Construction	扩建 Expansion	改建和技术改造 Reconstruction and Technical Transformation
全 国	**National Average**	**3.0**	**7.3**	**9.3**	**2.6**
农、林、牧、渔业	**Agriculture, Forestry, Animal Husbandry and Fishery**	**1.2**	**-1.3**	**-15.9**	**14.8**
农业	Farming	9.3	4.5	-20.1	41.4
林业	Forestry	1.5	2.3	-10.2	-11.3
畜牧业	Animal Husbandry	-18.2	-19.1	-8.7	-5.6
渔业	Fishery	8.7	9.1	-9.7	2.1
农、林、牧、渔专业及辅助性活动	Professional and Support Activities for Agriculture, Forestry, Animal Husbandry and Fishery	7.4	8.6	-29.5	6.8
采矿业	**Mining**	**2.1**	**21.4**	**4.0**	**1.2**
煤炭开采和洗选业	Mining and Washing of Coal	12.1	24.1	13.8	-1.4
石油和天然气开采业	Extraction of Petroleum and Natural Gas	15.2	16.0	18.5	10.5
黑色金属矿采选业	Mining and Processing of Ferrous Metal Ores	-6.8	8.5	-18.7	-14.3
有色金属矿采选业	Mining and Processing of Non-Ferrous Metal Ores	42.7	69.9	13.5	28.6
非金属矿采选业	Mining and Processing of Non-metal Ores	16.2	28.1	-21.3	3.3
开采专业及辅助性活动	Professional and Support Activities for Mining	-3.1	14.1	-29.4	-50.9
其他采矿业	Mining of Other Ores	-25.1	-40.2	104.8	-29.2
制造业	**Manufacturing**	**6.5**	**13.5**	**4.6**	**3.0**
农副食品加工业	Processing of Food from Agricultural Products	7.7	11.6	3.5	-0.4
食品制造业	Manufacture of Foods	12.5	14.1	14.9	9.8
酒、饮料和精制茶制造业	Manufacture of Alcohol, Beverages and Refined Tea	7.6	15.3	22.3	-12.2
烟草制品业	Manufacture of Tobacco	46.6	29.2	-16.3	52.6
纺织业	Manufacture of Textile	-0.4	0.8	6.7	-0.5
纺织服装、服饰业	Manufacture of Textile, Wearing Apparel and Accessories	-2.2	-0.3	15.2	-12.0
皮革、毛皮、羽毛及其制品和制鞋业	Manufacture of Leather, Fur, Feather and Related Products and Footware	-3.0	-8.9	0.8	3.4
木材加工和木、竹、藤、棕、草制品业	Processing of Timber, Manufacture of Wood, Bamboo, Rattan, Palm and Straw Products	2.8	5.7	2.9	-1.8
家具制造业	Manufacture of Furniture	-7.7	-5.3	-7.7	-13.5
造纸及纸制品业	Manufacture of Paper and Paper Products	10.1	15.5	17.2	-7.8
印刷和记录媒介复制业	Printing and Reproduction of Recording Media	-0.9	15.3	-4.2	-14.2
文教、工美、体育和娱乐用品制造业	Manufacture of Articles for Culture, Education, Arts and Crafts, Sport and Entertainment Activities	0.1	5.2	-9.2	-3.2
石油、煤炭及其他燃料加工业	Processing of Petroleum, Coal and Other Fuels	-18.9	-26.9	-18.0	-1.8
化学原料及化学制品制造业	Manufacture of Raw Chemical Materials and Chemical Products	13.4	17.6	8.9	7.4
医药制造业	Manufacture of Medicines	1.8	5.2	5.3	-6.2
化学纤维制造业	Manufacture of Chemical Fibres	-9.8	-7.4	-22.0	-3.0
橡胶和塑料制品业	Manufacture of Rubber and Plastics Products	4.6	12.0	-1.1	-4.7
非金属矿物制品业	Manufacture of Non-metallic Mineral Products	0.6	3.6	-4.4	-2.7
黑色金属冶炼和压延加工业	Smelting and Pressing of Ferrous Metals	0.2	6.5	-5.7	2.3
有色金属冶炼和压延加工业	Smelting and Pressing of Non-ferrous Metals	12.5	28.1	-8.6	0.7
金属制品业	Manufacture of Metal Products	3.5	6.5	0.2	-0.9
通用设备制造业	Manufacture of General Purpose Machinery	4.8	11.6	-4.3	-1.0
专用设备制造业	Manufacture of Special Purpose Machinery	10.4	12.5	12.6	6.8
汽车制造业	Manufacture of Automobiles	19.4	26.1	8.8	18.1
铁路、船舶、航空航天和其他运输设备制造业	Manufacture of Railway, Ship, Aerospace and Other Transport Equipments	3.1	2.7	-1.6	4.4
电气机械和器材制造业	Manufacture of Electrical Machinery and Apparatus	32.2	43.1	15.9	19.3
计算机、通信和其他电子设备制造业	Manufacture of Computers, Communication and Other Electronic Equipment	9.3	12.5	6.0	0.3
仪器仪表制造业	Manufacture of Measuring Instruments and Machinery	14.4	13.3	24.3	14.8
其他制造业	Other Manufacture	-22.0	21.9	-30.9	-6.0
废弃资源综合利用业	Utilization of Waste Resources	6.8	10.2	-21.1	9.8
金属制品、机械和设备修理业	Repair Service of Metal Products, Machinery and Equipment	71.4	72.8	114.5	-1.1
电力、热力、燃气及水生产和供应业	**Production and Supply of Electricity, Heat, Gas and Water**	**23.0**	**24.4**	**28.2**	**10.6**
电力、热力生产和供应业	Production and Supply of Electric Power and Heat Power	27.3	28.2	40.3	14.2
燃气生产和供应业	Production and Supply of Gas	16.7	16.6	9.0	21.4
水的生产和供应业	Production and Supply of Water	7.6	9.2	8.2	-3.1
建筑业	**Construction**	**22.5**	**17.9**		**-24.7**
房屋建筑业	Construction of Buildings	-6.1	-0.9	6.4	-46.0
土木工程建筑业	Civil Engineering	30.2	15.6		36.1
建筑安装业	Building Installation	29.8	29.1	61.2	-36.0
建筑装饰、装修和其他建筑业	Building Decoration and Other Constructions	37.4	129.6	-95.4	-79.5

10-13 续表 continued

单位：% (%)

指标	Item	全部投资 Total Investment in Fixed Assets	#新建 New Construction	扩建 Expansion	改建和技术改造 Reconstruction and Technical Transformation
批发和零售业	**Wholesale and Retail Trades**	**-0.4**	**1.8**	**-21.3**	**-18.2**
批发业	Wholesale Trade	3.6	7.5	-20.3	-26.5
零售业	Retail Trade	-3.3	-2.0	-22.5	-11.2
交通运输、仓储和邮政业	**Transport, Storage and Post**	**10.5**	**4.6**	**17.3**	**-12.2**
铁路运输业	Railway Transport	25.2	36.8	9.2	-21.9
道路运输业	Road Transport	-0.7	-1.4	24.1	-12.2
水上运输业	Water Transport	22.0	28.6	30.5	-15.4
航空运输业	Air Transport	4.1	-20.9	32.9	105.6
管道运输业	Transport Via Pipelines	2.0	4.8	215.7	-47.2
多式联运和运输代理业	Intermodality and Forwarding Agency	-5.6	-4.6	21.5	-41.8
装卸搬运和仓储业	Loading, Unloading and Storage	27.5	12.2	-14.3	2.2
邮政业	Post	-17.2	-15.9	-19.9	-43.3
住宿和餐饮业	**Hotels and Catering Services**	**8.2**	**6.2**	**8.6**	**22.6**
住宿业	Hotels	8.5	6.9	12.5	30.2
餐饮业	Catering Services	5.7	0.2	-7.6	-4.3
信息传输、软件和信息技术服务业	**Information Transmission, Software and Information Technology**	**13.8**	**8.5**	**25.7**	**-5.8**
电信、广播电视和卫星传输服务	Telecommunication, Radio and Television and Satellite Transmission Service	2.8	-1.1	38.4	-5.4
互联网和相关服务	Internet and Related Service	13.1	17.2	-6.5	35.3
软件和信息技术服务业	Software and Information Technology	14.6	11.3	24.8	-35.6
金融业	**Financial Intermediation**	**-11.9**	**-18.2**		**-46.2**
货币金融服务	Monetary and Financial Service	-21.5	-33.6		-47.4
资本市场服务	Capital Market Service	14.0	8.3		-65.8
保险业	Insurance	-2.5	-3.1	-45.8	38.8
其他金融业	Other Financial Activities	8.0	6.2	245.5	66.7
房地产业	**Real Estate**	**-8.1**	**2.9**	**-17.1**	**15.5**
租赁和商务服务业	**Leasing and Business Services**	**9.9**	**9.7**	**11.7**	**-2.1**
租赁业	Leasing	25.0	-25.8		203.4
商务服务业	Business Services	9.3	10.0	2.7	-4.1
科学研究和技术服务业	**Scientific Research and Technical Services**	**18.1**	**19.2**	**12.9**	**18.3**
研究和试验发展	Research and Experimental Development	8.6	11.7	2.5	0.0
专业技术服务业	Professional Technical Services	8.5	3.8	-9.6	43.6
科技推广和应用服务业	Science and Technology Popularization and Application Services	31.8	32.7	38.9	15.4
水利、环境和公共设施管理业	**Management of Water Conservancy, Environment and Public Facilities**	**0.1**	**0.5**	**-12.3**	**4.1**
水利管理业	Management of Water Conservancy	5.2	4.1	16.9	9.7
生态保护和环境治理业	Ecological Protection and Environmental Treatment	-2.9	-5.3	-13.6	19.7
公共设施管理业	Management of Public Facilities	-0.8	0.1	-17.2	2.1
土地管理业	Management of Land	47.9	53.5	-61.2	15.3
居民服务、修理和其他服务业	**Service to Households, Repair and Other Services**	**15.8**	**18.0**	**-4.6**	**10.0**
居民服务业	Services to Households	17.8	21.4	-13.9	15.2
机动车、电子产品和日用产品修理业	Repair of Motor Vehicles, Electronics and Household Products	-12.3	-16.4	58.8	28.5
其他服务业	Other Services	34.4	37.0	138.6	-40.1
教育	**Education**	**2.8**	**1.8**	**3.3**	**-2.2**
卫生和社会工作	**Health and Social Service**	**-3.8**	**-5.5**	**-2.0**	**-9.2**
卫生	Health	-4.4	-6.5	-0.4	-12.5
社会工作	Social Service	0.6	1.1	-22.3	22.3
文化、体育和娱乐业	**Culture, Sports and Entertainment**	**2.6**	**2.6**	**-11.6**	**-8.6**
新闻和出版业	Journalism and Publishing Activities	16.4	17.3	11.3	22.0
广播、电视、电影和影视录音制作业	Radio, Television, Motion Picture and Audio-visual Programme Production Services	-6.1	-1.3	81.5	-41.0
文化艺术业	Cultural and Art Activities	6.1	1.9	9.1	-2.9
体育	Sports Activities	-6.6	-6.6	-4.8	-0.7
娱乐业	Entertainment	3.7	5.7	-23.3	-15.2
公共管理、社会保障和社会组织	**Public Management, Social Security and Social Organization**	**-37.0**	**-40.3**	**-8.6**	**4.9**
中国共产党机关	Organs of Communist Party of China	4.8	15.4	-87.2	-29.6
国家机构	Government Agencies	-38.7	-42.6	1.6	9.8
人民政协、民主党派	People's Political Consultative Conference and Democratic Parties	63.4	77.6	-31.0	
社会保障	Social Security	6.5	20.2	-52.3	-38.8
群众团体、社会团体和其他成员组织	Mass Organizations, Social Organizations and Other Membership Organizations	2.7	2.8	18.3	-4.1
基层群众自治组织	Grass Roots Self-Governing Organizations	-39.3	-38.4	-53.5	-40.3
国际组织	**International Organizations**				

10-14 各行业按隶属关系分固定资产投资比上年增长情况(2023年)
Growth Rate of Total Investment in Fixed Assets over Preceding Year by Sector and Jurisdiction of Management (2023)

单位：% (%)

指标	Item	全部投资 Total Investment in Fixed Assets	中央 Central Government	地方 Local
全国	**National Average**	**3.0**	**11.3**	**1.3**
农、林、牧、渔业	**Agriculture, Forestry, Animal Husbandry and Fishery**	**1.2**	**30.9**	**-1.6**
农业	Farming	9.3	33.9	4.6
林业	Forestry	1.5	57.4	0.1
畜牧业	Animal Husbandry	-18.2	-10.5	-18.2
渔业	Fishery	8.7	89.5	8.7
农、林、牧、渔专业及辅助性活动	Professional and Support Activities for Agriculture, Forestry, Animal Husbandry and Fishery	7.4	-1.9	7.7
采矿业	**Mining**	**2.1**	**-4.2**	**10.4**
煤炭开采和洗选业	Mining and Washing of Coal	12.1	47.2	7.6
石油和天然气开采业	Extraction of Petroleum and Natural Gas	15.2	11.5	29.4
黑色金属矿采选业	Mining and Processing of Ferrous Metal Ores	-6.8	25.0	-15.5
有色金属矿采选业	Mining and Processing of Non-Ferrous Metal Ores	42.7	200.0	26.8
非金属矿采选业	Mining and Processing of Non-metal Ores	16.2	181.9	9.9
开采专业及辅助性活动	Professional and Support Activities for Mining	-3.1	-8.7	-0.2
其他采矿业	Mining of Other Ores	-25.1	-25.0	-38.7
制造业	**Manufacturing**	**6.5**	**-16.0**	**8.9**
农副食品加工业	Processing of Food from Agricultural Products	7.7	16.6	7.6
食品制造业	Manufacture of Foods	12.5	78.8	12.3
酒、饮料和精制茶制造业	Manufacture of Alcohol, Beverages and Refined Tea	7.6	12.2	7.6
烟草制品业	Manufacture of Tobacco	46.6	74.1	4.4
纺织业	Manufacture of Textile	-0.4	-37.8	-0.3
纺织服装、服饰业	Manufacture of Textile, Wearing Apparel and Accessories	-2.2	-14.5	-2.2
皮革、毛皮、羽毛及其制品和制鞋业	Manufacture of Leather, Fur, Feather and Related Products and Footware	-3.0	-22.2	-2.8
木材加工和木、竹、藤、棕、草制品业	Processing of Timber, Manufacture of Wood, Bamboo, Rattan, Palm and Straw Products	2.8	-31.8	2.9
家具制造业	Manufacture of Furniture	-7.7		-7.8
造纸及纸制品业	Manufacture of Paper and Paper Products	10.1		9.1
印刷和记录媒介复制业	Printing and Reproduction of Recording Media	-0.9	18.3	-1.1
文教、工美、体育和娱乐用品制造业	Manufacture of Articles for Culture, Education, Arts and Crafts, Sport and Entertainment Activities	0.1	-4.5	0.1
石油、煤炭及其他燃料加工业	Processing of Petroleum, Coal and Other Fuels	-18.9	-18.3	-19.0
化学原料及化学制品制造业	Manufacture of Raw Chemical Materials and Chemical Products	13.4	2.6	14.0
医药制造业	Manufacture of Medicines	1.8	-12.7	2.2
化学纤维制造业	Manufacture of Chemical Fibres	-9.8	-32.7	-8.8
橡胶和塑料制品业	Manufacture of Rubber and Plastics Products	4.6	56.8	4.5
非金属矿物制品业	Manufacture of Non-metallic Mineral Products	0.6	16.9	0.3
黑色金属冶炼和压延加工业	Smelting and Pressing of Ferrous Metals	0.2	-1.7	0.5
有色金属冶炼和压延加工业	Smelting and Pressing of Non-ferrous Metals	12.5	103.5	9.3
金属制品业	Manufacture of Metal Products	3.5	-26.7	3.8
通用设备制造业	Manufacture of General Purpose Machinery	4.8	42.8	4.5
专用设备制造业	Manufacture of Special Purpose Machinery	10.4	43.8	10.0
汽车制造业	Manufacture of Automobiles	19.4	28.6	19.0
铁路、船舶、航空航天和其他运输设备制造业	Manufacture of Railway, Ship, Aerospace and Other Transport Equipments	3.1	31.3	1.1
电气机械和器材制造业	Manufacture of Electrical Machinery and Apparatus	32.2	21.9	32.4
计算机、通信和其他电子设备制造业	Manufacture of Computers, Communication and Other Electronic Equipment	9.3	9.3	9.3
仪器仪表制造业	Manufacture of Measuring Instruments and Machinery	14.4	69.7	13.9
其他制造业	Other Manufacture	-22.0	-26.4	12.5
废弃资源综合利用业	Utilization of Waste Resources	6.8	6.7	6.8
金属制品、机械和设备修理业	Repair Service of Metal Products, Machinery and Equipment	71.4	47.2	74.7
电力、热力、燃气及水生产和供应业	**Production and Supply of Electricity, Heat, Gas and Water**	**23.0**	**26.5**	**21.2**
电力、热力生产和供应业	Production and Supply of Electric Power and Heat Power	27.3	27.0	27.5
燃气生产和供应业	Production and Supply of Gas	16.7	19.1	16.0
水的生产和供应业	Production and Supply of Water	7.6	8.5	7.6
建筑业	**Construction**	**22.5**	**10.7**	**24.8**
房屋建筑业	Construction of Buildings	-6.1	-73.9	-0.8
土木工程建筑业	Civil Engineering	30.2	29.9	30.2
建筑安装业	Building Installation	29.8		25.0
建筑装饰、装修和其他建筑业	Building Decoration and Other Constructions	37.4	-22.6	74.6

10-14 续表 continued

单位：% (%)

指 标	Item	全部投资 Total Investment in Fixed Assets	中央 Central Government	地方 Local
批发和零售业	**Wholesale and Retail Trades**	**-0.4**	**9.1**	**-0.7**
批发业	Wholesale Trade	3.6	1.4	3.6
零售业	Retail Trade	-3.3	17.5	-3.8
交通运输、仓储和邮政业	**Transport, Storage and Post**	**10.5**	**26.7**	**2.9**
铁路运输业	Railway Transport	25.2	26.2	24.2
道路运输业	Road Transport	-0.7	5.2	-1.2
水上运输业	Water Transport	22.0	29.8	21.5
航空运输业	Air Transport	4.1	-9.8	9.5
管道运输业	Transport Via Pipelines	2.0	15.3	-2.6
多式联运和运输代理业	Intermodality and Forwarding Agency	-5.6	-43.6	-4.7
装卸搬运和仓储业	Loading, Unloading and Storage	27.5	32.4	10.1
邮政业	Post	-17.2	12.3	-19.6
住宿和餐饮业	**Hotels and Catering Services**	**8.2**	**-23.7**	**8.7**
住宿业	Hotels	8.5	-28.1	9.2
餐饮业	Catering Services	5.7	131.2	5.2
信息传输、软件和信息技术服务业	**Information Transmission, Software and Information Technology**	**13.8**	**14.0**	**12.5**
电信、广播电视和卫星传输服务	Telecommunication, Radio and Television and Satellite Transmission Service	2.8	8.8	-5.3
互联网和相关服务	Internet and Related Service	13.1	6.6	14.2
软件和信息技术服务业	Software and Information Technology	14.6	14.3	21.0
金融业	**Financial Intermediation**	**-11.9**	**-12.0**	**-11.9**
货币金融服务	Monetary and Financial Service	-21.5	-25.6	-20.7
资本市场服务	Capital Market Service	14.0	155.7	7.9
保险业	Insurance	-2.5	41.3	-28.3
其他金融业	Other Financial Activities	8.0	-23.3	12.9
房地产业	**Real Estate**	**-8.1**	**-8.9**	**-8.1**
租赁和商务服务业	**Leasing and Business Services**	**9.9**	**12.4**	**9.8**
租赁业	Leasing	25.0	63.0	21.6
商务服务业	Business Services	9.3	7.2	9.3
科学研究和技术服务业	**Scientific Research and Technical Services**	**18.1**	**-11.2**	**21.3**
研究和试验发展	Research and Experimental Development	8.6	-9.2	11.6
专业技术服务业	Professional Technical Services	8.5	-18.9	13.7
科技推广和应用服务业	Science and Technology Popularization and Application Services	31.8	2.2	32.5
水利、环境和公共设施管理业	**Management of Water Conservancy, Environment and Public Facilities**	**0.1**	**13.0**	**-0.2**
水利管理业	Management of Water Conservancy	5.2	22.0	4.7
生态保护和环境治理业	Ecological Protection and Environmental Treatment	-2.9	-9.3	-2.6
公共设施管理业	Management of Public Facilities	-0.8	15.4	-1.2
土地管理业	Management of Land	47.9	-14.8	49.3
居民服务、修理和其他服务业	**Service to Households, Repair and Other Services**	**15.8**	**19.6**	**15.7**
居民服务业	Services to Households	17.8	40.7	17.3
机动车、电子产品和日用产品修理业	Repair of Motor Vehicles, Electronics and Household Products	-12.3		-12.4
其他服务业	Other Services	34.4	-36.7	38.6
教育	**Education**	**2.8**	**14.5**	**2.2**
卫生和社会工作	**Health and Social Service**	**-3.8**	**4.5**	**-4.0**
卫生	Health	-4.4	7.0	-4.7
社会工作	Social Service	0.6	-17.3	1.0
文化、体育和娱乐业	**Culture, Sports and Entertainment**	**2.6**	**-4.0**	**2.8**
新闻和出版业	Journalism and Publishing Activities	16.4	-42.2	17.1
广播、电视、电影和影视录音制作业	Radio, Television, Motion Picture and Audio-visual Programme Production Services	-6.1	-57.5	-4.1
文化艺术业	Cultural and Art Activities	6.1	-4.2	6.3
体育	Sports Activities	-6.6	12.7	-7.0
娱乐业	Entertainment	3.7	-4.4	3.8
公共管理、社会保障和社会组织	**Public Management, Social Security and Social Organization**	**-37.0**	**-91.2**	**-7.4**
中国共产党机关	Organs of Communist Party of China	4.8	183.6	2.3
国家机构	Government Agencies	-38.7	-91.7	-3.9
人民政协、民主党派	People's Political Consultative Conference and Democratic Parties	63.4		63.4
社会保障	Social Security	6.5	166.9	2.7
群众团体、社会团体和其他成员组织	Mass Organizations, Social Organizations and Other Membership Organizations	2.7	-27.7	3.2
基层群众自治组织	Grass Roots Self-Governing Organizations	-39.3	-14.2	-39.8
国际组织	**International Organizations**			

10−15 各行业按登记注册统计类别分固定资产投资比上年增长情况(2023年)
Growth Rate of Total Investment in Fixed Assets over Preceding Year by Sector and Registered Statistical Categories (2023)

单位：% (%)

指　　标	Item	全部投资 Total Investment in Fixed Assets	#内资 Domestic Invested	港澳台投资 Investment from Hong Kong, Macao and Taiwan	外商投资 Foreign Invested
全　国	**National Average**	**3.0**	**3.2**	**-2.7**	**0.6**
农、林、牧、渔业	**Agriculture, Forestry, Animal Husbandry and Fishery**	**1.2**	**-1.3**	**-14.3**	**-7.2**
农业	Farming	9.3	4.7	-23.9	-14.1
林业	Forestry	1.5	1.8		
畜牧业	Animal Husbandry	-18.2	-18.2	-2.1	-18.2
渔业	Fishery	8.7	7.7		89.0
农、林、牧、渔专业及辅助性活动	Professional and Support Activities for Agriculture, Forestry, Animal Husbandry and Fishery	7.4	7.2	-75.7	82.3
采矿业	**Mining**	**2.1**	**14.5**	**18.6**	**-36.4**
煤炭开采和洗选业	Mining and Washing of Coal	12.1	12.3	11.9	-8.6
石油和天然气开采业	Extraction of Petroleum and Natural Gas	15.2	13.9	28.1	-45.9
黑色金属矿采选业	Mining and Processing of Ferrous Metal Ores	-6.8	-5.1	-75.6	-39.2
有色金属矿采选业	Mining and Processing of Non-Ferrous Metal Ores	42.7	47.9	-12.0	-55.9
非金属矿采选业	Mining and Processing of Non-metal Ores	16.2	19.0	-81.4	-7.1
开采专业及辅助性活动	Professional and Support Activities for Mining	-3.1	-4.5		198.3
其他采矿业	Mining of Other Ores	-25.1	-3.4	-96.5	
制造业	**Manufacturing**	**6.5**	**9.8**	**-5.0**	**6.1**
农副食品加工业	Processing of Food from Agricultural Products	7.7	8.4	7.7	-9.2
食品制造业	Manufacture of Foods	12.5	15.3	-12.4	-15.2
酒、饮料和精制茶制造业	Manufacture of Alcohol, Beverages and Refined Tea	7.6	4.8	54.1	40.8
烟草制品业	Manufacture of Tobacco	46.6	47.5	-9.3	-1.2
纺织业	Manufacture of Textile	-0.4	0.3	2.3	-38.0
纺织服装、服饰业	Manufacture of Textile, Wearing Apparel and Accessories	-2.2	-1.9	-0.2	-12.0
皮革、毛皮、羽毛及其制品和制鞋业	Manufacture of Leather, Fur, Feather and Related Products and Footware	-3.0	-1.2	-32.2	-9.8
木材加工和木、竹、藤、棕、草制品业	Processing of Timber, Manufacture of Wood, Bamboo, Rattan, Palm and Straw Products	2.8	3.6	-1.7	-30.7
家具制造业	Manufacture of Furniture	-7.7	-8.6	45.3	-33.4
造纸及纸制品业	Manufacture of Paper and Paper Products	10.1	8.0	3.6	75.2
印刷和记录媒介复制业	Printing and Reproduction of Recording Media	-0.9	1.4	-3.3	-40.1
文教、工美、体育和娱乐用品制造业	Manufacture of Articles for Culture, Education, Arts and Crafts, Sport and Entertainment Activities	0.1	0.1	1.0	4.3
石油、煤炭及其他燃料加工业	Processing of Petroleum, Coal and Other Fuels	-18.9	-15.7	-49.1	74.1
化学原料及化学制品制造业	Manufacture of Raw Chemical Materials and Chemical Products	13.4	14.5	-13.6	16.7
医药制造业	Manufacture of Medicines	1.8	3.0	-17.8	5.7
化学纤维制造业	Manufacture of Chemical Fibres	-9.8	-10.3	6.4	-30.0
橡胶和塑料制品业	Manufacture of Rubber and Plastics Products	4.6	3.6	-27.6	76.6
非金属矿物制品业	Manufacture of Non-metallic Mineral Products	0.6	0.6	12.6	-11.6
黑色金属冶炼和压延加工业	Smelting and Pressing of Ferrous Metals	0.2	0.0	-1.9	15.4
有色金属冶炼和压延加工业	Smelting and Pressing of Non-ferrous Metals	12.5	10.9	65.4	69.2
金属制品业	Manufacture of Metal Products	3.5	4.6	-10.3	-20.0
通用设备制造业	Manufacture of General Purpose Machinery	4.8	4.3	12.5	11.8
专用设备制造业	Manufacture of Special Purpose Machinery	10.4	10.4	15.2	5.6
汽车制造业	Manufacture of Automobiles	19.4	22.9	-16.9	13.1
铁路、船舶、航空航天和其他运输设备制造业	Manufacture of Railway, Ship, Aerospace and Other Transport Equipments	3.1	3.7	-12.4	1.2
电气机械和器材制造业	Manufacture of Electrical Machinery and Apparatus	32.2	33.8	-14.4	35.7
计算机、通信和其他电子设备制造业	Manufacture of Computers, Communication and Other Electronic Equipment	9.3	13.2	-9.3	-4.4
仪器仪表制造业	Manufacture of Measuring Instruments and Machinery	14.4	13.1	67.1	-21.0
其他制造业	Other Manufacture	-22.0	13.2	-10.2	-28.3
废弃资源综合利用业	Utilization of Waste Resources	6.8	3.5	131.8	40.8
金属制品、机械和设备修理业	Repair Service of Metal Products, Machinery and Equipment	71.4	64.1	182.0	-13.0
电力、热力、燃气及水生产和供应业	**Production and Supply of Electricity, Heat, Gas and Water**	**23.0**	**22.7**	**42.2**	**3.8**
电力、热力生产和供应业	Production and Supply of Electric Power and Heat Power	27.3	26.8	52.7	4.7
燃气生产和供应业	Production and Supply of Gas	16.7	17.0	11.5	21.3
水的生产和供应业	Production and Supply of Water	7.6	8.0	6.6	-31.8
建筑业	**Construction**	**22.5**	**22.4**		
房屋建筑业	Construction of Buildings	-6.1	-7.1		
土木工程建筑业	Civil Engineering	30.2	30.2		
建筑安装业	Building Installation	29.8	29.8		
建筑装饰、装修和其他建筑业	Building Decoration and Other Constructions	37.4	36.9		

注：本表登记注册统计类别按《关于市场主体统计分类的划分规定》(国统字〔2023〕14号)执行。

a) The registered statistical categories of this table is implemented in accordance with the Regulations on the Classification of Market Entity Statistics (Guotongzi [2023] No. 14).

10−15 续表 continued

单位：% (%)

指标	Item	全部投资 Total Investment in Fixed Assets	#内资 Domestic Invested	港澳台投资 Investment from Hong Kong, Macao and Taiwan	外商投资 Foreign Invested
批发和零售业	**Wholesale and Retail Trades**	**-0.4**	**1.8**	**-46.7**	**-17.4**
批发业	Wholesale Trade	3.6	4.0	-12.2	1.7
零售业	Retail Trade	-3.3	0.0	-56.9	-25.7
交通运输、仓储和邮政业	**Transport, Storage and Post**	**10.5**	**4.7**	**-5.6**	**11.2**
铁路运输业	Railway Transport	25.2	25.2	5.4	-80.2
道路运输业	Road Transport	-0.7	-1.1	129.6	150.6
水上运输业	Water Transport	22.0	30.4	-60.0	-27.0
航空运输业	Air Transport	4.1	6.7	-23.0	-26.0
管道运输业	Transport Via Pipelines	2.0	5.7	37.3	-28.1
多式联运和运输代理业	Intermodality and Forwarding Agency	-5.6	-6.3	1.2	88.0
装卸搬运和仓储业	Loading, Unloading and Storage	27.5	11.1	0.4	0.8
邮政业	Post	-17.2	-17.3	-18.8	7.0
住宿和餐饮业	**Hotels and Catering Services**	**8.2**	**7.4**	**40.8**	**-14.8**
住宿业	Hotels	8.5	8.6	-6.1	-17.6
餐饮业	Catering Services	5.7	-1.5		20.5
信息传输、软件和信息技术服务业	**Information Transmission, Software and Information Technology**	**13.8**	**9.6**	**22.7**	**18.6**
电信、广播电视和卫星传输服务	Telecommunication, Radio and Television and Satellite Transmission Service	2.8	-1.7	10.1	23.7
互联网和相关服务	Internet and Related Service	13.1	18.3	-19.3	23.8
软件和信息技术服务业	Software and Information Technology	14.6	13.8	90.4	-24.9
金融业	**Financial Intermediation**	**-11.9**	**-14.7**	**137.9**	**69.7**
货币金融服务	Monetary and Financial Service	-21.5	-25.5		51.3
资本市场服务	Capital Market Service	14.0	4.5		169.0
保险业	Insurance	-2.5	-2.5		
其他金融业	Other Financial Activities	8.0	12.0	-86.8	
房地产业	**Real Estate**	**-8.1**	**-8.3**	**-9.2**	**-35.5**
租赁和商务服务业	**Leasing and Business Services**	**9.9**	**10.0**	**-6.4**	**43.8**
租赁业	Leasing	25.0	18.9	8.7	
商务服务业	Business Services	9.3	9.7	-7.5	18.2
科学研究和技术服务业	**Scientific Research and Technical Services**	**18.1**	**17.8**	**44.4**	**13.2**
研究和试验发展	Research and Experimental Development	8.6	7.5	66.9	5.4
专业技术服务业	Professional Technical Services	8.5	9.1	-2.2	-26.8
科技推广和应用服务业	Science and Technology Popularization and Application Services	31.8	31.5	19.1	77.0
水利、环境和公共设施管理业	**Management of Water Conservancy, Environment and Public Facilities**	**0.1**	**0.2**	**-12.9**	**-26.2**
水利管理业	Management of Water Conservancy	5.2	5.2	-23.9	196.6
生态保护和环境治理业	Ecological Protection and Environmental Treatment	-2.9	-2.8	68.5	-46.9
公共设施管理业	Management of Public Facilities	-0.8	-0.8	-29.7	-12.5
土地管理业	Management of Land	47.9	47.9		
居民服务、修理和其他服务业	**Service to Households, Repair and Other Services**	**15.8**	**17.9**	**-47.0**	**-51.4**
居民服务业	Services to Households	17.8	19.3	-85.2	-55.7
机动车、电子产品和日用产品修理业	Repair of Motor Vehicles, Electronics and Household Products	-12.3	-6.5	-54.9	-10.2
其他服务业	Other Services	34.4	34.1	42.3	241.2
教育	**Education**	**2.8**	**3.0**	**-37.4**	**58.5**
卫生和社会工作	**Health and Social Service**	**-3.8**	**-3.8**	**-34.6**	**-5.4**
卫生	Health	-4.4	-4.4	-25.6	3.6
社会工作	Social Service	0.6	1.0	-67.7	-23.4
文化、体育和娱乐业	**Culture, Sports and Entertainment**	**2.6**	**2.6**	**26.8**	**-8.1**
新闻和出版业	Journalism and Publishing Activities	16.4	16.4		
广播、电视、电影和影视录音制作业	Radio, Television, Motion Picture and Audio-visual Programme Production Services	-6.1	-6.0	-24.7	-98.5
文化艺术业	Cultural and Art Activities	6.1	6.1	4.1	-1.6
体育	Sports Activities	-6.6	-7.1	18.4	18.4
娱乐业	Entertainment	3.7	3.6	38.2	-10.4
公共管理、社会保障和社会组织	**Public Management, Social Security and Social Organization**	**-37.0**	**-37.0**		
中国共产党机关	Organs of Communist Party of China	4.8	4.8		
国家机构	Government Agencies	-38.7	-38.7		
人民政协、民主党派	People's Political Consultative Conference and Democratic Parties	63.4	63.4		
社会保障	Social Security	6.5	6.5		
群众团体、社会团体和其他成员组织	Mass Organizations, Social Organizations and Other Membership Organizations	2.7	2.7		
基层群众自治组织	Grass Roots Self-Governing Organizations	-39.3	-39.3		
国际组织	**International Organizations**				

10-16 各行业按控股情况分固定资产投资比上年增长情况(2023年)

Growth Rate of Total Investment in Fixed Assets over Preceding Year by Sector and Holding Type (2023)

单位：% (%)

指标	Item	全部投资 Total Investment in Fixed Assets	#国有控股 State-holding	集体控股 Collective-holding	私人控股 Private-holding
全国	**National Average**	**3.0**	**6.4**	**6.0**	**0.1**
农、林、牧、渔业	**Agriculture, Forestry, Animal Husbandry and Fishery**	**1.2**	**5.0**	**7.9**	**-5.4**
农业	Farming	9.3	15.3	4.1	-1.3
林业	Forestry	1.5	3.0	16.7	-2.5
畜牧业	Animal Husbandry	-18.2	-13.5	-15.0	-19.7
渔业	Fishery	8.7	-0.8	50.3	6.5
农、林、牧、渔专业及辅助性活动	Professional and Support Activities for Agriculture, Forestry, Animal Husbandry and Fishery	7.4	-1.5	43.3	27.4
采矿业	**Mining**	**2.1**	**21.3**	**-23.8**	**3.8**
煤炭开采和洗选业	Mining and Washing of Coal	12.1	19.5	-6.7	12.5
石油和天然气开采业	Extraction of Petroleum and Natural Gas	15.2	14.0	-52.2	39.8
黑色金属矿采选业	Mining and Processing of Ferrous Metal Ores	-6.8	28.5	-45.5	-24.7
有色金属矿采选业	Mining and Processing of Non-Ferrous Metal Ores	42.7	93.2	79.4	12.7
非金属矿采选业	Mining and Processing of Non-metal Ores	16.2	53.7	-17.3	-0.9
开采专业及辅助性活动	Professional and Support Activities for Mining	-3.1	-12.7	-72.4	25.9
其他采矿业	Mining of Other Ores	-25.1	37.4		-9.6
制造业	**Manufacturing**	**6.5**	**18.5**	**8.9**	**7.4**
农副食品加工业	Processing of Food from Agricultural Products	7.7	21.0	-2.3	6.4
食品制造业	Manufacture of Foods	12.5	53.3	-17.6	11.1
酒、饮料和精制茶制造业	Manufacture of Alcohol, Beverages and Refined Tea	7.6	11.0	13.2	3.9
烟草制品业	Manufacture of Tobacco	46.6	53.2	39.1	10.0
纺织业	Manufacture of Textile	-0.4	13.8		-1.4
纺织服装、服饰业	Manufacture of Textile, Wearing Apparel and Accessories	-2.2	4.8	101.4	-5.4
皮革、毛皮、羽毛及其制品和制鞋业	Manufacture of Leather, Fur, Feather and Related Products and Footware	-3.0	5.1	-37.2	-1.3
木材加工和木、竹、藤、棕、草制品业	Processing of Timber, Manufacture of Wood, Bamboo, Rattan, Palm and Straw Products	2.8	-4.2	85.6	4.6
家具制造业	Manufacture of Furniture	-7.7	20.0	-32.4	-8.3
造纸及纸制品业	Manufacture of Paper and Paper Products	10.1	68.2	9.7	7.2
印刷和记录媒介复制业	Printing and Reproduction of Recording Media	-0.9	22.6	67.9	1.0
文教、工美、体育和娱乐用品制造业	Manufacture of Articles for Culture, Education, Arts and Crafts, Sport and Entertainment Activities	0.1	73.8	9.3	-4.7
石油、煤炭及其他燃料加工业	Processing of Petroleum, Coal and Other Fuels	-18.9	-20.7	-56.2	-19.4
化学原料及化学制品制造业	Manufacture of Raw Chemical Materials and Chemical Products	13.4	7.3	14.5	11.8
医药制造业	Manufacture of Medicines	1.8	30.2	-9.2	-3.5
化学纤维制造业	Manufacture of Chemical Fibres	-9.8	-4.9	-44.0	-12.0
橡胶和塑料制品业	Manufacture of Rubber and Plastics Products	4.6	39.7	37.3	1.9
非金属矿物制品业	Manufacture of Non-metallic Mineral Products	0.6	19.3	-0.2	-1.6
黑色金属冶炼和压延加工业	Smelting and Pressing of Ferrous Metals	0.2	0.6	-44.6	2.2
有色金属冶炼和压延加工业	Smelting and Pressing of Non-ferrous Metals	12.5	51.7	29.1	2.8
金属制品业	Manufacture of Metal Products	3.5	10.9	44.4	4.7
通用设备制造业	Manufacture of General Purpose Machinery	4.8	6.0	-16.9	3.6
专用设备制造业	Manufacture of Special Purpose Machinery	10.4	30.7	27.0	7.2
汽车制造业	Manufacture of Automobiles	19.4	39.4	69.8	15.7
铁路、船舶、航空航天和其他运输设备制造业	Manufacture of Railway, Ship, Aerospace and Other Transport Equipments	3.1	3.0	39.8	0.8
电气机械和器材制造业	Manufacture of Electrical Machinery and Apparatus	32.2	60.8	-14.0	31.5
计算机、通信和其他电子设备制造业	Manufacture of Computers, Communication and Other Electronic Equipment	9.3	12.1	20.8	12.7
仪器仪表制造业	Manufacture of Measuring Instruments and Machinery	14.4	36.5	-25.0	11.0
其他制造业	Other Manufacture	-22.0	17.7	66.8	6.9
废弃资源综合利用业	Utilization of Waste Resources	6.8	6.0	-10.1	4.7
金属制品、机械和设备修理业	Repair Service of Metal Products, Machinery and Equipment	71.4	87.4	-88.6	58.3
电力、热力、燃气及水生产和供应业	**Production and Supply of Electricity, Heat, Gas and Water**	**23.0**	**24.5**	**47.9**	**14.9**
电力、热力生产和供应业	Production and Supply of Electric Power and Heat Power	27.3	29.2	80.2	17.4
燃气生产和供应业	Production and Supply of Gas	16.7	34.4	-58.1	-6.0
水的生产和供应业	Production and Supply of Water	7.6	6.5	13.9	10.0
建筑业	**Construction**	**22.5**	**23.0**	**46.1**	**15.6**
房屋建筑业	Construction of Buildings	-6.1	-20.3	122.9	-6.1
土木工程建筑业	Civil Engineering	30.2	35.2	141.9	11.9
建筑安装业	Building Installation	29.8	51.8	5.3	16.8
建筑装饰、装修和其他建筑业	Building Decoration and Other Constructions	37.4	-41.0		132.5

10-16 续表 continued

单位：% (%)

指　　标	Item	全部投资 Total Investment in Fixed Assets	#国有控股 State-holding	集体控股 Collective-holding	私人控股 Private-holding
批发和零售业	**Wholesale and Retail Trades**	**-0.4**	**16.6**	**-24.2**	**-1.7**
批发业	Wholesale Trade	3.6	10.8	-27.6	4.0
零售业	Retail Trade	-3.3	20.7	-22.6	-6.4
交通运输、仓储和邮政业	**Transport, Storage and Post**	**10.5**	**4.3**	**3.2**	**4.8**
铁路运输业	Railway Transport	25.2	25.6		0.0
道路运输业	Road Transport	-0.7	-2.3	-8.0	10.5
水上运输业	Water Transport	22.0	39.8		13.9
航空运输业	Air Transport	4.1	7.5		-23.6
管道运输业	Transport Via Pipelines	2.0	4.0	-19.0	2.2
多式联运和运输代理业	Intermodality and Forwarding Agency	-5.6	17.4	-33.7	-30.7
装卸搬运和仓储业	Loading, Unloading and Storage	27.5	17.7	-14.4	7.5
邮政业	Post	-17.2	14.7	154.3	-28.8
住宿和餐饮业	**Hotels and Catering Services**	**8.2**	**-2.7**	**-28.8**	**11.9**
住宿业	Hotels	8.5	-0.1	-29.6	12.8
餐饮业	Catering Services	5.7	-28.2	-22.9	5.9
信息传输、软件和信息技术服务业	**Information Transmission, Software and Information Technology**	**13.8**	**8.3**	**8.9**	**19.7**
电信、广播电视和卫星传输服务	Telecommunication, Radio and Television and Satellite Transmission Service	2.8	5.8	-65.1	-34.5
互联网和相关服务	Internet and Related Service	13.1	6.2	60.2	26.9
软件和信息技术服务业	Software and Information Technology	14.6	16.7	0.6	16.8
金融业	**Financial Intermediation**	**-11.9**	**-7.3**	**9.2**	**-30.9**
货币金融服务	Monetary and Financial Service	-21.5	-21.0	8.6	-50.0
资本市场服务	Capital Market Service	14.0	-4.0		-16.5
保险业	Insurance	-2.5	30.8		0.1
其他金融业	Other Financial Activities	8.0	32.9	-60.7	-23.2
房地产业	**Real Estate**	**-8.1**	**5.1**	**-20.6**	**-14.1**
租赁和商务服务业	**Leasing and Business Services**	**9.9**	**15.6**	**12.9**	**3.8**
租赁业	Leasing	25.0	58.1	138.9	10.1
商务服务业	Business Services	9.3	13.9	12.2	3.6
科学研究和技术服务业	**Scientific Research and Technical Services**	**18.1**	**18.1**	**-1.0**	**17.2**
研究和试验发展	Research and Experimental Development	8.6	6.9	-47.4	9.4
专业技术服务业	Professional Technical Services	8.5	1.7	9.3	17.5
科技推广和应用服务业	Science and Technology Popularization and Application Services	31.8	39.0	27.5	23.2
水利、环境和公共设施管理业	**Management of Water Conservancy, Environment and Public Facilities**	**0.1**	**0.3**	**-8.1**	**0.8**
水利管理业	Management of Water Conservancy	5.2	5.1	5.4	10.8
生态保护和环境治理业	Ecological Protection and Environmental Treatment	-2.9	-1.6	39.6	-12.6
公共设施管理业	Management of Public Facilities	-0.8	-0.9	-12.9	2.7
土地管理业	Management of Land	47.9	48.6	8.8	66.6
居民服务、修理和其他服务业	**Service to Households, Repair and Other Services**	**15.8**	**32.1**	**83.3**	**-2.7**
居民服务业	Services to Households	17.8	28.4	103.6	-0.7
机动车、电子产品和日用产品修理业	Repair of Motor Vehicles, Electronics and Household Products	-12.3	-15.8	118.3	-9.3
其他服务业	Other Services	34.4	81.3	-65.8	-1.0
教育	**Education**	**2.8**	**2.4**	**13.0**	**-0.1**
卫生和社会工作	**Health and Social Service**	**-3.8**	**-3.6**	**-15.3**	**-2.1**
卫生	Health	-4.4	-4.9	5.9	0.3
社会工作	Social Service	0.6	13.8	-41.4	-6.7
文化、体育和娱乐业	**Culture, Sports and Entertainment**	**2.6**	**-1.3**	**32.8**	**4.2**
新闻和出版业	Journalism and Publishing Activities	16.4	-2.6		-21.1
广播、电视、电影和影视录音制作业	Radio, Television, Motion Picture and Audio-visual Programme Production Services	-6.1	-1.0	-59.7	-4.2
文化艺术业	Cultural and Art Activities	6.1	1.7	89.6	8.9
体育	Sports Activities	-6.6	-7.6	-48.6	-7.8
娱乐业	Entertainment	3.7	-0.9	21.9	4.8
公共管理、社会保障和社会组织	**Public Management, Social Security and Social Organization**	**-37.0**	**-39.2**	**13.5**	**-5.5**
中国共产党机关	Organs of Communist Party of China	4.8	9.9		-99.6
国家机构	Government Agencies	-38.7	-40.1	12.4	-8.2
人民政协、民主党派	People's Political Consultative Conference and Democratic Parties	63.4	39.3		
社会保障	Social Security	6.5	-1.4	-4.4	
群众团体、社会团体和其他成员组织	Mass Organizations, Social Organizations and Other Membership Organizations	2.7	-4.6	21.9	29.8
基层群众自治组织	Grass Roots Self-Governing Organizations	-39.3	-47.5	9.1	-1.4
国际组织	**International Organizations**				

10-17 各行业实际到位资金比上年增长情况（2023年）

单位：%

指　　标	Item	本年实际到位资金 Actual Funds Available for Investment
全　国	**National Average**	**-1.4**
农、林、牧、渔业	**Agriculture, Forestry, Animal Husbandry and Fishery**	**-9.7**
农业	Farming	-1.7
林业	Forestry	-11.8
畜牧业	Animal Husbandry	-28.4
渔业	Fishery	-0.1
农、林、牧、渔专业及辅助性活动	Professional and Support Activities for Agriculture, Forestry, Animal Husbandry and Fishery	4.0
采矿业	**Mining**	**14.3**
煤炭开采和洗选业	Mining and Washing of Coal	13.0
石油和天然气开采业	Extraction of Petroleum and Natural Gas	15.9
黑色金属矿采选业	Mining and Processing of Ferrous Metal Ores	-2.8
有色金属矿采选业	Mining and Processing of Non-Ferrous Metal Ores	38.7
非金属矿采选业	Mining and Processing of Non-metal Ores	13.8
开采专业及辅助性活动	Professional and Support Activities for Mining	-4.7
其他采矿业	Mining of Other Ores	-29.2
制造业	**Manufacturing**	**8.9**
农副食品加工业	Processing of Food from Agricultural Products	5.4
食品制造业	Manufacture of Foods	12.3
酒、饮料和精制茶制造业	Manufacture of Alcohol, Beverages and Refined Tea	5.3
烟草制品业	Manufacture of Tobacco	60.9
纺织业	Manufacture of Textile	-0.4
纺织服装、服饰业	Manufacture of Textile, Wearing Apparel and Accessories	-6.6
皮革、毛皮、羽毛及其制品和制鞋业	Manufacture of Leather, Fur, Feather and Related Products and Footware	4.4
木材加工和木、竹、藤、棕、草制品业	Processing of Timber, Manufacture of Wood, Bamboo, Rattan, Palm and Straw Products	2.3
家具制造业	Manufacture of Furniture	-9.6
造纸及纸制品业	Manufacture of Paper and Paper Products	7.7
印刷和记录媒介复制业	Printing and Reproduction of Recording Media	-0.4
文教、工美、体育和娱乐用品制造业	Manufacture of Articles for Culture, Education, Arts and Crafts, Sport and Entertainment Activities	-1.7
石油、煤炭及其他燃料加工业	Processing of Petroleum, Coal and Other Fuels	-21.0
化学原料及化学制品制造业	Manufacture of Raw Chemical Materials and Chemical Products	11.6
医药制造业	Manufacture of Medicines	3.9
化学纤维制造业	Manufacture of Chemical Fibres	-5.7
橡胶和塑料制品业	Manufacture of Rubber and Plastics Products	8.7
非金属矿物制品业	Manufacture of Non-metallic Mineral Products	0.5
黑色金属冶炼和压延加工业	Smelting and Pressing of Ferrous Metals	-5.2
有色金属冶炼和压延加工业	Smelting and Pressing of Non-ferrous Metals	12.0
金属制品业	Manufacture of Metal Products	5.3
通用设备制造业	Manufacture of General Purpose Machinery	5.5
专用设备制造业	Manufacture of Special Purpose Machinery	13.6
汽车制造业	Manufacture of Automobiles	21.1
铁路、船舶、航空航天和其他运输设备制造业	Manufacture of Railway, Ship, Aerospace and Other Transport Equipments	5.4
电气机械和器材制造业	Manufacture of Electrical Machinery and Apparatus	33.5
计算机、通信和其他电子设备制造业	Manufacture of Computers, Communication and Other Electronic Equipment	6.5
仪器仪表制造业	Manufacture of Measuring Instruments and Machinery	16.8
其他制造业	Other Manufacture	14.2
废弃资源综合利用业	Utilization of Waste Resources	6.0
金属制品、机械和设备修理业	Repair Service of Metal Products, Machinery and Equipment	68.0
电力、热力、燃气及水生产和供应业	**Production and Supply of Electricity, Heat, Gas and Water**	**24.8**
电力、热力生产和供应业	Production and Supply of Electric Power and Heat Power	29.7
燃气生产和供应业	Production and Supply of Gas	17.1
水的生产和供应业	Production and Supply of Water	5.5
建筑业	**Construction**	**22.8**
房屋建筑业	Construction of Buildings	-10.0
土木工程建筑业	Civil Engineering	29.5
建筑安装业	Building Installation	3.0
建筑装饰、装修和其他建筑业	Building Decoration and Other Constructions	86.2

Growth Rate of Actual Funds Available for Investment over Preceding Year by Sector (2023)

(%)

国家预算资金 State Budget	国内贷款 Domestic Loans	利用外资 Foreign Investment	自筹资金 Self-raised Funds	其他资金 Other Funds
9.0	**5.1**	**-17.5**	**1.1**	**-13.4**
5.4	**-9.6**	**-44.2**	**-10.7**	**-30.1**
14.6	-4.2	-40.5	-4.5	-20.0
-13.7	14.9		-10.6	-36.5
4.9	-36.5	-75.3	-26.9	-57.4
-57.9	-50.9	-99.2	11.7	-47.9
1.4	7.3	-56.5	8.1	-6.4
55.9	**29.9**	**25.4**	**12.4**	**-9.3**
-35.5	0.4	63.8	19.8	-69.9
57.7	20.2	34.2	12.8	37.6
38.3	28.6		-3.9	-44.3
-99.6	160.2		22.6	93.2
143.7	39.3	-95.1	3.6	111.2
286.9			-5.3	-68.2
			-25.6	-91.7
69.4	**20.0**	**-21.2**	**8.6**	**-15.3**
55.8	27.5	-29.5	4.9	-23.8
145.0	57.0	87.8	8.7	-24.3
17.4	-3.4	21.1	8.6	-41.1
	-69.1		62.4	46.1
47.3	-2.0	-61.3	0.1	-16.4
-21.6	22.8	-8.0	-5.3	-34.7
-17.5	29.6	53.4	5.3	-23.5
-14.7	70.8	-65.7	-0.1	5.0
50.8	12.9	-54.9	-9.4	-41.9
100.5	12.7	-72.2	8.9	-26.5
	20.1	-54.8	-0.1	-32.3
54.7	5.0	-14.5	-2.7	-17.1
-55.3	-54.2	-72.7	-8.5	-53.3
82.6	-1.2	-29.4	14.9	15.4
88.7	23.0	-21.5	3.0	-33.6
24.8	-0.9	-93.7	-3.0	-31.7
	72.2	-52.4	6.3	-11.4
75.2	23.3	8.5	-0.3	-22.4
26.2	14.4	1.8	-3.2	-49.2
118.3	49.7	193.3	10.1	-19.3
70.9	30.9	-40.6	6.9	-45.2
144.5	11.9	-37.6	6.1	-32.3
173.9	23.8	-49.3	13.3	-19.8
231.4	58.0	175.3	18.7	-14.6
-44.1	104.5	130.0	0.5	1.8
83.1	72.4	28.3	33.0	-11.3
82.9	31.5	-35.5	2.9	7.2
2.5	38.3	132.3	21.4	-58.2
53.0	31.7	-22.1	-1.8	34.6
33.5	34.0		4.2	-4.4
	-4.7	-77.7	43.0	
15.9	**43.3**	**52.8**	**24.8**	**-25.7**
15.4	45.9	42.7	28.4	-25.3
31.2	27.6	-73.8	17.8	-19.3
15.2	11.4	158.4	6.7	-27.3
172.1			**-11.2**	**16.0**
-35.4	40.1		-1.5	-27.9
155.2			-21.2	60.4
			-33.4	-94.3
			67.4	

10-17 续表

单位：%

指　　标	Item	本年实际到位资金 Actual Funds Available for Investment
批发和零售业	**Wholesale and Retail Trades**	**-0.8**
批发业	Wholesale Trade	2.2
零售业	Retail Trade	-3.3
交通运输、仓储和邮政业	**Transport, Storage and Post**	**-1.9**
铁路运输业	Railway Transport	2.8
道路运输业	Road Transport	-4.9
水上运输业	Water Transport	17.8
航空运输业	Air Transport	-4.4
管道运输业	Transport Via Pipelines	-14.9
多式联运和运输代理业	Intermodality and Forwarding Agency	-3.2
装卸搬运和仓储业	Loading, Unloading and Storage	8.4
邮政业	Post	-6.2
住宿和餐饮业	**Hotels and Catering Services**	**-2.4**
住宿业	Hotels	-1.8
餐饮业	Catering Services	-8.4
信息传输、软件和信息技术服务业	**Information Transmission, Software and Information Technology**	**11.8**
电信、广播电视和卫星传输服务	Telecommunication, Radio and Television and Satellite Transmission Service	0.9
互联网和相关服务	Internet and Related Service	12.6
软件和信息技术服务业	Software and Information Technology	24.6
金融业	**Financial Intermediation**	**-4.5**
货币金融服务	Monetary and Financial Service	-13.4
资本市场服务	Capital Market Service	1.3
保险业	Insurance	-12.9
其他金融业	Other Financial Activities	26.4
房地产业	**Real Estate**	**-11.4**
租赁和商务服务业	**Leasing and Business Services**	**5.9**
租赁业	Leasing	29.4
商务服务业	Business Services	5.0
科学研究和技术服务业	**Scientific Research and Technical Services**	**11.4**
研究和试验发展	Research and Experimental Development	0.3
专业技术服务业	Professional Technical Services	-1.5
科技推广和应用服务业	Science and Technology Popularization and Application Services	27.4
水利、环境和公共设施管理业	**Management of Water Conservancy, Environment and Public Facilities**	**-2.4**
水利管理业	Management of Water Conservancy	-0.8
生态保护和环境治理业	Ecological Protection and Environmental Treatment	-5.6
公共设施管理业	Management of Public Facilities	-2.8
土地管理业	Management of Land	70.7
居民服务、修理和其他服务业	**Service to Households, Repair and Other Services**	**16.4**
居民服务业	Services to Households	19.2
机动车、电子产品和日用产品修理业	Repair of Motor Vehicles, Electronics and Household Products	-17.6
其他服务业	Other Services	28.4
教育	**Education**	**1.4**
卫生和社会工作	**Health and Social Service**	**-3.4**
卫生	Health	-3.4
社会工作	Social Service	-3.6
文化、体育和娱乐业	**Culture, Sports and Entertainment**	**-1.3**
新闻和出版业	Journalism and Publishing Activities	-10.8
广播、电视、电影和影视录音制作业	Radio, Television, Motion Picture and Audio-visual Programme Production Services	-18.1
文化艺术业	Cultural and Art Activities	3.1
体育	Sports Activities	-8.6
娱乐业	Entertainment	-0.9
公共管理、社会保障和社会组织	**Public Management, Social Security and Social Organization**	**-43.6**
中国共产党机关	Organs of Communist Party of China	-4.1
国家机构	Government Agencies	-45.5
人民政协、民主党派	People's Political Consultative Conference and Democratic Parties	
社会保障	Social Security	-8.2
群众团体、社会团体和其他成员组织	Mass Organizations, Social Organizations and Other Membership Organizations	11.4
基层群众自治组织	Grass Roots Self-Governing Organizations	-44.8
国际组织	**International Organizations**	

continued

(%)

国家预算资金 State Budget	国内贷款 Domestic Loans	利用外资 Foreign Investment	自筹资金 Self-raised Funds	其他资金 Other Funds
34.8	**-3.1**	**-53.1**	**2.6**	**-45.1**
53.6	-5.9	-94.1	6.2	-55.3
13.1	-1.6	-32.9	-0.4	-36.8
0.2	**3.7**	**-52.7**	**-4.3**	**-9.0**
23.5	-8.1	63.7	8.4	-5.5
-7.6	7.0	-73.3	-9.9	-13.2
50.8	40.7	-36.5	3.2	12.0
-24.1	-11.5	55.3	-4.9	151.5
75.1	9.3		-16.6	-84.3
46.0	-25.5	-47.6	-3.8	0.9
64.4	0.1	-48.9	7.4	-36.7
6.8	-60.9	-91.1	2.1	-77.9
-38.1	**1.4**	**-42.2**	**-0.9**	**-6.5**
-38.0	2.9	-42.2	-0.4	-3.7
-40.5	-15.0		-5.3	-38.1
50.9	**26.0**	**-19.6**	**10.7**	**-10.3**
-2.7	-9.6	-66.9	1.0	11.6
33.2	49.9	-9.2	10.3	-7.2
80.2	21.1	3.8	26.0	-24.4
-54.7	**122.0**		**-6.7**	**-49.9**
-45.9			-17.5	-84.9
36.6	-70.0		2.2	190.9
			-2.7	-54.3
-82.2	59.8		39.4	-15.8
17.3	**-9.5**	**-29.9**	**-13.1**	**-11.4**
23.8	**1.2**	**17.7**	**7.8**	**-24.6**
-62.7	74.9	-95.8	15.2	-20.0
24.1	-6.6	19.4	7.6	-24.8
7.0	**1.9**	**-61.0**	**20.4**	**-32.6**
2.2	9.3	18.5	1.4	-24.0
-26.9	-9.1	-52.1	22.3	-60.9
42.8	0.7	-93.8	35.5	-15.4
9.3	**-6.6**	**-14.9**	**-1.4**	**-29.5**
5.8	15.3	7.6	1.3	-26.3
-7.3	-27.5	-65.0	3.4	-21.2
11.5	-9.7	-3.3	-3.1	-31.5
39.3	211.1		97.0	15.3
103.5	**87.8**	**-67.7**	**6.3**	**-30.7**
77.6	72.3	-64.3	10.4	-18.2
			-5.3	-91.0
	151.4		-5.6	-5.5
18.6	**-3.9**	**20.4**	**-0.6**	**-29.0**
18.2	**-17.5**	**60.4**	**-12.3**	**-35.3**
17.8	-17.9	-38.3	-13.0	-37.3
25.1	-14.5	244.8	-9.5	-10.7
2.6	**-13.9**	**66.0**	**3.1**	**-24.7**
			-16.6	-98.8
-33.4	-26.2		4.0	-50.1
5.0	-6.2	-11.3	7.4	-13.7
3.2	-23.9		-11.4	-15.2
-4.2	-15.1	-40.0	4.5	-32.1
-56.5	**-21.8**		**-10.1**	**-32.6**
88.5	-70.1		-18.3	-42.3
-57.8	-25.0		-6.4	-31.9
-1.9	89.6		-40.5	27.7
-7.1			17.6	-8.0
-0.9			-53.8	-58.9

10–18 分地区各行业固定资产投资比上年增长情况(2023年)
Growth Rate of Total Investment in Fixed Assets over Preceding Year by Region and Sector (2023)

单位：% (%)

地 区	Region	全部投资 Total Investment in Fixed Assets	农、林、牧、渔业 Agriculture, Forestry, Animal Husbandry and Fishery	采矿业 Mining	制造业 Manufacturing	电力、热力、燃气及水生产和供应业 Production and Supply of Electricity, Heat, Gas and Water	建筑业 Construction	批发和零售业 Wholesale and Retail Trades
全 国	**National Average**	**3.0**	**1.2**	**2.1**	**6.5**	**23.0**	**22.5**	**-0.4**
北 京	Beijing	4.9	-43.5	-30.8	-1.6	1.3		1.5
天 津	Tianjin	-16.4	-6.0	16.5	-5.6	14.3	29.7	141.4
河 北	Hebei	6.3	-17.9	-16.9	12.6	-2.4	-85.2	76.7
山 西	Shanxi	-6.6	-5.8	21.3	-11.7	-7.6	-93.3	-8.0
内蒙古	Inner Mongolia	19.8	5.1	-2.4	46.4	27.6		8.2
辽 宁	Liaoning	4.0	7.6	20.3	14.0	25.4	131.2	-7.1
吉 林	Jilin	0.3	41.5	-26.0	3.9	7.9	6.7	-55.2
黑龙江	Heilongjiang	-14.8	-24.2	3.2	-34.1	-8.5		-10.5
上 海	Shanghai	13.8	11.1		6.7	-8.6	65.7	95.0
江 苏	Jiangsu	5.2	8.9	-18.3	9.1	10.7	47.6	4.9
浙 江	Zhejiang	6.1	34.2	-8.9	14.1	16.4	184.7	-3.4
安 徽	Anhui	4.0	13.5	57.0	20.0	32.0	-44.0	30.8
福 建	Fujian	2.5	20.6	30.0	11.6	16.0	-34.2	-4.7
江 西	Jiangxi	-5.9	-4.5	-13.3	-21.1	7.7		-42.0
山 东	Shandong	5.2	1.5	19.6	11.5	36.2	162.4	0.0
河 南	Henan	2.1	-21.1	6.1	7.4	18.0		-7.1
湖 北	Hubei	5.0	7.0	6.4	6.7	34.4	-25.2	0.8
湖 南	Hunan	-3.1	-17.9	14.4	4.4	33.3	95.1	0.5
广 东	Guangdong	2.5	0.2	64.5	20.7	21.8	24.0	-7.0
广 西	Guangxi	-15.5	-22.3	-25.6	-9.6	21.4	-49.3	-29.4
海 南	Hainan	1.1	-26.0	44.7	-15.6	21.8		-43.1
重 庆	Chongqing	4.3	17.4	3.9	13.5	16.7	-91.5	-7.5
四 川	Sichuan	2.4	12.2	5.5	21.6	29.7	-3.0	48.5
贵 州	Guizhou	-5.7	-25.4	-6.2	1.9	51.6	430.1	-1.4
云 南	Yunnan	-10.6	-7.5	9.1	11.8	33.1	-31.3	0.6
西 藏	Xizang	35.1	4.2	55.5	38.2	48.0	-45.5	-28.9
陕 西	Shaanxi	0.2	6.6	-1.8	9.4	1.9	58.3	-13.5
甘 肃	Gansu	5.9	-1.9	125.8	11.0	31.3	-34.9	84.7
青 海	Qinghai	-7.5	-7.0	-8.6	26.4	7.4	106.4	-58.5
宁 夏	Ningxia	5.5	-3.4	3.1	5.7	35.1		-4.2
新 疆	Xinjiang	12.4	9.0	24.9	1.5	72.4	-60.4	-8.1

10-18 续表 1 continued

单位：% (%)

地 区	Region	交通运输、仓储和邮政业 Transport, Storage and Post	住宿和餐饮业 Hotels and Catering Services	信息传输、软件和信息技术服务业 Information Transmission, Software and Information Technology	金融业 Financial Intermediation	房地产业 Real Estate	租赁和商务服务业 Leasing and Business Services	科学研究和技术服务业 Scientific Research and Technical Services
全 国	**National Average**	**10.5**	**8.2**	**13.8**	**-11.9**	**-8.1**	**9.9**	**18.1**
北 京	Beijing	10.1	2.9	47.1	-48.9	3.5	-2.3	0.8
天 津	Tianjin	-17.2	170.9	15.9	94.4	-38.8	8.3	26.3
河 北	Hebei	30.7	-0.6	25.0	-19.8	-0.5	-23.0	7.4
山 西	Shanxi	-17.6	46.4	0.7	-51.5	-1.4	-48.1	14.5
内蒙古	Inner Mongolia	4.5	111.6	146.8	89.5	-1.2	-0.6	156.7
辽 宁	Liaoning	7.0	46.8	14.1	8.7	-21.4	30.1	133.6
吉 林	Jilin	4.4	14.4	-12.0		-18.8	6.6	-2.3
黑龙江	Heilongjiang	6.2	-17.2	-10.8	-10.5	-25.4	-19.4	6.3
上 海	Shanghai	3.8	145.8	21.6	155.1	19.1	2.8	20.6
江 苏	Jiangsu	24.0	13.8	-6.0	-9.3	-3.0	33.3	7.3
浙 江	Zhejiang	3.9	-3.8	-2.3	8.0	2.4	9.7	42.5
安 徽	Anhui	27.1	38.0	9.7	-29.1	-15.0	8.2	68.8
福 建	Fujian	7.5	35.1	9.8	124.6	-11.5	21.2	7.0
江 西	Jiangxi	40.9	3.3	-33.2	-62.2	-8.8	-0.9	-0.4
山 东	Shandong	10.4	29.7	17.4	-16.7	-9.6	5.0	25.5
河 南	Henan	26.4	-1.5	0.4	21.1	-9.3	63.5	22.1
湖 北	Hubei	14.7	3.3	34.0	-10.7	-3.7	30.4	39.2
湖 南	Hunan	-24.0	17.2	0.5	-50.6	-13.9	9.3	1.7
广 东	Guangdong	-2.1	-19.8	-2.4	-21.1	-9.6	19.9	-3.4
广 西	Guangxi	-13.5	-18.8	-19.5	2.2	-30.7	-20.9	-7.3
海 南	Hainan	-15.4	-29.3	25.8	104.3	2.7	-9.4	40.9
重 庆	Chongqing	2.0	24.9	7.6		-11.0	22.0	49.3
四 川	Sichuan	1.2	-19.8	9.4	-68.3	-18.2	3.0	27.9
贵 州	Guizhou	3.3	-28.5	58.1	-75.8	-21.8	-14.9	-37.8
云 南	Yunnan	-18.9	13.6	16.6	-4.0	-31.8	3.0	36.5
西 藏	Xizang	37.3	20.6	-45.2		21.4	40.1	74.5
陕 西	Shaanxi	19.0	43.0	-8.9	-40.4	-9.7	9.9	17.3
甘 肃	Gansu	0.0	56.4	36.8	42.5	-12.7	-23.8	29.4
青 海	Qinghai	-36.3	-36.6	17.8		-26.5	-26.0	9.7
宁 夏	Ningxia	-15.4	17.9	27.6		3.4	34.0	34.5
新 疆	Xinjiang	12.2	27.8	14.4	-43.4	-1.0	-16.1	-9.4

10-18 续表 2 continued

单位：% (%)

地 区	Region	水利、环境和公共设施管理业 Management of Water Conservancy, Environment and Public Facilities	居民服务、修理和其他服务业 Service to Households, Repair and Other Services	教育 Education	卫生和社会工作 Health and Social Service	文化、体育和娱乐业 Culture, Sports and Entertainment	公共管理、社会保障和社会组织 Public Management, Social Security and Social Organization	国际组织 International Organizations
全 国	**National Average**	**0.1**	**15.8**	**2.8**	**-3.8**	**2.6**	**-37.0**	
北 京	Beijing	9.6	245.4	-11.8	-10.6	11.4	-50.5	
天 津	Tianjin	-17.9	7.2	33.5	6.5	-33.2	-40.6	
河 北	Hebei	17.5	103.5	5.5	12.7	4.4	43.3	
山 西	Shanxi	-18.2	0.8	5.9	-8.6	-15.4	39.1	
内蒙古	Inner Mongolia	-16.0	166.9	14.3	83.0	-22.6	57.4	
辽 宁	Liaoning	12.1	-13.3	16.7	9.6	102.4	14.6	
吉 林	Jilin	7.8	-46.5	52.0	8.1	16.5	17.0	
黑龙江	Heilongjiang	-22.4	-43.9	-12.3	-14.4	-39.6	5.5	
上 海	Shanghai	5.6	40.2	12.3	22.5	-8.9	-25.4	
江 苏	Jiangsu	-4.5	56.7	7.0	13.4	-7.4	-0.7	
浙 江	Zhejiang	-0.8	1.5	15.9	3.7	13.3	0.6	
安 徽	Anhui	-7.5	-0.4	1.7	-18.9	4.9	-24.7	
福 建	Fujian	3.2	41.1	-6.3	2.8	-1.6	27.5	
江 西	Jiangxi	14.3	-5.3	32.1	34.5	-11.1	8.9	
山 东	Shandong	24.7	-19.3	-4.6	-12.4	-19.2	-19.2	
河 南	Henan	-10.0	24.2	23.1	14.6	-17.0	-10.3	
湖 北	Hubei	0.1	0.6	9.6	-13.0	-2.1	3.9	
湖 南	Hunan	-7.9	-4.2	-4.4	-13.7	19.8	-7.0	
广 东	Guangdong	0.1	1.5	-0.3	-6.2	16.3	5.8	
广 西	Guangxi	-24.4	-22.6	-20.5	-21.6	-29.3	-21.7	
海 南	Hainan	7.9	283.7	-0.7	-23.4	6.5	35.1	
重 庆	Chongqing	9.3	80.4	18.5	19.1	13.5	-8.0	
四 川	Sichuan	19.9	46.9	-0.2	-5.5	34.2	-18.2	
贵 州	Guizhou	-20.9	-9.2	-11.8	3.3	-28.6	-48.5	
云 南	Yunnan	-24.8	14.8	-12.5	-19.1	28.9	-72.0	
西 藏	Xizang	37.6	51.6	91.6	-14.7	39.4	73.1	
陕 西	Shaanxi	3.4	82.6	-16.3	-6.8	-8.0	14.4	
甘 肃	Gansu	-0.2	-33.0	-4.6	24.8	-6.4	73.4	
青 海	Qinghai	1.5	-44.3	-5.9	13.2	0.2	-28.1	
宁 夏	Ningxia	-12.8	-11.3	5.0	-43.7	-6.5	-19.2	
新 疆	Xinjiang	-13.9	44.4	-2.2	-36.0	-3.0	-10.8	

10−19 农村农户固定资产投资比上年增长情况(2023年)
Growth Rate of Investment in Fixed Assets of Rural Households over Preceding Year (2023)

单位：% (%)

地 区	Region	全部投资 Total Investment in Fixed Assets	#竣工房屋投资 Investment in Buildings Completed	#住宅投资 Investment in Residential Buildings
全 国	**National Average**	**-10.0**	**0.9**	**-11.6**
北 京	Beijing	-29.9	-32.6	-32.9
天 津	Tianjin	117.7	40.0	35.5
河 北	Hebei	-4.8	-25.8	-30.8
山 西	Shanxi	19.7	29.1	29.3
内蒙古	Inner Mongolia	1.4	-0.3	-13.4
辽 宁	Liaoning	-5.2	3.4	-6.7
吉 林	Jilin	7.0	44.3	25.3
黑龙江	Heilongjiang	-25.1	52.4	145.3
上 海	Shanghai	76.4	25.1	19.2
江 苏	Jiangsu	-2.4	1.7	-2.2
浙 江	Zhejiang	-59.2	79.4	-52.5
安 徽	Anhui	5.2	-34.6	-37.9
福 建	Fujian	-12.7	-4.7	-5.1
江 西	Jiangxi	-5.0	-2.9	-4.7
山 东	Shandong	-42.6	-38.3	-33.2
河 南	Henan	-15.9	-18.1	-23.5
湖 北	Hubei	-7.3	-17.6	-16.8
湖 南	Hunan	-9.2	-9.3	-11.1
广 东	Guangdong	-21.2	-40.8	-43.1
广 西	Guangxi	-4.9	-20.5	-20.8
海 南	Hainan	41.3	27.1	29.8
重 庆	Chongqing	-3.5	-2.9	-3.0
四 川	Sichuan	7.6	21.3	28.4
贵 州	Guizhou	-11.3	16.1	12.8
云 南	Yunnan	7.5	18.3	25.9
西 藏	Xizang			
陕 西	Shaanxi	4.9	7.0	1.3
甘 肃	Gansu	1.5	7.9	8.3
青 海	Qinghai	116.1	130.3	134.9
宁 夏	Ningxia	-10.7	115.7	116.9
新 疆	Xinjiang	-3.4	59.4	-6.3

主要统计指标解释

全社会固定资产投资　是以货币形式表现的在一定时期内全社会建造和购置固定资产的工作量以及与此有关费用的总称。该指标是反映固定资产投资规模、结构和发展速度的综合性指标。全社会固定资产投资按登记注册类型可分为国有、集体、联营、股份制、私营和个体、港澳台商、外商、其他等。

固定资产投资（不含农户）　指城镇和农村各种登记注册统计类别的企业、事业、行政单位及城镇个体户进行的计划总投资 500 万元及以上的建设项目投资和房地产开发投资，包括原口径的城镇固定资产投资加上农村企事业组织项目投资，该口径自 2011 年起开始使用。

民间固定资产投资　指具有集体、私营、个人性质的内资调查单位以及由其控股（包括绝对控股和相对控股）的调查单位在中华人民共和国境内建造或购置固定资产的投资。

基础设施投资　指为社会生产和生活提供基础性、大众性服务的工程和设施，是社会赖以生存和发展的基本条件。包括以下行业投资：铁路运输业、道路运输业、水上运输业、航空运输业、管道运输业、多式联运和运输代理业、装卸搬运业、邮政业、电信广播电视和卫星传输服务业、互联网和相关服务业、水利管理业、生态保护和环境治理业、公共设施管理业。

实际到位资金　指用于固定资产投资的各种货币资金。包括国家预算资金、国内贷款、利用外资、自筹资金和其他资金。

国家预算资金　国家预算包括一般预算、政府性基金预算、国有资本经营预算和社保基金预算。各类预算中用于固定资产投资的资金全部作为国家预算资金填报，其中一般预算中用于固定资产投资的部分包括基建投资、车购税、灾后恢复重建基金和其他财政投资。各级政府债券也应归入国家预算资金。

国内贷款　指报告期固定资产投资项目单位向银行及非银行金融机构借入用于固定资产投资的各种国内借款，包括银行利用自有资金及吸收存款发放的贷款、上级拨入的国内贷款、国家专项贷款（包括煤代油贷款、劳改煤矿专项贷款等），地方财政专项资金安排的贷款、国内储备贷款、周转贷款等。

利用外资　指报告期收到的境外（包括外国及港澳台地区）资金(包括设备、材料、技术在内)。包括对外借款(外国政府贷款、国际金融组织贷款、出口信贷、外国银行商业贷款、对外发行债券和股票)、外商直接投资、外商其他投资(包括补偿贸易、加工装配由外商提供的设备价款、国际租赁、外商投资收益的再投资资金)。不包括我国自有外汇资金(国家外汇、地方外汇、留成外汇、调剂外汇和国内银行自有资金发放的外汇贷款等)。各类外资按报告期的外汇牌价（中间价）折成人民币计算。

自筹资金　指在报告期内筹集的用于项目建设和购置的资金。包括自有资金、股东投入资金和借入资金，但不包括各类财政性资金、从各类金融机构借入资金和国外资金。

其他资金来源　指在报告期收到的除以上各种资金之外的用于固定资产投资的资金。包括社会集资、个人资金、无偿捐赠的资金及其他单位拨入的资金等。

固定资产投资按国民经济行业分　指根据其从事的社会经济活动性质对各类单位进行的分类。应根据建设项目建成投产后的主要产品种类或主要用途及社会经济活动种类来划分，不能根据项目单位本身的行业类别来划分。如果项目投产后有几种产品，应根据主要产品来确定行业类别。一般情况下，一个建设项目只能属于一种国民经济行业。

固定资产投资按隶属关系分　是按建设单位或企业、事业、行政单位的主管上级机关确定的。

（1）中央　是指中共中央、人大常委会和国务院各部、委、局、总公司以及直属机构直接领导的建设项目和企业、事业、行政单位。这些单位的固定资产投资计划由国务院各部门直接编制和下达，统一组织或委托下级实施。包括有中央垂直管理的部门（如国家统计局各级调查队）和中央直属企业、事业单位（如工商银行、中国电信、中国石油）等。

（2）地方　是由省（自治区、直辖市）、地（区、市、州、盟）、县（区、市、旗）三级政府及业务主管部门直接领导和管理的建设项目、企业、事业、行政单位。地方项目还包括不隶属以上各级政府及主管部门的建设项目和企业、事业单位，如外商投资企业和无主管部门的企业等。

固定资产投资按建设性质分　按整个建设项目情况来确定。建设项目的性质一般分为新建、扩建、改建和技术改造、单纯建造生活设施、迁建、恢复、单纯购置。农户投资不划分建设性质。

（1）新建　指从无到有“平地起家”开始建设的项目。现有企业、事业、行政单位投资的项目一般不属于新建。但如有的单位原有基础很小，经过建设后新增的固定资产价值超过该企业、事业、行政单位原有固定资产价值（原值）三倍以上的，也应作为新建。

（2）扩建　指在厂内或其他地点，为扩大原有产品的生产能力（或效益）或增加新的产品生产能力，而增建的生产车间（或主要工程）、分厂、独立的生产线等项目。行政、事业单位在原单位增建业务性用房（如学校增建教学用房、医院增建门诊部、病房等）也作为扩建。

现有企、事业单位为扩大原有主要产品生产能力或增加新的产品生产能力，增建一个或几个主要生产车间（或主要工程）、分厂，同时进行一些更新改造工程的，也应作为扩建。

（3）改建和技术改造　指现有企业、事业单位对原有设施进行技术改造或更新（包括相应配套的辅助性生产、生活福利设施）的建设项目。改建项目包括企业、事业单位为适应市场变化的需要，而改变企业的主要产品种类（如军工企业转民用产品等）的建设项目；原有产品生产作业线由于各工序（车间）之间能力不平衡，为填平补齐充分发挥原有生产能力而增建但不增加主要产品生产能力的建设项目。技术改造是指企业、事业单位在现有基础上用先进的技术代替落后的技术，用先进的工艺和装备代替落后的工艺和装备，以改变企业落后的技术经济面貌，实现以内涵为主的扩大再生产，达到提高产品质量、促进产品更新换代、节约能源、降低消耗、扩大生产规模、全面提高社会经效益的目的。技术改造具体包括以下内容：机器设备和工具的更新改造；生产工艺改革、节约能源和原材料的改造；厂房建筑和公共设施的改造；保护环境进行的“三废”治理改造；劳动条件和生产环境的改造等。

固定资产投资按构成分

（1）建筑工程　指各种房屋、建筑物的建造工程。这部分投资额必须兴工动料，通过施工活动才能实现，是固定资产投资额的重要组成部分。

（2）安装工程　指各种设备、装置的安装工程。

在安装工程中，不包括被安装设备本身价值。

（3）设备工器具购置　指报告期内购置或自制的，达到固定资产标准的设备、工具、器具的价值。新建单位及扩建单位的新建车间，按照设计或计划要求购置或自制的全部设备、工具、器具，不论是否达到固定资产标准均计入“设备工器具购置”中。

（4）其他费用　指在固定资产建造和购置过程中发生的，除建筑安装工程和设备、工器具购置投资完成额以外的应当分摊计入固定资产投资的费用，不指经营中财务上的其他费用。

Explanatory Notes on Main Statistical Indicators

Total Investment in Fixed Assets in the Whole Country refers to the volume of activities in construction and purchases of fixed assets of the whole country and related fees, expressed in monetary terms during the reference period. It is a comprehensive indicator which shows the size, structure and growth of the investment in fixed assets, providing a basis for observing the progress of construction projects and evaluating results of investment. Total investment in fixed assets in the whole country includes, by type of ownership, the investment by State-owned units, collective-owned units, joint ownership units, share-holding units, private units, individuals as well as investments by entrepreneurs from Hong Kong, Macao and Taiwan, foreign investors and others.

Investment in Fixed Assets (Excluding Rural Households) refers to the investment in construction projects with a total planned investment of 5 million yuan and over by enterprises of various ownerships, institutions, administrative units and urban self-employed individuals, and the investment in real estate development in both urban and rural areas. Since 2011, it covers the urban investment in fixed assets under the previous statistical coverage plus project investments by rural enterprises and institutions.

Non-governmental Investment in Fixed Assets refers to the investment in the construction or purchase of fixed assets in the territory of the People's Republic of China by domestic-funded enterprises and institutions with collective, private and personal nature and by enterprises and institutions controlled by them (including absolute and relative holding).

Infrastructure Investment refers to projects and facilities that provide basic and popular services for social production and life. It is the basic condition for the survival and development of society. It includes: railway transport, road transport, water transport, air transport, pipeline transport, multimodal transport and transport agent Intermodality and Forwarding Agency, loading and unloading, posts, telecommunications, radio and television and satellite transmission services, Internet and related services, water management industry, ecological protection and environmental governance, public facilities management.

Actual Funds for Investment refer to all kinds of monetary funds used for fixed assets investment. It includes state budget funds, domestic loans, foreign capital utilization, self-raising funds and other funds.

Fund from the State Budget State budget consists of general budget, government fund budget, operation budget of state-owned assets and social security fund budget. Funds for investment in fixed assets from various budgets are reported as fund from the state budget, of which, the general budget utilized on fixed assets investment includes investment on infrastructure construction, vehicle purchase tax, post-disaster restoration and reconstruction funds and other financial investment. Government bonds at all levels should also be included.

Domestic Loans refer to loans of various forms borrowed by investing units from banks and non-bank financial institutions during the reference period for the purpose of investment in fixed assets, including loans issued by banks from their self-owned funds and deposit, loans appropriated by higher responsible authorities, special loans by government (including loan for substituting petroleum with coal, special loans for reform-through-labour coal mines), loans arranged by local government from special funds, domestic reserve loan, and revolving loan, etc.

Foreign Investment refers to overseas (including foreign countries, Hong Kong, Macao and Taiwan) funds received during the reference period (covering equipment, materials and technology), including foreign borrowings (loans from foreign governments and international financial institutions, export credit, commercial loans from foreign banks, issue of bonds and stocks overseas), foreign direct investment and other foreign investments (including funds from foreign direct investment income that are reinvested in fixed assets domestically). Excluded from this category is capital in foreign exchanges owned by China (foreign exchanges owned by the central and local governments, foreign exchanges retained by enterprises, foreign exchanges by enterprises through the regulating mechanism, loans in foreign exchanges issued by the Bank of China with its own fund, etc.). In calculating the utilization of foreign capital, foreign currencies are converted into Chinese Renminbi applying the exchange rate (central parity rate) at the end of the reference period.

Self-raised Funds refer to funds for investment in fixed assets received during the reference period by investing units, including investment in fixed assets using own funds of various enterprises and institutions or funds raised from other units other than financial funds, funds borrowed from financial institutions and overseas funds.

Other Funds refer to funds for investment in fixed assets received from sources other than those listed above, including funds raised from individuals and through donations, and funds transferred from other units.

Investment in Fixed Assets by Sector refers to the classification of investment by the nature of social economic activities the investing units are engaged in. The classification of construction projects by sector is determined by the major products or the purpose of the projects when they are put into production or use, and by the nature of their social economic activities, instead of being determined by industrial classification of the project enterprises. The project will be classified according to major product if there are several kinds of products yielded. In general, one project can only be classified into one sector.

Investment in Fixed Assets by Jurisdiction of Management refers to the classification of investment by the competent authorities under which investment is made by construction units, enterprises, institutions or administrative units.

(1) Central investment refers to the investment in projects or by enterprises, institutions or administrative units which are under the direct leadership and management of the State Council and of the national commissions, ministries, agencies and State-owned large corporations. Various ministries and departments of the State Council prepare and implement plans through unified organization or lower-level commissions, which include departments direct under central government (i.e. survey offices at all level of the National Bureau of Statistics) and enterprises and institutions directly under central government (like the Industrial and Commercial Bank of China, China Telecom and China National Petroleum Corporation).

(2) Local investment refers to the investment in projects or by enterprises, institutions or administrative units which are under the direct leadership and management of competent departments and governments at the level of province (autonomous regions and municipalities directly under the Central Government), prefecture （prefectures, cities and leagues） and county (districts, cities and banners). Also included are projects by foreign-invested enterprises and enterprises without competent managing authorities.

Investment in Fixed Assets by Type of Construction Construction projects in general can be classified, by the type of construction, into new construction, expansion, reconstruction and technical transformation, purely construction of living facilities, moving, restoration and purely purchasing. However, investment by type of construction is not applied to investment by real-estate development units and investment by rural households.

(1) New construction in general refers to construction projects, which start from scratch. The existing projects invested by enterprises, institutions and administrative agencies cannot be classified as new construction. In case the size of the existing unit is quite small, and the value of newly added fixed assets is more than three times of the original value, the expansion will be considered as new construction.

(2) Expansion refers to projects of construction of new production workshop, branch factory or independent production line within a factory or in other locations, for the purpose of increasing the production capacity (or improving efficiency) or adding new production capacity. Newly constructed accommodation for the operation of institutions and administrative organizations (such as newly constructed buildings for teaching in schools, buildings for clinics or wards in hospitals, etc.) are also classified as expansion.

Also included in expansion are investments by existing enterprises or institutions in building major production line(s) or branch factory (ies) along with some work on innovation, for the purpose of expanding the production capacity of original products or producing new products.

(3) Reconstruction and technical transformation refers to construction projects by existing enterprises or institutions in innovation or technical transformation of the old facilities (including auxiliary production equipment and welfare facilities). Also considered as reconstruction is the construction of new workshops by the existing enterprises or institutions to change the variety of products to meet the market demand (such as the production of civil products by defence industries), or to bring the designed production capacity into full play through a more balanced production process on production lines. Technical transformation refers to replacement of old technology or equipment by new technology or equipment, in order to expand the reproduction through improvement of technology contents in production, to improve product quality, to promote new products, to save energy, to reduce consumption, to expand the production scale and to improve overall social-economic efficiency. Contents of technical transformation include: updating of machinery, equipment and tools; reforming production process by using energy or materials saving technology; construction of factory workshops and transformation of public facilities; treatment transformation of “three wastes” (waste gas, waste water and industrial residue) aiming at environmental protection; improvement of working conditions and environment, etc.

Investment in Fixed Assets by Structure

(1) Construction refers to the construction of houses and buildings, also known as work volume of construction. This part of investment can only be achieved through construction activities, it is the major component of the total investment in fixed assets.

(2) Installation refers to the installation of various kinds of equipment and instruments, also known as work volume of installation.

The value of equipment installed itself is not included in the value of installation projects.

(3) Purchase of equipment and instruments refers to the total value of equipment, tools, and instruments purchased or self-produced which come up to the cut-off point for fixed assets during the reference period. Equipment, tools and instruments purchased or self-produced for new workshops by newly established or expanded units are categorized as “purchase of equipment and instruments” no matter whether they come up to the cut-off point for fixed assets.

(4) Other expenses refer to expenses arising during the construction or purchase of fixed assets other than those expenses on construction, installation and purchase of equipment and instruments. Other financial expenses arising in operation are not included.

11

对外经济贸易

International Trade and Economic Cooperation

简 要 说 明

本篇资料综合反映中国的货物贸易、服务进出口、利用外资、对外直接投资、对外经济合作的历年概况，重点反映对外经济贸易的近期发展状况。

一、货物贸易部分

主要内容包括进出口货物的品种、数(重)量、金额、国别(地区)、收发货人所在地、境内目的地和货源地等项目。

统计范围是按照联合国的国际货物贸易统计原则制定的，即凡能引起中华人民共和国关境内物质资源存量增加或减少的进出口货物，除制度另有规定者外，均列入该项统计。

资料来源于海关总署，调查方法是全面调查。

历年出口商品分类金额和历年进口商品分类金额按照联合国《国际贸易标准分类》(SITC)进行统计。进出口商品目录是在海关合作理事会（世界海关组织 WCO）制定的《商品名称和编码协调制度》(HS)的基础上，结合我国进出口实际情况制定的。

我国对各国(地区)进出口总额表中，出口货物按中华人民共和国关境外最终目的国(地区)，进口货物按中华人民共和国关境外原产国(地区)统计。各地区进出口商品总值分别按境内收发货人所在地、境内目的地和货源地列示。收发货人所在地是指中华人民共和国关境内进出口企业报关注册的登记地；境内货源地是指出口货物在中华人民共和国关境内的产地或原始发货地；境内目的地则指进口货物在中华人民共和国关境内的消费、使用地或最终运抵地。

二、服务进出口部分

主要内容包括服务提供者从中国关境内向其他国家或地区的服务消费者提供的服务，即服务出口；以及境外服务提供者从其他国家或地区向中国关境内的服务消费者提供的服务，即服务进口。

资料来源于商务部。

三、利用外资部分

主要内容包括外商直接投资情况和外商投资企业登记注册情况。

外商直接投资情况的统计范围是在中华人民共和国境内设立的外商投资企业和合作开发项目（包括港澳台地区投资企业）。资料来源于商务部。

外商投资企业登记注册情况的统计范围是经市场监督管理机关核准登记的外商投资企业，在境内从事经营活动的外国及港澳台地区企业以及外商投资企业分支机构。资料来源于国家市场监督管理总局。

特殊说明:利用外资统计 1985 年及以前为政府统计部门的调查汇总数，1986 年及以后全部来源于商务部（2003 年以前为对外贸易经济合作部）。

四、对外直接投资部分

主要内容包括对外直接投资流量、存量及非金融类对外直接投资流量。

统计范围主要包括境内投资者通过直接投资方式在境外拥有或控制 10%或以上股权、投票权或其他等价利益的各类公司型和非公司型的境外直接投资企业。

资料来源于商务部，调查方法是全面调查。

五、对外经济合作部分

主要内容包括对外承包工程的合同数、合同金额、完成营业额以及对外劳务合作派出人数、年末在外人数等。

统计范围是发生对外承包工程业务的企业或单位，有对外劳务合作经营资格的企业以及海员外派机构。

资料来源于商务部，调查方法是全面调查。

Brief Introduction

Data in this chapter provide summary data of China's international trade in goods and services, utilization of foreign capital, outward foreign direct investment, contracted projects and labour cooperation with foreign countries or territories over the years, focusing on the recent situation of international trade and economic cooperation.

I. Trade in Goods

Data mainly include: varieties of imports and exports, quantity (weight), value, countries (regions), import and export corporations, destination within territory, origin of goods within territory and so on.

The scope of statistics are designed according to United Nations' principles on international goods trade statistics, that is: all imports or exports that will lead to stock changes of material resources within the territory of the People's Republic of China; excluding goods by escape clause.

The data are from the General Administration of Customs of the People's Republic of China through a comprehensive reporting system.

Customs statistics in value terms for both imports and exports are compiled according to the classifications of *UN Standard International Trade Classification (SITC)*. The list of the imported and exported commodities is compiled based on the *Harmonized Commodity Description and Coding System (HS)* stipulated by the Customs Cooperation Council (World Customs Organization), taking into consideration of China's reality of imports and exports.

In the tables on China's total imports and exports with related countries and regions, the exported commodities are compiled by the countries (regions) of destination outside China's customs, and the imported commodities are compiled by the countries (regions) of origin outside China's customs. The total values of the imports and exports by region are compiled respectively at the provinces where the import or export corporations are located and at the provinces of destination or provinces of origin within the border of the People's Republic of China. The province where the import or export corporations are located refers to the province where the import or export corporations have declared to and have been registered at the Customs. The province of origin within the border of the Peoples Republic of China refers to the province where the export commodities are produced or originally delivered. The province of destination within the border of the People's Republic of China refers to the province where the imported commodities are consumed, used or transported to the destination.

II. Trade in Services

Data mainly include services provided by service providers to service consumers in other countries or regions from China's customs territory, that is, exports in services; And the services provided by overseas service providers from other countries or regions to service consumers within the customs territory of China, that is, imports in services.

The data are from the Ministry of Commerce.

III. Utilization of Foreign Capitals

Data mainly include: foreign direct investment of China and the basic condition of registration of foreign invested enterprises.

The statistical scope of foreign direct investment of China is the foreign invested enterprises and cooperative development projects (including enterprises with investment from Hong Kong, Macao and Taiwan) established within the territory of the People's Republic of China. The data are from the Ministry of Commerce.

The statistical scope of the basic condition of registration of foreign invested enterprises includes foreign invested enterprises approved and registered by the market supervision and administration organ, foreign and Hong Kong, Macao and Taiwan enterprises engaged in business activities in China and branches of foreign-invested enterprises. The data come from the State Administration for Market Regulation.

Special notice: data on utilization of foreign capitals before 1985 were survey results from governmental statistical agencies, since 1986 all data are from the Ministry of Commerce (formerly MOFTEC before 2003).

IV. Outward Foreign Direct Investment

Data mainly include: outward FDI flows, outward FDI stock and outward FDI flows of non-financial sector.

Statistics cover all types of overseas corporations and non-corporations that domestic investors own or control 10% or more equity, voting rights or other equivalent interests through direct investment.

Data are from the Ministry of Commerce through comprehensive survey.

V. Foreign Economic Cooperation

Data mainly include: number of contracts for overseas contracted projects, contracted volume, completed business turnover, and dispatched workers for overseas labour services, persons abroad by the end of year and so on.

Statistics in this aspect cover enterprises or units that have overseas contracted projects, enterprises with qualifications for overseas labour services and qualified agencies engaging in dispatching seamen.

The data are from the Ministry of Commerce through a comprehensive reporting system.

11－1　对外经济贸易基本情况
International Trade and Economic Cooperation

指　　标	Item	2019	2020	2021	2022	2023
货物进出口总额(亿元人民币)	**Import and Export of Goods (RMB 100 million)**	**315627.3**	**322215.2**	**387391.8**	**416727.8**	**417510.1**
出口总额	Exports	172373.6	179278.8	214255.2	236336.8	237656.4
进口总额	Imports	143253.7	142936.4	173136.6	180391.0	179853.7
进出口差额	Balance	29119.9	36342.4	41118.7	55945.8	57802.6
货物进出口总额 (亿美元)	**Import and Export of Goods (USD 100 million)**	**45778.9**	**46559.1**	**59954.3**	**62509.4**	**59359.8**
出口总额	Exports	24994.8	25899.5	33160.2	35444.3	33790.4
进口总额	Imports	20784.1	20659.6	26794.1	27065.1	25569.4
进出口差额	Balance	4210.7	5239.9	6366.1	8379.3	8221.0
服务进出口总额 (亿美元)	**Import and Export of Services (USD 100 million)**	**7850.0**	**6617.2**	**8212.5**	**8891.1**	**9331.2**
出口总额	Exports	2836.0	2806.3	3942.5	4240.6	3811.2
进口总额	Imports	5014.0	3810.9	4270.0	4650.5	5520.0
进出口差额	Balance	-2178.0	-1004.6	-327.5	-409.9	-1708.7
外商直接投资额 (亿美元)	**Inward Foreign Direct Investment (USD 100 million)**	**1412.2**	**1493.4**	**1809.6**	**1891.3**	**1632.5**
新设立外商直接投资企业数(个)	**Newly Established Foreign-Invested Enterprises (FIEs) (unit)**	**40910**	**38578**	**47647**	**38497**	**53766**
外资企业基本情况	**Registered Foreign-Invested Enterprises**					
年底登记户数 (户)	Number of Registered Enterprises (unit)	627223	635402	663562	674140	695695
投资总额 (亿美元)	Total Investment (USD 100 million)	88400.3	136437.0	179571.6	200425.0	293380.3
注册资本 (亿美元)	Registered Capital (USD 100 million)	50159.7	84334.2	111964.0	138731.0	316218.5
#外方	Foreign Capital	37894.5	62823.1	85597.0	109235.0	277534.4
对外直接投资流量 (亿美元)	**Outward Foreign Direct Investment(USD 100 million)**	**1369.1**	**1537.1**	**1788.2**	**1631.2**	**1772.9**
对外经济合作 (亿美元)	**Economic Cooperation with Foreign Countries & Regions (USD 100 million)**					
对外承包工程合同金额	Contracted Value of Contracted Projects	2602.5	2555.4	2584.9	2530.7	2645.1
对外承包工程完成营业额	Value of Turnover Fulfilled of Contracted Projects	1729.0	1559.4	1549.4	1549.9	1609.1

注：外资企业基本情况数据来自国家市场监督管理总局，数据包含港澳台投资企业。

a) Data of foreign-invested enterprises come from State Administration for Market Regulation and include the data of enterprises with investment from Hong Kong, Macao and Taiwan.

11-2 货物进出口总额
International Trade in Goods

年份 Year	亿元人民币 RMB 100 million				亿美元 USD 100 million			
	进出口总额 Total	出口总额 Exports	进口总额 Imports	差额 Balance	进出口总额 Total	出口总额 Exports	进口总额 Imports	差额 Balance
1978	355.0	167.7	187.4	-19.7	206.4	97.5	108.9	-11.5
1980	570.0	271.2	298.8	-27.6	381.4	181.2	200.2	-19.0
1985	2066.7	808.9	1257.9	-449.0	696.0	273.5	422.5	-149.0
1990	5560.1	2985.8	2574.3	411.6	1154.4	620.9	533.5	87.5
1991	7225.8	3827.1	3398.7	428.5	1356.3	718.4	637.9	80.5
1992	9119.6	4676.3	4443.3	233.0	1655.3	849.4	805.9	43.6
1993	11271.0	5284.8	5986.2	-701.4	1957.0	917.4	1039.6	-122.2
1994	20381.9	10421.8	9960.1	461.8	2366.2	1210.1	1156.2	53.9
1995	23499.9	12451.8	11048.1	1403.7	2808.6	1487.8	1320.8	167.0
1996	24133.9	12576.4	11557.4	1019.0	2898.8	1510.5	1388.3	122.2
1997	26967.2	15160.7	11806.6	3354.1	3251.6	1827.9	1423.7	404.2
1998	26849.7	15223.5	11626.1	3597.4	3239.5	1837.1	1402.4	434.8
1999	29896.2	16159.8	13736.5	2423.3	3606.3	1949.3	1657.0	292.3
2000	39273.3	20634.4	18638.8	1995.6	4743.0	2492.0	2250.9	241.1
2001	42183.6	22024.4	20159.2	1865.3	5096.5	2661.0	2435.5	225.5
2002	51378.2	26947.9	24430.3	2517.6	6207.7	3256.0	2951.7	304.3
2003	70483.5	36287.9	34195.6	2092.3	8509.9	4382.3	4127.6	254.7
2004	95539.1	49103.3	46435.8	2667.6	11545.5	5933.3	5612.3	321.0
2005	116921.8	62648.1	54273.7	8374.4	14219.1	7619.5	6599.5	1020.0
2006	140974.7	77597.9	63376.9	14221.0	17604.4	9689.8	7914.6	1775.2
2007	166924.1	93627.1	73296.9	20330.2	21761.8	12200.6	9561.2	2639.4
2008	179921.5	100394.9	79526.5	20868.4	25632.6	14306.9	11325.6	2981.3
2009	150648.1	82029.7	68618.4	13411.3	22075.4	12016.1	10059.2	1956.9
2010	201722.3	107022.8	94699.5	12323.3	29740.0	15777.5	13962.5	1815.1
2011	236402.0	123240.6	113161.4	10079.2	36418.6	18983.8	17434.8	1549.0
2012	244160.2	129359.3	114801.0	14558.3	38671.2	20487.1	18184.1	2303.1
2013	258168.9	137131.4	121037.5	16094.0	41589.9	22090.0	19499.9	2590.2
2014	264241.8	143883.8	120358.0	23525.7	43015.3	23422.9	19592.4	3830.6
2015	245502.9	141166.8	104336.1	36830.7	39530.3	22734.7	16795.6	5939.0
2016	243386.5	138419.3	104967.2	33452.1	36855.6	20976.3	15879.3	5097.1
2017	278099.2	153309.4	124789.8	28519.6	41071.4	22633.4	18437.9	4195.5
2018	305010.1	164128.8	140881.3	23247.5	46224.4	24867.0	21357.5	3509.5
2019	315627.3	172373.6	143253.7	29119.9	45778.9	24994.8	20784.1	4210.7
2020	322215.2	179278.8	142936.4	36342.4	46559.1	25899.5	20659.6	5239.9
2021	387391.8	214255.2	173136.6	41118.7	59954.3	33160.2	26794.1	6366.1
2022	416727.8	236336.8	180391.0	55945.8	62509.4	35444.3	27065.1	8379.3
2023	417510.1	237656.4	179853.7	57802.6	59359.8	33790.4	25569.4	8221.0

注：1.本表1978年为外贸业务统计数，1980年起为海关进出口统计数。
2.货物进出口差额负数为逆差。

a) Data in 1978 were from the Ministry of Foreign Trade; and data since 1980 are from China Customs statistics.
b) A negative balance indicates trade deficit. That is, imports surpassing exports.

11−3 按国际贸易标准分类分进出口商品金额(2023年)
International Trade in Goods by SITC (2023)

商品分类	Commodity (by SITC)	出口总额 Exports		进口总额 Imports	
		亿元人民币 RMB 100 million	亿美元 USD 100 million	亿元人民币 RMB 100 million	亿美元 USD 100 million
总额	**Total**	**237656.36**	**33790.44**	**179853.75**	**25569.41**
初级产品	**Primary Goods**	**11538.11**	**1640.77**	**76351.76**	**10862.17**
食品及活动物	**Food and Live Animals**	**5156.83**	**733.18**	**9064.66**	**1290.44**
活动物	Live Animals	34.89	4.96	33.06	4.71
肉及肉制品	Meat and Meat Preparations	200.50	28.51	1886.77	268.67
乳品及蛋品	Dairy Products and Birds' Eggs	34.92	4.96	515.50	73.50
鱼、甲壳及软体类动物及其制品	Fish, Crustaceans, Molluscs and Aquatic Invertebrates, and Preparations Thereof	1360.19	193.52	1350.75	192.29
谷物及其制品	Cereals and Cereal Preparations	186.13	26.41	1553.09	221.28
蔬菜及水果	Vegetables and Fruit	1920.55	272.84	1728.77	246.11
糖、糖制品及蜂蜜	Sugars, Sugar Preparations and Honey	250.92	35.65	286.79	40.53
咖啡、茶、可可、调味料及其制品	Coffee, Tea, Cocoa, Spices, and Manufactures Thereof	313.37	44.58	221.35	31.45
饲料(不包括未碾磨谷物)	Feeding Stuff For Animals(Not Including Unmilled Cereals)	277.34	39.48	586.73	83.63
杂项食品	Miscellaneous Edible Products And Preparations	578.02	82.26	901.85	128.27
饮料及烟类	**Beverages and Tobacco**	**266.37**	**37.81**	**555.50**	**78.99**
饮料	Beverages	206.13	29.26	401.16	56.87
烟草及其制品	Tobacco and Tobacco Manufactures	60.24	8.55	154.34	22.13
非食用原料(燃料除外)	**Crude Materials, Inedible, Except Fuels**	**1570.71**	**223.65**	**29481.73**	**4195.12**
生皮及生毛皮	Hides, Skins and Furskins, Raw	1.83	0.26	96.74	13.76
油籽及含油果实	Oil-seeds and Oleaginous Fruits	98.99	14.08	4660.19	663.48
生橡胶(包括合成橡胶及再生橡胶)	Crude Rubber (Including Synthetic and Reclaimed)	131.95	18.78	829.18	118.04
软木及木材	Cork and Wood	32.59	4.65	1157.85	165.00
纸浆及废纸	Pulp and Waste Paper	20.31	2.89	1673.66	238.48
纺织纤维及其废料	Textile Fibres and Their Wastes	316.47	45.05	628.00	88.98
天然肥料及矿物(煤、石油及宝石除外)	Crude Fertilizers, and Crude Minerals (Excluding Coal, Petroleum and Precious Stones)	258.32	36.80	1503.25	214.67
金属矿砂及金属废料	Metalliferous Ores and Metal Scrap	285.92	40.72	18692.09	2658.40
其他动、植物原料	Crude Animal and Vegetable Materials, n.e.s.	424.33	60.43	240.77	34.31
矿物燃料、润滑油及有关原料	**Mineral Fuels, Lubricants and Related Materials**	**4300.63**	**611.56**	**36292.63**	**5161.54**
煤、焦炭及煤砖	Coal, Coke and Briquettes	256.56	36.46	3743.03	532.49
石油、石油产品及有关原料	Petroleum, Petroleum Products and Related Materials	3667.31	521.45	26590.93	3781.41
天然气及人造气	Gas, Natural and Manufactured	256.02	36.48	5944.81	845.68
电流	Electric Current	120.74	17.16	13.86	1.97
动、植物油脂及蜡	**Animal and Vegetable Oils, Fats and Wax**	**243.57**	**34.58**	**957.24**	**136.07**
动物油、脂	Animal Oils and Fats	36.65	5.21	37.05	5.26
植物油、脂	Vegetable Oils and Fats	28.82	4.10	858.20	122.01
已加工的动植物油、脂及动植物蜡	Animal or Vegetable Fats and Oils, Processed; Waxes of Animal or Vegetable Origin	178.11	25.27	61.99	8.80

11-3 续表 continued

商品分类	Commodity (by SITC)	出口总额 Exports		进口总额 Imports	
		亿 元 人民币 RMB 100 million	亿美元 USD 100 million	亿 元 人民币 RMB 100 million	亿美元 USD 100 million
工业制品	**Manufactured Goods**	**226118.26**	**32149.66**	**103501.99**	**14707.24**
化学成品及有关产品	**Chemicals and Related Products**	**18251.85**	**2599.11**	**16795.99**	**2389.77**
有机化学品	Organic Chemicals	4857.41	692.02	3510.71	499.65
无机化学品	Inorganic Chemicals	2360.27	336.79	1775.48	253.10
染料、鞣料及着色料	Dyeing, Tanning and Colouring Materials	645.30	91.89	333.02	47.29
医药品	Medicinal and Pharmaceutical Products	1563.64	222.57	3612.08	513.49
精油、香料及盥洗、光洁制品	Essential Oils and Resinoids and Perfume Materials; Toilet, Polishing and Cleansing Preparations	880.11	125.04	1460.73	207.93
制成肥料	Fertilizers	681.31	96.73	393.08	56.04
初级形状的塑料	Plastics in Primary Forms	2239.08	319.07	3181.49	452.69
非初级形状的塑料	Plastics in Non-primary Forms	1842.31	262.01	826.22	117.30
其他化学原料及产品	Chemical Materials and Products	3182.41	452.99	1703.17	242.27
按原料分类的制成品	**Manufactured Goods Classified Chiefly by Material**	**38189.43**	**5434.68**	**11839.25**	**1682.50**
皮革、皮革制品及已鞣毛皮	Leather, Leather Manufactures and Dressed Furskins	185.98	26.45	168.73	23.96
橡胶制品	Rubber Manufactures	2116.29	301.00	320.30	45.51
软木及木制品(家具除外)	Cork and Wood Manufactures (Excluding Furniture)	1075.32	152.87	111.09	15.76
纸及纸板；纸浆、纸及纸板制品	Paper, Paperboard and Articles of Paper Pulp, of Paper or of Paperboard	2187.15	311.08	500.80	71.18
纺纱、织物、制成品及有关产品	Textile Yarn, Fabrics, Made-up Articles and Related Products	9436.10	1342.51	846.11	120.17
非金属矿物制品	Non-metallic Mineral Manufactures	4289.61	610.35	1168.66	166.59
钢铁	Iron and Steel	6215.97	886.49	2694.75	383.15
有色金属	Non-ferrous Metals	2593.20	369.32	5095.53	723.60
金属制品	Manufactures of Metals	10089.81	1434.61	933.27	132.58
机械及运输设备	**Machinery and Transport Equipment**	**115843.98**	**16466.67**	**58475.25**	**8301.95**
动力机械及设备	Power-generating Machinery and Equipment	3655.02	519.84	1865.79	264.92
特种工业专用机械	Machinery Specialized for Particular Industries	5797.32	824.44	4491.73	635.77
金工机械	Metalworking Machinery	1075.22	152.72	614.52	87.25
通用工业机械设备及零件	General Industrial Machinery and Equipment, and Machine Part	12538.25	1784.38	3508.90	498.38
办公用机械及自动数据处理设备	Office Machines and Automatic Data-processing Machines	13686.96	1946.62	3882.67	550.91
电信及声音的录制及重放装置设备	Telecommunications and Sound-recording and Reproducing Apparatus and Equipment	21730.45	3084.07	3266.97	463.35
电力机械、器具及其电气零件	Electrical Machinery, Apparatus and Appliances, and Electrical Parts Thereof	40592.94	5773.49	35004.04	4972.51
陆路车辆(包括气垫式)	Road Vehicles (Including Air-cushion Vehicles)	13932.71	1978.51	4980.93	706.03
其他运输设备	Other Transport Equipment	2835.11	402.62	859.70	122.83
杂项制品	**Miscellaneous Manufactured Articles**	**48662.25**	**6915.79**	**9186.05**	**1304.95**
活动房屋；卫生、水道、供热及照明装置	Prefabricated Buildings; Sanitary, Plumbing, Heating and Lighting Fixtures and Fittings	3741.35	531.51	57.10	8.10
家具及其零件；褥垫及类似填充制品	Furniture and Parts Thereof; Bedding, Mattresses, Mattress Supports, Cushions and Similar Stuffed Furnishings	5278.77	750.22	129.38	18.38
旅行用品、手提包及类似品	Travel Goods, Handbags and Similar Containers	2522.92	358.88	422.27	60.02
服装及衣着附件	Articles of Apparel and Clothing Accessories	11596.76	1646.99	720.52	102.28
鞋靴	Footwear	3726.91	529.92	440.07	62.51
专业、科学及控制用仪器和装置	Professional, Scientific and Controlling Instruments and Apparatus	3313.40	471.17	3930.10	558.21
摄影器材、光学物品及钟表	Photographic Apparatus, Equipment and Supplies and Optical Goods; Watches and Clocks	1513.72	215.18	1342.48	190.72
杂项制品	Miscellaneous Manufactured Articles	16968.41	2411.92	2144.12	304.72
未分类的商品	**Commodities and Transactions not classified elsewhere in the SITC**	**5170.75**	**733.41**	**7205.46**	**1028.06**

11-4 按商品类章分进出口商品金额(2023年)
International Trade in Goods by HS Section and Division (2023)

商品分类	Commodity (by HS Section and Division)	出口总额 Exports		进口总额 Imports	
		亿元人民币 RMB 100 million	亿美元 USD 100 million	亿元人民币 RMB 100 million	亿美元 USD 100 million
总　额	**Total**	**237656.36**	**33790.44**	**179853.75**	**25569.41**
第一类 活动物；动物产品	**Live Animals; Animal Products**	**1013.45**	**144.16**	**3884.67**	**553.20**
01章　活动物	Live Animals	34.89	4.96	33.06	4.71
02章　肉及食用杂碎	Meat and Edible Meat Offal	70.30	9.99	1877.42	267.34
03章　鱼、甲壳动物、软体动物及其他水生无脊椎动物	Fish and Crustaceans Molluscs and Other Aquatic Invertebrates	732.96	104.24	1317.49	187.56
04章　乳品；蛋品；天然蜂蜜；其他食用动物产品	Dairy Produce; Birds' Eggs; Natural Honey; Edible Products of Animal Origin, not Elsewhere Specified or Included	52.92	7.53	564.01	80.37
05章　其他动物产品	Products of Animal Origin, not Elsewhere Specified or Included	122.36	17.44	92.69	13.22
第二类 植物产品	**Vegetable Products**	**2045.63**	**290.43**	**8142.14**	**1159.54**
06章　活树及其他活植物；鳞茎、根及类似品；插花及装饰用簇叶	Live Tree and Other Plants; Bulbs, Roots and the Like; Cut Flowers and Ornamental Foliage	37.05	5.26	19.52	2.76
07章　食用蔬菜、根及块茎	Edible Vegetables and Certain Roots and Tubers	774.29	109.86	235.38	33.65
08章　食用水果及坚果；甜瓜或柑桔属水果的果皮	Edible Fruit and Nuts; Peel of Citrus Fruit or Melons	419.00	59.30	1323.25	188.32
09章　咖啡、茶、马黛茶及调味香料	Coffee, Tea, Mate and Spices	265.98	37.86	126.27	17.99
10章　谷物	Cereals	72.68	10.27	1440.74	205.40
11章　制粉工业产品；麦芽；淀粉；菊粉；面筋	Products of The Milling Industry; Malt; Starches; Inulin; Wheat Gluten	63.12	9.01	146.21	20.74
12章　含油子仁及果实；杂项子仁及果实；工业用或药用植物；稻草、秸秆及饲料	Oil Seeds and Oleaginous Fruits; Miscellaneous Grains, Seeds and Fruit; Industrial or Medicinal Plants; Straw and Fodder	232.09	33.01	4810.59	684.94
13章　虫胶；树胶、树脂及其他植物液、汁	Lac; Gums, Resins And Other Vegetable Saps and Extracts	162.71	23.19	29.60	4.22
14章　编结用植物材料；其他植物产品	Vegetable Plaiting Materials; Vegetable Products Not Elsewhere Specified or Included	18.72	2.67	10.56	1.50
第三类 动、植物油、脂及其分解产品；精制的食用油脂；动、植物蜡	**Animal or Vegetable Fats and Oils and their Cleavage Products; Prepared Edible Fats; Animal or Vegetable Waxes**	**246.32**	**34.97**	**1066.49**	**151.59**
15章　动、植物油、脂及其分解产品；精制的食用油脂；动、植物蜡	Animal or Vegetable Fats and Oils and Their Cleavage Products; Prepared Edible Fats; Animal or Vegetable Waxes	246.32	34.97	1066.49	151.59
第四类 食品；饮料、酒及醋；烟草、烟草及烟草代用品的制品	**Prepared Foodstuffs; Beverages, Spirits And Vinegar; Tobacco and Manufactured Tobacco Substitutes**	**3500.16**	**497.95**	**2543.51**	**361.46**
16章　肉、鱼、甲壳动物、软体动物及其他水生无脊椎动物的制品	Preparations of Meat, of Fish or of Crustaceans, Molluscs or other Aquatic Invertebrates	757.45	107.80	43.39	6.17
17章　糖及糖食	Sugars and Sugar Confectionery	211.87	30.10	273.13	38.58
18章　可可及可可制品	Cocoa and Cocoa Preparations	30.37	4.30	73.04	10.33
19章　谷物、粮食粉、淀粉或乳的制品；糕饼点心	Preparations of Cereals, Flour, Starch or Milk; Pastry-Cooks' Products	185.20	26.32	460.19	65.50

11-4 续表 1 continued

商品分类	Commodity (by HS Section and Division)	出口总额 Exports 亿元人民币 RMB 100 million	出口总额 Exports 亿美元 USD 100 million	进口总额 Imports 亿元人民币 RMB 100 million	进口总额 Imports 亿美元 USD 100 million
20章 蔬菜、水果、坚果或植物其他部分的制品	Preparations of Vegetables, Fruit, Nuts or Other Parts of Plants	694.72	99.05	155.83	22.10
21章 杂项食品	Miscellaneous Edible Preparations	487.44	69.39	430.76	61.18
22章 饮料、酒及醋	Beverages, Spirits and Vinegar	209.97	29.80	401.95	56.98
23章 食品工业的残渣及废料；配制的动物饲料	Residues and Waste from The Food Industries; Prepared Animal Fodder	277.16	39.46	547.91	78.08
24章 烟草、烟草及烟草代用品的制品	Tobacco, Tobacco and Manufactured Tobacco Substitutes	645.97	91.73	157.32	22.55
第五类 矿产品	**Mineral Products**	**4804.70**	**683.36**	**54588.94**	**7764.42**
25章 盐；硫磺；泥土及石料；石膏料、石灰及水泥	Salt; Sulphur; Earths and Stone; Plastering Materials, Lime and Cement	250.31	35.65	1503.83	214.76
26章 矿砂、矿渣及矿灰	Ores, Slag and Ash	253.65	36.14	16791.33	2387.96
27章 矿物燃料、矿物油及其蒸馏产品；沥青物质；矿物蜡	Mineral Fuels, Mineral Oils and Products of Their Distillation; Bituminous Substances; Mineral Waxes	4300.75	611.57	36293.77	5161.70
第六类 化学工业及其相关工业的产品	**Products of The Chemical or Industries Allied**	**13816.41**	**1967.76**	**12948.69**	**1842.57**
28章 无机化学品；贵金属、稀土金属、放射性元素及其同位素的有机及无机化合物	Inorganic Chemicals; Organic or Inorganic Compounds of Precious Metals, of Rare-Earth Metals, of Radioactive Elements or of Isotopes	2402.44	342.78	1833.78	261.37
29章 有机化学品	Organic Chemicals	5468.12	779.01	3415.04	485.86
30章 药品	Pharmaceutical Products	792.88	112.84	3029.16	430.77
31章 肥料	Fertilizers	683.62	97.06	393.81	56.14
32章 鞣料浸膏及染料浸膏；鞣酸及其衍生物；染料、颜料及其他着色料;油漆及清漆；油灰及其他类似胶粘剂；墨水、油墨	Tanning or Dyeing Extracts; Tannins and Their Derivatives; Dyes, Pigments and Other Colouring Matter; Paints and Varnishes; Putty and Other Mastics; Inks	665.37	94.74	339.58	48.23
33章 精油及香膏；芳香料制品及化妆盥洗品	Essential Oils and Retinoid; Perfumery, Cosmetic or Toilet Preparations	534.13	75.86	1240.93	176.67
34章 肥皂、有机表面活性剂、洗涤剂、润滑剂、人造蜡、调制蜡、光洁剂、蜡烛及类似品、塑型用膏、“牙科用蜡”及牙科用熟石膏制剂	Soap,Organic Surface-Active Agents,Washing Preparations, Lubricating Preparations, Artificial Waxes, Prepared Waxes, Polishing or Scouring Preparations, Candles and Similar Articles, Modelling Pastes, "Dental Waxes" And Dental Preparations With a Basis of Plast	494.30	70.26	391.84	55.71
35章 蛋白类物质；改性淀粉；胶；酶	Albuminoidal Substances; Modified Starches; Glues; Enzymes	316.87	45.08	290.79	41.32
36章 炸药；烟火制品；火柴；引火合金；易燃材料制品	Explosives; Pyrotechnic Products; Matches; Pyrophoric Alloys; Certain Combustible Preparations	79.15	11.26	8.53	1.21
37章 照相及电影用品	Photographic or Cinematographic Goods	89.07	12.67	236.62	33.61
38章 杂项化学产品	Miscellaneous Chemical Products	2290.46	326.19	1768.60	251.68
第七类 塑料及其制品；橡胶及其制品	**Plastics and Articles Thereof Rubber and Articles Thereof**	**11603.31**	**1650.73**	**5521.76**	**785.38**
39章 塑料及其制品	Plastics and Articles Thereof	9237.78	1314.27	4356.88	619.62
40章 橡胶及其制品	Rubber and Articles Thereof	2365.53	336.46	1164.88	165.75
第八类 生皮、皮革、毛皮及其制品；鞍具及挽具；旅行用品、手提包及类似品；动物肠线(蚕胶丝除外)制品	**Raw Hides and Skins, Leather, Fur Skins and Articles Thereof; Saddlery and Harness; Travel Goods, Handbags and Similar Containers; Articles of Animal Gut (Other Than Silk-Worm Gut)**	**2857.04**	**406.31**	**719.56**	**102.25**
41章 生皮(毛皮除外)及皮革	Raw Hides and Skins(Other Than Fur Skins) and Leather	63.30	9.01	204.94	29.16

11–4 续表 2 continued

	商品分类	Commodity (by HS Section and Division)	出口总额 Exports 亿元人民币 RMB 100 million	出口总额 Exports 亿美元 USD 100 million	进口总额 Imports 亿元人民币 RMB 100 million	进口总额 Imports 亿美元 USD 100 million
42章	皮革制品；鞍具及挽具；旅行用品、手提包及类似容器；动物肠线制品	Articles of Leather; Saddlery and Harness; Travel Goods, Handbags and Similar Containers; Articles of Animal Gut	2695.74	383.43	456.86	64.94
43章	毛皮、人造毛皮及其制品	Fur Skins and Artificial Fur; Manufactures Thereof	98.00	13.87	57.76	8.15
第九类	**木及木制品；木炭；软木及软木制品；稻草，秸秆、针茅或其他编结材料制品；篮筐及柳条编结品**	**Wood and Articles of Wood; Wood Charcoal; Cork and Articles of Cork; Manufactures of Straw, of Esparto or of Other Plaiting Materials; Basket Ware and Wickerwork**	**1218.02**	**173.19**	**1270.55**	**181.00**
44章	木及木制品；木炭	Wood and Articles of Wood; Wood Charcoal	1104.63	157.05	1266.23	180.38
45章	软木及软木制品	Cork and Articles of Cork	3.28	0.47	2.71	0.39
46章	稻草、秸秆、针茅或其他编结材料制品；篮筐及柳条编结品	Manufactures of Straw, of Esparto or of Other Plaiting Materials; Basket Ware and Wickerwork	110.11	15.68	1.61	0.23
第十类	**木浆及其他纤维状纤维素浆；回收(废碎)纸或纸板；纸板及其制品**	**Pulp of Wood or of Other Fibrous Cellulosic Material; Recycled Waste and Scrap of Paper or Paperboard; Paperboard and Articles Thereof**	**2344.48**	**333.40**	**2305.25**	**328.28**
47章	木浆及其他纤维状纤维素浆；回收(废碎)纸或纸板	Pulp of Wood or of Other Fibrous Cellulosic Material; Waste and Scrap of Paper or Paperboard	20.31	2.89	1673.66	238.48
48章	纸及纸板；纸浆、纸或纸板制品	Paper and Paperboard; Articles of Paper Pulp, of Paper or Paperboard	2040.75	290.25	487.32	69.27
49章	书籍、报纸、印刷图画及其他印制品；手稿、打字稿及设计图纸	Printed Books, Newspapers, Pictures and Other Products of The Printing Industry; Manuscripts, Typescripts and Plans	283.42	40.26	144.26	20.52
第十一类	**纺织原料及纺织制品**	**Textiles and Textile Articles**	**20441.84**	**2905.45**	**2105.28**	**298.73**
50章	蚕丝	Silk	56.35	8.02	5.68	0.80
51章	羊毛、动物细毛或粗毛；马毛纱线及其机织物	Wool, Fine or Coarse Animal Hair; Horsehair Yarn and Woven Fabric	143.90	20.55	195.64	27.86
52章	棉花	Cotton	747.52	106.43	634.90	89.86
53章	其他植物纺织纤维；纸纱线及其机织物	Other Vegetable Textile Fibres; Paper Yarn and Woven Fabrics of Paper Yarn	112.56	15.89	99.10	14.08
54章	化学纤维长丝；化学纤维纺织材料制扁条及类似品	Man-Made Filaments; Man-Made Textile Materials Making Flat Strips and Similar Products	2011.76	286.30	147.33	20.93
55章	化学纤维短纤	Man-Made Short Fibres	928.13	132.11	102.41	14.53
56章	絮胎、毡呢及无纺织物；特种纱线；线、绳、索、缆及其制品	Wadding, Felt and Nonwoven; Special Yarns; Twine, Cordage, Ropes and Cables and Articles Thereof	530.74	75.52	78.79	11.20
57章	地毯及纺织材料的其他铺地制品	Carpets and Other Textile Floor Coverings	281.32	40.01	6.34	0.90
58章	特种机织物；簇绒织物；花边；装饰毯；装饰带；刺绣品	Special Woven Fabrics; Tufted Textile Fabrics; Lace; Tapestries; Trimmings; Embroidery	399.02	56.76	20.35	2.89
59章	浸渍、涂布、包覆或层压的纺织物；工业用纺织制品	Impregnated, Coated, Covered or Laminated Textile Fabrics; Textile Articles of a Kind Suitable for Industrial Use	650.42	92.54	90.81	12.91
60章	针织物及钩编织物	Knitted or Crocheted Fabrics	1512.74	215.14	47.54	6.76
61章	针织或钩编的服装及衣着附件	Articles of Apparel and Clothing Accessories, Knitted or Crocheted	5796.87	822.94	278.94	39.63
62章	非针织或非钩编的服装及衣着附件	Articles of Apparel and Clothing Accessories, not Knitted or Crocheted	4937.85	701.51	373.74	53.00

11-4 续表 3 continued

商品分类		Commodity (by HS Section and Division)	出口总额 Exports		进口总额 Imports	
			亿 元 人民币 RMB 100 million	亿美元 USD 100 million	亿 元 人民币 RMB 100 million	亿美元 USD 100 million
63章	其他纺织制成品；成套物品；旧衣着及旧纺织品；碎织物	Other Made Up Textile Articles; Sets; Worn Clothing And Worn Textile Articles; Rags Articles; Rags	2332.68	331.73	23.74	3.38
第十二类	**鞋、帽、伞、杖、鞭及其零件；已加工的羽毛及其制品；人造花；人发制品**	**Footwear, Headgear, Umbrellas, Sun Umbrellas, Walking-Sticks, Seat-Sticks, Whips, Riding-Crops and Parts Thereof; Prepared Feathers and Articles Made Therewith; Artificial Flowers; Articles of Human Hair**	**5103.73**	**725.84**	**550.53**	**78.22**
64章	鞋靴、护腿和类似品及其零件	Footwear, Gaiters and The Like; Parts of Such Articles	3726.91	529.92	440.07	62.51
65章	帽类及其零件	Headgear and Parts Thereof	420.86	59.87	17.80	2.53
66章	雨伞、阳伞、手杖、鞭子、马鞭及其零件	Umbrellas, Sun Umbrellas, Walking-Sticks, Seat-Sticks, Whips, Riding-Crops And Parts Thereof	229.49	32.71	1.01	0.14
67章	已加工羽毛、羽绒及其制品；人造花；人发制品	Prepared Feathers and Down and Articles Made of Feathers or of Down; Artificial Flowers; Articles of Human Hair	726.47	103.33	91.65	13.04
第十三类	**石料、石膏、水泥、石棉、云母及类似材料的制品；陶瓷产品；玻璃及其制品**	**Articles of Stone, Plaster, Cement, Asbestos, Mica or Similar Materials; Ceramic Products; Glass and Glassware**	**4531.73**	**644.64**	**667.44**	**94.79**
68章	石料、石膏、水泥、石棉、云母及类似材料的制品	Articles of Stone, Plaster, Cement, Asbestos, Mica or Similar Materials; Ceramic Products; Glass and Glassware	915.45	130.40	124.31	17.68
69章	陶瓷产品	Ceramic Products	1833.57	260.58	99.55	14.15
70章	玻璃及其制品	Glass and Glassware	1782.71	253.66	443.58	62.97
第十四类	**天然或养殖珍珠、宝石或半宝石、贵金属、包贵金属及其制品；仿首饰；硬币**	**Natural or Cultured Pearls, Precious or Semi-Precious Stones, Precious Metals, Metals Clad With Precious Metal and Stones, Precious Metals, Metals Clad With Precious Metal and Articles Thereof; Imitation Jewellery; Coin**	**2197.18**	**312.30**	**7991.95**	**1140.06**
71章	天然或养殖珍珠、宝石或半宝石、 贵金属、包贵金属及其制品；仿首饰；硬币	Natural or Cultured Pearls, Precious or Semi-Precious Stones, Precious Metals, Metals Clad With Precious Metal and Articles Thereof; Imitation Jewellery; Coin	2197.18	312.30	7991.95	1140.06
第十五类	**贱金属及其制品**	**Base Metals and Articles of Base Metal**	**18830.78**	**2680.74**	**10039.85**	**1426.90**
72章	钢铁	Iron and Steel	4836.65	689.88	2582.71	367.25
73章	钢铁制品	Articles of Iron or Steel	6828.76	971.66	620.12	88.07
74章	铜及其制品	Copper and Articles Thereof	704.33	100.46	4414.02	627.32
75章	镍及其制品	Nickel and Articles Thereof	106.79	15.21	807.92	115.08
76章	铝及其制品	Aluminium and Articles Thereof	2452.73	348.91	870.25	123.44
78章	铅及其制品	Lead and Articles Thereof	33.37	4.72	7.56	1.07
79章	锌及其制品	Zinc and Articles Thereof	12.39	1.76	84.79	11.95
80章	锡及其制品	Tin and Articles Thereof	24.71	3.52	70.16	9.94
81章	其他贱金属、金属陶瓷及其制品	Other Base Metals; Cermets; Articles Thereof	344.60	49.05	283.44	40.32
82章	贱金属工具、器具、利口器、餐匙、餐叉及其零件	Tools, Implements, Cutlery, Spoons and Forks, of Base Metal; Parts Thereof of Base Metal	1653.80	235.10	182.40	25.92
83章	贱金属杂项制品	Miscellaneous Articles of Base Metal	1832.64	260.47	116.49	16.54

11–4 续表 4 continued

商品分类	Commodity (by HS Section and Division)	出口总额 Exports		进口总额 Imports	
		亿 元 人民币 RMB 100 million	亿美元 USD 100 million	亿 元 人民币 RMB 100 million	亿美元 USD 100 million
第十六类 机器、机械器具、电气设备及其零件；录音机及放声机、电视图像、声音的录制和重放设备及其零件、附件	**Machinery and Mechanical Appliances; Electrical Equipment; Parts Thereof; Sound Recorders and Reproducers, Television Image and Sound Recorders and Reproducers; and Parts and Accessories of Recorders and Reproducers; and Parts and Accessories of Such Artic**	**98942.63**	**14066.67**	**52507.12**	**7454.93**
84章 核反应堆、锅炉、机器、 机械器具及其零件	Nuclear Reactors, Boilers, Machinery and Mechanical Appliances; Parts Thereof	35892.05	5105.30	13901.82	1971.58
85章 电机、电气设备及其零件；录音机及放声机、电视图像、 声音的录制和重放设备及其零件、附件	Electrical Machinery and Equipment and Parts Thereof; Sound Recorders and Reproducers, Television Image and Sound Recorders and Reproducers, and Parts and Accessories of Such Articles	63050.58	8961.37	38605.30	5483.35
第十七类 车辆、航空器、船舶及有关运输设备	**Vehicles, Aircraft, Vessels And Associated Transport Equipment**	**17100.10**	**2428.33**	**5852.93**	**830.61**
86章 铁道及电车道机车、车辆及其零件；铁道及电车轨道固定装置及其零件、附件；各种机械(包括电动机械)交通信号设备	Railway or Tramway Locomotives, Rolling-Stock and Parts Thereof; Railway or Tramway Track Fixtures And Fittings and Parts Thereof; Mechanical(Including Electro-Mechanical) Traffic Signalling Equipment of All Kinds	824.27	117.37	40.42	5.75
87章 车辆及其零件、附件，但铁道及电车道车辆除外	Vehicles Other Than Railway or Tramway Rolling-Stock, and Parts and Accessories Thereof	13556.10	1924.87	4986.57	706.83
88章 航空器、航天器及其零件	Aircraft, Spacecraft, and Parts Thereof	474.60	67.39	788.78	112.72
89章 船舶及浮动结构体	Ships, Boats and Floating Structures	2245.14	318.71	37.17	5.30
第十八类 光学、照相、电影、计量、检验、医疗或外科用仪器及设备、精密仪器及设备；钟表；乐器；上述物品的零件、附件	**Optical, Photographic, Cinematographic, Measuring, Checking, Precision, Medical or Surgical Instruments and Apparatus; Clocks And Watches; Musical Instruments; Parts and Accessories Thereof**	**5364.29**	**762.72**	**5823.22**	**827.19**
90章 光学、照相、电影、计量、检验、医疗或外科用仪器及设备、精密仪器及设备；上述物品的零件、附件	Optical, Photographic, Cinematographic, Measuring, Checking, Precision Medical or Surgical Instruments and Apparatus; Parts and Accessories Thereof	4880.50	694.01	5461.37	775.77
91章 钟表及其零件	Clocks and Watches and Parts Thereof	337.37	47.92	326.70	46.42
92章 乐器及其零件、附件	Musical Instruments; Parts and Accessories of Such Articles	146.42	20.79	35.14	5.00
第十九类 武器、弹药及其零件、附件	**Arms and Ammunition; Parts and Accessories Thereof**	**14.66**	**2.08**	**1.01**	**0.14**
93章 武器、弹药及其零件、附件	Arms and Ammunition; Parts and Accessories Thereof	14.66	2.08	1.01	0.14
第二十类 杂项制品	**Miscellaneous Manufactured Articles**	**16705.35**	**2373.70**	**445.37**	**63.28**
94章 家具；寝具、褥垫、弹簧床垫、软坐垫及类似的填充制品；未列名灯具及照明装置；发光标志、发光名牌及类似品；活动房屋	Furniture; Bedding, Mattresses, Mattress Supports, Cushions and Similar Stuffed Furnishings; Lamps and Lighting Fittings, not Elsewhere Specified or Included; Illuminated Signs, Illuminated	8547.05	1214.47	172.50	24.49
95章 玩具、游戏品、运动用品及其零件、附件	Toys, Games and Sports Requisites; Parts and Accessories Thereof	6229.27	884.92	180.39	25.66
96章 杂项制品	Miscellaneous Manufactured Articles	1929.03	274.30	92.48	13.13
第二十一类 艺术品、收藏品及古物	**Works of Art, Collectors' Pieces and Antiques**	**79.31**	**11.23**	**112.80**	**15.97**
97章 艺术品、收藏品及古物	Works of Art, Collectors' Pieces and Antiques	79.31	11.23	112.80	15.97
第二十二类 特殊交易品及未分类商品	**Commodities and Transactions not Classified According to Kind**	**4895.22**	**694.49**	**764.69**	**108.88**
98章 特殊交易品及未分类商品	Commodities and Transactions not Classified According to Kind	4729.75	670.86	764.69	108.88
99章 跨境电商B2B简化申报商品	Simplified Declaration of Cross-border E-commerce B2B Commodities	165.47	23.63		

11−5 我国同各国(地区)海关货物进出口总额(2023年)
International Trade in Goods by Country (Region) of Origin/Destination(2023)

国 别（地区）	Country (Region)	万元人民币 (RMB 10 000)			万美元 (USD 10 000)		
		进出口总额 Total	出口总额 Exports	进口总额 Imports	进出口总额 Total	出口总额 Exports	进口总额 Imports
总 计	**Total**	**4175101094**	**2376563644**	**1798537451**	**593598478**	**337904357**	**255694121**
亚洲	**Asia**	**2065316488**	**1136299977**	**929016511**	**293601674**	**161564333**	**132037341**
阿富汗	Afghanistan	934540	889645	44896	133270	126879	6391
巴林	Bahrain	1218892	1084571	134320	173780	154630	19149
孟加拉国	Bangladesh	16835459	16113390	722069	2397848	2295248	102600
不丹	Bhutan	44415	42376	2038	6379	6089	290
文莱	Brunei	1978741	603676	1375065	280468	85761	194707
缅甸	Myanmar	14688965	8002142	6686822	2096006	1139822	956183
柬埔寨	Cambodia	10410723	8954272	1456451	1482230	1275200	207030
塞浦路斯	Cyprus	698847	673893	24954	99307	95753	3554
朝鲜	Korea DPR	1617144	1411423	205720	229437	200262	29175
中国香港	Hong Kong, China	202603839	193020339	9583500	28778536	27411468	1367069
印度	India	95806596	82781646	13024949	13621859	11766704	1855155
印度尼西亚	Indonesia	97938766	45857780	52080986	13926616	6519192	7407424
伊朗	Iran	10283912	7052526	3231386	1461792	1002479	459313
伊拉克	Iraq	34981866	10051684	24930182	4976087	1428532	3547555
以色列	Israel	16427170	10519606	5907564	2337906	1498449	839457
日本	Japan	223814801	110733858	113080943	31795305	15748580	16046725
约旦	Jordan	4064337	3571018	493319	578635	508042	70594
科威特	Kuwait	15725947	3672679	12053268	2238878	522423	1716455
老挝	Laos	5008267	2364634	2643634	710223	334830	375394
黎巴嫩	Lebanon	1711476	1666567	44910	243546	237131	6415
中国澳门	Macao, China	2700759	2643237	57522	383755	375605	8150
马来西亚	Malaysia	133872143	61419535	72452609	19029895	8736913	10292983
马尔代夫	Maldives	535451	535427	24	75712	75709	3
蒙古	Mongolia	11683296	2449219	9234077	1659382	346989	1312393
尼泊尔	Nepal	1268588	1244039	24550	179955	176473	3483
阿曼	Oman	24652284	2671972	21980312	3508068	379802	3128266
巴基斯坦	Pakistan	14601969	12171399	2430570	2074792	1729693	345099
巴勒斯坦	Palestine	115887	115852	35	16497	16492	5
菲律宾	Philippines	50492000	36793341	13698659	7187366	5239638	1947728
卡塔尔	Qatar	17258627	2560952	14697675	2456432	363599	2092833
沙特阿拉伯	Saudi Arabia	75308940	30134809	45174131	10721516	4285171	6436346
新加坡	Singapore	76132471	54037653	22094817	10833499	7690828	3142671
韩国	Republic of Korea	218451081	104661284	113789796	31069089	14897594	16171494
斯里兰卡	Sri Lanka	2896328	2646085	250244	411155	375543	35612
叙利亚	Syria	251084	249991	1093	35757	35601	155
泰国	Thailand	88739500	53214832	35524668	12627529	7572519	5055010
土耳其	Türkiye	30454562	27275618	3178944	4339133	3887138	451995
阿联酋	United Arab Emirates	66790675	39159069	27631606	9499468	5568201	3931267
也门	Yemen	1896097	1884243	11854	269306	267615	1690
越南	Vietnam	161814280	96828694	64985586	22973398	13760140	9213259
中国	P. R. China	73216925		73216925	10401866		10401866
中国台湾	Taiwan, China	188428286	48184658	140243627	26771116	6848122	19922994
东帝汶	Timor-Leste	236677	184046	52631	33646	26177	7469
哈萨克斯坦	Kazakhstan	28907748	17407537	11500211	4104309	2469589	1634720
吉尔吉斯斯坦	Kirghizia	13973496	13914413	59082	1980362	1972041	8321
塔吉克斯坦	Tadzhikistan	2760836	2585746	175090	392642	367661	24981
土库曼斯坦	Turkmenistan	7434237	672442	6761795	1059024	95684	963340
乌兹别克斯坦	Uzbekistan	9890223	8717104	1173119	1404026	1238066	165960
格鲁吉亚	Georgia	1437276	1357134	80142	204785	193373	11412
亚美尼亚	Armenia	1109161	420760	688401	157883	59790	98093
阿塞拜疆	Azerbaijan	1210685	1090947	119737	172172	155065	17107
亚洲其他国家（地区）	Other Asian Territories	215	214	1	31	31	0
非洲	**Africa**	**198203645**	**121393441**	**76810205**	**28197693**	**17273967**	**10923725**
阿尔及利亚	Algeria	7260983	6660751	600232	1030656	945715	84941
安哥拉	Angola	16240186	2904992	13335193	2305662	414022	1891640
贝宁	Benin	1208089	1139155	68935	172839	162994	9845
博茨瓦那	Botswana	498956	150799	348158	71095	21424	49672
布隆迪	Burundi	80078	73371	6707	11392	10439	953
喀麦隆	Cameroon	2974192	2608762	365430	423132	371428	51703
加那利群岛	Canary Is.	1521	1516	5	215	214	1

11−5 续表 1 continued

国 别（地区）	Country (Region)	万元人民币 (RMB 10 000)			万美元 (USD 10 000)		
		进出口总额 Total	出口总额 Exports	进口总额 Imports	进出口总额 Total	出口总额 Exports	进口总额 Imports
佛得角	Cape Verde	72517	72465	52	10326	10319	7
中非	Central Africa	58459	38250	20209	8329	5456	2873
塞卜泰(休达)	Ceuta	8	8	0	1	1	0
乍得	Chad	845521	265927	579594	120111	37771	82340
科摩罗	Comoros	77584	77538	46	11107	11100	7
刚果(布)	Congo	4888750	1053574	3835176	694853	149656	545197
吉布提	Djibouti	2442836	2359353	83483	348289	336368	11922
埃及	Egypt	11115610	10500597	615013	1581460	1493327	88134
赤道几内亚	Eq. Guinea	1104250	141573	962678	157286	20178	137109
埃塞俄比亚	Ethiopia	2123530	1817943	305586	302432	258878	43555
加蓬	Gabon	2665297	506757	2158540	379470	71940	307530
冈比亚	Gambia	361537	333744	27792	51392	47450	3942
加纳	Ghana	7769182	6483365	1285817	1104597	922364	182233
几内亚	Guinea	6360398	1861210	4499188	905126	264289	640837
几内亚比绍	Guinea-Bissau	44465	44464	1	6270	6269	0
科特迪瓦	Cote d'Ivoire	3707753	2957170	750582	527533	420689	106845
肯尼亚	Kenya	5698787	5539213	159574	810328	787562	22766
利比里亚	Liberia	6961261	6902868	58394	991887	983590	8296
利比亚	Libya	4282818	2748140	1534678	610054	390060	219994
马达加斯加	Madagascar	1172190	973059	199131	166895	138638	28257
马拉维	Malawi	168707	158734	9973	23957	22536	1421
马里	Mali	619749	564869	54880	88128	80288	7840
毛里塔尼亚	Mauritania	1578201	745440	832761	224682	105995	118687
毛里求斯	Mauritius	704690	688944	15746	100040	97796	2244
摩洛哥	Morocco	5225374	4537019	688355	743143	645215	97928
莫桑比克	Mozambique	3863589	2610606	1252983	548683	371425	177258
纳米比亚	Namibia	914217	390725	523493	130503	55722	74781
尼日尔	Niger	442042	226033	216009	63617	32444	31173
尼日利亚	Nigeria	15839729	14164060	1675668	2254727	2017313	237414
留尼汪	Reunion	171023	171020	3	24301	24300	0
卢旺达	Rwanda	388403	296209	92194	55183	42069	13114
圣多美和普林西比	Sao Tome & Principe	8169	8121	49	1163	1156	7
塞内加尔	Senegal	3912965	3676975	235990	556929	522805	34124
塞舌尔	Seychelles	73110	69631	3479	10420	9935	485
塞拉利昂	Sierra Leone	1158093	430262	727831	164732	61126	103607
索马里	Somalia	716304	711587	4717	101976	101304	672
南非	South Africa	39076599	16604788	22471811	5563955	2364768	3199187
西撒哈拉	Western Sahara	557	554	2	80	80	0
苏丹	Sudan	1511958	899703	612255	217042	128848	88194
坦桑尼亚	Tanzania	6184753	5695590	489164	877716	808856	68859
多哥	Togo	2771849	2655630	116219	394487	377620	16867
突尼斯	Tunisia	1594409	1422033	172375	226975	202452	24522
乌干达	Uganda	917371	868439	48932	130469	123502	6967
布基纳法索	Burkina Faso	417681	377931	39749	59438	53781	5657
刚果(金)	Congo, DR	13160868	3149271	10011597	1870391	448518	1421873
赞比亚	Zambia	3719950	702516	3017434	529861	99878	429983
津巴布韦	Zimbabwe	2159982	989214	1170768	306882	140713	166168
莱索托	Lesotho	90685	72248	18437	12943	10286	2656
梅利利亚	Melilla	65	63	2	9	9	0
斯威士兰	Swaziland	32541	32186	355	4616	4566	50
厄立特里亚	Eritrea	346499	97562	248937	49378	13896	35482
马约特	Mayotte	42789	42739	50	6067	6059	7
南苏丹共和国	Republic of South Sudan	367630	112822	254808	51570	16085	35485
法属南方领地	French Southern Territories	12		12	2		2
英属印度洋领地	British Indian Ocean Territory	535	535	0	75	75	0
圣赫勒拿	St. Helena	283	281	2	39	39	0
非洲其他国家（地区）	Other African Territories	5507	2537	2970	776	363	413
欧洲	**Europe**	**851509974**	**500835092**	**350674882**	**121062481**	**71216689**	**49845792**
比利时	Belgium	28199565	22855061	5344504	4015688	3255004	760683
丹麦	Denmark	9647318	5741166	3906151	1370888	815796	555092
英国	United Kingdom	68968076	54832095	14135981	9797288	7790194	2007094
德国	Germany	145425200	70683876	74741324	20674653	10055977	10618676
法国	France	55504778	29266348	26238430	7892661	4162253	3730408
爱尔兰	Ireland	15316344	3086361	12229983	2176041	438267	1737774
意大利	Italy	50454424	31283646	19170778	7174513	4452099	2722413
卢森堡	Luxembourg	504311	316512	187799	71715	44988	26727
荷兰	Netherlands	82313423	70370994	11942430	11709502	10019418	1690083
希腊	Greece	9542180	8958978	583202	1359499	1276260	83239
葡萄牙	Portugal	6120810	4069357	2051453	870396	579203	291193
西班牙	Spain	34132763	27907209	6225554	4856588	3970317	886271
阿尔巴尼亚	Albania	894468	767435	127033	127410	109401	18008

11–5 续表 2 continued

国　别（地区）	Country (Region)	万元人民币 (RMB 10 000) 进出口总额 Total	出口总额 Exports	进口总额 Imports	万美元 (USD 10 000) 进出口总额 Total	出口总额 Exports	进口总额 Imports
安道尔	Andorra	13704	13574	129	1969	1951	18
奥地利	Austria	8836090	3300994	5535096	1254643	469888	784755
保加利亚	Bulgaria	2964714	1857344	1107370	422074	264589	157485
芬兰	Finland	5759209	2298104	3461106	819933	326846	493087
直布罗陀	Gibraltar	5139	5136	2	732	732	0
匈牙利	Hungary	10215198	6887214	3327984	1452468	979536	472932
冰岛	Iceland	357223	187227	169996	50906	26676	24230
列支敦士登	Liechtenstein	178875	29100	149775	25467	4142	21325
马耳他	Malta	1740910	1288361	452549	247209	182888	64321
摩纳哥	Monaco	20807	7495	13313	2959	1068	1891
挪威	Norway	5423017	2479334	2943683	772824	352889	419934
波兰	Poland	29545763	26128638	3417126	4202222	3716322	485900
罗马尼亚	Romania	7420902	5435812	1985089	1055473	773273	282200
圣马力诺	San Marino	12750	8790	3960	1813	1248	565
瑞典	Sweden	13249313	6661307	6588006	1884337	946972	937365
瑞士	Switzerland	41691176	4030491	37660685	5949628	573499	5376130
爱沙尼亚	Estonia	822811	579398	243413	117010	82474	34535
拉脱维亚	Latvia	885337	694225	191112	125994	98798	27196
立陶宛	Lithuania	1472270	1377361	94909	209389	195935	13455
白俄罗斯	Byelorussia	5930865	4106066	1824799	844174	583728	260446
摩尔多瓦	Moldavia	244276	177363	66914	34612	25156	9455
俄罗斯	Russia	169249038	78187821	91061217	24023659	11091316	12932343
乌克兰	Ukraine	4772567	1962088	2810478	681163	278135	403028
斯洛文尼亚	Slovenia	4705214	4354099	351114	669701	619806	49895
克罗地亚	Croatia	1778952	1682470	96481	253298	239594	13705
捷克	Czech	15136636	11456610	3680025	2151321	1628889	522432
斯洛伐克	Slovak	8132969	3028443	5104525	1153383	429988	723394
北马其顿	North Macedonia	334312	198256	136056	47571	28198	19373
波黑	Bosnia & Herzegovina	253953	195584	58369	36171	27884	8288
梵蒂冈城国	Vatican City State	81	81	1	11	11	0
法罗群岛	Faroe Islands	67525	1512	66013	9606	215	9391
塞尔维亚	Serbia	3060516	1900368	1160148	434877	269920	164957
黑山	Montenegro	156014	127480	28535	22285	18226	4059
奥兰群岛	Åland Islands	108	108		15	15	
格恩西	Guernsey	121	121		17	17	
马恩岛	Isle of Man	47173	47171	2	6615	6615	0
泽西	Jersey	40	40	0	6	6	0
斯瓦尔巴群岛和扬马延岛	Svalbard Archipelago and Jan Mayen Island	3	3	0	0	0	0
欧洲其他国家（地区）	Other European Territories	745	465	280	105	66	39
拉丁美洲	**Latin America**	**344090677**	**172350734**	**171739943**	**48911606**	**24504198**	**24407408**
安提瓜和巴布达	Antigua and Barbuda	121116	117233	3882	17233	16684	549
阿根廷	Argentina	12192247	7544659	4647588	1734966	1073739	661228
阿鲁巴	Aruba	47208	47206	2	6696	6696	0
巴哈马	Bahamas	348201	347846	355	49397	49347	50
巴巴多斯	Barbados	114609	106389	8220	16348	15167	1180
伯利兹	Belize	164795	163727	1068	23455	23304	151
玻利维亚	Bolivia	1824919	797974	1026945	259238	113435	145803
巴西	Brazil	127982516	41582499	86400017	18172450	5910157	12262293
开曼群岛	Cayman Is.	112032	112026	6	16007	16006	1
智利	Chile	43900524	13710124	30190400	6251546	1950764	4300782
哥伦比亚	Colombia	13233625	8697453	4536172	1881812	1237045	644767
多米尼克	Dominica	51392	50898	494	7356	7286	70
哥斯达黎加	Costa Rica	4011299	1959247	2052052	570188	278402	291787
古巴	Cuba	603525	354495	249029	85823	50377	35446
库拉索	Curacao	41120	41087	33	5828	5824	5
多米尼加	Dominica	3490015	3048260	441755	496538	433516	63022
厄瓜多尔	Ecuador	9594907	4118717	5476190	1365811	586081	779730
法属圭亚那	French Guyana	35716	35713	2	5057	5057	0
格林纳达	Granada	16914	16910	4	2405	2404	1
瓜德罗普	Guadeloupe	50279	50276	3	7161	7161	0
危地马拉	Guatemala	3464118	3234640	229478	492652	459800	32853
圭亚那	Guyana	865027	558491	306536	123011	79243	43769
海地	Haiti	375760	370282	5478	53373	52599	774
洪都拉斯	Honduras	1343851	1287126	56725	190946	182830	8116
牙买加	Jamaica	900964	891529	9434	127980	126649	1331
马提尼克	Martinique	32014	31987	27	4551	4547	4

11−5 续表 3 continued

国别（地区）	Country (Region)	万元人民币 (RMB 10 000)			万美元 (USD 10 000)		
		进出口总额 Total	出口总额 Exports	进口总额 Imports	进出口总额 Total	出口总额 Exports	进口总额 Imports
墨西哥	Mexico	70478820	57295827	13182993	10018233	8145885	1872348
蒙特塞拉特	Montserrat	356	297	59	51	42	9
尼加拉瓜	Nicaragua	601179	581070	20109	85315	82452	2863
巴拿马	Panama	9096262	7961319	1134943	1293869	1132640	161228
巴拉圭	Paraguay	1590024	1554406	35618	225992	220911	5081
秘鲁	Peru	26486186	8518693	17967493	3767871	1210924	2556946
波多黎各	Puerto Rico	1560199	665153	895047	221941	94733	127208
圣卢西亚	Saint Lucia	31639	31586	53	4487	4479	8
法属圣马丁	Collectivité de Saint-Martin	4190	4189	1	596	595	0
圣文森特和格林纳丁斯	Saint Vincent & Grenadines	18289	18287	2	2604	2604	0
萨尔瓦多	El Salvador	1266908	1148489	118420	180226	163349	16877
苏里南	Suriname	270410	232064	38346	38415	32959	5456
特立尼达和多巴哥	Trinidad and Tobago	946439	394638	551801	134495	56111	78384
特克斯和凯科斯群岛	Turks & Caicos Is.	8003	8002	1	1129	1129	0
乌拉圭	Uruguay	3722055	2088793	1633262	529542	296897	232645
委内瑞拉	Venezuela	2954633	2435162	519471	419638	345055	74583
英属维尔京群岛	Virgin Is. (E)	50946	50910	36	7234	7228	5
圣其茨和尼维斯	St. Kitts and Nevis	17956	17809	147	2553	2532	21
博纳尔，圣俄斯塔休斯和萨巴	Bonaire, St. Eustatius and Saba	10819	10816	2	1561	1560	0
圣巴泰勒米	St. Barthélemy	565	565		80	80	
布维岛	Bouvet Island	207	207		30	30	
福克兰群岛(马尔维纳斯)	Falkland Islands (Malvinas)	342	342	0	48	48	0
南乔治亚岛和南桑德韦奇岛	South Georgia Island and South Sandwich Island	10	3	7	1	0	1
荷属圣马丁	Eilandgebied Sint Maarten	19588	19585	3	2758	2758	0
美属维尔京群岛	US Virgin Islands	30160	30153	6	4281	4280	1
安圭拉	Anguilla	4492	4267	225	643	611	32
拉丁美洲其他国家（地区）	Other Latin American Territories	1311	1308	2	185	185	0
北美洲	**North America**	**529880281**	**383712151**	**146168130**	**75345811**	**54539820**	**20805991**
加拿大	Canada	62606543	31703280	30903263	8900784	4507187	4393597
美国	United States	466946578	351949896	114996682	66398728	50024298	16374431
格陵兰	Greenland	270382	2218	268164	38272	311	37960
百慕大	Bermuda	55894	55893	1	7902	7902	0
圣皮埃尔和密克隆	Saint Pierre and Miquelon	6	6		1	1	
北美洲其他国家（地区）	Other North American Territories	878	858	20	124	121	3
大洋洲	**Oceania**	**184990701**	**61972000**	**123018702**	**26321263**	**8805315**	**17515948**
澳大利亚	Australia	161660729	51924210	109736519	23000310	7377839	15622471
库克群岛	Cook Is.	11790	10104	1686	1675	1430	244
斐济	Fiji	371161	356830	14331	52607	50578	2029
瑙鲁	Nauru	4187	4184	3	600	600	0
新喀里多尼亚	New Caledonia (Fr)	1177013	107958	1069055	167609	15354	152254
瓦努阿图	Vanuatu	97298	87480	9818	13809	12417	1392
新西兰	New Zealand	14996626	5544601	9452025	2135615	787523	1348092
诺福克岛	Norfolk Islands	227	227	0	32	32	0
巴布亚新几内亚	Papua New Guinea	3397732	907650	2490082	483481	128921	354560
所罗门群岛	Solomon Is.	375618	162099	213519	53447	23054	30394
汤加	Tonga	40492	40491	2	5759	5759	0
萨摩亚	Samoa	85097	84096	1001	12090	11949	141
基里巴斯	Kiribati	26695	26678	17	3782	3779	2
图瓦卢	Tuvalu	29500	29499	0	4190	4190	0
密克罗尼西亚联邦	Micronesia Commonwealth	39797	18185	21612	5699	2586	3113
马绍尔群岛	Marshall Is.	2468240	2467508	732	351008	350904	104
帕劳	Republic of Palau	29621	29616	6	4204	4203	1
法属波利尼西亚	Polynesia (F)	98595	90346	8249	13973	12830	1144
瓦利斯和富图纳	Wallis and Futuna	1545	1545	0	219	219	0
美属萨摩亚	American Samoa	19238	19230	8	2718	2717	1
科科斯(基林)群岛	Cocos (Keeling) Islands	0		0	0		0
圣诞岛	Christmas Island	2		2	0		0
关岛	Guam	45856	45855	1	6499	6499	0
北马里亚纳群岛	Northern Mariana Islands	8893	8891	2	1259	1259	0
纽埃	Niue	700	691	8	100	99	1
皮特凯恩	Pitcairn	63	62	0	9	9	0
托克劳	Tokelau	4	1	2	1	0	0
美国本土外小岛屿	US Minor Outlying Islands	2493	2474	20	354	352	3
大洋洲其他国家（地区）	Other Oceanian Territories	1489	1487	2	214	214	0
国别（地区）不明	**Others**	**1109328**	**249**	**1109079**	**157951**	**35**	**157916**

11-6 出口主要货物数量和金额(2023年)
Major Exported Commodities in Quantity and Value (2023)

品名		Commodity		数量 Quantity	金额 Value 万元人民币 RMB 10 000	万美元 USD 10 000
农产品		Agricultural Products			69581425	9892265
肉类(包含杂碎)	(万吨)	Meat (including entrails)	(10 000 tons)	44	1338828	190306
水产品	(万吨)	Aquatic Products	(10 000 tons)	370	13967147	1987152
食用水产品	(万吨)	Edible Aquatic Products	(10 000 tons)	370	13937928	1982977
蔬菜及食用菌	(万吨)	Vegetables and Edible Fungi	(10 000 tons)	1057	9399275	1334384
鲜或冷藏蔬菜	(万吨)	Fresh or Refrigerated Vegetables	(10 000 tons)	716	4890316	692955
干鲜瓜果及坚果	(万吨)	Dried and Fresh Fruits, Melons and Nuts	(10 000 tons)	404	4039820	571651
苹果	(万吨)	Apples	(10 000 tons)	80	683793	97039
茶叶	(吨)	Tea	(ton)	367542	1222969	173920
粮食	(万吨)	Grain	(10 000 tons)	262	1245491	176437
稻谷和大米	(万吨)	Paddy and Rice	(10 000 tons)	160	629764	88927
罐头	(吨)	Canned Food	(ton)	2493599	3111872	443986
蔬菜罐头	(吨)	Vegetable Can	(ton)	1892205	2410829	344342
酒类及饮料		Alcohol and Beverages			2691178	383017
果蔬汁	(万吨)	Fruit and vegetable juice	(10 000 tons)	35	629898	90424
啤酒	(万升)	Beer	(10 000 liters)	62103	318567	45176
烟草及其制品	(吨)	Tobacco and Tobacco Manufactures	(ton)	207245	591869	83997
烤烟	(吨)	Flue-cured Tobacco	(ton)	100058	268266	38199
卷烟	(万条)	Cigarettes	(10 000 units)	8395	198330	28018
制盐	(吨)	Salt and Pure Sodium Chloride	(ton)	1600017	91540	12988
水泥及水泥熟料	(万吨)	Cement and Cement Clinkers	(10 000 tons)	383	202587	28786
钨品	(吨)	Tungsten Products	(ton)	17510	479277	68333
煤及褐煤	(万吨)	Coal and Lignite	(10 000 tons)	447	809847	115049
焦炭及半焦炭	(万吨)	Coke and Semi-coke	(10 000 tons)	879	1755037	249475
成品油	(万吨)	Refined Oil Product	(10 000 tons)	6266	33998629	4832273
汽油	(万吨)	Gasoline	(10 000 tons)	1229	7018963	996891
航空煤油	(万吨)	Aviation Kerosene	(10 000 tons)	1582	9410945	1334019
柴油	(万吨)	Diesel Oil	(10 000 tons)	1381	8124320	1155357
氧化铝	(万吨)	Aluminum Oxide	(10 000 tons)	125	421663	59929
稀土及其制品	(吨)	Rare Earth and Its Products	(ton)	114258	3082640	439393
稀土	(吨)	Rare Earth	(ton)	52307	534171	76315
基本有机化学品		Basic Organic Chemicals			40354564	5750240
柠檬酸	(万吨)	Citric Acid	(10 000 tons)	117	688946	98253
医药材及药品	(吨)	Pharmaceutical Materials and Drugs	(ton)	1433606	16352028	2327361
中药材	(吨)	Traditional Chinese Medicine	(ton)	131589	702320	99814
中式成药	(吨)	Medicaments of Chinese Type	(ton)	12203	238220	33869
人用疫苗	(千克)	Human Vaccine	(kg)	161868	141233	20232
抗菌素(制剂除外)	(吨)	Antibiotics (except preparations)	(ton)	75850	2855492	406455
医用敷料	(吨)	Medical Dressing	(ton)	249341	1396321	198632
肥料	(万吨)	Chemical Fertilizers	(10 000 tons)	3150	6932030	984151
矿物肥料及化肥	(万吨)	Mineral fertilizers and chemical fertilizers	(10 000 tons)	3144	6920122	982451
尿素	(万吨)	Urea	(10 000 tons)	425	1144432	161143
硫酸铵	(万吨)	Ammonium Sulphate	(10 000 tons)	1377	1626339	230996
磷酸氢二铵	(万吨)	Diammonium Hydrogen Phosphate	(10 000 tons)	504	1902592	270508
磷酸二氢铵	(万吨)	Ammonium Dihydrogen Phosphate	(10 000 tons)	204	798901	113913
合成有机染料	(吨)	Synthetic Organic Dyestuffs	(ton)	245212	853020	121514
美容化妆品及洗护用品	(吨)	Beauty Cosmetics and Toiletries	(ton)	1102634	4575819	649628
烟花、爆竹	(吨)	Fireworks and Firecrackers	(ton)	363575	722223	102743
塑料制品		Plastic Articles			70754013	10060804
橡胶轮胎	(万吨)	Rubber Tire	(10 000 tons)	886	15580299	2216322
新的充气橡胶轮胎	(万吨)	New Pneumatic Rubber Tyres	(10 000 tons)	857	15010598	2135253

11-6 续表 1 continued

品名		Commodity		数量 Quantity	金额 Value 万元人民币 RMB 10 000	万美元 USD 10 000
皮革、毛皮及其制品		Leather, Fur and Their Products			3911781	556121
裘皮服装	(吨)	Fur Garment	(ton)	2160	550390	77583
箱包及类似容器	(万吨)	Luggage and Similar Containers	(10 000 tons)	331	25078081	3567335
皮革箱包及类似容器	(吨)	Leather Cases, Bags and Similar Containers	(ton)	62125	1334148	190241
木及其制品	(万吨)	Wood and Its Products	(10 000 tons)	1191	10934207	1554484
家用或装饰用木制品	(万吨)	Household or Decorative Wood Products	(10 000 tons)	81	2123332	301641
胶合板及类似多层板	(万立方米)	Plywood and Similar Multilayer Boards	(10 000 cbm)	1071	3386163	481410
植物材料编结品	(吨)	Plant Material Braid	(ton)	260479	1101075	156765
纸浆、纸及其制品	(万吨)	Pulp, Paper and Its Products	(10 000 tons)	1411	20610344	2931349
纺织原料	(万吨)	Textile Raw Materials	(10 000 tons)	181	2638366	375578
化学纤维纺织原料	(万吨)	Chemical Fiber Textile Raw Materials	(10 000 tons)	174	1801269	256382
纺织纱线、织物及其制品		Textile Yarn, Fabric and Its Products			94424362	13433201
纺织纱线		Textile Yarn			9616784	1370061
纺织织物		Textile Fabric			45707848	6502005
纺织制品		Textile Products			39099730	5561135
服装及衣着附件		Articles of Apparel and Clothing Accessories			111672674	15859033
服装		Garments			98279400	13957149
鞋靴	(万双)	Footwear	(10 000 pairs)	890533	34659948	4928198
帽类	(万个)	Hat Class	(10 000 units)	1212526	4083675	580955
伞	(万把)	Umbrellas	(10 000 units)	90832	1966096	280279
花岗岩石材及其制品	(万吨)	Granite Stone and Its Products	(10 000 tons)	386	2392053	341738
陶瓷产品	(万吨)	Ceramic Products	(10 000 tons)	1904	18335666	2605758
日用陶瓷	(万吨)	Household Ceramics	(10 000 tons)	475	11725894	1666270
建筑用陶瓷	(万吨)	Architectural Ceramics	(10 000 tons)	1396	6076880	863625
玻璃及其制品		Glass and Its Products			18194937	2588831
珍珠、宝石及半宝石		Pearls, Precious Stones and Semi Precious Stones			2072594	295540
贵金属或包贵金属的首饰	(吨)	Precious Metal or Jewelry Wrapped in Precious Metal	(ton)	966	10095451	1434444
铁合金	(万吨)	Ferroalloy	(10 000 tons)	68	1352993	193094
钢材	(万吨)	Rolled Steel	(10 000 tons)	9026	59279506	8453903
钢铁棒材	(万吨)	Steel Bar	(10 000 tons)	1081	5768937	822729
角钢及型钢	(万吨)	Angle Steel and Section Steel	(10 000 tons)	485	2599827	371133
钢铁板材	(万吨)	Steel Sheet	(10 000 tons)	5963	35233699	5023554
钢铁线材	(万吨)	Steel Wire Rod	(10 000 tons)	243	2374980	340402
未锻轧铜及铜材	(吨)	Unwrought Copper and Copper Products	(ton)	957213	6338866	904452
未锻轧铝及铝材	(吨)	Unwrought Aluminum and Aluminum Products	(ton)	5675028	13456330	1915917
家具及其零件		Furniture and Parts			45156561	6417533
玩具		Toys			28563175	4054314
体育用品及设备		Sporting Goods and Equipment			10731746	1526966
笔及其零件		Pen and Its Parts			2689963	382585
机电产品		Mechanical and Electrical Products			1391043627	197736388
机械基础件		Mechanical Foundation Parts			20581880	2927928
紧固件	(吨)	Fastener	(ton)	4977470	7791543	1109245
轴承	(吨)	Bearings	(ton)	768525	3461919	492653
手用或机用工具	(万吨)	Hand Tools and Tools for Machines	(10 000 tons)	224	11824624	1681013
农业机械		Agricultural Machinery			4048924	577349
拖拉机	(辆)	Tractors	(unit)	145526	689206	98361
食品加工机械	(万台)	Food Processing Machinery	(10 000 sets)	1275	1586860	225508
包装机械	(台)	Packaging Machinery	(set)	19227511	2750576	390591
印刷、装订机械及其零件		Printing and Binding Machinery and Its Parts			9804859	1396610

11-6 续表 2 continued

品名	Commodity	数量 Quantity	金额 Value 万元人民币 RMB 10 000	万美元 USD 10 000
打印机、复印机及一体机（台）	Printer, Copier and All-in-one Machine (set)	48435934	5737231	817728
通用机械设备	General Mechanical Equipment		39494587	5620156
泵（万台）	Pump (10 000 sets)	412266	6119660	870011
压缩机（万台）	Compressor (10 000 sets)	14591	5220863	742958
分离设备	Separation Equipment		4472824	636190
阀门及类似装置（万套）	Valves and Similar Devices (10 000 sets)	524083	11547979	1641488
纺织机械及其零件	Textile Machinery and Its Parts		3189801	453621
缝制机械及其零件	Sewing Machinery and Its Parts		1381477	196676
机床（台）	Machine Tool (set)	17058918	7411945	1052588
自动数据处理设备及其零部件	Automatic Data Processing Equipment and Its Parts		131808643	18742904
自动数据处理设备（万台）	Automatic Data Processing Equipment (10 000 sets)	26475	73600409	10468615
平板电脑（万台）	Tablet PC (10 000 sets)	11360	16413782	2336694
笔记本电脑（万台）	Notebook Computer (10 000 sets)	14061	53277461	7576341
中央处理部件（万台）	Central Processing Unit (10 000 sets)	3596	11732125	1669581
存储部件（万台）	Storage Unit (10 000 sets)	23084	8650406	1227425
自动数据处理设备的零件、附件（吨）	Parts and Accessories of Automatic Data Processing Equipment (ton)	514230	19335029	2750473
液晶监视器（万台）	LCD Monitor (10 000 sets)	9364	7088704	1007283
3D打印机（万台）	3D Printer (10 000 sets)	350	614878	87104
电工器材	Electrical Equipment		128531590	18281972
变压器（万个）	Transformer (10 000 units)	273605	3727463	529189
原电池（亿个）	Primary Cells and Batteries (100 million units)	290	1598546	227269
蓄电池（万个）	Electric Accumulators (10 000 units)	426494	48185261	6849500
锂离子蓄电池（万个）	Lithium-ion Battery (10 000 units)	362116	45735848	6500563
电气控制装置	Electrical Control Device		24469002	3479297
高压开关及控制装置	High Voltage Switch and Control Device		2325011	330131
低压开关及控制装置	Low Voltage Switch and Control Device		22143991	3149166
电线及电缆（万吨）	Wires and Cables (10 000 tons)	233	16257426	2311803
手机（万台）	Mobile Phone (10 000 sets)	80168	97920134	13872654
家用电器（万台）	Household Electric Appliances (10 000 sets)	370829	61731227	8776256
电扇（万台）	Fans (10 000 sets)	43002	4044693	578671
空调（万台）	Air Conditioner (10 000 sets)	4799	5179360	742354
冰箱（万台）	Refrigerator (10 000 sets)	6713	5871936	834219
洗衣机（万台）	Washing Machine (10 000 sets)	2878	2417095	343186
吸尘器（万台）	Vacuum Cleaner (10 000 sets)	13753	3836302	544318
微波炉（万个）	Microwave Oven (10 000 units)	6576	2341933	333400
电视机（万台）	TV (10 000 sets)	9924	9831809	1396812
液晶电视机（万台）	LCD TV (10 000 sets)	9851	9640818	1369709
音视频设备及其零件	Audio and Video Equipment and Its Parts		25218277	3582324
电视摄像机，数字照相机及视频摄录一体机（万台）	TV Camera, Digital Camera and Video Recorder (10 000 sets)	48587	7474677	1060413
数字照相机（万台）	Digital camera (10 000 sets)	1223	724009	102458
无线电广播接收设备（万台）	Radio Broadcasting Receiving Equipment(10 000 sets)	20751	2062415	293132
音视频设备的零件	Parts of Audio and Video Equipment		8019082	1139221
平板显示模组（万个）	Flat Panel Display Module (10 000 units)	201955	27270259	3875857
液晶平板显示模组（万个）	LCD Flat Panel Display Module (10 000 units)	169196	18728112	2662762
有机发光二极管(OLED)平板显示模组（万个）	Organic Light Emitting Diode Display Flat Panel Display Module (10 000 units)	27896	8145637	1156665
电子元件	Electronic Component		177597267	25268859
印刷电路（亿块）	Printed Circuit (100 million units)	404	12310011	1750681
二极管及类似半导体器件(亿个)	Diode and Semi Conductors (100 million units)	5924	42108032	6009995
太阳能电池（万个）	Solar Cell (10 000 units)	563663	30563637	4368141
集成电路（亿个）	Integrated Circuits (100 million units)	2670	95636179	13591603

11-6 续表 3 continued

品名	Commodity	数量 Quantity	金额 Value 万元人民币 RMB 10 000	万美元 USD 10 000
集装箱 (万个)	Containers (10 000 units)	231	5813012	827744
摩托车 (万辆)	Motorcycle (10 000 units)	2666	8149462	1158601
内燃机摩托车 (万辆)	Internal Combustion Engine Motorcycle(10 000 units)	1142	4915042	698654
电动摩托车及脚踏车 (万辆)	Electric Motorcycle and Bicycle (10 000 units)	1505	3205556	455768
自行车 (万辆)	Bicycles (10 000 units)	3961	1802934	257125
摩托车及自行车的零配件	Spare Parts for Motorcycles and Bicycles		7906141	1125065
汽车(包含底盘) (万辆)	Automobile (including chassis) (10 000 units)	522	71645883	10160493
乘用车 (辆)	Passenger Car (unit)	4430142	53267291	7552101
商用车 (辆)	Commercial Vehicle (unit)	787408	18378592	2608392
客车(十座及以上) (辆)	Passenger Cars (ten seats and above) (unit)	70688	3116816	441847
货车 (辆)	Trucks (unit)	519402	7263494	1031860
专用汽车 (辆)	Special Purpose Vehicle (unit)	35853	2110497	299682
汽车零配件	Auto Parts		61640179	8763476
车用发动机 (万台)	Vehicle Engine (10 000 sets)	317	1616834	229770
汽车轮胎 (吨)	Automobile Tire (ton)	7575447	12786573	1818937
婴孩车及其零件 (吨)	Baby Carriages and Parts (ton)	217793	1156153	164366
飞机及其他航空器 (万架)	Airplanes and Other Aircraft (10 000 units)	279	3325337	471930
无人驾驶航空器 (万架)	Unmanned Aerial Vehicles (10 000 units)	279	1274178	180521
船舶 (艘)	Shipping (unit)	4638	19442948	2757890
液货船 (艘)	Tanker (unit)	144	2965801	422357
集装箱船 (艘)	Container Ship (unit)	191	7075516	1000964
散货船 (艘)	Bulk Cargo Ship (unit)	333	4982933	709167
眼镜及其零件	Glasses and Parts Thereof		5200582	739553
计量检测分析自控仪器及器具	Automatic Control Instruments and Apparatus for Measurement, Detection and Analysis		21257857	3023363
分析仪器 (台)	Analysis instrument (set)	79628446	1709684	243211
医疗仪器及器械	Medical Instruments and Appliances		12943416	1839900
钟表及其零件	Clocks and Watches and Their Parts		3373712	479184
手表 (万只)	Wrist Watches (10 000 units)	53349	1441810	204550
灯具、照明装置及其零件	Lamps, Lighting Devices and Their Parts		29711412	4220106
游戏机及其零附件 (吨)	Game Console and Its Accessories (ton)	259228	13514331	1923860
高新技术产品	High-tech Products		592397694	84198675
生物技术	Biotechnology		1048560	149338
生命科学技术	Life Science and Technology		32062669	4563789
光电技术	Photoelectric Technology		25969780	3692087
计算机与通信技术	Computer and Communication Technology		325925915	46289772
电子技术	Electronic Technique		165866205	23600631
计算机集成制造技术	Computer Integrated Manufacturing Technology		23012394	3270308
材料技术 (吨)	Material Technology (ton)	587691	8803400	1253833
航空航天技术	Aviation and Aerospace Technology		8678632	1232808
其他技术	Other Technologies		1030138	146109
电动载人汽车 (辆)	Electric manned vehicle (unit)	1770250	29464529	4181213
混合动力客车(10座及以上)(辆)	Hybrid Bus (10 seats and above) (unit)	378	36002	5022
纯电动客车(10座及以上) (辆)	Pure Electric Bus (10 seats and above) (unit)	9677	1187667	168387
非插电式混合动力乘用车 (辆)	Non Plug-in Hybrid Passenger Vehicle (unit)	79011	1157981	162842
插电式混合动力乘用车 (辆)	Plug in Hybrid Passenger Car (unit)	138324	3052376	432073
纯电动乘用车 (辆)	Pure Electric Passenger Car (unit)	1542860	24030503	3412889
文化产品	Cultural Products		101800519	14458850
食品	Food		53821627	7651461

11-7 进口主要货物数量和金额(2023年)
Major Imported Commodities in Quantity and Value (2023)

品名		Commodity		数量 Quantity	金额 Value 万元人民币 RMB 10 000	万美元 USD 10 000
农产品		Agricultural Products			164080164	23351956
肉类(包含杂碎)	(万吨)	Meat (including entrails)	(10 000 tons)	738	19332607	2753058
牛肉及牛杂碎	(万吨)	Beef and Cattle Entrails	(10 000 tons)	277	10142882	1441158
牛肉	(万吨)	Beef	(10 000 tons)	274	10006840	1421780
猪肉及猪杂碎	(万吨)	Pork and Pig Entrails	(10 000 tons)	271	4516275	645069
猪肉	(万吨)	Pork	(10 000 tons)	155	2471033	353531
羊肉	(吨)	Mutton	(ton)	433643	1245751	177745
禽肉	(吨)	Meat of Poultry	(ton)	682881	1214579	173315
水产品	(万吨)	Aquatic Products	(10 000 tons)	501	13891471	1977774
食用水产品	(万吨)	Edible Aquatic Products	(10 000 tons)	487	13621845	1939120
冻鱼	(万吨)	Frozen Fish	(10 000 tons)	238	3370055	479629
乳品	(万吨)	Dairy Products	(10 000 tons)	287	8464378	1207169
奶粉	(万吨)	Milk Powder	(10 000 tons)	100	4990019	712638
干鲜瓜果及坚果	(万吨)	Dried and Fresh Fruits, Melons and Nuts	(10 000 tons)	774	12395076	1764946
粮食	(万吨)	Grain	(10 000 tons)	16116	57424355	8175041
薯类	(吨)	Tubers	(ton)	4578	1711	241
谷物及谷物粉	(万吨)	Cereals and Cereals Flour	(10 000 tons)	5908	14579389	2078309
小麦	(万吨)	Wheat	(10 000 tons)	1210	3082456	442041
大麦	(万吨)	Barley	(10 000 tons)	1132	2648798	377084
玉米	(万吨)	Corn	(10 000 tons)	2712	6336334	901213
稻谷及大米	(万吨)	Paddy and Rice	(10 000 tons)	263	1007329	144447
高粱	(万吨)	Jowar	(10 000 tons)	521	1289337	183071
豆类	(万吨)	Beans	(10 000 tons)	10206	42817747	6092873
大豆	(万吨)	Soybeans	(10 000 tons)	9861	41607810	5920839
食用油	(万吨)	Edible Oil	(10 000 tons)	1175	9091625	1292362
食用植物油	(万吨)	Edible Vegetable Oil	(10 000 tons)	978	7317021	1040442
豆油	(万吨)	Soybean Oil	(10 000 tons)	37	295390	41699
棕榈油	(万吨)	RBD Palm Oil	(10 000 tons)	433	2796745	396180
菜籽油及芥子油	(万吨)	Rapeseed Oil and Mustard Oil	(10 000 tons)	236	1879163	267546
食糖	(万吨)	Sugar	(10 000 tons)	397	1640184	230728
酒类及饮料		Alcohol and Beverages			4563676	647083
啤酒	(万升)	Beer	(10 000 liters)	41831	405754	57817
葡萄酒	(万升)	Wine	(10 000 liters)	24955	818269	116230
制盐	(吨)	Salt and Pure Sodium Chloride	(ton)	9249671	317542	45281
金属矿及矿砂	(万吨)	Metal Ore and Ore	(10 000 tons)	145752	168204542	23921192
铁矿砂及其精矿	(万吨)	Iron Ore and Concentrates	(10 000 tons)	117839	95363683	13561083
铜矿砂及其精矿	(万吨)	Copper Ores and Concentrates	(10 000 tons)	2753	42100155	5989500
铝矿砂及其精矿	(万吨)	Aluminum Ores and Concentrates	(10 000 tons)	14124	6033568	858906
煤及褐煤	(万吨)	Coal and Lignite	(10 000 tons)	47433	37301208	5306542
原油	(万吨)	Crude Oil	(10 000 tons)	56394	237541882	33780247
成品油	(万吨)	Refined Oil Product	(10 000 tons)	4777	19706145	2800871
石脑油	(万吨)	Naphtha	(10 000 tons)	1271	5890313	838247
航空煤油	(万吨)	Aviation Kerosene	(10 000 tons)	34	204460	28862
天然气	(万吨)	Natural Gas	(10 000 tons)	11986	45240712	6436106
液化天然气	(万吨)	Liquified Natural Gas	(10 000 tons)	7119	31598659	4494233
气态天然气	(万吨)	Natural Gas	(10 000 tons)	4867	13642052	1941873
多晶硅	(吨)	Polysilicon	(ton)	62895	1191313	170700
稀土	(吨)	Tombarthite	(ton)	175856	1550796	220670
基本有机化学品		Basic Organic Chemicals			33308999	4740601
二甲苯	(万吨)	Xylene	(10 000 tons)	920	6721806	957190
乙二醇	(万吨)	Ethylene Glycol	(10 000 tons)	715	2439820	346617
医药材及药品	(吨)	Pharmaceutical Materials and Drugs	(ton)	383752	36411006	5176337
中药材	(吨)	Traditional Chinese Medicine	(ton)	179190	289105	41234
人用疫苗	(千克)	Human Vaccine	(kg)	1758330	4380391	622524
肥料	(万吨)	Chemical Fertilizers	(10 000 tons)	1309	3898230	555817
矿物肥料及化肥	(万吨)	Mineral fertilizers and chemical fertilizers	(10 000 tons)	1308	3890957	554789
氯化钾	(万吨)	Potassium Chloride	(10 000 tons)	1157	3253049	463608
氮磷钾三元复合肥	(万吨)	N-P-K Compound Fertilizer	(10 000 tons)	121	524831	74996
美容化妆品及洗护用品	(吨)	Beauty Cosmetics and Toiletries	(ton)	358420	12599972	1793686
初级形状的塑料	(万吨)	Plastics in Primary Forms	(10 000 tons)	2960	31814920	4526905
塑料制品		Plastic Articles			12103091	1718910

11-7 续表 1 continued

品 名		Commodity		数 量 Quantity	金 额 Value 万元人民币 RMB 10 000	万美元 USD 10 000
天然及合成橡胶(包括胶乳)	(万吨)	Natural and Synthetic Rubber (including latex)	(10 000 tons)	795	8215632	1169604
皮革、毛皮及其制品		Leather, Fur and Their Products			4259703	605154
牛皮革及马皮革	(吨)	Cow Leather and Horse Leather	(ton)	511136	973363	138530
木及其制品	(万吨)	Wood and Its Products	(10 000 tons)	5250	10441170	1487774
原木	(万立方米)	Logs	(10 000 cbm)	3803	4473950	638315
锯材	(万立方米)	Wood Sawn	(10 000 cbm)	2772	4801708	684023
纸浆、纸及其制品	(万吨)	Pulp, Paper and Its Products	(10 000 tons)	4848	21526426	3065702
纸浆	(万吨)	Paper Pulp	(10 000 tons)	3666	16653214	2372972
纺织原料	(万吨)	Textile Raw Materials	(10 000 tons)	365	6221833	881563
羊毛及毛条	(吨)	Wool and Wool Tops	(ton)	296614	1427305	203507
棉花	(万吨)	Cotton	(10 000 tons)	196	2957126	417262
纺织纱线、织物及其制品		Textile Yarn, Fabric and Its Products			8267547	1174247
纺织纱线		Textile Yarn			4211805	597900
棉纱线	(万吨)	Cotton Yarn	(10 000 tons)	169	3093678	438959
合成纤维纱线	(吨)	Synthetic Fiber Yarn	(ton)	204428	734370	104380
服装及衣着附件		Clothing and Accessories			7021184	996679
玻璃及其制品		Glass and Its Products			4456415	632604
玻璃纤维及其制品	(吨)	Glass Fiber and Its Products	(ton)	124963	567004	80531
珍珠、宝石及半宝石		Pearls, Precious Stones and Semi Precious Stones			5218700	747182
钻石	(千克)	Diamonds	(kg)	2191	4180116	597194
钢材	(万吨)	Rolled Steel	(10 000 tons)	765	8912445	1267925
未锻轧铜及铜材	(吨)	Unwrought Copper and Copper Products	(ton)	5499955	33539620	4765127
未锻轧铝及铝材	(吨)	Unwrought Aluminum and Aluminum Products	(ton)	3059634	5748020	814568
机电产品		Mechanical and Electrical Products			653282030	92753676
机械基础件		Mechanical Foundation Parts			6808769	967414
农业机械		Agricultural Machinery			811530	115422
收获机械	(台)	Harvesting Machinery	(set)	3928	467485	66387
拖拉机	(辆)	Tractors	(unit)	1089	100264	14272
食品加工机械	(万台)	Food Processing Machinery	(10 000 sets)	21	558993	79038
包装机械	(台)	Packaging Machinery	(set)	32024	905121	128575
印刷、装订机械及其零件		Printing and Binding Machinery and Its Parts			3928752	559567
打印机、复印机及一体机	(台)	Printer, Copier and All-in-one Machine	(set)	9710567	1564030	222987
通用机械设备		General Mechanical Equipment			14401442	2046253
泵	(万台)	Pump	(10 000 sets)	8814	3102706	440576
压缩机	(万台)	Compressor	(10 000 sets)	622	1427743	202584
分离设备		Separation Equipment			2649514	376449
阀门及类似装置	(万套)	Valves and Similar Devices	(10 000 sets)	92826	5593508	795080
机床	(台)	Machine Tool	(set)	72854	4601172	652924
自动数据处理设备及其零部件		Automatic Data Processing Equipment and Its Parts			35549084	5042106
自动数据处理设备	(万台)	Automatic Data Processing Equipment	(10 000 sets)	475	1463706	207317
中央处理部件	(万台)	Central Processing Unit	(10 000 sets)	1437	3411937	484036
存储部件	(万台)	Storage Unit	(10 000 sets)	24014	11100203	1575344
自动数据处理设备的零件、附件	(吨)	Parts and Accessories of Automatic Data Processing Equipment	(ton)	41053	10518574	1495819
半导体制造设备	(台)	Semiconductor Manufacturing Equipment	(set)	54774	24810760	3502132
制造单晶柱或晶圆用的机器及装置	(台)	Machines and Devices for Manufacturing Single Crystal Columns or Wafers	(set)	2743	1242757	176290
制造半导体器件或集成电路用的机器及装置	(台)	Machines and Devices for Manufacturing Semiconductor Devices or Integrated Circuits	(set)	11865	19434562	2740972
制造平板显示器用的机器及装置	(台)	Machine and Device for Manufacturing Flat Panel Display	(set)	3574	1435270	202474
电工器材		Electrical Equipment			26340736	3743255
变压器	(万个)	Transformer	(10 000 units)	66649	413849	58876
蓄电池	(万个)	Electric Accumulators	(10 000 units)	83413	1837189	260930
锂离子蓄电池	(万个)	Lithium-ion Battery	(10 000 units)	80068	1659974	235692

11-7 续表 2 continued

品 名	Commodity	数 量 Quantity	金 额 Value 万元人民币 RMB 10 000	万美元 USD 10 000
电气控制装置	Electrical Control Device		12735354	1809736
电线及电缆 (万吨)	Wires and Cables (10 000 tons)	15	3162643	449819
家用电器 (万台)	Household Electric Appliances (10 000 sets)	2298	1453111	206387
电视机 (万台)	Televisions (10 000 sets)	32	135889	19258
液晶电视机 (万台)	LCD Televisions (10 000 sets)	30	122139	17309
音视频设备及其零件	Audio and Video Equipment and Its Parts		14282830	2023197
电视摄像机,数字照相机及视频摄录一体机 (万台)	TV Camera, Digital Camera and Video Recorder (10 000 sets)	2399	1613187	229055
音视频设备的零件	Parts of Audio and Video Equipment		12444329	1762061
平板显示模组 (万个)	Flat Panel Display Module (10 000 units)	177842	26396152	3739302
液晶平板显示模组 (万个)	LCD Flat Panel Display Module (10 000 units)	133445	8369792	1189762
有机发光二极管(OLED)平板显示模组 (万个)	Organic Light Emitting Diode Display Flat Panel Display Module (10 000 units)	43300	17538521	2480107
电子元件	Electronic Component		280090731	39795888
电容器 (万吨)	Electrical Capacitors (10 000 tons)	5	6245780	887698
印刷电路 (亿块)	Printed Circuit (100 million units)	309	5606846	796442
二极管及类似半导体器件(亿个)	Diode and Semi Conductor (100 million units)	4531	16556791	2354044
集成电路 (亿个)	Integrated Circuits (100 million units)	4791	245800638	34922819
汽车(包含底盘) (万辆)	Automobile (including chassis) (10 000 units)	80	33212587	4705380
乘用车 (辆)	Passenger Car (unit)	781640	32415832	4592137
商用车 (辆)	Commercial Vehicle (unit)	17200	796755	113243
货车 (辆)	Trucks (unit)	15256	673799	95842
专用汽车 (辆)	Special Purpose Vehicle (unit)	68	31667	4532
汽车零配件	Auto Parts		19351010	2745819
车用发动机 (万台)	Vehicle Engine (10 000 sets)	19	524080	74480
汽车轮胎 (吨)	Automobile Tire (ton)	85188	378020	53603
飞机及其他航空器 (架)	Aircraft and Others (unit)	60181	5781443	828230
空载重量超过2吨的飞机 (架)	Aircraft with an Unloaded Weight of More Than 2 Tons (unit)	146	5745445	823077
航空器零部件	Aircraft Parts		9117467	1294471
涡轮喷气发动机 (台)	Turbojet Engine (set)	819	3243890	460699
涡轮螺桨发动机 (台)	Turboprop Engine (set)	43	13878	1977
船舶 (艘)	Shipping (unit)	4161	320210	45785
计量检测分析自控仪器及器具	Automatic Control Instruments and Apparatus for Measurement, Detection and Analysis		29462629	4184294
医疗仪器及器械	Medical Instruments and Appliances		9695529	1377723
钟表及其零件	Clocks and Watches and Their Parts		3266975	464211
手表 (万只)	Wrist Watches (10 000 units)	1132	2884820	410031
电动手表 (万只)	Electric Watch (10 000 units)	972	685624	97725
机械手表 (万只)	Mechanical Watch (10 000 units)	160	2199196	312306
高新技术产品	High-tech Products		478780534	67993188
生物技术	Biotechnology		6265292	889131
生命科学技术	Life Science and Technology		36475890	5187038
光电技术	Photoelectric Technology		20219468	2870782
计算机与通信技术	Computer and Communication Technology		69599617	9873380
电子技术	Electronic Technique		278790298	39611653
计算机集成制造技术	Computer Integrated Manufacturing Technology		44008539	6227273
材料技术 (吨)	Material Technology (ton)	29332	4012508	570991
航空航天技术	Aviation and Aerospace Technology		18202666	2592461
其他技术	Other Technologies		1206257	170478
电动载人汽车 (辆)	Electric Manned Vehicle (unit)	150330	5726452	811489
混合动力客车(10座及以上) (辆)	Hybrid Bus(10 seats and above) (unit)			
纯电动客车(10座及以上) (辆)	Pure Electric Bus (10 seats and above) (unit)			
非插电式混合动力乘用车 (辆)	Non Plug-in Hybrid Passenger Vehicle (unit)	97308	2911251	412563
插电式混合动力乘用车 (辆)	Plug-in Hybrid Passenger Car (unit)	22898	1243637	176311
纯电动乘用车 (辆)	Pure Electric Passenger Car (unit)	30124	1571565	222615
文化产品	Cultural Products		12209046	1735150
食品	Food		145895561	20764906

11−8 分地区货物进出口总额(2023年)
International Trade in Goods by Region (2023)

单位：亿元人民币 (RMB 100 million)

地区	Region	按收发货人所在地分 By Location of Importers/Exporters			按境内目的地和货源地分 By Location of Domestic Consumers/Producers		
		进出口总额 Total	出口总额 Exports	进口总额 Imports	进出口总额 Total	出口总额 Exports	进口总额 Imports
全　国	**National Total**	**417510.1**	**237656.4**	**179853.7**	**417510.1**	**237656.4**	**179853.7**
北　京	Beijing	36448.5	5999.5	30449.1	9656.5	2062.5	7593.9
天　津	Tianjin	8008.6	3631.4	4377.2	10505.6	3768.7	6736.9
河　北	Hebei	5828.4	3504.2	2324.2	10422.6	5530.8	4891.8
山　西	Shanxi	1691.2	1050.3	640.9	1862.9	1324.8	538.2
内蒙古	Inner Mongolia	1960.0	781.0	1179.0	2456.0	861.2	1594.8
辽　宁	Liaoning	7667.3	3534.9	4132.4	10404.3	4431.4	5973.0
吉　林	Jilin	1678.8	627.0	1051.8	1698.5	653.1	1045.4
黑龙江	Heilongjiang	2980.1	760.6	2219.5	2592.0	681.6	1910.4
上　海	Shanghai	42135.3	17371.7	24763.6	40360.8	13916.0	26444.9
江　苏	Jiangsu	52495.4	33716.1	18779.3	58216.5	35463.8	22752.7
浙　江	Zhejiang	48997.6	35662.8	13334.8	46502.7	34105.1	12397.6
安　徽	Anhui	8053.0	5230.4	2822.6	8267.2	5727.8	2539.4
福　建	Fujian	19739.6	11765.4	7974.2	17249.5	11224.6	6024.9
江　西	Jiangxi	5686.3	3928.1	1758.2	5811.4	3989.3	1822.1
山　东	Shandong	32665.9	19428.6	13237.3	39731.8	21069.4	18662.4
河　南	Henan	8108.4	5280.0	2828.4	8846.2	5948.9	2897.3
湖　北	Hubei	6441.9	4325.3	2116.7	6013.3	3976.9	2036.4
湖　南	Hunan	6173.4	4008.6	2164.7	4265.3	3100.3	1165.0
广　东	Guangdong	83017.2	54374.3	28642.9	94112.2	58753.8	35358.4
广　西	Guangxi	6913.9	3625.4	3288.4	7797.8	2766.6	5031.3
海　南	Hainan	2313.9	740.3	1573.7	1835.4	588.3	1247.1
重　庆	Chongqing	7128.5	4776.5	2352.0	6399.3	4325.4	2073.9
四　川	Sichuan	9558.1	6031.0	3527.2	9877.5	5870.4	4007.1
贵　州	Guizhou	759.5	520.5	239.0	729.7	543.6	186.1
云　南	Yunnan	2588.0	925.9	1662.1	2808.7	1140.7	1668.0
西　藏	Xizang	109.8	98.2	11.5	43.4	39.2	4.2
陕　西	Shaanxi	4042.0	2630.6	1411.4	3678.5	2538.2	1140.3
甘　肃	Gansu	491.6	123.8	367.8	565.1	191.5	373.6
青　海	Qinghai	48.7	29.5	19.2	48.2	35.5	12.8
宁　夏	Ningxia	205.5	149.8	55.7	312.8	236.5	76.3
新　疆	Xinjiang	3573.6	3024.6	549.1	4438.2	2790.6	1647.6

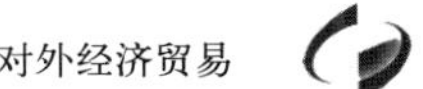

11–9 分地区货物进出口总额(2023年)
International Trade in Goods by Region (2023)

单位：亿美元 (USD 100 million)

地 区	Region	按收发货人所在地分 By Location of Importers/Exporters			按境内目的地和货源地分 By Location of Domestic Consumers/Producers		
		进出口总额 Total	出口总额 Exports	进口总额 Imports	进出口总额 Total	出口总额 Exports	进口总额 Imports
全 国	**National Total**	**59359.8**	**33790.4**	**25569.4**	**59359.8**	**33790.4**	**25569.4**
北 京	Beijing	5184.8	852.6	4332.2	1372.3	293.0	1079.3
天 津	Tianjin	1138.9	516.8	622.1	1495.1	536.9	958.2
河 北	Hebei	827.9	497.9	330.0	1482.0	786.3	695.7
山 西	Shanxi	240.0	149.0	91.0	264.4	187.9	76.4
内蒙古	Inner Mongolia	278.4	110.8	167.5	349.1	122.3	226.7
辽 宁	Liaoning	1090.6	502.7	587.9	1479.0	630.0	849.0
吉 林	Jilin	238.0	88.9	149.1	240.8	92.6	148.2
黑龙江	Heilongjiang	423.8	107.9	315.9	368.5	96.8	271.7
上 海	Shanghai	5992.2	2470.4	3521.9	5741.5	1979.2	3762.3
江 苏	Jiangsu	7461.5	4793.9	2667.6	8276.7	5042.7	3234.0
浙 江	Zhejiang	6967.7	5072.6	1895.1	6611.7	4850.2	1761.5
安 徽	Anhui	1144.0	743.4	400.7	1174.7	814.5	360.2
福 建	Fujian	2807.6	1672.5	1135.1	2451.7	1595.3	856.5
江 西	Jiangxi	810.8	561.0	249.8	827.8	568.8	259.0
山 东	Shandong	4643.8	2761.6	1882.2	5649.1	2995.2	2653.9
河 南	Henan	1151.7	750.1	401.6	1256.7	845.5	411.3
湖 北	Hubei	915.3	614.8	300.5	854.7	565.1	289.6
湖 南	Hunan	879.8	572.1	307.7	607.4	442.0	165.4
广 东	Guangdong	11799.2	7729.3	4069.9	13378.4	8352.2	5026.2
广 西	Guangxi	981.7	513.9	467.9	1108.4	392.5	715.8
海 南	Hainan	329.3	105.4	223.9	261.9	84.0	177.9
重 庆	Chongqing	1014.3	679.4	334.9	910.6	615.5	295.1
四 川	Sichuan	1358.8	857.7	501.1	1403.3	834.5	568.8
贵 州	Guizhou	107.8	73.9	33.9	103.7	77.1	26.5
云 南	Yunnan	367.7	131.5	236.3	399.2	162.0	237.2
西 藏	Xizang	15.4	13.8	1.6	6.1	5.5	0.6
陕 西	Shaanxi	575.4	374.4	200.9	523.5	361.1	162.4
甘 肃	Gansu	70.0	17.6	52.4	80.5	27.2	53.2
青 海	Qinghai	6.9	4.2	2.7	6.9	5.0	1.8
宁 夏	Ningxia	29.3	21.4	7.9	44.6	33.7	10.8
新 疆	Xinjiang	506.8	428.9	77.9	629.9	395.7	234.2

11-10 分地区外商投资企业货物进出口总额(2023年)
International Trade in Goods of Foreign-Invested Enterprises by Region (2023)

地 区	Region	万元人民币 (RMB 10 000)			万美元 (USD 10 000)		
		进出口总额 Total	出口总额 Exports	进口总额 Imports	进出口总额 Total	出口总额 Exports	进口总额 Imports
全 国	**National Total**	**1260673147**	**678625535**	**582047612**	**179288908**	**96533460**	**82755448**
北 京	Beijing	56838741	15051608	41787134	8070838	2136998	5933841
天 津	Tianjin	37176414	15755931	21420483	5288796	2242915	3045880
河 北	Hebei	10304629	7384288	2920341	1462977	1048838	414139
山 西	Shanxi	7086072	6724383	361689	1003695	952318	51377
内蒙古	Inner Mongolia	1222440	601681	620759	173549	85455	88094
辽 宁	Liaoning	28565957	13404647	15161309	4062341	1906491	2155850
吉 林	Jilin	6163422	1136666	5026756	873575	161442	712133
黑龙江	Heilongjiang	1066971	557285	509686	151736	79167	72569
上 海	Shanghai	247264697	87493737	159770959	35160396	12445179	22715216
江 苏	Jiangsu	243865080	146335836	97529244	34686491	20819913	13866578
浙 江	Zhejiang	62569554	39193009	23376545	8897621	5573995	3323626
安 徽	Anhui	17370625	11026545	6344080	2473782	1569663	904119
福 建	Fujian	38754288	22933369	15820919	5513557	3263177	2250380
江 西	Jiangxi	13985073	8440500	5544573	1993123	1203101	790022
山 东	Shandong	57353446	36975722	20377724	8164825	5264201	2900624
河 南	Henan	24846964	16492871	8354093	3546432	2358966	1187466
湖 北	Hubei	9069856	5679131	3390725	1289828	807540	482288
湖 南	Hunan	4777989	3299760	1478229	678550	468720	209830
广 东	Guangdong	279632405	171159354	108473051	39752438	24329742	15422695
广 西	Guangxi	8773244	4738336	4034908	1249154	673547	575606
海 南	Hainan	5754610	3700514	2054096	820138	527085	293053
重 庆	Chongqing	32765569	22755998	10009571	4663331	3236888	1426443
四 川	Sichuan	44679236	25368399	19310837	6349550	3607655	2741895
贵 州	Guizhou	283484	178871	104613	40392	25497	14895
云 南	Yunnan	460736	282739	177997	65085	39934	25151
西 藏	Xizang	1737	27	1710	245	4	241
陕 西	Shaanxi	19408541	11630908	7777633	2766740	1659072	1107668
甘 肃	Gansu	80977	33390	47587	11554	4786	6769
青 海	Qinghai	9164	8718	447	1309	1244	65
宁 夏	Ningxia	296465	200222	96243	42160	28520	13641
新 疆	Xinjiang	244762	81090	163671	34701	11408	23293

注：外商投资企业货物进出口数据来自海关总署，数据包含港澳台投资企业。

a) The import and export data of goods for foreign-invested enterprises come from General Administration of Customs, which include the data of enterprises with investment from Hong Kong, Macao and Taiwan.

11-11 服务进出口总额
International Trade in Services

年份 Year	亿美元 USD 100 million				亿元人民币 RMB 100 million			
	进出口 Total	出口 Exports	进口 Imports	差额 Balance	进出口 Total	出口 Exports	进口 Imports	差额 Balance
1982	46.9	26.7	20.2	6.5				
1983	47.6	27.7	19.9	7.7				
1984	59.5	30.9	28.6	2.3				
1985	56.2	31.0	25.2	5.8				
1986	61.4	38.6	22.8	15.9				
1987	65.7	40.8	24.9	16.0				
1988	87.0	51.0	36.0	15.0				
1989	101.1	62.0	39.1	22.9				
1990	124.2	80.7	43.5	37.1				
1991	136.7	95.5	41.2	54.3				
1992	220.1	125.8	94.3	31.5				
1993	266.2	145.8	120.4	25.5				
1994	365.0	202.0	163.0	39.0				
1995	496.4	244.2	252.2	-8.0				
1996	505.7	279.8	225.9	54.0				
1997	622.1	342.4	279.7	62.7				
1998	518.9	250.5	268.4	-17.9				
1999	610.2	293.7	316.5	-22.8				
2000	711.9	350.3	361.6	-11.3				
2001	784.5	391.8	392.7	-1.0				
2002	927.6	462.3	465.3	-3.0				
2003	1066.4	513.3	553.1	-39.8				
2004	1452.3	725.1	727.2	-2.2				
2005	1682.8	843.1	839.7	3.4				
2006	2038.2	1029.8	1008.4	21.4				
2007	2654.5	1353.2	1301.3	51.9				
2008	3222.6	1633.1	1589.5	43.7				
2009	3024.9	1435.7	1589.2	-153.5				
2010	3717.4	1783.4	1934.0	-150.6				
2011	4488.9	2010.5	2478.4	-468.0				
2012	4828.8	2015.8	2813.0	-797.3				
2013	5376.1	2070.1	3306.1	-1236.0				
2014	6520.2	2191.4	4328.8	-2137.4				
2015	6541.6	2186.2	4355.4	-2169.2				
2016	6616.3	2095.3	4521.0	-2425.7	43947.0	13918.0	30030.0	-16112.0
2017	6956.8	2280.9	4675.9	-2395.0	46991.1	15406.8	31584.3	-16177.4
2018	7918.8	2668.4	5250.4	-2582.0	52401.9	17658.0	34744.0	-17086.0
2019	7850.0	2836.0	5014.0	-2178.0	54152.9	19564.0	34588.9	-15024.9
2020	6617.2	2806.3	3810.9	-1004.6	45642.7	19356.7	26286.0	-6929.3
2021	8212.5	3942.5	4270.0	-327.5	52982.7	25435.0	27547.8	-2112.8
2022	8891.1	4240.6	4650.5	-409.9	59801.9	28522.4	31279.5	-2757.1
2023	9331.2	3811.2	5520.0	-1708.7	65754.3	26856.6	38897.7	-12041.1

注：服务进出口总额包含政府服务。

a) Total value of imports and exports of services includes government services.

11-12 服务进出口分类金额(2023年)
International Trade in Services by Sector (2023)

类别	Classification	亿美元 USD 100 million			亿元人民币 RMB 100 million		
		进出口 Total	出口 Exports	进口 Imports	进出口 Total	出口 Exports	进口 Imports
总额	**Total**	**9331.2**	**3811.2**	**5520.0**	**65754.3**	**26856.6**	**38897.7**
运输	Transport	2583.2	870.7	1712.5	18203.5	6135.8	12067.7
旅行	Travel	2108.2	145.6	1962.6	14856.2	1026.0	13830.2
建筑	Construction	392.9	314.1	78.7	2768.3	2213.7	554.6
保险服务	Insurance Services	243.8	71.1	172.7	1718.0	501.2	1216.8
金融服务	Financial Services	80.9	43.2	37.7	570.3	304.7	265.6
电信、计算机和信息服务	Telecommunications, Computer and Information Services	1290.1	903.4	386.7	9091.0	6366.2	2724.8
知识产权使用费	Fees for Use of Intellectual Property	534.7	109.7	424.9	3767.6	773.3	2994.3
个人、文化和娱乐服务	Personal, Cultural, and Recreational Services	58.5	18.2	40.3	412.3	128.1	284.2
维护和维修服务	Maintenance and Repair Services	158.4	99.8	58.6	1116.1	703.0	413.1
加工服务	Manufacturing Services on Physical Inputs Owned by Others	184.6	175.6	9.1	1301.2	1237.3	63.9
其他商业服务	Other Business Services	1651.1	1044.7	606.4	11634.6	7361.8	4272.8
政府服务	Government Services	44.7	15.0	29.7	315.2	105.6	209.6

11−13　外商直接投资情况
Foreign Direct Investment

年　份 Year	新设立企业 (个) Newly Establishment of Enterprises (unit)	实际使用外资金额 (亿美元) Total Amount of Foreign Investment Actually Utilized (USD 100 million)
1979−1982	920	17.7
1983	638	9.2
1984	2166	14.2
1985	3073	19.6
1986	1498	22.4
1987	2233	23.1
1988	5945	31.9
1989	5779	33.9
1990	7273	34.9
1991	12978	43.7
1992	48764	110.1
1993	83437	275.2
1994	47549	337.7
1995	37011	375.2
1996	24556	417.3
1997	21001	452.6
1998	19799	454.6
1999	16918	403.2
2000	22347	407.1
2001	26140	468.8
2002	34171	527.4
2003	41081	535.0
2004	43664	606.3
2005	44019	724.1
2006	41496	727.2
2007	37892	835.2
2008	27537	1083.1
2009	23442	940.6
2010	27420	1147.3
2011	27717	1239.9
2012	24934	1210.7
2013	22819	1239.1
2014	23794	1285.0
2015	26584	1355.8
2016	27908	1337.1
2017	35662	1363.2
2018	60560	1383.1
2019	40910	1412.2
2020	38578	1493.4
2021	47647	1809.6
2022	38497	1891.3
2023	53766	1632.5

注：2005年起，实际使用外资为包含银行、证券、保险领域全口径数据。

a) Since 2005, total amount of foreign investment actually utilized has included comprehensive data in the fields of banking, securities and insurance.

11-14 按国别(地区)分外商直接投资额
Foreign Direct Investment by Country (Region)

单位：万美元 (USD 10000)

国别(地区)	Country (Region)	2022	2023
总计	**Total**	**18913241**	**16325345**
亚洲	**Asia**	**16356555**	**13268648**
阿富汗	Afghanistan		181
孟加拉国	Bangladesh	100	6
文莱	Brunei	257	
柬埔寨	Cambodia	5217	5915
塞浦路斯	Cyprus	15075	1743
中国香港	Hong Kong, China	13724149	11117932
印度	India	225	481
印度尼西亚	Indonesia	3750	15203
伊拉克	Iraq	8	79
以色列	Israel	8101	5275
日本	Japan	460508	388932
约旦	Jordan	7	11
老挝	Laos	18	30
黎巴嫩	Lebanon	3	
中国澳门	Macao, China	124291	65752
马来西亚	Malaysia	112697	21069
蒙古	Mongolia	844	450
巴基斯坦	Pakistan		39
菲律宾	Philippines	1493	2205
卡塔尔	Qatar	24	15
沙特阿拉伯	Saudi Arabia	7898	9194
新加坡	Singapore	1059894	978222
韩国	Republic of Korea	659872	351421
叙利亚	Syria		1
泰国	Thailand	6809	5277
土耳其	Türkiye	1643	4401
阿联酋	United Arab Emirates	96424	220050
也门	Yemen	22	
越南	Vietnam	708	999
中国台湾	Taiwan, China	66110	73455
哈萨克斯坦	Kazakhstan		30
乌兹别克斯坦	Uzbekistan	408	280
亚洲其他国家(地区)	Other Asian Territories		
非洲	**Africa**	**33765**	**27358**
喀麦隆	Cameroon	664	1437
刚果(布)	Congo	24	22
埃塞俄比亚	Ethiopia	204	356
加纳	Ghana	28	3
利比里亚	Liberia		60
马里	Mali	43	27
毛里塔尼亚	Mauritania	200	650
毛里求斯	Mauritius	6594	9144
摩洛哥	Morocco	28	50
尼日利亚	Nigeria		131
卢旺达	Rwanda		22
塞舌尔	Seychelles	14572	12392

11-14 续表 1 continued

单位：万美元 (USD 10 000)

国别(地区)	Country (Region)	2022	2023
南非	South Africa	10319	633
坦桑尼亚	Tanzania	174	
乌干达	Uganda	1	123
刚果(金)	Congo DR		193
赞比亚	Zambia	133	764
津巴布韦	Zimbabwe		647
非洲其他国家(地区)	Other African Territories	781	704
欧洲	**Europe**	**1197604**	**1450858**
比利时	Belgium	18353	17769
丹麦	Denmark	42596	21379
英国	United Kingdom	159819	341303
德国	Germany	256643	192204
法国	France	75650	133629
爱尔兰	Ireland	17095	5451
意大利	Italy	14847	27992
卢森堡	Luxembourg	16059	26319
荷兰	Netherlands	449402	535506
希腊	Greece	9	327
葡萄牙	Portugal	810	292
西班牙	Spain	12335	11172
奥地利	Austria	15530	2980
保加利亚	Bulgaria	8	28
芬兰	Finland	1235	3588
匈牙利	Hungary	31	75
冰岛	Iceland	10	
列支敦士登	Liechtenstein	470	
马耳他	Malta		50
摩纳哥	Monaco	7	
挪威	Norway	6623	4627
波兰	Poland	1462	312
罗马尼亚	Romania	9	153
瑞典	Sweden	54233	44356
瑞士	Switzerland	39152	45457
爱沙尼亚	Estonia	10111	28543
拉脱维亚	Latvia		1
亚美尼亚	Armenia		19
阿塞拜疆	Azerbaijan		10
白俄罗斯	Byelorussia	17	266
俄罗斯联邦	Russian Federation	3895	3061
斯洛文尼亚	Slovenia	768	3400
克罗地亚	Croatia	11	5
捷克	Czech Rep.	391	582
斯洛伐克	Slovakia	21	
塞尔维亚	Serbia	2	2
欧洲其他国家(地区)	Other European Territories		
拉丁美洲	**Latin America**	**916876**	**1049394**
安提瓜和巴布达	Antigua and Barbuda	59	491
阿根廷	Argentina	15	
巴巴多斯	Barbados	1105	7047
伯利兹	Belize	3450	298
巴西	Brazil	2581	2334
开曼群岛	Cayman Islands	241631	351702
智利	Chile	205	794

11−14 续表 2 continued

单位：万美元 (USD 10 000)

国别（地区）	Country (Region)	2022	2023
多米尼加共和国	Dominican Republic	9	105
危地马拉	Guatemala	15	15
圭亚那	Guyana	5	
牙买加	Jamaica		65
墨西哥	Mexico	133	16
巴拿马	Panama	1072	85
秘鲁	Peru	104	126
特立尼达和多巴哥	Trinidad and Tobago		55
特克斯和凯科斯群岛	Turks & Caicos Is.	266	270
乌拉圭	Uruguay	332	5
英属维尔京群岛	Virgin Islands，British	663493	685580
圣其茨和尼维斯	St. Kitts-Nevis		147
拉丁美洲其他国家(地区)	Other Latin American Territories	2401	259
北美洲	**North America**	**287839**	**389585**
加拿大	Canada	16571	20745
美国	United States	221457	335970
百慕大	Bermuda	49811	32870
北美洲其他国家(地区)	Other North American Territories		
大洋洲	**Oceania**	**120516**	**139502**
澳大利亚	Australia	40211	44924
库克群岛	Cook Islands	132	
新西兰	New Zealand	1168	2391
萨摩亚	Samoa	74734	85659
马绍尔群岛	Marshall Islands	4271	6528
大洋洲其他国家(地区)	Other Oceanian Territories		
其他	**Others**	**86**	

11-15 按行业分外商直接投资（2023年）
Foreign Direct Investment by Sector (2023)

行　　业	Sector	设立企业（个）Establishment of Enterprises (unit)	实际使用外资金额（万美元）Total Amount of Foreign Investment Actually Utilized (USD 10 000)
总　　计	**Total**	**53766**	**16325345**
农、林、牧、渔业	Agriculture, Forestry, Animal Husbandry and Fishery	418	72190
采矿业	Mining	32	513686
制造业	Manufacturing	3624	4552686
电力、热力、燃气及水生产和供应业	Production and Supply of Electricity, Heat, Gas and Water	568	454463
建筑业	Construction	685	237235
批发和零售业	Wholesale and Retail Trades	18010	988812
交通运输、仓储和邮政业	Transport, Storage and Post	867	214028
住宿和餐饮业	Hotels and Catering Services	1211	39050
信息传输、软件和信息技术服务业	Information Transmission, Software and Information Technology	3764	1642694
金融业	Financial Intermediation	387	675697
房地产业	Real Estate	684	1172689
租赁和商务服务业	Leasing and Business Services	10673	2637742
科学研究和技术服务业	Scientific Research and Technical Services	9519	2938239
水利、环境和公共设施管理业	Management of Water Conservancy, Environment and Public Facilities	123	53498
居民服务、修理和其他服务业	Service to Households, Repair and Other Services	726	48692
教育	Education	109	6031
卫生和社会工作	Health and Social Service	143	29624
文化、体育和娱乐业	Culture, Sports and Entertainment	2223	43786
公共管理和社会组织	Public Management and Social Organizations	0	4503
国际组织	International Organizations		

注：本表行业类别按照《国民经济行业分类》(GB/T 4754-2017)划分。
a) Industries in this table are classified by Industrial Classification for National Economy Activities (GB/T 4754-2017).

11-16 按行业分外商投资企业年底注册登记情况（2023年）
Registration Status of Foreign Invested Enterprises by Sector at Year-end (2023)

行业	Sector	企业数(户) Number of Enterprises (unit)	投资总额(亿美元) Total Investment (USD 100 million)	注册资本(亿美元) Registered Capital (USD 100 million)	#外方 Foreign Capital
总计	**Total**	**695695**	**293380**	**316219**	**277534**
农、林、牧、渔业	Agriculture, Forestry, Animal Husbandry and Fishery	6796	35649	118157	117932
采矿业	Mining	758	274	182	119
制造业	Manufacturing	118058	32281	19627	13299
电力、热力、燃气及水生产和供应业	Production and Supply of Electricity, Heat, Gas and Water	6401	4356	2110	1377
建筑业	Construction	8140	2385	1894	1102
批发和零售业	Wholesale and Retail Trades	213945	19854	16237	12933
交通运输、仓储和邮政业	Transport, Storage and Post	14352	3068	1564	913
住宿和餐饮业	Hotels and Catering Services	48909	584	473	369
信息传输、软件和信息技术服务业	Information Transmission, Software and Information Technology	57009	20337	16834	15291
金融业	Financial Intermediation	15892	15338	15045	12789
房地产业	Real Estate	18497	22585	15021	12926
租赁和商务服务业	Leasing and Business Services	93092	59842	46802	35041
科学研究和技术服务业	Scientific Research and Technical Services	70330	65554	52349	47615
水利、环境和公共设施管理业	Management of Water Conservancy, Environment and Public Facilities	1705	4324	4163	677
居民服务、修理和其他服务业	Service to Households, Repair and Other Services	6791	1138	678	424
教育	Education	949	154	104	96
卫生和社会工作	Health and Social Service	1007	812	341	270
文化、体育和娱乐业	Culture, Sports and Entertainment	12546	1648	1469	1198
其他	Others	518	3198	3168	3163

注：本表数据来自国家市场监督管理总局，数据包含外商投资企业(包含港澳台投资企业)及其分支机构(以下相关表同)。

a) The data in this table come from the State Administration for Market Regulation, which include the data of foreign invested enterprises (including enterprises with investment from Hong Kong, Macao and Taiwan) and their branches. The same applies to the relevant following table.

11—17 分地区外商投资企业年底注册登记情况
Registration Status of Foreign Invested Enterprises by Region at Year-end

地区	Region	企业数（户） Number of Enterprises (unit)		投资总额（亿美元） Total Investment (USD 100 million)		注册资本（亿美元） Registered Capital (USD 100 million)		#外方 Foreign Capital	
		2022	2023	2022	2023	2022	2023	2022	2023
全国	**National Total**	**674140**	**695695**	**200425**	**293380**	**138731**	**316219**	**109235**	**277534**
北京	Beijing	34426	34871	7540	8099	5171	5715	3404	3963
天津	Tianjin	14616	14428	3057	3121	2612	2691	2015	1698
河北	Hebei	10494	10763	2667	2766	1446	1522	1167	1231
山西	Shanxi	3780	3879	617	617	617	617	586	587
内蒙古	Inner Mongolia	3186	3284	506	598	243	378	163	123
辽宁	Liaoning	16309	16178	5171	6161	2706	3326	2101	2297
吉林	Jilin	4221	4524	1264	1401	774	957	485	633
黑龙江	Heilongjiang	5853	5282	1798	1809	1581	1635	868	891
上海	Shanghai	98408	97479	12559	12733	8308	8492	6407	6560
江苏	Jiangsu	65078	65804	14916	15592	8826	8829	6845	7051
浙江	Zhejiang	46944	49281	7069	7423	4826	5096	3444	3615
安徽	Anhui	8407	8880	3387	3515	1656	2110	925	1344
福建	Fujian	33062	34828	3940	7896	2813	6884	1988	2259
江西	Jiangxi	7308	7318	1612	1898	1070	1296	789	991
山东	Shandong	37099	37304	25517	27481	19692	20446	15501	15990
河南	Henan	10217	10742	1030	10965	743	6228	574	6039
湖北	Hubei	13230	14145	2528	2467	1740	2808	1247	1162
湖南	Hunan	12599	13778	2464	2504	1345	1389	1022	1061
广东	Guangdong	189439	199057	24141	23059	11363	16253	8521	10947
广西	Guangxi	7276	7655	9707	9671	1580	1640	1343	1342
海南	Hainan	7161	8494	56704	97485	51985	92930	44045	84893
重庆	Chongqing	6936	7145	1560	1823	1100	1215	785	887
四川	Sichuan	14918	15711	2682	2779	1401	1557	1097	1232
贵州	Guizhou	3582	3860	2147	2142	1661	1671	1534	1548
云南	Yunnan	6322	7304	2369	2645	1487	1674	1238	1350
西藏	Xizang	288	296	27	32864	21	116316	18	116314
陕西	Shaanxi	7392	7572	2005	1927	1053	1150	540	637
甘肃	Gansu	2037	2062	410	410	333	335	269	271
青海	Qinghai	728	725	108	188	58	153	30	119
宁夏	Ningxia	865	872	304	286	159	135	105	90
新疆	Xinjiang	1959	2174	616	1055	360	770	180	411

11−18 对外直接投资
Outward Foreign Direct Investment

单位：亿美元 (USD 100 million)

年 份 Year	对外直接投资流量 Flow of Outward Foreign Direct Investment	#非金融类 Non-financial	年末对外直接投资存量 Stock of Outward Foreign Direct Investment at Year-end
2002	27.0	27.0	299.0
2003	28.5	28.5	332.0
2004	55.0	55.0	448.0
2005	122.6	122.6	572.0
2006	211.6	176.3	906.3
2007	265.1	248.4	1179.1
2008	559.1	418.6	1839.7
2009	565.3	478.0	2457.5
2010	688.1	601.8	3172.1
2011	746.5	685.8	4247.8
2012	878.0	777.3	5319.4
2013	1078.4	927.4	6604.8
2014	1231.2	1072.0	8826.4
2015	1456.7	1214.2	10978.6
2016	1961.5	1812.3	13573.9
2017	1582.9	1395.0	18090.4
2018	1430.4	1213.2	19822.7
2019	1369.1	1169.6	21988.8
2020	1537.1	1340.5	25806.6
2021	1788.2	1520.2	27851.5
2022	1631.2	1410.0	27548.1
2023	1772.9	1590.7	29554.0

注：2002—2005年流量数据为中国对外非金融类直接投资数据，2006—2023年为全行业对外直接投资数据。

a) The flow data from 2002 to 2005 are the data of China's outward non-financial direct investment, while the data from 2006 to 2023 are the data of all industries.

11-19 按主要国别(地区)分对外直接投资
Outward Foreign Direct Investment by Country (Region)

单位：万美元 (USD 10 000)

国家（地区）	Country or Region	对外直接投资流量 Flow of Outward Foreign Direct Investment		截至2023年对外直接投资存量 Stock of Outward Foreign Direct Investment at the End of 2023
		2022	2023	
合计	**Total**	**16312100**	**17728784**	**295539978**
亚洲	**Asia**	**12428354**	**14159587**	**201484334**
#中国香港	Hong Kong, China	9753423	10876698	175252154
印度	India	-33120	6037	320626
印度尼西亚	Indonesia	454960	313307	2634626
日本	Japan	39648	45842	576659
中国澳门	Macao, China	212752	75588	1394658
新加坡	Singapore	829538	1309714	8644682
韩国	Republic of Korea	53714	65945	698868
泰国	Thailand	127180	201759	1265743
越南	Vietnam	170301	259307	1359399
非洲	**Africa**	**181183**	**395882**	**4211535**
#阿尔及利亚	Algeria	2145	20928	169996
苏丹	Sudan	-17190	7656	95214
几内亚	Guinea	3911	2636	66086
马达加斯加	Madagascar	-6239	3304	25367
尼日利亚	Nigeria	11964	18558	266233
南非	South Africa	68309	35390	584164
欧洲	**Europe**	**1033598**	**996861**	**14767913**
#英国	United Kingdom	282306	166505	2925890
德国	Germany	197864	64133	1706352
法国	France	4848	-10902	462281
俄罗斯联邦	Russia	23362	62879	1066818
拉丁美洲	**Latin America**	**1634515**	**1347731**	**60080097**
#巴西	Brazil	22386	50674	394445
开曼群岛	Cayman Islands	576238	873084	22190516
墨西哥	Mexico	48852	107889	348822
英属维尔京群岛	Virgin Islands, British	911595	254610	35889354
北美洲	**North America**	**727119**	**778173**	**11010784**
#加拿大	Canada	14676	35368	1059734
美国	United States	729208	691293	8369426
大洋洲	**Oceania**	**307331**	**50550**	**3985316**
#澳大利亚	Australia	278588	54527	3477392
新西兰	New Zealand	11654	18856	260240

11–20 按行业分对外直接投资
Outward Foreign Direct Investment by Sector

单位：万美元 (USD 10 000)

行业	Sector	对外直接投资流量 Flow of Outward Foreign Direct Investment 2022	2023	截至2023年对外直接投资存量 Stock of Outward Foreign Direct Investment at the End of 2023
总　计	**Total**	**16312100**	**17728784**	**295539978**
农、林、牧、渔业	Agriculture, Forestry, Animal Husbandry and Fishery	51171	181628	2002101
采矿业	Mining	1510082	987878	19350973
制造业	Manufacturing	2715370	2734225	28340248
电力、热力、燃气及水生产和供应业	Production and Supply of Electricity, Heat, Gas and Water	544673	465403	5867936
建筑业	Construction	144150	285929	5249902
批发和零售业	Wholesale and Retail Trades	2116908	3882262	42140064
交通运输、仓储和邮政业	Transport, Storage and Post	1503813	844197	10426336
住宿和餐饮业	Hotels and Catering Services	1398	94745	435370
信息传输、软件和信息技术服务业	Information Transmission, Software and Information Technology	169329	228135	13310709
金融业	Financial Intermediation	2212554	1821852	32381953
房地产业	Real Estate	220654	141632	8851913
租赁和商务服务业	Leasing and Business Services	4347973	5416619	117910016
科学研究和技术服务业	Scientific Research and Technical Services	481719	504833	5852383
水利、环境和公共设施管理业	Management of Water Conservancy, Environment and Public Facilities	18270	23672	275293
居民服务、修理和其他服务业	Service to Households, Repair and Other Services	67915	104845	1413328
教育	Education	24093	8577	374908
卫生和社会工作	Health and Social Service	28626	16069	341463
文化、体育和娱乐业	Culture, Sports and Entertainment	153403	-13715	1015083
公共管理、社会保障和社会组织	Public Management, Social Security and Social Organization			

11-21 对外经济合作
Economic Cooperation with Foreign Countries or Regions

年 份 Year	对外承包工程 Contracted Projects					对外劳务合作 Labour Services	
	合同数 (份) Number of Contracts (unit)	合同金额 (亿美元) Contracted Value (USD 100 million)	完成营业额 (亿美元) Value of Turnover Fulfilled (USD 100 million)	派出人数 (万人) Dispatched Persons (10 000 persons)	年末在外人数 (万人) Persons Abroad by the End of Year (10 000 persons)	派出劳务人数 (万人) Dispatched Workers (10 000 persons)	年末在外人数 (万人) Workers Abroad by the End of Year (10 000 persons)
1979	27	0.33					
1980	138	1.40					
1981	250	2.76	1.23				
1982	195	3.46	1.89				
1983	280	7.99	3.16				
1984	344	15.38	4.94		2.19		2.76
1985	465	11.16	6.63		3.06		2.49
1986	486	11.89	8.19		2.74		1.90
1987	616	16.48	10.73		3.13		3.19
1988	642	18.13	12.53		3.00		3.98
1989	776	17.81	14.84		2.40		4.31
1990	920	21.25	16.44		2.18		3.61
1991	1171	25.24	19.70		2.15		6.83
1992	1164	52.51	24.03		2.54		10.56
1993	1393	51.89	36.69		3.42		13.09
1994	1702	60.28	48.83		3.83		18.43
1995	1558	76.65	52.41		3.84		22.59
1996	1634	79.93	59.85		3.88		24.66
1997	2085	88.07	62.18		4.78		28.55
1998	2322	93.83	78.58		6.11		29.08
1999	2527	103.70	86.12		5.53		32.65
2000	2597	119.52	85.13		5.56		36.93
2001	5836	131.27	89.62		6.00		41.47
2002	4036	151.37	112.80		7.85		41.04
2003	3708	178.40	139.22		9.40		42.97
2004	6694	241.95	176.15	7.38	11.47	17.30	41.94
2005	9502	299.68	219.90	8.95	14.48	18.34	41.87
2006	12996	664.16	303.21	13.48	19.86	21.48	47.52
2007	6282	786.32	411.26	15.48	23.60	21.49	50.51
2008	5411	1054.51	570.59	20.01	27.16	22.49	46.71
2009	7280	1262.10	777.06	21.42	32.69	18.01	45.03
2010	9544	1343.67	921.70	22.46	37.65	18.68	47.01
2011	6381	1423.32	1034.24	24.32	32.40	20.91	48.84
2012	6710	1565.29	1165.97	23.34	34.46	27.84	50.56
2013	11578	1716.29	1371.43	27.09	37.01	25.57	48.26
2014	7740	1917.56	1424.11	26.92	40.89	29.26	59.69
2015	8662	2100.74	1540.74	25.31	40.86	27.68	61.83
2016	19157	2440.10	1594.17	23.02	37.29	26.40	59.60
2017	22774	2652.76	1685.87	22.21	37.68	30.02	60.23
2018	10985	2418.04	1690.44	22.70	39.07	26.50	60.61
2019	11932	2602.45	1729.01	21.15	36.81	27.60	62.41
2020	9933	2555.40	1559.35	13.87	27.34	16.23	34.98
2021	10786	2584.94	1549.43	13.29	25.84	18.98	33.39
2022	9823	2530.70	1549.92	7.97	21.68	17.92	32.66
2023	9783	2645.14	1609.14	11.09	19.47	23.60	34.62

11-22 按国别(地区)分对外经济合作(2023年)
Economic Cooperation by Country (Region) (2023)

国别(地区)	Country (Region)	对外承包工程 Contracted Projects			对外劳务合作 Labour Services	
		完成营业额(万美元) Value of Turnover Fulfilled (USD 10 000)	派出人数(人) Dispatched Persons (person)	年末在外人数(人) Persons Abroad by the End of Year (person)	派出人数(人) Dispatched Workers (person)	年末在外人数(人) Workers Abroad by the End of Year (person)
总　计	**Total**	**16091443**	**110879**	**194746**	**235964**	**346189**
亚洲	**Asia**	**8564132**	**67900**	**103990**	**198928**	**293067**
阿富汗	Afghanistan	288	14	45		
巴林	Bahrain	26048	726	712		1
孟加拉国	Bangladesh	571129	3719	7820	73	294
文莱	Brunei	13937	1832	76		
缅甸	Myanmar	22391	1239	595	103	297
柬埔寨	Cambodia	239014	1620	3650	395	847
塞浦路斯	Cyprus	7704	72	81	427	426
中国香港	Hong Kong, China	861848	611	2215	50380	40878
印度	India	164006	433	700	51	58
印度尼西亚	Indonesia	845371	11134	17819	9622	5323
伊朗	Iran	63921	288	462	1	4
伊拉克	Iraq	421808	4471	8362	1330	1477
以色列	Israel	139371	2772	5262	6714	13299
日本	Japan	28259	2	4	13939	42594
约旦	Jordan	4208	3	94		
科威特	Kuwait	139806	2301	1404	91	86
老挝	Laos	126916	2548	4492	1506	1869
黎巴嫩	Lebanon	1747		13		29
中国澳门	Macao, China	200753	344	749	68441	115855
马来西亚	Malaysia	738792	2299	4081	810	1887
马尔代夫	Maldives	27030	178	366	44	75
蒙古	Mongolia	132304	2590	1867	595	545
尼泊尔联邦民主共和国	Nepal	57590	541	1278	19	153
阿曼	Oman	67473	72	213	14	84
巴基斯坦	Pakistan	321730	2859	4730	440	1008
巴勒斯坦	Palestine	31				
菲律宾	Philippines	274104	762	2101	189	610
卡塔尔	Qatar	38537	289	456	93	299
沙特阿拉伯	Saudi Arabia	927362	7906	10504	421	925
新加坡	Singapore	461381	733	1446	28382	45479
韩国	Republic of Korea	46049	1	77	1894	5960
斯里兰卡	Sri Lanka	59329	262	1341	83	151
叙利亚	Syria	256	11	17		
泰国	Thailand	334324	977	1413	132	96
土耳其	Türkiye	80875	813	897	320	192
阿联酋	United Arab Emirates	373994	1065	3526	397	1025
也门	Yemen	5551				
越南	Vietnam	194914	1025	1377	468	1778
中国台湾	Taiwan, China	13148	7	17	9050	7147
东帝汶	Timor-Leste	5319	84	297	9	9
哈萨克斯坦	Kazakhstan	135901	1682	2740	331	352
吉尔吉斯斯坦	Kirghizia	15224	55	506	428	376
塔吉克斯坦	Tadzhikistan	34468	1130	1691	249	384
土库曼斯坦	Turkmenistan	32677	173	253		15
乌兹别克斯坦	Uzbekistan	307244	8257	8241	1487	1180

11-22 续表 1 continued

国别(地区)	Country (Region)	对外承包工程 Contracted Projects 完成营业额(万美元) Value of Turnover Fulfilled (USD 10 000)	派出人数(人) Dispatched Persons (person)	年末在外人数(人) Persons Abroad by the End of Year (person)	对外劳务合作 Labour Services 派出人数(人) Dispatched Workers (person)	年末在外人数(人) Workers Abroad by the End of Year (person)
非洲	**Africa**	**3742527**	**23955**	**57080**	**15132**	**29998**
阿尔及利亚	Algeria	342122	1243	4275	723	1763
安哥拉	Angola	247658	1140	2339	641	4145
贝宁	Benin	47238	371	710	184	205
博茨瓦纳	Botswana	59927	148	354		4
布隆迪	Burundi	2298	67	150	8	16
喀麦隆	Cameroon	55443	478	1377	338	462
佛得角	Cape Verde	134		2		
中非	Central African	4784	37	99		
乍得	Chad	66688	729	937	84	194
科摩罗	Comoros	4977	11	102	10	49
刚果(布)	Congo	74224	187	672	365	656
吉布提	Djibouti	8163	136	295	54	317
埃及	Egypt	324157	1507	6884	905	1572
赤道几内亚	Eq.Guinea	39341	120	415	81	124
埃塞俄比亚	Ethiopia	192985	1893	3376	980	1612
加蓬	Gabon	16811	63	170	119	119
冈比亚	Gambia	3476	42	34		8
加纳	Ghana	93210	308	1013	203	375
几内亚	Guinea	147736	2626	4370	1410	2582
几内亚比绍	Guinea-Bissau	1757	21	55		
科特迪瓦	Cote d'Ivoire	144995	431	2033	138	319
肯尼亚	Kenya	158479	712	2759	93	660
利比里亚	Liberia	13840	247	402	2295	1895
利比亚	Libya	6566			21	2
马达加斯加	Madagascar	27495	131	291	64	132
马拉维	Malawi	18298	229	361	81	130
马里	Mali	11858	25	98	127	136
毛里塔尼亚	Mauritania	11490	50	192	75	197
毛里求斯	Mauritius	12429	67	165	27	26
摩洛哥	Morocco	39505	37	103	59	89
莫桑比克	Mozambique	63577	152	592	141	212
纳米比亚	Namibia	15478	77	214	28	37
尼日尔	Niger	95009	877	886	165	71
尼日利亚	Nigeria	397731	1919	4516	914	2609
卢旺达	Rwanda	17378	105	558	111	283
圣多美和普林西比	Sao Tome & Principe	2306				
塞内加尔	Senegal	85760	367	1328	363	773
塞舌尔	Seychelles	1239	25	42	11	58
塞拉利昂	Sierra Leone	13388	145	261	161	222
索马里	Somalia	1471				
南非	S. Africa	79636	392	462		5
苏丹	Sudan	17237	51	62	7	16
坦桑尼亚	Tanzania	146189	1242	2319	394	1110
多哥	Togo	6337	77	202	30	51
突尼斯	Tunisia	6796	11	91		
乌干达	Uganda	97981	1264	1812	207	381
布基纳法索	Burkina Faso	10612	72	278	31	85
赞比亚	Zambia	110606	605	2480	286	767
津巴布韦	Zimbabwe	46683	354	932	544	413
莱索托	Lesotho	16854	260	424	25	53
斯威士兰	Eswatini	255	4	5	4	4
厄立特里亚	Eritrea	17000	50	218	1	8
南苏丹共和国	Republic of South Sudan	22880	124	278	9	50
刚果(金)	Congo DR	292036	2726	5087	2615	5001

11-22 续表 2 continued

国别(地区)	Country (Region)	对外承包工程 Contracted Projects			对外劳务合作 Labour Services	
		完成营业额 (万美元) Value of Turnover Fulfilled (USD 10 000)	派出人数 (人) Dispatched Persons (person)	年末在外人数 (人) Persons Abroad by the End of Year (person)	派出人数 (人) Dispatched Workers (person)	年末在外人数 (人) Workers Abroad by the End of Year (person)
欧洲	**Europe**	**1712409**	**10730**	**14222**	**7465**	**8242**
比利时	Belgium	14392				3
丹麦	Denmark	1429		2	89	82
英国	United Kingdom	41330	30	91	1365	1105
德国	Germany	47706	32	66	249	1464
法国	France	53306	51	100	411	183
爱尔兰	Ireland	9337			60	323
意大利	Italy	27255	33	36	101	90
卢森堡	Luxembourg	1107	16	23		
荷兰	Netherlands	14535			222	218
希腊	Greece	10950	7	33	329	504
葡萄牙	Portugal	27476	2	5	19	14
西班牙	Spain	83259		6		7
阿尔巴尼亚	Albania	331			498	406
奥地利	Austria	7413	12	38	40	76
保加利亚	Bulgaria	6340		3		11
芬兰	Finland	4744		2	23	21
直布罗陀	Gibraltar	1629		3		
匈牙利	Hungary	45950	180	231	55	60
冰岛	Iceland				3	3
马耳他	Malta				14	62
摩纳哥	Monaco	27			161	75
挪威	Norway	11646		6	512	363
波兰	Poland	79093	79	141	4	4
罗马尼亚	Romania	9605	31	75		1
瑞典	Sweden	12758	24	42	1	1
瑞士	Switzerland	15073	16	47	85	72
爱沙尼亚	Estonia	90				
拉脱维亚	Latvia	275	1			
立陶宛	Lithuania	109				
格鲁吉亚	Georgia	57586	529	1797	354	390
亚美尼亚	Armenia	2032	15	66		
阿塞拜疆	Azerbaijan	64930	1	30		
白俄罗斯	Belorussia	62034	508	630	39	258
俄罗斯联邦	Russian Federation	648597	6924	5140	1544	1087
乌克兰	Ukraine	16484	36			
斯洛文尼亚	Slovenia	59			10	10
克罗地亚	Croatia	12953	1	63	4	5
捷克	Czech Rep.	8866			43	48
斯洛伐克	Slovak	4833			3	3
北马其顿共和国	Republic of North Macedonia	8442	68	101	9	44
波黑	Bosnia & Herzegovina	21783	329	400	7	23
塞尔维亚	Serbia	274069	1722	4893	1211	1226
黑山	Montenegro	2577	83	152		
拉丁美洲	**Latin America**	**1369236**	**7183**	**15526**	**7296**	**6766**
安提瓜和巴布达	Antigua & Barbuda	28		6		
阿根廷	Argentina	117094	2558	1450	107	167
巴哈马	Bahamas	820	7	17	303	206
巴巴多斯	Barbados	11278	80	404	52	135

11–22 续表 3 continued

国别(地区)	Country (Region)	对外承包工程 Contracted Projects			对外劳务合作 Labour Services	
		完成营业额(万美元) Value of Turnover Fulfilled (USD 10 000)	派出人数(人) Dispatched Persons (person)	年末在外人数(人) Persons Abroad by the End of Year (person)	派出人数(人) Dispatched Workers (person)	年末在外人数(人) Workers Abroad by the End of Year (person)
伯利兹	Belize				198	257
多民族玻利维亚国	Bolivia	72740	585	1171	156	177
巴西	Brazil	208023	70	106		3
开曼群岛	Cayman Is.				67	62
智利	Chile	72837	49	151		
哥伦比亚	Colombia	126415	60	440	22	36
多米尼克	Dominica	3111	218	213	174	170
哥斯达黎加	Costa Rica	12000	18	268		2
古巴	Cuba	5129		90	20	20
多米尼加共和国	Republic of Dominica	7547	95	196	71	156
厄瓜多尔	Ecuador	89967	122	296	18	51
格林纳达	Granada	2254				
危地马拉	Guatemala	638				
圭亚那	Guyana	27650	261	621	206	235
洪都拉斯	Honduras	971		10		8
牙买加	Jamaica	16773	47	142	78	112
墨西哥	Mexico	233829	222	559	20	48
尼加拉瓜	Nicaragua	778		24		
巴拿马	Panama	6313	3	260	5578	4511
巴拉圭	Paraguay	100				
秘鲁	Peru	319225	2583	8799	51	203
圣文森特和格林纳丁	Saint Vincent & Grenadines				130	116
萨尔瓦多	El Salvador	588	140	68		
苏里南	Suriname	2144	39	55		3
特立尼达和多巴哥	Trinidad & Tobago	4935	2	55	40	73
乌拉圭	Uruguay	9321	6	58		
委内瑞拉	Venezuela	16729	18	67	5	15
北美洲	**North America**	**109325**	**558**	**2315**	**2456**	**1743**
加拿大	Canada	33815		49	110	81
美国	United States	75511	558	2266	2314	1647
百慕大	Bermuda				32	15
大洋洲	**Oceanic**	**589975**	**553**	**1607**	**3344**	**4584**
澳大利亚	Australia	467400	10	24	514	706
库克群岛	Cook Is.					1
斐济	Fiji	13370	96	225	50	78
瑙鲁	Nauru	370	3	4		1
新喀里多尼亚	New Caledonia (Fr)			2		
瓦努阿图	Vanuatu	4332	60	109	1	16
新西兰	New Zealand	11222	11	28	1063	1851
巴布亚新几内亚	Papua New Guinea	78534	270	954	35	106
所罗门群岛	Solomon Is.	12175	62	120	51	64
汤加	Tonga	106	3	5		
萨摩亚	Samoa	1881	32	59	33	23
基里巴斯	Kiribati	169	2	32	1	35
图瓦卢	Tuvalu	7				36
密克罗尼西亚联邦	Micronesia Commonwealth	50		6		
马绍尔群岛	Republic of the Marshall Islands				1570	1638
帕劳	Republic of Palau					8
纽埃	Niue	361	4	39	26	21
其他	**Others**	**3840**		**6**	**1343**	**1789**

主要统计指标解释

货物进出口总额 指实际进出我国关境并改变我国境内物质存量的货物总金额，包括一般贸易进出口货物、加工贸易进出口货物、海关特殊监管区域、保税监管场所或经济特区进出境的货物、租赁期一年及以上的租赁贸易货物、外商投资企业进出口的货物、国际间无偿援助的物资以及捐赠品、免税品、边民互市进出口货物、低值快速货物以及以邮报或快件方式向海关申报的跨境电商包裹等，不包括过境货物、暂时进出境货物、进出境展览品、租赁期一年以下的租赁进出境货物、进出境货币及货币用金、进出境旅客的自用物品（汽车除外）、进出境运输工具在境外添装的燃料、物料和食品等。我国规定出口货物按离岸价格统计，进口货物按到岸价格统计，同时按照人民币和美元计价。

服务进出口 指常住单位与非常住单位之间相互提供的服务。包括运输，旅行，建筑，保险服务，金融服务，电信、计算机和信息服务，知识产权使用费，个人、文化和娱乐服务，维护和维修服务，加工服务，其他商业服务，政府服务。

外商投资 是指国外及港澳台地区的法人和自然人在中国大陆地区以现金、实物、无形资产、股权等方式进行投资。其中，外商直接投资是指国外及港澳台地区投资者在非上市公司中的全部投资及在单个外国投资者所占股权比例不低于10%的上市公司中的投资。

对外直接投资 是境内投资者以控制国（境）外企业的经营管理权为核心的经济活动，体现在一经济体通过投资于另一经济体而实现其持久利益的目标。

对外承包工程 根据《对外承包工程管理条例》，对外承包工程是指中国的企业或者其他单位承包境外建设工程项目的活动。

对外劳务合作 指组织劳务人员赴其他国家或地区为国外的企业或机构工作的经营性活动。

Explanatory Notes on Main Statistical Indicators

Import and Export of Goods refer to the value of commodities actually imported or exported across the border of China and changed the material stock within our country. They include general trade imports and exports, processing trade imported and exported goods, goods imported and exported from customs special supervision areas, bonded supervision places or economic special zones, leased trade goods with a lease term of one year or more, goods imported and exported by foreign invested enterprises, international free aid materials and donations, duty-free goods, border trade imported and exported goods, low value express goods, and cross-border e-commerce packages declared to customs by mail or express delivery. They do not include transit goods, temporary imported and exported goods, imported and exported exhibits, leased imported and exported goods with a lease term of less than one year, imported and exported currency and currency fees, personal belongings of inbound and outbound passengers (excluding cars), fuel, materials added to inbound and outbound transportation vehicles overseas, and food, etc. In accordance with the stipulation of the Chinese government, exports are calculated at FOB, while imports are calculated at CIF and simultaneously priced in both RMB and USD.

Import and Export of Services refer to services provided between resident and non-resident units, including transportation, travel, construction, insurance, finance, telecommunications, computer and information, professional and management consultancy, intellectual property fee, personal, cultural or recreational services, maintenance and repair, processing, other business services, and government services.

Foreign Investment refers to investment in China by legal or natural persons of foreign countries and of Hong Kong, Macao and Taiwan, in the form of cash、physical assets、intangible assets and equity and others. Foreign direct investment refers to investment by investors from foreign countries and from Hong Kong, Macao and Taiwan in a non-listed company, or the investment of over 10 percent or more in a listed company.

Outward Foreign Direct Investment refers to the economic activities of domestic investors focussing on controlling the operation and management of overseas enterprises. The content of overseas direct investment mainly reflects goal of lasting interest of one economic entity by investing in another economic entity.

Overseas Contracted Projects refer to activities of contracting overseas construction projects by Chinese enterprises or any other units, which are stipulated in the *Regulations on Administration of Foreign Contracted Project.*

Overseas Labour Services refer to operational activities of organizing labour force to go abroad providing services to foreign enterprises or agencies.

12

农　业

Agriculture

简 要 说 明

一、本篇资料的主要内容及统计范围

本篇资料全面反映我国农林牧渔业生产成果及农业生产条件情况，内容主要包括农林牧渔业产值、主要农产品产量、农业机械拥有量、水利设施与除涝治碱、国有农场基本情况等方面的统计资料。

农业统计范围包括全部农业生产经营户，各省、自治区、直辖市以及新疆生产建设兵团所属的各种经济组织类型、各个系统的全部农林牧渔业生产单位和非农行业单位附属的农林牧渔业生产活动单位，以及所经营的农作物种植地块、养殖场、牧场等，但不包括农业科学试验机构进行的农业生产。

1.农业：指对各种农作物的种植活动。包括谷物、豆类、薯类、棉花、油料、糖料、麻类、烟叶、蔬菜、园艺作物、水果、坚果、香料作物、中草药及其他作物的种植。

2.林业：包括林木的栽培(不包括茶园、桑园和果园的栽培、管理和收获等活动)，木材和竹材的采运，林产品的采集。

3.畜牧业：包括牲畜饲养和放牧，家禽饲养。

4.渔业：包括水生动物和海藻类植物的养殖和捕捞。

5.农、林、牧、渔专业及辅助性活动：指对农、林、牧、渔业生产活动进行的各种支持性服务。但不包括各种科学技术和专业性技术服务活动。

二、本篇的资料来源及统计调查方法

1.农林牧渔业产值情况资料由国家统计局农村社会经济调查司根据《农业产值和价格综合统计报表制度》的有关资料整理提供。

2.农业、畜牧业生产及农业生产条件情况资料，由国家统计局农村社会经济调查司根据《农林牧渔业统计报表制度》的有关资料整理提供。农业的稻谷、小麦、玉米等主要粮食作物生产情况实行抽样调查和遥感测量；畜牧业的猪、牛、羊、家禽等主要畜禽生产情况实行抽样调查；农业生产条件情况、其他农作物、园林作物、其他畜禽等生产情况实行全面统计。

3.林业和渔业生产情况资料，分别来自国家林业和草原局和农业农村部汇总的统计报表，统计调查方法由部门自行确定。

4.国有农场基本情况资料，来自农业农村部农垦局汇总的统计报表。其统计范围是全国31个省、自治区、直辖市。统计方法为逐级上报、全面汇总。

5.灌溉、水库等水利设施和除涝、治水、治碱情况资料，主要来源于水利部汇总的统计报表。其统计范围是全国31个省、自治区、直辖市。资料收集以县为基本统计单位，采取逐级汇总上报的方式。

三、数据使用注意事项

根据第三次全国农业普查结果，按照国际惯例，对2007年以后农业、畜牧业、渔业年报数据及农林牧渔业总产值等数据进行了修订。具体修订情况见相关表的标注。

Brief Introduction

I. Main Contents and Statistical Scopes

The data in this chapter show comprehensively the production results in agriculture, forestry, animal husbandry, fishery, as well as conditions of agricultural production, including output value of agriculture, forestry, animal husbandry and fishery, output of major products, quantity of agricultural machinery, facilities of water conservancy and efforts to eliminate water-logging and combat alkalinity, basic conditions of state-owned farms.

Statistics on agriculture cover all rural households engaged in production and operation, organizations for agriculture, forestry, animal husbandry, fishery of all types of economic organization and their branches; organizations engaged in agricultural production activities belonging to non-agricultural industry in each province, autonomous region, municipality, Xinjiang Production and Construction Corps; and all crop land, farms, pastures. Agricultural production activities undertaken by agriculture research institutions are not included.

(1) Agriculture: refers to cultivation of farm crops, including cereals, beans, tuber crops, cotton, oil-bearing crops, sugar crops, hemp, tobacco leaves, vegetables, gardening plants, fruits, nuts, crops for spices, medicinal herbs and other farm crops.

(2) Forestry: includes the planting of trees (excluding the operations of planting, management and harvesting on tea plantations, mulberry fields and orchards), cutting and transport of timber and bamboo and collection of forest products.

(3) Animal husbandry: includes the raising and grazing of domestic animals and poultry.

(4) Fishery: includes cultivation and catching of aquatic animals and seaweed.

(5) Professional and support activities for agriculture, forestry, animal husbandry and fishery: include supporting services to production activities in agriculture, forestry, animal husbandry and fishery, but do not include activities of science and technology and professional services.

II. Data Sources and Survey Methods

(1) Data on output value of agriculture, forestry, animal husbandry and fishery are provided by the Department of Rural Social and Economic Survey of the NBS using data from the *Statistical Reporting System on Agricultural Output and Price*.

(2) Data on production of agriculture, animal husbandry and the agricultural production conditions are provided by the Department of Rural Social and Economic Survey of the NBS using data from the *Statistical Reporting System on Agriculture, Forestry, Animal Husbandry and Fishery*. Data on major farm crops such as rice, wheat, corn are collected through sample surveys and measurement by remote sensing technology. Data on animal husbandry such as hog, cattle, sheep and poultry are collected from sample surveys. Data on conditions of agricultural production, and on other farm crops, garden crops, and other poultry are collected from comprehensive reporting system by using statistical reporting forms.

(3) Data on the basic conditions of forestry and fishery production come from statistical reports tabulated by the National Forestry and Grassland Administration and by the Ministry of Agriculture and Rural Affairs, with survey methods decided by them respectively.

(4) Data on the basic conditions of the state-owned farms come from the statistical reports tabulated by the Bureau of Reclamation of the Ministry of Agriculture and Rural Affairs. The statistical scope covers 31 provinces, autonomous regions and municipalities directly under the Central Government. Data are collected from the grassroots units in accordance with the statistical reporting scheme whereby reporting is done level by level for aggregation.

(5) Data on irrigation and reservoirs, data on efforts to eliminate water-logging, to prevent floods by water control and to combat alkalinity as well as data on the facilities of water conservancy and the area of water-logging eliminated and the improved area of saline-alkaline land come mainly from statistical reports of the Ministry of Water Resources, which covers 31 provinces, autonomous regions and municipalities directly under the Central Government. Data are collected from individual counties in accordance with the statistical reporting system and are tabulated and reported level by level.

III. Notes on Use of Data

According to the results of the Third National Agricultural Census and in line with international practices, data on gross output value of agriculture, forestry, animal husbandry and fishery after 2007 were revised. Please refer to the footnotes of relevant tables for detail.

12-1　农业生产条件与农作物播种面积
Conditions of Agricultural Production and Sown Area of Farm Crops

指　标	Item	2000	2010	2015	2020	2022	2023
农业机械总动力　（万千瓦）	Total Agricultural Machinery Power　(10 000 kW)	52573.6	92780.5	111728.1	105622.1	110597.2	113742.6
大中型拖拉机　（万台）	Number of Large and Medium-sized Tractors (10 000 units)	97.5	392.2	607.3	477.3	525.4	551.1
小型拖拉机　（万台）	Number of Small Tractors　(10 000 units)	1264.4	1785.8	1703.0	1727.6	1618.7	1562.4
大中型拖拉机配套农具（万部）	Number of Auxiliary Farm Machinery for Use with Large and Medium-sized　(10 000 units)	140.0	612.9	962.0	459.4	526.0	551.0
耕地灌溉面积　（千公顷）	Irrigated Area of Cultivated Land　(1 000 hectares)	53820	60348	65873	69161	70359	71644
农用化肥施用量　（万吨）	Consumption of Chemical Fertilizers　(10 000 tons)	4146.4	5561.7	6022.6	5250.7	5079.2	5021.7
农村用电量　（亿千瓦时）	Electricity Consumed in Rural Areas(100 million kW·h)	2421.3	6632.3	9026.9	6211.0	7765.6	7991.9
农作物总播种面积(千公顷)	Total Sown Area of Farm Crops　(1 000 hectares)	156300	158579	166829	167487	169991	171624
粮食	Grain Crops	108463	111695	118963	116768	118332	118969
谷物	Cereals	85264	92621	103225	97964	99269	99926
#稻谷	Rice	29962	30097	30784	30076	29450	28949
小麦	Wheat	26653	24442	24567	23380	23518	23627
玉米	Corn	23056	34977	44968	41264	43070	44219
豆类	Beans	12660	11053	8433	11593	11878	11994
#大豆	Soybeans	9307	8700	6827	9882	10244	10474
薯类	Tubers	10538	8021	7305	7210	7185	7048
油料	Oil-bearing Crops	15400	13695	13314	13129	13141	13922
#花生	Peanuts	4855	4374	4386	4731	4684	4798
油菜籽	Rapeseeds	7494	7316	7028	6765	7253	7805
芝麻	Sesame	784	357	301	292	269	280
棉花	Cotton	4041	4366	3775	3169	3000	2788
麻类	Fiber Crops	262	91	54	69	58	49
糖料	Sugar Crops	1514	1809	1573	1568	1453	1415
#甘蔗	Sugarcane	1185	1624	1476	1353	1289	1265
甜菜	Beetroots	329	185	96	213	163	149
烟叶	Tobacco	1437	1309	1254	1014	1044	1084
#烤烟	Flue-Cured Tobacco	1269	1209	1197	967	1001	1043
蔬菜	Vegetables	15237	17431	19613	21485	22434	22873
茶园面积　（千公顷）	Area of Tea Plantations　(1 000 hectares)	1089	1932	2641	3217	3393	3430
果园面积　（千公顷）	Area of Orchards　(1 000 hectares)	8932	10681	11212	12646	13010	12738

注：1.从2016年开始，农业机械总动力中不包括三轮汽车和低速载货汽车动力。

2.2018年，农业农村部修订制度，把大中型拖拉机和小型拖拉机的分类标准由发动机功率14.7千瓦改为22.1千瓦；大中型拖拉机配套农具口径改为“与58.8千瓦及以上拖拉机配套”。同时，取消小型拖拉机配套农具和农用排灌柴油机指标(以下相关表同)。

3.2020年起，“农村用电量”口径调整为农林牧渔业用电量+乡村居民生活用电量，数据来源于中国电力企业联合会(以下相关表同)。

a) Since 2016, total agricultural machinery power does not include power of three-wheeled vehicles and low-speed trucks.

b) In 2018, the Ministry of Agriculture revised the classification standard of large and medium-sized tractors and small tractors by changing the engine power from 14.7 kW to 22.1 kW; and the coverage of large and medium-sized tractor towing farm machinery was changed to "matching with 58.8 kW and above tractors". At the same time, indicators on small tractor towing farm machinery and diesel engines for irrigation were cancelled. The same applies to following tables.

c) From 2020, the caliber of "rural power consumption" is adjusted to agricultural, forestry, animal husbandry and fishery power consumption and rural residents'domestic power consumption, and the data is from the China Electricity Council. The same applies to following tables.

12-2 主要农牧渔业生产情况
Output of Agriculture, Animal Husbandry and Fishery

指 标	Item	2018	2019	2020	2021	2022	2023
农产品产量 (万吨)	Output of Farm Products (10 000 tons)						
粮食	Grain	65789.2	66384.3	66949.2	68284.7	68652.8	69541.0
谷物	Cereals	61003.6	61369.7	61674.3	63275.7	63324.3	64143.0
#稻谷	Rice	21212.9	20961.4	21186.0	21284.2	20849.5	20660.3
小麦	Wheat	13144.0	13359.6	13425.4	13694.4	13772.3	13659.0
玉米	Corn	25717.4	26077.9	26066.5	27255.1	27720.3	28884.2
豆类	Beans	1920.3	2131.9	2287.5	1965.5	2351.0	2384.1
#大豆	Soybeans	1596.7	1809.2	1960.2	1639.5	2028.3	2084.2
薯类	Tubers	2865.4	2882.7	2987.4	3043.5	2977.4	3013.9
油料	Oil-bearing Crops	3433.4	3493.0	3586.4	3613.2	3654.2	3863.7
#花生	Peanuts	1733.2	1752.0	1799.3	1830.8	1832.9	1923.1
油菜籽	Rapeseeds	1328.1	1348.5	1404.9	1471.4	1553.1	1631.7
芝麻	Sesame	43.1	46.7	45.7	45.5	43.5	45.3
棉花	Cotton	610.3	588.9	591.0	573.1	598.0	561.8
麻类	Fiber Crops	20.3	23.4	24.9	21.1	22.8	16.3
糖料	Sugar Crops	11937.4	12169.1	12014.0	11454.4	11236.5	11376.3
#甘蔗	Sugarcane	10809.7	10938.8	10812.1	10666.4	10338.1	10456.6
甜菜	Beetroots	1127.7	1227.3	1198.4	785.1	893.3	916.0
烟叶	Tobacco	224.1	215.3	213.4	212.8	218.8	229.7
#烤烟	Flue-cured Tobacco	211.0	202.1	202.2	202.1	208.0	219.1
蚕茧	Silkworm Cocoons	83.1	83.3	78.8	78.2	80.7	83.4
#桑蚕茧	Mulberry Silkworm Cocoons	76.4	77.2	73.5	72.7	74.8	77.2
茶叶	Tea	261.0	277.7	293.2	316.4	334.2	354.1
水果	Fruits	25688.4	27400.8	28692.4	29970.2	31296.2	32744.3
农产品单位面积产量 (公斤/公顷)	Output of Farm Products per Hectare (kg/hectare)						
粮食	Grain	5621	5720	5734	5805	5802	5845
谷物	Cereals	6120	6272	6296	6316	6379	6419
棉花	Cotton	1819	1764	1865	1893	1993	2015
花生	Peanuts	3752	3781	3803	3810	3913	4008
油菜籽	Rapeseeds	2027	2048	2077	2104	2141	2091
芝麻	Sesames	1645	1651	1564	1596	1620	1618
甘蔗	Sugarcane	76891	78655	79890	81047	80192	82652
甜菜	Beetroots	52174	56057	56307	55639	54855	61540
烤烟	Flue-Cured Tobacco	2103	2079	2091	2086	2079	2101
大牲畜年底头数(万头)	Number of Large Animals (year-end,10 000 heads)	9625.5	9877.4	10265.1	10486.8	10859.0	11115.4
#牛	Cattle and Buffaloes	8915.3	9138.3	9562.1	9817.2	10215.9	10508.5
马	Horses	347.3	367.1	367.2	372.5	366.7	359.1
驴	Donkeys	253.3	260.1	232.4	196.7	173.5	146.0
骡	Mules	75.8	71.4	62.3	54.2	48.8	43.8
骆驼	Camels	33.8	40.5	41.1	46.2	54.1	58.0
肉猪出栏头数 (万头)	Number of Slaughtered Fattened Hogs (10 000 heads)	69382.4	54419.2	52704.1	67128.0	69994.8	72662.4
猪年底头数 (万头)	Number of Hogs (year-end,10 000 heads)	42817.1	31040.7	40650.4	44922.4	45255.7	43422.3
羊年底只数 (万只)	Number of Sheep and Goats (year-end,10 000 heads)	29713.5	30072.1	30654.8	31969.3	32627.3	32232.6
山羊	Goats	13574.7	13723.2	13345.2	13331.6	13224.2	12934.2
绵羊	Sheep	16138.8	16349.0	17309.5	18637.7	19403.0	19298.4
肉类产量 (万吨)	Output of Meat (10 000 tons)	8624.6	7758.8	7748.4	8990.0	9328.4	9748.2
#猪牛羊肉	Pork, Beef and Mutton	6522.9	5410.1	5278.1	6507.5	6784.2	7078.3
猪肉	Pork	5403.7	4255.3	4113.3	5295.9	5541.4	5794.3
牛肉	Beef	644.1	667.3	672.4	697.5	718.3	752.7
羊肉	Mutton	475.1	487.5	492.3	514.1	524.5	531.3
奶类 (万吨)	Milk (10 000 tons)	3176.8	3297.6	3529.6	3778.1	4026.5	4281.3
#牛奶	Cow Milk	3074.6	3201.2	3440.1	3682.7	3931.6	4196.7
绵羊毛 (吨)	Sheep Wool (ton)	356608	341120	333625	356217	356194	367505
山羊粗毛 (吨)	Goat Raw Wool (ton)	26965	24875	24034	23332	24837	23123
山羊绒 (吨)	Cashmere (ton)	15438	14964	15244	15102	14649	17589
禽蛋 (万吨)	Poultry Eggs (10 000 tons)	3128.3	3309.0	3467.8	3408.8	3456.4	3563.0
水产品总产量 (万吨)	Total Output of Aquatic Products (10 000 tons)	6457.7	6480.4	6549.0	6690.3	6865.9	7116.2
海水产品	Seawater Aquatic Products	3301.4	3282.5	3314.4	3387.3	3459.5	3585.3
淡水产品	Freshwater Aquatic Products	3156.2	3197.9	3234.6	3303.1	3406.4	3530.9

12-3 农、林、牧、渔业总产值及指数
Gross Output Value of Agriculture, Forestry, Animal Husbandry and Fishery and Related Indices

年 份 地 区	Year Region	绝对数（亿元）Gross Output Value (100 million yuan)						指 数（上年=100）Indices of Gross Output (preceding year=100)					
		农林牧渔业总产值 Total	农 业 Farming	林 业 Forestry	牧 业 Animal Husbandry	渔 业 Fishery	农林牧渔专业及辅助性活动 Professional and Support Activities for Agriculture, Forestry, Animal Husbandry and Fishery	农林牧渔业总产值 Total	农 业 Farming	林 业 Forestry	牧 业 Animal Husbandry	渔 业 Fishery	农林牧渔专业及辅助性活动 Professional and Support Activities for Agriculture, Forestry, Animal Husbandry and Fishery
	1978	1397.0	1117.5	48.1	209.3	22.1							
	1980	1922.6	1454.1	81.4	354.2	32.9		101.4	99.7	112.2	107.0	107.7	
	1985	3619.5	2506.4	188.7	798.3	126.1		103.4	99.8	104.5	117.2	118.9	
	1990	7662.1	4954.3	330.3	1967.0	410.6		107.6	108.0	103.1	107.0	110.0	
	1995	20340.9	11884.6	709.9	6045.0	1701.3		110.9	107.9	105.0	114.8	119.4	
	2000	24915.8	13873.6	936.5	7393.1	2712.6		103.6	101.4	105.4	106.3	106.5	
	2005	39450.9	19613.4	1425.5	13310.8	4016.1	1085.1	105.7	104.1	103.2	107.8	106.5	106.7
	2006	40810.8	21522.3	1610.8	12083.9	3970.5	1623.4	105.4	105.4	105.6	105.0	106.0	108.7
	2007	48651.8	24444.7	1889.9	16068.6	4427.9	1820.6	103.9	103.7	109.8	103.2	104.0	109.1
	2008	57420.8	27679.9	2180.3	20354.2	5137.5	2068.8	105.6	104.6	108.0	106.7	105.8	106.4
	2009	59311.3	29983.8	2324.4	19184.6	5514.7	2303.8	104.6	103.4	106.7	105.5	105.6	105.5
	2010	67763.1	35909.1	2575.0	20461.1	6263.4	2554.6	104.4	104.3	103.5	104.2	105.4	106.6
	2011	78837.0	40339.6	3092.4	25194.2	7337.4	2873.4	104.4	105.6	107.6	101.7	104.1	107.0
	2012	86342.2	44845.7	3407.0	26491.2	8403.9	3194.3	104.9	104.3	106.7	105.2	105.0	107.1
	2013	93173.7	48943.9	3847.4	27572.4	9254.5	3555.5	104.0	104.4	107.4	102.0	105.1	107.8
	2014	97822.5	51851.1	4190.0	27963.4	9877.5	3940.5	104.3	104.9	106.4	102.6	104.0	108.7
	2015	101893.5	54205.3	4358.4	28649.3	10339.1	4341.3	104.0	105.4	106.1	100.5	104.3	108.5
	2016	106478.7	55659.9	4635.9	30461.2	10892.9	4828.9	103.5	104.2	108.2	101.1	102.9	108.3
	2017	109331.7	58059.8	4980.6	29361.2	11577.1	5353.1	104.0	104.7	106.9	102.1	102.8	108.6
	2018	113579.5	61452.6	5432.6	28697.4	12131.5	5865.4	103.5	103.9	106.5	101.7	102.7	107.8
	2019	123967.9	66066.5	5775.7	33064.3	12572.4	6489.0	102.8	104.6	105.2	97.9	102.5	107.4
	2020	137782.2	71748.2	5961.6	40266.7	12775.9	7029.8	103.4	104.1	104.3	102.0	102.2	105.7
	2021	147013.4	78339.5	6507.7	39910.8	14507.3	7748.1	107.9	104.5	104.4	115.6	104.1	107.7
	2022	156065.9	84438.6	6820.8	40652.4	15468.0	8686.2	104.4	104.0	105.7	104.5	103.8	108.9
	2023	158507.2	87073.4	7006.1	38964.6	16116.2	9346.9	104.2	103.6	106.2	104.5	104.5	107.1
北 京	Beijing	252.6	135.6	65.9	42.0	4.0	5.1	95.4	104.7	76.4	105.8	103.5	88.6
天 津	Tianjin	511.3	269.4	6.0	145.5	71.9	18.4	101.3	96.0	83.3	109.6	107.2	102.0
河 北	Hebei	7770.9	4081.0	259.1	2395.0	351.2	684.5	103.0	101.8	102.7	103.7	104.2	107.6
山 西	Shanxi	2291.7	1332.7	177.4	642.8	9.6	129.3	104.0	103.7	94.4	107.5	104.5	104.0
内蒙古	Inner Mongolia	4447.3	2288.0	116.9	1898.7	32.2	111.6	105.5	104.4	106.8	106.6	104.2	108.0
辽 宁	Liaoning	5266.8	2284.5	144.6	1691.5	957.0	189.2	104.7	104.1	103.9	105.8	105.0	102.2
吉 林	Jilin	3128.0	1494.5	70.1	1402.2	65.4	95.8	105.0	103.7	105.3	106.2	109.2	105.4
黑龙江	Heilongjiang	6492.5	4200.4	208.0	1722.9	155.1	206.2	102.6	101.7	106.1	103.7	106.2	104.8
上 海	Shanghai	269.6	145.2	7.2	47.0	52.7	17.5	99.3	98.7	86.9	107.2	97.7	94.5
江 苏	Jiangsu	8935.5	4844.1	188.4	1230.1	1903.2	769.7	103.9	102.9	104.9	105.0	104.0	108.1
浙 江	Zhejiang	3978.0	1871.9	198.3	393.2	1375.3	139.4	104.2	102.9	108.5	107.9	104.2	104.3
安 徽	Anhui	6247.9	2906.3	479.9	1746.3	689.5	425.9	104.4	102.9	106.8	105.6	104.2	107.6
福 建	Fujian	5729.2	2193.5	454.8	1083.4	1789.6	208.0	104.3	103.7	103.6	106.2	104.0	104.2
江 西	Jiangxi	4198.9	2003.4	399.8	978.3	554.1	263.3	104.2	103.9	107.9	102.1	104.8	108.1
山 东	Shandong	12531.9	6462.4	244.5	2973.7	1807.6	1043.7	105.1	104.1	109.9	106.4	104.4	108.2
河 南	Henan	10304.6	6471.2	162.2	2596.0	141.5	933.6	102.2	102.1	109.7	100.7	105.0	107.2
湖 北	Hubei	9106.9	4428.8	356.3	1934.3	1602.0	785.5	104.4	103.4	111.4	103.8	104.7	107.4
湖 南	Hunan	8199.4	4141.5	513.7	2232.1	635.0	677.1	103.7	104.1	108.3	100.6	105.9	108.4
广 东	Guangdong	9202.1	4431.0	562.7	1696.8	2005.3	506.3	105.1	103.5	108.2	107.0	104.9	110.6
广 西	Guangxi	7229.3	4253.5	543.7	1505.3	583.0	343.8	104.7	104.4	106.0	105.0	103.6	105.3
海 南	Hainan	2410.3	1319.7	111.4	334.2	523.0	121.9	104.8	103.4	101.3	107.1	106.4	111.1
重 庆	Chongqing	3154.3	1978.0	188.1	766.6	142.9	78.7	104.5	104.6	107.6	103.5	103.6	108.2
四 川	Sichuan	9977.8	5821.7	481.8	3035.6	359.1	279.6	104.0	104.9	109.9	101.6	104.7	104.2
贵 州	Guizhou	4953.6	3360.3	358.5	907.9	81.2	245.8	104.0	104.0	106.7	102.8	104.9	105.2
云 南	Yunnan	6834.5	4041.8	485.2	1969.3	125.4	212.8	104.3	104.5	107.0	103.4	103.9	105.5
西 藏	Xizang	320.1	132.6	9.5	170.0	0.3	7.8	113.1	107.9	134.4	116.7	125.2	108.3
陕 西	Shaanxi	4724.9	3468.1	96.4	864.4	36.7	259.4	104.0	104.0	102.6	104.0	106.2	104.6
甘 肃	Gansu	2927.7	2001.6	37.3	700.1	1.8	186.9	106.1	105.0	102.3	109.2	101.6	106.1
青 海	Qinghai	575.6	259.3	12.6	290.9	4.3	8.4	104.7	105.3	96.3	104.8	100.8	102.8
宁 夏	Ningxia	885.7	459.5	10.6	358.0	22.8	34.7	107.6	102.1	92.7	116.3	105.7	105.5
新 疆	Xinjiang	5648.3	3991.4	55.6	1210.6	33.6	357.1	106.5	106.0	108.8	107.7	108.8	108.3

注：本表绝对数按当年价格计算，指数按可比价格计算。2003年起总产值包括农林牧渔专业及辅助性活动产值。

a) Data in value terms in this table are calculated at current prices, while the indices are calculated at comparable prices. Since 2003, gross output value includes professional and support services for agriculture, forestry, animal husbandry and fishery.

12-4 主要农业机械拥有量（年底数）
Major Agricultural Machinery at Year-end

年份 Year / 地区 Region		农业机械总动力（万千瓦）Total Power of Agricultural Machinery (10 000 kW)	大中型拖拉机 Large and Medium-sized Tractors 数量（万台）Number (10 000 units)	大中型拖拉机 配套农具（万部）Towing Farm Machinery (10 000 units)	小型拖拉机 Small Tractors 数量（万台）Number (10 000 units)
	1978	11749.9	55.74	119.20	137.30
	1980	14745.7	74.49	136.90	187.40
	1985	20912.5	85.24	112.80	382.40
	1990	28707.7	81.35	97.40	698.10
	1995	36118.1	67.18	99.12	864.64
	2000	52573.6	97.45	139.99	1264.37
	2005	68397.8	139.60	226.20	1526.89
	2006	72522.1	171.82	261.50	1567.90
	2007	76589.6	206.27	308.28	1619.11
	2008	82190.4	299.52	435.36	1722.41
	2009	87496.1	351.58	542.06	1750.90
	2010	92780.5	392.17	612.86	1785.79
	2011	97734.7	440.65	698.95	1811.27
	2012	102559.0	485.24	763.52	1797.23
	2013	103906.8	527.02	826.62	1752.28
	2014	108056.6	567.95	889.64	1729.77
	2015	111728.1	607.29	962.00	1703.04
	2016	97245.6	645.35	1028.11	1671.61
	2017	98783.3	670.08	1070.03	1634.24
	2018	100371.7	421.99	422.57	1818.26
	2019	102758.3	443.86	436.47	1780.42
	2020	105622.1	477.27	459.44	1727.60
	2021	107764.3	498.07	479.69	1674.99
	2022	110597.2	525.36	526.00	1618.70
	2023	113742.6	551.09	550.99	1562.40
北 京	Beijing	123.9	0.45	0.16	0.18
天 津	Tianjin	368.8	1.02	1.69	0.14
河 北	Hebei	8403.8	35.28	46.21	99.57
山 西	Shanxi	1803.5	13.54	11.91	25.78
内蒙古	Inner Mongolia	4925.0	52.09	26.59	80.89
辽 宁	Liaoning	2823.9	24.50	18.44	35.40
吉 林	Jilin	4548.6	47.64	11.87	85.58
黑龙江	Heilongjiang	7339.6	72.55	76.91	83.55
上 海	Shanghai	105.4	0.72	0.51	0.17
江 苏	Jiangsu	5360.2	17.52	35.98	46.06
浙 江	Zhejiang	1794.0	1.63	1.89	2.96
安 徽	Anhui	7194.6	30.51	49.80	183.50
福 建	Fujian	1323.7	0.62	0.46	7.08
江 西	Jiangxi	2953.5	7.24	5.86	29.78
山 东	Shandong	11988.7	57.44	65.25	188.01
河 南	Henan	11118.4	47.93	73.48	271.25
湖 北	Hubei	4975.5	20.75	22.06	101.28
湖 南	Hunan	6839.5	9.87	14.29	17.85
广 东	Guangdong	2586.0	3.01	3.18	28.32
广 西	Guangxi	3850.9	5.84	3.72	45.21
海 南	Hainan	633.1	1.97	1.49	4.31
重 庆	Chongqing	1586.4	0.30	0.28	0.43
四 川	Sichuan	5027.2	7.69	2.82	12.47
贵 州	Guizhou	2869.0	1.78	0.31	9.71
云 南	Yunnan	3014.0	7.06	4.39	25.75
西 藏	Xizang	654.0	8.54	0.13	21.41
陕 西	Shaanxi	2520.8	12.97	13.30	17.12
甘 肃	Gansu	2638.7	15.69	11.05	71.86
青 海	Qinghai	517.8	1.58	1.53	24.35
宁 夏	Ningxia	673.2	5.68	3.32	15.57
新 疆	Xinjiang	3181.1	37.68	42.12	26.88

12-5 耕地灌溉面积和农用化肥施用量
Irrigated Area of Cultivated Land and Consumption of Chemical Fertilizers

年份 Year 地区 Region	耕地灌溉面积（千公顷）Irrigated Area of Cultivated Land (1 000 hectares)	农用化肥施用量（万吨）Consumption of Chemical Fertilizers (10 000 tons)	氮肥 Nitrogenous Fertilizer	磷肥 Phosphatic Fertilizer	钾肥 Potassic Fertilizer	复合肥 Compound Fertilizer
1978	44965.0	884.0				
1980	44888.1	1269.4	934.2	273.3	34.6	27.2
1985	44035.9	1775.8	1204.9	310.9	80.4	179.6
1990	47403.1	2590.3	1638.4	462.4	147.9	341.6
1995	49281.2	3593.7	2021.9	632.4	268.5	670.8
2000	53820.3	4146.4	2161.6	690.5	376.5	917.9
2005	55029.3	4766.2	2229.3	743.8	489.5	1303.2
2006	55750.5	4927.7	2262.5	769.5	509.7	1385.9
2007	56518.3	5107.8	2297.2	773.0	533.6	1503.0
2008	58471.7	5239.0	2302.9	780.1	545.2	1608.6
2009	59261.4	5404.4	2329.9	797.7	564.3	1698.7
2010	60347.7	5561.7	2353.7	805.6	586.4	1798.5
2011	61681.6	5704.2	2381.4	819.2	605.1	1895.1
2012	62490.5	5838.8	2399.9	828.6	617.7	1990.0
2013	63473.3	5911.9	2394.2	830.6	627.4	2057.5
2014	64539.5	5995.9	2392.9	845.3	641.9	2115.8
2015	65872.6	6022.6	2361.6	843.1	642.3	2175.7
2016	67140.6	5984.4	2310.5	830.0	636.9	2207.1
2017	67815.6	5859.4	2221.8	797.6	619.7	2220.3
2018	68271.6	5653.4	2065.4	728.9	590.3	2268.8
2019	68678.6	5403.6	1930.2	681.6	561.1	2230.7
2020	69160.5	5250.7	1833.9	653.8	541.9	2221.0
2021	69609.5	5191.3	1745.3	627.1	524.8	2294.0
2022	70358.9	5079.2	1654.2	563.2	493.2	2368.7
2023	71644.0	5021.7	1603.3	536.3	481.1	2401.0
北京 Beijing	118.0	6.7	1.9	0.3	0.3	4.2
天津 Tianjin	309.0	15.4	4.5	1.5	1.0	8.4
河北 Hebei	4122.0	266.4	87.7	19.4	18.5	140.7
山西 Shanxi	1490.9	103.2	17.7	7.8	7.1	70.6
内蒙古 Inner Mongolia	4809.0	220.8	70.6	15.0	15.3	119.9
辽宁 Liaoning	1721.2	129.5	39.8	7.8	9.9	72.0
吉林 Jilin	1949.3	222.5	37.8	4.8	11.6	168.3
黑龙江 Heilongjiang	6238.5	238.6	76.4	47.3	32.7	82.2
上海 Shanghai	161.6	6.4	2.4	0.3	0.1	3.6
江苏 Jiangsu	3856.7	267.0	124.6	23.0	14.2	105.2
浙江 Zhejiang	1240.7	65.8	20.5	3.2	4.6	37.5
安徽 Anhui	4679.1	278.0	65.7	10.2	13.5	188.6
福建 Fujian	858.8	89.2	31.3	12.2	17.3	28.3
江西 Jiangxi	2186.8	107.1	27.4	13.4	14.7	51.6
山东 Shandong	5241.7	354.8	94.7	29.6	27.2	203.3
河南 Henan	5666.7	584.0	152.4	68.5	46.3	316.8
湖北 Hubei	3220.2	254.4	84.4	32.9	21.9	115.2
湖南 Hunan	2917.6	213.3	62.9	15.6	29.4	105.4
广东 Guangdong	1560.2	206.8	77.2	24.8	39.9	64.8
广西 Guangxi	1695.6	247.6	64.4	26.6	49.1	107.4
海南 Hainan	334.5	37.5	9.7	2.4	6.8	18.5
重庆 Chongqing	681.1	88.4	41.8	15.2	5.1	26.3
四川 Sichuan	2994.2	202.2	74.5	31.4	14.0	82.3
贵州 Guizhou	1229.9	74.7	30.0	8.1	6.7	29.9
云南 Yunnan	2036.0	179.3	80.7	23.6	20.4	54.7
西藏 Xizang	304.6	2.8	0.8	0.5	0.1	1.4
陕西 Shaanxi	1181.2	193.7	71.8	16.2	19.3	86.3
甘肃 Gansu	1423.7	76.6	29.8	13.9	7.4	25.4
青海 Qinghai	222.1	4.5	1.8	0.4	0.1	2.2
宁夏 Ningxia	564.0	36.7	13.5	3.8	2.8	16.6
新疆 Xinjiang	6629.6	247.7	104.4	56.3	23.7	63.3

12–6 灌溉、水库和除涝治水情况
Irrigation, Reservoirs, Flood Prevention, Water and Soil Conservation

项　　目	Item	2005	2010	2015	2020	2022	2023
万亩以上灌区数　(处)	Number of Irrigated Areas over 10 000 Mu　(set)	5860	5795	7773	7713		
3.3万公顷以上	33 000 Hectares and Over	117	131	176	172		
2.0–3.3万公顷	20 000-33 000 Hectares	170	218	280	282		
灌区有效灌溉面积(万公顷)	Effective Irrigated Area　(10 000 hectares)	2641.9	2941.5	3230.2	3363.8		
3.3万公顷以上	33 000 Hectares and Over	1023.0	1091.8	1202.4	1234.4		
2.0–3.3万公顷	20 000-33 000 Hectares	408.0	474.0	566.3	547.8		
水库　(座)	Number of Reservoirs　(unit)	85108	87873	97988	98566	95296	94877
大型水库	Large Reservoir	470	552	707	774	814	836
中型水库	Medium-sized Reservoir	2934	3269	3844	4098	4192	4230
小型水库	Small Reservoir	81704	84052	93437	93694	90290	89811
水库库容量　(亿立方米)	Capacity of Reservoirs　(100 million cu.m)	5624	7162	8581	9306	9887	9999
大型水库	Large Reservoir	4197	5594	6812	7410	7979	8077
中型水库	Medium-sized Reservoir	826	930	1068	1179	1199	1210
小型水库	Small Reservoir	602	638	701	717	709	712
节水灌溉面积　(万公顷)	Water-saving Irrigated Area　(10 000 hectares)	2133.8	2731.4	3106.0	3779.6		
除涝面积　(万公顷)	Area with Flood Prevention Measures(10 000 hectares)	2133.9	2169.2	2271.3	2458.6	2412.9	2507.8
水土流失治理面积(万公顷)	Area with Soil Erosion under Control (10 000 hectares)	9465.0	10680.0	11557.8	14312.2	15603.0	16272.4
堤防长度　(万公里)	Total Length of Dikes　(10 000 km)	27.7	29.4	29.1	32.8	33.1	32.5
堤防保护面积　(万公顷)	Area of Land Protected by Dikes　(10 000 hectares)	4412.0	4683.1	4084.4	4216.8	4197.2	4174.8

注：1.大型水库库容：1亿立方米以上；中型水库库容：1千万至1亿立方米；小型水库库容：10万至1千万立方米。堤防长度为5级及以上堤防。
　　2.水利部2022年、2023年灌溉类相关数据暂未对外公布。

a) The capacity of the large-scale reservoir is over 100 million cubic meters, while that of the medium-scale one is from 10-100 million cubic meters, and that of the small-scale one is from 0.1-10 million cubic meters. The length of dikes is at Grade 5 and above.

b) The Ministry of Water Resources has not released the irrigation related data in 2022 and 2023.

12-7 分地区水利设施和除涝面积（2023年）
Water Conservancy Facilities and Area with Flood Prevention Measures by Region (2023)

地 区	Region	水库数（座）Number of Reservoirs (unit)	水库总库容量（亿立方米）Capacity of Reservoirs (100 million cu.m)	除涝面积（千公顷）Area with Flood Prevention Measures (1 000 hectares)	水土流失治理面积（千公顷）Area with Soil Erosion under Control (1 000 hectares)
全 国	**National Total**	**94877**	**9999**	**25078.3**	**162724.3**
北 京	Beijing	80	52	12.0	1003.8
天 津	Tianjin	21	25	362.1	105.0
河 北	Hebei	1013	207	1622.5	6573.3
山 西	Shanxi	623	72	89.3	8417.5
内蒙古	Inner Mongolia	472	214	277.0	17289.1
辽 宁	Liaoning	745	374	1220.1	6385.9
吉 林	Jilin	1245	325	1049.6	3457.2
黑龙江	Heilongjiang	794	207	3355.2	7219.7
上 海	Shanghai	5	6	50.4	
江 苏	Jiangsu	935	35	4034.4	979.9
浙 江	Zhejiang	4274	451	580.9	3789.9
安 徽	Anhui	5362	207	2548.1	2352.2
福 建	Fujian	3569	204	163.5	4401.3
江 西	Jiangxi	10623	357	499.5	6605.5
山 东	Shandong	5531	185	3268.5	4853.5
河 南	Henan	2540	438	2190.6	4399.7
湖 北	Hubei	6751	1263	1457.6	6894.2
湖 南	Hunan	13245	547	749.3	4595.5
广 东	Guangdong	7293	453	536.9	2171.8
广 西	Guangxi	4507	761	243.1	3622.1
海 南	Hainan	1112	121	41.6	167.5
重 庆	Chongqing	3085	130		4322.4
四 川	Sichuan	8281	764	103.6	12557.8
贵 州	Guizhou	2681	508	140.9	8550.4
云 南	Yunnan	7348	1181	335.7	12192.1
西 藏	Xizang	145	44	5.4	990.6
陕 西	Shaanxi	1063	118	103.2	8952.9
甘 肃	Gansu	355	115	15.5	12201.7
青 海	Qinghai	206	367		2077.1
宁 夏	Ningxia	328	26		2762.8
新 疆	Xinjiang	645	242	21.7	2832.0

12–8 农作物播种面积
Sown Areas of Farm Crops

单位：千公顷 (1 000 hectares)

年 份 Year 地 区 Region		农作物总播种面积 Total Sown Area	粮食作物播种面积 Sown Area of Grain Crops	谷 物 Cereals	#稻 谷 Rice	#小 麦 Wheat	#玉 米 Corn	豆 类 Beans	#大 豆 Soybeans
	1978	150104	120587		34421	29183	19961		7144
	1980	146380	117234		33878	28844	20087		7226
	1985	143626	108845		32070	29218	17694		7718
	1990	148362	113466		33064	30753	21401		7560
	1995	149879	110060	89310	30744	28860	22776	11232	8127
	2000	156300	108463	85264	29962	26653	23056	12660	9307
	2005	155488	104278	81874	28847	22793	26358	12901	9591
	2006	152149	104958	84931	28938	23613	28463	12149	9304
	2007	153010	105999	86388	28973	23762	30024	11708	8801
	2008	155566	107545	87499	29350	23704	30981	11988	9225
	2009	157242	110255	90383	29793	24425	32948	11785	9339
	2010	158579	111695	92621	30097	24442	34977	11053	8700
	2011	160360	112980	94615	30338	24507	36767	10367	8103
	2012	162071	114368	97142	30476	24551	39109	9405	7405
	2013	163702	115908	99288	30710	24440	41299	8893	7050
	2014	165183	117455	101087	30765	24443	42997	8824	7098
	2015	166829	118963	103225	30784	24567	44968	8433	6827
	2016	166939	119230	102702	30746	24666	44178	9287	7599
	2017	166332	117989	100765	30747	24478	42399	10051	8245
	2018	165902	117038	99671	30189	24266	42130	10186	8413
	2019	165931	116064	97847	29694	23728	41284	11075	9332
	2020	167487	116768	97964	30076	23380	41264	11593	9882
	2021	168695	117631	100177	29921	23567	43324	10121	8415
	2022	169991	118332	99269	29450	23518	43070	11878	10244
	2023	171624	118969	99926	28949	23627	44219	11994	10474
北 京	Beijing	159.0	89.5	82.9	0.3	25.0	56.1	4.5	4.3
天 津	Tianjin	453.1	390.0	382.0	53.9	122.9	194.2	5.8	5.7
河 北	Hebei	8098.2	6455.2	6083.3	73.5	2247.7	3442.2	138.9	113.6
山 西	Shanxi	3641.7	3161.0	2831.3	2.2	535.9	1842.2	150.3	117.0
内蒙古	Inner Mongolia	8808.9	6984.7	5417.9	103.4	401.0	4280.2	1319.4	1235.3
辽 宁	Liaoning	4361.4	3578.4	3395.8	500.5	2.0	2803.9	128.5	122.8
吉 林	Jilin	6292.5	5825.6	5425.3	828.8	5.0	4544.3	372.3	328.8
黑龙江	Heilongjiang	15304.2	14743.1	9762.6	3268.5	19.3	6451.7	4950.7	4886.9
上 海	Shanghai	273.2	127.2	126.5	104.3	18.7	0.7	0.6	0.6
江 苏	Jiangsu	7590.0	5458.9	5135.1	2221.0	2389.5	488.3	290.5	225.4
浙 江	Zhejiang	2041.4	1024.7	838.4	649.0	152.6	28.0	106.9	81.0
安 徽	Anhui	9044.0	7334.5	6594.4	2500.7	2862.7	1209.6	675.3	631.5
福 建	Fujian	1712.3	841.1	641.2	601.1	0.1	36.1	43.6	35.8
江 西	Jiangxi	5797.0	3774.3	3463.8	3383.9	11.3	60.6	155.7	112.7
山 东	Shandong	11002.7	8387.9	8026.2	101.0	4008.9	3881.1	236.0	232.4
河 南	Henan	14747.1	10785.3	10180.9	590.8	5686.1	3864.4	403.0	380.8
湖 北	Hubei	8309.2	4707.0	4103.5	2274.2	1038.4	765.3	271.8	242.2
湖 南	Hunan	8715.0	4763.5	4395.9	3947.0	22.7	407.0	178.2	139.7
广 东	Guangdong	4587.3	2229.5	1963.6	1827.6	0.7	134.0	45.6	35.9
广 西	Guangxi	6352.4	2834.7	2396.3	1760.8	4.6	616.5	168.6	110.1
海 南	Hainan	702.4	273.6	228.7	228.7			4.3	1.8
重 庆	Chongqing	3506.2	2025.9	1149.1	657.0	18.7	448.6	223.4	118.4
四 川	Sichuan	10264.4	6404.0	4473.2	1845.2	593.0	1866.0	725.0	554.0
贵 州	Guizhou	5344.3	2773.8	1534.9	573.7	110.5	687.1	369.2	238.3
云 南	Yunnan	7218.1	4243.2	3126.6	683.6	257.0	1943.7	503.2	175.2
西 藏	Xizang	281.4	194.6	188.4	0.9	33.0	4.9	4.7	0.0
陕 西	Shaanxi	4239.9	3023.0	2477.3	105.4	941.1	1212.3	223.1	177.0
甘 肃	Gansu	4139.6	2710.9	1985.7	2.3	740.2	1099.2	156.6	62.0
青 海	Qinghai	598.8	304.9	222.7		101.0	22.8	14.4	
宁 夏	Ningxia	1199.1	693.9	586.4	20.1	68.9	390.2	30.1	27.2
新 疆	Xinjiang	6839.8	2824.8	2706.5	39.7	1209.2	1437.7	93.8	77.5

12-8 续表 1 continued

单位：千公顷 (1 000 hectares)

年份 Year 地区 Region		薯类 Tubers	棉花 Cotton	油料 Oil-bearing Crops	#花生 Peanuts	#油菜籽 Rapeseeds	#芝麻 Sesame	麻类 Fiber Crops	糖料 Sugar Crops
	1978	11796	4866	6222	1768	2600	638	751	879
	1980	10153	4920	7928	2339	2844	776	666	922
	1985	8572	5140	11800	3318	4494	1052	1231	1525
	1990	9121	5588	10900	2907	5503	669	495	1679
	1995	9519	5422	13102	3809	6907	642	376	1820
	2000	10538	4041	15400	4855	7494	784	262	1514
	2005	9503	5062	14318	4662	7278	593	335	1564
	2006	7877	5816	11738	3956	5984	564	283	1567
	2007	7902	5199	12344	4128	6140	450	219	1756
	2008	8057	5278	13232	4362	6838	428	176	1926
	2009	8088	4485	13445	4281	7170	413	115	1804
	2010	8021	4366	13695	4374	7316	357	91	1809
	2011	7998	4524	13471	4336	7192	335	79	1834
	2012	7821	4360	13435	4401	7187	324	69	1887
	2013	7727	4162	13438	4396	7193	300	63	1844
	2014	7544	4176	13395	4370	7158	303	58	1737
	2015	7305	3775	13314	4386	7028	301	54	1573
	2016	7241	3198	13191	4448	6623	230	54	1555
	2017	7173	3195	13223	4608	6653	228	58	1546
	2018	7180	3354	12872	4620	6551	262	57	1623
	2019	7142	3339	12925	4633	6583	283	66	1610
	2020	7210	3169	13129	4731	6765	292	69	1568
	2021	7333	3028	13102	4805	6992	285	57	1458
	2022	7185	3000	13141	4684	7253	269	58	1453
	2023	7048	2788	13922	4798	7805	280	49	1415
北　京	Beijing	2.1	0.0	3.5	2.7	0.3	0.0		
天　津	Tianjin	2.2	1.1	1.5	0.6	0.7	0.0		0.0
河　北	Hebei	233.0	86.0	343.4	232.9	36.3	1.8	0.1	11.9
山　西	Shanxi	179.4	0.1	98.0	5.7	19.2	1.6	0.0	0.0
内蒙古	Inner Mongolia	247.4		834.2	44.8	263.6	0.0	1.9	66.2
辽　宁	Liaoning	54.1		320.2	317.3	0.2	0.0		0.1
吉　林	Jilin	28.1		237.4	226.9	0.0	0.0		0.3
黑龙江	Heilongjiang	29.7		45.6	27.8	0.1	0.4	10.0	4.2
上　海	Shanghai	0.1		2.3	0.1	2.2	0.0		0.0
江　苏	Jiangsu	33.4	3.5	311.5	95.1	208.9	7.2	0.2	2.9
浙　江	Zhejiang	79.3	2.4	160.4	16.3	138.0	5.9	0.0	5.9
安　徽	Anhui	64.8	22.7	643.5	147.8	469.7	17.9	1.8	2.1
福　建	Fujian	156.3		84.9	75.5	9.1	0.3		5.1
江　西	Jiangxi	154.8	19.4	808.2	182.3	592.8	32.8	2.4	13.3
山　东	Shandong	125.7	96.5	627.8	613.3	8.9	1.1	0.0	0.0
河　南	Henan	201.3	6.1	1610.2	1307.0	194.2	102.9	0.7	1.1
湖　北	Hubei	331.6	103.3	1567.4	256.2	1222.3	75.5	3.0	6.3
湖　南	Hunan	189.4	55.9	1614.8	118.9	1481.4	11.7	1.5	7.5
广　东	Guangdong	220.3		362.1	353.5	5.1	3.4	0.0	142.5
广　西	Guangxi	269.8	0.8	282.3	233.0	43.9	3.0	2.1	835.1
海　南	Hainan	40.6		30.8	30.2		0.7	0.0	13.3
重　庆	Chongqing	653.5		376.1	66.0	297.8	4.0	1.6	1.8
四　川	Sichuan	1205.8	0.2	1728.9	306.0	1413.8	1.9	19.4	9.6
贵　州	Guizhou	869.6	0.3	606.7	40.6	559.3	0.3	0.0	6.4
云　南	Yunnan	613.4		338.8	45.3	283.1	0.1	0.1	215.1
西　藏	Xizang	1.5		19.5	0.0	19.5			0.0
陕　西	Shaanxi	322.5	0.1	268.6	37.0	184.0	7.5	0.2	0.1
甘　肃	Gansu	568.6	20.4	277.6	0.1	160.7		0.4	2.4
青　海	Qinghai	67.8		147.2		146.2			
宁　夏	Ningxia	77.4		30.1	0.0	10.0			0.0
新　疆	Xinjiang	24.5	2369.3	138.1	14.8	33.3	0.2	3.7	61.6

12-8 续表 2 continued

单位：千公顷 (1 000 hectares)

年 份 Year 地 区 Region			烟 叶 Tobacco		蔬 菜 Vegetables	茶 园 Tea Plantations	果 园 Orchards
	#甘 蔗 Sugarcane	#甜 菜 Beetroots		#烤 烟 Flue-cured Tobacco			
1978	549	331	784	613	3331	1048	1657
1980	480	443	512	397	3163	1041	1783
1985	965	560	1313	1077	4753	1045	2736
1990	1009	670	1593	1342	6338	1061	5179
1995	1125	695	1470	1309	9515	1115	8091
2000	1185	329	1437	1269	15237	1089	8932
2005	1354	210	1363	1245	17721	1352	10035
2006	1378	189	1189	1088	16639	1431	10123
2007	1531	225	1180	1094	17557	1599	10119
2008	1709	218	1302	1219	17859	1716	10221
2009	1643	161	1329	1223	17818	1830	10454
2010	1624	185	1309	1209	17431	1932	10681
2011	1644	191	1418	1325	17910	2056	10808
2012	1696	191	1544	1446	18497	2201	10990
2013	1704	140	1552	1472	18836	2367	11043
2014	1638	99	1398	1330	19224	2526	11608
2015	1476	96	1254	1197	19613	2641	11212
2016	1402	154	1208	1153	19553	2723	10917
2017	1371	174	1131	1081	19981	2849	11149
2018	1406	216	1058	1003	20439	2986	11875
2019	1391	219	1027	972	20863	3105	12277
2020	1353	213	1014	967	21485	3217	12646
2021	1316	141	1013	969	21986	3308	12808
2022	1289	163	1044	1001	22434	3393	13010
2023	1265	149	1084	1043	22873	3430	12738
北 京 Beijing			0.0		51.5		28.4
天 津 Tianjin	0.0				55.0	0.0	14.3
河 北 Hebei	0.0	11.9	1.4	0.5	843.8	0.0	460.5
山 西 Shanxi		0.0	1.6	1.5	227.1	1.0	380.3
内蒙古 Inner Mongolia		65.9	0.9	0.5	218.7	0.0	99.5
辽 宁 Liaoning		0.1	4.0	2.9	343.5	0.0	340.4
吉 林 Jilin		0.3	7.9	4.1	142.2		28.3
黑龙江 Heilongjiang		4.2	9.9	9.3	193.9	0.0	44.8
上 海 Shanghai	0.0				85.6	0.2	10.8
江 苏 Jiangsu	0.6	2.4	0.0		1484.3	34.0	180.0
浙 江 Zhejiang	5.9		0.4	0.1	671.4	210.7	291.7
安 徽 Anhui	1.3		9.9	9.8	787.2	211.9	165.5
福 建 Fujian	5.1		62.9	62.8	641.0	248.5	383.8
江 西 Jiangxi	13.3		13.7	13.6	713.8	122.1	440.4
山 东 Shandong	0.0		20.6	20.6	1578.9	27.2	605.0
河 南 Henan	1.1		73.2	71.7	1799.4	116.8	386.7
湖 北 Hubei	6.3		41.2	36.2	1358.3	383.1	413.7
湖 南 Hunan	7.5		105.7	104.8	1433.5	216.1	588.6
广 东 Guangdong	142.5		15.1	14.2	1453.7	112.7	1094.9
广 西 Guangxi	835.1		11.9	10.5	1705.0	107.2	1406.0
海 南 Hainan	13.3		0.3	0.3	275.7	2.6	208.3
重 庆 Chongqing	1.8		29.1	25.1	829.0	56.0	373.9
四 川 Sichuan	9.6	0.0	79.7	74.4	1582.8	414.4	886.9
贵 州 Guizhou	6.4		142.2	137.6	1437.4	450.0	720.2
云 南 Yunnan	215.1		426.1	415.9	1339.0	535.5	767.8
西 藏 Xizang	0.0		0.0	0.0	28.7	3.8	7.4
陕 西 Shaanxi	0.1	0.0	24.5	24.4	558.3	163.3	1163.7
甘 肃 Gansu		2.4	1.7	1.6	485.7	12.9	331.3
青 海 Qinghai			0.0		43.8		2.6
宁 夏 Ningxia		0.0	0.2	0.2	133.6	0.0	96.1
新 疆 Xinjiang		61.6			371.4		816.1

12-9 主要农作物种植结构
Planting Structure of Major Farm Crops

单位：% (%)

项　目	Item	1995	2000	2005	2010	2015	2020	2022	2023
农作物总播种面积	**Total Sown Area of Farm Crops**	**100.00**	**100.00**	**100.00**	**100.00**	**100.00**	**100.00**	**100.00**	**100.00**
粮食作物	**Grain Crops**	**73.43**	**69.39**	**67.07**	**70.43**	**71.31**	**69.72**	**69.61**	**69.32**
谷物	Cereals	59.59	54.55	52.66	58.41	61.87	58.49	58.40	58.22
稻谷	Rice	20.51	19.17	18.55	18.98	18.45	17.96	17.32	16.87
小麦	Wheat	19.26	17.05	14.66	15.41	14.73	13.96	13.84	13.77
玉米	Corn	15.20	14.75	16.95	22.06	26.95	24.64	25.34	25.76
谷子	Millet	1.02	0.80	0.55	0.51	0.50	0.54	0.49	0.45
高粱	Jowar	0.81	0.57	0.37	0.32	0.25	0.38	0.40	0.40
其他谷物	Other Cereal	2.80	2.21	1.58	1.12	0.98	1.02	1.01	0.98
豆类	Beans	7.49	8.10	8.30	6.97	5.05	6.92	6.99	6.99
#大豆	Soybeans	5.42	5.95	6.17	5.49	4.09	5.90	6.03	6.10
杂豆	Miscellaneous Beans	2.07	2.15	2.13	1.48	0.96	1.02	0.96	0.89
薯类	Tubers	6.35	6.74	6.11	5.06	4.38	4.31	4.23	4.11
#马铃薯	Potato	2.29	3.02	3.14	3.08	2.87	2.78	2.67	2.60
油料作物	**Oil-bearing Crops**	**8.74**	**9.85**	**9.21**	**8.64**	**7.98**	**7.84**	**7.73**	**8.11**
#花生	Peanuts	2.54	3.11	3.00	2.76	2.63	2.82	2.76	2.80
油菜籽	Rapeseeds	4.61	4.79	4.68	4.61	4.21	4.04	4.27	4.55
芝麻	Sesame	0.43	0.50	0.38	0.23	0.18	0.17	0.16	0.16
胡麻籽	Benne Seeds	0.41	0.32	0.26	0.18	0.15	0.11	0.10	0.10
葵花籽	Sunflower Seeds	0.54	0.79	0.66	0.62	0.65	0.52	0.37	0.42
棉花	**Cotton**	**3.62**	**2.59**	**3.26**	**2.75**	**2.26**	**1.89**	**1.76**	**1.62**
麻类	**Fiber Crops**	**0.25**	**0.17**	**0.22**	**0.06**	**0.03**	**0.04**	**0.03**	**0.03**
糖料	**Sugar Crops**	**1.21**	**0.97**	**1.01**	**1.14**	**0.94**	**0.94**	**0.86**	**0.82**
甘蔗	Sugarcane	0.75	0.76	0.87	1.02	0.88	0.81	0.76	0.74
甜菜	Beetroots	0.46	0.21	0.14	0.12	0.06	0.13	0.10	0.09
烟叶	**Tobacco**	**0.98**	**0.92**	**0.88**	**0.83**	**0.75**	**0.61**	**0.61**	**0.63**
#烤烟	Flue-cured Tobacco	0.87	0.81	0.80	0.76	0.72	0.58	0.59	0.61
药材	**Medicinal Materials**	**0.19**	**0.43**	**0.78**	**0.80**	**1.12**	**1.73**	**1.86**	**1.89**
蔬菜	**Vegetables**	**6.35**	**9.75**	**11.40**	**10.99**	**11.76**	**12.83**	**13.20**	**13.33**
瓜果类	**Melon**	**0.73**	**1.31**	**1.42**	**1.40**	**1.32**	**1.29**	**1.25**	**1.26**
其他农作物	**Other Farm Crops**	**4.49**	**4.70**	**4.78**	**2.96**	**2.53**	**3.12**	**3.08**	**2.98**
#青饲料	Succulence	1.22	1.37	2.17	1.11	0.98	1.31	1.55	1.55

12-10 主要农产品产量
Output of Major Farm Products

单位：万吨 (10 000 tons)

年 份 地 区 Year Region	粮 食 Grain	谷 物 Cereals	#稻 谷 Rice	#小 麦 Wheat	#玉 米 Corn	豆 类 Beans	#大 豆 Soybeans	薯 类 Tubers
1978	30476.5		13693.0	5384.0	5594.5		756.5	3174.0
1980	32055.5		13990.5	5520.5	6260.0		794.0	2872.5
1985	37910.8		16856.9	8580.5	6382.6		1050.0	2603.6
1990	44624.3		18933.1	9822.9	9681.9		1100.0	2743.3
1995	46661.8	41611.6	18522.6	10220.7	11198.6	1787.5	1350.2	3262.6
2000	46217.5	40522.4	18790.8	9963.6	10600.0	2010.0	1540.9	3685.2
2005	48402.2	42776.0	18058.8	9744.5	13936.5	2157.7	1634.8	3468.5
2006	49804.2	45099.2	18171.8	10846.6	15160.3	2003.7	1508.2	2701.3
2007	50413.9	45963.0	18638.1	10949.2	15512.3	1709.1	1279.3	2741.8
2008	53434.3	48569.4	19261.2	11290.1	17212.0	2021.9	1570.9	2843.0
2009	53940.9	49243.3	19619.7	11579.6	17325.9	1904.6	1522.4	2792.9
2010	55911.3	51196.7	19722.6	11609.3	19075.2	1871.8	1541.0	2842.7
2011	58849.3	54061.7	20288.3	11857.0	21131.6	1863.3	1487.8	2924.3
2012	61222.6	56659.0	20653.2	12247.5	22955.9	1680.6	1343.6	2883.0
2013	63048.2	58650.4	20628.6	12363.9	24845.3	1542.4	1240.7	2855.4
2014	63964.8	59601.5	20960.9	12823.5	24976.4	1564.5	1268.6	2798.8
2015	66060.3	61818.4	21214.2	13255.5	26499.2	1512.5	1236.7	2729.3
2016	66043.5	61666.5	21109.4	13318.8	26361.3	1650.7	1359.5	2726.3
2017	66160.7	61520.5	21267.6	13424.1	25907.1	1841.6	1528.2	2798.6
2018	65789.2	61003.6	21212.9	13144.0	25717.4	1920.3	1596.7	2865.4
2019	66384.3	61369.7	20961.4	13359.6	26077.9	2131.9	1809.2	2882.7
2020	66949.2	61674.3	21186.0	13425.4	26066.5	2287.5	1960.2	2987.4
2021	68284.7	63275.7	21284.2	13694.4	27255.1	1965.5	1639.5	3043.5
2022	68652.8	63324.3	20849.5	13772.3	27720.3	2351.0	2028.3	2977.4
2023	69541.0	64143.0	20660.3	13659.0	28884.2	2384.1	2084.2	3013.9
北 京 Beijing	47.8	45.6	0.2	13.4	31.6	1.0	1.0	1.2
天 津 Tianjin	255.7	252.7	51.8	74.5	120.7	1.3	1.3	1.7
河 北 Hebei	3809.9	3626.0	48.9	1485.6	2014.3	29.8	24.5	154.1
山 西 Shanxi	1478.1	1393.4	1.5	247.1	1035.1	24.3	20.1	60.4
内蒙古 Inner Mongolia	3957.8	3572.0	82.1	132.5	3179.6	255.7	244.4	130.1
辽 宁 Liaoning	2563.4	2510.5	412.9	0.8	2057.4	29.0	28.0	23.9
吉 林 Jilin	4186.5	4087.0	682.1	1.7	3376.3	81.6	74.4	17.9
黑龙江 Heilongjiang	7788.2	6837.1	2440.0	7.5	4379.0	936.4	927.8	14.7
上 海 Shanghai	101.9	101.7	86.5	12.9	0.5	0.1	0.1	0.1
江 苏 Jiangsu	3797.7	3695.6	2003.2	1373.5	298.8	79.8	62.4	22.3
浙 江 Zhejiang	638.8	567.5	485.3	66.4	12.2	28.8	21.6	42.6
安 徽 Anhui	4150.8	4026.7	1609.8	1740.7	665.1	103.7	97.8	20.4
福 建 Fujian	511.0	412.4	394.6	0.0	16.3	12.5	10.1	86.1
江 西 Jiangxi	2198.3	2102.0	2070.7	3.5	26.5	37.4	29.4	59.0
山 东 Shandong	5655.3	5482.7	86.1	2673.8	2710.1	65.0	64.0	107.7
河 南 Henan	6624.3	6409.8	479.2	3549.7	2365.7	95.9	92.7	118.6
湖 北 Hubei	2777.0	2618.6	1880.4	410.4	318.2	47.4	42.8	111.1
湖 南 Hunan	3068.0	2919.9	2665.3	7.7	239.9	47.5	38.0	100.6
广 东 Guangdong	1285.2	1162.9	1096.9	0.2	65.5	12.4	9.6	109.9
广 西 Guangxi	1395.4	1312.4	1030.4	1.0	278.2	27.8	17.4	55.2
海 南 Hainan	147.0	128.1	128.1			0.9	0.4	18.0
重 庆 Chongqing	1095.9	765.8	492.0	6.2	258.6	46.4	24.4	283.7
四 川 Sichuan	3593.8	2904.2	1480.8	265.9	1097.2	163.1	124.7	526.5
贵 州 Guizhou	1119.7	791.3	366.1	27.6	343.4	45.6	27.2	282.8
云 南 Yunnan	1974.0	1628.6	455.5	55.4	1049.3	104.1	34.2	241.3
西 藏 Xizang	108.9	107.4	0.5	19.2	3.1	1.1	0.0	0.4
陕 西 Shaanxi	1323.7	1166.5	73.5	416.6	637.8	38.8	31.7	118.4
甘 肃 Gansu	1272.9	1014.3	1.4	299.2	672.6	36.5	11.5	222.1
青 海 Qinghai	116.2	82.7		39.7	15.2	3.7		29.8
宁 夏 Ningxia	378.8	345.0	16.2	23.4	294.9	3.8	3.4	30.0
新 疆 Xinjiang	2119.2	2072.9	38.3	702.8	1321.4	22.9	19.3	23.3

12-10 续表 1 continued

单位：万吨 (10 000 tons)

年 份 地 区	Year Region	棉 花 Cotton	油 料 Oil-bearing Crops	#花 生 Peanuts	#油菜籽 Rapeseeds	#芝 麻 Sesame	麻 类 Fiber Crops	糖 料 Sugar Crops	#甘 蔗 Sugarcane	#甜 菜 Beetroots
	1978	216.7	521.8	237.7	186.8	32.2	135.1	2381.9	2111.6	270.2
	1980	270.7	769.1	360.0	238.4	25.9	143.6	2911.3	2280.7	630.5
	1985	414.7	1578.4	666.4	560.7	69.1	444.8	6046.8	5154.9	891.9
	1990	450.8	1613.2	636.8	695.8	46.9	109.7	7214.5	5762.0	1452.5
	1995	476.8	2250.3	1023.5	977.7	58.3	89.7	7940.1	6541.7	1398.4
	2000	441.7	2954.8	1443.7	1138.1	81.1	52.9	7635.3	6828.0	807.3
	2005	571.4	3077.1	1434.2	1305.2	62.5	110.5	9451.9	8663.8	788.1
	2006	753.3	2640.3	1288.7	1096.6	66.2	89.1	10460.0	9709.2	750.8
	2007	759.7	2787.0	1381.5	1138.2	52.0	66.1	12082.4	11179.4	902.9
	2008	723.2	3036.8	1463.5	1240.3	51.5	56.1	13006.0	12152.1	853.9
	2009	623.6	3139.4	1460.4	1353.6	53.5	31.9	11746.9	11200.4	546.5
	2010	577.0	3156.8	1513.6	1278.8	46.2	24.2	11303.4	10598.2	705.1
	2011	651.9	3212.5	1530.2	1313.7	45.8	22.3	11663.1	10867.4	795.8
	2012	660.8	3285.6	1579.2	1340.1	46.6	19.6	12451.8	11574.6	877.2
	2013	628.2	3348.0	1610.9	1363.6	43.9	17.6	12555.0	11926.4	628.7
	2014	629.9	3371.9	1590.1	1391.4	43.7	16.5	12088.7	11578.8	509.9
	2015	590.7	3390.5	1596.1	1385.9	45.0	15.6	11215.2	10706.4	508.8
	2016	534.3	3400.0	1636.1	1312.8	35.2	18.1	11176.0	10321.5	854.5
	2017	565.3	3475.2	1709.2	1327.4	36.6	21.8	11378.8	10440.4	938.4
	2018	610.3	3433.4	1733.2	1328.1	43.1	20.3	11937.4	10809.7	1127.7
	2019	588.9	3493.0	1752.0	1348.5	46.7	23.4	12169.1	10938.8	1227.3
	2020	591.0	3586.4	1799.3	1404.9	45.7	24.9	12014.0	10812.1	1198.4
	2021	573.1	3613.2	1830.8	1471.4	45.5	21.1	11454.4	10666.4	785.1
	2022	598.0	3654.2	1832.9	1553.1	43.5	22.8	11236.5	10338.1	893.3
	2023	561.8	3863.7	1923.1	1631.7	45.3	16.3	11376.3	10456.6	916.0
北 京	Beijing	0.0	1.0	0.9	0.0	0.0				
天 津	Tianjin	0.1	0.4	0.2	0.1	0.0		0.0	0.0	
河 北	Hebei	10.4	118.3	94.2	6.3	0.2	0.0	65.5	0.1	65.5
山 西	Shanxi	0.0	17.9	1.7	2.9	0.2	0.0	0.1		0.1
内蒙古	Inner Mongolia		206.2	18.7	37.8	0.0	0.5	305.4		304.8
辽 宁	Liaoning		128.1	127.2	0.0	0.0		0.9		0.9
吉 林	Jilin		88.4	86.3	0.0	0.0		1.6		1.6
黑龙江	Heilongjiang		16.5	13.4	0.0	0.1	6.7	24.6		24.6
上 海	Shanghai		0.6	0.0	0.6	0.0		0.1	0.1	
江 苏	Jiangsu	0.5	103.4	40.7	61.3	1.3	0.0	5.3	3.5	1.8
浙 江	Zhejiang	0.3	35.6	5.1	29.4	1.0	0.0	37.7	37.7	
安 徽	Anhui	2.0	189.0	73.3	110.6	3.0	0.8	8.8	5.7	
福 建	Fujian		24.4	23.0	1.3	0.0		28.5	28.5	
江 西	Jiangxi	2.2	148.1	57.8	86.3	4.0	0.4	61.4	61.4	
山 东	Shandong	12.6	280.7	276.8	2.3	0.2	0.0	0.0	0.0	
河 南	Henan	0.7	703.0	638.9	45.8	16.8	0.3	8.0	8.0	
湖 北	Hubei	9.6	394.9	93.1	286.1	13.0	0.8	26.5	26.5	
湖 南	Hunan	7.6	293.1	32.2	258.8	1.8	0.4	35.0	35.0	
广 东	Guangdong		121.0	119.5	0.8	0.7	0.0	1271.1	1271.1	
广 西	Guangxi	0.1	80.8	75.5	4.1	0.9	0.7	7223.2	7223.2	
海 南	Hainan		7.9	7.9		0.1	0.0	86.5	86.5	
重 庆	Chongqing		77.5	15.1	60.7	0.5	0.3	8.4	8.4	
四 川	Sichuan	0.0	438.6	82.7	354.4	0.3	3.5	39.3	39.2	0.0
贵 州	Guizhou	0.0	111.0	10.4	99.4	0.0	0.0	34.7	34.7	
云 南	Yunnan		68.5	9.2	57.8	0.0	0.0	1586.9	1586.9	
西 藏	Xizang		5.0	0.0	5.0			0.0	0.0	
陕 西	Shaanxi	0.0	60.6	11.5	40.1	1.1	0.0	0.3	0.2	0.0
甘 肃	Gansu	4.2	63.1	0.1	37.6		0.1	16.9		16.9
青 海	Qinghai		32.1		31.9					
宁 夏	Ningxia		4.6	0.0	1.1			0.0		0.0
新 疆	Xinjiang	511.2	43.2	7.7	9.1	0.0	1.7	499.9		499.9

12-10 续表 2 continued

单位：万吨 (10 000 tons)

年 份 Year 地 区 Region	烟 叶 Tobacco	#烤 烟 Flue-cured Tobacco	蚕 茧 Silkworm Cocoons	#桑蚕茧 Mulberry Silkworm Cocoons	茶 叶 Tea	水 果 Fruits	#苹 果 Apples	#柑 橘 Citrus	#梨 Pears	#葡 萄 Grapes	#香 蕉 Bananas
1978	124.2	105.2	22.8	17.3	26.8	657.0	227.5	38.3	151.7	10.4	8.5
1980	84.5	71.7	32.6	25.0	30.4	679.3	236.3	71.3	146.6	11.0	6.1
1985	242.5	207.5	37.1	33.6	43.2	1163.9	361.4	180.8	213.7	36.1	63.1
1990	262.7	225.9	53.4	48.0	54.0	1874.4	431.9	485.5	235.3	85.9	145.6
1995	231.4	207.2	80.0	76.0	58.8	4214.6	1400.8	822.5	494.2	174.2	312.5
2000	255.2	223.8	54.8	50.1	68.3	6225.1	2043.1	878.3	841.2	328.2	494.1
2005	268.3	243.5	78.0	71.3	93.5	16120.1	2401.1	1591.9	1132.4	579.4	651.8
2006	245.6	225.5	87.9	82.0	102.8	17102.0	2605.9	1789.8	1198.6	627.1	690.1
2007	242.2	224.9	92.7	86.2	117.0	17659.4	2734.7	2036.4	1258.8	670.9	764.0
2008	275.9	258.2	88.2	80.5	125.5	18279.1	2899.5	2297.0	1296.4	698.2	748.4
2009	296.2	275.0	79.5	72.8	135.1	19093.7	3047.5	2471.7	1343.6	764.9	829.6
2010	283.2	261.2	82.7	75.5	146.2	20095.4	3164.9	2581.7	1409.5	813.5	884.1
2011	299.8	278.6	84.3	76.8	160.8	21018.6	3367.3	2864.1	1448.6	857.7	946.1
2012	324.6	302.3	83.7	76.7	176.1	22091.5	3581.4	3089.4	1550.4	1000.6	1036.0
2013	322.0	304.0	81.8	74.7	188.7	22748.1	3629.8	3196.4	1544.4	1088.5	1103.0
2014	284.7	269.7	81.5	74.4	204.9	23302.6	3735.4	3362.2	1581.9	1173.1	1062.2
2015	267.7	249.5	81.2	74.1	227.7	24524.6	3889.9	3617.5	1652.7	1316.4	1062.7
2016	257.4	244.5	80.3	73.8	231.3	24405.2	4039.3	3591.5	1596.3	1262.9	1094.0
2017	239.1	227.9	81.7	75.1	246.0	25241.9	4139.0	3816.8	1641.0	1308.3	1117.0
2018	224.1	211.0	83.1	76.4	261.0	25688.4	3923.3	4138.1	1607.8	1366.7	1122.2
2019	215.3	202.1	83.3	77.2	277.7	27400.8	4242.5	4584.5	1731.4	1419.5	1165.6
2020	213.4	202.2	78.8	73.5	293.2	28692.4	4406.6	5121.9	1781.5	1431.4	1151.3
2021	212.8	202.1	78.2	72.7	316.4	29970.2	4597.3	5595.6	1887.6	1499.8	1172.4
2022	218.8	208.0	80.7	74.8	334.2	31296.2	4757.2	6003.9	1926.5	1537.8	1177.7
2023	229.7	219.1	83.4	77.2	354.1	32744.3	4960.2	6433.8	1985.3	1616.6	1170.3
北 京 Beijing	0.0					41.8	3.0	0.0	3.5	0.9	0.0
天 津 Tianjin						42.3	2.0		3.5	4.4	
河 北 Hebei	0.4	0.1	0.0	0.0	0.0	1563.2	269.6		395.7	136.7	
山 西 Shanxi	0.5	0.5	0.2	0.2	0.2	1082.8	441.5		152.6	44.8	0.0
内蒙古 Inner Mongolia	0.4	0.2	0.2		0.0	213.3	35.7	0.0	8.0	4.8	
辽 宁 Liaoning	1.2	0.8	5.0	0.0	0.0	928.2	288.9		126.4	89.5	
吉 林 Jilin	2.1	1.0	0.4			157.2	8.6		7.1	7.7	
黑龙江 Heilongjiang	2.7	2.5	0.4		0.0	188.9	14.1		5.0	8.1	
上 海 Shanghai					0.0	31.7		5.8	3.1	3.6	
江 苏 Jiangsu	0.0		2.2	2.2	1.1	1015.2	57.3	3.4	78.6	69.8	
浙 江 Zhejiang	0.1	0.0	2.3	2.3	18.9	733.4	0.0	187.1	33.6	76.2	0.0
安 徽 Anhui	2.2	2.2	1.0	1.0	14.6	828.8	36.8	3.6	141.7	57.5	
福 建 Fujian	13.5	13.4			55.0	914.3		492.1	21.3	25.4	50.8
江 西 Jiangxi	2.9	2.8	0.2	0.2	7.9	799.0		504.2	16.4	11.9	
山 东 Shandong	5.5	5.5	0.2	0.2	3.1	3208.2	1039.8		136.6	126.3	
河 南 Henan	19.5	19.0	0.5	0.2	7.3	2561.6	422.4	5.2	150.3	91.4	
湖 北 Hubei	8.0	6.7	0.1	0.1	44.9	1191.5	0.2	570.9	44.7	33.6	
湖 南 Hunan	21.8	21.7	0.0	0.0	27.6	1266.1	0.0	678.3	21.4	28.9	
广 东 Guangdong	3.7	3.5	8.4	8.4	17.9	2127.8		591.8	14.0	6.9	478.3
广 西 Guangxi	2.4	2.1	46.1	46.1	12.0	3553.2		1894.6	53.4	74.7	302.0
海 南 Hainan	0.0	0.0	0.1	0.1	0.2	592.6		15.7		0.1	117.7
重 庆 Chongqing	5.7	4.7	1.3	1.3	5.6	645.9	0.6	397.5	36.0	13.9	0.1
四 川 Sichuan	17.3	15.7	10.4	10.4	42.5	1490.4	102.1	615.0	93.3	57.6	3.6
贵 州 Guizhou	23.8	23.0	0.2	0.2	28.8	756.7	34.0	132.2	54.3	44.0	9.1
云 南 Yunnan	89.6	87.1	3.6	3.6	55.7	1380.9	74.8	277.3	83.5	109.7	208.5
西 藏 Xizang	0.0	0.0			0.0	3.1	0.9	0.1	0.2	0.5	0.1
陕 西 Shaanxi	5.9	5.8	0.7	0.7	10.7	2335.5	1375.1	58.5	112.3	93.1	
甘 肃 Gansu	0.6	0.5	0.0	0.0	0.2	1044.0	511.9	0.4	25.5	26.9	
青 海 Qinghai	0.0					2.5	0.5		0.5	0.0	
宁 夏 Ningxia	0.0	0.0			0.0	310.5	24.5		1.9	19.9	
新 疆 Xinjiang			0.0	0.0		1733.8	216.0		160.9	347.7	

注：2003年起水果产量包括瓜果类产量。

a) Data of output of fruits include melons since 2003.

12-11 主要农产品单位面积产量
Output of Major Farm Products per Hectare

单位：公斤/公顷 (kg/hectare)

年份 Year / 地区 Region		粮食 Grain	谷物 Cereals	棉花 Cotton	花生 Peanuts	油菜籽 Rapeseeds	芝麻 Sesame	甘蔗 Sugarcane	甜菜 Beetroots	烤烟 Flue-cured Tobacco
	1978	2527		445	1344	718	506	38496	8166	1717
	1980	2734		550	1539	838	333	47562	14242	1806
	1985	3483		807	2008	1248	657	53430	15913	1927
	1990	3933		807	2191	1264	702	57118	21668	1683
	1995	4240	4659	879	2687	1415	908	58133	20132	1584
	2000	4261	4753	1093	2973	1519	1034	57626	24518	1763
	2005	4642	5225	1129	3076	1793	1054	63970	37523	1956
	2006	4745	5310	1295	3258	1833	1173	70450	39767	2072
	2007	4756	5321	1461	3347	1854	1156	73015	40097	2056
	2008	4969	5551	1370	3355	1814	1205	71122	39246	2118
	2009	4892	5448	1390	3411	1888	1295	68170	33845	2250
	2010	5006	5528	1322	3460	1748	1293	65271	38018	2160
	2011	5209	5714	1441	3529	1827	1366	66113	41720	2103
	2012	5353	5833	1516	3588	1865	1439	68264	45924	2090
	2013	5440	5907	1509	3664	1896	1464	69986	44801	2065
	2014	5446	5896	1508	3639	1944	1443	70682	51533	2027
	2015	5553	5989	1565	3640	1972	1495	72528	52751	2084
	2016	5539	6004	1671	3678	1982	1529	73638	55630	2121
	2017	5607	6105	1769	3709	1995	1610	76132	53843	2108
	2018	5621	6120	1819	3752	2027	1645	76891	52174	2103
	2019	5720	6272	1764	3781	2048	1651	78655	56057	2079
	2020	5734	6296	1865	3803	2077	1564	79890	56307	2091
	2021	5805	6316	1893	3810	2104	1596	81047	55639	2086
	2022	5802	6379	1993	3913	2141	1620	80192	54855	2079
	2023	5845	6419	2015	4008	2091	1618	82652	61540	2101
北京	Beijing	5341	5501	1071	3321	922	1024			
天津	Tianjin	6557	6616	1283	3349	1969	1808	67500		
河北	Hebei	5902	5961	1208	4043	1743	1312	52636	54903	2758
山西	Shanxi	4676	4921	1332	3021	1511	1180		31013	2994
内蒙古	Inner Mongolia	5666	6593		4179	1433	1057		46232	4211
辽宁	Liaoning	7164	7393		4009	1831	2324		64126	2805
吉林	Jilin	7186	7533		3804	2667	1243		52401	2332
黑龙江	Heilongjiang	5283	7003		4818	1425	1285		58860	2724
上海	Shanghai	8010	8039		2838	2794	1061	40421		
江苏	Jiangsu	6957	7197	1455	4279	2934	1867	62276	7411	
浙江	Zhejiang	6234	6768	1389	3111	2133	1734	63312		3057
安徽	Anhui	5659	6106	894	4958	2354	1667	45242		2270
福建	Fujian	6075	6432		3045	1453	1545	55882		2138
江西	Jiangxi	5824	6068	1135	3170	1456	1212	46039		2086
山东	Shandong	6742	6831	1304	4514	2616	2103	82695		2673
河南	Henan	6142	6296	1219	4888	2357	1633	72514		2657
湖北	Hubei	5900	6381	930	3634	2341	1721	42023		1857
湖南	Hunan	6441	6642	1360	2710	1747	1501	46298		2068
广东	Guangdong	5764	5923		3382	1504	1979	89176		2465
广西	Guangxi	4922	5477	1017	3240	940	3114	86496		1970
海南	Hainan	5374	5603		2603		1165	65127		1300
重庆	Chongqing	5409	6664		2289	2037	1212	45607		1884
四川	Sichuan	5612	6492	913	2703	2507	1596	40824	39697	2110
贵州	Guizhou	4037	5155	955	2561	1777	1277	54212		1671
云南	Yunnan	4652	5209		2032	2041	1012	73764		2094
西藏	Xizang	5595	5699		3126	2563		4800		2626
陕西	Shaanxi	4379	4709	1617	3116	2178	1538	39802	18609	2375
甘肃	Gansu	4695	5108	2080	3759	2343			71692	3350
青海	Qinghai	3812	3716			2183				
宁夏	Ningxia	5459	5884		2903	1083			29091	1906
新疆	Xinjiang	7502	7659	2158	5183	2749	1504		81172	

12-12 主要林产品产量
Output of Major Forestry Products

年 份 Year 地 区 Region		木 材 (万立方米) Timber (10 000 cu.m)	橡 胶 (吨) Rubber (ton)	竹 材 (万根) Bamboo (10 000 units)	核 桃 (吨) Walnut (ton)	油茶籽 (吨) Rapeseeds (ton)
	1978	5162.3	101600	11181	118650	478900
	1980	5359.3	112945	9621	118900	490350
	1985	6323.4	187901	5641	121917	619229
	1990	5571.0	264243	18714	149560	523313
	1995	6766.9	424025	44792	230867	623128
	2000	4724.0	480248	56183	309875	823224
	2005	5560.3	513618	115174	499074	875022
	2006	6611.8	537983	131176	475455	919947
	2007	6976.6	588390	139761	629986	939096
	2008	8108.3	547861	126220	828635	989859
	2009	7068.3	619138	135650	979366	1169289
	2010	8089.6	693022	143008	1284351	1092243
	2011	8145.9	750850	153929	1655508	1480044
	2012	8174.9	802255	164412	1979583	1727708
	2013	8438.5	864806	187685	2325010	1776506
	2014	8233.3	840171	222440	2713741	2023445
	2015	7200.3	816103	235466	3331703	2163492
	2016	7775.9	815918	250630	3645170	2164440
	2017	8398.2	817366	272013	4171386	2431647
	2018	8810.9	824093	315517	3820720	2629796
	2019	10045.9	809859	314480	4689184	2679270
	2020	10257.0	826348	324265	4795939	3141620
	2021	11589.1	871600	325568	5403500	3942376
	2022	12210.0	861675	421846	5934635	2946191
	2023	12700.9	897323	341798	5865974	3369641
北 京	Beijing				7863	
天 津	Tianjin	11.9			5	
河 北	Hebei	148.4			213594	
山 西	Shanxi	27.0			299564	
内蒙古	Inner Mongolia	144.2			1	
辽 宁	Liaoning	232.7			61295	
吉 林	Jilin	256.7			16700	
黑龙江	Heilongjiang	182.8			1132	
上 海	Shanghai					
江 苏	Jiangsu	181.9		483	113	
浙 江	Zhejiang	85.6		22916	595	109409
安 徽	Anhui	560.6		19483	27204	71810
福 建	Fujian	975.8		80792		171228
江 西	Jiangxi	454.9		30989	3	623005
山 东	Shandong	438.5			111408	
河 南	Henan	232.0		229	199153	53608
湖 北	Hubei	334.8		43608	69091	270957
湖 南	Hunan	517.6		28765	7099	1266388
广 东	Guangdong	1376.0	15984	43882		199441
广 西	Guangxi	4246.0		54355	8381	384532
海 南	Hainan	204.7	350092			3999
重 庆	Chongqing	63.4		1710	38997	23461
四 川	Sichuan	331.0		4636	697692	18432
贵 州	Guizhou	474.1		3946	78474	125109
云 南	Yunnan	1103.7	531247	5581	1987456	31493
西 藏	Xizang				2770	
陕 西	Shaanxi	25.1		422	414855	16768
甘 肃	Gansu	4.5			446150	
青 海	Qinghai				3258	
宁 夏	Ningxia				2804	
新 疆	Xinjiang	87.3			1170318	

12-13 牲畜饲养情况
Number of Livestock

单位：万头、万只 (10 000 heads)

年份 地区	Year Region	大牲畜年底头数 Large Animals (year-end)	牛 Cattle and Buffaloes	马 Horses	驴 Donkeys	骡 Mules	骆驼 Camels
	1996	13360.2	11031.8	871.5	944.4	478.0	34.5
	2000	14638.1	12353.2	876.6	922.7	453.0	32.6
	2005	12894.8	10990.8	740.0	777.2	360.4	26.6
	2006	12325.7	10503.1	719.3	730.9	345.5	26.9
	2007	11998.2	10397.5	646.7	638.9	291.0	24.1
	2008	11529.7	10068.0	594.7	600.4	243.8	22.8
	2009	11380.8	10035.9	562.3	540.4	219.7	22.6
	2010	11074.6	9820.0	529.9	510.1	191.5	23.0
	2011	10580.0	9384.0	515.4	485.3	171.1	24.3
	2012	10248.4	9137.3	465.2	462.4	159.0	24.5
	2013	10008.6	8985.8	431.7	425.7	138.0	27.4
	2014	9952.0	9007.3	415.8	383.6	117.4	28.0
	2015	9929.8	9055.8	397.5	342.4	104.1	30.1
	2016	9559.9	8834.5	351.2	259.3	84.5	30.5
	2017	9763.6	9038.7	343.6	267.8	81.1	32.3
	2018	9625.5	8915.3	347.3	253.3	75.8	33.8
	2019	9877.4	9138.3	367.1	260.1	71.4	40.5
	2020	10265.1	9562.1	367.2	232.4	62.3	41.1
	2021	10486.8	9817.2	372.5	196.7	54.2	46.2
	2022	10859.0	10215.9	366.7	173.5	48.8	54.1
	2023	11115.4	10508.5	359.1	146.0	43.8	58.0
北京	Beijing	8.5	8.3	0.0	0.1	0.0	
天津	Tianjin	32.4	31.4	0.1	0.9	0.0	0.0
河北	Hebei	439.3	414.6	9.2	12.7	2.7	0.1
山西	Shanxi	163.2	155.5	1.1	5.2	1.4	0.0
内蒙古	Inner Mongolia	1069.7	947.7	75.6	24.8	1.0	20.6
辽宁	Liaoning	316.7	290.2	3.8	20.6	2.0	0.0
吉林	Jilin	438.1	427.4	5.8	4.5	0.5	0.0
黑龙江	Heilongjiang	551.4	541.5	7.6	2.1	0.2	0.0
上海	Shanghai	6.2	6.1	0.1			
江苏	Jiangsu	31.5	31.3	0.0	0.1		
浙江	Zhejiang	15.1	15.1				
安徽	Anhui	109.8	109.3	0.1	0.5	0.0	0.0
福建	Fujian	30.9	30.9		0.0	0.0	
江西	Jiangxi	232.8	232.6	0.1	0.1		0.0
山东	Shandong	272.2	269.0	0.5	2.7	0.0	0.0
河南	Henan	382.8	380.7	0.3	1.7	0.1	
湖北	Hubei	234.3	234.0	0.1	0.1	0.0	0.0
湖南	Hunan	412.1	410.7	1.2	0.1	0.0	
广东	Guangdong	98.5	98.5	0.0			
广西	Guangxi	363.4	349.8	11.0	0.0	2.5	
海南	Hainan	47.6	47.6				
重庆	Chongqing	111.8	110.9	0.6	0.1	0.2	
四川	Sichuan	921.1	848.5	58.4	7.4	6.9	
贵州	Guizhou	514.3	503.6	10.2	0.1	0.4	
云南	Yunnan	943.5	897.4	11.2	16.8	18.1	0.0
西藏	Xizang	734.7	710.4	21.6	1.8	0.8	
陕西	Shaanxi	155.7	152.3	0.3	3.0	0.1	0.0
甘肃	Gansu	607.0	558.9	12.9	24.6	6.6	4.0
青海	Qinghai	647.5	632.0	13.5	0.2	0.2	1.6
宁夏	Ningxia	247.6	246.6	0.2	0.6	0.0	0.1
新疆	Xinjiang	975.9	815.6	113.5	15.2	0.1	31.6

12-13 续表 continued

单位：万头、万只 (10 000 heads)

年份 地区	Year Region	肉猪出栏头数 Slaughtered Hogs	猪年底头数 Hogs (year-end)	羊年底只数 Sheep and Goats (year-end)	山羊 Goats	绵羊 Sheep
	1996	41225.2	36283.6	23728.3	12315.8	11412.5
	2000	51862.3	41633.6	27948.2	14945.6	13002.6
	2005	60367.4	43319.1	29792.7	14659.0	15133.7
	2006	61209.0	41854.4	28337.6	13956.1	14381.5
	2007	56640.9	43933.2	28606.7	14564.1	14042.5
	2008	61278.9	46433.1	28823.7	15067.0	13756.7
	2009	64990.9	47177.2	29063.0	14734.0	14328.9
	2010	67332.7	46765.2	28730.2	14195.0	14535.2
	2011	67030.0	47074.8	28664.1	14087.4	14576.7
	2012	70724.5	48030.2	28512.7	13932.3	14580.4
	2013	72768.0	47893.1	28935.2	13657.5	15277.7
	2014	74951.5	47160.2	30391.3	14167.5	16223.8
	2015	72415.6	45802.9	31174.3	14507.5	16666.8
	2016	70073.9	44209.2	29930.5	13691.8	16238.8
	2017	70202.1	44158.9	30231.7	13823.8	16407.9
	2018	69382.4	42817.1	29713.5	13574.7	16138.8
	2019	54419.2	31040.7	30072.1	13723.2	16349.0
	2020	52704.1	40650.4	30654.8	13345.2	17309.5
	2021	67128.0	44922.4	31969.3	13331.6	18637.7
	2022	69994.8	45255.7	32627.3	13224.2	19403.0
	2023	72662.4	43422.3	32232.6	12934.2	19298.4
北 京	Beijing	32.9	26.7	22.0	7.5	14.5
天 津	Tianjin	205.4	117.0	51.3	9.0	42.3
河 北	Hebei	3648.4	1793.8	1414.4	346.7	1067.7
山 西	Shanxi	1276.1	814.1	1172.3	431.7	740.6
内蒙古	Inner Mongolia	910.2	629.9	6180.6	1518.3	4662.3
辽 宁	Liaoning	2970.5	1337.2	765.8	358.4	407.4
吉 林	Jilin	1927.7	1172.4	720.2	45.9	674.3
黑龙江	Heilongjiang	2414.3	1311.9	812.7	104.2	708.5
上 海	Shanghai	120.4	102.2	15.0	13.7	1.3
江 苏	Jiangsu	2408.5	1412.3	358.3	318.9	39.4
浙 江	Zhejiang	953.2	608.9	146.2	30.7	115.5
安 徽	Anhui	3075.5	1551.7	642.9	588.8	54.0
福 建	Fujian	1695.0	948.6	99.1	96.1	3.0
江 西	Jiangxi	3143.6	1676.0	144.3	129.2	15.1
山 东	Shandong	4659.7	2801.2	1353.2	485.4	867.9
河 南	Henan	6102.3	4039.0	1931.7	1596.8	334.9
湖 北	Hubei	4438.5	2595.3	527.1	527.1	
湖 南	Hunan	6286.3	3861.3	752.8	752.8	
广 东	Guangdong	3794.0	2049.2	83.8	83.8	0.1
广 西	Guangxi	3516.6	2268.5	276.6	255.5	21.1
海 南	Hainan	496.5	317.2	56.1	56.1	
重 庆	Chongqing	1974.9	1173.2	332.5	332.5	
四 川	Sichuan	6662.7	3855.0	1382.0	1196.1	185.9
贵 州	Guizhou	2048.0	1533.9	332.9	315.1	17.8
云 南	Yunnan	4627.0	3160.1	1406.5	1307.6	98.9
西 藏	Xizang	25.3	46.5	940.2	247.8	692.3
陕 西	Shaanxi	1298.3	890.2	916.7	756.5	160.2
甘 肃	Gansu	958.6	696.0	2805.8	392.1	2413.7
青 海	Qinghai	62.6	51.5	1344.8	40.8	1304.0
宁 夏	Ningxia	103.8	79.2	720.5	137.6	583.0
新 疆	Xinjiang	825.6	502.3	4524.4	451.5	4072.9

12–14 畜产品产量
Output of Livestock Products

年份 地区	Year Region	肉类 (万吨) Output of Meat (10 000 tons)	#猪牛羊肉 Output of Pork, Beef and Mutton	猪肉 Pork	牛肉 Beef	羊肉 Mutton	奶类 (万吨) Milk (10 000 tons)	#牛奶 Cow Milk
	1996	4584.0	3694.7	3158.0	355.7	181.0	735.8	629.4
	2000	6013.9	4743.2	3966.0	513.1	264.1	919.1	827.4
	2005	6938.9	5473.5	4555.3	568.1	350.1	2864.8	2753.4
	2006	7099.9	5608.4	4650.3	590.3	367.7	3051.6	2944.6
	2007	6916.4	5319.8	4307.9	626.2	385.7	3055.2	2947.1
	2008	7370.9	5692.9	4682.0	617.7	393.2	3236.2	3010.6
	2009	7706.7	5958.5	4932.8	626.2	399.4	3153.9	2995.1
	2010	7993.6	6173.5	5138.4	629.1	406.0	3211.3	3038.9
	2011	8023.0	6140.3	5131.6	610.7	398.0	3262.8	3109.9
	2012	8471.1	6462.8	5443.5	614.7	404.5	3306.7	3174.9
	2013	8632.8	6641.6	5618.6	613.1	409.9	3118.9	3000.8
	2014	8817.9	6864.2	5820.8	615.7	427.6	3276.5	3159.9
	2015	8749.5	6702.2	5645.4	616.9	439.9	3295.5	3179.8
	2016	8628.3	6502.6	5425.5	616.9	460.3	3173.9	3064.0
	2017	8654.4	6557.5	5451.8	634.6	471.1	3148.6	3038.6
	2018	8624.6	6522.9	5403.7	644.1	475.1	3176.8	3074.6
	2019	7758.8	5410.1	4255.3	667.3	487.5	3297.6	3201.2
	2020	7748.4	5278.1	4113.3	672.4	492.3	3529.6	3440.1
	2021	8990.0	6507.5	5295.9	697.5	514.1	3778.1	3682.7
	2022	9328.4	6784.2	5541.4	718.3	524.5	4026.5	3931.6
	2023	9748.2	7078.3	5794.3	752.7	531.3	4281.3	4196.7
北京	Beijing	4.2	3.4	2.7	0.5	0.2	26.5	26.5
天津	Tianjin	31.5	21.7	17.4	3.2	1.1	54.1	54.1
河北	Hebei	495.0	380.2	283.3	59.4	37.5	574.3	571.9
山西	Shanxi	155.0	121.7	99.5	10.2	12.0	147.5	147.1
内蒙古	Inner Mongolia	291.2	262.3	75.7	77.8	108.8	794.9	792.6
辽宁	Liaoning	473.7	287.9	249.1	32.0	6.8	136.0	135.4
吉林	Jilin	309.4	216.6	158.5	49.1	9.0	30.9	30.8
黑龙江	Heilongjiang	328.5	272.6	201.8	55.2	15.6	504.3	503.6
上海	Shanghai	12.2	11.0	10.7	0.0	0.2	30.7	30.7
江苏	Jiangsu	331.7	201.1	191.3	3.3	6.5	72.9	72.9
浙江	Zhejiang	119.9	84.8	80.8	1.5	2.5	20.9	20.9
安徽	Anhui	497.1	296.1	262.4	11.7	22.0	53.6	53.6
福建	Fujian	311.4	140.6	135.5	2.8	2.3	25.4	24.9
江西	Jiangxi	369.1	278.4	257.4	17.8	3.2	6.3	6.3
山东	Shandong	910.1	473.8	382.8	58.2	32.8	318.3	318.1
河南	Henan	679.1	530.6	465.3	38.0	27.3	241.8	237.5
湖北	Hubei	457.9	375.0	347.2	17.2	10.5	9.0	9.0
湖南	Hunan	582.6	499.1	461.8	20.4	16.9	8.0	7.8
广东	Guangdong	507.5	304.4	298.0	4.4	1.9	20.3	20.2
广西	Guangxi	478.9	295.6	276.0	15.3	4.3	13.8	13.8
海南	Hainan	76.4	45.2	42.1	2.0	1.1	0.3	0.3
重庆	Chongqing	215.8	173.6	158.2	8.5	6.9	3.1	3.1
四川	Sichuan	697.1	555.8	489.7	39.1	27.1	72.1	72.0
贵州	Guizhou	246.9	211.6	184.6	22.2	4.8	3.7	3.7
云南	Yunnan	536.1	472.4	405.4	44.7	22.3	73.9	72.6
西藏	Xizang	31.3	31.0	1.7	23.7	5.5	64.3	59.3
陕西	Shaanxi	135.7	123.8	104.5	9.0	10.4	163.9	109.1
甘肃	Gansu	157.4	143.4	72.7	29.8	40.9	102.8	101.8
青海	Qinghai	41.4	41.0	5.2	22.8	13.0	33.9	33.7
宁夏	Ningxia	41.4	38.1	8.6	14.4	15.1	430.6	430.6
新疆	Xinjiang	222.6	185.5	64.4	58.4	62.8	243.2	232.8

12-14 续表 continued

年 份 Year / 地 区 Region	绵羊毛 (吨) Sheep Wool (ton)	#细羊毛 Fine Wool	#半细羊毛 Semi-Fine Wool	山羊粗毛 (吨) Goat Raw Wool (ton)	山羊绒 (吨) Cashmere (ton)	禽 蛋 (万吨) Poultry Eggs (10 000 tons)	蜂 蜜 (万吨) Honey (10 000 tons)
1996	298102	121020	74099	35284	9585	1965.2	18.3
2000	292502	117386	84921	33266	11057	2182.0	24.6
2005	393172	127862	123068	36904	15435	2438.1	29.3
2006	387643	131543	116043	35171	16223	2424.0	33.4
2007	371075	124262	108635	35333	15665	2546.7	38.0
2008	369665	119279	105272	35477	16534	2699.6	38.5
2009	358121	124365	109013	35910	16593	2751.9	39.7
2010	385125	123504	113998	36226	17848	2776.9	38.2
2011	386487	132877	113305	38070	17126	2830.4	41.2
2012	393725	124716	127313	40505	17211	2885.4	43.8
2013	402081	131730	128335	40215	17307	2905.5	43.7
2014	407230	122251	132693	38655	18465	2930.3	46.3
2015	413134	130537	134905	35487	18684	3046.1	47.3
2016	411642	129164	137973	35785	18844	3160.5	55.5
2017	410523	127921	133458	32863	17852	3096.3	54.3
2018	356608	117891	120430	26965	15438	3128.3	44.7
2019	341120	108973	113284	24875	14964	3309.0	44.4
2020	333625	106109	116849	24034	15244	3467.8	45.8
2021	356217	98154	128262	23332	15102	3408.8	47.3
2022	356194	68799	155024	24837	14649	3456.4	46.2
2023	367505	80069	172286	23123	17589	3563.0	46.3
北 京 Beijing	3.9	0.4	1.3	3.1	1.4	9.1	0.1
天 津 Tianjin	462.1	35.4	426.8	6.6	0.1	23.2	0.0
河 北 Hebei	28417.5	6341.2	18892.8	2321.1	719.3	404.6	1.7
山 西 Shanxi	11883.6	3354.4	8135.4	2158.6	1526.8	126.7	0.8
内蒙古 Inner Mongolia	121190.8	27461.4	37509.3	5956.2	8635.8	67.2	0.2
辽 宁 Liaoning	6669.5	841.3	5828.2	1747.5	1391.5	311.8	0.2
吉 林 Jilin	14923.9	3148.9	11760.0	85.5	44.9	95.7	0.8
黑龙江 Heilongjiang	24300.0	3549.7	20750.3	440.2	46.6	107.4	1.4
上 海 Shanghai	9.3	8.1	1.3	51.7		3.6	0.1
江 苏 Jiangsu	318.2	74.7	243.4	3.5	0.1	235.3	0.5
浙 江 Zhejiang	1723.4		1723.4	36.2		36.3	5.0
安 徽 Anhui	307.5	226.9	80.5	23.1	14.8	206.3	1.3
福 建 Fujian	4.0	2.0	2.0			69.1	1.9
江 西 Jiangxi	26.3	6.2	20.1	6.3	2.7	73.2	1.7
山 东 Shandong	6706.8	655.9	5950.8	404.2	46.3	462.2	0.9
河 南 Henan	2634.1	525.1	1737.6	1560.5	148.2	441.2	4.9
湖 北 Hubei	24.9	16.7	8.2	26.4	0.4	216.3	2.0
湖 南 Hunan	0.2	0.0	0.1	3.9	1.3	119.6	1.8
广 东 Guangdong						49.9	3.2
广 西 Guangxi						33.4	3.1
海 南 Hainan						7.1	0.1
重 庆 Chongqing				0.2		53.1	2.2
四 川 Sichuan	4488.1	776.6	3711.4	228.8	58.4	181.1	6.7
贵 州 Guizhou	290.1	85.2	204.9	10.7	1.3	38.8	0.3
云 南 Yunnan	900.8	161.5	686.8	87.4	16.8	46.6	1.2
西 藏 Xizang	6235.8	3330.4	2174.4	708.3	718.4	1.4	0.0
陕 西 Shaanxi	3498.7	628.4	2642.6	1915.8	2018.8	65.2	1.7
甘 肃 Gansu	40731.5	11789.2	8438.5	1547.8	446.1	23.5	0.9
青 海 Qinghai	12649.8	2038.2	9942.3	363.3	174.1	1.7	0.0
宁 夏 Ningxia	8212.3	2515.5	5542.7	605.3	347.9	12.7	0.1
新 疆 Xinjiang	70892.2	12495.2	25871.1	2820.4	1227.4	39.9	1.5

12-15 水产品产量
Output of Aquatic Products

单位：万吨 (10,000 tons)

年份 地区	Year Region	水产品总产量 Total Aquatic Products	海水产品 Marine Aquatic Products	捕捞 Fishing Products	养殖 Aquacultural Products	鱼类 Fish	虾蟹类 Shrimps, Prawns and Crabs	贝类 Shellfish	藻类 Algae	其他 Others
	1978	465.4	359.5	314.5	45.0	256.1	50.6	26.8	26.0	
	1980	449.7	325.7	281.3	44.4	234.1	42.1	23.4	26.2	
	1985	705.2	419.7	348.5	71.2	274.5	70.6	47.3	27.3	
	1990	1427.3	895.7	611.5	284.2	423.1	107.0	147.3	27.5	8.2
	1995	2953.0	1861.3	1139.8	721.5	758.1	184.8	392.3	74.9	29.0
	2000	3706.2	2203.9	1275.9	928.0	896.7	257.9	901.7	106.1	41.5
	2005	4419.9	2465.9	1255.1	1210.8	913.9	281.3	1008.1	133.9	128.6
	2006	4583.6	2509.6	1245.5	1264.2	892.1	299.4	1046.7	137.6	133.8
	2007	4747.5	2550.9	1243.6	1307.3	891.3	298.9	1068.2	138.8	153.7
	2008	4895.6	2598.3	1258.0	1340.3	864.3	288.8	1072.5	142.3	122.1
	2009	5116.4	2681.6	1276.3	1405.2	880.8	303.6	1120.0	148.4	131.0
	2010	5373.0	2797.5	1315.2	1482.3	906.3	310.4	1170.4	156.6	142.1
	2011	5603.2	2908.0	1356.7	1551.3	1075.2	321.8	1212.8	162.9	135.3
	2012	5502.1	2889.6	1314.4	1575.2	957.3	345.7	1264.8	179.0	142.8
	2013	5744.2	2992.4	1327.7	1664.7	972.8	362.6	1327.6	188.5	140.9
	2014	6001.9	3136.3	1403.9	1732.4	1042.5	382.9	1371.7	202.9	136.2
	2015	6211.0	3232.3	1435.7	1796.6	1078.0	386.3	1414.0	211.5	142.5
	2016	6379.5	3301.3	1386.0	1915.3	1063.1	396.1	1476.9	219.3	145.8
	2017	6445.3	3321.7	1321.0	2000.7	1115.8	370.7	1481.4	224.8	129.0
	2018	6457.7	3301.4	1270.2	2031.2	1091.5	368.2	1487.0	236.2	118.5
	2019	6480.4	3282.5	1217.2	2065.3	1060.5	366.2	1480.2	255.6	120.1
	2020	6549.0	3314.4	1179.1	2135.3	1055.4	358.6	1516.3	263.7	120.4
	2021	6690.3	3387.3	1176.1	2211.1	1054.2	371.6	1562.0	273.5	125.9
	2022	6865.9	3459.5	1183.8	2275.7	1067.4	383.8	1605.9	273.3	129.1
	2023	7116.2	3585.3	1189.7	2395.6	1083.8	396.0	1681.2	289.5	134.8
北京	Beijing	19.0	17.9	17.9		17.9				
天津	Tianjin	29.1	4.5	3.4	1.1	3.1	1.1	0.2		0.0
河北	Hebei	114.7	83.7	22.9	60.8	15.5	11.1	47.4		9.7
山西	Shanxi	5.5								
内蒙古	Inner Mongolia	11.2								
辽宁	Liaoning	508.1	423.5	66.7	356.8	50.1	13.9	281.6	50.8	27.0
吉林	Jilin	25.5								
黑龙江	Heilongjiang	77.5								
上海	Shanghai	22.7	12.7	12.7		12.1	0.5	0.0		0.0
江苏	Jiangsu	522.1	142.0	46.9	95.1	34.4	23.4	75.4	3.7	5.1
浙江	Zhejiang	647.9	493.4	331.6	161.8	251.2	83.9	127.2	14.7	16.6
安徽	Anhui	254.0								
福建	Fujian	890.2	787.8	208.0	579.8	217.0	49.2	360.4	139.8	21.6
江西	Jiangxi	296.7								
山东	Shandong	913.9	790.5	209.5	581.0	166.0	46.2	473.8	73.6	30.9
河南	Henan	97.9								
湖北	Hubei	522.8								
湖南	Hunan	285.9								
广东	Guangdong	924.0	478.2	120.9	357.3	179.1	103.3	182.8	5.7	7.2
广西	Guangxi	378.6	222.4	49.2	173.2	42.3	45.9	127.6	0.1	6.5
海南	Hainan	175.2	128.7	100.0	28.7	95.1	17.4	4.9	1.1	10.2
重庆	Chongqing	58.9								
四川	Sichuan	178.9								
贵州	Guizhou	28.2								
云南	Yunnan	70.2								
西藏	Xizang	0.0								
陕西	Shaanxi	18.0								
甘肃	Gansu	1.5								
青海	Qinghai	1.9								
宁夏	Ningxia	17.5								
新疆	Xinjiang	18.4								

注：北京市水产品产量含中农发集团产量。
a) Data of aquatic products of Beijing include that of China National Agricultural Development Group Co., Ltd.

12-15 续表 continued

单位：万吨 (10 000 tons)

年份 Year / 地区 Region	淡水产品 Freshwater Aquatic Products	捕捞 Fishing Products	养殖 Aquacultural Products	鱼类 Fish	虾蟹类 Shrimps, Prawns and Crabs	贝类 Shellfish	其他 Others
1978	105.9	29.6	76.2	99.7	3.8	2.4	
1980	124.0	33.9	90.2	116.3	5.2	2.5	
1985	285.4	47.6	237.8	276.5	5.5	3.4	
1990	531.6	85.6	445.9	504.9	9.5	7.6	9.6
1995	1091.8	151.0	940.8	1018.6	27.3	20.5	25.3
2000	1502.3	193.4	1308.9	1358.4	76.3	40.0	27.7
2005	1954.0	221.0	1733.0	1737.2	140.3	46.3	30.2
2006	2074.0	220.4	1853.6	1822.5	167.8	50.9	32.8
2007	2196.6	225.6	1971.0	1908.5	202.1	50.5	35.5
2008	2297.3	224.8	2072.5	1998.5	210.1	50.1	38.7
2009	2434.9	218.4	2216.5	2109.9	228.8	52.0	44.2
2010	2575.5	228.9	2346.5	2225.6	248.1	53.8	47.9
2011	2695.2	223.2	2471.9	2343.7	248.8	53.9	48.8
2012	2612.5	204.0	2408.5	2235.9	268.7	54.0	54.0
2013	2751.9	204.2	2547.7	2366.5	277.0	52.8	55.5
2014	2865.7	202.5	2663.2	2470.7	288.7	51.4	54.8
2015	2978.7	199.3	2779.3	2571.9	300.2	51.6	54.9
2016	3078.2	200.3	2877.9	2653.8	316.1	52.5	55.8
2017	3123.6	218.3	2905.3	2702.6	320.8	46.7	53.6
2018	3156.2	196.4	2959.8	2691.4	369.7	40.8	54.4
2019	3197.9	184.1	3013.7	2686.4	416.5	39.4	55.5
2020	3234.6	145.8	3088.9	2697.3	442.0	35.8	59.6
2021	3303.1	119.8	3183.3	2732.3	470.7	33.7	66.3
2022	3406.4	116.6	3289.8	2800.3	501.9	32.1	72.0
2023	3530.9	116.9	3414.1	2862.2	544.8	32.5	91.4
北京 Beijing	1.1	0.1	1.0	1.1			
天津 Tianjin	24.6	0.3	24.4	19.6	5.0	0.0	0.0
河北 Hebei	31.0	4.1	26.9	28.0	2.8	0.0	0.2
山西 Shanxi	5.5	0.0	5.5	5.4	0.1	0.0	0.0
内蒙古 Inner Mongolia	11.2	1.0	10.2	10.6	0.2	0.0	0.4
辽宁 Liaoning	84.6	3.4	81.2	75.1	9.1		0.3
吉林 Jilin	25.5	1.9	23.7	24.0	0.7	0.0	0.9
黑龙江 Heilongjiang	77.5	5.1	72.5	74.8	2.1	0.1	0.5
上海 Shanghai	10.0	0.0	10.0	7.5	2.5		0.0
江苏 Jiangsu	380.1	18.0	362.1	267.2	101.4	8.5	2.9
浙江 Zhejiang	154.5	16.4	138.1	116.3	21.1	3.6	13.4
安徽 Anhui	254.0	9.9	244.1	158.9	82.2	5.4	7.5
福建 Fujian	102.4	7.3	95.1	82.9	13.5	4.9	1.1
江西 Jiangxi	296.7	3.2	293.5	253.2	28.2	3.9	11.3
山东 Shandong	123.4	10.5	112.9	102.1	19.5	0.4	1.4
河南 Henan	97.9	11.0	86.9	88.2	7.4	0.6	1.8
湖北 Hubei	522.8	2.2	520.6	363.2	145.7	0.6	13.4
湖南 Hunan	285.9	0.2	285.7	219.7	49.0	1.2	15.9
广东 Guangdong	445.9	7.4	438.4	400.5	36.9	1.0	7.6
广西 Guangxi	156.2	8.0	148.2	145.2	3.1	1.7	6.2
海南 Hainan	46.5	1.3	45.2	44.2	0.8	0.2	1.3
重庆 Chongqing	58.9		58.9	56.1	2.1	0.0	0.7
四川 Sichuan	178.9		178.9	168.0	8.8	0.2	1.9
贵州 Guizhou	28.2	0.4	27.7	27.0	0.4	0.1	0.7
云南 Yunnan	70.2	2.9	67.3	68.7	0.6	0.2	0.7
西藏 Xizang	0.0	0.0	0.0	0.0	0.0		0.0
陕西 Shaanxi	18.0		18.0	16.6	0.4		1.0
甘肃 Gansu	1.5		1.5	1.4	0.0		0.0
青海 Qinghai	1.9	0.4	1.5	1.9	0.0		
宁夏 Ningxia	17.5	0.7	16.8	17.2	0.1		0.2
新疆 Xinjiang	18.4	1.3	17.1	17.6	0.8		0.0

12-16 人均主要农产品产量
Per Capita Output of Major Farm Products

单位：公斤 (kg)

年份 地区	Year Region	粮食 Grain Crops	#谷物 Cereals	棉花 Cotton	油料 Oil-bearing Crops	猪牛羊肉 Pork, Beef and Mutton	水产品 Total Aquatic Products	牛奶 Cow Milk
	1978	319		2.3	5.5	9.1	4.9	
	1980	327		2.8	7.8	12.3	4.6	1.2
	1985	361		3.9	15.0	16.8	6.7	2.4
	1990	393		4.0	14.2	22.1	10.9	3.7
	1995	387	345	4.0	18.7	27.4	20.9	4.8
	2000	366	321	3.5	23.4	37.6	29.4	6.6
	2005	371	328	4.4	23.6	42.0	33.9	21.1
	2006	380	344	5.7	20.1	42.8	35.0	22.5
	2007	383	349	5.8	21.1	40.4	36.0	22.4
	2008	403	367	5.5	22.9	43.0	37.0	22.7
	2009	405	370	4.7	23.6	44.8	38.4	22.5
	2010	418	383	4.3	23.6	46.2	40.2	22.7
	2011	438	402	4.8	23.9	45.5	41.5	23.1
	2012	452	418	4.9	24.3	47.5	40.5	23.4
	2013	462	430	4.6	24.6	48.6	42.0	21.9
	2014	466	434	4.6	24.6	49.9	43.6	23.0
	2015	479	448	4.3	24.6	48.5	44.9	23.0
	2016	476	444	3.8	24.5	46.7	45.8	22.0
	2017	474	441	4.0	24.9	46.8	46.0	21.7
	2018	469	435	4.4	24.5	46.4	45.9	21.9
	2019	472	436	4.2	24.8	38.4	46.0	22.7
	2020	474	437	4.2	25.4	37.4	46.4	24.4
	2021	483	448	4.1	25.6	46.1	47.4	26.1
	2022	486	448	4.2	25.9	48.0	48.6	27.8
	2023	493	455	4.0	27.4	50.2	50.4	29.7
北京	Beijing	22	21	0.0	0.5	1.6	0.8	12.1
天津	Tianjin	188	185	0.1	0.3	15.9	21.4	39.7
河北	Hebei	514	490	1.4	16.0	51.3	15.5	77.2
山西	Shanxi	426	401	0.0	5.2	35.0	1.6	42.4
内蒙古	Inner Mongolia	1650	1489		86.0	109.4	4.7	330.4
辽宁	Liaoning	612	599		30.6	68.7	121.3	32.3
吉林	Jilin	1786	1744		37.7	92.4	10.9	13.2
黑龙江	Heilongjiang	2528	2219		5.4	88.5	25.2	163.5
上海	Shanghai	41	41		0.3	4.4	9.2	12.4
江苏	Jiangsu	446	434	0.1	12.1	23.6	61.3	8.6
浙江	Zhejiang	97	86	0.1	5.4	12.8	98.1	3.2
安徽	Anhui	678	658	0.3	30.9	48.4	41.5	8.8
福建	Fujian	122	99		5.8	33.6	212.7	5.9
江西	Jiangxi	486	465	0.5	32.8	61.6	65.6	1.4
山东	Shandong	558	541	1.2	27.7	46.7	90.1	31.4
河南	Henan	673	651	0.1	71.4	53.9	10.0	24.1
湖北	Hubei	475	448	1.6	67.6	64.2	89.5	1.5
湖南	Hunan	466	443	1.2	44.5	75.8	43.4	1.2
广东	Guangdong	101	92		9.5	24.0	72.9	1.6
广西	Guangxi	277	261	0.0	16.0	58.7	75.2	2.7
海南	Hainan	142	124		7.7	43.7	169.2	0.3
重庆	Chongqing	342	239		24.2	54.2	18.4	1.0
四川	Sichuan	429	347	0.0	52.4	66.4	21.4	8.6
贵州	Guizhou	290	205	0.0	28.7	54.8	7.3	1.0
云南	Yunnan	422	348		14.6	100.9	15.0	15.5
西藏	Xizang	299	295		13.7	85.0	0.1	162.8
陕西	Shaanxi	335	295	0.0	15.3	31.3	4.6	27.6
甘肃	Gansu	514	409	1.7	25.5	57.8	0.6	41.1
青海	Qinghai	196	139		53.9	69.0	3.2	56.7
宁夏	Ningxia	520	474		6.3	52.3	24.0	591.1
新疆	Xinjiang	817	800	197.2	16.7	71.6	7.1	89.8

注：因第七次全国人口普查后历史数据修订，2011—2019年人均主要农产品产量数据相应调整。

a) As the historical data are revised after the Seventh National Population Census, the per capita output of major agricultural products from 2011 to 2019 has been adjusted accordingly.

12−17 国有农场基本情况
Basic Statistics on State Farms

本表为农垦系统数据。
Data in this table are from land reclamation departments.

指 标	Item	2019	2020	2021	2022	2023
农场数 (个)	**Number of Farms (unit)**	**1834**	**1803**	**1799**	**1787**	**1776**
职工人数 (万人)	**Number of Staff and Workers (10 000 persons)**	**214.7**	**247.1**	**232.3**	**228.5**	**221.4**
耕地面积 (千公顷)	**Area of Cultivated Land (1 000 hectares)**	**6480.8**	**6516.6**	**6606.0**	**7038.9**	**7207.5**
农业机械总动力 (亿瓦)	**Total Agricultural Machinery Power (100 million watts)**	**311.9**	**320.9**	**330.8**	**343.0**	**348.1**
农业机械拥有量(万台、万辆)	**Possession of Agricultural Machinery(10 000 units)**					
大中型农用拖拉机	Large and Medium-sized Agricultural Tractors	22.8	23.1	23.8	24.5	25.2
小型及手扶拖拉机	Small and Walking Agricultural Tractors	29.1	28.2	28.1	26.9	25.6
农用排灌动力机械	Machinery for Agricultural Drainage and Irrigation	39.2	30.0	29.2	29.7	27.9
联合收割机	Combine Harvesters	6.5	6.8	7.1	7.5	7.5
农用运输汽车	Trucks for Agricultural Use	7.7				
农用化肥施用量 (万吨)	**Consumption of Chemical Fertilizers (10 000 tons)**	**252.3**	**242.8**	**238.0**	**242.0**	**236.7**
农业总产值 (亿元)	**Gross Agricultural Output Value (100 million yuan)**	**3862.1**	**4230.3**	**4634.8**	**4804.5**	**5000.8**
农作物总播种面积(千公顷)	**Total Sown Area of Farm Crops (1 000 hectares)**	**6789.1**	**6850.8**	**6995.9**	**7161.4**	**7330.3**
粮食作物	Grain Crops	4794.8	4807.8	4990.4	5108.4	5309.1
谷 物	Cereals	3766.1	3748.1	4092.5	3926.7	4097.3
棉 花	Cotton	1006.6	1016.2	1014.8	1032.3	935.6
油 料	Oil-bearing Crops	309.7	306.8	276.5	298.6	320.3
糖 料	Sugar Crops	97.3	95.0	81.7	81.5	78.9
麻 类	Fiber Crops	7.0	7.9	6.0	5.7	4.8
年底实有茶园面积	Area of Tea Plantations (year-end)	31.9	29.8	30.3	30.8	33.6
年底实有桑园面积	Area of Mulberry Plantations (year-end)	1.3	0.8	1.6	1.5	1.4
年底实有果园面积	Area of Orchards (year-end)	404.2	403.3	394.5	388.7	385.5
年底实有橡胶园面积	Area of Rubber Plantations (year-end)	425.4	407.3	401.4	397.9	394.5
主要农产品产量 (万吨)	**Output of Major Farm Products (10 000 tons)**					
粮食作物	Grain	3441.1	3562.7	3876.0	3848.6	3993.9
谷 物	Cereals	3154.2	3241.9	3585.8	3483.9	3652.5
棉 花	Cotton	244.7	261.8	263.3	270.7	244.3
油 料	Oil-bearing Crops	75.7	73.5	68.7	75.3	78.7
糖 料	Sugar Crops	746.5	712.5	613.2	598.5	595.5
麻 类	Fiber Crops	10.2	3.2	2.2	2.5	1.6
茶 叶	Tea	5.3	4.3	4.4	4.5	5.5
水 果	Fruits	784.2	817.0	831.2	825.7	849.3
干 胶	Rubber	28.5	25.6	27.3	28.6	28.0
畜牧业、渔业生产	**Production of Animal Husbandry and Fishery**					
大牲畜年底头数 (万头)	Number of Large Animals (year-end)(10 000 heads)	299.0	309.8	345.0	387.3	466.6
猪年底头数 (万头)	Number of Hogs (10 000 heads)	728.4	881.7	995.9	1111.8	1282.3
羊年底只数 (万只)	Number of Sheep and Goats (10 000 heads)	1118.5	1083.0	1084.7	1117.1	1112.7
#绵 羊	Sheep	916.7	931.1	933.2	976.9	959.3
畜产品产量 (万吨)	**Output of Livestock Products (10 000 tons)**					
猪牛羊肉	Pork, Beef and Mutton	139.0	129.0	159.6	183.4	221.0
#猪 肉	Pork	102.1	92.5	119.6	142.2	177.2
牛 奶	Milk	418.2	435.2	467.0	570.2	656.2
禽 蛋	Poultry Eggs	48.1	48.8	47.7	45.9	47.9
羊 毛	Sheep Wool	3.2	3.1	3.1	2.2	2.2
水产品总产量 (万吨)	**Total Output of Aquatic Products (10 000 tons)**	**161.4**	**176.7**	**177.1**	**180.0**	**182.0**

注：1.本表数据来自农业农村部农垦局。
2.从2020年起“职工人数”指标口径调整为“职工期末人数”；另外“农用运输汽车”取消调查。
3.2023年，农业农村部农垦局对2022年年底实有果园面积进行了修正。

a) The data in this table are from the Bureau of Land Reclamation of the Ministry of Agriculture and Rural Affairs.
b) From 2020, the indicator caliber of "number of employees" will be adjusted to "number of employees at the end of the period"; In addition, the investigation of "agricultural transport vehicles" was cancelled.
c) In 2023, the Bureau of Land Reclamation of the Ministry of Agriculture and Rural Affairs revised the area of orchards at year-end of 2022.

主要统计指标解释

农林牧渔业总产值 指以货币表现的农、林、牧、渔业全部产品和对农林牧渔业生产活动进行的各种支持性服务活动的价值总量，它反映一定时期内农林牧渔业生产总规模和总成果。1993年以前农林牧渔业总产值包括农、林、牧、副、渔五业，从1993年起取消副业，将野生动物的捕猎划入牧业，野生植物采集和农民家庭兼营商品性工业划归农业。从2003年起，执行新的国民经济行业分类标准，农林牧渔业总产值中包括了农、林、牧、渔及农林牧渔服务业产值，2018年以后农林牧渔服务业产值改称农林牧渔专业及辅助性活动产值。农业中取消了家庭兼营商品性工业产值，将野生林产品的采集划归林业。第一、二、三次农业普查以后，根据农业普查结果，对农业、牧业、渔业产值进行了修订。2010年执行《统计用产品分类目录》，对2009年的农业、林业产值做了相应调整。

农林牧渔业总产值采用“产品法”进行计算，通常是按农、林、牧、渔业产品及其副产品的产量分别乘以各自单位产品价格求得；少数生产周期较长，当年没有产品或产品产量不易统计的，则采用间接方法匡算其产值；然后将四业产品产值及农林牧渔专业及辅助性活动产值相加即为农林牧渔业总产值。

粮食产量 指日历年度内生产的全部粮食数量。按收获季节包括夏收粮食、早稻和秋收粮食，按作物品种包括谷物、豆类和薯类。其产量计算方法：谷物按脱粒后的原粮计算，豆类按去豆荚后的干豆计算；薯类(包括甘薯和马铃薯，不包括芋头和木薯)1964年以前按每4公斤鲜薯折1公斤粮食计算，从1964年开始改为按5公斤鲜薯折1公斤粮食计算；城市郊区作为蔬菜的薯类(如马铃薯等)按鲜品计算，并且不作粮食统计。1989年以前全国粮食产量数据主要靠全面报表取得，1989年开始使用抽样调查数据。

棉花产量 指全社会棉花的产量。包括春播棉和夏播棉。产量按皮棉计算。不包括木棉。

油料产量 指全部油料作物的生产量。包括花生、油菜籽、芝麻、向日葵籽、胡麻籽（亚麻籽）和其他油料。不包括大豆、木本油料和野生油料。花生以带壳干花生计算。

水产品产量 指渔业（捕捞和养殖）生产活动的最终有效成果，包括全部海水和淡水鱼类、甲壳类（虾、蟹）、贝类、头足类、藻类和其他类渔业产品的最终产量。水产品产量是通过各级渔业主管部门逐级上报取得数据。1995年及以前，贝类中牡蛎按鲜肉计算；蚶、蛤、蛙按5斤鲜品折1斤计算。1996年以后则统一按鲜品计算。

猪、牛、羊、禽肉产量 指当年出栏并已屠宰、除去头蹄下水后带骨肉(即胴体重)的重量。1996年以前为全面统计并逐级上报数据。1996年第一次农业普查以后，根据普查结果，对畜牧业主要年报数据进行了修正。1999年，国家统计局在部分地区开展了猪、牛、羊、禽等主要畜禽品种的抽样调查，并用抽样数据作为国家定案数据使用。未开展抽样调查的地区，仍使用各级统计部门逐级上报数据。2008年，建立了主要畜禽监测调查制度，猪、牛、羊、禽等主要畜禽数据均以抽样调查数为法定数据。

期初(末)畜禽存栏头(只)数 指报告期初(末)饲养的大牲畜、猪、羊、家禽等畜禽的数量。数据上报方式及数据调整情况同猪、牛、羊、禽肉产量。

农作物播种面积 指日历年度内收获农作物在全部土地（耕地或非耕地）上的播种或移植面积。凡是本年内收获的农作物，无论是本年还是上年播种，都算为播种面积，但不包括本年播种，下年收获的农作物面积。

耕地灌溉面积 指具有一定的水源，地块比较平整，灌溉工程或设备已经配套，在一般年景下能够进行正常灌溉的耕地面积。在一般情况下，耕地灌溉面积应等于灌溉工程或设备已经配套，能够进行正常灌溉的水田和水浇地面积之和。它是反映我国农田水利建设的重要指标。

农用化肥施用量（折纯） 指把氮肥、磷肥、钾肥分别按含氮、含五氧化二磷、含氧化钾的百分比进行折算后的数量。复合肥按其所含主要成分折算。计算公式为：

某种化肥折纯量=该种化肥实际施用量×折纯率（某种化肥有效成分含量的百分比）

农业机械总动力 指全部农业机械动力的额定功率之和。农业机械是指用于种植业、畜牧业、渔业、农产品初加工、农用运输和农田基本建设等活动的机械及设备。

本指标的统计数据来源于农业农村部。

Explanatory Notes on Main Statistical Indicators

Gross Output Value of Agriculture, Forestry, Animal Husbandry and Fishery refers to the total value of products (expressed in monetary terms) of agriculture, forestry, animal husbandry and fishery, and total value of services in support of agriculture, forestry, animal husbandry and fishery activities. It reflects the total scale and results of agricultural production during a given period. Before 1993, the gross output value of agriculture, forestry, animal husbandry and fishery included agriculture, forestry, animal husbandry, sideline and fishery. Since 1993, the subdivision of sideline occupations has been cancelled, and the hunting of wild animals has been classified into animal husbandry, and the gathering of wild plants and commodity industry run by rural household have been included in farming. A new industrial classification of economic activities was introduced in 2003. Under the new classification, the gross output value of agriculture included the value of farming, forestry, animal husbandry, and fishery, and included value of services to agriculture, forestry, animal husbandry and fishery. In 2018, the output value of services to agriculture, forestry, animal husbandry and fishery was renamed the output value of professional and support activities in agriculture, forestry, animal husbandry and fishery, value of industrial output by rural households is not included in agriculture. According to the result of the first, second and third agriculture census, efforts were made to adjust the output value of agriculture, animal husbandry and fishery output. In line with the *Classification of Products for Statistical Purposes* implemented in 2010, relevant revisions were made on the output value of agriculture and forestry in 2009.

Gross output value of agriculture is calculated by product method, and is obtained by multiplying the output of each product or by-product by its price, resulting in the output value of each single item. For a small number of products, annual output of which is not available or difficult to get due to the long production (growing) process involved, the output value is estimated through an indirect approach. The sum of output values of all products of agriculture, forestry, animal husbandry and fishery and professional and support activities in agriculture, forestry, animal husbandry and fishery is then equal to the gross output value of agriculture.

Grain Output refers to the total output of grains produced within a calendar year. It includes summer crops, early rice and autumn crops by harvest seasons; and covers cereals, beans and tubers by type of crops. Output of cereals cover husked grain only. Output of beans refers to dry beans without pods. The output of tubers (sweet potatoes and potatoes, not including taros and cassava) are converted with the ratio of 4:1, i.e. 4 kilograms of fresh tubers were equivalent to 1 kilogram of grain before 1964. Since 1964 the ratio has been changed to 5:1. Tubers consumed as vegetables (such as potatoes) in cities and suburbs are calculated as fresh vegetables and their output is not included in the output of grain. Data on grain production before 1989 were obtained through the comprehensive statistical reporting system. Since 1989, data from sample surveys are used.

Cotton Output refers to cotton production in the whole country including cotton planted in spring and in summer. Output is measured as the weight of ginned cotton. Ceiba is not included.

Output of Oil-bearing Crops refers to the total production of oil-bearing crops of various kinds, including peanuts (dry, in shell), rapeseeds, sesame, sunflower seeds, flax seeds, and other oil-bearing crops. Soybeans, oil-bearing woody plants, and wild oil-bearing crops are not included.

Output of Aquatic Products refers to final output actually yielded from fishing production (fishery and breeding), including all output of marine and freshwater fish, crustaceans (shrimps, crabs), shellfish, cephalopod, seaweed and other fishery products. Data on output of aquatic products are reported by fishery agencies level by level. Before 1995, among the shellfish, oyster was counted as fresh meat; and 5 kilograms of ark shell, clams and frogs were equivalent to 1 kilogram of fresh aquatic products; they have all been counted as fresh aquatic products since 1996.

Output of Pork, Beef, Mutton and Poultry refers to the meat of slaughtered hogs, cattle, sheep and goats with head, feet, and offal taken away. Before 1996, data were obtained through bottom-up comprehensive reporting system. The first agricultural census of China in 1996 revealed some discrepancy between the production of animal products from the annual reports and that from the census. Efforts were made to adjust the output value of animal husbandry to make the figures from the annual reports consistent with the census data. Since 1999, the NBS conducted sample surveys in selected regions for the major animal husbandry products, such as hogs, cattle, sheep and goats and fowls, and the data from sample surveys are used as finalized national data. Production of other regions which are not covered by the sample survey is still reported by statistical agencies level by level. A monitoring and survey program was set up in 2008 on main livestock, and data on the main livestock such as hog, cattle, sheep and poultry from the sample survey became the official data.

Number of Livestock or Poultry in Stock at Beginning/End of Period refers to the total number of large animals, pigs, sheep, fowls, etc. raised at the beginning/end of the reference period. Data reporting system and data adjustment are the same as that in the output of pork, beef, mutton and poultry.

Sown Area of Crops refers to area of all land (cultivated or non-cultivated area) sown or transplanted with crops that are harvested within the calendar year. All crops harvested within the year are counted as sown area, regardless of being sown in this year or the previous year. Crops sown this year but will be harvested in the coming year are excluded.

Irrigated Area of Cultivated Land refers to area of land that are effectively irrigated, i.e. relatively level land, where there are water sources or complete sets of irrigation facilities to lift and move adequate water for irrigation purpose under normal conditions. Under normal situations, irrigated area of cultivated land is the sum of watered fields and irrigated fields where irrigation systems or equipment have been installed for regular irrigation purpose. It is an important indicator to reflect the farmland water conservancy construction in China.

Consumption of Chemical Fertilizers in Agriculture (effective component) refers to the quantity of nitrogen fertilizer, phosphorus fertilizer, and potassium fertilizer converted based on the percentage of nitrogen, phosphorus pentoxide, and potassium oxide. Compound fertilizer is converted in regard to its major components. The formula is:

Volume of effective component of certain chemical fertilizer= actual application amount of certain chemical fertilizer× rate of effective component (effective component of certain chemical fertilizer)

Total Power of Agricultural Machinery refers to the total rated capacity of all agricultural machinery. Agricultural machinery refers to the machines and equipment which are used for activities of farming, animal husbandry, fishery, primary processing of agricultural products, agricultural transport and infrastructure construction of farmland.

Data are mainly from Ministry of Agriculture and Rural Affairs.

13

工　业

Industry

简 要 说 明

一、本篇资料的主要内容

本篇资料反映我国工业经济的基本情况，包括 31 个省、自治区、直辖市的主要工业经济统计数据：

1.全国规模以上工业企业主要经济指标，以及按工业门类、企业规模、登记注册统计类别、工业行业大类和按地区分组的主要经济指标；

2.国有控股、私营、外商投资和港澳台投资工业企业按工业行业大类和按地区分组的主要经济指标；

3.大中型工业企业按工业行业大类和按地区分组的主要经济指标；

4.主要工业产品产量和生产能力等。

二、本篇资料的统计范围

本篇资料中规模以上工业企业的统计范围：1998 年至2006年为全部国有和年主营业务收入500万元及以上的非国有工业法人单位；2007 年至 2010 年为年主营业务收入500万元及以上的工业法人单位；从2011年开始，为年主营业务收入 2000 万元及以上的工业法人单位。

本篇资料中工业行业分类按《国民经济行业分类》（GB/T 4754—2017）标准划分；企业规模划分按《统计上大中小微型企业划分办法（2017）》标准执行。

三、本篇的资料来源和统计调查方法

本篇工业企业统计数据主要根据工业统计年度报表有关资料整理汇总。

四、数据使用注意事项

2017 年以来全国规模以上工业企业主要经济指标数据与上年数据之间存在不可比因素，其主要原因是：（一）根据统计制度，每年定期对规模以上工业企业调查范围进行调整。每年有部分企业达到规模标准纳入调查范围，也有部分企业因规模变小而退出调查范围，还有新建投产企业、破产、注（吊）销企业等变化。（二）加强统计执法，对统计执法检查中发现的不符合规模以上工业统计要求的企业进行了清理，对相关基数依规进行了修正。（三）加强数据质量管理，剔除跨地区、跨行业重复统计数据。

Brief Introduction

I. Main Contents

Data in this chapter reflect the basic conditions of the industrial sector, presenting main industrial economic indicators of 31 provinces, autonomous regions and municipalities:

(1)The main economic indicators of industrial enterprises above designated size nationwide, as well as the main economic indicators grouped by industrial category, enterprise size, registered statistical categories, industrial industry category, and region.

(2) Main economic indicators and efficiency indicators of State-holding industrial enterprises, private industrial enterprises, foreign-funded industrial enterprises and industrial enterprises with funds from Hong Kong, Macao and Taiwan classified by branch of industry and by province.

(3) Main economic indicators and efficiency indicators of large and medium-sized industrial enterprises classified by branch of industry and by province.

(4) Output and production capacity of key industrial products.

II. Scopes of Statistics

The statistical scope of industrial enterprises above designated size in this article includes all state-owned and non-state-owned industrial legal entities with an annual main business income of 5 million yuan or more from 1998 to 2006; Industrial legal entities with an annual main business income of 5 million yuan or more from 2007 to 2010; Starting from 2011, it is an industrial legal entity with an annual main business income of 20 million yuan or more.

Data by branch of industry in this chapter are based on the *National Industrial Classification of all Economic Activities (GB/T 4754-2017)*, and data by size of enterprise are based on the 2017's *Standards of Enterprises by Size.*

III. Sources of Data and Methods of Survey

The data on industrial enterprises in this Chapter are compiled mainly on the basis of annual industrial statistics reporting forms.

IV. Data Usage Notes

Since 2017, data of main indicators of industrial enterprises above designated size nationwide are not comparable with previous years, the reasons are as following: (1) According to the statistical system, the investigation scope of industrial enterprises above designated size should be adjusted regularly every year. Every year, some enterprises meet the scale criteria to be included in the scope of investigation, some enterprises withdraw from the scope of investigation because of the smaller scale, and there are other changes: new enterprises, bankruptcy, annotation (cancellation) enterprises, etc. (2) Strengthening of statistical law enforcement, cleaning up enterprises found in the inspection of statistical law enforcement that do not meet the standard of industrial statistics above designated size, and amending the relevant cardinality in accordance with regulations. (3) Strengthening data quality management and eliminating duplicated statistical data across regions and across industries. According to the latest survey of organizational structure of enterprises carried out by the National Bureau of Statistics, the repeated calculation of enterprise groups (companies) across regions and industries is weighed.

13-1 规模以上工业企业主要指标（2023年）
Main Indicators of Industrial Enterprises above Designated Size (2023)

单位：亿元 (100 million yuan)

项 目	Item	企业单位数（个）Number of Enterprises (unit)	资产总计 Total Assets	营业收入 Business Revenue	利润总额 Total Profits
总 计	**Total**	**493161**	**1720755.8**	**1360317.1**	**82897.0**
按工业门类分	**Grouped by Industries**				
采矿业	Mining	12499	138876.3	62544.1	12770.2
制造业	Manufacturing	460054	1294372.5	1176215.8	63170.8
电力、热力、燃气及水生产和供应业	Production and Supply of Electricity, Heating, Gas and Water	20608	287507.0	121557.3	6956.0
按企业规模分	**Grouped by Size of Enterprises**				
大型企业	Large Enterprises	8216	789559.7	592007.8	40568.7
中型企业	Medium-sized Enterprises	35816	367897.9	290579.2	19127.5
小型企业	Small Enterprises	449129	563298.1	477730.2	23200.8
按登记注册统计类别分	**By Registered Statistical Categories**				
内资企业	**Domestic Invested Enterprises**	**451399**	**1421312.4**	**1091651.0**	**64453.0**
有限责任公司	Limited Liability Corporations	416684	1115230.7	910637.9	47632.9
股份有限公司	Share-holding Corporations Ltd.	22944	290624.7	168957.8	16052.4
非公司企业法人	Non Corporate Legal Entity	2120	11322.6	6040.6	399.8
个人独资企业	Sole Proprietorship Enterprises	8365	3288.4	4926.5	262.9
合伙企业	Partnership Enterprises	1270	802.2	1063.9	103.4
其他内资企业	Other Domestic Invested Enterprises	16	43.8	24.4	1.6
港澳台投资企业	**Enterprises with Investment from Hong Kong, Macao and Taiwan**	**19715**	**137382.0**	**112904.3**	**7357.0**
港澳台投资有限责任公司	Limited Liability Corporations with Investment from Hong Kong, Macao and Taiwan	18612	102377.2	93874.5	5223.3
港澳台投资股份有限公司	Share-holding Corporations Ltd. with Investment from Hong Kong, Macao and Taiwan	816	32400.0	16499.5	1703.7
港澳台投资合伙企业	Partnership Enterprises with Investment from Hong Kong, Macao and Taiwan	176	598.2	556.9	27.6
其他港澳台投资企业	Other Enterprises with Investment from Hong Kong, Macao and Taiwan	111	2006.7	1973.5	402.3
外商投资企业	**Foreign Invested Enterprises**	**21773**	**161754.0**	**155605.7**	**11080.1**
外商投资有限责任公司	Foreign Invested Limited Liability Corporations	20706	125830.8	133280.1	8558.7
外商投资股份有限公司	Foreign Invested Share-holding Corporations Ltd.	721	27847.9	14230.1	1337.6
外商投资合伙企业	Foreign Invested Partnership Enterprises	209	1210.4	1159.6	84.0
其他外商投资企业	Other Foreign Invested Enterprises	137	6864.9	6936.0	1099.8
其他统计类别	**Other Statistical Categories**	**274**	**307.4**	**156.1**	**7.0**

注：1.全国规模以上工业企业统计范围1998年至2006年为全部国有及年主营业务收入在500万元及以上非国有工业企业；2007年至2010年为年主营业务收入在500万元及以上的工业企业；2011年及以后年份为年主营业务收入在2000万元及以上的工业企业(以下相关表同)。
2.2017年以来规模以上工业企业数据与上年数据之间存在不可比因素，原因详见“简要说明四”(以下相关表同)。
3.本表登记注册统计类别按《关于市场主体统计分类的划分规定》(国统字〔2023〕14号)执行。
4.“其他统计类别”分组包括农民专业合作社(联合社)、个体工商户和其他市场主体。

a) Industrial enterprises above designated size covered all state-owned enterprises, and non-state owned enterprises with annual revenue from principal business of over 5 million yuan from 1998 to 2006.The coverage was adjusted to include all industrial enterprise with annual revenue from principal business of over 5 million yuan from 2007 to 2010, and further adjusted to include industrial enterprise with annual revenue from principal business of over 20 million yuan since 2011. The same applies to the relevant following tables.

b) Data of 2017 and of following years are not comparable with the preceeding year. See "Brief Introduction IV" for explanation. The same applies to the relevant following tables.

c) The registered statistical categories of this table is implemented in accordance with the Regulations on the Classification of Market Entity Statistics (Guotongzi [2023] No. 14).

d) The other statistical categories include professional farmers cooperatives, individual businesses and other market entities.

13-2 按行业分规模以上工业企业主要指标（2023年）

单位：亿元

行　　业	Sector	企　业 单位数 (个) Number of Enterprises (unit)	资产总计 Total Assets
总　　计	**National Total**	**493161**	**1720755.8**
煤炭开采和洗选业	Mining and Washing of Coal	5021	77496.4
石油和天然气开采业	Extraction of Petroleum and Natural Gas	164	25966.9
黑色金属矿采选业	Mining and Processing of Ferrous Metal Ores	1537	12806.6
有色金属矿采选业	Mining and Processing of Non-Ferrous Metal Ores	1306	7643.9
非金属矿采选业	Mining and Processing of Non-metal Ores	4078	10895.1
开采专业及辅助性活动	Professional and Support Activities for Mining	382	4043.4
其他采矿业	Mining of Other Ores	11	23.9
农副食品加工业	Processing of Food from Agricultural Products	25581	36630.7
食品制造业	Manufacture of Foods	10075	21639.0
酒、饮料和精制茶制造业	Manufacture of Alcohol, Beverages and Refined Tea	5860	23269.0
烟草制品业	Manufacture of Tobacco	194	10991.7
纺织业	Manufacture of Textile	20858	22906.5
纺织服装、服饰业	Manufacture of Textile, Wearing Apparel and Accessories	13346	10815.3
皮革、毛皮、羽毛及其制品和制鞋业	Manufacture of Leather, Fur, Feather and Related Products and Footwear	8566	6219.7
木材加工和木、竹、藤、棕、草制品业	Processing of Timber, Manufacture of Wood, Bamboo, Rattan, Palm and Straw Products	12887	6583.2
家具制造业	Manufacture of Furniture	7349	7358.6
造纸和纸制品业	Manufacture of Paper and Paper Products	7859	16868.2
印刷和记录媒介复制业	Printing and Reproduction of Recording Media	6696	7379.5
文教、工美、体育和娱乐用品制造业	Manufacture of Articles for Culture, Education, Arts and Crafts, Sport and Entertainment Activities	10505	9166.9
石油、煤炭及其他燃料加工业	Processing of Petroleum, Coal and Other Fuels	2324	42121.7
化学原料和化学制品制造业	Manufacture of Raw Chemical Materials and Chemical Products	25489	107977.7
医药制造业	Manufacture of Medicines	9563	49502.8
化学纤维制造业	Manufacture of Chemical Fibres	2362	11988.2
橡胶和塑料制品业	Manufacture of Rubber and Plastics Products	26495	31744.4
非金属矿物制品业	Manufacture of Non-metallic Mineral Products	49121	84383.5
黑色金属冶炼和压延加工业	Smelting and Pressing of Ferrous Metals	6203	73981.9
有色金属冶炼和压延加工业	Smelting and Pressing of Non-ferrous Metals	10005	52313.3
金属制品业	Manufacture of Metal Products	36000	43617.4
通用设备制造业	Manufacture of General Purpose Machinery	34915	64289.6
专用设备制造业	Manufacture of Special Purpose Machinery	27065	61497.3
汽车制造业	Manufacture of Automobiles	18899	107760.8
铁路、船舶、航空航天和其他运输设备制造业	Manufacture of Railway, Ship, Aerospace and Other Transport Equipments	6164	36368.6
电气机械和器材制造业	Manufacture of Electrical Machinery and Apparatus	34242	123839.6
计算机、通信和其他电子设备制造业	Manufacture of Computers, Communication and Other Electronic Equipment	27776	190720.0
仪器仪表制造业	Manufacture of Measuring Instruments and Machinery	7069	16122.5
其他制造业	Other Manufacture	2173	4503.6
废弃资源综合利用业	Utilization of Waste Resources	3578	6917.2
金属制品、机械和设备修理业	Repair Service of Metal Products, Machinery and Equipment	835	4894.3
电力、热力生产和供应业	Production and Supply of Electric Power and Heat Power	12947	236717.0
燃气生产和供应业	Production and Supply of Gas	3840	19076.6
水的生产和供应业	Production and Supply of Water	3821	31713.4

Main Indicators of Industrial Enterprises above Designated Size by Industrial Sector (2023)

(100 million yuan)

流动资产合计 Current Assets	应收账款 Accounts Receivable	存货 Inventories	#产成品 Finished Goods	负债合计 Total Liabilities
884380.2	**244492.6**	**166200.0**	**62372.9**	**986918.1**
34740.9	4996.1	1452.2	747.1	47118.6
4215.3	748.5	182.5	98.7	13528.5
4191.5	743.6	359.8	204.2	7317.6
2476.2	330.4	347.1	141.7	4499.7
4331.4	680.1	552.5	260.3	5913.4
2137.7	442.3	107.1	21.7	2297.3
8.6	1.1	0.4	0.3	17.6
22712.4	4057.8	6665.9	2804.7	22461.5
11827.7	2076.8	2445.7	1018.2	11316.4
13903.3	1530.1	4644.3	1277.0	10500.8
7668.6	447.7	4301.6	256.9	2258.5
13170.4	3285.3	3826.4	1997.8	13490.0
6996.3	1915.8	1804.6	935.7	5709.7
4283.7	1245.3	1057.7	465.7	3444.8
3828.8	1325.3	984.6	503.0	3860.5
4582.8	1265.6	958.3	405.7	4386.8
8512.0	2152.0	1772.9	705.7	9783.8
4294.7	1273.9	764.4	284.7	3424.1
6290.1	1507.5	2349.6	1247.2	5244.3
19115.6	2465.9	6270.9	1849.8	28188.8
48101.4	9797.3	9546.7	4152.2	58101.5
28344.0	5976.6	5417.0	2507.3	19692.7
5062.6	706.2	1269.4	714.6	7499.0
18706.7	6190.1	3801.2	1794.1	16065.8
48473.9	18607.0	7377.9	3320.1	48452.4
32399.2	4158.0	7854.9	2916.0	46945.2
28945.4	5685.7	7928.2	2129.4	31023.1
28979.8	9844.9	6301.4	2639.8	25730.7
44053.4	14234.8	9925.4	3546.2	35368.2
42741.7	12696.7	10165.8	3720.7	33149.4
67921.1	23293.3	8998.8	4106.3	67914.3
25213.2	6218.3	6226.0	1111.2	22812.2
81907.4	29130.7	12860.2	5893.6	74699.2
118855.1	40570.0	20252.3	6843.6	104362.6
11389.7	3575.3	2402.9	832.3	7420.7
2497.0	565.5	526.8	149.1	2909.6
4065.8	1092.1	972.2	429.3	4368.1
2342.0	631.8	504.6	58.7	2427.1
48365.3	16032.4	2255.7	79.9	143098.4
7100.7	1199.2	436.8	152.9	11292.5
9627.1	1796.1	327.5	49.5	18822.8

13-2 续表

单位：亿元

行　　业	Sector	营业收入 Business Revenue	营业成本 Business Cost
总　　计	**National Total**	**1360317.1**	**1145830.7**
煤炭开采和洗选业	Mining and Washing of Coal	35780.0	22957.0
石油和天然气开采业	Extraction of Petroleum and Natural Gas	11761.8	6314.5
黑色金属矿采选业	Mining and Processing of Ferrous Metal Ores	4829.5	3690.7
有色金属矿采选业	Mining and Processing of Non-Ferrous Metal Ores	3497.1	2207.9
非金属矿采选业	Mining and Processing of Non-metal Ores	3768.7	2639.4
开采专业及辅助性活动	Professional and Support Activities for Mining	2888.3	2678.5
其他采矿业	Mining of Other Ores	18.7	12.9
农副食品加工业	Processing of Food from Agricultural Products	54735.6	50225.9
食品制造业	Manufacture of Foods	21142.5	16520.6
酒、饮料和精制茶制造业	Manufacture of Alcohol, Beverages and Refined Tea	15365.4	9664.0
烟草制品业	Manufacture of Tobacco	13519.3	4059.3
纺织业	Manufacture of Textile	23059.5	20258.4
纺织服装、服饰业	Manufacture of Textile, Wearing Apparel and Accessories	11977.2	10018.3
皮革、毛皮、羽毛及其制品和制鞋业	Manufacture of Leather, Fur, Feather and Related Products and Footwear	8173.0	6951.8
木材加工和木、竹、藤、棕、草制品业	Processing of Timber, Manufacture of Wood, Bamboo, Rattan, Palm and Straw Products	9040.4	7971.2
家具制造业	Manufacture of Furniture	6755.0	5522.1
造纸和纸制品业	Manufacture of Paper and Paper Products	14086.2	12292.4
印刷和记录媒介复制业	Printing and Reproduction of Recording Media	6370.9	5258.1
文教、工美、体育和娱乐用品制造业	Manufacture of Articles for Culture, Education, Arts and Crafts, Sport and Entertainment Activities	12235.5	10502.3
石油、煤炭及其他燃料加工业	Processing of Petroleum, Coal and Other Fuels	62741.9	53398.3
化学原料和化学制品制造业	Manufacture of Raw Chemical Materials and Chemical Products	87344.9	74672.3
医药制造业	Manufacture of Medicines	25009.1	14142.4
化学纤维制造业	Manufacture of Chemical Fibres	11042.8	10163.0
橡胶和塑料制品业	Manufacture of Rubber and Plastics Products	28773.8	23951.4
非金属矿物制品业	Manufacture of Non-metallic Mineral Products	56947.9	47284.6
黑色金属冶炼和压延加工业	Smelting and Pressing of Ferrous Metals	85471.8	80587.1
有色金属冶炼和压延加工业	Smelting and Pressing of Non-ferrous Metals	76411.0	70365.5
金属制品业	Manufacture of Metal Products	46083.7	39959.0
通用设备制造业	Manufacture of General Purpose Machinery	48433.4	38930.6
专用设备制造业	Manufacture of Special Purpose Machinery	37387.9	28744.6
汽车制造业	Manufacture of Automobiles	101678.2	87752.8
铁路、船舶、航空航天和其他运输设备制造业	Manufacture of Railway, Ship, Aerospace and Other Transport Equipments	21364.0	18090.4
电气机械和器材制造业	Manufacture of Electrical Machinery and Apparatus	110663.8	93766.8
计算机、通信和其他电子设备制造业	Manufacture of Computers, Communication and Other Electronic Equipment	152540.3	131787.4
仪器仪表制造业	Manufacture of Measuring Instruments and Machinery	10472.8	7709.4
其他制造业	Other Manufacture	2885.3	2398.9
废弃资源综合利用业	Utilization of Waste Resources	12112.6	11328.9
金属制品、机械和设备修理业	Repair Service of Metal Products, Machinery and Equipment	2390.2	2008.7
电力、热力生产和供应业	Production and Supply of Electric Power and Heat Power	97986.1	88326.8
燃气生产和供应业	Production and Supply of Gas	18789.9	17171.6
水的生产和供应业	Production and Supply of Water	4781.3	3545.2

注：“管理费用”包含“研发费用”(以下相关表同)。

continued

(100 million yuan)

销售费用 Selling Expenses	管理费用 Management Expenses	财务费用 Financial Expenses	利润总额 Total Profits	平均用工人数（万人） Annual Average Employees (10 000 persons)
31601.3	**76300.0**	**9530.3**	**82897.0**	**7734.1**
434.1	2349.9	599.3	7990.6	267.2
36.8	893.4	131.4	2898.3	51.7
50.6	316.1	132.7	583.9	26.2
19.8	301.5	60.0	804.3	25.1
157.7	317.5	73.8	449.4	27.4
5.9	139.6	6.4	44.8	28.9
1.2	3.4	0.1	-1.1	0.1
989.2	1597.4	300.4	1790.8	263.4
1766.1	1229.4	65.5	1737.3	169.3
1182.9	859.5	13.1	3159.0	100.8
164.4	695.0	-89.6	1556.4	18.2
402.8	1277.4	211.2	935.9	257.5
470.3	855.6	45.6	641.7	214.6
186.6	547.8	31.8	491.3	144.1
146.5	364.9	54.1	461.9	95.6
284.0	550.7	38.8	404.4	96.0
374.5	801.2	157.8	550.7	94.5
175.5	554.3	32.1	393.9	77.5
314.2	749.8	56.4	621.0	147.9
275.9	1235.6	371.4	591.4	78.3
1927.0	4814.8	760.0	4893.0	344.2
4281.4	3250.2	51.2	3496.4	207.8
77.0	398.9	119.4	297.4	44.9
800.5	2137.3	164.5	1804.5	288.1
1768.4	3590.0	517.4	3634.0	442.1
484.7	2578.7	471.7	935.2	193.8
315.3	1818.6	381.5	3464.3	162.5
831.8	2839.0	274.7	2141.4	381.6
1632.5	4348.4	183.4	3522.6	430.3
1703.8	3949.9	158.0	3060.8	348.5
1920.1	5912.5	129.6	5413.9	466.9
367.4	1803.7	-0.7	1176.4	155.9
3495.8	6624.6	222.0	6621.4	609.8
3246.9	11612.5	306.5	7599.4	921.3
572.4	1247.9	25.7	1079.3	102.2
64.9	268.2	4.7	169.9	34.7
76.9	283.0	65.4	348.0	25.7
26.7	216.0	19.5	177.3	27.4
79.0	2067.6	3021.3	5601.9	266.9
289.5	447.9	115.1	903.4	37.7
200.8	450.3	247.3	450.8	57.4

a) Management expenses include R&D expenses. The same applies to the relevant tables following.

13-3 规模以上工业企业主要指标
Main Indicators of Industrial Enterprises above Designated Size

单位：亿元 (100 million yuan)

年份 地区	Year Region	企业单位数(个) Number of Enterprises (unit)	资产总计 Total Assets	流动资产合计 Current Assets	应收账款 Accounts Receivable	存货 Inventories	#产成品 Finished Goods	负债合计 Total Liabilities
	1998	165080	108821.9	46600.9	12612.7	15054.0	5975.0	69363.8
	2000	162885	126211.2	54338.2	14789.8	16034.1	6293.2	76743.8
	2005	271835	244784.3	111031.4	26646.2	31379.1	11087.6	141509.8
	2006	301961	291214.5	132310.1	31692.2	36999.3	13141.4	167322.2
	2007	336768	353037.4	163259.6	38690.6	45288.7	16024.4	202913.7
	2008	426113	431305.6	195681.8	43933.8	54108.6	19518.9	248899.4
	2009	434364	493692.9	223038.7	51399.8	56724.8	20495.0	285732.8
	2010	452872	592881.9	279227.3	61441.2	69790.1	23841.1	340396.4
	2011	325609	675796.9	327778.7	70502.0	80583.1	28478.6	392644.6
	2012	343769	768421.2	368200.7	84043.1	88324.7	31919.2	445371.8
	2013	369813	870751.1	413490.9	97402.7	97119.2	34535.8	505694.3
	2014	377888	956777.2	445742.4	107437.0	102874.4	38359.5	547031.4
	2015	383148	1023398.1	469207.3	117246.3	102804.0	39501.2	579310.5
	2016	378599	1085865.9	500852.8	126847.2	106962.7	40492.8	606641.5
	2017	372729	1121909.6	534080.9	135645.1	113305.4	42393.7	628016.3
	2018	374964	1153251.2	565178.3	146083.8	118974.9	43987.7	653871.3
	2019	377815	1205868.9	591231.3	156298.4	119225.7	44060.2	681085.1
	2020	399375	1303499.3	648817.5	167496.2	125903.8	46626.5	735385.9
	2021	441517	1466716.3	751807.2	194094.2	151021.6	55352.3	828485.4
	2022	472009	1601925.7	832270.4	221462.5	163927.3	61149.7	920053.6
	2023	493161	1720755.8	884380.2	244492.6	166200.0	62372.9	986918.1
北京	Beijing	3145	72994.0	30386.3	7083.1	4012.0	1408.7	32590.1
天津	Tianjin	5850	26841.9	13671.1	3893.7	2747.9	949.2	15307.0
河北	Hebei	18114	65216.6	32231.6	8473.0	5641.8	2012.8	41383.1
山西	Shanxi	8126	61369.2	28811.6	6508.9	3071.9	1287.3	41519.0
内蒙古	Inner Mongolia	3797	48562.0	17882.4	3679.0	2615.0	951.1	27764.6
辽宁	Liaoning	9271	47229.6	24561.2	5704.6	5654.2	1749.2	28571.7
吉林	Jilin	3234	20275.3	9480.7	2088.7	1713.6	540.0	11500.0
黑龙江	Heilongjiang	4613	20964.6	10290.7	1996.7	1942.8	633.1	12985.7
上海	Shanghai	9327	58723.8	34087.6	9920.8	6725.7	2043.2	28549.3
江苏	Jiangsu	66571	190299.0	114687.7	39290.8	22338.8	9542.4	104210.7
浙江	Zhejiang	56845	137869.2	77306.7	23111.2	15437.5	6335.3	76755.3
安徽	Anhui	22521	62936.0	33563.1	10800.5	5815.6	2314.6	36168.1
福建	Fujian	21177	54246.5	28582.1	6962.9	5761.1	2353.2	30015.0
江西	Jiangxi	18178	37901.5	20448.6	5970.1	4200.6	1548.0	22437.2
山东	Shandong	39472	130627.9	69215.4	16804.5	14036.0	5581.7	80091.9
河南	Henan	25618	59760.5	30037.1	8893.3	5668.1	1946.1	36406.8
湖北	Hubei	19219	60439.9	27681.3	7491.6	5621.6	2045.1	32674.7
湖南	Hunan	21491	40265.3	19251.8	5796.2	3888.9	1368.1	21286.8
广东	Guangdong	71973	211484.2	126344.5	35063.4	22865.8	8650.8	124245.1
广西	Guangxi	9361	28770.6	13911.4	4260.6	2952.8	1226.3	19000.5
海南	Hainan	715	5110.4	1946.4	481.4	403.0	124.6	3134.9
重庆	Chongqing	7725	29091.6	15568.1	4781.8	2486.4	1020.2	16462.5
四川	Sichuan	18557	74351.9	34100.9	8828.8	6977.3	2258.7	41696.8
贵州	Guizhou	5040	20819.8	9447.5	2114.0	2347.9	511.5	13162.8
云南	Yunnan	5257	29640.7	11554.1	2378.6	3077.6	974.9	16225.2
西藏	Xizang	191	2477.8	525.9	97.8	58.4	19.2	1281.0
陕西	Shaanxi	8066	49576.1	22829.3	5460.6	3707.6	1272.5	27501.0
甘肃	Gansu	2858	17681.1	6428.6	1679.4	1407.8	453.5	10675.9
青海	Qinghai	638	8490.8	3086.6	747.9	354.8	123.2	5260.9
宁夏	Ningxia	1500	13972.0	4577.9	1191.0	836.2	402.3	9364.8
新疆	Xinjiang	4711	32766.2	11882.0	2937.8	1831.5	726.3	18689.7

13-3 续表 continued

单位：亿元 (100 million yuan)

年 份 Year 地 区 Region	营业收入 Business Revenue	营业成本 Business Cost	销售费用 Selling Expenses	管理费用 Management Expenses	财务费用 Financial Expenses	利润总额 Total Profits	平均用工人数(万人) Annual Average Employees (10 000 persons)
1998	64148.9	52797.5	2290.7	4644.7	2415.7	1458.1	6195.8
2000	84151.8	68654.0	2985.8	5414.2	1961.0	4393.5	5559.4
2005	248544.0	209862.5	7209.4	10950.3	2671.0	14802.5	6896.0
2006	313592.5	264696.6	8592.7	12807.2	3375.2	19504.4	7358.4
2007	399717.1	334598.6	10728.1	15943.7	4287.9	27155.2	7875.2
2008	500020.1	423295.8	12893.3	20199.8	6021.8	30562.4	8837.6
2009	542522.4	457510.0	14137.4	22169.7	5898.9	34542.2	8831.2
2010	697744.0	585256.8	17520.3	28873.0	7024.7	53049.7	9544.7
2011	841830.2	708092.0	20259.6	32165.2	8913.5	61396.3	9167.3
2012	929291.5	784541.2	22908.7	35888.1	11295.6	61910.1	9567.3
2013	1038659.5	880679.7	25945.2	39431.9	12008.3	68378.9	9791.5
2014	1107032.5	943369.6	28001.1	41121.0	13482.3	68154.9	9977.2
2015	1109853.0	944857.3	29150.2	43125.3	13494.2	66187.1	9775.0
2016	1158998.5	984668.4	31174.9	45490.7	12650.6	71921.4	9475.6
2017	1133160.8	956120.0	31343.8	46717.8	12832.9	74916.3	8957.9
2018	1057327.3	880806.8	31007.9	48152.5	11856.5	71608.9	8356.4
2019	1067397.2	891095.0	31362.4	54801.7	11371.1	65799.0	7929.1
2020	1083658.4	903752.5	30777.8	58274.7	11687.7	68465.0	7756.1
2021	1314557.3	1095044.2	32672.0	69764.4	11428.3	92933.0	7951.0
2022	1333214.4	1121897.1	30431.7	72256.2	9628.1	84162.5	7764.1
2023	1360317.1	1145830.7	31601.3	76300.0	9530.3	82897.0	7734.1
北 京 Beijing	28950.6	24419.1	1277.2	1826.3	209.7	1684.1	80.6
天 津 Tianjin	24354.4	20813.6	447.2	1195.8	114.7	1501.1	93.8
河 北 Hebei	52787.2	46692.8	919.8	2327.8	526.9	1280.3	259.2
山 西 Shanxi	35862.1	29538.7	450.9	1744.1	591.5	3034.3	197.2
内蒙古 Inner Mongolia	29741.6	23553.2	596.3	1189.1	375.1	3284.3	103.5
辽 宁 Liaoning	37335.1	32039.1	794.4	1601.4	306.7	1635.4	185.3
吉 林 Jilin	14025.4	11933.8	259.6	825.8	124.7	806.7	72.3
黑龙江 Heilongjiang	12711.0	10727.5	252.8	696.2	150.9	416.5	83.5
上 海 Shanghai	45961.3	38038.3	1551.8	3394.2	25.6	2546.2	172.2
江 苏 Jiangsu	171068.5	145263.1	3942.9	10138.9	795.2	9950.7	953.1
浙 江 Zhejiang	111422.3	94640.6	2800.3	7439.1	721.9	6050.9	758.9
安 徽 Anhui	51322.1	44117.9	1068.3	2723.2	298.8	2580.3	291.3
福 建 Fujian	56668.8	48409.7	1255.9	2599.1	274.7	3956.8	364.5
江 西 Jiangxi	42012.4	36889.3	605.8	1722.6	239.5	2375.6	219.2
山 东 Shandong	115672.0	99695.0	2161.0	5524.6	809.8	5874.4	589.6
河 南 Henan	49278.6	43015.6	839.5	2207.6	482.1	2152.7	322.9
湖 北 Hubei	46973.8	39120.8	1075.8	2739.7	364.9	2831.8	279.5
湖 南 Hunan	39814.0	32042.0	1089.7	2866.4	287.9	2377.6	290.4
广 东 Guangdong	185496.9	154245.3	6069.9	13767.3	685.4	11595.2	1308.5
广 西 Guangxi	23495.3	20827.8	355.5	848.4	232.2	822.4	141.6
海 南 Hainan	3539.3	2914.1	117.9	153.1	44.6	189.6	12.4
重 庆 Chongqing	27534.9	23313.1	674.3	1446.6	101.6	1476.8	149.5
四 川 Sichuan	50393.3	40861.7	1313.7	2477.5	421.8	4607.1	304.4
贵 州 Guizhou	10623.9	7971.4	249.4	678.8	165.6	1281.5	80.4
云 南 Yunnan	19734.2	15619.8	364.0	785.8	234.6	1665.6	83.4
西 藏 Xizang	564.0	415.0	11.1	48.3	16.9	51.6	2.9
陕 西 Shaanxi	31186.9	24212.8	524.5	1596.1	258.7	3646.3	159.0
甘 肃 Gansu	11298.6	9606.5	138.6	429.6	147.6	580.1	51.2
青 海 Qinghai	4241.6	3445.4	37.6	171.8	71.6	493.0	16.7
宁 夏 Ningxia	7922.7	6819.6	89.0	307.5	166.8	368.1	32.9
新 疆 Xinjiang	18324.6	14628.4	266.8	827.4	282.8	1780.1	74.5

注：2017年及以前为主营业务收入和主营业务成本，2018年及以后为营业收入和营业成本(以下相关表同)。

a) The revenue and cost indicators were revenue from principal business and cost of principal business in 2017 and before, and are revised to business revenue and business cost since 2018. The same applies to the following tables.

13-4 按行业分国有控股工业企业主要指标（2023年）

单位：亿元

行业	Sector	企业单位数（个）Number of Enterprises (unit)	资产总计 Total Assets
总　计	**National Total**	**28688**	**650249.3**
煤炭开采和洗选业	Mining and Washing of Coal	1014	56730.3
石油和天然气开采业	Extraction of Petroleum and Natural Gas	118	21889.3
黑色金属矿采选业	Mining and Processing of Ferrous Metal Ores	131	8615.4
有色金属矿采选业	Mining and Processing of Non-Ferrous Metal Ores	257	4135.4
非金属矿采选业	Mining and Processing of Non-metal Ores	575	5721.9
开采专业及辅助性活动	Professional and Support Activities for Mining	45	3423.5
农副食品加工业	Processing of Food from Agricultural Products	850	2802.9
食品制造业	Manufacture of Foods	395	2180.2
酒、饮料和精制茶制造业	Manufacture of Alcohol, Beverages and Refined Tea	357	10151.7
烟草制品业	Manufacture of Tobacco	85	10742.9
纺织业	Manufacture of Textile	153	1091.8
纺织服装、服饰业	Manufacture of Textile, Wearing Apparel and Accessories	239	427.7
皮革、毛皮、羽毛及其制品和制鞋业	Manufacture of Leather, Fur, Feather and Related Products and Footwear	23	99.9
木材加工和木、竹、藤、棕、草制品业	Processing of Timber, Manufacture of Wood, Bamboo, Rattan, Palm and Straw Products	82	319.9
家具制造业	Manufacture of Furniture	23	243.8
造纸和纸制品业	Manufacture of Paper and Paper Products	110	1631.1
印刷和记录媒介复制业	Printing and Reproduction of Recording Media	294	1110.1
文教、工美、体育和娱乐用品制造业	Manufacture of Articles for Culture, Education, Arts and Crafts, Sport and Entertainment Activities	67	352.5
石油、煤炭及其他燃料加工业	Processing of Petroleum, Coal and Other Fuels	259	21953.7
化学原料和化学制品制造业	Manufacture of Raw Chemical Materials and Chemical Products	1372	28955.4
医药制造业	Manufacture of Medicines	544	7430.2
化学纤维制造业	Manufacture of Chemical Fibres	77	2275.0
橡胶和塑料制品业	Manufacture of Rubber and Plastics Products	316	2293.3
非金属矿物制品业	Manufacture of Non-metallic Mineral Products	2587	17527.3
黑色金属冶炼和压延加工业	Smelting and Pressing of Ferrous Metals	295	29690.1
有色金属冶炼和压延加工业	Smelting and Pressing of Non-ferrous Metals	619	18614.1
金属制品业	Manufacture of Metal Products	741	6502.4
通用设备制造业	Manufacture of General Purpose Machinery	901	13992.6
专用设备制造业	Manufacture of Special Purpose Machinery	924	11967.1
汽车制造业	Manufacture of Automobiles	936	39269.8
铁路、船舶、航空航天和其他运输设备制造业	Manufacture of Railway, Ship, Aerospace and Other Transport Equipments	686	24847.8
电气机械和器材制造业	Manufacture of Electrical Machinery and Apparatus	776	11176.0
计算机、通信和其他电子设备制造业	Manufacture of Computers, Communication and Other Electronic Equipment	1014	33164.9
仪器仪表制造业	Manufacture of Measuring Instruments and Machinery	286	2736.9
其他制造业	Other Manufacture	78	2587.8
废弃资源综合利用业	Utilization of Waste Resources	256	1150.7
金属制品、机械和设备修理业	Repair Service of Metal Products, Machinery and Equipment	199	3700.0
电力、热力生产和供应业	Production and Supply of Electric Power and Heat Power	7497	201950.3
燃气生产和供应业	Production and Supply of Gas	1104	10002.2
水的生产和供应业	Production and Supply of Water	2400	26779.3

Main Indicators of State-holding Industrial Enterprises by Industrial Sector (2023)

(100 million yuan)

流动资产合计 Current Assets	应收账款 Accounts Receivable	存货 Inventories	#产成品 Finished Goods	负债合计 Total Liabilities
242945.6	**54332.3**	**41561.3**	**10822.6**	**374844.7**
23048.9	3105.9	586.3	249.6	35768.1
3484.3	477.9	142.2	88.1	10051.9
2131.7	341.9	61.4	30.0	4605.8
1133.2	125.6	128.4	46.8	2381.7
2226.7	214.1	287.1	95.3	2834.4
1750.7	249.0	71.8	16.7	1930.5
1690.4	186.1	574.5	261.9	1899.3
1080.3	210.1	195.8	91.4	1109.8
6445.1	430.9	1827.8	378.9	3678.9
7463.5	405.6	4264.2	238.2	2114.9
468.7	65.9	130.8	78.7	565.2
275.7	30.0	44.1	24.0	176.7
58.6	14.4	10.8	7.1	33.0
150.2	27.0	32.9	14.7	194.2
188.0	60.3	12.2	3.3	189.5
739.8	76.8	158.0	47.7	1042.9
651.3	110.6	108.6	38.6	342.1
291.5	20.9	148.3	41.0	192.7
7964.2	875.9	2927.3	647.4	12473.5
9347.4	1324.4	1644.8	711.0	17024.3
3843.9	703.2	730.2	284.6	2590.7
833.3	85.2	218.3	97.4	1331.2
1135.9	268.2	220.5	127.1	1096.5
8676.7	2737.2	1108.2	434.1	9666.2
9381.8	1177.8	2617.5	603.6	17544.0
8599.7	1183.2	2873.7	537.1	10382.0
4130.6	1192.7	934.0	323.6	4111.9
9382.0	2404.1	1915.1	565.4	8727.5
8213.0	2502.6	2137.4	762.4	7668.9
22996.3	6692.5	2597.3	1358.0	23853.4
17394.2	3914.9	4719.9	609.5	16285.2
7519.6	2963.4	1294.1	512.1	7317.5
17459.5	4697.7	3602.7	1116.7	17477.0
1811.5	558.6	290.7	79.4	1404.9
1237.4	239.5	269.8	49.1	1923.3
728.7	192.2	112.3	53.3	728.3
1552.1	339.4	354.6	36.0	1800.1
36140.1	12331.5	1732.6	51.8	120468.0
3430.1	478.9	197.7	71.4	5915.7
7884.3	1316.1	277.7	39.3	15934.4

13-4 续表

单位：亿元

行业	Sector	营业收入 Business Revenue	营业成本 Business Cost
总 计	**National Total**	**384563.9**	**320636.1**
煤炭开采和洗选业	Mining and Washing of Coal	20777.3	12548.4
石油和天然气开采业	Extraction of Petroleum and Natural Gas	9250.5	5359.0
黑色金属矿采选业	Mining and Processing of Ferrous Metal Ores	1867.2	1322.8
有色金属矿采选业	Mining and Processing of Non-Ferrous Metal Ores	1521.3	859.5
非金属矿采选业	Mining and Processing of Non-metal Ores	1020.2	697.4
开采专业及辅助性活动	Professional and Support Activities for Mining	2536.2	2381.2
农副食品加工业	Processing of Food from Agricultural Products	3962.0	3728.1
食品制造业	Manufacture of Foods	1670.8	1379.8
酒、饮料和精制茶制造业	Manufacture of Alcohol, Beverages and Refined Tea	5371.4	2645.5
烟草制品业	Manufacture of Tobacco	13216.2	3849.6
纺织业	Manufacture of Textile	642.7	593.1
纺织服装、服饰业	Manufacture of Textile, Wearing Apparel and Accessories	238.5	174.1
皮革、毛皮、羽毛及其制品和制鞋业	Manufacture of Leather, Fur, Feather and Related Products and Footwear	72.1	57.3
木材加工和木、竹、藤、棕、草制品业	Processing of Timber, Manufacture of Wood, Bamboo, Rattan, Palm and Straw Products	167.4	149.3
家具制造业	Manufacture of Furniture	197.7	162.9
造纸和纸制品业	Manufacture of Paper and Paper Products	778.8	711.0
印刷和记录媒介复制业	Printing and Reproduction of Recording Media	618.9	486.7
文教、工美、体育和娱乐用品制造业	Manufacture of Articles for Culture, Education, Arts and Crafts, Sport and Entertainment Activities	1012.9	955.3
石油、煤炭及其他燃料加工业	Processing of Petroleum, Coal and Other Fuels	37797.9	31146.6
化学原料和化学制品制造业	Manufacture of Raw Chemical Materials and Chemical Products	18930.6	16516.8
医药制造业	Manufacture of Medicines	2821.2	1451.1
化学纤维制造业	Manufacture of Chemical Fibres	1529.9	1395.3
橡胶和塑料制品业	Manufacture of Rubber and Plastics Products	1351.0	1140.5
非金属矿物制品业	Manufacture of Non-metallic Mineral Products	7311.8	6208.5
黑色金属冶炼和压延加工业	Smelting and Pressing of Ferrous Metals	28832.0	27644.8
有色金属冶炼和压延加工业	Smelting and Pressing of Non-ferrous Metals	25891.2	24039.0
金属制品业	Manufacture of Metal Products	4221.7	3772.6
通用设备制造业	Manufacture of General Purpose Machinery	6849.7	5753.5
专用设备制造业	Manufacture of Special Purpose Machinery	5737.6	4762.7
汽车制造业	Manufacture of Automobiles	35102.0	30772.0
铁路、船舶、航空航天和其他运输设备制造业	Manufacture of Railway, Ship, Aerospace and Other Transport Equipments	12448.6	10759.4
电气机械和器材制造业	Manufacture of Electrical Machinery and Apparatus	7636.6	6658.5
计算机、通信和其他电子设备制造业	Manufacture of Computers, Communication and Other Electronic Equipment	16191.4	13471.6
仪器仪表制造业	Manufacture of Measuring Instruments and Machinery	1287.4	1016.1
其他制造业	Other Manufacture	830.4	709.2
废弃资源综合利用业	Utilization of Waste Resources	2283.4	2167.5
金属制品、机械和设备修理业	Repair Service of Metal Products, Machinery and Equipment	1366.5	1177.5
电力、热力生产和供应业	Production and Supply of Electric Power and Heat Power	86672.4	79056.0
燃气生产和供应业	Production and Supply of Gas	10907.2	10171.1
水的生产和供应业	Production and Supply of Water	3635.1	2779.7

continued

(100 million yuan)

销售费用 Selling Expenses	管理费用 Management Expenses	财务费用 Financial Expenses	利润总额 Total Profits	平均用工人数（万人） Annual Average Employees (10 000 persons)
4490.8	**17517.4**	**4458.0**	**23855.9**	**1371.3**
155.6	1683.2	508.2	4987.9	194.1
32.4	853.7	110.0	1563.0	49.7
5.8	139.4	86.8	353.3	10.1
3.5	150.2	30.4	417.7	11.7
18.1	82.9	34.2	140.5	6.0
1.6	111.5	1.8	27.6	24.1
53.7	87.1	27.2	64.7	13.0
93.7	91.3	7.1	158.3	12.1
338.3	302.5	-34.9	1933.9	25.1
150.5	661.6	-88.7	1511.6	14.3
7.9	29.0	12.9	5.7	7.2
3.7	61.5	-1.7	5.5	5.8
1.0	10.0	0.1	4.1	1.2
2.4	10.4	3.6	2.9	1.9
2.6	23.7	-0.2	22.5	0.7
10.8	54.1	12.5	4.4	4.8
10.2	85.2	-6.3	43.8	7.1
10.0	11.8	1.4	44.8	1.3
92.7	638.0	160.0	527.3	39.8
220.8	965.7	251.9	846.1	64.2
552.6	344.7	-1.3	542.7	23.6
11.6	68.0	22.9	39.5	7.1
37.8	100.9	5.1	70.2	11.1
118.5	519.7	73.6	421.3	42.6
106.7	792.8	226.2	74.2	57.1
47.6	542.2	138.6	1270.2	44.9
44.0	292.3	23.6	154.5	25.6
187.6	614.3	-1.1	375.9	39.1
174.9	526.1	47.9	217.9	35.4
698.1	1710.8	-64.7	1691.4	83.0
173.4	1064.3	-28.3	512.6	71.3
207.6	483.7	29.2	246.8	29.9
473.5	1771.2	94.0	333.0	81.0
55.1	143.9	4.2	119.9	9.0
4.0	94.5	-2.5	45.5	7.4
8.7	35.6	9.3	53.8	3.3
8.2	128.7	14.1	97.5	14.2
44.4	1681.7	2496.7	4281.2	229.0
140.5	194.2	60.9	411.9	16.4
180.8	354.3	193.0	232.5	46.3

13-5 国有控股工业企业主要指标
Main Indicators of State-holding Industrial Enterprises

单位：亿元 (100 million yuan)

年份 Year 地区 Region	企业单位数(个) Number of Enterprises (unit)	资产总计 Total Assets	流动资产合计 Current Assets	应收账款 Accounts Receivable	存货 Inventories	#产成品 Finished Goods	负债合计 Total Liabilities
1998	64737	74916.3	29559.0	7769.5	9163.7	3439.6	48144.4
2000	53489	84014.9	32628.8	8396.6	8849.7	3242.0	51239.6
2005	27477	117629.6	42155.3	6842.3	11841.6	3278.1	66653.6
2006	24961	135153.4	46713.1	7129.9	12787.5	3630.9	76012.5
2007	20680	158187.9	54997.5	8536.2	15262.8	4166.6	89372.3
2008	21313	188811.4	65494.0	9660.7	18031.6	5094.7	111374.7
2009	20510	215742.0	74114.0	11705.1	19373.6	5057.3	130098.9
2010	20253	247759.9	90810.2	13054.2	23692.7	6109.7	149432.1
2011	17052	281673.9	106550.4	15432.8	27478.6	7460.2	172289.9
2012	17851	312094.4	115385.6	19061.3	29261.6	8010.9	191350.0
2013	18574	343985.9	124529.4	22513.9	31551.6	8458.4	214230.6
2014	18808	371308.8	131827.3	24270.9	32852.1	9278.6	230132.1
2015	19273	397403.7	138438.2	26553.5	31760.2	9128.1	246147.1
2016	19022	417704.2	147311.8	28354.4	32462.3	9304.8	257235.4
2017	19022	439622.9	160206.5	29239.4	34082.7	9704.9	266097.9
2018	19250	456504.2	166576.0	30722.4	34736.5	9581.6	268477.9
2019	20683	469679.9	165149.7	31388.5	32761.0	8892.8	271603.0
2020	22072	500461.0	177774.4	32849.0	32479.2	8933.5	289137.0
2021	25180	565082.1	212832.8	40194.1	38356.2	10303.4	327576.1
2022	27065	604246.8	228878.4	48596.7	40041.2	10809.9	351497.6
2023	28688	650249.3	242945.6	54332.3	41561.3	10822.6	374844.7
北　京 Beijing	688	51323.1	16076.9	4003.5	1869.1	578.4	21690.4
天　津 Tianjin	520	10458.1	4450.2	995.0	752.9	211.6	5762.6
河　北 Hebei	1181	23837.6	8602.3	2210.9	1439.9	415.0	15225.6
山　西 Shanxi	1515	39070.5	16478.5	3483.2	1170.7	387.3	27135.7
内蒙古 Inner Mongolia	925	23596.0	6865.0	1611.4	953.9	228.2	13685.1
辽　宁 Liaoning	861	20700.2	8323.7	1513.9	1821.3	373.9	12255.7
吉　林 Jilin	436	12394.6	5235.8	943.9	746.4	186.4	6794.5
黑龙江 Heilongjiang	574	13002.5	5743.9	897.4	781.0	198.5	7951.6
上　海 Shanghai	706	26115.7	11759.7	2418.7	2348.9	504.6	13105.3
江　苏 Jiangsu	1710	32412.7	14594.4	4253.9	2681.4	852.1	18077.0
浙　江 Zhejiang	975	19004.2	5907.9	1536.2	1330.7	315.6	10468.6
安　徽 Anhui	1185	21683.8	8281.1	1755.2	1271.9	369.4	11192.9
福　建 Fujian	662	14682.5	4221.8	855.5	907.3	181.4	8383.0
江　西 Jiangxi	888	10257.0	4306.5	1014.3	871.9	173.5	5966.5
山　东 Shandong	2234	44076.6	17192.6	3665.1	2675.5	878.3	28548.9
河　南 Henan	1252	23241.8	9580.8	2188.3	1818.6	520.9	15248.9
湖　北 Hubei	1056	26642.7	10981.2	2188.1	2039.7	514.1	14687.2
湖　南 Hunan	1035	15984.4	6878.9	1934.8	1524.6	315.4	9426.2
广　东 Guangdong	1623	47170.6	16915.0	3668.0	3089.1	816.6	27303.6
广　西 Guangxi	816	13181.6	4715.3	1483.3	868.9	244.7	8738.4
海　南 Hainan	113	2349.6	424.1	101.7	122.2	27.5	1596.9
重　庆 Chongqing	674	12369.7	5621.7	1229.6	791.5	279.2	6959.5
四　川 Sichuan	1674	38648.7	14667.3	2860.8	2890.1	634.0	22716.5
贵　州 Guizhou	796	12897.9	5291.1	965.5	1286.1	166.5	7969.0
云　南 Yunnan	806	18976.4	5675.6	951.4	1674.0	287.2	10152.9
西　藏 Xizang	76	1673.1	288.9	56.5	22.8	8.3	804.5
陕　西 Shaanxi	1223	31487.3	11996.0	2519.6	2051.8	629.3	17538.2
甘　肃 Gansu	775	12575.7	3960.6	916.1	858.8	203.7	7568.3
青　海 Qinghai	224	6058.0	1882.5	423.1	163.7	45.9	3808.4
宁　夏 Ningxia	282	5748.7	1234.9	451.9	149.8	51.0	3799.4
新　疆 Xinjiang	1203	18628.2	4791.6	1235.7	586.7	224.1	10283.9

13-5 续表 continued

单位：亿元 (100 million yuan)

年份 Year / 地区 Region		营业收入 Business Revenue	营业成本 Business Cost	销售费用 Selling Expenses	管理费用 Management Expenses	财务费用 Financial Expenses	利润总额 Total Profits	平均用工人数（万人） Annual Average Employees (10 000 persons)
	1998	33566.1	27092.5	979.3	2961.1	1596.6	525.1	3747.8
	2000	42203.1	33473.6	1178.1	3304.5	1228.8	2408.3	2995.2
	2005	85574.2	69302.4	1869.7	4912.0	1166.7	6519.8	1874.9
	2006	101404.6	81957.8	2081.3	5293.5	1416.8	8485.5	1804.0
	2007	122617.1	98515.1	2487.6	6350.0	1724.2	10795.2	1743.0
	2008	147507.9	122504.2	2753.1	7378.6	2477.6	9063.6	1794.1
	2009	151700.6	124590.5	3042.1	8002.8	2409.0	9287.0	1803.4
	2010	194339.7	158727.4	3739.5	9714.5	2681.3	14737.7	1836.3
	2011	228900.1	187783.8	4255.9	10623.1	3430.9	16457.6	1812.0
	2012	245076.0	202600.4	4794.4	11198.7	4396.4	15176.0	1892.8
	2013	257816.9	213204.7	5201.2	11567.9	4513.2	15917.7	1889.5
	2014	262692.3	217409.7	5552.9	11413.2	5331.7	14508.0	1842.7
	2015	241668.9	199927.3	5245.5	11191.5	5420.7	11416.7	1777.8
	2016	238990.2	196284.8	5507.3	11340.5	4877.6	12324.3	1695.9
	2017	265393.0	216186.1	5802.9	11981.9	5012.5	17215.5	1595.8
	2018	290753.9	236355.9	6077.3	12594.4	4977.8	19284.7	1524.1
	2019	287707.7	235523.0	5814.3	13600.6	4922.5	16067.8	1418.5
	2020	279606.8	229113.5	5386.6	13932.1	4821.0	15346.1	1382.8
	2021	350557.9	286649.2	5061.9	16694.7	4891.8	24435.2	1390.3
	2022	375590.1	311172.5	4288.3	16961.2	4849.0	24399.4	1369.5
	2023	384563.9	320636.1	4490.8	17517.4	4458.0	23855.9	1371.3
北 京	Beijing	17108.7	15132.0	325.1	699.8	233.0	1079.9	34.3
天 津	Tianjin	7428.8	6630.4	45.2	302.4	61.4	198.0	20.6
河 北	Hebei	15545.6	13622.9	135.0	634.4	247.0	393.8	60.8
山 西	Shanxi	16184.3	12401.5	119.2	967.0	417.1	2034.0	103.6
内蒙古	Inner Mongolia	12489.4	9788.7	64.7	467.7	242.7	1216.0	43.4
辽 宁	Liaoning	14655.0	12803.3	100.5	534.1	139.4	574.1	61.7
吉 林	Jilin	8674.3	7416.4	78.3	477.2	45.3	564.6	31.6
黑龙江	Heilongjiang	6802.9	5565.0	56.4	404.5	85.9	238.9	47.1
上 海	Shanghai	16904.9	14452.5	241.6	1005.8	2.0	627.5	32.8
江 苏	Jiangsu	23888.5	20357.4	345.4	998.9	148.8	1289.7	65.3
浙 江	Zhejiang	14182.8	12278.8	126.7	435.6	135.5	667.1	27.0
安 徽	Anhui	14426.6	12389.9	170.1	654.2	105.3	684.3	53.0
福 建	Fujian	9964.7	8770.5	91.6	330.5	131.8	606.1	27.1
江 西	Jiangxi	8355.0	7191.5	91.3	346.3	64.9	352.4	27.7
山 东	Shandong	28417.8	24040.3	358.1	1302.0	308.2	1582.1	105.4
河 南	Henan	14710.3	12655.9	123.2	739.5	261.0	461.4	83.6
湖 北	Hubei	14692.6	12244.1	208.2	793.5	157.4	669.4	54.2
湖 南	Hunan	10665.9	8427.1	145.4	621.0	85.7	558.4	44.6
广 东	Guangdong	35370.7	30519.9	497.1	1477.7	239.7	1626.9	79.9
广 西	Guangxi	9376.8	8201.2	93.8	303.5	106.0	259.9	30.5
海 南	Hainan	1644.6	1372.6	12.8	42.7	21.7	76.8	3.0
重 庆	Chongqing	8000.4	6686.5	240.0	460.4	47.7	272.3	31.1
四 川	Sichuan	18163.4	14272.0	337.0	912.2	241.8	1741.6	75.4
贵 州	Guizhou	6083.4	4300.4	60.0	376.7	107.2	1036.9	33.5
云 南	Yunnan	10370.6	7737.7	98.5	378.7	174.9	933.3	29.7
西 藏	Xizang	314.7	275.6	4.4	29.8	9.3	-20.9	1.8
陕 西	Shaanxi	16222.0	11931.2	133.0	842.1	204.4	2226.2	75.8
甘 肃	Gansu	8308.4	6986.0	63.4	274.3	106.0	480.7	32.0
青 海	Qinghai	2424.8	1872.9	10.4	102.9	56.2	349.4	9.0
宁 夏	Ningxia	3238.5	2641.8	16.6	114.6	87.4	207.4	11.9
新 疆	Xinjiang	9947.5	7670.2	98.2	487.4	183.6	867.9	34.4

13-6 按行业分私营工业企业主要指标（2023年）

单位：亿元

行 业	Sector	企业单位数（个）Number of Enterprises (unit)	资产总计 Total Assets
总 计	**National Total**	**368946**	**492856.1**
煤炭开采和洗选业	Mining and Washing of Coal	3240	9154.0
石油和天然气开采业	Extraction of Petroleum and Natural Gas	21	120.0
黑色金属矿采选业	Mining and Processing of Ferrous Metal Ores	1169	2607.3
有色金属矿采选业	Mining and Processing of Non-Ferrous Metal Ores	789	1644.6
非金属矿采选业	Mining and Processing of Non-metal Ores	2828	3333.6
开采专业及辅助性活动	Professional and Support Activities for Mining	286	380.5
其他采矿业	Mining of Other Ores	8	11.6
农副食品加工业	Processing of Food from Agricultural Products	19942	19057.6
食品制造业	Manufacture of Foods	7141	7834.2
酒、饮料和精制茶制造业	Manufacture of Alcohol, Beverages and Refined Tea	4104	5611.2
烟草制品业	Manufacture of Tobacco	88	160.4
纺织业	Manufacture of Textile	18237	14599.9
纺织服装、服饰业	Manufacture of Textile, Wearing Apparel and Accessories	10735	5593.2
皮革、毛皮、羽毛及其制品和制鞋业	Manufacture of Leather, Fur, Feather and Related Products and Footwear	7357	3463.4
木材加工和木、竹、藤、棕、草制品业	Processing of Timber, Manufacture of Wood, Bamboo, Rattan, Palm and Straw Products	12141	4921.4
家具制造业	Manufacture of Furniture	6280	4295.3
造纸和纸制品业	Manufacture of Paper and Paper Products	6406	5762.5
印刷和记录媒介复制业	Printing and Reproduction of Recording Media	5390	3752.5
文教、工美、体育和娱乐用品制造业	Manufacture of Articles for Culture, Education, Arts and Crafts, Sport and Entertainment Activities	8483	5360.1
石油、煤炭及其他燃料加工业	Processing of Petroleum, Coal and Other Fuels	1601	8724.6
化学原料和化学制品制造业	Manufacture of Raw Chemical Materials and Chemical Products	17734	31976.0
医药制造业	Manufacture of Medicines	6112	16483.7
化学纤维制造业	Manufacture of Chemical Fibres	1893	4444.0
橡胶和塑料制品业	Manufacture of Rubber and Plastics Products	21438	16824.0
非金属矿物制品业	Manufacture of Non-metallic Mineral Products	40059	41046.8
黑色金属冶炼和压延加工业	Smelting and Pressing of Ferrous Metals	5040	25174.0
有色金属冶炼和压延加工业	Smelting and Pressing of Non-ferrous Metals	7820	14584.2
金属制品业	Manufacture of Metal Products	29974	24088.6
通用设备制造业	Manufacture of General Purpose Machinery	27522	27568.5
专用设备制造业	Manufacture of Special Purpose Machinery	20445	25928.2
汽车制造业	Manufacture of Automobiles	12497	21148.7
铁路、船舶、航空航天和其他运输设备制造业	Manufacture of Railway, Ship, Aerospace and Other Transport Equipments	4370	5903.8
电气机械和器材制造业	Manufacture of Electrical Machinery and Apparatus	26207	52996.7
计算机、通信和其他电子设备制造业	Manufacture of Computers, Communication and Other Electronic Equipment	17624	50071.4
仪器仪表制造业	Manufacture of Measuring Instruments and Machinery	4983	7085.8
其他制造业	Other Manufacture	1673	1008.3
废弃资源综合利用业	Utilization of Waste Resources	2623	3730.0
金属制品、机械和设备修理业	Repair Service of Metal Products, Machinery and Equipment	436	543.9
电力、热力生产和供应业	Production and Supply of Electric Power and Heat Power	2467	12302.1
燃气生产和供应业	Production and Supply of Gas	1225	2330.8
水的生产和供应业	Production and Supply of Water	558	1228.8

注：“私营工业企业”包含《关于市场主体统计分类的划分规定》(国统字〔2023〕14号)中的“私营有限责任公司”“私营股份有限公司”“个人独资公司”“合伙企业”。

Main Indicators of Private Enterprises by Industrial Sector (2023)

(100 million yuan)

流动资产合计 Current Assets	应收账款 Accounts Receivable	存货 Inventories	#产成品 Finished Goods	负债合计 Total Liabilities
305916.5	**93273.9**	**64496.5**	**28553.3**	**288903.6**
5481.1	1028.1	589.7	351.4	5481.4
63.3	12.1	1.7	0.4	43.6
1308.9	252.8	209.6	125.2	1793.5
787.7	149.2	131.9	66.6	991.4
1417.6	331.1	182.4	114.3	1929.3
246.8	117.3	23.7	3.5	235.5
3.7	0.9	0.1	0.1	9.0
11825.6	2238.9	3598.4	1537.5	11464.1
4315.1	642.0	1182.5	461.4	4018.9
3159.5	434.9	1242.9	510.4	2863.7
138.8	32.0	24.7	11.5	99.6
8493.7	2250.0	2629.6	1387.4	9343.4
3622.1	974.7	1036.8	530.7	3172.2
2306.6	740.7	644.1	282.4	2080.2
2974.3	1112.9	776.7	405.2	2976.7
2668.4	697.8	617.7	265.6	2540.4
3177.4	903.1	839.5	367.1	3516.4
2134.4	724.4	449.7	167.0	2076.2
3470.6	876.5	1127.5	526.3	3135.2
5355.0	749.7	1522.2	583.5	6887.9
17496.2	4323.0	3418.9	1596.1	16671.8
9476.0	2330.8	1919.9	936.1	6782.1
2303.8	355.2	609.9	376.1	2833.0
10374.7	3653.1	2201.4	1024.0	9373.9
26260.9	12104.9	4248.8	1997.4	25371.1
12993.2	1887.2	3249.3	1593.8	16985.5
9482.8	2179.5	2596.3	1027.0	9533.6
16363.3	5987.3	3502.9	1536.8	14635.8
18753.9	6659.5	4223.6	1699.0	14840.9
18082.8	5767.8	4267.3	1613.9	13716.9
13664.7	5015.2	2469.8	1177.9	13368.8
3967.2	1280.2	828.4	313.2	3331.8
36676.8	13154.3	5943.4	2900.2	31355.7
32800.9	10143.6	6016.9	2257.9	28091.0
5090.1	1659.9	1077.4	407.2	3275.4
621.9	186.6	147.2	65.1	589.2
2164.9	643.7	615.0	269.6	2333.3
334.3	127.9	60.6	12.8	280.5
4573.4	1235.8	177.5	16.2	8658.9
999.5	177.0	68.9	30.0	1480.1
484.8	132.5	21.9	5.6	736.2

a) The private industrial enterprises include private limited liability corporations, private share-holding limited corporations, sole proprietorship companies and partnership enterprises as defined in the Regulations on the Classification of Market Entity Statistics (Guotongzi [2023] No. 14).

13-6 续表

单位：亿元

行　业	Sector	营业收入 Business Revenue	营业成本 Business Cost
总　计	**National Total**	**494375.9**	**418535.6**
煤炭开采和洗选业	Mining and Washing of Coal	9098.1	7027.9
石油和天然气开采业	Extraction of Petroleum and Natural Gas	46.8	30.6
黑色金属矿采选业	Mining and Processing of Ferrous Metal Ores	2013.2	1636.9
有色金属矿采选业	Mining and Processing of Non-Ferrous Metal Ores	1109.1	854.3
非金属矿采选业	Mining and Processing of Non-metal Ores	1943.6	1422.8
开采专业及辅助性活动	Professional and Support Activities for Mining	260.1	225.0
其他采矿业	Mining of Other Ores	12.3	7.3
农副食品加工业	Processing of Food from Agricultural Products	28824.0	26110.9
食品制造业	Manufacture of Foods	8280.8	6725.5
酒、饮料和精制茶制造业	Manufacture of Alcohol, Beverages and Refined Tea	3972.9	2863.7
烟草制品业	Manufacture of Tobacco	214.0	153.0
纺织业	Manufacture of Textile	16489.1	14474.8
纺织服装、服饰业	Manufacture of Textile, Wearing Apparel and Accessories	7450.8	6299.9
皮革、毛皮、羽毛及其制品和制鞋业	Manufacture of Leather, Fur, Feather and Related Products and Footwear	5486.5	4728.0
木材加工和木、竹、藤、棕、草制品业	Processing of Timber, Manufacture of Wood, Bamboo, Rattan, Palm and Straw Products	7963.0	7054.9
家具制造业	Manufacture of Furniture	4495.0	3706.8
造纸和纸制品业	Manufacture of Paper and Paper Products	6903.7	6040.2
印刷和记录媒介复制业	Printing and Reproduction of Recording Media	4027.7	3361.5
文教、工美、体育和娱乐用品制造业	Manufacture of Articles for Culture, Education, Arts and Crafts, Sport and Entertainment Activities	7294.2	6205.2
石油、煤炭及其他燃料加工业	Processing of Petroleum, Coal and Other Fuels	11413.8	10212.6
化学原料和化学制品制造业	Manufacture of Raw Chemical Materials and Chemical Products	30049.9	25456.8
医药制造业	Manufacture of Medicines	9410.3	5914.1
化学纤维制造业	Manufacture of Chemical Fibres	4997.5	4527.7
橡胶和塑料制品业	Manufacture of Rubber and Plastics Products	17903.1	15093.3
非金属矿物制品业	Manufacture of Non-metallic Mineral Products	34600.6	28897.2
黑色金属冶炼和压延加工业	Smelting and Pressing of Ferrous Metals	34375.1	32062.5
有色金属冶炼和压延加工业	Smelting and Pressing of Non-ferrous Metals	30245.4	27943.9
金属制品业	Manufacture of Metal Products	29096.0	25152.0
通用设备制造业	Manufacture of General Purpose Machinery	23321.2	18620.6
专用设备制造业	Manufacture of Special Purpose Machinery	18083.3	13778.1
汽车制造业	Manufacture of Automobiles	18537.6	15725.5
铁路、船舶、航空航天和其他运输设备制造业	Manufacture of Railway, Ship, Aerospace and Other Transport Equipments	5016.1	4160.9
电气机械和器材制造业	Manufacture of Electrical Machinery and Apparatus	52514.1	44018.8
计算机、通信和其他电子设备制造业	Manufacture of Computers, Communication and Other Electronic Equipment	39032.5	31287.3
仪器仪表制造业	Manufacture of Measuring Instruments and Machinery	4739.0	3428.9
其他制造业	Other Manufacture	1307.9	1097.5
废弃资源综合利用业	Utilization of Waste Resources	6827.9	6374.0
金属制品、机械和设备修理业	Repair Service of Metal Products, Machinery and Equipment	422.3	338.9
电力、热力生产和供应业	Production and Supply of Electric Power and Heat Power	3820.0	3109.4
燃气生产和供应业	Production and Supply of Gas	2433.5	2162.1
水的生产和供应业	Production and Supply of Water	343.8	244.2

continued

(100 million yuan)

销售费用 Selling Expenses	管理费用 Management Expenses	财务费用 Financial Expenses	利润总额 Total Profits	平均用工人数(万人) Annual Average Employees (10 000 persons)
13460.5	**31721.6**	**3111.7**	**26744.3**	**3725.1**
212.2	331.3	44.6	1174.3	39.6
0.1	2.0	0.6	8.6	0.3
30.4	106.6	33.2	124.9	10.9
11.1	77.2	13.5	125.7	8.1
103.9	162.0	24.1	176.0	16.0
3.1	20.0	3.2	9.0	3.6
1.2	2.4		0.8	0.1
536.3	973.6	177.7	980.2	162.2
400.8	536.0	52.6	591.4	87.0
237.2	271.8	36.4	414.6	36.1
9.1	25.2	-0.5	23.6	2.8
266.5	918.6	160.0	673.9	184.0
268.9	491.6	37.5	360.7	136.4
113.9	338.5	28.4	263.2	91.6
115.3	295.6	41.4	410.0	84.9
185.3	352.2	29.1	224.3	66.6
167.6	386.8	56.1	274.7	57.2
110.3	317.1	35.0	209.5	48.1
197.7	458.2	43.7	382.3	89.3
103.9	262.2	64.1	43.7	21.1
746.1	1889.7	196.4	1650.2	163.4
1230.6	1160.1	47.8	1088.9	88.4
37.4	194.0	46.9	195.3	22.9
432.9	1276.1	125.0	1020.9	178.8
1272.8	2154.0	316.6	1798.6	299.0
240.4	1023.4	145.2	529.6	84.7
163.8	717.9	128.1	1137.6	74.8
546.5	1781.1	197.6	1301.7	255.8
796.1	2219.7	153.2	1557.4	253.7
836.3	2004.7	101.1	1450.1	195.4
417.9	1378.4	132.2	836.4	168.5
109.1	432.8	28.4	296.6	54.0
1816.5	3376.5	137.5	3147.6	320.5
1292.8	4553.9	181.3	2914.6	296.8
273.2	624.1	19.9	446.3	53.6
39.5	100.0	8.7	63.8	18.0
52.6	173.0	35.5	209.4	15.5
11.2	42.7	2.5	25.0	6.8
17.5	174.2	192.9	436.5	18.1
44.9	82.3	21.0	119.4	6.8
7.6	34.1	13.2	47.6	3.7

13-7 私营工业企业主要指标
Main Indicators of Private Industrial Enterprises

单位：亿元 (100 million yuan)

年份 地区	Year Region	企业单位数(个) Number of Enterprises (unit)	资产总计 Total Assets	流动资产合计 Current Assets	应收账款 Accounts Receivable	存货 Inventories	#产成品 Finished Goods	负债合计 Total Liabilities
	1998	10667	1487.0	776.5	222.3	301.9	148.2	909.4
	2000	22128	3873.8	1910.8	556.9	683.8	333.3	2208.8
	2005	123820	30325.1	16426.0	4333.8	4709.3	2198.3	18038.9
	2006	149736	40514.8	22035.6	5737.7	6198.8	2877.7	23946.8
	2007	177080	53305.0	29412.6	7500.2	8122.1	3762.3	31120.2
	2008	245850	75879.6	40572.4	10375.8	11220.3	5115.4	42825.3
	2009	256031	91175.6	47550.4	11944.2	12276.0	5876.1	50495.5
	2010	273259	116867.8	61798.7	15137.7	15004.2	6601.2	64068.4
	2011	180612	127749.9	69059.5	16244.4	16614.1	7388.3	69744.8
	2012	189289	152548.1	81049.1	19819.7	19166.3	8659.6	82699.3
	2013	208409	187704.4	99272.0	24676.2	23118.9	10101.7	101334.0
	2014	213789	213114.4	108457.8	27805.4	25066.2	11435.3	111130.1
	2015	216506	229006.5	114893.2	30628.4	26063.5	12075.1	118651.5
	2016	214309	239542.7	120053.6	32257.5	27468.5	12364.8	121386.1
	2017	215138	242636.7	127828.0	35237.1	29635.9	12840.8	127610.5
	2018	235424	263450.6	149298.6	41768.4	34157.6	14574.8	148739.5
	2019	243640	282829.6	164720.6	48769.7	37116.5	15814.1	162348.9
	2020	286430	345022.8	205754.1	60158.7	45126.9	19293.7	198275.5
	2021	325752	409303.1	249374.7	72447.7	56354.6	23935.2	236427.1
	2022	349269	446756.6	277687.1	82011.8	61788.0	26965.9	266324.9
	2023	368946	492856.1	305916.5	93273.9	64496.5	28553.3	288903.6
北京	Beijing	1131	4299.0	2710.1	804.7	457.0	171.3	1870.9
天津	Tianjin	3927	6316.1	4007.5	1226.6	885.6	344.6	3595.4
河北	Hebei	14295	21072.4	12695.0	3765.5	2502.0	988.9	13291.2
山西	Shanxi	5398	11195.5	6470.3	1640.2	1236.5	611.6	7928.6
内蒙古	Inner Mongolia	1814	7905.3	3947.3	799.6	697.7	343.3	4736.1
辽宁	Liaoning	6133	9224.3	6288.2	1816.4	1637.0	649.6	5848.2
吉林	Jilin	2075	3470.9	2070.6	530.2	526.0	182.7	2113.9
黑龙江	Heilongjiang	3270	4009.0	2466.2	641.1	691.3	278.4	2474.8
上海	Shanghai	5264	10559.9	7565.6	2607.9	1460.3	611.6	4964.6
江苏	Jiangsu	52177	81989.7	52943.2	18042.5	10962.4	5259.8	45957.9
浙江	Zhejiang	47280	55140.7	35376.8	11506.7	7322.5	3178.0	32929.4
安徽	Anhui	16745	15389.3	9906.6	4000.3	2148.2	992.2	9054.8
福建	Fujian	17235	24825.7	15524.6	3860.5	3165.9	1480.7	14009.5
江西	Jiangxi	14150	12238.1	7338.6	2285.0	1729.1	788.4	7055.7
山东	Shandong	29197	40739.9	25689.6	6733.2	5813.2	2550.7	25894.5
河南	Henan	20380	15136.1	8955.3	2914.9	1964.5	834.0	8473.3
湖北	Hubei	14772	17904.0	8674.7	2850.9	2077.2	934.8	8861.7
湖南	Hunan	17795	14325.8	7082.5	2221.8	1612.6	730.2	6623.6
广东	Guangdong	50821	68973.2	47432.6	13559.8	9243.9	3695.0	42025.7
广西	Guangxi	6780	6940.0	4653.6	1547.5	1132.3	627.2	4985.8
海南	Hainan	347	689.4	494.4	117.6	102.6	30.2	430.8
重庆	Chongqing	6389	12496.8	7087.3	2338.0	1203.2	521.1	7347.6
四川	Sichuan	13296	15204.5	8554.3	2564.0	1923.8	837.3	7883.4
贵州	Guizhou	3281	3452.1	2089.7	613.9	515.6	205.5	2411.8
云南	Yunnan	3747	6251.2	3723.7	854.7	1039.1	537.4	3800.3
西藏	Xizang	69	95.0	56.9	17.9	11.7	7.2	59.9
陕西	Shaanxi	5526	9063.8	5474.8	1495.8	870.7	398.3	4968.5
甘肃	Gansu	1682	2511.1	1364.0	446.1	315.4	147.4	1596.2
青海	Qinghai	248	621.7	391.6	109.2	58.0	29.8	439.0
宁夏	Ningxia	976	4696.2	1860.2	601.6	457.5	278.1	3461.1
新疆	Xinjiang	2746	6119.5	3020.9	760.1	733.9	308.5	3809.0

注：“私营工业企业”2023年包含《关于市场主体统计分类的划分规定》(国统字〔2023〕14号)中的“私营有限责任公司”“私营股份有限公司”“个人独资公司”“合伙企业”。

a) The private industrial enterprises include private limited liability corporations, private share-holding limited corporations, sole proprietorship companies and partnership enterprises as defined in the Regulations on the Classification of Market Entity Statistics (Guotongzi [2023] No. 14) for 2023.

13-7 续表 continued

单位：亿元 (100 million yuan)

年 份 地 区	Year Region	营业收入 Business Revenue	营业成本 Business Cost	销售费用 Selling Expenses	管理费用 Management Expenses	财务费用 Financial Expenses	利润总额 Total Profits	平均用工人数（万人） Annual Average Employees (10 000 persons)
	1998	1846.3	1563.2	74.0	75.2	43.4	67.3	160.8
	2000	4791.5	4122.0	178.4	180.3	72.0	189.7	346.4
	2005	45801.4	39914.5	1185.5	1469.7	465.9	2120.7	1692.1
	2006	64817.7	56316.2	1610.1	1972.0	632.5	3191.1	1971.0
	2007	90277.8	77335.8	2136.1	2734.1	903.3	5053.7	2252.9
	2008	131525.4	112220.3	3076.1	4135.6	1389.4	8302.1	2871.9
	2009	156603.6	134374.6	3539.4	4941.5	1442.0	9677.7	2973.8
	2010	207838.2	177049.5	4573.6	7179.9	1921.4	15102.5	3312.1
	2011	247277.9	210191.5	5083.5	7751.2	2415.9	18155.5	2956.4
	2012	285621.5	243192.1	5976.6	9025.3	2921.5	20191.9	3121.3
	2013	342002.6	293764.8	7161.7	10719.7	3471.6	23327.1	3359.4
	2014	372175.7	322482.8	7956.3	11266.7	3717.7	23550.4	3505.3
	2015	386394.6	334569.2	8618.5	12278.5	3603.0	24249.7	3464.0
	2016	410188.1	355823.8	9202.5	13142.6	3506.2	25494.9	3397.8
	2017	381034.4	329585.7	9217.5	13430.1	3550.8	23043.0	3230.0
	2018	343843.2	293245.3	9260.3	14366.8	3263.4	21762.8	3318.6
	2019	361133.2	307940.3	9929.3	17991.7	3198.0	20650.8	3245.4
	2020	413564.0	351705.6	11356.7	21954.8	3718.9	23800.5	3574.4
	2021	517444.3	439256.1	13194.9	27875.0	3913.1	31774.1	3824.0
	2022	487258.5	416289.6	12224.4	28170.0	3116.9	25945.8	3698.2
	2023	494375.9	418535.6	13460.5	31721.6	3111.7	26744.3	3725.1
北 京	Beijing	1821.6	1347.1	144.9	243.1	6.4	104.2	13.2
天 津	Tianjin	7576.5	6849.6	142.5	385.7	27.7	199.9	36.7
河 北	Hebei	22186.3	19944.9	356.1	900.5	163.5	412.8	126.9
山 西	Shanxi	11123.1	10012.3	233.1	403.2	96.7	280.3	51.6
内蒙古	Inner Mongolia	6030.4	5002.2	119.4	280.6	54.7	505.6	24.4
辽 宁	Liaoning	7768.1	6793.8	181.8	460.5	62.1	238.5	63.7
吉 林	Jilin	2239.6	1887.7	90.6	159.1	37.1	74.0	22.5
黑龙江	Heilongjiang	2996.0	2676.0	84.0	154.3	30.0	27.4	21.7
上 海	Shanghai	8034.6	6418.6	333.4	838.1	31.0	487.9	54.7
江 苏	Jiangsu	77194.7	65296.2	1868.6	5114.6	452.1	4393.1	526.9
浙 江	Zhejiang	49989.3	42191.5	1377.7	3936.3	376.3	2321.0	496.9
安 徽	Anhui	16206.7	13988.8	424.3	964.0	108.1	702.4	133.8
福 建	Fujian	32380.2	27511.1	797.8	1508.8	99.9	2320.2	233.4
江 西	Jiangxi	18500.6	16270.4	299.3	757.2	89.9	1055.1	116.6
山 东	Shandong	45217.1	39126.5	905.3	2310.7	271.5	2125.9	286.7
河 南	Henan	14826.8	12854.5	390.5	741.6	93.3	623.1	134.1
湖 北	Hubei	19202.8	15949.3	507.1	1177.6	127.7	1357.4	145.5
湖 南	Hunan	21191.9	17066.2	718.6	1678.3	161.3	1319.3	183.2
广 东	Guangdong	68727.7	55918.5	2773.1	6516.3	360.8	4273.6	593.2
广 西	Guangxi	7208.8	6502.4	148.8	286.5	59.2	195.1	69.1
海 南	Hainan	544.5	438.1	33.7	36.8	3.6	33.1	4.0
重 庆	Chongqing	13176.4	11010.1	346.0	772.2	60.5	756.8	90.8
四 川	Sichuan	14311.1	11492.2	515.6	829.1	99.9	1172.2	130.5
贵 州	Guizhou	2244.6	1801.3	117.1	166.7	25.8	98.8	27.8
云 南	Yunnan	6227.7	5292.7	157.8	272.1	47.3	436.2	37.8
西 藏	Xizang	51.8	37.3	1.4	3.8	0.4	8.4	0.3
陕 西	Shaanxi	8068.9	6639.1	203.8	429.4	28.5	802.7	47.4
甘 肃	Gansu	1756.2	1556.6	45.8	89.9	24.1	37.8	12.4
青 海	Qinghai	553.8	503.2	14.0	21.2	5.9	11.3	2.5
宁 夏	Ningxia	2847.4	2594.9	48.5	115.4	50.0	45.1	13.2
新 疆	Xinjiang	4170.8	3562.6	79.9	168.2	56.3	325.1	23.9

13-8 按行业分外商投资和港澳台投资工业企业主要指标（2023年）

单位：亿元

行业	Sector	企业单位数（个）Number of Enterprises (unit)	资产总计 Total Assets
总　计	**National Total**	**41488**	**299136.0**
煤炭开采和洗选业	Mining and Washing of Coal	32	3500.8
石油和天然气开采业	Extraction of Petroleum and Natural Gas	10	3420.7
黑色金属矿采选业	Mining and Processing of Ferrous Metal Ores	19	264.6
有色金属矿采选业	Mining and Processing of Non-Ferrous Metal Ores	29	270.4
非金属矿采选业	Mining and Processing of Non-metal Ores	46	161.2
开采专业及辅助性活动	Professional and Support Activities for Mining	6	138.6
农副食品加工业	Processing of Food from Agricultural Products	1247	6873.1
食品制造业	Manufacture of Foods	1094	6330.9
酒、饮料和精制茶制造业	Manufacture of Alcohol, Beverages and Refined Tea	606	3553.1
烟草制品业	Manufacture of Tobacco	5	19.2
纺织业	Manufacture of Textile	1456	3762.7
纺织服装、服饰业	Manufacture of Textile, Wearing Apparel and Accessories	1591	3155.9
皮革、毛皮、羽毛及其制品和制鞋业	Manufacture of Leather, Fur, Feather and Related Products and Footwear	829	1665.3
木材加工和木、竹、藤、棕、草制品业	Processing of Timber, Manufacture of Wood, Bamboo, Rattan, Palm and Straw Products	198	381.9
家具制造业	Manufacture of Furniture	545	1318.1
造纸和纸制品业	Manufacture of Paper and Paper Products	654	6440.0
印刷和记录媒介复制业	Printing and Reproduction of Recording Media	494	1504.4
文教、工美、体育和娱乐用品制造业	Manufacture of Articles for Culture, Education, Arts and Crafts, Sport and Entertainment Activities	1424	2582.9
石油、煤炭及其他燃料加工业	Processing of Petroleum, Coal and Other Fuels	112	2779.7
化学原料和化学制品制造业	Manufacture of Raw Chemical Materials and Chemical Products	2490	20275.1
医药制造业	Manufacture of Medicines	758	11174.0
化学纤维制造业	Manufacture of Chemical Fibres	185	1990.5
橡胶和塑料制品业	Manufacture of Rubber and Plastics Products	2748	7298.6
非金属矿物制品业	Manufacture of Non-metallic Mineral Products	1427	8510.6
黑色金属冶炼和压延加工业	Smelting and Pressing of Ferrous Metals	300	8260.2
有色金属冶炼和压延加工业	Smelting and Pressing of Non-ferrous Metals	453	7266.9
金属制品业	Manufacture of Metal Products	2428	6184.0
通用设备制造业	Manufacture of General Purpose Machinery	3382	14065.8
专用设备制造业	Manufacture of Special Purpose Machinery	2596	12431.1
汽车制造业	Manufacture of Automobiles	3068	42421.9
铁路、船舶、航空航天和其他运输设备制造业	Manufacture of Railway, Ship, Aerospace and Other Transport Equipments	536	3339.0
电气机械和器材制造业	Manufacture of Electrical Machinery and Apparatus	3047	19740.3
计算机、通信和其他电子设备制造业	Manufacture of Computers, Communication and Other Electronic Equipment	4518	60998.8
仪器仪表制造业	Manufacture of Measuring Instruments and Machinery	800	2689.6
其他制造业	Other Manufacture	264	610.9
废弃资源综合利用业	Utilization of Waste Resources	101	327.1
金属制品、机械和设备修理业	Repair Service of Metal Products, Machinery and Equipment	91	677.3
电力、热力生产和供应业	Production and Supply of Electric Power and Heat Power	971	13898.8
燃气生产和供应业	Production and Supply of Gas	604	6016.7
水的生产和供应业	Production and Supply of Water	324	2835.4

注：本表登记注册统计类别按《关于市场主体统计分类的划分规定》(国统字〔2023〕14号)执行。

Main Indicators of Industrial Enterprises with Investment from Hong Kong, Macao, Taiwan and Foreign Funds by Industrial Sector (2023)

(100 million yuan)

流动资产合计 Current Assets	应收账款 Accounts Receivable	存货 Inventories	#产成品 Finished Goods	负债合计 Total Liabilities
176773.5	**53731.9**	**31348.6**	**11508.2**	**157683.1**
1181.8	69.5	24.6	13.0	2166.2
360.0	239.8	36.1	9.4	3327.8
117.8	32.8	16.7	6.2	133.6
93.8	4.2	11.2	3.1	149.5
69.1	11.8	9.5	4.8	88.7
70.3	36.5	3.1	0.2	69.5
4508.5	719.5	1289.7	508.4	4073.6
3795.4	820.2	541.9	247.7	3190.4
2020.5	460.3	465.1	147.4	1583.2
11.6	3.6	3.2	1.1	8.7
2292.7	580.1	588.2	265.0	1697.6
2014.8	592.7	447.4	209.4	1571.9
1230.3	340.9	240.3	99.2	891.6
212.3	56.0	63.2	29.5	179.7
886.3	237.6	163.4	71.2	702.3
3260.9	862.3	503.1	176.6	3410.8
913.8	237.8	115.4	43.3	494.4
1896.6	453.2	827.4	557.6	1429.4
1089.1	244.4	448.0	86.8	1616.6
9675.1	2299.7	1777.3	784.8	9320.8
6920.0	1373.0	1416.5	698.3	4038.2
911.2	122.1	263.1	138.8	1267.7
4359.9	1431.0	860.9	376.2	2876.2
4548.1	997.8	588.0	274.8	3421.8
3897.8	408.8	921.1	210.8	5150.6
3959.9	641.7	995.4	189.6	3977.4
4164.8	1400.8	862.9	339.8	2904.4
10356.8	3188.5	2529.9	805.3	7175.4
8765.4	2426.4	1807.3	595.7	5450.1
28693.5	10258.1	3579.7	1498.9	27192.0
2385.1	542.0	433.1	108.2	1797.0
13274.6	4526.8	2083.7	768.0	10703.3
39362.9	15312.4	6232.9	1947.3	31168.7
2015.0	603.9	517.1	168.8	1123.9
462.6	103.7	73.0	24.6	246.3
160.6	23.7	16.0	9.7	142.2
426.2	141.1	134.8	17.3	369.9
3437.5	1270.7	286.5	14.9	7771.7
2058.6	396.8	142.2	43.3	3240.2
912.5	259.8	29.7	13.4	1560.2

a) The registered statistical categories of this table is implemented in accordance with the Regulations on the Classification of Market Entity Statistics (Guotongzi [2023] No. 14).

13–8 续表

单位：亿元

行　　业	Sector	营业收入 Business Revenue	营业成本 Business Cost
总　　计	**National Total**	**268510.0**	**226023.4**
煤炭开采和洗选业	Mining and Washing of Coal	1140.6	707.9
石油和天然气开采业	Extraction of Petroleum and Natural Gas	2320.5	853.5
黑色金属矿采选业	Mining and Processing of Ferrous Metal Ores	194.3	160.2
有色金属矿采选业	Mining and Processing of Non-Ferrous Metal Ores	92.4	52.4
非金属矿采选业	Mining and Processing of Non-metal Ores	62.9	39.6
开采专业及辅助性活动	Professional and Support Activities for Mining	36.4	28.0
农副食品加工业	Processing of Food from Agricultural Products	9774.7	9134.2
食品制造业	Manufacture of Foods	6243.3	4510.7
酒、饮料和精制茶制造业	Manufacture of Alcohol, Beverages and Refined Tea	3787.8	2695.5
烟草制品业	Manufacture of Tobacco	13.9	10.8
纺织业	Manufacture of Textile	3085.7	2640.0
纺织服装、服饰业	Manufacture of Textile, Wearing Apparel and Accessories	2927.0	2440.0
皮革、毛皮、羽毛及其制品和制鞋业	Manufacture of Leather, Fur, Feather and Related Products and Footwear	1960.9	1621.7
木材加工和木、竹、藤、棕、草制品业	Processing of Timber, Manufacture of Wood, Bamboo, Rattan, Palm and Straw Products	239.6	205.4
家具制造业	Manufacture of Furniture	1022.9	830.6
造纸和纸制品业	Manufacture of Paper and Paper Products	4147.2	3551.7
印刷和记录媒介复制业	Printing and Reproduction of Recording Media	953.7	766.1
文教、工美、体育和娱乐用品制造业	Manufacture of Articles for Culture, Education, Arts and Crafts, Sport and Entertainment Activities	2920.1	2491.9
石油、煤炭及其他燃料加工业	Processing of Petroleum, Coal and Other Fuels	4467.9	3831.3
化学原料和化学制品制造业	Manufacture of Raw Chemical Materials and Chemical Products	17274.2	14600.0
医药制造业	Manufacture of Medicines	6440.7	3543.4
化学纤维制造业	Manufacture of Chemical Fibres	2097.5	1903.2
橡胶和塑料制品业	Manufacture of Rubber and Plastics Products	5674.4	4516.7
非金属矿物制品业	Manufacture of Non-metallic Mineral Products	4542.4	3602.7
黑色金属冶炼和压延加工业	Smelting and Pressing of Ferrous Metals	10043.2	9619.4
有色金属冶炼和压延加工业	Smelting and Pressing of Non-ferrous Metals	6790.2	6012.4
金属制品业	Manufacture of Metal Products	5804.8	4906.1
通用设备制造业	Manufacture of General Purpose Machinery	12450.5	9876.9
专用设备制造业	Manufacture of Special Purpose Machinery	7808.9	5892.1
汽车制造业	Manufacture of Automobiles	50206.4	42614.8
铁路、船舶、航空航天和其他运输设备制造业	Manufacture of Railway, Ship, Aerospace and Other Transport Equipments	2404.3	1964.7
电气机械和器材制造业	Manufacture of Electrical Machinery and Apparatus	18145.3	15207.8
计算机、通信和其他电子设备制造业	Manufacture of Computers, Communication and Other Electronic Equipment	59621.0	53828.2
仪器仪表制造业	Manufacture of Measuring Instruments and Machinery	2538.7	1902.8
其他制造业	Other Manufacture	470.3	371.0
废弃资源综合利用业	Utilization of Waste Resources	283.7	252.9
金属制品、机械和设备修理业	Repair Service of Metal Products, Machinery and Equipment	713.1	597.9
电力、热力生产和供应业	Production and Supply of Electric Power and Heat Power	4780.8	3927.8
燃气生产和供应业	Production and Supply of Gas	4478.3	3973.1
水的生产和供应业	Production and Supply of Water	549.6	338.4

continued

(100 million yuan)

销售费用 Selling Expenses	管理费用 Management Expenses	财务费用 Financial Expenses	利润总额 Total Profits	平均用工人数(万人) Annual Average Employees (10 000 persons)
8002.7	**14982.9**	**556.1**	**18437.0**	**1435.0**
15.1	72.6	18.3	432.1	7.7
3.8	33.2	22.6	1261.0	1.6
1.4	8.4	2.4	21.6	0.7
0.4	9.0	1.2	27.3	0.7
3.5	5.7	0.7	12.4	0.5
0.3	2.6	0.6	4.4	0.2
179.3	212.4	28.8	424.7	29.9
844.6	370.2	-9.3	582.3	37.0
466.2	147.9	-4.5	433.1	21.7
0.2	1.7	0.1	1.0	0.2
71.6	205.8	15.2	154.9	36.6
123.3	214.9	2.7	181.2	50.3
60.6	145.8	2.0	181.0	39.4
9.4	16.8	2.4	6.8	2.8
39.5	87.9	4.1	94.7	14.5
147.7	242.4	55.8	195.8	18.9
33.9	94.0	-2.0	71.0	13.3
71.6	223.7	6.6	128.6	46.2
21.3	89.8	20.6	-18.5	3.7
669.1	884.4	82.8	975.1	46.1
1188.6	850.9	-6.0	920.6	36.9
19.9	74.9	22.1	81.0	7.5
223.2	481.2	7.3	464.2	64.5
130.7	293.7	5.7	540.5	33.1
41.9	252.1	42.5	-4.0	19.8
33.7	189.5	48.4	407.5	14.3
139.2	395.0	13.0	369.8	53.2
445.3	1008.2	1.8	1121.6	83.4
412.9	778.0	-10.9	833.6	61.6
938.6	2660.9	-33.1	3274.8	152.0
49.0	167.6	-4.5	238.8	17.3
505.6	1158.2	18.2	1260.2	117.7
834.9	2933.7	-36.6	2332.1	342.3
115.5	237.1	-2.4	303.5	21.2
15.8	49.0	-2.5	34.4	6.3
2.4	13.6	2.9	16.3	1.0
5.2	46.1	3.6	60.4	4.3
5.1	125.5	192.4	574.8	11.0
116.9	151.2	19.6	300.6	12.1
15.4	47.2	23.6	136.2	3.9

13–9 外商投资和港澳台投资工业企业主要指标
Main Indicators of Industrial Enterprises with Investment from Hong Kong, Macao, Taiwan and Foreign Funds

单位：亿元 (100 million yuan)

年份 Year / 地区 Region		企业单位数(个) Number of Enterprises (unit)	资产总计 Total Assets	流动资产合计 Current Assets	应收账款 Accounts Receivable	存货 Inventories	#产成品 Finished Goods	负债合计 Total Liabilities
	1998	26442	21327.0	9971.9	3071.2	3233.0	1151.1	12481.6
	2000	28445	25714.1	12849.5	4045.9	4078.4	1417.6	14658.9
	2005	56387	64308.5	35304.0	11422.0	10093.4	3258.3	36459.4
	2006	60872	77108.7	42674.9	13655.9	12167.9	3954.6	43398.6
	2007	67456	96367.0	53781.5	16785.3	15126.2	4862.9	55168.2
	2008	77847	112145.0	60340.2	17123.6	16801.2	5782.2	62831.0
	2009	75376	124477.6	69082.1	20860.9	16469.7	5634.6	69928.8
	2010	74045	148552.3	84328.6	24176.3	20623.8	6588.1	82038.8
	2011	57216	161987.7	95334.6	27132.0	23075.2	7973.7	92130.8
	2012	56908	172320.3	100289.9	29850.6	23510.8	8199.6	97414.1
	2013	57368	188661.4	108770.2	32460.7	24399.1	8389.9	106197.3
	2014	55172	198162.1	113723.6	34419.4	24840.3	9023.0	109924.4
	2015	52758	201302.7	114481.0	35955.1	23622.2	8933.8	109679.8
	2016	49554	212744.4	122079.2	39362.5	23936.7	8829.7	114911.3
	2017	47458	215998.1	128098.4	41604.2	25712.3	9696.0	116678.1
	2018	44624	219165.4	131316.6	42574.5	26854.3	10306.4	118559.0
	2019	43588	228743.9	135590.5	43145.4	25934.3	9880.4	123011.5
	2020	43026	248426.9	149146.4	45399.7	27714.3	10616.4	133713.8
	2021	43455	279178.6	168071.2	51032.7	33303.5	12194.6	148646.1
	2022	43260	292953.6	177252.1	54436.2	34046.1	12516.0	156831.6
	2023	41488	299136.0	176773.5	53731.9	31348.6	11508.2	157683.1
北京	Beijing	580	14984.9	10403.2	2762.6	1427.2	623.4	8627.2
天津	Tianjin	1037	8963.4	4323.3	1433.4	934.2	339.0	5015.8
河北	Hebei	592	8867.1	4700.1	1095.9	648.5	246.6	5382.2
山西	Shanxi	140	2502.8	1366.0	393.5	121.9	30.4	1372.9
内蒙古	Inner Mongolia	124	3409.3	1080.2	262.9	172.9	58.8	1604.9
辽宁	Liaoning	1048	9359.6	5414.4	1339.8	1261.9	408.5	5114.2
吉林	Jilin	230	3545.8	2334.7	429.7	332.2	85.1	2352.9
黑龙江	Heilongjiang	159	1500.6	869.5	185.6	177.7	47.4	954.4
上海	Shanghai	2814	22109.9	14154.7	4449.0	2900.5	919.2	11272.9
江苏	Jiangsu	8824	51445.4	32236.7	11105.7	6074.9	2237.0	24604.4
浙江	Zhejiang	3898	24964.5	14891.1	4014.2	2498.2	1040.1	11916.2
安徽	Anhui	861	7562.5	4229.5	1497.9	679.3	219.0	4221.7
福建	Fujian	2551	11406.6	7000.4	1787.5	1375.1	550.3	5722.2
江西	Jiangxi	709	5755.8	3164.6	757.8	505.5	165.8	3050.0
山东	Shandong	2769	21307.9	11500.2	2936.3	1983.7	772.3	11263.4
河南	Henan	491	6604.3	3694.8	1572.9	484.7	113.9	3802.6
湖北	Hubei	800	7191.9	3944.0	1062.2	638.2	217.8	4235.2
湖南	Hunan	491	4428.9	1895.5	531.0	260.6	93.8	2015.7
广东	Guangdong	11217	59859.6	36944.3	11681.7	6839.2	2650.7	32562.0
广西	Guangxi	414	3956.5	2501.3	1046.8	319.7	139.2	2815.3
海南	Hainan	69	1271.6	483.2	152.9	119.2	27.1	617.7
重庆	Chongqing	397	4781.9	2932.4	1086.6	466.0	177.9	2727.6
四川	Sichuan	573	5855.9	3430.2	1468.4	517.6	187.7	3443.6
贵州	Guizhou	106	908.3	367.1	124.1	69.1	14.0	443.0
云南	Yunnan	171	1214.0	612.8	129.6	79.9	30.1	543.6
西藏	Xizang	5	32.9	24.3	7.1	1.2	0.2	16.9
陕西	Shaanxi	234	2297.6	1132.0	237.8	353.0	75.5	717.9
甘肃	Gansu	57	519.2	221.9	75.8	30.2	9.2	285.2
青海	Qinghai	16	135.7	38.4	16.2	0.8	0.2	64.0
宁夏	Ningxia	40	1330.3	396.9	45.8	37.6	11.1	685.1
新疆	Xinjiang	71	1061.6	485.8	41.6	38.2	16.9	232.6

注：本表登记注册统计类别2023年按《关于市场主体统计分类的划分规定》(国统字〔2023〕14号)执行。

a)The registered statistical categories of this table is implemented in accordance with the Regulations on the Classification of Market Entity Statistics (Guotongzi [2023] No. 14) for 2023.

13-9 续表 continued

单位：亿元 (100 million yuan)

年份 地区	Year Region	营业收入 Business Revenue	营业成本 Business Cost	销售费用 Selling Expenses	管理费用 Management Expenses	财务费用 Financial Expenses	利润总额 Total Profits	平均用工人数（万人） Annual Average Employees (10 000 persons)
	1998	15604.6	13023.6	763.9	964.3	477.7	418.6	775.2
	2000	22545.7	18583.3	1044.8	1236.8	393.6	1282.5	853.0
	2005	78564.5	67863.0	2818.6	3084.6	468.0	4140.8	1899.6
	2006	98936.1	84903.3	3369.7	3733.3	684.4	5384.1	2118.1
	2007	125498.0	106981.4	4206.0	4655.2	808.3	7527.4	2353.0
	2008	146613.6	125931.6	4858.7	5830.8	1033.8	8242.6	2579.4
	2009	150263.1	127247.8	4965.8	5991.9	1145.4	10107.1	2450.4
	2010	188729.4	159273.1	5948.1	7544.3	1137.0	15019.6	2645.7
	2011	216304.3	183931.7	6859.4	8281.0	1164.5	15494.2	2574.1
	2012	221948.8	189558.5	7104.4	8982.6	1709.7	13965.9	2573.8
	2013	242964.2	207255.7	7832.2	9878.3	1443.0	15802.6	2536.1
	2014	252630.1	215004.2	8123.6	10365.1	1562.8	16577.3	2472.4
	2015	245697.6	208266.5	8006.4	10541.3	1703.9	15905.8	2355.4
	2016	250393.0	211127.9	8253.7	10794.7	1536.3	17597.5	2182.4
	2017	247619.7	208242.5	8328.5	10999.2	1417.1	18412.4	2052.3
	2018	236958.7	198405.2	8141.6	11270.4	1289.3	16943.5	1856.9
	2019	234409.8	195620.0	8103.6	12236.7	1149.1	16483.0	1748.3
	2020	243188.6	202461.0	8146.0	12518.0	1276.8	18167.4	1672.0
	2021	282716.2	235850.3	8763.9	14440.4	896.9	22795.8	1668.0
	2022	277775.5	234458.5	8140.3	14741.8	422.3	19700.9	1580.6
	2023	268510.0	226023.4	8002.7	14982.9	556.1	18437.0	1435.0
北 京	Beijing	10593.5	8536.1	715.5	579.2	-32.8	731.7	22.9
天 津	Tianjin	9119.1	7150.4	196.8	424.0	25.3	1244.8	30.1
河 北	Hebei	7059.7	6211.0	168.3	351.5	31.5	249.9	26.8
山 西	Shanxi	1771.5	1513.9	17.6	43.9	11.4	179.7	8.1
内蒙古	Inner Mongolia	2192.6	1778.8	118.0	82.5	-2.7	300.2	5.3
辽 宁	Liaoning	9213.9	7551.3	363.5	376.7	16.0	741.3	35.0
吉 林	Jilin	4836.7	4054.7	26.6	248.0	6.9	402.7	10.0
黑龙江	Heilongjiang	1083.4	902.2	64.3	47.4	10.2	55.2	4.4
上 海	Shanghai	22504.5	18715.6	847.8	1578.0	-16.2	1282.8	78.7
江 苏	Jiangsu	47958.5	40262.0	1341.2	2975.8	96.4	3316.2	266.5
浙 江	Zhejiang	18378.9	15267.1	638.1	1349.8	40.6	1407.6	106.2
安 徽	Anhui	6579.1	5688.0	186.6	316.4	13.6	351.2	29.2
福 建	Fujian	11324.2	9572.1	304.6	585.0	35.2	855.4	85.2
江 西	Jiangxi	5094.1	4506.7	76.0	213.9	20.9	397.6	26.0
山 东	Shandong	16438.7	14002.3	411.4	792.0	76.8	1327.5	88.1
河 南	Henan	7333.1	6658.2	111.1	163.5	33.3	405.2	29.9
湖 北	Hubei	7619.8	6478.2	171.8	349.3	25.1	371.0	31.8
湖 南	Hunan	2563.6	2059.1	77.4	209.8	22.7	142.1	25.1
广 东	Guangdong	56027.3	46899.7	1678.8	3532.9	67.0	3512.0	436.7
广 西	Guangxi	3132.7	2817.4	61.0	129.3	14.6	115.6	14.9
海 南	Hainan	1185.2	998.3	21.4	33.0	12.1	41.9	1.8
重 庆	Chongqing	6140.5	5525.8	133.7	227.6	0.7	192.0	22.1
四 川	Sichuan	6618.2	5972.5	103.9	173.7	24.0	357.7	31.3
贵 州	Guizhou	346.4	248.2	18.7	20.1	8.0	40.4	3.5
云 南	Yunnan	592.7	455.9	32.0	31.7	4.2	73.5	3.8
西 藏	Xizang	7.8	4.5	1.0	0.6	0.0	1.8	0.1
陕 西	Shaanxi	1592.1	1254.1	83.8	102.6	2.1	148.5	6.6
甘 肃	Gansu	322.2	273.4	10.9	8.3	4.1	25.1	1.1
青 海	Qinghai	30.0	24.5	1.2	2.6	0.6	1.0	0.1
宁 夏	Ningxia	397.5	308.0	4.6	19.1	8.9	56.9	2.1
新 疆	Xinjiang	452.7	333.6	15.1	14.9	-4.7	108.5	1.8

13-10 按行业分大中型工业企业主要指标（2023年）

单位：亿元

行业	Sector	企业单位数 (个) Number of Enterprises (unit)	资产总计 Total Assets
总计	**National Total**	**44032**	**1157457.7**
煤炭开采和洗选业	Mining and Washing of Coal	1523	67328.8
石油和天然气开采业	Extraction of Petroleum and Natural Gas	52	23440.3
黑色金属矿采选业	Mining and Processing of Ferrous Metal Ores	182	9935.0
有色金属矿采选业	Mining and Processing of Non-Ferrous Metal Ores	207	4876.4
非金属矿采选业	Mining and Processing of Non-metal Ores	94	2156.4
开采专业及辅助性活动	Professional and Support Activities for Mining	65	3545.6
农副食品加工业	Processing of Food from Agricultural Products	1580	14707.1
食品制造业	Manufacture of Foods	1190	13493.3
酒、饮料和精制茶制造业	Manufacture of Alcohol, Beverages and Refined Tea	522	16369.4
烟草制品业	Manufacture of Tobacco	90	10639.5
纺织业	Manufacture of Textile	1669	10884.9
纺织服装、服饰业	Manufacture of Textile, Wearing Apparel and Accessories	1365	5621.9
皮革、毛皮、羽毛及其制品和制鞋业	Manufacture of Leather, Fur, Feather and Related Products and Footwear	850	3130.4
木材加工和木、竹、藤、棕、草制品业	Processing of Timber, Manufacture of Wood, Bamboo, Rattan, Palm and Straw Products	197	1160.2
家具制造业	Manufacture of Furniture	534	3907.4
造纸和纸制品业	Manufacture of Paper and Paper Products	534	11668.7
印刷和记录媒介复制业	Printing and Reproduction of Recording Media	441	2866.6
文教、工美、体育和娱乐用品制造业	Manufacture of Articles for Culture, Education, Arts and Crafts, Sport and Entertainment Activities	842	4332.2
石油、煤炭及其他燃料加工业	Processing of Petroleum, Coal and Other Fuels	456	37876.8
化学原料和化学制品制造业	Manufacture of Raw Chemical Materials and Chemical Products	2232	72224.6
医药制造业	Manufacture of Medicines	1534	35467.9
化学纤维制造业	Manufacture of Chemical Fibres	258	9338.6
橡胶和塑料制品业	Manufacture of Rubber and Plastics Products	1503	15221.9
非金属矿物制品业	Manufacture of Non-metallic Mineral Products	2245	33627.7
黑色金属冶炼和压延加工业	Smelting and Pressing of Ferrous Metals	784	67039.8
有色金属冶炼和压延加工业	Smelting and Pressing of Non-ferrous Metals	961	38805.3
金属制品业	Manufacture of Metal Products	1978	18865.5
通用设备制造业	Manufacture of General Purpose Machinery	2419	37328.7
专用设备制造业	Manufacture of Special Purpose Machinery	2073	33927.8
汽车制造业	Manufacture of Automobiles	3022	86905.5
铁路、船舶、航空航天和其他运输设备制造业	Manufacture of Railway, Ship, Aerospace and Other Transport Equipments	904	29775.8
电气机械和器材制造业	Manufacture of Electrical Machinery and Apparatus	3784	90813.2
计算机、通信和其他电子设备制造业	Manufacture of Computers, Communication and Other Electronic Equipment	5105	157315.8
仪器仪表制造业	Manufacture of Measuring Instruments and Machinery	699	8976.1
其他制造业	Other Manufacture	192	3459.4
废弃资源综合利用业	Utilization of Waste Resources	95	1688.5
金属制品、机械和设备修理业	Repair Service of Metal Products, Machinery and Equipment	183	4155.5
电力、热力生产和供应业	Production and Supply of Electric Power and Heat Power	1090	143370.6
燃气生产和供应业	Production and Supply of Gas	205	7047.3
水的生产和供应业	Production and Supply of Water	373	14161.5

注：从2017年开始，工业企业年报规模划分按《统计上大中小微型企业划分办法(2017)》执行。大中型工业企业为从业人员300人及以上并且主营业务收入在2000万元及以上的工业企业。

Main Indicators of Large and Medium-sized Industrial Enterprises by Industrial Sector (2023)

(100 million yuan)

流动资产合计 Current Assets	应收账款 Accounts Receivable	存货 Inventories	#产成品 Finished Goods	负债合计 Total Liabilities
569299.3	**138677.1**	**104239.5**	**36321.4**	**646808.5**
28922.2	3725.0	835.0	357.9	40331.0
3498.7	664.3	173.1	93.5	12415.6
2850.1	473.4	135.6	73.5	5312.7
1348.8	130.5	153.3	47.2	2682.4
812.0	82.7	58.9	33.5	894.8
1823.8	283.7	86.9	17.1	1989.0
8783.4	1231.9	2250.4	1037.0	8776.6
7293.0	1269.8	1159.5	470.4	6877.7
10182.1	790.2	3318.7	729.2	6709.9
7421.9	388.8	4261.6	234.5	2149.1
5879.1	1171.5	1588.2	842.4	5783.0
3629.1	952.5	874.5	504.9	2604.7
2178.6	585.7	458.5	207.5	1539.4
590.6	146.9	137.0	60.6	601.1
2390.5	590.2	369.9	147.9	2238.1
5345.3	1101.9	955.5	372.1	6473.6
1649.2	451.2	270.0	98.5	1159.8
3096.5	595.7	1354.1	801.2	2362.8
16528.3	1775.0	5612.8	1517.0	25235.0
27896.2	4468.9	5401.1	2191.8	39524.0
20121.7	3904.3	3554.9	1646.6	12646.5
3561.0	397.3	849.1	460.0	5825.1
8139.2	2288.0	1526.1	763.7	6949.1
16515.8	3436.6	2551.9	1235.2	16127.4
27739.9	3101.4	6535.7	2269.5	42144.9
19649.8	3424.5	5618.6	1135.2	21650.5
11837.5	3310.1	2662.7	1083.4	10337.3
25197.7	7334.1	5573.6	1912.2	20122.9
23297.1	6436.8	5792.0	2179.7	17580.1
54651.5	17900.2	6563.6	3028.5	54743.9
20778.1	4802.3	5189.7	804.7	18895.7
58356.7	19100.9	8571.9	4109.1	55250.5
96162.8	32207.4	15728.1	5100.6	86452.3
6224.2	1799.8	1283.1	461.0	3989.8
1831.0	357.7	356.9	83.8	2305.6
947.1	241.4	259.9	95.6	953.5
1836.2	434.3	412.8	39.5	2002.1
24514.3	6377.2	1466.0	26.0	80473.7
2102.3	341.9	141.7	29.0	4145.6
3715.9	601.3	146.8	20.6	8552.0

a) Since 2017, sizes in industrial enterprises annual reporting forms are based on the 2017's Standards of Enterprises by Size. Large and medium-sized enterprises refer to enterprises with engaged persons over 300 and revenue from principal business above 20 million yuan.

13-10 续表

单位：亿元

行 业	Sector	营业收入 Business Revenue	营业成本 Business Cost
总 计	**National Total**	**882586.9**	**738222.4**
煤炭开采和洗选业	Mining and Washing of Coal	25990.3	15314.8
石油和天然气开采业	Extraction of Petroleum and Natural Gas	10995.5	5886.4
黑色金属矿采选业	Mining and Processing of Ferrous Metal Ores	2779.6	1975.0
有色金属矿采选业	Mining and Processing of Non-Ferrous Metal Ores	1984.2	1106.1
非金属矿采选业	Mining and Processing of Non-metal Ores	661.4	438.4
开采专业及辅助性活动	Professional and Support Activities for Mining	2586.3	2419.0
农副食品加工业	Processing of Food from Agricultural Products	19574.2	17960.2
食品制造业	Manufacture of Foods	13361.8	10215.3
酒、饮料和精制茶制造业	Manufacture of Alcohol, Beverages and Refined Tea	10516.2	5911.7
烟草制品业	Manufacture of Tobacco	13318.9	3928.8
纺织业	Manufacture of Textile	9927.4	8632.8
纺织服装、服饰业	Manufacture of Textile, Wearing Apparel and Accessories	5323.4	4279.9
皮革、毛皮、羽毛及其制品和制鞋业	Manufacture of Leather, Fur, Feather and Related Products and Footwear	3657.5	3039.2
木材加工和木、竹、藤、棕、草制品业	Processing of Timber, Manufacture of Wood, Bamboo, Rattan, Palm and Straw Products	931.0	776.5
家具制造业	Manufacture of Furniture	3131.6	2490.4
造纸和纸制品业	Manufacture of Paper and Paper Products	7716.5	6688.9
印刷和记录媒介复制业	Printing and Reproduction of Recording Media	2272.8	1829.9
文教、工美、体育和娱乐用品制造业	Manufacture of Articles for Culture, Education, Arts and Crafts, Sport and Entertainment Activities	5394.2	4599.7
石油、煤炭及其他燃料加工业	Processing of Petroleum, Coal and Other Fuels	57299.7	48442.7
化学原料和化学制品制造业	Manufacture of Raw Chemical Materials and Chemical Products	52179.7	44752.8
医药制造业	Manufacture of Medicines	16894.3	8679.6
化学纤维制造业	Manufacture of Chemical Fibres	8334.4	7727.0
橡胶和塑料制品业	Manufacture of Rubber and Plastics Products	11593.0	9460.7
非金属矿物制品业	Manufacture of Non-metallic Mineral Products	19203.8	15636.9
黑色金属冶炼和压延加工业	Smelting and Pressing of Ferrous Metals	73388.1	69304.7
有色金属冶炼和压延加工业	Smelting and Pressing of Non-ferrous Metals	44868.0	40644.3
金属制品业	Manufacture of Metal Products	17471.5	15012.6
通用设备制造业	Manufacture of General Purpose Machinery	25156.7	20165.4
专用设备制造业	Manufacture of Special Purpose Machinery	18794.1	14355.6
汽车制造业	Manufacture of Automobiles	83296.4	71956.8
铁路、船舶、航空航天和其他运输设备制造业	Manufacture of Railway, Ship, Aerospace and Other Transport Equipments	16694.5	14217.5
电气机械和器材制造业	Manufacture of Electrical Machinery and Apparatus	77712.8	65501.2
计算机、通信和其他电子设备制造业	Manufacture of Computers, Communication and Other Electronic Equipment	125396.1	108574.9
仪器仪表制造业	Manufacture of Measuring Instruments and Machinery	5349.7	3961.2
其他制造业	Other Manufacture	1615.5	1338.2
废弃资源综合利用业	Utilization of Waste Resources	2259.2	2074.3
金属制品、机械和设备修理业	Repair Service of Metal Products, Machinery and Equipment	1782.2	1498.2
电力、热力生产和供应业	Production and Supply of Electric Power and Heat Power	76742.6	71969.9
燃气生产和供应业	Production and Supply of Gas	4230.0	3759.0
水的生产和供应业	Production and Supply of Water	2202.0	1696.1

continued

(100 million yuan)

销售费用 Selling Expenses	管理费用 Management Expenses	财务费用 Financial Expenses	利润总额 Total Profits	平 均 用工人数 (万人) Annual Average Employees (10 000 persons)
20284.3	**46584.6**	**4878.7**	**59696.2**	**4318.3**
212.7	2024.5	541.9	6796.2	241.8
31.7	844.4	123.8	2657.5	50.5
16.6	207.8	110.1	485.7	16.0
6.2	174.7	37.0	599.0	14.9
21.3	57.9	9.1	109.4	5.9
3.0	119.3	2.2	29.9	26.0
375.0	521.1	108.4	835.4	109.8
1378.0	664.2	10.1	1255.8	90.8
980.3	556.1	-24.8	2728.1	60.8
157.0	662.6	-87.2	1528.1	16.6
191.8	538.5	88.4	510.0	116.0
299.4	391.5	10.3	388.7	97.2
93.9	264.7	6.1	299.1	72.7
30.6	54.9	6.5	60.8	10.3
154.6	258.5	12.4	268.7	41.5
215.3	424.3	107.9	364.8	39.1
65.8	206.5	2.3	200.0	26.5
141.6	318.2	15.9	335.9	62.0
207.0	1056.5	334.9	554.5	66.0
989.0	2581.4	531.0	3164.3	170.4
3351.3	2236.2	-18.2	2857.9	129.3
48.4	267.7	93.9	199.4	29.8
346.8	805.1	39.8	1021.8	107.6
414.8	1171.7	112.2	1894.8	144.5
375.2	2247.7	420.7	750.9	158.1
176.5	1127.6	287.6	2745.5	98.5
311.3	1036.1	73.2	1100.7	137.9
898.5	2039.1	26.5	2178.0	184.8
929.5	1776.3	23.7	1868.7	153.2
1576.6	4503.4	-7.4	4792.6	314.8
264.9	1349.8	-33.0	954.0	108.3
2726.9	4239.3	37.2	5278.7	369.8
2639.4	9146.9	191.4	6779.4	708.8
298.7	564.2	-0.2	628.7	49.0
29.1	167.3	-3.8	106.0	18.6
7.7	61.5	15.1	105.2	5.9
15.7	164.7	16.0	144.2	21.0
34.4	1388.0	1515.2	2755.1	201.7
126.1	159.6	46.2	219.4	14.7
142.2	204.8	96.8	143.3	27.3

13-11 大中型工业企业主要指标

Main Indicators of Large and Medium-sized Industrial Enterprises

单位：亿元 (100 million yuan)

年份 Year / 地区 Region		企业单位数(个) Number of Enterprises (unit)	资产总计 Total Assets	流动资产合计 Current Assets	应收账款 Accounts Receivable	存货 Inventories	#产成品 Finished Goods	负债合计 Total Liabilities
	1998	23408	76095.8	30719.9	8127.9	9481.4	3481.6	47836.5
	2000	21724	87309.8	35282.9	9238.3	9918.3	3614.9	52083.9
	2005	29774	178816.9	77623.7	17018.8	21879.5	7026.0	102529.7
	2006	32930	212410.4	92049.1	20206.2	25788.9	8341.8	121016.5
	2007	36506	257015.6	113694.5	24735.1	31839.6	10245.5	147160.5
	2008	40392	305328.8	132898.8	26679.9	36825.6	12227.3	177416.3
	2009	41290	351080.5	152364.1	32208.4	38724.5	12448.6	206323.4
	2010	46648	427451.6	195899.0	39220.0	49505.4	15465.7	249848.2
	2011	61347	505941.0	240505.3	47882.1	59552.6	19535.3	299089.3
	2012	63314	564360.4	264650.9	55981.3	63992.4	21459.0	333780.3
	2013	65514	626731.5	288989.1	63297.6	68989.0	22891.6	370709.3
	2014	65301	679436.7	311020.9	69442.3	72064.1	24966.9	397804.3
	2015	63703	718838.6	325464.4	75915.9	70757.8	25130.0	416708.3
	2016	62312	767059.8	350655.7	83000.2	73915.5	26096.8	438442.2
	2017	58854	797736.2	372934.5	87351.7	77583.6	27525.5	451584.5
	2018	51073	820351.3	391077.9	92501.9	81197.0	28317.7	463975.9
	2019	48184	840682.6	396805.1	95719.6	78716.2	27422.3	469324.8
	2020	47045	897779.2	428512.6	98509.7	81448.0	28358.8	498299.2
	2021	47427	995876.2	491227.2	111670.9	97426.0	33431.6	550415.9
	2022	45061	1075852.4	537931.8	128251.4	103811.1	36230.7	602627.4
	2023	44032	1157457.7	569299.3	138677.1	104239.5	36321.4	646808.5
北京	Beijing	534	63974.9	24516.3	5200.0	2901.0	1002.3	28401.2
天津	Tianjin	567	17554.8	7920.8	2202.0	1607.4	549.9	9930.5
河北	Hebei	1331	42553.9	19878.1	4097.5	3527.4	1204.8	26313.2
山西	Shanxi	1215	46644.2	21742.9	4126.4	1901.7	698.3	30989.1
内蒙古	Inner Mongolia	658	33934.8	11776.9	1509.7	1885.3	609.3	18255.5
辽宁	Liaoning	1126	34183.9	16884.4	3311.0	3963.6	1099.4	20462.7
吉林	Jilin	416	14668.7	6616.8	1197.8	1059.0	300.6	7847.8
黑龙江	Heilongjiang	406	14463.9	6762.7	915.9	1039.3	278.1	8546.8
上海	Shanghai	1074	43126.2	22819.5	6035.8	4522.2	1215.6	21027.4
江苏	Jiangsu	5387	117920.6	68547.2	22058.0	13118.4	5461.7	62931.7
浙江	Zhejiang	4578	83489.0	44303.2	12107.0	8583.7	3516.8	44025.7
安徽	Anhui	1587	40557.1	20675.8	6022.6	3323.5	1191.6	22567.1
福建	Fujian	2011	36303.8	18550.5	4032.1	3479.4	1328.3	20106.6
江西	Jiangxi	1140	20879.1	11014.5	2962.4	2235.3	668.9	12030.8
山东	Shandong	3425	87249.8	43733.9	8710.4	8940.2	3357.5	51637.0
河南	Henan	1571	40247.4	19646.5	5412.1	3685.6	1168.8	24592.8
湖北	Hubei	1517	38753.3	17587.7	4072.5	3579.7	1071.9	20899.6
湖南	Hunan	1456	23869.9	11935.9	3527.4	2428.1	688.1	13025.3
广东	Guangdong	7781	151540.8	87533.2	22307.9	14924.8	5635.5	87439.7
广西	Guangxi	784	17183.0	7903.9	2022.7	1726.5	606.2	11281.2
海南	Hainan	83	3246.5	1083.5	241.0	257.9	67.3	2024.7
重庆	Chongqing	927	19426.7	10782.8	3137.1	1614.2	655.6	11096.9
四川	Sichuan	1605	47235.5	22057.7	5284.5	4594.6	1399.9	25922.5
贵州	Guizhou	490	13052.5	6030.1	1077.8	1687.2	257.8	7723.7
云南	Yunnan	490	19451.9	6942.6	1148.1	2168.0	528.8	9916.5
西藏	Xizang	13	1474.5	223.1	16.1	25.5	1.6	606.5
陕西	Shaanxi	821	37612.9	16546.8	3419.9	2728.5	863.6	20241.9
甘肃	Gansu	272	11166.8	3524.9	586.0	917.5	209.9	6389.5
青海	Qinghai	86	5467.9	1967.8	271.3	252.8	74.9	3242.3
宁夏	Ningxia	215	9407.6	2869.3	496.0	560.8	267.4	6363.1
新疆	Xinjiang	466	20815.5	6920.3	1168.1	1000.8	341.2	10969.4

13-11 续表 continued

单位：亿元 (100 million yuan)

年份 Year / 地区 Region		营业收入 Business Revenue	营业成本 Business Cost	销售费用 Selling Expenses	管理费用 Management Expenses	财务费用 Financial Expenses	利润总额 Total Profits	平均用工人数（万人）Annual Average Employees (10 000 persons)
	1998	37130.6	29949.7	1275.5	2987.3	1591.8	881.9	3412.8
	2000	50120.3	39768.9	1717.4	3502.6	1313.0	3183.3	2880.6
	2005	169237.9	141880.2	4949.2	7511.1	1878.3	11011.8	3798.9
	2006	210877.1	176592.3	5884.6	8722.2	2368.0	14363.2	4116.5
	2007	264015.8	219425.5	7367.6	10826.3	2946.3	19626.7	4403.1
	2008	318812.5	268933.2	8488.7	13207.5	4060.6	19929.2	4759.7
	2009	335751.1	280972.6	9342.3	14443.7	3927.4	22265.7	4831.3
	2010	439013.7	365216.5	11654.8	18908.2	4677.8	34977.2	5390.2
	2011	554055.8	463087.0	13900.0	22320.7	6091.1	41743.8	6177.8
	2012	603021.4	506604.0	15840.2	24431.7	7784.7	40570.2	6394.5
	2013	665283.3	561075.8	17589.4	26147.9	7998.1	44007.2	6457.2
	2014	705027.1	595485.7	19091.3	27390.3	9013.3	44152.9	6435.2
	2015	693927.8	585638.3	19566.0	28370.0	8869.5	41564.9	6245.2
	2016	722934.4	607782.7	20902.9	29838.9	8206.7	46192.8	6051.6
	2017	721344.7	600748.0	21141.3	30767.4	8380.8	51361.5	5664.9
	2018	702409.1	578893.4	21412.4	31955.5	7622.0	50370.7	5138.2
	2019	691560.6	570797.2	21105.2	35067.1	6993.1	46023.0	4732.8
	2020	695028.4	573691.0	20402.5	36719.4	7144.6	47198.6	4582.6
	2021	839140.1	690060.8	20914.4	43273.9	6476.3	66715.0	4611.1
	2022	865859.5	723033.5	19393.1	44364.7	4939.3	59996.0	4360.3
	2023	882586.9	738222.4	20284.3	46584.6	4878.7	59696.2	4318.3
北 京	Beijing	23760.7	20298.3	1016.6	1286.1	189.8	1410.2	54.8
天 津	Tianjin	15077.3	12498.1	269.7	739.0	59.2	1236.3	54.9
河 北	Hebei	35625.4	31638.3	582.7	1497.6	294.7	865.6	149.3
山 西	Shanxi	24949.0	19783.6	235.7	1346.1	419.4	2662.0	151.5
内蒙古	Inner Mongolia	21940.2	17405.5	456.8	865.4	221.8	2467.0	79.0
辽 宁	Liaoning	27717.4	23700.8	537.7	1015.0	202.4	1264.4	119.6
吉 林	Jilin	10830.7	9207.5	154.8	626.0	60.8	711.6	49.2
黑龙江	Heilongjiang	8900.4	7342.8	166.8	499.4	75.7	344.0	60.3
上 海	Shanghai	32682.6	27192.9	1074.3	2184.1	-21.6	1769.5	99.5
江 苏	Jiangsu	104603.9	89000.6	2413.6	5513.3	299.3	6483.9	489.2
浙 江	Zhejiang	64612.1	54658.1	1676.2	3834.5	269.1	4114.5	343.1
安 徽	Anhui	32366.2	27744.3	620.6	1576.5	121.4	1768.7	151.6
福 建	Fujian	31531.3	26479.1	757.8	1481.7	130.2	2586.4	179.1
江 西	Jiangxi	20417.6	17856.0	262.5	857.1	98.3	1195.3	106.2
山 东	Shandong	77405.2	66410.8	1402.4	3341.2	462.5	4245.1	332.6
河 南	Henan	33910.4	29634.4	503.7	1419.3	306.3	1537.1	190.6
湖 北	Hubei	27312.6	22741.8	561.2	1538.5	191.0	1529.8	142.1
湖 南	Hunan	19724.7	15825.7	500.2	1235.7	97.9	1192.9	131.3
广 东	Guangdong	125402.7	102526.9	4459.3	9336.4	308.0	9596.9	769.7
广 西	Guangxi	14523.1	12830.4	197.4	497.6	121.4	487.3	66.9
海 南	Hainan	2384.0	1933.9	85.4	89.9	28.2	135.9	7.3
重 庆	Chongqing	19102.8	16272.4	471.1	925.0	30.9	991.5	86.5
四 川	Sichuan	34019.1	27546.0	864.0	1547.3	176.9	3345.0	175.5
贵 州	Guizhou	7178.7	5103.5	145.6	464.9	90.0	1121.7	51.9
云 南	Yunnan	13587.7	10418.0	224.5	505.9	131.5	1248.3	49.6
西 藏	Xizang	350.7	271.1	3.5	31.3	8.8	29.0	1.7
陕 西	Shaanxi	23402.9	17974.7	334.1	1131.7	149.8	2935.7	107.1
甘 肃	Gansu	8123.8	6871.3	74.0	286.7	74.6	426.0	34.7
青 海	Qinghai	3094.6	2507.2	17.1	125.7	31.1	400.0	12.5
宁 夏	Ningxia	5748.9	4952.1	52.3	211.6	101.8	257.8	23.7
新 疆	Xinjiang	12300.4	9596.4	162.8	574.1	147.6	1337.1	47.5

13-12 主要工业产品产量
Output of Main Industrial Products

产品名称		Item		2022	2023
原盐	(万吨)	Salt	(10 000 tons)	5359.88	5268.58
精制食用植物油	(万吨)	Refined Edible Vegetable Oil	(10 000 tons)	4881.87	4685.94
成品糖	(万吨)	Refined Sugar	(10 000 tons)	1486.75	1291.49
罐头	(万吨)	Canned Food	(10 000 tons)	889.73	681.23
啤酒	(万千升)	Beer	(10 000 kiloliter)	3568.67	3641.14
卷烟	(亿支)	Cigarettes	(100 million pieces)	24321.50	24406.26
纱	(万吨)	Yarn	(10 000 tons)	2720.25	2388.16
布	(亿米)	Cloth	(100 million m)	467.74	318.94
机制纸及纸板	(万吨)	Machine-made Paper and Paperboard	(10 000 tons)	13691.36	15129.38
硫酸(折100%)	(万吨)	Sulfuric Acid (Converted to 100%)	(10 000 tons)	9504.58	9770.86
烧碱(折100%)	(万吨)	Caustic Soda (Converted to 100%)	(10 000 tons)	3980.53	4169.06
纯碱(碳酸钠)	(万吨)	Soda Ash (Sodium Carbonate)	(10 000 tons)	2920.21	3282.81
乙烯	(万吨)	Ethylene	(10 000 tons)	2897.51	3413.64
合成氨	(万吨)	Synthetic Ammonia	(10 000 tons)	5321.01	5806.02
农用氮、磷、钾化肥	(万吨)	Chemical Nitrogen, Phosphate and Potash Fertilizers for Agricultural Use	(10 000 tons)	5573.38	5683.83
#氮肥	(万吨)	Nitrogen Fertilizers	(10 000 tons)	3821.29	3966.29
磷肥	(万吨)	Phosphate Fertilizers	(10 000 tons)	984.02	985.73
化学农药原药	(万吨)	Chemical Pesticides	(10 000 tons)	249.71	372.28
初级形态塑料	(万吨)	Primary Plastics	(10 000 tons)	11488.10	12857.45
合成橡胶	(万吨)	Synthetic Rubber	(10 000 tons)	836.21	952.03
合成洗涤剂	(万吨)	Synthetic Detergents	(10 000 tons)	1071.45	1224.63
化学药品原药	(万吨)	Chemical Medicines	(10 000 tons)	370.78	323.24
中成药	(万吨)	Traditional Chinese Medicine	(10 000 tons)	244.66	235.18
化学纤维	(万吨)	Chemical Fiber	(10 000 tons)	6697.84	7566.45
橡胶轮胎外胎	(万条)	Rubber Outer Tires	(10 000 tires)	85919.41	116980.06
水泥	(万吨)	Cement	(10 000 tons)	212927.18	201940.15
平板玻璃	(万重量箱)	Plate Glass	(10 000 weight cases)	101668.65	98752.75
生铁	(万吨)	Pig Iron	(10 000 tons)	86382.78	87210.79
粗钢	(万吨)	Crude Steel	(10 000 tons)	101795.90	102885.97
钢材	(万吨)	Rolled Steel	(10 000 tons)	134033.48	138378.70
#重轨	(万吨)	Heavy Rail	(10 000 tons)	355.49	324.80
大型型钢	(万吨)	Rolled-steel, Large	(10 000 tons)	2234.39	2450.30
中小型型钢	(万吨)	Rolled-steel, Medium and Small	(10 000 tons)	5206.36	4306.30
棒材	(万吨)	Steel Bar	(10 000 tons)	8692.32	9214.35
钢筋	(万吨)	Corrugated Steel Bar	(10 000 tons)	23762.81	22643.23
线材(盘条)	(万吨)	Wire Rod	(10 000 tons)	14136.79	13768.71
特厚板	(万吨)	Heavy Steel Plate	(10 000 tons)	1138.68	1118.03
厚钢板	(万吨)	Thick Steel Plate	(10 000 tons)	3812.54	4010.27
中厚宽钢带	(万吨)	Medium Wide Steel Belt	(10 000 tons)	18779.96	20593.65

注：1.主要工业产品产量2023年数据统计范围为规模以上工业企业，即年主营业务收入2000万元及以上的工业企业。
2.纱包括棉纱、棉混纺纱、纯化纤纱，不包括棉线、代用纤维纱和手工纺纱。
3.布包括棉布、棉混纺布、纯化纤布，不包括代用纤维布、手工织布。
4.农用氮、磷、钾化肥按有效成分100%计算。
5.橡胶轮胎外胎包括摩托车充气橡胶轮胎外胎。

a) The statistical scope of the main industrial product output in 2023 includes industrial enterprises above designated size, which have an annual main business income of 20 million yuan or more.
b) Yarn includes pure and blended cotton yarn, pure chemical-fiber yarn, but excludes cotton thread, substitute fiber yarn and hand-made yarn.
c) Cloth includes pure and blended cotton cloth, pure chemical-fiber cloth and canvas, but excludes substitute fiber cloth, hand-woven cloth and cord fabric.
d) The output of chemical nitrogen, phosphate and potash fertilizers for agricultural use is calculated on the basis of 100% effective content.
e) Tires include pneumatic tires of motorcycle.

13-12 续表 continued

产品名称	Item	2022	2023
热轧薄宽钢带 (万吨)	Hot-rolled Thin Wide Steel Belt (10 000 tons)	10588.16	10755.39
冷轧薄宽钢带 (万吨)	Cold-rolled Thin Wide Steel Belt (10 000 tons)	6890.68	6907.49
镀层板(带) (万吨)	Plated Plate(Belt) (10 000 tons)	7299.77	8118.04
无缝钢管 (万吨)	Seamless Steel Pipe (10 000 tons)	3217.65	3550.09
十种有色金属 (万吨)	Ten Kinds of Nonferrous Metals (10 000 tons)	6789.82	7499.07
#精炼铜 (万吨)	Refined Copper (10 000 tons)	1111.53	1325.57
原铝(电解铝) (万吨)	Electrolyzed Aluminum (10 000 tons)	4014.43	4197.97
氧化铝 (万吨)	Aluminum Oxide (10 000 tons)	8186.18	8251.17
发动机 (万千瓦)	Engines (10 000 kW)	226890.99	240064.42
金属切削机床 (万台)	Metal-cutting Machine Tools (10 000 units)	57.33	69.10
矿山专用设备 (万吨)	Special Equipment for Mining (10 000 tons)	725.66	821.76
炼油、化工生产专用设备(万吨)	Equipment for Oil Refining and Chemical Production (10 000 tons)	152.69	182.35
大中型拖拉机 (万台)	Large and Medium Tractors (10 000 sets)	39.95	42.45
铁路客车 (辆)	Railway Passenger Coaches (unit)	473	1250
铁路货车 (万辆)	Railway Freight Wagons (10 000 units)	4.13	3.80
汽车 (万辆)	Motor Vehicles (10 000 sets)	2713.63	3009.89
#轿车 (万辆)	Cars (10 000 sets)	1044.95	1181.09
客车 (万辆)	Buses (10 000 sets)	40.65	45.06
载货汽车 (万辆)	Trucks (10 000 sets)	263.70	350.73
摩托车整车 (万辆)	Motorcycle (10 000 sets)	2640.24	2754.50
两轮脚踏自行车 (万辆)	Pedal Bicycles with Two Wheels (10 000 sets)	4351.22	3072.17
发电机组(发电设备) (万千瓦)	Power Generation Equipment (10 000 kW)	18371.09	26815.85
家用电冰箱 (万台)	Household Refrigerators (10 000 sets)	8664.43	9942.25
房间空气调节器 (万台)	Air Conditioners (10 000 sets)	22247.34	25088.67
家用电风扇 (万台)	Household Electric Fans (10 000 sets)	19780.71	21706.80
家用吸排油烟机 (万台)	Household Kitchen Ventilators (10 000 sets)	3970.66	3179.90
家用洗衣机 (万台)	Household Washing Machines (10 000 sets)	9106.32	10529.38
家用吸尘器 (万台)	Household Vacuum Cleaners (10 000 sets)	10585.09	10444.05
移动通信手持机 (万台)	Mobile Phones (10 000 sets)	156079.96	155652.28
#智能手机 (万台)	Smartphone (10 000 sets)	116577.65	114745.46
微型计算机设备 (万台)	Micro Computer Equipment (10 000 units)	43418.16	32855.14
#笔记本计算机 (万台)	Notebook PCs (10 000 units)	22717.83	17922.19
显示器 (万台)	Display (10 000 units)	18230.13	15811.98
集成电路 (亿块)	Integrated Circuits (100 million units)	3241.85	3946.78
彩色电视机 (万台)	Color Television Sets (10 000 sets)	19578.26	19807.81
组合音响 (万台)	Hi-Fi Stereo Component Players (10 000 sets)	21915.16	20594.58
照相机 (万台)	Cameras (10 000 sets)	1012.27	1726.53
#数码照相机 (万台)	Digital Cameras (10 000 sets)	588.97	761.03
复印和胶版印制设备 (万台)	Xerox and Hectograph Printing Equipment(10 000 sets)	255.18	259.83

注：1.金属切削机床不包括台钻、砂轮机、抛光机。
2.拖拉机是指14.7千瓦及以上的轮式和履带式拖拉机。用本厂自产的拖拉机装配的推土机，只计推土机产量，不计拖拉机产量。
3.发电机组(发电设备)指500千瓦以上的水轮发电机组、汽轮发电机和燃气轮发电机等。

a) Metal-cutting machine tools do not include bench drills, grinders and polishing machines.
b) Tractors refer to both wheel and crawler tractors with a haulage capacity of 14.7 kW and over. The tractors which are refitted into bulldozers by the same tractor factories are deducted.
c) Power generating equipment refers to units with a generating capacity of 500 kW and over, including hydroturbine generating units, steam turbine generating units and gas turbine generating units.

13-13 分地区主要工业产品产量
Output of Main Industrial Products by Region

年份 Year 地区 Region		原盐 (万吨) Salt (10 000 tons)	成品糖 (万吨) Refined Sugar (10 000 tons)	啤酒 (万千升) Beer (10 000 kiloliter)	卷烟 (亿支) Cigarettes (100 million pieces)	布 (亿米) Cloth (100 million m)
	1978	1953.00	227.00	40.00	1182.00	110.30
	1980	1728.00	257.00	69.00	1520.00	134.70
	1985	1479.00	451.00	310.00	2370.00	146.70
	1990	2023.00	582.00	692.00	3298.00	188.80
	1995	2977.72	558.64	1568.82	3485.02	260.18
	2000	3128.00	700.00	2231.32	3397.00	277.00
	2005	4661.06	912.37	3126.05	19389.08	484.39
	2006	5663.13	949.07	3543.58	20218.13	598.55
	2007	6166.97	1271.38	3954.07	21438.84	675.26
	2008	6664.43	1432.61	4156.91	22199.20	723.05
	2009	6662.79	1338.35	4162.18	22901.50	753.42
	2010	7037.76	1117.59	4490.16	23752.60	800.00
	2011	6742.16	1187.43	4834.50	24474.00	814.14
	2012	6911.78	1409.47	4778.58	25160.90	848.94
	2013	7367.60	1592.76	4982.79	25603.86	897.59
	2014	7049.71	1642.67	4936.29	26098.49	893.68
	2015	6665.54	1474.11	4715.60	25890.70	892.58
	2016	6620.10	1443.30	4506.44	23825.76	906.75
	2017	6654.17	1472.04	4401.49	23448.25	691.05
	2018	6363.61	1198.77	3800.83	23375.59	698.47
	2019	6701.44	1389.39	3765.29	23642.49	555.19
	2020	5852.68	1431.30	3411.11	23863.73	459.19
	2021	5706.51	1449.74	3562.43	24182.36	501.95
	2022	5359.88	1486.75	3568.67	24321.50	467.74
	2023	5268.58	1291.49	3641.14	24406.26	318.94
北京	Beijing			112.61	160.29	
天津	Tianjin	168.99		11.37	210.66	0.22
河北	Hebei	230.33	60.50	177.87	791.58	8.71
山西	Shanxi			17.06	154.00	0.13
内蒙古	Inner Mongolia	121.13	51.96	63.96	321.64	
辽宁	Liaoning	121.69		166.90	280.17	0.84
吉林	Jilin			64.70	551.12	0.28
黑龙江	Heilongjiang		7.91	115.86	397.50	
上海	Shanghai			21.92	928.38	0.46
江苏	Jiangsu	666.63	20.53	228.04	1060.92	59.51
浙江	Zhejiang		1.34	277.39	957.78	71.92
安徽	Anhui	145.54		69.48	1227.12	4.60
福建	Fujian	28.39	35.41	164.52	904.61	22.55
江西	Jiangxi	108.22		58.51	643.23	6.50
山东	Shandong	1030.56	76.37	485.37	1293.08	48.46
河南	Henan	74.62		132.45	1582.88	6.87
湖北	Hubei	545.93		156.36	1352.91	36.52
湖南	Hunan	449.50	1.18	58.28	1668.41	2.15
广东	Guangdong	1.44	103.40	454.46	1302.28	16.30
广西	Guangxi		622.14	117.28	720.98	0.33
海南	Hainan		7.22	2.02	117.00	
重庆	Chongqing	158.94		76.17	569.07	1.29
四川	Sichuan	432.33	1.55	268.71	913.92	10.27
贵州	Guizhou		0.42	65.00	1184.16	0.55
云南	Yunnan	168.05	240.92	86.21	3562.97	
西藏	Xizang			12.44		
陕西	Shaanxi	74.69		65.78	818.66	6.10
甘肃	Gansu		4.56	38.52	470.00	
青海	Qinghai	315.48		1.52		
宁夏	Ningxia	106.79		17.56	80.00	0.53
新疆	Xinjiang	319.32	56.08	52.82	180.95	13.84

注：1.本表部分指标存在总计不等于分项之和情况，是数据四舍五入所致，未作机械调整。
2.分地区主要工业产品产量2023年数据统计范围为规模以上工业企业，即年主营业务收入2000万元及以上的工业企业。
3.成品糖1997年及以前名称为糖，产量包括土糖，1998—2004年名称为机制糖。
4.啤酒2003年及以前计量单位为万吨。
5.卷烟2003年及以前计量单位为万箱。

a) The total of some indicators in this table is not equal to the sum of sub items, which is caused by the rounding of data, and no mechanical adjustment has been made.
b) The statistical scope of 2023 data on the production of major industrial products by region includes industrial enterprises above designated size, which have an annual main business income of 20 million yuan or more.
c) Refined sugar was called sugar in 1997 and before, in which the homemade sugar was included. During 1998-2004, it was called machine-made sugar.
d) Unit of beer in 2003 and before was 10 000 tons.
e) Unit of cigarettes in 2003 and before was 10 000 boxes.

13-13 续表 1 continued

年份 地区	Year Region	机制纸及纸板(万吨) Machine-made Paper and Paperboards (10 000 tons)	硫酸(折100%)(万吨) Sulfuric Acid (Converted to 100%) (10 000 tons)	烧碱(折100%)(万吨) Caustic Soda (Converted to 100%) (10 000 tons)	纯碱(万吨) Soda Ash (10 000 tons)	乙烯(万吨) Ethylene (10 000 tons)	农用氮、磷、钾化肥(万吨) Chemical Nitrogen, Phosphate and Potash Fertilizers for Agricultural Use (10 000 tons)
	1978	439.00	661.00	164.00	132.90	38.03	869.30
	1980	535.00	764.30	192.30	161.30	48.99	1232.10
	1985	911.00	676.40	235.30	201.10	65.21	1322.20
	1990	1372.00	1196.90	335.40	379.50	157.20	1879.70
	1995	2812.30	1811.00	531.82	597.71	240.10	2548.14
	2000	2486.93	2427.00	667.88	834.00	470.00	3186.00
	2005	6205.42	4544.66	1239.98	1421.08	755.54	5177.86
	2006	6863.02	5033.17	1511.78	1560.03	940.51	5345.05
	2007	7792.43	5412.56	1759.29	1765.00	1027.80	5824.98
	2008	8404.30	5097.95	1926.01	1854.60	987.58	6028.05
	2009	8965.13	5960.91	1832.37	1944.77	1072.62	6385.01
	2010	9832.63	7090.47	2228.39	2034.82	1421.34	6337.86
	2011	11010.89	7482.70	2473.52	2294.03	1527.50	6419.39
	2012	10956.54	7876.63	2696.82	2395.93	1486.80	6832.10
	2013	11323.06	8154.49	2927.44	2431.63	1599.31	7026.18
	2014	11785.80	8901.55	3063.51	2525.84	1696.69	6876.85
	2015	11742.77	8975.70	3020.66	2591.80	1714.60	7431.99
	2016	12319.22	9133.03	3201.68	2584.98	1781.14	6629.62
	2017	12542.01	9212.92	3329.17	2767.14	1821.84	5891.71
	2018	12045.97	9209.27	3475.47	2647.96	1861.76	5403.51
	2019	12515.30	9119.24	3457.89	2986.46	2052.29	5731.18
	2020	12700.63	9238.18	3673.87	2812.37	2159.96	5495.97
	2021	13583.87	9382.70	3891.31	2913.25	2825.67	5543.58
	2022	13691.36	9504.58	3980.53	2920.21	2897.51	5573.38
	2023	15129.38	9770.86	4169.06	3282.81	3413.64	5683.83
北 京	Beijing	3.07		0.29		69.76	
天 津	Tianjin	257.73	20.38	93.88	79.23	147.62	60.95
河 北	Hebei	436.19	180.53	162.90	215.20		219.67
山 西	Shanxi	177.40	68.71	93.09			406.78
内蒙古	Inner Mongolia	8.72	621.53	370.40	146.48		485.90
辽 宁	Liaoning	228.12	173.97	78.33		389.18	38.13
吉 林	Jilin	54.62	110.49	12.97		74.93	32.41
黑龙江	Heilongjiang	32.65	62.66	20.89		105.91	89.67
上 海	Shanghai	24.20	5.88	73.12		145.02	0.84
江 苏	Jiangsu	1680.04	262.52	334.00	388.02	644.26	187.05
浙 江	Zhejiang	1768.16	287.41	243.34	33.61	278.94	36.29
安 徽	Anhui	483.80	659.13	86.00	86.06	31.14	237.21
福 建	Fujian	908.86	297.06	68.06		274.82	23.15
江 西	Jiangxi	466.65	339.93	96.03	69.79	0.49	93.73
山 东	Shandong	2637.23	635.83	1111.77	464.41	281.40	472.69
河 南	Henan	433.41	545.58	187.49	695.80	26.14	391.51
湖 北	Hubei	703.55	1059.36	98.38	185.62	101.74	610.55
湖 南	Hunan	438.96	212.00	75.83	34.64	1.13	58.48
广 东	Guangdong	2509.21	260.86	34.73	64.56	501.57	12.80
广 西	Guangxi	656.87	486.18	121.14			27.80
海 南	Hainan	187.37					65.45
重 庆	Chongqing	397.61	107.06	36.52	134.16		257.82
四 川	Sichuan	365.33	499.08	155.77	128.54		286.73
贵 州	Guizhou	79.25	610.20				228.77
云 南	Yunnan	85.06	1563.76	28.79			250.72
西 藏	Xizang						
陕 西	Shaanxi	45.64	129.24	119.66	33.85	78.00	156.45
甘 肃	Gansu	5.11	401.07	52.77	18.66	60.79	21.00
青 海	Qinghai		15.52	32.84	464.14		476.80
宁 夏	Ningxia	17.42	67.21	80.72	40.03		73.91
新 疆	Xinjiang	37.15	87.71	299.35		200.80	380.56

13-13 续表 2 continued

年份 地区	Year Region	化学农药原药(万吨) Chemical Pesticide (10 000 tons)	初级形态塑料(万吨) Primary Plastics (10 000 tons)	化学纤维(万吨) Chemical Fiber (10 000 tons)	水泥(万吨) Cement (10 000 tons)	平板玻璃(万重量箱) Plate Glass (10 000 weight cases)	生铁(万吨) Pig Iron (10 000 tons)	粗钢(万吨) Crude Steel (10 000 tons)	钢材(万吨) Rolled Steel (10 000 tons)
	1978	53.30	67.90	28.46	6524.00	1784.00	3479.00	3178.00	2208.00
	1980	53.70	89.80	45.03	7986.00	2466.00	3802.00	3712.00	2716.00
	1985	21.10	123.40	94.78	14595.00	4942.00	4384.00	4679.00	3693.00
	1990	22.80	227.00	165.42	20971.00	8067.00	6238.00	6635.00	5153.00
	1995	41.65	516.87	341.17	47560.59	15731.71	10529.27	9535.99	8979.80
	2000	60.70	1087.51	694.00	59700.00	18352.20	13101.48	12850.00	13146.00
	2005	114.73	2308.86	1664.79	106884.79	40210.24	34375.19	35323.98	37771.14
	2006	138.46	2602.60	2073.18	123676.48	46574.70	41245.19	41914.85	46893.36
	2007	176.48	3184.54	2413.78	136117.25	53918.07	47651.63	48928.80	56560.87
	2008	209.99	3680.23	2453.29	142355.73	59890.39	47824.42	50305.75	60460.29
	2009	208.92	3629.97	2747.28	164397.78	58574.07	55283.46	57218.23	69405.40
	2010	223.52	4432.59	3090.00	188191.17	66330.80	59733.34	63722.99	80276.58
	2011	230.00	4992.31	3390.07	209925.86	79107.55	64050.88	68528.31	88619.57
	2012	290.88	5330.92	3837.37	220984.08	75050.50	66354.40	72388.22	95577.83
	2013	303.14	6293.03	4160.28	241923.89	79285.80	71149.88	81313.89	108200.54
	2014	374.40	7088.84	4389.75	249207.08	83128.16	71374.78	82230.63	112513.12
	2015	374.00	7807.66	4831.71	235918.83	78651.63	69141.30	80382.50	103468.41
	2016	320.97	8307.81	4886.36	241030.98	80408.45	70227.33	80760.94	104813.45
	2017	250.74	8458.08	4877.05	233084.06	83765.80	71361.93	87074.09	104642.05
	2018	240.02	8854.87	5418.02	223609.62	93963.26	77987.63	92903.84	113287.33
	2019	211.81	9743.65	5883.37	234430.62	94461.22	80849.38	99541.89	120456.94
	2020	214.80	10542.20	6124.68	239470.83	95227.79	88897.61	106476.68	132489.18
	2021	249.85	11198.41	6708.47	237724.49	101727.37	86856.78	103524.26	133666.83
	2022	249.71	11488.10	6697.84	212927.18	101668.65	86382.78	101795.90	134033.48
	2023	372.28	12857.45	7566.45	201940.15	98752.75	87210.79	102885.97	138378.70
北京	Beijing		103.88	0.39	199.96	48.48			183.23
天津	Tianjin	1.87	405.96	0.08	483.97	2975.77	1895.29	1644.48	6001.64
河北	Hebei	10.29	182.03	115.27	10130.59	13401.62	19549.41	21050.63	29891.02
山西	Shanxi	0.57	117.24	2.48	4667.02	2258.40	6022.46	6292.02	6888.82
内蒙古	Inner Mongolia	18.62	912.69	0.64	3793.08	1118.72	2347.91	3266.93	3387.94
辽宁	Liaoning	3.80	670.29	16.22	3831.44	5517.09	6960.06	7344.09	7864.72
吉林	Jilin	2.90	154.79	58.42	2043.04	1183.57	1359.89	1452.50	1483.37
黑龙江	Heilongjiang	1.55	199.97	3.37	1949.54	481.79	699.71	956.35	933.09
上海	Shanghai	1.35	322.37	19.98	441.65		1460.38	1573.33	1980.10
江苏	Jiangsu	69.90	1294.73	2327.87	14368.85	3297.38	9852.89	11859.15	16631.46
浙江	Zhejiang	48.16	1779.89	3533.20	12727.86	3854.52	873.57	1445.75	3335.20
安徽	Anhui	26.13	378.44	51.29	13356.67	5032.63	3111.24	3891.46	4228.95
福建	Fujian	2.65	634.83	786.47	7154.44	5304.43	1486.08	3469.70	4270.63
江西	Jiangxi	2.66	64.22	111.59	8422.85	394.12	2446.70	2659.60	3666.46
山东	Shandong	65.41	1406.70	103.46	12969.65	8680.82	7293.92	7455.90	11341.77
河南	Henan	14.25	163.77	69.66	9620.95	1453.50	2819.11	3374.30	3528.03
湖北	Hubei	16.92	241.48	45.06	9803.35	10655.84	2863.83	3640.91	3868.36
湖南	Hunan	12.05	43.39	41.99	8234.19	4286.51	2180.78	2415.55	3080.31
广东	Guangdong	3.84	946.19	71.85	14251.58	8931.64	2437.57	4448.54	6192.39
广西	Guangxi	8.20	101.65		9999.99	3333.54	3401.97	3816.57	5236.50
海南	Hainan	1.74	107.47		1545.43	1146.84			
重庆	Chongqing	1.48	21.33	32.69	5477.81	2122.72	651.60	889.68	2154.53
四川	Sichuan	32.98	236.35	62.74	12379.41	6546.00	1984.78	2688.79	4224.90
贵州	Guizhou		2.47	1.50	5941.42	1345.81	388.95	443.55	580.87
云南	Yunnan	0.11	42.25	4.05	9295.82	1158.13	1472.06	2309.61	2475.02
西藏	Xizang				1196.63				
陕西	Shaanxi	0.26	788.40	8.25	5803.93	2008.43	1317.34	1426.55	1628.75
甘肃	Gansu	9.27	159.09	0.06	4178.11	776.88	814.70	1108.86	1179.41
青海	Qinghai		76.04		1192.17	48.81	67.11	73.84	70.63
宁夏	Ningxia	14.75	493.41	11.06	1671.29	401.86	326.37	596.22	582.16
新疆	Xinjiang	0.56	806.12	86.84	4807.43	986.90	1125.10	1291.10	1488.48

注：初级形态塑料2004年及以前名称为塑料树脂及共聚物，简称塑料。

a) Before 2004, the primary plastics was called plastic colophony copolymer, or plastics in short.

13-13 续表 3 continued

年 份 地 区	Year Region	金属切削机床(万台) Metal-cutting Machine Tools (10 000 units)	大中型拖拉机(万台) Large and Medium-sized Tractors (10 000 units)	汽 车(万辆) Motor Vehicles (10 000 units)	#轿 车 Cars	发电机组(万千瓦) Power Generation Equipment (10 000 kW)	家用电冰箱(万台) Household Refrigerators (10 000 units)	房间空气调节器(万台) Air Conditioners (10 000 units)
	1978	18.32	11.35	14.91		483.80	2.80	0.02
	1980	13.36	9.77	22.23	0.54	419.30	4.90	1.32
	1985	16.72	4.50	43.72	0.90	563.60	144.81	12.35
	1990	13.45	3.94	51.40	3.50	1225.40	463.06	24.07
	1995	20.34	6.33	145.27	33.70	1667.90	918.54	682.56
	2000	17.66	4.10	207.00	60.70	1249.00	1279.00	1826.67
	2005	51.14	16.33	570.49	277.01	9200.00	2987.06	6764.57
	2006	57.30	19.93	727.89	386.94	11694.27	3530.89	6849.42
	2007	64.69	20.31	888.89	479.78	12990.98	4397.13	8014.28
	2008	71.73	28.44	930.59	503.81	13942.42	4799.95	8147.37
	2009	58.55	37.13	1379.53	748.48	11729.25	5930.45	8078.25
	2010	69.73	33.68	1826.53	957.59	12880.21	7295.72	10887.47
	2011	88.68	40.19	1841.64	1012.67	14410.52	8699.20	13912.50
	2012	88.23	52.73	1927.62	1077.00	13005.52	8427.00	12398.72
	2013	87.55	66.56	2212.09	1210.43	14197.66	9255.74	13069.30
	2014	85.80	64.37	2372.52	1248.31	15053.02	8796.09	14463.27
	2015	75.50	68.82	2450.35	1162.97	12431.38	7992.75	14200.35
	2016	67.28	61.84	2811.91	1211.12	13119.78	8481.57	14342.37
	2017	60.85	34.44	2901.81	1194.54	11822.93	8314.48	17861.53
	2018	54.07	26.21	2782.74	1217.38	10903.07	8108.79	20955.68
	2019	42.10	28.08	2567.67	1028.49	9073.69	7904.25	21866.16
	2020	43.89	34.52	2532.49	923.98	13384.46	9014.71	21035.25
	2021	60.17	41.17	2625.70	970.62	15976.44	8992.11	21835.70
	2022	57.33	39.95	2713.63	1044.95	18371.09	8664.43	22247.34
	2023	69.10	42.45	3009.89	1181.09	26815.85	9942.25	25088.67
北 京	Beijing	0.58		100.27	49.59	1876.27		
天 津	Tianjin	0.17	0.29	89.46	23.07	230.66		229.74
河 北	Hebei	0.26	0.26	86.20	8.71	117.48		1081.18
山 西	Shanxi			10.66	4.34	32.20		
内蒙古	Inner Mongolia			10.59	10.57	698.29		
辽 宁	Liaoning	3.03	0.41	94.34	48.28	155.57	179.17	96.93
吉 林	Jilin	0.01		155.89	79.89	461.70		
黑龙江	Heilongjiang	0.13	0.53	8.74	8.15	2842.75		
上 海	Shanghai	0.48		215.62	92.25	2816.13		169.81
江 苏	Jiangsu	9.18	7.19	195.23	72.88	3073.28	1535.66	965.69
浙 江	Zhejiang	18.59	1.21	152.59	84.68	1258.59	461.75	2440.94
安 徽	Anhui	2.53		208.80	56.54		3166.93	2832.18
福 建	Fujian	1.38		33.34	13.37	236.89		221.05
江 西	Jiangxi	1.10	0.02	47.97	4.69	36.35	77.49	773.63
山 东	Shandong	7.28	21.78	194.54	37.06	605.63	964.22	1448.29
河 南	Henan	0.36	9.95	78.21	27.50	85.76	61.65	1238.25
湖 北	Hubei	0.77	0.68	178.88	66.89	1.97	612.39	2250.38
湖 南	Hunan	1.14		45.41	17.59	1493.16		774.78
广 东	Guangdong	17.19		518.30	269.74	1685.65	2195.00	7438.47
广 西	Guangxi	0.12	0.09	97.52	45.69	56.67	205.88	386.36
海 南	Hainan			3.02		12.70		
重 庆	Chongqing	0.55		231.62	67.87	116.24	150.33	2182.91
四 川	Sichuan	0.36	0.04	97.20	47.30	4512.41	140.02	526.24
贵 州	Guizhou	0.05		4.76	0.16		169.96	
云 南	Yunnan	2.82		1.82	1.15	66.29		
西 藏	Xizang							
陕 西	Shaanxi	0.65		147.01	42.50	1972.88	21.61	31.51
甘 肃	Gansu	0.16				932.48		
青 海	Qinghai					69.81		
宁 夏	Ningxia	0.21				242.82		0.36
新 疆	Xinjiang			1.90	0.63	1125.22	0.18	

13-13 续表 4 continued

年份 Year / 地区 Region	家用洗衣机(万台) Household Washing Machines (10 000 units)	移动通信手持机(万台) Mobile Phones (10 000 units)	微型计算机设备(万台) Micro-Computer Equipment (10 000 units)	集成电路(亿块) Integrated Circuit (100 million units)	彩色电视机(万台) Color Television Sets (10 000 units)
1978	0.04			0.30	0.38
1980	24.53			0.17	3.21
1985	887.20			0.64	435.28
1990	662.68		8.21	1.08	1033.04
1995	948.40		83.57	55.17	2057.74
2000	1442.98	5247.88	672.00	58.80	3936.00
2005	3035.52	30354.21	8084.89	269.97	8283.22
2006	3560.50	48013.79	9336.44	335.75	8375.40
2007	4005.10	54857.86	12073.38	411.62	8478.01
2008	4447.00	55945.10	15853.65	438.77	9187.14
2009	4973.63	68193.37	18215.07	414.40	9898.79
2010	6247.73	99827.36	24584.46	652.50	11830.03
2011	6715.94	113257.71	32036.93	719.52	12231.34
2012	6791.12	118154.57	31806.71	779.61	12823.52
2013	7300.53	152343.90	35348.41	903.46	12745.21
2014	7114.40	168202.75	35079.63	1015.53	14128.90
2015	7274.50	181261.40	31418.70	1087.20	14475.73
2016	7620.85	184845.66	29008.51	1317.95	15769.64
2017	7500.88	188982.37	30678.37	1564.58	15932.62
2018	7261.50	180050.62	31580.23	1852.60	19695.03
2019	7432.99	169603.36	34163.22	2018.22	18999.06
2020	8041.87	146961.78	37800.41	2614.23	19626.24
2021	8618.54	166151.58	46691.98	3594.35	18496.53
2022	9106.32	156079.96	43418.16	3241.85	19578.26
2023	10529.38	155652.28	32855.14	3946.78	19807.81
北京 Beijing		10286.76	615.83	219.13	360.60
天津 Tianjin	226.00			27.36	
河北 Hebei				0.37	
山西 Shanxi		2009.21	21.37	1.52	
内蒙古 Inner Mongolia					106.70
辽宁 Liaoning		5.09		6.53	
吉林 Jilin					
黑龙江 Heilongjiang			1.00	3.12	
上海 Shanghai	115.74	2398.32	1903.79	350.12	59.15
江苏 Jiangsu	3516.48	7996.15	2428.50	1298.56	694.33
浙江 Zhejiang	1062.97	3052.37	151.03	314.26	26.90
安徽 Anhui	3031.35	15.82	2125.82	60.64	835.68
福建 Fujian		913.21	465.20	19.42	1011.22
江西 Jiangxi		9418.89	2370.78	30.62	18.33
山东 Shandong	935.34	316.49	0.20	40.93	2431.62
河南 Henan	3.47	14689.89	165.62	0.12	6.80
湖北 Hubei		5455.61	1347.21	1.04	188.68
湖南 Hunan		1581.34	141.76	27.27	4.61
广东 Guangdong	785.56	65066.15	7458.10	697.80	11211.09
广西 Guangxi	227.63	2266.06	173.36	16.01	573.05
海南 Hainan		0.47			
重庆 Chongqing	545.79	8537.59	7400.53	37.50	2.53
四川 Sichuan	25.35	12155.32	5337.78	116.48	1918.26
贵州 Guizhou		1458.00	2.77	3.11	342.41
云南 Yunnan		4195.75	743.78	2.71	9.31
西藏 Xizang					
陕西 Shaanxi	50.24	3583.25	0.12	67.68	5.92
甘肃 Gansu				604.09	
青海 Qinghai		235.04			
宁夏 Ningxia				0.39	
新疆 Xinjiang	3.47	15.50	0.58		0.64

13–14 人均主要工业产品产量
Per Capita Output of Main Industrial Products

年 份 Year	纱 (公斤) Yarn (kg)	布 (米) Cloth (m)	机制纸及纸板 (公斤) Machine-made Paper and Paperboard (kg)	水 泥 (公斤) Cement (kg)	粗 钢 (公斤) Crude Steel (kg)
1978	2.49	11.54	4.59	68.23	33.24
1980	2.98	13.73	5.45	81.39	37.83
1985	3.36	13.96	8.67	138.86	44.52
1990	4.08	16.63	12.09	184.74	58.45
1995	4.50	21.59	23.34	394.74	79.15
1996	4.21	17.17	21.67	403.42	83.15
1997	4.55	20.23	22.22	416.02	88.57
1998	4.36	19.41	17.12	431.58	93.07
1999	4.53	19.96	17.24	457.40	99.19
2000	5.20	21.94	19.70	472.82	101.77
2001	5.98	22.80	29.70	519.75	119.22
2002	6.64	25.18	36.45	566.23	142.43
2003	7.63	27.44	37.64	669.11	172.57
2004	9.96	37.20	41.77	745.96	218.28
2005	11.13	37.15	47.60	819.84	270.95
2006	13.29	45.66	52.35	943.36	319.71
2007	14.86	51.24	59.13	1032.85	371.27
2008	15.52	54.58	63.45	1074.66	379.76
2009	17.02	56.59	67.34	1234.90	429.81
2010	19.23	59.80	73.50	1406.82	476.36
2011	20.21	60.53	81.86	1560.75	509.49
2012	22.04	62.69	80.91	1631.85	534.55
2013	23.47	65.84	83.06	1774.62	596.48
2014	24.63	65.14	85.91	1816.56	599.41
2015	25.64	64.69	85.10	1709.73	582.54
2016	26.90	65.34	88.77	1736.80	581.94
2017	22.86	49.49	89.83	1669.40	623.64
2018	21.95	49.79	85.87	1594.07	662.29
2019	20.08	39.44	88.90	1665.29	707.10
2020	18.55	32.54	90.01	1697.05	754.57
2021	20.35	35.54	96.18	1683.17	732.99
2022	19.26	33.12	96.95	1507.80	720.84
2023	16.93	22.61	107.25	1431.48	729.32

注：1.人均主要工业产品产量2023年数据统计范围为规模以上工业企业，即年主营业务收入2000万元及以上的工业企业。
2.2011–2019年数据根据第七次全国人口普查结果修订数修订。

a) The statistical scope of 2023 data on per capita output of main industrial products by region includes industrial enterprises above designated size, which have an annual main business income of 20 million yuan or more.
b) The data from 2011 to 2019 were revised according to the results of the seventh National Population Census.

13-15 全国规模以上工业主要产品生产能力
Production Capacity of Main Industrial Products of Industrial Enterprises above Designated Size

产品名称		Item		2022	2023
天然原油	(万吨)	Natural Crude Oil	(10 000 tons)	21729.67	22158.22
卷烟	(亿支)	Cigarettes	(100 million pieces)	27817.68	27771.58
原油加工能力	(万吨)	Crude Oil Processing Capacity	(10 000 tons)	83898.24	85064.46
焦炭	(万吨)	Coke	(10 000 tons)	56003.42	56775.14
烧碱	(万吨)	Caustic Soda	(10 000 tons)	4364.68	4539.66
碳化钙(电石，折300升/千克)	(万吨)	Calsium Carbide (converted to 300 litres/kg)	(10 000 tons)	3625.71	3852.53
农用氮、磷、钾化学肥料总计(折纯)	(万吨)	Chemical Nitrogen, Phosphate and Potash Fertilizers for Agricultural Use (converted pure quantity)	(10 000 tons)	9789.86	8436.65
初级形态塑料	(万吨)	Primary Plastics	(10 000 tons)	14616.81	16333.62
化学纤维	(万吨)	Chemical Fibre	(10 000 tons)	9040.01	9220.93
水泥	(万吨)	Cement	(10 000 tons)	357543.13	351083.23
平板玻璃	(万重量箱)	Plate Glass	(10 000 weight cases)	116284.54	118230.27
粗钢	(万吨)	Crude Steel	(10 000 tons)	110186.18	110804.10
钢材	(万吨)	Rolled Steel	(10 000 tons)	176195.93	182129.71
原铝(电解铝)	(万吨)	Electrolyzed Aluminum	(10 000 tons)	4793.48	4722.51
金属切削机床	(万台)	Metal-cutting Machine Tools	(10 000 sets)	89.17	108.01
汽车	(万辆)	Motor Vehicles	(10 000 sets)	4234.92	4350.31
家用电冰箱	(万台)	Household Refrigerators	(10 000 sets)	13056.55	13487.37
房间空气调节器	(万台)	Air Conditioners	(10 000 sets)	34051.55	33814.00
微型计算机设备	(万台)	Micro Computer Equipment	(10 000 sets)	63786.69	50867.07
移动通信手持机(手机)	(万台)	Mobile Phones	(10 000 sets)	210973.23	228951.72
彩色电视机	(万台)	Color TV Set	(10 000 sets)	27469.97	27547.75
发电设备容量总计	(万千瓦)	Installed Capacity of Power Generation	(10 000 kW)	202885.92	220884.21
#火电设备容量	(万千瓦)	Thermal Power	(10 000 kW)	121136.61	127284.66
水电设备容量	(万千瓦)	Hydropower	(10 000 kW)	32512.18	35205.68
核电设备容量	(万千瓦)	Nuclear Power	(10 000 kW)	5557.13	5675.93
风电设备容量	(万千瓦)	Wind Power	(10 000 kW)	27166.54	32775.48

主要统计指标解释

工业　指从事自然资源的开采，对采掘品和农产品进行加工和再加工的物质生产部门。具体包括：(1)对自然资源的开采，如采矿、晒盐等(但不包括禽兽捕猎和水产捕捞)；(2)对农副产品的加工、再加工，如粮油加工、食品加工、缫丝、纺织、制革等；(3)对采掘品的加工、再加工，如炼铁、炼钢、化工生产、石油加工、机器制造、木材加工等，以及电力、燃气及水的生产和供应等；(4)对工业品的修理、翻新，如机器设备的修理等。

工业统计调查单位为工业法人单位。

工业法人单位指从事工业生产经营活动的法人单位。工业法人单位应同时具备以下条件：①依法成立，有自己的名称、组织机构和场所，能够独立承担民事责任；②独立拥有（或授权）使用资产，承担负债，有权与其他单位签订合同；③具有包括资产负债表在内的账户，或者能够根据需要编制账户。

国有控股企业　即原来的国有及国有控股企业，根据企业实收资本中国有经济成分的出资人的实际投资情况，或国有经济成分的出资人对企业资产的实际控制、支配程度进行分类。以下情况为国有控股：(1) 在企业的全部实收资本中，国有经济成分的出资人拥有的实收资本（股本）所占企业全部实收资本（股本）的比例大于50%的国有绝对控股。(2) 在企业的全部实收资本中，国有经济成分的出资人拥有的实收资本（股本）所占比例虽未大于50%，但相对大于其他任何一方经济成分的出资人所占比例的国有相对控股；或者虽不大于其他经济成分，但根据协议规定拥有企业实际控制权的国有协议控股。(3) 投资双方各占50%，且未明确由谁绝对控股的企业，若其中一方为国有经济成分的，一律按国有控股处理。

资产总计　指企业过去的交易或者事项形成的、由企业拥有或者控制的、预期会给企业带来经济利益的资源。包括企业拥有的土地、办公楼、厂房、机器、运输工具、存货等实物资产和现金、存款、应收账款和预付账款等金融资产。资产一般按流动性分为流动资产和非流动资产。其中流动资产可分为货币资金、交易性金融资产、应收票据、应收账款、预付款项、其他应收款、存货等；非流动资产可分为长期股权投资、固定资产、无形资产及其他非流动资产等。来源于会计“资产负债表”中“资产总计”项目的期末余额数。

流动资产合计　资产满足以下条件之一应归为流动资产：(1) 预计在一个正常营业周期中变现、出售或耗用，主要包括存货、应收账款等；(2) 主要为交易目的而持有；(3) 预计在资产负债表日起一年内（含一年）变现；(4) 自资产负债表日起一年内，交换其他资产或清偿负债的能力不受限制的现金或现金等价物。包括货币资金、应收票据、应收账款、存货等项目。来源于会计“资产负债表”中“流动资产合计”项目的期末余额数。

负债合计　指企业过去的交易或者事项形成的，预期会导致经济利益流出企业的现时义务。包括银行贷款、借款、应付账款、应付职工工资、应付职工福利费、应交税金等企业负有偿还责任的债务。负债一般按偿还期长短分为流动负债和非流动负债。来源于会计“资产负债表”中“负债合计”项目的期末余额数。

应收账款　指资产负债表日以摊余成本计量的、企业因销售商品、提供服务等经营活动应收取的款项。来源于会计“资产负债表”中“应收账款”项目的期末余额数。

存货　指企业在日常活动中持有以备出售的产成品或商品、处在生产过程中的在产品、在生产过程或提供劳务过程中耗用的材料或物料等，通常包括原材料、在产品、半成品、产成品、商品以及周转材料等。来源于会计“资产负债表”中“存货”项目的期末余额数。

产成品　指企业已经完成全部生产过程并验收入库，可以按照合同规定的条件送交订货单位，或者可以作为商品对外销售的产品；以及外购或委托加工完成验收入库用于销售的各种商品。如果会计“资产负债表”列示“产成品”或“库存商品”项目，则根据其期末余额填报；或者，根据会计“产成品”或“库存商品”科目的期末借方余额，减去为“产成品”或“库存商品”计提的存货跌价准备等填报。

营业收入　指企业从事销售商品、提供劳务和让渡资产使用权等生产经营活动形成的经济利益流入。营业收入包括“主营业务收入”和“其他业务收入”。来源于会计“利润表”中“营业收入”项目的本年累计数。

营业成本　指企业从事销售商品、提供劳务和让渡资产使用权等生产经营活动发生的实际成本。包括企业（单位）在报告期内从事销售商品、提供劳务等日常活动发生的各种耗费。包括“主营业务成本”和“其他业务成本”。来源于会计“利润表”中“营业成本”项目的本年累计数。

销售费用　指企业在销售商品和材料、提供劳务的过程中发生的各种费用，包括保险费、包装费、展览费和广告费、商品维修费、预计产品质量保证损失、运输费、装卸费等以及为销售本企业商品而专设的销售机构（含销售网点、售后服务网点等）的职工薪酬、业务费、折旧费等经营费用。

管理费用　指企业为组织和管理企业生产经营所发生的费用，包括企业在筹建期间内发生的开办费、董事会和行政管理部门在企业经营管理中发生的，或者应当由企业统一负担的公司经费等。来源于会计“利润表”中“管理费用”项目的本年累计数。

财务费用　指企业为筹集生产经营所需资金等而发生的筹资费用，包括企业生产经营期间发生的利息支出（减利息收入）、汇兑损失（减汇兑收益）以及相关的手续费等。来源于会计“利润表”中“财务费用”项目的本年累计数。

利润总额　指企业在一定会计期间的经营成果，是生产经营过程中各种收入扣除各种耗费后的盈余，反映企业在报告期内实现的盈亏总额。来源于会计“利润表”中“利润总额”项目的本年累计数。

平均用工人数　指报告期企业平均实际拥有的、参与本企业生产经营活动的人员数。

Explanatory Notes on Main Statistical Indicators

Industry refers to the material production sector which is engaged in the extraction of natural resources and processing and reprocessing of minerals and agricultural products, including (1) extraction of natural resources, such as mining, salt production (but not including hunting and fishing); (2) processing and reprocessing of farm and sideline produces, such as grain and oil processing, food processing, silk reeling, spinning and weaving and leather making; (3) processing and reprocessing of mineral products, such as steel making, iron smelting, chemicals manufacturing, petroleum processing, machine building, timber processing, and production and supply of electricity, gas and water; (4) repairing and renovating of industrial products such as the machinery.

In industrial surveys, the units of enquiry are industrial corporate units.

Industrial corporate units refer to corporate units engaging in industrial production and operation activities, which meet the following requirements: (1) They are established legally, having their own names, organizations, location, and are able to take civil liability independently; (2) They possess (or are authorized to use) assets independently, assume liabilities and are entitled to sign contracts with other units; (3) They have accounts including the balance sheets or can compile the accounts according to the need.

State-holding Enterprises cover the original state-owned enterprises and state-holding enterprises. They are classified according to the actual investment made by the contributors of state-owned part in the paid-in capital of the enterprises, or the degree of control or dominance of the contributor on the assets of the enterprises. The following cases are regarded as state-holding: (1) Absolute state-holding in which the contributors of state-owned parts possess more than 50% of all the paid-in capital (stocks) of the enterprises; (2) Relative state-holding in which the contributors of state-owned parts possess no more than 50% of the paid-in capital (stocks) of the enterprises, but more than that of any other contributors; or agreed state-holding in which the contributors of state-owned parts possess no more than other contributors but have actual control over the enterprises according to agreements; (3) In case both contributors possess 50% and it is not clear which one is in absolute holding position, the enterprise is regarded as state-holding enterprise if one of the contributor has state-owned elements.

Total Assets refer to all resources that are owned or controlled by enterprises through previous trades or transactions, with expectation of making economic profits to enterprises. Included are all assets owned by enterprises such as land, office buildings, factories, machines, vehicles, inventories and other physical assets as well as cash, deposits, accounts receivable, prepayments and other financial assets. Classified by the degree of liquidity, total assets include current assets and non-current assets. Current assets can be classified into monetary capital, trading financial assets, notes receivable, accounts receivable, advanced payments, other receivables and inventories. Non-current assets can be divided into long-term equity investment, fixed assets, intangible assets and other non-current assets. Data on this indicator can be obtained from the year-end figures of total assets in the *Balance Sheet* of accounting records.

Current Assets refer to the assets that meet one of the following requirements: (1) expected to be cashed, sold or used in a normal operation cycle, mainly including inventory and accounts receivable; (2) owned for transaction purpose mainly; (3) expected to be cashed within one year (including one year) from the day of the *Balance Sheet*; (4) unlimited cash or cash equivalents that can be exchanged with other assets or capable of settling debts during one year since the day of the *Balance Sheet*. Included are monetary capital, notes receivable, accounts receivable and inventories. Data on this indicator can be obtained from the year-end figures of total current assets in the *Balance Sheet* of accounting records.

Total Liabilities refer to payable liabilities of enterprises that are accumulated from earlier transactions with expectation of leaking out of economic profits. Included are debts that enterprises are responsible for repaying such as bank loans, borrowings, accounts payable, wages payable, employee benefits payable, taxes payable, etc. In terms of payment, it can be divided into liquid liabilities and long-term liabilities. Data on this indicator can be obtained from the year-end figures of total liabilities in the *Balance Sheet* of accounting records.

Accounts Receivable refers to creditor's rights through business activities such as selling goods and providing labor. It comes from the ending balance of accounts receivable in balance sheet.

Inventories refers to finished goods or commodities held in preparation for sale in enterprises' daily activities, goods in the production process, material or the physical materials consumed in the production process or in the process of providing labor, usually include raw materials, goods in the production process, semi-finished products, finished products, goods and materials in flow. It comes from the ending balance of inventory in balance sheet.

Finished Goods refers to products that have completed the entire production process and have been accepted for storage by the enterprise, and can be delivered to the ordering unit according to the conditions stipulated in the contract, or can be sold as commodities to the outside world; and various goods purchased or commissioned for processing, acceptance and storage for sale. If the accounting "balance sheet" lists "finished products" or "inventory goods" items, report them based on their ending balance; alternatively, based on the ending debit balance of the accounting "finished products" or "inventory goods" account, subtract the provision for inventory depreciation made for "finished products" or "inventory goods".

Business Revenue refers to the inflow of economic benefits through production and operation activities of enterprises, such as selling commodities, providing labor services and transferring the right to use of assets. Business revenue includes "revenue from principal business" and " revenue from other business". It comes from current year's cumulative report of "business revenue" items from the "income statement".

Business Cost refers to the actual costs incurred by the enterprises in such production and operation activities as selling commodities, providing labor services and transferring the right to use of assets. It includes various expenditures incurred by enterprises (units) in their daily activities of selling goods and providing labour services during the reporting period. It includes "cost of principal business" and "cost of other business". It comes from current year's cumulative report of "operating cost" items from the "income statement".

Selling Expenses refer to the cost during the sale of goods and materials, providing labour services, including insurance, packing, exhibition fees and advertising fees, merchandise maintenance costs, expected product quality guarantee loss, transportation fees, handling fees, and operating expenses for the sales of the company's products, such as employee compensation, business expenses, depreciation costs for dedicated sales offices (including sales outlets, after-sales service outlets, etc.).

Management Expenses refer to the expenses for the organization and management of enterprise operation, including the start-up costs during the construction of enterprises, funds occurred during enterprises operation by board of directors and executive management in the enterprise management, and other costs to be paid by enterprises. It comes from current year's cumulative amount of management cost in income statement.

Financial Expenses refer to cost of fund-raising for enterprises to raise funds for production and operation, including interest payments (a reduction in interest income), exchange loss (less exchange gains) and related fees during the period of production. It comes from current year's cumulative amount of financial expenses in income statement.

Total Profits refer to the operational results in a certain accounting period, and it is the balance of various incomes minus various spending in the course of operation, reflecting the total profits and losses of enterprises in reference period. Data are obtained from current year's cumulative amount of total profits in the profit statement of the accounting record of enterprise.

Annual Average Employees refer to the number of persons engaged in the production and operation activities of enterprises in the reporting period, which are actually employed by the enterprises.

14

建筑业

Construction

简要说明

一、本篇资料主要内容

本篇资料反映我国建筑业概况和发展情况。包括建筑业企业基本情况和生产经营情况。主要指标有企业个数、从业人员数、建筑业总产值、房屋建筑面积、利润、税金、劳动生产率等。此外，还包括勘察设计、建设工程监理单位和人员情况的主要指标。

二、本篇资料统计范围

根据建筑业发展的实际情况，建筑业统计范围从2002年年报起由原具有建筑业资质等级四级及四级以上的独立核算的建筑业企业调整为具有建筑业资质的独立核算建筑业企业。

三、本篇资料来源及统计调查方法

本篇建筑业企业统计数据根据国家统计局制定的《建筑业统计报表制度》整理汇总。建筑业统计报表由国家统计局根据企业实际情况采取全面调查的方法布置、收集，由资质内建筑业企业通过联网直报系统上报。

勘察设计单位和人员表依据住房和城乡建设部制定的《勘察设计报表制度》中有关年报资料编制，由住房和城乡建设部提供。

四、本篇资料的数据情况说明

本篇资料对 2019—2022 年建筑业总产值等相关指标数据进行了修订，主要原因是：（一）加强统计执法，对统计执法检查中发现的问题数据，按照相关规定进行了改正。（二）加强数据质量管理，剔除主营业务为非建筑业企业在库数据。

Brief Introduction

I. Main Contents

Data in this chapter show the general situation and the development of the construction industry in China. They cover the situation of production and management of construction enterprises, including the number of enterprises; number of employed persons; gross output value and value added of the construction industry; floor space of buildings under construction; profits and taxes; and labour productivity etc. Also included in this chapter are main indicators on the situation of prospecting and designing institutions，construction project supervision unit and personnel.

II. Scope of Statistics

In view of the development of the construction industry, starting from 2002 the scope of construction statistics has been adjusted to include all the construction enterprises of various types of ownership with qualification certificates and independent accounting systems, replacing the previous criteria that required construction enterprises of various types of ownership to have qualification certificates at or above Grade 4 with independent accounting systems.

III. Sources of Data and Methods of Survey

Data on construction enterprises are collected in accordance with the *Statistical Reporting System of Construction* stipulated by the National Bureau of Statistics. Report forms of construction statistics are distributed and collected through comprehensive survey by National Bureau of Statistics in accordance with the real conditions of the enterprises, and they are directly reported by qualified construction enterprises through internet.

Data on prospecting and designing institutions and their personnel are provided by the Ministry of Housing and Urban-Rural Development, based on the requirements on the annual reporting specified in the *Statistical Reporting Form System of Prospecting and Designing* stipulated by the Ministry of Housing and Urban-Rural Development.

IV. Explanation of Data Situation

This article has revised the data of relevant indicators such as the total output value of the construction industry from 2019 to 2022, mainly due to: (1) Strengthen statistical law enforcement and correct the problem data found in statistical law enforcement inspections in accordance with relevant regulations. （2） Strengthen management of data quality and remove non construction enterprise data from the database as the main business.

14-1 建筑业企业概况
Main Indicators of Construction Enterprises

年　份 Year	总　计 Total	内资企业 Domestic Invested Enterprises	港澳台投资企业 Enterprises with Investment from Hong Kong, Macao and Taiwan	外商投资企业 Foreign Invested Enterprises
企业单位数（个） Number of Enterprises (unit)				
1980	6604	6604		
1985	11150	11150		
1990	13327	13327		
1995	24133	23492	329	312
2000	47518	46564	635	319
2005	58750	57846	516	388
2010	71863	71116	416	331
2011	72280	71584	393	303
2012	75280	74600	385	295
2013	78919	78257	390	272
2014	81141	80511	369	261
2015	80911	80319	343	249
2016	83017	82469	326	222
2017	88074	87522	334	218
2018	96544	96075	266	203
2019	103805	103370	245	190
2020	116722	116304	235	183
2021	128743	128327	227	189
2022	142906	142475	230	201
2023	159140	158707	262	171
从业人员（万人） Number of Employed Persons (10 000 persons)				
1980	648.0	648.0		
1985	911.5	911.5		
1990	1010.7	1010.7		
1995	1497.9	1487.5	5.0	5.4
2000	1994.3	1981.7	8.2	4.4
2005	2699.9	2680.5	8.6	10.8
2010	4160.4	4138.5	12.2	9.8
2011	3852.5	3831.3	11.3	9.9
2012	4267.2	4244.0	13.0	10.3
2013	4528.4	4501.8	16.5	10.1
2014	4537.0	4512.9	15.4	8.6
2015	5093.7	5066.6	17.9	9.2
2016	5184.5	5159.7	16.1	8.7
2017	5529.6	5502.9	19.0	7.7
2018	5305.2	5280.0	17.6	7.6
2019	5427.1	5406.0	14.3	6.8
2020	5367.0	5341.2	18.0	7.8
2021	5282.4	5260.5	14.7	7.2
2022	5063.4	5038.9	17.3	7.2
2023	5043.5	5022.6	14.4	6.5
建筑业总产值（亿元） Gross Output Value (100 million yuan)				
1980	286.93	286.93		
1985	675.10	675.10		
1990	1345.01	1345.01		
1995	5793.75	5726.96	33.60	33.19
2000	12497.60	12330.93	99.18	67.49
2005	34552.10	34130.53	172.54	249.03
2010	96031.13	95147.50	443.96	439.68
2011	116463.32	115192.47	612.68	658.17
2012	137217.86	136091.13	649.74	476.99
2013	160366.06	159136.38	621.96	607.72
2014	176713.42	175408.54	661.67	643.20
2015	180757.47	179457.89	693.34	606.24
2016	193566.78	192357.58	683.99	525.21
2017	213943.56	212596.90	799.36	547.30
2018	225816.86	224434.08	743.74	639.04
2019	244816.92	243472.22	750.80	593.89
2020	256553.18	254379.39	1211.48	962.32
2021	281238.66	278984.04	1295.66	958.96
2022	298675.15	296336.77	1455.59	882.79
2023	314393.53	312216.62	1455.85	721.06

注：1.1980—1992年数据为全民和集体所有制建筑业企业数据；1993—1995年数据为各种经济成分的建制镇以上企业数据；1996—2001年数据为资质等级(旧资质)四级及四级以上建筑业企业数据；2002年及以后为所有具有资质等级的施工总承包、专业承包建筑业企业数据。

2.从业人员数1993年至1997年为年平均人数，其余年份为年末人数。

3.本表登记注册统计类别按《关于市场主体统计分类的划分规定》(国统字〔2023〕14号)执行。

a) Data from 1980 to 1992 were construction enterprises owned by the whole people or under collective ownership. Data from 1993 to 1995 were enterprises above the designated town in diverse economic sectors. Data from 1996 to 2001 included construction enterprises at fourth or higher quality grades(old classification of grades). Data since 2002 included all general contracting and professional contracting construction enterprises which possess qualification certificates.

b) For 1993-1997,the number of employed persons refers to the annual average, and for other years, it refers to employed persons at the end of the year.

c) The registered statistical categories of this table is implemented in accordance with the Regulations on the Classification of Market Entity Statistics (Guotongzi [2023] No. 14).

14–2 按登记注册统计类别分建筑业企业主要经济指标（2023年）
Main Economic Indicators of Construction Enterprises by Registered Statistical Categories (2023)

指　标	Item	总　计 Total	内资企业 Domestic Invested Enterprises	港澳台投资企　业 Enterprises with Investment from Hong Kong, Macao and Taiwan	外商投资企　业 Foreign Invested Enterprises
企业单位数　（个）	Number of Construction Enterprises (unit)	159140	158707	262	171
从业人员　（万人）	Number of Employed Persons (10 000 persons)	5043	5023	14	6
固定资产原价　（亿元）	Fixed Assets (original value) (100 million yuan)	24848	24664	77	107
建筑业总产值　（亿元）	Gross Output Value of Construction (100 million yuan)	314394	312217	1456	721
房屋施工面积(万平方米)	Floor Space of Buildings under Construction (10 000 sq.m)	1530925	1515914	12634	2377
房屋竣工面积(万平方米)	Floor Space of Buildings Completed (10 000 sq.m)	393401	390126	2466	809
利润总额　（亿元）	Total Profits (100 million yuan)	8902	8793	62	47
税金总额　（亿元）	Total Tax (100 million yuan)	7019	6973	30	16
按总产值计算的劳动生产率　（元/人）	Overall Labour Productivity In Terms of Gross Output Value (yuan/person)	475594	474966	576748	608399
房屋建筑面积竣工率(%)	Rate of Floor Space of Buildings Completed (%)	25.7	25.7	19.5	34.0
产值利润率　(%)	Ratio of Profit to Gross Output Value (%)	2.8	2.8	4.3	6.5
产值利税率　(%)	Ratio of Pre-tax Profit to Gross Output Value (%)	5.1	5.0	6.3	8.7

注：本表登记注册统计类别按《关于市场主体统计分类的划分规定》(国统字〔2023〕14号)执行。

a) The registered statistical categories of this table is implemented in accordance with the Regulations on the Classification of Market Entity Statistics (Guotongzi [2023] No. 14).

14–3 分地区建筑业劳动生产率(2023年)
Labor Productivity of Construction Industry by Region (2023)

单位：元/人 (yuan/person)

地区	Region	按建筑业总产值计算的劳动生产率 Labor Productivity in Terms of Total Output Value of Construction	#内资企业 Domestic Invested Enterprises
全国	**National Average**	**475594**	**474966**
北京	Beijing	627924	631308
天津	Tianjin	652617	652181
河北	Hebei	542192	541990
山西	Shanxi	457916	457917
内蒙古	Inner Mongolia	490250	490250
辽宁	Liaoning	611814	609611
吉林	Jilin	498218	496772
黑龙江	Heilongjiang	379288	379626
上海	Shanghai	681208	684650
江苏	Jiangsu	401167	400541
浙江	Zhejiang	417772	416257
安徽	Anhui	488250	486312
福建	Fujian	330854	330493
江西	Jiangxi	502886	502948
山东	Shandong	523282	522688
河南	Henan	414855	414866
湖北	Hubei	705214	704568
湖南	Hunan	486576	486484
广东	Guangdong	579361	575211
广西	Guangxi	474994	475006
海南	Hainan	587768	588029
重庆	Chongqing	438009	437702
四川	Sichuan	409397	409402
贵州	Guizhou	482147	482147
云南	Yunnan	470784	470784
西藏	Xizang	518669	518669
陕西	Shaanxi	506639	507106
甘肃	Gansu	501958	501961
青海	Qinghai	562467	562467
宁夏	Ningxia	371744	371188
新疆	Xinjiang	451814	451814

14-4 分地区按登记注册统计类别分建筑业企业单位数（2023年）
Number of Construction Enterprises by Registered Statistical Categories and Region (2023)

单位：个 (unit)

地 区	Region	总 计 Total	内资企业 Domestic Invested Enterprises	港澳台投资企业 Enterprises with Investment from Hong Kong, Macao and Taiwan	外商投资企业 Foreign Invested Enterprises
全 国	**National Total**	**159140**	**158707**	**262**	**171**
北 京	Beijing	2706	2664	22	20
天 津	Tianjin	3379	3367	3	9
河 北	Hebei	4118	4114	3	1
山 西	Shanxi	3834	3833	1	
内蒙古	Inner Mongolia	1135	1135		
辽 宁	Liaoning	5962	5940	9	13
吉 林	Jilin	2664	2661	2	1
黑龙江	Heilongjiang	2097	2093	1	3
上 海	Shanghai	2460	2380	40	40
江 苏	Jiangsu	14815	14757	28	30
浙 江	Zhejiang	10827	10810	15	2
安 徽	Anhui	9009	8999	7	3
福 建	Fujian	9281	9257	21	3
江 西	Jiangxi	6910	6903	5	2
山 东	Shandong	12570	12551	11	8
河 南	Henan	10042	10033	2	7
湖 北	Hubei	6945	6941	1	3
湖 南	Hunan	4213	4209	3	1
广 东	Guangdong	11576	11484	78	14
广 西	Guangxi	2869	2868	1	
海 南	Hainan	390	389	1	
重 庆	Chongqing	3924	3921	2	1
四 川	Sichuan	9372	9367	3	2
贵 州	Guizhou	2356	2356		
云 南	Yunnan	4616	4616		
西 藏	Xizang	525	525		
陕 西	Shaanxi	4334	4325	3	6
甘 肃	Gansu	2760	2759		1
青 海	Qinghai	625	625		
宁 夏	Ningxia	772	771		1
新 疆	Xinjiang	2054	2054		

注：本表登记注册统计类别按《关于市场主体统计分类的划分规定》(国统字〔2023〕14号)执行。

a) The registered statistical categories of this table is implemented in accordance with the Regulations on the Classification of Market Entity Statistics (Guotongzi [2023] No. 14).

14-5 分地区按登记注册统计类别分建筑业企业从业人员（2023年）
Number of Employed Persons in Construction Enterprises by Registered Statistical Categories and Region (2023)

单位：人 (person)

地 区	Region	总 计 Total	内资企业 Domestic Invested Enterprises	港澳台投资企业 Enterprises with Investment from Hong Kong, Macao and Taiwan	外商投资企业 Foreign Invested Enterprises
全 国	**National Total**	**50434857**	**50225641**	**144351**	**64865**
北 京	Beijing	537874	526851	7611	3412
天 津	Tianjin	532612	531854	179	579
河 北	Hebei	790340	783527	6768	45
山 西	Shanxi	822086	822083	3	
内蒙古	Inner Mongolia	206213	206213		
辽 宁	Liaoning	465991	462578	2891	522
吉 林	Jilin	314469	313538	596	335
黑龙江	Heilongjiang	151998	151594	15	389
上 海	Shanghai	719485	706593	5804	7088
江 苏	Jiangsu	7528633	7512204	4645	11784
浙 江	Zhejiang	4967325	4923226	31476	12623
安 徽	Anhui	2335857	2324482	11122	253
福 建	Fujian	4575818	4529768	45606	444
江 西	Jiangxi	1608328	1603292	1050	3986
山 东	Shandong	3074544	3066916	3261	4367
河 南	Henan	2431461	2429321	638	1502
湖 北	Hubei	2367797	2366892	220	685
湖 南	Hunan	2514923	2508050	2348	4525
广 东	Guangdong	3700643	3672863	18462	9318
广 西	Guangxi	1346948	1346918	30	
海 南	Hainan	58895	58779	116	
重 庆	Chongqing	1854216	1853640	66	510
四 川	Sichuan	3411084	3410659	284	141
贵 州	Guizhou	563922	563922		
云 南	Yunnan	1167781	1167781		
西 藏	Xizang	35024	35024		
陕 西	Shaanxi	1384880	1381850	1160	1870
甘 肃	Gansu	428772	428769		3
青 海	Qinghai	61125	61125		
宁 夏	Ningxia	96325	95841		484
新 疆	Xinjiang	379488	379488		

注：本表登记注册统计类别按《关于市场主体统计分类的划分规定》(国统字〔2023〕14号)执行。
a) The registered statistical categories of this table is implemented in accordance with the Regulations on the Classification of Market Entity Statistics (Guotongzi [2023] No. 14).

14-6 建筑业企业技术装备情况
Machinery and Equipment Owned by Construction Enterprises

年 份 Year 地 区 Region	自有施工机械设备年末总台数(台) Number of Machinery and Equipment Owned (set)	自有施工机械设备年末总功率(万千瓦) Total Power of Machinery and Equipment Owned (10 000 kW)	自有施工机械设备年末净值(万元) Year-end Net Value of Machinery and Equipment Owned (10 000 yuan)	技术装备率(元/人) Value of Machinery per Worker (yuan/person)	动力装备率(千瓦/人) Power of Machines per Worker (kW/person)
1992	2531578	4431.9	3147398	2719	3.8
1995	3482784	7056.5	6386383	4264	4.7
2000	6259885	9228.1	12572317	6304	4.6
2005	8798527	13765.6	25037702	9273	5.1
2006	8973042	14156.3	26217542	9109	4.9
2007	9487515	15579.4	28856331	9208	5.0
2008	9448056	18195.4	32869151	9915	5.5
2009	9734910	19022.6	37049784	10088	5.2
2010	11209484	19386.4	39719872	9547	4.7
2011	10054231	21822.4	46327127	12025	5.7
2012	10157280	24275.3	57070804	13374	5.7
2013	11467280	25424.0	60941736	13458	5.6
2014	12030587	29602.2	56797668	12519	6.5
2015	9643725	26736.8	56619984	11116	5.2
2016	9579327	25365.3	56021121	10805	4.9
2017	10225555	25500.6	54818437	9914	4.6
2018	10923709	25757.7	62464586	11774	4.9
2019	9833258	25117.8	58450114	10770	4.6
2020	8166436	27321.8	52494828	9781	5.1
2021	7394261	22920.9	45635349	8639	4.3
2022	5629429	16709.1	36567627	7222	3.3
2023	5232523	14844.5	36920143	7320	2.9
北 京 Beijing	68413	546.7	863227	16049	10.2
天 津 Tianjin	57173	228.3	1040052	19527	4.3
河 北 Hebei	210639	581.8	939274	11884	7.4
山 西 Shanxi	175027	722.8	1333064	16216	8.8
内蒙古 Inner Mongolia	32000	178.8	397356	19269	8.7
辽 宁 Liaoning	70792	258.3	453950	9742	5.5
吉 林 Jilin	37703	100.5	308046	9796	3.2
黑龙江 Heilongjiang	57220	135.6	271501	17862	8.9
上 海 Shanghai	29406	156.4	756427	10514	2.2
江 苏 Jiangsu	1241458	3239.1	8084297	10738	4.3
浙 江 Zhejiang	538373	933.2	2312154	4655	1.9
安 徽 Anhui	117157	243.8	628831	2692	1.0
福 建 Fujian	202742	651.6	1517539	3316	1.4
江 西 Jiangxi	111159	317.9	743277	4621	2.0
山 东 Shandong	428196	860.4	3066192	9973	2.8
河 南 Henan	320119	919.0	1942365	7989	3.8
湖 北 Hubei	266800	735.8	2182970	9219	3.1
湖 南 Hunan	289554	795.8	1502951	5976	3.2
广 东 Guangdong	246955	685.9	2390059	6459	1.9
广 西 Guangxi	81311	130.7	293806	2181	1.0
海 南 Hainan	3789	8.4	12162	2065	1.4
重 庆 Chongqing	88490	320.7	954534	5148	1.7
四 川 Sichuan	174552	698.7	1483575	4349	2.0
贵 州 Guizhou	27057	154.0	294724	5226	2.7
云 南 Yunnan	119983	257.9	732842	6276	2.2
西 藏 Xizang	1553	9.3	24318	6943	2.6
陕 西 Shaanxi	101652	601.8	1362681	9840	4.3
甘 肃 Gansu	70380	149.8	353864	8253	3.5
青 海 Qinghai	10402	46.2	115172	18842	7.6
宁 夏 Ningxia	19327	28.5	83105	8628	3.0
新 疆 Xinjiang	33141	146.8	475829	12539	3.9

注：从2004年起，自有机械设备情况统计改为自有施工机械设备情况统计。

a) Starting from 2004, statistics on machinery and equipment owned refer to construction machinery and equipment owned.

14–7 分地区建筑业总产值（2023年）
Total Output Value of Construction by Region (2023)

单位：万元 (10 000 yuan)

地 区	Region	建筑业总产值 Total Output Value of Construction	建筑工程产值 Output Value of Construction	安装工程产值 Output Value of Installation	其 他 Others
全 国	**National Total**	**3143935311**	**2787259803**	**264549353**	**92126156**
北 京	Beijing	143184759	134405539	7526451	1252769
天 津	Tianjin	51035739	45533568	3942921	1559250
河 北	Hebei	72590170	61228651	9728822	1632696
山 西	Shanxi	61596340	54789361	5495748	1311231
内蒙古	Inner Mongolia	14992590	13622526	824423	545641
辽 宁	Liaoning	43378557	35928208	5521655	1928694
吉 林	Jilin	22191409	18754092	2444301	993016
黑龙江	Heilongjiang	14571878	11853378	1745344	973157
上 海	Shanghai	100833022	87067380	11164026	2601616
江 苏	Jiangsu	422512502	390821491	29102297	2588714
浙 江	Zhejiang	244557965	217058970	21731473	5767522
安 徽	Anhui	124042767	106157667	9385324	8499776
福 建	Fujian	173954614	160836229	10177164	2941221
江 西	Jiangxi	108020454	94615394	7469487	5935573
山 东	Shandong	187818935	157661754	25310075	4847106
河 南	Henan	114932006	98554928	12184869	4192209
湖 北	Hubei	207787842	184951661	17567255	5268926
湖 南	Hunan	151591737	130135165	13806559	7650014
广 东	Guangdong	253992051	225931247	21860027	6200778
广 西	Guangxi	56893532	50224016	3608232	3061283
海 南	Hainan	4925728	4292527	404313	228887
重 庆	Chongqing	95361470	84952604	6699766	3709100
四 川	Sichuan	172725363	152520577	12941360	7263425
贵 州	Guizhou	39429279	33325422	4324477	1779380
云 南	Yunnan	78839434	70084968	5364609	3389857
西 藏	Xizang	2509839	2195436	188747	125656
陕 西	Shaanxi	103153580	91547833	7977840	3627906
甘 肃	Gansu	26974787	23355849	2623388	995550
青 海	Qinghai	6257834	5559289	497892	200652
宁 夏	Ningxia	7438553	6568822	722418	147312
新 疆	Xinjiang	35840580	32725249	2208089	907241

14-8 分地区按登记注册统计类别分建筑业总产值（2023年）
Total Output Value of Construction by Registered Statistical Categories and Region (2023)

单位：万元 (10 000 yuan)

地 区	Region	总 计 Total	内资企业 Domestic Invested Enterprises	港澳台投资企业 Enterprises with Investment from Hong Kong, Macao and Taiwan	外商投资企业 Foreign Invested Enterprises
全 国	**National Total**	**3143935311**	**3122166185**	**14558505**	**7210621**
北 京	Beijing	143184759	142049442	635171	500146
天 津	Tianjin	51035739	50938222	10909	86608
河 北	Hebei	72590170	69089042	3499805	1322
山 西	Shanxi	61596340	61596327	13	
内蒙古	Inner Mongolia	14992590	14992590		
辽 宁	Liaoning	43378557	43005811	341956	30790
吉 林	Jilin	22191409	22094478	84953	11978
黑龙江	Heilongjiang	14571878	14564112	266	7500
上 海	Shanghai	100833022	99171948	691146	969928
江 苏	Jiangsu	422512502	419473664	455439	2583399
浙 江	Zhejiang	244557965	240976224	3431160	150581
安 徽	Anhui	124042767	122977966	1029208	35593
福 建	Fujian	173954614	172626763	1123424	204427
江 西	Jiangxi	108020454	107756131	141803	122520
山 东	Shandong	187818935	186853320	722434	243181
河 南	Henan	114932006	114843163	11661	77182
湖 北	Hubei	207787842	207527601	2812	257429
湖 南	Hunan	151591737	151234341	139937	217460
广 东	Guangdong	253992051	250467097	2105011	1419943
广 西	Guangxi	56893532	56893469	63	
海 南	Hainan	4925728	4920863	4864	
重 庆	Chongqing	95361470	95205860	4642	150968
四 川	Sichuan	172725363	172695392	21468	8503
贵 州	Guizhou	39429279	39429279		
云 南	Yunnan	78839434	78839434		
西 藏	Xizang	2509839	2509839		
陕 西	Shaanxi	103153580	102950716	100363	102501
甘 肃	Gansu	26974787	26974660		127
青 海	Qinghai	6257834	6257834		
宁 夏	Ningxia	7438553	7410018		28535
新 疆	Xinjiang	35840580	35840580		

注：本表登记注册统计类别按《关于市场主体统计分类的划分规定》(国统字〔2023〕14号)执行。

a) The registered statistical categories of this table is implemented in accordance with the Regulations on the Classification of Market Entity Statistics (Guotongzi [2023] No. 14).

14–9 分地区按行业分建筑业总产值（2023年）
Total Output Value of Construction by Branch and Region (2023)

单位：万元 (10 000 yuan)

地区	Region	建筑业总产值 Total Output Value of Construction	房屋建筑业 Construction of Buildings	土木工程建筑业 Civil Engineering	建筑安装业 Building Installation	建筑装饰、装修和其他建筑业 Building Decoration and Other Construction
全国	**National Total**	**3143935311**	**1875370690**	**954082341**	**153920355**	**160561925**
北京	Beijing	143184759	75655361	47182034	9743659	10603704
天津	Tianjin	51035739	17533775	27618847	3570596	2312520
河北	Hebei	72590170	40165397	23556142	7003545	1865086
山西	Shanxi	61596340	29226984	27471486	3074198	1823672
内蒙古	Inner Mongolia	14992590	8563593	4829480	348559	1250957
辽宁	Liaoning	43378557	16031975	20676892	3629980	3039710
吉林	Jilin	22191409	10482253	9664675	1168046	876436
黑龙江	Heilongjiang	14571878	5509572	7706305	596018	759983
上海	Shanghai	100833022	57282872	26880254	6709416	9960480
江苏	Jiangsu	422512502	303033532	67809070	29444762	22225138
浙江	Zhejiang	244557965	157445875	57181944	12276254	17653891
安徽	Anhui	124042767	65597924	47180886	5557450	5706506
福建	Fujian	173954614	127014688	38037086	3365486	5537354
江西	Jiangxi	108020454	68770636	31656210	2348972	5244636
山东	Shandong	187818935	111443869	54062534	13107123	9205409
河南	Henan	114932006	62245044	37753384	5601650	9331929
湖北	Hubei	207787842	116980023	77504029	8199520	5104270
湖南	Hunan	151591737	108725998	35764749	4241194	2859797
广东	Guangdong	253992051	129524673	84420336	13026522	27020521
广西	Guangxi	56893532	34767141	20449489	905348	771554
海南	Hainan	4925728	3541673	682104	337866	364085
重庆	Chongqing	95361470	63064263	25445180	2897525	3954502
四川	Sichuan	172725363	104583994	58335455	5303458	4502456
贵州	Guizhou	39429279	19874711	15771712	1936856	1846000
云南	Yunnan	78839434	49016526	25294440	2217258	2311211
西藏	Xizang	2509839	1576931	878153	10693	44062
陕西	Shaanxi	103153580	46012730	50483884	4319621	2337345
甘肃	Gansu	26974787	14104332	10599304	1749625	521527
青海	Qinghai	6257834	1802011	4063595	328158	64070
宁夏	Ningxia	7438553	4193631	3050727	122469	71726
新疆	Xinjiang	35840580	21598706	12071956	778527	1391390

14-10 分地区建筑业企业签订合同和承包工程完成情况（2023年）
Contracts Signed and Completion of Contracted Projects by Construction Enterprises by Region (2023)

单位：万元 (10 000 yuan)

地区	Region	合同总额 Total Value of Contracts	上年结转合同额 Value from Contracts Signed in Last Year	本年新签合同额 Value from New Contracts Signed in This Year	直接从建设单位承揽工程完成的产值 Completed Output Value of Projects Contracted Directly from Investors	自行完成施工产值 Own-completed Output Value	分包出去工程的产值 Output Value of Out-subcontracted Projects	从建设单位以外承揽工程完成的产值 Completed Output Value of Projects Contracted from Non-investors
全国	**National Total**	**7287919324**	**3724428011**	**3563491314**	**3007619739**	**2865061632**	**142558107**	**278873679**
北京	Beijing	501539885	304763886	196775998	147547131	118068486	29478645	25116273
天津	Tianjin	175481285	89150044	86331241	52960657	45391898	7568759	5643841
河北	Hebei	175218099	91020795	84197305	70394862	69229011	1165851	3361159
山西	Shanxi	138419448	62195788	76223660	58188783	57268424	920359	4327916
内蒙古	Inner Mongolia	40167954	20191787	19976167	15224405	14675776	548629	316814
辽宁	Liaoning	86248845	36197214	50051631	40397860	39590102	807758	3788454
吉林	Jilin	45595898	22144471	23451428	19652577	19479553	173024	2711856
黑龙江	Heilongjiang	33932543	17336187	16596356	14437054	14306862	130192	265016
上海	Shanghai	385477214	232073191	153404023	110182001	84351329	25830672	16481694
江苏	Jiangsu	641820444	266379594	375440850	387472539	385214294	2258245	37298208
浙江	Zhejiang	477681953	248497146	229184807	229982140	224750062	5232078	19807903
安徽	Anhui	271340323	123427841	147912481	109402054	107455465	1946589	16587301
福建	Fujian	313339965	146872024	166467941	162400688	161928504	472184	12026110
江西	Jiangxi	185332487	78699693	106632794	103729944	102384435	1345508	5636018
山东	Shandong	407200077	187861500	219338577	188844739	174412588	14432151	13406348
河南	Henan	268176939	137942264	130234675	111329641	110283722	1045919	4648284
湖北	Hubei	566074549	294565453	271509096	198464407	195717649	2746758	12070192
湖南	Hunan	320550336	159700306	160850030	145362372	144292590	1069782	7299147
广东	Guangdong	757962233	438234579	319727654	254612873	222445070	32167803	31546982
广西	Guangxi	121041528	72504648	48536880	53005290	51003187	2002102	5890345
海南	Hainan	15826567	8944857	6881710	5122138	4703492	418646	222236
重庆	Chongqing	173048589	80378183	92670406	86722394	84992538	1729856	10368932
四川	Sichuan	458931769	247166314	211765455	166696679	160258486	6438193	12466876
贵州	Guizhou	133944807	83798302	50146505	38270767	38180957	89809	1248321
云南	Yunnan	152928729	72316688	80612041	69753702	69438374	315328	9401060
西藏	Xizang	4810568	2772132	2038436	2497813	2416512	81302	93327
陕西	Shaanxi	263327241	114748394	148578847	88746545	88048679	697867	15104901
甘肃	Gansu	60715751	28305360	32410391	26584491	26332010	252481	642777
青海	Qinghai	22976985	11677423	11299562	6380041	6125342	254699	132492
宁夏	Ningxia	13426175	5570137	7856038	7819904	7302187	517717	136366
新疆	Xinjiang	75380138	38991809	36388330	35433250	35014048	419202	826532

14-11 分地区按登记注册统计类别分建筑业企业实收资本（2023年）

Paid-in Capitals of Construction Enterprises by Registered Statistical Categories and Region (2023)

单位：万元 (10 000 yuan)

地区	Region	总计 Total	内资企业 Domestic Invested Enterprises	港澳台投资企业 Enterprises with Investment from Hong Kong, Macao and Taiwan	外商投资企业 Foreign Invested Enterprises
全国	**National Total**	**433260405**	**429712989**	**2373567**	**1173849**
北京	Beijing	33144257	32921661	106255	116341
天津	Tianjin	11016737	10960947	25389	30401
河北	Hebei	10696406	10496068	196338	4000
山西	Shanxi	12403435	12401636	1799	
内蒙古	Inner Mongolia	4211592	4211592		
辽宁	Liaoning	9311483	9066653	230305	14525
吉林	Jilin	4777823	4762223	15600	
黑龙江	Heilongjiang	4016614	4011124	166	5324
上海	Shanghai	15818525	15534330	128421	155774
江苏	Jiangsu	46267308	45979185	152014	136109
浙江	Zhejiang	28490516	28159689	320242	10585
安徽	Anhui	12995089	12835367	140398	19323
福建	Fujian	15052068	14962055	90014	
江西	Jiangxi	10528175	10495532	14645	17998
山东	Shandong	27143433	26976019	153039	14374
河南	Henan	19273160	19237028	4598	31534
湖北	Hubei	21895883	21881363	4200	10320
湖南	Hunan	12188596	12171038	11866	5691
广东	Guangdong	37208833	36095905	561682	551247
广西	Guangxi	9053637	9053637		
海南	Hainan	999739	999216	523	
重庆	Chongqing	8349844	8150968	188876	10000
四川	Sichuan	22075307	22057610	11697	6000
贵州	Guizhou	6325313	6325313		
云南	Yunnan	20365805	20365805		
西藏	Xizang	636655	636655		
陕西	Shaanxi	14377381	14358078	15500	3803
甘肃	Gansu	6377661	6377161		500
青海	Qinghai	1511643	1511643		
宁夏	Ningxia	1507528	1477528		30000
新疆	Xinjiang	5239962	5239962		

注：本表登记注册统计类别按《关于市场主体统计分类的划分规定》(国统字〔2023〕14号)执行。

a) The registered statistical categories of this table is implemented in accordance with the Regulations on the Classification of Market Entity Statistics (Guotongzi [2023] No. 14).

14-12 分地区建筑业企业资产（2023年）
Assets of Construction Enterprises by Region (2023)

单位：万元 (10 000 yuan)

地 区	Region	资产总计 Total Assets	#流动资产 Current Assets	#固定资产 Fixed Assets	#在建工程 Projects Under Construction
全 国	**National Total**	**3817408224**	**2980936341**	**248479659**	**38621883**
北 京	Beijing	351376758	220227746	11138105	572286
天 津	Tianjin	96088473	75150327	7902936	322263
河 北	Hebei	95140699	79344617	8197298	662245
山 西	Shanxi	107475468	80278315	7636794	1286934
内蒙古	Inner Mongolia	25183479	20211125	2967824	327254
辽 宁	Liaoning	71918606	60406013	7049409	482845
吉 林	Jilin	36111007	29825392	3732790	460137
黑龙江	Heilongjiang	27177996	23360751	2286254	158294
上 海	Shanghai	159604392	125630290	8988011	579908
江 苏	Jiangsu	316175895	266591477	30741140	3609425
浙 江	Zhejiang	211566396	175234896	16673363	2721194
安 徽	Anhui	134326959	107649703	7816623	1478416
福 建	Fujian	106280575	84257737	8039079	936910
江 西	Jiangxi	99418201	79080598	6606958	1459529
山 东	Shandong	261767197	213912129	18590850	3124825
河 南	Henan	143895425	114716888	12104378	1110683
湖 北	Hubei	220878518	168212045	13540029	2273146
湖 南	Hunan	108137578	80190245	9046126	1404922
广 东	Guangdong	357463092	293447831	14887499	2301105
广 西	Guangxi	60430722	47874023	3058787	1957383
海 南	Hainan	8841128	7729923	264103	110964
重 庆	Chongqing	86777805	64282696	5686410	1833156
四 川	Sichuan	245077354	182641892	14092180	4048427
贵 州	Guizhou	97823367	81677376	2270817	1098369
云 南	Yunnan	105777470	72587079	6047216	1246006
西 藏	Xizang	7252049	5731093	368888	38272
陕 西	Shaanxi	144148335	119931457	7939551	504963
甘 肃	Gansu	55833542	41249727	4370906	1537351
青 海	Qinghai	10736572	7879790	915537	64322
宁 夏	Ningxia	9099157	7624775	881569	50797
新 疆	Xinjiang	55624006	43998384	4638231	859554

14−13 分地区建筑业企业负债及所有者权益（2023年）
Liabilities and Owners' Equity of Construction Enterprises by Region (2023)

单位：万元 (10 000 yuan)

地 区	Region	负债合计 Total Liabilities	流动负债合计 Current Liabilities	非流动负债合计 Non-current Liabilities	所有者权益 Owners' Equity	#实收资本 Paid-in Capitals
全 国	**National Total**	**2786050425**	**2371040467**	**184362601**	**1031357798**	**433260405**
北 京	Beijing	244387936	218763318	23875051	106988822	33144257
天 津	Tianjin	74956363	67664607	4535741	21132111	11016737
河 北	Hebei	72496122	60568065	4539542	22644578	10696406
山 西	Shanxi	80747198	70231627	7678736	26728270	12403435
内蒙古	Inner Mongolia	17678151	14789163	550314	7505328	4211592
辽 宁	Liaoning	54796450	46427608	3283791	17122156	9311483
吉 林	Jilin	25588590	21257402	857001	10522417	4777823
黑龙江	Heilongjiang	21408111	18856499	826015	5769885	4016614
上 海	Shanghai	126227279	117925426	3133309	33377113	15818525
江 苏	Jiangsu	191929183	168176575	9076434	124246712	46267308
浙 江	Zhejiang	150531734	136130258	6791414	61034661	28490516
安 徽	Anhui	102960653	84507255	5417263	31366306	12995089
福 建	Fujian	65593309	46707598	5700572	40687266	15052068
江 西	Jiangxi	72383465	53830360	4597327	27034736	10528175
山 东	Shandong	203015491	170704033	9489313	58751706	27143433
河 南	Henan	101742415	83599708	5273741	42153010	19273160
湖 北	Hubei	162067913	133482682	17191065	58810606	21895883
湖 南	Hunan	76150255	58742216	6113648	31987323	12188596
广 东	Guangdong	276591542	244141757	18418637	80871550	37208833
广 西	Guangxi	45874469	38628409	3708815	14556254	9053637
海 南	Hainan	6713814	5669146	220975	2127315	999739
重 庆	Chongqing	63192626	49261573	4260344	23585179	8349844
四 川	Sichuan	181940631	144352105	16963528	63136723	22075307
贵 州	Guizhou	77726806	65888170	4216916	20096561	6325313
云 南	Yunnan	72491636	63418311	3745713	33285834	20365805
西 藏	Xizang	4776921	3389927	360277	2475129	636655
陕 西	Shaanxi	114255540	102388096	5166539	29892795	14377381
甘 肃	Gansu	40641787	33673152	3826063	15191755	6377661
青 海	Qinghai	7731898	6466065	712332	3004674	1511643
宁 夏	Ningxia	6526774	5589733	266671	2572383	1507528
新 疆	Xinjiang	42925366	35809624	3565515	12698641	5239962

14-14 分地区按登记注册统计类别分建筑业企业资产（2023年）
Assets of Construction Enterprises by Registered Statistical Categories and Region (2023)

单位：万元 (10 000 yuan)

地区	Region	总计 Total	内资企业 Domestic Invested Enterprises	港澳台投资企业 Enterprises with Investment from Hong Kong, Macao and Taiwan	外商投资企业 Foreign Invested Enterprises
全国	**National Total**	**3817408224**	**3766631784**	**32132680**	**18643759**
北京	Beijing	351376758	349293382	866314	1217063
天津	Tianjin	96088473	95793493	137945	157036
河北	Hebei	95140699	89930073	5199319	11308
山西	Shanxi	107475468	107472660	2808	
内蒙古	Inner Mongolia	25183479	25183479		
辽宁	Liaoning	71918606	70912564	937114	68928
吉林	Jilin	36111007	35982429	107262	21316
黑龙江	Heilongjiang	27177996	27139112	9224	29660
上海	Shanghai	159604392	157011430	1002077	1590885
江苏	Jiangsu	316175895	311128530	1162043	3885323
浙江	Zhejiang	211566396	206765954	4741353	59089
安徽	Anhui	134326959	131190250	3005942	130766
福建	Fujian	106280575	105375558	579761	325256
江西	Jiangxi	99418201	99118394	89273	210534
山东	Shandong	261767197	259827408	987397	952392
河南	Henan	143895425	143475936	93568	325921
湖北	Hubei	220878518	220736885	12905	128728
湖南	Hunan	108137578	107710341	51945	375292
广东	Guangdong	357463092	336760276	12103879	8598937
广西	Guangxi	60430722	60430657	66	
海南	Hainan	8841128	8837878	3251	
重庆	Chongqing	86777805	85730579	854605	192621
四川	Sichuan	245077354	244955618	83028	38708
贵州	Guizhou	97823367	97823367		
云南	Yunnan	105777470	105777470		
西藏	Xizang	7252049	7252049		
陕西	Shaanxi	144148335	143942006	101603	104726
甘肃	Gansu	55833542	55830913		2629
青海	Qinghai	10736572	10736572		
宁夏	Ningxia	9099157	8882515		216643
新疆	Xinjiang	55624006	55624006		

注：本表登记注册统计类别按《关于市场主体统计分类的划分规定》(国统字〔2023〕14号)执行。

a) The registered statistical categories of this table is implemented in accordance with the Regulations on the Classification of Market Entity Statistics (Guotongzi [2023] No. 14).

14-15 分地区按登记注册统计类别分建筑业企业负债（2023年）
Liabilities of Construction Enterprises by Registered Statistical Categories and Region (2023)

单位：万元 (10 000 yuan)

地 区	Region	总 计 Total	内资企业 Domestic Invested Enterprises	港澳台投资企业 Enterprises with Investment from Hong Kong, Macao and Taiwan	外商投资企业 Foreign Invested Enterprises
全 国	**National Total**	**2786050425**	**2747934518**	**24530480**	**13585428**
北 京	Beijing	244387936	242718003	600461	1069472
天 津	Tianjin	74956363	74762569	107076	86718
河 北	Hebei	72496122	67860183	4635204	734
山 西	Shanxi	80747198	80745259	1939	
内蒙古	Inner Mongolia	17678151	17678151		
辽 宁	Liaoning	54796450	54312251	428728	55472
吉 林	Jilin	25588590	25507489	65808	15293
黑龙江	Heilongjiang	21408111	21375430	7041	25640
上 海	Shanghai	126227279	124371898	666195	1189186
江 苏	Jiangsu	191929183	188986831	758941	2183412
浙 江	Zhejiang	150531734	146677302	3807361	47071
安 徽	Anhui	102960653	100221129	2669682	69842
福 建	Fujian	65593309	65029265	426652	137392
江 西	Jiangxi	72383465	72163641	36628	183196
山 东	Shandong	203015491	201714072	662076	639344
河 南	Henan	101742415	101422404	83368	236644
湖 北	Hubei	162067913	161955701	5599	106612
湖 南	Hunan	76150255	75901318	34885	214052
广 东	Guangdong	276591542	260796461	8800442	6994639
广 西	Guangxi	45874469	45874403	65	
海 南	Hainan	6713814	6711086	2728	
重 庆	Chongqing	63192626	62447205	585594	159827
四 川	Sichuan	181940631	181858221	68662	13748
贵 州	Guizhou	77726806	77726806		
云 南	Yunnan	72491636	72491636		
西 藏	Xizang	4776921	4776921		
陕 西	Shaanxi	114255540	114148578	75346	31616
甘 肃	Gansu	40641787	40641784		3
青 海	Qinghai	7731898	7731898		
宁 夏	Ningxia	6526774	6401258		125517
新 疆	Xinjiang	42925366	42925366		

注：本表登记注册统计类别按《关于市场主体统计分类的划分规定》(国统字〔2023〕14号)执行。

a) The registered statistical categories of this table is implemented in accordance with the Regulations on the Classification of Market Entity Statistics (Guotongzi [2023] No. 14).

14-16 分地区按登记注册统计类别分建筑业企业所有者权益（2023年）
Owners' Equity of Construction Enterprises by Registered Statistical Categories and Region (2023)

单位：万元 (10 000 yuan)

地 区	Region	总 计 Total	内资企业 Domestic Invested Enterprises	港澳台投资企业 Enterprises with Investment from Hong Kong, Macao and Taiwan	外商投资企业 Foreign Invested Enterprises
全 国	**National Total**	**1031357798**	**1018697266**	**7602200**	**5058332**
北 京	Beijing	106988822	106575379	265853	147591
天 津	Tianjin	21132111	21030924	30869	70318
河 北	Hebei	22644578	22069890	564115	10574
山 西	Shanxi	26728270	26727401	869	
内蒙古	Inner Mongolia	7505328	7505328		
辽 宁	Liaoning	17122156	16600314	508386	13456
吉 林	Jilin	10522417	10474940	41454	6023
黑龙江	Heilongjiang	5769885	5763682	2183	4020
上 海	Shanghai	33377113	32639532	335882	401699
江 苏	Jiangsu	124246712	122141699	403102	1701911
浙 江	Zhejiang	61034661	60088652	933992	12018
安 徽	Anhui	31366306	30969121	336260	60925
福 建	Fujian	40687266	40346293	153108	187865
江 西	Jiangxi	27034736	26954753	52645	27338
山 东	Shandong	58751706	58113337	325321	313048
河 南	Henan	42153010	42053531	10201	89278
湖 北	Hubei	58810606	58781184	7306	22116
湖 南	Hunan	31987323	31809023	17060	161240
广 东	Guangdong	80871550	75963815	3303437	1604298
广 西	Guangxi	14556254	14556254	0	
海 南	Hainan	2127315	2126792	523	
重 庆	Chongqing	23585179	23283374	269011	32794
四 川	Sichuan	63136723	63097398	14366	24960
贵 州	Guizhou	20096561	20096561		
云 南	Yunnan	33285834	33285834		
西 藏	Xizang	2475129	2475129		
陕 西	Shaanxi	29892795	29793428	26257	73110
甘 肃	Gansu	15191755	15189129		2626
青 海	Qinghai	3004674	3004674		
宁 夏	Ningxia	2572383	2481257		91126
新 疆	Xinjiang	12698641	12698641		

注：本表登记注册统计类别按《关于市场主体统计分类的划分规定》(国统字〔2023〕14号)执行。

a) The registered statistical categories of this table is implemented in accordance with the Regulations on the Classification of Market Entity Statistics (Guotongzi [2023] No. 14).

14-17 分地区建筑业企业营业收入（2023年）
Business Revenue of Construction Enterprises by Region (2023)

单位：万元 (10 000 yuan)

地 区	Region	营业收入 Business Revenue	主营业务收入 Revenue from Principal Business	#主营业务成本 Costs of Principal Business	#主营业务利润 Profits from Principal Business	其他业务收入 Revenue from Other Businesses	#其他业务利润 Profits from Other Businesses
全 国	**National Total**	**2842348252**	**2764691901**	**2511242389**	**87876740**	**77656352**	**2046701**
北 京	Beijing	175929475	174750638	159742367	6347828	1178837	160100
天 津	Tianjin	55669841	54907769	50237998	1069737	762071	47748
河 北	Hebei	64757423	64212641	58701881	1241511	544782	31172
山 西	Shanxi	66332381	64749336	55951443	1629892	1583044	84011
内蒙古	Inner Mongolia	16623166	16244834	14765827	470210	378331	17205
辽 宁	Liaoning	40091354	38457440	32288586	477638	1633914	28087
吉 林	Jilin	21148262	19571034	17847169	570629	1577228	16390
黑龙江	Heilongjiang	16914847	15925029	14708081	344837	989819	23328
上 海	Shanghai	140084038	139086165	129975102	2311089	997873	138863
江 苏	Jiangsu	353992060	349158620	315732210	14173803	4833441	225766
浙 江	Zhejiang	202353627	200657585	186653976	3154412	1696041	202140
安 徽	Anhui	107243952	104944570	96203032	3275189	2299382	58371
福 建	Fujian	133667449	126948194	115111847	5088592	6719255	48075
江 西	Jiangxi	71263927	67961651	61750732	2712455	3302276	49653
山 东	Shandong	181643655	176164240	161031019	5684991	5479415	147059
河 南	Henan	98084713	95546907	85313792	3186885	2537805	60396
湖 北	Hubei	173242219	171237753	154834966	6844071	2004466	69482
湖 南	Hunan	121397684	109618857	97591759	4458312	11778827	24424
广 东	Guangdong	251672434	243274222	224241406	5066729	8398212	148839
广 西	Guangxi	40638978	39765029	35940256	1623354	873950	23338
海 南	Hainan	5415999	5296897	4834055	192533	119102	5627
重 庆	Chongqing	73837948	70137729	62812959	2798200	3700220	45180
四 川	Sichuan	160014768	155644347	140563043	6279107	4370421	133730
贵 州	Guizhou	34836240	32830057	29967401	1127959	2006183	21089
云 南	Yunnan	56592439	56166067	49913494	2735765	426372	135118
西 藏	Xizang	2960512	2431435	2204401	91386	529077	351
陕 西	Shaanxi	94541081	91214573	83478878	2943841	3326509	49586
甘 肃	Gansu	27484007	25790597	23641998	877539	1693410	16199
青 海	Qinghai	8966388	8738099	8040398	177013	228289	6145
宁 夏	Ningxia	8173305	8113001	7539058	153981	60304	2136
新 疆	Xinjiang	36774085	35146587	29623257	767257	1627499	27091

14-18 分地区按登记注册统计类别分建筑业企业营业收入（2023年）
Business Revenue of Construction Enterprises by Registered Statistical Categories and Region (2023)

单位：万元 (10 000 yuan)

地 区	Region	总 计 Total	内资企业 Domestic Invested Enterprises	港澳台投资企业 Enterprises with Investment from Hong Kong, Macao and Taiwan	外商投资企业 Foreign Invested Enterprises
全 国	**National Total**	**2842348252**	**2819042267**	**15020452**	**8285533**
北 京	Beijing	175929475	174246850	767002	915622
天 津	Tianjin	55669841	55542814	18726	108300
河 北	Hebei	64757423	62063648	2692323	1451
山 西	Shanxi	66332381	66332368	13	
内蒙古	Inner Mongolia	16623166	16623166		
辽 宁	Liaoning	40091354	39846272	214199	30883
吉 林	Jilin	21148262	21037470	99291	11500
黑龙江	Heilongjiang	16914847	16888862	266	25719
上 海	Shanghai	140084038	137321623	823112	1939303
江 苏	Jiangsu	353992060	350981501	710510	2300048
浙 江	Zhejiang	202353627	199182155	3050581	120891
安 徽	Anhui	107243952	106187903	1020456	35593
福 建	Fujian	133667449	132528051	1002098	137300
江 西	Jiangxi	71263927	71051691	138344	73892
山 东	Shandong	181643655	180900658	636944	106053
河 南	Henan	98084713	97995074	11807	77832
湖 北	Hubei	173242219	173104718	2714	134788
湖 南	Hunan	121397684	121043056	137168	217460
广 东	Guangdong	251672434	246554816	3502042	1615576
广 西	Guangxi	40638978	40638913	66	
海 南	Hainan	5415999	5411537	4463	
重 庆	Chongqing	73837948	73636449	35900	165599
四 川	Sichuan	160014768	159924994	74901	14873
贵 州	Guizhou	34836240	34836240		
云 南	Yunnan	56592439	56592439		
西 藏	Xizang	2960512	2960512		
陕 西	Shaanxi	94541081	94347365	77526	116190
甘 肃	Gansu	27484007	27483891		116
青 海	Qinghai	8966388	8966388		
宁 夏	Ningxia	8173305	8036760		136545
新 疆	Xinjiang	36774085	36774085		

注：本表登记注册统计类别按《关于市场主体统计分类的划分规定》(国统字〔2023〕14号)执行。

a) The registered statistical categories of this table is implemented in accordance with the Regulations on the Classification of Market Entity Statistics (Guotongzi [2023] No. 14).

14-19 分地区建筑业企业利税总额（2023年）
Total Pre-tax Profits of Construction Enterprises by Region (2023)

地区	Region	利税总额 合计（万元） Total Pre-tax Profits (10 000 yuan)	利润总额 Total Profits	税金总额 Total Tax	产值利税率(%) Ratio of Pre-tax Profits to Output Value (%)	资产利税率(%) Ratio of Pre-tax Profits to Assets (%)
全国	**National Total**	**159210875**	**89022677**	**70188198**	**5.1**	**4.2**
北京	Beijing	9127958	6532376	2595582	6.4	2.6
天津	Tianjin	2039941	1113426	926515	4.0	2.1
河北	Hebei	2711099	1259130	1451969	3.7	2.9
山西	Shanxi	3262808	1713696	1549112	5.3	3.0
内蒙古	Inner Mongolia	982824	475977	506847	6.6	3.9
辽宁	Liaoning	1619128	517378	1101750	3.7	2.3
吉林	Jilin	1232287	566194	666093	5.6	3.4
黑龙江	Heilongjiang	871792	360454	511338	6.0	3.2
上海	Shanghai	4532571	2496711	2035860	4.5	2.8
江苏	Jiangsu	23895656	14192844	9702811	5.7	7.6
浙江	Zhejiang	8560784	3521183	5039602	3.5	4.0
安徽	Anhui	5950979	3374535	2576444	4.8	4.4
福建	Fujian	8769990	5143034	3626956	5.0	8.3
江西	Jiangxi	4624565	2622986	2001579	4.3	4.7
山东	Shandong	10243082	5789890	4453192	5.5	3.9
河南	Henan	5959501	3152295	2807206	5.2	4.1
湖北	Hubei	11742449	6861341	4881108	5.7	5.3
湖南	Hunan	8332385	4473336	3859049	5.5	7.7
广东	Guangdong	10088627	4988471	5100156	4.0	2.8
广西	Guangxi	2597458	1615775	981683	4.6	4.3
海南	Hainan	367793	198269	169524	7.5	4.2
重庆	Chongqing	5414848	2814557	2600290	5.7	6.2
四川	Sichuan	10511518	6370039	4141479	6.1	4.3
贵州	Guizhou	2119468	1116883	1002584	5.4	2.2
云南	Yunnan	4642435	2839551	1802884	5.9	4.4
西藏	Xizang	180832	88273	92559	7.2	2.5
陕西	Shaanxi	4795904	2913949	1881955	4.6	3.3
甘肃	Gansu	1738209	840427	897783	6.4	3.1
青海	Qinghai	374331	177408	196923	6.0	3.5
宁夏	Ningxia	350828	147207	203622	4.7	3.9
新疆	Xinjiang	1568829	745083	823746	4.4	2.8

14-20 分地区按登记注册统计类别分建筑业企业税金总额（2023年）
Taxes of Construction Enterprises by Registered Statistical Categories and by Region (2023)

单位：万元 (10 000 yuan)

地 区	Region	总 计 Total	内资企业 Domestic Invested Enterprises	港澳台投资企 业 Enterprises with Investment from Hong Kong, Macao and Taiwan	外商投资企 业 Foreign Invested Enterprises
全 国	**National Total**	**70188198**	**69731343**	**299026**	**157829**
北 京	Beijing	2595582	2568836	12963	13783
天 津	Tianjin	926515	922633	587	3295
河 北	Hebei	1451969	1406180	45763	26
山 西	Shanxi	1549112	1549111	1	
内蒙古	Inner Mongolia	506847	506847		
辽 宁	Liaoning	1101750	1096589	3812	1349
吉 林	Jilin	666093	658300	7427	366
黑龙江	Heilongjiang	511338	509861	2	1474
上 海	Shanghai	2035860	1995547	17645	22668
江 苏	Jiangsu	9702811	9653421	6795	42595
浙 江	Zhejiang	5039602	5004870	32040	2692
安 徽	Anhui	2576444	2499317	76273	854
福 建	Fujian	3626956	3602633	22164	2159
江 西	Jiangxi	2001579	1997016	2168	2396
山 东	Shandong	4453192	4442581	8228	2383
河 南	Henan	2807206	2802199	1163	3844
湖 北	Hubei	4881108	4868656	328	12124
湖 南	Hunan	3859049	3840703	5374	12972
广 东	Guangdong	5100156	5026795	51532	21829
广 西	Guangxi	981683	981682	0	
海 南	Hainan	169524	169523	0	
重 庆	Chongqing	2600290	2596659	2191	1441
四 川	Sichuan	4141479	4140490	494	495
贵 州	Guizhou	1002584	1002584		
云 南	Yunnan	1802884	1802884		
西 藏	Xizang	92559	92559		
陕 西	Shaanxi	1881955	1876280	2075	3601
甘 肃	Gansu	897783	897781		1
青 海	Qinghai	196923	196923		
宁 夏	Ningxia	203622	198139		5483
新 疆	Xinjiang	823746	823746		

注：本表登记注册统计类别按《关于市场主体统计分类的划分规定》(国统字〔2023〕14号)执行。

a) The registered statistical categories of this table is implemented in accordance with the Regulations on the Classification of Market Entity Statistics (Guotongzi [2023] No. 14).

14–21 分地区按登记注册统计类别分建筑业企业利润总额（2023年）
Total Profits of Construction Enterprises by Registered Statistical Categories and Region (2023)

单位：万元 (10 000 yuan)

地 区	Region	总 计 Total	内资企业 Domestic Invested Enterprises	港澳台投资企业 Enterprises with Investment from Hong Kong, Macao and Taiwan	外商投资企业 Foreign Invested Enterprises
全 国	**National Total**	**89022677**	**87930519**	**620704**	**471454**
北 京	Beijing	6532376	6476597	52047	3731
天 津	Tianjin	1113426	1106204	-898	8120
河 北	Hebei	1259130	1191305	67724	101
山 西	Shanxi	1713696	1713698	-1	
内蒙古	Inner Mongolia	475977	475977		
辽 宁	Liaoning	517378	492202	19543	5633
吉 林	Jilin	566194	556639	9042	513
黑龙江	Heilongjiang	360454	360207	2	245
上 海	Shanghai	2496711	2313801	42647	140262
江 苏	Jiangsu	14192844	13979315	52719	160811
浙 江	Zhejiang	3521183	3527166	-6238	255
安 徽	Anhui	3374535	3175315	186203	13017
福 建	Fujian	5143034	5120137	17688	5209
江 西	Jiangxi	2622986	2605663	19427	-2103.8
山 东	Shandong	5789890	5741619	27986	20285
河 南	Henan	3152295	3142464	-69	9899
湖 北	Hubei	6861341	6850185	10	11146
湖 南	Hunan	4473336	4419365	12069	41902
广 东	Guangdong	4988471	4872179	117493	-1201
广 西	Guangxi	1615775	1615826	-50	
海 南	Hainan	198269	198288	-18	
重 庆	Chongqing	2814557	2810463	-4095	8189
四 川	Sichuan	6370039	6365810	3549	680
贵 州	Guizhou	1116883	1116883		
云 南	Yunnan	2839551	2839551		
西 藏	Xizang	88273	88273		
陕 西	Shaanxi	2913949	2893564	3924	16461
甘 肃	Gansu	840427	840422		5
青 海	Qinghai	177408	177408		
宁 夏	Ningxia	147207	118911		28296
新 疆	Xinjiang	745083	745083		

注：本表登记注册统计类别按《关于市场主体统计分类的划分规定》(国统字〔2023〕14号)执行。
a) The registered statistical categories of this table is implemented in accordance with the Regulations on the Classification of Market Entity Statistics (Guotongzi [2023] No. 14).

14–22 分地区按登记注册统计类别分建筑业企业主营业务利润（2023年）
Profits from Principal Business of Construction Enterprises by Registered Statistical Categories and Region (2023)

单位：万元 (10 000 yuan)

地 区	Region	总 计 Total	内资企业 Domestic Invested Enterprises	港澳台投资企业 Enterprises with Investment from Hong Kong, Macao and Taiwan	外商投资企业 Foreign Invested Enterprises
全 国	**National Total**	**87876740**	**86824260**	**590246**	**462234**
北 京	Beijing	6347828	6292638	51128	4063
天 津	Tianjin	1069737	1062393	-611	7955
河 北	Hebei	1241511	1175688	65740	84
山 西	Shanxi	1629892	1629893	-1	
内蒙古	Inner Mongolia	470210	470210		
辽 宁	Liaoning	477638	471178	975	5485
吉 林	Jilin	570629	561949	8171	508
黑龙江	Heilongjiang	344837	347087	2	-2252
上 海	Shanghai	2311089	2135469	41212	134408
江 苏	Jiangsu	14173803	13963710	52901	157192
浙 江	Zhejiang	3154412	3165562	-11491	341
安 徽	Anhui	3275189	3076757	185686	12746
福 建	Fujian	5088592	5066043	17557	4991
江 西	Jiangxi	2712455	2695523	19036	-2104
山 东	Shandong	5684991	5635545	28587	20859
河 南	Henan	3186885	3176673	-71	10283
湖 北	Hubei	6844071	6832915	10	11146
湖 南	Hunan	4458312	4404006	12394	41912
广 东	Guangdong	5066729	4954197	115985	-3453
广 西	Guangxi	1623354	1623404	-50	
海 南	Hainan	192533	192560	-26	
重 庆	Chongqing	2798200	2794992	-4328	7535
四 川	Sichuan	6279107	6274960	3519	628
贵 州	Guizhou	1127959	1127959		
云 南	Yunnan	2735765	2735765		
西 藏	Xizang	91386	91386		
陕 西	Shaanxi	2943841	2923828	3922	16091
甘 肃	Gansu	877539	877534		5
青 海	Qinghai	177013	177013		
宁 夏	Ningxia	153981	120169		33812
新 疆	Xinjiang	767257	767257		

注：本表登记注册统计类别按《关于市场主体统计分类的划分规定》(国统字〔2023〕14号)执行。

a) The registered statistical categories of this table is implemented in accordance with the Regulations on the Classification of Market Entity Statistics (Guotongzi [2023] No. 14).

14−23 建筑业企业房屋建筑面积
Floor Space of Buildings Constructed by Construction Enterprises

单位：万平方米 (10 000 sq.m)

年份 地区	Year Region	房屋建筑施工面积 Floor Space under Construction of Buildings Constructed	房屋建筑竣工面积 Floor Space Completed of Buildings Constructed
	1985	35491.8	17072.7
	1990	37923.0	19552.5
	1995	89862.8	35666.3
	2000	160141.1	80714.9
	2005	352744.7	159406.2
	2006	410154.4	179673.0
	2007	482005.5	203992.7
	2008	530518.6	223592.0
	2009	588593.9	245401.6
	2010	708023.5	277450.2
	2011	851828.1	316429.3
	2012	986427.5	358736.2
	2013	1132002.9	401520.9
	2014	1249826.3	423357.3
	2015	1239717.6	420784.9
	2016	1264216.3	422382.3
	2017	1318374.1	419072.3
	2018	1371994.7	411498.0
	2019	1441504.7	402335.5
	2020	1494753.7	384821.5
	2021	1575463.8	408027.5
	2022	1536111.4	396363.4
	2023	1530925.3	393400.9
北京	Beijing	88152.7	13823.6
天津	Tianjin	17885.3	3539.6
河北	Hebei	34046.6	7922.8
山西	Shanxi	22404.3	4229.0
内蒙古	Inner Mongolia	6871.3	1336.4
辽宁	Liaoning	11758.7	3545.0
吉林	Jilin	6197.8	2133.4
黑龙江	Heilongjiang	3604.9	1184.6
上海	Shanghai	55422.3	9788.5
江苏	Jiangsu	259218.3	73100.1
浙江	Zhejiang	168024.3	46600.4
安徽	Anhui	59857.7	16164.7
福建	Fujian	99066.6	20000.7
江西	Jiangxi	37076.1	12937.7
山东	Shandong	97991.5	23384.5
河南	Henan	61392.7	13419.4
湖北	Hubei	80348.8	26976.5
湖南	Hunan	76671.8	25599.4
广东	Guangdong	117914.6	27198.6
广西	Guangxi	27563.2	5950.7
海南	Hainan	2123.3	520.6
重庆	Chongqing	31600.8	11839.9
四川	Sichuan	65039.5	18709.6
贵州	Guizhou	14416.5	2524.7
云南	Yunnan	16797.2	5659.7
西藏	Xizang	366.5	223.1
陕西	Shaanxi	39662.6	7785.2
甘肃	Gansu	11417.1	2190.8
青海	Qinghai	877.3	240.6
宁夏	Ningxia	1716.8	584.6
新疆	Xinjiang	15438.3	4286.7

14–24 勘察设计单位基本情况（2023年）
Conditions of Prospecting and Designing Institutions (2023)

地 区	Region	单位数（个）Number of Institutions (unit)	年末从业人员数（人）Number of Employed Persons at Year-end (person)	#高级职称 Senior Title	#中级职称 Middle Title	#初级职称 Junior Title	营业收入（万元）Business Revenue (10 000 yuan)
全 国	**National Total**	**29352**	**4827324**	**576157**	**873992**	**623768**	**941545133**
北 京	Beijing	1272	378665	68593	89236	57895	129341742
天 津	Tianjin	505	99550	24148	23176	16813	40878142
河 北	Hebei	1021	171745	24541	36111	25203	33285522
山 西	Shanxi	1200	101566	15372	25133	17189	17134083
内蒙古	Inner Mongolia	289	15657	3788	4624	1817	1892490
辽 宁	Liaoning	763	60280	13783	16681	8249	5150293
吉 林	Jilin	640	35380	10214	9797	3709	2822957
黑龙江	Heilongjiang	326	21906	7616	6708	2494	3344736
上 海	Shanghai	1333	282160	34417	63602	52844	113702309
江 苏	Jiangsu	3114	655332	39190	69454	58339	80991278
浙 江	Zhejiang	1431	479931	32300	48398	36654	55727831
安 徽	Anhui	1096	249331	18491	33077	34991	50540617
福 建	Fujian	1518	339221	13767	33160	24678	31002005
江 西	Jiangxi	505	90577	6897	10846	8035	11871130
山 东	Shandong	2072	268986	35665	57852	46716	62335007
河 南	Henan	1495	139452	19190	33841	19084	16006603
湖 北	Hubei	1261	242447	35493	52030	40032	65018891
湖 南	Hunan	483	117339	15049	28986	14980	32996284
广 东	Guangdong	1666	386014	36291	61062	50180	79034673
广 西	Guangxi	606	70296	11767	19431	11408	9848484
海 南	Hainan	230	11480	1945	3000	1517	896822
重 庆	Chongqing	658	59529	12475	14439	7775	6886970
四 川	Sichuan	1458	204557	26612	42253	27949	40201252
贵 州	Guizhou	772	45229	9689	13291	6246	5182872
云 南	Yunnan	865	62763	12889	16004	10431	9223676
西 藏	Xizang	54	2139	324	696	288	105219
陕 西	Shaanxi	1753	131811	24326	33882	21949	25035075
甘 肃	Gansu	293	52948	11341	14104	9352	5456158
青 海	Qinghai	169	8487	1913	2090	1226	845674
宁 夏	Ningxia	271	7791	1312	2728	1135	444884
新 疆	Xinjiang	233	34755	6759	8300	4590	4341453

14−25 建设工程监理企业基本情况(2023年)
Conditions of Construction Project Supervision Enterprises (2023)

行业 地区	Sector Region	企业单位数(个) Number of Enterprises (unit)	年末从业人数(人) Employed Persons (year-end) (person)	#高、中级职称人员 Persons with Senior or Middle Certificates	年末注册执业人数(人) Registered Professionals (year-end) (person)	#注册监理工程师 Registered Supervisory Engineers	营业收入(万元) Business Revenue (10 000 yuan)
合计	**Total**	**19717**	**2107974**	**746590**	**713759**	**339003**	**158280227**
按行业分	**By Sector**						
房屋建筑工程	Housing Construction Projects	14542	1344489	418820	429378	199905	79353554
冶炼工程	Metallurgical Projects	25	13811	8310	2860	926	4042355
矿山工程	Mining Projects	84	14751	5260	3500	1859	626982
化工石油工程	Chemical and Petroleum Projects	183	43752	23108	14087	5987	8117807
水利水电工程	Water Conservancy and Hydro-power Projects	125	33226	12941	11643	3003	7783146
电力工程	Power Projects	666	92597	36781	30306	12739	18247829
农林工程	Agriculture and Forestry Projects	9	491	235	253	151	24542
铁路工程	Railway Projects	60	23926	14138	7377	4014	1285379
公路工程	Highway Projects	60	10624	5776	3641	1626	1150828
港口与航道工程	Harbour and Navigation Projects	14	2198	1104	1598	1069	81890
航天航空工程	Air and Space Projects	10	1808	872	706	461	47825
通信工程	Communications Projects	92	21017	7612	5570	2512	1932404
市政公用工程	Civil and Public Utility Projects	3450	233318	83197	79642	34471	18419108
机电安装工程	Machinery and Electric Installation Projects	47	9030	4375	2262	825	3367595
综合资质	Comprehensive Qualification	349	262926	124054	120933	69452	13798887
事务所资质	Office Qualification	1	10	7	3	3	97
按地区分	**By Region**						
北京	Beijing	430	114872	59380	38706	16924	7827071
天津	Tianjin	160	23849	13797	8383	4411	1527096
河北	Hebei	662	49092	22810	21039	11352	1785163
山西	Shanxi	340	30570	15315	12201	7088	2060879
内蒙古	Inner Mongolia	154	9943	5880	4329	2887	318753
辽宁	Liaoning	354	28289	16092	10466	6147	2282077
吉林	Jilin	292	19876	11230	7088	3410	1592519
黑龙江	Heilongjiang	278	17844	11044	6771	3989	690162
上海	Shanghai	283	65888	29597	25307	12990	6014422
江苏	Jiangsu	1568	147794	65066	78655	35096	14536491
浙江	Zhejiang	1901	300085	61325	69546	31214	20755478
安徽	Anhui	1685	126671	28220	35076	14106	7506001
福建	Fujian	1777	274134	41624	41596	17778	19934592
江西	Jiangxi	616	32638	10208	13711	6355	3218954
山东	Shandong	1088	106996	46022	49821	25466	8902461
河南	Henan	624	71472	30290	27892	14839	4367519
湖北	Hubei	758	87879	41197	28964	12213	12526205
湖南	Hunan	454	58663	28296	20318	10235	3690198
广东	Guangdong	1355	179269	56712	54898	28177	12468748
广西	Guangxi	586	38483	19139	17634	7994	2517253
海南	Hainan	154	6257	2701	2522	1302	456317
重庆	Chongqing	518	49380	18926	21279	8564	4525714
四川	Sichuan	978	115805	43969	55813	25483	9820364
贵州	Guizhou	322	21216	11099	8820	4064	1939574
云南	Yunnan	464	24130	11437	10202	4903	1909176
西藏	Xizang	92	1891	535	875	539	50849
陕西	Shaanxi	1018	59883	26843	25522	11885	3986486
甘肃	Gansu	195	7169	3311	3467	1991	203689
青海	Qinghai	278	15102	2488	3234	1344	231836
宁夏	Ningxia	165	6886	3508	2570	1653	106848
新疆	Xinjiang	168	15948	8529	7054	4604	527333

主要统计指标解释

建筑业统计单位 指从事房屋、构筑物建造和设备安装活动的法人企业。建筑业法人企业应具有建筑业资质并能够独立核算，同时还应具备以下条件：①依法成立，有自己的名称、组织机构和场所，能够承担民事责任；②独立拥有和使用资产，承担负债，有权与其他单位签订合同；③独立核算盈亏，能够编制资产负债表。

建筑业总产值 是以货币形式表现的建筑业企业在一定时期内生产的建筑业产品和提供服务的总和。建筑业总产值包括：

⑴建筑工程产值：指列入建筑工程预算内的各种工程价值。

⑵安装工程产值：指设备安装工程价值以及将预制部品部件安装成建筑工程产品的价值，不包括被安装设备本身的价值。

⑶其他产值：建筑业总产值中除建筑工程、安装工程以外的产值。包括房屋构筑物修理产值、非标准设备制造产值、总包企业向分包企业收取的管理费以及不能明确划分的施工活动所完成的产值。

a.房屋构筑物修理产值：指房屋和构筑物修理所完成的产值，但不包括被修理房屋、构筑物本身价值和生产设备的修理价值。

b.非标准设备制造产值：指加工制造没有定型的非标准生产设备的加工费和原材料价值(如化工厂、炼油厂用的各种罐、槽，矿井生产统一使用的各种漏斗、三角槽、阀门等)以及附属加工厂为本企业承建工程制作的非标准设备的价值。

房屋施工面积 指报告期内施工的全部房屋建筑面积，包括本期新开工的房屋建筑面积、上期跨入本期继续施工的房屋建筑面积、上期停缓建在本期恢复施工的房屋建筑面积、本期竣工的房屋建筑面积及本期施工后又停缓建的房屋建筑面积。

房屋竣工面积 指报告期内房屋建筑按照设计要求已全部完工，达到住人和使用条件，经验收鉴定合格或达到竣工验收标准，可正式移交使用的各栋房屋建筑面积的总和。

Explanatory Notes on Main Statistical Indicators

Statistical Units in the Construction Industry refer to corporate enterprises engaged in the construction of buildings and structures and in the installation of equipment. A corporate construction enterprise should have qualification certificates with independent accounting system, and should meet the following 3 requirements: a) being set up in line with relevant legal basis, having its full name, organization and location, and capable of taking civil liabilities; b) independently possessing and using its assets and assuming its liabilities, and entitled to sign contracts with other institutions; c) making independent accounts of its profits and losses, and capable of compiling its own balance sheet.

Gross Output Value of Construction refers to total of construction products and services, expressed in monetary terms, produced or rendered by construction and installation enterprises during a given period of time. It includes:

(1) Output value of construction projects: the value of projects covered by the project budgets;

(2) Output value of installation projects: the value of the installation of equipment, and the value of installing prefabricated components into construction engineering products (excluding the value of the equipment to be installed);

(3) Other output values: the output value of construction industry apart from that of construction projects and installation projects. It includes: output value of repair of buildings and structures; output value of manufacturing of non-standard equipment; overhead expenses received by contracted enterprises from the sub-contracted enterprises, and the completed output value of construction activities for which there is no clear definition.

a. Output value of repair of buildings and structures: the value created through the repairs of buildings or structures. It does not include the value of buildings or structures being repaired and the value of the repair of production equipment.

b. Output value of manufactured non-standard equipment: refers to the value of non-standard production equipment, including raw materials and manufacturing cost, (i.e., kettles or tanks used by chemical plant or refinery; various fillers, triangle tanks, valves used in mines). It also includes the output value of non-standard equipment manufactured made by its subsidiary workshops for undertaking projects.

Floor Space of Buildings under Construction refers to the total floor space area of buildings under construction in the reference period. It includes buildings new started; buildings started earlier and continued during the reference period; buildings suspended earlier but restarted during the reference period; buildings completed during the reference period; and buildings under construction but suspended during the reference period.

Floor Space of Buildings Completed refers to the total floor space area of buildings that have been completed in the reference period in accordance with the requirements of the design, up to the standard for accommodation or putting into use, and have been checked and accepted by departments concerned as qualified or up to the standard of buildings completed and can be handed over for putting into use.

15

批发和零售业

Wholesale and Retail Trades

简 要 说 明

一、本篇资料的主要内容

本篇资料主要反映批发和零售业的发展与经营状况，同时反映国内商品流通、商品消费、市场运行态势以及流通现代化进程。主要内容包括：限额以上批发和零售业基本情况、商品流转情况、财务状况；零售连锁经营情况；亿元商品交易市场成交情况；社会消费品零售总额等。

二、本篇资料的统计范围

限额以上批发和零售业的法人企业、个体经营户，零售连锁集团，成交额在亿元以上的商品交易市场，以及参与商品零售、餐饮经营活动的各行业法人企业、产业活动单位和个体经营户。限额以上批发和零售业统计单位是指年主营业务收入 2000 万元及以上的批发业统计单位和年主营业务收入 500 万元及以上的零售业统计单位。

三、本篇的资料来源

本篇资料是根据《批发和零售业统计报表制度》进行搜集和加工整理而得。

四、本篇的统计调查方法

本篇资料中限额以上批发和零售业法人企业、个体经营户、其他行业附营的批发和零售业产业活动单位，以及零售连锁集团、亿元商品交易市场等资料采用全面调查方法取得；限额以下法人企业及个体经营户等资料采用抽样调查方法推算。

Brief Introduction

I. Main Contents

Data in this chapter reflect the development and operation of enterprises above designated size of wholesale and retail trades, highlighting commodity circulation, consumption, market operation, and modernization of logistics of China's domestic trade. Main contents include the basic conditions of the wholesale and retail trades above designated size; circulation of commodities; financial status; total retail sales of consumer goods; turnover of large commodity transaction markets with transaction over 100 million yuan; development of chain stores of retail trades, etc.

II. Scope of Statistics

Data in this chapter cover corporate enterprises and self-employed individuals above the designated size engaged in wholesale and retail trades; chain enterprises; large commodity markets with transaction value over 100 million yuan; and corporate enterprises, establishments and self-employed individuals of other industries that are involved in retail trades and catering services. The criteria for wholesale and retail sale trades above designated size are as follows: wholesale trade with annual principal business sales over 20 million yuan; and retail trade, with annual principal business sales over 5 million yuan.

III. Sources of Data

Data in this chapter are collected and processed in accordance with *Statistical Reporting System on Wholesale and Retail Trades* by the Department of Trade and External Economic Relations of the National Bureau of Statistics.

IV. Methods of Survey

Data on main indicators for all enterprises of wholesale and retail trades above designated size, self-employed individuals, the establishments of other industries involved in the wholesale and retail trades, chain enterprises of wholesale and retail trades, large commodity markets with transaction value over 100 million yuan are collected through comprehensive reporting system. Data on corporate enterprises and self-employed individuals below the designated size are collected by sample surveys.

15-1 限额以上批发和零售业企业主要指标
Main Indicators of Enterprises above Designated Size of Wholesale and Retail Trade

指标	Item	2019	2020	2021	2022	2023
批发和零售业	**Wholesale and Retail Trade**					
法人企业 (个)	Number of Corporate Enterprises (unit)	242544	276499	318134	364480	424885
年末从业人数 (万人)	Employed Persons at Year-end (10 000 persons)	1213.9	1235.0	1286.7	1306.1	1340.9
商品购进额 (亿元)	Total Purchases Value (100 million yuan)	709505.3	800298.9	1037966.3	1132163.4	1235724.8
#进口额 (亿元)	Imports (100 million yuan)	51415.4	54162.1	68022.2	69512.4	69486.7
商品销售额 (亿元)	Total Sales Value (100 million yuan)	782518.3	864261.2	1107727.2	1201793.5	1307419.9
#出口额 (亿元)	Exports (100 million yuan)	27436.1	27553.6	33537.3	37513.4	38135.4
期末商品库存额 (亿元)	Total Stock at Year-end (100 million yuan)	46410.0	52982.9	54539.4	57573.9	61714.3
批发业	**Wholesale Trade**					
法人企业 (个)	Number of Corporate Enterprises (unit)	140075	168738	200137	230637	268609
年末从业人数 (万人)	Employed Persons at Year-end (10 000 persons)	568.5	595.7	635.4	655.0	683.9
商品购进额 (亿元)	Total Purchases Value (100 million yuan)	601908.8	689230.3	911849.7	998326.8	1091915.9
#进口额 (亿元)	Imports (100 million yuan)	48241.8	50884.0	64339.2	65947.7	66135.2
商品销售额 (亿元)	Total Sales Value (100 million yuan)	652164.1	733272.8	959635.2	1047569.5	1140285.4
#出口额 (亿元)	Exports (100 million yuan)	27346.3	27464.2	33460.1	37438.3	38014.0
期末商品库存额 (亿元)	Total Stock at Year-end (100 million yuan)	35036.0	40336.2	43152.6	45005.6	48563.6
零售业	**Retail Trade**					
法人企业 (个)	Number of Corporate Enterprises (unit)	102469	107761	117997	133843	156276
年末从业人数 (万人)	Employed Persons at Year-end (10 000 persons)	645.4	639.2	651.3	651.1	657.0
商品购进额 (亿元)	Total Purchases Value (100 million yuan)	107596.6	111068.6	126116.6	133836.6	143808.9
#进口额 (亿元)	Imports (100 million yuan)	3173.6	3278.1	3683.0	3564.7	3351.5
商品销售额 (亿元)	Total Sales Value (100 million yuan)	130354.1	130988.4	148091.9	154224.0	167134.5
#出口额 (亿元)	Exports (100 million yuan)	89.8	89.4	77.2	75.1	121.4
期末商品库存额 (亿元)	Total Stock at Year-end (100 million yuan)	11374.0	12646.7	11386.7	12568.3	13150.7
年末零售营业面积 (万平方米)	Business Area of Retail at Year-end (10 000 sq.m)	36744.8	38243.7	39617.9	41246.1	43208.1

15−2 按登记注册统计类别和行业分限额以上批发业企业主要指标(2023年)

单位：亿元

指标	Item	法人企业(个) Number of Corporate Enterprises (unit)	年末从业人数(人) Employed Persons at Year-end (person)	商品购进额 Total Purchases Value	#进口 Imports
批发业合计	**Wholesale Trade**	**268609**	**6839205**	**1091915.9**	**66135.2**
按登记注册统计类别分	**By Registered Statistical Categories**				
内资企业	**Domestic Invested Enterprises**	**257897**	**5877151**	**968540.9**	**40894.2**
有限责任公司	Limited Liability Corporations	252591	5299303	897233.9	37989.0
股份有限公司	Share-holding Corporations Ltd.	2798	323227	49669.3	2704.3
非公司企业法人	Non Corporate Legal Entity	1093	237045	20600.0	191.1
个人独资企业	Sole Proprietorship Enterprises	1214	14212	723.2	6.7
合伙企业	Partnership Enterprises	198	3322	313.9	3.2
其他内资企业	Other Domestic Invested Enterprises	3	42	0.6	
港澳台投资企业	**Enterprises with Investment from Hong Kong, Macao and Taiwan**	**4350**	**395108**	**46570.0**	**5761.7**
外商投资企业	**Foreign Invested Enterprises**	**5351**	**549845**	**76383.1**	**19477.3**
其他统计类别	**Other Statistical Categories**	**1011**	**17101**	**421.9**	**2.0**
按国民经济行业分	**By Sector**				
农、林、牧、渔产品批发	Wholesale of Agricultural, Forestry, Livestock and Fishery Products	12211	216929	35513.3	3458.6
食品、饮料及烟草制品批发	Wholesale of Food, Beverages and Tobaccos	28900	1320868	74828.6	5088.6
#米、面制品及食用油批发	Wholesale of Rice, Flour and Edible Oil	4418	144181	13692.2	1434.2
烟草制品批发	Wholesale of Tobaccos	499	244121	16021.5	39.0
纺织、服装及家庭用品批发	Wholesale of Textiles, Wearing Apparel and Household Articles	26409	965752	62926.0	3178.4
#服装批发	Wholesale of Garments	4672	248413	10096.5	591.1
日用家电批发	Wholesale of Household Electrical Appliances	3316	143201	16878.2	144.0
文化、体育用品及器材批发	Wholesale of Culture, Sports Appliances and Equipments	6927	245719	15977.8	631.6
医药及医疗器材批发	Wholesale of Medicines and Medical Appliances	17656	962780	45451.4	3411.0
矿产品、建材及化工产品批发	Wholesale of Mineral Products, Building Materials and Chemical Products	123349	1712082	688256.5	30527.6
#煤炭及制品批发	Wholesale of Coal and Related Products	11700	198269	79449.5	2768.3
石油及制品批发	Wholesale of Petroleum and Related Products	10177	297795	119021.9	7995.6
金属及金属矿批发	Wholesale of Metal Materials	44438	444417	329503.3	13363.9
建材批发	Wholesale of Building Materials	22064	292142	35345.4	778.2
化肥批发	Wholesale of Chemical Fertilizer	2257	46875	8314.7	771.3
机械设备、五金产品及电子产品批发	Wholesale of Machinery, Hardware and Electronic Products	43902	1222203	138590.7	17860.3
#汽车及零配件批发	Wholesale of Motor Vehicles and Their Parts	7863	204469	51694.3	4649.6
计算机、软件及辅助设备批发	Wholesale of Computer, Software and Auxiliary Appliances	4127	125927	15569.0	5575.2
贸易经纪与代理	Trade Broker and Agency	1171	26546	5127.0	1499.7
其他批发业	Other Wholesale not Classified Elsewhere	8084	166326	25244.5	479.4

注：1.限额以上批发业企业中，由于包含了部分视同法人单位，因此财务指标数据资产≠负债+所有者权益。
2.本表登记注册统计类别按《关于市场主体统计分类的划分规定》(国统字〔2023〕14号)执行。
3.“其他统计类别”分组包括农民专业合作社(联合社)和其他市场主体(以下相关表同)。

Main Indicators of Enterprises above Designated Size of Wholesale Trade by Registered Statistical Categories and Sector (2023)

(100 million yuan)

商 品 销售额 Total Sales Value	#出口 Exports	期末商品库存额 Stock (year-end)	资产总计 Total Assets	#流动资产合 计 Total Current Assets	#固定资产净 额 Net Value of Fixed Assets	负债合计 Total Liabilities	所有者权益合计 Total Owners' Equities	营业收入 Business Revenue	营业成本 Business Cost	税金及附加 Taxes and Other Charges	利润总额 Total Profits
1140285.4	**38014.0**	**48563.6**	**516805.7**	**399437.1**	**9859.2**	**372582.2**	**144413.6**	**1014698.9**	**962943.0**	**3597.5**	**20681.6**
1007221.0	**31170.0**	**40368.1**	**443822.0**	**343970.0**	**8206.5**	**325130.3**	**118881.9**	**891498.8**	**851743.6**	**3370.5**	**16044.6**
929796.0	29711.3	36827.4	391708.3	313184.4	6984.2	298506.1	93192.5	824897.2	792142.9	1324.3	12791.8
49855.1	1413.7	2318.8	44279.6	24135.7	754.7	24095.9	20383.5	42065.2	40029.2	60.6	1333.2
26392.4	36.1	1179.9	7472.4	6341.2	451.5	2256.9	5215.5	23454.6	18574.7	1982.1	1871.9
819.0	5.1	28.4	244.3	200.3	14.4	173.7	70.6	760.3	710.3	2.8	20.2
357.9	3.8	13.5	115.4	106.6	1.8	96.7	18.6	320.9	285.9	0.7	27.6
0.6		0.1	2.1	1.8	0.0	0.9	1.2	0.6	0.6	0.0	-0.1
51041.8	**1543.2**	**3384.8**	**32871.3**	**25688.8**	**526.3**	**22019.0**	**10852.3**	**46679.0**	**42133.3**	**85.2**	**1757.3**
81546.6	**5300.4**	**4799.2**	**39950.7**	**29663.9**	**1112.0**	**25338.0**	**14612.6**	**76056.2**	**68647.4**	**140.7**	**2853.1**
476.0	**0.3**	**11.5**	**161.7**	**114.3**	**14.4**	**94.9**	**66.8**	**464.9**	**418.8**	**1.0**	**26.6**
35760.6	242.6	3550.1	21624.0	16041.5	700.6	16343.1	5280.9	32478.7	31484.3	33.9	401.5
87639.1	1051.6	7281.7	45615.6	37203.0	1501.4	29334.1	16281.1	80060.0	67830.4	2491.2	4710.2
14086.3	124.6	2063.3	8575.2	6725.0	327.2	6779.5	1795.4	12970.8	12394.8	15.6	134.6
22732.9	48.8	1155.9	7308.0	6145.4	444.9	1472.4	5835.6	20236.2	14578.6	2374.9	2127.8
69634.2	9943.1	4487.7	37283.0	30010.5	696.7	27224.6	10058.3	63480.0	56058.5	100.9	2327.4
11672.0	2993.8	974.6	6983.3	5524.8	152.2	4678.9	2304.3	10762.9	9237.0	19.9	448.9
17625.7	573.0	1171.8	9803.9	7971.1	115.7	7624.0	2179.9	15862.2	14456.8	21.0	722.4
17434.6	976.3	1631.3	11486.4	8563.8	248.2	7519.4	3966.8	15809.2	14468.5	31.6	481.6
51447.7	584.6	5188.5	35895.3	30441.6	684.9	25918.7	9976.6	46575.1	40338.4	121.4	1595.1
698533.6	8658.3	16945.8	267488.5	196371.1	4451.1	192333.8	75347.1	615473.7	601999.2	553.0	7399.9
82554.4	178.4	1781.5	45966.7	29326.4	712.9	30118.2	15843.5	71568.6	69385.5	108.5	2329.6
116997.7	1338.2	3493.4	34189.5	24546.6	1564.7	24726.3	9682.7	106499.8	104188.7	81.9	925.1
333141.1	3134.1	6918.3	106339.5	81895.3	1016.8	79930.4	26408.8	289399.0	285539.5	209.7	2029.9
37082.4	750.8	1357.1	29387.0	24246.6	489.0	22812.6	6574.3	33261.1	31633.5	51.1	608.3
8624.3	321.3	655.5	4690.7	3284.4	98.4	3282.2	1408.4	7735.2	7451.5	10.5	157.8
147921.7	14700.6	8449.1	82285.1	68565.1	1329.9	62510.3	19776.3	131748.7	123223.6	200.0	3087.2
55371.6	4354.8	3062.3	28562.8	23888.8	284.4	23361.6	5203.0	49307.4	46936.3	84.8	660.2
16181.4	1044.5	1076.6	6973.4	6228.0	86.6	5373.3	1600.1	14697.2	13832.6	16.1	294.2
5318.5	747.3	213.9	4528.5	3817.2	34.4	3438.6	1089.9	4627.6	4374.4	4.7	161.0
26595.2	1109.6	815.5	10599.3	8423.3	212.1	7959.7	2636.5	24446.0	23165.6	60.8	517.6

a) For the financial data of wholesale enterprises above designated size, total assets may not equal to liabilities plus total owner's equities, due to the fact that there are some establishments which are regarded as enterprises.

b) The registered statistical categories of this table is implemented in accordance with the Regulations on the Classification of Market Entity Statistics (Guotongzi [2023] No. 14).

c) The other statistical categories includes professional farmers cooperatives and other market entities. The same applies to the relevant following tables.

15-3 分地区限额以上批发业企业主要指标(2023年)
Main Indicators of Enterprises above Designated Size of Wholesale Trade by Region (2023)

单位：亿元 (100 million yuan)

地区	Region	法人企业(个) Number of Corporate Enterprises (unit)	年末从业人数(人) Employed Persons at Year-end (person)	商品购进额 Total Purchases Value	#进口 Imports	商品销售额 Total Sales Value	#出口 Exports	期末商品库存额 Stock (year-end)
全　国	**National Total**	**268609**	**6839205**	**1091915.9**	**66135.2**	**1140285.4**	**38014.0**	**48563.6**
北　京	Beijing	9223	432911	80392.3	12520.5	83648.4	2085.2	6751.1
天　津	Tianjin	8840	146216	43550.7	1180.6	44853.4	627.8	1350.9
河　北	Hebei	4760	126059	19926.5	195.8	20865.1	206.5	675.4
山　西	Shanxi	4513	122737	20051.5	195.5	21097.7	63.8	697.3
内蒙古	Inner Mongolia	1946	53000	7512.0	344.0	7572.4	96.5	494.5
辽　宁	Liaoning	5175	103788	21625.1	815.5	22564.0	592.4	885.8
吉　林	Jilin	1282	48562	3983.4	32.7	4376.8	10.9	326.7
黑龙江	Heilongjiang	2024	59144	8043.3	338.7	8819.3	71.3	433.0
上　海	Shanghai	13534	718675	135851.0	19633.0	144819.3	5872.7	7462.0
江　苏	Jiangsu	36177	663150	102002.0	4270.8	106321.4	4960.7	3793.8
浙　江	Zhejiang	26792	579777	136644.7	5836.8	139764.6	8110.9	3993.7
安　徽	Anhui	5343	150943	17664.1	482.4	19243.6	630.6	764.3
福　建	Fujian	16263	316721	67749.6	4051.8	70426.5	2591.6	2049.0
江　西	Jiangxi	5722	128824	11331.0	53.2	12490.6	365.0	497.0
山　东	Shandong	27394	485687	75798.4	2745.7	78876.1	2589.4	2979.7
河　南	Henan	9280	205809	17941.7	211.7	19061.2	244.1	893.3
湖　北	Hubei	7364	213807	20357.9	273.4	21839.9	498.1	911.9
湖　南	Hunan	4807	157126	11219.3	567.5	11351.5	298.1	575.8
广　东	Guangdong	45291	1145296	141856.2	7014.3	146030.6	5727.6	5939.8
广　西	Guangxi	3876	94441	16834.2	559.0	17471.9	92.6	562.2
海　南	Hainan	1603	36641	21119.8	982.6	21682.7	259.0	468.3
重　庆	Chongqing	3873	113051	16340.3	662.5	17278.0	778.0	688.3
四　川	Sichuan	8033	259384	24658.1	349.0	26202.1	260.9	1594.9
贵　州	Guizhou	2325	75809	7213.6	83.8	8436.5	31.9	488.2
云　南	Yunnan	3278	99335	12372.4	454.2	13489.9	320.9	694.5
西　藏	Xizang	140	8178	970.4		1094.9	0.2	53.4
陕　西	Shaanxi	3656	121111	19923.0	384.7	20837.5	448.9	1005.6
甘　肃	Gansu	1206	47683	9121.5	64.9	9510.6	26.7	247.6
青　海	Qinghai	318	12205	1569.5	11.6	1733.6	3.1	43.7
宁　夏	Ningxia	463	17361	2039.8	5.9	1616.0	0.5	70.5
新　疆	Xinjiang	4108	95774	16252.6	1812.8	16909.1	148.3	1171.6

15—3 续表 continued

单位：亿元 (100 million yuan)

地 区	Region	资产总计 Total Assets	#流动资产合计 Total Current Assets	#固定资产净额 Net Value of Fixed Assets	负债合计 Total Liabilities	所有者权益合计 Total Owners' Equities	营业收入 Business Revenue	营业成本 Business Cost	税金及附加 Taxes and Other Charges	利润总额 Total Profits
全 国	**National Total**	**516805.7**	**399437.1**	**9859.2**	**372582.2**	**144413.6**	**1014698.9**	**962943.0**	**3597.5**	**20681.6**
北 京	Beijing	59767.4	40243.8	889.1	38864.6	20904.5	71072.3	66646.0	128.6	2658.6
天 津	Tianjin	13973.3	11967.0	144.3	11000.3	2972.9	39687.8	38754.2	86.3	259.2
河 北	Hebei	9329.1	7749.3	160.1	7013.3	2315.8	18450.8	17581.4	122.2	281.0
山 西	Shanxi	14290.0	10531.8	262.8	10379.0	3911.0	18620.2	17785.7	79.5	584.9
内蒙古	Inner Mongolia	4760.3	2964.9	140.8	2964.7	1793.9	6850.1	6474.5	60.3	183.7
辽 宁	Liaoning	6888.5	5684.7	431.5	5179.5	1697.3	20334.7	19684.1	81.5	131.7
吉 林	Jilin	2715.6	2021.0	137.4	1990.3	725.3	3560.0	3269.1	41.5	44.7
黑龙江	Heilongjiang	3873.7	3080.1	121.9	2928.9	944.8	7937.8	7587.7	49.8	60.1
上 海	Shanghai	58644.7	45445.2	696.0	39332.9	19311.7	128331.8	119696.5	191.2	2730.6
江 苏	Jiangsu	50270.0	40286.4	1133.4	38225.3	12041.3	94890.1	89230.3	280.2	2488.8
浙 江	Zhejiang	49952.8	40307.4	724.1	38002.2	11950.6	125955.0	121881.4	270.6	1866.6
安 徽	Anhui	9274.5	7643.6	189.2	7071.3	2203.3	17410.8	16244.7	133.5	288.6
福 建	Fujian	27478.0	20537.8	373.6	19734.4	7743.5	60406.8	57893.3	142.1	1157.4
江 西	Jiangxi	6440.2	5397.3	158.6	4802.7	1637.2	11544.7	10587.1	94.6	339.9
山 东	Shandong	36240.2	29845.0	699.6	28738.0	7501.9	70519.6	67875.2	189.6	809.4
河 南	Henan	8565.3	7171.1	189.5	6142.6	2416.9	17102.7	15992.0	160.6	354.0
湖 北	Hubei	9861.9	7653.0	306.7	7072.1	2789.3	20155.7	18505.1	129.8	848.9
湖 南	Hunan	5452.0	4304.6	145.6	3877.7	1583.9	10400.4	9414.4	168.4	336.7
广 东	Guangdong	63549.9	51850.0	940.3	48822.2	14727.7	131909.5	126270.8	337.4	1365.9
广 西	Guangxi	8534.0	6154.4	192.2	5983.3	2472.5	15397.5	14857.2	86.5	153.5
海 南	Hainan	5852.9	4597.8	68.1	4061.5	1791.4	18738.1	18216.0	40.1	293.2
重 庆	Chongqing	6920.6	5717.3	201.2	4848.5	2154.9	15564.9	14387.7	129.3	464.0
四 川	Sichuan	15927.7	11952.1	427.0	10634.2	5293.5	23244.1	21492.3	163.2	783.1
贵 州	Guizhou	7772.2	5195.1	109.2	4404.6	3340.7	7581.1	6349.3	94.8	867.7
云 南	Yunnan	6589.6	4871.9	206.7	4273.6	2316.1	12045.9	11150.3	113.8	455.5
西 藏	Xizang	437.3	398.4	9.4	243.6	193.7	863.3	728.0	14.4	29.4
陕 西	Shaanxi	7380.3	5821.6	170.5	5060.1	2320.1	18671.2	17942.8	88.5	363.7
甘 肃	Gansu	3303.6	1768.9	190.3	2093.8	1209.8	8951.6	8676.7	45.3	97.0
青 海	Qinghai	1937.7	865.6	49.6	1010.5	927.2	1708.8	1642.3	12.3	15.2
宁 夏	Ningxia	634.7	479.5	35.9	673.6	207.5	1454.5	1372.3	13.4	27.4
新 疆	Xinjiang	10187.8	6930.7	354.8	7153.0	3013.2	15337.0	14754.7	48.0	341.3

15-4 按登记注册统计类别和行业分限额以上零售业企业主要指标(2023年)

单位：亿元

指标	Item	法人企业(个) Number of Corporate Enterprises (unit)	年末从业人数(人) Employed Persons at Year-end (person)	商品购进额 Total Purchases Value	#进口 Imports
零售业合计	**Retail Trade**	**156276**	**6569928**	**143808.9**	**3351.5**
按登记注册统计类别分	**By Registered Statistical Categories**				
内资企业	**Domestic Invested Enterprises**	**152847**	**5780906**	**122588.8**	**2002.2**
有限责任公司	Limited Liability Corporations	139150	5206818	111547.6	1970.3
股份有限公司	Share-holding Corporations Ltd.	1201	390112	8583.2	29.9
非公司企业法人	Non Corporate Legal Entity	1297	46392	764.6	0.9
个人独资企业	Sole Proprietorship Enterprises	10222	123873	1493.1	0.9
合伙企业	Partnership Enterprises	971	13532	197.4	0.3
其他内资企业	Other Domestic Invested Enterprises	6	179	2.9	
港澳台投资企业	**Enterprises with Investment from Hong Kong, Macao and Taiwan**	**1762**	**431682**	**10084.8**	**671.3**
外商投资企业	**Foreign Invested Enterprises**	**1170**	**350033**	**11051.0**	**677.7**
其他统计类别	**Other Statistical Categories**	**497**	**7307**	**84.3**	**0.3**
按国民经济行业分	**By Sector**				
综合零售	General Retail	17136	1733504	18842.4	592.2
#百货零售	Retail of General Merchandise	6832	634750	8817.0	551.2
超级市场零售	Retail of Supermarkets	8178	989594	8909.6	40.0
食品、饮料及烟草制品专门零售	Special Retail of Food, Beverages and Tobaccos	17729	449982	6061.4	29.3
纺织、服装及日用品专门零售	Special Retail of Textiles, Garments and Daily Consumer Articles	7206	521359	5441.0	461.7
#服装零售	Retail of Garments	2984	314808	2968.6	339.2
文化、体育用品及器材专门零售	Special Retail of Culture, Sports Appliances and Equipments	6451	255035	3525.9	152.4
#体育用品及器材零售	Retail of Sports Appliances and Equipments	353	19511	194.8	18.3
图书、报刊零售	Retail of Books, Newspapers and Magazines	1485	113944	1386.7	58.3
医药及医疗器材专门零售	Special Retail of Medicines and Medical Appliances	6881	867882	4961.1	17.1
#西药零售	Retail of Western Medicines	5591	811395	4581.5	7.3
汽车、摩托车、零配件和燃料及其他动力销售	Retail of Motor Vehicles, Motorcycles, Parts, and Fuel and Other Powers	56592	1790943	71081.8	1898.1
#汽车新车零售	Retail of New Motor Vehicles	36237	1288301	51805.3	1883.1
机动车燃油零售	Retail of Fuel Oil of Motor Vehicles	16245	433212	17456.1	3.2
家用电器及电子产品专门零售	Special Retail of Household Electric Appliances and Electronic Products	16268	340817	7167.9	46.7
#日用家电零售	Retail of Household Electric Appliances	6869	124511	2406.6	12.3
计算机、软件及辅助设备零售	Retail of Computer, Software and Assistant Appliances	3305	64635	1687.2	4.5
通信设备零售	Retail of Communication Equipments	3062	89787	1898.4	22.6
五金、家具及室内装饰材料专门零售	Special Retail of Hardware, Furniture and Interior Decoration Materials	8723	128474	1662.5	17.8
货摊、无店铺及其他零售业	Stalls, Non-shop and Other Retails	19290	481932	25065.1	136.3
#互联网零售	Retails on the Internet	16820	413655	24184.0	107.1

注：1.限额以上零售业企业中，由于包含了部分视同法人单位，因此财务指标数据资产≠负债+所有者权益。
2.本表登记注册统计类别按《关于市场主体统计分类的划分规定》(国统字〔2023〕14号)执行。

Main Indicators of Enterprises above Designated Size of Retail Trade by Registered Statistical Categories and Sector (2023)

(100 million yuan)

商品销售额 Total Sales Value	#出口 Exports	期末商品库存额 Stock (year-end)	资产总计 Total Assets	#流动资产合计 Total Current Assets	#固定资产净额 Net Value of Fixed Assets	负债合计 Total Liabilities	所有者权益合计 Total Owners' Equities	营业收入 Business Revenue	营业成本 Business Cost	税金及附加 Taxes and Other Charges	利润总额 Total Profits
167134.5	**121.4**	**13150.7**	**81730.5**	**56436.9**	**5361.9**	**60827.3**	**21293.3**	**151112.0**	**130871.5**	**503.0**	**2828.6**
136854.2	**104.5**	**11236.1**	**66156.9**	**46908.1**	**4190.1**	**50005.2**	**16551.2**	**124430.4**	**109140.8**	**394.6**	**1949.7**
122155.1	104.2	10581.0	56820.7	42118.4	3285.1	44471.9	12378.5	111438.6	97720.9	336.9	1517.7
11554.8	0.3	528.8	8152.9	4070.0	759.0	5015.4	3509.9	10184.4	9016.9	37.0	283.5
1228.0		44.0	548.9	330.6	64.2	199.4	347.0	1066.8	936.1	10.2	38.2
1688.1	0.0	74.1	556.6	341.8	72.9	278.1	278.4	1533.3	1291.5	9.4	98.6
225.1	0.0	7.9	76.7	46.3	8.9	40.1	36.6	204.5	172.9	1.1	11.6
3.1		0.2	1.1	1.0	0.0	0.3	0.8	2.7	2.5	0.0	0.0
12689.8	**14.7**	**1024.7**	**7068.7**	**4748.4**	**436.0**	**5418.5**	**1650.2**	**11791.4**	**9282.6**	**60.3**	**436.5**
17487.0	**2.0**	**887.3**	**8458.0**	**4753.2**	**729.9**	**5382.7**	**3065.8**	**14792.5**	**12363.9**	**47.9**	**434.4**
103.6	**0.2**	**2.7**	**46.9**	**27.2**	**6.0**	**20.8**	**26.1**	**97.7**	**84.1**	**0.3**	**8.0**
22739.1	0.4	1951.4	19733.0	11295.9	1703.9	15086.8	4658.0	19961.7	15933.9	130.9	495.3
11382.8	0.4	764.3	12084.5	6531.1	1124.2	8306.1	3779.3	9176.0	7107.0	99.8	423.0
9983.3	0.0	709.9	6740.5	4140.8	515.2	5975.9	771.3	9503.5	7824.9	27.3	61.7
7187.1	2.4	550.2	4773.0	3414.6	269.2	2983.5	1789.4	6650.9	5443.9	27.8	348.2
8499.5	6.4	1155.6	5367.9	4044.3	258.6	4038.5	1329.4	7583.0	4723.7	44.0	511.2
4753.7	3.2	714.0	3250.5	2371.5	172.1	2436.6	813.9	4244.2	2607.5	21.4	225.4
4357.4	10.1	809.0	4293.5	3167.8	290.3	2527.0	1766.4	4091.6	3087.7	34.8	237.9
315.7	0.7	46.6	191.5	140.0	10.1	149.3	42.2	296.0	176.6	1.4	32.4
1597.7	1.1	234.1	2267.5	1609.1	229.9	1241.3	1026.2	1569.1	1155.7	4.9	119.2
6239.6	0.0	749.3	4003.6	2976.8	107.4	3090.3	913.4	5756.4	4440.2	15.6	164.6
5731.7	0.0	694.0	3670.1	2721.8	96.1	2851.2	818.8	5290.4	4092.1	14.1	147.7
79116.3	63.4	5904.8	29868.4	20181.3	2284.3	22190.3	8058.6	71703.3	66662.5	179.1	533.2
51575.9	55.8	5233.7	19327.5	15463.1	1032.7	16207.0	3120.5	47673.6	44745.0	132.1	-141.3
25580.8	0.0	500.8	9214.4	3797.8	1132.1	5006.3	4511.1	22177.2	20264.8	42.8	635.0
7922.1	10.9	723.5	4120.2	3415.5	96.3	3078.3	1041.9	7095.1	6272.6	14.7	129.0
2578.3	1.5	302.7	1903.6	1601.8	45.4	1451.3	452.3	2295.7	2014.6	5.3	23.2
1982.9	6.6	116.8	795.0	574.1	15.4	506.6	288.4	1740.2	1529.2	3.4	56.5
2042.5	0.3	181.0	744.2	677.9	8.9	613.7	130.6	1881.6	1709.1	2.1	18.5
1985.4	6.9	184.6	1367.4	948.3	139.5	1053.0	314.4	1832.2	1464.7	9.3	57.3
29088.0	20.9	1122.2	8203.4	6992.4	212.5	6779.6	1422.0	26437.9	22842.3	46.8	352.0
28011.6	20.0	1062.0	7468.2	6512.6	138.6	6312.8	1155.4	25439.3	22053.5	43.0	300.3

a) For the financial data of retail enterprises above designated size, total assets may not equal to liabilities plus total owner's equities, due to the fact that there are some establishments which are regarded as enterprises.

b) The registered statistical categories of this table is implemented in accordance with the Regulations on the Classification of Market Entity Statistics (Guotongzi [2023] No. 14).

15-5 分地区限额以上零售业企业主要指标(2023年)
Main Indicators of Enterprises above Designated Size of Retail Trade by Region (2023)

单位：亿元 (100 million yuan)

地区	Region	法人企业(个) Number of Corporate Enterprises (unit)	年末从业人数(人) Employed Persons at Year-end (person)	商品购进额 Total Purchases Value	#进口 Imports	商品销售额 Total Sales Value	#出口 Exports	期末商品库存额 Stock (year-end)
全　国	**National Total**	**156276**	**6569928**	**143808.9**	**3351.5**	**167134.5**	**121.4**	**13150.7**
北　京	Beijing	2803	213132	9975.5	242.8	10950.7	7.5	862.0
天　津	Tianjin	1326	87039	2324.5	31.5	2544.6	2.3	205.3
河　北	Hebei	3858	262810	4217.6	59.9	4607.0	0.5	443.0
山　西	Shanxi	3340	136111	2297.9	26.6	2567.9	0.1	242.2
内蒙古	Inner Mongolia	1412	79250	1490.6	13.2	1739.6	0.1	141.7
辽　宁	Liaoning	2675	157711	3522.9	52.7	3861.6	0.3	314.4
吉　林	Jilin	1435	76676	1346.0	22.0	1689.1	0.0	138.4
黑龙江	Heilongjiang	1962	90280	1666.6	17.4	1889.4	0.7	152.0
上　海	Shanghai	2922	350582	9558.5	918.5	12722.4	3.9	1270.3
江　苏	Jiangsu	18488	550811	14088.5	242.8	15972.9	2.7	1099.6
浙　江	Zhejiang	8719	367573	11248.8	273.7	13262.7	11.4	897.7
安　徽	Anhui	5742	233915	4182.4	42.3	4844.5	0.8	360.3
福　建	Fujian	8960	287824	5764.7	89.5	6808.4	2.0	382.1
江　西	Jiangxi	7112	196623	3223.2	32.3	3962.7	1.4	249.7
山　东	Shandong	12809	481533	8808.5	118.3	10006.8	0.7	822.6
河　南	Henan	9947	317631	5254.9	73.0	5776.6	2.0	550.6
湖　北	Hubei	10587	359664	6831.7	56.2	7808.4	1.7	919.5
湖　南	Hunan	8368	296147	4379.7	51.8	5770.6	0.5	316.2
广　东	Guangdong	12106	671373	16528.9	412.5	19527.7	25.1	1357.8
广　西	Guangxi	3634	138584	2100.9	28.2	2269.8	44.7	230.0
海　南	Hainan	640	46598	1413.9	206.9	1605.5	2.0	243.3
重　庆	Chongqing	4274	179274	3847.8	50.0	4440.1	5.2	263.6
四　川	Sichuan	7030	343219	7942.5	146.2	8584.1	4.8	539.5
贵　州	Guizhou	2634	99093	2331.9	35.3	2891.0	0.4	248.0
云　南	Yunnan	3605	159118	2454.7	37.1	3068.5	0.1	234.2
西　藏	Xizang	299	8863	235.6	1.1	314.7	0.0	18.3
陕　西	Shaanxi	5373	187177	3333.9	43.4	3899.7	0.1	297.9
甘　肃	Gansu	1559	75177	1273.2	10.3	1399.7		110.4
青　海	Qinghai	294	14511	232.3	1.6	254.5		27.9
宁　夏	Ningxia	397	22768	352.1	1.0	371.7		43.8
新　疆	Xinjiang	1966	78861	1578.7	13.3	1721.6	0.2	168.6

15-5 续表 continued

单位：亿元 (100 million yuan)

地区	Region	资产总计 Total Assets	#流动资产合计 Total Current Assets	#固定资产净额 Net Value of Fixed Assets	负债合计 Total Liabilities	所有者权益合计 Total Owners' Equities	营业收入 Business Revenue	营业成本 Business Cost	税金及附加 Taxes and Other Charges	利润总额 Total Profits
全　国	**National Total**	**81730.5**	**56436.9**	**5361.9**	**60827.3**	**21293.3**	**151112.0**	**130871.5**	**503.0**	**2828.6**
北　京	Beijing	5313.5	3996.9	230.2	4070.4	1243.2	10017.6	8803.9	33.5	72.7
天　津	Tianjin	1246.8	875.9	97.0	1005.1	241.7	2339.4	2029.1	7.1	11.6
河　北	Hebei	2179.7	1481.4	192.7	1570.8	606.7	4182.3	3739.5	13.9	45.5
山　西	Shanxi	1227.1	852.6	97.0	1086.6	140.6	2320.2	2122.9	5.2	-11.8
内蒙古	Inner Mongolia	689.8	460.4	76.1	596.0	103.7	1568.1	1410.2	3.6	15.7
辽　宁	Liaoning	2164.5	1455.3	182.1	1674.0	480.3	3250.7	2908.3	11.8	18.3
吉　林	Jilin	1116.8	771.9	120.9	811.2	306.5	1513.0	1343.1	5.3	6.9
黑龙江	Heilongjiang	911.3	655.1	87.7	757.6	153.7	1710.1	1533.9	5.1	17.4
上　海	Shanghai	6590.2	4848.8	275.3	5186.7	1403.4	11651.5	8578.2	57.0	450.7
江　苏	Jiangsu	8023.8	5537.3	479.1	5696.8	2317.4	14291.7	12566.8	36.6	332.1
浙　江	Zhejiang	5497.7	3838.1	349.5	4222.7	1274.9	11322.3	9901.1	33.7	106.2
安　徽	Anhui	2319.8	1626.8	141.6	1620.0	693.6	4399.5	3886.4	11.6	62.3
福　建	Fujian	2782.1	1853.6	181.0	1953.7	828.3	6291.2	5355.1	18.5	187.7
江　西	Jiangxi	1887.4	1328.4	122.7	1291.6	595.8	3606.6	3135.0	11.4	121.8
山　东	Shandong	5325.1	3769.4	394.1	4571.9	883.5	8959.2	7907.5	25.7	136.6
河　南	Henan	2767.5	1995.7	208.1	2090.4	803.4	5308.5	4640.7	15.6	153.4
湖　北	Hubei	3654.4	2327.0	330.4	2689.6	964.7	7036.9	5990.4	32.3	285.7
湖　南	Hunan	2995.9	1631.7	239.1	1890.2	1105.7	5293.0	4592.3	29.6	196.0
广　东	Guangdong	9737.7	7175.5	366.0	7213.8	2524.0	17875.7	15501.0	53.5	68.3
广　西	Guangxi	1293.2	913.4	88.5	959.6	340.4	2078.6	1836.2	4.8	-0.5
海　南	Hainan	935.0	653.8	51.2	649.3	285.7	1485.6	1254.4	18.2	45.8
重　庆	Chongqing	1936.8	1196.4	165.9	1432.7	651.2	4072.9	3602.6	11.9	91.9
四　川	Sichuan	3671.8	2327.7	283.4	2564.1	1107.7	7855.6	6982.2	21.7	183.6
贵　州	Guizhou	1737.5	1109.2	116.4	1092.4	645.1	2610.7	2296.0	6.3	103.7
云　南	Yunnan	1579.5	974.2	126.7	1067.8	511.7	2785.1	2462.0	7.3	36.3
西　藏	Xizang	154.3	100.2	16.8	100.1	58.3	290.4	261.4	0.5	6.9
陕　西	Shaanxi	1971.0	1345.1	133.5	1478.9	491.9	3570.1	3170.4	11.1	44.2
甘　肃	Gansu	647.8	429.0	62.1	456.7	181.1	1285.6	1149.4	3.6	23.6
青　海	Qinghai	152.6	103.7	19.5	123.6	31.9	232.3	207.9	0.8	1.0
宁　夏	Ningxia	267.5	149.8	23.9	190.5	77.0	326.2	283.6	1.3	2.0
新　疆	Xinjiang	952.7	652.8	103.5	712.5	240.2	1581.2	1420.0	4.7	13.4

15-6 按登记注册统计类别分连锁零售企业基本情况(2023年)
Main Indicators of Chain Retail Enterprises by Registered Statistical Categories (2023)

指　标	Item	总店数(个) Number of Head Stores (unit)	门店总数(个) Number of Stores (unit)	年末从业人数(万人) Employed Persons at Year-end (10 000 persons)	年末零售营业面积(万平方米) Operating Area of Retail Enterprises at Year-end (10 000 sq.m)	商品销售额(亿元) Total Sales of Commodities (100 million yuan)	商品购进总额(亿元) Total Purchases Value (100 million yuan)	统一配送商品购进额(亿元) Centralized Purchase and Delivery (100 million yuan)
合　计	**Total**	**5033**	**398343**	**235.9**	**18671.9**	**42577.5**	**34509.0**	**24458.8**
内资企业	**Domestic Invested Enterprises**	**4659**	**342281**	**175.8**	**12226.0**	**24448.5**	**19642.4**	**14842.8**
有限责任公司	Limited Liability Corporations	4290	294548	139.9	7639.8	14800.9	12242.3	9416.6
股份有限公司	Share-holding Corporations Ltd.	302	45215	34.1	4352.4	8637.4	6778.7	4879.9
非公司企业法人	Non Corporate Legal Entity	38	1581	1.4	220.7	988.0	605.3	531.3
个人独资企业	Sole Proprietorship Enterprises	28	558	0.2	9.1	15.7	11.8	10.8
合伙企业	Partnership Enterprises							
其他内资企业	Other Domestic Invested Enterprises	NA	379	0.1	4.0	6.6	4.1	4.1
港澳台投资企业	**Enterprises with Investment from Hong Kong, Macao and Taiwan**	**159**	**22157**	**32.2**	**2489.2**	**4972.4**	**4315.4**	**1683.6**
外商投资企业	**Foreign Invested Enterprises**	**215**	**33905**	**27.9**	**3956.7**	**13156.7**	**10551.2**	**7932.4**
其他统计类别	**Other Statistical Categories**							

注：1.本表登记注册统计类别按《关于市场主体统计分类的划分规定》(国统字〔2023〕14号)执行。
2.NA表示企业个数小于或等于3(以下相关表同)。
3.2023年，根据第五次全国经济普查有关资料，更加全面掌握连锁企业的经营情况，统计单位增加较多。

a) The registered statistical categories of this table is implemented in accordance with the Regulations on the Classification of Market Entity Statistics (Guotongzi [2023] No. 14).
b) NA refers to less than or equal to three. The same applies to the tables following.
c) In 2023, according to the relevant data of the fifth national economic census, a more comprehensive understanding of the operation of chain enterprises has been obtained and the number of statistical units has increased significantly.

15-7 按行业和业态分连锁零售企业基本情况(2023年)
Main Indicators of Chain Retail Enterprises by Sector and Business Categories (2023)

指标	Item	总店数(个) Number of Head Stores (unit)	门店总数(个) Number of Stores (unit)	年末从业人数(万人) Employed Persons at Year-end (10 000 persons)	年末零售营业面积(万平方米) Operating Area of Retail Enterprises at Year-end (10 000 sq.m)	商品销售额(亿元) Total Sales of Commodities (100 million yuan)	商品购进总额(亿元) Total Purchases Value (100 million yuan)	统一配送商品购进额(亿元) Centralized Purchase and Delivery (100 million yuan)
总计	**Total**	**5033**	**398343**	**235.9**	**18671.9**	**42577.5**	**34509.0**	**24458.8**
按行业分	**By Sector**							
#综合零售	General Retail	1129	77960	96.8	8388.5	11534.0	10352.8	5490.7
食品、饮料及烟草制品专门零售	Special Retail of Food, Beverages and Tobaccos	293	21126	7.8	114.1	669.5	501.0	406.5
纺织、服装及日用品专门零售	Special Retail of Textiles, Garments and Daily Consumer Articles	239	23526	14.8	585.4	2115.2	1218.6	624.8
文化、体育用品及器材专门零售	Special Retail of Culture, Sports Appliances and Equipments	122	5921	5.6	288.5	1348.4	1219.6	1186.8
医药及医疗器材专门零售	Special Retail of Medicines and Medical Appliances	2312	195374	70.2	2096.5	4130.6	3191.4	2804.6
汽车、摩托车、燃料及零配件专门零售	Special Retail of Motor Vehicles, Motorcycles, Fuel and Parts	266	18649	10.8	3047.0	9252.8	6251.5	4886.9
家用电器及电子产品专门零售	Special Retail of Household Electric Appliances and Electronic Products	187	3915	5.0	428.5	2262.3	1956.6	1014.4
五金、家具及室内装饰材料专门零售	Special Retail of Hardware, Furniture and Interior Decoration Materials	16	465	0.7	80.4	129.5	92.0	76.3
货摊、无店铺及其他零售业	Stalls, Non-Shop and Other Retails	25	677	0.3	8.1	88.3	85.6	82.4
按业态分	**By Business Categories**							
便利店	Convenience Store	234	45292	12.5	416.5	811.8	652.0	508.9
超市	Supermarket	679	26622	63.7	5113.9	7346.2	6982.2	3461.2
折扣店	Discount Store	10	485	0.2	24.7	52.2	49.8	11.7
仓储会员店	Warehouse Club	18	971	3.0	124.4	406.3	395.0	190.4
百货店	Department Store	106	4523	13.2	2186.4	2048.0	1556.1	719.4
购物中心	Shopping Mall	26	418	1.2	231.4	257.6	209.4	95.7
专业店	Specialty Store	3332	263336	108.1	9537.4	25561.8	20217.4	17211.1
#加油站	Gas Station	371	34163	19.4	5463.2	17219.2	13225.5	11240.5
品牌专卖店	Brand Exclusive Store	536	45740	27.4	877.7	4999.8	3607.0	1589.5
集合店	Multi-brands Store	37	2283	1.1	66.7	83.0	48.2	40.0
无人值守商店	Unmanned Store							
其他	Other Store	55	8673	5.4	92.7	1010.8	791.7	630.8

15-8 分地区连锁零售企业基本情况
Main Indicators of Chain Retail Enterprises by Region

年 份 Year 地 区 Region		总店数 (个) Number of Head Stores (unit)	门店总数 (个) Number of Stores (unit)	年末从业人数 (万人) Employed Persons at Year-end (10 000 persons)	年末零售营业面积 (万平方米) Operating Area of Retail Enterprises at Year-end (10 000 sq.m)	商品销售额 (亿元) Total Sales of Commodities (100 million yuan)	商品购进总额 (亿元) Total Purchases Value (100 million yuan)	统一配送商品购进额 (亿元) Centralized Purchase and Delivery (100 million yuan)
	2005	1416	90476	148.8	8202.7	10668.4	9044.1	7036.8
	2006	1696	123690	176.5	9549.7	15548.9	13511.8	10807.2
	2007	1729	145366	186.2	10044.0	17754.3	15917.0	12542.4
	2008	2457	168502	197.1	10197.8	20466.5	17193.1	13782.1
	2009	2327	175677	210.9	11809.2	22240.0	19343.7	14723.1
	2010	2361	176792	225.2	12756.8	27385.4	24044.6	17412.5
	2011	2411	195779	249.1	13670.7	34510.7	29653.0	22919.6
	2012	2524	192870	256.3	14765.9	35462.1	30825.5	23975.8
	2013	2649	204090	255.9	15640.3	38006.9	32258.7	25341.8
	2014	2663	206415	250.2	16221.3	37340.6	31298.5	24582.4
	2015	2690	209812	248.1	16862.4	35400.4	30556.8	23379.9
	2016	2726	232444	245.0	17960.1	35922.9	31036.9	24173.7
	2017	2871	236103	234.9	17329.6	36630.7	31396.4	24613.2
	2018	2934	249711	239.0	17924.7	38012.7	32133.0	24294.4
	2019	2897	252656	226.6	18384.9	37256.9	31358.0	23356.3
	2020	3082	269345	220.2	18276.6	33903.9	27830.2	20250.8
	2021	3169	292383	221.7	18695.9	38400.2	31440.7	22389.1
	2022	3214	296605	205.7	18604.3	39030.1	32394.7	22539.2
	2023	5033	398343	235.9	18671.9	42577.5	34509.0	24458.8
北 京	Beijing	182	9545	10.0	743.9	3112.0	2601.9	1413.7
天 津	Tianjin	64	3506	2.5	131.7	519.5	459.7	351.8
河 北	Hebei	256	14859	7.4	714.2	1152.8	940.4	691.0
山 西	Shanxi	107	11235	5.6	267.0	451.0	365.4	236.0
内蒙古	Inner Mongolia	58	4051	1.6	62.8	83.4	64.4	64.3
辽 宁	Liaoning	197	13047	6.1	455.2	831.8	661.9	476.5
吉 林	Jilin	93	5606	2.3	87.9	261.6	107.7	83.9
黑龙江	Heilongjiang	137	6395	3.2	100.8	431.0	396.5	227.4
上 海	Shanghai	186	24359	22.6	1459.8	5128.5	4457.4	2619.9
江 苏	Jiangsu	252	25511	15.1	1638.2	3489.1	3199.3	2876.0
浙 江	Zhejiang	300	22688	10.3	1033.2	2850.8	2594.9	2306.5
安 徽	Anhui	156	12838	6.7	645.2	1270.8	1108.2	1042.7
福 建	Fujian	230	18403	18.2	1348.7	2304.4	1774.1	519.6
江 西	Jiangxi	104	7199	4.4	308.1	1030.5	410.7	343.4
山 东	Shandong	439	30354	20.5	2601.2	2890.7	2409.1	1395.1
河 南	Henan	206	14852	8.7	638.4	1099.5	874.6	557.8
湖 北	Hubei	211	16303	11.1	530.3	1726.1	1356.1	1041.6
湖 南	Hunan	180	18616	10.3	895.4	1713.6	1081.1	844.6
广 东	Guangdong	574	46734	24.4	1487.5	4696.0	3296.2	2063.1
广 西	Guangxi	153	13962	5.3	580.4	1077.4	960.3	931.0
海 南	Hainan	18	2207	0.9	122.9	329.4	315.4	307.9
重 庆	Chongqing	67	8323	6.1	455.7	1057.4	967.2	732.1
四 川	Sichuan	306	27169	12.1	516.4	1387.6	1177.8	892.2
贵 州	Guizhou	55	3699	1.5	78.8	164.6	161.6	156.2
云 南	Yunnan	61	13230	4.7	268.0	590.7	309.8	283.6
西 藏	Xizang	5	139	0.1	3.5	5.3	2.9	2.8
陕 西	Shaanxi	146	8749	6.1	439.3	960.0	772.3	541.7
甘 肃	Gansu	70	3601	1.9	130.3	353.6	304.7	254.1
青 海	Qinghai	20	552	0.3	14.5	21.5	16.4	12.1
宁 夏	Ningxia	62	2278	1.7	235.2	412.7	350.2	209.7
新 疆	Xinjiang	138	8333	3.9	677.5	1174.1	1010.8	980.6

注：门店总数全国总计中包括开设在港澳台地区和国外的门店。

a) Total number of stores includes those located in Hong Kong, Macao and Taiwan province and foreign countries.

15-9 亿元以上商品交易市场基本情况(2023年)

Main Indicators of Commodity Exchange Markets with Transaction Value over 100 Million Yuan by Type of Market (2023)

市场	Market Category	市场数量(个) Number of Markets (unit)	摊位数(个) Number of Booths (unit)	营业面积(万平方米) Operating Area (10 000 sq.m)	成交额(亿元) Turnover (100 million yuan)	批发市场 Whole-sale	零售市场 Retail
总计	**Total**	**3555**	**2618959**	**29825.8**	**109570.7**	**98541.9**	**11028.8**
综合市场	**General Markets**	**1088**	**979229**	**8813.7**	**28176.9**	**25068.3**	**3108.6**
生产资料综合市场	Comprehensive Markets for Means of Production	36	54997	1084.7	1364.6	1321.3	43.3
工业消费品综合市场	Industrial Consumable Comprehensive Markets	158	301839	2507.7	6948.7	6262.4	686.3
农产品综合市场	Comprehensive Markets for Agricultural Products	621	348720	2754.3	15488.7	13952.7	1536.0
其他综合市场	Other Comprehensive Markets	273	273673	2467.0	4374.9	3531.8	843.1
专业市场	**Specialized Markets**	**2467**	**1639730**	**21012.1**	**81393.8**	**73473.6**	**7920.2**
生产资料市场	Markets for Means of Production	425	229301	5130.0	27224.8	27140.4	84.4
农业生产用具市场	Markets for Agricultural Production Equipment	7	3526	74.3	178.6	178.6	
农用生产资料市场	Markets for Means of Agricultural Production	10	1710	30.5	29.2	29.2	
煤炭市场	Coal and Charcoal Markets	1	32	304.8	22.0	22.0	
木材市场	Wood Markets	22	7122	166.2	213.6	213.6	
建材市场	Building Material Markets	164	96676	2023.7	1796.8	1712.4	84.4
化工材料及制品市场	Chemical Materials and Products Markets	18	12854	148.4	4044.7	4044.7	
金属材料市场	Metal Materials Markets	140	65377	1888.6	18843.5	18843.5	
机械设备市场	Mechanical Equipment Markets	34	25987	299.1	738.3	738.3	
其他生产资料市场	Others	29	16017	194.6	1358.1	1358.1	
农产品市场	Agricultural Products Markets	728	412436	4519.3	21453.4	20761.4	691.9
粮油市场	Grain and Oil Markets	63	17223	283.4	1188.5	1184.9	3.5
肉禽蛋市场	Meat, Poultry and Eggs Markets	81	36947	413.4	1922.3	1760.7	161.5
水产品市场	Aquatic Products Markets	132	55404	525.2	3920.7	3796.8	123.9
蔬菜市场	Vegetables Markets	196	134715	1419.7	4267.3	4162.1	105.2
干鲜果品市场	Dried and Fresh Melons and Fruits Markets	111	68107	967.8	5978.4	5975.2	3.1
棉麻土畜、烟叶市场	Markets for Cotton, Local & Livestock Products, and Tobacco Leaves	9	12307	115.6	399.6	383.6	16.0
其他农产品市场	Others	136	87733	794.3	3776.7	3498.0	278.7
食品、饮料及烟酒市场	Markets for Food, Beverages, Tobacco and Alcohol	82	36755	333.2	1181.9	1098.2	83.6
食品饮料市场	Food and Beverages Markets	22	7716	71.1	227.5	203.5	23.9
茶叶市场	Tea Markets	30	12666	135.3	455.1	418.4	36.7
烟酒市场	Tobacco and Alcohol Markets	5	1308	15.0	53.2	49.5	3.6
其他食品饮料及烟酒市场	Others	25	15065	111.8	446.1	426.8	19.3
纺织、服装、鞋帽市场	Markets for Textiles, Clothing, Shoes and Hats	323	467027	3604.5	15759.3	15133.8	625.6
布料及纺织品市场	Cloth and Textiles Markets	46	89527	1075.2	7979.8	7975.7	4.2
服装市场	Clothing Markets	214	291685	1878.6	5881.8	5394.9	486.9
鞋帽市场	Footwear and Hats Markets	25	16210	107.1	246.7	246.7	
其他纺织服装鞋帽市场	Others	38	69605	543.5	1651.0	1516.5	134.5
日用品及文化用品市场	Markets for Daily Use Articles and Cultural Goods	60	45367	358.0	858.1	807.7	50.4

15–9 续表 continued

市　　场	Market Category	市场数量(个) Number of Markets (unit)	摊位数(个) Number of Booths (unit)	营业面积(万平方米) Operating Area (10 000 sq.m)	成交额(亿元) Turnover (100 million yuan)	批发市场 Whole-sale	零售市场 Retail
小商品市场	Small Merchandise Markets	28	19405	150.7	287.0	262.1	24.9
箱包市场	Luggage Markets	3	8913	73.4	221.0	221.0	
玩具市场	Toys Markets	3	1288	32.3	24.5	24.5	
文具市场	Stationary Markets						
图书、报刊杂志市场	Markets for Books, Newspapers and Magazines	5	785	6.8	34.2	15.9	18.4
音像制品及电子出版物市场	Markets for Video and E-book Products	1	113	0.7	4.6		4.6
体育用品市场	Sports Article Markets						
其他日用品及文化用品市场	Others	20	14863	94.3	286.8	284.2	2.5
黄金、珠宝、玉器等首饰市场	Gold, Jewelry, Jade Markets	17	17926	186.4	855.7	826.0	29.7
电器、通讯器材、电子设备市场	Markets for Electrical Appliances, Communication Appliances and Electronical Appliances	74	33824	268.1	566.5	379.8	186.8
家电市场	Household Appliances Markets	18	7374	130.9	131.3	121.5	9.8
通讯器材市场	Communication Appliances Markets	12	7604	26.8	123.2	115.4	7.8
照相、摄像器材市场	Cameras and Video Equipments Markets	3	513	3.3	6.9	3.9	3.0
计算机及辅助设备市场	Computer and Auxiliary Equipments Markets	38	16642	99.0	285.8	120.6	165.1
其他电器、通讯器材、电子设备市场	Others	3	1691	8.2	19.4	18.3	1.1
医药、医疗用品及器材市场	Markets for Medicine, Medical Materials and Medical Instruments	22	52357	327.5	2027.4	1912.4	115.0
中药材市场	Chinese Medicine Markets	20	51797	312.4	1986.9	1871.9	115.0
其他医药、医疗用品及器材市场	Others	2	560	15.1	40.5	40.5	
家具、五金及装饰材料市场	Markets for Furniture, Hardware and Decoration Materials	440	238445	4295.6	4420.1	3007.6	1412.5
家具市场	Furniture Markets	139	66683	1584.8	1266.1	809.6	456.4
装饰材料市场	Decoration Materials Markets	163	77135	1381.1	1321.7	669.8	651.9
灯具市场	Lamps Markets	10	5433	90.7	191.1	185.3	5.8
厨具、盥洗设备市场	Markets for Kitchen Utensils and Washing Equipment	3	1304	34.8	29.8	28.8	1.0
五金材料市场	Hardware Materials Markets	62	48785	616.9	1176.2	1136.6	39.5
其他装修市场	Others	63	39105	587.4	435.2	177.4	257.8
汽车、摩托车及零配件市场	Markets for Cars, Motorcycles and Spare Parts	241	66658	1434.9	5551.7	989.8	4562.0
汽车市场	Cars Markets	180	41510	1128.2	4789.2	299.8	4489.4
摩托车市场	Motorcycles Markets	4	1076	8.9	8.0	2.9	5.1
机动车零配件市场	Vehicle Spare Parts Markets	57	24072	297.8	754.5	687.1	67.4
花、鸟、鱼、虫市场	Markets for Flower, Bird, Fish and Insects	21	19542	254.7	639.5	606.4	33.1
花卉市场	Flower Markets	18	18824	249.6	618.4	591.5	26.9
鸟市场	Bird Markets						
观赏鱼市场	Markets for Fish for Display						
其他花鸟鱼虫市场	Others	3	718	5.1	21.1	14.9	6.2
旧货市场	Second-hand Articles Markets	4	1529	7.5	12.8		12.8
古玩、古董、字画市场	Markets for Antiques, Calligraphy and Painting						
邮票、硬币市场	Stamps and Coins Markets						
其他旧货市场	Markets for Others Second-hand Articles	4	1529	7.5	12.8		12.8
其他专业市场	Other Specialized Markets	30	18563	292.3	842.5	810.0	32.5

15-10 亿元以上商品交易市场摊位分类情况（2023年）

Main Indicators of Commodity Exchange Markets with Transaction Value over 100 Million Yuan by Commodity (2023)

类别	Commodity Category	摊位数（个）Number of Booths (unit)	成交额（亿元）Turnover (100 million yuan)	批发市场 Wholesale Markets	零售市场 Retail Markets
总计	**Total**	**2618959**	**109570.7**	**98541.9**	**11028.8**
粮油、食品类	Grain and Oil, Food	779760	37211.8	34786.9	2425.0
#粮油类	Grain and Oil	74625	3911.5	3681.0	230.5
肉禽蛋类	Meat, Poultry and Eggs	109560	4771.1	4052.4	718.7
水产品类	Aquatic Products	111333	7105.1	6534.7	570.4
蔬菜类	Vegetables	273217	9435.7	8939.7	495.9
干鲜果品类	Dried and Fresh Melons and Fruits	147208	9887.4	9651.4	236.0
饮料类	Beverages	37497	1356.9	1259.7	97.3
烟酒类	Tobacco and Alcohol	22981	921.2	836.3	84.9
服装鞋帽、针、纺织品类	Clothing, Shoes, Hats and Textiles	632441	17877.7	16946.8	930.9
服装类	Clothing	388834	6959.9	6283.1	676.8
鞋帽类	Footwear and Hats	81817	1325.6	1176.5	149.1
针、纺织品类	Knitwear and Textiles	161790	9592.2	9487.1	105.0
化妆品类	Cosmetics	16771	301.7	259.5	42.2
金银珠宝类	Gold, Silver and Jewellery	27519	1211.0	1154.9	56.1
日用品类	Articles for Daily Use	115850	2437.6	2215.0	222.6
五金、电料类	Hardware & Electrical Materials	107043	2372.2	2177.2	195.0
体育、娱乐用品类	Sports & Recreational Articles	7887	125.7	103.7	22.0
#照相器材类	Photographic Equipment	867	9.3	4.8	4.6
书报杂志类	Newspapers and Magazines	2027	64.4	49.6	14.8
电子出版物及音像制品类	E-book and Video Products	1731	41.7	28.8	12.8
家用电器和音像器材类	Household Appliances and Audio-visual Equipment	27022	514.6	449.7	64.9
中西药品类	Traditional Chinese and Western Medicine	36231	2058.3	1916.1	142.2
#西药类	Western Medicine	715	37.0	17.2	19.8
中草药及中成药类	Traditional Chinese Medicine	34387	1976.4	1859.7	116.7
文化办公用品类	Cultural and Office Goods	39148	818.1	651.7	166.4
#计算机及其配套产品	Computer and Related Equipment	14303	286.5	160.6	125.9
家具类	Furniture	97176	1748.8	1173.0	575.8
通讯器材类	Communication Appliances	16392	344.2	292.5	51.7
煤炭及制品类	Coal and Related Products	269	63.7	62.4	1.4
木材及制品类	Wood and Wooden Products	18899	450.8	394.7	56.1
石油及制品类	Petroleum and Related Products	766	1044.8	1043.2	1.6
化工材料及制品类	Raw Chemical Materials and Related Products	20230	4268.9	4242.8	26.2
#化肥类	Fertilizer	2044	31.0	27.6	3.4
金属材料类	Metal Materials	79425	19275.4	19218.9	56.5
建筑及装潢材料类	Building and Decoration Materials	233929	3894.5	2976.6	917.9
机电产品及设备类	Mechanical & Electrical Products	45002	1401.8	1368.5	33.2
#农机类	Agricultural Machinery	3074	176.2	168.0	8.2
汽车类	Automobile	79185	5815.9	1210.3	4605.7
种子饲料类	Seed and Feedstuff	4476	94.3	88.7	5.7
棉麻类	Cotton and Hemp	1538	182.4	180.8	1.6
其他类	Others	167764	3671.5	3453.3	218.3

15-11 分地区亿元以上商品交易市场基本情况
Main Indicators of Commodity Exchange Markets with Transaction Value over 100 Million Yuan by Region

年份 Year 地区 Region	市场数量(个) Number of Markets (unit)	摊位数(个) Number of Booths (unit)	营业面积(万平方米) Operating Area (10 000 sq.m)	成交额(亿元) Turnover (100 million yuan)	批发市场 Wholesale	零售市场 Retail
2000	3087	2115115	8261.6	16358.9	11648.0	4710.9
2005	3323	2248803	13140.8	30020.9	24544.2	5476.7
2006	3876	2527987	18072.3	37137.5	29679.9	7457.5
2007	4121	2681630	19814.6	44085.1	35871.5	8213.6
2008	4567	2839070	21225.2	52458.0	43120.0	9337.9
2009	4687	2994781	23230.3	57963.8	48308.2	9655.5
2010	4940	3193365	24832.3	72703.5	60954.9	11748.6
2011	5075	3334787	26234.5	82017.3	69390.8	12626.5
2012	5194	3494122	27899.4	93023.8	80141.8	12882.0
2013	5089	3488170	28868.3	98365.1	84628.3	13736.8
2014	5023	3534757	29567.9	100309.9	86323.7	13986.2
2015	4952	3468638	30065.7	100133.8	85836.9	14296.8
2016	4861	3457899	30023.4	102139.7	87859.3	14280.4
2017	4617	3347936	29691.8	108247.6	93996.9	14250.7
2018	4296	3178423	29190.6	109373.3	95323.2	14050.1
2019	4037	3045931	28447.4	112016.8	98733.4	13283.4
2020	3891	2877393	29114.7	105748.7	93874.6	11874.1
2021	3753	2794347	29134.6	115462.2	103547.7	11914.4
2022	3659	2665088	29471.2	106316.3	95455.4	10860.9
2023	3555	2618959	29825.8	109570.7	98541.9	11028.8
北京 Beijing	67	43572	530.4	3178.5	2470.8	707.7
天津 Tianjin	42	26791	466.2	1271.2	1241.2	30.0
河北 Hebei	148	199639	2338.1	6028.7	5879.3	149.4
山西 Shanxi	29	20073	237.3	649.8	614.3	35.5
内蒙古 Inner Mongolia	39	21817	644.6	660.5	619.9	40.6
辽宁 Liaoning	118	99620	1049.1	3098.1	2820.9	277.2
吉林 Jilin	31	30926	288.9	398.7	345.4	53.3
黑龙江 Heilongjiang	27	16033	178.9	390.9	363.9	26.9
上海 Shanghai	87	37337	340.3	8464.3	7993.6	470.7
江苏 Jiangsu	334	283608	3466.4	20382.0	19094.8	1287.2
浙江 Zhejiang	593	344176	3156.1	18115.3	15610.7	2504.7
安徽 Anhui	86	93389	1159.6	2499.6	2213.4	286.2
福建 Fujian	95	37969	273.0	1160.3	976.8	183.5
江西 Jiangxi	101	78953	902.4	2413.4	2176.3	237.1
山东 Shandong	501	270551	4006.3	10018.0	9159.1	858.9
河南 Henan	84	75674	1146.3	3025.9	2749.9	276.0
湖北 Hubei	88	55778	652.0	2183.3	1898.2	285.1
湖南 Hunan	245	169073	1316.3	6065.8	5133.3	932.5
广东 Guangdong	247	180857	1740.2	5379.2	4764.6	614.6
广西 Guangxi	58	50615	360.2	1076.3	885.9	190.4
海南 Hainan	5	4282	88.6	126.9	122.6	4.3
重庆 Chongqing	125	77847	832.9	3355.5	2847.6	507.9
四川 Sichuan	102	133509	1203.2	3609.2	3444.5	164.7
贵州 Guizhou	42	34548	567.5	1084.6	936.1	148.5
云南 Yunnan	25	38262	206.1	378.0	336.2	41.8
西藏 Xizang	3	2217	3.9	23.4	19.7	3.7
陕西 Shaanxi	45	37523	534.5	1070.5	999.7	70.8
甘肃 Gansu	37	24221	282.8	440.8	289.7	151.2
青海 Qinghai	6	6076	47.2	105.3	99.5	5.8
宁夏 Ningxia	32	23396	284.6	365.9	341.0	24.9
新疆 Xinjiang	113	100627	1521.8	2551.0	2093.1	457.9

15-12 社会消费品零售总额
Total Retail Sales of Consumer Goods

地区	Region	2022 社会消费品零售总额(亿元) Total Retail Sales of Consumer Goods (100 million yuan)	2022 比上年增长(%) Growth Rate (%)	2023 社会消费品零售总额(亿元) Total Retail Sales of Consumer Goods (100 million yuan)	2023 比上年增长(%) Growth Rate (%)
全 国	**National Total**	**439732.5**	**-0.2**	**471495.2**	**7.2**
北 京	Beijing	13794.2	-7.2	14462.7	4.8
天 津	Tianjin	3572.0	-5.2	3820.7	7.0
河 北	Hebei	13720.1	1.6	15040.5	9.6
山 西	Shanxi	7562.7	-2.4	7981.8	5.5
内蒙古	Inner Mongolia	4971.4	-1.8	5374.3	8.1
辽 宁	Liaoning	9526.2	-2.6	10362.1	8.8
吉 林	Jilin	3807.7	-9.7	4150.4	9.0
黑龙江	Heilongjiang	5210.0	-6.0	5634.2	8.1
上 海	Shanghai	16442.1	-9.1	18515.5	12.6
江 苏	Jiangsu	42752.1	0.1	45547.5	6.5
浙 江	Zhejiang	30467.2	4.3	32550.2	6.8
安 徽	Anhui	21518.4	0.2	23008.3	6.9
福 建	Fujian	21050.1	3.3	22109.6	5.0
江 西	Jiangxi	12853.5	5.3	13659.8	6.3
山 东	Shandong	33236.2	-1.4	36141.8	8.7
河 南	Henan	24407.4	0.1	26004.4	6.5
湖 北	Hubei	22164.8	2.8	24041.9	8.5
湖 南	Hunan	19050.7	2.4	20203.3	6.1
广 东	Guangdong	44882.9	1.6	47494.9	5.8
广 西	Guangxi	8539.1	0.0	8651.6	1.3
海 南	Hainan	2268.4	-9.2	2511.3	10.7
重 庆	Chongqing	13926.1	-0.3	15130.3	8.6
四 川	Sichuan	24104.6	-0.1	26313.4	9.2
贵 州	Guizhou	8507.1	-4.5	9011.2	5.9
云 南	Yunnan	10838.8	1.0	11560.7	6.7
西 藏	Xizang	726.5	-10.3	879.8	21.1
陕 西	Shaanxi	10401.6	1.5	10759.0	3.4
甘 肃	Gansu	3922.2	-2.8	4329.7	10.4
青 海	Qinghai	842.1	-11.2	987.7	17.3
宁 夏	Ningxia	1338.4	0.2	1354.9	1.2
新 疆	Xinjiang	3240.5	-9.6	3849.7	18.8

15-13 分地区网上零售额(2023年)
Online Retail Sales by Region (2023)

地 区	Region	网上零售额 Online Retail Sales		#实物商品网上零售额 Online Retail Sales in Goods	
		绝对值 (亿元) Value (100 million yuan)	比上年增长 (%) Growth Rate (%)	绝对值 (亿元) Value (100 million yuan)	比上年增长 (%) Growth Rate (%)
全 国	**National Total**	**154264.2**	**11.0**	**130173.8**	**8.4**
北 京	Beijing	12017.4	-2.6	8700.0	-6.9
天 津	Tianjin	2053.9	3.4	1695.2	-3.7
河 北	Hebei	4654.6	10.6	4214.6	8.1
山 西	Shanxi	1094.5	22.1	876.1	18.4
内蒙古	Inner Mongolia	647.2	21.5	449.0	22.1
辽 宁	Liaoning	2439.3	10.5	2023.3	8.8
吉 林	Jilin	726.3	24.0	513.6	19.8
黑龙江	Heilongjiang	872.2	13.5	661.8	4.6
上 海	Shanghai	12680.8	11.2	10203.1	6.0
江 苏	Jiangsu	13091.1	9.5	11156.2	6.5
浙 江	Zhejiang	20867.8	10.6	18492.9	11.0
安 徽	Anhui	3985.4	14.5	3406.9	12.0
福 建	Fujian	8009.5	7.7	7267.1	6.3
江 西	Jiangxi	3107.6	13.8	2734.5	11.8
山 东	Shandong	7728.5	11.0	6723.1	8.6
河 南	Henan	4605.3	22.5	3813.0	21.0
湖 北	Hubei	4347.7	9.0	3657.3	6.7
湖 南	Hunan	3040.6	15.6	2432.0	12.1
广 东	Guangdong	31484.1	9.4	28410.4	7.5
广 西	Guangxi	1299.1	13.2	941.5	9.5
海 南	Hainan	1319.4	100.3	1088.1	108.9
重 庆	Chongqing	2066.8	22.8	1502.6	14.5
四 川	Sichuan	4855.0	12.8	3725.3	5.8
贵 州	Guizhou	897.7	40.8	660.3	48.9
云 南	Yunnan	1329.8	17.2	916.7	8.6
西 藏	Xizang	173.1	89.7	142.4	92.1
陕 西	Shaanxi	2142.0	28.7	1709.2	23.8
甘 肃	Gansu	370.6	22.5	235.6	3.2
青 海	Qinghai	149.8	72.0	102.5	84.5
宁 夏	Ningxia	174.9	2.1	108.8	-0.7
新 疆	Xinjiang	546.4	46.6	368.8	32.4
不分地区	Not Classified by Region	1485.8		1241.9	

15-14 乘用车销售情况
Sales of Passenger Cars

年 份 Year	乘用车合计 Total Passenger Cars		#轿车 Cars		#MPV		#SUV	
	绝对量 (万辆) Number (10 000 units)	同比增速 (%) Growth Rate (%)	绝对量 (万辆) Number (10 000 units)	同比增速 (%) Growth Rate (%)	绝对量 (万辆) Number (10 000 units)	同比增速 (%) Growth Rate (%)	绝对量 (万辆) Number (10 000 units)	同比增速 (%) Growth Rate (%)
2007	594.0	17.9	442.1	19.0	21.7	23.1	34.2	55.7
2008	643.3	8.3	476.3	7.7	18.9	-12.7	42.5	24.3
2009	1026.6	59.6	738.2	55.0	24.5	29.6	69.9	64.5
2010	1332.5	29.8	925.9	25.4	43.3	76.5	123.2	76.4
2011	1367.1	2.6	951.6	2.8	51.1	17.8	150.3	22.0
2012	1465.9	7.2	1015.5	6.7	92.0	80.1	183.3	21.9
2013	1724.3	17.6	1156.7	13.9	130.1	41.5	283.7	54.8
2014	1898.9	10.1	1209.8	4.6	185.3	42.4	383.9	35.3
2015	2060.9	8.5	1145.2	-5.3	212.2	14.5	608.5	58.5
2016	2383.8	15.7	1203.5	5.1	245.2	15.6	874.1	43.6
2017	2418.4	1.5	1163.4	-3.3	201.6	-17.8	1006.9	15.2
2018	2275.1	-5.9	1116.6	-4.0	167.7	-16.8	953.4	-5.3
2019	2102.9	-7.6	1014.5	-9.1	137.7	-17.9	916.6	-3.9
2020	1960.7	-6.8	925.0	-8.8	109.0	-20.8	894.8	-2.4
2021	2048.6	4.4	984.6	6.4	107.9	-1.0	922.1	3.0
2022	2082.4	1.6	1019.3	3.5	94.2	-12.7	940.6	1.9
2023	2192.9	5.3	1022.4	0.3	109.3	15.9	1038.2	10.3

数据来源：中国汽车流通协会。
Source: China Automobile Dealers Association.

15-15 二手乘用车销售情况
Sales of Second-hand Passenger Cars

年 份 Year	二手乘用车合计 Total Second-hand Passenger Cars		#轿车 Cars		#MPV		#SUV	
	绝对量 (万辆) Number (10 000 units)	同比增速 (%) Growth Rate (%)	绝对量 (万辆) Number (10 000 units)	同比增速 (%) Growth Rate (%)	绝对量 (万辆) Number (10 000 units)	同比增速 (%) Growth Rate (%)	绝对量 (万辆) Number (10 000 units)	同比增速 (%) Growth Rate (%)
2009	196.3	21.4	171.8	20.4	12.0	25.4	6.4	31.3
2010	238.7	21.6	209.8	22.1	14.9	23.6	7.1	10.9
2011	422.0		370.7		26.7		12.3	
2012	514.7	22.0	452.5	22.1	31.3	17.3	18.4	49.3
2013	573.9	11.5	496.5	9.7	36.6	16.9	27.2	47.9
2014	625.7	9.0	534.0	7.5	44.6	21.9	30.9	13.7
2015	677.7	8.3	564.1	5.6	35.5	-20.4	47.3	53.1
2016	788.0	16.3	628.0	11.3	58.9	66.0	68.1	44.1
2017	931.6	18.2	737.0	17.4	72.3	22.8	86.8	27.4
2018	1045.0	12.2	822.2	11.6	78.2	8.1	113.6	30.8
2019	1142.5	9.3	861.4	4.8	95.7	22.4	148.1	30.4
2020	1112.9	-2.6	858.7	-0.3	83.2	-13.1	137.1	-7.4
2021	1397.8	25.6	1059.1	23.3	100.9	21.2	197.6	44.2
2022	1288.2	-7.8	952.4	-10.1	96.9	-3.9	203.8	3.1
2023	1841.3	14.9	1089.7	14.4	114.1	17.8	237.8	16.7

注：1.2011年开始为全口径统计数据，之前两年为600家重点企业调查数据。
　　2.数据来源：中国汽车流通协会。
a) Data of 2009 and 2010 were from the survey data of 600 key enterprises. Since 2011, the data are all-inclusive statistics.
b) Source: China Automobile Dealers Association.

主要统计指标解释

批发业　指向其他批发或零售单位（含个体经营者）及其他企事业单位、机关团体等批量销售生活用品、生产资料的活动，以及从事进出口贸易和贸易经纪与代理的活动，包括拥有货物所有权，并以本单位（公司）的名义进行交易活动，也包括不拥有货物的所有权，收取佣金的商品代理、商品代售活动；还包括各类商品批发市场中固定摊位的批发活动，以及以销售为目的的收购活动。

零售业　指百货商店、超级市场、专门零售商店、品牌专卖店、售货摊等主要面向最终消费者（如居民等）的销售活动，以互联网、邮政、电话、售货机等方式的销售活动，还包括在同一地点，后面加工生产，前面销售的店铺（如面包房）；谷物、种子、饲料、牲畜、矿产品、生产用原料、化工原料、农用化工产品、机械设备（乘用车、计算机及通信设备除外）等生产资料的销售不作为零售活动；多数零售商对其销售的货物拥有所有权，但有些则是充当委托人的代理人，进行委托销售或以收取佣金的方式进行销售。

批发和零售业商品购进、销售、库存额　指各种登记注册统计类别的批发和零售业企业从国内、国外市场购进的商品总价，销售和出口的商品总价，库存的商品总价等情况。该指标可以反映商品流转过程中商品购进、销售、库存之间的比例关系和存在的问题。

商品购进额　指从本企业以外的单位和个人购进（包括从国外直接进口）作为转卖或加工后转卖的商品金额（含增值税）。商品购进包括：（1）从工农业生产者、批发和零售业、住宿和餐饮业、出版社或报社的出版发行部门和其他服务业等企事业单位和个体经营户购进的商品；（2）从机关、社会团体购进的商品；（3）从海关、市场管理部门购进的缉私和没收的商品；（4）从居民收购的废旧商品等。不包括：（1）企业为本单位自身经营用，不是作为转卖而购进的商品，如材料物资、包装物、低值易耗品、办公用品等；（2）未通过买卖行为而收入的商品，如接受其他部门移交的商品、借入的商品、收入代其他单位保管的商品、其他单位赠送的样品、加工回收的成品等；（3）经本单位介绍，由买卖双方直接结算，本单位只收取手续费的业务；（4）销售退回和买方拒付货款的商品；（5）商品溢余；（6）期货交易商品。

进口　指直接从国外进口或委托外贸企业代理进口的商品金额，不包括从国内有关单位购进的进口商品。对外贸易企业只统计自主经营进口的商品，不统计受托代理进口的商品。

商品销售额　指对本单位以外的单位和个人出售的商品金额（含增值税），以及出售给本单位且开具增值税发票的商品金额。商品销售包括：（1）售给个人和社会集团消费用的商品；（2）售给农业、工业、建筑业、服务业等国民经济各行业用于生产、经营用的商品，包括售予批发和零售业作为转卖或加工后转卖的商品；（3）对国（境）外直接出口的商品。不包括：（1）未通过买卖行为付出的商品，如因机构变动移交给其他企业单位的商品、借出的商品、归还受其他单位委托代保管的商品、付出的加工原料和赠送给其他单位的样品等；（2）促销返券所销售的、不计入营业收入的商品；（3）经本单位介绍，由买卖双方直接结算，本单位只收取手续费的业务；（4）未发生所有权转移的商品预付卡销售，如加油卡；（5）汽车维修、电话卡销售等服务性经济活动；（6）购货退回的商品；（7）商品损耗和损失；（8）出售本单位自用的废旧物资；（9）期货交易商品；（10）自来水供应企业、电力企业、天然气供应企业提供的水、电、气。

出口　指直接向国（境）外出口商品和委托外贸企业代理出口的商品金额，商品出口不包括售给外贸企业出口或加工后出口的商品，以及在国内市场以外币销售的商品。外贸企业只统计自主经营出口的商品，不包括受托代理出口的商品。

期末商品库存额　对于批发和零售业法人单位和个体经营户，是指报告期末取得所有权的全部商品金额（含增值税）；对于批发和零售业产业活动单位，是指报告期末实际在库且归属法人具有所有权的全部商品金额（含增值税）。库存商品包括：（1）存放在本单位（如门市部、批发站、采购站、经营处）的仓库、货场、货柜和货架中的商品；（2）挑选、整理、包装中的商品；（3）已记入购进而尚未运到本单位的商品，即发货单或银行承兑凭证已到而货未到的商品；（4）寄放他处的商品，如因购货方拒绝付款而暂时存在购货方的商品；（5）委托其他单位代销（未作销售或调出）尚未售出的商品；（6）代其他单位购进尚未交付的商品。不包括：（1）所有权不属于本单位的商品，如商品已做销售但买方尚未取走的商品，代替他人保管、运输、加工的商品，代其他单位销售（未做购进或调入）而未售出的商品；（2）委托外单位加工的商品（包括本单位所属加工厂和其他生产单位加工生产尚未收回成品的商品）；（3）外贸企业代理其他单位从国外进口，尚未付给订货单位的商品；（4）代国家储备部门保管的商品。

连锁总店（总部）　指负责连锁企业资源（商号、商誉、经营模式、服务标准、管理模式等）的开发、配置、控制或使用等功能的企业核心管理机构。连锁经营是指经营同类商品或服务，使用统一商号的若干店铺，在同一总店（总部）的管理下，采取统一采购或特许经营等方式，实现规模效益的组织形式，包括直营连锁、特许连锁和自愿连锁三种形式。其中，直营连锁是指连锁店铺由连锁公司全资或控股开设，在总部的直接控制下，开展统一经营的连锁经营形式；特许连锁是指拥有注册商标、企业标志、专利、专有技术等经营资源的企业（特许人），以合同形式将其拥有的经营资源许

可其他经营者（被特许人）使用，被特许人按合同约定在统一的经营模式下开展经营，并向特许人支付特许经营费用的连锁经营形式；自愿连锁是指若干个店铺或企业自愿组合起来，在不改变各自资产所有权关系的情况下，以同一个品牌形象面对消费者，以共同进货为纽带开展的连锁经营形式。

亿元以上商品交易市场 指年成交额在亿元及以上的商品交易市场。商品交易市场是指经有关部门和组织批准设立，有固定场所、设施，有经营管理部门和监管人员，若干市场经营者入内，常年或实际开业三个月以上，集中、公开、独立地进行生活消费品、生产资料等现货商品交易以及提供相关服务的交易场所，包括各类消费品市场、生产资料市场等。

社会消费品零售总额 指企业（单位、个体户）通过交易直接售给个人、社会集团非生产、非经营用的实物商品金额，以及提供餐饮服务所取得的收入金额。个人包括城乡居民和入境人员，社会集团包括机关、社会团体、部队、学校、企事业单位、居委会或村委会等。

网上零售额 指通过公共网络交易平台（包括自建网站和第三方平台）实现的商品和服务零售额之和。商品和服务包括实物商品和非实物商品（如虚拟商品、服务类商品等）。

Explanatory Notes on Main Statistical Indicators

Wholesale Trade refers to the activities of selling wholesale commodities for daily use and capital goods to other enterprises of wholesale and retail trades (including self-employed individuals) and other enterprises, institutions and government agencies and organizations, and the activities of engaging in import and export and acting as a trade agent. The wholesaler may have the ownership of the commodities for wholesale and trade in the name of its own (a company), and the wholesaler can act as commission agent or commodity broker without the ownership of commodities. Also included are the wholesale activities at the fixed stalls in wholesale market and the acquisition for sales purpose.

Retail Trade refers to the activities of department stores, supermarkets, franchised stores, brand stores, retail stalls and on-the-spot-making-selling stores selling commodities to the final consumers (residents) by any means, including internet, post, telephone, sales machine. It also includes shops with sales and production located in the same places (such as bakeries). Retail trade excludes the activities of sales of capital goods such as grain, seed, feed, livestock, mineral products, raw material for production, industrial chemicals, chemical products for agricultural use, machine and equipment (excluding vehicles, computers and communication equipment). Most retailers have the ownership of commodities to sell, but some are acting as agents or brokers to make transactions for a commission.

Purchase, Sales and Stock of Commodities by Wholesale and Retail Trades refer to the total volume of commodities purchased, total volume of sales and exports, and the stock of commodities by wholesale and retail enterprises (establishments) of different statistical categories of registration from domestic and overseas markets. This indicator reflects the relationship among purchase, sales and stock of commodities in the circulation of goods and reveals the existing problems.

Total Purchases of Commodities refer to the total value of purchases of commodities by enterprises (establishments) from other establishments or individuals (including direct import from abroad) for the purpose of re-selling, either with or without further processing of the commodities purchased. The commodities include: (1) commodities purchased from agricultural and industrial producers, wholesalers, retailers, hotels and catering services, publishing houses and other enterprises, institutions and individual operators of service business; (2) commodities purchased from institutions and government departments; (3) smuggled or confiscated goods purchased from the customs authorities or market regulation agencies; (4) second-hand goods purchased from households. The commodities exclude (1) commodities purchased by enterprises (establishments) for use in their own business operation, commodities obtained without buying or selling procedures, such as materials, consumable goods of low value, office appliance, etc. (2) received goods without trading, such as goods handed over from others, borrowed goods, goods kept for others, donated goods from others, processed and retrieved goods, etc. (3) goods of direct settlement between buyer and seller with handling fees introduced by others, (4) goods returned or refused to pay by the buyer, (5) excessive goods, (6) futures trading commodities.

Import refers to the amount of goods imported directly from abroad or imported entrusted to foreign trade enterprises as agents, excluding imports purchased from relevant domestic units. Foreign trade enterprises only count imported goods independently, not imported goods entrusted by agents.

Total Sales of Commodities refer to value of commodities sold by the establishments to other establishments and individuals(including VAT), and the value of commodities sold to the establishments themselves and invoiced for VAT. The commodities include: (1) commodities sold to individuals and social groups for their consumption; (2) commodities sold to establishments in all industries for their production and operation, including agriculture, industry, construction, and catering services, including commodities sold to wholesale and retail establishments for re-selling, with or without further processing; (3) commodities for direct export to abroad. Excluded are (1) extended commodities without trading, such as goods handed over to other enterprises and institutions because of the change of organizations, lent goods, return of goods kept for others, extended processing materials and samples donated to others, (2) goods sold by coupon rebates that are not included in business income, (3) goods of direct settlement between buyer and seller with handling fees introduced by others, (4) prepaid cards for goods without transfer of ownership, such as gas cards, (5) Service-oriented economic activities such as automobile maintenance and telephone card sales, (6) goods returned after purchase, (7) damaged and spoiled goods, (8) waste and used goods of self-use, (9) futures trading commodities, (10) water, electricity and gas supplied by water supply enterprises, electric power enterprises and natural gas supply enterprises.

Export refers to the amount of goods exported directly to foreign countries (or customers outside the borders), or exported entrusted to foreign trade enterprises as agents. Commodity export does not include goods sold to foreign trade enterprises for export or exported after processing, as well as goods sold in foreign currencies in the domestic market. Foreign trade enterprises only count the goods they export independently, excluding those exported by trusted agents.

Total Stock of Commodities at End of Period For corporate units and self-employed individuals engaged in wholesale and retail trade, it refers to total value (including

VAT) of commodities possessed at the end of the reference period; and for wholesale and retail establishments, it refers to the value (including VAT) of all commodities actually in stock and owned by their corporate units at the end of reference period. The commodities in stock includes: (1) commodities located in storage, garages, counters, and shelves of operating places of wholesale and retail trades (such as sale stores, wholesale centres, procurement stations and operating offices); (2) commodities in the process of being selected, sorted, and packed; (3) commodities not arrived but recorded as purchased in the account, i.e. commodities not arrived but payment receipts for the commodities from the sellers or the banks arrived; (4) commodities deposited in other places rather than places mentioned above, for instance: commodities in the hold of purchasers temporarily due to the refusal of payment; (5) commodities entrusted to other units to sell but not sold yet; (6) commodities purchased for other units but not delivered yet. Commodities not included as stock are those not owned by the enterprises (units), commodities on commission for processing, imported commodities of agency of foreign trade enterprise but not yet delivered to ordering units and finally those put in stock on behalf of the state reserves units.

Chain Head Stores (Headquarters) refer to the core leading stores responsible for development, allocation, administration and utilization of resources (name of stores, brand of stores, operation model, service standard, management way, etc.) of chain stores. Chain stores refer to the stores engaged in providing homogeneous commodities or services, with the central leadership of the head stores (headquarters) and guided by common policies, conduct centralized purchase and distributed selling of commodities, in order to gain better efficiency through standardized operation. The chain stores include regular chain stores, franchise chain stores and voluntary chain stores.

Regular Chain store refers to chain stores that are invested or controlled by the headquarters. They operate under direct and unified management from the headquarters.

Franchise chain store refers to the chain stores (franchisees) which are franchised with operation resources such as trade marks, names, patent and operation know-how by the franchisors in form of contract, and pay the operation fees to the franchisors.

Voluntary chain store refers to the stores operating jointly on the voluntary basis while maintaining their status of independent legal entities with full ownership of their assets. They sell goods of same brand from same channel of resources to the consumers.

Large Commodity Markets with Transaction Value over 100 Million Yuan refers to the commodity markets with an annual transaction at and above 100 million. The commodity markets refer to markets approved and managed by related departments, where there are fixed sites, facilities, managers and administrative offices, where there are a certain number of traders to operate for at least three months or all the year, where the commodities, including articles for daily consumption and capital goods and services, are traded in a centralized, independent and open way. Such markets include markets for daily goods, markets of capital goods, etc.

Total Retail Sales of Consumer Goods refer to the revenue received by enterprises (units, self-employed individuals) through direct sales of non-production and non-business physical commodities to individuals and social institutions, and revenue from providing catering services. Individuals include rural and urban households, population from abroad, social institutions include government agencies, social organizations, military units, schools, institutions, neighbourhood (village) committees, etc.

Online Retail Sales refer to the total retail sales of goods and services through public online trading platforms (including self-built websites and third-party platforms). Goods and services include physical goods and non-physical goods (such as virtual goods, service goods, etc.).

16

运输、邮电和软件业

Transport, Postal and Telecommunication Services, and Software Industry

简 要 说 明

一、本篇资料的主要内容

本篇资料反映我国交通运输业和邮政、电信、软件业发展的基本状况以及企业信息化和电子商务应用情况。

交通运输业资料主要包括：五种运输方式的线路里程、运输设备拥有量、技术质量情况，各种运输方式完成的货物运输量和旅客运输量，全国港口码头长度、泊位数量及货物吞吐量等资料。

邮政、电信、软件业资料主要包括：全国营业网点及邮政邮路情况，电信主要通信能力，主要的邮电业务完成情况，邮电通信发展水平，软件和信息技术服务业主要经济指标等资料。

企业信息化及电子商务情况资料主要包括：企业在生产经营中应用信息技术的基本情况和电子商务交易活动情况。

二、本篇资料的统计范围

1.铁路资料：包括国家铁路（含控股合资）、地方铁路和非控股合资铁路运营情况，不含军用铁路及由厂矿企事业单位自建的铁路专用线和不办理公共营业的专用铁路。国家铁路（含控股合资）和非控股合资铁路运营资料来源于各铁路局及所属运输企业(公司)。地方铁路运营概况资料来源于各省地方铁路管理部门。

2.公路、水运、港口资料：(1)公路和水路线路里程为年末通车和通航里程数，不含未正式投入使用的公路和航道里程；(2)民用汽车拥有量及机动车和汽车驾驶员人数，根据公安部交通管理局所属各省车管部门登记注册的车辆资料和驾驶员资料整理，不含军用车辆；(3)公路营运汽车拥有量，根据各省道路运输主管部门登记注册的从事公路运输的营业性运输车辆资料整理，属于民用汽车的一部分；(4)营业性运输船舶拥有量，根据各省交通运输主管部门登记注册的从事水上客、货运输的营业性船舶资料整理，不含非运输船舶及农业、渔业生产船舶；(5)公路、水路客货运输量资料，由交通运输部负责收集整理；(6)公路、水路运输量统计包括全面调查和非全面调查两种方式，统计范围是在各省交通运输主管部门登记注册的从事公路、水路客、货运输的营业性的车辆和船舶所完成的运输量；(7)港口的统计范围为所有取得港口经营许可的业户。

3.管道运输资料：包括输原油、输成品油、输天然气及输其他气体的运输量。管道运输统计数据主要来源于中国石油天然气集团有限公司、中国石油化工集团公司、中国海洋石油集团有限公司和国家管网集团公司所属的管道运输企业，由四家集团公司分别负责收集审核本部门统计数据。

4.民航运输资料：统计对象为在我国境内注册从事民用航空运输飞行和通用飞行的航空运输企业和定期航班通航机场，不包括在我国境内运输飞行的外国航空公司。统计范围为各航空公司从事国内运输、港澳台运输、国际运输的定期航班航线条数及里程、运输量及飞机构成和运营情况、通用航空飞行完成情况等。

5.邮政、电信、软件业资料：包括邮政企业和获得快递业务经营许可的快递企业，以及从事电信运营的中国电信集团有限公司、中国移动通信集团有限公司、中国联合网络通信集团有限公司三家基础电信企业（不含专用网业务资料）。软件和信息技术服务业统计范围：（1）主要从事软件和信息技术服务业务、主营业务年收入2000万元以上且软件业务收入(包括但不限于嵌入式系统软件）占企业主营业务收入比例不低于30%、具有独立法人资格的企业；（2）主要从事集成电路设计的企业或其集成电路设计收入占本企业主营业务收入60%以上、主营业务年收入500万元以上的独立法人单位；(3)主要从事基础软件、工业软件、信息安全、工业互联网平台服务或数据服务，且主营业务年收入500万元以上的独立法人单位。邮电业务量按业务种类分为邮政业务量和电信业务量。

6.企业信息化及电子商务情况资料：包括规模以上工业、有资质的建筑业、限额以上批发和零售业、限额以上住宿和餐饮业、有开发经营活动的全部房地产开发经营业和规模以上服务业的法人单位。

三、本篇的资料来源

本篇资料由国家统计局服务业统计司负责整理、编辑。有关交通运输资料分别来源于交通运输部、中国民用航空局、国家铁路局、中国国家铁路集团有限公司、中国石油天然气集团有限公司、中国石油化工集团有限公司、中国海洋石油集团有限公司、国家管网集团公司和公安部交通管理局所属各省车管部门。有关邮政、电信、软件资料分别来源于工业和信息化部、国家邮政局、中国互联网络信息中心。企业信息化及电子商务情况资料是由国家统计局服务业统计司根据《一套表统计调查制度》调查资料加工整理而得。

Brief Introduction

I. Main Contents

Data in this chapter present the development of transport, post, telecommunications, software industry, as well as informatization and e-commerce of enterprises in China.

Data on transport cover mainly the length of the routes of five means of transportation, the possession of transport equipment, the condition of technological quality, freight traffic and passenger traffic accomplished by various means of transportation, the length of quay lines, number of berths and cargo handled in the ports.

Data on post, telecommunications and software industry cover mainly the situation of post and telecommunication offices and postal routes; main telecommunication capacity; business volume of postal and telecommunication services achieved; the level of development of postal and telecommunication services, and the main economic indicators of software and IT service industry.

Data on informatization and e-commerce of enterprises cover mainly the situation of informatization and e-commerce of enterprises in business production and operation.

II. Scope of Statistics

1. Data on railway transportation: including the operation and management of the national, local and joint-venture railways but not including railways for military purpose, lines built by industrial and mining enterprises and special railways not for commercial use. Data on the operation and management of the national railways and joint-venture railways come from local railway bureaus and transport enterprises subordinate to them. Data on the operation and management of local railways come from the provincial administrative departments managing the local railways.

2. Data on highways, waterways and ports: (1) The length of highways and waterways refer to the length open to traffic or navigation at the end of the year, but not including the highways and waterways under construction or not officially in operation. (2) Data on the possession of civil motor vehicles and the number of drivers are provided by offices of vehicle management under the provincial departments of traffic management, and they do not include vehicles for military use. (3) Data on possession of highway vehicles for business are provided by the offices of vehicle management under provincial departments of traffic management, and they are part of the civil motor vehicles. (4) Data on possession of ships are provided by the offices of navigation or ports management under provincial departments of communications, and they do not include ships for non-transport purpose, ships for agriculture and fishery. (5) Data on passenger and freight traffic by highways and waterways are collected and prepared by the Ministry of Transport. (6) Data on highway and waterway transport are collected through both comprehensive reporting system and non-comprehensive reporting system. They cover passenger and freight transport undertaken by all vehicles and vessels registered at the provincial departments of transport. (7) Data on ports cover all operators with port business permits.

3. Data on pipeline transport: The data on pipeline transport cover the volume transported of petroleum (crude oil) pipelines, petroleum products pipelines, natural gas pipelines and other gas pipelines. Data sources of the pipeline transport statistics are mainly from enterprises engaged in the pipeline transport subordinate to the China National Petroleum Corporation, Sinopec Group, China National Offshore Oil Corporation and China Oil & Gas Pipeline Network Corporation. The four corporations collect and examine the statistical data submitted to them from their subordinate units respectively.

4. Data on civil aviation transport: The respondents of statistical collection are enterprises registered for engagement in civil aviation transport flights and flights for general purposes and general aviation airports with scheduled flights. Excluded are foreign companies which operate flights within Chinese territory. The scope of statistics include number of routes, mileage flown, transport volume, composition of the fleets, operational situation of the airlines, performance of general purpose flights.

5. Data on post, telecommunications and software industry: Data in this category cover postal enterprises and express delivery companies that obtained express business permits, the three major telecommunication enterprises: China Telecom, China Mobile and China Unicom (not including services provided through dedicated networks).Statistical scope of Software and IT service industry: (1) Enterprises mainly engaged in software and information technology services, with an annual revenue of over 20 million yuan in their main business, and software business revenue (including but not limited to embedded system software) accounting for no less than 30% of the enterprise's main business revenue, and possessing independent legal personality; (2) Enterprises mainly engaged in integrated circuit design or independent legal entities with integrated circuit design revenue accounting for over 60% of their main business revenue and annual main business revenue of over 5 million yuan; (3) An independent legal entity mainly engaged in basic software, industrial software, information security, industrial internet platform services or data services, with an annual revenue of over 5 million yuan in its main business. By types of business, the business volume of post and telecommunications is divided into postal services and telecommunication services.

6. Data on informatization and e-commerce of enterprises: Data in this category include industrial enterprises above designated size, construction enterprises with qualification certificates, enterprises of wholesale and retail trades above designated size, enterprises of hotel and catering services above designated size, corporate units with development activities in real estate development and corporate units above designated size in service industries.

III. Sources of Data

Data in this chapter are processed and compiled by the Department of Service Statistics, NBS. Data on transportation are from Ministry of Transport, Civil Aviation Administration of China, National Railway Administration, China State Railway Group Co., Ltd., China National Petroleum Corporation, Sinopec Group, China National Offshore Oil Corporation, China Oil & Gas Pipeline Network Corporation, offices of vehicle management of the provincial departments of vehicle administration, which are subordinate to the Traffic Management Bureau, Ministry of Public Security. Data on post, telecommunication and software come from the Ministry of Industry and Information, China Post, and CNNIC separately. Data on informatization and e-commerce of enterprises are processed and compiled by the Department of Service Statistics, NBS from the survey data based on the *Integrated Statistical Questionnaires for Enterprises*.

16–1 分地区交通运输、仓储和邮政业就业人员数(2023年底)
Number of Employed Persons in Transport, Storage and Post by Region (End of 2023)

单位：人 (person)

地　区	Region	铁路运输业 Railway Transport	道路运输业 Road Transport	水上运输业 Water Transport	航空运输业 Air Transport	管道运输业 Pipeline Transport	多式联运和运输代理业 Multimodal and Forwarding Agencies	装卸搬运和仓储业 Loading, Unloading and Storage	邮政业 Post
全　国	**National Total**	**1781369**	**3268056**	**263567**	**594526**	**37582**	**329088**	**461232**	**943352**
北　京	Beijing	86792	199292	236	79781	11041	26791	9733	62369
天　津	Tianjin	25837	59302	8037	8562	826	10343	10792	18492
河　北	Hebei	70771	119299	17386	5873	5783	1914	15504	39303
山　西	Shanxi	97072	89464	5	5541	2358	1664	10333	23756
内蒙古	Inner Mongolia	102219	66023		7095	178	1915	5292	15510
辽　宁	Liaoning	96564	99778	16489	11460	181	10250	24450	23598
吉　林	Jilin	53448	50415	33	4039	67	1796	14395	13487
黑龙江	Heilongjiang	122852	41538	1282	8531		737	13513	28966
上　海	Shanghai	31841	130200	24068	89743	953	97340	31017	28954
江　苏	Jiangsu	48377	228477	31027	6280	5184	18766	69970	69877
浙　江	Zhejiang	34097	180744	25729	14921	217	17782	23981	81771
安　徽	Anhui	37159	154448	6002	3850	15	6922	12569	46281
福　建	Fujian	33065	75728	14980	25944	89	9463	14332	29659
江　西	Jiangxi	52642	78931	2642	124	42	940	7366	19079
山　东	Shandong	86446	182503	36165	10847	1596	19967	38609	62559
河　南	Henan	98711	182885	613	10457	171	3624	16786	45552
湖　北	Hubei	73503	142182	10450	7050	747	5534	16289	39759
湖　南	Hunan	69036	105022	3022	7666	479	3146	18238	24890
广　东	Guangdong	71703	341882	38733	116491	939	60325	50557	59581
广　西	Guangxi	60422	59830	9411	2837	73	2488	8624	34679
海　南	Hainan	6471	16307	4846	28263	172	1807	2810	9592
重　庆	Chongqing	27001	108961	10766	14761	73	3833	5206	27663
四　川	Sichuan	68799	172739	722	43602	1788	6233	12606	52310
贵　州	Guizhou	32349	49334	511	12316	91	478	4623	17616
云　南	Yunnan	41019	65716	111	27563	262	2399	5472	15640
西　藏	Xizang	1779	7170		7684		7	328	5656
陕　西	Shaanxi	85230	109430	144	13224	614	8360	8087	15817
甘　肃	Gansu	59570	42703	100	4368	433	666	3813	9911
青　海	Qinghai	25103	16704		2827		230	1280	3495
宁　夏	Ningxia	18754	13134	13	2328		552	691	3150
新　疆	Xinjiang	62737	77912	45	10500	3210	2818	3968	14379

16-2 交通运输业基本情况
Basic Conditions of Transport

指 标	Item	2020	2021	2022	2023
运输线路长度 （万公里）	**Length of Transport Routes (10 000 km)**				
铁路营业里程	Railways in Operation	14.63	15.07	15.49	15.87
公路里程	Highways	519.81	528.07	535.48	543.68
#高速公路	Expressway	16.10	16.91	17.73	18.36
内河航道里程	Navigable Inland Waterways	12.77	12.76	12.80	12.82
定期航班航线里程	Regular Civil Aviation Routes	942.63	689.78	699.89	875.96
输油(气)管道里程	Petroleum and Gas Pipelines	12.87	13.12	13.64	14.76
客运量总计 （万人）	**Total Passenger Traffic (10 000 persons)**	**966540**	**830257**	**558738**	**1574331**
铁路	Railways	220350	261171	167296	385450
公路	Highways	689425	508693	354643	1101153
水路	Waterways	14987	16337	11627	25771
民航	Civil Aviation	41778	44056	25171	61958
旅客周转量总计 （亿人公里）	**Total Passenger-Kilometers(100 million passenger-km)**	**19251.5**	**19758.1**	**12921.5**	**29832.2**
铁路	Railways	8266.2	9567.8	6577.5	14729.4
公路	Highways	4641.0	3627.5	2407.5	4740.0
水路	Waterways	33.0	33.1	22.6	53.8
民航	Civil Aviation	6311.3	6529.7	3913.9	10309.0
货运量总计 （万吨）	**Total Freight Traffic (10 000 tons)**	**4725862**	**5298499**	**5152571**	**5570636**
铁路	Railways	455236	477372	498424	503535
公路	Highways	3426413	3913889	3711928	4033681
水路	Waterways	761630	823973	855352	936746
民航	Civil Aviation	676.6	731.8	607.6	735.4
管道	Petroleum and Gas Pipelines	81907	82534	86260	95939
货物周转量 （亿吨公里）	**Total Freight Ton-Kilometers (100 million ton-km)**	**201946**	**223600**	**231783**	**247745**
铁路	Railways	30514.5	33238.0	35945.7	36460.4
公路	Highways	60171.8	69087.7	68958.0	73950.2
水路	Waterways	105834.4	115577.5	121003.1	129951.5
民航	Civil Aviation	240.20	278.16	254.10	283.62
管道	Petroleum and Gas Pipelines	5185	5419	5622	7100
民用汽车拥有量 （万辆）	**Possession of Civil Motor Vehicles (10 000 units)**	**27340.92**	**29418.59**	**31184.44**	**32911.55**
#私人汽车	Private Vehicles	24291.19	26152.02	27792.11	29356.89
其他机动车拥有量 （万辆）	**Possession of Other Motor Vehicles (10 000 units)**	**7266.91**	**8292.62**	**8791.99**	**9039.90**
民用运输船舶拥有量 （艘）	**Possession of Civil Transport Vessels (unit)**	**126805**	**125890**	**121868**	**124665**
机动船	Motor Vessels	117931	118025	114507	118284
驳船	Barges	8874	7865	7361	6381
沿海港口货物吞吐量 （万吨）	**Volume of Freight Handled in Coastal Ports (10 000 tons)**	**948002**	**997259**	**1013102**	**1083471**

注：1.港口统计范围为全国所有获得港口经营许可的业户(以下相关表同)。
2.2023年起，公路营业性客运量包括班车包车客运量、公共汽电车城际城乡客运量、出租汽车(含巡游出租汽车、网络预约出租汽车)城际城乡客运量(以下相关表同)。
3.2023年起，公路客运周转量包括班车包车客运周转量、公共汽电车城际城乡客运周转量、出租汽车(含巡游出租汽车、网络预约出租汽车)城际城乡客运周转量(以下相关表同)。

a) The statistical coverage refers to all the operators having port business permits. The same applies to the relevant following tables.

b) Since 2023, the commercial passenger traffic volume of highways includes the passenger traffic volume of shuttle buses and charter passenger transportation, intercity urban and rural passenger traffic volume of public buses and trams and intercity urban and rural passenger traffic volume of taxis (including cruising taxis and online reservation taxis). The same applies to the relevant following tables.

c) Since 2023, the passenger-kilometers of highways includes the passenger-kilometers of shuttle bus and charter passenger transportation, intercity urban and rural passenger-kilometers of public buses and trams and intercity urban and rural passenger-kilometers of taxis (including cruising taxis and online reservation taxis). The same applies to the relevant following tables.

16–3 运输线路长度
Length of Transport Routes

单位：万公里 (10 000 km)

年份 Year	铁路营业里程 Length of Railways in Operation	#铁路电气化里程 Electrified Railways	公路里程 Length of Highways	#高速公路 Expressway	内河航道里程 Length of Navigable Inland Waterways	定期航班航线里程 Length of Regular Civil Aviation Routes	#国际航线 International Routes	输油(气)管道里程 Length of Petroleum and Gas Pipelines
1978	5.17	0.10	89.02		13.60	14.89	5.53	0.83
1980	5.33	0.17	88.83		10.85	19.53	8.12	0.87
1985	5.52	0.41	94.24		10.91	27.72	10.60	1.17
1990	5.79	0.69	102.83	0.05	10.92	50.68	16.64	1.59
1991	5.78	0.78	104.11	0.06	10.97	55.91	17.74	1.62
1992	5.81	0.84	105.67	0.07	10.97	83.66	30.30	1.59
1993	5.86	0.89	108.35	0.11	11.02	96.08	27.87	1.64
1994	5.90	0.90	111.78	0.16	11.02	104.56	35.19	1.68
1995	6.24	0.97	115.70	0.21	11.06	112.90	34.82	1.72
1996	6.49	1.01	118.58	0.34	11.08	116.65	38.63	1.93
1997	6.60	1.20	122.64	0.48	10.98	142.50	50.44	2.04
1998	6.64	1.30	127.85	0.87	11.03	150.58	50.44	2.31
1999	6.74	1.40	135.17	1.16	11.65	152.22	52.33	2.49
2000	6.87	1.49	167.98	1.63	11.93	150.29	50.84	2.47
2001	7.01	1.69	169.80	1.94	12.15	155.36	51.69	2.76
2002	7.19	1.74	176.52	2.51	12.16	163.77	57.45	2.98
2003	7.30	1.81	180.98	2.97	12.40	174.95	71.53	3.26
2004	7.44	1.86	187.07	3.43	12.33	204.94	89.42	3.82
2005	7.54	1.94	334.52	4.10	12.33	199.85	85.59	4.40
2006	7.71	2.34	345.70	4.53	12.34	211.35	96.62	4.81
2007	7.80	2.40	358.37	5.39	12.35	234.30	104.74	5.45
2008	7.97	2.50	373.02	6.03	12.28	246.18	112.02	5.83
2009	8.55	3.02	386.08	6.51	12.37	234.51	91.99	6.91
2010	9.12	3.27	400.82	7.41	12.42	276.51	107.02	7.85
2011	9.32	3.43	410.64	8.49	12.46	349.06	149.44	8.33
2012	9.76	3.55	423.75	9.62	12.50	328.01	128.47	9.16
2013	10.31	3.60	435.62	10.44	12.59	410.60	150.32	9.85
2014	11.18	3.69	446.39	11.19	12.63	463.72	176.72	10.57
2015	12.10	7.47	457.73	12.35	12.70	531.72	239.44	10.87
2016	12.40	8.03	469.63	13.10	12.71	634.81	282.80	11.34
2017	12.70	8.66	477.35	13.64	12.70	748.30	324.59	11.93
2018	13.17	9.22	484.65	14.26	12.71	837.98	359.89	12.23
2019	13.99	10.04	501.25	14.96	12.73	948.22	401.47	12.66
2020	14.63	10.63	519.81	16.10	12.77	942.63	382.87	12.87
2021	15.07	11.08	528.07	16.91	12.76	689.78	131.96	13.12
2022	15.49	11.45	535.48	17.73	12.80	699.89	153.74	13.64
2023	15.87	11.94	543.68	18.36	12.82	875.96	284.31	14.76

注：1.铁路营业里程为全国铁路营业里程；铁路电气化里程2014年及以前为国家铁路电气化里程，2015年起为全国铁路电气化里程。
2.2005年起公路里程包括村道(以下相关表同)。
3.2004年起内河航道里程为内河航道通航里程数(以下相关表同)。
4.2011年起民航航线里程改为定期航班航线里程(以下相关表同)。
5.2013年管道运输统计口径有所调整，2012年管道数据按同口径调整(以下相关表同)。

a) Length of railways in operation refers to railways of the whole country. Length of electrified railways refers to national electrified railways before 2014, and refers to electrified railways of the whole country since 2015.
b) Length of highways include the village road since 2005. The same applies to the relevant following tables.
c) Since 2004, length of inland waterways refer to navigable inland waterways. The same applies to the relevant following tables.
d) Since 2011, length of civil aviation routes has been change to regular civil aviation routes. The same applies to the relevant following tables.
e) In 2013, the pipelines transport statistics were adjusted, the 2012 data on pipelines transport are adjusted for data comparability. The same applies in the relevant following tables.

16-4 分地区运输线路长度(2023年底)
Length of Transport Routes by Region (End of 2023)

单位：公里 (km)

地 区	Region	铁路营业里程 Length of Railways in Operation	内河航道里程 Length of Navigable Inland Waterways	公路里程 Total Length of Highways	等级公路 Expressway and Class I to IV Highways	#高速 Expressway	#一级 Class I	#二级 Class II	等外公路 Highways Below Class IV
全 国	**National Total**	**158737**	**128153**	**5436845**	**5270055**	**183645**	**139833**	**438746**	**166790**
北 京	Beijing	1534		22433	22433	1211	1458	4020	
天 津	Tianjin	1287	52	15221	15221	1358	1432	1993	
河 北	Hebei	8488	34	211107	211107	8408	8083	22380	
山 西	Shanxi	6348	467	146545	146115	6188	3147	15824	430
内蒙古	Inner Mongolia	14201	2403	219407	216120	7863	9213	22458	3287
辽 宁	Liaoning	6825	413	132371	129772	4409	4328	19021	2599
吉 林	Jilin	5157	1456	110465	107881	4644	2271	10072	2584
黑龙江	Heilongjiang	7230	5098	169273	147940	5037	3494	12739	21333
上 海	Shanghai	491	1817	12989	12989	881	466	3923	
江 苏	Jiangsu	4708	24408	158734	158734	5128	16543	24005	
浙 江	Zhejiang	3853	9787	121408	121408	5510	9349	11159	
安 徽	Anhui	5528	5673	239129	239106	5804	7098	14153	23
福 建	Fujian	4573	3245	115645	105713	5964	1667	11969	9932
江 西	Jiangxi	5337	5638	209560	205380	6742	3221	12556	4180
山 东	Shandong	7694	1117	293411	293411	8433	12993	27029	
河 南	Henan	6762	1491	281101	279937	8321	5227	31979	1164
湖 北	Hubei	5679	8496	307566	305336	7849	8591	25053	2231
湖 南	Hunan	6097	11496	242769	232205	7530	3254	16976	10564
广 东	Guangdong	5737	12265	223391	223383	11481	13710	18066	8
广 西	Guangxi	5672	5707	183618	179629	9067	2074	17265	3989
海 南	Hainan	1033	434	41817	41737	1399	507	2346	80
重 庆	Chongqing	2768	4352	186598	177545	4142	1310	9677	9054
四 川	Sichuan	6471	10817	418254	409359	9806	5278	18778	8895
贵 州	Guizhou	4270	3954	219839	204918	8784	1565	11337	14920
云 南	Yunnan	5224	4670	329344	315819	10466	1780	13315	13525
西 藏	Xizang	1188		122712	106416	407	587	1112	16296
陕 西	Shaanxi	5603	1146	187831	180259	6735	2408	10484	7572
甘 肃	Gansu	5591	911	158219	155294	6181	1772	11187	2925
青 海	Qinghai	2975	674	89416	79421	4022	987	9235	9995
宁 夏	Ningxia	1726	130	38739	38739	2122	2019	4385	
新 疆	Xinjiang	8689		227934	206728	7757	4001	24251	21205

16-5 运输线路质量
Quality of Transport Routes

指 标		Item		2000	2010	2020	2022	2023
铁路营业里程	**(公里)**	**Length of Railways in Operation**	**(km)**	**58656**	**66239**	**146330**	**154907**	**158737**
#复线里程	(公里)	Double-Tracking Length	(km)	21408	29684	86587	92429	95765
复线里程比重	(%)	Proportion	(%)	36.5	44.8	59.2	59.7	60.3
公路里程	**(公里)**	**Length of Highways**	**(km)**	**1679848**	**4008229**	**5198120**	**5354837**	**5436845**
#等级公路里程	(公里)	Expressway and Class I to IV Highways	(km)	1315931	3304709	4944489	5162473	5270055
等级公路里程比重	(%)	Proportion	(%)	78.3	82.4	95.1	96.4	96.9
内河航道里程	**(公里)**	**Length of Navigable Inland Waterways**	**(km)**	**119325**	**124242**	**127686**	**127968**	**128153**
#等级航道里程	(公里)	Standard Waterways	(km)	61367	62290	67269	67475	67826
等级航道里程比重	(%)	Proportion	(%)	51.4	50.1	52.7	52.7	52.9

注：铁路营业里程2014年及以前为国家铁路营业里程，2015年起为全国铁路营业里程。

a) Length of railways in operation refers to that of national railways before 2015, and refers to railways of the whole country since 2015.

16-6 客运量
Passenger Traffic

单位：万人 (10 000 persons)

年份 Year	客运量 总计 Total	铁路 Railways	公路 Highways	水路 Waterways	民航 Civil Aviation
1978	253993	81491	149229	23042	231
1980	341785	92204	222799	26439	343
1985	620206	112110	476486	30863	747
1990	772682	95712	648085	27225	1660
1991	806048	95080	682681	26109	2178
1992	860855	99693	731774	26502	2886
1993	996634	105458	860719	27074	3383
1994	1092882	108738	953940	26165	4039
1995	1172596	102745	1040810	23924	5117
1996	1245357	94797	1122110	22895	5555
1997	1326094	93308	1204583	22573	5630
1998	1378717	95085	1257332	20545	5755
1999	1394413	100164	1269004	19151	6094
2000	1478573	105073	1347392	19386	6722
2001	1534122	105155	1402798	18645	7524
2002	1608150	105606	1475257	18693	8594
2003	1587497	97260	1464335	17142	8759
2004	1767453	111764	1624526	19040	12123
2005	1847018	115583	1697381	20227	13827
2006	2024158	125656	1860487	22047	15968
2007	2227761	135670	2050680	22835	18576
2008	2867892	146193	2682114	20334	19251
2009	2976898	152451	2779081	22314	23052
2010	3269508	167609	3052738	22392	26769
2011	3526319	186226	3286220	24556	29317
2012	3804035	189337	3557010	25752	31936
2013	2122992	210597	1853463	23535	35397
2014	2032218	230460	1736270	26293	39195
2015	1943271	253484	1619097	27072	43618
2016	1900194	281405	1542759	27234	48796
2017	1848620	308379	1456784	28300	55156
2018	1793820	337495	1367170	27981	61174
2019	1760436	366002	1301173	27267	65993
2020	966540	220350	689425	14987	41778
2021	830257	261171	508693	16337	44056
2022	558738	167296	354643	11627	25171
2023	1574331	385450	1101153	25771	61958

注：1.从1979年起，公路运输包括社会车辆完成数量，从1984年起，还包括私营运输完成的数量(以下相关表同)。从2008年起，公路、水路运输量统计口径有调整，公路运输量统计范围原则上为营运车辆，水路运输量统计范围为在交通运输主管部门审批、备案、从事营业性旅客和货物运输生产的船舶(以下相关表同)。

2.2013年公路水路客货运输数据，源自2013年交通运输业经济统计专项调查，统计范围口径有所调整(以下相关表同)。

3.2014年、2015年公路水路运输量统计数据根据2015年开展的公路水路运输量小样本抽样调查结果进行了调整。

a) Since 1979, passenger traffic by highways included the quantities transported by vehicles of non-highway departments. Since 1984, it also included the quantities transported by private vehicles. The same applies to following tables. Data since 2008 on total passenger traffic and freight traffic of highway and waterways were adjusted, passenger traffic by highways refers to all operational vehicles. Statistical coverage of passenger traffic by waterways includes vessels engaged in passengers and goods transport for business purpose, with approval and registertion by the transportation departments. The same applies to the relevant following tables.

b) The 2013 figures on passenger traffic and freight traffic are calculated with the data from the 2013 survey of transport economics, and have different coverages. The same applies to the relevant following tables.

c) Data of transport of highways and waterways in 2014 and 2015 are adjusted according to small-sized sample survey on transport of highways and waterways conducted in 2015.

16−7 旅客周转量
Passenger-Kilometers

单位：亿人公里 (100 million passenger-km)

年 份 Year	旅客周转量 总 计 Total	铁 路 Railways	公 路 Highways	水 路 Waterways	民 航 Civil Aviation
1978	1743.1	1093.2	521.3	100.6	27.9
1980	2281.3	1383.2	729.5	129.1	39.6
1985	4435.4	2416.1	1724.9	178.7	115.7
1990	5628.4	2612.6	2620.3	164.9	230.5
1991	6178.3	2828.1	2871.7	177.2	301.3
1992	6949.4	3152.2	3192.6	198.4	406.1
1993	7858.0	3483.3	3700.7	196.4	477.6
1994	8591.4	3636.0	4220.3	183.5	551.6
1995	9001.9	3545.7	4603.1	171.8	681.3
1996	9164.8	3347.6	4908.8	160.6	747.8
1997	10055.5	3584.9	5541.4	155.7	773.5
1998	10636.7	3773.4	5942.8	120.3	800.2
1999	11299.7	4135.9	6199.2	107.3	857.3
2000	12261.1	4532.6	6657.4	100.5	970.5
2001	13155.1	4766.8	7207.1	89.9	1091.4
2002	14125.6	4969.4	7805.8	81.8	1268.7
2003	13810.5	4788.6	7695.6	63.1	1263.2
2004	16309.1	5712.2	8748.4	66.3	1782.3
2005	17466.7	6062.0	9292.1	67.8	2044.9
2006	19197.2	6622.1	10130.8	73.6	2370.7
2007	21592.6	7216.3	11506.8	77.8	2791.7
2008	23196.7	7778.6	12476.1	59.2	2882.8
2009	24834.9	7878.9	13511.4	69.4	3375.2
2010	27894.3	8762.2	15020.8	72.3	4039.0
2011	30984.0	9612.3	16760.2	74.5	4537.0
2012	33383.1	9812.3	18467.5	77.5	5025.7
2013	27571.7	10595.6	11250.9	68.3	5656.8
2014	28647.1	11241.9	10996.8	74.3	6334.2
2015	30058.9	11960.6	10742.7	73.1	7282.6
2016	31258.5	12579.3	10228.7	72.3	8378.1
2017	32812.8	13456.9	9765.2	77.7	9513.0
2018	34218.2	14146.6	9279.7	79.6	10712.3
2019	35349.2	14706.6	8857.1	80.2	11705.3
2020	19251.5	8266.2	4641.0	33.0	6311.3
2021	19758.1	9567.8	3627.5	33.1	6529.7
2022	12921.5	6577.5	2407.5	22.6	3913.9
2023	29832.2	14729.4	4740.0	53.8	10309.0

16–8 货运量
Freight Traffic

单位：万吨 (10 000 tons)

年 份 Year	货运量总计 Total	铁 路 Railways	公 路 Highways	水 路 Waterways	#海 洋 Ocean	民 航 Civil Aviation	管 道 Petroleum and Gas Pipelines
1978	319431	110119	151602	47357	3659	6.4	10347
1980	310841	111279	142195	46833	4292	8.9	10525
1985	745763	130709	538062	63322	6627	19.5	13650
1990	970602	150681	724040	80094	9408	37.0	15750
1991	985793	152893	733907	83370	10567	45.2	15578
1992	1045899	157627	780941	92490	11191	57.5	14783
1993	1115902	162794	840256	97938	12508	69.4	14845
1994	1180396	163216	894914	107091	13421	82.9	15092
1995	1234938	165982	940387	113194	15251	101.1	15274
1996	1298421	171024	983860	127430	14213	115.0	15992
1997	1278218	172149	976536	113406	20287	124.7	16002
1998	1267427	164309	976004	109555	18892	140.1	17419
1999	1293008	167554	990444	114608	22621	170.4	20232
2000	1358682	178581	1038813	122391	22949	196.7	18700
2001	1401786	193189	1056312	132675	27573	171.0	19439
2002	1483447	204956	1116324	141832	29896	202.1	20133
2003	1564492	224248	1159957	158070	34002	219.0	21998
2004	1706412	249017	1244990	187394	39469	276.7	24734
2005	1862066	269296	1341778	219648	48549	306.7	31037
2006	2037060	288224	1466347	248703	54413	349.4	33436
2007	2275822	314237	1639432	281199	58903	401.8	40552
2008	2585937	330354	1916759	294510	42352	407.6	43906
2009	2825222	333348	2127834	318996	51733	445.5	44598
2010	3241807	364271	2448052	378949	58054	563.0	49972
2011	3696961	393263	2820100	425968	63542	557.5	57073
2012	4100436	390438	3188475	458705	65815	545.0	62274
2013	4098900	396697	3076648	559785	71156	561.3	65209
2014	4167296	381334	3113334	598283	74733	594.1	73752
2015	4175886	335801	3150019	613567	74685	629.3	75870
2016	4386763	333186	3341259	638238	79769	668.0	73411
2017	4804850	368865	3686858	667846	76030	705.9	80576
2018	5152732	402631	3956871	702684	76969	738.5	89807
2019	4713624	438904	3435480	747225	83243	753.1	91261
2020	4725862	455236	3426413	761630	380087	676.6	81907
2021	5298499	477372	3913889	823973	405095	731.8	82534
2022	5152571	498424	3711928	855352	415145	607.6	86260
2023	5570636	503535	4033681	936746	457658	735.4	95939

注：1.2019年起铁路货运量和货物周转量数据来自国家铁路局，与以往年份相比统计范围增加部分地方铁路(以下相关表同)。
2.1993年起铁路货物运输增加行包运量(以下相关表同)。
3.2019年公路货运量及货物周转量统计口径，根据2019年道路货物运输量专项调查进行了调整，数据与上年不可比(以下相关表同)。按照调整后可比口径计算，2019年公路货运量、货物周转量比上年分别增长4.2%和0.4%。
4.2020年起，沿海和远洋合并为海洋；2019年及以前年份为远洋运输数据(以下相关表同)。

a) Since 2019, data on railway freight traffic and freight ton-kilometers are from national railway administration. Compared with previous years, statistical coverages include some local railways. The same applies to the relevant following tables.
b) Railways freight includes the freight of packages since 1993. The same applies to the following tables.
c) In 2019, statistical coverages of highway freight traffic and freight ton-kilometers are changed according to the 2019 suvery of road freight transport volume, so the data are not comparable with previous year. The same applies to the relevant following tables. When adjusted to comparable coverages, the 2019 highway freight traffic and freight ton-kilometers increased over the previous year 4.2% and 0.4% respectively.
d) Since 2020, the freight traffic of ocean includes the volume of coastal and ocean freight traffic, and in the previous years, it only refers to the volume of ocean freight traffic. The same applies to the following table.

16–9 货物周转量
Freight Ton-Kilometers

单位：亿吨公里 (100 million ton-km)

年份 Year	货物周转量总计 Total	铁路 Railways	公路 Highways	水路 Waterways	#海洋 Ocean	民航 Civil Aviation	管道 Petroleum and Gas Pipelines
1978	9928	5345.2	350.3	3801.8	2487	0.97	430
1980	11629	5717.5	342.9	5076.5	3532	1.41	491
1985	18365	8125.7	1903.0	7729.3	5329	4.15	603
1990	26208	10622.4	3358.1	11591.9	8141	8.18	627
1991	27987	10972.0	3428.0	12955.4	8990	10.10	621
1992	29218	11575.6	3755.4	13256.2	9034	13.42	617
1993	30647	12090.9	4070.5	13860.8	9134	16.61	608
1994	33435	12632.0	4486.3	15686.6	10268	18.58	612
1995	35909	13049.5	4694.9	17552.2	11938	22.30	590
1996	36590	13106.2	5011.2	17862.5	11254	24.93	585
1997	38385	13269.9	5271.5	19235.0	14875	29.10	579
1998	38089	12560.1	5483.4	19405.8	14920	33.45	606
1999	40568	12910.3	5724.3	21262.8	17014	42.34	628
2000	44321	13770.5	6129.4	23734.2	17073	50.27	636
2001	47710	14694.1	6330.4	25988.9	20873	43.72	653
2002	50686	15658.4	6782.5	27510.6	21733	51.55	683
2003	53859	17246.7	7099.5	28715.8	22305	57.90	739
2004	69445	19288.8	7840.9	41428.7	32255	71.80	815
2005	80258	20726.0	8693.2	49672.3	38552	78.90	1088
2006	88840	21954.4	9754.2	55485.7	42577	94.28	1551
2007	101419	23797.0	11354.7	64284.8	48686	116.39	1866
2008	110300	25106.3	32868.2	50262.7	32851	119.60	1944
2009	122133	25239.2	37188.8	57556.7	39524	126.23	2022
2010	141837	27644.1	43389.7	68427.5	45999	178.90	2197
2011	159324	29465.8	51374.7	75423.8	49355	173.91	2885
2012	173804	29187.1	59534.9	81707.6	53412	163.89	3211
2013	168014	29173.9	55738.1	79435.7	48705	170.29	3496
2014	181668	27530.2	56846.9	92774.6	55935	187.77	4328
2015	178356	23754.3	57955.7	91772.5	54236	208.07	4665
2016	186629	23792.3	61080.1	97338.8	58075	222.45	4196
2017	197373	26962.2	66771.5	98611.2	55084	243.55	4784
2018	204686	28821.0	71249.2	99052.8	51927	262.50	5301
2019	199394	30182.0	59636.4	103963.0	54057	263.20	5350
2020	201946	30514.5	60171.8	105834.4	89897	240.20	5185
2021	223600	33238.0	69087.7	115577.5	97842	278.16	5419
2022	231783	35945.7	68958.0	121003.1	101977	254.10	5622
2023	247745	36460.4	73950.2	129951.5	109179	283.62	7100

16-10 旅客运输平均运距
Average Transport Distance of Passengers

单位：公里 (km)

年 份 Year	所有运输方式平均运距 Average Transport Distance	铁 路 Railways	公 路 Highways	水 路 Waterways	民 航 Civil Aviation
1978	69	134	35	44	1208
1980	67	150	33	49	1153
1985	72	216	36	58	1563
1990	73	273	40	61	1388
1991	77	297	42	68	1383
1992	81	316	44	75	1407
1993	79	330	43	73	1412
1994	79	334	44	70	1366
1995	77	345	44	72	1331
1996	74	353	44	70	1346
1997	76	384	46	69	1374
1998	77	397	47	59	1391
1999	81	413	49	56	1407
2000	83	431	49	52	1444
2001	86	453	51	48	1450
2002	88	471	53	44	1476
2003	87	492	53	37	1442
2004	92	511	54	35	1470
2005	95	524	55	34	1479
2006	95	527	54	33	1485
2007	97	532	56	34	1503
2008	81	532	47	29	1497
2009	83	517	49	31	1464
2010	85	523	49	32	1509
2011	88	516	51	30	1548
2012	88	518	52	30	1574
2013	130	503	61	29	1598
2014	141	488	63	28	1616
2015	155	472	66	27	1670
2016	165	447	66	27	1717
2017	177	436	67	27	1725
2018	191	419	68	28	1751
2019	201	402	68	29	1774
2020	199	375	67	22	1511
2021	238	366	71	20	1482
2022	231	393	68	19	1555
2023	189	382	43	21	1664

16-11 货物运输平均运距
Average Transport Distance of Freight

单位：公里 (km)

年份 Year	所有运输方式平均运距 Average Transport Distance	铁路 Railways	公路 Highways	水路 Waterways	民航 Civil Aviation	管道 Petroleum and Gas Pipelines
1978	395	485	32	873	1516	416
1980	220	514	20	1184	1580	467
1985	246	622	35	1221	2129	442
1990	270	705	46	1447	2211	398
1991	284	718	47	1554	2234	399
1992	279	734	48	1433	2335	417
1993	275	743	48	1415	2394	410
1994	283	774	50	1465	2241	406
1995	291	786	50	1551	2206	386
1996	282	766	51	1402	2168	366
1997	300	771	54	1696	2334	362
1998	301	764	56	1771	2388	348
1999	314	771	58	1855	2485	310
2000	326	771	59	1939	2555	340
2001	340	761	60	1959	2556	336
2002	342	764	61	1940	2551	339
2003	344	769	61	1817	2643	336
2004	407	775	63	2211	2595	329
2005	431	770	65	2261	2572	350
2006	436	762	67	2231	2698	464
2007	446	757	69	2286	2896	460
2008	427	760	171	1707	2934	443
2009	432	757	175	1804	2833	453
2010	438	759	177	1806	3177	440
2011	431	749	182	1771	3120	506
2012	424	748	187	1781	3007	516
2013	410	735	181	1419	3034	536
2014	436	722	183	1551	3161	587
2015	427	707	184	1496	3306	615
2016	425	714	183	1525	3330	572
2017	411	731	181	1477	3450	594
2018	397	716	180	1410	3554	590
2019	423	688	174	1391	3495	586
2020	427	670	176	1390	3550	633
2021	422	696	177	1403	3801	657
2022	450	721	186	1415	4182	652
2023	445	724	183	1387	3857	740

16−12 分地区客运量(2023年)
Passenger Traffic by Region (2023)

单位：万人 (10 000 persons)

地 区	Region	合 计 Total	铁 路 Railways	公 路 Highways	水 路 Waterways
全 国	**National Total**	**1574331**	**385450**	**1101153**	**25771**
北 京	Beijing	75655	15165	60489	
天 津	Tianjin	16441	4969	11310	162
河 北	Hebei	41973	12388	29585	
山 西	Shanxi	31382	8514	22662	206
内蒙古	Inner Mongolia	24877	5060	19817	
辽 宁	Liaoning	60234	11187	48517	530
吉 林	Jilin	35932	5933	29873	127
黑龙江	Heilongjiang	44507	8161	36114	232
上 海	Shanghai	20548	13007	6908	633
江 苏	Jiangsu	109961	31821	75309	2831
浙 江	Zhejiang	103647	26686	71866	5094
安 徽	Anhui	62177	15191	46763	223
福 建	Fujian	40941	12471	27381	1089
江 西	Jiangxi	41623	12702	28693	228
山 东	Shandong	78752	21003	55197	2552
河 南	Henan	81138	20224	60622	291
湖 北	Hubei	56087	17042	38328	718
湖 南	Hunan	80916	17552	62006	1358
广 东	Guangdong	100636	36939	60923	2774
广 西	Guangxi	40504	12078	27532	893
海 南	Hainan	12336	3035	7017	2284
重 庆	Chongqing	43461	9538	33050	872
四 川	Sichuan	92804	21927	69769	1108
贵 州	Guizhou	46122	8067	37709	345
云 南	Yunnan	43992	9442	33934	616
西 藏	Xizang	1571	421	1150	
陕 西	Shaanxi	39820	12057	27670	92
甘 肃	Gansu	31128	6200	24770	157
青 海	Qinghai	10040	1033	8878	129
宁 夏	Ningxia	8543	1053	7264	226
新 疆	Xinjiang	34628	4583	30045	
不分地区	Not Classified by Region	61958			

注：不分地区合计数为民航完成数(以下相关表同)。
a) The total passenger traffic not classified by region refers to that completed by civil aviation. The same applies to the relevant following table.

16−13 分地区旅客周转量(2023年)
Passenger-kilometers by Region (2023)

单位：亿人公里 (100 million passenger-km)

地区	Region	合计 Total	铁路 Railways	公路 Highways	水路 Waterways
全国	**National Total**	**29832.15**	**14729.36**	**4740.04**	**53.77**
北京	Beijing	295.37	163.18	132.19	
天津	Tianjin	233.18	178.84	54.10	0.24
河北	Hebei	1118.16	1003.91	114.25	
山西	Shanxi	316.20	231.88	84.24	0.07
内蒙古	Inner Mongolia	252.96	184.17	68.80	
辽宁	Liaoning	698.59	553.21	141.61	3.76
吉林	Jilin	335.83	225.41	110.32	0.09
黑龙江	Heilongjiang	342.01	229.63	112.08	0.30
上海	Shanghai	191.66	118.96	71.80	0.89
江苏	Jiangsu	1353.90	1052.55	300.24	1.12
浙江	Zhejiang	995.36	739.34	250.33	5.69
安徽	Anhui	1050.66	883.72	166.61	0.33
福建	Fujian	494.05	378.58	114.48	0.99
江西	Jiangxi	864.63	749.06	115.22	0.34
山东	Shandong	1053.39	810.86	234.16	8.37
河南	Henan	1543.30	1124.62	418.24	0.44
湖北	Hubei	915.00	743.23	167.83	3.94
湖南	Hunan	1218.74	967.78	248.90	2.07
广东	Guangdong	1315.17	1014.11	292.51	8.56
广西	Guangxi	663.57	467.48	192.53	3.56
海南	Hainan	105.36	47.77	53.39	4.20
重庆	Chongqing	411.69	267.33	138.84	5.52
四川	Sichuan	814.18	529.03	284.14	1.01
贵州	Guizhou	544.53	370.70	173.19	0.64
云南	Yunnan	469.55	294.46	174.09	1.00
西藏	Xizang	47.11	22.35	24.75	
陕西	Shaanxi	673.77	528.42	145.19	0.15
甘肃	Gansu	519.54	402.35	116.98	0.21
青海	Qinghai	147.53	86.94	60.45	0.14
宁夏	Ningxia	85.70	43.27	42.29	0.14
新疆	Xinjiang	452.47	316.20	136.27	
不分地区	Not Classified by Region	10308.98			

16-14 分地区货运量(2023年)
Freight Traffic by Region (2023)

单位：万吨 (10 000 tons)

地 区	Region	合 计 Total	铁 路 Railways	公 路 Highways	水 路 Waterways
全 国	**National Total**	**5570636**	**503535**	**4033681**	**936746**
北 京	Beijing	19707	308	19399	
天 津	Tianjin	56073	11673	33742	10659
河 北	Hebei	253091	30124	217492	5475
山 西	Shanxi	222753	101001	121751	1
内蒙古	Inner Mongolia	236621	90250	146372	
辽 宁	Liaoning	179704	20073	153305	6325
吉 林	Jilin	54410	5376	49034	
黑龙江	Heilongjiang	54458	12137	41619	701
上 海	Shanghai	153213	547	50436	102230
江 苏	Jiangsu	310363	9315	183485	117563
浙 江	Zhejiang	344881	5565	222803	116512
安 徽	Anhui	422888	8054	260939	153895
福 建	Fujian	178749	5211	110497	63040
江 西	Jiangxi	209403	5131	188006	16267
山 东	Shandong	346633	35842	285567	25224
河 南	Henan	283056	12521	251333	19202
湖 北	Hubei	248947	6159	173045	69743
湖 南	Hunan	228497	5091	200674	22732
广 东	Guangdong	371033	12344	252809	105880
广 西	Guangxi	228355	11503	172005	44846
海 南	Hainan	35987	890	7774	27324
重 庆	Chongqing	141104	2518	117584	21001
四 川	Sichuan	201400	8437	185814	7148
贵 州	Guizhou	102678	6503	95909	266
云 南	Yunnan	144427	6226	137540	661
西 藏	Xizang	5058	104	4954	
陕 西	Shaanxi	180282	46129	134102	51
甘 肃	Gansu	79807	9905	69902	
青 海	Qinghai	21605	3622	17983	
宁 夏	Ningxia	54996	9935	45061	
新 疆	Xinjiang	103783	21041	82742	
不分地区	Not Classified by Region	96674			

注：不分地区合计数中包括民航、管道等完成数(以下相关表同)。
a) The freight ton-kilometers not classified by region refers to that completed by civil aviation and pipelines,etc. The same applies to the following table.

16-15 分地区货物周转量(2023年)
Freight Ton-kilometers by Region (2023)

单位：亿吨公里 (100 million ton-km)

地 区	Region	合 计 Total	铁 路 Railways	公 路 Highways	水 路 Waterways
全 国	**National Total**	**247745.32**	**36460.39**	**73950.21**	**129951.52**
北 京	Beijing	1062.60	805.67	256.93	
天 津	Tianjin	2785.84	566.62	690.04	1529.18
河 北	Hebei	14796.92	5436.68	8472.24	888.00
山 西	Shanxi	6877.42	3494.20	3383.22	0.00
内蒙古	Inner Mongolia	5556.14	3195.70	2360.44	
辽 宁	Liaoning	4685.93	1196.64	2869.10	620.19
吉 林	Jilin	2012.99	572.20	1440.79	
黑龙江	Heilongjiang	1942.22	1011.88	891.37	38.96
上 海	Shanghai	32789.82	22.10	895.42	31872.31
江 苏	Jiangsu	13232.13	368.72	3459.48	9403.93
浙 江	Zhejiang	15062.19	277.98	3142.23	11641.99
安 徽	Anhui	12097.16	833.61	3792.65	7470.90
福 建	Fujian	12230.90	214.59	1319.11	10697.20
江 西	Jiangxi	5348.05	598.15	4256.76	493.14
山 东	Shandong	15043.18	1868.77	7999.35	5175.05
河 南	Henan	12228.82	2696.26	8183.17	1349.39
湖 北	Hubei	8593.36	1172.25	2424.33	4996.79
湖 南	Hunan	3036.90	1015.42	1574.36	447.12
广 东	Guangdong	29304.37	370.84	2850.49	26083.05
广 西	Guangxi	5589.63	772.43	2000.37	2816.83
海 南	Hainan	11713.20	12.65	45.31	11655.24
重 庆	Chongqing	3928.52	334.82	1126.59	2467.11
四 川	Sichuan	3434.43	1159.93	1983.93	290.57
贵 州	Guizhou	1468.67	678.48	783.92	6.26
云 南	Yunnan	2062.09	515.37	1538.58	8.14
西 藏	Xizang	161.55	36.06	125.49	
陕 西	Shaanxi	4478.08	2547.79	1930.13	0.16
甘 肃	Gansu	4245.68	2155.17	2090.51	
青 海	Qinghai	803.38	593.86	209.52	
宁 夏	Ningxia	946.62	281.36	665.26	
新 疆	Xinjiang	2843.32	1654.18	1189.14	
不分地区	Not Classified by Region	7383.20			

16−16 按货类分全国铁路货物运输量
Railway Freight Traffic by Category of Cargo

项　　目	Item	2022			2023		
		货运量（万吨）Freight Traffic (10 000 tons)	货物周转量（百万吨公里）Freight Ton-kilometers (million ton-kilometers)	平均运距（公里）Average Transport Distance (km)	货运量（万吨）Freight Traffic (10 000 tons)	货物周转量（百万吨公里）Freight Ton-kilometers (million ton-kilometers)	平均运距（公里）Average Transport Distance (km)
总　　计	**Total**	**498327**	**3592893**	**721**	**503417**	**3643939**	**724**
#煤	Coal	272951	1720630	630	278101	1779007	640
焦　　炭	Coke	9092	79672	876	7882	69027	876
石　　油	Petroleum	12378	79726	644	13050	86573	663
钢铁及有色金属	Steel, Iron and Non-ferrous Metal	22655	178074	786	20796	164609	792
金属矿石	Metal Ores	55167	251392	456	54342	241457	444
非金属矿石	Non-metal Ores	9166	44448	485	7966	36879	463
磷 矿 石	Phosphorus Ore	1249	9209	737	1403	9707	692
矿建材料	Mineral Building Materials	11235	33262	296	11695	31842	272
水　　泥	Cement	1589	4525	285	1357	3732	275
木　　材	Timber	938	6930	739	814	7118	874
粮　　食	Grain	7440	145904	1961	6847	139877	2043
零　　担	Less-Than-Truckload	0	0	354			
集 装 箱	Containers	73631	714814	971	79111	760561	961

注：本表货运量和货物周转量不包括行包运量。
a) Freight traffic and freight ton-kilometers in the table do not include package freight.

16-17 国家铁路地区间货物交流(2023年)
Cross-region Freight Transport of National Railways (2023)

单位：万吨 (10 000 tons)

发送省 Sender		到达省 Receiver									
		合计 Total	北京 Beijing	天津 Tianjin	河北 Hebei	山西 Shanxi	内蒙古 Inner Mongolia	辽宁 Liaoning	吉林 Jilin	黑龙江 Heilongjiang	上海 Shanghai
总　计	**National Total**	**389597**	**1469**	**13774**	**77646**	**15106**	**18377**	**24184**	**9978**	**12852**	**1032**
北　京	Beijing	274	9	5	61	28	36	6	9	1	
天　津	Tianjin	10541	42	7140	1291	164	1315	26	9	8	1
河　北	Hebei	21802	864	2516	12292	1646	178	439	96	111	13
山　西	Shanxi	88066	120	1810	48171	6784	543	2313	209	55	39
内蒙古	Inner Mongolia	46333	164	1332	9602	2084	13863	4019	5283	5857	16
辽　宁	Liaoning	18058	65	241	628	73	1115	12133	1979	1102	19
吉　林	Jilin	5074	34	117	65	7	120	1499	1314	520	5
黑龙江	Heilongjiang	11677	43	103	140	20	242	3250	823	4851	8
上　海	Shanghai	527	4	4	1	3	6	9	5	2	3
江　苏	Jiangsu	6993	2	5	7	288	40	12	19	11	308
浙　江	Zhejiang	4574	2	3	4	2	40	13	14	17	184
安　徽	Anhui	8051	3	6	6	7	17	11	3	5	59
福　建	Fujian	4292			2	1	8	2	2	1	27
江　西	Jiangxi	5071	1		2	1	9	2	1	2	42
山　东	Shandong	25341	43	29	2546	2714	120	40	21	66	13
河　南	Henan	10864	4	40	139	59	54	142	33	43	88
湖　北	Hubei	5194	13	6	35	3	26	26	49	50	12
湖　南	Hunan	4961	6	3	15	2	40	3	3	6	18
广　东	Guangdong	8436	6	1	7	3	57	29	1		9
广　西	Guangxi	11501			2	1	3	2			3
海　南	Hainan	890					2				
重　庆	Chongqing	1907	2	5	10	3	11	10		1	4
四　川	Sichuan	6310	11	4	21	6	17	15	10	4	22
贵　州	Guizhou	6037	1	1	19	14	14	3	3	37	1
云　南	Yunnan	5933	1	8	65	4	31	10	10	33	22
西　藏	Xizang	103	1		1						1
陕　西	Shaanxi	33979	16	74	2053	1066	55	53	12	10	21
甘　肃	Gansu	9770	2	41	55	5	51	8	4	5	40
青　海	Qinghai	3277		4	117	40	251	29	42	26	
宁　夏	Ningxia	3314	3	81	200	11	45	42	12	19	13
新　疆	Xinjiang	20449	8	198	92	69	66	38	11	8	39

16-17 续表 1 continued

单位：万吨 (10 000 tons)

发送省 Sender		到达省 Receiver										
		江苏 Jiangsu	浙江 Zhejiang	安徽 Anhui	福建 Fujian	江西 Jiangxi	山东 Shandong	河南 Henan	湖北 Hubei	湖南 Hunan	广东 Guangdong	广西 Guangxi
总　计	**National Total**	**9359**	**6129**	**12762**	**3588**	**9789**	**32054**	**18219**	**12469**	**11067**	**8882**	**10548**
北　京	Beijing	2	3	4	1	1	11	16	11	5	6	1
天　津	Tianjin	7	8	4	2	7	12	22	16	17	9	4
河　北	Hebei	100	35	167	8	103	1170	972	179	148	74	27
山　西	Shanxi	2255	271	1915	183	597	11896	4163	2170	1436	170	205
内蒙古	Inner Mongolia	219	109	162	31	293	829	567	317	308	61	18
辽　宁	Liaoning	44	28	41	3	23	206	118	38	31	2	1
吉　林	Jilin	56	45	202	17	114	110	164	137	96	13	4
黑龙江	Heilongjiang	86	50	163	33	72	313	308	159	128	22	7
上　海	Shanghai	88	49	31	4	7	12	14	11	11	57	3
江　苏	Jiangsu	2051	97	1400	20	131	72	1227	41	74	77	12
浙　江	Zhejiang	67	2928	59	16	590	9	27	8	21	91	21
安　徽	Anhui	1292	356	4521	70	360	169	96	404	81	49	52
福　建	Fujian	7	177	6	2024	1726	6	8	7	7	206	1
江　西	Jiangxi	30	480	58	492	2524	6	4	114	529	536	19
山　东	Shandong	228	28	516	17	290	12142	3134	199	117	117	40
河　南	Henan	689	196	1218	244	587	507	2322	1107	575	279	315
湖　北	Hubei	28	164	426	82	76	55	189	1696	295	241	173
湖　南	Hunan	44	94	9	10	218	16	12	76	2926	950	175
广　东	Guangdong	10	16	7	3	313	17	26	109	1204	3820	1299
广　西	Guangxi	3	16	5	5	34	3	19	19	411	1191	6183
海　南	Hainan					2		1		3	50	5
重　庆	Chongqing	2	21	13	2	6	12	16	2	20	46	215
四　川	Sichuan	10	15	9	2	12	41	35	89	17	67	214
贵　州	Guizhou	10	12	3	116	54	41	71	215	209	162	500
云　南	Yunnan	66	61	17	29	31	91	28	42	47	207	738
西　藏	Xizang	3	1	1			1	19	2		1	1
陕　西	Shaanxi	1014	286	1145	86	1242	3344	3285	4017	1902	94	127
甘　肃	Gansu	317	68	400	11	164	299	593	676	198	45	27
青　海	Qinghai	53	22	93	8	44	85	136	179	32	10	46
宁　夏	Ningxia	153	99	47	18	40	221	72	124	71	48	49
新　疆	Xinjiang	423	392	120	49	126	356	554	302	147	182	68

16-17 续表 2 continued

单位：万吨 (10 000 tons)

发送省 Sender		到达省 Receiver 海南 Hainan	重庆 Chongqing	四川 Sichuan	贵州 Guizhou	云南 Yunnan	西藏 Xizang	陕西 Shaanxi	甘肃 Gansu	青海 Qinghai	宁夏 Ningxia	新疆 Xinjiang
总 计	**National Total**	**936**	**7988**	**17780**	**7174**	**9206**	**627**	**10791**	**6925**	**2348**	**3055**	**13483**
北 京	Beijing	1	12	8	1	1		12	8	5	5	5
天 津	Tianjin		16	38	6	7		22	36	10	280	22
河 北	Hebei		106	182	45	67	5	54	73	17	69	45
山 西	Shanxi	1	602	998	401	169	1	225	36	23	189	118
内蒙古	Inner Mongolia	1	168	341	40	67	3	264	91	50	132	41
辽 宁	Liaoning		14	68	16	23		32	4	1	1	9
吉 林	Jilin		30	113	118	136	1	21	10	1	1	5
黑龙江	Heilongjiang		107	337	130	178	13	50	18	4	13	6
上 海	Shanghai	1	24	68	11	16	3	27	4	3	2	45
江 苏	Jiangsu	1	36	149	48	76	8	462	151	18	8	138
浙 江	Zhejiang	1	73	64	30	58	7	44	33	5	3	142
安 徽	Anhui		50	109	92	85	3	63	26	3	2	49
福 建	Fujian		12	20	9	12	1	7	2		1	8
江 西	Jiangxi		31	40	66	44	1	15	2	1	2	17
山 东	Shandong		116	405	99	134	5	1057	277	82	225	520
河 南	Henan	1	289	647	297	265	23	148	146	75	7	325
湖 北	Hubei	8	123	501	258	175	4	269	56	8	12	133
湖 南	Hunan	9	90	60	62	59		6	3	3	3	39
广 东	Guangdong	80	79	184	619	387	1	32	3	1	2	109
广 西	Guangxi	21	313	492	925	1749	1	11	11	3	1	76
海 南	Hainan	785	1	13	13	14						
重 庆	Chongqing	1	86	1011	61	97	1	11	57	82		97
四 川	Sichuan	3	594	4015	201	651	17	49	34	8	1	115
贵 州	Guizhou	4	784	1127	1442	916		58	138	41	3	41
云 南	Yunnan	8	201	878	551	2562	1	19	39	20	12	100
西 藏	Xizang			1		1	18		25	23		
陕 西	Shaanxi	1	2593	3066	958	346	36	6597	138	71	34	236
甘 肃	Gansu		442	1080	300	185	148	417	3202	287	497	203
青 海	Qinghai	2	100	154	32	40	202	25	260	1154	42	45
宁 夏	Ningxia		156	519	58	118	20	254	307	65	426	27
新 疆	Xinjiang	5	738	1092	287	567	103	540	1735	283	1082	10767

16−18 全国铁路运输设备基本情况
Basic Statistics on Railways Transport Equipment

项　目		Item		2019	2020	2021	2022	2023
机　车	**（台）**	**Locomotives**	**(unit)**	**21733**	**21865**	**21741**	**22063**	**22396**
内燃机车		Diesel Locomotives		8048	8013	7805	7839	7751
电力机车		Electric Locomotives		13665	13841	13916	14213	14634
客　车	**（辆）**	**Passenger Coaches**	**(coach)**	**74848**	**76033**	**77572**	**77341**	**78274**
软卧车		Soft Berth Coaches		4841	4889	4861	4873	4924
硬卧车		Hard Berth Coaches		19430	19093	19128	19035	18830
软座车		Soft Seat Coaches		28578	30516	32292	32668	34158
硬座车		Hard Seat Coaches		15864	15603	15272	14964	14467
货　车	**（辆）**	**Freight Wagons**	**(coach)**	**877134**	**912735**	**966361**	**997312**	**1007473**

16−19 高速铁路基本情况
Basic Statistics of High Speed Railway

年　份 Year	营业里程 （公里） Length in Operation (km)	占铁路营业里程比重 (%) Percentage of Length of Railways in Operation (%)	客运量 （万人） Passenger Traffic (10 000 persons)	占铁路客运量比重 (%) Percentage of Railway Passenger Traffic (%)	旅客周转量 （亿人公里） Passenger-kilometers (100 million passenger-km)	占铁路客运周转量比重 (%) Percentage of Railway Passenger-kilometers (%)
2008	672	0.8	734	0.5	15.6	0.2
2009	2699	3.2	4651	3.1	162.2	2.1
2010	5133	5.6	13323	8.0	463.2	5.3
2011	6601	7.1	28552	15.8	1058.4	11.0
2012	9356	9.6	38815	20.5	1446.1	14.7
2013	11028	10.7	52962	25.1	2141.1	20.2
2014	16456	14.7	70378	30.5	2825.0	25.1
2015	19838	16.4	96139	37.9	3863.4	32.3
2016	22980	18.5	122128	43.4	4641.0	36.9
2017	25164	19.8	175216	56.8	5875.6	43.7
2018	29904	22.7	205430	60.9	6871.9	48.6
2019	35388	25.3	235833	64.4	7746.7	52.7
2020	37929	25.9	155707	70.7	4844.9	58.6
2021	40139	26.6	192236	73.6	6064.2	63.4
2022	42241	27.3	127533	76.2	4386.1	66.7
2023	45036	28.4	289788	75.2	9834.1	66.8

16–20 民用汽车拥有量
Possession of Civil Vehicles

年 份 Year 地 区 Region		民用汽车总计(万辆) Total (10 000 units)	载客汽车(万辆) Passenger Vehicles (10 000 units)	大 型 Large	中 型 Medium	小 型 Small	微 型 Minicar	载货汽车(万辆) Trucks (10 000 units)
	1978	135.84	25.90					100.17
	1980	178.29	35.08					129.90
	1985	321.12	79.45					223.20
	1990	551.36	162.19					368.48
	1995	1040.00	417.90					585.43
	2000	1608.91	853.73					716.32
	2005	3159.66	2132.46	82.13	131.65	1618.35	300.32	955.55
	2006	3697.35	2619.57	87.34	137.00	2083.40	311.83	986.30
	2007	4358.36	3195.99	93.82	140.52	2646.47	315.18	1054.06
	2008	5099.61	3838.92	100.39	143.19	3271.14	324.19	1126.07
	2009	6280.61	4845.09	107.95	145.80	4246.90	344.44	1368.60
	2010	7801.83	6124.13	116.44	146.07	5498.36	363.25	1597.55
	2011	9356.32	7478.37	126.54	147.41	6827.54	376.88	1787.99
	2012	10933.09	8943.01	128.13	131.78	8302.63	380.47	1894.75
	2013	12670.14	10561.78	131.38	117.06	9951.46	361.87	2010.62
	2014	14598.11	12326.70	139.61	112.06	11748.19	326.84	2125.46
	2015	16284.45	14095.88	140.07	89.66	13580.48	285.66	2065.62
	2016	18574.54	16278.24	146.03	83.82	15813.84	234.55	2171.89
	2017	20906.67	18469.54	152.94	78.95	18038.69	198.96	2338.85
	2018	23231.23	20555.40	158.33	75.40	20135.22	186.46	2567.82
	2019	25376.38	22474.27	160.58	72.08	22069.74	171.88	2782.84
	2020	27340.92	24166.18	157.01	68.29	23782.77	158.12	3042.64
	2021	29418.59	26015.84	153.00	65.45	25651.99	145.40	3258.47
	2022	31184.44	27715.55	147.57	61.91	27372.59	133.47	3317.65
	2023	32911.55	29395.59	143.06	58.03	29074.95	119.55	3358.94
北 京	Beijing	639.98	573.77	5.76	8.47	557.48	2.08	59.69
天 津	Tianjin	418.59	376.61	2.30	1.00	371.60	1.71	39.63
河 北	Hebei	2017.92	1759.85	6.10	1.66	1734.67	17.42	248.40
山 西	Shanxi	925.94	822.40	3.38	1.04	808.20	9.78	99.06
内蒙古	Inner Mongolia	749.07	657.28	2.91	1.11	648.81	4.45	87.76
辽 宁	Liaoning	1101.81	983.31	6.50	2.87	970.11	3.83	113.57
吉 林	Jilin	571.80	513.63	3.27	1.05	507.40	1.92	55.46
黑龙江	Heilongjiang	659.57	573.87	4.33	1.79	565.90	1.85	82.15
上 海	Shanghai	535.82	497.99	4.25	1.74	491.53	0.47	35.14
江 苏	Jiangsu	2422.70	2256.53	9.94	2.87	2238.31	5.41	154.42
浙 江	Zhejiang	2156.76	1976.09	6.92	2.63	1960.79	5.75	173.68
安 徽	Anhui	1188.79	1043.04	5.23	1.76	1034.00	2.04	139.50
福 建	Fujian	871.59	775.48	3.34	1.63	768.48	2.02	92.65
江 西	Jiangxi	799.24	707.09	2.82	1.06	701.95	1.26	88.01
山 东	Shandong	3033.54	2687.67	12.33	3.36	2648.96	23.03	331.11
河 南	Henan	2103.46	1897.36	6.72	2.72	1877.36	10.56	197.41
湖 北	Hubei	1133.76	1017.64	5.62	2.09	1008.72	1.21	109.16
湖 南	Hunan	1154.16	1053.84	5.74	3.15	1043.07	1.88	95.46
广 东	Guangdong	3068.22	2772.92	14.05	3.58	2750.29	4.99	284.88
广 西	Guangxi	942.01	833.78	3.34	1.35	826.33	2.77	104.53
海 南	Hainan	198.08	175.75	1.34	0.47	173.68	0.26	21.42
重 庆	Chongqing	606.79	549.51	2.94	0.86	545.31	0.40	54.72
四 川	Sichuan	1542.23	1392.21	6.84	1.72	1379.65	4.00	143.44
贵 州	Guizhou	692.85	613.66	2.66	1.40	608.68	0.92	76.53
云 南	Yunnan	956.15	819.54	2.98	1.61	811.67	3.29	132.48
西 藏	Xizang	78.35	55.16	0.46	0.25	54.31	0.14	22.55
陕 西	Shaanxi	904.95	815.20	3.86	1.29	806.49	3.56	83.70
甘 肃	Gansu	460.72	385.23	2.30	0.86	381.23	0.84	72.50
青 海	Qinghai	154.93	128.22	0.93	0.51	126.38	0.41	25.47
宁 夏	Ningxia	210.36	167.02	0.98	0.30	165.14	0.60	41.72
新 疆	Xinjiang	611.38	513.94	2.93	1.80	508.48	0.73	92.73

16–20 续表 continued

年份 Year 地区 Region	载货汽车（万辆）Trucks (10 000 units) 重型 Heavy	中型 Medium	轻型 Light	微型 Mini	其他汽车（万辆）Others (10 000 units)	机动车驾驶员（万人）Number of Motor Drivers (10 000 persons)	#汽车驾驶员 Automobile Drivers
1978							192.45
1980							245.23
1985							462.14
1990						1635.85	790.96
1995						3501.52	1673.39
2000						7655.56	3746.51
2005	168.07	236.66	484.51	66.31	71.66	13069.52	8017.76
2006	174.01	235.39	532.13	44.76	91.49	14213.87	9317.24
2007	186.74	243.46	587.22	36.63	108.31	15363.88	10567.15
2008	200.84	249.73	644.96	30.54	134.62	17336.56	12276.80
2009	315.08	262.21	765.33	25.97	66.92	19167.58	13740.73
2010	394.80	269.75	911.88	21.12	80.14	20068.47	15129.89
2011	460.58	267.80	1042.07	17.54	89.96	22817.62	17416.76
2012	472.51	229.20	1179.65	13.40	95.33	25250.83	20028.52
2013	501.97	196.40	1300.02	12.23	97.75	26955.93	21742.70
2014	533.67	188.09	1385.77	17.93	145.95	29892.32	24812.07
2015	530.05	148.87	1375.79	10.90	122.95	32853.05	28012.99
2016	569.48	138.69	1455.29	8.43	124.41	35876.98	30328.77
2017	635.41	130.68	1566.30	6.46	98.28	36016.94	31658.20
2018	709.53	124.39	1728.53	5.37	108.00	41030.16	36923.42
2019	761.70	116.27	1900.76	4.11	119.27	43636.74	39752.86
2020	840.64	106.19	2092.72	3.09	132.09	45702.49	41794.89
2021	907.09	95.88	2253.26	2.25	144.28	48113.64	44379.72
2022	894.15	86.29	2335.60	1.61	151.24	50178.05	46434.41
2023	881.94	77.40	2398.01	1.59	157.02	52319.46	48617.16
北京 Beijing	10.24	1.48	47.74	0.22	6.52	1237.05	1226.78
天津 Tianjin	8.78	0.57	30.25	0.04	2.34	550.82	549.78
河北 Hebei	75.07	2.59	170.68	0.06	9.66	2788.30	2749.24
山西 Shanxi	39.30	0.80	58.94	0.02	4.48	1280.68	1264.60
内蒙古 Inner Mongolia	25.90	1.06	60.79	0.01	4.04	929.83	897.50
辽宁 Liaoning	36.63	3.55	73.39	0.01	4.93	1527.25	1469.73
吉林 Jilin	17.75	1.33	36.38	0.00	2.70	871.66	818.33
黑龙江 Heilongjiang	24.14	3.25	54.75	0.00	3.55	1043.54	1013.59
上海 Shanghai	22.63	3.03	9.49		2.69	1002.01	988.86
江苏 Jiangsu	57.78	8.22	88.38	0.03	11.76	3470.07	3328.07
浙江 Zhejiang	32.63	2.94	138.09	0.03	7.00	2834.59	2727.34
安徽 Anhui	44.99	2.39	92.07	0.06	6.25	1920.16	1855.95
福建 Fujian	16.30	1.47	74.87	0.01	3.47	1593.23	1368.31
江西 Jiangxi	27.40	2.15	58.45	0.01	4.14	1618.72	1395.36
山东 Shandong	98.06	5.07	227.78	0.20	14.76	3750.02	3675.25
河南 Henan	55.29	2.01	140.03	0.08	8.68	3619.65	3527.26
湖北 Hubei	28.82	3.64	76.67	0.03	6.96	2035.81	1877.07
湖南 Hunan	19.06	3.08	73.23	0.09	4.87	2023.50	1814.26
广东 Guangdong	54.15	8.23	221.89	0.62	10.42	5301.88	4832.23
广西 Guangxi	27.67	3.01	73.83	0.02	3.69	1802.52	1493.34
海南 Hainan	2.21	0.72	18.48	0.00	0.92	361.21	289.08
重庆 Chongqing	15.97	1.63	37.11	0.01	2.56	1101.82	990.00
四川 Sichuan	34.97	4.08	104.37	0.02	6.59	2875.57	2503.21
贵州 Guizhou	9.82	1.44	65.28	0.00	2.66	1309.26	1115.58
云南 Yunnan	17.63	2.22	112.62	0.01	4.13	1808.60	1403.29
西藏 Xizang	4.32	1.60	16.63	0.00	0.64	89.63	83.02
陕西 Shaanxi	24.13	1.31	58.25	0.02	6.05	1437.36	1369.68
甘肃 Gansu	11.83	1.56	59.10	0.00	2.99	779.39	694.89
青海 Qinghai	4.17	0.57	20.73	0.00	1.24	188.33	187.29
宁夏 Ningxia	11.03	0.54	30.15	0.00	1.62	275.52	269.13
新疆 Xinjiang	23.26	1.88	67.58	0.00	4.72	891.51	839.14

注：1.小轿车包括在载客汽车中（以下相关表同）。
2.从2002年起，载客汽车和载货汽车的其中分项、其他汽车统计口径有调整与以前年份不可比（以下相关表同）。

a) Cars are included in passenger vehicles. The same applies to the following tables.

b) Since 2002, there has been adjustment to the statistical coverages of some detailed items of passenger vehicles, trucks and other vehicles, the data are hence not comparable with those in previous years. The same applies to the following tables.

16-21 私人汽车拥有量
Possession of Private Vehicles

单位：万辆 (10 000 units)

年份/地区	Year/Region	汽车总计 Total	载客汽车 Passenger Vehicles	大型 Large	中型 Medium	小型 Small	微型 Minicar
	1985	28.49	1.93				
	1990	81.62	24.07				
	1995	249.96	114.15				
	2000	625.33	365.09				
	2005	1848.07	1383.93	7.61	50.88	1079.78	245.66
	2006	2333.32	1823.57	11.19	56.20	1491.18	265.00
	2007	2876.22	2316.91	7.91	55.73	1984.29	268.98
	2008	3501.39	2880.50	8.57	57.97	2533.28	280.68
	2009	4574.91	3808.33	8.72	59.96	3436.26	303.39
	2010	5938.71	4989.50	9.34	61.00	4593.46	325.70
	2011	7326.79	6237.46	9.99	62.34	5823.62	341.52
	2012	8838.60	7637.87	8.26	55.43	7226.48	347.71
	2013	10501.68	9198.23	6.95	46.95	8810.51	333.83
	2014	12339.36	10945.39	7.70	42.10	10590.75	304.83
	2015	14099.10	12737.23	8.27	28.89	12432.26	267.81
	2016	16330.22	14896.27	4.99	24.84	14645.61	220.83
	2017	18515.11	17001.51	4.58	22.17	16788.42	186.35
	2018	20574.93	18930.29	4.48	20.39	18731.80	173.62
	2019	22508.99	20710.58	4.21	18.99	20527.27	160.11
	2020	24291.19	22333.81	3.82	17.65	22165.13	147.21
	2021	26152.02	24074.19	3.24	16.66	23919.16	135.14
	2022	27792.11	25662.21	2.77	15.35	25520.30	123.78
	2023	29356.89	27195.00	2.29	13.88	27068.69	110.14
北　京	Beijing	545.53	510.09	0.29	5.41	502.36	2.02
天　津	Tianjin	368.07	345.56	0.07	0.35	343.48	1.65
河　北	Hebei	1840.09	1661.39	0.28	0.38	1644.75	15.98
山　西	Shanxi	825.48	769.75	0.05	0.15	760.29	9.26
内蒙古	Inner Mongolia	688.29	620.76	0.08	0.35	616.02	4.31
辽　宁	Liaoning	984.02	913.25	0.38	1.05	908.20	3.62
吉　林	Jilin	512.57	474.55	0.20	0.29	472.26	1.80
黑龙江	Heilongjiang	601.20	540.79	0.34	0.59	538.08	1.78
上　海	Shanghai	421.85	420.87	0.04	0.36	420.04	0.43
江　苏	Jiangsu	2072.13	1997.03	0.02	0.43	1991.61	4.98
浙　江	Zhejiang	1911.97	1807.93	0.03	0.36	1802.48	5.05
安　徽	Anhui	1059.82	981.38	0.03	0.28	979.12	1.95
福　建	Fujian	761.28	704.59	0.02	0.18	702.50	1.89
江　西	Jiangxi	726.66	673.98	0.01	0.07	672.70	1.19
山　东	Shandong	2689.96	2480.42	0.15	1.12	2458.76	20.38
河　南	Henan	1941.05	1811.51	0.03	0.18	1801.04	10.27
湖　北	Hubei	1022.98	950.52	0.02	0.18	949.18	1.14
湖　南	Hunan	1074.41	998.41	0.02	0.23	996.41	1.74
广　东	Guangdong	2705.70	2559.41	0.08	0.71	2554.15	4.47
广　西	Guangxi	873.43	796.68	0.02	0.20	793.73	2.72
海　南	Hainan	174.79	160.35	0.01	0.06	160.05	0.23
重　庆	Chongqing	539.43	507.23	0.01	0.09	506.77	0.37
四　川	Sichuan	1362.52	1274.39	0.02	0.11	1271.14	3.13
贵　州	Guizhou	642.60	577.61	0.01	0.08	576.63	0.89
云　南	Yunnan	885.95	771.13	0.02	0.11	767.82	3.18
西　藏	Xizang	67.79	49.00	0.00	0.02	48.85	0.13
陕　西	Shaanxi	818.06	756.56	0.01	0.04	753.13	3.38
甘　肃	Gansu	397.06	345.66	0.01	0.09	344.92	0.65
青　海	Qinghai	131.78	113.04	0.00	0.06	112.72	0.26
宁　夏	Ningxia	190.93	156.76	0.01	0.07	156.09	0.59
新　疆	Xinjiang	519.50	464.42	0.02	0.28	463.42	0.70

16-21 续表 continued

单位：万辆 (10 000 units)

年份 地区	Year Region	载货汽车 Trucks	重型 Heavy	中型 Medium	轻型 Light	微型 Mini	其他汽车 Others
	1985	26.48					
	1990	57.48					
	1995	131.83					
	2000	259.09					
	2005	452.11	62.50	100.34	243.29	45.98	12.04
	2006	494.91	64.23	108.64	288.94	33.09	14.84
	2007	539.45	68.89	110.44	332.69	27.43	19.86
	2008	596.39	73.28	115.68	384.12	23.31	24.50
	2009	753.40	108.73	129.59	494.97	20.12	13.17
	2010	931.52	141.44	140.52	632.77	16.78	17.69
	2011	1067.43	164.28	144.52	744.39	14.24	21.90
	2012	1175.63	168.13	128.51	867.64	11.35	25.09
	2013	1275.49	174.39	111.85	978.73	10.52	27.95
	2014	1352.78	182.68	104.90	1050.60	14.59	41.20
	2015	1330.65	173.86	86.62	1060.70	9.47	31.22
	2016	1401.16	184.82	79.77	1129.13	7.45	32.79
	2017	1478.40	193.98	73.22	1205.66	5.54	35.19
	2018	1605.10	208.78	68.59	1323.25	4.48	39.55
	2019	1753.66	218.11	63.07	1469.04	3.44	44.76
	2020	1907.28	222.62	55.58	1626.49	2.60	50.10
	2021	2022.34	227.97	47.48	1745.07	1.82	55.49
	2022	2072.26	229.27	41.41	1800.36	1.22	57.64
	2023	2102.74	225.31	34.94	1841.55	0.95	59.15
北京	Beijing	32.51	0.53	0.12	31.69	0.16	2.94
天津	Tianjin	21.75	0.35	0.07	21.31	0.02	0.77
河北	Hebei	174.68	33.67	1.33	139.63	0.04	4.01
山西	Shanxi	53.91	9.05	0.23	44.61	0.02	1.82
内蒙古	Inner Mongolia	65.70	14.01	0.54	51.14	0.01	1.84
辽宁	Liaoning	68.80	11.01	2.02	55.75	0.00	1.97
吉林	Jilin	37.04	7.58	0.78	28.68	0.00	0.98
黑龙江	Heilongjiang	59.28	11.56	2.11	45.60	0.00	1.13
上海	Shanghai	0.70	0.19	0.07	0.44		0.29
江苏	Jiangsu	71.41	17.41	3.20	50.78	0.02	3.69
浙江	Zhejiang	102.35	2.96	0.74	98.63	0.01	1.69
安徽	Anhui	76.12	3.93	0.95	71.23	0.01	2.32
福建	Fujian	55.82	2.01	0.47	53.34	0.00	0.86
江西	Jiangxi	51.39	3.46	1.14	46.78	0.01	1.29
山东	Shandong	202.17	10.85	1.96	189.28	0.07	7.38
河南	Henan	125.59	6.02	0.83	118.72	0.02	3.95
湖北	Hubei	70.07	10.03	2.02	57.99	0.02	2.39
湖南	Hunan	73.94	10.86	2.19	60.89	0.01	2.06
广东	Guangdong	143.28	7.17	2.86	132.78	0.46	3.02
广西	Guangxi	75.05	10.69	1.94	62.41	0.01	1.71
海南	Hainan	14.16	0.65	0.44	13.07	0.00	0.28
重庆	Chongqing	31.35	1.74	0.69	28.91	0.00	0.85
四川	Sichuan	85.84	6.47	1.72	77.64	0.01	2.29
贵州	Guizhou	63.73	4.87	0.78	58.08	0.00	1.26
云南	Yunnan	112.91	9.52	1.58	101.81	0.00	1.91
西藏	Xizang	18.59	3.66	1.41	13.52	0.00	0.20
陕西	Shaanxi	59.41	12.09	0.63	46.68	0.02	2.09
甘肃	Gansu	50.19	3.97	0.93	45.30	0.00	1.21
青海	Qinghai	18.17	1.24	0.31	16.62	0.00	0.57
宁夏	Ningxia	33.32	6.33	0.37	26.62	0.00	0.86
新疆	Xinjiang	53.53	1.43	0.51	51.58	0.00	1.55

16-22 新注册民用汽车数量
Statistics on New Registrations of Civil Vehicles

单位：辆 (unit)

年份 地区	Year Region	民用汽车总计 Total	载客汽车 Passenger Vehicles	大型 Large	中型 Medium	小型 Small	微型 Minicar
	2002	3371951	2294649	97200	145062	1491479	560908
	2005	5286287	4157504	99489	105314	3712056	240645
	2006	5730432	4678667	95428	82758	4382206	118275
	2007	6079209	5000042	91087	72059	4772468	64428
	2008	7631839	6226814	112811	64024	5928095	121884
	2009	12459452	10248554	114984	69548	9794452	269570
	2010	15288186	12546891	148234	76519	12086273	235865
	2011	16242474	13694540	163258	76472	13244774	210036
	2012	17725011	15248801	163517	71013	14875884	138387
	2013	20309394	17522965	168946	81160	17173792	99067
	2014	22051905	19366787	151405	79646	19050695	85041
	2015	23317507	21202815	191034	67080	20862002	82699
	2016	27244374	24648115	194829	59767	24338735	54784
	2017	28003955	24802416	171474	46657	24507374	76911
	2018	26521129	23139385	155760	39514	22876458	67653
	2019	25445941	21845871	133357	35844	21648138	28532
	2020	24001366	19724444	86902	23424	19608897	5221
	2021	26179642	21961429	81366	28291	21850635	1137
	2022	23191805	20695447	66735	17677	20610868	167
	2023	24529995	21813708	63508	17697	21732451	52
北京	Beijing	525877	474853	3796	3633	467424	
天津	Tianjin	354988	328166	701	289	327176	
河北	Hebei	1366404	1136578	3167	517	1132892	2
山西	Shanxi	600574	483826	1051	439	482335	1
内蒙古	Inner Mongolia	424137	354044	818	339	352887	
辽宁	Liaoning	611420	551772	2361	417	548994	
吉林	Jilin	374582	340862	1240	219	339403	
黑龙江	Heilongjiang	356529	309544	782	277	308485	
上海	Shanghai	625662	596365	3076	694	592595	
江苏	Jiangsu	2088775	1939188	4915	999	1933273	1
浙江	Zhejiang	1861913	1724539	5229	1770	1717540	
安徽	Anhui	960338	848919	2651	379	845887	2
福建	Fujian	617033	549813	1545	768	547500	
江西	Jiangxi	592128	536999	1233	321	535445	
山东	Shandong	1841761	1599276	3319	548	1595391	18
河南	Henan	1542920	1366294	1938	413	1363924	19
湖北	Hubei	909666	825224	2655	394	822175	
湖南	Hunan	801215	726279	2520	691	723068	
广东	Guangdong	2505037	2326904	4332	810	2321762	
广西	Guangxi	526384	466827	1179	323	465325	
海南	Hainan	202306	182752	485	104	182160	3
重庆	Chongqing	505609	455458	1433	265	453759	1
四川	Sichuan	1238826	1104789	4093	600	1100096	
贵州	Guizhou	523702	460653	1105	310	459238	
云南	Yunnan	632901	527434	2039	546	524846	3
西藏	Xizang	66932	46768	168	122	46478	
陕西	Shaanxi	741001	661413	1750	449	659212	2
甘肃	Gansu	341626	275132	884	236	274012	
青海	Qinghai	113259	84794	714	111	83969	
宁夏	Ningxia	152357	114823	1094	90	113639	
新疆	Xinjiang	524133	413420	1235	624	411561	

16-22 续表 continued

单位：辆 (unit)

年份 地区	Year Region	载货汽车 Trucks	重型 Heavy	中型 Medium	轻型 Light	微型 Mini	其他汽车 Others
	2002	993761	186498	220969	501985	84309	83541
	2005	1024034	162859	175576	639557	46042	104749
	2006	925294	139120	147689	616910	21575	126471
	2007	917603	155155	157867	591014	13567	161564
	2008	1168226	236749	185338	733343	12796	236799
	2009	2148355	500593	242679	1391249	13834	62543
	2010	2637605	769644	238595	1614803	14563	103690
	2011	2442601	726854	173140	1535590	7017	105333
	2012	2386173	560063	139793	1681908	4409	90037
	2013	2689898	739027	133402	1814385	3084	96531
	2014	2542287	630588	104425	1805471	1803	142831
	2015	2043257	454979	72274	1513773	2231	71435
	2016	2507282	649352	77114	1779643	1173	88977
	2017	3087575	980068	66974	2037906	2627	113964
	2018	3238847	967089	49591	2220492	1675	142897
	2019	3434877	1041421	55776	2337472	208	165193
	2020	4102293	1436723	58835	2606241	494	174629
	2021	4038153	1370833	68424	2598107	789	180060
	2022	2379396	417423	36220	1924343	1410	116962
	2023	2601817	563705	36294	1997845	3973	114470
北 京	Beijing	40207	5301	484	34288	134	10817
天 津	Tianjin	25579	5268	330	19888	93	1243
河 北	Hebei	220997	72997	1772	146115	113	8829
山 西	Shanxi	112488	59680	669	52098	41	4260
内蒙古	Inner Mongolia	67137	11252	706	55157	22	2956
辽 宁	Liaoning	57751	17007	1243	39483	18	1897
吉 林	Jilin	32343	5731	453	26154	5	1377
黑龙江	Heilongjiang	45119	6348	1127	37635	9	1866
上 海	Shanghai	27520	15980	1111	10429		1777
江 苏	Jiangsu	141442	36816	3915	100510	201	8145
浙 江	Zhejiang	132189	17688	1676	112670	155	5185
安 徽	Anhui	106201	24512	1405	79853	431	5218
福 建	Fujian	64805	9215	1195	54349	46	2415
江 西	Jiangxi	52212	9466	914	41809	23	2917
山 东	Shandong	232670	57491	3152	171474	553	9815
河 南	Henan	171670	40099	1807	129168	596	4956
湖 北	Hubei	79389	12752	1066	65516	55	5053
湖 南	Hunan	72563	9008	1510	61303	742	2373
广 东	Guangdong	171107	21635	4133	144878	461	7026
广 西	Guangxi	57790	8991	801	47961	37	1767
海 南	Hainan	18803	1567	239	16966	31	751
重 庆	Chongqing	48405	8189	666	39531	19	1746
四 川	Sichuan	128990	26046	1246	101581	117	5047
贵 州	Guizhou	61568	6185	685	54683	15	1481
云 南	Yunnan	103603	8606	708	94273	16	1864
西 藏	Xizang	19527	814	386	18327		637
陕 西	Shaanxi	75160	16380	1060	57693	27	4428
甘 肃	Gansu	64337	7401	449	56480	7	2157
青 海	Qinghai	27590	3140	297	24148	5	875
宁 夏	Ningxia	36171	15949	131	20091		1363
新 疆	Xinjiang	106484	22191	958	83334	1	4229

16-23 公路营运汽车拥有量
Possession of Vehicles for Highway Transport Business

年份 地区	Year Region	汽车总计（万辆）Total (10 000 units)	载客汽车 Passenger Vehicles 辆数（万辆）Number (10 000 units)	客位（万客位）Number of Seats (10 000 seats)	载货汽车 Trucks 辆数（万辆）Number (10 000 units)	#普通载货汽车 Ordinary Trucks	吨位（万吨）Capacity (10 000 tons)	#普通载货汽车 Ordinary Trucks
	2010	1133.32	83.13	2017.09	1050.19	996.43	5999.82	5223.23
	2011	1263.75	84.34	2086.66	1179.41	1116.36	7261.20	6273.51
	2012	1339.89	86.71	2166.55	1253.19	1184.58	8062.14	6963.29
	2013	1504.73	85.26	2170.26	1419.48	1080.75	9613.91	5008.34
	2014	1537.93	84.58	2189.55	1453.36	1091.32	10292.47	5241.45
	2015	1473.12	83.93	2148.58	1389.19	1011.87	10366.50	4982.50
	2016	1435.77	84.00	2140.26	1351.77	946.03	10826.78	4843.83
	2017	1450.22	81.61	2099.18	1368.62	902.90	11774.81	4868.40
	2018	1435.48	79.66	2048.11	1355.82	816.76	12872.97	4791.21
	2019	1165.49	77.67	2002.53	1087.82	489.77	13587.00	4479.25
	2020	1171.54	61.26	1840.89	1110.28	414.14	15784.17	4660.76
	2021	1231.96	58.70	1751.03	1173.26	406.94	17099.50	4923.43
	2022	1222.08	55.42	1647.24	1166.66	387.69	16967.33	4716.19
	2023	1226.20	55.24	1638.29	1170.97	358.71	17216.71	4434.51
北京	Beijing	13.00	1.35	59.88	11.65	5.41	102.93	53.96
天津	Tianjin	12.67	0.85	35.39	11.82	2.04	169.90	22.69
河北	Hebei	120.91	1.50	48.35	119.41	19.43	1958.82	255.36
山西	Shanxi	61.27	0.94	28.44	60.33	8.87	946.64	122.65
内蒙古	Inner Mongolia	28.90	1.01	33.80	27.89	5.27	351.61	63.06
辽宁	Liaoning	53.25	1.97	73.71	51.28	16.07	733.42	172.72
吉林	Jilin	26.70	1.09	35.59	25.61	10.04	306.13	109.48
黑龙江	Heilongjiang	34.57	1.36	44.68	33.20	11.03	435.78	128.83
上海	Shanghai	27.95	0.87	38.39	27.08	8.87	402.22	98.71
江苏	Jiangsu	78.45	2.92	120.84	75.52	32.78	1056.60	375.11
浙江	Zhejiang	38.40	1.67	61.27	36.73	12.00	552.58	157.10
安徽	Anhui	63.69	1.40	48.32	62.29	11.15	885.13	146.43
福建	Fujian	23.98	1.38	43.24	22.61	6.46	366.87	79.69
江西	Jiangxi	38.67	1.05	32.55	37.62	10.26	593.00	146.03
山东	Shandong	143.21	1.78	67.23	141.42	34.60	2171.97	441.90
河南	Henan	85.71	2.81	88.06	82.90	20.83	1306.62	321.91
湖北	Hubei	35.49	2.46	65.75	33.03	14.68	467.95	179.76
湖南	Hunan	28.99	2.75	71.71	26.23	11.65	374.84	137.67
广东	Guangdong	56.72	3.27	129.30	53.45	18.60	819.45	237.05
广西	Guangxi	37.54	1.90	61.63	35.64	16.23	508.77	201.26
海南	Hainan	3.45	0.54	17.58	2.91	1.26	40.04	13.13
重庆	Chongqing	24.12	1.41	36.15	22.71	12.17	278.86	121.73
四川	Sichuan	46.98	4.62	103.32	42.36	18.44	610.17	226.41
贵州	Guizhou	11.28	2.21	53.48	9.07	4.82	122.55	61.19
云南	Yunnan	28.15	3.76	68.13	24.38	13.95	322.24	161.76
西藏	Xizang	5.13	0.43	8.10	4.71	3.74	59.18	45.34
陕西	Shaanxi	30.32	1.61	48.27	28.71	9.34	407.09	115.59
甘肃	Gansu	13.39	1.46	33.07	11.93	5.60	157.99	68.04
青海	Qinghai	4.99	0.43	11.93	4.56	2.11	62.91	26.43
宁夏	Ningxia	14.69	0.42	12.63	14.28	2.00	185.80	25.35
新疆	Xinjiang	33.63	4.00	57.50	29.63	9.01	458.64	118.16

注：1.小轿车包括在载客汽车中。
2.从2013年起，公路营运载货汽车包括货车、牵引车和挂车，统计口径发生调整，数据与上年同期不可比。

a) Passenger vehicles include cars.

b) Since 2013, the coverage of highway business trucks has changed to include trucks, towing vehicles and trailers. So it is not comparable with data of previous year.

16–24 民用运输船舶拥有量
Possession of Civil Transport Vessels

年份 Year 地区 Region		机动船 Motor Vessels				驳船 Barges		
		艘数 (艘) Number (unit)	净载重量 (吨位) Dead Weight Tonnage (ton)	载客量 (客位) Passenger Capacity (seat)	拖船功率 (千瓦) Drawing Power (kW)	艘数 (艘) Number (unit)	净载重量 (吨位) Dead Weight Tonnage (ton)	载客量 (客位) Passenger Capacity (seat)
	1980	29588	12207808	455454	914704	71604	4743905	89584
	1985	260296	20898230	877963	1666163	132682	8670224	99643
	1990	325888	29090082	1138937	1750351	82482	9066738	62926
	1995	299717	40940087	979985	1707115	57998	9449652	17722
	2000	185018	42640605	1014013	1439743	44658	8640504	18258
	2005	165900	90756392	977846	1480381	41394	11030057	33496
	2006	157805	98241489	1025861	1538957	36555	12015595	33355
	2007	157544	106441173	1004546	1520924	34227	12373412	22316
	2008	152247	111047702	994495	1564439	31943	13121439	14050
	2009	149367	133384848	979384	1120381	27565	12702991	2166
	2010	155624	168985654	1001395	1410719	22783	11422911	2260
	2011	157950	202602789	1004622	1600896	21292	10040453	3768
	2012	158309	218793742	1021260	1531873	20282	9692502	3798
	2013	155340	234317614	1031711	1235661	17214	9692720	1287
	2014	154974	247399826	1030973	1424950	17003	10452402	1334
	2015	149659	261434867	1015939	1424426	16246	11007996	1391
	2016	144568	255170820	999008	1445786	15576	11056320	3124
	2017	131746	246750827	964377	1532698	13178	9765519	3122
	2018	125754	242447129	960245	1465403	11221	8705726	3044
	2019	121440	248626381	882764	1422199	10115	8223366	3044
	2020	117931	263138418	857098	1586411	8874	7463162	2846
	2021	118025	276926929	856146	1888557	7865	7399347	1622
	2022	114507	290687729	861574	2029434	7361	7070420	200
	2023	118284	300520668	812477	2231706	6381	6550573	0
北京	Beijing							
天津	Tianjin	316	4826542	2792	464965	7	189346	
河北	Hebei	497	2662159	15703	1940			
山西	Shanxi	236	7761	4552				
内蒙古	Inner Mongolia							
辽宁	Liaoning	367	1332485	31694	21699	8	24212	
吉林	Jilin	263	5260	9661	440	10	5260	
黑龙江	Heilongjiang	1049	196285	23595	22859	217	146165	
上海	Shanghai	1452	28087647	32804	212949	9	42461	
江苏	Jiangsu	26188	38045007	34800	461429	2053	2553027	
浙江	Zhejiang	12369	33161780	97318	239713			
安徽	Anhui	24310	57662669	14484	23485	523	291677	
福建	Fujian	1774	19813937	29034	21390			
江西	Jiangxi	2496	7375383	14865	8018			
山东	Shandong	8757	14238572	65897	399662	2404	2647103	
河南	Henan	5363	12414319	16832	3374	314	302979	
湖北	Hubei	2811	7230771	39436	36311	64	175749	
湖南	Hunan	3524	4955852	51573	2398	8	20600	
广东	Guangdong	6102	19267601	79023	212751	5	25147	
广西	Guangxi	8577	20114163	32553		1	3758	
海南	Hainan	673	15668844	41102	55682			
重庆	Chongqing	2636	11657281	33568	16912	18	32406	
四川	Sichuan	3935	1428718	31320	23565	733	87155	
贵州	Guizhou	1810	166590	47994	202	4	3278	
云南	Yunnan	971	171274	24215	676	2	130	
西藏	Xizang							
陕西	Shaanxi	560	27972	11657	272	1	120	
甘肃	Gansu	434	1796	9671				
青海	Qinghai	147		3653				
宁夏	Ningxia	667		12681	1014			
新疆	Xinjiang							
不分地区	Not Classified by Region							

16–25 全国沿海和内河港口分货类吞吐量(2023年)
Volume of Freight Handled in Coastal Ports and Inland River Ports by Type of Freight (2023)

单位：万吨　　(10 000 tons)

货物种类	Type of Freight	沿海港口 Coastal Ports			内河港口 Inland River Ports		
		合计 Total	出港 Outbound	进港 Inbound	合计 Total	出港 Outbound	进港 Inbound
总计	**Total**	**1083471**	**485955**	**597516**	**613855**	**268016**	**345839**
#煤炭及制品	Coal and Related Products	193179	100264	92916	110438	34809	75629
石油、天然气及制品	Petroleum, Natural Gas and Related Products	127504	35081	92423	15901	5599	10301
金属矿石	Metal Ores	172987	32046	140941	88608	28550	60058
钢铁	Steel and Iron	38217	24830	13387	31913	14699	17215
矿建材料	Mineral Building Materials	105288	63297	41991	202788	94471	108317
水泥	Cement	8765	2388	6377	36831	28588	8243
木材	Timber	7463	1233	6230	3308	871	2437
非金属矿石	Non-metal Ores	38390	15014	23376	31796	16760	15036
化肥和农药	Chemical Fertilizers and Pesticides	3736	2453	1283	3338	1914	1424
盐	Salt	1594	504	1090	1837	972	865
粮食	Grain	26044	7903	18141	16929	5262	11668
其他	Others	300857	169466	131391	49660	26163	23497

16–26 沿海港口货物吞吐量
Volume of Freight Handled in Coastal Ports

单位：万吨　　(10 000 tons)

港口	Seaport	1990	1995	2000	2005	2010	2015	2020	2022	2023
总计	**Total**	**48321**	**80166**	**125603**	**292777**	**548358**	**784578**	**948002**	**1013102**	**1083471**
#大连	Dalian	4952	6417	9084	17085	31399	41482	33401	30613	31588
营口	Yingkou	237	1156	2268	7537	22579	33849	23821	21118	22448
秦皇岛	Qinhuangdao	6945	8382	9743	16900	26297	25309	20061	19269	18964
天津	Tianjin	2063	5787	9566	24069	41325	54051	50290	54902	55881
烟台	Yantai	668	1361	1774	4506	15033	25163	39935	46257	48465
威海	Weihai	100	379	669	1015	2407	4213	3863	4520	5154
青岛	Qingdao	3034	5103	8636	18678	35012	48453	60459	65754	68367
日照	Rizhao	925	1452	2674	8421	22597	33707	49615	57057	59284
上海	Shanghai	13959	16567	20440	44317	56320	64906	65105	66832	75277
连云港	Lianyungang	1137	1716	2708	6016	12739	19756	24182	30111	32149
宁波-舟山	Ningbo-Zhoushan	2554	6853	11547	26881	63300	88929	117240	126134	132370
台州	Taizhou			950	2067	4706	6237	5091	6241	7380
温州	Wenzhou	307	601	859	3097	6408	8490	7401	8479	8813
福州	Fuzhou	561	1032	2426	7443	7125	13967	24897	30164	33202
厦门	Xiamen	529	1314	1965	4771	12728	21023	20750	21940	22020
汕头	Shantou	279	716	1284	1736	3509	5181	3351	4019	3879
深圳	Shenzhen			5697	15351	22098	21706	26506	27243	28664
广州	Guangzhou	4163	7299	11128	25036	41095	50053	61239	62906	64283
湛江	Zhanjiang	1557	1885	2038	4647	13638	22036	23391	25376	28273
北海	Beihai	82	201	265	437	1251	2468	3736	4418	5301
防城	Fangcheng					7650	11504	12182	15359	19389
海口	Haikou	288	468	808	2118	5700	9204	11781	11118	12369
八所	Basuo	431	275	378	486	893	1767	1501	1646	1692

注：1.从2006年起，宁波－舟山港包括原宁波港和舟山港，以往年度数据为原宁波港数据。
2.从2007年起，烟台港包括原烟台港和龙口港，以往年度数据为原烟台港数据。
3.从2011年起，厦门港统计范围包括原厦门港和漳州港，以往年度数据为原厦门港数据。
4.从2009年起，沿海规模以上港口统计范围为年吞吐量1000万吨以上的沿海港口，内河规模以上港口统计范围为年吞吐量200万吨以上的内河港口(以下相关表同)。

a) Since 2006, data of Ningbo-Zhoushan Port include those of Ningbo Port and Zhoushan Port, whereas data for earlier years refer to Ningbo Port.
b) Since 2007, data of Yantai Port include those of Yantai Port and Longkou Port, whereas data for earlier years refer to Yantai Port.
c) Since 2011, data of Xiamen Port include Xiamen Port and Zhangzhou Port, and are data of Xiamen Port before 2011.
d) Since 2009, statistical coverage above designated size refers to coastal ports with capacity over 10 million tons yearly and inland ports over 2 million tons yearly. The same applies to the relevant following tables.

16–27 沿海港口码头泊位数(2023年底)
Number of Berths in Coastal Ports (End of 2023)

名 称	Name	总计 Total			生产用 For Productive Use			非生产用 For Non-productive Use	
		码头长度(米) Length of Quay Line (m)	泊位个数(个) Number of Berths (unit)	#万吨级 10 000 Ton Class	码头长度(米) Length of Quay Line (m)	泊位个数(个) Number of Berths (unit)	#万吨级 10 000 Ton Class	码头长度(米) Length of Quay Line (m)	泊位个数(个) Number of Berths (unit)
总 计	**Total**	**1021083**	**6580**	**2409**	**956806**	**5590**	**2409**	**64276**	**990**
#大 连	Dalian	48211	257	114	44334	232	114	3877	25
营 口	Yingkou	19994	93	63	19260	86	63	734	7
秦 皇 岛	Qinhuangdao	17246	93	44	16013	73	44	1233	20
天 津	Tianjin	48356	221	132	42278	165	132	6078	56
烟 台	Yantai	43305	247	111	42175	237	111	1130	10
威 海	Weihai	14394	86	39	13524	81	39	870	5
青 岛	Qingdao	34379	132	100	33258	126	100	1121	6
日 照	Rizhao	25335	93	81	25029	92	81	306	1
上 海	Shanghai	109339	1002	189	77317	561	189	32022	441
连 云 港	Lianyungang	23483	107	78	23186	105	78	297	2
宁波–舟山	Ningbo-Zhoushan	113363	777	214	107845	671	214	5518	106
台 州	Taizhou	12258	106	11	12258	106	11		
温 州	Wenzhou	16289	158	22	16151	157	22	138	1
福 州	Fuzhou	31628	182	83	31284	176	83	344	6
厦 门	Xiamen	33911	200	80	32887	181	80	1024	19
汕 头	Shantou	6178	36	15	6178	36	15		
深 圳	Shenzhen	35269	172	77	33728	160	77	1541	12
广 州	Guangzhou	42398	541	86	40848	342	86	1550	199
湛 江	Zhanjiang	24182	166	64	23147	153	64	1035	13
北 海	Beihai	9270	70	18	9210	69	18	60	1
防 城	Fangcheng	20826	148	56	20766	143	56	60	5
海 口	Haikou	9842	70	35	9651	69	35	191	1
八 所	Basuo	2488	12	9	2488	12	9		

16–28 内河港口码头泊位数(2023年底)
Number of Berths in Ports of Inland Rivers (End of 2023)

名 称	Name	总计 Total			生产用 For Productive Use			非生产用 For Non-productive Use	
		码头长度(米) Length of Quay Line (m)	泊位个数(个) Number of Berths (unit)	#万吨级 10 000 Ton Class	码头长度(米) Length of Quay Line (m)	泊位个数(个) Number of Berths (unit)	#万吨级 10 000 Ton Class	码头长度(米) Length of Quay Line (m)	泊位个数(个) Number of Berths (unit)
总 计	**Total**	**1211809**	**16906**	**469**	**1180144**	**16433**	**469**	**31664**	**473**
#重 庆	Chongqing	53424	558		46136	437		7288	121
宜 昌	Yichang	30392	196		29947	193		445	3
武 汉	Wuhan	21620	171		18783	148		2837	23
黄 石	Huangshi	5315	48		5145	47		170	1
九 江	Jiujiang	22866	350	1	22625	348	1	241	2
安 庆	Anqing	4594	42		4152	38		442	4
池 州	Chizhou	8990	85		8990	85			
铜 陵	Tongling	7025	66	3	6980	65	3	45	1
芜 湖	Wuhu	14267	128	13	14267	128	13		
马 鞍 山	Maanshan	9327	109	1	9327	109	1		
南 京	Nanjing	24675	190	58	24675	190	58		
镇 江	Zhenjiang	24904	168	56	24650	164	56	254	4
泰 州	Taizhou	25407	176	74	25267	172	74	140	4
扬 州	Yangzhou	10228	53	32	10228	53	32		
江 阴	Jiangyin	22705	164	40	21187	149	40	1518	15
常 州	Changzhou	3746	27	9	3746	27	9		
南 通	Nantong	21852	129	46	21508	125	46	344	4
上海(内河)	Shanghai(Inland Rivers)	39844	775		39299	763		545	12

16-29 民用航空航线及飞机架数
Number of Civil Aviation Routes and Civil Aircrafts

指　　标	Item	2000	2010	2020	2021	2022	2023
定期航班航线条数　（条）	**Number of Regular Civil Aviation Routes (line)**	**1165**	**1880**	**5581**	**4864**	**4670**	**5206**
国际航线	International Routes	133	302	895	279	336	623
国内航线	Domestic Routes	1032	1578	4686	4585	4334	4583
#港澳台地区航线	Routes of Hong Kong, Macao and Taiwan	42	85	94	25	27	65
定期航班航线里程（公里）	**Length of Regular Civil Aviation Routes (km)**	**1502887**	**2765147**	**9426313**	**6897750**	**6998940**	**8759598**
国际航线	International Routes	508405	1070167	3828748	1319643	1537440	2843094
国内航线	Domestic Routes	994482	1694980	5597565	5578107	5461500	5916504
#港澳台地区航线	Routes of Hong Kong, Macao and Taiwan	55759	121437	136783	29426	35407	101639
定期航班通航机场　（个）	**Number of Regular Civil Airports Opened(unit)**	**139**	**175**	**240**	**248**	**253**	**259**
民用飞机期末架数　（架）	**Number of Civil Aircraft (unit)**	**982**	**2405**	**6795**	**7072**	**7351**	**7573**
运输飞机	Aero Transport	527	1597	3903	4054	4165	4270
大中型飞机	Large and Medium Aircrafts	462	1453	3701	3840	3919	4003
#波音747	Boeing 747	19	40	23	23	23	23
波音737	Boeing 737	186	650	1500	1506	1484	1468
波音757	Boeing 757	48	48	54	58	67	70
波音767	Boeing 767	16	18	8	13	19	25
A320	Airbus A320	60	281	1045	1129	1171	1217
小型飞机	Small Aircrafts	65	144	202	214	246	267
#ARJ21-700	ARJ21-700			42	58	90	113
通用航空飞机	General Aircrafts	301	606	2892	3018	3186	3303

注：1.1992年以前，民航机场和飞机架数为民航总局直属企业数，1992年起为民航全行业数字。
2.1997年以前，地区航线含民航至香港、澳门航线,与国内航线、国际航线并列。1997年起，民航至香港航线统计在国内航线中，航线里程及运输量统计口径也做同样调整。1999年起，地区航线为国内航线的其中项，仍含民航至香港、澳门航线及运量(以下相关表同)。
3.2011年起民用航空航线条数改为定期航班航线条数，民用通航机场改为定期航班通航机场。

a) Before 1992, the number of civil airports and aircrafts refered to those owned by enterprises directly under CAAC. Since 1992, it refers to those owned by all enterprises of civil aviation. The same applies to following tables.

b) Before 1997, regional routes included the routes to and from Hong Kong, Macao, and were listed as parallel items to the items of domestic routes and international routes. Since 1997, regional routes to and from Hong Kong are taken as domestic routes, and adjustment are also made on the length of aviation routes and traffic volume accordingly. Since 1999, regional routes are taken as a part of domestic routes, and include the aviation routes to and from Hong Kong and Macao. The same applies to the following tables.

c) Since 2011, civil aviation routes are changed to regular civil aviation routes, civil airports opened are changed to regular civil airports opened.

16-30 民用航空运输量及通用航空飞行时间
Civil Aviation Traffic and Flying Time of General Aviation

指　　标	Item	2000	2010	2020	2021	2022	2023
客运量　　　（万人）	**Passenger Traffic　　(10 000 persons)**	**6722**	**26769**	**41778**	**44056**	**25171**	**61958**
国际航线	International Routes	690	1931	957	148	186	2906
国内航线	Domestic Routes	6031	24838	40821	43908	24985	59052
#港澳台地区航线	Routes of Hong Kong, Macao and Taiwan	403	672	96	59	47	668
旅客周转量（万人公里）	**Passenger-kilometers (10 000 person-km)**	**9705437**	**40389960**	**63112770**	**65296813**	**39138743**	**103089790**
国际航线	International Routes	2328154	7589325	4424091	905627	1088690	12295209
国内航线	Domestic Routes	7377283	32800635	58688680	64391186	38050053	90794580
#港澳台地区航线	Routes of Hong Kong, Macao and Taiwan	502405	981817	128296	81928	65140	935537
货(邮)运量　　（吨）	**Freight Traffic　　(ton)**	**1967123**	**5630371**	**6766070**	**7318402**	**6076086**	**7353824**
国际航线	International Routes	492356	1926315	2230742	2667008	2638211	2789940
国内航线	Domestic Routes	1474767	3704056	4535328	4651394	3437875	4563884
#港澳台地区航线	Routes of Hong Kong, Macao and Taiwan	135442	216603	175781	189891	147439	151155
货邮周转量（万吨公里）	**Freight Ton-kilometers(10 000 ton-km)**	**502683**	**1788982**	**2402014**	**2781579**	**2540958**	**2836204**
国际航线	International Routes	291550	1253028	1723269	2075723	2017943	2131522
国内航线	Domestic Routes	211133	535954	678745	705856	523035	704681
#港澳台地区航线	Routes of Hong Kong, Macao and Taiwan	19495	28700	20662	22901	17258	18362
总周转量（万吨公里）	**Total Air Traffic Ton-kilometers (10 000 ton-km)**	**1225007**	**5384490**	**7985060**	**8567493**	**5992786**	**11883381**
国际航线	International Routes	465190	1929689	2108328	2156119	2114179	3210124
国内航线	Domestic Routes	759818	3454801	5876731	6411375	3878607	8673256
#港澳台地区航线	Routes of Hong Kong, Macao and Taiwan	56878	115895	31866	30129	23020	99960
通用航空飞行时间（小时）	**Flying Time of General Aviation　(hr)**	**48707**	**391135**	**983988**	**1178412**	**1219450**	**1370602**

16-31 邮电业务基本情况
Basic Conditions of Postal and Telecommunication Services

指 标	Item	2020	2021	2022	2023
邮政业务量	**Business Volume of Postal Services**				
函件 (亿件)	Number of Letters (100 million pcs)	14.2	10.9	9.4	9.7
包裹 (万件)	Packages (10 000 pcs)	2030.6	1822.9	1757.3	2472.6
快递 (万件)	Express Deliveries (10 000 pcs)	8335789.4	10829641.3	11058122.0	13207461.0
报刊期发数 (万份)	Issue of Newspapers and Magazines (10 000 copies)	11210.4	10907.7	10755.1	10703.4
汇兑 (万笔)	Postal Remittance Transactions (10 000 times)	960.7	646.0	433.3	348.9
纪特邮票 (万枚)	Commemorative and Special Stamps (10 000 pcs)	71371.8	58335.0	53876.4	58607.1
营业网点 (处)	Number of Business Outlets (unit)	349075	412522	433525	467634
平均每一营业网点服务面积 (平方公里)	Average Area Served by Each Postal Office (sq.km)	27.5	23.3	22.1	20.5
电信业务量	**Business Volume of Telecommunication Services**				
电信业务总量 (亿元)	Business Volume of Telecommunication Services (100 million yuan)	136763.3	17197.5	17501.1	18359.3
移动电话通话时长 (亿分钟)	Length of Calls of Mobile Phones (100 million minutes)	44964.5	45592.0	46267.9	45205.4
移动短信业务量 (亿条)	Short Message Services (100 million messages)	17795.7	17619.5	18748.1	18693.2
互联网上网人数 (万人)	Number of Internet Users (10 000 persons)	98899	103195	106744	109225
互联网普及率 (%)	Popularization Rate of Internet (%)	70.4	73.0	75.6	77.5
移动电话用户 (万户)	Number of Mobile Phone Subscribers(10 000 subscribers)	159407.0	164282.5	168344.3	174358.1
#5G移动电话用户 (万户)	5G Mobile Phone Subscribers (10 000 subscribers)		35484.6	56071.8	82196.9
移动电话漫游国家和地区(个)	Countries (regions) with Mobile Phone Roaming (unit)	264	264	264	264
固定电话用户 (万户)	Number of Fixed Telephone Subscribers (10 000 subscribers)	18190.8	18070.1	17941.4	17332.6
移动电话交换机容量 (万户)	Capacity of Mobile Phone Exchanges(10 000 subscribers)	274567.1	275690.8	275194.1	275458.0
长途光缆线路长度 (万公里)	Length of Long-distance Optical Cable Lines (10 000 km)	111.8	112.1	109.5	114.0
互联网宽带接入端口 (万个)	Broadband Subscribers Port of Internet (10 000 ports)	94604.7	101784.7	107104.2	113589.7
IPv4地址数 (万个)	Number of IPv4 Addresses (10 000 units)	34066.8	34388.1	34322.8	34312.9
IPv6地址数 (块/32)	Number of IPv6 Addresses (unit/32)	54593	59995	64318	64403

注：1.电信业务总量2000年及以前按1990年不变价格计算，2001—2010年按2000年不变价格计算，2011—2015年按2010年不变价格计算，2016—2020年按2015年不变价格计算，2021年起按上年不变价格计算(以下相关表同)。
2.快递业务量2006年及以前为邮政特快专递，2007年起为规模以上(年业务收入200万元以上)快递服务企业，2013年起为获得快递业务经营许可的快递服务企业业务量(以下相关表同)。
3.营业网点1998年及以前为邮电局所，1999—2006年为邮政局所；统计口径从2002年起为邮政局所和邮政代办点，2007年起为规模以上邮政业法人企业办理业务的场所(以下相关表同)。
4.2015年移动电话用户统计口径有调整，与往年不可比(以下相关表同)。
5.自2023年起，移动电话用户、5G移动电话用户将中国广电数据纳入行业汇总数据。

a) The total amount of telecommunication services in 2000 and before was calculated at the same price in 1990, 2001-2010 at the same price in 2000, 2011-2015 at the same price in 2010, 2016-2020 at the same price in 2015, and 2021 at the same price in the previous year. The same applies to the following table.
b) Business volume of express delivery services covered express mail service in 2006 and before, changed to express delivery service by enterprises above designated size (with business revenue over 2 million yuan) since 2007, and refers to express delivery service by enterprises with business license since 2013. The same applies to the following table.
c) Data on number of postal offices referred to postal and communication offices before 1998,and referred to postal offices from 1999 to 2006. It included postal offices and postal sub-stations since 2002, and was the business sites of postal enterprises above designated size since 2007. The same applies to the following table.
d) In 2015, coverage of mobile phone users was adjusted, so the data are not compared with previous years. The same applies to the following table.
e) Since 2023, mobile phone subscribers and 5G mobile phone subscribers have include China Broadcast Network data in industry summary data.

16-32 邮政和电信业务量
Business Volume of Postal Services and Telecommunication Services

年份 地区	Year Region	函件 (亿件) Letters (100 million pcs)	包裹 (万件) Packages (10 000 pcs)	报刊期发数 (万份) Issue of Newspapers and Magazines (10 000 copies)	订销报纸累计数 (万份) Cumulative Number of Newspaper Subscribed and Sold (10 000 copies)
	1978	28.35	7400.5	11250.0	1394729.8
	1980	33.13	7153.2	16431.0	1604235.2
	1985	46.78	7612.7	30172.0	2293065.2
	1990	54.87	9690.1	20078.0	1548568.5
	1995	79.55	15641.0	21689.0	1985894.5
	2000	77.71	9600.3	20089.7	1844607.1
	2005	73.51	9531.8	14601.3	1502669.3
	2006	71.31	9317.5	14372.7	1538987.5
	2007	69.50	9103.3	13030.6	1505639.6
	2008	73.63	7936.7	15658.3	1626004.2
	2009	75.32	7229.6	13909.5	1621040.2
	2010	74.01	6642.5	17158.3	1717080.6
	2011	73.78	6883.0	15007.7	1817050.7
	2012	70.74	6875.5	15401.6	1892652.5
	2013	63.41	6924.9	15140.9	1942934.7
	2014	56.10	6024.2	14936.8	1912277.3
	2015	45.81	4243.4	15539.5	1880361.3
	2016	36.19	2794.0	13617.5	1786989.7
	2017	31.48	2657.2	12572.8	1766328.4
	2018	26.71	2407.6	12458.2	1727899.1
	2019	21.71	2155.0	11429.0	1680708.2
	2020	14.18	2030.6	11210.4	1654230.4
	2021	10.88	1822.9	10907.7	1638906.5
	2022	9.41	1757.3	10755.1	1655562.6
	2023	9.66	2472.6	10703.4	1669549.7
北京	Beijing	1.06	132.2	394.8	60572.2
天津	Tianjin	0.15	33.4	86.6	12959.2
河北	Hebei	0.13	142.3	452.1	68768.6
山西	Shanxi	0.06	39.8	326.8	58065.0
内蒙古	Inner Mongolia	0.05	26.8	171.6	29467.4
辽宁	Liaoning	0.14	64.1	398.1	44845.7
吉林	Jilin	0.06	30.3	182.4	24741.9
黑龙江	Heilongjiang	0.13	70.4	219.7	32578.6
上海	Shanghai	1.40	124.7	362.7	66733.2
江苏	Jiangsu	1.32	147.2	809.7	148831.2
浙江	Zhejiang	1.10	223.7	726.8	118861.4
安徽	Anhui	0.48	102.4	424.7	59744.9
福建	Fujian	0.28	86.9	382.5	62464.8
江西	Jiangxi	0.07	81.1	289.8	50849.4
山东	Shandong	0.38	172.8	644.5	108243.7
河南	Henan	0.30	163.2	781.7	104080.1
湖北	Hubei	0.26	66.4	341.5	61834.6
湖南	Hunan	0.09	62.7	426.0	60885.4
广东	Guangdong	1.14	317.8	566.3	66689.0
广西	Guangxi	0.15	36.4	231.2	33858.8
海南	Hainan	0.02	18.0	88.9	15849.8
重庆	Chongqing	0.13	56.1	258.7	25576.8
四川	Sichuan	0.24	84.9	662.7	102894.1
贵州	Guizhou	0.21	15.9	196.4	36412.4
云南	Yunnan	0.06	20.5	232.1	43711.2
西藏	Xizang	0.01	26.5	81.3	16028.2
陕西	Shaanxi	0.09	41.8	354.2	46997.5
甘肃	Gansu	0.07	37.1	205.0	37395.8
青海	Qinghai	0.01	13.5	57.8	10758.5
宁夏	Ningxia	0.02	8.4	50.0	8091.0
新疆	Xinjiang	0.06	25.2	297.0	50759.5

16-32 续表 1 continued

年份 地区	Year Region	订销杂志累计数(万份) Cumulative Number of Magazines Subscribed and Sold (10 000 copies)	汇兑(万笔) Postal Remittance Transactions (10 000 times)	纪特邮票(万枚) Commemorative and Special Stamps (10 000 pieces)	快递(万件) Express Deliveries (10 000 pcs)	快递业务收入(万元) Revenue from Express Delivery Service (10 000 yuan)
	1978	64099.2	11852.4			
	1980	105525.0	13557.0			
	1985	208015.7	16355.1			
	1990	116652.0	16555.8	71233.0	343.3	
	1995	125473.4	23985.1	239250.0	5562.7	
	2000	124449.8	22475.0	453500.0	11031.4	
	2005	100314.6	16052.0	121214.0	22880.3	
	2006	100466.5	18928.0	104580.9	26988.0	
	2007	98104.1	22875.2	113656.7	120189.6	3425851.6
	2008	104220.0	26404.2	131873.0	151329.3	4084274.6
	2009	102073.1	27177.4	110088.5	185785.8	4790030.7
	2010	104756.3	28043.2	114622.5	233892.0	5746029.8
	2011	107701.6	26474.3	102857.5	367311.1	7579878.2
	2012	112009.7	22913.4	118276.0	568548.0	10553324.2
	2013	113720.0	18520.6	118335.3	918674.9	14416815.3
	2014	107618.1	12527.4	138990.4	1395925.3	20453586.2
	2015	99977.1	8241.7	157000.8	2066636.8	27696465.9
	2016	84415.0	5804.4	154320.6	3128315.1	39743601.3
	2017	79261.4	3743.4	140219.4	4005591.9	49571088.8
	2018	77496.9	2520.0	118076.4	5071042.8	60384253.8
	2019	72997.1	1639.7	91800.9	6352291.0	74978235.2
	2020	71321.3	960.7	71371.8	8335789.4	87954342.4
	2021	68740.3	646.0	58335.0	10829641.3	103323162.0
	2022	69216.6	433.3	53876.4	11058122.0	105667264.6
	2023	65147.1	348.9	58607.1	13207461.0	120742722.0
北京	Beijing	2296.8	22.6	4800.2	227115.2	3110046.2
天津	Tianjin	677.8	2.5	1412.5	145024.6	1574105.6
河北	Hebei	2813.6	5.9	2563.3	660073.0	4640536.3
山西	Shanxi	1644.4	11.3	1666.6	110445.8	1102995.0
内蒙古	Inner Mongolia	1008.7	1.3	1309.6	36570.5	633503.8
辽宁	Liaoning	2536.8	10.9	2213.2	218251.4	2002710.9
吉林	Jilin	1327.0	1.1	1305.4	76909.0	831265.1
黑龙江	Heilongjiang	1857.3	1.8	2461.9	94611.7	1059756.0
上海	Shanghai	1471.1	63.5	2689.7	370311.3	20893619.4
江苏	Jiangsu	4389.9	45.2	4253.4	994563.8	8947869.0
浙江	Zhejiang	3933.7	28.3	2475.8	2631955.2	13058532.1
安徽	Anhui	2936.6	4.0	2382.8	410386.5	2663482.9
福建	Fujian	2054.4	8.8	1915.5	498673.2	3886669.4
江西	Jiangxi	1842.0	3.9	1773.7	227930.8	1868015.4
山东	Shandong	4067.4	8.7	3362.0	706967.5	5265683.5
河南	Henan	3179.5	16.0	2405.9	604600.4	4252916.8
湖北	Hubei	1983.9	4.2	2354.1	376892.1	3073467.4
湖南	Hunan	3270.9	5.0	2381.1	310320.8	2174929.9
广东	Guangdong	5226.5	7.6	3453.6	3456729.0	28265755.0
广西	Guangxi	1753.5	6.0	899.6	129972.5	1308869.2
海南	Hainan	448.8	0.4	385.6	21434.9	375450.8
重庆	Chongqing	2842.3	4.2	1235.1	140857.6	1357974.7
四川	Sichuan	3343.0	17.6	2035.1	349483.7	3243577.4
贵州	Guizhou	1751.3	5.6	981.0	66135.7	895716.1
云南	Yunnan	1393.5	36.0	1252.3	109034.5	1140203.6
西藏	Xizang	517.1	3.9	111.2	2192.0	60880.7
陕西	Shaanxi	1328.6	6.7	1484.3	152267.6	1590640.3
甘肃	Gansu	1020.9	5.5	1014.2	29225.0	522921.2
青海	Qinghai	340.2	3.5	328.4	4922.9	127070.1
宁夏	Ningxia	339.2	0.4	633.0	13098.8	193202.4
新疆	Xinjiang	1550.6	6.5	1067.3	30504.0	620356.1

16-32 续表 2 continued

年份 地区	Year Region	电信业务总量 (亿元) Business Volume of Telecommunication Services (100 million yuan)	移动短信业务量 (亿条) Short Message Service (100 million messages)	移动电话用户 (万户) Number of Mobile Phone Subscribers (10 000 subscribers)	#5G移动电话用户 5G Mobile Phone Subscribers	#4G移动电话用户 4G Mobile Phone Subscribers
	1978	19.17				
	1980	22.01				
	1985	36.51				
	1990	109.59		1.8		
	1995	875.51		362.9		
	2000	4559.90		8453.3		
	2005	11403.02	3046.3	39340.6		
	2006	14595.38	4295.4	46105.8		
	2007	18591.33	5945.8	54730.6		
	2008	22247.72	6996.9	64124.5		
	2009	25553.58	7726.5	74721.4		
	2010	29993.18	8277.5	85900.3		
	2011	11725.78	8790.0	98625.3		
	2012	12982.44	8973.1	111215.5		
	2013	15707.15	8921.0	122911.3		
	2014	18138.33	7674.2	128609.3		9728.4
	2015	23346.30	6991.8	127139.7		43038.1
	2016	15616.95	6670.9	132193.4		76994.9
	2017	27596.74	6641.4	141748.7		99688.9
	2018	65633.91	11398.6	156609.8		116546.4
	2019	106810.67	15066.4	160134.5		128197.5
	2020	136763.33	17795.7	159407.0		128876.4
	2021	17197.45	17619.5	164282.5	35484.6	106862.9
	2022	17501.05	18748.1	168344.3	56071.8	94273.0
	2023	18359.30	18693.2	174358.1	82196.9	77914.2
北京	Beijing	633.32	2601.1	4096.0	2061.4	1663.8
天津	Tianjin	205.92	134.7	1907.5	867.6	880.3
河北	Hebei	783.54	763.2	8851.6	4013.3	4352.6
山西	Shanxi	363.57	348.4	4228.7	2061.8	1953.2
内蒙古	Inner Mongolia	333.59	214.5	3052.1	1387.8	1490.5
辽宁	Liaoning	420.19	324.4	5254.0	2247.7	2577.5
吉林	Jilin	244.18	242.8	3055.3	1460.5	1380.0
黑龙江	Heilongjiang	273.28	171.0	3947.8	1740.8	1773.9
上海	Shanghai	645.98	923.5	4691.8	1973.5	2061.7
江苏	Jiangsu	1468.30	1006.4	11027.3	5271.0	4579.2
浙江	Zhejiang	1161.21	781.7	9403.2	4692.8	3711.0
安徽	Anhui	640.56	518.4	6617.9	3122.8	2902.2
福建	Fujian	536.43	1218.3	4970.3	2328.5	2279.7
江西	Jiangxi	459.21	251.7	4851.0	2318.0	1898.4
山东	Shandong	1131.04	1251.0	12139.3	5422.5	5545.5
河南	Henan	1043.12	968.9	10932.1	5387.3	4835.9
湖北	Hubei	601.68	521.3	6320.2	2845.0	2916.7
湖南	Hunan	720.88	629.4	7731.8	3656.9	3497.4
广东	Guangdong	2024.09	2079.6	17237.3	8872.2	7736.3
广西	Guangxi	528.37	331.0	6121.8	2692.8	2938.6
海南	Hainan	154.20	112.7	1206.8	619.5	497.6
重庆	Chongqing	397.13	400.4	4385.6	1966.7	1933.1
四川	Sichuan	994.84	825.3	9701.8	4468.1	4682.1
贵州	Guizhou	463.86	221.1	4554.5	2177.1	2065.5
云南	Yunnan	502.93	307.5	5213.0	2434.4	2182.8
西藏	Xizang	60.85	20.3	342.5	165.3	106.1
陕西	Shaanxi	472.86	850.8	4954.2	2376.7	2110.8
甘肃	Gansu	300.42	208.6	2894.0	1333.1	1356.5
青海	Qinghai	96.19	76.6	739.1	396.8	315.3
宁夏	Ningxia	117.01	98.5	918.0	484.6	377.1
新疆	Xinjiang	372.53	263.4	3011.4	1350.4	1313.0

注：电信业务总量、移动短信业务量全国与分地区合计之差为集团总部及直属部分(以下相关表同)。

a) The difference between the business volume of telecommunication services and the total amount of mobile short message service for nationwide and by region is the difference between the group headquarters and its directly affiliated parts. The same applies to the relevant following tables.

16-32 续表 3 continued

年份 地区	Year Region	移动电话通话时长(亿分钟) Length of Calls of Mobile Phone Subscribers (100 million minutes)	#去话通话时长 Length of Outgoing Calls	固定电话用户(万户) Number of Fixed Telephone Subscribers (10 000 subscribers)
	1978			192.5
	1980			214.1
	1985			312.0
	1990			685.0
	1995	113.4		4070.6
	2000	1845.3		14482.9
	2005	12507.4		35044.5
	2006	16870.7		36778.6
	2007	23061.3		36563.7
	2008	29355.6		34035.9
	2009	35351.0		31373.2
	2010	43261.2	21129.0	29434.2
	2011	50472.6	25056.0	28509.8
	2012	55444.9	27603.5	27815.3
	2013	58229.7	28987.7	26698.5
	2014	59012.7	29270.1	24943.0
	2015	57648.9	28499.9	23099.6
	2016	56599.0	28072.8	20662.4
	2017	54004.7	26904.2	19375.7
	2018	51125.2	25441.5	19208.5
	2019	47826.2	23929.2	19103.3
	2020	44964.5	22448.5	18190.8
	2021	45592.0	22691.1	18070.1
	2022	46267.9	23022.8	17941.4
	2023	45205.4	22397.0	17332.6
北京	Beijing	792.7	400.5	467.4
天津	Tianjin	518.2	263.3	321.6
河北	Hebei	2037.4	991.7	586.8
山西	Shanxi	1290.4	640.4	278.7
内蒙古	Inner Mongolia	880.1	439.5	196.9
辽宁	Liaoning	1348.7	667.3	555.9
吉林	Jilin	763.0	378.1	356.9
黑龙江	Heilongjiang	937.6	461.0	333.3
上海	Shanghai	781.3	397.2	610.7
江苏	Jiangsu	2570.6	1268.3	1153.4
浙江	Zhejiang	2306.9	1136.1	1062.2
安徽	Anhui	1440.1	699.8	510.4
福建	Fujian	1421.1	704.4	671.0
江西	Jiangxi	1086.1	529.6	448.1
山东	Shandong	3767.6	1864.8	1101.6
河南	Henan	2818.0	1377.7	581.8
湖北	Hubei	1482.3	728.2	434.3
湖南	Hunan	2227.3	1102.4	548.7
广东	Guangdong	3626.8	1836.1	1783.7
广西	Guangxi	1090.1	536.7	477.6
海南	Hainan	343.0	211.5	178.6
重庆	Chongqing	1291.4	643.3	594.7
四川	Sichuan	3073.6	1514.2	1942.9
贵州	Guizhou	1570.4	781.0	224.7
云南	Yunnan	1799.1	889.8	247.2
西藏	Xizang	141.8	71.8	88.5
陕西	Shaanxi	1285.8	635.2	664.3
甘肃	Gansu	781.9	383.4	306.6
青海	Qinghai	169.8	86.1	155.9
宁夏	Ningxia	227.3	114.6	48.8
新疆	Xinjiang	1335.2	642.9	399.3

16–33 邮政业网点及邮递线路数(年底数)
Postal Offices and Postal Delivery Routes (Year-end Figure)

年份 地区	Year Region	营业网点 (处) Number of Offices (unit)	信筒信箱 (个) Number of Post Boxes (unit)	邮政普遍服务网路条数 (条) Number of Postal Universal Service Networks (line)	快递服务网路条数 (条) Number of Express Delivery Service Networks (line)
	1978	49623	156398		
	1980	49471	159009		
	1985	53107	174678		
	1990	53629	181877		
	1995	61898	203011		
	2000	58437	239356		
	2005	65917	202259		
	2006	62799	197491		
	2007	70655	195336		
	2008	69146	224023		
	2009	65672	206597		
	2010	75739	171043		
	2011	78667	148206		
	2012	95572	150271		
	2013	125115	147351		
	2014	137562	142330		
	2015	188637	129572		
	2016	216708	127678		
	2017	278025	125409		
	2018	274635	122060		
	2019	318516	119234		
	2020	349075	99582		
	2021	412522	95186		
	2022	433525	92475		
	2023	467634	91249	39566	227508
北京	Beijing	5138	3756	752	15085
天津	Tianjin	7237	2476	321	2292
河北	Hebei	20781	2689	1343	5224
山西	Shanxi	15750	1782	885	3097
内蒙古	Inner Mongolia	7546	1545	1031	2562
辽宁	Liaoning	10952	2275	1474	8001
吉林	Jilin	7222	1368	551	2392
黑龙江	Heilongjiang	11196	1832	813	4298
上海	Shanghai	7843	2540	888	12993
江苏	Jiangsu	30459	5172	3093	23232
浙江	Zhejiang	34261	9931	2474	22022
安徽	Anhui	18952	2171	1173	9694
福建	Fujian	16873	7231	1055	7315
江西	Jiangxi	14682	2031	918	4610
山东	Shandong	28782	3416	2934	11587
河南	Henan	24967	2913	1797	5271
湖北	Hubei	17087	2163	1728	8203
湖南	Hunan	17208	2722	1547	6619
广东	Guangdong	47694	4106	3670	35527
广西	Guangxi	14967	2306	1060	5364
海南	Hainan	3004	2723	406	1338
重庆	Chongqing	11440	1969	661	4162
四川	Sichuan	31829	6662	2911	8718
贵州	Guizhou	15439	1909	843	4636
云南	Yunnan	13613	1858	2019	3977
西藏	Xizang	1182	5399	254	349
陕西	Shaanxi	16616	2114	703	3963
甘肃	Gansu	6901	1784	770	1431
青海	Qinghai	1893	480	461	446
宁夏	Ningxia	2274	380	316	461
新疆	Xinjiang	3846	1546	715	2639

16—34 电信主要通信能力(年底数)
Main Communication Capacity of Telecommunications (Year-end Figure)

年份 Year 地区 Region		移动电话交换机容量(万户) Capacity of Mobile Phone Exchanges (10 000 subscribers)	移动电话基站(万个) Base Stations of Mobile Phones (10 000)	光缆线路长度(公里) Length of Optical Cable Lines (km)	#长途光缆线路长度 Length of Long Distance Optical Cable Lines
	1978				
	1980				
	1985				
	1990	5.1			3334
	1995	796.7			106882
	2000	13985.6	8.3	1212358	286642
	2005	48241.7	36.2	4072788	723040
	2006	61032.0	44.2	4279559	722439
	2007	85496.1	54.6	5777289	792154
	2008	114531.4	69.0	6778496	797979
	2009	144084.7	111.9	8294565	831011
	2010	150284.9	139.8	9962467	818133
	2011	171636.0	175.2	12119303	842341
	2012	184023.8	206.6	14793300	868175
	2013	196557.3	241.0	17453709	890018
	2014	205024.9	350.8	20612529	928398
	2015	218150.0	465.6	24863348	965283
	2016	218540.0	559.4	30420755	994092
	2017	242185.8	618.7	37801073	1044998
	2018	259453.1	667.2	43167888	994130
	2019	272523.7	841.0	47412442	1084937
	2020	274567.1	931.0	51692051	1117923
	2021	275690.8	996.3	54808233	1120837
	2022	275194.1	1083.4	59580032	1094864
	2023	275458.0	1162.0	64317941	1139873
北 京	Beijing	10750.0	32.9	528411	4366
天 津	Tianjin	3366.0	15.6	373817	4653
河 北	Hebei	15609.7	55.1	2728695	38967
山 西	Shanxi	7251.2	32.9	1650832	35555
内蒙古	Inner Mongolia	5863.0	24.0	1688029	75252
辽 宁	Liaoning	6478.6	36.3	1831541	23036
吉 林	Jilin	4183.0	16.3	872212	26413
黑龙江	Heilongjiang	7213.0	22.4	1361903	55123
上 海	Shanghai	7099.0	23.9	786850	4832
江 苏	Jiangsu	21969.1	78.1	4508664	42280
浙 江	Zhejiang	15009.0	73.2	4420720	32424
安 徽	Anhui	11181.3	40.5	2857668	41502
福 建	Fujian	7817.5	41.7	1825282	31167
江 西	Jiangxi	6718.0	34.6	2561057	29588
山 东	Shandong	14713.4	71.4	3717944	36223
河 南	Henan	12919.5	57.4	2426681	42508
湖 北	Hubei	13282.0	41.7	2514594	35887
湖 南	Hunan	10436.6	45.6	3171735	46193
广 东	Guangdong	24521.6	102.4	4101779	66124
广 西	Guangxi	10677.0	35.5	2689019	45392
海 南	Hainan	1964.0	10.0	423739	2893
重 庆	Chongqing	5285.0	29.5	1642354	8193
四 川	Sichuan	16935.6	59.4	4499875	63317
贵 州	Guizhou	5350.0	35.4	1973514	34958
云 南	Yunnan	7424.3	42.4	3085616	64416
西 藏	Xizang	3380.0	6.3	367442	44840
陕 西	Shaanxi	5071.3	37.4	2077741	58412
甘 肃	Gansu	5009.1	22.4	1171319	43970
青 海	Qinghai	927.0	6.9	480753	41990
宁 夏	Ningxia	1343.0	6.3	333735	10603
新 疆	Xinjiang	5710.4	24.7	1644421	48794
不分地区	Not Classified by Region				

16–35 电信通信服务水平(年底数)
Telecommunication Services Available at Year-end

年份 Year / 地区 Region		电话普及率(包括移动电话)(部/百人) Popularization Rate of Telephones (Include Mobile Phones) (set/100 persons)	固定电话普及率 Popularization Rate of Fixed Line Telephones	移动电话普及率 Popularization Rate of Mobile Phones
	1978	0.38	0.38	
	1980	0.43	0.43	
	1985	0.60	0.60	
	1990	1.11	1.11	
	1995	4.66	4.36	0.30
	2000	19.10	12.38	6.72
	2005	57.22	26.96	30.26
	2006	63.40	28.10	35.30
	2007	69.45	27.81	41.64
	2008	74.29	25.76	48.53
	2009	79.89	23.62	56.27
	2010	86.41	22.05	64.36
	2011	94.81	21.26	73.55
	2012	103.10	20.60	82.50
	2013	109.95	19.62	90.33
	2014	112.26	18.24	94.03
	2015	109.30	16.80	92.49
	2016	110.55	14.94	95.60
	2017	115.91	13.94	101.97
	2018	126.00	13.77	112.23
	2019	128.02	13.64	114.38
	2020	125.80	12.89	112.91
	2021	129.09	12.79	116.30
	2022	131.95	12.71	119.25
	2023	135.98	12.30	123.69
北　京	Beijing	208.78	21.39	187.39
天　津	Tianjin	163.43	23.58	139.85
河　北	Hebei	127.67	7.94	119.73
山　西	Shanxi	130.05	8.04	122.01
内蒙古	Inner Mongolia	135.60	8.22	127.38
辽　宁	Liaoning	138.92	13.29	125.63
吉　林	Jilin	145.86	15.26	130.60
黑龙江	Heilongjiang	139.82	10.89	128.93
上　海	Shanghai	213.17	24.55	188.62
江　苏	Jiangsu	142.87	13.53	129.34
浙　江	Zhejiang	157.92	16.03	141.89
安　徽	Anhui	116.46	8.34	108.12
福　建	Fujian	134.86	16.04	118.82
江　西	Jiangxi	117.37	9.92	107.44
山　东	Shandong	130.80	10.88	119.92
河　南	Henan	117.31	5.93	111.38
湖　北	Hubei	115.70	7.44	108.26
湖　南	Hunan	126.07	8.35	117.72
广　东	Guangdong	149.70	14.04	135.66
广　西	Guangxi	131.28	9.50	121.78
海　南	Hainan	132.81	17.12	115.69
重　庆	Chongqing	156.05	18.64	137.42
四　川	Sichuan	139.16	23.22	115.94
贵　州	Guizhou	123.65	5.81	117.84
云　南	Yunnan	116.85	5.29	111.56
西　藏	Xizang	118.07	24.24	93.83
陕　西	Shaanxi	142.17	16.81	125.36
甘　肃	Gansu	129.82	12.44	117.38
青　海	Qinghai	150.68	26.25	124.43
宁　夏	Ningxia	132.63	6.70	125.93
新　疆	Xinjiang	131.28	15.37	115.91

注：2015年移动电话用户口径有调整，移动电话普及率与往年不可比。

a) In 2015, coverage of mobile phone users was adjusted, hence the popularization rate of mobile phones is not comparable with previous years.

16-36 邮政通信服务水平(年底数)
Postal Services Available at Year-end

年 份 地 区	Year Region	平均每一营业网点服务面积(平方公里) Average Area Served by Each Postal Office (sq.km)	平均每一营业网点服务人口(万人) Average Population Served by Each Postal Office (10 000 persons)	平均每人每年发函件数(件) Annual Average Number of Letters Mailed per Capita (piece)	平均每百人每年订报刊数(份) Annual Average Number of Newspaper and Magazine Subscribed per 100 Persons (piece)	已通邮的行政村比重(%) Percentage of Administrative Villages with Access to Postal Service (%)
	1978	193.5	1.94	2.95	11.7	
	1980	194.1	1.98	3.36	16.7	96.5
	1985	180.8	1.97	4.48	28.8	96.3
	1990	179.0	2.13	4.82	17.6	96.4
	1995	155.1	1.95	6.61	18.0	
	2000	135.3	1.77	6.40	16.4	
	2005	145.6	1.97	5.66	11.2	99.0
	2006	152.9	2.09	5.50	11.2	99.4
	2007	135.9	1.90	5.30	9.9	98.4
	2008	138.8	1.90	5.60	11.9	98.5
	2009	146.2	2.03	5.66	10.4	98.8
	2010	126.8	1.77	5.52	12.8	99.0
	2011	122.0	1.71	5.50	11.1	98.0
	2012	100.4	1.42	5.22	11.4	99.1
	2013	76.7	1.09	4.66	11.0	99.2
	2014	69.8	0.99	4.10	10.9	99.4
	2015	50.9	0.73	3.30	11.3	99.8
	2016	44.3	0.64	2.65	9.9	99.4
	2017	34.5	0.50	2.26	9.0	100.0
	2018	35.0	0.51	1.91	8.9	100.0
	2019	30.1	0.44	1.55	8.2	100.0
	2020	27.5	0.44	1.00	7.9	100.0
	2021	23.3	0.34	0.77	7.7	100.0
	2022	22.1	0.33	0.67	7.6	100.0
	2023	20.5	0.30	0.69	7.6	100.0
北 京	Beijing	3.3	0.43	4.86	18.1	100.0
天 津	Tianjin	1.5	0.19	1.07	6.4	100.0
河 北	Hebei	9.1	0.36	0.18	6.1	100.0
山 西	Shanxi	9.5	0.22	0.18	9.4	100.0
内蒙古	Inner Mongolia	145.8	0.32	0.21	7.2	100.0
辽 宁	Liaoning	13.7	0.38	0.34	9.5	100.0
吉 林	Jilin	24.9	0.32	0.24	7.8	100.0
黑龙江	Heilongjiang	41.1	0.27	0.42	7.2	100.0
上 海	Shanghai	0.7	0.32	5.64	14.6	100.0
江 苏	Jiangsu	3.3	0.28	1.55	9.5	100.0
浙 江	Zhejiang	2.9	0.19	1.66	11.0	100.0
安 徽	Anhui	6.9	0.32	0.78	6.9	100.0
福 建	Fujian	7.1	0.25	0.68	9.1	100.0
江 西	Jiangxi	10.9	0.31	0.16	6.4	100.0
山 东	Shandong	5.2	0.35	0.38	6.4	100.0
河 南	Henan	6.4	0.39	0.30	8.0	100.0
湖 北	Hubei	10.5	0.34	0.44	5.8	100.0
湖 南	Hunan	12.2	0.38	0.13	6.5	100.0
广 东	Guangdong	3.8	0.27	0.89	4.5	100.0
广 西	Guangxi	15.4	0.34	0.30	4.6	100.0
海 南	Hainan	11.3	0.35	0.20	8.5	100.0
重 庆	Chongqing	7.2	0.28	0.41	8.1	100.0
四 川	Sichuan	15.1	0.26	0.28	7.9	100.0
贵 州	Guizhou	11.0	0.25	0.54	5.1	100.0
云 南	Yunnan	27.9	0.34	0.14	5.0	100.0
西 藏	Xizang	1015.2	0.31	0.31	22.3	100.0
陕 西	Shaanxi	11.4	0.24	0.22	9.0	100.0
甘 肃	Gansu	56.5	0.36	0.27	8.3	100.0
青 海	Qinghai	380.3	0.31	0.21	9.7	100.0
宁 夏	Ningxia	29.0	0.32	0.28	6.9	100.0
新 疆	Xinjiang	416.0	0.68	0.23	11.4	100.0

16–37 互联网主要指标发展情况(年底数)
Main Indicators on Internet Development (Year-end Figure)

年 份 地 区	Year Region	域名数 (万个) Number of Domain Names (10 000)	网页数 (万个) Number of Webpages (10 000 pages)	IPv4地址数 (万个) IPv4 Addresses (10 000)	互联网宽带接入端口 (万个) Broadband Subscribers Port of Internet (10 000 ports)	移动互联网用户 (万户) Mobile Internet Subscribers (10 000 subscribers)
	1995					
	2000					
	2005	259.2		7439.1	4874.7	
	2006	410.9	447257.8	9801.6	6486.4	
	2007	1193.1	847108.5	13527.5	8539.3	
	2008	1682.6	1608637.0	18127.3	10890.4	
	2009	1681.8	3360173.2	23244.6	13835.7	
	2010	865.6	6000806.0	27763.7	18781.1	
	2011	774.8	8658229.8	33044.0	23239.4	
	2012	1341.2	12274681.7	33053.5	32108.4	
	2013	1843.6	15004076.3	33030.8	35945.3	
	2014	2059.6	18991864.9	33198.8	40546.1	87522.1
	2015	3101.4	21229622.4	33652.0	57709.4	96447.2
	2016	4227.6	23599758.4	33810.3	71276.9	109395.0
	2017	3848.0	26039903.0	33870.5	77599.1	127153.7
	2018	3792.8	28162240.6	33892.5	86752.3	127481.5
	2019	5094.2	29782991.5	33909.3	91578.0	131852.6
	2020	4197.8	31550109.8	34066.8	94604.7	134851.9
	2021	3593.1	33496371.3	34388.1	101784.7	141564.9
	2022	3440.0	35878144.3	34322.8	107104.2	145385.1
	2023	3159.6	38201004.1	34312.9	113589.7	152439.8
北 京	Beijing	589.9	14090056.7	8643.4	2112.3	3364.7
天 津	Tianjin	20.7	634426.7	356.9	1517.3	1644.7
河 北	Hebei	53.0	1468672.3	964.2	5480.5	7892.9
山 西	Shanxi	34.8	436562.0	432.3	2828.3	3721.2
内蒙古	Inner Mongolia	12.2	24420.2	264.2	1792.7	2661.5
辽 宁	Liaoning	36.3	349035.4	1128.9	3720.7	4475.9
吉 林	Jilin	16.8	210693.6	411.8	1923.9	2547.1
黑龙江	Heilongjiang	26.5	199769.5	408.3	2207.7	3229.4
上 海	Shanghai	121.2	2694852.8	1533.8	2560.5	3877.9
江 苏	Jiangsu	123.3	1676782.0	1612.7	8009.1	9386.5
浙 江	Zhejiang	120.1	4582769.1	2192.6	6952.9	8016.0
安 徽	Anhui	73.8	322125.2	559.3	4696.1	5763.1
福 建	Fujian	204.3	1160896.9	658.8	3833.2	4433.9
江 西	Jiangxi	44.9	297612.3	586.7	2834.5	4173.6
山 东	Shandong	151.5	742282.6	1657.3	7657.3	10421.4
河 南	Henan	91.9	2275317.8	892.1	6624.9	9729.6
湖 北	Hubei	67.7	335315.9	813.2	4431.3	5465.5
湖 南	Hunan	78.2	219464.9	799.5	4181.6	6692.6
广 东	Guangdong	769.3	4865059.9	3235.7	10395.2	15814.7
广 西	Guangxi	52.6	273983.0	466.7	4099.3	5450.6
海 南	Hainan	13.2	191580.7	161.3	1142.5	1094.0
重 庆	Chongqing	38.9	61855.7	569.6	2744.5	3686.1
四 川	Sichuan	97.1	651455.0	940.2	6732.5	8843.1
贵 州	Guizhou	175.2	14834.9	151.0	2622.4	4167.2
云 南	Yunnan	27.3	185706.2	329.4	3142.2	4497.4
西 藏	Xizang	1.2	537.7	44.6	311.9	317.8
陕 西	Shaanxi	39.1	198724.4	552.4	3277.1	4346.5
甘 肃	Gansu	19.6	20615.2	161.3	1958.6	2613.3
青 海	Qinghai	1.7	3677.2	58.3	463.0	686.2
宁 夏	Ningxia	4.1	2228.3	92.6	707.9	819.1
新 疆	Xinjiang	8.0	9690.3	205.9	2627.9	2606.4
不分地区	Not Classified by Region	45.3		3431.3		

注：1.各地区IPv4地址数是根据各地区占全国的比例推算数据。
2.自2023年起，移动互联网用户将中国广电数据纳入行业汇总数据。

a) The number of IPv4 addresses in each region is calculated according to the proportion of the regions in the whole country.

b) Since 2023, mobile phone subscribers have include China Broadcast Network data in industry summary data.

16-37 续表 continued

年 份 地 区	Year Region	移动互联网接入流量(万GB) Flow Accessed to Mobile Internet (10 000 GB)	互联网宽带接入用户(万户) Broadband Subscribers of Internet (10 000 subscribers)	#城市宽带接入用户 Urban Broadband Subscribers	#农村宽带接入用户 Rural Broadband Subscribers	#家庭宽带接入用户 Household Broadband Subscribers	#政企宽带接入用户 Government and Enterprise Broadband Subscribers
	1995						
	2000						
	2005		3735.0				
	2006		5085.3				
	2007		6641.4				
	2008		8287.9				
	2009		10397.8				
	2010		12629.1	9963.5	2475.7		
	2011		15000.1	11691.4	3308.8		
	2012		17518.3	13442.4	4075.9		
	2013		18890.9	14153.6	4737.3		
	2014	206193.6	20048.3	15174.6	4873.7	16333.6	3714.8
	2015	418753.3	25946.6	19547.2	6398.4	21716.4	4230.2
	2016	937863.5	29720.7	22266.6	7454.0	24926.8	4793.9
	2017	2459380.3	34854.0	25476.7	9377.3	29552.2	5301.8
	2018	7090039.3	40738.2	28996.5	11741.7	35351.6	5386.6
	2019	12199200.6	44927.9	31450.5	13477.3	38857.8	6070.1
	2020	16556817.2	48355.0	34165.3	14189.7	41833.9	6521.1
	2021	22163224.3	53578.7	37808.2	15770.5	46368.7	7210.0
	2022	26175867.1	58964.8	41332.6	17632.2	50699.5	8265.3
	2023	30253953.8	63630.6	44441.4	19189.2		
北 京	Beijing	668029.5	933.4	855.6	77.8	792.1	85.1
天 津	Tianjin	324323.9	673.4	628.9	44.5	569.8	61.3
河 北	Hebei	1205637.5	3179.7	1912.1	1267.6	2661.8	330.8
山 西	Shanxi	617431.8	1605.1	1320.3	284.9	1305.7	164.9
内蒙古	Inner Mongolia	503971.3	948.5	826.7	121.8	758.1	109.9
辽 宁	Liaoning	665842.9	1689.8	1472.6	217.2	1421.7	148.1
吉 林	Jilin	459703.8	850.8	687.1	163.7	695.2	84.0
黑龙江	Heilongjiang	472928.9	1211.0	952.4	258.6	1008.1	122.3
上 海	Shanghai	546309.7	1205.5	1173.2	32.3	954.9	116.3
江 苏	Jiangsu	2003868.2	4754.6	3207.7	1546.9	3758.1	693.5
浙 江	Zhejiang	1868939.9	3608.5	2094.7	1513.8	2688.6	711.5
安 徽	Anhui	1122600.7	2947.1	1903.2	1043.9	2157.5	509.2
福 建	Fujian	791942.4	2261.2	1436.4	824.8	1811.5	333.8
江 西	Jiangxi	809621.3	2091.3	1440.8	650.5	1636.5	321.7
山 东	Shandong	1875046.5	4581.9	3403.4	1178.5	3730.8	534.0
河 南	Henan	1979683.0	4260.6	3044.1	1216.4	3491.3	443.5
湖 北	Hubei	999160.1	2494.2	1736.3	757.9	1921.7	369.1
湖 南	Hunan	1430400.0	2744.1	1846.7	897.4	2183.0	292.1
广 东	Guangdong	3431672.7	4824.0	3704.2	1119.7	3915.6	713.1
广 西	Guangxi	1070320.8	2315.4	1327.2	988.3	1830.6	223.6
海 南	Hainan	282405.3	578.1	344.6	233.5	433.8	74.4
重 庆	Chongqing	736887.7	1552.8	1121.9	430.8	1271.2	190.3
四 川	Sichuan	1739903.7	3767.8	2190.8	1577.0	3089.2	476.9
贵 州	Guizhou	954356.9	1568.3	1055.8	512.5	1222.8	161.3
云 南	Yunnan	1118034.5	1778.3	1197.6	580.7	1339.0	288.2
西 藏	Xizang	99386.9	145.5	120.5	25.0	107.1	23.2
陕 西	Shaanxi	876588.3	1921.3	1341.3	580.0	1550.0	210.4
甘 肃	Gansu	522490.1	1186.7	749.5	437.2	868.9	223.8
青 海	Qinghai	202283.8	290.6	210.5	80.1	209.4	40.3
宁 夏	Ningxia	208706.4	373.0	293.4	79.6	310.6	38.8
新 疆	Xinjiang	665475.2	1288.3	841.9	446.4	1005.1	169.7

注：1.家庭宽带接入用户、政企宽带接入用户分省数据为2022年数据。
2.自2023年起，移动互联网接入流量将中国广电数据纳入行业汇总数据。

a) The data for household broadband subscribers and government and enterprise broadband subscribers by region are in 2022.
b) Since 2023, the flow accessed to mobile internet has include China Broadcast Network data in industry summary data.

16–38 软件和信息技术服务业主要经济指标
Main Indicators on Software and Information Technology Services

年 份 地 区	Year Region	软件业务收入（亿元） Income from Software Related Business (100 million yuan)	#软件产品收入 Income from Software Products	#信息技术服务收入 Income from IT Services	#信息安全收入 Income from Information Safety	#嵌入式系统软件收入 Income from Embedded Systems and Software	其中：软件业务出口（亿美元） Of which: Export of Software (100 million USD)
	2010	13588.55	4930.53	6529.69		2128.33	267.35
	2011	18848.99	6192.15	9583.07		3073.77	346.19
	2012	24793.75	7857.24	12944.90		3991.61	394.24
	2013	30587.47	9876.84	16030.53		4680.10	469.14
	2014	37026.42	12198.50	18711.09		6116.83	486.71
	2015	42847.92	13656.14	22210.95		6980.82	494.87
	2016	48232.22	15027.83	26090.42		7113.98	499.46
	2017	55103.12	16983.57	30603.71		7515.84	541.16
	2018	61908.73	17378.56	37563.08	1162.92	5804.18	510.66
	2019	72071.87	20857.20	43580.34	1301.78	6332.55	569.39
	2020	81585.91	21045.01	52588.01	1293.78	6659.12	620.17
	2021	95501.99	22970.36	62691.04	1397.04	8443.54	629.91
	2022	107790.13	24862.99	70597.57	1468.93	10860.64	642.65
	2023	123642.74	27714.48	81761.15	1475.57	12691.54	632.00
北 京	Beijing	26693.27	6372.12	19692.29	509.49	119.37	78.97
天 津	Tianjin	3119.48	670.62	2394.68	2.26	51.91	2.49
河 北	Hebei	657.21	69.96	557.71	2.30	27.24	0.01
山 西	Shanxi	112.46	18.93	86.91	2.47	4.15	
内蒙古	Inner Mongolia	9.42	1.50	7.61		0.31	
辽 宁	Liaoning	2334.70	1287.44	906.67	54.23	86.36	30.92
吉 林	Jilin	555.63	117.25	315.80	28.18	94.39	1.16
黑龙江	Heilongjiang	69.10	23.79	36.72	0.69	7.91	0.01
上 海	Shanghai	10789.80	2076.13	8674.11	36.41	3.14	85.31
江 苏	Jiangsu	14386.27	3257.46	8266.22	165.10	2697.48	97.75
浙 江	Zhejiang	9372.63	1691.61	7098.70	35.74	546.58	31.98
安 徽	Anhui	1094.74	503.15	392.36	8.79	190.45	7.09
福 建	Fujian	3073.72	782.28	2018.13	18.07	255.24	8.13
江 西	Jiangxi	269.28	120.26	137.58	1.77	9.67	1.44
山 东	Shandong	12919.85	2871.05	5971.04	229.91	3847.85	15.39
河 南	Henan	767.06	177.10	498.38	9.25	82.33	1.74
湖 北	Hubei	3044.07	600.03	2341.41	18.98	83.65	3.54
湖 南	Hunan	1181.79	325.12	626.92	6.37	223.38	2.98
广 东	Guangdong	20428.87	3875.86	13977.58	126.02	2449.42	233.26
广 西	Guangxi	567.05	26.97	537.12	0.73	2.22	0.11
海 南	Hainan	129.21	12.00	116.73	0.48		0.20
重 庆	Chongqing	3161.83	812.76	2070.44	67.89	210.73	3.79
四 川	Sichuan	5490.63	1618.95	3441.34	139.67	290.67	18.06
贵 州	Guizhou	851.13	65.99	769.32	6.60	9.21	0.07
云 南	Yunnan	141.80	16.36	123.85	1.09	0.50	
西 藏	Xizang						
陕 西	Shaanxi	2300.89	293.92	609.60	1.60	1395.77	7.63
甘 肃	Gansu	45.90	11.66	33.14	0.60	0.50	
青 海	Qinghai	4.91		4.91			
宁 夏	Ningxia	42.24	11.17	29.61	0.52	0.94	
新 疆	Xinjiang	27.82	3.02	24.27	0.36	0.16	

注：2021年及以前本表统计口径为主营业务收入500万元以上的软件和信息技术服务业等企业。2022年起本表统计口径为：(1)主要从事软件和信息技术服务业务、主营业务年收入2000万元以上且软件业务收入(包括但不限于嵌入式系统软件)占企业主营业务收入比例不低于30%、具有独立法人资格的企业；(2)主要从事集成电路设计的企业或其集成电路设计收入占本企业主营业务收入60%以上、主营业务年收入500万元以上的独立法人单位；(3)主要从事基础软件、工业软件、信息安全、工业互联网平台服务或数据服务，且主营业务年收入500万元以上的独立法人单位。

a) The data in 2021 and before covered software and IT service enterprises with revenue from principal business of over 5 million yuan. Since 2022, the data covers software and IT service enterprises for which (1) enterprises mainly engaged in software and information technology services, with an annual revenue of over 20 million yuan in their main business, and software business revenue (including but not limited to embedded system software) accounting for no less than 30% of the enterprise's main business revenue, and possessing independent legal personality; (2) enterprises mainly engaged in integrated circuit design or independent legal entities with integrated circuit design revenue accounting for over 60% of their their main business revenue and annual main business revenue of over 5 million yuan;(3) an independent legal entity mainly engaged in basic software, industrial software, information security, industrial internet platform services or data services, with an annual revenue of over 5 million yuan in its main business.

16-39 按行业分企业信息化及电子商务情况(2023年)
Informatization and E-Commerce of Enterprises by Industrial Sector (2023)

行业	Industrial Sector	企业数(个) Number of Enterprises (unit)	期末使用计算机数(台) Computers Used at the End of Period (unit)	每百人使用计算机数(台) Computers Used Per 100 Persons (unit)	企业拥有网站数(个) Websites of All Enterprises (unit)	每百家企业拥有网站数(个) Websites Per 100 Enterprises (unit)
总　计	**Total**	**1482250**	**65643734**	**39**	**609867**	**41**
采矿业	Mining	11768	1170780	28	3103	26
制造业	Manufacturing	444631	23785176	36	263147	59
电力、热力、燃气及水生产和供应业	Production and Supply of Electricity, Heat, Gas and Water	20207	2867627	81	8710	43
建筑业	Construction	168243	5053012	17	44726	27
批发和零售业	Wholesale and Retail Trades	408349	7926316	59	114307	28
交通运输、仓储和邮政业	Transport, Storage and Post	44522	3378233	41	15603	35
住宿和餐饮业	Hotels and Catering Services	93686	1266809	24	26101	28
信息传输、软件和信息技术服务业	Information Transmission, Software and Information Technology	30694	8204271	126	31652	103
房地产业	Real Estate	119290	2536771	38	33595	28
租赁和商务服务业	Leasing and Business Services	60672	2796520	22	24991	41
科学研究和技术服务业	Scientific Research and Technical Services	31387	3671102	91	20769	66
水利、环境和公共设施管理业	Management of Water Conservancy, Environment and Public Facilities	6258	254153	15	2693	43
居民服务、修理和其他服务业	Service to Households, Repair and Other Services	11724	202941	13	3397	29
教育	Education	5694	945648	114	3793	67
卫生和社会工作	Health and Social Service	8537	930593	62	5756	67
文化、体育和娱乐业	Culture, Sports and Entertainment	16588	653782	69	7524	45

注：1.分行业企业数根据《信息通信技术应用和数字化转型情况》2023年度调查结果汇总。
　　2.有电子商务交易活动的企业是指通过互联网开展电子商务销售或电子商务采购的企业(以下相关表同)。

a) The number of enterprises by sector is summarized according to the survey result of Data on ICT Usage and Digital Transformation in 2023.

b) Enterprises with E-commerce transactions refers to those enterprises which carry out sales or purchases through Internet. The same applies to the following tables.

16-39 续表 continued

行 业	Industry	有电子商务交易活动 With E-Commerce Transactions		企业电子商务销售额(亿元) Sales of Enterprises Through E-commerce (100 million yuan)	企业电子商务采购额(亿元) Purchases of Enterprises Through E-commerce (100 million yuan)
		企业数(个) Enterprises (unit)	比重(%) Proportion (%)		
总 计	**Total**	**203411**	**13.7**	**363802.1**	**186368.8**
采矿业	Mining	510	4.3	2490.6	1405.8
制造业	Manufacturing	57062	12.8	119800.6	76175.5
电力、热力、燃气及水生产和供应业	Production and Supply of Electricity, Heat, Gas and Water	2006	9.9	12231.2	3074.6
建筑业	Construction	4796	2.9	268.1	10582.3
批发和零售业	Wholesale and Retail Trades	70075	17.2	169720.3	84281.9
交通运输、仓储和邮政业	Transport, Storage and Post	4527	10.2	18023.6	3312.7
住宿和餐饮业	Hotels and Catering Services	37608	40.1	3068.4	126.9
信息传输、软件和信息技术服务业	Information Transmission, Software and Information Technology	6758	22.0	25714.0	2790.6
房地产业	Real Estate	3796	3.2	1030.7	142.5
租赁和商务服务业	Leasing and Business Services	5239	8.6	7706.5	3316.7
科学研究和技术服务业	Scientific Research and Technical Services	2390	7.6	1401.6	955.2
水利、环境和公共设施管理业	Management of Water Conservancy, Environment and Public Facilities	803	12.8	268.5	32.5
居民服务、修理和其他服务业	Service to Households, Repair and Other Services	1237	10.6	205.0	38.2
教育	Education	657	11.5	498.5	6.9
卫生和社会工作	Health and Social Service	1511	17.7	218.0	77.5
文化、体育和娱乐业	Culture, Sports and Entertainment	4436	26.7	1156.4	49.0

16-40 分地区企业信息化及电子商务情况(2023年)
Informatization and E-Commerce of Enterprises by Region (2023)

地 区	Region	企业数(个) Number of Enterprises (unit)	期末使用计算机数(台) Computers Used at the End of Period (unit)	每百人使用计算机数(台) Computers Used Per 100 Persons (unit)	企业拥有网站数(个) Websites of All Enterprises (unit)	每百家企业拥有网站数(个) Websites Per 100 Enterprises (unit)	有电子商务交易活动 With E-commerce Transactions 企业数(个) Enter-prises (unit)	比重(%) Propor-tion (%)	企业电子商务销售额(亿元) Sales of Enterprises Through E-commerce (100 million yuan)	企业电子商务采购额(亿元) Purchases of Enterprises Through E-commerce (100 million yuan)
全 国	**National Total**	**1482250**	**65643734**	**39**	**609867**	**41**	**203411**	**13.7**	**363802.1**	**186368.8**
北 京	Beijing	44193	5149193	78	23000	52	10415	23.6	42301.7	22713.0
天 津	Tianjin	26563	1177617	48	8377	32	2553	9.6	8267.5	4556.8
河 北	Hebei	40506	1587107	35	16431	41	3955	9.8	3920.8	1979.6
山 西	Shanxi	27433	974350	29	5350	20	2337	8.5	6351.2	2206.3
内蒙古	Inner Mongolia	12433	646400	38	3480	28	1386	11.1	5316.7	2198.4
辽 宁	Liaoning	31568	1432853	40	10854	34	2730	8.6	7841.3	4025.1
吉 林	Jilin	12758	560264	40	3864	30	964	7.6	1250.9	1247.3
黑龙江	Heilongjiang	14317	626951	45	4262	30	1257	8.8	1469.7	573.8
上 海	Shanghai	51776	5078350	70	31121	60	7661	14.8	47257.7	38057.2
江 苏	Jiangsu	174340	6912347	34	76980	44	20931	12.0	28716.5	13372.8
浙 江	Zhejiang	128374	5568544	36	56199	44	19299	15.0	23463.9	7757.3
安 徽	Anhui	54942	1943200	30	24347	44	7565	13.8	10202.2	4987.1
福 建	Fujian	68109	2154786	29	22056	32	8857	13.0	12541.3	2862.4
江 西	Jiangxi	49923	1246822	29	18284	37	6790	13.6	5007.8	1411.3
山 东	Shandong	120269	3856707	34	50724	42	22920	19.1	33152.4	13864.8
河 南	Henan	71075	1966765	30	25170	35	6438	9.1	9813.3	3953.7
湖 北	Hubei	64218	2250768	34	28337	44	8971	14.0	10550.6	4446.9
湖 南	Hunan	54358	1693084	29	24406	45	7742	14.2	6322.3	3866.5
广 东	Guangdong	195868	11026304	45	93839	48	28076	14.3	53154.0	29140.7
广 西	Guangxi	27680	1017919	35	7460	27	3447	12.5	4022.6	1976.2
海 南	Hainan	6179	266051	47	2160	35	950	15.4	2441.0	636.0
重 庆	Chongqing	27777	1319054	32	11734	42	4790	17.2	9406.9	4917.8
四 川	Sichuan	63196	2793689	36	25153	40	9046	14.3	11126.7	5846.1
贵 州	Guizhou	19084	629810	36	4934	26	2521	13.2	4963.9	1321.5
云 南	Yunnan	24877	887615	38	7484	30	3450	13.9	3135.2	1063.8
西 藏	Xizang	1744	49637	41	664	38	222	12.7	326.1	98.5
陕 西	Shaanxi	30460	1440424	43	13039	43	4093	13.4	5467.2	2906.5
甘 肃	Gansu	12252	428512	33	3700	30	1317	10.7	1403.5	1039.6
青 海	Qinghai	2735	139496	41	867	32	368	13.5	483.8	353.3
宁 夏	Ningxia	4392	205282	36	1540	35	544	12.4	751.0	482.9
新 疆	Xinjiang	18851	613833	33	4051	21	1816	9.6	3372.3	2505.3

主要统计指标解释

铁路营业里程 又称营业长度，指投入客货运输营业或临时营业的线路长度。

电气化里程 指具备了电力机车牵引条件，并已交付运营的线路里程。

公路里程 指报告期末公路的实际长度。统计范围：包括城间、城乡间、乡（村）间能行驶汽车的公共道路，公路通过城镇街道的里程，公路桥梁长度、隧道长度、渡口宽度。不包括城市街道里程，断头路里程，农（林）业生产用道路里程，工（矿）企业等内部道路里程。统计原则：按已竣工验收或交付使用的实际里程计算；两条或多条公路共同经由同一路段的重复里程，只计算一次。

内河航道里程 指在一定时期内，能通航运输船舶及排筏的天然河流、湖泊水库、运河及通航渠道的长度。包括全年季节性通航累计三个月以上的航道，不包括仅供零散流放竹、木排的河道。两省以河为界的航道里程，双方均按一半计算，以免重复。

定期航班航线里程 指定期航班营运里程的总长度，以万公里为计算单位。航线里程的统计分为按重复距离计算和按不重复距离计算两种形式。“按重复距离计算”是指不同航线的相同航段距离可以重复累加；“按不重复距离计算”则不同航线相同航段只统计一次。

输油(气)管道里程 指油、气、成品油等各类介质实际输送距离，是反映运输管线长度的指标，也是计算周转量的依据。对于有复线和备用线的地段，原则上按单线计算管输里程。双线同时输送又不能分开计量的情况下，管输里程为双线长度之和除以2。

货(客)运量 指在一定时期内，各种运输工具实际运送的货物重量(旅客数量)。货运按吨计算，客运按人计算。货物不论运输距离长短、货物类别，均按实际重量统计。旅客不论行程远近或票价多少，均按一人一次客运量统计；半价票、儿童票也按一人统计。

货物(旅客)周转量 指在一定时期内，由各种运输工具运送的货物(旅客)数量与其相应运输距离的乘积之总和。该指标可以反映运输业生产的总成果，也是编制和检查运输生产计划，计算运输效率、劳动生产率以及核算运输单位成本的主要基础资料。计算货物周转量通常按发出站与到达站之间的最短距离，也就是计费距离计算。计算公式为：

货物（旅客）周转量=Σ（货物（旅客）运输量×运输距离）

港口货物吞吐量 指经由水路进、出港区范围，并经过装卸的货物数量。按货物流向分为进港吞吐量和出港吞吐量，按货物的贸易性质分为内贸和外贸吞吐量。货物类别根据现行的交通行业《运输货物分类和代码》标准分类。

民用运输船舶拥有量 指报告期末在水路运输管理部门注册登记的从事水上客、货运输活动的我国企业或私人拥有的营业性运输船舶（含我国企业或私人拥有的悬挂外国旗的船舶）数量。不包括非运输船舶及农业、渔业生产船舶。

民用汽车拥有量 指报告期末，在公安交通管理部门按照《机动车注册登记工作规范》，已注册登记领有民用车辆牌照的全部汽车数量。汽车拥有量统计的主要分类：根据汽车结构分为载客汽车、载货汽车及其他汽车；根据汽车所有者不同分为个人(私人)汽车、单位汽车；根据汽车的使用性质分为营运汽车、非营运汽车；根据汽车大小规格不同，载客汽车分为大型、中型、小型和微型，载货汽车分为重型、中型、轻型和微型。

电信业务总量 指以货币形式表示的电信通信企业为社会提供各类电信通信服务的总数量。计算方法为各类业务的实物量分别乘以相应的不变单价，求出各类业务的货币量加总求得。没有不变单价的业务按其业务收入直接相加。

移动电话用户 指在电信运营企业营业网点办理开户登记手续，通过移动电话交换机进入移动电话网，占用移动电话号码的各类电话用户。包括各类签约用户、智能网预付费用户、无线上网卡用户。

互联网上网人数 指过去半年内使用过互联网的6周岁及以上中国居民人数。

固定电话用户 指在电信企业营业网点办理开户登记手续并已接入固定电话网上的全部电话用户。

移动电话交换机容量 指移动电话交换机根据一定话务模型和交换机处理能力计算出来的最大同时服务用户的数量。按报告期末已割接入网正式投入使用的设备实际容量统计。

互联网宽带接入端口 指用于接入互联网用户的各类实际安装运行的接入端口的数量，包括xDSL用户接入端口、LAN接入端口、其他类型接入端口等，不包括窄带拨号接入端口。

计算机（数） 指报告期末企业（单位）使用的计算机数量，包括台式机、笔记本电脑和平板电脑。

互联网 指在世界范围内的公共计算机网络。它提供一系列通信服务（包括万维网）的接入，并传送电子邮件、新闻、娱乐和数据文件等。

网站 指在公共互联网上，面向公众使用的，基于TCP/IP协议的计算机系统，以域名本身或者“WWW.+域名”为网址的web站点，由地址、软件、硬件和内容组成。

电子商务销售额 指报告期内企业（单位）借助网络订单而销售的商品和服务总额（包含增值税），借助网络订单

指通过网络接受订单，付款和配送可以不借助于网络。自2022年起，该指标包括“通过网站或APP实现的销售额”以及“EDI类型的商品或服务销售额”。

电子商务采购额　指报告期内企业（单位）借助网络订单而采购的商品和服务总额（包含增值税），借助网络订单指通过网络发送订单，付款和配送可以不借助于网络。自2022年起，该指标包括“通过网站或APP实现的采购额”以及“EDI类型的商品或服务采购额”。

Explanatory Notes on Main Statistical Indicators

Length of Railways in Operation refers to the total length of the trunk line for passenger and freight transportation in full operation or temporary operation.

Length of Electrified Trunk Line refers to the length of the trunk line put into operation, capable for the running of electrified locomotives.

Length of Highways refers to the actual length of highways at the end of reference period. It covers public roads running vehicles between cities, between urban and rural areas, and between townships (villages), as well as highways passing through streets at small cities and towns, length of bridges and tunnels, width of ferry piers. It does not include the length of streets in cities, dead end highways, the length of streets built for agricultural (forest) production and inside factories (mines). Mileage can only be included when the road is completed, checked and accepted or put into operation. If two or more highways use the same section, the length of the section is counted only once.

Length of Navigable Inland Waterways refers to the length of natural rivers, lakes, reservoirs and canals that are open to navigation for ships and rafts during a given period. It includes the channels with annual seasonal navigation for more than three months, excluding waterways for scattered bamboo and wooden rafts. If two provinces share one river as the border, the length of waterways will be equally divided for each province to avoid duplication.

Length of Regular Civil Aviation Routes refers to the total length of all routes for scheduled flights, which is calculated using 10,000 kilometres as the measuring unit. There are usually two ways to calculate the route length: duplicated calculation and non-duplicated calculation. Duplicated calculation means that the same segment of different routes can be added with duplication, while the non-duplicated calculation allows the same segment of different routes to be counted only once.

Length of Oil (Gas) Pipelines refers to the actual transport distance of oil, gas and oil products, an indicator to reflect the length of pipeline routes and a reference to calculate the freight-kilometers. For those sections with double pipelines and alternate pipelines, the length will be calculated according to the length of single pipeline in principle. If the double pipelines perform the transportation at the same time and is unable to be counted separately, the length of pipelines will be the length of double pipelines divided by 2.

Freight (Passenger) Traffic refers to the weight of freight (number of passengers) transported with various means within a specific period of time. Freight transport is calculated in tons and passenger traffic is calculated in terms of number of persons. Freight transport is calculated in terms of the actual weight of the goods, irrespective of the type of freight and distance of transport. Passenger traffic is calculated by the principle that one person can be counted only once in one trip, irrespective of travelling distance and ticket price. The passengers who travel with a discounted ticket or a children ticket is also calculated as one person.

Freight Ton-kilometres (Passenger-kilometres) refers to the sum of the product of the volume of transported cargo (passengers) multiplied by the transport distance. AS an indicator to reflect the achievement of the transportation industry, this is an important indicator to show the total results of the transport industry; to prepare and examine the transport plan; and to serve as the main basic data for calculating the efficiency, labour productivity and unit cost of transport. Normally, the shortest distance between the departure station and the destination station (i.e., the payable distance) is the basis in calculating the freight ton-kilometres. The formula is as follows:

$$\frac{\text{Freight ton - kilometres}}{\text{(passenger - kilometres)}} = \sum \frac{\text{freight}}{\text{(passenger)traffic}} \times \frac{\text{distance of}}{\text{transportation}}$$

Volume of Freight Handled in Coastal Ports refers to the volume of cargo passing in and out of the harbour area of the major coastal ports and having been loaded and unloaded. The volume of freight handled may be classified by direction of cargo flow as inbound freight and outbound freight, or by nature of trading as freight for domestic trade and freight for foreign trade. It can also be classified by type of freight based on the existing standard classification for transportation industry "*Classification and Coding for Freight*".

Possession of Civil Transport Vessels refers to the total number of operating transport vessels at the end of reference period, owned by Chinese enterprises or privately, that are registered in the water transport management agencies and permitted to perform cargo or passenger transport activities (including vessels with foreign flags but owned by Chinese enterprises or citizens). Non-transport vessels and vessels used for agriculture and fishery are not included.

Possession of Civil Motor Vehicles refer to the total numbers of vehicles at the end of the reference period that are registered and received vehicles license according to the *Working Regulations for Motor Vehicle Registration* formulated by the transport management offices. Motor vehicles are classified into different categories. By the structure of motor vehicles, they are divided into passenger vehicles, trucks and others; by ownership, into private vehicles and vehicles for the unit's use; by usage, into business vehicles and non-business vehicles; and by size of vehicles, into large passenger vehicles, medium-sized passenger vehicles, small passenger vehicles and mini passenger vehicles, heavy trucks, light-heavy trucks, light trucks and mini-trucks.

Business Volume of Telecommunications refers to the total amount of telecommunication services, expressed in value terms, provided by the telecommunications departments for the society. Business volume of telecommunications is the sum of each service in kind multiplying with its correspondent unit price (constant price). For business activities without constant price, the business revenue is added up directly.

Mobile Phone Subscribers refer to persons who have gone through registration procedures in the operation outlets of enterprises engaged in telecommunications and are hence connected with the mobile phone communication network through the mobile phone switchboards and occupy mobile phone numbers. Included are various types of contracted subscribers, prepaid users for intelligent network and wireless network card users.

Internet Users refer to the number of Chinese citizens aged 6 and over who use the Internet in the past six months.

Fixed Telephone Subscribers refer to all subscribers who have gone through registration procedures in the operation outlets of enterprises engaged in telecommunications and are hence connected to the local telecommunications service provider through fixed line network.

Capacity of Mobile Phone Exchanges refers to the capacity of the maximum services provided to subscribers at any one time as computed based on a certain model of calls distribution and transacting capacity of the mobile phone exchanges. It is calculated based on the actual capacity of equipment connected to network through cutover and put into operation officially at the end of the reference period.

Broadband Connection Terminals refer to the connection terminals to internet users actually installed and put into operation, including connection terminals for XDSL, connection terminals for LAN, and other types of connection terminals. N-ISDN connection terminals are not included.

Number of Computers refer to the number of computers used by enterprises (entities) at the end of reference period, including desktop computers, notebook computers and tablet computers.

Internet refers to the worldwide public computer network which provides access to a range of communication services (including the World Wide Web) and transmits e-mail, news, entertainment, data files, etc.

Websites refer to the computer system based on TCP / IP protocol, which is used by the public on the public Internet. It takes the domain name or "www. + domain name" as the website address and is composed of address, software, hardware and content.

Sales Through E-commerce refer to the total value of goods and services (including value-added tax) sold by enterprises (entities) with the help of online orders during the reference period. With the help of online orders means receiving orders by internet or public networks automatically, while payments and distributions may not need the help of network. Since 2022, this indicator has consisted of two types: Sales made through websites or APPs and EDI-type sales of goods or services.

Purchases Through E-commerce refer to the total value of goods and services (including value-added tax) purchased by enterprises (entities) with the help of online orders during the reference period. With the help of online orders means placing orders by internet or public networks automatically, while payments and distributions may not need the help of network. Since 2022, this indicator has consisted of two types: Purchases made through websites or APPs and EDI-type purchases of goods or services.

17

住宿、餐饮业和旅游

Hotels, Catering Services and Tourism

简 要 说 明

一、本篇资料的主要内容

本篇资料主要反映住宿和餐饮业的发展与经营情况以及旅游产业的发展状况。主要内容包括：限额以上住宿和餐饮业基本情况、经营情况、财务状况；连锁餐饮业经营情况；旅行社、星级饭店基本情况；入境、出境旅游人数，国内出游人数，以及国内游客出游总花费、入境游客总花费等。

二、本篇资料的统计范围

限额以上住宿和餐饮业法人企业、个体经营户，餐饮业连锁总店（总部），旅行社，星级饭店和旅游者。限额以上住宿和餐饮业统计单位是指年主营业务收入 200 万元及以上的住宿和餐饮业统计单位。

三、本篇的资料来源

本篇资料中住宿和餐饮业统计数据是根据《住宿和餐饮业统计报表制度》进行搜集和加工整理而得；旅游产业统计数据主要根据文化和旅游部、国家移民管理局有关资料编制而成。

四、本篇的统计调查方法

本篇资料中限额以上住宿和餐饮业法人企业、个体经营户，以及餐饮业连锁总店（总部）资料采用全面调查方法取得；限额以下法人企业和个体经营户资料采用抽样调查方法推算。旅游数据中国内游客出游总花费、入境游客总花费和国内出游人数等指标采用抽样调查方法推算，其余数据均为全面调查统计取得。

Brief Introduction

I. Main Contents

Data in this chapter reflect the development of hotel and catering services and tourism in China. They mainly include: basic conditions, operating and financial status of hotel and catering services above the designated size; operating status of chain catering services; basic conditions of travel agencies and star-rated hotels; number of international tourists and Chinese residents going abroad, number of domestic tourists and total expenses of international and domestic tourism.

II. Scope of Statistics

Data in this chapter cover the corporate enterprises of hotel and catering services above the designated size, self-employed households of hotel and catering services; headquarters of chain catering services, travel agencies, star-rated hotels and tourists; The statistical units of the enterprises of hotel and catering services above the designated size refer to those with an annual income from main business at and over 2 million yuan.

III. Sources of Data

Data on hotels and catering services in this chapter are collected and compiled according to the *Statistical Reporting System on Hotels and Catering Services*. Data on tourism are from Ministry of Culture and Tourism and National Immigration Administration.

IV. Methods of Survey

Data on corporate enterprises of hotel and catering services above the designated size and headquarters of chain catering services are collected from the comprehensive reporting system. Data on the enterprises of hotel and catering services below the designated size and self-employed households are compiled from the results of sample survey. Data on tourism are from the comprehensive reporting system, except for those on total expenses of international and domestic tourism and number of domestic tourists, which are from sample surveys.

17-1 限额以上住宿和餐饮业企业主要指标
Main Indicators of Enterprises above Designated Size of Hotels and Catering Services

指 标		Item		2019	2020	2021	2022	2023
住宿和餐饮业		**Hotels and Catering Services**						
法人企业	(个)	Number of Corporate Enterprises	(unit)	53711	58182	65666	77628	97971
年末从业人数	(万人)	Employed Persons at Year-end	(10 000 persons)	434.8	424.3	451.1	453.8	528.7
营业额	(亿元)	Business Revenue	(100 million yuan)	10901.0	9367.0	12044.0	11902.6	15966.5
#餐费收入	(亿元)	From Meals	(100 million yuan)	7349.5	6545.7	8498.4	8436.0	11205.5
住宿业		**Hotels**						
法人企业	(个)	Number of Corporate Enterprises	(unit)	23793	25281	27766	30829	36317
年末从业人数	(万人)	Employed Persons at Year-end	(10 000 persons)	182.0	166.6	166.1	161.8	178.5
营业额	(亿元)	Business Revenue	(100 million yuan)	4343.6	3329.7	4071.6	3831.8	5314.0
#客房收入	(亿元)	From Hotel Rooms	(100 million yuan)	2345.6	1777.8	2236.9	2203.4	3202.6
餐费收入	(亿元)	From Meals	(100 million yuan)	1463.0	1100.0	1290.1	1120.9	1480.0
客房数	(万间)	Number of Rooms	(10 000 rooms)	422.8	450.2	525.3	532.7	575.5
床位数	(万位)	Number of Beds	(10 000 beds)	677.5	715.1	796.1	817.1	879.6
餐饮业		**Catering Services**						
法人企业	(个)	Number of Corporate Enterprises	(unit)	29918	32901	37900	46799	61654
年末从业人数	(万人)	Employed Persons at Year-end	(10 000 persons)	252.8	257.7	285.0	292.0	350.2
营业额	(亿元)	Business Revenue	(100 million yuan)	6557.4	6037.3	7972.4	8070.8	10652.5
#餐费收入	(亿元)	From Meals	(100 million yuan)	5886.6	5445.7	7208.3	7315.2	9725.4

17-2 按登记注册统计类别和行业分限额以上住宿业企业主要指标(2023年)

单位：亿元

指标	Item	法人企业(个) Number of Corporate Enterprises (unit)	年末从业人数(人) Employed Persons at Year-end (person)	营业额 Business Revenue	#客房收入 From Hotel Rooms	#餐费收入 From Meals
住宿业合计	**Hotels**	**36317**	**1785144**	**5314.0**	**3202.6**	**1480.0**
按登记注册统计类别分	**By Registered Statistical Categories**					
内资企业	**Domestic Invested Enterprises**	**35575**	**1664216**	**4812.8**	**2944.1**	**1340.0**
有限责任公司	Limited Liability Corporations	33179	1546007	4502.5	2787.9	1238.0
股份有限公司	Share-holding Corporations Ltd.	148	17099	49.4	23.4	15.4
非公司企业法人	Non Corporate Legal Entity	628	62863	156.5	66.2	55.3
个人独资企业	Sole Proprietorship Enterprises	1403	31717	87.6	55.9	26.6
合伙企业	Partnership Enterprises	215	6466	16.6	10.6	4.7
其他内资企业	Other Domestic Invested Enterprises	2	64	0.1	0.0	0.0
港澳台投资企业	**Enterprises with Investment from Hong Kong, Macao and Taiwan**	**508**	**81174**	**328.2**	**169.9**	**100.2**
外商投资企业	**Foreign Invested Enterprises**	**230**	**39681**	**172.9**	**88.6**	**39.8**
其他统计类别	**Other Statistical Categories**	**4**	**73**	**0.1**	**0.1**	**0.0**
按国民经济行业分	**By Sector**					
旅游饭店	Tourist Hotel	14902	1156897	3495.4	1828.4	1174.0
一般旅馆	General Hotels	19313	564909	1647.1	1262.4	261.4
民宿服务	Home Lodging Services	751	12338	33.1	23.9	7.6
露营地服务	Campground Services	37	764	1.9	1.1	0.5
其他住宿业	Others	1314	50236	136.4	86.8	36.5

注：1.本表登记注册统计类别按《关于市场主体统计分类的划分规定》(国统字〔2023〕14号)执行。
2.“其他统计类别”分组包括农民专业合作社(联合社)和其他市场主体(以下相关表同)。

Main Indicators of Enterprises above Designated Size of Hotels by Registered Statistical Categories and Sector (2023)

(100 million yuan)

资产总计 Total Assets	#流动资产合计 Total Current Assets	#固定资产净额 Net Value of Fixed Assets	负债合计 Total Liabilities	所有者权益合计 Total Owners' Equities	营业收入 Business Revenue	营业成本 Business Cost	税金及附加 Taxes and Other Charges	利润总额 Total Profits
17937.5	**7332.4**	**3512.6**	**14538.0**	**3401.8**	**5127.0**	**2379.8**	**70.4**	**-39.3**
14939.9	**6051.7**	**2909.6**	**12401.7**	**2540.3**	**4644.7**	**2200.2**	**57.1**	**-55.3**
14053.5	5755.5	2673.7	11899.0	2156.6	4347.1	2062.8	51.5	-47.7
298.2	99.9	45.1	123.4	174.8	48.4	22.5	0.9	-0.5
446.6	139.9	162.1	295.1	151.6	149.6	56.2	3.6	-14.9
116.7	45.2	23.8	67.7	49.0	83.8	50.2	0.9	7.1
24.7	11.2	4.9	16.4	8.3	15.8	8.4	0.2	0.7
0.1	0.1	0.0	0.1	0.0	0.1	0.1	0.0	0.0
1725.8	**721.4**	**402.2**	**1384.8**	**340.9**	**313.4**	**113.7**	**9.1**	**8.6**
1271.8	**559.2**	**200.7**	**751.3**	**520.4**	**168.8**	**65.9**	**4.1**	**7.4**
0.1	**0.1**	**0.1**	**0.0**	**0.1**	**0.1**	**0.0**	**0.0**	**0.0**
13719.1	5439.9	2918.1	11004.7	2715.1	3378.2	1499.2	57.5	-54.3
3654.2	1668.4	497.0	3109.7	546.1	1582.3	787.2	11.2	12.3
104.5	44.2	18.2	56.5	48.1	32.5	19.1	0.2	0.7
18.8	8.7	1.8	12.4	6.4	1.9	1.4	0.0	-0.4
440.9	171.3	77.4	354.8	86.1	132.1	72.9	1.4	2.3

a) The registered statistical categories of this table is implemented in accordance with the Regulations on the Classification of Market Entity Statistics (Guotongzi [2023] No. 14).

b) The other statistical categories includes professional farmers cooperatives and other market entities. The same applies to the relevant following tables.

17-3　分地区限额以上住宿业企业主要指标(2023年)
Main Indicators of Enterprises above Designated Size of Hotels by Region (2023)

单位：亿元　(100 million yuan)

地　区	Region	法人企业(个) Number of Corporate Enterprises (unit)	年末从业人数(人) Employed Persons at Year-end (person)	营业额 Business Revenue	#客房收入 From Hotel Rooms	#餐费收入 From Meals	资产总计 Total Assets	#流动资产合计 Total Current Assets	#固定资产净额 Net Value of Fixed Assets
全　国	**National Total**	**36317**	**1785144**	**5314.0**	**3202.6**	**1480.0**	**17937.5**	**7332.4**	**3512.6**
北　京	Beijing	1262	86715	455.8	267.5	88.0	1667.6	584.4	393.8
天　津	Tianjin	419	15789	49.2	34.7	10.1	273.7	138.8	41.0
河　北	Hebei	713	45876	99.4	47.7	38.7	379.2	155.0	78.9
山　西	Shanxi	714	37756	70.0	39.8	21.2	253.0	79.6	65.7
内蒙古	Inner Mongolia	428	20549	47.8	29.5	14.4	132.5	44.2	36.6
辽　宁	Liaoning	594	29297	79.9	47.6	20.4	251.4	96.5	52.3
吉　林	Jilin	253	15835	36.3	21.4	10.0	160.3	66.0	46.2
黑龙江	Heilongjiang	307	13741	31.5	20.4	7.0	115.1	39.1	40.4
上　海	Shanghai	1089	71996	392.6	233.2	79.6	1501.9	718.3	203.0
江　苏	Jiangsu	2577	117704	381.5	224.9	124.7	1318.0	532.0	221.1
浙　江	Zhejiang	2338	141250	458.8	253.0	151.9	1536.3	573.1	358.1
安　徽	Anhui	965	45722	105.2	56.1	32.9	334.1	135.5	60.6
福　建	Fujian	1518	91486	301.1	160.3	117.3	1001.9	421.1	175.3
江　西	Jiangxi	1589	53063	137.8	88.2	40.6	362.3	124.0	71.1
山　东	Shandong	2376	102094	278.3	167.3	82.0	727.3	326.2	141.0
河　南	Henan	2018	77740	149.7	84.5	50.8	451.1	186.5	83.7
湖　北	Hubei	1838	62078	175.7	117.3	45.2	416.2	152.5	87.0
湖　南	Hunan	1599	65702	192.1	115.7	63.3	423.0	136.4	78.4
广　东	Guangdong	4105	223763	674.4	412.7	164.6	2232.7	1116.6	320.9
广　西	Guangxi	1115	50172	108.0	74.9	23.9	371.6	143.5	67.8
海　南	Hainan	375	40975	147.7	99.3	33.3	726.6	271.9	242.4
重　庆	Chongqing	729	35956	109.4	70.2	30.5	380.9	185.2	57.5
四　川	Sichuan	2258	100088	261.7	163.4	77.0	866.9	359.5	178.4
贵　州	Guizhou	1017	39145	85.5	61.1	16.7	353.9	154.6	56.9
云　南	Yunnan	1161	56972	137.8	96.8	27.9	507.6	181.9	95.1
西　藏	Xizang	142	5237	14.3	10.8	2.3	61.9	16.7	13.3
陕　西	Shaanxi	1406	72321	180.3	101.3	67.8	602.2	193.8	119.1
甘　肃	Gansu	532	25171	55.2	37.2	15.5	198.8	84.2	43.2
青　海	Qinghai	153	5957	12.6	9.9	2.1	61.5	24.0	12.3
宁　夏	Ningxia	101	4649	10.0	5.7	2.8	29.9	9.7	12.5
新　疆	Xinjiang	626	30345	74.3	50.3	17.5	238.1	81.8	58.9

17-3 续表 continued

单位：亿元 (100 million yuan)

地 区	Region	负债合计 Total Liabilities	所有者权益合计 Total Owners' Equities	营业收入 Business Revenue	营业成本 Business Cost	税金及附加 Taxes and Other Charges	利润总额 Total Profits
全 国	**National Total**	**14538.0**	**3401.8**	**5127.0**	**2379.8**	**70.4**	**-39.3**
北 京	Beijing	1189.8	477.8	432.2	169.3	11.3	29.5
天 津	Tianjin	258.9	14.8	48.5	17.6	0.8	-3.5
河 北	Hebei	381.6	-2.4	95.1	42.7	1.7	-16.8
山 西	Shanxi	241.6	11.5	67.3	35.9	1.1	-10.5
内蒙古	Inner Mongolia	118.1	14.4	45.5	16.8	0.6	-1.7
辽 宁	Liaoning	258.7	-7.3	79.9	33.7	1.5	-3.4
吉 林	Jilin	139.1	21.2	34.6	14.9	0.7	-3.8
黑龙江	Heilongjiang	97.0	18.1	30.2	10.3	0.6	-2.5
上 海	Shanghai	1175.6	326.3	380.0	167.6	6.0	8.3
江 苏	Jiangsu	1035.8	282.3	368.6	167.6	1.6	-3.9
浙 江	Zhejiang	1267.9	268.4	434.5	170.4	4.8	-24.8
安 徽	Anhui	244.0	90.9	101.6	49.4	0.9	-0.1
福 建	Fujian	619.8	382.1	299.4	156.0	4.0	4.7
江 西	Jiangxi	283.5	78.9	134.7	72.6	1.2	4.0
山 东	Shandong	625.2	102.1	265.8	122.3	2.8	2.4
河 南	Henan	341.5	109.6	145.3	70.0	1.7	-1.0
湖 北	Hubei	318.2	98.0	168.6	88.7	1.8	12.9
湖 南	Hunan	321.1	101.9	184.4	106.5	3.0	10.5
广 东	Guangdong	2061.0	172.2	644.1	298.1	7.4	-31.5
广 西	Guangxi	298.4	73.7	104.0	45.2	1.1	-7.2
海 南	Hainan	660.1	66.5	142.0	49.8	3.7	-0.5
重 庆	Chongqing	292.0	89.0	107.8	55.3	1.4	3.6
四 川	Sichuan	725.9	141.0	255.5	130.2	2.5	4.6
贵 州	Guizhou	274.9	79.2	85.8	46.1	1.0	-2.2
云 南	Yunnan	382.1	125.4	133.2	68.5	2.4	1.4
西 藏	Xizang	27.4	34.5	13.8	7.0	0.1	0.2
陕 西	Shaanxi	524.0	78.2	175.7	89.4	2.5	-5.2
甘 肃	Gansu	130.3	68.5	53.8	26.9	0.7	0.6
青 海	Qinghai	42.2	19.4	12.5	6.7	0.3	-1.8
宁 夏	Ningxia	24.6	5.3	9.5	4.9	0.1	-0.4
新 疆	Xinjiang	178.0	60.1	73.2	39.5	1.2	-0.9

17–4 按登记注册统计类别和行业分限额以上餐饮业企业主要指标(2023年)

单位：亿元

指 标	Item	法人企业(个) Number of Corporate Enterprises (unit)	年末从业人数(人) Employed Persons at Year-end (person)	营业额 Business Revenue	#餐费收入 From Meals
餐饮业合计	**Catering Services**	**61654**	**3502009**	**10652.5**	**9725.4**
按登记注册统计类别分	**By Registered Statistical Categories**				
内资企业	**Domestic Invested Enterprises**	**60496**	**2665542**	**8471.4**	**7676.1**
有限责任公司	Limited Liability Corporations	54360	2483889	7817.7	7092.0
股份有限公司	Share-holding Corporations Ltd.	195	57492	251.1	214.8
非公司企业法人	Non Corporate Legal Entity	271	15286	46.7	37.2
个人独资企业	Sole Proprietorship Enterprises	4770	89057	293.1	271.5
合伙企业	Partnership Enterprises	897	19730	62.3	60.2
其他内资企业	Other Domestic Invested Enterprises	3	88	0.5	0.4
港澳台投资企业	**Enterprises with Investment from Hong Kong, Macao and Taiwan**	**767**	**426355**	**1122.7**	**1034.3**
外商投资企业	**Foreign Invested Enterprises**	**380**	**409722**	**1056.9**	**1014.0**
其他统计类别	**Other Statistical Categories**	**11**	**390**	**1.4**	**1.1**
按国民经济行业分	**By Sector**				
正餐服务	Restaurant	53687	2220018	6802.0	6174.4
快餐服务	Fast Food	2762	736051	1933.3	1826.7
饮料及冷饮服务	Beverages and Cold Drinks	1384	168902	741.4	674.8
餐饮配送及外卖送餐服务	Catering Distribution and Delivery Service	2410	204394	649.6	562.0
其他餐饮业	Others	1411	172644	526.2	487.5

注：本表登记注册统计类别按《关于市场主体统计分类的划分规定》(国统字〔2023〕14号)执行。

Main Indicators of Enterprises above Designated Size of Catering Services by Registered Statistical Categories and Sector (2023)

(100 million yuan)

资产总计 Total Assets	#流动资产合计 Total Current Assets	#固定资产净额 Net Value of Fixed Assets	负债合计 Total Liabilities	所有者权益合计 Total Owners' Equities	营业收入 Business Revenue	营业成本 Business Cost	税金及附加 Taxes and Other Charges	利润总额 Total Profits
8811.3	**4616.4**	**934.2**	**6721.2**	**2095.7**	**10124.3**	**5737.4**	**27.3**	**459.2**
7103.3	**3923.8**	**762.2**	**5583.3**	**1525.4**	**8064.4**	**4797.6**	**25.7**	**302.6**
6490.6	3617.3	704.9	5251.2	1244.6	7446.5	4378.2	22.4	254.7
353.8	186.5	21.0	185.7	168.0	236.8	169.2	0.8	17.0
56.5	30.3	6.9	45.1	11.7	43.8	26.3	0.3	-0.1
176.5	74.8	24.7	84.5	91.9	278.3	192.3	2.0	27.2
25.9	14.9	4.6	16.7	9.2	58.8	31.5	0.2	3.8
0.0	0.0	0.0	0.1	0.0	0.2	0.1	0.0	0.0
951.2	**357.2**	**111.7**	**624.5**	**326.6**	**1059.8**	**424.8**	**0.9**	**52.0**
754.7	**334.4**	**60.3**	**512.5**	**242.4**	**998.9**	**514.3**	**0.7**	**104.5**
2.1	**1.0**	**0.1**	**0.9**	**1.2**	**1.1**	**0.7**	**0.0**	**0.0**
6357.9	3296.4	739.6	4990.9	1370.8	6476.2	3673.1	23.8	244.8
1172.2	435.0	135.1	855.0	317.3	1820.5	974.6	1.4	108.2
546.4	338.3	22.8	348.9	199.4	711.0	322.9	0.5	46.4
390.2	303.4	26.2	279.5	110.6	616.2	479.6	1.0	8.7
344.6	243.3	10.5	247.0	97.6	500.4	287.2	0.6	51.1

a) The registered statistical categories of this table is implemented in accordance with the Regulations on the Classification of Market Entity Statistics (Guotongzi [2023] No. 14).

17-5 分地区限额以上餐饮业企业主要指标(2023年)
Main Indicators of Enterprises above Designated Size of Catering Services by Region (2023)

单位：亿元 (100 million yuan)

地 区	Region	法人企业(个) Number of Corporate Enterprises (unit)	年末从业人数(人) Employed Persons at Year-end (person)	营业额 Business Revenue	#餐费收入 From Meals	资产总计 Total Assets	#流动资产合计 Total Current Assets	#固定资产净额 Net Value of Fixed Assets
全 国	**National Total**	**61654**	**3502009**	**10652.5**	**9725.4**	**8811.3**	**4616.4**	**934.2**
北 京	Beijing	2531	292634	1093.6	1008.6	640.0	384.1	47.3
天 津	Tianjin	720	64568	182.8	164.5	120.5	62.0	9.3
河 北	Hebei	900	44163	124.3	103.4	182.3	104.6	13.3
山 西	Shanxi	1109	66056	136.4	119.5	191.3	96.3	29.1
内蒙古	Inner Mongolia	330	26979	59.2	47.2	87.4	37.9	17.4
辽 宁	Liaoning	564	70165	154.4	139.6	119.8	53.9	16.2
吉 林	Jilin	248	14449	38.8	36.0	37.3	20.2	6.5
黑龙江	Heilongjiang	280	10137	25.3	23.4	20.6	10.0	3.6
上 海	Shanghai	2413	318813	1255.9	1189.2	883.1	557.0	39.6
江 苏	Jiangsu	6452	340114	1067.5	966.4	1008.2	509.3	108.6
浙 江	Zhejiang	3480	214551	737.3	662.1	648.3	292.7	76.3
安 徽	Anhui	2092	117523	344.7	303.1	319.8	152.2	27.7
福 建	Fujian	2902	126737	466.6	438.9	211.4	106.3	26.4
江 西	Jiangxi	2553	69843	219.9	201.8	184.0	86.2	30.6
山 东	Shandong	5161	199664	528.7	466.9	555.8	264.6	105.4
河 南	Henan	2132	70227	168.2	159.1	132.3	71.0	16.2
湖 北	Hubei	4981	177024	511.3	466.2	377.7	159.4	58.3
湖 南	Hunan	2627	97318	318.4	288.1	215.3	91.7	27.5
广 东	Guangdong	8142	585683	1656.2	1521.2	1270.1	742.4	90.7
广 西	Guangxi	1119	53844	126.0	109.7	125.5	63.2	17.2
海 南	Hainan	179	12709	36.9	33.0	26.2	15.9	2.4
重 庆	Chongqing	1547	61662	222.1	199.2	180.9	85.6	20.2
四 川	Sichuan	3699	230397	590.1	547.4	593.4	302.6	68.5
贵 州	Guizhou	910	32136	70.3	64.3	121.7	83.1	4.3
云 南	Yunnan	1477	52821	135.5	125.0	116.0	70.9	11.4
西 藏	Xizang	33	1886	5.0	4.0	15.5	3.9	3.5
陕 西	Shaanxi	1907	93106	243.7	220.7	202.1	98.3	26.4
甘 肃	Gansu	590	28342	63.8	55.9	79.1	36.5	13.9
青 海	Qinghai	65	3146	5.6	4.3	9.7	4.3	2.6
宁 夏	Ningxia	91	4183	8.6	7.1	10.7	4.2	2.1
新 疆	Xinjiang	420	21129	55.5	49.7	125.3	46.3	11.8

17-5 续表 continued

单位：亿元 (100 million yuan)

地 区	Region	负债合计 Total Liabilities	所有者权益合计 Total Owners' Equities	营业收入 Business Revenue	营业成本 Business Cost	税金及附加 Taxes and Other Charges	利润总额 Total Profits
全 国	**National Total**	**6721.2**	**2095.7**	**10124.3**	**5737.4**	**27.3**	**459.2**
北 京	Beijing	558.9	81.6	1026.8	502.8	1.2	31.0
天 津	Tianjin	98.7	21.4	174.4	100.4	0.3	8.1
河 北	Hebei	179.5	2.8	118.4	77.8	0.5	-2.4
山 西	Shanxi	167.6	23.2	129.8	77.9	0.6	-1.2
内蒙古	Inner Mongolia	77.5	9.9	56.6	27.2	0.3	0.4
辽 宁	Liaoning	119.6	3.5	146.5	82.7	0.4	6.0
吉 林	Jilin	33.6	3.7	37.5	24.2	0.1	0.8
黑龙江	Heilongjiang	15.3	5.4	24.3	13.8	0.1	0.7
上 海	Shanghai	666.7	216.4	1200.0	571.6	0.8	32.2
江 苏	Jiangsu	758.4	249.8	1020.4	578.1	2.3	58.6
浙 江	Zhejiang	582.6	66.1	671.4	369.3	1.5	19.1
安 徽	Anhui	215.6	104.2	330.0	200.8	1.1	17.3
福 建	Fujian	141.8	69.5	449.8	303.0	1.0	25.7
江 西	Jiangxi	113.4	70.6	212.7	142.3	1.0	17.8
山 东	Shandong	450.1	105.7	505.1	310.3	2.4	28.4
河 南	Henan	83.4	49.0	160.6	93.8	0.5	10.7
湖 北	Hubei	223.8	153.8	490.9	295.4	2.5	46.7
湖 南	Hunan	136.8	78.6	304.6	196.3	2.5	26.5
广 东	Guangdong	1006.6	265.3	1573.5	864.3	2.7	20.3
广 西	Guangxi	95.3	30.9	120.9	75.8	0.4	1.4
海 南	Hainan	20.9	5.3	34.7	18.2	0.1	1.4
重 庆	Chongqing	99.2	81.7	207.2	145.0	1.1	17.5
四 川	Sichuan	410.6	182.8	568.2	300.5	1.7	71.5
贵 州	Guizhou	101.8	19.8	68.2	47.2	0.2	0.1
云 南	Yunnan	66.3	49.7	129.9	88.4	0.5	8.9
西 藏	Xizang	5.1	10.5	4.9	2.6	0.0	0.2
陕 西	Shaanxi	137.4	64.6	228.5	144.3	0.9	10.3
甘 肃	Gansu	58.4	20.7	61.0	38.1	0.3	1.4
青 海	Qinghai	8.8	0.9	5.2	3.0	0.0	-0.2
宁 夏	Ningxia	7.7	3.0	8.2	4.6	0.0	0.1
新 疆	Xinjiang	79.8	45.4	54.1	37.5	0.3	-0.2

17–6 按登记注册统计类别分连锁餐饮企业基本情况(2023年)
Main Indicators of Chain Catering Enterprises by Registered Statistical Categories (2023)

指　标	Item	总店数 (个) Number of Head Stores (unit)	门店总数 (个) Number of Stores (unit)	年末从业人数 (万人) Employed Persons at Year-end (10 000 persons)	年末餐饮营业面积 (万平方米) Operating Area of Catering Enterprises at Year-end (10 000 sq.m)	餐位数 (万个) Number of Dining -seats (10 000 units)	营业额 (亿元) Business Revenue (100 million yuan)	商品购进总额 (亿元) Total Purchases Value (100 million yuan)	统一配送商品购进额 (亿元) Centralized Purchase and Delivery (100 million yuan)
合　计	**Total**	**970**	**64693**	**117.9**	**1638.4**	**499.0**	**3239.0**	**1049.6**	**771.3**
内资企业	**Domestic Invested Enterprises**	**722**	**27055**	**42.1**	**713.3**	**229.7**	**1389.9**	**497.6**	**356.6**
有限责任公司	Limited Liability Corporations	683	25102	36.2	589.8	199.4	1220.9	429.2	306.7
股份有限公司	Share-holding Corporations Ltd.	25	1865	5.8	118.9	29.3	165.0	66.2	48.7
非公司企业法人	Non Corporate Legal Entity	NA	6	0.0	0.7	0.2	0.7	0.4	
个人独资企业	Sole Proprietorship Enterprises	10	57	0.1	3.7	0.7	2.8	1.6	1.0
合伙企业	Partnership Enterprises	NA	25	0.0	0.1	0.0	0.5	0.2	0.2
其他内资企业	Other Domestic Invested Enterprises								
港澳台投资企业	**Enterprises with Investment from Hong Kong, Macao and Taiwan**	**136**	**18285**	**36.3**	**455.9**	**131.0**	**875.5**	**231.4**	**163.4**
外商投资企业	**Foreign Invested Enterprises**	**112**	**19353**	**39.4**	**469.1**	**138.4**	**973.5**	**320.6**	**251.3**
其他统计类别	**Other Statistical Categories**								

注：1.本表登记注册统计类别按《关于市场主体统计分类的划分规定》(国统字〔2023〕14号)执行。
　　2.NA表示企业个数小于或等于3(以下相关表同)。
　　3.2023年，根据第五次全国经济普查有关资料，更加全面掌握连锁企业的经营情况，统计单位增加较多。

a) The registered statistical categories of this table is implemented in accordance with the Regulations on the Classification of Market Entity Statistics (Guotongzi [2023] No. 14).

b) NA refers to less than or equal to three. The same applies to the tables following.

c) In 2023, according to the relevant data of the fifth national economic census, a more comprehensive understanding of the operation of chain enterprises has been obtained and the number of statistical units has increased significantly.

17–7 按行业分连锁餐饮企业基本情况(2023年)
Main Indicators of Chain Catering Enterprises by Division of Economic Activity (2023)

指　标	Item	总店数 (个) Number of Head Stores (unit)	门店总数 (个) Number of Stores (unit)	年末从业人数 (万人) Employed Persons at Year-end (10 000 persons)	年末餐饮营业面积 (万平方米) Operating Area of Catering Enterprises at Year-end (10 000 sq.m)	餐位数 (万个) Number of Dining -seats (10 000 units)	营业额 (亿元) Business Revenue (100 million yuan)	商品购进总额 (亿元) Total Purchases Value (100 million yuan)	统一配送商品购进额 (亿元) Centralized Purchase and Delivery (100 million yuan)
总　计	**Total**	**970**	**64693**	**117.9**	**1638.4**	**499.0**	**3239.0**	**1049.6**	**771.3**
正餐服务	Restaurant	508	12481	34.9	589.7	189.7	1004.5	340.0	228.1
快餐服务	Fast Food	255	29221	62.9	744.0	224.4	1501.2	486.3	363.9
饮料及冷饮服务	Beverages and Cold Drinks	153	20733	12.6	229.6	60.2	540.6	153.4	113.3
餐饮配送及外卖送餐服务	Catering Distribution and Delivery Service	8	138	0.2	4.3	1.1	3.9	2.1	2.1
其他餐饮业	Others	46	2120	7.5	70.7	23.6	188.8	67.8	63.8

17-8 分地区连锁餐饮企业基本情况
Main Indicators of Chain Catering Enterprises by Region

年 份 地 区	Year Region	总店数 (个) Number of Head Stores (unit)	门店总数 (个) Number of Stores (unit)	年末从业人数 (万人) Employed Persons at Year-end (10 000 persons)	年末餐饮营业面积 (万平方米) Operating Area of Catering Enterprises at Year-end (10 000 sq.m)	餐位数 (万个) Number of Dining-seats (10 000 units)	营业额 (亿元) Business Revenue (100 million yuan)	商品购进总额 (亿元) Total Purchases Value (100 million yuan)	统一配送商品购进额 (亿元) Centralized Purchase and Delivery (100 million yuan)
	2005	300	9748	50.1	478.1	245.8	454.4	171.5	109.1
	2006	349	11360	55.7	588.2	274.8	563.8	201.2	127.5
	2007	358	12743	62.6	629.2	280.0	640.0	274.9	168.8
	2008	453	12561	66.1	651.9	253.1	806.9	271.6	192.5
	2009	426	13739	65.2	691.6	248.9	879.3	362.0	239.8
	2010	415	15333	70.6	742.6	263.8	955.4	455.8	298.8
	2011	428	16285	83.3	821.4	277.1	1120.4	518.9	343.1
	2012	456	18153	80.6	869.2	286.5	1283.3	561.4	388.5
	2013	454	20554	80.3	937.1	319.5	1319.6	571.2	400.7
	2014	465	22494	78.0	1020.0	338.6	1391.0	583.4	413.9
	2015	455	23721	71.4	970.9	333.6	1526.6	577.0	462.5
	2016	459	25634	75.6	1036.9	341.1	1635.2	612.4	494.1
	2017	463	27478	78.0	1075.4	337.9	1735.5	613.3	489.5
	2018	482	31001	89.3	1075.0	332.6	1950.0	674.0	504.1
	2019	495	34356	93.5	1151.5	346.6	2234.5	774.3	563.6
	2020	504	37217	97.2	1216.2	381.2	2019.3	655.9	464.9
	2021	553	43250	106.0	1339.2	398.5	2525.2	834.6	588.9
	2022	564	47631	98.4	1395.1	461.4	2332.8	766.6	573.5
	2023	970	64693	117.9	1638.4	499.0	3239.0	1049.6	771.3
北 京	Beijing	112	8680	16.9	228.7	60.9	520.1	152.2	131.2
天 津	Tianjin	22	1255	3.4	42.9	11.4	74.8	27.6	7.7
河 北	Hebei	9	142	0.2	7.7	1.4	5.1	1.9	0.5
山 西	Shanxi	6	286	0.7	7.9	2.4	14.4	5.9	5.9
内蒙古	Inner Mongolia	6	127	0.3	4.1	1.2	6.4	2.9	2.7
辽 宁	Liaoning	20	1625	4.5	52.1	14.3	74.5	21.8	19.9
吉 林	Jilin	NA	96	0.0	1.7	0.2	1.2	0.5	0.5
黑龙江	Heilongjiang	5	135	0.2	4.5	1.2	6.1	2.2	1.8
上 海	Shanghai	136	13119	18.6	254.8	83.2	599.4	177.2	133.1
江 苏	Jiangsu	47	4051	7.8	90.2	30.7	213.3	78.4	34.8
浙 江	Zhejiang	48	3583	6.3	90.8	26.4	204.6	63.4	43.6
安 徽	Anhui	21	1649	2.9	45.8	20.3	93.7	43.8	35.0
福 建	Fujian	33	2191	4.1	43.7	12.1	83.3	24.0	20.0
江 西	Jiangxi	20	532	0.8	11.5	3.7	19.9	9.8	9.0
山 东	Shandong	48	2056	3.2	74.1	17.0	88.7	24.3	21.5
河 南	Henan	12	669	1.0	15.2	6.6	24.7	10.2	8.6
湖 北	Hubei	56	3175	5.1	80.9	23.5	135.8	65.2	19.3
湖 南	Hunan	35	2542	4.7	77.5	28.1	97.9	31.8	28.7
广 东	Guangdong	208	10757	19.3	258.2	67.4	517.9	151.0	116.8
广 西	Guangxi	19	825	1.0	11.4	3.5	21.9	7.3	6.4
海 南	Hainan	13	267	0.4	8.2	2.5	13.1	4.9	4.8
重 庆	Chongqing	13	2021	3.4	63.3	18.1	95.9	36.9	24.9
四 川	Sichuan	23	2663	9.7	110.4	50.1	242.4	78.5	69.8
贵 州	Guizhou	7	149	0.2	3.4	0.7	4.3	0.3	0.3
云 南	Yunnan	9	253	0.5	6.4	2.0	13.8	3.5	3.5
西 藏	Xizang								
陕 西	Shaanxi	23	1156	1.8	24.9	6.8	48.8	16.5	14.2
甘 肃	Gansu	4	119	0.3	3.7	1.2	5.8	2.8	2.8
青 海	Qinghai								
宁 夏	Ningxia								
新 疆	Xinjiang	11	569	0.6	14.4	1.9	11.0	4.7	4.3

注：门店总数全国总计中包括开设在港澳台地区和国外的门店。
a) Total number of stores includes those located in Hong Kong, Macao and Taiwan province and in foreign countries.

17–9 旅游发展情况
Main Indicators of Tourism

指　　标	Item	2019	2020	2021	2022	2023
旅行社数（个）	**Number of Travel Agencies (unit)**	**38943**	**31074**	**31001**	**32603**	**39580**
星级饭店数（个）	**Number of Star-rated Hotels (unit)**	**10130**	**8430**	**7676**	**7337**	**7245**
入境游客（万人次）	**Number of Overseas Visitor Arrivals(10 000 person-times)**	**14530.78**				**8202.54**
外国人	Foreigners	3188.34				1378.38
港澳同胞	Chinese Compatriots from Hong Kong and Macao	10729.01				6627.05
台湾同胞	Chinese Compatriots from Taiwan Province	613.42				197.10
#入境过夜游客	Overnight Tourists	6572.52				3431.05
国内居民出境人数(万人次)	**Number of Chinese Outbound Visitors(10 000 person-times)**	**16920.54**				**10096.50**
#因私出境人数	For Private Purpose	16211.43				9684.49
国内游客（亿人次）	**Number of Domestic Visitors (100 million person-times)**	**60.06**	**28.79**	**32.46**	**25.30**	**48.91**
旅游总花费	**Total Expenses of Tourism**					
入境游客总花费（亿美元）	Total Expenses of Inbound Tourists (100 million USD)	1312.54				529.60
国内游客出游总花费(亿元)	Total Travel Expenses of Domestic Tourists(100 million yuan)	57250.92	22286.00	29190.75	20444.00	49133.10

17–10 国内旅游情况
Domestic Tourism

年　份 Year	国内出游人数（百万人次） Number of Domestic Tourists (million person-times)	城镇居民 Urban Residents	农村居民 Rural Residents	国内游客出游总花费（亿元） Total Travel Expenses of Domestic Tourists (100 million yuan)	城镇居民 Urban Residents	农村居民 Rural Residents	人均花费（元） Per Capita Expenditure (yuan)	城镇居民 Urban Residents	农村居民 Rural Residents
1994	524	205	319	1023.5	848.2	175.3	195.3	414.7	54.9
1995	629	246	383	1375.7	1140.1	235.6	218.7	464.0	61.5
1996	639	256	383	1638.4	1368.4	270.0	256.2	534.1	70.5
1997	644	259	385	2112.7	1551.8	560.9	328.1	599.8	145.7
1998	694	250	445	2391.2	1515.1	876.1	345.0	607.0	197.0
1999	719	284	435	2831.9	1748.2	1083.7	394.0	614.8	249.5
2000	744	329	415	3175.5	2235.3	940.3	426.6	678.6	226.6
2001	784	375	409	3522.4	2651.7	870.7	449.5	708.3	212.7
2002	878	385	493	3878.4	2848.1	1030.3	441.8	739.7	209.1
2003	870	351	519	3442.3	2404.1	1038.2	395.7	684.9	200.0
2004	1102	459	643	4710.7	3359.0	1351.7	427.5	731.8	210.2
2005	1212	496	716	5285.9	3656.1	1629.7	436.1	737.1	227.6
2006	1394	576	818	6229.7	4414.7	1815.0	446.9	766.4	221.9
2007	1610	612	998	7770.6	5550.4	2220.2	482.6	906.9	222.5
2008	1712	703	1009	8749.3	5971.7	2777.6	511.0	849.4	275.3
2009	1902	903	999	10183.7	7233.8	2949.9	535.4	801.1	295.3
2010	2103	1065	1038	12579.8	9403.8	3176.0	598.2	883.0	306.0
2011	2641	1687	954	19305.4	14808.6	4496.8	731.0	877.8	471.4
2012	2957	1933	1024	22706.2	17678.0	5028.2	767.9	914.5	491.0
2013	3262	2186	1076	26276.1	20692.6	5583.5	805.5	946.6	518.9
2014	3611	2483	1128	30311.9	24219.8	6092.1	839.7	975.4	540.2
2015	3990	2802	1188	34195.1	27610.9	6584.2	857.0	985.5	554.2
2016	4435	3195	1240	39389.8	32241.9	7147.9	888.2	1009.1	576.4
2017	5001	3677	1324	45660.8	37673.0	7987.7	913.0	1024.6	603.3
2018	5539	4119	1420	51278.3	42590.0	8688.3	925.8	1034.0	611.9
2019	6006	4471	1535	57250.9	47509.0	9741.9	953.3	1062.6	634.7
2020	2879	2065	814	22286.3	17966.5	4319.8	774.1	870.3	530.5
2021	3246	2342	904	29190.7	23644.2	5546.6	899.3	1009.6	613.6
2022	2530	1928	601	20444.0	16881.3	3562.7	808.1	875.6	592.8
2023	4891	3758	1133	49133.1	41780.5	7352.6	1004.6	1111.8	649.0

17−11 入境游客总花费及构成

Total Expenses of Inbound Tourists and Composition

指 标	Item	2018		2019	
		数 额 (亿美元) Value (100 million USD)	比 重 (%) Percentage (%)	数 额 (亿美元) Value (100 million USD)	比 重 (%) Percentage (%)
总计	**Total**	**1271.03**	**100.0**	**1312.54**	**100.0**
长途交通	Long Distance Transportation	366.31	28.8	401.91	30.6
民航	Civil Aviation	333.53	26.2	369.02	28.1
铁路	Railway	13.52	1.1	14.10	1.1
汽车	Highway	13.72	1.1	15.93	1.2
轮船	Waterway	5.54	0.4	2.85	0.2
游览	Sightseeing	53.71	4.2	58.66	4.5
住宿	Accommodation	181.09	14.2	200.49	15.3
餐饮	Food and Beverage	142.55	11.2	160.41	12.2
商品销售	Shopping	327.61	25.8	302.97	23.1
娱乐	Entertainment	45.82	3.6	44.21	3.4
邮电通讯	Postal and Communication Services	11.62	0.9	7.47	0.6
市内交通	Local Transportation	27.76	2.2	34.53	2.6
其他服务	Other Service	114.54	9.0	101.89	7.8

17−12 入境外国游客分组构成

Number of Overseas Visitor Arrivals by Gender, Age and Purpose

指 标	Item	2018		2019	
		人 数 (万人次) Persons (10 000 person-times)	比 重 (%) Percentage (%)	人 数 (万人次) Persons (10 000 person-times)	比 重 (%) Percentage (%)
总 计	**Total**	**4795.11**	**100.0**	**4911.36**	**100.0**
按性别分	By Gender				
男	Male	2859.71	59.6	2881.29	58.7
女	Female	1935.39	40.4	2030.07	41.3
按年龄分	By Age				
14岁及以下	14 and under	161.18	3.4	184.92	3.8
15至24岁	15-24	656.71	13.7	686.20	14.0
25至44岁	25-44	2394.69	49.9	2439.71	49.7
45至64岁	45-64	1363.24	28.4	1365.75	27.8
65岁以上	65 and Over	219.28	4.6	234.77	4.8
按事由分类	By Purpose				
会议/商务	Meeting /Business	614.70	12.8	628.47	12.8
观光休闲	Sightseeing and Leisure	1608.57	33.5	1740.31	35.4
探亲访友	Visiting Relatives and Friends	132.24	2.8	143.17	2.9
服务员工	Worker and Crew	744.86	15.5	714.01	14.5
其他	Others	1694.74	35.3	1685.40	34.3

注：本表中入境外国游客含边民入境人数。

a) Visitor arrivals include arrivals of population inhabitating in border areas to China.

主要统计指标解释

住宿业　指为旅行者提供短期留宿场所的活动，有些单位只提供住宿，也有些单位提供住宿、饮食、商务、娱乐一体的服务，不包括主要按月或按年长期出租房屋住所的活动。

餐饮业　指通过即时制作加工、商业销售和服务性劳动等，向消费者提供食品和消费场所及设施的服务。

营业额　指本单位在经营活动中，因提供服务或销售商品等取得的全部收入（含增值税），收入主要来源于提供客房及餐饮服务、商品销售和其他服务，如商务服务。不包括多产业法人企业附营的其他行业产业活动单位的餐费收入、商品销售收入等各项收入。其中，客房收入指本单位在经营活动中因提供住宿服务取得的收入（含增值税）。不包括多产业法人企业附营的其他行业产业活动单位的客房收入。餐费收入指本单位为顾客提供就餐服务取得的收入（含增值税）。包括：经烹饪、调制加工后出售的各种食品，如主食、炒菜、凉拌菜等的收入。不包括多产业法人企业附营的其他行业产业活动单位的餐费收入。

入境游客　指报告期内来中国（大陆）观光、度假、探亲访友、就医疗养、购物、参加会议或从事经济、文化、体育、宗教活动的外国人、港澳台同胞等游客（即入境旅游人数）。统计时，入境游客按每入境一次统计 1 人次。入境游客包括入境过夜游客和入境一日游游客。

出境人数（出境游客）　指中国（大陆）居民因公或因私出境前往其他国家、中国香港特别行政区、澳门特别行政区和台湾省观光、度假、探亲访友、就医疗养、购物、参加会议或从事经济、文化、体育、宗教活动的人数（即出境游客）。统计时，出境游客按每出境一次统计 1 人次。

国内出游人数　指报告期内在中国（大陆）观光游览、度假、探亲访友、就医疗养、购物、参加会议或从事经济、文化、体育、宗教活动的中国（大陆）居民人数，其出游的目的不是通过所从事的活动谋取报酬。统计时，国内游客按每出游一次统计 1 人次。

入境游客总花费　指入境游客在中国(大陆)境内旅行、游览过程中用于交通、参观游览、住宿、餐饮、购物、娱乐等全部花费。

国内游客出游总花费　指国内游客在国内旅行、游览过程中用于交通、参观游览、住宿、餐饮、购物、娱乐等全部花费。

星级饭店　指设备、设施、服务符合《旅游饭店星级的划分与评定》（GB/T14308-2010）标准，经过有关旅游管理权威部门评定（验收）后授予“星级”称号的饭店。

Explanatory Notes on Main Statistical Indicators

Hotel Services refer to short-term accommodation services provided to visitors. Some units may provide only accommodation while others provide a combination of accommodation, meals, business services and recreational facilities. It excludes activities related to the provision of long-term primary residences, typically leased on a monthly or annual basis.

Catering Services refer to the activities of providing foods, serving locations and facilities to customers through instant processing, commercial sales and service-type labor.

Business Revenue refers to total revenue (including VAT) received from providing services or selling commodities through business activities. Revenue comes mainly from providing hotels and catering services, selling of commodities and other services, such as commodity services. It does not include revenue from providing meals or selling of commodities by establishments affiliated to other multi-industrial corporate enterprises. Income from hotel rooms refers to income (including VAT) from providing lodging services through business activities. Income from meals refers to income (including VAT) from providing catering services, including selling of cooked or prepared foods, such as staple food, cooked dishes, or cold dishes. It does not include income from meals provided by establishments affiliated to other multi-industrial corporate enterprises.

Overseas Visitor Arrivals refer to the number of tourists of foreigners, Chinese compatriots from Hong Kong, Macao and Taiwan who come to China (mainland) within the reference period for sight-seeing, vacation, visiting relatives, medical treatment, shopping, attending conference, or to engage in economic, cultural, sports and religious activities (namely the number of overseas visitor arrivals). In compiling statistics, each arrival is counted as one person-time. Overseas visitor arrivals includes inbound overnight tourists and one-day tourists.

Number of Chinese Residents Going Abroad (Chinese Outbound Visitors) refers to the number of Chinese (mainland) residents going to other countries, Hong Kong Special Administrative Region, Macao Special Administrative Region and Taiwan Province on official or private purposes, for sight-seeing, vacation, visiting relatives, medical treatment, shopping, attending conference, or to engage in economic, cultural, sports and religious activities (namely the Chinese outbound visitors). In compiling statistics, each outbound travel is counted as one person-time.

Number of Domestic Tourists refers to the number of Chinese (mainland) residents who travel within China (mainland) for sight-seeing, vacation, visiting relatives, medical treatment, shopping, attending conference, or to engage in economic, cultural, sports and religious activities. In compiling statistics, each travel is counted as one person-time.

Total Expenses of International Tourism refer to the total expenses of overseas visitors during their stay in the mainland of China on transportation, sighting, accommodation, food, shopping and entertainment.

Total Expenses of Domestic Tourism refer to the total expenses of domestic tourists on transportation, sighting, accommodation, food, shopping and entertainment while they travel.

Star-rated Hotels refer to hotels rated with stars as evaluated (accepted) by the relevant tourism authorities according to GB/T14308-2010 standard with reference to their infrastructure, facilities and service levels.

18

金融业

Financial Intermediation

简 要 说 明

一、本篇资料的主要内容

本篇反映我国金融、证券和保险业发展情况。有以下四个部分：一是金融机构金融活动情况，二是存贷款利率调整情况，三是直接融资情况，四是保险业务情况。

二、本篇各部分资料来源

1.反映金融机构活动情况的资料包括：金融机构人民币信贷收支表(资金来源)、金融机构人民币信贷收支表(资金运用)、货币供应量（年底余额）、货币供应量同比增长率、黄金和外汇储备、人民币汇率(年平均价)、货币当局资产负债表（年底余额)、其他存款性公司资产负债表（年底余额)、外资银行资产负债表（年底余额)、社会融资规模增量及构成、社会融资规模存量及增长率。金融机构信贷收支表的统计范围包括中国人民银行、银行业存款类金融机构、银行业非存款类金融机构。银行业存款类金融机构包括银行、信用社和财务公司；银行业非存款类金融机构包括信托投资公司、金融租赁公司、汽车金融公司和贷款公司。中国人民银行总行根据金融机构的基层单位全面填报、并按各自系统汇总的资料，进行归并和汇总，最后得到金融机构的信贷收支表。人民币汇率（年平均价）、黄金和外汇储备表由国家外汇管理局提供，其中黄金和外汇储备表中的资料取自于官方储备资产表。

2.反映存贷款利率调整情况的金融机构人民币存款基准利率、人民币贷款基准利率和贷款市场报价利率，数据由中国人民银行提供。

3.反映直接融资情况的证券市场基本情况、上市公司数量、证券市场发行情况、股票交易情况，资料由中国证券监督管理委员会提供。

4.反映保险业务情况的保险公司业务经济技术指标、保险公司资产情况、保险公司资金运用情况、各地区原保险保费收入和赔付支出情况，数据由国家金融监督管理总局提供。

Brief Introduction

I. Main Contents

Data in this chapter reflect the development of China's financial, securities and insurance industries, in the following four aspects: (1) the financial activities of the financial institutions; (2) the adjustment of deposit and loan interest rates; (3) the situation regarding direct financing; (4) the situation regarding the insurance business.

II. Sources of Data

(1) Data on the activities of financial institutions are balance sheet of RMB credit funds of financial institutions (funds sources), balance sheet of RMB credit funds of financial institutions (funds uses), money supply (balance at year-end), growth rate of money supply over the previous corresponding period, gold and foreign exchange reserves, RMB exchange rate (annual average price), balance sheet of monetary authority (balance at year-end), balance sheet of other depository corporations (balance at year-end), balance sheet of foreign-funded banks at year-end, statistics on increment of all-system financing aggregates and composition, statistics on stock of all-system financing aggregates and composition. Statistical scope of balance sheet of credit funds of financial institutions and data on cash income and expenditure cover the People's Bank of China, banking depository financial institutions, banking non-depository financial institutions. Banking depository financial institutions include banks, credit cooperatives and finance companies; Banking non-depository financial institutions include financial trust and investment companies, financial leasing companies, auto financing companies and loan companies. The grassroots units of the above financial institutions fill out the questionnaires and report to the higher authority. The higher authorities tabulate the data level by level. Finally, the Head Office of the People's Bank of China tabulates the data to obtain the national total. The RMB exchange rate (annual average price), gold and foreign exchange reserve table are provided by the State Administration of Foreign Exchange, and the data in the gold and foreign exchange reserve table are taken from the official reserve asset table.

(2) The data of RMB statutory deposit benchmark interest rate, RMB loan benchmark interest rate and loan market quoted interest rate of financial institutions reflecting the adjustment of deposit and loan interest rate shall be provided by the People's Bank of China.

(3) General statistics on securities markets, the number of listed companies, the issuance of securities markets and statistics of stock trading show the situation regarding direct financing. Data are provided by China Securities Regulatory Commission.

(4) Economic and technical indicators of insurance companies, situations of assets of insurance company, fund uses of insurance company, premium of primary insurance and payment by region show the business situation of the insurance industry, with data from the insurance statistics compiled by the China Securities Regulatory Commission.

18-1 货币供应量（年底余额）
Money Supply at Year-end

单位：亿元 (100 million yuan)

年 份 Year	货币和准货币 (M_2) Money and Quasi-money (M_2)	货 币			准货币			
		(M_1) Money (M_1)	流通中货币 (M_0) Currency in Circulation (M_0)	单位活期存款 Corporate Demand Deposits	Quasi-money	单位定期存款 Corporate Time Deposits	个人存款 Personal Deposits	其他存款 Other Deposits
1990	15293.4	6950.7	2644.4	4306.3	8342.7			
1991	19349.9	8633.3	3177.8	5455.5	10716.6			
1992	25402.2	11731.5	4336.0	7395.2	13670.7			
1993	34879.8	16280.4	5864.7	10415.7	18599.4	1247.9	15203.5	2148.0
1994	46923.5	20540.7	7288.6	13252.1	26382.8	1943.1	21518.8	2920.9
1995	60750.5	23987.1	7885.3	16101.8	36763.4	3324.2	29662.2	3777.0
1996	76094.9	28514.8	8802.0	19712.8	47580.1	5041.9	38520.8	4017.4
1997	90995.3	34826.3	10177.6	24648.7	56169.1	6738.5	46279.8	3150.7
1998	104498.5	38953.7	11204.2	27749.5	65544.9	8301.9	53407.5	3835.5
1999	119897.9	45837.3	13455.5	32381.8	74060.6	9476.8	59621.8	4962.0
2000	134610.3	53147.2	14652.7	38494.5	81463.1	11261.1	64332.4	5869.7
2001	158301.9	59871.6	15688.8	44182.8	98430.3	14180.1	73762.4	10487.8
2002	185007.0	70881.8	17278.0	53603.8	114125.2	16433.8	86910.7	10780.7
2003	221222.8	84118.6	19746.0	64372.6	137104.3	20940.4	103617.7	12546.2
2004	253207.7	95970.8	21468.3	74501.4	158137.2	25382.2	119555.4	13199.7
2005	298755.5	107278.6	24031.7	83247.1	191476.9	33100.0	141051.0	17325.9
2006	345577.9	126028.1	27072.6	98955.4	219549.9	38715.9	161587.3	19246.7
2007	403401.3	152519.2	30334.3	122184.9	250882.1	46932.5	172534.2	31415.4
2008	475166.6	166217.1	34219.0	131998.2	308949.5	60103.1	217885.4	30961.1
2009	610224.5	221445.8	38247.0	183198.8	388778.7	84819.5	260752.7	43206.5
2010	725851.8	266621.5	44628.2	221993.4	459230.3	105858.7	303302.5	50069.1
2011	851590.9	289847.7	50748.5	239099.2	561743.2	166616.0	352797.5	42329.7
2012	974148.8	308664.2	54659.8	254004.5	665484.6	195940.1	411362.6	58181.9
2013	1106525.0	337291.1	58574.4	278716.6	769233.9	232696.6	467031.1	69506.2
2014	1228374.8	348056.4	60259.5	287796.9	880318.4	264055.7	508878.1	107384.6
2015	1392278.1	400953.4	63216.6	337736.9	991324.7	288240.7	552073.5	151010.5
2016	1550066.7	486557.2	68303.9	418253.4	1063509.4	307989.6	603504.2	152015.6
2017	1690235.3	543790.1	70645.6	473144.5	1146445.2	320196.2	649341.5	176907.4
2018	1826744.2	551685.9	73208.4	478477.5	1275058.3	340178.9	721688.6	213190.8
2019	1986488.8	576009.2	77189.5	498819.7	1410479.7	363486.0	819161.8	227831.8
2020	2186795.9	625581.0	84314.5	541266.5	1561214.9	383837.3	932966.3	244411.2
2021	2382899.6	647443.4	90825.2	556618.2	1735456.2	412951.6	1032441.2	290063.5
2022	2664320.8	671674.8	104706.0	566968.7	1992646.1	462001.6	1211692.8	318951.6
2023	2922713.3	680542.5	113444.6	567097.9	2242170.8	520995.5	1378566.9	342608.4

注：1.1997年初，中国人民银行对金融统计制度进行了调整，因此自1997年起的数据与历史数据不完全可比。
2.2001年6月起，将证券公司客户保证金计入货币供应量(M_2)，含在其他存款项内。
3.2010年金融机构会计科目变动，因此对2009年末数据进行了相应调整。
4.自2011年10月起，货币供应量已包含住房公积金中心存款和非存款类金融机构在存款类金融机构的存款。
5.2018年1月，人民银行完善货币供应量中货币市场基金部分的统计方法，用非存款机构部门持有的货币市场基金取代货币市场基金存款(含存单)。表中2017年以来的M_2数据均为统计方法完善后的可比数据。
6.自2022年12月起，“流通中货币(M_0)”含流通中数字人民币。

a) The People's Bank of China (PBC) made some adjustments to the monetary statistics system at the beginning of 1997, hence the statistics since 1997 are not fully comparable to historical statistics.
b) Since June 2001, the customer margin of security companies maintained with financial institutions are included in money supply (M_2), as part of other deposits.
c) Due to adjustments in the accounting subjects of financial institutions in 2010, data at the end of 2009 are updated correspondingly.
d) Since October 2011, money supply includes deposits of Housing Provident Fund Management Center and deposits of non-depository corporations in depository corporations.
e) The PBC improved the method of data compiling in money supply statistics in January 2018. Specifically, as a result of improvement, the item of money market funds, which was treated as deposits of money market funds (CD included), is now treated as the total of money market fund units held by the non-deposit taking financial institutions, household sector and non-financial companies. After applying the new method, monthly M_2 growth rates since 2017 are updated correspondingly.
f) From December 2022, e-CNY in Circulation is covered in Currency in Circulation.

18–2 货币供应量同比增长率
Growth Rate of Money Supply

单位：% (%)

年 份 Year	货币和准货币 (M_2) Money and Quasi-money (M_2)	货 币 (M_1) Money (M_1)	流通中货币 (M_0) Currency in Circulation (M_0)	单位活期存款 Corporate Demand Deposits	准货币 Quasi-money	单位定期存款 Corporate Time Deposits	个人存款 Personal Savings Deposits	其他存款 Other Deposits
1991	26.5	24.2	20.2	26.7	28.5			
1992	31.3	35.9	36.4	35.6	27.6			
1993								
1994	34.5	26.2	24.3	27.2	41.9	55.7	41.5	36.0
1995	29.5	16.8	8.2	21.5	39.4	71.1	37.9	29.3
1996	25.3	18.9	11.6	22.4	29.4	51.7	29.9	6.4
1997	17.3	16.5	15.6	16.9	17.8	24.5	19.3	-8.9
1998	14.8	11.9	10.1	12.6	16.7	23.2	15.4	21.7
1999	14.7	17.7	20.1	16.7	13.0	14.2	11.6	29.3
2000	12.3	16.0	8.9	18.9	10.0	18.8	7.9	18.3
2001	14.4	12.7	7.1	14.8	15.5	25.9	14.7	9.1
2002	16.8	16.8	10.1	19.2	16.8	21.8	17.8	2.8
2003	19.6	18.7	14.3	20.3	20.1	27.4	19.2	16.4
2004	14.7	13.6	8.7	15.1	15.3	21.2	15.4	5.2
2005	17.6	11.8	11.9	11.7	21.1	30.4	18.0	31.3
2006	16.9	17.5	12.7	18.9	16.6	17.1	14.6	36.2
2007	16.7	21.1	12.2	23.5	14.3	21.2	6.8	63.2
2008	17.8	9.1	12.7	8.2	23.2	28.1	26.3	-1.5
2009	28.5	33.2	11.8	38.8	26.0	42.0	19.7	39.6
2010	19.7	21.2	16.7	22.1	18.9	28.7	16.3	16.0
2011	13.6	7.9	13.8	6.7	16.8	18.1	16.2	17.7
2012	13.8	6.5	7.7	6.2	17.6	17.6	16.6	25.1
2013	13.6	9.3	7.2	9.7	15.6	18.8	13.5	19.5
2014	12.2	3.2	2.9	3.3	14.4	13.5	9.0	54.5
2015	13.3	15.2	4.9	17.4	12.6	9.2	8.5	40.6
2016	11.3	21.4	8.1	23.8	7.3	6.9	9.3	0.7
2017	8.2	11.8	3.4	13.1	6.4	4.0	7.6	6.5
2018	8.1	1.5	3.6	1.1	11.2	6.2	11.1	20.5
2019	8.7	4.4	5.4	4.3	10.6	6.9	13.5	6.9
2020	10.1	8.6	9.2	8.5	10.7	5.6	13.9	7.3
2021	9.0	3.5	7.7	2.8	11.2	7.6	10.7	18.7
2022	11.8	3.7	15.3	1.9	14.8	11.9	17.4	10.0
2023	9.7	1.3	8.3	0.0	12.5	12.8	13.8	7.4

注：同比增长率按可比口径计算。1993年口径调整，未按可比口径计算增长率。

a) Growth rate is calculated on the basis of comparable coverage. As the statistical coverage before 1992 was not comparable to that of 1993, the growth rate in 1993 was not calculated.

18–3 社会融资规模增量及构成
Statistics on Aggregate Financing to the Real Economy (Flow) and Composition

单位：亿元 (100 million yuan)

年份 Year	社会融资规模增量 AFRE (flow)	#人民币贷款 RMB Loans	#外币贷款（折合人民币） Foreign Currency-denominated Loans (RMB equivalent)	#委托贷款 Entrusted Loans	#信托贷款 Trust Loans	#未贴现银行承兑汇票 Undiscounted Bankers' Acceptances	#企业债券 Net Financing of Corporate Bonds	#政府债券 Government Bonds	#非金融企业境内股票融资 Equity Financing on the Domestic Stock Market by Non-financial Enterprises
2002	20112	18475	731	175		-695	367		628
2003	34113	27652	2285	601		2010	499		559
2004	28629	22673	1381	3118		-290	467		673
2005	30008	23544	1415	1961		24	2010		339
2006	42696	31523	1459	2695	825	1500	2310		1536
2007	59663	36323	3864	3371	1702	6701	2284		4333
2008	69802	49041	1947	4262	3144	1064	5523		3324
2009	139104	95942	9265	6780	4364	4606	12367		3350
2010	140191	79451	4855	8748	3865	23346	11063		5786
2011	128286	74715	5712	12962	2034	10271	13658		4377
2012	157631	82038	9163	12838	12845	10499	22551		2508
2013	173169	88916	5848	25466	18404	7756	18111		2219
2014	158761	97452	1235	21740	5174	-1198	24329		4350
2015	154063	112693	-6427	15911	434	-10567	29388		7590
2016	177999	124372	-5640	21854	8593	-19514	29865		12416
2017	261536	138432	18	7994	22232	5364	6244	55804	8759
2018	224920	156712	-4201	-16062	-6975	-6343	26318	48531	3606
2019	256735	168835	-1275	-9396	-3467	-4757	33384	47204	3479
2020	347917	200310	1450	-3954	-11020	1746	43748	83217	8923
2021	313407	199403	1715	-1696	-20074	-4916	32866	70154	12133
2022	320101	209149	-5254	3579	-6003	-3411	20508	71228	11757
2023	355799	222240	-2206	199	1576	-1782	16254	96045	7931

注：1.社会融资规模增量是指一定时期内实体经济从金融体系获得的资金额。

2.数据来源于中国人民银行、国家金融监督管理总局、中国证券监督管理委员会、中央国债登记结算有限责任公司和银行间市场交易商协会等。

3.2019年12月起，将“国债”和“地方政府一般债券”纳入社会融资规模统计，与原有“地方政府专项债券”合并为“政府债券”指标。指标数值为托管机构的托管面值。2019年9月起，将“交易所企业资产支持证券”纳入“企业债券”指标。2018年9月起，人民银行将“地方政府专项债券”纳入社会融资规模统计。2018年7月起，将“存款类金融机构资产支持证券”和“贷款核销”纳入社会融资规模统计，在“其他融资”项下单独列示。可比口径数据追溯到2017年1月，详见中国人民银行官网社会融资规模数据表附注。

4.自2023年1月起，人民银行将消费金融公司、理财公司和金融资产投资公司等三类银行业非存款类金融机构纳入金融统计范围。由此，对社会融资规模中“对实体经济发放的人民币贷款”和“贷款核销”数据进行调整。2023年1月末，上述三类机构对实体经济发放的人民币贷款余额8410亿元，当月增加57亿元；贷款核销余额1706亿元，当月增加30亿元。2023年1月以来数据为可比口径计算。

a) AFRE(flow) refers to the total volume of financing provided by the financial system to the real economy during a certain period of time.

b) In the calculation of AFRE, data are from the PBC, NFRA, CSRC, CCDC and NAFMII.

c) Since December 2019, "Treasury Bonds" and "Local Government General Bonds" were newly introduced into AFRE and merged with "Local Government Special Bonds" into "Government Bonds " ,which is recorded at face value at depositories. Since September 2019, the People's Bank of China incorporated "Asset-backed Securities of Non-Financial Enterprises" into "Net Financing of Corporate Bonds". Since September 2018, the People's Bank of China incorporated "Local Government Special Bonds" into AFRE. Since July 2018, the People's Bank of China incorporated "Asset-backed Securities of Depository Financial Institutions" and "Loans Written off" into AFRE, which is reflected as a sub-item of "Other Financing". Data is comparably adjusted as of January, 2017.Please refer to the notes of the AFRE release on the website of PBC for details.

d) As of January 2023, three kinds of non-depository financial institutions, i.e., the Consumer Finance Companies, the Wealth Management Companies and the Financial Asset Investment Companies were included in the coverage of financial statistics of PBC. Thereby, the item “RMB loans to real economy” and “Loans written-off” in AFRE were adjusted accordingly. At the end of January, 2023, the balance of RMB loans to real economy by the three institutions amounted to 841 billion yuan, increased by 5.7 billion yuan compared with the end of last month. The balance of loans written-off reached 170.6 billion yuan, increased by 3 billion yuan compared with the end of last month.The data is calculated on a comparative basis as of January, 2023.

18-4 社会融资规模存量及增长率

Statistics on Aggregate Financing to the Real Economy (Stock) and Growth Rate

年份 Year	社会融资规模存量(亿元) AFRE (stock) (100 million yuan)	社会融资规模存量同比增速(%) Year-on-year Growth (%)	#人民币贷款 RMB Loans	#外币贷款(折合人民币) Foreign Currency-denominated Loans (RMB equivalent)	#委托贷款 Entrusted Loans	#信托贷款 Trust Loans	#未贴现银行承兑汇票 Undiscounted Bankers' Acceptances	#企业债券 Net Financing of Corporate Bonds	#政府债券 Government Bonds	#非金融企业境内股票融资 Equity Financing on the Domestic Stock Market by Non-financial Enterprises
2002	148532									
2003	181655	22.3	21.4	26.6	13.3		126.0	132.9		8.0
2004	204143	14.9	14.3	16.8	61.6		-8.0	4.0		8.5
2005	224265	13.5	13.3	11.0	11.8		0.7	129.1		4.2
2006	264500	18.1	16.3	9.0	20.0		44.9	68.7		12.5
2007	321326	21.5	16.4	21.9	29.9	84.0	138.4	41.0		45.8
2008	379765	20.5	18.7	5.1	29.1	84.3	9.2	78.7		17.7
2009	511835	34.8	31.3	55.5	35.8	63.4	36.5	86.2		18.3
2010	649869	27.0	19.9	15.9	44.2	34.4	135.5	42.3		30.9
2011	767791	18.3	16.1	13.1	21.2	13.5	25.6	36.2		17.7
2012	914675	19.1	15.0	27.2	17.1	75.0	21.0	44.4		8.6
2013	1075217	17.6	14.2	7.2	39.7	61.1	12.7	24.2		6.7
2014	1229386	14.3	13.6	4.1	29.2	10.8	-1.1	25.8		11.8
2015	1382824	12.5	13.9	-13.0	18.0	2.0	-14.8	25.1		20.2
2016	1559884	12.8	13.4	-12.9	19.8	15.8	-33.3	22.4		27.6
2017	2059098	14.1	13.2	-5.8	5.9	35.9	13.7	3.9	24.7	15.2
2018	2270356	10.3	13.2	-10.7	-11.5	-8.0	-14.3	9.8	17.2	5.4
2019	2514071	10.7	12.5	-4.6	-7.6	-4.4	-12.5	13.8	14.3	5.0
2020	2847526	13.3	13.2	-0.6	-3.4	-14.8	5.3	16.9	22.1	12.1
2021	3141163	10.3	11.6	6.3	-1.6	-31.3	-14.0	8.6	15.2	14.7
2022	3442180	9.6	10.9	-17.4	3.4	-14.0	-11.6	3.6	13.4	12.4
2023	3780839	9.5	10.4	-10.2	0.2	4.2	-6.7	0.3	16.0	7.5

注：1.社会融资规模存量是指一定时期末实体经济从金融体系获得的资金余额。存量数据基于账面值或面值计算。

2.数据来源于中国人民银行、国家金融监督管理总局、中国证券监督管理委员会、中央国债登记结算有限责任公司和银行间市场交易商协会等。

3.2019年12月起，将“国债”和“地方政府一般债券”纳入社会融资规模统计，与原有“地方政府专项债券”合并为“政府债券”指标。指标数值为托管机构的托管面值。2019年9月起，将“交易所企业资产支持证券”纳入“企业债券”指标。2018年9月起，人民银行将“地方政府专项债券”纳入社会融资规模统计。2018年7月起，将“存款类金融机构资产支持证券”和“贷款核销”纳入社会融资规模统计，在“其他融资”项下单独列示。可比口径数据追溯到2017年1月，详见中国人民银行官网社会融资规模数据表附注。

4.自2023年1月起，人民银行将消费金融公司、理财公司和金融资产投资公司等三类银行业非存款类金融机构纳入金融统计范围。由此，对社会融资规模中“对实体经济发放的人民币贷款”和“贷款核销”数据进行调整。2023年1月末，上述三类机构对实体经济发放的人民币贷款余额8410亿元，当月增加57亿元；贷款核销余额1706亿元，当月增加30亿元。2023年1月以来数据为可比口径计算。

a) AFRE(Stock) refers to the outstanding of financing provided by the financial system to the real economy at the end of a period.Stock figures were based on book-value or face-value.

b) In the calculation of AFRE, data are from the PBC, NFRA, CSRC, CCDC and NAFMII.

c) Since December 2019, "Treasury Bonds" and "Local Government General Bonds" were newly introduced into AFRE and merged with "Local Government Special Bonds" into "Government Bonds " ,which is recorded at face value at depositories. Since September 2019, the People's Bank of China incorporated "Asset-backed Securities of Non-Financial Enterprises" into "Net Financing of Corporate Bonds". Since September 2018, the People's Bank of China incorporated "Local Government Special Bonds" into AFRE. Since July 2018, the People's Bank of China incorporated "Asset-backed Securities of Depository Financial Institutions" and "Loans Written off" into AFRE, which is reflected as a sub-item of "Other Financing". Data is comparably adjusted as of January, 2017.Please refer to the notes of the AFRE release on the website of PBC for details.

d) As of January 2023, three kinds of non-depository financial institutions, i.e., the Consumer Finance Companies, the Wealth Management Companies and the Financial Asset Investment Companies were included in the coverage of financial statistics of PBC. Thereby, the item" RMB loans to real economy" and "Loans written-off" in AFRE were adjusted accordingly. At the end of January, 2023, the balance of RMB loans to real economy by the three institutions amounted to 841 billion yuan, increased by 5.7 billion yuan compared with the end of last month. The balance of loans written -off reached 170.6 billion yuan, increased by 3 billion yuan compared with the end of last month.The data is calculated on a comparative basis as of January, 2023.

18-5 金融机构人民币存款基准利率
RMB Deposit Benchmark Interest Rates in Financial Institutions

单位：年利率% (% p.a.)

项 目	Item	2010.10.20 Oct.20,2010	2010.12.26 Dec.26,2010	2011.02.09 Feb.09,2011	2011.04.06 Apr.06,2011	2011.07.07 July.07,2011	2012.06.08 Jun.08,2012
活期	Demand	0.36	0.36	0.40	0.50	0.50	0.40
定期	Time						
三个月	3-Month	1.91	2.25	2.60	2.85	3.10	2.85
半年	6-Month	2.20	2.50	2.80	3.05	3.30	3.05
一年	1-Year	2.50	2.75	3.00	3.25	3.50	3.25
二年	2-Year	3.25	3.55	3.90	4.15	4.40	4.10
三年	3-Year	3.85	4.15	4.50	4.75	5.00	4.65
五年	5-Year	4.20	4.55	5.00	5.25	5.50	5.10

18-5 续表 continued

单位：年利率% (% p.a.)

项 目	Item	2012.07.06 July.06,2012	2014.11.22 Nov.22,2014	2015.03.01 Mar.01,2015	2015.05.11 May.11,2015	2015.06.28 Jun.28,2015	2015.08.26 Aug.26,2015	2015.10.24 Oct.24,2015
活期	Demand	0.35	0.35	0.35	0.35	0.35	0.35	0.35
定期	Time							
三个月	3-Month	2.60	2.35	2.10	1.85	1.60	1.35	1.10
半年	6-Month	2.80	2.55	2.30	2.05	1.80	1.55	1.30
一年	1-Year	3.00	2.75	2.50	2.25	2.00	1.75	1.50
二年	2-Year	3.75	3.35	3.10	2.85	2.60	2.35	2.10
三年	3-Year	4.25	4.00	3.75	3.50	3.25	3.00	2.75
五年	5-Year	4.75						

注：自2014年11月22日起，人民银行不再公布金融机构人民币五年期定期存款基准利率。
a) Since Nov.22,2014, the People's Bank of China stopped to publish official benchmark interest rates of 5-Year time deposits of financial institutions.

18–6 金融机构人民币贷款基准利率
Loans Benchmark Interest Rates in Financial Institutions

单位：年利率% (%, p.a.)

项　目	Item	2010.12.26 Dec.26, 2010	2011.02.09 Feb.09, 2011	2011.04.06 Apr.06, 2011	2011.07.07 July.07, 2011	2012.06.08 June.08, 2012	2012.07.06 July.06, 2012
短期贷款	Short-term						
六个月	6-Month	5.35	5.60	5.85	6.10	5.85	5.60
一年	1-Year	5.81	6.06	6.31	6.56	6.31	6.00
中长期贷款	Medium and Long-term						
一年以上至三年	1-Year to 3-Year	5.85	6.10	6.40	6.65	6.40	6.15
三年以上至五年	3-Year to 5-Year	6.22	6.45	6.65	6.90	6.65	6.40
五年以上	Longer than 5-Year	6.40	6.60	6.80	7.05	6.80	6.55

18–6 续表 continued

单位：年利率% (%, p.a.)

项　目	Item	2014.11.22 Nov.22, 2014	2015.03.01 Mar.01, 2015	2015.05.11 May.11, 2015	2015.06.28 June.28, 2015	2015.08.26 Aug.26, 2015	2015.10.24 Oct.24, 2015
短期贷款	Short-term						
六个月 一年	6-Month 1-Year	5.60	5.35	5.10	4.85	4.60	4.35
中长期贷款	Medium and Long-term						
一年以上至三年 三年以上至五年	1-Year to 3-Year 3-Year to 5-Year	6.00	5.75	5.50	5.25	5.00	4.75
五年以上	Longer than 5-Year	6.15	5.90	5.65	5.40	5.15	4.90

注：自2014年11月22日起，贷款基准利率期限档次简并为一年期以内(含一年)、一至五年(含五年)和五年以上三个档次。

a) Since Nov.22,2014, the term grades of benchmark interest rate of loans are simply divided into three grades: within one year (including one year), one to five years (including five years) and more than five years.

18–7 贷款市场报价利率(LPR)
Loan Prime Rate

单位：% (%)

日　期 Date	1年期 1-year	5年期以上 over 5-year
2023.1.20	3.65	4.30
2023.2.20	3.65	4.30
2023.3.20	3.65	4.30
2023.4.20	3.65	4.30
2023.5.22	3.65	4.30
2023.6.20	3.55	4.20
2023.7.20	3.55	4.20
2023.8.21	3.45	4.20
2023.9.20	3.45	4.20
2023.10.20	3.45	4.20
2023.11.20	3.45	4.20
2023.12.20	3.45	4.20

18-8 黄金和外汇储备
Gold and Foreign Exchange Reserves

年 份 Year	黄金储备 (万盎司) Gold Reserves (10 000 oz.)	外汇储备 (亿美元) Foreign Exchange Reserves (USD 100 million)	年 份 Year	黄金储备 (万盎司) Gold Reserves (10 000 oz.)	外汇储备 (亿美元) Foreign Exchange Reserves (USD 100 million)
1978	1280	1.67	2001	1608	2121.65
1979	1280	8.40	2002	1929	2864.07
1980	1280	-12.96	2003	1929	4032.51
1981	1267	27.08	2004	1929	6099.32
1982	1267	69.86	2005	1929	8188.72
1983	1267	89.01	2006	1929	10663.44
1984	1267	82.20	2007	1929	15282.49
1985	1267	26.44	2008	1929	19460.30
1986	1267	20.72	2009	3389	23991.52
1987	1267	29.23	2010	3389	28473.38
1988	1267	33.72	2011	3389	31811.48
1989	1267	55.50	2012	3389	33115.89
1990	1267	110.93	2013	3389	38213.15
1991	1267	217.12	2014	3389	38430.18
1992	1267	194.43	2015	5666	33303.62
1993	1267	211.99	2016	5924	30105.17
1994	1267	516.20	2017	5924	31399.49
1995	1267	735.97	2018	5956	30727.12
1996	1267	1050.29	2019	6264	31079.24
1997	1267	1398.90	2020	6264	32165.22
1998	1267	1449.59	2021	6264	32501.66
1999	1267	1546.75	2022	6464	31276.91
2000	1267	1655.74	2023	7187	32379.77

18-9 人民币汇率（年平均价）
Exchange Rate of Renminbi (Period Average)

单位：人民币元 (RMB yuan)

年 份 Year	100美元 100 US Dollars	100日元 100 Japanese Yen	100港元 100 Hong Kong Dollars	100欧元 100 Euros
1985	293.67	1.2457	37.57	
1986	345.28	2.0694	44.22	
1987	372.21	2.5799	47.74	
1988	372.21	2.9082	47.70	
1989	376.51	2.7360	48.28	
1990	478.32	3.3233	61.39	
1991	532.33	3.9602	68.45	
1992	551.46	4.3608	71.24	
1993	576.20	5.2020	74.41	
1994	861.87	8.4370	111.53	
1995	835.10	8.9225	107.96	
1996	831.42	7.6352	107.51	
1997	828.98	6.8600	107.09	
1998	827.91	6.3488	106.88	
1999	827.83	7.2932	106.66	
2000	827.84	7.6864	106.18	
2001	827.70	6.8075	106.08	
2002	827.70	6.6237	106.07	800.58
2003	827.70	7.1466	106.24	936.13
2004	827.68	7.6552	106.23	1029.00
2005	819.17	7.4484	105.30	1019.53
2006	797.18	6.8570	102.62	1001.90
2007	760.40	6.4632	97.46	1041.75
2008	694.51	6.7427	89.19	1022.27
2009	683.10	7.2986	88.12	952.70
2010	676.95	7.7279	87.13	897.25
2011	645.88	8.1050	82.97	900.11
2012	631.25	7.9037	81.38	810.67
2013	619.32	6.3323	79.85	822.19
2014	614.28	5.8196	79.22	816.51
2015	622.84	5.1543	80.34	691.41
2016	664.23	6.1243	85.58	734.26
2017	675.18	6.0244	86.64	763.03
2018	661.74	5.9890	84.43	780.16
2019	689.85	6.3347	88.05	772.55
2020	689.76	6.4626	88.93	787.55
2021	645.15	5.8735	83.00	762.93
2022	672.61	5.1261	85.89	707.21
2023	704.67	5.0350	90.02	764.25

18－10　货币当局资产负债表（年底余额）
Balance Sheet of Monetary Authority (Balance at Year-end)

单位：亿元 (100 million yuan)

项　　目	Item	2021	2022	2023
总资产	**Total Assets**	**395702.2**	**416783.8**	**456944.1**
国外资产	Foreign Assets	225102.8	226906.6	233548.5
外汇	Foreign Exchange	212867.2	214712.3	220453.9
货币黄金	Monetary Gold	2855.6	3106.6	4052.9
其他国外资产	Other Foreign Assets	9380.0	9087.7	9041.8
对政府债权	Claims on Government	15240.7	15240.7	15240.7
对其他存款性公司债权	Claims on Other Depository Corporations	128645.5	143132.3	185561.0
对其他金融性公司债权	Claims on Other Financial Corporations	4125.2	1557.0	1310.9
对非金融部门债权	Claims on Non-financial Sectors			
其他资产	Other Assets	22588.1	29947.3	21283.0
总负债	**Total Liabilities**	**395702.2**	**416783.8**	**456944.1**
储备货币	Reserve Money	329487.3	360956.0	389036.9
货币发行	Currency Issue	96164.8	110012.6	118660.9
其他存款性公司存款	Deposits of Other Depository Corporations	212392.9	227876.5	245687.4
非金融机构存款	Deposits of Non-financial Institutions	20929.6	23066.9	24688.5
不计入储备货币的金融性公司存款	Deposits of Financial Corporations not Included in Reserve Money	6053.4	5208.4	6038.4
发行债券	Bond Issue	950.0	950.0	1250.0
国外负债	Foreign Liabilities	998.2	1574.5	3062.3
政府存款	Deposits of Government	42931.7	41272.9	46291.7
自有资金	Own Capital	219.8	219.8	219.8
其他负债	Other Liabilities	15061.9	6602.2	11045.0

注：1.自2017年起，对国际金融组织相关本币账户以净头寸反映。
　　2.“非金融机构存款”为支付机构交存人民银行的客户备付金存款。

a) Since 2017, RMB accounts with international financial organiztions have been calculated on a net basis.

b) Deposits of non-financial Institutions refers to the customer provision deposits of paying institutions at the PBC.

18－11　其他存款性公司资产负债表（年底余额）
Balance Sheet of Other Depository Corporations (Balance at Year-end)

单位：亿元 (100 million yuan)

项　　目	Item	2021	2022	2023
总资产	**Total Assets**	**3430395.1**	**3766294.0**	**4132768.6**
国外资产	Foreign Assets	73885.9	78345.0	77476.0
储备资产	Reserve Assets	222500.4	236791.0	253765.0
准备金存款	Deposits with Central Bank	217160.8	231484.5	248548.7
库存现金	Cash in Vault	5339.7	5306.5	5216.3
对政府债权	Claims on Government	412863.0	475892.8	553947.9
对中央银行债权	Claims on Central Bank	21.2	133.0	224.2
对其他存款性公司债权	Claims on Other Depository Corporations	311829.9	350308.2	382273.4
对其他金融性公司债权	Claims on Other Financial Corporations	246908.2	254785.9	279680.7
对非金融性公司债权	Claims on Non-financial Sectors	1333788.5	1501256.9	1671554.0
对其他居民部门债权	Claims on Other Resident Sectors	703434.3	742025.4	782471.9
其他资产	Other Assets	125163.7	126755.8	131375.3
总负债	**Total Liabilities**	**3430395.1**	**3766294.0**	**4132768.6**
对非金融机构及住户负债	Liabilities to Non-financial & Households Institutions	2116898.6	2340881.2	2556823.9
纳入广义货币的存款	Deposits Included in Broad Money	2002010.9	2240663.2	2466660.3
单位活期存款	Corporate Demand Deposits	556618.2	566968.7	567097.9
单位定期存款	Corporate Time Deposits	412951.6	462001.6	520995.5
个人存款	Personal Deposits	1032441.2	1211692.8	1378566.9
不纳入广义货币的存款	Deposits Excluded from Broad Money	59378.6	56100.7	52672.9
可转让存款	Transferable Deposits	26309.2	23349.3	21613.5
其他存款	Other Deposits	33069.4	32751.4	31059.4
其他负债	Other Liabilities	55509.1	44117.4	37490.7
对中央银行负债	Liabilities to Central Bank	118576.2	134995.7	180439.6
对其他存款性公司负债	Liabilities to Other Depository Corporations	112651.9	122637.0	129084.5
对其他金融性公司负债	Liabilities to Other Financial Corporations	253973.5	274424.0	296667.9
#计入广义货币的存款	Deposits Included in Broad Money	249744.1	270433.2	293323.5
国外负债	Foreign Liabilities	14995.8	14547.3	15094.1
债券发行	Bond Issue	350551.7	382522.4	421556.6
实收资本	Paid-in Capital	81208.2	84516.0	57163.4
其他负债	Other Liabilities	381539.2	411770.2	475938.6

18-12 外资银行资产负债表（年底余额）
Balance Sheet of Foreign-funded Banks (Balance at Year-end)

单位：亿元 (100 million yuan)

项 目	Item	2021	2022	2023
总资产	**Total Assets**	**48091**	**49366**	**50680**
国外资产	Foreign Assets	3767	3297	3027
储备资产	Reserve Assets	2578	2800	2888
准备金	Deposits with Central Bank	2575	2798	2885
库存现金	Cash in Vault	3	3	2
对政府债权	Claims on Government	4421	5107	5990
对中央银行债权	Claims on Central Bank	6		15
对其他存款性公司债权	Claims on Other Depository Corporations	4540	4179	4263
对其他金融性公司债权	Claims on Other Financial Corporations	4781	4857	5177
对非金融性公司债权	Claims on Non-financial Sectors	13267	13444	12910
对其他居民部门债权	Claims on Other Resident Sectors	2212	2186	2052
其他资产	Other Assets	12519	13494	14358
总负债	**Total Liabilities**	**48091**	**49366**	**50680**
对非金融机构及住户负债	Liabilities to Non-financial & Households Institutions	21225	21554	21613
纳入广义货币的存款	Deposits Included in Broad Money	15681	16014	15673
单位活期存款	Corporate Demand Deposits	5516	5636	5908
单位定期存款	Corporate Time Deposits	8781	8799	7785
个人存款	Personal Deposits	1383	1579	1981
不纳入广义货币的存款	Deposits Excluded from Broad Money	4192	4001	4332
可转让存款	Transferable Deposits	2649	2381	2138
其他存款	Other Deposits	1544	1620	2194
其他负债	Other Liabilities	1352	1539	1608
对中央银行负债	Liabilities to Central Bank	331	215	589
对其他存款性公司负债	Liabilities to Other Depository Corporations	2735	2190	2960
对其他金融性公司负债	Liabilities to Other Financial Corporations	2067	2469	2255
#计入广义货币的存款	Deposits Included in Broad Money	1859	2301	2118
国外负债	Foreign Liabilities	4066	3877	3371
债券发行	Bond Issue	884	1020	1082
实收资本	Paid-in Capital	2019	2054	2054
其他负债	Other Liabilities	14765	15988	16756

18-13 金融机构人民币信贷收支表(年底余额)(资金来源)

Balance Sheet of RMB Credit Funds of Financial Institutions at Year-end (Funds Sources)

单位：亿元 (100 million yuan)

项　目	Item	2021	2022	2023
资金来源合计	**Total Funds Sources**	**2831289**	**3121815**	**3450554**
各项存款	Total Deposits	2322500	2584998	2842623
境内存款	Domestic Deposits	2307172	2568007	2824093
住户存款	Deposits of Households	1025012	1203387	1369895
非金融企业存款	Deposits of Non-financial Enterprises	696695	746574	787756
机关团体存款	Deposits of Government Departments & Organizations	311530	329814	353261
财政性存款	Fiscal Deposits	50389	50013	57937
非银行业金融机构存款	Deposits of Non-banking Financial Institutions	223546	238219	255244
境外存款	Overseas Deposits	15329	16991	18531
金融债券	Financial Bonds	122954	126587	138622
流通中货币	Currency in Circulation	90825	104706	113445
对国际金融机构负债	Liabilities to International Financial Institutions	5	5	5
其他	Others	295005	305518	355858

注：1.本表机构包括中国人民银行、银行业存款类金融机构、银行业非存款类金融机构(以下相关表同)。
2.银行业存款类金融机构包括银行、信用社和财务公司。银行业非存款类金融机构包括信托投资公司、金融租赁公司、汽车金融公司和贷款公司等银行业非存款类金融机构(以下相关表同)。
3.自2015年起，“各项存款”含非银行业金融机构存放款项，“各项贷款”含拆放给非银行业金融机构款项(以下相关表同)。

a) Institutions in this table include the People's Bank of China, depository financial institutions of banks, non-depository financial institutions of banks. The same applies to following tables.

b) Depository financial institutions of banks include banks, credit cooperatives and financial corporations. Non-depository financial institutions of banks include trust and investment companies, financial leasing companies, motor vehicle financing companies, and loans companies.The same applies to following tables.

c) Since 2015, Total Deposits include Deposits of Non-banking Financial Institutions, and Total Loans include those lent to non-banking financial institutions. The same applies to following tables.

18-14 金融机构人民币信贷收支表(年底余额)(资金运用)

Balance Sheet of RMB Credit Funds of Financial Institutions at Year-end (Funds Uses)

单位：亿元 (100 million yuan)

项　目	Item	2021	2022	2023
资金运用合计	**Total Funds Uses**	**2831289**	**3121815**	**3450554**
各项贷款	Total Loans	1926903	2139853	2375905
境内贷款	Domestic Loans	1919855	2130060	2362901
住户贷款	Loans to Households	711043	749323	800921
企(事)业单位贷款	Loans to Non-financial Enterprises and Government Departments & Organizations	1204537	1375208	1554232
非银行业金融机构贷款	Loans to Non-banking Financial Institutions	4275	5529	7748
境外贷款	Overseas Loans	7048	9792	13005
债券投资	Portfolio Investments	503154	572977	654241
股权及其他投资	Shares and Other Investments	181387	186779	191322
黄金占款	Position for Bullion Purchase	2856	3107	4053
中央银行外汇占款	Foreign Exchange	212867	214712	220454
在国际金融机构资产	Assets with International Financial Institutions	4123	4387	4578

18-15 证券市场基本情况
General Statistics on Securities Markets

项　　目	Item	2022	2023
沪深股市上市公司数(A、B股)　(家)	Number of Listed Companies (A and B Shares) on Shanghai&Shenzhen Stock Markets (unit)	4917	5107
沪深股市上市外资股公司数(B股)(家)	Number of Listed Companies of Foreign Fund (B Shares) on Shanghai&Shenzhen Stock Markets (unit)	86	85
北交所市场上市公司数　(家)	Number of Listed Companies on Beijing Stock Exchange (unit)	162	239
境外上市公司数(H股)　(家)	Number of Listed Companies (H Shares) on Hong Kong Market (unit)	316	339
沪深股市股票总发行股本　(亿股)	Volume Issued on Shanghai&Shenzhen Markets (100 million shares)	73311.67	75489.40
#流通股本　(亿股)	Negotiable Shares (100 million shares)	64245.31	68142.40
北交所市场股票总发行股本　(亿股)	Volume Issued on Beijing Stock Exchange (100 million shares)	213.54	318.04
#流通股本　(亿股)	Negotiable Shares (100 million shares)	110.99	169.16
沪深股市股票市价总值　(亿元)	Total Market Capitalization on Shanghai&Shenzhen Markets (100 million yuan)	788005.91	773130.71
#股票流通市值　(亿元)	Negotiable Market Capitalization (100 million yuan)	663428.88	674341.52
北交所市场股票市价总值　(亿元)	Total Market Capitalization on Beijing Stock Exchange (100 million yuan)	2110.29	4496.41
#股票流通市值　(亿元)	Negotiable Market Capitalization (100 million yuan)	1148.06	2263.28
沪深股市股票成交量　(亿股)	Stock Trading Volume on Shanghai&Shenzhen Markets (100 million shares)	185725.37	170809.11
北交所市场股票成交量　(亿股)	Stock Trading Volume on Beijing Stock Exchange (100 million shares)	158.53	615.42
沪深股市股票成交金额　(亿元)	Turnover of Stock Trading on Shanghai&Shenzhen Markets (100 million yuan)	2245094.74	2122109.53
北交所市场股票成交金额　(亿元)	Turnover of Stock Trading on Beijing Stock Exchange (100 million yuan)	1980.13	7272.23
上证综合指数(收盘)	Shanghai Composite Index (Close)	3089.26	2974.93
深证综合指数(收盘)	Shenzhen Composite Index (Close)	1975.61	1837.85
期末投资者数　(万个)	Number of Investors at the End of This Period (10 000 units)	21214	22406
静态市盈率(平均市盈率)	Average P/E Ratio		
上海	Shanghai	12.78	11.92
深圳	Shenzhen	23.44	21.61
北京	Beijing	18.87	24.20
年换手率(平均换手率)　(%)	Average Turnover Rate (%)		
上海	Shanghai	239.84	207.76
深圳	Shenzhen	470.35	448.22
北京	Beijing	172.95	419.20
债券发行金额　(亿元)	Amount of Bonds Issued (100 million yuan)	614458.47	708262.75
银行间市场债券成交金额　(亿元)	Bonds Trading Turnover in the Interbank Market (100 million yuan)	16513779.25	19815308.85
银行间市场债券现货成交金额(亿元)	Turnover of Spots Trading of Bonds in the Interbank Market (100 million yuan)	2712234.55	3073049.31
银行间市场债券回购成交金额(亿元)	Turnover of Repurchase Trading of Bonds in the Interbank Market(100 million yuan)	13801546.70	16742259.54
交易所市场债券成交金额　(亿元)	Bonds Trading Turnover in the Exchange Market (100 million yuan)	4565584.88	5224160.58
交易所市场债券现货成交金额(亿元)	Turnover of Spots Trading of Bonds in the Exchange Market (100 million yuan)	381136.30	468031.92
交易所市场债券回购成交金额(亿元)	Turnover of Repurchase Trading of Bonds in the Exchange Market(100 million yuan)	4184448.58	4756128.66
证券投资基金只数　(只)	Number of Securities Investment Funds (unit)	10375	11528
证券投资基金规模　(亿份)	Capital of Securities Investment Funds (100 million units)	256437.54	264134.76
证券投资基金成交金额　(亿元)	Turnover of Securities Investment Funds (100 million yuan)	231161.00	275992.96
期货总成交量　(万手)	Trading Volume of Futures (10 000 pieces)	634241.92	737871.19
期货总成交额　(亿元)	Trading Turnover of Futures (100 million yuan)	5343025.26	5675693.72
期货交易所期权总成交量　(万手)	Trading Volume of Options Listed on Futures Exchange (10 000 pieces)	42588.25	112260.37
期货交易所期权总成交额　(亿元)	Trading Turnover of Options Listed on Futures Exchange (100 million yuan)	6372.21	9403.00

注：1.银行间市场债券指银行间市场交易的各类债券。包括记账式国债、地方政府债券、政策性银行债券、商业银行债券、非银行金融机构债券、资产支持证券、同业存单、政府支持机构债、企业债券、非金融企业债务融资工具、国际机构债券。
2.交易所债券包含由中国证监会审批或备案的公司债、可转债、可交换债、可分离债、企业资产支持证券，以及交易所招标发行的地方政府债、政策性金融债。
3.期末投资者数量指持有未注销、未休眠的A股、B股、信用账户、衍生品合约账户的一码通账户数量。
4.期货、期权成交数据按单边口径统计，包括商品和金融期货、期权(自2022年起将商品期权和金融期权纳入统计口径，不包含沪深证券交易所金融期权产品)。
5.计算市盈率时剔除亏损企业。

a) Debt securities traded in Inter-Bank Market, including book-entry treasury bonds, local government bonds, policy bank bonds, commercial bank bonds, non-banking financial institution bonds, asset-backed securities, negotiable certificates of deposits, government-backed agency bonds, enterprise bonds, financing instruments of non-financial enterprise, and international agency bonds.
b) Exchange bonds include corporate bonds, convertible bonds, exchangeable bonds, separable bonds, and enterprise asset-backed securities approved or filed by CSRC, and local government bonds and policy-based financial bonds tendered and issued by the exchange.
c) Number of investors at the end of this period refers to the number of one-way accounts holding unregistered, dormant A-shares, B-shares, credit accounts and derivatives contract accounts.
d) Futures trading data are counted by unilateral caliber, including commodity futures and financial futures.(Commodity options and financial options are included in the statistical caliber from 2022, excluding financial option products from the Shanghai and Shenzhen exchanges.)
e) Loss-making companies are excluded when calculating average P/E ratio.

18-16 上市公司数量
Number of Listed Companies

单位：个 (unit)

年 份 Year	全国合计 National Total	上交所 Shanghai Stock Exchange	深交所 Shenzhen Stock Exchange	北交所 Beijing Stock Exchange	发A股公司 A Shares	发B股公司 B Shares	同时发A股、B股公司 A&B Shares
1990	10	8	2				
1991	13	7	6				
1992	53	29	24		53	18	18
1993	183	106	77		177	41	35
1994	291	171	120		287	58	54
1995	323	188	135		311	70	58
1996	530	293	237		514	85	69
1997	745	383	362		720	101	76
1998	852	438	414		826	106	80
1999	949	484	465		922	108	81
2000	1088	572	516		1060	114	86
2001	1160	646	514		1140	112	92
2002	1224	715	509		1213	111	100
2003	1287	780	507		1277	111	101
2004	1377	837	540		1363	110	96
2005	1381	834	547		1358	109	86
2006	1434	842	592		1411	109	86
2007	1550	860	690		1527	109	86
2008	1625	864	761		1602	109	86
2009	1718	870	848		1696	108	86
2010	2063	894	1169		2041	108	86
2011	2342	931	1411		2320	108	86
2012	2494	954	1540		2472	107	85
2013	2489	953	1536		2468	106	85
2014	2613	995	1618		2592	104	83
2015	2827	1081	1746		2808	101	82
2016	3052	1182	1870		3034	100	82
2017	3485	1396	2089		3467	100	82
2018	3584	1450	2134		3567	99	82
2019	3777	1572	2205		3760	97	80
2020	4154	1800	2354		4140	96	82
2021	4697	2037	2578	82	4685	90	78
2022	5079	2174	2743	162	5067	86	74
2023	5346	2263	2844	239	5335	85	74

注：发A股公司包括既发A股又发B股的公司，发B股公司包括既发A股又发B股的公司。

a) A-share issuing companies include both A-share and B-share issuing companies, and B-share issuing companies include both A-share and B-share issuing companies.

18-17 证券市场发行情况
Share Issued on Securities Markets

单位：亿元 (100 million yuan)

年 份 Year	境内发行金额 Proceeds Raised in Domestic Capital Markets				境外股票发行金额 Proceeds Raised in Foreign Capital Markets	新三板股票发行金额 Proceeds Raised in NEEQ	合 计 Total
	小 计 Subtotal	沪深股市股票发行金额 Proceeds Raised in Shanghai&Shenzhen Stock Markets	北交所市场股票发行金额 Proceeds Raised in Beijing Stock Markets	交易所市场债券发行金额 Proceeds Raised in Bond Markets			
1992	68.91	68.91					68.91
1993	245.02	245.02			60.84		305.86
1994	213.63	213.63			188.75		402.38
1995	99.78	99.78			31.53		131.31
1996	308.04	308.04			100.57		408.61
1997	859.98	859.98			387.91		1247.89
1998	787.44	787.44			37.83		825.27
1999	873.63	873.63			47.11		920.74
2000	1515.82	1515.82			562.08		2077.90
2001	1238.14	1238.14			73.00		1311.14
2002	720.05	720.05			192.28		912.33
2003	665.51	665.51			537.32		1202.83
2004	650.53	650.53			647.72		1298.25
2005	339.03	339.03			1666.25		2005.28
2006	2374.50	2374.50			3072.57		5447.07
2007	8222.02	7814.74		407.28	927.46		9149.48
2008	4310.44	3312.39		998.05	311.38		4621.82
2009	5645.85	4834.34		811.51	1067.66		6713.51
2010	11120.10	9799.80		1320.30	2343.11		13463.21
2011	8884.13	7154.43		1729.70	732.41	6.48	9623.02
2012	7313.28	4542.40		2770.88	997.83	8.59	8319.70
2013	8086.40	4131.46		3954.94	1060.24	10.02	9156.66
2014	12671.90	8498.26		4173.64	2253.40	132.09	15057.39
2015	37983.36	16361.62		21621.74	7090.12	1216.17	46289.65
2016	56965.75	20297.39		36668.36	1271.48	1390.89	59628.12
2017	54681.89	15534.98		39146.91	1829.19	1336.25	57847.33
2018	68255.59	11377.88		56877.71	1387.61	604.43	70247.63
2019	84525.53	12538.82		71986.71	781.65	264.63	85571.81
2020	98998.96	14221.61		84777.35	1513.64	338.50	100851.10
2021	101974.58	15400.13	21.32	86553.13	1035.33	259.67	103269.58
2022	78836.21	14175.45	166.99	64493.77	1096.39	231.66	80164.26
2023	145317.18	9902.04	154.32	135260.82	354.18	180.19	145851.55

注：1.境内股票发行金额包括首发筹资金额和再筹资金额，均按股份上市日统计，再筹资包含公开增发、定向增发、配股、权证和优先股，其中权证为2008年之后开展的业务，优先股为2014年之后开展的业务。

2.境外股票发行金额指在港交所上市的H股的筹资金额，不含可转债。

3.新三板股票发行金额中不含优先股。

4.交易所债券发行包含国债、企业债、资产支持证券、政策性金融债、地方政府债、公司债、可转债、可交换债，其中企业债2023年纳入统计，企业债包含职责划转前国家发展改革委注册项目。

a) Proceeds raised in domestic capital markets include proceeds raised by IPO and proceeds raised by subsequent offerings, and are counted by the date of listing. Proceeds raised by subsequent offerings include public issue, directional issue, allotment, warrant and preferred stock. The warrant is the business started after 2008, and preferred stock is the business started after 2014.

b) Proceeds raised in foreign capital market refer to the amount of money raised by H-shares listed in Hong Kong Stock Exchange, excluding convertible bonds.

c) Proceeds raised in NEEQ do not include preferred stock.

d) The issuance of exchange bonds includes treasury bond, corporate bonds, asset-backed securities, policy financial bonds, local government bonds, corporate bonds, convertible bonds, and exchangeable bonds, of which corporate bonds will be included in the statistics in 2023, and corporate bonds include projects registered by the National Development and Reform Commission before the transfer of responsibilities.

18-18 股票交易情况

项　目	Item	2016
沪深股市上市公司数　（家）	**Number of Listed Companies on Shanghai&Shenzhen Markets　(unit)**	**3052**
北交所市场上市公司数　（家）	**Number of Listed Companies on Beijing Stock Exchange　(unit)**	
沪深股市上市股票数　（只）	**Number of Listed Stocks on Shanghai&Shenzhen Markets　(unit)**	**3134**
A股	A Shares	3034
B股	B Shares	100
北交所市场上市股票数　（只）	**Number of Listed Stocks on Beijing Stock Exchange　(unit)**	
沪深股市股票总发行股本　（亿股）	**Total Issued Capital on Shanghai&Shenzhen Markets (100 million shares)**	**48750**
A股	A Shares	48468
B股	B Shares	282
#流通股本	Negotiable Shares	41136
A股	A Shares	40855
B股	B Shares	281
北交所市场股票总发行股本（亿股）	**Total Issued Capital on Beijing Stock Exchange　(100 million shares)**	
#流通股本	Negotiable Shares	
沪深股市股票市价总值　（亿元）	**Total Market Capitalization on Shanghai&Shenzhen Markets (100 million yuan)**	**507686**
A股	A Shares	505773
B股	B Shares	1913
#股票流通市值	Negotiable Market Capitalization	393402
A股	A Shares	391499
B股	B Shares	1903
北交所市场股票市价总值（亿元）	**Total Market Capitalization on Beijing Stock Exchange (100 million yuan)**	
#股票流通市值	Negotiable Market Capitalization	
沪深股市股票成交金额　（亿元）	**Total Turnover on Shanghai&Shenzhen Markets　(100 million yuan)**	**1277680**
A股	A Shares	1276194
B股	B Shares	1486
北交所市场股票成交金额（亿元）	**Total Turnover on Beijing Stock Exchange　(100 million yuan)**	
沪深股市总成交股数　（亿股）	**Trading Volume on Shanghai&Shenzhen Markets　(100 million shares)**	**95525**
A股	A Shares	94481
B股	B Shares	210
北交所市场总成交股数　（亿股）	**Trading Volume on Beijing Stock Exchange　(100 million shares)**	
上证综合指数	**Shanghai Composite Index**	
最高	Highest	3538.69
最低	Lowest	2638.30
收盘	Close	3103.64
深证综合指数	**Shenzhen Composite Index**	
最高	Highest	2304.49
最低	Lowest	1618.12
收盘	Close	1969.11

注：1.股票总成交金额中包含约定购回式证券成交金额，故总成交金额大于A股B股成交金额之和。
2.指数最高、最低点为盘中最高、最低点。

Trading Summary of Stocks

2017	2018	2019	2020	2021	2022	2023
3485	**3584**	**3777**	**4154**	**4615**	**4917**	**5107**
				82	**162**	**239**
3567	**3666**	**3857**	**4233**	**4693**	**4991**	**5181**
3467	3567	3760	4140	4603	4905	5096
100	99	97	93	90	86	85
				82	**162**	**239**
53747	**57581**	**61720**	**65479**	**70694**	**73312**	**75489**
53462	57290	61428	65174	70390	73018	75193
285	291	292	305	304	294	297
45045	49048	52488	56354	60755	64245	68142
44761	48758	52197	56073	60475	63975	67869
283	289	291	281	281	270	272
				123	**214**	**318**
				57	111	169
567086	**434924**	**592935**	**797238**	**916088**	**788006**	**773131**
565255	433548	591623	796024	914671	786558	771834
1831	1376	1311	1214	1418	1448	1297
449298	353794	483461	643605	751556	663429	674342
447476	352428	482158	642396	750255	662159	673244
1822	1366	1304	1209	1301	1269	1098
				2723	**2110**	**4496**
				1074	1148	2263
1124625	**901739**	**1274159**	**2068253**	**2579734**	**2245095**	**2122110**
1123648	901103	1273572	2067632	2579050	2244412	2121682
977	636	587	621	684	683	427
				667	**1980**	**7272**
87781	**82037**	**126624**	**167452**	**187426**	**185725**	**170809**
87629	81927	126509	167324	187280	185588	170722
152	110	116	128	146	137	87
				37	**159**	**615**
3450.50	3587.03	3288.45	3474.92	3731.69	3651.89	3418.95
3016.53	2449.20	2440.91	2646.80	3312.72	2863.65	2882.02
3307.17	2493.90	3050.12	3473.07	3639.78	3089.26	2974.93
2054.02	1966.15	1799.10	2340.89	2571.27	2542.99	2200.22
1753.53	1212.23	1231.83	1552.96	2130.09	1724.92	1760.70
1899.34	1267.87	1722.95	2329.37	2530.14	1975.61	1837.85

a) Total turnover of stocks includes the turnover of Appointed Repurchase Securities, so it is larger than the sum of A shares and B shares turnover.
b) The high and low points of the index are the highest and lowest points in the stock market.

18–19 保险公司业务经济技术指标
Economic and Technical Indicators of Insurance Companies

单位：亿元 (100 million yuan)

项　　目	Item	2022		2023	
		保　费 Premium	赔款及给付 Claim and Payment	保　费 Premium	赔款及给付 Claim and Payment
合　　计	**Total**	**46957.2**	**15485.1**	**51246.7**	**18883.0**
财产保险公司	**Property Insurance Companies**	**14866.5**	**9078.2**	**15867.8**	**10694.0**
企业财产保险	Enterprise Property Insurance	553.4	256.8	595.8	293.8
家庭财产保险	Family Property Insurance	164.1	32.5	247.0	61.2
机动车辆保险	Motor Vehicle Insurance	8210.2	5138.1	8672.6	5932.6
工程保险	Engineering Insurance	145.1	71.4	170.1	76.3
责任保险	Liability Insurance	1147.5	508.0	1268.5	661.2
信用保险	Export Credit Insurance	236.8	105.6	292.3	191.9
保证保险	Guarantee Insurance	551.7	512.1	296.9	486.3
船舶保险	Ship Insurance	66.2	33.9	72.6	40.9
货物运输保险	Freight Transport Insurance	177.9	82.5	226.5	121.5
特殊风险保险	Special Risks Insurance	61.0	27.9	64.9	27.3
农业保险	Agriculture Insurance	1219.3	868.9	1429.7	1106.9
健康险	Health Insurance	1580.1	1121.9	1751.7	1293.6
意外伤害保险	Accident Injury Insurance	574.1	199.3	509.1	229.0
其他险	Other Insurance	179.1	119.2	270.3	171.5
人身保险公司	**Personal Insurance Companies**	**32090.6**	**6407.0**	**35378.9**	**8188.7**
寿险	Life Insurance	24518.6	3791.4	27646.4	5505.0
健康险	Health Insurance	7072.8	2477.7	7282.9	2537.0
人身意外伤害险	Personal Accident Insurance	499.2	137.9	449.6	147.0

注：1.本表人身保险公司中包括中华控股寿险业务。
2.2022、2023年数据不包含风险处置机构。

a) Personal insurance companies include life insurance of China United Insurance Holding Company.
b) The 2022 and 2023 data do not include risk disposal institutions.

18-20 保险公司资产情况
Assets of Insurance Companies

单位：亿元 (100 million yuan)

年 份 Year	总资产 Total Assets	#财产险公司 Property Insurance Companies	#寿险公司 Life Insurance Companies	#再保险公司 Reinsurance Companies	#中资公司 Domestic Funded Insurance Companies	#外资公司 Foreign-funded Insurance Companies
2002	6320.00	948.00	5161.00	211.00		
2003	9088.00	1176.00	7657.00	255.00		
2004	11953.68	1411.38	8352.90	262.37	11540.63	413.05
2005	15286.44	1718.81	13458.27	292.70	14630.97	665.64
2006	19704.19	2340.45	17446.26	311.31	18862.60	862.66
2007	28912.78	3880.51	23249.16	877.26	27656.26	1256.51
2008	33418.83	4687.03	27138.45	994.45	31893.93	1524.91
2009	40634.75	4892.62	33655.05	1162.01	38582.37	2052.39
2010	50481.61	5833.52	42642.66	1151.79	47860.49	2621.12
2011	59828.94	7919.95	49798.19	1579.11	56822.12	3006.83
2012	73545.73	9477.47	60991.22	1845.25	70080.33	3465.40
2013	82886.95	10941.45	68250.07	2103.93	78551.67	4335.28
2014	101591.47	14061.48	82487.20	3513.56	94950.98	6640.49
2015	123597.76	18481.13	99324.83	5187.38	115057.96	6539.80
2016	153764.66	23849.82	126557.51	2765.61	144646.59	9118.07
2017	169377.32	24901.04	131885.05	3150.32	158956.86	10420.46
2018	183305.24	23502.73	146032.48	3633.48	171695.83	11609.41
2019	205644.90	22939.60	169575.17	4261.12	192052.69	13592.21
2020	232984.30	23422.59	199789.74	4956.29	216367.12	17076.79
2021	248874.05	24512.74	213894.93	6057.45	228766.77	20107.28
2022	271467.47	26707.95	233744.86	6719.45	248909.94	22557.53
2023	299573.16	27593.20	259285.55	7471.48	275602.90	23970.26

注：2021、2022、2023年汇总数据不包含风险处置机构。
a) The data of 2021, 2022 and 2023 do not include risk disposal institutions.

18-21 保险公司资金运用情况
Fund Uses of Insurance Companies

单位：亿元 (100 million yuan)

年 份 Year	资金运用余额 Balance of Fund Uses	#银行存款 Deposits	#国债 Government and Public Bonds	#金融债券 Financial Bonds	#企业债券 Net Financing of Corporate Bonds	#证券投资基金 Securities Investment Funds
2004	10778.62	5071.10	2618.44	1026.25	639.73	666.32
2005	14092.69	5165.55	3590.65	1804.71	1204.55	1107.00
2006	17785.40	5989.11	3647.01	2754.25	2121.56	912.08
2007	26647.81	6503.44	3956.56	4897.84	2799.76	2519.41
2008	30552.83	8087.49	4208.26	8754.06	4598.46	1646.46
2009	37417.12	10519.68	4053.82	8746.10	6074.56	2758.78
2010	46046.62	13909.97	4815.78	10038.75	7935.69	2620.73
2011	55192.98	17692.69	4741.90	12418.80	8755.86	2909.92
2012	68542.58	23446.00	4795.02	14832.57	10899.98	3625.58
2013	76873.41	22640.98	4776.73	14811.84	13727.75	3575.52
2014	93314.43	25310.73	5009.88	15067.12	15465.13	4714.28
2015	111795.49	24349.67	5831.12	15215.31	17307.38	8856.50
2016	133910.67	24844.21	7796.24	16260.35	18627.99	8554.46
2017	149206.21	19274.07	10167.99	19153.05	19436.76	7524.77
2018	164088.38	24363.50	14027.62	20215.82	21011.68	8650.55
2019	185270.58	25227.42	20672.01	20658.19	21462.84	9423.29
2020	216801.13	25973.45	32069.60	20940.95	23654.17	11040.41
2021	232280.06	26178.59	43054.84	20627.14	22639.22	12248.02
2022	250508.92	28347.87	51139.60	22254.57	22478.13	13971.79
2023	276738.24	27243.40	63193.74	30322.54	22187.46	15302.46

注：2021、2022、2023年汇总数据不包含风险处置机构。
a) The data of 2021, 2022 and 2023 do not include risk disposal institutions.

18−22 分地区原保险保费收入和赔付支出情况（2023年）
Premium of Primary Insurance and Claim Payment by Region (2023)

单位：亿元 (100 million yuan)

地 区	Region	原保险保费收入 Premium of Primary Insurance			赔付支出 Claim Payment		
		小计 Sub-total	财产险业务 Property Insurance	人身险业务 Life Insurance	小计 Sub-total	财产险业务 Property Insurance	人身险业务 Life Insurance
全 国	**National Total**	**51246.71**	**13606.98**	**37639.73**	**18882.98**	**9171.35**	**9711.63**
北 京	Beijing	3204.70	517.91	2686.79	250.41	106.81	143.60
天 津	Tianjin	731.41	167.26	564.15	843.42	470.82	372.60
山 西	Shanxi	1106.66	267.21	839.44	304.90	168.25	136.65
河 北	Hebei	2136.28	626.14	1510.14	369.58	171.85	197.73
内蒙古	Inner Mongolia	718.73	241.79	476.94	460.27	223.71	236.56
辽 宁	Liaoning	1118.48	327.60	790.88	147.48	59.04	88.44
#大 连	Dalian	451.22	97.21	354.01	293.48	150.09	143.39
吉 林	Jilin	721.28	199.69	521.59	430.67	160.66	270.01
黑龙江	Heilongjiang	1026.03	238.74	787.29	783.37	365.35	418.02
上 海	Shanghai	2470.74	640.42	1830.32	1646.33	778.08	868.26
江 苏	Jiangsu	4790.30	1193.36	3596.94	1085.76	610.26	475.50
浙 江	Zhejiang	3098.75	881.25	2217.50	183.59	128.39	55.21
#宁 波	Ningbo	455.22	197.79	257.43	644.19	343.19	301.00
安 徽	Anhui	1494.88	514.16	980.71	434.12	215.64	218.48
福 建	Fujian	1211.86	292.31	919.55	94.64	56.76	37.88
#厦 门	Xiamen	297.15	79.63	217.52	411.45	218.13	193.32
江 西	Jiangxi	1007.72	327.51	680.21	1110.88	513.40	597.49
山 东	Shandong	3100.09	763.75	2336.34	200.23	108.90	91.33
#青 岛	Qingdao	541.06	143.44	397.62	1004.10	458.63	545.47
河 南	Henan	2399.87	617.83	1782.05	761.09	310.60	450.49
湖 北	Hubei	2118.06	462.97	1655.10	684.26	320.15	364.11
湖 南	Hunan	1693.99	465.44	1228.55	1634.78	783.07	851.71
广 东	Guangdong	4836.48	1236.66	3599.81	561.57	264.54	297.03
#深 圳	Shenzhen	1719.56	442.69	1276.87	328.65	178.89	149.76
广 西	Guangxi	844.77	283.89	560.87	85.10	56.05	29.06
海 南	Hainan	209.85	85.86	123.99	443.76	172.97	270.79
重 庆	Chongqing	1055.76	244.40	811.37	974.49	424.29	550.21
四 川	Sichuan	2483.51	633.83	1849.67	241.93	158.92	83.01
贵 州	Guizhou	537.90	245.47	292.44	336.47	180.19	156.28
云 南	Yunnan	760.30	285.93	474.37	32.35	25.33	7.02
西 藏	Xizang	47.06	32.00	15.06	461.74	193.83	267.91
陕 西	Shaanxi	1192.65	294.17	898.48	213.48	104.72	108.76
甘 肃	Gansu	534.25	150.63	383.62	51.14	34.01	17.12
青 海	Qinghai	117.99	50.74	67.24	93.06	53.20	39.86
宁 夏	Ningxia	244.59	79.31	165.28	341.46	201.43	140.03
新 疆	Xinjiang	724.30	250.34	473.96	60.43	56.10	4.33
集团、总公司本级	Head Offices	43.27	27.65	15.62	878.36	345.15	533.21

注：1.本表数据为各公司上报中国保险统计信息系统年报数据，未经审计。
2.集团、总公司本级是指集团、总公司直接开展的业务，不计入任何地区。
3.2023年数据不包含风险处置机构。

a) Data in this table are collected through China Insurance Statistical Information System reported by insurance companies, and have not been audited.
b) Data of head offices refer to business conducted directly by head offices, and are not allocated to any region.
c) The 2023 data do not include risk disposal institutions.

主要统计指标解释

各项存款 金融机构资金来源的主要项目，包括住户存款、非金融企业存款、机关团体存款、财政性存款、非银行业金融机构存款和境外存款。

各项贷款 金融机构资金运用的主要项目，包括住户贷款、企（事）业单位贷款、非银行业金融机构贷款和境外贷款。

保险公司 在中国境内的、经过保险监督管理部门批准设立，并依法登记注册的各类商业保险公司。

保险金额 指保险人承担赔偿或者给付保险金责任的最高限额。

保费 指投保人为取得保险人在约定范围内所承担赔偿责任而支付给保险人的费用。

赔款 指保险人根据保险合同的规定，向被保险人支付的赔偿保险责任损失的金额，包括公司财产保险、意外伤害保险、一年期以内(含一年)的健康保险业务按保险合同约定支付的赔款。

给付 包括死伤医疗给付、满期给付和年金给付。死伤医疗给付是指保险人根据人寿保险及长期健康保险合同的规定，因被保险人在保险期内发生保险责任范围内的保险事故支付给被保险人(或受益人)的金额。满期给付是指被保险人生存期满，保险人按人寿保险合同规定支付给被保险人的满期保险金额。年金给付是指公司因年金保险业务的被保险人生存至规定的年龄，按保险合同约定支付给被保险人的给付金额。

社会融资规模增量 指一定时期内实体经济从金融体系获得的资金额。主要包括：人民币贷款、外币贷款（折合人民币）、委托贷款、信托贷款、未贴现的银行承兑汇票、企业债券、政府债券、非金融企业境内股票融资、投资性房地产、保险公司赔偿等。

社会融资规模存量 指一定时期末实体经济从金融体系获得的资金余额。主要包括：人民币贷款、外币贷款（折合人民币）、委托贷款、信托贷款、未贴现的银行承兑汇票、企业债券、政府债券、非金融企业境内股票融资、投资性房地产等。

沪深股市上市公司数 指在统计期末其发行的股票在上交所、深交所上市的股份有限公司的数量。以股票上市日进行统计，同时发行A、B股的上市公司，按一家计算。

北交所市场上市公司数 指在统计期末其发行的股票在北交所上市的股份有限公司的数量。以股票上市日进行统计。

沪深股市股票总发行股本 指统计期末上市公司在沪、深股市发行的全部股份数量合计，包括A股股本、B股股本和其他不流通的境内股本。

北交所市场股票总发行股本 指统计期末上市公司在北交所发行的全部股份数量合计。

沪深股市股票市价总值 指统计期末根据沪、深股市上市公司股票价格和对应股票数量计算的股权价值合计。具体统计口径和计算方法如下：如当日无交易价格，采用最后交易日的收盘价；暂停上市股票的价格以零计算；未股改公司的非流通股以流通A股价格计算市值；仅发行B股的上市公司，其非流通股不进行股票市值计算；对当日除权股票进行市值计算时需要包含在途股份（已登记未上市）的市值。

北交所市场股票市价总值 指统计期末根据北交所上市公司股票价格和对应股票数量计算的股权价值合计。

债券发行金额 报告期各类债券发行金额的合计。包括国债、地方政府债券、中央银行票据、金融债券、公司信用类债券、国际机构债券。

证券投资基金只数 指统计期末基金市场上基金产品的只数。自基金合同生效日（基金成立日）纳入统计，自基金合同终止日从统计中剔除。一般根据证监会主代码（基金主合同）口径统计。

Explanatory Notes on Main Statistical Indicators

Total Deposits are the main items of financial sources of financial institutions, which include deposits of households, deposits of non-financial enterprises, deposits of government departments & organizations, fiscal deposits, deposits of non-banking financial institutions and overseas deposits.

Total Loans are the main items of financial uses of financial institutions, which include loans to households, loans to non-financial enterprises and government departments & organizations, loans to non-banking financial institutions and overseas loans.

Insurance Companies refer to commercial insurance companies of various forms registered by law and established in China with the approval of insurance regulatory agencies.

Amount Insured refers to the maximum that the insurant will get for the claim of the case insured.

Premium is the fee paid by the insurant to the insurer to obtain the obligation of compensation from the insurance within the agreed terms.

Settled Claim is the compensation paid by the insurer to the insurant in accordance with the insurance contract, including company property insurance, accidental injury insurance, and health insurance business within one year (including one year), the compensation paid according to the insurance contract.

Payment includes payment for death, injury or medical treatment, payment at maturity and annuity payment. Payment for death, injury or medical treatment refers to the money paid to the insurant (or the beneficiary) in accordance with the life or health insurance contract when the insurant encounters accidents within the insured period covered in the contract. Payment at maturity refers to the payment to the insurant in accordance with the life insurance contract at the end of the insured period. Annuity payment refers to the amount paid by a company to the insured in accordance with the insurance contract for the insured who has lived up to the specified age in the annuity insurance business.

Aggregate Financing to the Real Economy (Flow) refers to the total volume of financing provided by the financial system to the real economy over a period of time. It includes: RMB loans, foreign currency-denominated loans (RMB equivalent), entrusted loans, credit loans, undiscounted banker's acceptances, corporate bonds, government bonds, domestic equity financing of non-financial enterprises, investment real estate, premium of insurance, etc.

Aggregate Financing to the Real Economy (Stock) refers to the total volume of financing provided by the financial system to the real economy at the end of a period. It includes: RMB loans, foreign currency-denominated loans (RMB equivalent), credit loans, entrusted loans, undiscounted banker's acceptances, corporate bonds, government bonds, domestic equity financing of non-financial enterprises, investment real estate, etc.

Number of Listed Companies on the Shanghai and Shenzhen Stock Exchange refers to the number of limited companies whose stocks issued are listed on the Shanghai or Shenzhen exchanges at the end of the statistical period. A listed company that issues both A and B shares at the same time are counted as one company by the date of listing.

Number of Listed Companies on the Beijing Stock Exchange refers to the number of limited liability companies whose issued stocks are listed on the Beijing Stock Exchange at the end of the statistical period. Conduct statistics based on the date of stock listing.

Total Issued Share Capital of Shanghai and Shenzhen Stock Exchange also known as total stock of listed companies, refers to the total number of shares issued by domestic listed companies at the end of the statistical period, including A share capital, B share capital and other non-tradable domestic equity.

Total Issued Share Capital of the Beijing Stock Exchange refers to the total number of shares issued by listed companies on the exchange at the end of the period.

Total Market Capitalization of Shanghai and Shenzhen Stock Markets refers to the total equity value calculated based on the stock prices and corresponding quantities of shares issued by listed companies in the Shanghai and Shenzhen Stock Exchange at the end of the statistical period. Specific statistical coverage and calculation methods are as follows: if there is no trading price on the day, the closing price on the last trading day shall be adopted; the price of suspended listed shares shall be calculated at zero; the non-tradable shares of non-equity-restructured companies shall be calculated at the price of circulating A shares; the non-tradable shares of listed companies that issue only B shares shall not be calculated at the market value of their non-tradable shares on the same day. When calculating the market value of the right stock, the market value of the shares in transit (registered and unlisted) should be included.

Total Market Capitalization on the Beijing Stock Exchange refers to the total equity value calculated based on the stock prices of listed companies on the exchange and the corresponding number of stocks at the end of the statistical period.

Bonds Trading Turnover refers to the total amount of all kinds of bonds traded during the statistical period, including government bonds, local government bonds, central bank bills, financial bonds, corporate credit bonds, and international institution bonds.

Number of Securities Investment Funds refers to the number of fund products in the fund market at the end of the period. It is counted since the effective date of the fund contract (the establishment date of the fund), and is excluded from the statistics since the termination date of the fund contract. It is generally counted at the coverage of the main code of the Securities Regulatory Commission (the main contract of the fund).

19

房地产

Real Estate

简 要 说 明

一、本篇资料的主要内容及统计范围

本篇资料通过对一定时期内房地产开发企业开发经营活动的数量方面的描述，反映报告期内房地产开发企业投资总规模及完成情况、实际到位资金情况、房屋建筑面积和造价情况、房屋新开工面积情况、商品房销售情况以及资产负债和经营情况。

本篇资料的统计范围包括有开发经营活动的全部房地产开发经营业法人单位。

二、本篇的资料来源及统计调查方法

本篇统计资料是根据《房地产开发统计报表制度》进行搜集和加工整理而得，全部数据采用全面调查的统计方法。

三、本篇资料的数据情况说明

本篇资料对2010年度以来房地产开发投资、新建商品房销售等指标数据进行了修订，主要原因是：（一）加强在建房地产开发项目审核，剔除单纯一级土地开发等非房地产开发项目。（二）加强商品房销售数据审核，剔除退房和具有抵押性质等非商品房销售数据。(三)加强统计执法，对发现的问题数据按照相关规定进行了改正。

Brief Introduction

I. Main Contents and Scope of Statistics

Data in this chapter describe activities of real estate development enterprises during a given period of time, and reflect total size and completed investment, actual funds in place, floor space and cost of buildings constructed, floor space started in the year, sales of commercial buildings, assets and liabilities, and operation status of real estate developers during report period.

Data in this chapter covers all corporate units with development and operating activities engaged in real estate development.

II. Sources of Data

Data in this chapter are collected and compiled in accordance with the *Statistical Reporting System on Real Estate Development* collected through comprehensive survey.

III. Explanation of Data Situation

This document has revised the data on indicators such as real estate development investment and sales area of newly-built commercial housing since 2010. The main reason is: (1) strengthen the review of real estate development projects under construction, and eliminate non real estate development projects such as pure primary land development. (2) Strengthen the review of sales data for commercial housing, exclude non commercial housing sales data such as check-out and those with mortgage properties. (3) strengthen statistical law enforcement and made corrections to the problem data discovered in accordance with relevant regulations.

19-1 房地产开发企业主要指标
Main Indicators of Enterprises for Real Estate Development

指 标	Item	2020	2021	2022	2023
企业个数 （个）	**Number of Enterprises (unit)**	**103262**	**105434**	**102852**	**100111**
内资企业	Domestic Invested Enterprises	99150	101374	99054	96929
港澳台投资企业	Enterprises with Investment from Hong Kong, Macao and Taiwan	2759	2703	2550	2448
外商投资企业	Foreign Invested Enterprises	1353	1357	1248	734
平均从业人数 （万人）	**Average Number of Employed Persons (10 000 persons)**	**290.13**	**280.16**	**244.67**	**200.23**
内资企业	Domestic Invested Enterprises	274.65	265.76	232.80	191.42
港澳台投资企业	Enterprises with Investment from Hong Kong, Macao and Taiwan	10.19	9.24	7.82	6.72
外商投资企业	Foreign Invested Enterprises	5.29	5.15	4.05	2.09
本年完成投资 （亿元）	**Investment Completed in the Year (100 million yuan)**	**132013.7**	**137633.3**	**123847.8**	**112142.3**
#住宅	Residential Buildings	97122.1	103281.5	93420.1	84961.2
本年实际到位资金 （亿元）	**Actual Funds in Place in the Year (100 million yuan)**	**193114.9**	**201132.2**	**148209.6**	**129766.3**
#国内贷款	Domestic Loans	26675.9	23295.8	17424.2	16212.5
利用外资	Foreign Investment	192.0	107.4	78.0	43.1
自筹资金	Self-raised Fund	63376.6	65427.7	52406.1	42698.7
房屋建筑面积 （万平方米）	**Floor Space of Buildings (10 000 sq.m)**				
施工面积	Floor Space under Construction	926759.2	975386.5	904499.7	840156.9
竣工面积	Floor Space Completed	91218.2	101411.9	85358.0	101999.1
本年新开工面积	Floor Space Started in the Year	224433.1	198895.0	119944.0	95958.0
#住宅	Residential Buildings	164328.5	146378.6	87620.7	69669.1
新建商品房销售面积（万平方米）	**Floor Space of Newly-built Commercial Buildings Sold (10 000 sq.m)**	**158819.3**	**161354.0**	**122154.5**	**111761.6**
#住宅	Residential Buildings	139926.6	141006.7	103305.8	94818.9
新建商品房平均销售价格 （元/平方米）	**Average Selling Price of Newly-built Commercial Buildings (yuan/sq.m)**	**10248**	**10546**	**10210**	**10438**
#住宅	Residential Buildings	10385	10825	10608	10864
实收资本 （亿元）	**Paid-in Capital (100 million yuan)**	**116652.0**	**127272.2**	**134049.7**	**139206.3**
资产负债率 （%）	**Assets-liability Ratio (%)**	**80.7**	**80.3**	**79.1**	**78.0**
主营业务收入 （亿元）	**Revenue from Principal Business (100 million yuan)**	**118582.1**	**134342.2**	**123052.0**	**143273.6**
#土地转让收入	Revenue from Land Transfer	747.8	769.3	709.1	674.4

注：1.本表登记注册统计类别按《关于市场主体统计分类的划分规定》(国统字〔2023〕14号)执行。
2.商品房平均销售价格由报告期内新建商品房销售额除以销售面积计算而成。不同时期的商品房平均销售价格可能会受商品房区域、房屋类型等各种因素的影响(以下相关表同)。

a) The registered statistical categories of this table is implemented in accordance with the Regulations on the Classification of Market Entity Statistics (Guotongzi [2023] No. 14).

b) Average selling price of commercial buildings is calculated by total value of sale of newly-built commercial buildings divided by floor space sold during report period.Selling prices of buildings during different periods are affected by location and type of buildings etc. The same applies to the relevant following tables.

19–2 房地产开发企业个数
Number of Enterprises for Real Estate Development

单位：个 (unit)

年份 地区	Year Region	企业个数 Number of Enterprises	内资企业 Domestic Invested Enterprises	港澳台投资企业 Enterprises with Investment from Hong Kong, Macao and Taiwan	外商投资企业 Foreign Invested Enterprises
	1998	24378	19960	3214	1204
	2000	27303	23277	2899	1127
	2005	56290	50957	3443	1890
	2006	58710	53268	3519	1923
	2007	62518	56965	3524	2029
	2008	87562	81282	3916	2364
	2009	80407	74674	3633	2100
	2010	85218	79489	3677	2052
	2011	88419	83011	3565	1843
	2012	89859	84695	3451	1713
	2013	91444	86379	3391	1674
	2014	94197	89218	3414	1565
	2015	93426	88773	3235	1418
	2016	94948	90408	3232	1308
	2017	95897	91608	3066	1223
	2018	97937	94063	2719	1155
	2019	99544	95691	2664	1189
	2020	103262	99150	2759	1353
	2021	105434	101374	2703	1357
	2022	102852	99054	2550	1248
	2023	100111	96929	2448	734
北 京	Beijing	1171	1116	27	28
天 津	Tianjin	1084	1029	35	20
河 北	Hebei	3840	3810	20	10
山 西	Shanxi	2766	2757	6	3
内蒙古	Inner Mongolia	1696	1695		1
辽 宁	Liaoning	2581	2410	131	40
吉 林	Jilin	1345	1337	5	3
黑龙江	Heilongjiang	1297	1284	9	4
上 海	Shanghai	2528	2209	227	92
江 苏	Jiangsu	6922	6378	423	121
浙 江	Zhejiang	6142	5957	126	59
安 徽	Anhui	3682	3635	36	11
福 建	Fujian	3148	2986	131	31
江 西	Jiangxi	2853	2790	55	8
山 东	Shandong	7882	7590	219	73
河 南	Henan	8337	8276	46	15
湖 北	Hubei	4180	4109	60	11
湖 南	Hunan	4383	4314	55	14
广 东	Guangdong	9603	8902	589	112
广 西	Guangxi	3060	3018	36	6
海 南	Hainan	1256	1204	43	9
重 庆	Chongqing	2121	2031	68	22
四 川	Sichuan	4671	4612	43	16
贵 州	Guizhou	2594	2576	12	6
云 南	Yunnan	2808	2780	21	7
西 藏	Xizang	121	121		
陕 西	Shaanxi	2968	2941	18	9
甘 肃	Gansu	1666	1664	1	1
青 海	Qinghai	306	305		1
宁 夏	Ningxia	572	569	2	1
新 疆	Xinjiang	2528	2524	4	

注：本表登记注册统计类别按《关于市场主体统计分类的划分规定》(国统字〔2023〕14号)执行。

a) The registered statistical categories of this table is implemented in accordance with the Regulations on the Classification of Market Entity Statistics (Guotongzi [2023] No. 14).

19-3 房地产开发企业从业人员数
Number of Employed Persons in Enterprises for Real Estate Development

单位：人 (person)

年份 Year / 地区 Region		平均从业人数 Average Number of Employed Persons	内资企业 Domestic Invested Enterprises	港澳台投资企业 Enterprises with Investment from Hong Kong, Macao and Taiwan	外商投资企业 Foreign Invested Enterprises
	1998	825888	708738	83784	33366
	2000	971942	862245	79066	30631
	2005	1516150	1366743	90674	58733
	2006	1600930	1442158	97688	61084
	2007	1719666	1541336	100398	77932
	2008	2100362	1906029	109246	85087
	2009	1949295	1763867	109965	75463
	2010	2091147	1908969	105846	76332
	2011	2256964	2075474	112990	68500
	2012	2386772	2199815	116849	70108
	2013	2591814	2397762	121807	72245
	2014	2760070	2561817	129287	68966
	2015	2738454	2551484	124494	62476
	2016	2752298	2576545	118495	57258
	2017	2830960	2663954	113221	53785
	2018	2889165	2735301	104378	49486
	2019	2937379	2784130	103746	49503
	2020	2901253	2746467	101924	52862
	2021	2801571	2657629	92414	51528
	2022	2446671	2328044	78151	40476
	2023	2002341	1914210	67184	20947
北　京	Beijing	33612	30942	1843	827
天　津	Tianjin	21102	19144	1582	376
河　北	Hebei	87560	86705	453	402
山　西	Shanxi	52836	52624	77	135
内蒙古	Inner Mongolia	26932	26919		13
辽　宁	Liaoning	35493	32033	2606	854
吉　林	Jilin	23414	23147	164	103
黑龙江	Heilongjiang	17245	16966	212	67
上　海	Shanghai	43745	33241	7652	2852
江　苏	Jiangsu	122415	110195	9102	3118
浙　江	Zhejiang	92465	87766	2833	1866
安　徽	Anhui	70008	68843	981	184
福　建	Fujian	63262	59355	3358	549
江　西	Jiangxi	62190	60711	1362	117
山　东	Shandong	167833	160578	5812	1443
河　南	Henan	150121	148753	1039	329
湖　北	Hubei	103094	100190	2561	343
湖　南	Hunan	99572	97382	1810	380
广　东	Guangdong	198518	177713	16321	4484
广　西	Guangxi	58157	57106	969	82
海　南	Hainan	28718	27602	953	163
重　庆	Chongqing	59184	55791	2290	1103
四　川	Sichuan	116843	115116	1094	633
贵　州	Guizhou	48261	48015	185	61
云　南	Yunnan	68996	67895	988	113
西　藏	Xizang	2343	2343		
陕　西	Shaanxi	57892	56962	618	312
甘　肃	Gansu	32805	32798	6	1
青　海	Qinghai	6229	6209		20
宁　夏	Ningxia	12083	11953	113	17
新　疆	Xinjiang	39413	39213	200	

注：本表登记注册统计类别按《关于市场主体统计分类的划分规定》(国统字〔2023〕14号)执行。

a) The registered statistical categories of this table is implemented in accordance with the Regulations on the Classification of Market Entity Statistics (Guotongzi [2023] No. 14).

19-4 房地产开发企业投资总规模及完成情况(2023年)
Total Size and Completed Investment of Enterprises for Real Estate Development (2023)

单位：亿元 (100 million yuan)

地区	Region	计划总投资 Total Investment Planned	自开始建设至本年底累计完成投资 Accumulative Investment Completed from Starting of Construction Till the End of the Year	本年完成投资 Investment Completed in the Year	建筑安装工程 Construction and Installation	设备工器具购置 Purchase of Equipment and Instruments	其他费用 Others	土地购置费 Value of Land Purchased
全国	**National Total**	**1017306.92**	**688412.66**	**112142.25**	**66077.23**	**985.94**	**45079.08**	**39058.00**
北京	Beijing	29098.03	24563.79	4202.41	1358.91	3.45	2840.05	2507.93
天津	Tianjin	23315.30	16542.71	1232.04	691.46	2.94	537.65	359.23
河北	Hebei	29434.16	16131.10	3094.45	2072.28	20.15	1002.02	837.93
山西	Shanxi	17394.64	9636.71	1760.08	1281.23	14.63	464.22	333.65
内蒙古	Inner Mongolia	9239.72	5795.46	1009.68	746.76	2.58	260.34	218.98
辽宁	Liaoning	21727.14	16091.65	1742.80	1328.16	17.98	396.67	312.02
吉林	Jilin	9328.93	6154.89	823.04	561.69	1.84	259.50	229.52
黑龙江	Heilongjiang	6764.59	4549.85	458.04	346.41	5.91	105.71	69.00
上海	Shanghai	50157.85	30994.57	6062.04	2452.49	14.71	3594.84	3066.65
江苏	Jiangsu	99112.98	60966.84	11932.12	6654.57	109.79	5167.76	4695.29
浙江	Zhejiang	77145.09	52348.35	13319.18	5239.62	43.00	8036.56	7226.55
安徽	Anhui	41196.13	29464.62	4676.52	2808.14	17.72	1850.66	1697.52
福建	Fujian	29935.77	25084.42	4413.89	2081.74	38.71	2293.44	2194.91
江西	Jiangxi	20730.36	11263.83	1604.88	1181.42	25.29	398.16	358.79
山东	Shandong	69979.51	42661.21	8541.23	5763.24	69.36	2708.63	2381.79
河南	Henan	49232.14	30143.04	4225.18	3487.35	34.01	703.82	595.42
湖北	Hubei	43999.49	28719.92	5467.61	3377.90	81.95	2007.76	1780.65
湖南	Hunan	31454.89	20974.34	3852.23	2749.19	120.27	982.77	845.60
广东	Guangdong	137490.32	102751.49	13693.33	7121.28	118.97	6453.08	5293.26
广西	Guangxi	27263.17	18984.66	1336.75	1039.22	10.30	287.23	198.02
海南	Hainan	14230.06	10730.35	1169.29	851.45	6.25	311.58	214.99
重庆	Chongqing	30331.99	27076.98	2796.71	2060.91	86.52	649.27	515.56
四川	Sichuan	42945.53	28082.64	5322.02	3487.58	63.49	1770.95	1578.03
贵州	Guizhou	22423.98	14587.28	1190.82	946.14	8.36	236.32	187.39
云南	Yunnan	22876.19	17979.06	1718.50	1509.84	6.91	201.75	160.18
西藏	Xizang	538.37	433.30	79.41	58.00	0.57	20.84	18.29
陕西	Shaanxi	33719.48	19717.50	3278.40	2354.95	33.57	889.89	661.30
甘肃	Gansu	9353.11	5623.43	1264.00	963.19	12.40	288.41	240.22
青海	Qinghai	2649.19	1738.46	201.35	166.38	1.84	33.13	28.07
宁夏	Ningxia	3582.33	2267.65	436.22	354.01	3.37	78.84	62.32
新疆	Xinjiang	10656.47	6352.58	1238.01	981.70	9.08	247.24	188.93

19-5 按用途分房地产开发企业完成投资
Investment Completed by Enterprises for Real Estate Development by Use

单位：亿元 (100 million yuan)

年 份 地 区	Year Region	本年完成投资 Investment Completed in the Year	#住宅 Residential Buildings	#办公楼 Office Buildings	#商业营业用房 Buildings for Business Use
	1998	3614.23	2081.56	433.80	475.83
	2000	4984.05	3311.98	297.85	579.99
	2005	15909.25	10860.93	763.07	2039.53
	2006	19422.92	13638.41	928.06	2353.88
	2007	25288.84	18005.42	1035.04	2785.65
	2008	31203.19	22440.87	1167.17	3354.48
	2009	36241.81	25613.69	1377.21	4180.66
	2010	47562.35	33477.25	1794.57	5555.40
	2011	60145.57	43014.19	2521.56	7194.18
	2012	69210.92	47417.35	3293.18	8900.66
	2013	82197.73	56155.84	4521.90	11257.15
	2014	90247.21	60950.57	5452.85	13390.06
	2015	90911.49	61056.93	5970.83	13572.49
	2016	96900.01	64809.07	6258.18	14634.57
	2017	103427.38	70683.79	6459.16	14396.79
	2018	112740.23	79643.61	5725.76	13003.55
	2019	123610.14	90462.96	5875.28	12111.72
	2020	132013.68	97122.10	6179.88	11952.40
	2021	137633.32	103281.53	5684.84	11363.40
	2022	123847.80	93420.11	5034.77	9722.17
	2023	112142.25	84961.22	4571.05	8067.20
北 京	Beijing	4202.41	2714.42	268.74	189.98
天 津	Tianjin	1232.04	973.70	32.12	62.94
河 北	Hebei	3094.45	2607.48	37.64	144.77
山 西	Shanxi	1760.08	1421.86	22.79	121.78
内蒙古	Inner Mongolia	1009.68	787.83	10.68	78.20
辽 宁	Liaoning	1742.80	1377.29	54.24	163.42
吉 林	Jilin	823.04	613.42	16.51	77.90
黑龙江	Heilongjiang	458.04	372.73	4.45	39.54
上 海	Shanghai	6062.04	3466.79	772.74	489.80
江 苏	Jiangsu	11932.12	9622.98	371.27	812.98
浙 江	Zhejiang	13319.18	9273.88	571.76	845.55
安 徽	Anhui	4676.52	3772.31	85.28	356.28
福 建	Fujian	4413.89	3207.63	117.78	275.16
江 西	Jiangxi	1604.88	1340.21	34.36	135.44
山 东	Shandong	8541.23	6934.60	320.06	523.36
河 南	Henan	4225.18	3673.64	101.01	214.73
湖 北	Hubei	5467.61	4356.88	244.43	407.86
湖 南	Hunan	3852.23	3140.13	81.98	339.50
广 东	Guangdong	13693.33	9942.27	864.80	1041.90
广 西	Guangxi	1336.75	1056.99	24.99	91.48
海 南	Hainan	1169.29	841.58	73.80	104.63
重 庆	Chongqing	2796.71	2109.64	45.29	294.49
四 川	Sichuan	5322.02	4006.34	188.68	421.54
贵 州	Guizhou	1190.82	983.97	10.17	86.69
云 南	Yunnan	1718.50	1284.40	49.43	173.51
西 藏	Xizang	79.41	60.44	4.45	10.80
陕 西	Shaanxi	3278.40	2615.02	117.99	189.65
甘 肃	Gansu	1264.00	1029.53	17.69	87.70
青 海	Qinghai	201.35	158.50	4.40	20.73
宁 夏	Ningxia	436.22	346.21	2.52	40.38
新 疆	Xinjiang	1238.01	868.57	18.98	224.54

19-6 房地产开发企业实际到位资金
Actual Funds in Place of Enterprises for Real Estate Development

单位：亿元 (100 million yuan)

年份 地区	Year Region	本年实际到位资金 Actual Funds in Place in the Year	国内贷款 Domestic Loans	利用外资 Foreign Investment	自筹资金 Self-raised Funds	定金及预收款 Deposit and Advance Payment	个人按揭贷款 Individual Mortgage Loans	其他到位资金 Others
	1998	4414.94	1053.17	361.76	1166.98			
	2000	5997.63	1385.08	168.70	1614.21			
	2005	21397.84	3918.08	257.81	7000.39	6954.23	1341.18	1926.15
	2006	27135.55	5356.98	400.15	8597.09	8192.65	2588.38	2000.30
	2007	37477.96	7015.64	641.04	11772.53	10663.20	5080.43	2305.12
	2008	39619.36	7605.69	728.22	15312.10	9756.68	3886.04	2330.63
	2009	57799.04	11364.51	479.39	17949.12	16217.49	8561.65	3226.88
	2010	72944.04	12563.70	790.68	26637.21	19275.15	9523.77	4153.53
	2011	85688.73	13056.80	785.15	35004.57	22470.32	8678.37	5693.53
	2012	96536.81	14778.39	402.09	39081.96	26558.02	10523.78	5192.57
	2013	122122.47	19672.66	534.17	47424.95	34498.97	14033.26	5958.47
	2014	121991.48	21242.61	639.26	50419.80	30237.51	13665.45	5786.85
	2015	125203.06	20214.38	296.53	49037.56	32520.34	16661.65	6472.61
	2016	144214.05	21512.40	140.44	49132.85	41952.14	24402.94	7073.29
	2017	156052.62	25241.76	168.19	50872.22	48693.57	23906.31	7170.58
	2018	166407.11	24132.14	114.02	55754.79	55748.16	23643.06	7014.94
	2019	178608.59	25228.77	175.72	58157.84	61358.88	27281.03	6406.34
	2020	193114.85	26675.94	192.00	63376.65	66546.83	29975.81	6347.62
	2021	201132.21	23295.79	107.36	65427.69	73945.65	32388.19	5967.53
	2022	148209.59	17424.17	77.97	52406.09	49085.11	23655.31	5560.95
	2023	129766.29	16212.53	43.13	42698.67	43620.90	21709.02	5482.04
北京	Beijing	5849.22	740.78		1217.58	2849.18	522.06	519.61
天津	Tianjin	2703.25	274.24		684.47	1318.42	321.24	104.88
河北	Hebei	3806.95	295.02		1315.13	1300.03	782.92	113.86
山西	Shanxi	1990.34	66.02		691.48	773.66	400.76	58.41
内蒙古	Inner Mongolia	1168.95	37.22		386.54	513.66	201.99	29.53
辽宁	Liaoning	1901.24	146.72	0.80	779.92	671.02	262.53	40.25
吉林	Jilin	848.92	35.00	0.21	431.65	198.63	138.74	44.69
黑龙江	Heilongjiang	559.80	42.60		224.28	177.71	79.73	35.49
上海	Shanghai	6077.40	1469.91	1.51	2376.03	1732.68	320.23	177.04
江苏	Jiangsu	14391.61	2401.06	10.47	3905.49	4821.02	2583.74	669.84
浙江	Zhejiang	13383.71	1901.99	4.23	4267.24	4787.51	1999.40	423.34
安徽	Anhui	5614.30	522.34	0.03	1653.94	1824.14	1230.18	383.66
福建	Fujian	4614.92	507.26	1.93	2289.72	1116.91	484.52	214.57
江西	Jiangxi	2132.64	190.31	0.33	575.02	649.11	632.60	85.27
山东	Shandong	8757.32	796.55	0.22	3059.69	2967.66	1495.90	437.28
河南	Henan	4432.51	367.69		2262.24	1022.80	695.39	84.40
湖北	Hubei	4521.99	545.82	2.88	1472.67	1238.52	936.43	325.66
湖南	Hunan	4216.27	540.72		1419.87	1230.63	854.92	170.14
广东	Guangdong	18186.79	2857.43	17.89	5993.29	6020.35	2775.16	522.68
广西	Guangxi	2009.31	186.74		495.90	607.70	501.43	217.54
海南	Hainan	1718.02	315.58		603.88	635.69	80.65	82.22
重庆	Chongqing	2846.91	464.46	0.02	843.15	881.87	506.39	151.02
四川	Sichuan	7318.99	703.15		2168.92	2891.35	1463.71	91.86
贵州	Guizhou	1336.62	78.63		315.91	400.02	471.05	71.00
云南	Yunnan	1905.46	99.46	2.60	557.99	671.39	494.60	79.41
西藏	Xizang	64.54	3.81		14.86	16.51	28.85	0.51
陕西	Shaanxi	4140.07	443.89		1652.40	1197.84	614.94	230.99
甘肃	Gansu	1052.94	48.80		451.90	309.62	220.48	22.13
青海	Qinghai	216.45	18.32		54.44	85.81	43.39	14.48
宁夏	Ningxia	627.87	55.21		92.18	216.58	244.66	19.24
新疆	Xinjiang	1371.00	55.76		440.91	492.89	320.42	61.02

19–7 房地产开发企业房屋建筑面积和造价
Floor Space and Cost of Buildings Constructed by Enterprises for Real Estate Development

年份 地区	Year Region	房屋施工面积(万平方米) Floor Space of Buildings under Construction (10 000 sq.m)	房屋竣工面积(万平方米) Floor Space of Buildings Completed (10 000 sq.m)	房屋建筑面积竣工率(%) Rate of Floor Space of Buildings Completed (%)	房屋竣工价值(亿元) Value of Buildings Completed (100 million yuan)	房屋竣工造价(元/平方米) Cost of Buildings Completed (yuan/sq.m)
	1998	50770.14	17566.60	34.6	2139.19	1218
	2000	65896.92	25104.86	38.1	2859.35	1139
	2005	166053.26	53417.04	32.2	7752.24	1451
	2006	194786.42	55830.92	28.7	8729.35	1564
	2007	236318.24	60606.68	25.6	10039.89	1657
	2008	283266.18	66544.77	23.5	11947.57	1795
	2009	320368.16	72677.43	22.7	14689.37	2021
	2010	405356.40	78743.88	19.4	17542.73	2228
	2011	506775.48	92619.94	18.3	21975.91	2373
	2012	573417.52	99424.96	17.3	24836.62	2498
	2013	665571.89	101434.99	15.2	26805.38	2643
	2014	726482.34	107459.05	14.8	30261.99	2816
	2015	735693.37	100039.10	13.6	30552.38	3054
	2016	758974.80	106127.71	14.0	32252.13	3039
	2017	781483.73	101486.41	13.0	31512.46	3105
	2018	822299.56	94421.15	11.5	30309.07	3210
	2019	893820.89	95941.53	10.7	34045.90	3549
	2020	926759.19	91218.23	9.8	34493.83	3781
	2021	975386.51	101411.94	10.4	39458.15	3891
	2022	904499.67	85357.96	9.4	34940.22	4093
	2023	840156.92	101999.09	12.1	42326.64	4150
北京	Beijing	12531.34	2112.42	16.9	1014.25	4801
天津	Tianjin	9587.14	1864.41	19.4	670.69	3597
河北	Hebei	31697.17	3447.23	10.9	1241.27	3601
山西	Shanxi	24601.25	2363.85	9.6	634.19	2683
内蒙古	Inner Mongolia	14169.98	1309.56	9.2	462.77	3534
辽宁	Liaoning	20845.01	2243.45	10.8	807.92	3601
吉林	Jilin	10514.27	688.93	6.6	209.99	3048
黑龙江	Heilongjiang	9084.79	840.14	9.2	262.13	3120
上海	Shanghai	17618.37	2112.35	12.0	1463.75	6930
江苏	Jiangsu	57414.73	8942.76	15.6	4517.75	5052
浙江	Zhejiang	55986.18	10094.63	18.0	5294.35	5245
安徽	Anhui	34953.76	5741.84	16.4	2113.97	3682
福建	Fujian	27695.65	4310.59	15.6	1717.94	3985
江西	Jiangxi	21594.82	1994.25	9.2	654.09	3280
山东	Shandong	71309.86	8964.87	12.6	3337.57	3723
河南	Henan	52064.48	6193.15	11.9	1720.53	2778
湖北	Hubei	31528.21	3865.82	12.3	1634.28	4228
湖南	Hunan	31958.71	4374.32	13.7	1468.70	3358
广东	Guangdong	82899.11	8283.72	10.0	4813.82	5811
广西	Guangxi	29555.08	2650.60	9.0	959.28	3619
海南	Hainan	9098.09	751.78	8.3	494.71	6580
重庆	Chongqing	20497.57	3302.02	16.1	1571.15	4758
四川	Sichuan	47766.63	4371.32	9.2	1665.76	3811
贵州	Guizhou	24780.43	1585.41	6.4	445.17	2808
云南	Yunnan	24983.98	3331.68	13.3	1014.43	3045
西藏	Xizang	647.00	67.61	10.4	27.80	4111
陕西	Shaanxi	28579.86	2196.82	7.7	811.05	3692
甘肃	Gansu	12115.10	1241.19	10.2	476.38	3838
青海	Qinghai	3149.59	269.82	8.6	101.64	3767
宁夏	Ningxia	4861.39	1048.40	21.6	319.57	3048
新疆	Xinjiang	16067.36	1434.19	8.9	399.76	2787

19-8 按用途分房地产开发企业房屋新开工面积
Floor Space of Buildings Started in the Year by Enterprises for Real Estate Development by Use

单位：万平方米 (10 000 sq.m)

年份 Year 地区 Region	本年房屋新开工面积 Floor Space of Buildings Started in the Year	#住宅 Residential Buildings	#办公楼 Office Buildings	#商业营业用房 Buildings for Business Use
1998	20387.90	16637.50	871.50	1938.65
2000	29582.64	24401.15	898.81	3034.77
2005	68064.44	55185.07	1671.10	7675.47
2006	79252.83	64403.80	2134.94	8473.23
2007	95401.53	78795.51	2141.44	9093.89
2008	102553.37	83642.12	2471.95	10040.69
2009	116422.05	93298.41	2860.76	12415.03
2010	163646.87	129359.31	3668.07	17472.58
2011	191236.87	147163.11	5399.20	20730.78
2012	177333.62	130695.42	5986.46	22006.85
2013	201207.84	145844.80	6887.24	25902.00
2014	179592.49	124877.00	7349.10	25047.73
2015	154453.68	106651.30	6569.12	22530.29
2016	166928.13	115910.60	6415.29	22316.63
2017	178653.77	128097.78	6139.66	20483.93
2018	209537.16	153485.36	6101.51	19995.39
2019	227153.58	167463.43	7083.59	18936.28
2020	224433.13	164328.53	6603.71	18012.32
2021	198895.05	146378.56	5223.89	14105.53
2022	119943.95	87620.71	3175.20	8120.50
2023	95957.96	69669.14	2619.80	6493.42
北京 Beijing	1257.14	715.06	73.24	59.15
天津 Tianjin	1037.28	735.63	15.27	54.58
河北 Hebei	4966.66	3986.64	44.02	173.50
山西 Shanxi	2499.46	2013.06	27.37	126.32
内蒙古 Inner Mongolia	1614.17	1213.11	21.38	94.49
辽宁 Liaoning	1577.68	1254.70	17.36	103.50
吉林 Jilin	949.24	722.93	9.67	88.85
黑龙江 Heilongjiang	738.43	617.55	4.66	52.02
上海 Shanghai	2388.19	1370.91	195.64	124.51
江苏 Jiangsu	8209.51	5785.36	244.66	542.29
浙江 Zhejiang	7718.60	4764.75	356.43	543.33
安徽 Anhui	5197.02	3854.18	103.94	306.32
福建 Fujian	3535.58	2303.05	113.41	217.86
江西 Jiangxi	2694.15	2157.43	68.66	218.86
山东 Shandong	7937.57	5801.30	244.56	532.39
河南 Henan	5629.64	4788.28	43.71	306.66
湖北 Hubei	3596.22	2832.74	72.27	220.63
湖南 Hunan	3883.00	3115.69	33.73	287.76
广东 Guangdong	6883.83	4726.95	382.69	515.54
广西 Guangxi	1869.71	1432.75	14.38	97.94
海南 Hainan	1054.72	726.90	55.03	82.17
重庆 Chongqing	1974.78	1362.74	11.37	164.64
四川 Sichuan	5803.82	3898.54	248.32	458.39
贵州 Guizhou	1809.31	1331.22	21.86	125.70
云南 Yunnan	2148.75	1510.52	39.13	186.77
西藏 Xizang	44.24	31.64	0.80	8.22
陕西 Shaanxi	4290.58	3229.23	118.98	223.21
甘肃 Gansu	1581.55	1210.56	10.74	121.28
青海 Qinghai	232.89	195.64	0.33	16.09
宁夏 Ningxia	765.09	600.21	0.75	46.02
新疆 Xinjiang	2069.14	1379.87	25.44	394.42

19-9 按用途分新建商品房销售面积
Floor Space of Newly-built Commercial Buildings Sold by Use

单位：万平方米 (10 000 sq.m)

年份 Year 地区 Region	新建商品房销售面积 Floor Space of Newly-built Commercial Buildings Sold	#住宅 Residential Buildings	#办公楼 Office Buildings	#商业营业用房 Buildings for Business Use
1998	12185.30	10827.10	400.60	810.80
2000	18637.13	16570.28	436.98	1399.31
2005	55486.22	49587.83	1096.23	4081.38
2006	61857.07	55422.95	1231.04	4337.79
2007	77354.72	70135.88	1465.23	4644.61
2008	65969.83	59280.35	1157.05	4206.06
2009	94755.00	86184.89	1544.43	5328.03
2010	103818.91	92592.44	1889.97	6879.02
2011	107498.82	95030.58	1988.91	7599.82
2012	108540.85	96185.10	2217.99	7419.95
2013	125306.90	111215.06	2804.47	7986.26
2014	115291.30	100757.54	2431.12	8448.16
2015	121512.12	106544.46	2804.08	8515.38
2016	145972.62	127816.43	3630.55	9784.81
2017	155400.38	133187.10	4404.58	11449.28
2018	156188.72	134910.12	4023.75	10590.60
2019	155415.79	136265.02	3420.18	8989.53
2020	158819.29	139926.57	3056.74	8172.05
2021	161354.02	141006.67	3087.61	7933.82
2022	122154.48	103305.77	2985.91	7228.28
2023	111761.62	94818.89	2715.38	6359.64
北京 Beijing	1131.82	818.25	75.66	51.79
天津 Tianjin	1178.51	1110.25	7.00	39.31
河北 Hebei	4338.53	4085.48	43.69	104.37
山西 Shanxi	2356.05	2257.88	5.80	65.25
内蒙古 Inner Mongolia	1543.98	1426.51	7.40	85.97
辽宁 Liaoning	2067.02	1860.99	13.13	132.32
吉林 Jilin	1047.34	977.88	18.67	39.33
黑龙江 Heilongjiang	855.32	769.43	6.14	62.94
上海 Shanghai	1811.71	1456.96	86.43	55.19
江苏 Jiangsu	11024.25	9073.40	308.87	750.13
浙江 Zhejiang	6107.04	5113.32	297.91	389.93
安徽 Anhui	4674.14	4210.03	86.44	177.76
福建 Fujian	4224.95	3072.08	153.66	244.69
江西 Jiangxi	3417.68	2901.59	91.50	299.36
山东 Shandong	11285.01	9441.97	336.18	675.77
河南 Henan	6966.64	6520.56	122.13	250.09
湖北 Hubei	5259.22	4536.11	152.71	320.17
湖南 Hunan	5626.48	5093.57	63.47	331.98
广东 Guangdong	9582.01	7665.55	332.41	581.05
广西 Guangxi	2878.41	2304.81	36.73	170.97
海南 Hainan	905.82	780.08	43.18	48.80
重庆 Chongqing	3557.25	2258.06	71.10	323.96
四川 Sichuan	8005.48	6364.98	191.43	480.26
贵州 Guizhou	2214.68	2028.46	19.54	127.57
云南 Yunnan	2488.53	2099.24	51.20	155.23
西藏 Xizang	80.25	68.80	3.90	7.53
陕西 Shaanxi	2718.94	2453.62	60.39	101.11
甘肃 Gansu	1498.12	1428.22	6.71	50.79
青海 Qinghai	238.27	223.13	5.00	8.70
宁夏 Ningxia	691.10	637.37	2.91	48.03
新疆 Xinjiang	1987.11	1780.31	14.08	179.30

注：2004年及以前的销售数据仅包括现房；2005年及以后的销售数据包括期房和现房(以下相关表同)。

a) Data on floor space of buildings sold for 2004 and earlier years refer to completed buildings, while data since 2005 refer to both completed and future buildings. The same applies to the relevant following tables .

19-10 按用途分新建商品房销售额
Sales of Newly-built Commercial Buildings by Use

单位：亿元 (100 million yuan)

年份 地区	Year Region	新建商品房销售额 Total Sale of Newly-built Commercial Buildings	#住宅 Residential Buildings	#办公楼 Office Buildings	#商业营业用房 Buildings for Business Use
	1998	2513.30	2006.87	222.41	257.06
	2000	3935.44	3228.60	207.63	456.23
	2005	17576.13	14563.76	758.87	2049.57
	2006	20825.96	17287.81	991.33	2275.87
	2007	29889.12	25565.81	1269.91	2681.72
	2008	25068.18	21196.00	969.36	2475.85
	2009	44355.17	38432.90	1638.41	3660.67
	2010	52381.16	43871.54	2155.71	5341.70
	2011	57876.98	47788.66	2454.09	6425.19
	2012	63382.29	52766.29	2741.25	6698.41
	2013	79299.42	66133.41	3688.54	7834.34
	2014	74092.97	60938.80	2913.12	8341.42
	2015	84230.01	70558.86	3687.48	8200.45
	2016	112385.35	95010.47	5346.06	9703.56
	2017	126804.48	105122.66	6174.57	12035.51
	2018	141267.49	119884.33	5991.30	11763.12
	2019	150335.88	131727.35	5075.46	10041.29
	2020	162752.25	145319.73	4798.24	8896.85
	2021	170158.66	152636.66	4459.72	8702.23
	2022	124720.39	109583.35	4295.10	7298.06
	2023	116660.90	103013.19	3742.11	6628.31
北京	Beijing	4255.10	3828.00	178.69	79.64
天津	Tianjin	1895.87	1812.37	9.10	53.82
河北	Hebei	3548.78	3383.44	21.71	99.92
山西	Shanxi	1597.30	1514.06	3.84	68.28
内蒙古	Inner Mongolia	1019.83	927.93	6.08	72.42
辽宁	Liaoning	1555.66	1402.35	13.63	116.12
吉林	Jilin	725.05	665.97	22.56	32.01
黑龙江	Heilongjiang	553.39	487.44	6.59	50.91
上海	Shanghai	7277.69	6701.64	300.80	138.39
江苏	Jiangsu	12690.29	11268.76	337.57	737.34
浙江	Zhejiang	11509.69	10152.78	539.43	563.31
安徽	Anhui	3872.25	3561.51	75.51	174.42
福建	Fujian	4653.99	3805.37	164.61	286.64
江西	Jiangxi	2469.38	2091.70	74.37	250.67
山东	Shandong	9530.01	8163.56	377.68	666.71
河南	Henan	4547.52	4210.55	124.04	183.86
湖北	Hubei	4616.73	3971.27	198.55	329.89
湖南	Hunan	3688.86	3291.92	70.59	272.77
广东	Guangdong	15103.05	12976.46	725.28	865.00
广西	Guangxi	1666.93	1420.48	26.77	144.39
海南	Hainan	1500.99	1297.57	78.44	100.43
重庆	Chongqing	2450.32	1932.37	59.91	249.34
四川	Sichuan	7173.77	6289.94	174.66	476.64
贵州	Guizhou	1251.82	1123.79	13.82	105.63
云南	Yunnan	1700.42	1483.94	38.09	128.14
西藏	Xizang	67.19	55.46	2.58	9.14
陕西	Shaanxi	2978.32	2725.63	74.02	114.50
甘肃	Gansu	902.15	847.03	6.08	45.50
青海	Qinghai	167.96	155.57	3.71	8.28
宁夏	Ningxia	480.04	441.66	1.89	36.04
新疆	Xinjiang	1210.53	1022.64	11.52	168.18

19-11 按用途分新建商品房平均销售价格
Average Selling Price of Newly-built Commercial Buildings by Use

单位：元/平方米 (yuan/sq.m)

年份 Year 地区 Region	新建商品房平均销售价格 Average Selling Price of Newly-built Commercial Buildings	#住宅 Residential Buildings	#办公楼 Office Buildings	#商业营业用房 Buildings for Business Use
1998	2063	1854	5552	3170
2000	2112	1948	4751	3260
2005	3168	2937	6923	5022
2006	3367	3119	8053	5247
2007	3864	3645	8667	5774
2008	3800	3576	8378	5886
2009	4681	4459	10608	6871
2010	5045	4738	11406	7765
2011	5384	5029	12339	8454
2012	5839	5486	12359	9028
2013	6328	5946	13152	9810
2014	6427	6048	11983	9874
2015	6932	6622	13150	9630
2016	7699	7433	14725	9917
2017	8160	7893	14019	10512
2018	9045	8886	14890	11107
2019	9673	9667	14840	11170
2020	10248	10385	15697	10887
2021	10546	10825	14444	10969
2022	10210	10608	14385	10097
2023	10438	10864	13781	10422
北京 Beijing	37595	46783	23616	15378
天津 Tianjin	16087	16324	12995	13692
河北 Hebei	8180	8282	4968	9573
山西 Shanxi	6780	6706	6630	10464
内蒙古 Inner Mongolia	6605	6505	8222	8424
辽宁 Liaoning	7526	7536	10383	8775
吉林 Jilin	6923	6810	12085	8140
黑龙江 Heilongjiang	6470	6335	10731	8089
上海 Shanghai	40170	45997	34804	25076
江苏 Jiangsu	11511	12420	10929	9829
浙江 Zhejiang	18847	19856	18107	14446
安徽 Anhui	8284	8460	8735	9812
福建 Fujian	11015	12387	10713	11714
江西 Jiangxi	7225	7209	8128	8374
山东 Shandong	8445	8646	11235	9866
河南 Henan	6528	6457	10157	7352
湖北 Hubei	8778	8755	13002	10304
湖南 Hunan	6556	6463	11121	8216
广东 Guangdong	15762	16928	21819	14887
广西 Guangxi	5791	6163	7290	8445
海南 Hainan	16571	16634	18167	20579
重庆 Chongqing	6888	8558	8426	7697
四川 Sichuan	8961	9882	9124	9925
贵州 Guizhou	5652	5540	7070	8280
云南 Yunnan	6833	7069	7438	8255
西藏 Xizang	8373	8061	6615	12147
陕西 Shaanxi	10954	11109	12256	11324
甘肃 Gansu	6022	5931	9072	8957
青海 Qinghai	7049	6972	7415	9517
宁夏 Ningxia	6946	6929	6494	7503
新疆 Xinjiang	6092	5744	8180	9380

19-12 房地产开发企业资产负债
Assets and Liabilities of Enterprises for Real Estate Development

单位：亿元 (100 million yuan)

年份 Year / 地区 Region		实收资本 Paid-in Capital	资产总计 Total Assets	累计折旧 Total Depreciation	#本年折旧 Depreciation in the Year	负债合计 Total Liabilities	所有者权益合计 Total Owners' Equity	资产负债率 (%) Assets-liability Ratio (%)
	1998	5778.73	19526.18	191.04	39.02	14857.25	4668.92	76.1
	2000	5302.91	25185.99	299.28	57.72	19032.10	6153.88	75.6
	2005	13926.98	72193.64	737.01	157.35	52520.71	19672.93	72.7
	2006	16172.37	88397.99	875.67	191.58	65476.67	22921.32	74.1
	2007	19438.00	111078.20	1025.65	231.59	82680.23	28397.97	74.4
	2008	27561.90	144833.55	1414.14	340.19	104782.31	40051.24	72.3
	2009	28966.02	170184.24	1469.96	320.41	125042.73	45141.51	73.5
	2010	36767.41	224467.14	1758.34	379.81	167297.41	57170.12	74.5
	2011	46430.63	284359.44	2113.63	427.26	214469.96	69889.73	75.4
	2012	54735.36	351858.65	2360.92	525.35	264597.55	87261.10	75.2
	2013	59987.59	425243.89	2871.45	626.74	323228.24	102015.65	76.0
	2014	76566.04	498749.92	3099.89	616.67	384095.53	114654.40	77.0
	2015	78329.42	551968.06	3265.20	596.61	428729.90	123238.16	77.7
	2016	79278.30	625733.70	3658.29	640.50	489750.32	135983.38	78.3
	2017	85649.75	722236.02	3909.38	657.18	571274.85	150961.17	79.1
	2018	95324.97	852720.54	4358.86	904.59	674333.36	178382.98	79.1
	2019	105248.81	947935.60	4521.18	841.78	762035.19	185900.41	80.4
	2020	116652.02	1062327.43	4845.32	842.32	857043.72	205283.71	80.7
	2021	127272.18	1133856.73	5216.62	886.40	910483.55	223373.18	80.3
	2022	134049.68	1126529.36	5532.21	898.56	891499.10	235030.25	79.1
	2023	139206.27	1119129.49	6048.68	991.19	873174.59	245954.90	78.0
北 京	Beijing	7233.74	52300.06	206.53	22.85	41898.26	10401.80	80.1
天 津	Tianjin	4281.01	25148.31	113.70	17.40	19614.69	5533.62	78.0
河 北	Hebei	2909.86	30415.82	125.73	21.13	26820.52	3595.29	88.2
山 西	Shanxi	1422.01	17274.23	73.38	10.55	15679.30	1594.94	90.8
内蒙古	Inner Mongolia	738.30	9235.94	52.82	8.31	8153.90	1082.04	88.3
辽 宁	Liaoning	3006.55	19668.97	200.02	25.69	15903.53	3765.44	80.9
吉 林	Jilin	695.42	8092.25	48.67	9.92	6938.34	1153.91	85.7
黑龙江	Heilongjiang	826.68	9237.23	52.12	5.15	6274.34	2962.89	67.9
上 海	Shanghai	15136.93	80881.24	643.64	80.14	55207.88	25673.37	68.3
江 苏	Jiangsu	17929.91	108784.50	600.60	129.31	81500.18	27284.32	74.9
浙 江	Zhejiang	12593.29	91323.48	295.00	51.39	69607.14	21716.34	76.2
安 徽	Anhui	4321.84	36785.23	186.65	34.25	27699.84	9085.39	75.3
福 建	Fujian	5493.82	43087.98	115.38	21.64	31229.83	11858.15	72.5
江 西	Jiangxi	1835.15	21145.03	120.51	23.91	16580.80	4564.23	78.4
山 东	Shandong	8292.39	80576.61	497.65	96.06	64664.32	15912.29	80.3
河 南	Henan	4005.44	50607.55	234.84	36.24	42473.18	8134.37	83.9
湖 北	Hubei	5120.21	42419.51	241.67	46.28	32088.71	10330.80	75.6
湖 南	Hunan	2332.87	24825.27	141.75	28.77	20212.22	4613.05	81.4
广 东	Guangdong	18956.27	151413.25	829.01	131.24	117863.01	33550.24	77.8
广 西	Guangxi	1876.23	22665.64	108.96	16.21	17429.56	5236.09	76.9
海 南	Hainan	2008.93	14401.86	102.09	20.00	11228.86	3173.00	78.0
重 庆	Chongqing	3647.92	31822.38	182.30	21.23	23220.45	8601.92	73.0
四 川	Sichuan	4959.58	49462.73	304.85	42.62	39265.17	10197.57	79.4
贵 州	Guizhou	2045.04	20514.01	81.41	12.53	16392.90	4121.12	79.9
云 南	Yunnan	2327.36	22759.32	149.80	21.60	19418.98	3340.34	85.3
西 藏	Xizang	183.04	1320.89	6.51	1.36	890.24	430.65	67.4
陕 西	Shaanxi	2891.74	29015.31	97.91	18.81	24555.99	4459.32	84.6
甘 肃	Gansu	658.69	9641.36	68.01	13.81	8171.56	1469.80	84.8
青 海	Qinghai	162.97	1966.98	17.23	2.86	1741.01	225.96	88.5
宁 夏	Ningxia	363.51	3169.24	48.02	7.00	2662.76	506.48	84.0
新 疆	Xinjiang	949.57	9167.32	101.93	12.93	7787.13	1380.19	84.9

19−13 房地产开发企业经营情况
Operating Statistics on Enterprises for Real Estate Development

单位：亿元 (100 million yuan)

年份 地区	Year Region	主营业务收入 Revenue from Principal Business	土地转让收入 Revenue from Land Transfer	商品房销售收入 Revenue from Commercial Buildings Sold	房屋出租收入 Revenue from House Leasing	其他收入 Others	税金及附加 Taxes and Other Charges	营业利润 Operating Profit
	1992	528.56	42.74	426.59	5.96	53.26		63.52
	1995	1731.66	194.40	1258.28	25.79	253.19		143.41
	2000	4515.71	129.61	3896.82	95.32	393.96		73.28
	2005	14769.35	341.43	13316.77	290.29	820.86		1109.19
	2006	18046.76	300.65	16621.36	316.79	807.96		1669.89
	2007	23397.13	427.92	21604.21	386.81	978.19		2436.61
	2008	26696.84	466.85	24394.12	521.47	1314.40		3432.23
	2009	34606.23	498.05	32507.83	544.27	1056.08		4728.58
	2010	42996.48	519.19	40585.33	742.92	1149.04		6111.48
	2011	44491.28	664.66	41697.91	904.28	1224.43	3959.67	5798.58
	2012	51028.41	819.39	47463.49	1151.55	1593.98	4731.04	6001.33
	2013	70706.67	671.42	66697.99	1364.01	1973.25	6322.76	9562.67
	2014	66463.80	571.95	62535.06	1464.10	1892.69	6239.00	6143.13
	2015	70174.34	600.54	65861.30	1600.42	2112.08	6412.80	6165.54
	2016	90091.51	666.32	85163.32	1786.97	2474.89	6875.67	8673.23
	2017	95896.90	838.42	90609.15	1568.32	2881.01	6307.36	11728.11
	2018	112924.68	1207.38	106688.38	1484.30	3544.62	7299.72	18543.71
	2019	110239.78	874.14	104126.42	1539.29	3699.94	7420.57	15439.35
	2020	118582.08	747.84	112267.54	1504.88	4061.83	6925.34	14022.99
	2021	134342.24	769.29	127444.89	1651.80	4476.26	6723.74	11834.02
	2022	123051.98	709.12	115936.21	1646.11	4760.53	5607.22	9262.81
	2023	143273.58	674.39	135045.71	1896.88	5656.60	5632.14	11047.41
北京	Beijing	4456.62	57.31	3832.15	134.46	432.69	204.94	92.44
天津	Tianjin	2217.66	16.76	2092.50	30.44	77.96	71.44	-147.61
河北	Hebei	3806.58	3.83	3605.64	10.98	186.13	161.67	259.98
山西	Shanxi	1864.28	6.83	1782.07	13.36	62.02	62.06	75.11
内蒙古	Inner Mongolia	1408.74	3.31	1366.30	6.12	33.02	48.32	115.26
辽宁	Liaoning	2391.75	24.97	2296.41	17.59	52.78	82.54	22.55
吉林	Jilin	977.19	1.15	957.25	4.30	14.48	21.67	49.74
黑龙江	Heilongjiang	823.20	1.49	803.40	5.25	13.06	28.89	48.23
上海	Shanghai	6354.99	21.31	5425.49	570.05	338.15	547.46	1044.04
江苏	Jiangsu	17708.28	97.99	17001.92	124.78	483.59	472.15	1436.93
浙江	Zhejiang	16854.40	55.79	16155.34	102.99	540.29	469.55	1442.03
安徽	Anhui	5447.87	21.27	5108.83	28.72	289.05	119.37	384.25
福建	Fujian	4967.61	20.90	4462.42	46.79	437.50	131.48	480.02
江西	Jiangxi	3504.86	38.13	3311.15	11.93	143.65	83.04	319.82
山东	Shandong	11268.75	52.33	10603.36	69.20	543.86	402.13	817.11
河南	Henan	6386.04	13.33	6065.54	34.93	272.24	191.93	395.83
湖北	Hubei	6202.62	13.19	5929.97	51.12	208.33	251.15	616.29
湖南	Hunan	4147.84	64.50	3984.80	26.19	72.36	146.76	295.33
广东	Guangdong	16339.14	25.08	15596.76	338.47	378.82	1053.49	1726.43
广西	Guangxi	2331.93	8.57	2235.57	25.93	61.86	61.96	26.48
海南	Hainan	1532.37	27.41	1328.13	8.24	168.59	197.34	170.05
重庆	Chongqing	3008.44	29.18	2791.74	63.77	123.74	91.75	268.69
四川	Sichuan	7653.62	48.42	7256.73	63.99	284.48	317.13	554.62
贵州	Guizhou	2070.26	2.01	1985.47	13.79	68.99	45.38	141.86
云南	Yunnan	2592.21	9.02	2476.97	42.08	64.13	148.32	-5.75
西藏	Xizang	91.61	0.02	87.78	1.96	1.84	3.03	13.86
陕西	Shaanxi	3363.89	2.20	3124.79	16.17	220.73	108.97	262.17
甘肃	Gansu	1160.34	4.82	1098.83	8.88	47.82	27.90	46.49
青海	Qinghai	253.83	0.20	247.95	1.56	4.12	7.22	8.46
宁夏	Ningxia	684.33	1.28	669.37	6.02	7.66	21.12	66.85
新疆	Xinjiang	1402.34	1.78	1361.10	16.79	22.67	51.99	19.84

19−14 分地区按项目规模分房地产开发完成投资（2023年）
Investment Completed by Enterprises for Real Estate Development by Size of Projects and Region (2023)

单位：亿元 (100 million yuan)

地 区	Region	500万元以下 Less Than 5 Million Yuan	500−1000万元 5-10 Million Yuan	1000−3000万元 10-30 Million Yuan	3000−5000万元 30-50 Million Yuan	5000万−1亿元 50-100 Million Yuan	1-5亿元 100-500 Million Yuan	5-10亿元 500-1000 Million Yuan	10亿元以上 1 Billion Yuan and More
全 国	**National Total**	**0.14**	**3.13**	**53.67**	**132.68**	**639.15**	**11479.58**	**18026.17**	**81807.73**
北 京	Beijing						27.48	63.98	4110.95
天 津	Tianjin				0.22	0.67	41.37	119.23	1070.54
河 北	Hebei		0.07	1.03	5.00	31.75	959.38	957.11	1140.10
山 西	Shanxi		0.06	1.50	5.81	32.55	411.86	442.19	866.13
内蒙古	Inner Mongolia		0.14	3.78	7.54	36.67	335.76	271.02	354.78
辽 宁	Liaoning		0.16	1.61	2.62	15.42	367.29	409.34	946.36
吉 林	Jilin		0.05	2.21	3.29	11.15	200.36	148.06	457.92
黑龙江	Heilongjiang	0.02	0.17	3.10	7.27	25.91	127.78	68.57	225.22
上 海	Shanghai			0.04	0.18	0.14	74.17	252.36	5735.15
江 苏	Jiangsu			1.42	3.18	22.96	555.68	1471.68	9877.21
浙 江	Zhejiang	0.09	0.02	1.23	3.70	18.84	609.97	1494.17	11191.16
安 徽	Anhui		0.08	0.71	2.58	13.22	366.43	1091.60	3201.90
福 建	Fujian		0.34	1.93	2.54	14.24	326.26	809.00	3259.58
江 西	Jiangxi		0.08	2.65	7.09	25.12	397.97	497.04	674.93
山 东	Shandong	0.01	0.04	3.14	10.12	50.94	1264.41	2114.91	5097.66
河 南	Henan			1.53	5.06	34.31	748.20	1148.23	2287.86
湖 北	Hubei		0.10	2.23	4.56	21.30	390.58	668.12	4380.71
湖 南	Hunan		0.11	1.62	6.49	33.67	538.82	764.67	2506.87
广 东	Guangdong		0.07	4.03	8.49	37.39	639.53	1096.70	11907.13
广 西	Guangxi		0.11	1.85	2.85	18.04	269.07	304.52	740.31
海 南	Hainan			0.64	1.57	6.13	135.53	246.40	779.04
重 庆	Chongqing	0.02	0.05	0.44	0.82	8.00	162.00	346.25	2279.14
四 川	Sichuan		0.09	1.10	2.66	24.59	639.78	1250.38	3403.42
贵 州	Guizhou		0.05	0.44	1.29	10.84	226.16	252.28	699.76
云 南	Yunnan		0.06	2.03	3.76	27.28	332.28	385.29	967.79
西 藏	Xizang		0.05	0.53	0.06	1.11	21.18	17.65	38.84
陕 西	Shaanxi		0.23	1.38	6.73	23.33	343.56	539.07	2364.10
甘 肃	Gansu		0.08	2.50	6.05	22.93	292.43	350.88	589.12
青 海	Qinghai			0.59	1.42	3.67	46.87	39.95	108.86
宁 夏	Ningxia		0.09	0.95	1.72	5.35	124.08	113.47	190.57
新 疆	Xinjiang		0.83	7.47	18.00	61.64	503.35	292.06	354.66

19-15 房地产开发企业成套住宅竣工与销售情况
Number of Flats of Residential Buildings Completed and Sold by Enterprises for Real Estate Development

单位：套 (sets)

年份 Year 地区 Region		住宅竣工套数合计 Total Number of Flats of Residential Buildings Completed	住宅销售套数合计 Total Number of Flats of Residential Buildings Sold
2000		2139702	
2005		3682523	4235372
2006		4005305	5049094
2007		4401203	6251263
2008		4939189	5565827
2009		5548897	8040470
2010		6019767	8732798
2011		7219163	8981696
2012		7642379	9217894
2013		7493133	10609988
2014		7659418	9675509
2015		7050109	10036148
2016		7455409	11937330
2017		6770598	12325337
2018		6229216	12170240
2019		6452838	12045714
2020		5976595	12309379
2021		6468266	12404016
2022		6277094	9062682
2023		6606549	8258625
北京	Beijing	113479	76747
天津	Tianjin	133526	105709
河北	Hebei	235905	348077
山西	Shanxi	155035	194539
内蒙古	Inner Mongolia	81733	116174
辽宁	Liaoning	162195	170353
吉林	Jilin	48276	92634
黑龙江	Heilongjiang	65454	74093
上海	Shanghai	123857	145839
江苏	Jiangsu	548567	767360
浙江	Zhejiang	762357	429315
安徽	Anhui	375560	394920
福建	Fujian	270801	283444
江西	Jiangxi	129493	244339
山东	Shandong	558894	765593
河南	Henan	419267	558590
湖北	Hubei	268090	388566
湖南	Hunan	260151	396537
广东	Guangdong	492875	707378
广西	Guangxi	170692	212084
海南	Hainan	51639	72699
重庆	Chongqing	229601	226898
四川	Sichuan	259230	588412
贵州	Guizhou	92788	176230
云南	Yunnan	203834	174600
西藏	Xizang	4054	5900
陕西	Shaanxi	143662	200762
甘肃	Gansu	83062	122274
青海	Qinghai	19402	18985
宁夏	Ningxia	60171	50413
新疆	Xinjiang	82899	149161

19–16 35个大中城市主要指标完成情况（2023年）
Main Indicators of Real Estate Projects in 35 Large and Medium-sized Cities (2023)

城市	City	本年完成投资（亿元）Investment Completed in the Year (100 million yuan)	#住宅 Residential Buildings	#办公楼 Office Buildings	#商业营业用房 Buildings for Business Use	房屋施工面积（万平方米）Floor Space of Buildings under Construction (10 000 sq.m)	房屋竣工面积（万平方米）Floor Space of Buildings Completed (10 000 sq.m)	#住宅 Residential Buildings
总计	**Total**	**56550.32**	**40105.15**	**3507.67**	**4151.84**	**309189.54**	**38647.23**	**25460.33**
北京	Beijing	4202.41	2714.42	268.74	189.98	12531.34	2112.42	1164.89
天津	Tianjin	1232.04	973.70	32.12	62.94	9587.14	1864.41	1462.18
石家庄	Shijiazhuang	521.01	446.61	11.53	18.97	3806.50	604.72	505.72
太原	Taiyuan	518.23	408.26	9.76	37.70	7723.63	196.74	178.03
呼和浩特	Hohhot	234.58	171.78	0.99	18.83	2919.84	345.07	248.35
沈阳	Shenyang	610.86	492.75	17.89	57.16	6061.97	867.39	617.55
大连	Dalian	458.13	331.41	31.59	50.19	3383.46	324.60	241.58
长春	Changchun	551.16	394.61	16.41	52.21	6409.17	300.94	236.85
哈尔滨	Harbin	228.21	178.57	3.66	24.63	4933.32	366.57	275.57
上海	Shanghai	6062.04	3466.79	772.74	489.80	17618.37	2112.35	1186.19
南京	Nanjing	2764.36	2076.61	130.85	219.64	7467.23	997.50	641.72
杭州	Hangzhou	4400.69	2829.59	322.64	298.75	14362.92	1662.21	939.12
宁波	Ningbo	2218.61	1503.79	74.81	156.24	9569.29	2972.07	1814.90
合肥	Hefei	1544.63	1197.82	50.04	110.18	7412.33	2345.19	1523.13
福州	Fuzhou	1085.97	791.23	40.63	77.98	6152.58	1002.43	632.09
厦门	Xiamen	1435.60	1034.62	33.33	67.16	3443.31	332.71	138.42
南昌	Nanchang	496.63	393.61	25.71	41.59	4728.09	510.64	361.43
济南	Jinan	1489.24	1084.29	138.27	111.86	8137.75	985.50	692.47
青岛	Qingdao	1729.32	1376.68	86.07	86.82	10443.78	2104.47	1384.06
郑州	Zhengzhou	1863.87	1546.88	85.21	93.42	17151.32	2012.79	1476.10
武汉	Wuhan	3446.88	2581.16	225.83	278.78	14456.27	1195.35	869.83
长沙	Changsha	1888.70	1473.96	72.98	186.53	9763.72	1356.65	957.36
广州	Guangzhou	3311.45	2411.91	227.18	193.83	12676.79	1013.04	510.07
深圳	Shenzhen	3787.46	2410.43	420.37	396.79	10995.05	970.65	531.04
南宁	Nanning	496.41	363.79	18.49	30.72	9555.77	1065.72	786.29
海口	Haikou	482.25	345.08	30.91	32.62	3810.50	110.37	47.32
重庆	Chongqing	2796.71	2109.64	45.29	294.49	20497.57	3302.02	2285.46
成都	Chengdu	2449.59	1721.27	143.29	183.13	17764.84	1746.16	1019.95
贵阳	Guiyang	417.78	354.77	6.54	21.64	6930.79	529.06	428.41
昆明	Kunming	634.26	452.31	38.31	56.67	10361.00	1018.63	680.15
西安	Xi'an	2052.03	1593.68	95.78	112.65	13712.30	710.84	486.57
兰州	Lanzhou	401.54	314.36	10.27	24.26	4351.16	387.05	277.40
西宁	Xining	113.17	88.34	4.08	9.03	1909.76	189.78	136.95
银川	Yinchuan	266.42	209.41	2.36	22.59	3094.76	736.12	539.88
乌鲁木齐	Urumqi	358.08	261.01	12.98	42.07	5465.92	295.09	183.27

19–16 续表 continued

城市 City		新建商品房销售面积(万平方米) Floor Space of Newly-built Commercial Buildings Sold (10 000 sq.m)	#住宅 Residential Buildings	新建商品房平均销售价格(元/平方米) Average Selling Price of Newly-built Commercial Buildings (yuan/sq.m)	#住宅 Residential Buildings
总计	**Total**	**35015.71**	**27998.76**	**16780**	**18402**
北京	Beijing	1131.82	818.25	37595	46783
天津	Tianjin	1178.51	1110.25	16087	16324
石家庄	Shijiazhuang	586.75	565.93	10599	10743
太原	Taiyuan	532.78	511.32	10193	10105
呼和浩特	Hohhot	187.79	180.43	10855	10845
沈阳	Shenyang	530.33	461.22	10749	11219
大连	Dalian	309.03	266.74	11676	11899
长春	Changchun	570.74	534.14	8455	8300
哈尔滨	Harbin	388.65	343.05	8586	8434
上海	Shanghai	1811.71	1456.96	40170	45997
南京	Nanjing	906.77	797.08	22599	23643
杭州	Hangzhou	1447.34	1202.16	31536	33047
宁波	Ningbo	901.56	730.46	18025	19546
合肥	Hefei	1109.25	937.61	14365	15530
福州	Fuzhou	877.41	628.17	12629	14297
厦门	Xiamen	603.79	346.73	21035	31054
南昌	Nanchang	717.77	548.17	10447	10733
济南	Jinan	1170.22	825.52	13275	14758
青岛	Qingdao	1454.85	1209.64	13926	13952
郑州	Zhengzhou	2027.80	1823.13	8619	8614
武汉	Wuhan	1972.96	1583.96	14305	14883
长沙	Changsha	1556.78	1363.06	11091	11239
广州	Guangzhou	1404.49	1067.71	29040	32433
深圳	Shenzhen	762.00	584.33	45524	50010
南宁	Nanning	952.23	574.74	7602	9917
海口	Haikou	325.79	263.35	15826	16561
重庆	Chongqing	3557.25	2258.06	6888	8558
成都	Chengdu	2204.57	1786.19	17329	19517
贵阳	Guiyang	478.21	412.06	9208	9463
昆明	Kunming	749.49	528.88	9275	11005
西安	Xi'an	1265.33	1045.51	15836	17084
兰州	Lanzhou	335.75	315.22	8656	8453
西宁	Xining	106.15	96.36	8882	8925
银川	Yinchuan	350.85	324.44	8565	8509
乌鲁木齐	Urumqi	549.00	497.93	8959	8586

主要统计指标解释

土地购置费 指房地产开发企业通过各种方式取得土地使用权而支付的费用。土地购置费按实际发生额填报，分期付款的应分期计入。项目分期开发的，只计入与本期项目有关的土地购置费。前期支付的土地购置费，项目纳入统计后计入。

计划总投资 指房地产开发企业在建的建设工程按照总体设计（或按设计概算或预算）规定的内容全部建成计划需要的总投资。

自开始建设累计完成投资 指房地产开发企业在建的房屋建设工程或正在开发的土地开发工程从开始建设到本年末止累计完成的全部投资。

房地产开发投资 指房地产开发企业本年完成的全部用于房屋建设工程、土地开发工程的投资额以及公益性建筑和土地购置费等的投资。

本年实际到位资金 指房地产开发企业本年实际到位的，用于房地产开发的各种货币资金。包括国内贷款、利用外资、自筹资金、定金及预收款、个人按揭贷款和其他资金。

房屋施工面积 指房地产开发企业本年施工的全部房屋建筑面积。包括本年新开工的房屋建筑面积、上年跨入本年继续施工的房屋建筑面积、上年停缓建在本年恢复施工的房屋建筑面积、本年竣工的房屋建筑面积以及本年施工后又停缓建的房屋建筑面积。多层建筑应填各层建筑面积之和。

房屋新开工面积 指房地产开发企业本年新开工建设的房屋建筑面积，以单位工程为核算对象。不包括在上年开工跨入本年继续施工的房屋建筑面积和上年停缓建而在本年恢复施工的房屋建筑面积。房屋的开工应以房屋正式开始破土刨槽（地基处理或打永久桩）的日期为准。房屋新开工面积指整栋房屋的全部建筑面积，不能分割计算。

房屋竣工面积 指房地产开发企业本年按照设计要求已全部完工，达到住人和使用条件，经验收鉴定合格或达到竣工验收标准，可正式移交使用的各栋房屋建筑面积的总和。

新建商品房销售面积 指房地产开发企业本年出售商品房屋的合同总面积(即双方签署的正式买卖合同中所确定的建筑面积)。

新建商品房销售额 指房地产开发企业本年出售商品房屋的合同总价款(即双方签署的正式买卖合同中所确定的合同总价)。该指标与商品房销售面积同口径。

Explanatory Notes on Main Statistical Indicators

Value of Land Purchased refers to the payment made by real estate development enterprises for land use rights. The actual payment of land purchased is recorded. If the payment is by installments, it should be recorded when occurring. If the project is developed by stages, the value of land purchased only related to the current project. The value of land purchased in the early stage should be recorded after the project is included in the statistics.

Total Investment Planned refers to the total investment required for the completion of the activities according to the planned design or budget for the project under construction by real estate development enterprises.

Accumulative Investment Completed from Starting of Construction refers to all the investment accomplished by real estate development enterprises in the construction of buildings or the development of land from the beginning of project to the end of the year.

Investment in Real Estate Development refers to the investment made by real estate development enterprises in the construction of buildings, development of land, nonprofit buildings and value of land purchased.

Total Actual Funds in Place in the Year refers to the total amount available for real estate development regardless of kinds of currencies. It includes domestic loans, foreign investment, self-raised funds, deposit and advance payment, personal mortgage loan and others.

Floor Space of Buildings under Construction refers to the total space area of the buildings under construction in the year by real estate development enterprises. It includes buildings started in the year, continued from the previous year, suspended in earlier years but restarted in the year, completed in the year, and buildings under construction but suspended in the year. The floor space of a multi-storied building should be the sum of floor space of all the stories.

Floor Space of Buildings Started in the Year refers to the total floor space area of the buildings started in the year by real estate development enterprises. It excludes the buildings started in previous years and continued in the year, and the buildings suspended in previous years but restarted in the year. The start of a construction is defined by the date of ground breaking or pile driving. The floor space of the buildings started in the year includes that of the entire building.

Floor Space of Buildings Completed refers to the total floor space area of each building completed in the year by real estate development enterprises, which meet the requirements as designed, up to the standard for being resided in and put into use, has been checked and accepted by departments concerned as qualified or up to the standard of buildings completed and can be handed over for putting into use.

Floor Space of Newly-built Commercial Buildings Sold refers to total contracted area of commercial buildings (i.e. area of floor space as designated in the formal contracts signed by both sides) sold by real estate development enterprises in the year.

Total Sale of Newly-built Commercial Buildings refers to the total contracted value (i.e. value of sales/purchase for selling/ purchase of commercial buildings as designated in the contract signed by both sides) received from the sales of the buildings by real estate development enterprises in the year. This indicator has the same statistical coverage as the area of commercial buildings sold.

20

科学技术

Science and Technology

简 要 说 明

本篇资料主要反映我国科学技术活动和企业创新活动开展的基本情况。

一、本篇资料的主要内容

包括全社会以及规模以上工业法人单位、政府属研究机构、高等学校的研究与试验发展（R&D）活动情况；规模以上工业法人单位创新活动开展情况；国内外专利申请和授权情况；高技术企业研发活动情况；科技论文收录情况；高新技术产品进出口贸易情况；技术市场交易情况；高新区企业主要经济指标；科协系统科技活动情况；测绘、地震、气象和质量监督等综合技术服务部门业务机构及业务活动情况等。

二、本篇资料的统计范围

科技活动统计资料范围为全社会有研究与试验发展（R&D）活动的企事业单位，具体包括工业法人单位、地级及以上独立核算的政府属科学研究与技术开发机构及科技信息与文献机构、全日制普通高等学校及附属医院以及研究与试验发展（R&D）活动相对密集行业（包括农、林、牧、渔业，建筑业，交通运输、仓储和邮政业，信息传输、软件和信息技术服务业，金融业，租赁和商务服务业，科学研究和技术服务业，水利、环境和公共设施管理业，卫生和社会工作，文化、体育和娱乐业等）中从事研究与试验发展（R&D）活动的企事业单位。创新活动统计资料范围为规模以上工业法人单位。

三、本篇的资料来源

全国综合资料由国家统计局根据科技综合统计报表的有关资料整理汇总，工业法人单位、非工业（包括建筑业，交通运输、仓储和邮政业，信息传输、软件和信息技术服务业，租赁和商务服务业，科学研究和技术服务业，水利、环境和公共设施管理业，卫生和社会工作，文化、体育和娱乐业）法人单位科技活动情况由国家统计局根据企业（单位）研发活动统计报表的有关资料整理汇总；农、林、牧、渔业，金融业等行业的企事业单位由国家统计局根据最近年份的调查数据进行推算；规模以上工业法人单位创新活动情况由国家统计局根据企业创新调查的有关资料整理汇总；政府属研究机构资料由科技部和国家国防科技工业局调查提供；科学研究和技术服务业事业的研究与试验发展（R&D）活动情况资料，以及科技论文资料由科技部调查提供；技术市场资料、高新区企业资料由工信部调查提供；高等学校资料由教育部调查提供；高新技术产品进出口贸易资料由海关总署调查提供；科协系统科技活动资料由中国科协调查提供；专利、测绘、地震、气象和产品质量监督等资料，分别由国家知识产权局、自然资源部、中国地震局、中国气象局、国家市场监督管理总局等部门调查提供。

四、本篇资料的统计调查方法

研究与试验发展(R&D)活动情况采用全面调查取得；创新活动情况采用全面调查取得；科协、专利、测绘、地震、气象和产品质量监督资料采用抽样等多种调查方法取得。

Brief Introduction

Statistics in this chapter reflect the basic information on scientific and technological activities and innovation activities of enterprises in China.

I. Main Contents

Data on research and experimental development (R&D) activities of the whole society, industrial corporate units above designated size, scientific and technological institutions under the government and institutions of higher education; data on innovation activities of industrial corporate units above designated size; data on domestic and foreign patents application accepted and granted; data on research and experimental development activities of high-technology industry (manufacturing industry) enterprises; data on scientific and technological papers; data on import and export trade of high-technological products; data on technological markets transactions; main economic indicators of enterprises in high-tech development zones; data on the scientific and technological activities in the system of associations for science and technology; data on comprehensive technical service departments' operation institutions and activities, such as surveying and mapping, earthquake, meteorology, and product quality supervision.

II.Scope of Statistics

Data on scientific and technological activities cover research and experimental development (R&D) activities of enterprises and institutions of whole society, mainly including industrial corporate units, scientific research and technological development institutions and scientific and technological information and literature institutions of prefecture level and above under the government with independent accounting, full-time universities and colleges, affiliated hospitals, and enterprises and institutions engaged in R&D activities in relatively R&D-intensive industries (such as agriculture, forestry, animal husbandry, fishery, construction, transport, storage and post, information transmission, software and information technology service, finance, leasing and business services, scientific research and technical services, management of water conservancy, environment and public facilities, health and social service, culture, sports and entertainment). Data on innovation activities cover industrial corporate units above designated size.

III.Sources of Data

National Bureau of Statistics provides national comprehensive data on the basis of comprehensive reporting forms of science and technology; data on scientific and technological activities of industrial corporate units, and non-industrial corporate units (including construction, transport, storage and post, information transmission, information technology service, leasing and business services, scientific research and technical services, management of water conservancy, environment and public facilities, health and social service, culture, sports and entertainment) based on reporting forms of enterprises'(units') R&D activities. National Bureau of Statistics is responsible for providing estimation on enterprises and institutions in agriculture, forestry, animal husbandry, fishery, finance based on recent surveys. Data on innovation activities of industrial corporate units above designated size is also from the National Bureau of Statistics based on business innovation survey. Ministry of Science and Technology and State Administration of Science, Technology and Industry for National Defense provide information on scientific and technological institutions under the government; Ministry of Science and Technology provides information on R&D activities of scientific research and technical service enterprises and institutions, scientific and technological papers; Ministry of Industry and Information Technology provides information on technological markets and enterprises in high-tech development zones; Ministry of Education provides information on scientific and technological activities in institutions of higher education; General Administration of Customs provides information on import and export trade of high-technological products; China Association for Science and Technology provides data on the scientific and technological activities of associations for science and technology; State Intellectual Property Office, Ministry of Natural Resources, China Earthquake Administration, China Meteorological Administration, State Administration for Market Regulation respectively provide data on patents, surveying and mapping, earthquake, meteorology and product quality supervision.

IV.Statistical Methodology

Data on R&D activities are collected through complete surveys. Data on innovation activities are collected through complete survey. Data on scientific and technological associations, patents, surveying and mapping, earthquake, meteorology and product quality supervision are collected through sample surveys and other surveys.

20-1 科技活动基本情况
Basic Statistics on Scientific and Technological Activities

指　标	Item	2019	2020	2021	2022	2023
研究与试验发展(R&D)投入情况	**Statistics on R&D Input**					
R&D人员折合全时当量(万人年)	Full-time Equivalent of R&D Personnel(10 000 man-years)	480.1	523.5	571.6	635.4	724.1
#基础研究	Basic Research	39.2	42.7	47.2	50.9	57.5
应用研究	Applied Research	61.5	64.3	69.1	74.1	77.7
试验发展	Experimental Development	379.4	416.5	455.3	510.3	588.9
R&D经费支出 (亿元)	Expenditure on R&D (100 million yuan)	22143.6	24393.1	27956.3	30782.9	33357.1
#基础研究	Basic Research	1335.6	1467.0	1817.0	2023.5	2259.1
应用研究	Applied Research	2498.5	2757.2	3145.4	3482.5	3661.5
试验发展	Experimental Development	18309.5	20168.9	22995.9	25276.9	27436.5
#政府资金	Government Funds	4537.3	4825.6	5299.7	5470.9	5693.4
企业资金	Enterprises Funds	16887.2	18895.0	21808.8	24323.9	26443.7
R&D经费支出与国内生产总值之比 (%)	Ratio of Expenditure on R&D to GDP (%)	2.24	2.41	2.43	2.56	2.65
科技产出及成果情况	**Statistics on S&T Outputs and Results**					
发表科技论文 (万篇)	Scientific Papers Issued (10 000 pieces)	195	195	203	215	217
出版科技著作 (种)	Publications on Science and Technology (kind)	52067	49634	50580	46968	49978
科技成果登记数 (项)	Number of Major Achievements in Science and Technology (item)	68562	76521	78655	84324	93406
国家技术发明奖 (项)	Number of National Invention Prizes Awarded (item)	65	61			62
国家科学技术进步奖 (项)	Number of National Scientific and Technological Progress Prizes Awarded (item)	185	157			139
专利申请数 (件)	Number of Patent Applications (piece)	4380468	5194154	5243592	5364639	5561990
#发明专利	Invention Patents	1400661	1497159	1585663	1619268	1677701
专利授权数 (件)	Number of Patent Grants (piece)	2591607	3639268	4601457	4323409	3649072
#发明专利	Invention Patents	452804	530127	695946	798347	920797
高技术产品进出口及技术市场情况	**Statistics on Export and Import of High-tech Products and Technical Market**					
高新技术产品进出口额(亿美元)	Total Value of Export and Import of High and New-tech Products (USD 100 million)	13685	14584	18091	17073	15219
高新技术产品出口额	Export	7307	7763	9749	9467	8420
高新技术产品进口额	Import	6378	6821	8342	7606	6799
技术市场成交额 (亿元)	Transaction Value in Technical Market(100 million yuan)	22398	28252	37294	47791	61476

注：1.2017年起专利申请受理数改为专利申请数(以下相关表同)。
2.R&D经费支出与国内生产总值之比，根据国内生产总值最新核实数据作了相应修正。

a) Since 2017, number of patent applications accepted change to number of patent applications.The same applies to the relevant tables following.
b) Ratio of expenditure on R&D to GDP was revised by use of lastest updated data of GDP.

20-2 科学研究与开发机构基本情况
Basic Statistics on Scientific Research and Development Institutions

指 标	Item	2019	2020	2021	2022	2023
机构基本情况	**Basic Statistics on Institutions**					
机构数 (个)	Number of R&D Institutions (unit)	3217	3109	2962	2871	2890
#中央属	At National Level	726	731	746	743	751
地方属	At Local Levels	2491	2378	2216	2128	2139
研究与试验发展(R&D)投入情况	**Statistics on R&D Input**					
R&D人员 (万人)	R&D Personnel (10 000 persons)	48.5	51.9	52.9	55.9	57.9
R&D人员全时当量 (万人年)	Full-time Equivalent of R&D Personnel (10 000 man-years)	42.5	45.4	46.1	48.7	50.5
#基础研究	Basic Research	9.2	10.3	10.9	12.0	13.0
应用研究	Applied Research	14.8	15.5	16.1	16.9	18.2
试验发展	Experimental Development	18.4	19.6	19.1	19.9	19.3
R&D经费支出 (亿元)	Expenditure on R&D (100 million yuan)	3080.8	3408.8	3717.9	3814.4	3856.3
#基础研究	Basic Research	510.3	573.9	646.1	725.1	799.6
应用研究	Applied Research	933.6	1084.5	1196.3	1266.9	1367.4
试验发展	Experimental Development	1636.9	1750.4	1877.4	1822.4	1689.3
#政府资金	Government Funds	2582.4	2847.4	3007.1	2996.2	2991.3
企业资金	Enterprises Funds	118.7	135.1	203.9	210.9	206.8
R&D项目(课题)情况	**Statistics on R&D Projects**					
R&D项目(课题)数 (项)	Number of R&D Projects (item)	125642	130089	135867	142572	153419
R&D项目(课题)人员全时当量 (万人年)	Participants (Full-time Equivalent) (10 000 man-years)	37.8	39.6	40.7	42.3	43.5
R&D项目(课题)经费支出 (亿元)	Expenditure on R&D Projects (100 million yuan)	2119.5	2420.4	2577.0	2683.5	2610.4
科技产出及成果情况	**Statistics on S&T Outputs and Results**					
发表科技论文 (篇)	Scientific Papers Issued (piece)	185978	193947	195668	199791	198342
#国外发表	Published in Foreign Periodicals	68776	77414	79623	91405	91270
出版科技著作 (种)	Publications on Science and Technology (kind)	5469	5706	5619	5397	5340
专利申请数 (件)	Number of Patent Applications (piece)	67302	74601	81879	89945	97006
#发明专利	Inventions	52185	57477	64132	71636	80764
专利授权数 (件)	Number of Patent Grants (piece)	38476	47029	55387	62590	69254
#发明专利	Inventions	24486	29205	35838	43341	54110

20-3 高等学校科技活动情况
Basic Statistics on Science and Technology Activities by Higher Education Institutions

指　　标	Item	2019	2020	2021	2022	2023
高等学校基本情况	**Basic Statistics on Institutions of Higher Education**					
学校数　(个)	Number of Institutions　(unit)	2688	2738	2756	2760	2822
#理工农医	Natural Sciences & Technology	2294	2342	2381	2451	2579
#人文社科	Social Sciences & Humanities	2376	2447	2546	2509	2658
R&D机构　(个)	R&D Institutions　(unit)	18379	19988	22859	24745	26881
研究与试验发展(R&D)投入情况	**Statistics on R&D Input**					
R&D人员　(万人)	R&D Personnel　(10 000 persons)	123.3	127.4	140.8	151.9	185.5
R&D人员全时当量　(万人年)	Full-time Equivalent of R&D Personnel　(10 000 man-years)	56.5	61.5	67.2	72.6	83.7
#基础研究	Basic Research	26.7	28.5	31.9	34.8	40.4
应用研究	Applied Research	25.8	28.9	30.7	32.8	36.8
试验发展	Experimental Development	4.1	4.1	4.6	4.9	6.5
R&D经费支出　(亿元)	Expenditure on R&D　(100 million yuan)	1796.6	1882.5	2180.5	2412.4	2753.3
#基础研究	Basic Research	722.2	724.8	904.5	997.0	1138.9
应用研究	Applied Research	879.3	964.2	1054.1	1177.1	1295.3
试验发展	Experimental Development	195.1	193.5	221.9	238.3	319.1
#政府资金	Government Funds	1048.5	1128.0	1249.2	1384.2	1560.3
企业资金	Enterprises Funds	471.0	666.0	710.4	779.7	866.7
R&D项目(课题)情况	**Statistics on R&D Projects**					
R&D项目(课题)数　(项)	Number of R&D Projects　(item)	1188769	1288633	1436251	1539845	1701829
R&D项目(课题)人员全时当量(万人年)	Participants(Full-time Equivalent)(10 000 man-years)	56.5	61.5	67.2	72.6	83.5
R&D项目(课题)经费支出　(亿元)	Expenditure on R&D Projects　(100 million yuan)	1154.0	1202.2	1343.6	1441.3	1711.3
科技产出及成果情况	**Statistics on S&T Outputs and Results**					
发表科技论文　(篇)	Scientific Papers Issued　(piece)	1447336	1503531	1577932	1657992	1707581
#国外发表	Published in Foreign Periodicals	542557	595080	683991	797869	851635
出版科技著作　(种)	Publications on Science and Technology　(kind)	43331	42970	44039	40646	43464
专利申请数　(件)	Number of Patent Applications　(piece)	340685	340360	381565	354852	346835
#发明专利	Inventions	210885	194612	220640	235572	254978
专利授权数　(件)	Number of Patent Grants　(piece)	213163	278016	319514	300633	274057
#发明专利	Inventions	92394	116633	145352	177413	184693

20-4 规模以上工业企业的科技活动基本情况
Basic Statistics on Science and Technology Activities of Industrial Enterprises above Designated Size

指　标	Item	2004	2009	2022	2023
企业基本情况	**Statistics on Industrial Enterprises**				
有R&D活动企业数 (个)	Number of Enterprises with R&D Activities (unit)	17075	36387	175619	151290
有R&D活动企业所占比重 (%)	Percentage of Enterprises with R&D Activities to Total Number of Enterprises (%)	6.2	8.5	37.3	30.7
R&D活动情况	**Statistics on R&D Activities**				
R&D人员全时当量 (万人年)	Full-time Equivalent of R&D Personnel (10 000 man-years)	54.2	144.7	421.5	481.7
R&D经费支出 (亿元)	Expenditure on R&D (100 million yuan)	1104.5	3775.7	19361.8	20969.9
R&D经费支出与营业收入之比(%)	Percentage of Expenditure on R&D to Sales Revenue (%)	0.56	0.69	1.39	1.55
企业办R&D机构情况	**Statistics on R&D Institutions**				
机构数 (个)	Number of R&D Institutions (unit)	17555	29879	136836	149068
机构人员数 (万人)	R&D Personnel (10 000 persons)	64.4	155.0	441.9	458.9
机构经费支出 (亿元)	Expenditure on R&D Institutions (100 million yuan)	841.6	2983.6	18161.3	19626.4
新产品开发及生产情况	**Statistics on Development and Production of New Products**				
新产品开发项目数 (个)	Number of Projects on New Products Development (unit)	76176	237754	1093975	1204643
新产品开发经费支出 (亿元)	Expenditure on New Products Development (100 million yuan)	965.7	4482.0	25540.0	27563.8
新产品销售收入 (亿元)	Sales Revenue of New Products (100 million yuan)	22808.6	65838.2	327983.0	341334.0
#新产品出口	Exports	5312.2	11572.5	55859.8	55479.8
专利情况	**Statistics on Patents**				
专利申请数 (件)	Number of Patent Applications (piece)	64569	265808	1507296	1565960
#发明专利	Inventions	20456	92450	554615	613602
有效发明专利数 (件)	Number of Effective Invention Patents (piece)	30315	118245	1981098	2227602
技术获取和技术改造情况	**Statistics on Technology Acquisition and Technology Transformation**				
引进国外技术经费支出 (亿元)	Expenditure for Acquisition of Foreign Technology(100 million yuan)	397.4	422.2	356.3	390.2
引进技术消化吸收经费支出(亿元)	Expenditure for Assimilation of Imported Technology(100 million yuan)	61.2	182.0	85.8	60.1
购买国内技术经费支出 (亿元)	Expenditure for Purchase of Domestic Technology(100 million yuan)	82.5	203.4	600.0	471.9
技术改造经费支出 (亿元)	Expenditure for Technical Renovation (100 million yuan)	2953.5	4344.7	3968.4	3332.6

注：从2011年起，规模以上工业企业的统计范围从年主营业务收入为500万元及以上的法人工业企业调整为年主营业务收入为2000万元及以上的法人工业企业(以下相关表同)。

a) From 2011, the statistics coverage of the industrial enterprises above designated size has been changed from the industrial enterprises with the sales revenue above 5 million RMB to the industrial enterprises with the sales revenue above 20 million RMB. The same applies to the following tables.

20–5 按登记注册统计类别分规模以上工业企业研究与试验发展(R&D)活动及专利情况(2023年)

Statistics on R&D Activities and Patents of Industrial Enterprises above Designated Size by Registered Statistical Categories (2023)

登记注册统计类别	Registered Statistical Categories	R&D人员全时当量(人年) Full-time Equivalent of R&D Personnel (man-year)	R&D经费(万元) Expenditure on R&D (10 000 yuan)	专利申请数(件) Number of Patent Applications (piece)	#发明专利 Inventions	有效发明专利数(件) Number of Effective Inventions (piece)
合　计	**Total**	**4816705**	**209698997**	**1565960**	**613602**	**2227602**
#大中型工业企业	Large and Medium-sized Industrial Enterprises	2943115	149458752	786384	399241	1315227
内资企业	**Domestic Invested Enterprises**	**3978276**	**172123465**	**1364273**	**527996**	**1900810**
有限责任公司	Limited Liability Corporations	3118129	132458049	1052619	376668	1383927
股份有限公司	Share-holding Corporations Ltd.	825412	38281464	303740	147744	505901
非公司企业法人	Non Corporate Legal Entity	21005	974247	5940	3195	9296
个人独资企业	Sole Proprietorship Enterprises	11270	333126	1441	256	1177
合伙企业	Partnership Enterprises	2401	75828	522	131	496
其他内资企业	Other Domestic Invested Enterprises	59	752	11	2	13
港澳台投资企业	**Enterprises with Investment from Hong Kong, Macao and Taiwan**	**458589**	**18361276**	**102724**	**41888**	**165138**
港澳台投资有限责任公司	Limited Liability Corporations with Investment from Hong Kong, Macao and Taiwan	357640	13294223	66036	24448	99311
港澳台投资股份有限公司	Share-holding Corporations Ltd. with Investment from Hong Kong, Macao and Taiwan	89957	4553088	33704	15913	58547
港澳台投资合伙企业	Partnership Enterprises with Investment from Hong Kong, Macao and Taiwan	6026	249243	1869	1163	6339
其他港澳台投资企业	Other Enterprises with Investment from Hong Kong, Macao and Taiwan	4966	264722	1115	364	941
外商投资企业	**Foreign Invested Enterprises**	**379840**	**19214256**	**98963**	**43718**	**161654**
外商投资有限责任公司	Foreign Invested Limited Liability Corporations	299289	14904762	70472	29151	113555
外商投资股份有限公司	Foreign Invested Share-holding Corporations Ltd.	68733	3611038	25264	13001	44194
外商投资合伙企业	Foreign Invested Partnership Enterprises	8154	365962	850	292	1271
其他外商投资企业	Other Foreign Invested Enterprises	3664	332495	2377	1274	2634

注：本表登记注册统计类别按《关于市场主体统计分类的划分规定》(国统字〔2023〕14号)执行。

a) The registered statistical categories of this table is implemented in accordance with the Regulations on the Classification of Market Entity Statistics (Guotongzi [2023] No. 14).

20-6 按行业分规模以上工业企业研究与试验发展(R&D)活动及专利情况(2023年)

Statistics on R&D Activities and Patents of Industrial Enterprises above Designated Size by Industrial Sector (2023)

行业	Sector	R&D人员全时当量(人年) Full-time Equivalent of R&D Personnel (man-year)	R&D经费(万元) Expenditure on R&D (10 000 yuan)	专利申请数(件) Number of Patent Applications (piece)	#发明专利 Inventions	有效发明专利数(件) Number of Effective Inventions (piece)
全国总计	**Total**	**4816705**	**209698997**	**1565960**	**613602**	**2227602**
煤炭开采和洗选业	Mining and Washing of Coal	58330	2206325	6614	2128	3769
石油和天然气开采业	Extraction of Petroleum and Natural Gas	19281	1375573	5247	3849	9071
黑色金属矿采选业	Mining and Processing of Ferrous Metal Ores	6169	451033	1567	719	3103
有色金属矿采选业	Mining and Processing of Non-ferrous Metal Ores	8740	386433	1683	463	1633
非金属矿采选业	Mining and Processing of Non-metal Ores	8306	293974	1670	478	1465
农副食品加工业	Processing of Food from Agricultural Products	80884	3165903	16990	4610	20586
食品制造业	Manufacture of Foods	65026	1868130	15884	5204	23987
酒、饮料和精制茶制造业	Manufacture of Alcohol, Beverages and Refined Tea	26968	872397	6457	1617	6961
烟草制品业	Manufacture of Tobacco	7629	363548	11044	4060	10651
纺织业	Manufacture of Textile	121957	2812582	21268	4909	22655
纺织服装、服饰业	Manufacture of Textile, Wearing Apparel and Accessories	54113	1015887	8824	1622	7054
皮革、毛皮、羽毛及其制品和制鞋业	Manufacture of Leather, Fur, Feather and Related Products and Footwear	51201	1044149	8367	1152	5205
木材加工和木、竹、藤、棕、草制品业	Processing of Timber, Manufacture of Wood, Bamboo, Rattan, Palm and Straw Products	29199	849720	5774	1376	5478
家具制造业	Manufacture of Furniture	43813	947892	17590	2358	10191
造纸和纸制品业	Manufacture of Paper and Paper Products	49745	1793057	10689	2324	11963
印刷和记录媒介复制业	Printing and Reproduction of Recording Media	38746	929706	10655	2307	12245
文教、工美、体育和娱乐用品制造业	Manufacture of Articles for Culture, Education, Arts and Crafts, Sport and Entertainment Activities	58523	1208160	17635	2720	14228
石油、煤炭及其他燃料加工业	Processing of Petroleum, Coal and Other Fuels	26470	1914042	5266	2098	7921
化学原料及化学制品制造业	Manufacture of Raw Chemical Materials and Chemical Products	251646	12162533	66480	28055	113474
医药制造业	Manufacture of Medicines	191292	10963162	34308	17766	81600
化学纤维制造业	Manufacture of Chemical Fibres	33918	1721998	5194	1743	7523
橡胶和塑料制品业	Manufacture of Rubber and Plastics Products	170960	5332732	54614	12981	60608
非金属矿物制品业	Manufacture of Non-metallic Mineral Products	207903	7240261	61783	16490	68978
黑色金属冶炼和压延加工业	Smelting and Pressing of Ferrous Metals	101794	9678563	26053	11221	31917
有色金属冶炼和压延加工业	Smelting and Pressing of Non-ferrous Metals	102235	6423964	25074	8299	31028
金属制品业	Manufacture of Metal Products	213223	7231794	69091	15528	74624
通用设备制造业	Manufacture of General Purpose Machinery	358481	12189227	136327	41253	169207
专用设备制造业	Manufacture of Special Purpose Machinery	321797	11642127	146402	50378	187218
汽车制造业	Manufacture of Automobiles	385540	18022429	108329	44398	107857
铁路、船舶、航空航天和其他运输设备制造业	Manufacture of Railway, Ship, Aerospace and Other Transport Equipments	118087	6231313	29716	10567	40155
电气机械和器材制造业	Manufacture of Electrical Machinery and Apparatus	489251	23773955	239281	86380	271989
计算机、通信和其他电子设备制造业	Manufacture of Computers, Communication and Other Electronic Equipment	875515	43927705	271007	160017	652396
仪器仪表制造业	Manufacture of Instruments and Meters	116909	3575131	45748	17801	59786
其他制造业	Other Manufacturing	22738	1034717	5512	1327	5511
金属制品、机械和设备修理业	Repair Service of Metal Products, Machinery and Equipment	7317	256136	2211	635	2107
电力、热力生产和供应业	Production and Supply of Electric Power and Heat Power	50319	2675077	54785	40126	69637
燃气生产和供应业	Production and Supply of Gas	8911	435884	1491	343	1293
水的生产和供应业	Production and Supply of Water	10128	323876	2350	724	2582

20−7 分地区规模以上工业企业研究与试验发展(R&D)活动及专利情况(2023年)

Statistics on R&D Activities and Patents of Industrial Enterprises above Designated Size by Region (2023)

地 区	Region	R&D人员全时当量(人年) Full-time Equivalent of R&D Personnel (man-year)	R&D经费(万元) Expenditure on R&D (10 000 yuan)	专利申请数(件) Number of Patent Applications (piece)	#发明专利 Inventions	有效发明专利数(件) Number of Effective Inventions (piece)
全 国	**National Total**	**4816705**	**209698997**	**1565960**	**613602**	**2227602**
北 京	Beijing	59993	4410019	31980	20643	80347
天 津	Tianjin	56539	2959946	19635	7249	30392
河 北	Hebei	128602	7035030	34738	13170	44210
山 西	Shanxi	42266	2175885	9698	4017	13426
内蒙古	Inner Mongolia	26554	1919744	11056	4064	9468
辽 宁	Liaoning	67329	3922250	19606	6927	34185
吉 林	Jilin	16859	1036767	13009	8420	11455
黑龙江	Heilongjiang	21864	1060212	6186	2930	10546
上 海	Shanghai	112518	8110336	45050	19761	88728
江 苏	Jiangsu	721248	33016934	234666	83835	328671
浙 江	Zhejiang	651025	18275760	180387	48296	181101
安 徽	Anhui	196251	9269647	82018	34015	101197
福 建	Fujian	211921	9172900	59409	23148	63781
江 西	Jiangxi	126157	4840718	34785	12220	26071
山 东	Shandong	444404	18693400	123645	43358	156453
河 南	Henan	182729	9142432	45208	12661	49860
湖 北	Hubei	183963	8956266	63597	27742	97938
湖 南	Hunan	209066	9419834	40317	16701	60535
广 东	Guangdong	920359	34266367	366916	164853	661500
广 西	Guangxi	33516	1551896	11790	5136	15301
海 南	Hainan	5700	190844	1685	701	3024
重 庆	Chongqing	86802	4999041	27116	11321	29767
四 川	Sichuan	128074	5718223	41770	17184	62570
贵 州	Guizhou	27878	1261991	8290	3883	8168
云 南	Yunnan	37271	2101472	13189	5256	14217
西 藏	Xizang	236	11538	128	46	265
陕 西	Shaanxi	71868	3765593	18424	7791	24558
甘 肃	Gansu	17229	782290	7154	2285	6664
青 海	Qinghai	2137	151826	1744	896	1352
宁 夏	Ningxia	12038	668838	5486	1955	5295
新 疆	Xinjiang	14308	811001	7278	3138	6557

20－8 按登记注册统计类别分规模以上工业企业新产品开发及生产情况(2023年)

New Products Development and Production of Industrial Enterprises above Designated Size by Registered Statistical Categories (2023)

登记注册统计类别	Registered Statistical Categories	新产品开发项目数(项) Number of Projects on New Products Development (unit)	新产品开发经费支出(万元) Expenditure on New Products Development (10 000 yuan)	新产品销售收入(万元) Sales Revenue of New Products (10 000 yuan)	#出口 Exports
合　计	**Total**	**1204643**	**275638464**	**3413340364**	**554797551**
#大中型工业企业	Large and Medium-sized Industrial Enterprises	373518	183058075	2487564696	475853430
内资企业	**Domestic Invested Enterprises**	**1069652**	**223568696**	**2711802539**	**340978745**
有限责任公司	Limited Liability Corporations	895861	171716465	2077958607	235103936
股份有限公司	Share-holding Corporations Ltd.	165216	50258562	615774343	104823734
非公司企业法人	Non Corporate Legal Entity	3747	925393	10172157	797481
个人独资企业	Sole Proprietorship Enterprises	3831	548468	6877162	160055
合伙企业	Partnership Enterprises	977	118743	1007562	89156
其他内资企业	Other Domestic Invested Enterprises	20	1064	12708	4383
港澳台投资企业	**Enterprises with Investment from Hong Kong, Macao and Taiwan**	**66855**	**24912212**	**352470969**	**112757495**
港澳台投资有限责任公司	Limited Liability Corporations with Investment from Hong Kong, Macao and Taiwan	54478	18446043	273703061	90864554
港澳台投资股份有限公司	Share-holding Corporations Ltd. with Investment from Hong Kong, Macao and Taiwan	10368	5788643	71010301	19023637
港澳台投资合伙企业	Partnership Enterprises with Investment from Hong Kong, Macao and Taiwan	1116	357683	4405850	2417977
其他港澳台投资企业	Other Enterprises with Investment from Hong Kong, Macao and Taiwan	893	319843	3351756	451328
外商投资企业	**Foreign Invested Enterprises**	**68136**	**27157556**	**349066856**	**101061311**
外商投资有限责任公司	Foreign Invested Limited Liability Corporations	55496	20842917	275211772	85228072
外商投资股份有限公司	Foreign Invested Share-holding Corporations Ltd.	10777	5342484	58236528	11222364
外商投资合伙企业	Foreign Invested Partnership Enterprises	1031	450855	6178064	4202438
其他外商投资企业	Other Foreign Invested Enterprises	832	521300	9440492	408437

注：本表登记注册统计类别按《关于市场主体统计分类的划分规定》(国统字〔2023〕14号)执行。

a) The registered statistical categories of this table is implemented in accordance with the Regulations on the Classification of Market Entity Statistics (Guotongzi [2023] No. 14).

20-9 按行业分规模以上工业企业新产品开发及生产情况(2023年)
New Products Development and Production of Industrial Enterprises above Designated Size by Industrial Sector (2023)

行　业	Sector	新产品开发项目数(项) Projects for New Products Development (unit)	新产品开发经费支出(万元) Expenditure on New Products Development (10 000 yuan)	新产品销售收入(万元) Sales Revenue of New Products (10 000 yuan)	#出口 Exports
全国总计	**Total**	**1204643**	**275638464**	**3413340364**	**554797551**
煤炭开采和洗选业	Mining and Washing of Coal	2998	1082227	7460251	
石油和天然气开采业	Extraction of Petroleum and Natural Gas	939	482290	1494026	
黑色金属矿采选业	Mining and Processing of Ferrous Metal Ores	882	310814	3976132	2219
有色金属矿采选业	Mining and Processing of Non-ferrous Metal Ores	1329	317939	3897239	23048
非金属矿采选业	Mining and Processing of Non-metal Ores	1717	298725	4817117	58465
农副食品加工业	Processing of Food from Agricultural Products	25943	4849945	73961611	2214681
食品制造业	Manufacture of Foods	21050	2880018	36555365	3140461
酒、饮料和精制茶制造业	Manufacture of Alcohol, Beverages and Refined Tea	7712	1330739	18597986	420108
烟草制品业	Manufacture of Tobacco	2218	406237	8473870	750785
纺织业	Manufacture of Textile	29727	4309865	55085742	8044827
纺织服装、服饰业	Manufacture of Textile, Wearing Apparel and Accessories	12121	1580761	21559439	4035738
皮革、毛皮、羽毛及其制品和制鞋业	Manufacture of Leather, Fur, Feather and Related Products and Footwear	10844	1478450	16158164	3149245
木材加工和木、竹、藤、棕、草制品业	Processing of Timber, Manufacture of Wood, Bamboo, Rattan, Palm and Straw Products	8388	1194531	17512626	1047763
家具制造业	Manufacture of Furniture	13459	1613569	18765994	4276509
造纸及纸制品业	Manufacture of Paper and Paper Products	13381	2734531	44388762	2620101
印刷和记录媒介复制业	Printing and Reproduction of Recording Media	11257	1377677	16645074	2238353
文教、工美、体育和娱乐用品制造业	Manufacture of Articles for Culture, Education, Arts and Crafts, Sport and Entertainment Activities	17116	1970785	21594765	6551156
石油、煤炭及其他燃料加工业	Processing of Petroleum, Coal and Other Fuels	5135	2874527	72668181	1768973
化学原料及化学制品制造业	Manufacture of Raw Chemical Materials and Chemical Products	73792	15167831	250029188	19814824
医药制造业	Manufacture of Medicines	62793	13293840	89334805	9001593
化学纤维制造业	Manufacture of Chemical Fibres	6322	2000006	34526022	2350390
橡胶和塑料制品业	Manufacture of Rubber and Plastics Products	59633	7611773	90073208	16894346
非金属矿物制品业	Manufacture of Non-metallic Mineral Products	59050	9836847	129220885	6564085
黑色金属冶炼和压延加工业	Smelting and Pressing of Ferrous Metals	18824	15090033	196720033	7503715
有色金属冶炼和压延加工业	Smelting and Pressing of Non-ferrous Metals	22629	8303384	165679614	6787935
金属制品业	Manufacture of Metal Products	73339	9502391	116655350	15497140
通用设备制造业	Manufacture of General Purpose Machinery	117031	16589195	173817059	23032597
专用设备制造业	Manufacture of Special Purpose Machinery	107200	16701444	145002534	21044090
汽车制造业	Manufacture of Automobiles	67596	24912899	357616419	38154657
铁路、船舶、航空航天和其他运输设备制造业	Manufacture of Railway, Ship, Aerospace and Other Transport Equipments	25885	4953279	59026855	15192865
电气机械和器材制造业	Manufacture of Electrical Machinery and Apparatus	127563	31532337	463318737	79635682
计算机、通信和其他电子设备制造业	Manufacture of Computers, Communication and Other Electronic Equipment	133541	59052432	617246770	245412488
仪器仪表制造业	Manufacture of Instruments and Meters	36078	5174401	37543998	4793726
其他制造业	Other Manufacturing	5445	564116	5940009	1895683
金属制品、机械和设备修理业	Repair Service of Metal Products, Machinery and Equipment	1849	299483	2075338	650802
电力、热力生产和供应业	Production and Supply of Electric Power and Heat Power	11332	2120912	8638395	84778
燃气生产和供应业	Production and Supply of Gas	1687	398319	8733809	22454
水的生产和供应业	Production and Supply of Water	1813	262761	1509144	3399

20-10 分地区规模以上工业企业新产品开发及生产情况(2023年)
New Products Development and Production of Industrial Enterprises above Designated Size by Region (2023)

地区	Region	新产品开发项目数(项) Projects for New Products Development (unit)	新产品开发经费支出(万元) Expenditure on New Products Development (10 000 yuan)	新产品销售收入(万元) Sales Revenue of New Products (10 000 yuan)	#出口 Exports
全国	**National Total**	**1204643**	**275638464**	**3413340364**	**554797551**
北京	Beijing	18031	7032647	56484637	8982306
天津	Tianjin	17475	3060245	41246491	6385926
河北	Hebei	39967	9014152	111738833	11013762
山西	Shanxi	8629	1909004	33068331	4210583
内蒙古	Inner Mongolia	5477	1949972	25748596	1320288
辽宁	Liaoning	17457	3927147	44915467	6311439
吉林	Jilin	5287	2138062	18184662	840264
黑龙江	Heilongjiang	7235	939316	10539364	495623
上海	Shanghai	29520	12572812	103849988	17792835
江苏	Jiangsu	141304	40743988	495617097	114808572
浙江	Zhejiang	207990	29587234	418362856	82909771
安徽	Anhui	45238	11570656	195925423	22760235
福建	Fujian	35207	9216778	77141442	16641154
江西	Jiangxi	38801	6785937	124701285	16547101
山东	Shandong	120033	24971529	471245878	53348886
河南	Henan	30162	6115299	94255387	25187682
湖北	Hubei	32209	10682056	147224070	5771171
湖南	Hunan	53825	11203893	156312569	7371846
广东	Guangdong	241406	58461092	518774584	130155246
广西	Guangxi	12372	2368579	29752124	1971036
海南	Hainan	2535	435042	3116309	440408
重庆	Chongqing	23069	5534886	75867349	12903945
四川	Sichuan	32723	5926139	60814817	3389225
贵州	Guizhou	5920	836460	11072480	477236
云南	Yunnan	7108	1872295	22045901	253018
西藏	Xizang	118	13731	146836	
陕西	Shaanxi	16419	3459332	32682050	1600948
甘肃	Gansu	2830	631067	13770262	597185
青海	Qinghai	364	211329	2056030	22957
宁夏	Ningxia	2699	802872	8138665	156921
新疆	Xinjiang	3233	1664914	8540581	129984

20-11 按行业分规模以上工业企业产品和工艺创新情况(2023年)
Industrial Enterprises above Designated Size with Product or Process Innovation by Industrial Sector (2023)

行业	Sector	有产品或工艺创新活动的企业数(个) Number of Enterprises with Product or Process Innovation Activities (unit)	有产品或工艺创新活动的企业占规模以上工业企业的比重(%) As Percentage of Industrial Enterprises above Designated Size (%)	#实现产品创新的企业所占比重 With Product Innovation	#实现工艺创新的企业所占比重 With Process Innovation
总计	**Total**	**291129**	**60.5**	**37.5**	**42.3**
采矿业	Mining	3477	29.0	8.1	21.4
煤炭开采和洗选业	Mining and Washing of Coal	1150	23.8	2.9	19.6
石油和天然气开采业	Extraction of Petroleum and Natural Gas	89	54.9	6.2	42.0
黑色金属矿采选业	Mining and Processing of Ferrous Metal Ores	436	29.1	9.9	22.7
有色金属矿采选业	Mining and Processing of Non-ferrous Metal Ores	499	39.5	10.5	28.3
非金属矿采选业	Mining and Processing of Non-metal Ores	1164	30.2	13.0	19.8
开采专业及辅助性活动	Professional and Support Activities for Mining	133	35.1	9.5	24.0
其他采矿业	Mining of Other Ores	6	54.5	18.2	36.4
制造业	Manufacturing	282005	62.8	39.8	43.8
农副食品加工业	Processing of Food from Agricultural Products	12288	49.6	28.9	33.3
食品制造业	Manufacture of Foods	6207	63.2	40.3	41.9
酒、饮料和精制茶制造业	Manufacture of Alcohol, Beverages and Refined Tea	3236	57.3	32.4	37.7
烟草制品业	Manufacture of Tobacco	159	86.4	59.2	61.4
纺织业	Manufacture of Textile	11296	55.8	34.2	40.6
纺织服装、服饰业	Manufacture of Textile, Wearing Apparel and Accessories	5122	40.2	23.3	27.3
皮革、毛皮、羽毛及其制品和制鞋业	Manufacture of Leather, Fur, Feather and Related Products and Footware	4294	52.3	33.2	30.8
木材加工和木、竹、藤、棕、草制品业	Processing of Timber, Manufacture of Wood, Bamboo, Rattan, Palm and Straw Products	5042	40.6	24.2	28.6
家具制造业	Manufacture of Furniture	3955	56.0	37.7	37.3
造纸和纸制品业	Manufacture of Paper and Paper Products	4032	52.8	31.4	37.9
印刷和记录媒介复制业	Printing and Reproduction of Recording Media	3830	57.9	32.9	43.3
文教、工美、体育和娱乐用品制造业	Manufacture of Articles for Culture, Education, Arts and Crafts, Sport and Entertainment Activities	5696	56.3	37.1	38.9
石油、煤炭及其他燃料加工业	Processing of Petroleum, Coal and Other Fuels	1172	52.4	25.9	38.3
化学原料和化学制品制造业	Manufacture of Raw Chemical Materials and Chemical Products	17510	70.1	43.8	48.8
医药制造业	Manufacture of Medicines	7735	82.2	46.6	56.6
化学纤维制造业	Manufacture of Chemical Fibres	1571	67.7	40.1	50.3
橡胶和塑料制品业	Manufacture of Rubber and Plastics Products	16190	62.2	39.5	43.4
非金属矿物制品业	Manufacture of Non-metallic Mineral Products	22733	47.5	25.7	33.1
黑色金属冶炼和压延加工业	Smelting and Pressing of Ferrous Metals	2891	47.7	26.7	36.1
有色金属冶炼和压延加工业	Smelting and Pressing of Non-ferrous Metals	5630	58.2	33.8	43.2
金属制品业	Manufacture of Metal Products	20766	58.9	35.4	41.9
通用设备制造业	Manufacture of General Purpose Machinery	25988	75.6	51.4	53.4
专用设备制造业	Manufacture of Special Purpose Machinery	21219	79.5	53.7	54.9
汽车制造业	Manufacture of Automobiles	13395	72.4	49.5	51.9
铁路、船舶、航空航天和其他运输设备制造业	Manufacture of Railway, Ship, Aerospace and Other Transport Equipments	4161	71.3	47.0	49.6
电气机械和器材制造业	Manufacture of Electrical Machinery and Apparatus	24808	73.4	50.7	51.1
计算机、通信和其他电子设备制造业	Manufacture of Computers, Communication and Other Electronic Equipment	21671	80.2	55.7	55.7
仪器仪表制造业	Manufacture of Measuring Instruments and Machinery	6023	86.5	62.1	58.6
其他制造业	Other Manufacture	1354	63.8	40.0	42.6
废弃资源综合利用业	Utilization of Waste Resources	1624	46.9	20.8	33.5
金属制品、机械和设备修理业	Repair Service of Metal Products, Machinery and Equipment	407	51.1	19.2	34.9
电力、热力、燃气及水生产和供应业	Production and Supply of Electricity, Heat, Gas and Water	5647	27.7	4.8	20.0
电力、热力生产和供应业	Production and Supply of Electric Power and Heat Power	3554	27.8	4.4	20.1
燃气生产和供应业	Production and Supply of Gas	874	22.9	4.9	16.9
水的生产和供应业	Production and Supply of Water	1219	32.3	6.3	22.7

20-12 按登记注册统计类别分规模以上工业企业产品和工艺创新情况(2023年)

Industrial Enterprises above Designated Size with Product or Process Innovation by Registered Statistical Categories (2023)

登记注册统计类别	Registered Statistical Categories	有产品或工艺创新活动的企业数(个) Number of Enterprises with Product or Process Innovation Activities (unit)	有产品或工艺创新活动的企业占规模以上工业企业的比重(%) As Percentage of Industrial Enterprises above Designated Size (%)	#实现产品创新的企业所占比重 With Product Innovation	#实现工艺创新的企业所占比重 With Process Innovation
总　计	**Total**	**291129**	**60.5**	**37.5**	**42.3**
内资企业	**Domestic Invested Enterprises**	**267359**	**60.7**	**37.6**	**42.4**
有限责任公司	Limited Liability Corporations	242808	59.8	36.5	41.6
股份有限公司	Share-holding Corporations Ltd.	20148	88.7	65.7	64.8
非公司企业法人	Non Corporate Legal Entity	895	42.7	22.4	28.4
个人独资企业	Sole Proprietorship Enterprises	2986	36.3	20.9	23.9
合伙企业	Partnership Enterprises	514	40.7	21.0	26.6
其他内资企业	Other Domestic Invested Enterprises	8	71.4	28.6	28.6
港澳台投资企业	**Enterprises with Investment from Hong Kong, Macao and Taiwan**	**11410**	**58.5**	**37.1**	**41.5**
港澳台投资有限责任公司	Limited Liability Corporations with Investment from Hong Kong, Macao and Taiwan	10385	57.2	35.7	40.4
港澳台投资股份有限公司	Share-holding Corporations Ltd. with Investment from Hong Kong, Macao and Taiwan	749	87.9	66.5	64.9
港澳台投资合伙企业	Partnership Enterprises with Investment from Hong Kong, Macao and Taiwan	162	57.0	36.3	37.7
其他港澳台投资企业	Other Enterprises with Investment from Hong Kong, Macao and Taiwan	114	57.9	38.1	40.1
外商投资企业	**Foreign Invested Enterprises**	**12360**	**58.5**	**36.6**	**40.7**
外商投资有限责任公司	Foreign Invested Limited Liability Corporations	11390	57.3	35.4	39.6
外商投资股份有限公司	Foreign Invested Share-holding Corporations Ltd.	657	91.9	74.1	72.7
外商投资合伙企业	Foreign Invested Partnership Enterprises	196	60.5	34.9	38.3
其他外商投资企业	Other Foreign Invested Enterprises	117	55.2	26.9	39.6

注：本表登记注册统计类别按《关于市场主体统计分类的划分规定》(国统字〔2023〕14号)执行。

a) The registered statistical categories of this table is implemented in accordance with the Regulations on the Classification of Market Entity Statistics (Guotongzi [2023] No. 14).

20-13 按行业分规模以上工业企业组织(管理)和营销创新情况(2023年)
Industrial Enterprises above Designated Size with Organizational or Marketing Innovation by Industrial Sector (2023)

行业	Sector	实现组织(管理)或营销创新的企业数(个) Number of Enterprises with Organizational or Marketing Innovation (unit)	实现组织(管理)或营销创新的企业占规模以上工业企业的比重(%) As Percentage of Industrial Enterprises above Designated Size (%)	#实现组织(管理)创新的企业所占比重 With Organizational Innovation	#实现营销创新的企业所占比重 With Marketing Innovation
总计	**Total**	**170751**	**35.5**	**26.4**	**26.9**
采矿业	Mining	2097	17.5	15.6	7.1
煤炭开采和洗选业	Mining and Washing of Coal	692	14.3	12.9	5.1
石油和天然气开采业	Extraction of Petroleum and Natural Gas	49	30.2	28.4	9.3
黑色金属矿采选业	Mining and Processing of Ferrous Metal Ores	245	16.4	15.0	6.4
有色金属矿采选业	Mining and Processing of Non-ferrous Metal Ores	281	22.3	20.1	6.9
非金属矿采选业	Mining and Processing of Non-metal Ores	737	19.1	16.6	10.0
开采专业及辅助性活动	Professional and Support Activities for Mining	89	23.5	22.4	6.1
其他采矿业	Mining of Other Ores	4	36.4	18.2	36.4
制造业	Manufacturing	165139	36.8	27.2	28.4
农副食品加工业	Processing of Food from Agricultural Products	8986	36.3	22.8	31.7
食品制造业	Manufacture of Foods	4727	48.1	29.5	43.1
酒、饮料和精制茶制造业	Manufacture of Alcohol, Beverages and Refined Tea	2622	46.4	27.5	42.3
烟草制品业	Manufacture of Tobacco	111	60.3	43.5	50.5
纺织业	Manufacture of Textile	5702	28.1	21.2	21.1
纺织服装、服饰业	Manufacture of Textile, Wearing Apparel and Accessories	2975	23.3	16.5	18.4
皮革、毛皮、羽毛及其制品和制鞋业	Manufacture of Leather, Fur, Feather and Related Products and Footware	2081	25.4	17.4	20.4
木材加工和木、竹、藤、棕、草制品业	Processing of Timber, Manufacture of Wood, Bamboo, Rattan, Palm and Straw Products	2941	23.7	17.4	19.6
家具制造业	Manufacture of Furniture	2409	34.1	23.1	29.4
造纸和纸制品业	Manufacture of Paper and Paper Products	2504	32.8	22.8	25.9
印刷和记录媒介复制业	Printing and Reproduction of Recording Media	2277	34.4	25.0	26.5
文教、工美、体育和娱乐用品制造业	Manufacture of Articles for Culture, Education, Arts and Crafts, Sport and Entertainment Activities	3518	34.7	21.8	30.2
石油、煤炭及其他燃料加工业	Processing of Petroleum, Coal and Other Fuels	708	31.7	25.0	21.2
化学原料和化学制品制造业	Manufacture of Raw Chemical Materials and Chemical Products	10014	40.1	29.6	30.9
医药制造业	Manufacture of Medicines	4910	52.2	36.8	42.6
化学纤维制造业	Manufacture of Chemical Fibres	788	34.0	26.0	25.5
橡胶和塑料制品业	Manufacture of Rubber and Plastics Products	8888	34.2	24.7	27.0
非金属矿物制品业	Manufacture of Non-metallic Mineral Products	12918	27.0	21.1	18.7
黑色金属冶炼和压延加工业	Smelting and Pressing of Ferrous Metals	1641	27.1	22.8	17.9
有色金属冶炼和压延加工业	Smelting and Pressing of Non-ferrous Metals	2946	30.4	24.6	20.5
金属制品业	Manufacture of Metal Products	11227	31.8	24.5	23.6
通用设备制造业	Manufacture of General Purpose Machinery	14479	42.1	31.6	32.5
专用设备制造业	Manufacture of Special Purpose Machinery	12342	46.2	35.2	35.8
汽车制造业	Manufacture of Automobiles	7175	38.8	31.2	26.4
铁路、船舶、航空航天和其他运输设备制造业	Manufacture of Railway, Ship, Aerospace and Other Transport Equipments	2309	39.6	30.6	27.3
电气机械和器材制造业	Manufacture of Electrical Machinery and Apparatus	14861	43.9	32.4	34.8
计算机、通信和其他电子设备制造业	Manufacture of Computers, Communication and Other Electronic Equipment	13337	49.4	38.6	37.1
仪器仪表制造业	Manufacture of Measuring Instruments and Machinery	3739	53.7	40.9	41.9
其他制造业	Other Manufacture	837	39.4	26.2	33.6
废弃资源综合利用业	Utilization of Waste Resources	933	26.9	23.7	15.6
金属制品、机械和设备修理业	Repair Service of Metal Products, Machinery and Equipment	234	29.4	26.7	11.7
电力、热力、燃气及水生产和供应业	Production and Supply of Electricity, Heat, Gas and Water	3515	17.2	15.6	5.7
电力、热力生产和供应业	Production and Supply of Electric Power and Heat Power	2092	16.3	15.0	4.6
燃气生产和供应业	Production and Supply of Gas	747	19.6	16.7	9.4
水的生产和供应业	Production and Supply of Water	676	17.9	16.3	5.8

20-14　按登记注册统计类别分规模以上工业企业组织(管理)和营销创新情况(2023年)

Industrial Enterprises above Designated Size with Organizational or Marketing Innovation by Registered Statistical Categories (2023)

登记注册统计类别	Registered Statistical Categories	实现组织(管理)或营销创新的企业数(个) Number of Enterprises with Organizational or Marketing Innovation (unit)	实现组织(管理)或营销创新的企业占规模以上工业企业的比重(%) As Percentage of Industrial Enterprises above Designated Size (%)	#实现组织(管理)创新的企业所占比重 With Organizational Innovation	#实现营销创新的企业所占比重 With Marketing Innovation
总　计	**Total**	**170751**	**35.5**	**26.4**	**26.9**
内资企业	**Domestic Invested Enterprises**	**157581**	**35.8**	**26.7**	**27.3**
有限责任公司	Limited Liability Corporations	142518	35.1	26.1	26.7
股份有限公司	Share-holding Corporations Ltd.	12647	55.7	43.4	43.9
非公司企业法人	Non Corporate Legal Entity	476	22.7	18.0	14.5
个人独资企业	Sole Proprietorship Enterprises	1651	20.1	14.1	15.7
合伙企业	Partnership Enterprises	287	22.7	16.0	17.5
其他内资企业	Other Domestic Invested Enterprises	NA	14.3	14.3	14.3
港澳台投资企业	**Enterprises with Investment from Hong Kong, Macao and Taiwan**	**6515**	**33.4**	**24.2**	**24.4**
港澳台投资有限责任公司	Limited Liability Corporations with Investment from Hong Kong, Macao and Taiwan	5879	32.4	23.3	23.5
港澳台投资股份有限公司	Share-holding Corporations Ltd. with Investment from Hong Kong, Macao and Taiwan	480	56.3	44.2	42.8
港澳台投资合伙企业	Partnership Enterprises with Investment from Hong Kong, Macao and Taiwan	95	33.5	20.1	27.8
其他港澳台投资企业	Other Enterprises with Investment from Hong Kong, Macao and Taiwan	61	31.0	23.4	24.9
外商投资企业	**Foreign Invested Enterprises**	**6655**	**31.5**	**23.0**	**21.7**
外商投资有限责任公司	Foreign Invested Limited Liability Corporations	6037	30.4	22.1	20.8
外商投资股份有限公司	Foreign Invested Share-holding Corporations Ltd.	449	62.8	49.1	47.3
外商投资合伙企业	Foreign Invested Partnership Enterprises	95	29.3	18.8	21.9
其他外商投资企业	Other Foreign Invested Enterprises	74	34.9	26.4	21.2

注：本表登记注册统计类别按《关于市场主体统计分类的划分规定》(国统字〔2023〕14号)执行。

a) The registered statistical categories of this table is implemented in accordance with the Regulations on the Classification of Market Entity Statistics (Guotongzi [2023] No. 14).

20-15 按行业分规模以上工业企业创新费用支出情况(2023年)
Expenditure on Innovation of Industrial Enterprises above Designated Size by Industrial Sector (2023)

行 业	Sector	创新费用支出合计(亿元) Total Innovation Expenditure (100 million yuan)	在创新费用合计中占比(%) As Percentage of Total Innovation Expenditure(%)			
			内部R&D In-house R&D	外部R&D Contracted out R&D	获得机器设备和软件 Acquisition of Machinery, Equipment and Software	从外部获取相关技术 Acquisition of Other External Technoogy
总 计	**Total**	**32593.5**	**64.1**	**4.3**	**29.0**	**2.6**
采矿业	Mining	819.6	63.2	5.1	31.6	0.1
煤炭开采和洗选业	Mining and Washing of Coal	392.7	56.2	4.0	39.6	0.2
石油和天然气开采业	Extraction of Petroleum and Natural Gas	198.0	69.5	9.5	21.0	
黑色金属矿采选业	Mining and Processing of Ferrous Metal Ores	62.7	71.6	3.2	25.0	0.2
有色金属矿采选业	Mining and Processing of Non-ferrous Metal Ores	61.3	63.0	3.3	33.8	
非金属矿采选业	Mining and Processing of Non-metal Ores	44.1	66.7	1.1	32.0	0.2
开采专业及辅助性活动	Professional and Support Activities for Mining	60.6	77.7	4.3	18.0	
制造业	Manufacturing	30993.9	64.6	4.1	28.7	2.6
农副食品加工业	Processing of Food from Agricultural Products	486.8	65.0	0.5	33.9	0.6
食品制造业	Manufacture of Foods	313.8	59.5	2.5	35.8	2.1
酒、饮料和精制茶制造业	Manufacture of Alcohol, Beverages and Refined Tea	199.3	43.8	1.2	52.1	2.9
烟草制品业	Manufacture of Tobacco	185.0	19.6	3.1	61.5	15.7
纺织业	Manufacture of Textile	423.5	66.4	0.5	32.8	0.3
纺织服装、服饰业	Manufacture of Textile, Wearing Apparel and Accessories	160.1	63.5	0.6	35.7	0.2
皮革、毛皮、羽毛及其制品和制鞋业	Manufacture of Leather, Fur, Feather and Related Products and Footware	137.3	76.0	0.8	23.2	
木材加工和木、竹、藤、棕、草制品业	Processing of Timber, Manufacture of Wood, Bamboo, Rattan, Palm and Straw Products	120.5	70.5	0.3	29.0	0.2
家具制造业	Manufacture of Furniture	146.8	64.6	1.8	33.5	0.1
造纸和纸制品业	Manufacture of Paper and Paper Products	284.3	63.1	0.3	36.6	0.1
印刷和记录媒介复制业	Printing and Reproduction of Recording Media	151.9	61.2	0.5	37.4	0.9
文教、工美、体育和娱乐用品制造业	Manufacture of Articles for Culture, Education, Arts and Crafts, Sport and Entertainment Activities	181.2	66.7	0.6	32.5	0.3
石油、煤炭及其他燃料加工业	Processing of Petroleum, Coal and Other Fuels	574.0	33.2	0.8	64.7	1.3
化学原料和化学制品制造业	Manufacture of Raw Chemical Materials and Chemical Products	1970.0	61.7	1.5	36.1	0.7
医药制造业	Manufacture of Medicines	1601.0	68.5	9.7	18.6	3.3
化学纤维制造业	Manufacture of Chemical Fibres	218.5	78.8	0.5	20.0	0.6
橡胶和塑料制品业	Manufacture of Rubber and Plastics Products	772.8	69.0	1.6	28.2	1.2
非金属矿物制品业	Manufacture of Non-metallic Mineral Products	1144.4	63.3	0.6	35.7	0.5
黑色金属冶炼和压延加工业	Smelting and Pressing of Ferrous Metals	2183.2	44.3	0.5	50.3	4.8
有色金属冶炼和压延加工业	Smelting and Pressing of Non-ferrous Metals	1074.4	59.8	1.0	38.9	0.4
金属制品业	Manufacture of Metal Products	1017.0	70.7	0.6	28.0	0.7
通用设备制造业	Manufacture of General Purpose Machinery	1734.5	70.2	2.1	26.3	1.4
专用设备制造业	Manufacture of Special Purpose Machinery	1627.3	71.5	2.2	25.5	0.8
汽车制造业	Manufacture of Automobiles	2963.2	60.7	9.4	23.8	6.2
铁路、船舶、航空航天和其他运输设备制造业	Manufacture of Railway, Ship, Aerospace and Other Transport Equipments	704.9	85.7	8.0	1.8	4.6
电气机械和器材制造业	Manufacture of Electrical Machinery and Apparatus	3221.8	73.8	2.9	22.1	1.2
计算机、通信和其他电子设备制造业	Manufacture of Computers, Communication and Other Electronic Equipment	6655.9	65.6	7.2	23.2	4.0
仪器仪表制造业	Manufacture of Measuring Instruments and Machinery	504.0	70.2	3.3	25.9	0.5
其他制造业	Other Manufacture	78.1	91.8	6.9		1.3
废弃资源综合利用业	Utilization of Waste Resources	111.2	79.7	1.2	19.0	0.2
金属制品、机械和设备修理业	Repair Service of Metal Products, Machinery and Equipment	47.2	53.2	1.1	34.7	11.0
电力、热力、燃气及水生产和供应业	Production and Supply of Electricity, Heat, Gas and Water	780.0	43.4	9.7	41.7	5.2
电力、热力生产和供应业	Production and Supply of Electric Power and Heat Power	670.0	39.2	10.9	43.9	6.1
燃气生产和供应业	Production and Supply of Gas	64.0	68.1	3.0	28.9	
水的生产和供应业	Production and Supply of Water	46.0	70.4	1.7	27.6	0.2

20−16 按登记注册统计类别分规模以上工业企业创新费用支出情况(2023年)
Expenditure on Innovation of Industrial Enterprises above Designated Size by Registered Statistical Categories (2023)

登记注册统计类别	Registered Statistical Categories	创新费用支出合计(亿元) Total Core Innovation Expenditure (100 million yuan)	在创新费用合计中占比(%) As Percentage of Total Innovation Expenditure(%)			
			内部R&D In-house R&D	外部R&D Contracted out R&D	获得机器设备和软件 Acquisition of Machinery, Equipment and Software	从外部获取相关技术 Acquisition of Other External Knowledge
总　计	**Total**	**32593.5**	**64.1**	**4.3**	**29.0**	**2.6**
内资企业	**Domestic Invested Enterprises**	**26684.0**	**64.2**	**4.3**	**29.6**	**1.9**
有限责任公司	Limited Liability Corporations	20364.9	64.6	4.4	29.0	2.0
股份有限公司	Share-holding Corporations Ltd.	6108.7	62.7	3.9	31.7	1.7
非公司企业法人	Non Corporate Legal Entity	147.8	65.9	7.0	25.5	1.6
个人独资企业	Sole Proprietorship Enterprises	51.2	65.0	1.0	33.8	0.2
合伙企业	Partnership Enterprises	11.4	66.7	0.9	32.5	
其他内资企业	Other Domestic Invested Enterprises	0.1			100.0	
港澳台投资企业	**Enterprises with Investment from Hong Kong, Macao and Taiwan**	**2703.7**	**67.6**	**3.4**	**27.4**	**1.6**
港澳台投资有限责任公司	Limited Liability Corporations with Investment from Hong Kong, Macao and Taiwan	2009.0	65.8	3.2	29.6	1.5
港澳台投资股份有限公司	Share-holding Corporations Ltd. with Investment from Hong Kong, Macao and Taiwan	613.0	74.3	3.0	20.7	2.1
港澳台投资合伙企业	Partnership Enterprises with Investment from Hong Kong, Macao and Taiwan	42.4	58.7	14.9	25.7	0.7
其他港澳台投资企业	Other Enterprises with Investment from Hong Kong, Macao and Taiwan	39.3	64.9	10.7	24.4	
外商投资企业	**Foreign Invested Enterprises**	**3205.8**	**59.9**	**4.9**	**25.6**	**9.6**
外商投资有限责任公司	Foreign Invested Limited Liability Corporations	2528.2	59.0	5.1	24.9	11.0
外商投资股份有限公司	Foreign Invested Share-holding Corporations Ltd.	562.5	64.2	4.1	29.8	1.9
外商投资合伙企业	Foreign Invested Partnership Enterprises	53.2	68.8	3.9	16.0	11.3
其他外商投资企业	Other Foreign Invested Enterprises	61.9	53.6	5.0	23.4	17.9

注：本表登记注册统计类别按《关于市场主体统计分类的划分规定》(国统字〔2023〕14号)执行。

a) The registered statistical categories of this table is implemented in accordance with the Regulations on the Classification of Market Entity Statistics (Guotongzi [2023] No. 14).

20−17 高技术产业(制造业)企业R&D及相关活动情况
Statistics on R&D and Related Activities of Enterprises in High Technology Industry (Manufacturing Industry)

指　标	Item	2005	2010	2015	2020	2022	2023
R&D机构数 (个)	R&D Institutions (unit)	1619	3184	11265	20185	25084	25821
R&D人员全时当量(万人年)	Full-time Equivalent of R&D Personnel(10 000 man-years)	17.3	39.9	72.7	99.0	125.4	139.8
R&D经费支出 (亿元)	Expenditure on R&D (100 million yuan)	362.5	967.8	2626.7	4649.1	6507.7	6960.2
新产品开发经费支出(亿元)	Expenditure on New Products Development (100 million yuan)	415.7	1006.9	3030.6	6152.4	8590.6	9022.8
专利申请数 (件)	Number of Patent Applications (piece)	16823	59683	158463	348522	434039	444950
有效发明专利数 (件)	Number of Effective Invention Patents (piece)	6658	50166	241404	570905	809824	892210

注：2005年与2010年数据为大中型高技术产业(制造业)企业数据。

a) The data for 2005 and 2010 are for large and medium-sized enterprises in high technology industry (manufacturing industry).

20-18 高技术产业(制造业)相关情况（2023年）

行业	Industry	R&D 机构数 (个) R&D Institutions (unit)
合计	**Total**	**25821**
医药制造业	**Manufacture of Medicines**	**4745**
#化学药品制造	Manufacture of Chemical Medicine	1699
中成药生产	Manufacture of Finished Traditional Chinese Herbal Medicine	809
生物药品制品制造	Manufacture of Biopharmaceutical Products	622
电子及通信设备制造业	**Manufacture of Electronic Equipment and Communication Equipment**	**14376**
#电子工业专用设备制造	Manufacture of Special Equipment for Electronic Industry	1057
光纤光缆及锂离子电池制造	Manufacture of Optical Fiber and Cable, and Lithium Ion Battery	1144
#锂离子电池制造	Manufacture of Lithium Ion Batteries	920
通信设备、雷达及配套设备制造	Manufacture of Communication Equipment, Radar and Matching Equipment	1446
#通信系统设备制造	Manufacture of Communication System Equipment	711
通信终端设备制造	Manufacture of Communication Terminal Equipment	655
雷达及配套设备制造	Manufacture of Radar and Related Equipment	80
广播电视设备制造	Manufacture of Broadcasting and TV Equipment	304
非专业视听设备制造	Manufacture of Non-professional Audio-visual Equipment	587
电子器件制造	Manufacture of Electronic Appliances	3253
#电子真空器件制造	Manufacture of Electronic Vacuum Appliances	194
半导体分立器件制造	Manufacture of Semiconductor Discreting Appliances	275
集成电路制造	Manufacture of Integrated Circuit	759
光电子器件制造	Manufacture of Optoelectronic Devices	599
电子元件及电子专用材料制造	Manufacture of Electronic Components and Electronic Specialized Materials	4917
#电阻电容电感元件制造	Manufacture of Resistance, Capacitance and Inductance Components	609
电子电路制造	Manufacture of Electronic Circuit	987
电子专用材料制造	Manufacture of Electronic Specialized Materials	1425
智能消费设备制造	Manufacturing of Intelligent Consumption Equipment	912
其他电子设备制造	Other Electronic Equipment	756
计算机及办公设备制造业	**Manufacture of Computers and Office Equipments**	**1555**
#计算机整机制造	Manufacture of Entire Computer	182
计算机零部件制造	Manufacture of Parts and Fixture for Computer	460
计算机外围设备制造	Manufacture of Computer Peripheral Equipment	455
办公设备制造	Manufacture of Office Equipment	141
医疗仪器设备及仪器仪表制造业	**Manufacture of Medical Equipments and Meters**	**4834**
#医疗仪器设备及器械制造	Manufacture of Medical Equipment and Appliances	1575
#医疗诊断、监护及治疗设备制造	Manufacture of Medical Diagnosis, Monitoring and Treatment Equipment	527
医疗、外科及兽医用器械制造	Manufacture of Medical, Surgical and Veterinary Instruments	389
通用仪器仪表制造	Manufacture of General Measuring Instruments and Machinery	2221
专用仪器仪表制造	Manufacture of Special Measuring Instruments and Machinery	626
信息化学品制造业	**Manufacture of Information Chemicals**	**96**

注：本表的数据口径为规模以上工业企业。

Statistics on High-tech Industry (Manufacturing Industry) (2023)

R&D人员折合 全时当量 (人年) Full-time Equivalent of R&D Personnel (man-year)	R&D 经费支出 (万元) Expenditure on R&D (10 000 yuan)	R&D 项目数 (个) R&D Projects (unit)	新产品开发 项目数 (项) Number of Projects on New Products Development (unit)
1397796	**69602196**	**140650**	**281742**
191292	**10963162**	**31730**	**62793**
86015	5017268	14654	27703
32177	1204168	5475	10356
35347	3576026	5180	10738
898893	**46453804**	**71314**	**138673**
42148	1705134	5011	11004
75931	4378300	5796	9999
69273	3953940	4728	8275
250009	16175596	8314	15255
71932	3589472	4137	7963
172284	12326579	3463	6095
5793	259544	714	1197
15281	477559	1368	2899
31154	1228124	2418	5050
194906	11232092	17538	34727
5347	200244	695	1456
11149	458732	1318	2493
63329	5707060	5217	10575
24917	1150415	2902	5777
207164	8057518	23462	43502
20420	599358	2585	4945
52696	1458610	4473	8349
50555	3568374	7776	12917
52685	1990075	4316	9209
29615	1209406	3091	7028
97368	**3566177**	**7926**	**16120**
23136	1225445	1392	2737
22866	648505	2164	3869
19452	560078	1968	4343
6257	173848	522	1186
170193	**5851919**	**25209**	**56468**
57698	2355837	8878	21774
25978	1137739	3354	8380
13511	465123	2122	5063
73500	2257063	11069	23576
22494	688580	3233	6994
2547	**117503**	**397**	**673**

a) Data in this table cover industrial enterprises above designated size.

20-18 续表

行 业	Industry	新产品开发经费支出（万元）Expenditure on New Products Development (10 000 yuan)
合计	**Total**	**90228012**
医药制造业	**Manufacture of Medicines**	**13293840**
#化学药品制造	Manufacture of Chemical Medicine	5920978
中成药生产	Manufacture of Finished Traditional Chinese Herbal Medicine	1419257
生物药品制品制造	Manufacture of Biopharmaceutical Products	4393163
电子及通信设备制造业	**Manufacture of Electronic Equipment and Communication Equipment**	**62171007**
#电子工业专用设备制造	Manufacture of Special Equipment for Electronic Industry	2516910
光纤光缆及锂离子电池制造	Manufacture of Optical Fiber and Cable and Lithium Ion Battery	5494344
#锂离子电池制造	Manufacture of Lithium Ion Batteries	5024803
通信设备、雷达及配套设备制造	Manufacture of Communication Equipment, Radar and Matching Equipment	21884673
#通信系统设备制造	Manufacture of Communication System Equipment	5673924
通信终端设备制造	Manufacture of Communication Terminal Equipment	16068256
雷达及配套设备制造	Manufacture of Radar and Related Equipment	142493
广播电视设备制造	Manufacture of Broadcasting and TV Equipment	653064
非专业视听设备制造	Manufacture of Non-professional Audio-visual Equipment	1610029
电子器件制造	Manufacture of Electronic Appliances	15119171
#电子真空器件制造	Manufacture of Electronic Vacuum Appliances	220186
半导体分立器件制造	Manufacture of Semiconductor Discreting Appliances	643716
集成电路制造	Manufacture of Integrated Circuit	8046966
光电子器件制造	Manufacture of Optoelectronic Devices	1462238
电子元件及电子专用材料制造	Manufacture of Electronic Components and Electronic Specialized Materials	10235249
#电阻电容电感元件制造	Manufacture of Resistance, Capacitance and Inductance Components	758513
电子电路制造	Manufacture of Electronic Circuit	2006248
电子专用材料制造	Manufacture of Electronic Specialized Materials	4217868
智能消费设备制造	Manufacture of Intelligent Consumption Equipment	2982609
其他电子设备制造	Other Electronic Equipment	1674957
计算机及办公设备制造业	**Manufacture of Computers and Office Equipments**	**4892703**
#计算机整机制造	Manufacture of Entire Computer	1650460
计算机零部件制造	Manufacture of Parts and Components for Computer	864351
计算机外围设备制造	Manufacture of Computer Peripheral Equipment	957187
办公设备制造	Manufacture of Office Equipment	238548
医疗仪器设备及仪器仪表制造业	**Manufacture of Medical Equipments and Instruments and Meters**	**8839768**
#医疗仪器设备及器械制造	Manufacture of Medical Equipments and Appliances	3799975
#医疗诊断、监护及治疗设备制造	Manufacture of Medical Diagnosis, Monitoring and Treatment Equipment	1947929
医疗、外科及兽医用器械制造	Manufacture of Medical, Surgical and Veterinary Instruments	720916
通用仪器仪表制造	Manufacture of General Instruments	3389156
专用仪器仪表制造	Manufacture of Special Instruments	1009264
信息化学品制造业	**Manufacture of Information Chemicals**	**145192**

continued

新产品销售收入(万元) Sales Revenue of New Products (10 000 yuan)	#出口 Export	专利申请数(件) Patent Applications (piece)	#发明专利 Inventions	有效发明专利数(件) Number of Effective Inventions (piece)
858901500	**277967894**	**444950**	**237589**	**892210**
89334805	**9001593**	**34308**	**17766**	**81600**
45870568	6105765	12425	7499	33435
19020247	151053	5165	2433	15729
10937908	861515	6389	4178	15575
637578743	**218867798**	**305356**	**174373**	**653879**
17145842	1451143	21119	8136	24251
76302674	13242783	40746	20026	27483
69184025	12757252	38332	18783	23035
198339997	91575072	77323	63947	315481
40310749	12612881	22133	16640	101818
157508838	78951678	53913	46616	211825
520409	10514	1277	691	1838
6829740	1965923	5613	2338	7584
29202799	11833205	8622	3666	16458
117495997	38007515	70068	43458	155861
2920455	318700	5490	4119	8607
4856484	639653	3366	1535	4161
41063766	8636055	22841	17073	54679
11565732	3722880	11039	5362	17924
136951485	36003531	50951	21078	74442
8227742	2734938	5206	1590	6506
26133099	12028448	8096	2999	10681
61446499	5044022	16986	9157	25603
42128105	22089684	18963	7692	18954
13182104	2698941	11951	4032	13365
74255405	**41849710**	**25541**	**12704**	**49735**
47109670	31787160	7700	5249	19271
10220281	4504513	5202	2110	7432
8864452	3474008	6497	2336	9996
1786825	693174	1591	750	3919
52672900	**7742840**	**74901**	**30697**	**99831**
16236015	3363664	30862	13223	41540
7476482	1834283	14391	7297	20187
4560331	698413	5730	2062	8372
27013135	2915316	30348	12077	39980
6074336	824208	8178	3063	10580
2305182	**179152**	**794**	**388**	**1347**

20−19 国内外三种专利申请数和授权数
Three Kinds of Domestic and Foreign Patent Applications and Authorizations

单位：件 (piece)

指　标	Item	申请数 Applications		授权数 Authorizations	
		2022	2023	2022	2023
合　计	**Total**	**5364639**	**5561990**	**4323409**	**3649072**
发　明	**Inventions**	**1619268**	**1677701**	**798347**	**920797**
国　内	Domestic	1464605	1522292	695591	819234
职　务	Official	1410074	1505921	682618	806180
高等院校	Institutions of Higher Education	265072	266112	171779	172984
科研单位	Research Institutions	68258	79691	39917	45341
企　业	Enterprises	1042541	1131693	457968	571807
机关团体	Government Agencies and Organizations	34203	28425	12954	16048
非职务	Non-official	54531	16371	12973	13054
国　外	Foreign	154663	155409	102756	101563
职　务	Official	152567	153348	101388	100467
非职务	Non-official	2096	2061	1368	1096
实用新型	**Utility Models**	**2950653**	**3063928**	**2804155**	**2090331**
国　内	Domestic	2944139	3057150	2796049	2084664
职　务	Official	2603825	2844120	2582572	1966198
高等院校	Institutions of Higher Education	112471	104070	98971	60063
科研单位	Research Institutions	21907	22771	21581	16500
企　业	Enterprises	2377721	2607158	2384678	1831617
机关团体	Government Agencies and Organizations	91726	110121	77342	58018
非职务	Non-official	340314	213030	213477	118466
国　外	Foreign	6514	6778	8106	5667
职　务	Official	6207	6525	7727	5464
非职务	Non-official	307	253	379	203
外观设计	**Appearance Designs**	**794718**	**820361**	**720907**	**637944**
国　内	Domestic	777663	804007	709563	628384
职　务	Official	502902	565872	456445	422952
高等院校	Institutions of Higher Education	17730	22070	16506	18121
科研单位	Research Institutions	1543	1898	1367	1420
企　业	Enterprises	480352	537996	435817	400499
机关团体	Government Agencies and Organizations	3277	3908	2755	2912
非职务	Non-official	274761	238135	253118	205432
国　外	Foreign	17055	16354	11344	9560
职　务	Official	16383	15745	10716	9119
非职务	Non-official	672	609	628	441

20–20 分地区国内三种专利申请数和授权数（2023年）
Three Kinds of Domestic Patent Applications and Authorizations by Region (2023)

单位：件 (piece)

地 区	Region	申请数 Applications	发 明 Inventions	实用新型 Utility Models	外观设计 Appearance Designs	授权数 Authorizations	发 明 Inventions	实用新型 Utility Models	外观设计 Appearance Designs
全 国	**National Total**	**5383449**	**1522292**	**3057150**	**804007**	**3532282**	**819234**	**2084664**	**628384**
北 京	Beijing	318984	205179	90710	23095	193973	107875	68901	17197
天 津	Tianjin	91141	24263	61494	5384	59154	14319	40991	3844
河 北	Hebei	149855	28929	98499	22427	92009	14213	61202	16594
山 西	Shanxi	45179	11387	30582	3210	28463	6557	19483	2423
内蒙古	Inner Mongolia	39138	8248	28596	2294	22258	3391	17085	1782
辽 宁	Liaoning	105912	25496	73141	7275	67632	13069	49755	4808
吉 林	Jilin	46407	17576	25652	3179	26637	7619	16473	2545
黑龙江	Heilongjiang	47168	14726	28676	3766	27588	8035	16303	3250
上 海	Shanghai	246656	97066	125155	24435	159115	44345	95380	19390
江 苏	Jiangsu	684579	191877	443900	48802	447006	107899	302132	36975
浙 江	Zhejiang	553317	117996	297814	137507	381835	64760	211193	105882
安 徽	Anhui	242322	67093	158533	16696	142638	30526	99086	13026
福 建	Fujian	171901	33730	100245	37926	120264	17858	72127	30279
江 西	Jiangxi	92239	20186	48066	23987	60120	10375	29885	19860
山 东	Shandong	424640	96906	293289	34445	273523	55318	192463	25742
河 南	Henan	176579	30637	126741	19201	109957	17531	78574	13852
湖 北	Hubei	213714	59068	140329	14317	135211	29025	94533	11653
湖 南	Hunan	109198	35007	55640	18551	74940	20133	39760	15047
广 东	Guangdong	963732	240223	427462	296047	703695	143141	324931	235623
广 西	Guangxi	49188	12471	29261	7456	34115	6717	20675	6723
海 南	Hainan	21029	4681	14443	1905	10963	2273	7347	1343
重 庆	Chongqing	92060	30517	53346	8197	54136	13600	34110	6426
四 川	Sichuan	180303	53454	106935	19914	113073	33339	63767	15967
贵 州	Guizhou	36997	11954	18987	6056	22149	4712	12920	4517
云 南	Yunnan	54207	12493	37818	3896	32718	5907	23959	2852
西 藏	Xizang	3486	625	2502	359	1877	299	1385	193
陕 西	Shaanxi	117687	41729	69078	6880	71562	22020	43732	5810
甘 肃	Gansu	32916	7052	23942	1922	20903	3568	15763	1572
青 海	Qinghai	7686	1790	5588	308	3987	561	3265	161
宁 夏	Ningxia	16788	3518	12639	631	10363	1522	8469	372
新 疆	Xinjiang	30662	5484	23318	1860	19124	2398	15569	1157
香 港	Hong Kong	3291	1334	859	1098	2301	752	598	951
澳 门	Macao	245	175	50	20	134	69	50	15
台 湾	Taiwan	14243	9422	3860	961	8859	5508	2798	553

20-21 按国别(地区)分国外三种专利申请数及授权数（2023年）
Three Kinds of Foreign Patent Applications and Authorizations by Country (Region) (2023)

单位：件 (piece)

国别(地区)	Country (Region)	申请数 Applications	发明 Inventions	实用新型 Utility Models	外观设计 Appearance Designs	授权数 Authorizations	发明 Inventions	实用新型 Utility Models	外观设计 Appearance Designs
总　　计	**Total**	**178541**	**155409**	**6778**	**16354**	**116790**	**101563**	**5667**	**9560**
澳大利亚	Australia	1005	703	42	260	550	326	37	187
奥地利	Austria	1097	1036	15	46	744	701	16	27
比利时	Belgium	934	833	44	57	561	483	25	53
巴　西	Brazil	248	206	6	36	138	110	3	25
加拿大	Canada	1140	949	45	146	730	631	34	65
塞浦路斯	Cyprus	23	23			15	15		
捷　克	Czech	67	51		16	63	39	7	17
丹　麦	Denmark	1210	1029	44	137	661	523	20	118
芬　兰	Finland	1152	1031	36	85	687	601	34	52
法　国	France	5606	4724	325	557	4054	3234	290	530
德　国	Germany	17493	15472	641	1380	11116	9444	605	1067
荷　兰	Holland	3815	3331	168	316	2424	1996	171	257
匈牙利	Hungary	37	31	1	5	27	25		2
印　度	India	355	326	10	19	190	167	14	9
爱尔兰	Ireland	629	585	13	31	396	364	17	15
以色列	Israel	1219	1112	38	69	653	583	26	44
意大利	Italy	2483	1905	133	445	1694	1139	114	441
日　本	Japan	50874	46236	1301	3337	36047	32929	1135	1983
列支敦士登	Liechtenstein	179	166	7	6	143	135	4	4
卢森堡	Luxembourg	302	246	12	44	228	187	8	33
马来西亚	Malaysia	133	71	23	39	68	31	14	23
摩纳哥	Monaco	45	10		35	44	4		40
新西兰	New Zealand	286	176	33	77	135	83	29	23
挪　威	Norway	298	277	2	19	184	164	3	17
波　兰	Poland	103	89	2	12	72	47	3	22
韩　国	Republic of Korea	23200	20016	1334	1850	14820	12623	937	1260
俄罗斯联邦	Russia	235	193	24	18	155	126	15	14
新加坡	Singapore	2280	1720	209	351	1240	908	154	178
南　非	South Africa	43	39		4	18	18		
西班牙	Spain	611	467	36	108	362	225	18	119
瑞　典	Sweden	2769	2366	84	319	1916	1639	72	205
瑞　士	Switzerland	5399	4684	184	531	2853	2331	135	387
泰　国	Thailand	186	87	49	50	82	47	5	30
英　国	United Kingdom	3861	3147	103	611	2110	1735	71	304
美　国	United States	46823	40380	1436	5007	27101	24005	1329	1767
其　他	Others	2401	1692	378	331	4509	3945	322	242

20-22 按国际标准分类的发明和实用新型专利申请数与授权数
Inventions and Utility Models of Patent Applications and Authorizations by International Classifications

单位：件 (piece)

分类	Item	2022		2023	
		分类申请数 Application Accepted by Technology Theme	分类授权数 Authorizations Granted by Technology Theme	分类申请数 Application Accepted by Technology Theme	分类授权数 Authorizations Granted by Technology Theme
合计	**Total**	**4602161**	**3602502**	**4679215**	**3011128**
A 部(人类生活需要)	**Section A: Human Necessities**	**620433**	**461639**	**556789**	**358557**
农、林、牧、渔	Agriculture, Forestry, Animal Husbandry and Fishery	113582	96000	113216	73523
烘烤、食用面团	Baking and Edible Doughs	4855	4255	5465	3309
屠宰、加工	Butchering and Meat Processing	3875	3472	4480	2886
食品、食物及处理	Foods or Foodstuffs and Their Treatment	29857	17746	28929	15385
烟类及用品	Tobacco, Cigars and Cigarettes	11124	9572	11488	8305
服　装	Clothing	16774	12395	13109	8389
帽类制品	Headwear	2678	1970	2393	1497
鞋　类	Footwear	8173	6833	8493	5689
男用服饰用品、珠宝	Haberdashery and Jewelry	3934	3562	3631	2727
手携及旅行用品	Hand Carried or Traveling Articles	10844	9681	10536	7316
刷类用品	Brushware	1713	1599	1615	1195
家具、家庭日用品或设备	Furniture, Domestic Articles and Appliances	105192	93883	94883	65189
医学、兽医学、卫生学	Medicine, Veterinary Medicine and Hygienics	240444	168351	222455	138817
救生、消防	Life-saving and Fire-fighting	11913	10368	12569	8139
体育、游戏、娱乐活动	Sports, Games, and Recreation	28529	21951	23527	16191
本部其他类目中不包括的技术主题	Subject Matter Not Otherwise Provided for in This Section	26946	1		
B 部(作业、运输)	**Section B: Industrial and Transportation**	**1405011**	**1230234**	**1505955**	**986687**
物理或化学的方法或装置	Physical or Chemical Processes or Apparatus	188504	161086	197757	129585
破碎、研磨、粉碎	Crushing, Pulverizing, Disintegrating	36104	32337	40126	25417
分选、分离	Separation of Solid Materials, Electrostatic Separation	6770	5991	7643	4955
离心装置、离心机	Centrifugal Apparatus or Equipment	3485	3122	4015	2527
喷射、雾化	Spraying or Atomizing General	39597	36375	43729	30858
机械振动的产生和传递	Generation or Transmission of Mechanical Vibrations	452	436	481	295
固体分离、分选	Separating Solids from Solid Wastes	32011	28288	35570	22364
清　洁	Cleaning	46609	41915	49067	31568
固体废料的处理	Disposal of Solid Waste	8980	6454	7655	5128
金属加工、冲裁	Mechanical Metal-working and Stamping	67004	58996	72926	46680
铸造、粉末冶金	Casting and Powder Metallurgy	22029	17940	22642	15471
机床、其他金属加工	Machine Tools, Other Metal Processing	154949	136269	173563	109717
磨削、抛光	Grinding and Polishing	52336	44345	61027	36924
简单工具	Simple Tools	63718	56022	71220	47836
手工、切割工具、切断	Hand Cutting Tools, Cutting, and Severing	31607	28917	35637	23438
木材加工、保存、钉钉机	Wood Processing, Preservation and Nailing or Stapling Machines	10706	10194	10861	7952
加工水泥、粘土和石料	Cement, Clay and Stone	29366	26271	32355	21429
塑料制品的加工	Plastics	79694	68197	87648	56126
压力机	Presses	7629	7036	7878	5485
纸品制作、纸的加工	Paper Making and Processing Paper	9465	8822	10123	7140
叠层产品	Layered Products	20550	16889	16890	11639
增材制造技术	Additive Manufacturing Technology	32	10		7
装订、图册、文件夹	Bookbinding, Albums, and Files	3710	3372	3202	2235

注：1.分类指专利分类部门对每一件发明专利申请或实用新型专利申请的技术主题进行分类，给出完整的代表发明或实用新型的发明情报的分类号。
2.本表不包括外观设计分类。
3.因专利分类工作流程优化，2023年A部(人类生活需要)中不存在未能划分技术领域的申请。因此“本部其他类目中不包括的技术主题”指标数据为0。

a) Classification refers to the classifying number of every patent assigned according to the technical theme of inventions and utility models of patents by patent classification department.
b) Designs patents are not included in this table.
c) Due to the optimization of the patent classification workflow, there were no applications in Section A (Human Necessities) in 2023 that could not be classified into technical fields. Therefore, the index data for "technical topics not included in other categories of this section" is 0.

20−22 续表 1 continued

单位：件 (piece)

分类	Item	2022 分类申请数 Application Accepted by Technology Theme	2022 分类授权数 Authorizations Granted by Technology Theme	2023 分类申请数 Application Accepted by Technology Theme	2023 分类授权数 Authorizations Granted by Technology Theme
绘图具、办公附属用品	Drawing Tools, Office Accessories	4929	3386	3793	2172
装饰艺术	Decorative Arts	4189	3846	3881	2605
一般车辆	Vehicles in General	79925	65769	85654	53855
铁　路	Railways	7774	7025	7879	5520
无轨陆用车辆	Trackless Land Vehicles	40343	36844	41054	28277
船舶、船只、有关设备	Ships and Related Equipment	12883	10276	14128	8509
飞行器、航空、宇宙航行	Aircraft and Aviation	15953	12789	16564	10753
输送、包装、存贮、搬运	Conveying, Packaging, Storage and Handling	243599	219014	254687	172150
卷扬、提升、牵引	Hoisting, Lifting and Hauling	49823	43636	55281	36068
液体的贮运	Opening or Closing Bottles, Jars or Similar Containers	8413	8086	8756	6020
鞍具、室内装潢	Saddlery ; Upholstery	223	218	236	148
微观结构技术	Micro-structural Technology	674	315	693	633
超微观技术	Nano-Technology	60	28	16	22
C 部（化学、冶金）	**Section C: Chemistry and Metallurgy**	**281609**	**210328**	**277327**	**185766**
无机化学	Inorganic Chemistry	12580	8649	12938	9143
水、废污水、泥浆的处理	Treatment of Water, Waste Water, Sewage or Sludge	51850	44345	51723	31135
玻璃、石棉和渣棉	Glass, Asbestos, and Slag Cotton	8849	8385	8812	6618
水泥、陶瓷等、隔音材料	Cement, Ceramics, etc., Sound Insulation Materials	12299	9559	11347	7143
肥料及制造	Fertilizers and Related Products	4581	2746	4319	1830
炸药、火柴	Explosives and Matches	515	379	524	318
有机化学	Organic Chemistry	31483	23365	28240	23675
有机高分子化合物	Organic Macromolecular Compounds	28224	20226	26319	21119
染料、涂料、抛光剂等	Dyes, Paints, Polishes, Resins, and Adhesives	19933	12892	18838	11414
石油、煤气及炼焦工业	Petroleum, Gas and Coking Industries	7740	6425	7687	4725
动植物油、脂类	Animal or Vegetable Oils, Fats	3522	2247	3364	1799
生化、酒、醋、酶	Biochemistry, Beer, Spirits, Wine, Vinegar	44895	31175	45476	30841
糖或淀粉工业	Sugar Industry	206	178	177	145
大小原皮、毛皮、皮革	Raw Leather, Fur, Leather	1137	1248	1303	854
黑色冶金	Ferrous Metallurgy	12181	9583	12324	8222
冶金学、合金或有色合金	Metallurgy, Ferrous or Non-ferrous Alloys	12274	8476	11865	6346
金属加工涂料、防腐防锈	Coating Metallic Materials	13655	9858	14500	9873
电解电泳方法及设备	Electrolytic or Electrophoretic Processes	11905	8062	13471	7970
晶体生长	Crystal Growth	3687	2463	4010	2524
组合技术	Combinatorial Technology	93	67	90	72
D 部（纺织、造纸）	**Section D: Textiles and Papers Making**	**57265**	**49876**	**60492**	**41576**
线、纤维、纺纱	Natural or Artificial Threads or Fibers, Spinning	8285	7340	8837	6245
纺纱、整经或络经	Spinning, Warping or Winding	3043	2193	2590	1601
织　造	Weaving	3481	3036	3703	2426
编带、花边、针织、整理	Braiding, Lace-Making, Knitting	5273	4514	5270	3889
缝纫、绣花、簇绒	Sewing, Embroidery, Tufting	5555	5769	5915	4319
织物等的处理、洗涤	Treatment of Textiles, Laundering	26570	22265	28738	19269
绳、除电缆外的缆绳	Ropes, Cordage other than Electric Cables	818	808	698	569
造纸、纤维素的生产	Paper Making, Production of Cellulose	4240	3951	4741	3258
E 部（固定建筑物）	**Section E: Fixed Construction**	**319145**	**283566**	**330331**	**218375**
道路、铁路和桥梁的建筑	Construction of Roads, Railways, or Bridges	49693	42873	51744	32206
水利工程、基础、运土	Hydraulic Engineering, Foundations, Soil-shifting	50320	43896	53884	34675
给水、排水	Water Supply, Sewage	19572	17569	19959	12994

20-22 续表 2 continued

单位：件 (piece)

分 类	Item	2022 分类申请数 Application Accepted by Technology Theme	2022 分类授权数 Authorizations Granted by Technology Theme	2023 分类申请数 Application Accepted by Technology Theme	2023 分类授权数 Authorizations Granted by Technology Theme
建筑物	Building	119568	109321	123391	82980
锁、钥匙、门窗、保险箱	Locks, Keys, Windows or Door Fittings; Safes	16172	15961	16673	12858
一般门、窗、百叶窗、梯子	Doors, Windows, Shutters, Roller Blinds, Ladders in General	21619	20321	19493	14812
钻井、采矿	Well Drilling, Mining	42201	33625	45187	27850
F 部(机械工程)	**Section F: Mechanical Engineering**	**464282**	**403931**	**478070**	**311844**
一般机器、发动机、蒸汽机	Machines, Engines, Steam Engines in General	10712	9856	9952	7134
内燃机等	Combustion Engines	12298	11358	11449	7978
液力机械和其他发动机	Machines or Engines for Liquids	8974	5960	8876	4916
液体变容机械、泵	Positive-displacement Machines for Liquids; Pumps for Liquid or Elastic Fluids	37378	32623	38841	25148
液压调节器、液压技术	Fluid-pressure Actuators, Hydraulic or Pneumatics	9383	8566	9335	6486
工程元件或部件	Engineering Elements or Parts	174296	150928	183460	117441
气体或液体的贮藏或分配	Storage or Distribution of Gases or Liquids	9255	7901	11157	6539
照 明	Lighting	38969	35113	36749	25329
蒸汽的生产	Steam Generation	3894	3264	3650	2626
燃烧设备、燃烧技术	Combustion Apparatus; Combustion Processes	14783	13014	15033	10719
采暖、炉灶、通风	Heating, Stove, Ventilation	58962	51461	56066	35849
制冷气体的液化和固化	Refrigeration or Cooling, Heat Pump Systems	22141	18527	24406	16139
干 燥	Drying	28121	24193	29813	19309
炉、窑、灶、罐	Furnaces, Kilns, Ovens	14170	12537	16904	10765
一般热交换	Heat Exchange in General	13912	12440	15023	10352
武 器	Weapons	3643	3277	3603	2469
弹药、爆破	Ammunition, Blasting Caps	3391	2913	3753	2645
G 部(物理)	**Section G: Physics**	**849383**	**520748**	**841822**	**506785**
测量、测试	Measurements, Testing	344761	256759	344976	220459
光学技术	Optical Technology	35815	30333	34694	25126
照相术、电影术、电刻术	Photography, Cinematography, Electrography	10915	8796	10265	7254
测时技术	Horology	2405	1958	2245	1532
控制、调节技术	Controlling, Regulating	32068	21424	29602	16638
计算、推算、计数技术	Computing, Calculating, Counting	313142	130283	319808	177818
核算装置	Measurement Devices	13934	11110	11296	7277
信号装置	Signaling	20243	14666	19020	11313
教育、密码、显示、广告等	Education, Cryptogram, Displays, Advertisements,etc	47373	31427	39045	22041
乐器、声学	Musical Instruments, Acoustics	9520	5541	9505	6279
信息的存储	Information Storage	6051	3128	5892	3531
仪器的零部件	Components and Parts of Instrument	164	160	107	90
特别适用于特定应用领域的信息通信技术	Ict is particularly Suitable for Specific Application Areas	10519	3405	12884	5859
其他的技术主题	Subject Matter not Otherwise Provided for in This Section	2473	1758	2483	1568
H 部(电学)	**Section H: Electricity**	**605033**	**442180**	**628429**	**401538**
基本电器元件	Basic Electric Elements	225317	162948	223091	144327
电力的发电、变电或配电	Generation, Conversion, or Distribution of Electric Power	152664	110634	162977	98196
基本电子电路	Basic Electronic Circuitry	10126	6429	10820	9391
电信技术	Telecommunications Techniques	150653	113382	151243	99961
其他类不包括的电技术	Electric Techniques Not Otherwise Provided for	66252	48787	68415	43379

20–23 国外主要检索工具收录我国科技论文按学科分布(2022年)
Chinese Scientific Papers Taken by Major Foreign Referencing Systems by Discipline (2022)

学科	Discipline	篇数 pieces			位次 Precedence		
		SCI	EI	CPCI-S	SCI	EI	CPCI-S
合计	**Total**	**681884**	**435547**	**30390**			
数学	Mathematics	14646	8628	12	16	17	24
力学	Mechanics	6600	9164	6	20	16	27
信息、系统科学	Information, Systems Science	2351	1056	118	30	23	13
物理学	Physics	40360	24647	1260	6	7	5
化学	Chemistry	72737	19158	15	2	11	23
天文学	Astronomy	2916	2550	22	25	20	22
地学	Earth Science	30878	37586	970	9	2	6
生物学	Biology	68529	66932	97	3	1	15
预防医学与卫生学	Protective Medicine and Hygienics	17350		80	15	33	18
基础医学	Basic Medicine	28201	588	832	10	25	7
药学	Pharmacy	19500		71	13	33	19
临床医学	Clinical Medicine	80714		2655	1	33	3
中医学	Traditional Chinese Medicine	3456			24	33	33
军事医学与特种医学	Military Medicine and Special Medicine	4373		6	21	33	27
农学	Agriculture	10271	498	54	18	27	20
林学	Forestry	1855			34	33	33
畜牧、兽医科学	Livestock, Veterinary Medicine	3633			23	33	33
水产学	Aquatic	2688			26	33	33
测绘科学技术	Surveying and Mapping Technology	2	6146		40	18	33
材料科学	Material Science	53777	29239	221	4	6	11
工程与技术基础学科	Engineering & Basic Technology Science	3863	9733	385	22	14	9
矿山工程技术	Mining	1553	1867	11	36	22	25
能源科学技术	Energy	23065	24418	1501	11	8	4
冶金、金属学	Metallurgy, Metallography	2375	21200		29	10	33
机械、仪表	Machinery, Instrument	8993	13893	536	19	13	8
动力与电气	Power & Electrical Engineering	1188	31236	193	38	5	12
核科学技术	Nuclear Technology	1964	453	95	33	28	16
电子、通讯与自动控制	Electronics, Communication & Automation	42610	31967	8522	5	4	2
计算技术	Computing Technology	31250	23619	12197	8	9	1
化工	Chemical Engineering	20509	560	36	12	26	21
轻工、纺织	Light Industry & Textile Industry	1987	697		32	24	33
食品	Food	18592	73	3	14	31	32
土木建筑	Civil Construction	11730	35165	285	17	3	10
水利	Water Conservancy	2634	3	5	27	32	29
交通运输	Transportation	2468	9672	100	28	15	14
航空航天	Aviation and Aerospace	2206	4310	11	31	19	25
环境	Environment	36616	17459	4	7	12	31
安全科学技术	Security	497	374		39	29	33
管理	Management Science	1674	2472	82	35	21	17
其他	Others	1273	184	5	37	30	29

注：SCI指科学引文索引(美国)，EI指工程索引(美国)，CPCI–S(原ISTP)指科学会议录引文索引。
a) SCI refers to Science Citation Index, EI refers to Engineering Index, and CPCI-S refers to Conference Proceedings Citation Index-Science.

20−24 高新技术产品、工业制品和初级产品的进出口贸易额
Imports and Exports of High and New-tech Products, Manufactured Goods and Primary Goods

项　　目	Item	1995	2000	2005	2010	2015	2020	2022	2023
绝对数　　（亿美元）	**Value　　(USD 100 million)**								
商品进出口贸易总额	Total Value of Imports and Exports	2809	4743	14219	29728	39569	46559	62701	59360
工业制品	Manufactured Goods	2350	4021	12252	24585	33799	38534	50118	46857
#高新技术产品	High and New-tech Products			4159	9051	12033	14584	17073	15219
初级产品	Primary Goods	459	722	1968	5143	5770	8025	12583	12503
商品出口贸易总额	Total Value of Exports	1488	2492	7620	15779	22749	25900	35605	33790
工业制品	Manufactured Goods	1273	2237	7129	14962	21710	24743	33914	32150
#高新技术产品	High and New-tech Products			2182	4924	6552	7763	9467	8420
初级产品	Primary Goods	215	255	490	817	1040	1156	1691	1641
商品进口贸易总额	Total Value of Imports	1321	2251	6600	13948	16820	20660	27096	25569
工业制品	Manufactured Goods	1077	1784	5122	9623	12089	13791	16204	14707
#高新技术产品	High and New-tech Products			1977	4127	5481	6821	7606	6799
初级产品	Primary Goods	244	467	1477	4326	4730	6869	10891	10862
商品进出口贸易差额	Balance of Imports and Exports	167	241	1020	1831	5930	5240	8510	8221
工业制品	Manufactured Goods	196	454	2007	5339	9620	10953	17710	17443
#高新技术产品	High and New-tech Products			206	797	1072	942	1861	1621
初级产品	Primary Goods	-29	-213	-987	-3508	-3690	-5713	-9200	-9221
构成　　（%）	**Percentage　　(%)**								
商品进出口贸易总额=100	Total Value of Imports and Exports=100								
工业制品	Manufactured Goods	83.6	84.8	86.2	82.7	85.4	82.8	79.9	78.9
#高新技术产品	High and New-tech Products			29.2	30.4	30.4	31.3	27.2	25.6
初级产品	Primary Goods	16.3	15.2	13.8	17.3	14.6	17.2	20.1	21.1
商品出口贸易总额=100	Total Value of Export=100								
工业制品	Manufactured Goods	85.6	89.8	93.6	94.8	95.4	95.5	95.3	95.1
#高新技术产品	High and New-tech Products			28.6	31.2	28.8	30.0	26.6	24.9
初级产品	Primary Goods	14.4	10.2	6.4	5.2	4.6	4.5	4.7	4.9
商品进口贸易总额=100	Total Value of Import=100								
工业制品	Manufactured Goods	81.5	79.2	77.6	69.0	71.9	66.8	59.8	57.5
#高新技术产品	High and New-tech Products			30.0	29.6	32.6	33.0	28.1	26.6
初级产品	Primary Goods	18.5	20.8	22.4	31.0	28.1	33.2	40.2	42.5

20–25 国家级高新区企业主要经济指标（2023年）
Major Indicators of Enterprises in High-Technology Industrial Development Zones (2023)

开发区	Development Zones	企业数（个）Number of Enterprises (unit)	从业人员（人）Number of Employed Persons (person)	营业收入（万元）Business Revenue (10 000 yuan)	出口总额（万元）Exports (10 000 yuan)
合　　计	**Total**	**223573**	**26804953**	**5501494037**	**582161020**
中关村国家自主创新示范区	Zhongguancun Science Park	24294	3221028	917724957	33772901
天津滨海高新技术产业开发区	Tianjin Binhai High-tech Industrial Development Zone	4680	242310	60087592	4138971
石家庄高新技术产业开发区	Shijiazhuang High-tech Industrial Development Zone	2733	230672	37103796	1141364
唐山高新技术产业开发区	Tangshan High-tech Industrial Development Zone	496	38106	5123965	360030
保定国家高新技术产业开发区	Baoding High-tech Industrial Development Zone	1089	141987	32348048	4452106
承德高新技术产业开发区	Chengde High-tech Industrial Development Zone	211	20373	2668443	18586
燕郊高新技术产业开发区	Yanjiao High-tech Industrial Development Zone	291	29068	6686513	56541
太原高新技术产业开发区	Taiyuan High-tech Industrial Development Zone	1748	144292	39490563	292200
长治高新技术产业开发区	Changzhi High-tech Industrial Development Zone	243	45220	5473243	24151
呼和浩特金山高新技术产业开发区	Hohhot Jinshan High-tech Industrial Development Zone	126	21690	9416300	68832
包头稀土高新技术产业开发区	Baotou Rare Earth High-tech Industrial Development Zone	575	118474	38943032	1114138
鄂尔多斯高新技术产业开发区	Eerduosi High-tech Industrial Development Zone	132	11324	1897779	258765
沈阳高新技术产业开发区	Shenyang High-tech Industrial Development Zone	2134	177016	48573243	991890
大连高新技术产业园区	Dalian High-tech Industrial Development Zone	3980	280081	49080973	6941664
鞍山高新技术产业开发区	Anshan High-tech Industrial Development Zone	507	51703	10270563	438922
本溪高新技术产业开发区	Benxi High-tech Industrial Development Zone	98	9799	940157	33116
锦州高新技术产业开发区	Jinzhou High-tech Industrial Development Zone	196	26318	3935227	343777
营口高新技术产业开发区	Yingkou High-tech Industrial Development Zone	196	22198	6350085	1104077
阜新高新技术产业开发区	Fuxin High-tech Industrial Development Zone	221	25051	3071873	190345
辽阳高新技术产业开发区	Liaoyang High-tech Industrial Development Zone	68	20726	5811510	267152
长春高新技术产业开发区	Changchun High-tech Industrial Development Zone	1031	138232	48454081	319277
长春净月高新技术产业开发区	Changchun Jingyue High-tech Industrial Development Zone	785	37504	9969538	1956052
吉林高新技术产业开发区	Jilin High-tech Industrial Development Zone	236	53863	8267196	76971
通化国家医药高新技术产业开发区	Tonghua Medicine High-tech Industrial Development Zone	112	13799	1608172	61098
延吉高新技术产业开发区	Yanji High-tech Industrial Development Zone	132	8614	2154086	25914
哈尔滨高新技术产业开发区	Haerbin High-tech Industrial Development Zone	1525	95729	26456202	457741
齐齐哈尔高新技术产业开发区	Qiqihaer High-tech Industrial Development Zone	200	29130	5460761	349290
大庆高新技术产业开发区	Daqing High-tech Industrial Development Zone	505	58610	15387120	403950
上海张江高新技术产业开发区	Shanghai Zhangjiang High-tech Industrial Development Zone	17122	1941340	474221916	54381372
上海紫竹高新技术产业开发区	Shanghai Zizhu High-tech Industrial Development Zone	542	48555	9339296	589705
南京高新技术产业开发区	Nanjing High-tech Industrial Development Zone	10362	737348	129290282	13317482
无锡国家高新技术产业开发区	Wuxi High-tech Industrial Development Zone	2064	308647	58552924	16671084
江阴高新技术产业开发区	Jiangyin High-tech Industrial Development Zone	774	116422	25584810	3197516
徐州高新技术产业开发区	Xuzhou High-tech Industrial Development Zone	765	86282	25086732	1095680
常州高新技术产业开发区	Changzhou High-tech Industrial Development Zone	2225	248146	43428854	7279126
武进国家高新技术产业开发区	Wujin High-tech Industrial Development Zone	1015	145137	25838788	2852465
苏州国家高新技术产业开发区	Suzhou High-tech Industrial Development Zone	2543	229701	43849999	15810699
昆山高新技术产业开发区	Kunshan High-tech Industrial Development Zone	1613	216282	36640305	17204282
苏州工业园区	Suzhou Industrial Park	4390	332694	76367516	23972156
常熟高新技术产业开发区	Changshu High-tech Industrial Development Zone	726	92071	17669043	3061030
南通高新技术产业开发区	Nantong High-tech Industrial Development Zone	643	117386	24447654	2813075
连云港高新技术产业开发区	Lianyungang High-tech Industrial Development Zone	369	57493	8581652	375207
淮安高新技术产业开发区	Huaian High-tech Industrial Development Zone	474	69245	8405360	758228
盐城高新技术产业开发区	Yancheng High-tech Industrial Development Zone	1116	102290	13129003	1023208
扬州高新技术产业开发区	Yangzhou High-tech Industrial Development Zone	507	47668	6675435	921769
镇江高新技术产业开发区	Zhenjiang High-tech Industrial Development Zone	571	66913	10226440	735370
泰州医药高新技术产业开发区	Taizhou Medical High-tech Industrial Development Zone	821	104858	18828083	1731123
宿迁高新技术产业开发区	Suqian Medicine High-tech Industrial Development Zone	292	53038	6918023	389395
杭州高新技术产业开发区	Hangzhou High-tech Industrial Development Zone	3846	474474	106544294	8774786
萧山临江高新技术产业开发区	Xiaoshan Linjiang High-tech Industrial Development Zone	1768	205280	39046053	4760203
宁波国家高新技术产业开发区	Ningbo High-tech Industrial Development Zone	3276	395871	79372967	13183399
温州高新技术产业开发区	Wenzhou High-tech Industrial Development Zone	1052	205470	21182168	3061748
嘉兴秀洲高新技术产业开发区	Jiaxing Xiuzhou High-tech Industrial Development Zone	237	79854	13716948	2716706

20-25 续表 1 continued

开发区	Development Zones	企业数（个）Number of Enterprises (unit)	从业人员（人）Number of Employed Persons (person)	营业收入（万元）Business Revenue (10 000 yuan)	出口总额（万元）Exports (10 000 yuan)
莫干山高新技术产业开发区	Moganshan High-tech Industrial Development Zone	449	66444	10037971	1678881
绍兴国家高新技术产业开发区	Shaoxing High-tech Industrial Development Zone	827	95185	13475345	1954084
衢州高新技术开发区	Quzhou High-tech Industrial Development Zone	905	129427	25070248	2149664
合肥高新技术产业开发区	Hefei High-tech Industrial Development Zone	3514	342510	86712244	13111981
芜湖国家高新技术产业开发区	Wuhu High-tech Industrial Development Zone	546	101837	17957510	1571218
蚌埠国家高新技术产业开发区	Bengbu High-tech Industrial Development Zone	226	49622	14324907	336847
淮南高新技术产业开发区	Huainan High-tech Industrial Development Zone	265	23832	3851110	52819
马鞍山慈湖高新技术产业开发区	Maanshan Cihu High-tech Industrial Development Zone	413	45883	19287855	542535
铜陵狮子山高新技术产业开发区	Tongling Shizishan High-tech Industrial Development Zone	177	16243	5950924	443934
安庆高新技术产业开发区	AnQing High-tech Industrial Development Zone	266	33957	5727975	284203
滁州高新技术产业开发区	Chuzhou High-tech Industrial Development Zone	498	46887	11140329	330894
福州高新技术产业开发区	Fuzhou High-tech Industrial Development Zone	1714	151624	20949065	1692594
厦门火炬高技术产业开发区	Xiamen Torch High-tech Industrial Development Zone	2793	281804	45111890	9980508
莆田高新技术产业开发区	Putian High-tech Industrial Development Zone	352	91688	13579313	933841
三明高新技术产业开发区	Sanming High-tech Industrial Development Zone	147	21058	4582412	204011
泉州高新技术产业开发区	Quanzhou High-tech Industrial Development Zone	861	119801	9366851	1174895
漳州高新技术产业开发区	Zhangzhou High-tech Industrial Development Zone	824	80675	11100176	805845
龙岩高新技术产业开发区	Longyan High-tech Industrial Development Zone	223	22686	3313353	49472
南昌高新技术产业开发区	Nanchang High-tech Industrial Development Zone	917	178851	51674087	4843468
景德镇高新技术产业开发区	Jingdezhen High-tech Industrial Development Zone	311	57646	10689373	978070
九江共青城高新技术产业开发区	Jiujiang Gongqingcheng High-tech Industrial Development Zone	270	27414	3304476	81279
新余高新技术企业开发区	Xinyu High-tech Industrial Development Zone	306	71546	11189617	1293554
鹰潭国家高新技术产业开发区	Yingtan High-tech Industrial Development Zone	266	26459	12090064	683996
赣州高新技术产业开发区	Ganzhou High-tech Industrial Development Zone	506	54111	10928720	576306
吉安高新技术产业开发区	Jian High-tech Industrial Development Zone	205	46761	4768596	2934979
宜春丰城高新技术产业开发区	Yichun Fengcheng High-tech Industrial Development Zone	274	28706	7526901	138574
抚州高新技术产业开发区	Fuzhou High-tech Industrial Development Zone	253	44284	9621763	619096
济南高新技术产业开发区	Jinan High-tech Industrial Development Zone	2926	264298	45487868	1894087
青岛高新技术产业开发区	Qingdao High-tech Industrial Development Zone	2862	258939	63300965	10162175
淄博高新技术产业开发区	Zibo High-tech Industrial Development Zone	840	175770	31657002	3032243
枣庄高新技术产业开发区	Zaozhuang High-tech Industrial Development Zone	212	27091	5458298	305424
黄河三角洲农业高新技术产业示范区	Huanghesanjiaozhou Agricultural High-tech Industrial Development Zone	60	4859	4317774	9093
烟台高新技术产业开发区	Yantai High-tech Industrial Development Zone	541	54496	8994357	890528
潍坊高新技术产业开发区	Weifang High-tech Industrial Development Zone	853	252854	61123034	8213620
济宁高新技术产业开发区	Jining High-tech Industrial Development Zone	639	149717	32755335	1467790
泰安高新技术产业开发区	Taian High-tech Industrial Development Zone	524	58973	9885138	399528
威海火炬高技术产业开发区	Weihai Torch High-tech Industrial Development Zone	560	145235	18952535	3618653
莱芜高新技术产业开发区	Laiwu High-tech Industrial Development Zone	359	42082	12753578	484789
临沂高新技术产业开发区	Linyi High-tech Industrial Development Zone	490	67423	10229704	485699
德州高新技术产业开发区	Dezhou High-tech Industrial Development Zone	279	21445	2995313	295346
郑州高新技术产业开发区	Zhengzhou High-tech Industrial Development Zone	3614	282046	44856956	3791182
洛阳高新技术产业开发区	Luoyang High-tech Industrial Development Zone	1427	197898	30165660	1571337
平顶山高新技术产业开发区	Pingdingshan High-tech Industrial Development Zone	275	33434	7856553	421453
安阳高新技术产业开发区	Anyang High-tech Industrial Development Zone	427	88182	14073889	244294
新乡高新技术产业开发区	Xinxiang High-tech Industrial Development Zone	451	65455	10260843	539202
焦作高新技术产业开发区	Jiaozuo High-tech Industrial Development Zone	305	41590	6878662	758941
许昌高新技术产业开发区	Xuchang High-tech Industrial Development Zone	75	5522	821834	7074
南阳高新技术产业开发区	Nanyang High-tech Industrial Development Zone	583	96985	8506860	788050
信阳高新技术产业开发区	Xinyang High-tech Industrial Development Zone	144	19905	4616001	60470
武汉东湖新技术开发区	Wuhan Donghu New Technology Development Zone	6214	627853	132417460	8504370
黄石大冶湖高新技术产业开发区	Huangshi Dazhi High-tech Industrial Development Zone	589	77512	13339047	490083
宜昌高新技术产业开发区	Yichang High-tech Industrial Development Zone	1138	171480	32639116	2066951
襄阳高新技术产业开发区	Xiangyang High-tech Industrial Development Zone	1199	187608	34923272	1019946
荆门高新技术产业开发区	Jingmen High-tech Industrial Development Zone	593	113662	22281422	1174381
孝感高新技术产业开发区	Xiaogan High-tech Industrial Development Zone	868	124690	19281407	474885
荆州高新技术产业开发区	Jingzhou High-tech Industrial Development Zone	496	62402	7647257	228838
黄冈高新技术产业开发区	Huanggang High-tech Industrial Development Zone	1105	110909	17438994	509277
咸宁高新技术产业开发区	Xianning High-tech Industrial Development Zone	638	83413	14837974	888135
随州高新技术产业开发区	Suizhou High-tech Industrial Development Zone	420	50716	8702350	666321
仙桃高新技术产业开发区	Xiantao High-tech Industrial Development Zone	462	75876	6931268	843267
潜江高新技术产业开发区	Qianjiang High-tech Industrial Development Zone	316	43690	6811622	134473

20-25 续表 2 continued

开发区	Development Zones	企业数 (个) Number of Enterprises (unit)	从业人员 (人) Number of Employed Persons (person)	营业收入 (万元) Business Revenue (10 000 yuan)	出口总额 (万元) Exports (10 000 yuan)
长沙高新技术产业开发区	Changsha High-tech Industrial Development Zone	3659	406221	61737642	4040433
宁乡高新技术产业开发区	Ningxiang High-tech Industrial Development Zone	170	28823	6436437	685623
株洲高新技术产业开发区	Zhuzhou High-tech Industrial Development Zone	749	186659	36239970	1147662
湘潭高新技术产业开发区	Xiangtan High-tech Industrial Development Zone	532	100666	18790275	962247
衡阳高新技术产业开发区	Hengyang High-tech Industrial Development Zone	516	57287	9557664	1349737
常德高新技术产业开发区	Changde High-tech Industrial Development Zone	571	56690	8234837	194660
益阳高新技术产业开发区	Yiyang High-tech Industrial Development Zone	499	61629	10880253	699264
郴州高新技术产业开发区	Chenzhou High-tech Industrial Development Zone	252	24813	5252950	386991
怀化高新技术产业开发区	Huaihua High-tech Industrial Development Zone	216	13990	1632000	36733
广州高新技术产业开发区	Guangzhou High-tech Industrial Development Zone	6347	772401	146240246	12709287
深圳高新技术产业开发区	Shenzhen High-tech Industrial Development Zone	9963	1374717	270387317	65189843
珠海高新技术产业开发区	Zhuhai High-tech Industrial Development Zone	2278	299844	41007957	8188454
汕头高新技术产业开发区	Shantou High-tech Industrial Development Zone	305	26961	3059239	386356
佛山高新技术产业开发区	Foshan High-tech Industrial Development Zone	2301	354289	57182708	12047759
江门高新技术产业开发区	Jiangmen High-tech Industrial Development Zone	1041	129373	16051229	5009896
湛江高新技术产业开发区	Zhanjiang High-tech Industrial Development Zone	249	34287	21880900	1898311
茂名高新技术产业开发区	Maoming High-tech Industrial Development Zone	212	29186	8398075	147813
肇庆高新技术产业开发区	Zhaoqing High-tech Industrial Development Zone	462	72485	13497370	882809
惠州仲恺高新技术产业开发区	Huizhou Zhongkai High-tech Industrial Development Zone	1245	258473	34229476	10330284
源城高新技术产业开发区	Yuancheng High-tech Industrial Development Zone	204	55349	5861333	801047
清远高新技术产业开发区	Qingyuan High-tech Industrial Development Zone	272	65398	12168481	743323
东莞松山湖高新技术产业开发区	Dongguan Songshanhu High-tech Industrial Development Zone	1104	162755	48038520	5000047
中山国家高新技术产业开发区	Zhongshan High-tech Industrial Development Zone	913	143317	18977213	5947622
南宁高新技术产业开发区	Nanning High-tech Industrial Development Zone	1234	192842	25811911	3277873
柳州高新技术产业开发区	Liuzhou High-tech Industrial Development Zone	813	136628	26272109	2848648
桂林国家高新技术产业开发区	Guilin High-tech Industrial Development Zone	973	124298	12607840	1132994
北海高新技术产业开发区	Beihai High-tech Industrial Development Zone	179	51012	12741031	1280999
海口国家高新技术产业开发区	Haikou High-tech Industrial Development Zone	490	49822	13333402	459987
重庆高新技术产业开发区	Chongqing High-tech Industrial Development Zone	2409	299304	48493834	10840887
璧山高新技术产业开发区	Bishan High-tech Industrial Development Zone	550	89965	10411076	1318975
荣昌高新技术产业开发区	Rongchang High-tech Industrial Development Zone	390	40759	3372523	139353
永川高新技术产业开发区	Yongchuan High-tech Industrial Development Zone	408	91857	16327468	778913
成都高新技术产业开发区	Chengdu High-tech Industrial Development Zone	5421	544602	95962648	37906450
自贡高新技术产业开发区	Zigong High-tech Industrial Development Zone	510	59360	6415286	267711
攀枝花高新技术产业开发区	Panzhihua High-tech Industrial Development Zone	259	48414	11368853	72745
泸州高新技术产业开发区	Luzhou High-tech Industrial Development Zone	444	63468	13671830	271959
德阳高新技术产业开发区	Deyang High-tech Industrial Development Zone	336	52909	8261955	288184
绵阳国家高新技术产业开发区	Mianyang High-tech Industrial Development Zone	565	125212	20111726	4145328
内江高新技术产业开发区	Neijiang High-tech Industrial Development Zone	223	32785	4035588	132061
乐山高新技术产业开发区	Leshan High-tech Industrial Development Zone	363	67720	13850195	551736
贵阳国家高新技术产业开发区	Guiyang High-tech Industrial Development Zone	1101	190913	30352143	640990
遵义高新技术产业开发区	Zunyi High-tech Industrial Development Zone	173	25493	3892836	73028
安顺高新技术产业开发区	Anshun High-tech Industrial Development Zone	241	29897	2899040	66238
昆明国家高新技术产业开发区	Kunming High-tech Industrial Development Zone	737	112904	32665987	249515
玉溪高新技术产业开发区	Yuxi High-tech Industrial Development Zone	157	26805	10643328	34603
楚雄高新技术产业开发区	Chuxiong High-tech Industrial Development Zone	117	15994	3588350	5536
拉萨高新技术产业开发区	Lhasa High-tech Industrial Development Zone	45	4641	540879	15728
西安高新技术产业开发区	Xi'an High-tech Industrial Development Zone	7576	649983	116219485	6944387
宝鸡高新技术产业开发区	Baoji High-tech Industrial Development Zone	987	131820	19783184	828956
杨凌农业高新技术产业示范区	Lhasa High-tech Industries Demonstration Zone	260	25395	3656888	63216
咸阳高新技术产业开发区	Xianyang High-tech Industrial Development Zone	297	44437	11359751	1219643
渭南国家高新技术产业开发区	Weinan High-tech Industrial Development Zone	266	24139	5448981	376212
榆林高新科技产业园区	Yulin High-tech Industrial Development Zone	416	43340	19769906	5200
安康高新技术产业开发区	Ankang High-tech Industrial Development Zone	298	37529	7312033	147305
兰州高新技术产业开发区	Lanzhou High-tech Industrial Development Zone	807	129685	22043799	165894
白银高新技术产业开发区	Baiyin High-tech Industrial Development Zone	321	73901	15753099	71329
青海高新技术产业开发区	Qinghai High-tech Industrial Development Zone	135	11739	767726	6199
银川高产业开发区	Yinchuan High-tech Industrial Development Zone	193	13407	3342837	34067
宁夏石嘴山高新技术产业开发区	Ningxia Shizuishan High-tech Industrial Development Zone	145	18113	2614439	121773
乌鲁木齐高新技术产业开发区	Wulumuqi High-tech Industrial Development Zone	541	194522	52136347	79299
克拉玛依高新技术产业开发区	Karamay High-tech Industrial Development Zone	159	21218	1939865	381
昌吉高新技术产业开发区	Changji High-tech Industrial Development Zone	307	14475	4324992	274918
石河子高新技术产业开发区	Shihezi High-tech Industrial Development Zone	125	32291	8577998	6912
阿克苏阿拉尔高新技术产业开发区	Aksu Alaer High-tech Industrial Development Zone	94	15932	2220747	2598

20-26 分地区技术市场成交额
Transaction Value in Technical Markets by Region

单位：万元 (10 000 yuan)

地　区	Region	2016	2017	2018	2019	2020	2021	2022	2023
全　国	**National Total**	**114069816**	**134242245**	**176974213**	**223983882**	**282515092**	**372943030**	**477910166**	**614756578**
北　京	Beijing	39409752	44868872	49578246	56952843	63161622	70056517	79475111	85369394
天　津	Tianjin	5526361	5514411	6855875	9092549	10895598	12568262	16508667	19285572
河　北	Hebei	589959	889245	2759840	3811904	5549646	7473182	10038253	17830882
山　西	Shanxi	425622	941471	1507567	1095227	449791	1344737	1614346	2238585
内蒙古	Inner Mongolia	120492	196087	198398	224793	359540	411478	512988	609824
辽　宁	Liaoning	3232180	3858317	4744910	5575904	6328126	7551240	9713459	12890739
吉　林	Jilin	1164198	2199199	3419460	4741327	4621541	1081468	369481	839977
黑龙江	Heilongjiang	1258091	1467121	1659200	2328823	2652015	3501428	4601814	1128827
上　海	Shanghai	7809858	8106177	12251857	14223539	15832248	25454910	38707329	46423364
江　苏	Jiangsu	6356425	7784223	9914475	14715193	20878468	26061663	29867776	33310038
浙　江	Zhejiang	1983716	3247310	5906641	8880078	14033228	18557774	24350738	43237082
安　徽	Anhui	2173748	2495697	3213131	4496068	6595728	17877084	28754545	35975671
福　建	Fujian	432204	754634	845235	1395883	1635367	1967976	2595179	3290010
江　西	Jiangxi	790077	962096	1158231	1486137	2334099	4093849	7338839	15848723
山　东	Shandong	3959453	5116448	8199520	11100178	19038906	24777895	32318349	45546684
河　南	Henan	587075	768528	1492840	2318885	3797786	6073260	10207498	13626332
湖　北	Hubei	9038371	10330773	12040937	14298358	16658080	20907763	30099979	47711723
湖　南	Hunan	1056287	2031915	2816126	4906932	7359497	12612640	25428885	39897680
广　东	Guangdong	7581650	9370755	13654186	22230844	32672142	40996121	39674797	38667832
广　西	Guangxi	339922	394228	614077	775572	916691	9405765	2269901	889320
海　南	Hainan	34431	41079	69407	91077	201902	284162	315522	525900
重　庆	Chongqing	1471870	513581	1883529	566518	1177865	1845180	5594685	7184904
四　川	Sichuan	2993006	4058307	9967010	12119539	12445928	13886947	16435301	19421478
贵　州	Guizhou	204437	807409	1710975	2271758	2491150	2892651	3907245	4820184
云　南	Yunnan	582559	847625	894879	827040	499498	1060953	2189452	2688786
西　藏	Xizang		440	394	9577	7783	17269	62143	81681
陕　西	Shaanxi	8027887	9209395	11252908	14673473	17587198	23434411	30487345	41184641
甘　肃	Gansu	1506615	1629587	1808778	1964171	2331559	2803921	3358410	4648103
青　海	Qinghai	569190	677186	793553	90969	105626	141042	160342	193042
宁　夏	Ningxia	40526	66679	121058	149033	168054	250947	340474	402960
新　疆	Xinjiang	42755	57554	39215	78214	151123	188537	311791	735844
港澳台	Hong Kong, Macao and Taiwan	678396	604530	174241	864897	271843	599483	1696168	2461829
国　外	Foreign	4082703	4431367	5427512	5626577	9305442	12762515	18603353	25788966

20–27 按技术合同构成分全国技术市场成交合同金额
Value of Contract Deals in Domestic Technical Markets by Type of Contracts

单位：万元 (10 000 yuan)

项　目	Item	2017	2018	2019	2020	2021	2022	2023
合　计	**Total**	**134242245**	**176974213**	**223983882**	**282515092**	**372943030**	**477910166**	**614756578**
一、按技术性收入的类型分	**By Type of Technical Revenue**							
技术开发	Technology Development	47485447	58885455	71773214	88740760	116739293	140108266	179651089
委托开发	Commissioned Development	40029867	49362634	60129654	73465753	99600809	120362954	161688026
合作开发	Cooperated Development	7455580	9522821	11643559	15275007	17138484	19745311	17963063
技术转让	Technology Transfer	14002811	16096954	21888778	23976580	32465629	40015953	28150220
#技术秘密转让	Technical Secrets Transfer	6792785	6868054	7165852	8497844	14387474	19258600	17172062
专利实施许可转让	Patent License Transfer	2922040	4550718	3810624	8157296	9584003	10843211	2237380
专利权转让	Patent Right Transfer	1383493	1692490	8188387	4571110	5242740	5898827	5903432
专利申请权转让	Patent Application Right Transfer	90058	130087	162206	162062	865065	712923	500391
计算机软件著作权转让	Computer Software Copyright Transfer	366011	603217	1829127	765616	789610	993253	700864
集成电路布图设计专有权转让	Exclusive Right Transfer of Integrated Circuit Layout Design	141781	6722	7404	34050	4938	3364	9024
植物新品种权转让	New Species of Plants Patent Right Transfer	121273	70916	122216	97456	202499	101361	120649
生物、医药新品种权转让	New Species of Biology and Medicine Patent Right Transfer	155789	245353	554764	750359	493967	832285	154533
技术咨询	Technology Consultation	4492289	5646121	6141064	11045590	9511586	9666998	12858770
技术服务	Technology Service	68261698	96345683	124180826	158752162	214226522	287189135	368966858
一般性技术服务	General Technology Service	66742900	95686432	122954691	158070665	213454236	286137477	367928097
技术中介	Technology Intermediary	179426	320246	173636	67533	150361	122263	269650
技术培训	Technology Training	1339371	339005	1052500	613964	621925	929395	769112
二、按知识产权构成分	**By Intellectual Right**							
技术秘密	Technology Secrets	29912687	34926639	46731818	53812813	63391085	81901970	92074212
专利	Patents	14204704	20945087	30857642	37903761	54402645	72957791	89352420
发明专利	Inventions Patents	8706940	14363204	17414736	23261556	30618844	48145611	57544709
实用新型专利	Utility Model Patents	5313921	6215502	13239858	14274242	23515257	24650254	31365276
外观设计专利	Appearance Design Patents	183844	366381	203048	367963	268544	161926	442435
计算机软件	Computer Software	8526746	8793395	12028361	14818532	19522592	18206295	22186476
植物新品种	New Species of Plants	328249	229036	260925	243499	371673	477064	457876
集成电路布图设计	IC Layout Design	533307	378028	497789	1340403	753842	424511	432263
生物、医药新品种	New Species of Biology and Medicine	1197028	1432862	1454721	2839086	2245032	2192915	5193470
未涉及知识产权	Others	78735493	108840079	131114916	169977388	230116586	297864963	398143498

20–27 续表 continued

单位：万元 (10 000 yuan)

项　目	Item	2017	2018	2019	2020	2021	2022	2023
三、按技术领域分	**By Technical Field**							
电子信息技术	IT Technology	38607227	45051745	56366799	63239892	84986682	96196349	119855294
航空航天技术	Aviation and Aerospace Technology	4254075	4082361	5403232	4583747	7404529	9131646	13572518
先进制造技术	Advanced Manufacture Technology	15843314	24908842	29517064	41949439	58193317	83423043	116619845
生物、医药和医疗器械技术	Biology, Medicine and Medical Machine Technology	7502520	8391509	10579333	17690387	22355590	24429912	34483952
新材料及其应用	Advanced Material and Application	5010016	6724306	8711065	12200630	20794696	31070871	38553700
新能源与高效节能	New Energy and Power Saving	12021350	15400556	28135523	28543702	30090682	47475336	70722407
环境保护与资源综合利用技术	Environment Protection and Resource Application Technology	10698894	13269314	16234919	18458047	23745047	26998535	29046121
核应用技术	Nuclear Application Technology	292010	2660383	1192283	779457	648906	952991	2227058
农业技术	Agriculture Technology	4074813	4208292	5002269	7476774	8885729	12129050	16860890
现代交通	Modern Traffic	16653203	25427249	20775555	32559757	39556256	48703523	46763385
城市建设与社会发展	Urban Construction and Social Development	19284823	26849657	42065841	55033260	76281596	97398909	126051409
四、按社会经济目标分	**By Social and Economic Objectives**							
农林牧渔业发展	Agriculture, Forestry , Animal Husbandry and Fishery Development	4204404	4689757	5529437	7178247	8613132	11277037	15885295
工商业发展	Industry and Commerce Development	19246645	24484176	31211072	42238960	62274659	75014447	109434765
能源生产、分配和合理利用	Energy Production, Distribution and Application	11150576	16276268	22550167	25813656	27116137	46863126	58359592
基础设施以及城市和农村规划	Infrastructure, Urban and Rural Planning	19033606	30297060	34186555	45092915	60450633	71801519	83595951
环境保护、生态建设及污染防治	Environmental Protection, Ecological Building and Pollution Prevention	10517303	13219134	16520526	16462018	23206472	27099495	33031292
卫生事业发展	Sanitation Development	4378747	4990593	6486663	12029398	13872474	15367337	18403573
社会发展和社会服务	Social Development and Social Service	38821539	41718264	52897407	68363721	87739354	114493539	143755199
地球和大气层的探索与利用	Earth and Atmosphere Exploration and Utility	119448	105352	186924	126319	160439	278920	410819
教育事业发展	Education Development	717617	1079244	1853943	1922472	1962236	1852751	2277562
民用空间探测及开发	Civil Aerospace Exploration and Development	505418	519280	629062	650756	880305	764373	1055587
国防	National Defense	2975035	3906405	4209612	4266412	6758128	7810793	12461846
其他民用目标	Other Civil Purpose	20063635	29048652	38765858	43662157	60836405	83264147	111482402
非定向研究	Non-directive Research	2508271	6640029	8956657	14708059	19072655	22022683	24602697

20–28 分地区测绘资料提供情况（2023年）

Statistics on Output of Surveying and Mapping Materials by Region (2023)

地 区	Region	地形图合计 (张) Topographic Maps (unit)	1:10000 (scale)	1:50000 (scale)	测绘基准成果 (点) Surveying and Mapping Datum Product (point)	航摄成果 (GB) Aerial Photograph (GB)
全 国	**National Total**	**226563**	**51287**	**7563**	**237474**	**572196**
北 京	Beijing	1427	10		4801	
天 津	Tianjin				85	
河 北	Hebei	1362	1200	162	1112	247944
山 西	Shanxi	18952	18605	347	1016	
内蒙古	Inner Mongolia				18298	
辽 宁	Liaoning				2858	
吉 林	Jilin	113		113	1427	
黑龙江	Heilongjiang	773	651	122	4692	
上 海	Shanghai	166190			30760	
江 苏	Jiangsu	70	66	4	5231	
浙 江	Zhejiang	67		67	1377	34606
安 徽	Anhui	57		57	3071	
福 建	Fujian	9		9	1325	
江 西	Jiangxi	159	151	8	695	
山 东	Shandong	25		25	2084	
河 南	Henan	53		53	7451	
湖 北	Hubei				285	
湖 南	Hunan	1		1	3447	
广 东	Guangdong	427	409	18	3509	
广 西	Guangxi	2		2	19064	22886
海 南	Hainan				504	
重 庆	Chongqing	124	99	25	404	
四 川	Sichuan				1239	
贵 州	Guizhou				9744	75056
云 南	Yunnan	1720	1510	210	9778	
西 藏	Xizang	16619	13510	3109	1235	
陕 西	Shaanxi				11851	18750
甘 肃	Gansu	8612	7585	995	31969	
青 海	Qinghai	189		189	12090	
宁 夏	Ningxia	152	90	62	19865	
新 疆	Xinjiang	7769	7401	364	4097	14141
国家基础地理信息中心	National Geomatics Center of China	1691		1621	22110	158812

注：全国数据包括计划单列市数据。
a) The national data include data of cities with independent planning authority.

20–29 分地区地震监测情况（2023年）
Earthquake Monitoring by Region (2023)

单位：个 (unit)

地区	Region	地震台数总数 Number of Seismic Stations	全国地震监测台站 National Earthquake Monitoring Stations: 国家地震台 Number of National Seismic Stations	省地震台 Number of Provincial Seismic Stations	中心站 Number of Central Stations	一般监测站 Number of General Monitoring Stations	市、县级台 Municipality/County-level Stations: 市、县级台 Number of Municipality/County-level Stations	企业台 Number of Enterprise Stations	宏观观测点 Number of Macro-observation Spots
全国	**National Total**	**5948**	**1**	**31**	**140**	**3676**	**1737**	**363**	**43304**
北京	Beijing	301	1	1	1	280	18		129
天津	Tianjin	230		1	2	227			168
河北	Hebei	144		1	7	60	74	2	5194
山西	Shanxi	210		1	5	102	96	6	1661
内蒙古	Inner Mongolia	86		1	7	32	46		1607
辽宁	Liaoning	82		1	6	25	49	1	773
吉林	Jilin	101		1	3	52	45		843
黑龙江	Heilongjiang	89		1	5	38	43	2	1804
上海	Shanghai	83		1	1	74	7		
江苏	Jiangsu	159		1	5	14	138	1	717
浙江	Zhejiang	121		1	3	2	102	13	464
安徽	Anhui	158		1	5	55	97		947
福建	Fujian	310		1	5	267	25	12	290
江西	Jiangxi	36		1	3	29	3		695
山东	Shandong	221		1	7	18	190	5	1851
河南	Henan	122		1	5	10	89	17	3178
湖北	Hubei	92		1	4	50	12	25	460
湖南	Hunan	58		1	2	8	34	13	490
广东	Guangdong	368		1	5	262	95	5	155
广西	Guangxi	143		1	4	56	42	40	970
海南	Hainan	41		1	3	26	11		353
重庆	Chongqing	48		1	1	38	1	7	3292
四川	Sichuan	509		1	7	416	80	5	3970
贵州	Guizhou	146		1	1	134	5	5	2085
云南	Yunnan	974		1	8	605	191	169	1614
西藏	Xizang	21		1	3	17			223
陕西	Shaanxi	259		1	5	159	86	8	1271
甘肃	Gansu	444		1	8	351	77	7	2800
青海	Qinghai	107		1	5	69	12	20	83
宁夏	Ningxia	92		1	3	75	13		306
新疆	Xinjiang	193		1	11	125	56		4911

20–30 中国科协系统科技活动情况(2023年)

指 标		Item		总计 Total
机构和人员		**Associations or Academic Societies and Personnel**		
机构数	(个)	Number of Associations or Academic Societies	(unit)	7879
从业人员	(人)	Number of Employed Persons	(person)	47809
学会数	(个)	Number of Academic Societies	(unit)	23209
学会个人会员	(万人)	Number of Individual Members of Academic Societies	(10000 persons)	1289
学会秘书处从业人员	(人)	Number of Employed Persons of Academic Societies' Secretariat	(person)	47128
企业/科技园区科协	(个)	Number of S&T Associations in Enterprises and Science Park	(unit)	32033
个人会员	(万人)	Number of Individual Members	(10000 persons)	608
高等/科研院所院校科协	(个)	Number of S&T Associations in Institutions of Higher Education and Scientific Research Institution	(unit)	1966
个人会员	(万人)	Number of Individual Members	(10000 persons)	94
乡镇/街道科协	(个)	Number of S&T Associations in Township and Subdistrict	(unit)	28907
个人会员	(万人)	Number of Individual Members	(10000 persons)	145
农技协	(个)	Number of Rural Professional and Technical Associations	(unit)	17561
个人会员	(万人)	Number of Individual Members	(10000 persons)	293
学术交流活动		**Academic Exchange**		
学术交流活动	(次)	Number of Academic Exchanges	(time)	18499
参加人数	(万人)	Number of Participants	(10000 person)	36473
科学技术普及活动		**S&T Popularization Activities**		
举办科普活动	(场)	Number of S&T Popularization Activities	(show)	503398
科普活动受众人数	(万人)	Number of Participants	(10000 person)	754339
实用技术培训人次	(万人次)	Number of Practical Technology Training Participating in Activities	(10000 person-times)	1432
推广新技术、新品种	(项)	Number of Items Promoting New Technologies and Varieties	(item)	7058
参加活动科技人员、专家人次	(万人次)	Number of S&T Personnel and Experts Participating in Activities	(10000 person-times)	188
青少年科技教育		**Teenagers' Education of S&T**		
举办青少年科技竞赛	(次)	Number of Teenagers' S&T Competition Activities	(time)	7886
参赛人数	(万人次)	Number of Participants	(10000 person-times)	3788
举办青少年科学营	(次)	Number of Teenagers' S&T Camp	(time)	881
参加营员人数	(万人次)	Number of Participants	(10000 person-times)	9
科技开放与交流		**Opening-up and Exchange of S&T**		
参加双边科技人文交流活动人次	(人次)	Participants to Bilateral S&T Activities	(person-time)	340969
邀请、接待境外代表团来访人次	(人次)	Inviting and Receiving Overseas Delegations	(person-time)	2725
为科技工作者服务		**Services for the S&T Workers**		
反映科技工作者建议篇数	(篇)	Number of S&T Workers' Proposals Forwarded	(piece)	9941
表彰奖励科技工作者	(人次)	Number of Recognitions and Awards to S&T Workers	(person-time)	178965
#女性科技工作者		Number of Recognitions and Awards to Female S&T Workers		44884
科技期刊与科技传播		**Scientific Journals and S&T Diffusion**		
主办学术期刊	(种)	Number of S&T Journals	(kind)	1711
期刊总印数	(万册)	Printed Copies of Journals	(10000 copies)	4015
主办科技(普)报纸	(种)	Number of S&T Newspaper	(kind)	352
报纸总印数	(万份)	Printed Copies of Newspaper	(10000 copies)	4656
编著科技(普)图书	(个)	Compilation of S&T Publications	(kind)	6605
图书总印数	(万册)	Printed Copies of books	(10000 copies)	2047
科普基础设施建设		**S&T Infrastructure Construction**		
科技馆	(个)	Number of S&T Museums	(unit)	1073
全年参观人数	(万人次)	Annual Number of Visitors	(10000 person-times)	5352
科普大篷车行驶里程	(公里)	Science Popularization Caravan Mileage	(km)	7229647

Basic Statistics on Scientific and Technological Activities of China Associations for Science and Technology (2023)

科协小计 Total Number of Associations	学会小计 Total Number of Academic Societies	全国学会 National Societies	省级学会 Provincial Societies
3195	4684	214	4470
47809			
23209			
	1289	636	653
	47128	4178	42950
32033			
608			
1966			
94			
28907			
145			
17561			
293			
1951	16548	4158	12390
5908	30564	23807	6757
297150	206248	145085	61163
492757	261581	226141	35440
823	609	268	341
4599	2459	392	2067
62	126	97	29
5531	2355	1165	1190
2091	1697	253	1444
662	219	41	178
6	4	1	2
19132	321837	253725	68112
730	1995	1101	894
7151	2790	730	2060
29991	148974	46587	102387
11122	33762	7827	25935
67	1644	1004	640
847	3168	2254	915
280	72	8	64
4079	577	161	416
4978	1627	363	1264
1506	541	129	412
955	118	20	98
5110	243	11	232
7229647			

20-31 分地区气象业务站点及观测项目情况（2023年）
Status of Operational Meteorological Stations and Observation Items by Region (2023)

单位：个 (unit)

地区和单位	Region and Units	地面观测业务 Surface Observation Stations	高空探测业务 Upper-air Observation Stations	省级常规气象观测站 Provincial Conventional Meteorological Observation Stations	天气雷达观测业务 Weather Radar Observation Stations	农业气象观测站 Agro-Meteorological Observation Stations	环境气象观测站 Environmental Meteorological Observation Stations	闪电定位监测业务 Lightning Position Monitoring Stations	卫星云图接收业务 Satellite Cloud Images Receiving Stations
全　国	**National Total**	**10939**	**120**	**55760**	**634**	**653**	**1786**	**541**	**241**
北　京	Beijing	55	1	570	12	7	56	2	1
天　津	Tianjin	36		290	3	5	31	2	3
河　北	Hebei	410	3	2636	23	30	72	12	7
山　西	Shanxi	262	1	1682	18	31	77	8	2
内蒙古	Inner Mongolia	706	12	1826	21	29	43	53	11
辽　宁	Liaoning	298	2	1507	14	25	77	10	2
吉　林	Jilin	388	3	1035	16	22	33	8	8
黑龙江	Heilongjiang	485	4	439	17	36	49	31	7
上　海	Shanghai	46	1	230	5	1	30		4
江　苏	Jiangsu	263	3	1660	19	19	188	21	8
浙　江	Zhejiang	263	3	5115	38	13	233	12	4
安　徽	Anhui	294	2	2194	29	22	38	8	2
福　建	Fujian	299	3	1945	20	23	44	10	8
江　西	Jiangxi	379	2	2178	26	18	49	13	11
山　东	Shandong	426	3	1490	11	19	55	14	9
河　南	Henan	369	3	2477	17	35	100	20	21
湖　北	Hubei	326	3	2413	18	30	84	14	14
湖　南	Hunan	421	3	1641	13	22	18	11	10
广　东	Guangdong	433	4	987	62	26	121	10	10
广　西	Guangxi	518	6	2629	18	24	30	12	11
海　南	Hainan	125	3	439	8	6	42	7	5
重　庆	Chongqing	159	1	2071	15	13	24	6	5
四　川	Sichuan	504	7	6089	55	45	50	79	7
贵　州	Guizhou	364	2	2114	23	18	17	13	10
云　南	Yunnan	571	5	3559	26	22	25	23	11
西　藏	Xizang	501	5	442	19	4	25	25	10
陕　西	Shaanxi	392	4	1360	22	21	39	12	12
甘　肃	Gansu	341	9	1791	16	23	30	21	10
青　海	Qinghai	234	7	756	9	17	35	34	2
宁　夏	Ningxia	112	1	872	7	7	12	6	7
新　疆	Xinjiang	714	14	1323	24	40	52	39	9
其　他	Others	245			10		3	5	

20–32　产品质量监督抽查情况(2023年)
Results of Sampling Check under Supervision on the Quality of Products (2023)

项　目	Item	抽查企业（家）Number of Enterprises Selected for Supervision (unit)	检验产品（批次）Examined Products (batch-time)	不合格产品（批次）Unqualified Products (batch-time)
产品质量国家监督抽查合计	**Total of Sampling Check under Supervision on the Quality of Products**	**26472**	**28265**	**3476**
食品相关产品	Food-related Products	1607	1620	46
工业品	Industrial Products	24865	26645	3430

注：2023年数据指产品质量国家监督抽查结果，不含地方抽查结果数据。
a) The 2023 data refers to the results of national supervision and spot checks on product quality, excluding local spot check results.

20–33　分地区产品质量情况
Quality of Products by Region

单位：%　　(%)

地　区	Region	产品质量合格率 Qualification Rate of Products 2022	2023
全　国	**National Total**	**93.29**	**93.65**
北　京	Beijing	96.87	96.75
天　津	Tianjin	95.46	95.36
河　北	Hebei	92.49	93.27
山　西	Shanxi	92.79	93.12
内蒙古	Inner Mongolia	93.42	93.22
辽　宁	Liaoning	94.03	93.86
吉　林	Jilin	92.37	91.62
黑龙江	Heilongjiang	92.53	91.89
上　海	Shanghai	96.04	96.33
江　苏	Jiangsu	94.59	94.98
浙　江	Zhejiang	93.61	93.44
安　徽	Anhui	95.33	94.73
福　建	Fujian	94.52	95.09
江　西	Jiangxi	92.95	93.30
山　东	Shandong	94.12	93.97
河　南	Henan	92.86	93.08
湖　北	Hubei	93.58	93.95
湖　南	Hunan	93.90	93.93
广　东	Guangdong	94.49	94.75
广　西	Guangxi	91.49	91.22
海　南	Hainan	92.08	91.55
重　庆	Chongqing	93.33	93.47
四　川	Sichuan	93.21	93.86
贵　州	Guizhou	91.10	91.17
云　南	Yunnan	92.45	92.08
西　藏	Xizang	87.12	87.18
陕　西	Shaanxi	91.65	91.71
甘　肃	Gansu	91.69	91.37
青　海	Qinghai	88.64	88.73
宁　夏	Ningxia	89.06	88.76
新　疆	Xinjiang	90.64	90.66

注：本资料由75个重点工业城市抽样数据汇总而成。
a) Data in this table are collected from samples of 75 key industrial cities.

主要统计指标解释

研究与试验发展(R&D) 指为增加知识存量（也包括有关人类、文化和社会的知识）以及设计已有知识的新应用而进行的创造性、系统性工作，包括基础研究、应用研究和试验发展三种类型。国际上通常采用R&D活动的规模和强度指标反映一国的科技实力和核心竞争力。

基础研究 指一种不预设任何特定应用或使用目的的实验性或理论性工作，其主要目的是为获得（已发生）现象和可观察事实的基本原理、规律和新知识。其成果通常表现为提出一般原理、理论或规律，并以论文、著作、研究报告等形式为主。

应用研究 指为获取新知识，达到某一特定的实际目的或目标而开展的初始性研究。应用研究是为了确定基础研究成果的可能用途，或确定实现特定和预定目标的新方法。其研究成果以论文、著作、研究报告、原理性模型或发明专利等形式为主。

试验发展 指利用从科学研究、实际经验中获取的知识和研究过程中产生的其他知识，开发新的产品、工艺或改进现有产品、工艺而进行的系统性研究。其研究成果以专利、专有技术，以及具有新颖性的产品原型、原始样机及装置等形式为主。

产品创新 指企业推出了全新的或有重大改进的产品。产品创新的“新”要体现在产品的功能或特性上，包括技术规范、材料、组件、用户友好性等方面的重大改进。不包括产品仅有外观变化或其他微小改变的情况，也不包括直接转销。此处的“新”是指该产品对本企业而言必须是新的，但对于其他企业或整个市场而言不一定是新的。这里的产品既包括货物，也包括服务。货物方面产品创新的例子有新能源汽车、新功能手机等；服务方面产品创新的例子有新的保修服务，如显著延长的新产品保修期限等。

工艺创新 指企业采用了全新的或有重大改进的生产方法、工艺设备或辅助性活动。工艺创新的“新”要体现在技术、设备或流程上；它对本企业而言必须是新的，但对于其他企业或整个市场而言不一定是新的。不包括单纯的组织管理方式的变化。此处的辅助性活动指企业的采购、物流、财务、信息化等活动。

组织（管理）创新 指企业采取了此前从未使用过的全新的组织管理方式，主要涉及企业的经营模式、组织结构或外部关系等方面。不包括单纯的合并或收购。组织（管理）创新应是企业管理层战略决策的结果。此处的“新”是指它对本企业而言必须是新的，但对于其他企业或整个市场而言不一定是新的。

营销创新 指企业采用了此前从未使用过的全新的营销概念或营销策略，主要涉及产品（服务）设计或包装、产品（服务）推广、产品（服务）销售渠道、产品（服务）定价等方面。不包括季节性、周期性变化和其他常规的营销方式变化。此处的“新”是指它对本企业而言必须是新的，但对于其他企业或整个市场而言不一定是新的。

R&D人员 指报告期R&D活动单位中从事基础研究、应用研究和试验发展活动的人员。包括直接参加上述三类R&D活动的人员，以及与上述三类R&D活动相关的管理人员和直接服务人员，即直接为R&D活动提供资料文献、材料供应、设备维护等服务的人员。不包括为R&D活动提供间接服务的人员，如餐饮服务、安保人员等。

R&D人员全时当量 指报告期R&D人员按实际从事R&D活动时间计算的工作量，以“人年”为计量单位。为国际上比较科技人力投入而制定的可比指标。

R&D经费支出 指报告期调查单位内部为实施R&D活动而实际发生的全部经费，按支出性质分为日常性支出和资产性支出。不包括调查单位委托其他单位或与其他单位合作开展R&D活动而转拨给其他单位的全部经费。

R&D经费支出中政府资金 指R&D经费支出中来自各级政府财政的各类资金，包括财政科学技术支出和财政其他功能支出的资金用于R&D活动的实际支出。

R&D经费支出中企业资金 指R&D经费支出中来自企业的各类资金。对企业而言，企业资金指企业自有资金、接受其他企业委托开展R&D活动而获得的资金，以及从金融机构贷款获得的开展R&D活动的资金；对科研院所、高校等事业单位而言，企业资金是指因接受从企业委托开展R&D活动而获得的各类资金。

R&D项目（课题）数 R&D项目（课题）是进行R&D活动的基本组织形式，通常由R&D活动执行单位依据项目立项书或合同书等形式明确项目任务、目标、人员和经费等。

R&D项目（课题）人员全时当量 指实际参加研发项目（课题）活动人员折合的全时当量。

R&D项目（课题）经费支出 指调查单位内部在报告年度进行研发项目（课题）研究和试制等的实际支出。包括劳务费、其他日常支出、固定资产购建费、外协加工费等，不包括委托或与外单位合作进行项目（课题）研究而拨付给对方使用的经费。

新产品销售收入 指报告期企业销售新产品实现的销售收入。新产品是指采用新技术原理、新设计构思研制、生产的全新产品，或在结构、材质、工艺等某一方面比原有产品有明显改进，从而显著提高了产品性能或扩大了使用功能的产品。既包括经政府有关部门认定并在有效期内的新产品，也包括企业自行研制开发，未经政府有关部门认定，从投产之日起一年之内的新产品。

专利 是专利权的简称，是对发明人的发明创造经审查合格后，由国家知识产权局依据专利法授予发明人和设计人对该项发明创造享有的专有权。包括发明、实用新型和外观设计。反映拥有自主知识产权的科技和设计成果情况。

发明（专利） 指对产品、方法或者其改进所提出的新的技术方案。是国际通行的反映拥有自主知识产权技术的核心指标。

实用新型（专利） 指对产品的形状、构造或者其结合所提出的适于实用的新的技术方案。反映具有一定技术含量的技术成果情况。

外观设计（专利） 指对产品的形状、图案、色彩或者其结合所作出的富有美感并适于工业上应用的新设计。反映拥有自主知识产权的外观设计成果情况。

Explanatory Notes on Main Statistical Indicators

Research and Experimental Development (R&D) refers to creative and systematic work undertaken in order to increase the stock of knowledge (including knowledge of humankind, culture and society) and to devise new applications of available knowledge. R&D includes 3 categories of activities: basic research, applied research and experimental development. The scale and intensity of R&D are widely used internationally to reflect the strength of S&T and the core competitiveness of a country in the world.

Basic Research refers to experimental or theoretical work undertaken primarily to acquire new knowledge of the underlying foundations of phenomena and observable facts, without any particular application or use in view. Basic research usually formulates hypotheses, theories or laws, and its results are mainly released or disseminated in the form of scientific papers or monographs or research reports.

Applied Research refers to original investigation undertaken in order to acquire new knowledge. It is directed primarily towards a specific, practical aim or objective. Purpose of the applied research is to identify the possible uses of results from basic research, or to explore new (fundamental) methods or new approaches. Results of applied research are expressed in the form of scientific papers, monographs, fundamental models or invention patents.

Experimental Development refers to systematic work, drawing on knowledge gained from research and practical experience and producing additional knowledge, which is directed to producing new products or processes or to improving existing products or processes. Results of experimental development activities are embodied in patents, exclusive technology, and monotype of new products or equipment.

Product Innovation refers to the introduction of new or significantly improved products by enterprises. The innovation should be reflected by the functions or features of the products, including improvement on technical specifications, materials, parts, user-friendliness etc. Simple appearance change or other subtle changes are not included, neither is direct reselling. The product must be new to the enterprise, but it is not necessarily new to other enterprises or the whole market.The products here cover both goods and services. Examples of innovation on goods include new energy vehicles and mobile phones with new functions; examples of innovation on services include new warranty service, such as significantly extended new warranty period of products.

Process Innovation refers to the implementation of new or significantly improved production methods, process equipments or supporting activities by enterprises. The innovation should be reflected by technology, equipment or process. It must be new to the enterprise, but it is not necessarily new to other enterprises or the whole market. Simple change of organization and management mode is not included. Supporting activities cover purchase, logistics, account and compute activities.

Organizational (management) Innovation refers to the adoption of a completely new organizational management mode, which has never been used before. It mainly involves the business model, organizational structure or external relations of enterprises. It does not include pure mergers or acquisitions. Organizational (management) innovation should be the result of strategic decision-making of enterprise management. The term "new" here means that it must be new to the enterprise, but not necessarily new to other enterprises or the whole market.

Marketing Innovation refers to the implementation of completely new marketing concepts or marketing strategies that have never been used before. It mainly involves product (service) design or packaging, product (service) promotion, product (service) sales channels, product (service) pricing and so on. It does not include seasonal, cyclical and other conventional marketing changes. The term "new" here means that it must be new to the enterprise, but not necessarily new to other enterprises or the whole market.

R&D Personnel refer to persons of R&D activities units engaged in basic research, applied research, and experimental development at the reference period, including persons of directly participating in the three activities above, as well as management and direct service staff related to R&D activities, such as literature provision, material supply, equipment maintenance staff, it excludes persons providing indirect support and ancillary services, such as canteen and security staff.

Full-time Equivalent of R&D Personnel refers to the ratio of working hours actually spent on R&D during a specific reference period (usually a calendar year) divided by the total number of hours conventionally worked in the same period by an individual or by a group. The measurement unit of the ratio is “man-years”. This is an internationally comparable indicator of S&T manpower input.

Expenditure on R&D refers to the real expenditure of surveyed units on their own R&D activities in reporting period. It is divided into current expenditures and gross fixed capital expenditures for R&D according to the nature of expenditure. It doesn’t include the fees transferred to cooperated or entrusted agencies on R&D activities.

Expenditure on R&D from Government Funds refers to the expenditure of funds on R&D activities from government agencies at different levels, including appropriate funds on

science and technology from financial departments, and the real expenditure of other fiscal functional funds on R&D activities from government agencies.

Expenditure on R&D from Enterprises Funds refers to the expenditure of all kinds of funds on R&D activities from enterprises. In terms of enterprises, it refers to the expenditure of self-raised funds of enterprises, funds from other enterprises through entrustment, loans from financial institutions on R&D activities. In terms of public institutions, such as institution of scientific research and universities, it refers to the expenditure of funds from enterprises through entrustment.

Number of R&D Projects (subjects) R&D Projects (subjects) are the basic forms of R&D activities, The project task, target, personnel and expenditure are usually defined by R&D activity execution unit according to project approval specification or contract document.

Full-time Equivalent of Personnel on R&D Projects (subjects) refers to the full-time equivalent of persons actually engaged in R&D projects (subjects).

Expenditure on R&D Projects (subjects) refers to the real expenditure of internal funds of the surveyed units on research and test of R&D projects (subjects) at the reference year, including service fee, other daily expenditure, cost for fixed assets, cost of external process, it excludes expenditure of funds transferred to other cooperated or entrusted units of the projects.

Sales Income of New Products refers to the sales income of new products of the enterprises at the reference period. New products refer to products developed and produced with new technologies and designs or improved in structure, material, process or other aspects so that their performance are improved or their functions expanded. New products include those affirmed by government authorities in their validity period and also those developed by enterprises without the affirmation of government authorities within one year after they are put into production.

Patent is an abbreviation for the patent right and refers to the exclusive right of ownership by the inventors or designers for the creation or inventions, given from the China National Intellectual Property Administration after due process of assessment and approval in accordance with the Patent Law. Patents are granted for inventions, utility models and designs. This indicator reflects the achievements of S&T and design with independent intellectual property.

Patented Inventions refer to new technical proposals to the products or methods or their modifications. This is universal core indicator reflecting the technologies with independent intellectual property.

Patented Utility Models refer to the practical and new technical proposals on the shape and structure of the product or the combination of both. This indicator reflects the condition of technological results with certain technical content.

Designs refer to the aesthetics and industrially applicable new designs for the shape, pattern and colour of the product, or their combinations. This indicator reflects the appearance design achievements with independent intellectual property.

21

教　育

Education

简 要 说 明

一、本篇资料的主要内容

本篇主要反映我国教育事业发展基本情况。

包括高等教育、高中阶段教育、义务教育阶段教育、特殊教育、学前教育以及教育经费等资料。主要指标包括学校数、在校生数、招生数、毕业生数、教职工数、专任教师数、教育经费总投入及国家财政性教育经费等。

二、本篇的资料来源

教育事业统计资料、教育经费统计资料由教育部提供；技工学校资料由人力资源和社会保障部提供。

详细资料分别见《中国教育统计年鉴》（教育部发展规划司编）和《中国教育经费统计年鉴》（教育部财务司编）。

Brief Introduction

I. Main Content of Data on Education

Data in this chapter reflect the development of China's education.

Data on education cover the situations on higher education, high school level education, compulsory education, special education, pre-school education and educational finance. The main indicators include number of schools, number of enrolments, entrants, graduates, number of educational personnel and full-time teachers, total educational finance, government appropriation for education and so on.

II. Sources of Data on Education

The Ministry of Education provides statistical data on educational undertakings and educational finance. Data on skilled workers schools are provided by the Ministry of Human Resources and Social Security.

For detailed information please refer to "*Educational Statistics Yearbook of China*" compiled by Department of Development & Planning, Ministry of Education; and the "*China Educational Finance Statistical Yearbook*" compiled by Department of Finance, Ministry of Education.

21-1 各级各类学校和教职工情况（2023年）
Number of Schools and Educational Personnel by Type and Level (2023)

项　目	Item	学校数(所) Schools (unit)	教职工数(人) Educational Personnel (person)
高等教育学校	**Higher Education Schools**	**3074**	**2946431**
普通本科学校	HEIs Offering Degree Programs	1242	1996956
#独立学院	Independent Institutions	164	83136
本科层次职业学校	Undergraduate Level Vocational Schools	33	38470
高职(专科)学校	Higher Vocational (Specialist) Schools	1547	884563
成人高等学校	Adult HEIs	252	26442
高中阶段学校	**Senior Secondary Schools**	**22466**	**4184538**
普通高中	Regular Senior Secondary Schools	15381	3319638
完全中学	Combined Secondary Schools	5277	1199867
高级中学	Regular High Schools	8308	1634154
十二年一贯制学校	12-Year Schools	1796	485617
中等职业教育	Secondary Vocational Education	7085	864900
中等职业学校	Secondary Vocational Schools	7085	854455
其他中职机构	Other Secondary Vocational Institutions	(234)	10445
义务教育阶段学校	**Compulsory Education Schools**	**195820**	**11079310**
初中学校	Junior Secondary Schools	52348	4819200
初级中学	Regular Junior Secondary Schools	34014	2968264
九年一贯制学校	9-Year Schools	18330	1850868
职业初中	Vocational Junior Secondary Schools	4	68
普通小学	Regular Primary Schools	143472	6260110
小学	Primary Schools	143472	5958062
小学教学点	External Teaching Sites	(66009)	302048
特殊教育学校	**Schools for Special Education**	**2345**	**90370**
幼儿园	**Kindergarten**	**274414**	**5514369**
专门学校	**Specialized Schools**	**150**	**4532**

注：1.完全中学的学校数和教职工数计入高中阶段教育，九年一贯制学校的校数和教职工数计入初中阶段教育，十二年一贯制学校的校数和教职工数计入高中阶段教育(以下相关表同)。

2.2021年起，中等职业教育数据不含人社部管理的技工学校(以下相关表同)。

3.“()”内数据为不计校数(以下相关表同)。

a) Number of combined secondary schools and their educational personnel are classified into the number of senior secondary education, the number of 9-year schools and their educational personnel are classified into the number of junior secondary education, the number of 12-year schools and their educational personnel are classified into the number of senior secondary education. The full-time teachers are classified by educational level. The same applies to the relevant following tables.

b) Since 2021, Secondary Vocational Education data do not include Technical Schools managed by the Ministry of Human Resources and Social Security. The same applies to the relevant following tables.

c) Data within “( )” do not include the number of schools. The same applies to the relevant following tables.

21–2 各级各类学历教育学生情况（2023年）
Number of Students of Formal Education by Type and Level (2023)

单位：人 (person)

项 目	Item	毕业生数 Graduates	招生数 Entrants	在校生数 Enrolment
高等教育	**Higher Education**			
研究生	Postgraduates	1014755	1301679	3882940
博 士	Doctor's Degree	87126	153275	612489
硕 士	Master's Degree	927629	1148404	3270451
普通本科	Undergraduates	4897422	4781609	20346933
职业本专科	Vocational Undergraduates	5572836	5640597	17403213
本 科	Bachelor Degree	39924	89899	324692
专 科	Short-cycle Courses	5532912	5550698	17078521
成人本专科	Undergraduates in Adult HEIs	3631278	4454878	10082275
本 科	Bachelor Degree	1947475	2702145	6000262
专 科	Short-cycle Courses	1683803	1752733	4082013
网络本专科生	Web-based Undergraduates	2633542	1634220	7399703
本 科	Bachelor Degree	1100611	607030	2890562
专 科	Short-cycle Courses	1532931	1027190	4509141
高中阶段教育	**High School Level Education**	**12758618**	**14218362**	**41020889**
普通高中	Regular Senior Secondary Schools	8604097	9678010	28036268
完全中学	Combined Secondary Schools	2584182	2840146	8297472
高级中学	Regular High Schools	5535595	6176251	17943270
十二年一贯制学校	12-Year Schools	460101	628523	1711473
附设普通高中班	Subsidiary Regular Senior Secondary School Class	24219	33090	84053
中等职业教育	Secondary Vocational Education	4154521	4540352	12984621
中等职业学校	Secondary Vocational Schools	3810165	4305502	12161274
附设中职班	Subsidiary Secondary Vocational Class	344356	234850	823347
义务教育阶段教育	**Compulsory Education**	**33870737**	**36325096**	**160797169**
初中阶段	Junior Secondary Schools	16235844	17546266	52436916
初级中学	Regular Junior Secondary Schools	10845995	11715815	35108702
九年一贯制学校	9-Year Schools	2863914	3248910	9549400
十二年一贯制学校	12-Year Schools	542827	499262	1555185
完全中学	Combined Secondary Schools	1949666	2050720	6129698
职业初中	Junior Secondary Vocational Schools	116	89	305
附设普通初中班	Junior Secondary Classes Attached	33309	31470	93590
附设职业初中班	Vocational Junior Secondary Classes Attached	17		36
小学阶段	Primary Education	17634893	18778830	108360253
小学	Primary Schools	14768984	15742385	91044804
九年一贯制学校	9-Year Schools	2229796	2351382	13391091
十二年一贯制学校	12-Year Schools	283640	251204	1600192
小学教学点	External Teaching Sites	277229	416231	2150227
附设小学班	Subsidiary Primary School Classes	75244	17628	173939
特殊教育	**Special Education**	**173140**	**154977**	**911981**
#特殊教育学校	Special Education Schools	55188	52132	341248
学前教育	**Pre-school Education**	**18044024**	**11812117**	**40929784**
幼儿园	Kindergartens	16926231	11189350	39126337
附设幼儿班	Subsidiary Toddler Class	1117793	622767	1803447
专门学校	**Specialized Schools**	**5753**	**8420**	**9891**

注：1.2017年起，研究生招生数包含全日制和非全日制研究生，在校生数包含全日制、非全日制研究生和在职人员攻读硕士学位学生(以下相关表同)。
2.2023年，高中阶段教育学生数不含国家开放大学中职部(以下相关表同)。
3.完全中学、九年一贯制学校、十二年一贯制学校和附设教学班的学生数按教育层次分别计入对应教育阶段的学生数中(以下相关表同)。
4.特殊教育涵盖特殊教育学校、附设特教班、随班就读和送教上门等各类形式(以下相关表同)。
5.2019年起，学前教育招生数仅包括首次入园的适龄儿童，不再包括复学、转入等情况(以下相关表同)。

a) Since 2017, the number of postgraduate entrants includes full-time and part-time postgraduates, the number of enrolment includes full-time, part-time postgraduates and on-the-job students. The same applies to the relevant following tables.
b) In 2023, number of students in high school level education does not include secondary vocational department of National Open University. The same applies to the relevant following tables.
c) Number of the students in Combined Secondary Schools, 9-Year Schools, 12-Year Schools and subsidiary class are classified by educational level.
d) Special education covers various forms including special education schools, attached special education classes, regular classes and 'home delivery' teaching. The same applies to the relevant following tables.
e) From 2019, the number of entrants of the pre-school education only includes the school-age children who enter the kindergarten for the first time, and does not include the situation of returning to school and transferring in. The same applies to the relevant following tables.

21-3 各级各类民办学校和教职工情况（2023年）
Number of Non-government Schools and Educational Personnel by Type and Level (2023)

项　　目	Item	学校数(所) Schools (unit)	教职工数(人) Educational Personnel (person)
高等教育学校	**Higher Education Schools**	**789**	**571795**
普通本科学校	HEIs Offering Degree Programs	391	345455
#独立学院	Independent Institutions	164	83136
本科层次职业学校	Undergraduate Level Vocational Schools	22	23736
高职(专科)学校	Higher Vocational (Specialist) Schools	374	202572
成人高等学校	Adult HEIs	2	32
高中阶段学校	**Senior Secondary Schools**	**6695**	**1016097**
普通高中	Regular Senior Secondary Schools	4567	838630
完全中学	Combined Secondary Schools	819	173031
高级中学	Regular High Schools	2397	287022
十二年一贯制学校	12-Year Schools	1351	378577
中等职业教育	Secondary Vocational Education	2128	177467
义务教育阶段学校	**Compulsory Education Schools**	**10110**	**853150**
初中学校	Junior Secondary Schools	5342	616423
初级中学	Regular Junior Secondary Schools	955	90913
九年一贯制学校	9-Year Schools	4386	525510
职业初中	Vocational Junior Secondary Schools	1	
普通小学	Regular Primary Schools	4768	236727
特殊教育学校	**Schools for Special Education**	**78**	**2641**
幼儿园	**Kindergarten**	**149476**	**2731279**
专门学校	**Specialized Schools**	**10**	**329**

21-4 各级各类民办教育学生情况（2023年）
Statistics on Students of Non-government Education by Type and Level (2023)

单位：人 (person)

项　目	Item	毕业生数 Graduates	招生数 Entrants	在校生数 Enrolment
高等教育	**Higher Education**			
研究生	Postgraduates	1261	1834	4430
普通本科	Undergraduates	1354335	1180192	5475270
职业本专科	Vocational Undergraduates	1289208	1587610	4468538
本　科	Bachelor Degree	38597	59785	233072
专　科	Short-cycle Courses	1250611	1527825	4235466
成人本专科	Undergraduates in Adult HEIs	390663	568200	1158031
本　科	Bachelor Degree	69993	142946	264962
专　科	Short-cycle Courses	320670	425254	893069
高中阶段教育	**High School Level Education**	**2296216**	**2945802**	**8141981**
普通高中	Regular Senior Secondary Schools	1448166	2019599	5477609
完全中学	Combined Secondary Schools	332168	386305	1103503
高级中学	Regular High Schools	757604	1141216	3032142
十二年一贯制学校	12-Year Schools	358394	492078	1341964
中等职业教育	Secondary Vocational Education	848050	926203	2664372
义务教育阶段教育	**Compulsory Education**	**3516437**	**2515038**	**12219867**
初中阶段	Junior Secondary Schools	2027383	1632387	5304172
初级中学	Regular Junior Secondary Schools	404614	296517	969008
九年一贯制学校	9-Year Schools	882385	791923	2489314
十二年一贯制学校	12-Year Schools	425461	343817	1125157
完全中学	Combined Secondary Schools	314906	200130	720657
职业初中	Junior Secondary Vocational Schools	17		36
小学阶段	Primary Education	1489054	882651	6915695
小学	Primary Schools	584281	340013	2731385
九年一贯制学校	9-Year Schools	679627	401067	3098989
十二年一贯制学校	12-Year Schools	225146	141571	1085321
特殊教育	**Special Education**	**1598**	**1783**	**9801**
学前教育	**Pre-school Education**	**8222918**	**4800043**	**17916228**
专门学校	**Specialized Schools**	**504**	**743**	**1185**

21-5 各级各类教育专任教师情况（2023年）
Number of Full-time Teachers of Education by Type and Level (2023)

单位：人 (person)

项 目	Item	专任教师数 Full-time Teachers	#民办 Civilian-run
高等教育学校	**Higher Education Schools**	**2074943**	**435169**
普通本科学校	HEIs Offering Degree Programs	1345486	254947
#独立学院	Independent Institutions	60686	60686
本科层次职业学校	Undergraduate Level Vocational Schools	30823	19283
高职(专科)学校	Higher Vocational (Specialist) Schools	684584	160929
成人高等学校	Adult HEIs	14050	10
高中阶段教育	**High School Level Education**	**2949646**	**548368**
普通高中	Regular Senior Secondary Schools	2214804	406117
完全中学	Combined Secondary Schools	630448	79249
高级中学	Regular High Schools	1442126	221024
十二年一贯制学校	12-Year Schools	135758	103876
附设普通高中班	Subsidiary Regular Senior Secondary School Class	6472	1968
中等职业教育	Secondary Vocational Education	734842	142251
中等职业学校	Secondary Vocational Schools	704741	130647
附设中职班	Subsidiary Secondary Vocational Class	30101	11604
义务教育阶段教育	**Compulsory Education**	**10739319**	**852120**
初中阶段	Junior Secondary Education	4083058	400809
初级中学	Regular Junior Secondary Schools	2721710	69254
九年一贯制学校	9-Year Schools	784536	188814
十二年一贯制学校	12-Year Schools	122488	88163
完全中学	Combined Secondary Schools	446969	53215
职业初中	Vocational Junior Secondary Schools	52	
附设初中班	Junior Secondary Classes Attached	7303	1363
小学阶段	Primary Education	6656261	451311
小学	Primary Schools	5458669	171978
九年一贯制学校	9-Year Schools	821055	198166
十二年一贯制学校	12-Year Schools	106937	78632
小学教学点	External Teaching Sites	259394	131
附设小学班	Subsidiary Primary School Classes	10206	2404
特殊教育	**Special Education**	**77047**	**1758**
#特殊教育学校	Special Education Schools	76135	8
学前教育	**Pre-school Education**	**3073704**	**1370269**
幼儿园	Kindergartens	2962814	1365593
附设幼儿班	Subsidiary Toddler Class	110890	4676
专门学校	**Specialized Schools**	**2790**	**162**

注：完全中学、九年一贯制学校、十二年一贯制学校和附设教学班的专任教师数按教育层次分别计入对应教育阶段的专任教师数中(以下相关表同)。

a) Numbers of full-time teachers in combined secondary schools, 9-year schools, 12-year schools and subsidiary class are classified by educational levels. The same applies to the relevant following tables.

21-6 各级各类学校校数情况
Number of Schools by Type and Level

单位：所 (unit)

年 份 Year	普通、职业高等学校 Regular and Vocational HEIs	#高职(专科)学校 Higher Vocational (Specialist) Schools	普通高中 Regular Senior Secondary Schools	中等职业教育 Secondary Vocational Education	初中学校 Junior Secondary Schools	普通小学 Regular Primary Schools	特殊教育学校 Special Education Schools	幼儿园 Kindergarten
1978	598		49215	2760	113130	949323	292	163952
1980	675		31300	3459	87077	917316	292	170419
1985	1016		17318	14190	77529	832309	375	172262
1990	1075		15678	20763	73462	766072	746	172322
1995	1054		13991	22072	68564	668685	1379	180438
2000	1041	442	14564	19727	63898	553622	1539	175836
2001	1225	628	14907	17580	66590	491273	1531	111706
2002	1396	767	15406	15919	65645	456903	1540	111752
2003	1552	908	15779	14682	64730	425846	1551	116390
2004	1731	1047	15998	14454	63757	394183	1560	117899
2005	1792	1091	16092	14466	62486	366213	1593	124402
2006	1867	1147	16153	14693	60885	341639	1605	130495
2007	1908	1168	15681	14832	59384	320061	1618	129086
2008	2263	1184	15206	14847	57914	300854	1640	133722
2009	2305	1215	14607	14388	56320	280184	1672	138209
2010	2358	1246	14058	13862	54890	257410	1706	150420
2011	2409	1280	13688	13083	54117	241249	1767	166750
2012	2442	1297	13509	12654	53216	228585	1853	181251
2013	2491	1321	13352	12262	52804	213529	1933	198553
2014	2529	1327	13253	11878	52623	201377	2000	209881
2015	2560	1341	13240	11202	52405	190525	2053	223683
2016	2596	1359	13383	10893	52118	177633	2080	239812
2017	2631	1388	13555	10671	51894	167009	2107	254950
2018	2663	1418	13737	10229	51982	161811	2152	266677
2019	2688	1423	13964	10078	52415	160148	2192	281174
2020	2738	1468	14235	9896	52805	157979	2244	291715
2021	2756	1486	14585	7294	52871	154279	2288	294832
2022	2760	1489	15026	7201	52480	149117	2314	289222
2023	2822	1547	15381	7085	52348	143472	2345	274414

21-7 各级各类教育专任教师情况
Number of Full-time Teachers of Education by Type and Level

单位：万人 (10 000 persons)

年 份 Year	普通、职业高等学校 Regular and Vocational HEIs	#高职(专科)学校 Higher Vocational (Specialist) Schools	普通高中 Regular Senior Secondary Schools	中等职业教育 Secondary Vocational Education	初中阶段 Junior Secondary Education	小学阶段 Primary Education	特殊教育 Special Education	学前教育 Pre-school Education
1978	20.6		74.1	9.9	244.1	522.6	0.4	27.7
1980	24.7		57.1	13.3	244.9	549.9	0.5	41.1
1985	34.4		49.2	35.5	216.0	537.7	0.7	55.0
1990	39.5		56.2	66.3	249.9	558.2	1.4	75.0
1995	40.1		55.1	74.0	282.1	566.4	2.5	87.5
2000	46.3	8.7	75.7	79.7	328.7	586.0	3.2	85.6
2001	53.2	12.4	84.0	73.8	338.6	579.8	2.9	54.6
2002	61.8	15.6	94.6	69.1	346.8	577.9	3.0	57.1
2003	72.5	19.7	107.1	71.3	349.8	570.3	3.0	61.3
2004	85.8	23.8	119.1	73.6	350.0	562.9	3.1	65.6
2005	96.6	26.8	129.9	75.0	349.2	559.2	3.2	72.2
2006	107.6	31.6	138.7	79.9	347.5	558.8	3.3	77.6
2007	116.8	35.5	144.3	85.9	347.3	561.3	3.5	82.7
2008	123.7	37.7	147.6	89.5	347.6	562.2	3.6	89.9
2009	129.5	39.5	149.3	86.7	351.8	563.3	3.8	98.6
2010	134.3	40.4	151.8	87.1	352.5	561.7	4.0	114.4
2011	139.3	41.3	155.7	88.1	352.5	560.5	4.1	131.6
2012	144.0	41.3	159.5	88.0	350.4	558.5	4.4	147.9
2013	149.7	43.7	162.9	86.8	348.1	558.5	4.6	166.3
2014	153.5	43.8	166.3	85.8	348.8	563.4	4.8	184.4
2015	157.3	45.5	169.5	84.4	347.6	568.5	5.0	205.1
2016	160.2	46.7	173.3	84.0	348.8	578.9	5.3	223.2
2017	163.3	48.2	177.4	83.9	354.9	594.5	5.6	243.2
2018	167.3	49.8	181.3	83.4	363.9	609.2	5.9	258.1
2019	174.0	51.4	185.9	84.3	374.7	626.9	6.2	276.3
2020	183.3	55.6	193.3	85.7	386.1	643.4	6.6	291.3
2021	186.6	57.0	202.8	69.5	397.1	660.1	6.9	319.1
2022	196.3	62.0	213.3	71.8	402.5	662.9	7.3	324.4
2023	206.1	68.5	221.5	73.5	408.3	665.6	7.7	307.4

21-8 各级各类教育毕业生情况
Number of Graduates of Formal Education by Type and Level

单位：万人 (10 000 persons)

年 份 Year	研究生 Post-Graduates	普通、职业本专科 Undergraduate in Regular and Vocational HEIs	#专科 Short-cycle Courses	普通高中 Regular Senior Secondary Schools	中等职业教育 Secondary Vocational Education	初中阶段 Junior Secondary Education	小学阶段 Primary Education	特殊教育 Special Education	学前教育 Pre-school Education
1978	0.0	16.5	0.8	682.7	40.3	1692.6	2287.9	0.3	
1980	0.0	14.7		616.2	73.3	964.8	2053.3	0.4	
1985	1.7	31.6	14.4	196.6	92.5	1007.2	1999.9	0.4	
1990	3.5	61.4	30.6	233.0	240.6	1123.0	1863.1	0.5	
1995	3.2	80.5	48.0	201.6	348.4	1244.4	1961.5	1.9	
2000	5.9	95.0	17.9	301.5	476.7	1633.5	2419.2	4.3	
2001	6.8	103.6	19.3	340.5	430.6	1731.5	2396.9	4.6	1160.2
2002	8.1	133.7	27.7	383.8	380.1	1903.7	2351.9	4.4	1152.7
2003	11.1	187.7	94.8	458.1	346.4	2018.5	2267.9	4.5	1072.0
2004	15.1	239.1	119.5	546.9	359.2	2087.3	2135.2	4.7	1059.7
2005	19.0	306.8	160.2	661.6	418.2	2123.4	2019.5	4.3	1025.4
2006	25.6	377.5	204.8	727.1	479.1	2071.6	1928.5	4.5	1045.1
2007	31.2	447.8	248.2	788.3	530.9	1963.7	1870.2	5.0	1049.1
2008	34.5	511.9	286.3	836.1	580.7	1868.0	1865.0	5.2	1040.5
2009	37.1	531.1	285.6	823.7	624.9	1797.7	1805.2	5.7	1040.6
2010	38.4	575.4	316.4	794.4	665.0	1750.4	1739.6	5.9	1057.6
2011	43.0	608.2	328.5	787.7	660.0	1736.7	1662.8	4.4	1184.7
2012	48.6	624.7	320.9	791.5	674.6	1660.8	1641.6	4.9	1433.6
2013	51.4	638.7	318.7	799.0	674.4	1561.5	1581.1	5.1	1491.7
2014	53.6	659.4	318.0	799.6	622.9	1413.5	1476.6	4.9	1527.2
2015	55.2	680.9	322.3	797.7	567.9	1417.6	1437.3	5.3	1590.3
2016	56.4	704.2	329.8	792.4	533.6	1423.9	1507.4	5.9	1623.2
2017	57.8	735.8	351.6	775.7	496.9	1397.5	1565.9	6.9	1652.7
2018	60.4	753.3	366.5	779.2	487.3	1367.8	1616.5	8.1	1790.6
2019	64.0	758.5	363.8	789.2	493.5	1454.1	1647.9	9.8	1765.2
2020	72.9	797.2	376.7	786.5	484.9	1535.3	1640.3	12.1	1779.4
2021	77.3	826.5	398.4	780.2	375.4	1587.1	1718.0	14.6	1714.8
2022	86.2	967.3	494.8	824.1	399.3	1623.9	1740.6	15.9	1678.3
2023	101.5	1047.0	553.3	860.4	415.5	1623.6	1763.5	17.3	1804.4

21-9 各级各类教育招生情况
Number of Entrants of Formal Education by Type and Level

单位：万人　　(10 000 persons)

年 份 Year	研究生 Post-Graduates	普通、职业本专科 Undergraduate in Regular and Vocational HEIs	#专科 Short-cycle Courses	普通高中 Regular Senior Secondary Schools	中等职业教育 Secondary Vocational Education	初中阶段 Junior Secondary Education	小学阶段 Primary Education	特殊教育 Special Education	学前教育 Pre-school Education
1978	1.1	40.2	12.4	692.9	44.7	2006.0	3315.4	0.6	
1980	0.4	28.1	7.7	383.4	58.3	1557.6	2942.3	0.6	
1985	4.7	61.9	30.2	257.5	234.2	1367.0	2298.2	0.9	
1990	3.0	60.9	29.2	249.8	286.1	1389.3	2064.0	1.6	
1995	5.1	92.6	47.8	273.6	498.6	1781.1	2531.8	5.6	1972.4
2000	12.8	220.6	48.7	472.7	408.3	2295.6	1946.5	5.3	1531.1
2001	16.5	268.3	66.6	558.0	399.9	2287.9	1944.2	5.6	1398.2
2002	20.3	320.5	89.1	676.7	473.6	2281.8	1952.8	5.3	1373.6
2003	26.9	382.2	199.6	752.1	515.8	2220.1	1829.4	4.9	1316.8
2004	32.6	447.3	237.4	821.5	566.2	2094.6	1747.0	5.1	1350.3
2005	36.5	504.5	268.1	877.7	655.7	1987.6	1671.7	4.9	1356.2
2006	39.8	546.1	293.0	871.2	747.8	1929.5	1729.4	5.0	1391.3
2007	41.9	565.9	283.8	840.2	810.0	1868.5	1736.1	6.3	1433.6
2008	44.6	607.7	310.6	837.0	812.1	1859.6	1695.7	6.2	1482.7
2009	51.1	639.5	313.4	830.3	868.2	1788.5	1637.8	6.4	1546.9
2010	53.8	661.8	310.5	836.2	870.4	1716.6	1691.7	6.5	1700.4
2011	56.0	681.5	324.9	850.8	813.9	1634.7	1736.8	6.4	1827.3
2012	59.0	688.8	314.8	844.6	754.1	1570.8	1714.7	6.6	1911.9
2013	61.1	699.8	318.4	822.7	674.8	1496.1	1695.4	6.6	1970.0
2014	62.1	721.4	338.0	796.6	619.8	1447.8	1658.4	7.1	1987.8
2015	64.5	737.8	348.4	796.6	601.2	1411.0	1729.0	8.3	2008.8
2016	66.7	748.6	343.2	802.9	593.3	1487.2	1752.5	9.2	1922.1
2017	80.6	761.5	350.7	800.1	582.4	1547.2	1766.6	11.1	1938.0
2018	85.8	791.0	368.8	792.7	557.0	1602.6	1867.3	12.4	1863.9
2019	91.7	914.9	483.6	839.5	600.4	1638.8	1869.0	14.4	1688.2
2020	110.7	967.5	524.3	876.4	644.7	1632.1	1808.1	14.9	1791.4
2021	117.7	1001.3	552.6	905.0	489.0	1705.4	1782.6	14.9	1526.2
2022	124.2	1014.5	539.0	947.5	484.8	1731.4	1701.4	14.6	1360.4
2023	130.2	1042.2	555.1	967.8	454.0	1754.6	1877.9	15.5	1181.2

21-10 各级各类教育在校生情况
Number of Enrolments of Formal Education by Type and Level

单位：万人 (10 000 persons)

年 份 Year	研究生 Post-Graduates	普通、职业本专科 Undergraduate in Regular and Vocational HEIs	#专科 Short-cycle Courses	普通高中 Regular Senior Secondary Schools	中等职业教育 Secondary Vocational Education	初中阶段 Junior Secondary Education	小学阶段 Primary Education	特殊教育 Special Education	学前教育 Pre-school Education
1978	1.1	85.6	38.0	1553.1	212.8	4995.2	14624.0	3.1	787.7
1980	2.2	114.4	28.2	969.8	586.3	4551.8	14627.0	3.3	1150.8
1985	8.7	170.3	58.0	741.1	476.1	4010.1	13370.2	4.2	1479.7
1990	9.3	206.3	74.3	717.3	763.5	3916.6	12241.4	7.2	1972.2
1995	14.5	290.6	126.8	713.2	1230.2	4727.5	13195.2	29.6	2711.2
2000	30.1	556.1	100.9	1201.3	1284.5	6256.3	13013.3	37.8	2244.2
2001	39.3	719.1	146.8	1405.0	1164.9	6514.4	12543.5	38.6	2021.8
2002	50.1	903.4	193.4	1683.8	1190.8	6687.4	12156.7	37.5	2036.0
2003	65.1	1108.6	479.4	1964.8	1256.7	6690.8	11689.7	36.5	2003.9
2004	82.0	1333.5	595.7	2220.4	1409.2	6527.5	11246.2	37.2	2089.4
2005	97.9	1561.8	713.0	2409.1	1600.0	6214.9	10864.1	36.4	2179.0
2006	110.5	1738.8	795.5	2514.5	1809.9	5957.9	10711.5	36.3	2263.9
2007	119.5	1884.9	860.6	2522.4	1987.0	5736.2	10564.0	41.9	2348.8
2008	128.3	2021.0	916.8	2476.3	2087.1	5585.0	10331.5	41.7	2475.0
2009	140.5	2144.7	964.8	2434.3	2195.2	5440.9	10071.5	42.8	2657.8
2010	153.8	2231.8	966.2	2427.3	2238.5	5279.3	9940.7	42.6	2976.7
2011	164.6	2308.5	958.9	2454.8	2205.3	5066.8	9926.4	39.9	3424.5
2012	172.0	2391.3	964.2	2467.2	2113.7	4763.1	9695.9	37.9	3685.8
2013	179.4	2468.1	973.6	2435.9	1923.0	4440.1	9360.5	36.8	3894.7
2014	184.8	2547.7	1006.6	2400.5	1755.3	4384.6	9451.1	39.5	4050.7
2015	191.1	2625.3	1048.6	2374.4	1656.7	4312.0	9692.2	44.2	4264.8
2016	198.1	2695.8	1082.9	2366.6	1599.0	4329.4	9913.0	49.2	4413.9
2017	264.0	2753.6	1105.0	2374.5	1592.5	4442.1	10093.7	57.9	4600.1
2018	273.1	2831.0	1133.7	2375.4	1555.3	4652.6	10339.3	66.6	4656.4
2019	286.4	3031.5	1280.7	2414.3	1576.5	4827.1	10561.2	79.5	4713.9
2020	314.0	3285.3	1459.5	2494.5	1663.4	4914.1	10725.4	88.1	4818.3
2021	333.2	3496.1	1590.1	2605.0	1311.8	5018.4	10779.9	92.0	4805.2
2022	365.4	3659.4	1670.9	2713.9	1339.3	5120.6	10732.1	91.9	4627.5
2023	388.3	3775.0	1707.9	2803.6	1298.5	5243.7	10836.0	91.2	4093.0

21-11 技工学校情况
Statistics on Skilled Workers Schools

年 份 Year	学校数 (所) Schools (unit)	教职工数 (万人) Educational Personnel (10 000 persons)	毕业生数 (万人) Graduates (10 000 persons)	招生数 (万人) Entrants (10 000 persons)	在校生数 (万人) Enrolment (10 000 persons)
1985	3548	21.5	22.6	35.5	74.2
1986	3765	24.4	23.3	39.4	89.2
1987	3952	26.2	26.5	42.3	103.1
1988	3996	28.0	31.1	46.1	116.1
1989	4102	29.6	36.8	47.0	125.8
1990	4184	30.8	41.3	50.6	133.2
1991	4269	32.5	45.4	54.4	142.2
1992	4392	33.6	45.7	60.2	155.6
1993	4477	33.5	49.7	66.4	171.7
1994	4430	34.0	55.7	71.4	187.1
1995	4521	33.7	68.5	74.6	189.0
1996	4467	33.5	68.1	72.7	191.8
1997	4395	31.0	69.9	73.4	193.1
1998	4362	31.0	68.2	59.4	181.3
1999	4098	26.9	66.2	51.5	156.0
2000	3792	24.0	64.6	50.4	140.1
2001	3470	22.0	47.7	55.1	134.7
2002	3075	20.3	45.4	73.3	153.0
2003	2970	20.2	45.3	91.6	193.1
2004	2884	20.4	53.5	109.7	234.4
2005	2855	20.4	69.0	118.4	275.3
2006	2880	21.5	86.4	134.8	320.8
2007	2995	24.0	99.7	158.5	367.1
2008	3075	24.7	109.0	161.4	397.5
2009	3064	25.8	115.2	156.4	414.3
2010	2998	26.5	121.3	158.6	421.0
2011	2914	26.5	118.9	163.5	429.4
2012	2892	26.7	120.2	156.8	422.8
2013	2882	26.9	116.9	133.5	386.6
2014	2818	26.5	106.8	124.4	339.0
2015	2545	26.0	94.6	121.4	321.5
2016	2526	26.5	93.1	127.2	323.2
2017	2490	26.9	90.5	130.9	338.2
2018	2379	26.7	90.3	128.5	341.6
2019	2392	27.2	98.4	143.0	360.3
2020	2423	27.9	101.4	160.1	395.5
2021	2492	29.8	108.7	167.2	426.7
2022	2551	31.3	120.0	166.0	445.4
2023	2468	30.0	121.7	162.5	439.5

21-12 进城务工人员子女和农村留守儿童在校情况（2023年）
Statistics on Children of Migrant Workers and Rural Left Behind Children in Schools (2023)

单位：人 (person)

项 目	Item	进城务工人员随迁子女 Children of Migrant Workers	外省迁入 From Other Provinces	本省外县迁入 From Other Counties of the Same Province	农村留守儿童 Rural Left-Behind Children
普通小学	**Regular Primary Schools**				
毕业生数	Graduates	1522476	653241	869235	1118451
招生数	Entrants	1529258	628344	900914	795246
在校生数	Enrolment	9526484	4009995	5516489	6078723
#女	Female	4364155	1821255	2542900	2808250
初中	**Junior Secondary Schools**				
毕业生数	Graduates	1162268	456411	705857	1216860
招生数	Entrants	1355916	553542	802374	1191945
在校生数	Enrolment	4013377	1613364	2400013	3742758
#女	Female	1807730	716481	1091249	1731130

21-13 义务教育巩固率、高中阶段和高等教育毛入学率
Consolidation Rate of Compulsory Education, Gross Enrollment Rate of High School Education and Higher Education

单位：%　　(%)

年 份 Year	九年义务教育巩固率 Consolidation Rate of 9-year Compulsory Education	高中阶段毛入学率 Gross Enrollment Rate of High School Education	高等教育毛入学率 Gross Enrollment Rate of Higher Education
1995		33.6	7.2
1996		38.0	8.3
1997		40.6	9.1
1998		40.7	9.8
1999		41.0	10.5
2000		42.8	12.5
2001		42.8	13.3
2002		42.8	15.0
2003		43.8	17.0
2004		48.1	19.0
2005		52.7	21.0
2006		59.8	22.0
2007		66.0	23.0
2008		74.0	23.3
2009		79.2	24.2
2010	91.1	82.5	26.5
2011	91.5	84.0	26.9
2012	91.8	85.0	30.0
2013	92.3	86.0	34.5
2014	92.6	86.5	37.5
2015	93.0	87.0	40.0
2016	93.4	87.5	42.7
2017	93.8	88.3	45.7
2018	94.2	88.8	48.1
2019	94.8	89.5	51.6
2020	95.2	91.2	54.4
2021	95.4	91.4	57.8
2022	95.5	91.6	59.6
2023	95.7	91.8	60.2

21-14 分地区普通、职业本专科学生情况（2023年）
Number of Students Enrolled in Normal and Short-cycle Courses in Regular and Vocational Higher Education Institutions by Region (2023)

单位：人 (person)

地 区	Region	招生数 Entrants	普通本科 Undergraduates	职业本科 Vocational Undergraduates	专科 Short-cycle Courses	在校生数 Enrolment	普通本科 Undergraduates	职业本科 Vocational Undergraduates	专科 Short-cycle Courses
全 国	**National Total**	**10422206**	**4781609**	**89899**	**5550698**	**37750146**	**20346933**	**324692**	**17078521**
北 京	Beijing	172852	144457		28395	644532	568295		76237
天 津	Tianjin	164836	94514		70322	596569	380429		216140
河 北	Hebei	524442	233553	8863	282026	1839836	985569	18085	836182
山 西	Shanxi	239418	125285	6255	107878	962859	550715	22436	389708
内蒙古	Inner Mongolia	141705	65375		76330	540063	293820		246243
辽 宁	Liaoning	313324	184841	1670	126813	1153492	774231	5977	373284
吉 林	Jilin	212078	132373		79705	821534	542597		278937
黑龙江	Heilongjiang	260643	143488		117155	935330	601630		333700
上 海	Shanghai	152689	104537	2344	45808	572443	424483	6012	141948
江 苏	Jiangsu	631910	306815	4299	320796	2299046	1277612	13365	1008069
浙 江	Zhejiang	328579	171681	4806	152092	1291463	731380	16356	543727
安 徽	Anhui	421044	184840		236204	1579570	787849		791721
福 建	Fujian	314836	139086	2573	173177	1139877	598927	10831	530119
江 西	Jiangxi	450383	180195	7360	262828	1546344	739124	25206	782014
山 东	Shandong	748512	286097	9603	452812	2672548	1259763	41585	1371200
河 南	Henan	846824	326198	4370	516256	2956157	1428713	17103	1510341
湖 北	Hubei	522296	240098		282198	1839906	1030857		809049
湖 南	Hunan	531206	230573	1709	298924	1778008	913956	3739	860313
广 东	Guangdong	739429	311217	7945	420267	2601372	1375855	30376	1195141
广 西	Guangxi	422744	153574	7258	261912	1483170	659755	30790	792625
海 南	Hainan	77228	31913	2514	42801	272595	133821	13648	125126
重 庆	Chongqing	282960	123062	3561	156337	1100170	550830	13788	535552
四 川	Sichuan	606744	266344	2680	337720	2164130	1142291	10337	1011502
贵 州	Guizhou	259468	92503	2457	164508	907193	411369	7532	488292
云 南	Yunnan	292734	126150		166584	1137073	567069		570004
西 藏	Xizang	11367	7479		3888	43092	30574		12518
陕 西	Shaanxi	339759	184320	3971	151468	1316232	792256	15197	508779
甘 肃	Gansu	162317	78598	3666	80053	662493	338906	15000	308587
青 海	Qinghai	24649	12270		12379	82765	48758		34007
宁 夏	Ningxia	44423	26198		18225	177330	107224		70106
新 疆	Xinjiang	180807	73975	1995	104837	632954	298275	7329	327350

21-14 续表 continued

单位：人 (person)

地区	Region	毕业生数 Graduates	普通本科 Under-graduates	职业本科 Vocational Undergraduates	专科 Short-cycle Courses	授予学位数 Degrees Conferred	预计毕业生数 Estimated Graduates	普通本科 Under-graduates	职业本科 Vocational Undergraduates	专科 Short-cycle Courses
全国	**National Total**	**10470258**	**4897422**	**39924**	**5532912**	**4919700**	**11002391**	**5288254**	**71120**	**5643017**
北京	Beijing	158866	135534		23332	135869	168010	142743		25267
天津	Tianjin	168571	91377		77194	91474	169730	96991		72739
河北	Hebei	508940	243685		265255	243229	528934	256061		272873
山西	Shanxi	263140	138436		124704	137718	281714	146862	2856	131996
内蒙古	Inner Mongolia	151077	74608		76469	74409	165357	79532		85825
辽宁	Liaoning	369127	182360	35	186732	182135	320015	198216	2001	119798
吉林	Jilin	203922	130255		73667	129977	232515	139140		93375
黑龙江	Heilongjiang	254642	144972		109670	144672	266686	152703		113983
上海	Shanghai	148421	98285	107	50029	97676	159211	110457	654	48100
江苏	Jiangsu	630104	304220	1327	324557	302851	650347	323540	2601	324206
浙江	Zhejiang	358969	174640	311	184018	174122	389133	192314	3157	193662
安徽	Anhui	449901	195681		254220	194825	509414	203231		306183
福建	Fujian	297789	143409	1997	152383	145140	328408	156271	2783	169354
江西	Jiangxi	422680	174979	4173	243528	178110	435404	185526	5288	244590
山东	Shandong	745225	321685	6377	417163	329003	783183	336487	11861	434835
河南	Henan	832925	349800	3002	480123	352620	889059	379838	5184	504037
湖北	Hubei	504940	255222		249718	253300	522078	269401		252677
湖南	Hunan	462819	204927		257892	203794	479096	219784	327	258985
广东	Guangdong	860826	329217	6509	525100	336173	768656	364517	9351	394788
广西	Guangxi	369168	154815	3911	210442	157807	441013	176847	6431	257735
海南	Hainan	74291	32060	3200	39031	34722	74891	34679	4064	36148
重庆	Chongqing	299414	132447	2916	164051	134881	330313	148187	3145	178981
四川	Sichuan	552236	265688	2186	284362	267795	607721	297077	2859	307785
贵州	Guizhou	252900	105794		147106	104606	271853	111283		160570
云南	Yunnan	322518	136288		186230	135726	355176	154302		200874
西藏	Xizang	11632	6851		4781	6741	11138	7505		3633
陕西	Shaanxi	374774	188126	2997	183651	189651	402316	208790	3870	189656
甘肃	Gansu	189459	84330		105129	83878	196593	87653	2920	106020
青海	Qinghai	22194	11402		10792	11336	21836	10603		11233
宁夏	Ningxia	45232	23688		21544	23479	55796	26642		29154
新疆	Xinjiang	163556	62641	876	100039	61981	186795	71072	1768	113955

21-15 分地区普通、职业高等学校情况（2023年）
Statistics on Regular and Vocational Higher Education Institutions by Region (2023)

单位：人 (person)

地 区	Region	学校数(所) Institutions (unit)	教职工数 Educational Personnel	#专任教师 Full-time Teachers	正高级 Senior	副高级 Sub-senior	中级 Middle	初级 Junior	未定职级 No Rank	#行政人员 Administrative Personnel	#教辅人员 Supporting Staff	#工勤人员 Workers
全 国	**National Total**	**2822**	**2919989**	**2060893**	**255618**	**591427**	**757964**	**240974**	**214910**	**400555**	**239994**	**109618**
北 京	Beijing	92	160678	77202	22523	28847	21873	1852	2107	29830	20167	10414
天 津	Tianjin	56	49937	34599	5152	10918	13954	3096	1479	8671	4562	1114
河 北	Hebei	128	131186	98699	10731	26934	38158	9556	13320	16058	8762	5642
山 西	Shanxi	83	64510	44317	3240	12499	18929	6812	2837	8260	6621	2562
内蒙古	Inner Mongolia	54	42764	28804	3544	9299	11682	2019	2260	7142	3994	1492
辽 宁	Liaoning	114	98659	66049	9996	21460	27034	4754	2805	16773	10253	3835
吉 林	Jilin	66	57761	37871	6662	12654	13466	3978	1111	10531	5818	2718
黑龙江	Heilongjiang	78	76309	51527	8657	16670	18095	4582	3523	12253	6098	4073
上 海	Shanghai	68	87554	51328	10365	16761	19104	3392	1706	16534	11956	2496
江 苏	Jiangsu	168	183446	130368	19309	43350	49071	10842	7796	27296	14635	5125
浙 江	Zhejiang	109	118588	82525	12254	22722	34135	6590	6824	18661	10081	1908
安 徽	Anhui	121	103214	80581	8154	21249	29342	12576	9260	10763	5730	3090
福 建	Fujian	89	84281	59277	6807	17978	20606	8635	5251	13766	6512	2332
江 西	Jiangxi	109	101588	77858	5719	17779	27230	11760	15370	8800	9764	3056
山 东	Shandong	156	189835	144793	15709	42773	55857	20597	9857	21446	14791	3959
河 南	Henan	168	196143	152847	10484	36653	58645	28934	18131	19835	9149	8288
湖 北	Hubei	132	147270	100063	13830	32762	33052	10801	9618	21661	14540	6266
湖 南	Hunan	137	120418	89820	9872	24950	35426	7951	11621	14182	8710	4262
广 东	Guangdong	162	205665	143477	16926	36129	52583	14795	23044	27702	16618	7148
广 西	Guangxi	87	87675	65973	6310	16717	24033	3947	14966	11685	5734	3769
海 南	Hainan	22	21334	14425	1734	3968	4947	1486	2290	2987	2028	1477
重 庆	Chongqing	72	78289	60407	6720	16168	23429	7008	7082	9574	4139	2041
四 川	Sichuan	137	155115	110182	10934	27378	40010	21171	10689	18980	11385	6650
贵 州	Guizhou	77	60400	46145	4550	13008	14595	6243	7749	7373	4367	1917
云 南	Yunnan	88	65386	47349	4804	12831	16138	7095	6481	8473	5058	3310
西 藏	Xizang	7	4084	2937	410	855	1110	450	112	634	235	153
陕 西	Shaanxi	97	115463	80981	11099	25906	28670	9083	6223	17156	9981	3973
甘 肃	Gansu	50	47346	35952	4848	11445	12383	4495	2781	5087	2832	1583
青 海	Qinghai	12	8410	5119	665	1494	1594	752	614	1384	788	812
宁 夏	Ningxia	21	13313	9509	1338	2639	2982	1747	803	2070	1006	350
新 疆	Xinjiang	62	43368	29909	2272	6631	9831	3975	7200	4988	3680	3803

21-16 分地区普通高中情况（2023年）
Statistics on Regular Senior Secondary Schools by Region (2023)

单位：人 (person)

地区	Region	学校数(所) Schools (unit)	教职工数 Educational Personnel	#专任教师 Full-time Teachers	毕业生数 Graduates	招生数 Entrants	在校生数 Enrolment
全国	**National Total**	**15381**	**3319638**	**2214804**	**8604097**	**9678010**	**28036268**
北京	Beijing	363	71689	23786	59193	79716	216891
天津	Tianjin	205	36054	18863	67176	78985	221427
河北	Hebei	818	209191	143188	556851	629833	1826292
山西	Shanxi	510	105468	65051	221425	211836	677700
内蒙古	Inner Mongolia	318	63150	42117	142561	145856	428434
辽宁	Liaoning	436	68673	54714	202603	208373	621038
吉林	Jilin	265	47893	35391	147922	138568	436985
黑龙江	Heilongjiang	365	59069	45532	191950	168106	544476
上海	Shanghai	294	39288	21236	59074	75519	207861
江苏	Jiangsu	664	163582	128075	414857	505021	1431830
浙江	Zhejiang	650	104573	79897	277867	307946	887644
安徽	Anhui	676	132039	92196	387947	423931	1232813
福建	Fujian	598	125444	61391	219650	289859	803669
江西	Jiangxi	568	128488	87550	380301	402305	1222717
山东	Shandong	782	204610	166895	611440	715743	1985425
河南	Henan	1098	249834	193068	774723	900599	2622690
湖北	Hubei	577	107595	80325	313514	369665	1058079
湖南	Hunan	750	144332	106416	440247	502641	1473029
广东	Guangdong	1165	319755	172114	664568	784251	2228677
广西	Guangxi	548	126383	88451	394734	445026	1291996
海南	Hainan	142	36369	16574	64063	75550	215363
重庆	Chongqing	280	83297	45327	214581	231430	678960
四川	Sichuan	817	212412	115660	470064	510643	1500614
贵州	Guizhou	505	101204	72889	318658	326917	944983
云南	Yunnan	650	119497	77280	336112	372271	1063293
西藏	Xizang	40	9678	6965	25244	26710	79427
陕西	Shaanxi	445	88559	58595	211239	256682	721635
甘肃	Gansu	368	64568	48361	171028	178684	529748
青海	Qinghai	101	14915	10698	43261	45726	134532
宁夏	Ningxia	70	15878	13302	56270	58154	173608
新疆	Xinjiang	313	66151	42897	164974	211464	574432

21－17 分地区中等职业教育情况（2023年）
Statistics on Secondary Vocational Education by Region (2023)

单位：人 (person)

地 区	Region	学校数（所）Schools (unit)	教职工数 Educational Personnel	#专任教师 Full-time Teachers	毕业生数 Graduates	招生数 Entrants	在校生数 Enrolment	预计毕业生数 Estimated Graduates for Next Year
全 国	**National**	**7085**	**864900**	**734842**	**4154521**	**4540352**	**12984621**	**4212849**
北 京	Beijing	76	8128	5703	15527	20637	58508	15931
天 津	Tianjin	59	7209	5366	30262	27969	82710	28188
河 北	Hebei	628	69494	58440	315575	318570	892031	325261
山 西	Shanxi	337	31820	26316	104653	109521	330986	113710
内蒙古	Inner Mongolia	171	18064	14620	57881	65247	186579	61388
辽 宁	Liaoning	264	26235	20514	87543	86470	265921	86441
吉 林	Jilin	213	17594	13280	42502	35641	123115	46874
黑龙江	Heilongjiang	183	15542	12159	55712	44248	158467	57430
上 海	Shanghai	76	10224	7658	41624	39476	107747	34997
江 苏	Jiangsu	211	54331	47512	208127	232065	679094	221587
浙 江	Zhejiang	246	42764	39058	184148	167860	502536	173769
安 徽	Anhui	245	35244	31539	248619	246578	659728	224580
福 建	Fujian	167	23250	20536	116258	142531	409032	129581
江 西	Jiangxi	272	28009	23962	163273	162487	533712	187760
山 东	Shandong	413	66107	59389	290260	300762	882941	285878
河 南	Henan	546	61413	55777	379808	381896	1119505	390225
湖 北	Hubei	252	28817	23880	141791	139507	425182	146666
湖 南	Hunan	497	46354	40428	226885	230421	703675	236363
广 东	Guangdong	372	59122	47182	277277	336508	965071	300955
广 西	Guangxi	241	28330	21547	161201	195407	510918	148676
海 南	Hainan	57	5193	3890	36841	47092	131330	41694
重 庆	Chongqing	129	22140	19826	113077	130888	378800	120466
四 川	Sichuan	341	52626	45091	283033	299764	867123	289568
贵 州	Guizhou	184	21138	17789	105322	309014	687403	126024
云 南	Yunnan	293	21066	18898	190339	146282	392245	138876
西 藏	Xizang	13	3317	2528	9261	10805	31947	10943
陕 西	Shaanxi	228	23123	18995	89485	101629	305390	95040
甘 肃	Gansu	177	15961	13585	51561	65069	181352	47830
青 海	Qinghai	30	2777	2392	27631	31174	86864	22313
宁 夏	Ningxia	31	4297	3781	22641	24556	76090	24289
新 疆	Xinjiang	133	15211	13201	76404	90278	248619	79546

21-18 分地区初中情况（2023年）
Statistics on Junior Secondary Schools by Region (2023)

单位：人 (person)

地 区	Region	初中学校数（所）Junior Secondary Schools (unit)	初中阶段专任教师数 Full-time Teachers in Junior Secondary Schools	城区 City	镇区 Township	乡村 Rural	初中阶段在校生数 Enrolment in Junior Secondary Schools	城区 City	镇区 Township	乡村 Rural
全 国	**National Total**	**52348**	**4083058**	**1689924**	**1897107**	**496027**	**52436916**	**22273999**	**24412633**	**5750284**
北 京	Beijing	324	40382	34051	3329	3002	370920	326593	23572	20755
天 津	Tianjin	346	31754	23848	5504	2402	381796	296025	60740	25031
河 北	Hebei	2525	244726	77453	130988	36285	3332508	1078481	1778750	475277
山 西	Shanxi	1346	103536	44447	47662	11427	1121739	536950	480708	104081
内蒙古	Inner Mongolia	715	65005	26097	34674	4234	663109	298323	331844	32942
辽 宁	Liaoning	1529	98482	56500	31945	10037	932323	595240	262040	75043
吉 林	Jilin	1183	65229	27559	25827	11843	590957	299635	222190	69132
黑龙江	Heilongjiang	1398	82764	37862	35293	9609	792899	427683	310038	55178
上 海	Shanghai	606	48642	43614	4029	999	567211	517623	40246	9342
江 苏	Jiangsu	2336	232510	121447	102385	8678	2772879	1438377	1243542	90960
浙 江	Zhejiang	1794	138107	81976	48000	8131	1734735	1046512	594543	93680
安 徽	Anhui	2763	169734	49244	93171	27319	2312674	694762	1290638	327274
福 建	Fujian	1281	118095	51424	51117	15554	1577017	739274	669253	168490
江 西	Jiangxi	2249	155780	52090	80480	23210	2080579	734053	1079899	266627
山 东	Shandong	3327	315640	144784	145330	25526	4003470	1872940	1828567	301963
河 南	Henan	4626	366068	102924	199613	63531	5081295	1506094	2790630	784571
湖 北	Hubei	2176	146365	69801	62639	13925	1882355	921499	798458	162398
湖 南	Hunan	3390	202032	64480	107886	29666	2707785	915712	1465336	326737
广 东	Guangdong	3945	341084	202760	108341	29983	4766647	2800753	1560582	405312
广 西	Guangxi	1764	165963	51952	96273	17738	2455916	775315	1442254	238347
海 南	Hainan	396	31876	13815	13715	4346	415652	186869	177315	51468
重 庆	Chongqing	843	84572	42476	35038	7058	1046154	566343	398619	81192
四 川	Sichuan	3233	224090	82304	117719	24067	2755193	1085040	1428325	241828
贵 州	Guizhou	1870	134816	38792	79553	16471	1974519	580215	1168566	225738
云 南	Yunnan	1708	138805	33708	70252	34845	1886645	463760	964634	458251
西 藏	Xizang	106	13143	3604	7126	2413	157638	43907	83335	30396
陕 西	Shaanxi	1666	109552	47364	53703	8485	1352382	661239	607419	83724
甘 肃	Gansu	1437	83961	22076	48911	12974	951952	281311	561353	109288
青 海	Qinghai	263	17198	5747	8336	3115	237475	78969	117470	41036
宁 夏	Ningxia	254	21430	9362	9530	2538	289410	133718	126446	29246
新 疆	Xinjiang	949	91717	26363	38738	26616	1241082	370784	505321	364977

21－19 分地区小学情况（2023年）
Statistics on Primary Schools by Region (2023)

单位：人 (person)

地区	Region	普通小学数（所） Regular Primary Schools (unit)	小学阶段专任教师数 Full-time Teachers in Primary Schools	城区 City	镇区 Township	乡村 Rural	小学阶段在校生数 Enrolment in Primary Schools	城区 City	镇区 Township	乡村 Rural
全 国	**National Total**	**143472**	**6656261**	**2752411**	**2446562**	**1457288**	**108360253**	**49685145**	**40288637**	**18386471**
北 京	Beijing	714	78879	67542	6028	5309	1161797	1023993	75650	62154
天 津	Tianjin	873	51484	40246	4986	6252	818370	676704	72424	69242
河 北	Hebei	11313	405702	119768	162876	123058	6531750	2230890	2679538	1621322
山 西	Shanxi	3805	166104	67894	67121	31089	2318407	1182376	913087	222944
内蒙古	Inner Mongolia	1635	112055	40810	53552	17693	1408425	656837	630460	121128
辽 宁	Liaoning	2320	139545	80148	38947	20450	1993743	1433195	403991	156557
吉 林	Jilin	1574	98251	39518	35958	22775	1095277	579509	408646	107122
黑龙江	Heilongjiang	1315	94994	43400	38808	12786	1059686	627140	371238	61308
上 海	Shanghai	664	66965	60009	5813	1143	937129	843859	78618	14652
江 苏	Jiangsu	4009	364112	206486	137807	19819	5885320	3408397	2209708	267215
浙 江	Zhejiang	3144	238447	144211	72961	21275	4113670	2566490	1232096	315084
安 徽	Anhui	6218	268243	83551	120042	64650	4722273	1652766	2241948	827559
福 建	Fujian	4886	209007	93109	78998	36900	3697864	1761280	1438705	497879
江 西	Jiangxi	5830	238843	78805	106485	53553	3750629	1435198	1762726	552705
山 东	Shandong	8654	477406	217360	175130	84916	8120924	3965939	2989107	1165878
河 南	Henan	16429	601010	159628	248870	192512	9628783	3040171	4269731	2318881
湖 北	Hubei	5145	224303	107479	79248	37576	3895006	2035405	1392612	466989
湖 南	Hunan	6604	310354	107986	142482	59886	5184911	2027438	2471692	685781
广 东	Guangdong	10690	613411	369787	145383	98241	11105243	6922537	2725928	1456778
广 西	Guangxi	7858	301442	88969	108236	104237	5162921	1702526	1954520	1505875
海 南	Hainan	1294	58141	22510	20004	15627	870602	392424	310345	167833
重 庆	Chongqing	2567	134488	69599	44355	20534	2058660	1237916	640382	180362
四 川	Sichuan	5119	352007	135572	157031	59404	5490451	2424666	2365791	699994
贵 州	Guizhou	6156	217558	61369	96450	59739	3945252	1228653	1839785	876814
云 南	Yunnan	9913	232114	54280	71974	105860	3864564	1038408	1265290	1560866
西 藏	Xizang	825	26630	5210	7303	14117	383510	82888	103581	197041
陕 西	Shaanxi	4191	190664	87674	78625	24365	3031907	1613756	1188614	229537
甘 肃	Gansu	4465	152108	34886	68185	49037	2040393	631339	1003332	405722
青 海	Qinghai	698	29944	9009	11359	9576	520101	162642	209404	148055
宁 夏	Ningxia	1037	35872	14328	12469	9075	621276	289687	218428	113161
新 疆	Xinjiang	3527	166178	41268	49076	75834	2941409	810116	821260	1310033

21-20 分地区特殊教育情况（2023年）
Statistics on Special Education by Region (2023)

单位：人 (person)

地 区	Region	学校数（所）Schools (unit)	专任教师数 Full-time Teachers	毕业生数 Graduates	招生数 Entrants	在校生数 Enrolment	# 女 Female
全 国	**National Total**	**2345**	**77047**	**173140**	**154977**	**911981**	**331793**
北 京	Beijing	20	1121	1788	1296	7825	2620
天 津	Tianjin	20	689	743	583	4444	1516
河 北	Hebei	163	3865	6918	5127	37471	13934
山 西	Shanxi	88	2236	4312	3807	20123	7754
内蒙古	Inner Mongolia	54	2066	2638	2267	13465	5162
辽 宁	Liaoning	86	2340	2307	2181	15786	5433
吉 林	Jilin	54	1821	2264	1942	12279	4328
黑龙江	Heilongjiang	75	2327	2699	1599	14139	4986
上 海	Shanghai	31	1698	1870	1343	9315	3239
江 苏	Jiangsu	108	4190	7892	8283	45063	15267
浙 江	Zhejiang	87	3444	4777	5332	27069	9400
安 徽	Anhui	81	2393	6625	6821	42075	14814
福 建	Fujian	76	2843	5172	5502	30602	10107
江 西	Jiangxi	91	2313	8996	6663	37603	13334
山 东	Shandong	161	6856	10612	9554	54572	18997
河 南	Henan	153	4645	8814	10072	68332	26015
湖 北	Hubei	88	2170	4396	4151	28503	9546
湖 南	Hunan	98	3201	8244	7980	51740	17842
广 东	Guangdong	154	8099	12048	13657	76278	25193
广 西	Guangxi	95	2774	7608	7600	44154	15871
海 南	Hainan	17	568	1075	1136	6600	2054
重 庆	Chongqing	39	1189	5923	4453	25459	9665
四 川	Sichuan	138	3957	16877	12571	64055	24830
贵 州	Guizhou	78	2172	8298	7541	40692	15593
云 南	Yunnan	86	2592	10925	7849	44794	17912
西 藏	Xizang	7	328	1410	1347	7080	3363
陕 西	Shaanxi	81	1890	4301	2965	17935	6860
甘 肃	Gansu	47	1202	3658	3294	19789	7733
青 海	Qinghai	17	240	1838	1377	7446	3126
宁 夏	Ningxia	16	432	1899	1488	6811	2671
新 疆	Xinjiang	36	1386	6213	5196	30482	12628

21－21　各级教育生师比
Student-Teacher Ratio of Regular Education by Level

(教师人数=1)　　(number of teachers=1)

年　份 Year 地　区 Region		小学阶段 Primary Education	初中阶段 Junior Secondary Education	普通高中 Regular Senior Secondary Schools	中等职业教育 Secondary Vocational Education	高等教育 Higher Education
	2005	19.43	17.80	18.54	21.34	16.85
	2006	19.17	17.15	18.13	22.65	17.93
	2007	18.82	16.52	17.48	23.13	17.28
	2008	18.38	16.07	16.78	23.32	17.23
	2009	17.88	15.47	16.30	25.27	17.27
	2010	17.70	14.98	15.99	25.69	17.33
	2011	17.71	14.38	15.77	25.01	17.42
	2012	17.36	13.59	15.47	24.19	17.52
	2013	16.76	12.76	14.95	22.97	17.53
	2014	16.78	12.57	14.44	21.34	17.68
	2015	17.05	12.41	14.01	20.47	17.73
	2016	17.12	12.41	13.65	19.84	17.07
	2017	16.98	12.52	13.39	18.98	17.52
	2018	16.97	12.79	13.10	19.10	17.56
	2019	16.85	12.88	12.99	18.94	17.95
	2020	16.67	12.73	12.90	19.54	18.37
	2021	16.33	12.64	12.84	18.86	18.54
	2022	16.19	12.72	12.72	18.65	18.32
	2023	16.28	12.84	12.66	17.67	17.98
北　京	Beijing	14.73	9.19	9.12	10.26	15.98
天　津	Tianjin	15.90	12.02	11.74	15.41	18.04
河　北	Hebei	16.10	13.62	12.75	15.26	17.49
山　西	Shanxi	13.96	10.83	10.42	12.58	20.73
内蒙古	Inner Mongolia	12.57	10.20	10.17	12.76	17.78
辽　宁	Liaoning	14.29	9.47	11.35	12.96	18.53
吉　林	Jilin	11.15	9.06	12.35	9.27	20.45
黑龙江	Heilongjiang	11.16	9.58	11.96	13.03	17.54
上　海	Shanghai	13.99	11.66	9.79	14.07	15.17
江　苏	Jiangsu	16.16	11.93	11.18	14.29	16.65
浙　江	Zhejiang	17.25	12.56	11.11	12.87	15.78
安　徽	Anhui	17.60	13.63	13.37	20.92	18.88
福　建	Fujian	17.69	13.35	13.09	19.92	17.11
江　西	Jiangxi	15.70	13.36	13.97	22.27	18.21
山　东	Shandong	17.01	12.68	11.90	14.87	17.20
河　南	Henan	16.02	13.88	13.58	20.07	18.15
湖　北	Hubei	17.36	12.86	13.17	17.80	18.54
湖　南	Hunan	16.71	13.40	13.84	17.41	18.04
广　东	Guangdong	18.10	13.97	12.95	20.45	17.88
广　西	Guangxi	17.13	14.80	14.61	23.71	19.52
海　南	Hainan	14.97	13.04	12.99	33.76	18.17
重　庆	Chongqing	15.31	12.37	14.98	19.11	17.69
四　川	Sichuan	15.60	12.30	12.97	19.23	18.97
贵　州	Guizhou	18.13	14.65	12.96	38.64	18.27
云　南	Yunnan	16.65	13.59	13.76	20.76	21.44
西　藏	Xizang	14.40	11.99	11.40	12.64	17.49
陕　西	Shaanxi	15.90	12.34	12.32	16.08	18.23
甘　肃	Gansu	13.41	11.34	10.95	13.35	19.04
青　海	Qinghai	17.37	13.81	12.58	36.31	18.63
宁　夏	Ningxia	17.32	13.50	13.05	20.12	19.17
新　疆	Xinjiang	17.70	13.53	13.39	18.83	20.08

21−22 每十万人口各级教育平均在校生数
Average Education Enrolment per 100 000 Population by Level

单位：人 (person)

年份 Year / 地区 Region		学前教育 Pre-school Education	小学阶段 Primary Education	初中阶段 Junior Secondary Education	高中阶段 Senior Secondary Education	高等教育 Higher Education
	1990	1725	10707	3426	1337	326
	1995	2262	11010	3945	1610	457
	2000	1782	10335	4969	2000	723
	2005	1676	8358	4781	3070	1613
	2006	1731	8192	4557	3321	1816
	2007	1787	8037	4364	3409	1924
	2008	1873	7819	4227	3463	2042
	2009	2001	7584	4097	3495	2128
	2010	2230	7448	3955	3504	2189
	2011	2554	7403	3779	3495	2253
	2012	2736	7196	3535	3411	2335
	2013	2876	6913	3279	3227	2418
	2014	2977	6946	3222	3100	2488
	2015	3118	7086	3152	2965	2524
	2016	3211	7211	3150	2887	2530
	2017	3327	7300	3213	2861	2576
	2018	3350	7438	3347	2828	2658
	2019	3378	7569	3459	2850	2857
	2020	3441	7661	3510	2948	3126
	2021	3403	7634	3554	2774	3301
	2022	3276	7597	3625	2895	3510
	2023	2899	7676	3714	2906	3663
北 京	Beijing	2359	5320	1698	1261	5584
天 津	Tianjin	2128	6004	2801	2231	5559
河 北	Hebei	2688	8803	4491	3664	3190
山 西	Shanxi	2638	6660	3222	2898	3528
内蒙古	Inner Mongolia	2308	5866	2762	2561	2523
辽 宁	Liaoning	1737	4750	2221	2113	3963
吉 林	Jilin	1508	4665	2517	2385	5839
黑龙江	Heilongjiang	1244	3419	2559	2268	3817
上 海	Shanghai	1956	3786	2292	1275	3936
江 苏	Jiangsu	2465	6912	3256	2479	3845
浙 江	Zhejiang	2700	6255	2638	2122	2839
安 徽	Anhui	2943	7707	3775	3089	3469
福 建	Fujian	3234	8830	3766	2896	3462
江 西	Jiangxi	2925	8283	4595	3879	4510
山 东	Shandong	3023	7991	3939	2822	3909
河 南	Henan	3278	9754	5147	3791	3801
湖 北	Hubei	2657	6665	3221	2538	4483
湖 南	Hunan	2782	7851	4100	3296	3965
广 东	Guangdong	3623	8774	3766	2523	3144
广 西	Guangxi	3826	10230	4866	3572	3819
海 南	Hainan	3539	8477	4047	3376	3169
重 庆	Chongqing	2726	6407	3256	3292	4012
四 川	Sichuan	2765	6557	3290	2827	3278
贵 州	Guizhou	3968	10231	5121	4233	2641
云 南	Yunnan	3580	8235	4020	3102	3184
西 藏	Xizang	4180	10536	4331	3060	1612
陕 西	Shaanxi	3026	7664	3419	2596	4624
甘 肃	Gansu	3435	8188	3820	2854	3376
青 海	Qinghai	3425	8741	3991	3721	1813
宁 夏	Ningxia	3303	8534	3975	3430	3338
新 疆	Xinjiang	2774	11370	4797	3181	2956

注：1.高等教育在校生数包括研究生、普通本科、职业本专科、成人本专科，不含网络本专科生。
2.2021年起，高中阶段在校生数不含人社部管理的技工学校。

a) The number of students in higher education includes postgraduates, regular undergraduates, vocational undergraduates and adult undergraduates, excluding web-based undergraduates.

b) Since 2021, the number of students in Senior Secondary Education data do not include Technical Schools managed by the Ministry of Human Resources and Social Security.

21-23 教育经费情况
Basic Statistics on Educational Finance

单位：万元 (10 000 yuan)

年 份 Year 地 区 Region	合 计 Total	国家财政性教育经费 Government Appropriation for Education	#一般公共预算教育经费 General Public Budget Expenditure on Education	民办学校中举办者投入 Funds from Sponsors of Non-public Schools	捐 赠 收 入 Donation Revenues	事业收入 Income from Teaching Research and Other Auxiliary Activities	#学费 Tuition	其他教育经费 Other Educational Funds
1992	8670491	7287506	5649364		696285		439319	247380
1995	18779501	14115233	10929473	203672	1628414		2012423	819760
2000	38490806	25626056	21917652	858537	1139557	9382717	5948304	1483939
2005	84188391	51610759	49460379	4522185	931613	23399991	15530545	3723842
2006	98153087	63483648	61353481	5490583	899078	24073042	15523301	4206736
2007	121480663	82802142	80943369	809337	930584	31772357	21309082	5166242
2008	145007374	104496296	102129675	698479	1026663	33670711	23492983	5115225
2009	165027065	122310935	119749753	749829	1254991	35275939	25155983	5435371
2010	195618471	146700670	141639029	1054254	1078839	41060664	30155593	5724045
2011	238692936	185867009	178217380	1119320	1118675	44246927	33169742	6341005
2012	286553052	231475698	203141685	1281753	956919	46198404	35048301	6640278
2013	303647182	244882177	214056715	1474089	855445	49262087	37376869	7173384
2014	328064609	264205821	225760099	1313476	796700	54271581	40530393	7477031
2015	361291927	292214511	258618740	1876620	869960	58097239	43173611	8233597
2016	388883850	313962519	277006325	2032733	810447	62768292	47709339	9309860
2017	425620069	342077546	299197838	2250061	849974	69575734	52932815	10866754
2018	461429980	369957704	319927298	2406210	947574	77382499	58958343	10735993
2019	501781166	400465452	346485685	2201304	1013752	87235021	66863024	10865637
2020	530338681	429081543	363104728	2292516	1172355	87041177	67614302	10751091
2021	578736693	458353089	374633647	2423821	1426654	104575160	81306525	11957969
2022	613291382	484729094	392569627	1882765	1543121	108318215	84516216	16818187
中 央 Central Government	57787503	42422445	16816279		622611	11684144	4073421	3058303
地 方 Local Governments	555503878	442306649	375753347	1882765	920510	96634071	80442794	13759884
北 京 Beijing	15854348	13736713	11609960	9662	5577	1966234	1636322	136162
天 津 Tianjin	6565887	5392187	4748759	31159	5087	998910	837760	138544
河 北 Hebei	24395755	19640362	17546049	58758	103611	4346161	3710470	246864
山 西 Shanxi	12125465	10101087	8558450	25473	10271	1861448	1466243	127186
内蒙古 Inner Mongolia	9230537	8286826	6742091	34322	10875	795200	680318	103314
辽 宁 Liaoning	11674506	9225509	7431780	9533	5333	2264766	1833490	169365
吉 林 Jilin	7484068	6031448	4973524	11284	4452	1221906	1050908	214977
黑龙江 Heilongjiang	8806510	7386673	6146837	6059	2585	1197877	1023664	213315
上 海 Shanghai	16916927	13919603	10930909	2562	9464	2654225	2222669	331074
江 苏 Jiangsu	38820349	30682348	25443278	100757	166702	6328518	5239337	1542024
浙 江 Zhejiang	34440066	26041786	21825484	163150	70270	6772035	5374692	1392825
安 徽 Anhui	20532087	16580173	14200714	59545	5990	3368366	2779777	518013
福 建 Fujian	17625677	14198649	11967707	29330	93644	2932711	2469080	371343
江 西 Jiangxi	18915971	14987656	13171484	166329	15714	2948209	2368778	798063
山 东 Shandong	37144368	29500836	25969681	153760	49844	6711254	5658243	728675
河 南 Henan	29695708	22412360	18456526	238422	36165	6518768	5472555	489992
湖 北 Hubei	19405534	14726548	12797954	69891	27649	4087444	3422774	494001
湖 南 Hunan	22100519	16530549	15302896	58039	21580	4481740	3695088	1008611
广 东 Guangdong	61902003	45712767	38631327	259331	121423	14994003	13168894	814479
广 西 Guangxi	17038772	13618238	11411905	38290	7627	2968766	2366762	405851
海 南 Hainan	4833662	3862257	3062853	15986	297	891659	730855	63463
重 庆 Chongqing	13146996	10589502	8276631	33245	11111	2129341	1687112	383797
四 川 Sichuan	28294459	21693844	18562582	169136	42067	5300669	4382116	1088743
贵 州 Guizhou	15801330	13268794	11528125	48201	7653	2001255	1672599	475427
云 南 Yunnan	17068501	14383782	11587534	51251	38466	2313366	1950326	281636
西 藏 Xizang	3643259	3611421	3166656		920	25878	12440	5040
陕 西 Shaanxi	14954384	11569592	10523390	19057	17635	2914113	2215712	433986
甘 肃 Gansu	9055895	8192054	6984296	8031	9886	750613	622801	95311
青 海 Qinghai	3085235	2901473	2309228	2042	7751	129139	94633	44830
宁 夏 Ningxia	3332220	2792247	2136159	3008	2502	338951	275925	195511
新 疆 Xinjiang	11612882	10729367	9748579	7152	8358	420546	320452	447460

注：1.“民办学校中举办者投入”1993-2006年数据为社会团体和公民个人办学总经费。
2.从2017年起，“公共财政教育经费”改为“一般公共预算教育经费”。“一般公共预算教育经费”数据1992-2011年包括教育事业费、基本建设经费、教育费附加、科研经费和其他经费，2012年起仅包括教育事业费、基本建设经费和教育费附加，2015年起教育事业费包含地方教育附加和土地出让收益计提的教育资金。
3.“其他教育经费”数据1992-1997年包含扣除“学费”后的事业收入。

a) "Funds from sponsors of non-public schools" from 1993 to 2006 cover funds from social organizations and from citizens for running schools.

b) Since 2017, the "public expenditure on education" has been changed to "general public budget expenditure on education". From 1992 to 2011, the "general public budget expenditure on education" included the appropriated funds for education, capital construction, education surcharges, scientific research, and other funds. Since 2012, it only includes the appropriated funds for education, capital construction, and education surcharges. Since 2015, the "appropriated funds for education" includes the education funds accrued from local education surcharges and land transfer income.

c) The "other education funds" includes career income after deducting "tuition fees" from 1992 to 1997.

主要统计指标解释

普通、职业高等学校　指国家依法审批的，实施高等学历教育的全日制大学、独立设置的学院、独立学院、本科层次职业学校、高等专科学校及高等职业学校。

大学、独立设置的学院主要实施普通本科及本科层次以上的教育。独立学院主要实施普通本科层次的教育。本科层次职业学校主要实施本科层次职业教育。高等专科学校、高等职业学校实施专科层次的教育。

成人高等学校　指国家依法审批的，招收具有高中毕业或同等学力的人员为主要培养对象，利用函授、业余、脱产等多种形式，对其实施高等学历教育的学校。包括：职工高等学校、农民高等学校、管理干部学院、教育学院、独立函授学院、广播电视大学、其他成人高教机构等。其他成人高教机构是指承担国家成人招生计划任务不计校数的机构。

国家财政性教育经费　包括一般公共预算安排的教育经费，政府性基金预算安排的教育经费，企业办学中的企业拨款，校办产业和社会服务收入用于教育的经费，其他属于国家财政性教育经费。

Explanatory Notes on Main Statistical Indicators

Regular and Vocational Higher Education Institutions refer to full-time universities, independently established schools, independent colleges, undergraduate level vocational schools, higher professional colleges and higher vocational colleges approved by the state according to law and implementing higher academic education..

Universities and independently established schools primarily provide normal courses at undergraduate and higher levels. Independent colleges mainly provide normal undergraduate courses. Undergraduate level vocational schools primarily provide undergraduate level vocational courses. Higher professional colleges and higher vocational colleges primarily provide undergraduate of short-cycle courses.

Adults Higher Education Institutions refer to educational establishments approved by the state according to law, enrolling personnel graduated from senior secondary school or with equivalent education, and providing higher education courses in forms of correspondence, spare time or full time, for adults. Adults higher education institutions include schools of higher education for staff and workers, schools of higher education for peasants, institutions of administration, educational colleges, independent correspondence colleges, radio and television universities and other educational establishments of higher education for adult. Other educational establishments of higher education for adult refer undertakings to enrol adult students under the State Plan but not enumerated in the number of schools.

Government Appropriation for Education refers to the general public budget appropriation fund for education, educational funds budgeted by government funds, enterprise appropriation for enterprise-run schools, income from school-run enterprises and social services that are used for education purpose and other government appropriations for education.

22

卫生和社会服务

Public Health and Social Services

简 要 说 明

一、本篇资料的主要内容

本篇主要反映卫生、社会服务、残疾人事业的发展情况。

卫生统计资料主要包括医疗卫生机构、卫生人员、医疗服务、卫生设施、妇幼保健、疾病控制、卫生费用等情况。

社会服务统计资料主要包括社会组织和自治组织情况，民政机构床位情况，社会救助情况，孤儿和收养登记情况，婚姻登记情况，医疗救助情况和福利彩票销售情况等。

残疾人统计资料主要包括残疾人康复、教育、就业、社会保障、维权和组织建设情况。

二、本篇的资料来源

卫生统计资料由国家卫生健康委员会和国家疾病预防控制局提供。社会服务统计资料由民政部和国家医疗保障局提供。残疾人统计资料由中国残疾人联合会提供。

详细资料分别见《中国卫生健康统计年鉴》（国家卫生健康委员会编）、《中国民政统计年鉴》（中华人民共和国民政部编）、《中国医疗保障统计年鉴》（国家医疗保障局编）、《中国残疾人事业统计年鉴》（中国残疾人联合会编）。

Brief Introduction

I. Main Contents

Data in this chapter mainly reflect the development of health, social services, and work for persons with disability.

Data on health include mainly the number of health care institutions, health personnel, health services, health facility, maternal and child health care, disease control and health expenditure.

Data on social services include the statistics of social organizations and autonomous organizations, beds of civil affairs institutions, social assistance, orphans and children adoption registration, marriage registration service, medical aid, and welfare lottery.

Data on work for persons with disability cover information on the rehabilitation, education, employment, social security, rights protection and organizations development.

II. Sources of Data

Data on health are provided by the National Health Commission and National Bureau of Disease Control and Prevention. Data on social services are provided by the Ministry of Civil Affairs and National Healthcare Security Administration. Data on work for persons with disability are provided by the China Disabled Persons' Federation.

For detailed information please refer to *China Health Statistical Yearbook* compiled by the National Health Commission, *China Civil Affairs Statistical Yearbook* compiled by the Ministry of Civil Affairs, *China Healthcare Security Statistical Yearbook* compiled by the National Healthcare Security Administration and *China Statistical Yearbook on the Work for Persons with Disability* compiled by China Disabled Persons' Federation.

22-1 医疗卫生机构
Health Care Institutions

单位：个 (unit)

年份 Year / 地区 Region	合计 Total	#医院 Hospitals	#综合医院 General Hospitals	#中医医院 Traditional Chinese Medicine Hospitals	#专科医院 Specialized Hospitals	#基层医疗卫生机构 Health Care Institutions at Grass-root Level	#社区卫生服务中心(站) Community Health Service Centers (Stations)	#乡镇卫生院 Township Health Centers
1978	169732	9293	7539	447	643			55018
1980	180553	9902	7859	678	694			55413
1985	978540	11955	9197	1485	938			47387
1990	1012690	14377	10424	2115	1362			47749
1995	994409	15663	11586	2361	1445			51797
2000	1034229	16318	11872	2453	1543	1000169		49229
2005	882206	18703	12982	2620	2682	849488	17128	40907
2010	936927	20918	13681	2778	3956	901709	32739	37836
2011	954389	21979	14328	2831	4283	918003	32860	37295
2012	950297	23170	15021	2889	4665	912620	33562	37097
2013	974398	24709	15887	3015	5127	915368	33965	37015
2014	981432	25860	16524	3115	5478	917335	34238	36902
2015	983528	27587	17430	3267	6023	920770	34321	36817
2016	983394	29140	18020	3462	6642	926518	34327	36795
2017	986649	31056	18921	3695	7220	933024	34652	36551
2018	997433	33009	19693	3977	7900	943639	34997	36461
2019	1007579	34354	19963	4221	8531	954390	35013	36112
2020	1022922	35394	20133	4426	9021	970036	35365	35762
2021	1030935	36570	20307	4630	9699	977790	36160	34943
2022	1032918	36976	20190	4779	10000	979768	36448	33917
2023	1070785	38355	20497	5053	10581	1016238	37177	33753
北京 Beijing	11487	682	205	192	216	10505	2034	
天津 Tianjin	6799	458	286	62	105	6184	701	126
河北 Hebei	92825	2487	1616	301	504	89576	1631	1965
山西 Shanxi	37849	1383	628	219	488	35984	1087	1285
内蒙古 Inner Mongolia	25685	851	393	166	185	24328	1267	1240
辽宁 Liaoning	34137	1536	785	226	487	32005	1419	1001
吉林 Jilin	26161	870	403	167	288	24905	338	762
黑龙江 Heilongjiang	21417	1249	793	195	244	19623	648	973
上海 Shanghai	6514	467	182	26	150	5796	1192	
江苏 Jiangsu	39536	2173	981	166	562	36378	2690	905
浙江 Zhejiang	37679	1606	631	192	614	35405	3955	1045
安徽 Anhui	31361	1354	733	152	368	29340	1825	1311
福建 Fujian	30023	731	388	92	229	28845	739	877
江西 Jiangxi	40129	1139	664	140	287	38292	706	1603
山东 Shandong	88186	2847	1463	397	830	84426	2499	1449
河南 Henan	85044	2527	1400	478	562	81645	1993	1987
湖北 Hubei	38586	1245	602	161	443	36735	1136	1107
湖南 Hunan	57503	1781	841	225	666	55110	1053	2071
广东 Guangdong	62819	1875	974	199	629	59874	2794	1164
广西 Guangxi	34888	892	452	119	285	33497	362	1266
海南 Hainan	6538	240	128	25	77	6143	217	303
重庆 Chongqing	23389	862	434	142	213	22279	637	804
四川 Sichuan	74975	2479	1423	277	676	71581	1104	2762
贵州 Guizhou	30695	1543	1021	140	351	28750	1093	1313
云南 Yunnan	28765	1409	860	170	352	26745	668	1361
西藏 Xizang	7058	190	116		16	6745	16	674
陕西 Shaanxi	35133	1292	747	180	340	33334	752	1509
甘肃 Gansu	25375	737	357	120	205	24200	744	1348
青海 Qinghai	6950	243	131	17	38	6536	282	407
宁夏 Ningxia	4863	220	133	31	50	4514	244	205
新疆 Xinjiang	18416	987	727	76	121	16958	1351	930

注：1.村卫生室数计入医疗卫生机构数中。
2.2002年起，医疗卫生机构数不再包括高中等医学院校本部、药检机构、国境卫生检疫所和非卫生部门举办的计划生育指导站。
3.2013年起，医疗卫生机构数包括原计生部门主管的计划生育技术服务机构。
4.1996年以前，门诊部(所)不包括私人诊所。

a) Number of village clinics was included in health care institutions.
b) Since 2002, health care institutions no longer includes headquarters of higher and secondary medical schools, drug test institutions, frontier health and quarantine institutions and family planning service stations run by non-health departments.
c) Since 2013, health care institutions include family planning technical services institutions managed by original family planning department.
d) Before 1996, outpatient departments did not include private clinics.

22-1 续表 continued

单位：个 (unit)

年份 地区	Year Region	#村卫生室 Village Clinics	#门诊部(所) Outpatient Departments	#专业公共卫生机构 Specialized Public Health Institutions	#疾病预防控制中心 Centers for Disease Control	#专科疾病防治院(所/站) Specialized Disease Prevention & Treatment Institutions	#妇幼保健院(所/站) Maternal and Children Care Centers	#卫生监督所(中心) Health Inspection Institutions (Centers)
	1978		94395		2989	887	2571	
	1980		102474		3105	1138	2745	
	1985	777674	126604		3410	1566	2996	
	1990	803956	129332		3618	1781	3148	
	1995	804352	104406		3729	1895	3179	
	2000	709458	240934	11386	3741	1839	3163	
	2005	583209	207457	11177	3585	1502	3021	1702
	2010	648424	181781	11835	3513	1274	3025	2992
	2011	662894	184287	11926	3484	1294	3036	3022
	2012	653419	187932	12083	3490	1289	3044	3088
	2013	648619	195176	31155	3516	1271	3144	2967
	2014	645470	200130	35029	3490	1242	3098	2975
	2015	640536	208572	31927	3478	1234	3078	2986
	2016	638763	216187	24866	3481	1213	3063	2986
	2017	632057	229221	19896	3456	1200	3077	2992
	2018	622001	249654	18033	3443	1161	3080	2949
	2019	616094	266659	15958	3403	1128	3071	2869
	2020	608828	289542	14492	3384	1048	3052	2934
	2021	599292	306883	13276	3376	932	3032	3010
	2022	587749	321123	12436	3386	856	3031	2944
	2023	581964	362847	12121	3426	823	3063	2791
北　京	Beijing	2774	5697	93	27	16	17	18
天　津	Tianjin	2196	3156	72	20	3	17	17
河　北	Hebei	59321	26659	633	187	13	184	178
山　西	Shanxi	22566	10824	428	132	6	129	120
内蒙古	Inner Mongolia	12812	9009	438	121	9	118	117
辽　宁	Liaoning	16401	13168	440	123	39	96	91
吉　林	Jilin	8799	15006	282	67	54	70	49
黑龙江	Heilongjiang	10325	7676	474	145	22	117	117
上　海	Shanghai	1118	3486	104	19	15	19	17
江　苏	Jiangsu	14671	18105	508	115	25	119	108
浙　江	Zhejiang	11581	18816	414	103	14	96	99
安　徽	Anhui	15546	10652	485	128	42	130	108
福　建	Fujian	16487	10742	324	102	19	94	86
江　西	Jiangxi	27059	8917	529	152	78	115	111
山　东	Shandong	51541	28881	601	194	75	158	115
河　南	Henan	59447	18207	724	185	21	164	176
湖　北	Hubei	22459	12006	469	119	61	104	107
湖　南	Hunan	36126	15858	511	146	67	140	122
广　东	Guangdong	25127	30783	690	147	123	133	106
广　西	Guangxi	18589	13280	427	123	26	106	111
海　南	Hainan	2663	2957	128	29	16	28	13
重　庆	Chongqing	9496	11339	156	41	11	41	39
四　川	Sichuan	42301	25398	677	211	20	201	156
贵　州	Guizhou	19643	6660	333	101	4	99	75
云　南	Yunnan	13588	11101	539	149	25	147	135
西　藏	Xizang	5236	819	121	82		28	3
陕　西	Shaanxi	21611	9433	391	121	4	118	116
甘　肃	Gansu	16272	5833	413	105	9	99	94
青　海	Qinghai	4469	1378	168	54	2	52	46
宁　夏	Ningxia	2142	1923	104	26		25	24
新　疆	Xinjiang	9598	5078	445	152	4	99	117

22-2 卫生人员
Statistics on Health Personnel

单位：人 (person)

年 份 地 区	Year Region	卫生人员 Health Personnel	卫生技术人员 Health Technical Personnel	#执业(助理)医师 Licensed (Assistant) Physicians	#执业医师 Licensed Physicians	#注册护士 Registered Nurses	#药师(士) Pharmacists	乡村医生和卫生员 Village Doctors and Assistants	其他技术人员 Other Technical Personnel	管理人员 Administrative Staffs	工勤技能人员 Logistics Technical Workers
	1978	7883041	2463931	978152	609608	405223	266570	4777469	22950	298104	320587
	1980	7355483	2798241	1153234	709473	465798	308438	3820776	27834	310805	397827
	1985	5606105	3410910	1413281	724238	636974	365145	1293094	46052	358812	497237
	1990	6137711	3897921	1763086	1302997	974541	405978	1231510	85504	396694	526082
	1995	6704395	4256923	1917772	1454926	1125661	418520	1331017	120782	450013	545660
	2000	6910383	4490803	2075843	1603266	1266838	414408	1319357	157533	426789	515901
	2005	6447246	4564050	2042135	1622684	1349589	349533	916532	225697	312826	428141
	2010	8207502	5876158	2413259	1972840	2048071	353916	1091863	290161	370548	578772
	2011	8616040	6202858	2466094	2020154	2244020	363993	1126443	305981	374885	605873
	2012	9115705	6675549	2616064	2138836	2496599	377398	1094419	319117	372997	653623
	2013	9790483	7210578	2794754	2285794	2783121	395578	1081063	359819	420971	718052
	2014	10234213	7589790	2892518	2374917	3004144	409595	1058182	379740	451250	755251
	2015	10693881	8007537	3039135	2508408	3241469	423294	1031525	399712	472620	782487
	2016	11172945	8454403	3191005	2651398	3507166	439246	1000324	426171	483198	808849
	2017	11748972	8988230	3390034	2828999	3804021	452968	968611	451480	509093	831558
	2018	12300325	9529179	3607156	3010376	4098630	467685	907098	476569	529045	858434
	2019	12928335	10154010	3866916	3210515	4445047	483420	842302	503947	543750	884326
	2020	13474992	10678019	4085689	3401672	4708717	496793	795510	529601	561157	910705
	2021	13985363	11244217	4287604	3590846	5019422	520865	696749	599026	460012	985359
	2022	14410844	11657878	4434728	3721811	5224244	531221	664543	605684	492467	990272
	2023	15237463	12488283	4782086	4009658	5637142	569481	622079	614547	515527	997027
北 京	Beijing	389020	312758	121550	114956	134646	16982	2273	20423	20670	32896
天 津	Tianjin	165384	133656	56468	53123	52051	8136	2641	8739	10162	10186
河 北	Hebei	790666	644925	289780	224708	269708	23715	53117	30206	21189	41229
山 西	Shanxi	374803	298173	118428	100253	132685	12601	24099	16795	13236	22500
内蒙古	Inner Mongolia	284106	234507	92704	78884	101220	12243	12114	13656	10592	13237
辽 宁	Liaoning	442605	357550	137914	124244	167895	14161	14490	19009	16922	34634
吉 林	Jilin	294224	232250	92276	79946	106986	9071	11697	14594	12853	22830
黑龙江	Heilongjiang	335659	267541	103732	88488	118794	11494	11855	13761	15137	27365
上 海	Shanghai	297704	245752	89072	85454	110968	11568	46	13124	13089	25693
江 苏	Jiangsu	910971	743324	290096	247688	333420	37770	19476	43847	31854	72470
浙 江	Zhejiang	785789	662556	265975	238284	292265	34911	6319	31904	25042	59968
安 徽	Anhui	590238	509859	200567	164082	241447	19620	22681	20019	13856	23823
福 建	Fujian	397110	325816	123317	106471	144733	18103	14760	17122	11084	28328
江 西	Jiangxi	439075	361613	134825	111420	169354	18172	27506	14001	11038	24917
山 东	Shandong	1135939	934661	371920	306629	417633	43091	63961	55599	30815	50903
河 南	Henan	1069794	866110	346557	262578	383863	33907	62598	45607	31904	63575
湖 北	Hubei	602208	497181	190424	160105	230596	19972	27374	25774	20560	31319
湖 南	Hunan	682963	569682	219647	174338	270469	24861	26473	25316	20133	41359
广 东	Guangdong	1169128	976091	357885	307084	450163	52372	18289	36565	41198	96985
广 西	Guangxi	536134	433491	145146	120565	200913	24506	26760	21031	14680	40172
海 南	Hainan	106097	86544	31456	27302	41211	3962	2385	3942	4844	8382
重 庆	Chongqing	334725	272035	102267	86095	128142	11066	12586	10041	15040	25023
四 川	Sichuan	926093	740444	279437	234510	335453	33895	39924	34962	34322	76441
贵 州	Guizhou	430549	354783	125958	101520	163692	12933	23268	13528	17010	21960
云 南	Yunnan	512722	425232	146724	120660	203577	15746	28713	20746	11739	26292
西 藏	Xizang	46320	29531	12289	9804	9820	1412	9990	2573	1264	2962
陕 西	Shaanxi	471012	391726	133291	109331	169607	16799	16872	5209	26597	30608
甘 肃	Gansu	268421	221119	78030	65313	100397	9365	16061	11533	6486	13222
青 海	Qinghai	72697	57975	21604	18339	23710	3117	5683	4026	1483	3530
宁 夏	Ningxia	78053	65731	24266	21362	30046	3552	2477	2379	2657	4809
新 疆	Xinjiang	297254	235667	78481	66122	101678	10378	15591	18516	8071	19409

注：1.卫生人员和卫生技术人员中包括获得“卫生监督员”证书的公务员1万人。
2.2013年起，卫生人员数包括原卫生计生部门主管的计划生育技术服务机构人员数。
3.执业(助理)医师数包括村卫生室执业(助理)医师数。
4.1985年以前乡村医生和卫生员系赤脚医生数。
5.2021年起，管理人员指仅从事管理的人员数，不含同时担负临床或监督工作的管理人员。

a) Health personnel and health technical personnel include 10 000 civil servants who obtain the Certificate of Health Supervisor.
b) Since 2013, health personnel include personnel of family planning technical service institutions managed by family planning departments.
c) Licensed Physicians & physician assistants include those in village clinics.
d) Before 1985, village doctors and assistants referred to barefoot doctors.
e) Since 2021, administrative staffs refer to the number of personnel who are only engaged in management, excluding those who are also responsible for clinical or supervision work.

22-3 每千人口卫生技术人员
Health Technical Personnel in Health Care Institutions per 1000 Persons

单位：人 (person)

年份 Year / 地区 Region	卫生技术人员 Health Technical Personnel			执业(助理)医师 Licensed (Assistant) Physicians			注册护士 Registered Nurses		
	合计 Total	城市 Urban	农村 Rural	合计 Total	城市 Urban	农村 Rural	合计 Total	城市 Urban	农村 Rural
1980	2.85	8.03	1.81	1.17	3.22	0.76	0.47	1.83	0.20
1985	3.28	7.92	2.09	1.36	3.35	0.85	0.61	1.85	0.30
1990	3.45	6.59	2.15	1.56	2.95	0.98	0.86	1.91	0.43
1995	3.59	5.36	2.32	1.62	2.39	1.07	0.95	1.59	0.49
2000	3.63	5.17	2.41	1.68	2.31	1.17	1.02	1.64	0.54
2005	3.50	5.82	2.69	1.56	2.46	1.26	1.03	2.10	0.65
2006	3.60	6.09	2.70	1.60	2.56	1.26	1.09	2.22	0.66
2007	3.72	6.44	2.69	1.61	2.61	1.23	1.18	2.42	0.70
2008	3.90	6.68	2.80	1.66	2.68	1.26	1.27	2.54	0.76
2009	4.15	7.15	2.94	1.75	2.83	1.31	1.39	2.82	0.81
2010	4.39	7.62	3.04	1.80	2.97	1.32	1.53	3.09	0.89
2011	4.58	7.90	3.19	1.82	3.00	1.33	1.66	3.29	0.98
2012	4.94	8.54	3.41	1.94	3.19	1.40	1.85	3.65	1.09
2013	5.27	9.18	3.64	2.04	3.39	1.48	2.04	4.00	1.22
2014	5.56	9.70	3.77	2.12	3.54	1.51	2.20	4.30	1.31
2015	5.84	10.21	3.90	2.22	3.72	1.55	2.37	4.58	1.39
2016	6.12	10.42	4.08	2.31	3.79	1.61	2.54	4.75	1.50
2017	6.47	10.87	4.28	2.44	3.97	1.68	2.74	5.01	1.62
2018	6.83	10.91	4.63	2.59	4.01	1.82	2.94	5.08	1.80
2019	7.26	11.10	4.96	2.77	4.10	1.96	3.18	5.22	1.99
2020	7.57	11.46	5.18	2.90	4.25	2.06	3.34	5.40	2.10
2021	7.97	9.87	6.27	3.04	3.73	2.42	3.56	4.58	2.64
2022	8.27	10.20	6.55	3.15	3.84	2.53	3.71	4.74	2.79
2023	8.87	10.89	7.07	3.40	4.13	2.74	4.00	5.08	3.05
北京 Beijing	14.31	14.31		5.56	5.56		6.16	6.16	
天津 Tianjin	9.80	9.80		4.14	4.14		3.82	3.82	
河北 Hebei	8.72	11.75	7.08	3.92	5.06	3.30	3.65	5.20	2.80
山西 Shanxi	8.60	12.14	6.11	3.42	4.62	2.57	3.83	5.80	2.44
内蒙古 Inner Mongolia	9.79	12.81	7.73	3.87	4.88	3.18	4.22	5.95	3.05
辽宁 Liaoning	8.55	10.47	5.73	3.30	3.98	2.30	4.01	5.08	2.45
吉林 Jilin	9.93	10.65	9.32	3.95	4.11	3.81	4.57	5.15	4.08
黑龙江 Heilongjiang	8.74	11.06	6.53	3.39	4.17	2.64	3.88	5.26	2.57
上海 Shanghai	9.88	9.88		3.58	3.58		4.46	4.46	
江苏 Jiangsu	8.72	10.04	7.07	3.40	3.81	2.90	3.91	4.62	3.03
浙江 Zhejiang	10.00	11.95	8.22	4.01	4.68	3.40	4.41	5.38	3.52
安徽 Anhui	8.33	10.86	6.67	3.28	4.12	2.73	3.94	5.31	3.05
福建 Fujian	7.79	10.22	5.80	2.95	3.92	2.16	3.46	4.65	2.49
江西 Jiangxi	8.01	10.94	6.40	2.99	4.01	2.43	3.75	5.31	2.90
山东 Shandong	9.23	11.76	7.12	3.67	4.64	2.87	4.13	5.41	3.06
河南 Henan	8.82	13.48	6.81	3.53	5.15	2.83	3.91	6.43	2.82
湖北 Hubei	8.52	10.88	6.79	3.26	4.02	2.71	3.95	5.27	2.99
湖南 Hunan	8.67	12.60	7.07	3.34	4.68	2.80	4.12	6.21	3.26
广东 Guangdong	7.68	8.33	6.03	2.82	3.10	2.09	3.54	3.86	2.73
广西 Guangxi	8.62	11.32	6.65	2.89	3.99	2.08	4.00	5.40	2.97
海南 Hainan	8.30	9.75	6.95	3.02	3.54	2.53	3.95	4.77	3.19
重庆 Chongqing	8.53	8.52	8.54	3.20	3.21	3.19	4.02	4.06	3.85
四川 Sichuan	8.85	11.01	7.08	3.34	4.07	2.74	4.01	5.23	3.01
贵州 Guizhou	9.18	11.81	8.00	3.26	4.37	2.76	4.24	5.61	3.62
云南 Yunnan	9.10	13.14	7.83	3.14	4.74	2.64	4.36	6.53	3.67
西藏 Xizang	8.09	17.43	4.98	3.37	7.14	2.11	2.69	7.07	1.23
陕西 Shaanxi	9.91	10.99	8.71	3.37	3.89	2.80	4.29	5.07	3.42
甘肃 Gansu	8.97	12.34	6.95	3.17	4.31	2.48	4.07	5.96	2.94
青海 Qinghai	9.76	13.72	7.22	3.64	5.01	2.75	3.99	6.27	2.53
宁夏 Ningxia	9.02	11.09	6.56	3.33	4.15	2.35	4.12	5.19	2.85
新疆 Xinjiang	9.07	12.98	8.18	3.02	4.84	2.61	3.91	5.92	3.46

注：1.2002年以前，执业(助理)医师系医生，执业医师系医师，注册护士系护师(士)。

2.城市包括直辖市区和地级市辖区，农村包括县及县级市。

3.合计项分母系常住人口数，分城乡项分母2020年及以前系推算户籍人口数，2021年起系推算常住人口数。

a) Before 2002, licensed physician assistants referred to doctors, licensed physicians referred to physicians, registered nurses referred to nurses.

b) Urban area includes districts of municipalities and prefecture-level cities, rural area includes counties and cities at county level.

c) The denominator of the total item is the number of permanent population. In 2020 and before, the denominator of urban and rural items is the estimated number of registered population, and from 2021, it is the estimated number of permanent population.

22-4 村卫生室情况
Statistics on Village Clinics

单位：个 (unit)

年份 地区	Year Region	村卫生室 Village Clinics	村办 Village-run	乡卫生院设点 Outlets of Township Health Centers	联合办 Joint-run	私人办 Private-run	其他 Others
	1985	777674	305537	29769	88803	323904	29661
	1990	803956	266137	29963	87149	381844	38863
	1995	804352	297462	36388	90681	354981	22876
	2000	709458	300864	47101	89828	255179	16486
	2005	583209	313633	32396	38561	180403	18216
	2006	609128	333790	34803	36805	186524	17206
	2007	613855	340082	33633	33649	186841	19650
	2008	613143	342692	40248	31698	180157	18348
	2009	632770	350515	45434	31035	183699	22087
	2010	648424	365153	49678	32650	177080	23863
	2011	662894	372661	56128	33639	175747	24719
	2012	653419	370099	58317	32278	167025	25700
	2013	648619	371579	59896	32690	158811	25643
	2014	645470	349428	59396	29180	160549	46917
	2015	640536	353196	60231	29208	153353	44548
	2016	638763	351016	60419	29336	152164	45828
	2017	632057	349025	63598	28687	147046	43701
	2018	622001	342062	65495	28353	141623	44468
	2019	616094	339525	69091	27626	134575	45277
	2020	608828	337868	71858	26817	125503	46782
	2021	599292	338065	67551	26751	118322	48603
	2022	587749	335704	64325	25367	109640	52713
	2023	581964	340502	62695	24630	102409	51728
北京	Beijing	2774	2586	12	1	161	14
天津	Tianjin	2196	561	808	111	98	618
河北	Hebei	59321	33386	3124	1217	17147	4447
山西	Shanxi	22566	15684	993	517	2210	3162
内蒙古	Inner Mongolia	12812	4721	2861	255	3646	1329
辽宁	Liaoning	16401	7949	416	164	6814	1058
吉林	Jilin	8799	3980	1657	1069	1667	426
黑龙江	Heilongjiang	10325	7468	1283	139	761	674
上海	Shanghai	1118	939				179
江苏	Jiangsu	14671	7742	3748	1765	38	1378
浙江	Zhejiang	11581	6001	2711	129	1553	1187
安徽	Anhui	15546	9252		2513	702	3079
福建	Fujian	16487	10642	1026	208	2957	1654
江西	Jiangxi	27059	12590	964	1465	10825	1215
山东	Shandong	51541	28019	11626	3976	4865	3055
河南	Henan	59447	36197	1274	2787	14381	4808
湖北	Hubei	22459	15053	2982	2469	802	1153
湖南	Hunan	36126	24545	1574	690	5918	3399
广东	Guangdong	25127	12696	2684	198	5444	4105
广西	Guangxi	18589	13127	1086	38	4178	160
海南	Hainan	2663	952	365	22	1075	249
重庆	Chongqing	9496	6758	845	205	726	962
四川	Sichuan	42301	23709	3196	1290	8981	5125
贵州	Guizhou	19643	12069	244	264	3729	3337
云南	Yunnan	13588	10115	1713	576	162	1022
西藏	Xizang	5236	2158	2221	21		836
陕西	Shaanxi	21611	20473	124	131	803	80
甘肃	Gansu	16272	5868	6013	773	1965	1653
青海	Qinghai	4469	1806	813	584	646	620
宁夏	Ningxia	2142	1711	177	249		5
新疆	Xinjiang	9598	1745	6155	804	155	739

22-5 各类医疗卫生机构医疗服务及床位利用情况(2023年)
Statistics on Health Services and Utilization of Beds in Health Care Institutions (2023)

机构名称	Institutions	诊疗人次数(万人次) Visits (10 000 person-times)	入院人次数(万人次) Inpatients (10 000 person-times)	医师日均担负诊疗人次(人次) Daily Visits per Physician (person-time)	实际开放总床日数(万日) Days of Total Beds Actually Opened (10 000 days)	平均开放病床(万张) Average Beds Opened (10 000 beds)
总计	**Total**	**955088**	**30187**	**7.5**	**351327**	**963**
医院	Hospitals	426118	24500	6.6	278825	764
综合医院	General Hospitals	298560	17776	6.8	172260	472
中医医院	Traditional Chinese Medicine Hospitals	67867	3509	6.7	40160	110
中西医结合医院	Hospital of Integrated Traditional Chinese and Western Medicine	9183	420	6.5	5222	14
民族医院	Nationalities Hospitals	1583	103	4.2	1458	4
专科医院	Specialized Hospitals	48601	2645	5.6	55222	151
护理院	Nursing Hospitals	324	48	1.3	4502	12
基层医疗卫生机构	Health Care Institutions at Grass-root Level	494486	4545	9.0	60781	167
社区卫生服务中心(站)	Community Health Service Centers (Stations)	103543	487	15.1	9071	25
卫生院	Health Centers	132705	4032	9.2	51696	142
街道卫生院	Sub-district Health Centers	1809	40	10.4	558	2
乡镇卫生院	Township Health Centers	130896	3992	9.2	51138	140
村卫生室	Village Clinics	140050				
门诊部	Outpatient Departments	25438	26	4.5		
诊所(医务室、护理站)	Clinics (Infirmaries, Nursing Stations)	92750		7.3	14	
专业公共卫生机构	Specialized Public Health Institutions	34319	1112	7.3	11024	30
#专科疾病防治院(所、站)	Specialized Disease Prevention & Treatment Institutions	1707	40	5.4	1329	4
妇幼保健院(所、站)	Maternal and Children Care Centers	31385	1072	7.4	9695	27
其他医疗卫生机构	Other Health Care Institutions	164	30	2.3	697	2

22-5 续表 continued

机构名称	Institutions	病床周转次数(次) Turnover of Hospital Beds (time)	病床工作日(日) Working Days of Hospital Beds (day)	病床使用率(%) Occupancy Rate of Hospital Beds (%)	平均住院日(日) Average Length of Stay in Hospital (day)
总计	**Total**	**31.3**	**270.9**	**74.2**	**8.4**
医院	Hospitals	32.0	289.9	79.4	8.8
综合医院	General Hospitals	37.7	293.9	80.5	7.7
中医医院	Traditional Chinese Medicine Hospitals	31.8	289.7	79.4	8.9
中西医结合医院	Hospital of Integrated Traditional Chinese and Western Medicine	29.3	283.2	77.6	9.4
民族医院	Nationalities Hospitals	25.6	246.7	67.6	9.3
专科医院	Specialized Hospitals	17.2	283.4	77.7	15.7
护理院	Nursing Hospitals	3.7	238.9	65.5	49.4
基层医疗卫生机构	Health Care Institutions at Grass-root Level	27.2	192.6	52.8	6.6
社区卫生服务中心(站)	Community Health Service Centers (Stations)	19.5	181.7	49.8	8.6
卫生院	Health Centers	28.4	194.5	53.3	6.4
街道卫生院	Sub-district Health Centers	25.8	203.3	55.7	7.4
乡镇卫生院	Township Health Centers	28.4	194.4	53.3	6.4
村卫生室	Village Clinics				
门诊部	Outpatient Departments				
诊所(医务室、护理站)	Clinics (Infirmaries, Nursing Stations)	1.5	117.1	32.1	29.1
专业公共卫生机构	Specialized Public Health Institutions	36.7	228.4	62.6	6.0
#专科疾病防治院(所、站)	Specialized Disease Prevention & Treatment Institutions	10.8	244.2	66.9	20.3
妇幼保健院(所、站)	Maternal and Children Care Centers	40.2	226.2	62.0	5.5
其他医疗卫生机构	Other Health Care Institutions	15.7	176.2	48.3	9.9

22–6 医疗卫生机构床位
Number of Beds in Health Care Institutions

单位：万张 (10 000 beds)

年份 Year 地区 Region	合计 Total	#医院 Hospitals	#基层医疗卫生机构 Health Care Institutions at Grass-root Level	#社区卫生服务中心(站) Community Health Service Centers (Stations)	#乡镇卫生院 Township Health Centers	#专业公共卫生机构 Specialized Public Health Institutions	#妇幼保健院(所、站) Maternal and Children Care Centers	#专科疾病防治院(所、站) Specialized Disease Prevention & Treatment Institutions
1978	204.17	110.00			74.73		1.16	2.63
1980	218.44	119.58			77.54		1.64	2.73
1985	248.71	150.86			72.06		3.46	2.95
1990	292.54	186.89			72.29		4.66	3.10
1995	314.06	206.33			73.31		5.13	3.07
2000	317.70	216.67	76.65		73.48	11.86	7.12	2.84
2005	336.75	244.50	72.58	2.50	67.82	13.58	9.41	3.34
2006	351.18	256.04	76.19	4.12	69.62	13.50	9.93	2.80
2007	370.11	267.51	85.03	7.66	74.72	13.29	10.62	2.59
2008	403.87	288.29	97.10	9.80	84.69	14.66	11.73	2.64
2009	441.66	312.08	109.98	13.13	93.34	15.40	12.61	2.71
2010	478.68	338.74	119.22	16.88	99.43	16.45	13.44	2.93
2011	515.99	370.51	123.37	18.71	102.63	17.81	14.59	3.14
2012	572.48	416.15	132.43	20.32	109.93	19.82	16.16	3.57
2013	618.19	457.86	134.99	19.42	113.65	21.49	17.55	3.85
2014	660.12	496.12	138.12	19.59	116.72	22.30	18.48	3.76
2015	701.52	533.06	141.38	20.10	119.61	23.63	19.54	4.03
2016	741.05	568.89	144.19	20.27	122.39	24.72	20.65	4.00
2017	794.03	612.05	152.85	21.84	129.21	26.26	22.11	4.08
2018	840.41	651.97	158.36	23.13	133.39	27.44	23.28	4.08
2019	880.70	686.65	163.11	23.74	136.99	28.50	24.32	4.11
2020	910.07	713.12	164.94	23.83	139.03	29.61	25.29	4.23
2021	945.01	741.42	169.98	25.17	141.74	30.16	26.01	4.06
2022	974.99	766.29	175.11	26.31	145.59	31.36	27.35	3.91
2023	1017.37	800.45	182.02	28.52	150.45	32.51	28.54	3.87
北京 Beijing	13.88	13.08	0.55	0.55		0.25	0.19	0.06
天津 Tianjin	7.25	6.67	0.53	0.19	0.33	0.03		0.03
河北 Hebei	53.40	41.49	10.11	0.95	8.98	1.73	1.71	0.01
山西 Shanxi	23.23	19.04	3.73	0.49	2.98	0.46	0.43	0.04
内蒙古 Inner Mongolia	17.31	13.94	2.82	0.56	2.19	0.53	0.49	0.04
辽宁 Liaoning	33.42	29.45	3.52	0.71	2.78	0.28	0.20	0.07
吉林 Jilin	18.37	16.20	1.78	0.33	1.45	0.26	0.17	0.09
黑龙江 Heilongjiang	27.33	23.34	3.36	0.74	2.46	0.61	0.39	0.22
上海 Shanghai	17.50	15.70	1.58	1.58		0.13	0.11	0.02
江苏 Jiangsu	57.88	45.65	10.82	2.44	8.20	1.13	0.98	0.14
浙江 Zhejiang	40.61	36.17	3.09	1.07	1.99	1.21	1.17	0.04
安徽 Anhui	45.35	34.84	9.26	1.15	7.99	1.16	0.95	0.21
福建 Fujian	24.21	19.28	4.04	0.53	3.51	0.85	0.68	0.16
江西 Jiangxi	34.07	24.79	7.17	0.44	6.56	1.84	1.48	0.36
山东 Shandong	73.86	57.13	13.63	2.45	10.57	2.76	2.23	0.54
河南 Henan	77.74	57.88	16.90	2.44	14.31	2.93	2.75	0.17
湖北 Hubei	47.61	34.04	11.37	1.88	9.37	2.17	1.91	0.26
湖南 Hunan	53.39	38.98	12.54	1.88	10.50	1.84	1.44	0.40
广东 Guangdong	62.86	51.56	7.78	0.98	6.75	3.47	2.86	0.61
广西 Guangxi	36.20	25.17	9.24	0.41	8.82	1.70	1.66	0.04
海南 Hainan	6.09	4.68	1.14	0.13	0.91	0.26	0.26	0.00
重庆 Chongqing	25.56	18.99	6.00	1.37	4.59	0.53	0.52	0.01
四川 Sichuan	70.86	53.32	15.88	2.33	13.45	1.50	1.43	0.06
贵州 Guizhou	31.54	25.55	4.82	0.83	3.87	1.14	1.12	0.03
云南 Yunnan	35.99	27.58	7.18	0.67	6.34	1.15	1.07	0.06
西藏 Xizang	2.16	1.70	0.43	0.01	0.39	0.03	0.03	
陕西 Shaanxi	30.62	25.26	4.28	0.46	3.76	1.01	0.92	0.09
甘肃 Gansu	20.40	15.61	3.77	0.51	3.22	0.95	0.87	0.08
青海 Qinghai	4.57	3.90	0.59	0.06	0.51	0.08	0.08	0.00
宁夏 Ningxia	4.35	3.74	0.44	0.06	0.36	0.16	0.16	
新疆 Xinjiang	19.75	15.71	3.67	0.33	3.32	0.34	0.32	0.01

22–7 分城乡医疗卫生机构床位数
Number of Beds in Health Institutions by Urban and Rural Areas

单位：张 (bed)

年份 地区	Year Region	医疗卫生机构床位数 Beds of Health Institutions			每千人口医疗卫生机构床位 Beds of Health Care Institutions per 1000 Population		
		合计 Total	城市 Urban	农村 Rural	合计 Total	城市 Urban	农村 Rural
	2010	4786831	2302297	2484534	3.58	5.94	2.60
	2011	5159889	2475222	2684667	3.84	6.24	2.80
	2012	5724775	2733403	2991372	4.24	6.88	3.11
	2013	6181891	2948465	3233426	4.55	7.36	3.35
	2014	6601214	3169880	3431334	4.85	7.84	3.54
	2015	7015214	3418194	3597020	5.11	8.27	3.71
	2016	7410453	3654956	3755497	5.37	8.41	3.91
	2017	7940252	3922024	4018228	5.72	8.75	4.19
	2018	8404088	4141427	4262661	6.03	8.70	4.56
	2019	8806956	4351540	4455416	6.30	8.78	4.81
	2020	9100700	4502529	4598171	6.46	8.81	4.95
	2021	9450110	4970374	4479736	6.70	7.47	6.01
	2022	9749933	5090352	4659581	6.92	7.66	6.25
	2023	10173727	5322366	4851361	7.23	8.02	6.52
北　京	Beijing	138823	138823		6.35	6.35	
天　津	Tianjin	72505	72505		5.32	5.32	
河　北	Hebei	534036	223564	310472	7.22	8.58	6.48
山　西	Shanxi	232339	123924	108415	6.70	8.65	5.33
内蒙古	Inner Mongolia	173136	88748	84388	7.23	9.15	5.92
辽　宁	Liaoning	334223	221739	112484	7.99	8.91	6.64
吉　林	Jilin	183671	91670	92001	7.85	8.55	7.26
黑龙江	Heilongjiang	273327	167593	105734	8.93	11.23	6.74
上　海	Shanghai	174966	174966		7.04	7.04	
江　苏	Jiangsu	578826	355449	223377	6.79	7.53	5.87
浙　江	Zhejiang	406088	236353	169735	6.13	7.48	4.90
安　徽	Anhui	453525	217856	235669	7.41	9.01	6.36
福　建	Fujian	242062	124295	117767	5.79	6.62	5.11
江　西	Jiangxi	340712	150878	189834	7.55	9.45	6.51
山　东	Shandong	738564	390643	347921	7.30	8.48	6.31
河　南	Henan	777415	320418	456997	7.92	10.80	6.67
湖　北	Hubei	476130	226347	249783	8.16	9.19	7.40
湖　南	Hunan	533935	205546	328389	8.13	10.79	7.04
广　东	Guangdong	628584	448403	180181	4.95	4.91	5.04
广　西	Guangxi	362013	175329	186684	7.20	8.26	6.43
海　南	Hainan	60929	30316	30613	5.84	6.03	5.67
重　庆	Chongqing	255591	190561	65030	8.01	7.54	9.79
四　川	Sichuan	708592	348851	359741	8.47	9.26	7.82
贵　州	Guizhou	315372	118217	197155	8.16	9.87	7.39
云　南	Yunnan	359916	104220	255696	7.70	9.34	7.19
西　藏	Xizang	21551	11926	9625	5.90	13.09	3.51
陕　西	Shaanxi	306176	169290	136886	7.75	8.11	7.34
甘　肃	Gansu	203974	99028	104946	8.27	10.74	6.80
青　海	Qinghai	45712	22470	23242	7.70	9.69	6.42
宁　夏	Ningxia	43499	28596	14903	5.97	7.23	4.47
新　疆	Xinjiang	197535	43842	153693	7.60	9.11	7.26

注：每千人口床位数合计项分母系常住人口数，分城乡项分母2020年及以前系推算户籍人口数，2021年起系推算常住人口数。

a) For the number of beds per 1000 population, the denominator of the total item is the number of permanent population. In 2020 and before, the denominator of urban and rural items is the estimated number of registered population, and from 2021, it is the estimated number of permanent population.

22-8 分地区医院床位利用情况(2023年)
Occupancy of Hospital Beds by Region (2023)

地 区	Region	病床工作日(日) Working Days of Hospital Beds (day)			病床使用率(%) Occupancy Rate of Hospital Beds (%)			出院者平均住院日(日) Average Length of Stay in Hospital (day)		
		合计 Total	公立 Public Hospitals	民营 Non-public Hospitals	合计 Total	公立 Public Hospitals	民营 Non-public Hospitals	合计 Total	公立 Public Hospitals	民营 Non-public Hospitals
总 计	**National Total**	**289.9**	**314.0**	**231.9**	**79.4**	**86.0**	**63.5**	**8.8**	**8.4**	**10.7**
北 京	Beijing	293.1	314.2	226.6	80.3	86.1	62.1	8.6	8.2	10.8
天 津	Tianjin	272.3	296.1	175.9	74.6	81.1	48.2	7.7	7.5	9.7
河 北	Hebei	261.2	284.2	207.3	71.6	77.9	56.8	8.7	8.4	9.7
山 西	Shanxi	260.0	284.0	195.8	71.2	77.8	53.7	9.6	9.4	10.4
内蒙古	Inner Mongolia	246.4	269.6	134.8	67.5	73.8	36.9	8.7	8.7	8.0
辽 宁	Liaoning	258.7	284.4	203.7	70.9	77.9	55.8	9.4	9.1	10.2
吉 林	Jilin	259.8	284.6	203.2	71.2	78.0	55.7	9.3	8.9	11.1
黑龙江	Heilongjiang	263.4	276.1	226.3	72.2	75.6	62.0	9.0	8.7	10.4
上 海	Shanghai	332.0	353.9	287.8	91.0	97.0	78.8	11.5	9.8	31.1
江 苏	Jiangsu	296.0	331.7	242.8	81.1	90.9	66.5	8.7	8.1	10.7
浙 江	Zhejiang	308.6	336.9	253.5	84.5	92.3	69.4	8.5	7.2	16.5
安 徽	Anhui	277.5	307.6	211.9	76.0	84.3	58.1	8.6	8.2	9.8
福 建	Fujian	290.6	312.4	231.3	79.6	85.6	63.4	8.7	8.2	11.4
江 西	Jiangxi	282.9	300.2	244.7	77.5	82.2	67.0	8.9	8.3	11.1
山 东	Shandong	289.2	314.2	222.9	79.2	86.1	61.1	8.2	7.9	9.9
河 南	Henan	303.3	330.0	235.8	83.1	90.4	64.6	8.9	8.7	9.7
湖 北	Hubei	309.4	333.1	225.0	84.8	91.3	61.6	8.9	8.7	10.2
湖 南	Hunan	290.6	314.0	234.0	79.6	86.0	64.1	9.2	8.8	10.8
广 东	Guangdong	287.7	306.7	233.3	78.8	84.0	63.9	8.3	7.8	12.2
广 西	Guangxi	306.6	324.4	257.3	84.0	88.9	70.5	8.6	7.9	13.0
海 南	Hainan	259.5	282.8	192.3	71.1	77.5	52.7	8.5	8.1	11.6
重 庆	Chongqing	299.0	335.9	225.7	81.9	92.0	61.8	9.3	9.5	8.6
四 川	Sichuan	313.9	345.1	254.6	86.0	94.5	69.7	9.7	9.2	11.2
贵 州	Guizhou	292.5	319.0	258.0	80.1	87.4	70.7	8.4	8.0	9.3
云 南	Yunnan	291.2	322.2	220.2	79.8	88.3	60.3	8.2	8.0	8.9
西 藏	Xizang	198.4	191.5	217.5	54.4	52.5	59.6	8.2	8.9	6.9
陕 西	Shaanxi	295.7	316.1	246.8	81.0	86.6	67.6	8.7	8.4	9.7
甘 肃	Gansu	274.4	287.2	213.0	75.2	78.7	58.4	8.4	8.4	8.3
青 海	Qinghai	265.9	280.0	195.6	72.9	76.7	53.6	9.7	8.8	16.2
宁 夏	Ningxia	291.0	320.5	200.0	79.7	87.8	54.8	8.1	8.0	8.7
新 疆	Xinjiang	323.3	339.0	222.3	88.6	92.9	60.9	7.9	8.0	7.2

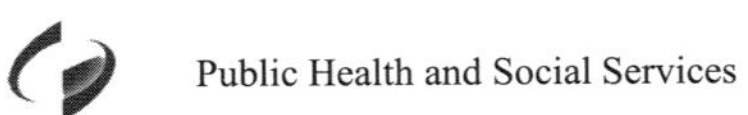

22–9 分地区医疗卫生机构门诊服务情况(2023年)
Outpatient Services of Health Institutions by Region (2023)

地 区	Region	诊 疗 人次数 (亿人次) Visits (100 million person-times)	#门急诊 Outpatient and Emergency Visits	观察室留观病例数 (万例) Cases in Observation Rooms (10 000 cases)	健康检查人次数 (万人次) Number of Health Examinations (10 000 person-times)	急诊病死率 (%) Fatality Rate among Emergency Admissions (%)	观察室病死率 (%) Fatality Rate in Observation Rooms (%)	居民年平均就诊次数 (次) Average Number of Visits of Residents (time)
总 计	**National Total**	**95.51**	**90.88**	**3995.71**	**52479.78**	**0.07**	**0.11**	**6.78**
北 京	Beijing	2.75	2.74	170.94	1160.89	0.12	0.33	12.60
天 津	Tianjin	1.19	1.13	153.18	544.00	0.08	0.11	8.70
河 北	Hebei	5.04	4.75	125.11	2065.18	0.16	0.17	6.82
山 西	Shanxi	1.46	1.36	51.99	1088.33	0.13	0.32	4.22
内蒙古	Inner Mongolia	1.18	1.09	45.59	748.40	0.13	0.26	4.94
辽 宁	Liaoning	1.94	1.82	210.97	1102.44	0.14	0.12	4.64
吉 林	Jilin	1.13	0.97	58.75	624.43	0.11	0.16	4.82
黑龙江	Heilongjiang	1.20	1.08	27.44	682.26	0.14	0.79	3.92
上 海	Shanghai	2.60	2.55	18.98	1387.68	0.14	1.48	10.46
江 苏	Jiangsu	6.42	6.22	161.14	3807.54	0.05	0.06	7.53
浙 江	Zhejiang	7.53	7.25	124.92	3777.55	0.03	0.25	11.36
安 徽	Anhui	3.89	3.63	81.56	2216.21	0.06	0.05	6.35
福 建	Fujian	2.91	2.74	58.69	1424.77	0.03	0.06	6.95
江 西	Jiangxi	2.56	2.44	108.64	1522.43	0.03	0.03	5.67
山 东	Shandong	7.82	7.35	269.66	3392.54	0.14	0.25	7.72
河 南	Henan	6.84	6.50	158.80	3230.64	0.08	0.06	6.97
湖 北	Hubei	3.68	3.47	198.81	1992.10	0.07	0.05	6.30
湖 南	Hunan	4.04	3.69	352.21	2139.40	0.03	0.03	6.15
广 东	Guangdong	9.06	8.80	342.75	6245.66	0.03	0.06	7.13
广 西	Guangxi	2.62	2.56	73.63	1747.78	0.04	0.06	5.22
海 南	Hainan	0.55	0.51	24.31	272.63	0.03	0.00	5.28
重 庆	Chongqing	2.15	2.08	179.30	1067.33	0.06	0.01	6.74
四 川	Sichuan	5.90	5.54	258.06	3299.25	0.07	0.08	7.05
贵 州	Guizhou	2.09	2.05	159.78	1162.17	0.04	0.03	5.41
云 南	Yunnan	3.18	3.09	350.46	1448.77	0.03	0.05	6.80
西 藏	Xizang	0.16	0.14	8.76	191.09	0.04	0.17	4.30
陕 西	Shaanxi	2.17	2.13	20.17	1244.70	0.08	0.19	5.50
甘 肃	Gansu	1.21	1.14	70.43	840.44	0.08	0.02	4.91
青 海	Qinghai	0.29	0.27	29.89	220.78	0.12	0.21	4.85
宁 夏	Ningxia	0.51	0.49	44.74	331.45	0.11	0.01	6.96
新 疆	Xinjiang	1.43	1.30	56.03	1500.95	0.20	0.36	5.50

22-10　分地区医疗卫生机构住院服务情况(2023年)
Hospitalization Services in Health Care Institutions by Region (2023)

地　区	Region	入院人次数(万人次) Inpatients (10 000 person-times)	出院人次数(万人次) Patients Discharged (10 000 person-times)	住院病人手术人次(万人次) Surgical Operations of Inpatients (10 000 person-times)	病死率(%) Fatality Rate (%)	每床出院人次数(人次) Patients Discharged per Bed (person-time)	每百门急诊入院人次数(人次) Inpatients per 100 Outpatient and Emergency Visits (person-time)	居民年住院率(%) Annual Hospitalization Rate of Residents (%)
总　计	**National Total**	**30187.3**	**30126.2**	**9638.7**	**0.4**	**29.7**	**4.5**	**21.4**
北　京	Beijing	445.1	444.3	190.7	1.2	32.1	1.7	20.4
天　津	Tianjin	213.3	214.2	109.8	0.7	29.6	2.2	15.6
河　北	Hebei	1294.1	1290.6	293.9	0.4	24.2	4.7	17.5
山　西	Shanxi	544.1	523.7	155.1	0.3	22.6	5.0	15.7
内蒙古	Inner Mongolia	408.2	406.4	98.7	0.8	23.5	4.5	17.0
辽　宁	Liaoning	779.7	779.3	220.6	1.2	23.4	5.0	18.6
吉　林	Jilin	420.8	418.1	105.4	1.2	22.9	5.4	18.0
黑龙江	Heilongjiang	672.9	671.9	195.5	1.1	24.6	7.2	22.0
上　海	Shanghai	533.1	530.8	642.1	1.5	30.3	2.2	21.4
江　苏	Jiangsu	1711.9	1708.9	613.2	0.2	29.7	3.4	20.1
浙　江	Zhejiang	1324.1	1324.2	470.3	0.4	32.7	2.3	20.0
安　徽	Anhui	1160.5	1164.7	316.1	0.4	25.8	4.5	19.0
福　建	Fujian	675.7	672.3	254.2	0.2	28.0	3.5	16.2
江　西	Jiangxi	940.4	945.1	238.4	0.2	27.8	5.8	20.8
山　东	Shandong	2349.3	2335.9	652.9	0.5	31.7	5.2	23.2
河　南	Henan	2294.1	2290.5	559.0	0.3	29.5	5.0	23.4
湖　北	Hubei	1487.5	1494.0	418.7	0.4	31.4	6.0	25.5
湖　南	Hunan	1606.5	1604.6	362.3	0.2	30.1	7.0	24.5
广　东	Guangdong	2019.5	2020.0	1159.8	0.6	32.2	3.0	15.9
广　西	Guangxi	1304.8	1303.7	278.6	0.3	36.0	6.5	26.0
海　南	Hainan	146.3	145.8	59.2	0.3	24.1	3.4	14.0
重　庆	Chongqing	836.1	837.4	212.5	0.4	32.8	6.3	26.2
四　川	Sichuan	2254.6	2260.0	823.2	0.4	32.0	5.9	26.9
贵　州	Guizhou	1045.5	1037.3	250.2	0.2	32.9	6.6	27.1
云　南	Yunnan	1162.4	1158.1	287.7	0.3	32.2	5.2	24.9
西　藏	Xizang	35.4	35.4	8.8	0.3	16.4	3.3	9.7
陕　西	Shaanxi	944.9	940.7	336.1	0.3	30.7	6.0	23.9
甘　肃	Gansu	591.9	587.2	107.0	0.2	28.8	6.7	24.0
青　海	Qinghai	120.2	119.1	27.5	0.4	26.1	5.9	20.2
宁　夏	Ningxia	141.6	141.0	38.2	0.2	32.5	3.6	19.4
新　疆	Xinjiang	722.7	720.9	152.9	0.4	36.6	6.5	27.8

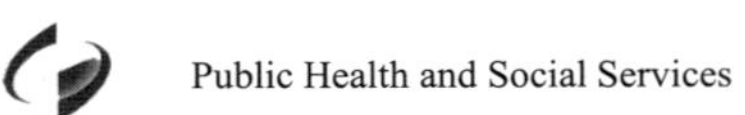

22-11 社区卫生服务中心(站)医疗服务情况
Health Services of Community Health Centers (Stations)

年份 Year 地区 Region	社区卫生服务中心 Community Health Service Centers					社区卫生服务站 Community Health Service Stations	
	诊疗人次数 (万人次) Visits (10 000 person-times)	入院人次数 (万人次) Inpatients (10 000 person-times)	病床使用率 (%) Occupancy Rate of Hospital Beds (%)	平均住院日 (日) Average Length of Stay in Hospital (day)	医师日均担负诊疗人次(人次) Daily Visits per Physician (person-time)	诊疗人次数 (万人次) Visits (10 000 person-times)	医师日均担负诊疗人次(人次) Daily Visits per Physician (person-time)
2004	4615.6	15.2	61.2	21.0	13.0	5095.5	11.1
2005	5938.5	26.6	60.7	17.2	13.7	6281.5	11.0
2006	8285.5	43.6	57.9	15.5	13.0	9378.9	13.1
2007	12712.4	74.3	59.6	13.1	13.1	9875.0	14.6
2008	17247.3	103.3	58.7	13.4	12.9	8425.1	12.5
2009	26080.2	164.2	59.8	10.6	14.0	11617.3	13.7
2010	34740.4	218.1	56.1	10.4	13.6	13711.1	13.6
2011	40950.0	247.3	54.4	10.2	14.0	13703.8	13.7
2012	45475.1	268.7	55.5	10.1	14.8	14393.6	14.0
2013	50788.6	292.1	57.0	9.8	15.7	14921.2	14.3
2014	53618.8	298.1	55.6	9.9	16.1	14912.0	14.4
2015	55902.6	305.5	54.7	9.8	16.3	14742.5	14.1
2016	56327.0	313.7	54.6	9.7	15.9	15561.9	14.5
2017	60743.2	344.2	54.8	9.5	16.2	15982.4	14.1
2018	63897.9	339.5	52.0	9.9	16.1	16011.5	13.7
2019	69110.7	339.5	49.7	9.7	16.5	16805.7	14.0
2020	62068.4	292.7	42.8	10.3	13.9	13403.7	10.8
2021	69596.6	319.3	43.2	9.8	14.6	14005.9	11.0
2022	69330.3	333.8	41.1	9.9	13.9	13919.9	11.0
2023	82909.0	480.4	50.2	8.7	15.5	20634.0	13.7
北京 Beijing	7244.6	2.4	28.6	18.8	20.1	1239.9	25.3
天津 Tianjin	1709.6	0.3	15.6	14.8	16.3	171.8	21.4
河北 Hebei	1158.7	6.5	31.5	9.2	9.7	1099.5	8.3
山西 Shanxi	545.5	3.3	29.9	11.0	8.0	504.0	6.8
内蒙古 Inner Mongolia	867.9	3.3	20.3	6.7	9.9	365.6	6.5
辽宁 Liaoning	1367.7	3.7	20.9	9.5	11.3	634.5	9.6
吉林 Jilin	660.2	1.7	20.5	10.8	7.9	42.9	8.0
黑龙江 Heilongjiang	877.6	4.5	18.9	8.0	7.5	34.5	4.4
上海 Shanghai	7271.9	5.5	74.3	76.6	19.4		
江苏 Jiangsu	7736.0	46.1	50.1	8.6	14.6	1297.1	18.3
浙江 Zhejiang	11907.8	16.4	56.4	11.1	21.7	438.9	25.0
安徽 Anhui	2344.0	11.6	34.5	7.4	14.9	1365.6	12.4
福建 Fujian	3246.1	7.1	34.5	8.1	23.9	405.4	11.8
江西 Jiangxi	606.9	4.6	33.3	6.2	10.6	376.5	11.7
山东 Shandong	4781.3	50.5	55.3	8.2	13.7	2653.8	16.8
河南 Henan	3402.8	34.7	45.3	8.5	12.1	1054.2	11.0
湖北 Hubei	2146.5	37.4	57.9	8.4	10.3	621.6	15.2
湖南 Hunan	2923.2	40.6	49.9	6.9	13.4	575.6	12.1
广东 Guangdong	10651.6	13.4	43.5	9.2	20.5	4089.8	23.9
广西 Guangxi	1034.2	10.8	59.3	7.1	12.3	213.9	11.3
海南 Hainan	178.3	0.6	14.6	6.0	9.7	259.3	15.0
重庆 Chongqing	1678.4	45.5	70.7	7.4	11.3	244.9	12.2
四川 Sichuan	3884.9	69.3	70.5	7.6	14.5	527.4	14.3
贵州 Guizhou	1292.2	30.2	66.1	5.7	10.4	475.4	10.1
云南 Yunnan	971.6	14.1	51.0	7.7	12.7	357.4	10.1
西藏 Xizang	31.0		11.8		10.0	5.0	5.5
陕西 Shaanxi	821.4	7.1	36.3	7.4	12.1	405.4	10.4
甘肃 Gansu	503.4	5.5	51.1	7.3	9.5	310.6	9.3
青海 Qinghai	107.6	1.0	42.4	8.1	8.3	155.7	13.3
宁夏 Ningxia	234.8	0.2	13.8	13.2	19.1	377.5	28.9
新疆 Xinjiang	721.2	2.3	28.9	7.8	15.7	330.1	6.3

22-12 乡镇卫生院医疗服务情况
Statistics on Health Services in Township Health Centers

年份 Year 地区 Region	诊疗人次数(亿人次) Visits (100 million person-times)	入院人次数(万人次) Inpatients (10 000 person-times)	病床使用率(%) Occupancy Rate of Hospital Beds (%)	平均住院日(日) Average Length of Stay in Hospital (day)
1981	14.38	2123.5	53.5	6.3
1985	11.00	1771.2	46.0	5.9
1990	10.65	1958.1	43.4	5.2
1995	9.38	1959.8	40.2	4.6
2000	8.24	1708.3	33.2	4.6
2005	6.79	1621.9	37.7	4.6
2006	7.01	1836.1	39.4	4.6
2007	7.59	2662.2	48.4	4.8
2008	8.27	3312.7	55.8	4.4
2009	8.77	3807.7	60.7	4.8
2010	8.74	3630.4	59.0	5.2
2011	8.66	3448.8	58.1	5.6
2012	9.68	3907.5	62.1	5.7
2013	10.07	3937.2	62.8	5.9
2014	10.29	3732.6	60.5	6.3
2015	10.55	3676.1	59.9	6.4
2016	10.82	3799.9	60.6	6.4
2017	11.11	4047.2	61.3	6.3
2018	11.16	3985.1	59.6	6.4
2019	11.75	3909.4	57.5	6.5
2020	10.95	3383.3	50.4	6.6
2021	11.61	3223.0	48.2	6.6
2022	12.08	3239.0	46.9	6.5
2023	13.09	3992.1	53.3	6.4
北 京 Beijing				
天 津 Tianjin	0.08	1.5	11.7	6.8
河 北 Hebei	0.55	117.1	31.2	7.0
山 西 Shanxi	0.17	24.5	21.6	7.8
内蒙古 Inner Mongolia	0.11	32.0	26.4	4.5
辽 宁 Liaoning	0.12	28.8	27.4	7.4
吉 林 Jilin	0.08	9.5	23.6	7.5
黑龙江 Heilongjiang	0.07	31.5	27.9	5.8
上 海 Shanghai				
江 苏 Jiangsu	1.02	208.5	60.0	7.6
浙 江 Zhejiang	1.10	37.8	51.1	8.3
安 徽 Anhui	0.77	130.7	39.9	6.6
福 建 Fujian	0.42	67.9	37.2	6.4
江 西 Jiangxi	0.47	152.5	43.8	5.5
山 东 Shandong	0.95	329.3	64.1	7.1
河 南 Henan	1.52	316.0	51.8	7.1
湖 北 Hubei	0.55	291.1	66.3	6.6
湖 南 Hunan	0.66	359.1	60.9	5.9
广 东 Guangdong	0.85	185.2	48.8	5.8
广 西 Guangxi	0.52	367.1	62.4	5.2
海 南 Hainan	0.11	6.3	25.1	10.3
重 庆 Chongqing	0.24	177.8	71.5	6.6
四 川 Sichuan	0.88	479.2	73.3	6.9
贵 州 Guizhou	0.41	183.3	72.1	5.1
云 南 Yunnan	0.66	179.6	49.3	5.7
西 藏 Xizang	0.03	0.4	9.3	4.1
陕 西 Shaanxi	0.22	75.9	40.7	7.0
甘 肃 Gansu	0.14	80.1	53.5	5.4
青 海 Qinghai	0.03	7.8	37.2	6.7
宁 夏 Ningxia	0.07	5.6	35.4	7.2
新 疆 Xinjiang	0.29	105.8	62.0	5.6

注：1993年以前的诊疗人次及入院人数系推算数据。

a) Number of visits and inpatients before 1993 are estimated.

22-13 甲乙类法定报告传染病发病及死亡人数(2023年)
Number of Reported Cases and Deaths of Class A and B Notifiable Infectious Diseases (2023)

单位：人 (person)

顺位 No.	发病 Diseases			死亡 Deaths		
	疾病名称	Diseases	发病人数 Number of Cases	疾病名称	Diseases	死亡人数 Number of Deaths
1	病毒性肝炎	Viral Hepatitis	1278473	艾滋病	AIDS	22137
2	肺结核	Pulmonary Tuberculosis	613091	病毒性肝炎	Viral Hepatitis	2397
3	梅毒	Syphilis	530116	肺结核	Pulmonary Tuberculosis	2167
4	淋病	Gonorrhea	103613	狂犬病	Hydrophobia	111
5	布鲁氏菌病	Brucellosis	70439	梅毒	Syphilis	16
6	艾滋病	AIDS	58903	流行性出血热	Hemorrhage Fever	12
7	百日咳	Pertussis	41124	疟疾	Malaria	12
8	细菌性和阿米巴性痢疾	Dysentery	37114	流行性乙型脑炎	Encephalitis B	7
9	猩红热	Scarlet Fever	25819	百日咳	Pertussis	5
10	登革热	Dengue Fever	19541	细菌性和阿米巴性痢疾	Dysentery	2
11	伤寒和副伤寒	Typhoid and Paratyphoid Fever	5542	炭疽	Anthrax	2
12	流行性出血热	Hemorrhage Fever	5360	登革热	Dengue Fever	1
13	疟疾	Malaria	2313	伤寒和副伤寒	Typhoid and Paratyphoid Fever	1
14	麻疹	Measles	621	流行性脑脊髓膜炎	Epidemic Encephalitis	1
15	炭疽	Anthrax	434	鼠疫	The Plague	1
16	猴痘	Mpox	407	淋病	Gonorrhea	
17	钩端螺旋体病	Leptospirosis	302	布鲁氏菌病	Brucellosis	
18	流行性乙型脑炎	Encephalitis B	205	猩红热	Scarlet Fever	
19	狂犬病	Hydrophobia	122	麻疹	Measles	
20	流行性脑脊髓膜炎	Epidemic Encephalitis	90	猴痘	Mpox	
21	霍乱	Cholera	29	钩端螺旋体病	Leptospirosis	
22	新生儿破伤风	Newborn Tetanus	21	霍乱	Cholera	
23	血吸虫病	Schistosomiasis	13	新生儿破伤风	Newborn Tetanus	
24	鼠疫	The Plague	5	血吸虫病	Schistosomiasis	
25	人感染高致病性禽流感	HpAI	1	人感染高致病性禽流感	HpAI	
26	传染性非典型肺炎	SARS		传染性非典型肺炎	SARS	
27	脊髓灰质炎	Poliomyelitis		脊髓灰质炎	Poliomyelitis	
28	白喉	Diphtheria		白喉	Diphtheria	
29	人感染H7N9禽流感	Avian Influenza H7N9		人感染H7N9禽流感	Avian Influenza H7N9	

注：1.空格系无报告发病或死亡病例(以下相关表同)。
2.疟疾数据系按照终审日期以及按照报告地区统计的中国籍病例(以下相关表同)。
3.猴痘于2023年9月20日纳入乙类传染病管理(以下相关表同)。
4.新型冠状病毒感染相关数据由中国疾病预防控制中心定期发布(以下相关表同)。

a) Blank cell means no infections or death cases reported. The same applies to the relevant following table.
b) Data on malaria are the Chinese cases counted on the date of final review and the reporting area. The same applies to the relevant following table.
c) Mpox was included in Class B infectious diseases on September 20, 2023. The same applies to the relevant following table.
d) Data related to novel coronavirus infection are regularly released by the Chinese Center for Disease Control and Prevention. The same applies to the relevant following table.

22-14 甲乙类法定报告传染病发病率及死亡率(2023年)
Reported Morbidity and Mortality Rates of Class A and B Notifiable Infectious Diseases (2023)

顺位 No.	发病 Diseases			死亡 Deaths		
	疾病名称	Diseases	发病率(1/10万) Morbidity Rate (1/100 000)	疾病名称	Diseases	死亡率(1/10万) Mortality Rate (1/100 000)
1	病毒性肝炎	Viral Hepatitis	90.6879	艾滋病	AIDS	1.5703
2	肺结核	Pulmonary Tuberculosis	43.4893	病毒性肝炎	Viral Hepatitis	0.1700
3	梅毒	Syphilis	37.6036	肺结核	Pulmonary Tuberculosis	0.1537
4	淋病	Gonorrhea	7.3497	狂犬病	Hydrophobia	0.0079
5	布鲁氏菌病	Brucellosis	4.9966	梅毒	Syphilis	0.0011
6	艾滋病	AIDS	4.1783	流行性出血热	Hemorrhage Fever	0.0009
7	百日咳	Pertussis	2.9171	疟疾*	Malaria	0.0009
8	细菌性和阿米巴性痢疾	Dysentery	2.6327	流行性乙型脑炎	Encephalitis B	0.0005
9	猩红热	Scarlet Fever	1.8315	百日咳	Pertussis	0.0004
10	登革热	Dengue Fever	1.3861	细菌性和阿米巴性痢疾	Dysentery	0.0001
11	伤寒和副伤寒	Typhoid and Paratyphoid Fever	0.3931	登革热	Dengue Fever	0.0001
12	流行性出血热	Hemorrhage Fever	0.3802	伤寒和副伤寒	Typhoid and Paratyphoid Fever	0.0001
13	疟疾	Malaria	0.1641	炭疽	Anthrax	0.0001
14	麻疹	Measles	0.0441	流行性脑脊髓膜炎	Epidemic Encephalitis	0.0001
15	炭疽	Anthrax	0.0308	鼠疫	The Plague	0.0001
16	猴痘	Mpox	0.0289	淋病	Gonorrhea	
17	钩端螺旋体病	Leptospirosis	0.0214	布鲁氏菌病	Brucellosis	
18	流行性乙型脑炎	Encephalitis B	0.0145	猩红热	Scarlet Fever	
19	狂犬病	Hydrophobia	0.0087	麻疹	Measles	
20	流行性脑脊髓膜炎	Epidemic Encephalitis	0.0064	猴痘	Mpox	
21	霍乱	Cholera	0.0021	钩端螺旋体病	Leptospirosis	
22	新生儿破伤风	Newborn Tetanus	0.0015	霍乱	Cholera	
23	血吸虫病	Schistosomiasis	0.0009	新生儿破伤风	Newborn Tetanus	
24	鼠疫	The Plague	0.0004	血吸虫病	Schistosomiasis	
25	人感染高致病性禽流感	HpAI	0.0001	人感染高致病性禽流感	HpAI	
26	传染性非典型肺炎	SARS		传染性非典型肺炎	SARS	
27	脊髓灰质炎	Poliomyelitis		脊髓灰质炎	Poliomyelitis	
28	白喉	Diphtheria		白喉	Diphtheria	
29	人感染H7N9禽流感	Avian Influenza H7N9		人感染H7N9禽流感	Avian Influenza H7N9	

22–15 监测地区儿童和孕产妇死亡率
Mortality Rate of Maternity Female and Children in Surveillance Areas

年份 Year	新生儿死亡率(‰) Neonatal Mortality Rate(‰)			婴儿死亡率(‰) Infant Mortality Rate(‰)			5岁以下儿童死亡率(‰) Mortality Rate of Children under 5(‰)			孕产妇死亡率(1/10万) Maternal Mortality Rate (1/100 000)		
	合计 Total	城市 Urban	农村 Rural	合计 Total	城市 Urban	农村 Rural	合计 Total	城市 Urban	农村 Rural	合计 Total	城市 Urban	农村 Rural
1991	33.1	12.5	37.9	50.2	17.3	58.0	61.0	20.9	71.1	80.0	46.3	100.0
1992	32.5	13.9	36.8	46.7	18.4	53.2	57.4	20.7	65.6	76.5	42.7	97.9
1993	31.2	12.9	35.4	43.6	15.9	50.0	53.1	18.3	61.6	67.3	38.5	85.1
1994	28.5	12.2	32.3	39.9	15.5	45.6	49.6	18.0	56.9	64.8	44.1	77.5
1995	27.3	10.6	31.1	36.4	14.2	41.6	44.5	16.4	51.1	61.9	39.2	76.0
1996	24.0	12.2	26.7	36.0	14.8	40.9	45.0	16.9	51.4	63.9	29.2	86.4
1997	24.2	10.3	27.5	33.1	13.1	37.7	42.3	15.5	48.5	63.6	38.3	80.4
1998	22.3	10.0	25.1	33.2	13.5	37.7	42.0	16.2	47.9	56.2	28.6	74.1
1999	22.2	9.5	25.1	33.3	11.9	38.2	41.4	14.3	47.7	58.7	26.2	79.7
2000	22.8	9.5	25.8	32.2	11.8	37.0	39.7	13.8	45.7	53.0	29.3	69.6
2001	21.4	10.6	23.9	30.0	13.6	33.8	35.9	16.3	40.4	50.2	33.1	61.9
2002	20.7	9.7	23.2	29.2	12.2	33.1	34.9	14.6	39.6	43.2	22.3	58.2
2003	18.0	8.9	20.1	25.5	11.3	28.7	29.9	14.8	33.4	51.3	27.6	65.4
2004	15.4	8.4	17.3	21.5	10.1	24.5	25.0	12.0	28.5	48.3	26.1	63.0
2005	13.2	7.5	14.7	19.0	9.1	21.6	22.5	10.7	25.7	47.7	25.0	53.8
2006	12.0	6.8	13.4	17.2	8.0	19.7	20.6	9.6	23.6	41.1	24.8	45.5
2007	10.7	5.5	12.8	15.3	7.7	18.6	18.1	9.0	21.8	36.6	25.2	41.3
2008	10.2	5.0	12.3	14.9	6.5	18.4	18.5	7.9	22.7	34.2	29.2	36.1
2009	9.0	4.5	10.8	13.8	6.2	17.0	17.2	7.6	21.1	31.9	26.6	34.0
2010	8.3	4.1	10.0	13.1	5.8	16.1	16.4	7.3	20.1	30.0	29.7	30.1
2011	7.8	4.0	9.4	12.1	5.8	14.7	15.6	7.1	19.1	26.1	25.2	26.5
2012	6.9	3.9	8.1	10.3	5.2	12.4	13.2	5.9	16.2	24.5	22.2	25.6
2013	6.3	3.7	7.3	9.5	5.2	11.3	12.0	6.0	14.5	23.2	22.4	23.6
2014	5.9	3.5	6.9	8.9	4.8	10.7	11.7	5.9	14.2	21.7	20.5	22.2
2015	5.4	3.3	6.4	8.1	4.7	9.6	10.7	5.8	12.9	20.1	19.8	20.2
2016	4.9	2.9	5.7	7.5	4.2	9.0	10.2	5.2	12.4	19.9	19.5	20.0
2017	4.5	2.6	5.3	6.8	4.1	7.9	9.1	4.8	10.9	19.6	16.6	21.1
2018	3.9	2.2	4.7	6.1	3.6	7.3	8.4	4.4	10.2	18.3	15.5	19.9
2019	3.5	2.0	4.1	5.6	3.4	6.6	7.8	4.1	9.4	17.8	16.5	18.6
2020	3.4	2.1	3.9	5.4	3.6	6.2	7.5	4.4	8.9	16.9	14.1	18.5
2021	3.1	1.9	3.6	5.0	3.2	5.8	7.1	4.1	8.5	16.1	15.4	16.5
2022	3.1	1.8	3.6	4.9	3.1	5.7	6.8	4.2	8.0	15.7	14.3	16.6
2023	2.8	1.7	3.2	4.5	2.9	5.2	6.2	3.9	7.2	15.1	12.5	17.0

22-16 分地区儿童健康情况(2023年)
Health Status of Children by Region (2023)

单位：%　　　　(%)

地区	Region	新生儿访视率 Visit Rate to the Newborn	3岁以下儿童系统管理率 System Management Rate for Children under 3 Years Old	7岁以下儿童健康管理率 Health Management Rate for Children under 7 Years old	0-6岁儿童眼保健和视力检查覆盖率 Coverage Rate of Eye Care and Vision Examination for Children Aged 0-6
全　国	**National Total**	**97.4**	**94.3**	**95.9**	**95.1**
北　京	Beijing	98.0	97.0	99.4	99.3
天　津	Tianjin	98.1	96.9	95.0	96.3
河　北	Hebei	96.0	93.6	95.3	94.0
山　西	Shanxi	96.5	92.8	94.4	93.6
内蒙古	Inner Mongolia	98.0	96.1	95.7	94.2
辽　宁	Liaoning	96.7	94.1	94.6	93.6
吉　林	Jilin	99.8	97.1	98.3	97.7
黑龙江	Heilongjiang	98.0	95.8	96.2	95.2
上　海	Shanghai	98.5	97.8	99.6	99.6
江　苏	Jiangsu	98.6	98.4	99.2	98.7
浙　江	Zhejiang	99.4	97.3	98.6	97.9
安　徽	Anhui	96.4	92.5	94.1	93.5
福　建	Fujian	97.0	94.7	95.8	93.7
江　西	Jiangxi	98.1	95.2	95.7	94.3
山　东	Shandong	98.4	97.1	97.7	98.4
河　南	Henan	95.0	91.7	93.7	93.3
湖　北	Hubei	97.4	94.4	96.0	94.5
湖　南	Hunan	98.6	95.4	96.1	95.7
广　东	Guangdong	97.1	92.6	96.0	95.8
广　西	Guangxi	97.8	89.0	95.8	95.6
海　南	Hainan	98.0	92.2	95.8	94.8
重　庆	Chongqing	96.4	93.9	95.5	95.2
四　川	Sichuan	97.5	95.3	95.8	94.6
贵　州	Guizhou	96.6	94.0	95.1	94.7
云　南	Yunnan	98.1	94.0	95.2	94.9
西　藏	Xizang	94.6	91.1	93.1	50.5
陕　西	Shaanxi	98.2	96.3	97.0	96.4
甘　肃	Gansu	97.2	93.5	95.2	93.9
青　海	Qinghai	95.8	94.7	92.7	91.7
宁　夏	Ningxia	99.4	96.9	97.0	97.0
新　疆	Xinjiang	99.1	97.5	95.9	95.3

22-17 分地区孕产妇健康情况(2023年)
Health status of Maternity Female by Region (2023)

单位：% (%)

地区	Region	产前检查率 Prenatal Examination Rate	孕产妇系统管理率 Maternal Systematic Management Rate	孕产妇建卡率 Card Establishment Rate for Maternal Health	住院分娩率 Institutional Delivery Rate	产后访视率 Postnatal Visit Rate
全　国	**National Total**	**98.2**	**94.5**	**95.6**	**99.9**	**97.0**
北　京	Beijing	98.4	97.9	94.6	100.0	98.2
天　津	Tianjin	98.9	95.3	98.7	100.0	98.0
河　北	Hebei	97.9	93.7	95.1	100.0	95.5
山　西	Shanxi	98.3	92.4	90.7	100.0	96.0
内蒙古	Inner Mongolia	98.4	96.1	97.3	100.0	97.4
辽　宁	Liaoning	98.5	93.0	91.8	100.0	96.2
吉　林	Jilin	98.4	96.4	97.7	100.0	98.6
黑龙江	Heilongjiang	98.6	95.4	96.6	100.0	97.2
上　海	Shanghai	98.4	97.0	98.6	100.0	98.5
江　苏	Jiangsu	98.8	96.1	95.8	100.0	98.1
浙　江	Zhejiang	98.4	97.1	98.7	100.0	98.4
安　徽	Anhui	97.4	92.7	93.8	99.9	96.2
福　建	Fujian	98.3	93.6	94.8	100.0	96.5
江　西	Jiangxi	98.4	96.8	98.3	100.0	97.7
山　东	Shandong	98.4	96.7	98.5	100.0	97.6
河　南	Henan	97.0	90.4	92.4	100.0	95.2
湖　北	Hubei	98.1	95.8	96.8	100.0	97.1
湖　南	Hunan	98.4	96.6	97.2	100.0	97.7
广　东	Guangdong	98.3	94.8	95.9	99.9	97.1
广　西	Guangxi	98.1	94.9	97.7	99.9	98.3
海　南	Hainan	99.0	92.0	93.2	99.9	97.8
重　庆	Chongqing	98.5	94.0	97.1	99.9	95.7
四　川	Sichuan	98.1	95.5	95.8	99.8	96.9
贵　州	Guizhou	97.8	93.6	95.5	99.9	96.2
云　南	Yunnan	98.8	92.1	93.4	99.9	97.7
西　藏	Xizang	92.1	81.9	83.7	99.2	94.5
陕　西	Shaanxi	98.8	96.7	98.2	100.0	97.6
甘　肃	Gansu	98.4	93.4	92.6	99.9	96.8
青　海	Qinghai	97.0	92.8	91.8	99.9	95.5
宁　夏	Ningxia	99.0	97.9	99.0	100.0	98.8
新　疆	Xinjiang	99.0	95.4	97.6	99.8	98.2

22-18 卫生总费用
Total Health Expenditure

年份 Year	卫生总费用（亿元） Total Health Expenditure (100 million yuan)	政府卫生支出 Government Health Expenditure		社会卫生支出 Social Health Expenditure		个人卫生支出 Personal Health Expenditure		人均卫生总费用（元） Per Capita Health Expenditure (yuan)	卫生总费用占GDP的比重(%) Health Expenditure as Percentage of GDP (%)
		绝对数（亿元） Value (100 million yuan)	占卫生总费用比重(%) As Percentage of Health Expenditure	绝对数（亿元） Value (100 million yuan)	占卫生总费用比重(%) As Percentage of Health Expenditure	绝对数（亿元） Value (100 million yuan)	占卫生总费用比重(%) As Percentage of Health Expenditure		
1978	110.21	35.44	32.16	52.25	47.41	22.52	20.43	11.45	3.00
1979	126.19	40.64	32.21	59.88	47.45	25.67	20.34	12.94	3.08
1980	143.23	51.91	36.24	60.97	42.57	30.35	21.19	14.51	3.12
1981	160.12	59.67	37.27	62.43	38.99	38.02	23.74	16.00	3.24
1982	177.53	68.99	38.86	70.11	39.49	38.43	21.65	17.46	3.30
1983	207.42	77.63	37.43	64.55	31.12	65.24	31.45	20.14	3.44
1984	242.07	89.46	36.96	73.61	30.41	79.00	32.64	23.20	3.33
1985	279.00	107.65	38.58	91.96	32.96	79.39	28.46	26.36	3.07
1986	315.90	122.23	38.69	110.35	34.93	83.32	26.37	29.38	3.04
1987	379.58	127.28	33.53	137.25	36.16	115.05	30.31	34.73	3.12
1988	488.04	145.39	29.79	189.99	38.93	152.66	31.28	43.96	3.21
1989	615.50	167.83	27.27	237.84	38.64	209.83	34.09	54.61	3.58
1990	747.39	187.28	25.06	293.10	39.22	267.01	35.73	65.37	3.96
1991	893.49	204.05	22.84	354.41	39.67	335.02	37.50	77.14	4.06
1992	1096.86	228.61	20.84	431.55	39.34	436.70	39.81	93.61	4.03
1993	1377.78	272.06	19.75	524.75	38.09	580.97	42.17	116.25	3.86
1994	1761.24	342.28	19.43	644.91	36.62	774.06	43.95	146.95	3.62
1995	2155.13	387.34	17.97	767.81	35.63	999.98	46.40	177.93	3.51
1996	2709.42	461.61	17.04	875.66	32.32	1372.15	50.64	221.38	3.77
1997	3196.71	523.56	16.38	984.06	30.78	1689.09	52.84	258.58	4.01
1998	3678.72	590.06	16.04	1071.03	29.11	2017.63	54.85	294.86	4.32
1999	4047.50	640.96	15.84	1145.99	28.31	2260.56	55.85	321.78	4.47
2000	4586.63	709.52	15.47	1171.94	25.55	2705.17	58.98	361.88	4.57
2001	5025.93	800.61	15.93	1211.43	24.10	3013.88	59.97	393.80	4.53
2002	5790.03	908.51	15.69	1539.38	26.59	3342.14	57.72	450.75	4.76
2003	6584.10	1116.94	16.96	1788.50	27.16	3678.67	55.87	509.50	4.79
2004	7590.29	1293.58	17.04	2225.35	29.32	4071.35	53.64	583.92	4.69
2005	8659.91	1552.53	17.93	2586.41	29.87	4520.98	52.21	662.30	4.62
2006	9843.34	1778.86	18.07	3210.92	32.62	4853.56	49.31	748.84	4.49
2007	11573.97	2581.58	22.31	3893.72	33.64	5098.66	44.05	875.96	4.29
2008	14535.40	3593.94	24.73	5065.60	34.85	5875.86	40.42	1094.52	4.55
2009	17541.92	4816.26	27.46	6154.49	35.08	6571.16	37.46	1314.49	5.03
2010	19980.39	5732.49	28.69	7196.61	36.02	7051.29	35.29	1490.06	4.85
2011	24345.91	7464.18	30.66	8416.45	34.57	8465.28	34.77	1804.52	4.99
2012	28119.00	8431.98	29.99	10030.70	35.67	9656.32	34.34	2068.76	5.22
2013	31668.95	9545.81	30.14	11393.79	35.98	10729.34	33.88	2316.23	5.34
2014	35312.40	10579.23	29.96	13437.75	38.05	11295.41	31.99	2565.45	5.49
2015	40974.64	12475.28	30.45	16506.71	40.29	11992.65	29.27	2962.18	5.95
2016	46344.88	13910.31	30.01	19096.68	41.21	13337.90	28.78	3328.61	6.21
2017	52598.28	15205.87	28.91	22258.81	42.32	15133.60	28.77	3756.72	6.32
2018	59121.91	16399.13	27.74	25810.78	43.66	16911.99	28.61	4206.74	6.43
2019	65841.39	18016.95	27.36	29150.57	44.27	18673.87	28.36	4669.34	6.67
2020	72175.00	21941.90	30.40	30273.67	41.94	19959.43	27.65	5112.34	7.12
2021	76844.99	20676.06	26.91	34963.26	45.50	21205.67	27.60	5439.97	6.69
2022	85327.49	24040.89	28.17	38345.67	44.94	22940.94	26.89	6044.09	7.08
2023	90575.81	24147.89	26.66	41676.80	46.01	24751.13	27.33	6425.32	7.19

注：1.本表系按当年价格核算数，2023年为初步测算数。

2.2001年起卫生总费用不含高等医学教育经费，2006年起包括城乡医疗救助经费。

a) Data in this table are at current prices. Data of 2022 are preliminary data.

b) Since 2001, total health expenditure does not include expenditure on higher medical education. Since 2006, it includes expenditure on medical aid in urban and rural areas.

22-19 分地区民政机构床位数(2023年)
Beds of Civil Affairs Institutions by Region (2023)

单位：万张 (10 000 beds)

地 区	Region	提供住宿的民政机构床位数 Number of Beds of Civil Affairs Institutions with Accommodations	养老 Elderly Care Institutions	儿童福利和救助 Child Welfare and Assistance Institutions	精神疾病 Mental Illness Service Institutions	其他 Other Institutions	每千老年人口养老床位数(张) Elderly Care Beds per 1 000 Elderly Population (bed)
全 国	**National Total**	**543.58**	**517.22**	**9.88**	**7.30**	**9.18**	**27.7**
北 京	Beijing	11.85	11.37	0.28	0.01	0.20	26.0
天 津	Tianjin	6.06	5.90	0.06	0.06	0.05	21.0
河 北	Hebei	24.87	24.42	0.12	0.10	0.24	28.0
山 西	Shanxi	9.02	8.47	0.14	0.18	0.23	22.0
内蒙古	Inner Mongolia	8.82	8.32	0.19	0.17	0.15	39.0
辽 宁	Liaoning	20.32	19.81	0.13		0.39	21.0
吉 林	Jilin	15.51	14.55	0.30	0.47	0.19	26.0
黑龙江	Heilongjiang	19.01	18.08	0.23	0.48	0.22	25.0
上 海	Shanghai	16.49	15.88	0.11	0.18	0.31	28.0
江 苏	Jiangsu	47.32	45.81	0.45	0.52	0.55	36.0
浙 江	Zhejiang	24.67	23.84	0.41	0.05	0.37	26.0
安 徽	Anhui	33.03	32.02	0.55		0.46	30.0
福 建	Fujian	13.42	12.59	0.18	0.39	0.26	40.0
江 西	Jiangxi	18.88	18.46	0.13	0.07	0.21	32.0
山 东	Shandong	44.36	43.74	0.39		0.23	30.0
河 南	Henan	39.61	38.48	0.41	0.10	0.62	27.0
湖 北	Hubei	30.43	29.48	0.41	0.17	0.37	37.0
湖 南	Hunan	24.51	23.04	0.33	0.52	0.63	28.0
广 东	Guangdong	25.82	24.29	0.60	0.17	0.76	24.0
广 西	Guangxi	10.12	9.14	0.37	0.36	0.25	28.0
海 南	Hainan	1.08	1.00	0.01		0.07	9.0
重 庆	Chongqing	13.58	12.78	0.25	0.32	0.23	27.0
四 川	Sichuan	35.64	32.40	0.78	1.74	0.72	21.0
贵 州	Guizhou	9.34	8.17	0.50	0.42	0.26	22.0
云 南	Yunnan	10.54	9.84	0.29	0.18	0.23	18.0
西 藏	Xizang	1.68	1.16	0.48		0.03	36.0
陕 西	Shaanxi	12.03	11.29	0.31	0.08	0.36	26.0
甘 肃	Gansu	4.02	3.35	0.26	0.09	0.32	32.0
青 海	Qinghai	1.14	0.89	0.20		0.06	24.0
宁 夏	Ningxia	2.94	2.73	0.12	0.03	0.05	32.0
新 疆	Xinjiang	7.44	5.95	0.89	0.45	0.16	27.0

注：1.老年人口指60岁及以上人口。
2.全国数据含部本级单位。

a) The elderly refer to population aged 60 and over.
b) The national data includes ministerial level units.

22–20 分地区孤儿和收养登记情况(2023年)
Orphans and Children Adoption Registration by Region (2023)

单位：人 (person)

地 区	Region	孤儿数 Number of Orphans	集中养育 Institutional Rearing	社会散居 Family Rearing	被收养儿童 Number of Children Adopted	社会福利机构抚养的儿童 Children Raised in Social Welfare Institutions
全 国	**National Total**	**144447**	**42311**	**102136**	**8162**	**1594**
北 京	Beijing	1096	931	165	16	2
天 津	Tianjin	491	324	167	41	1
河 北	Hebei	4591	1451	3140	250	53
山 西	Shanxi	3951	1944	2007	221	39
内蒙古	Inner Mongolia	1805	614	1191	87	6
辽 宁	Liaoning	2407	848	1559	44	16
吉 林	Jilin	2997	1211	1786	22	5
黑龙江	Heilongjiang	2567	584	1983	77	8
上 海	Shanghai	951	833	118	18	
江 苏	Jiangsu	4771	1832	2939	426	205
浙 江	Zhejiang	2186	1154	1032	258	128
安 徽	Anhui	4595	1382	3213	320	26
福 建	Fujian	2137	899	1238	283	24
江 西	Jiangxi	3490	1053	2437	276	30
山 东	Shandong	7354	1590	5764	276	4
河 南	Henan	14815	3405	11410	892	157
湖 北	Hubei	4290	1004	3286	417	46
湖 南	Hunan	9284	1380	7904	516	55
广 东	Guangdong	10500	5166	5334	645	140
广 西	Guangxi	8050	1381	6669	1101	452
海 南	Hainan	577	175	402	54	3
重 庆	Chongqing	3061	528	2533	137	19
四 川	Sichuan	16396	1870	14526	512	77
贵 州	Guizhou	8179	1152	7027	172	18
云 南	Yunnan	7158	953	6205	254	
西 藏	Xizang	4031	3202	829	17	2
陕 西	Shaanxi	3718	1653	2065	305	35
甘 肃	Gansu	4553	1110	3443	223	18
青 海	Qinghai	883	267	616	128	6
宁 夏	Ningxia	620	204	416	12	5
新 疆	Xinjiang	2943	2211	732	162	14

22–21 社会救助情况
Statistics on Social Assistance

单位：万人 (10 000 persons)

年 份 Year / 地 区 Region		城市最低生活保障人数 Number of Urban Residents Entitled to Minimum Living Allowance	农村最低生活保障人数 Number of Rural Residents Entitled to Minimum Living Allowance	农村特困人员集中供养人数 Rural Households in Extreme Difficulty with Centralized Living Arrangement	农村特困人员分散供养人数 Rural Households in Extreme Difficulty with Decentralized Living Arrangement
	2007	2272.1	3566.3	138.0	393.3
	2008	2334.8	4305.5	155.6	393.0
	2009	2345.6	4760.0	171.8	381.6
	2010	2310.5	5214.0	177.4	378.9
	2011	2276.8	5305.7	184.5	366.5
	2012	2143.5	5344.5	185.3	360.3
	2013	2064.0	5388.0	183.5	353.8
	2014	1877.0	5207.0	174.3	354.8
	2015	1701.1	4903.6	162.3	354.4
	2016	1480.2	4586.5	139.7	357.2
	2017	1261.0	4045.2	99.6	367.2
	2018	1007.0	3519.1	86.2	368.8
	2019	860.9	3455.4	75.0	364.1
	2020	805.1	3620.8	73.9	372.4
	2021	737.8	3474.5	69.2	368.1
	2022	682.4	3349.6	64.4	370.1
	2023	663.6	3399.7	61.4	374.0
北 京	Beijing	6.9	3.5	0.2	0.3
天 津	Tianjin	6.2	5.7	0.1	0.9
河 北	Hebei	13.8	147.9	2.6	22.3
山 西	Shanxi	16.0	86.3	1.4	11.0
内蒙古	Inner Mongolia	24.2	132.5	1.0	7.6
辽 宁	Liaoning	25.4	61.0	1.5	11.1
吉 林	Jilin	28.0	51.7	1.0	6.6
黑龙江	Heilongjiang	42.4	87.3	1.1	8.1
上 海	Shanghai	12.4	3.0	0.1	0.1
江 苏	Jiangsu	8.2	56.4	3.1	16.0
浙 江	Zhejiang	5.6	50.0	1.3	1.8
安 徽	Anhui	26.2	167.8	4.6	26.9
福 建	Fujian	7.1	52.7	1.2	5.0
江 西	Jiangxi	29.1	144.3	3.1	9.2
山 东	Shandong	9.0	130.7	5.2	28.4
河 南	Henan	30.6	275.8	6.7	40.4
湖 北	Hubei	23.7	125.1	4.0	19.7
湖 南	Hunan	32.3	147.1	4.2	31.1
广 东	Guangdong	14.6	109.9	1.4	18.5
广 西	Guangxi	40.7	242.8	0.5	23.7
海 南	Hainan	3.2	14.6	0.2	2.2
重 庆	Chongqing	21.1	56.7	1.0	9.0
四 川	Sichuan	51.4	358.2	6.4	33.7
贵 州	Guizhou	57.7	171.5	1.5	8.6
云 南	Yunnan	37.5	232.5	1.5	10.8
西 藏	Xizang	2.3	14.2	0.6	0.6
陕 西	Shaanxi	15.7	109.2	3.6	9.0
甘 肃	Gansu	30.9	159.1	0.9	8.8
青 海	Qinghai	7.2	28.5	0.3	1.3
宁 夏	Ningxia	7.5	36.7	0.3	0.5
新 疆	Xinjiang	26.5	137.0	1.0	0.6

22-22　分地区医疗救助情况(2023年)
Statistics on Medical Aid by Region (2023)

地　区	Region	资助参加基本医疗保险人数(万人) Number of People Subsidized to Participate in Basic Medical Insurance (10 000 persons)	门诊和住院医疗救助人次数(万人次) Outpatients and Inpatients Receiving Medical Aid (10 000 person-times)	资助参加基本医疗保险资金数(万元) Expenses on Subsidy to Participation in Basic Medical Insurance (10 000 yuan)	门诊和住院医疗救助资金数(万元) Expenses on Medical Aid for Outpatients and Inpatients (10 000 yuan)
全　国	**National Total**	**8020.4**	**15340.2**	**1891031.0**	**5112185.6**
北　京	Beijing	10.1	399.1	4396.0	40035.0
天　津	Tianjin	13.4	107.2	4032.8	24703.5
河　北	Hebei	364.1	924.9	105171.2	230299.7
山　西	Shanxi	143.1	163.5	42310.6	81667.6
内蒙古	Inner Mongolia	163.3	261.6	28306.9	108764.7
辽　宁	Liaoning	114.1	240.0	40605.6	98651.5
吉　林	Jilin	87.1	161.8	13643.5	89386.6
黑龙江	Heilongjiang	168.4	345.0	43859.6	199653.4
上　海	Shanghai	12.5	368.6	7587.1	69428.2
江　苏	Jiangsu	332.3	2441.5	118964.5	402956.9
浙　江	Zhejiang	60.8	1543.2	43501.0	198449.0
安　徽	Anhui	341.6	928.6	106708.5	350587.0
福　建	Fujian	121.5	471.9	43368.7	104998.9
江　西	Jiangxi	172.8	767.6	56206.8	260838.0
山　东	Shandong	179.9	591.2	53603.9	188570.2
河　南	Henan	378.3	477.1	99500.9	259434.6
湖　北	Hubei	245.2	562.8	57786.1	226493.2
湖　南	Hunan	288.1	256.8	70908.1	208510.3
广　东	Guangdong	234.7	709.7	87078.0	259257.6
广　西	Guangxi	304.8	525.0	67891.4	299299.4
海　南	Hainan	18.3	111.5	5875.6	18050.5
重　庆	Chongqing	135.7	398.0	43004.0	60893.0
四　川	Sichuan	798.8	642.1	180889.2	339907.7
贵　州	Guizhou	851.9	333.3	122526.5	174114.9
云　南	Yunnan	988.4	605.4	133644.0	232379.7
西　藏	Xizang	48.2	33.0	16353.0	8901.9
陕　西	Shaanxi	186.0	222.2	34905.6	112427.3
甘　肃	Gansu	675.0	383.3	112936.7	219331.5
青　海	Qinghai	47.2	61.4	9736.0	77665.0
宁　夏	Ningxia	105.3	86.4	25023.8	35585.5
新　疆	Xinjiang	429.4	216.3	110705.3	130943.5

22–23 社会组织情况
Statistics on Social Organizations

单位：个 (unit)

年份 Year 地区 Region	社会组织 Social Organizations	社会团体 Social Groups	民办非企业单位 Private Non-Enterprise Units	基金会 Foundations
2000	153322	130668	22654	
2005	319762	171150	147637	975
2006	354393	191946	161303	1144
2007	386916	211661	173915	1340
2008	413660	229681	182382	1597
2009	431069	238747	190479	1843
2010	445631	245256	198175	2200
2011	461971	254969	204388	2614
2012	499268	271131	225108	3029
2013	547245	289026	254670	3549
2014	606048	309736	292195	4117
2015	662425	328500	329141	4784
2016	702405	335932	360914	5559
2017	761539	354794	400438	6307
2018	817360	366234	444092	7034
2019	866335	371638	487112	7585
2020	894162	374771	510959	8432
2021	901870	371110	521883	8877
2022	891267	370093	511855	9319
2023	881574	372662	499295	9617
中央级 Central-level	2295	1996	86	213
北京 Beijing	12407	4306	7262	839
天津 Tianjin	6571	2658	3800	113
河北 Hebei	38635	12923	25185	527
山西 Shanxi	18940	8101	10670	169
内蒙古 Inner Mongolia	16840	7717	8929	194
辽宁 Liaoning	26812	6853	19853	106
吉林 Jilin	12741	5584	7036	121
黑龙江 Heilongjiang	19719	6876	12722	121
上海 Shanghai	17283	4307	12349	627
江苏 Jiangsu	75771	29644	45318	809
浙江 Zhejiang	68787	26395	41213	1179
安徽 Anhui	38736	18908	19621	207
福建 Fujian	33358	18701	14130	527
江西 Jiangxi	28652	13411	15131	110
山东 Shandong	67680	22625	44721	334
河南 Henan	50117	14663	35300	154
湖北 Hubei	31173	12849	18111	213
湖南 Hunan	36842	16042	20373	427
广东 Guangdong	71358	32713	37194	1451
广西 Guangxi	28368	12191	16060	117
海南 Hainan	8993	3697	5165	131
重庆 Chongqing	17955	8313	9542	100
四川 Sichuan	44692	20880	23608	204
贵州 Guizhou	15411	7481	7855	75
云南 Yunnan	22417	12294	10011	112
西藏 Xizang	745	644	79	22
陕西 Shaanxi	30688	16854	13647	187
甘肃 Gansu	19034	11855	7088	91
青海 Qinghai	5745	3991	1719	35
宁夏 Ningxia	4439	2565	1812	62
新疆 Xinjiang	8370	4625	3705	40

22-24 婚姻登记情况
Statistics on Marriage Registration

年 份 Year / 地 区 Region	结婚登记 (万对) Total Number of Marriage Registration (10 000 couples)	内地居民 Mainland Residents	涉外、华侨及港澳台居民 Involving Foreigners, Overseas Chinese or Residents of Hong Kong, Macao, Taiwan	初 婚 (万人) First Marriages (10 000 persons)	再 婚 (万人) Re-marriages (10 000 persons)	离 婚 (万对) Divorces (10 000 couples)	离婚率 (‰) Divorce Rate (‰)
1985	831.30	829.06	2.22	1607.63	50.48	45.79	0.44
1990	951.10	948.69	2.38	1819.13	78.24	80.00	0.69
1995	934.10	929.71	4.40	1776.07	83.35	105.60	0.88
2000	848.50	842.00	6.49	1581.39	102.62	121.29	0.96
2005	823.10	816.60	6.43	1483.00	163.10	178.50	1.37
2006	945.00	938.20	6.82	1705.60	184.40	191.30	1.46
2007	991.40	986.30	5.11	1779.70	203.10	209.80	1.59
2008	1098.30	1093.20	5.10	1972.50	224.10	226.90	1.71
2009	1212.40	1207.50	4.92	2168.80	256.00	246.80	1.85
2010	1241.00	1236.10	4.90	2200.90	281.10	267.80	2.00
2011	1302.36	1297.48	4.88	2309.88	294.85	287.40	2.13
2012	1323.59	1318.27	5.33	2361.17	286.02	310.38	2.29
2013	1346.93	1341.43	5.50	2385.96	307.89	350.01	2.57
2014	1306.74	1302.04	4.70	2286.81	326.68	363.68	2.67
2015	1224.71	1220.59	4.12	2108.97	340.44	384.14	2.79
2016	1142.82	1138.61	4.22	1913.26	372.39	415.82	3.02
2017	1063.10	1059.04	4.05	1746.33	379.86	437.40	3.15
2018	1013.94	1009.11	4.84	1598.67	429.22	446.08	3.20
2019	927.33	922.39	4.94	1398.71	455.94	470.06	3.36
2020	814.33	812.60	1.74	1228.60	400.07	433.90	3.09
2021	764.30	762.70	1.60	1157.80	370.80	283.93	2.01
2022	683.50	681.86	1.64	1051.76	315.24	287.92	2.04
2023	768.21	763.25	4.97	1193.98	342.45	360.53	2.56
北 京 Beijing	13.73	13.67	0.07	19.52	7.95	5.49	2.51
天 津 Tianjin	8.38	8.35	0.03	13.69	3.06	4.94	3.62
河 北 Hebei	37.11	36.98	0.13	56.82	17.40	17.77	2.40
山 西 Shanxi	20.59	20.56	0.03	34.02	7.17	7.38	2.12
内蒙古 Inner Mongolia	14.24	14.21	0.03	19.78	8.69	7.06	2.94
辽 宁 Liaoning	22.84	22.76	0.08	36.14	9.54	12.03	2.87
吉 林 Jilin	13.79	13.74	0.05	20.61	6.97	8.02	3.42
黑龙江 Heilongjiang	17.94	17.87	0.07	21.26	14.62	11.32	3.68
上 海 Shanghai	10.42	10.29	0.13	15.26	5.59	4.30	1.73
江 苏 Jiangsu	45.28	45.13	0.15	75.89	14.68	21.36	2.51
浙 江 Zhejiang	30.06	29.82	0.24	48.16	11.95	12.34	1.87
安 徽 Anhui	35.54	35.27	0.27	53.07	18.01	18.18	2.97
福 建 Fujian	18.08	17.52	0.57	27.86	8.30	9.02	2.16
江 西 Jiangxi	22.16	21.98	0.19	35.50	8.83	10.59	2.34
山 东 Shandong	48.16	48.02	0.14	71.92	24.40	21.97	2.17
河 南 Henan	57.40	57.20	0.20	96.77	18.03	27.07	2.75
湖 北 Hubei	29.33	29.17	0.16	46.72	11.94	15.30	2.62
湖 南 Hunan	30.27	30.00	0.28	45.49	15.06	16.57	2.52
广 东 Guangdong	63.22	62.23	0.99	107.11	19.33	22.61	1.78
广 西 Guangxi	25.17	24.90	0.27	39.87	10.48	11.60	2.30
海 南 Hainan	5.69	5.65	0.04	9.37	2.01	2.10	2.03
重 庆 Chongqing	18.37	18.29	0.08	25.32	11.41	10.72	3.35
四 川 Sichuan	48.02	47.83	0.18	70.29	25.75	25.16	3.01
贵 州 Guizhou	29.46	29.39	0.07	45.47	13.45	14.13	3.66
云 南 Yunnan	28.81	28.40	0.41	44.51	13.11	12.66	2.70
西 藏 Xizang	2.95	2.95	0.00	5.41	0.49	0.70	1.93
陕 西 Shaanxi	23.50	23.43	0.07	36.25	10.75	9.59	2.43
甘 肃 Gansu	16.42	16.40	0.02	27.78	5.07	5.79	2.34
青 海 Qinghai	4.71	4.71	0.00	7.54	1.87	1.79	3.01
宁 夏 Ningxia	5.07	5.06	0.01	7.99	2.14	2.10	2.89
新 疆 Xinjiang	21.51	21.50	0.01	28.61	14.42	10.88	4.20

22-25 福利彩票销售情况
Statistics on Welfare Lottery

年份 地区	Year Region	福利彩票发行单位 (个) Welfare Lottery Issuing Units (unit)	福利彩票销售额 (亿元) Sales of Welfare Lottery (100 million yuan)	提取公益金 (亿元) Withdraws of Public Welfare Fund from Welfare Lottery (100 million yuan)	公益金支出 (亿元) Expenditure of Public Welfare Fund from Welfare Lottery (100 million yuan)
	2000	1253	89.9	24.2	38.7
	2005	1113	411.2	143.7	52.3
	2006	989	495.7	171.6	52.6
	2007	985	631.6	217.0	77.6
	2008	999	604.0	211.4	119.2
	2009	988	756.0	248.0	113.4
	2010	993	968.0	297.1	121.2
	2011	974	1278.0	388.7	127.9
	2012	955	1510.3	449.4	159.0
	2013	940	1765.3	510.7	195.5
	2014	893	2060.0	585.7	231.3
	2015	861	2015.1	563.8	288.9
	2016	788	2064.9	591.5	268.3
	2017	729	2169.8	631.1	275.2
	2018	700	2245.6	643.6	251.7
	2019	702	1912.4	557.3	259.9
	2020	688	1444.9	444.6	229.9
	2021	655	1422.5	443.6	196.8
	2022	642	1481.3	461.0	212.9
	2023	621	1944.4	580.1	234.4
北京	Beijing	2	51.6	15.4	5.9
天津	Tianjin	3	17.3	5.3	2.5
河北	Hebei	17	60.0	19.0	9.0
山西	Shanxi	11	32.5	9.7	5.6
内蒙古	Inner Mongolia	15	38.8	11.9	5.9
辽宁	Liaoning	15	69.3	20.9	5.3
吉林	Jilin	42	29.3	8.5	3.1
黑龙江	Heilongjiang	15	30.7	9.3	3.4
上海	Shanghai	17	56.5	16.8	9.0
江苏	Jiangsu	72	133.1	37.9	11.4
浙江	Zhejiang	31	163.8	47.3	18.4
安徽	Anhui	43	71.3	21.4	9.2
福建	Fujian	11	56.9	17.1	6.2
江西	Jiangxi	10	40.6	12.4	5.9
山东	Shandong	17	110.2	33.7	11.0
河南	Henan	34	62.4	19.5	11.8
湖北	Hubei	25	72.7	22.3	8.7
湖南	Hunan	74	80.3	24.2	11.0
广东	Guangdong	47	216.7	61.9	22.7
广西	Guangxi	16	46.3	13.2	6.4
海南	Hainan	6	7.2	2.0	0.9
重庆	Chongqing	1	44.1	13.3	4.6
四川	Sichuan	1	96.6	29.6	14.8
贵州	Guizhou	11	35.9	11.2	5.0
云南	Yunnan	14	94.4	30.7	5.6
西藏	Xizang	2	8.9	2.5	5.3
陕西	Shaanxi	20	77.0	23.2	8.5
甘肃	Gansu	14	26.7	8.3	4.2
青海	Qinghai	6	12.7	3.9	2.1
宁夏	Ningxia	13	17.5	5.4	2.1
新疆	Xinjiang	15	83.2	22.4	8.6

注：全国数据含部本级单位。

a) The national data includes ministerial level units.

22-26 残疾人事业基本情况
Basic Statistics on the Work for Persons with Disability

项　目	Item	2022	2023
康复	**Rehabilitation**		
视力残疾康复服务人数 (万人)	Rehabilitation of Persons with Visual Disability (10 000 persons)	75.5	72.5
听力残疾康复服务人数 (万人)	Rehabilitation of Persons with Hearing Disability (10 000 persons)	67.4	69.5
言语残疾康复服务人数 (万人)	Rehabilitation of Persons with Speaking Disability(10 000 persons)	5.6	5.9
肢体残疾康复服务人数 (万人)	Rehabilitation of Persons with Physical Disability (10 000 persons)	414.3	415.7
智力残疾康复服务人数 (万人)	Rehabilitation of Persons with Mental Disability (10 000 persons)	65.6	70.1
精神残疾康复服务人数 (万人)	Prevention and Rehabilitation of Mental Illness (PRMI) (10 000 persons)	157.0	159.9
残疾人康复机构 (个)	Rehabilitation Institutions for Persons with Disability (unit)	11661	12463
辅助器具服务机构 (个)	Auxiliary Appliance Service Agencies (unit)	2000	1938
教育	**Education**		
特殊教育普通高中在校生 (人)	Students at Senior Secondary Schools with Special Education (person)	11431	12429
高等院校录取残疾考生人数 (人)	Disabled Students Admitted to Higher Education Institutions (person)	30035	30810
就业	**Employment**		
城乡持证残疾人就业人数 (万人)	Employed Persons with Disability Certificates (10 000 persons)	905.5	906.1
残疾人实用技术培训 (万人次)	Vocational Skills Training for Persons with Disability (10 000 person-times)	28.5	25.9
社会保障	**Social Security**		
残疾居民参加城乡基本养老保险人数(万人)	Disabled Residents Covered by Pension Insurance (10 000 persons)	2761.7	2749.0
维权	**Rights Protection**		
残疾人法律救助工作协调机构 (个)	Legal Assistance Stations for Persons with Disability (unit)	2869	2901
残疾人机动轮椅车燃油补贴 (万人)	Subsidy for Fuel of Motor Wheelchairs of Persons with Disability (10 000 persons)	26.3	22.5
组织建设	**Organization Development**		
残疾人专职委员 (万人)	Full-time Committee Members with Disability (10 000 persons)	55.7	56.0
残疾人人口库持证残疾人 (万人)	Persons with Disability Certificates in the Database of PWDs (10 000 persons)	3768.2	3779.4

注：2022年起，高等院校录取残疾考生人数含普通高等院校和高等特殊教育院校。

a) From 2022, the number of disabled students admitted to higher education institutions includes regular higher education institutions and higher special education institutions.

主要统计指标解释

医疗卫生机构 指从卫生健康行政部门取得《医疗机构执业许可证》，或从民政、工商行政、机构编制管理部门取得法人单位登记证书，为社会提供医疗保健、疾病控制、卫生监督服务或从事医学科研和医学在职培训等工作的单位。医疗卫生机构包括医院、基层医疗卫生机构、专业公共卫生机构、其他医疗卫生机构。

医院 包括综合医院、中医医院、中西医结合医院、民族医院、各类专科医院和护理院，不包括专科疾病防治院、妇幼保健院和疗养院。

基层医疗卫生机构 包括社区卫生服务中心（站）、街道卫生院、乡镇卫生院、村卫生室、门诊部、诊所（医务室）。

专业公共卫生机构 包括疾病预防控制中心、专科疾病防治机构、妇幼保健机构、健康教育机构、急救中心（站）、采供血机构、卫生监督机构、卫生健康部门主管的计划生育技术服务机构。不包括传染病院、结核病医院、血防医院、精神病医院、卫生监督（监测、检测）机构。

卫生人员 指在医院、基层医疗卫生机构、专业公共卫生机构及其他医疗卫生机构工作的职工，包括卫生技术人员、乡村医生和卫生员、其他技术人员、管理人员和工勤人员。一律按支付年底工资的在岗职工统计，包括各类聘任人员（含合同工）及返聘本单位半年以上人员，不包括临时工、离退休人员、退职人员、离开本单位仍保留劳动关系人员、本单位返聘和临聘不足半年人员。

卫生技术人员 包括执业医师、执业助理医师、注册护士、药师（士）、检验技师（士）、影像技师、卫生监督员和见习医（药、护、技）师（士）等卫生专业人员。不包括从事管理工作的卫生技术人员(如院长、副院长、党委书记等)。

执业医师 指《医师执业证》“级别”为“执业医师”且实际从事医疗、预防保健工作的人员，不包括实际从事管理工作的执业医师。执业医师类别分为临床、中医、口腔和公共卫生四类。

执业助理医师 指《医师执业证》“级别”为“执业助理医师”且实际从事医疗、预防保健工作的人员，不包括实际从事管理工作的执业助理医师。执业助理医师类别分为临床、中医、口腔和公共卫生四类。

每千人口卫生技术人员 每千人口卫生技术人员=卫生技术人员数/人口数×1000。

每千人口执业(助理)医师 每千人口执业(助理)医师=(执业医师数+执业助理医师数）/人口数×1000。

床位数 指年末医疗卫生机构实有床位，又称实有床位数、病床数。实有床位包括正规床、简易床、监护床、超过半年的加床、正在消毒和修理的床位、因扩建或大修而停用的床位。不包括产科新生儿床、接产室待产床、库存床、观察床、临时加床和病人家属陪待床。

每千人口医疗卫生机构床位 每千人口医疗卫生机构床位=年末医疗卫生机构床位数/年末人口数×1000。

甲乙类法定报告传染病发病率 是指某年每10万人口中甲乙类法定报告传染病发病数。即甲乙类法定传染病发病率=甲乙类法定报告传染病发病数/人口数×100000。

甲乙类法定报告传染病死亡率 是指某年每10万人口中甲乙类法定报告传染病死亡数。即甲乙类法定报告传染病死亡率=甲乙类法定报告传染病死亡数/人口数×100000。

孕产妇死亡率 指年内每10万名孕产妇的死亡人数。孕产妇死亡指从妊娠期至产后42天内，由于任何妊娠或妊娠处理有关的原因导致的死亡，但不包括意外原因死亡者。按国际通用计算方法，“孕产妇总数”以“活产数”代替计算。

5岁以下儿童死亡率 指年内未满5岁儿童死亡人数与活产数之比，一般以‰表示。

新生儿死亡率 指年内新生儿死亡数与活产数之比。一般以‰表示。新生儿死亡指出生至28天以内（即0–27天）死亡人数。

新生儿访视率 指年内新生儿出院后1周内接受1次及1次以上访视的新生儿人数与活产数之比。

3岁以下儿童系统管理率 指年内3岁以下儿童系统管理人数与3岁以下儿童数之比。

7岁以下儿童健康管理率 指年内7岁以下儿童健康管理人数与7岁以下儿童数之比。

0—6岁儿童眼保健和视力检查覆盖率 指年内接受1次及以上眼保健和视力检查的0—6岁儿童数与0—6岁儿童数之比。

产前检查率 指年内接受过1次及以上产前检查的产妇人数与活产数之比。

孕产妇系统管理率 指年内孕产妇系统管理人数与活产数之比。

住院分娩率 指年内在取得助产技术资质的机构分娩的活产数与所有活产数之比。

产后访视率 指年内接受过1次及以上产后访视的产妇人数与活产数之比。

卫生总费用 指一个国家或地区在一定时期内，为开展卫生服务活动从全社会筹集的卫生资源的货币总额，按来源法核算。它反映一定经济条件下，政府、社会和居民个人对卫生保健的重视程度和费用负担水平，以及卫生筹资模式的主要特征和卫生筹资的公平性合理性。

政府卫生支出 指各级政府用于医疗卫生服务、医疗保障补助、卫生和医疗保障行政管理、人口与计划生育事务支出等各项事业的经费。

社会卫生支出 指政府支出外的社会各界对卫生事业的资金投入。包括社会医疗保障支出、商业健康保险费、社会办医支出、社会捐赠援助、行政事业性收费收入等。

个人卫生支出 指城乡居民在接受各类医疗卫生服务时的现金支付，包括享受各种医疗保险制度的居民就医时自付的费用。可分为城镇居民、农村居民个人现金卫生支出，反映城乡居民医疗卫生费用的负担程度。

人均卫生总费用 即某年卫生总费用与同期平均人口数之比。

卫生总费用占 GDP 比重 指某年卫生总费用与同期国内生产总值（GDP）之比。是用来反映一定时期国家对卫生事业的资金投入力度，以及政府和全社会对卫生事业、居民健康的重视程度。

提供住宿的民政机构 指能为老年人、残疾人、智障与精神病人、儿童等人员提供住宿的社会服务机构数。包括社会福利院、特困人员救助供养机构、其他各类养老机构、社会福利医院、儿童福利院、未成年人救助保护中心、流浪乞讨人员救助管理机构、安置农场以及其他提供住宿的机构。

孤儿数 指失去父母或查找不到生父母的未满18周岁的未成年人的人数。由地方县级以上民政部门依据有关规定和条件认定的，并已经领取了孤儿补助费的孤儿。

被收养儿童 指通过收养登记被家庭收养儿童人数的总和，包括国内外收养中国儿童的总人数。

城市最低生活保障人数 指在报告期末纳入当地城市最低生活保障范围、并已发放补助经费的人数。

农村最低生活保障人数 指在报告期末纳入当地农村最低生活保障范围、并已发放补助经费的人数。

农村特困人员 指无劳动能力、无生活来源、无法定赡养、抚养、扶养义务人或者其法定义务人无履行义务能力的农村老年人、残疾人以及未满 16 周岁的未成年人被依法纳入特困人员救助供养范围、享受供养待遇的人员。

离婚率 指某地区当年离婚对数占该地区年平均人口的比重。计算公式为：

$$离婚率=\frac{当年离婚对数}{年平均人口数}\times 1000‰$$

残疾人就业人数 指截止到本年度 12 月 31 日，以各种就业形式实际在业的城乡持证残疾人数。

Explanatory Notes on Main Statistical Indicators

Health Care Institutions refer to the units which have been qualified with the Certification of Health Care Institution,, or qualified with the Certification of Corporate Unit by the civil affairs, administration for industry and commerce, and engaging in medical care services, disease control services, health supervision services, or medicine research and on-job training, etc., including: hospitals, health care institutions at grass-root level, specialized public health institutions, and other health care institutions.

Hospitals include general hospitals, traditional Chinese medicine hospitals, hospitals of integrated traditional Chinese and western medicine, nationalities hospitals, specialized hospitals and nursing hospitals, as well as affiliated hospitals of medical colleges, excluding specialized disease prevention and treatment institutes, maternal and child health centers and convalescent hospitals.

Health Care Institutions at Grass-root Level include community health service centers (stations), sub-district health centers, township health centers, village clinics, outpatient departments and clinics.

Specialized Public Health Institutions include CDC, specialized disease prevention and treatment institutions, maternal and children health centers, health education institutions, emergency centers (first-aid stations), blood gathering and supplying institutions, health inspection institutions, and family planning technical service institutions headed by the health department. It does not include infectious hospital, tuberculosis hospital, schistosomiasis control hospital, mental hospital, health supervision (monitoring and testing) institution.

Health Personnel refer to all employees engaged in the health care institutions, such as hospitals, health care institutions at grass-root level, specialized public health institutions, and other health care institutions, including health technical personnel, village doctors and assistants, other technical personnel, administrative staffs and logistics technical workers. Data are based on the year end payroll, including personnel employed (including contract workers) and re-employed after retirement by the institution for more than 6 months, excluding temporary workers, retired personnel, resigned personnel, personnel who have left the institution but kept the contract relation and personnel who are re-employed after retirement or temporarily employed for less than 6 months.

Health Technical Personnel refer to the professional staff engaged in health care, including licensed physicians and physician assistants, registered nurses, pharmacists, laboratory and imaging technicians, health care supervisors and intern doctors, pharmacists, nurses, and technical personnel, excluding health technical personnel engaged in management (e.g. president, vice president and secretary of the party committee etc).

Licensed Physicians refer to the medical workers with licenses of qualified doctors and are employed in medical treatment, disease prevention or healthcare institutions, excluding the licensed doctors engaged in management. The physicians are divided into 4 categories: clinician, Chinese medicine, stomatology and public health.

Licensed Physician Assistants refer to the medical workers with licenses of qualified assistant doctors and are employed in medical treatment, disease prevention or healthcare institutions, excluding the licensed assistant doctors engaged in management. Physician assistants are divided into 4 categories: clinician, Chinese medicine, stomatology and public health.

Number of Health Technical Personnel per 1000 Population The formula is:

Number of health technical personnel per 1000 population = number of health technical personnel / population ×1000

Number of Licensed Physicians & Physician Assistants per 1000 Population The formula is:

Number of licensed physicians & physician assistants per 1000 population = (number of licensed physicians + number of licensed physician assistants) / population ×1000

Number of Beds refer to the actual number of beds in health care institutions at year-end, also known as the actual number of beds or hospital beds, including regular beds, simple beds, monitoring beds, extra bed over 6 months, beds under disinfection or repairing, beds deactivated due to expansion or overhaul, not including neonatal beds, pre-delivery beds, inventory beds, observation beds, temporary beds and family accompany beds.

Number of Beds of Health Care Institutions per 1000 Population the formula is:

Number of beds of health care institutions per 1000 population = number of beds of health care institutions at year-end / population at year-end ×1000

Morbidity Rate of Class A and B Notifiable Infectious Diseases refers to the number of cases of Class A and B notifiable infectious diseases per 100 thousand population in the reference year. The formula is:

Morbidity rate of Class A and B notifiable infectious diseases = number of cases of Class A and B notifiable infectious diseases / population 100000

Mortality Rate of Class A and B Notifiable Infectious Diseases refers to the number of deaths of Class A and B notifiable infectious diseases per 100 thousand population in the reference year. The formula is:

Mortality rate of Class A and B notifiable infectious diseases= number of deaths of Class A and B notifiable

infectious diseases / population ×100000

Maternal Mortality Rate refers to number of maternal deaths per 100,000 maternal. It generally refers to maternal mortality from the start of pregnancy to 42 days after parturition, due to pregnancy or any treatment of pregnancy. However, accidental deaths are not included. According to internationally accepted approach, the live births are used to represent the total number of maternity.

Mortality Rate of Children under 5 refers to the ratio of deaths of children under 5 in a year to the number of live births, and usually is presented by ‰.

Neonatal Mortality Rate refers to the ratio of neonatal deaths in a year to the number of live births, and usually is presented by ‰. Neonatal deaths refer to the deaths of new-birth within 28 days (0-27 days).

Visit Rate to the Newborn refers to the ratio of the number of newborns who receive one or more visits within one week after discharge within a year to the number of live births.

System Management Rate for Children under 3 Years Old refers to the ratio of the number of children under 3 years old managed by the system to the number of children under 3 years old during the year.

Health Management Rate for Children under 7 Years Old refers to the ratio of the number of children under 7 years old who are under health management to the number of children under 7 years old during the year.

Coverage Rate of Eye Care and Vision Examination for Children Aged 0-6 refers to the ratio of the number of children aged 0-6 who receive one or more eye care and vision examinations within a year to the number of children aged 0-6.

Prenatal Examination Rate refers to the ratio of the number of pregnant women who have undergone one or more prenatal examinations within a year to the number of live births.

Maternal Systematic Management Rate refers to the ratio of the number of maternal system management personnel to the number of live births within a year.

Institutional Delivery Rate refers to the ratio of live births to all live births in institutions that have obtained midwifery technical qualifications within a year.

Postnatal Visit Rate refers to the ratio of the number of mothers who have received one or more postpartum visits within a year to the number of live births.

Total Health Expenditure refers to the total monetary value of health resources in a country or a region mobilized by the whole society for public health, calculated based on source approach. It reflects the attention and affordability of the government, society and individuals for public health, and the major characteristics, justice and rationality of the health fund-raising model under certain economic circumstance.

Government Health Expenditure refers to the expenditure of the governments at all levels on medical and health care services, medical subsidies, health administration and health security management, and undertakings of family planning etc.

Social Health Expenditure refers to all inputs of the society except the government in public health, including the expenditures on social medical security, commercial health insurance, private expenditure on of medical and health care operation, social donation and contribution, and income from administrative fees etc.

Out-of-Pocket Health Expenditure refers to expenditure in cash on various health services by rural and urban residents, including self payments of residents within various medical insurance systems. It can be categorized as cash expenditure on health by urban and rural residents and reflects their affordability of public health.

Per Capita Health Expenditure refers to the ratio of total health expenditure in a year to the average population.

Proportion of Total Health Expenditure to GDP refers to the ratio of total health expenditure in a year to GDP, which indicates the financial support given by a nation to health work and the attention paid on the public health and the health of residents by the government and society.

Number of Civil Affairs Institutions with Accommodations refers to the number of social service institutions that can provide accommodations for the elderly, the disabled, the mentally handicapped and the mentally ill, and children. It includes social welfare institutions, assistance and support institutions for people in extreme difficulty, other pension institutions, social welfare hospitals, children's welfare homes, assistance and protection centers for minors, relief and management institutions for vagrants and beggars, resettlement farms and other institutions providing accommodations.

Number of Orphans refers to juveniles under the age of 18 that have lost or cannot find their parents. Orphans are affirmed by departments of civil affairs at county level according to relevant regulations, and receive orphan subsidies.

Number of Children Adopted refers to the total number of children adopted by families through adoption registration, including the total number of Chinese children adopted at home and abroad.

Number of Urban Residents Entitled to Minimum Living Allowances refers to the number of urban residents who have been included in the scope of local urban minimum living guarantee and have been granted subsidies by the end of the reporting period.

Number of Rural Residents Entitled to Minimum Living Allowances refers to the number of rural residents who have been included in the scope of local rural minimum living guarantee and have been granted subsidies by the end of the reporting period.

Rural Residents in Special Hardship refers to the rural elderly, disabled persons and minors under the age of 16 who have no working ability, no source of income, no regular maintenance, upbringing and support obligations, or their legal obligations have no ability to perform their obligations, and are included in the scope of assistance and support for people in special hardship and enjoy support treatment according to law.

Divorce Rate refers to ratio of divorced couples to the annual average population in a certain region for the reference year, the formula is:

$$\text{Divorce Rate} = \frac{\text{number of couples divorced for the reference year}}{\text{annual average population}} \times 1000‰$$

Number of Employed Person with Disabilities refers to the number of urban and rural persons with disability certificates who are actually employed through various forms of employment.

23

文化和体育

Culture and Sports

简 要 说 明

一、本篇资料的主要内容

本篇主要反映新闻出版、广电、文化、文物、档案、体育事业发展情况。

内容包括全国及各地区图书、期刊、报纸、音像制品的出版、印刷以及引进和输出版权情况；全国及各地区广播影视宣传、覆盖、技术等方面的情况；全国及各地区艺术表演团体、公共图书馆、群众文化机构、博物馆以及国家档案馆等单位的机构、人员、经费和业务活动情况；全国及分地区规模以上文化及相关产业企业主要情况；全国体育系统机构人员情况；运动员获世界冠军、创世界纪录情况。

二、本篇的资料来源

新闻出版资料来自国家新闻出版署；电影资料来自国家电影局；广播、电视资料来自国家广播电视总局；文化资料来自文化和旅游部；文物资料来自国家文物局；档案资料来自国家档案局；体育资料来自国家体育总局。

详细资料分别见《中国新闻出版统计资料汇编》（国家新闻出版署编）、《全国广播电视服务业统计数据》（国家广播电视总局编）、《中国文化文物和旅游统计年鉴》（中华人民共和国文化和旅游部编）。

三、数据使用注意事项

规模以上文化企业主要指标数据与上年数据之间存在不可比因素，主要原因是有部分企业达到规模以上标准纳入调查范围，也有部分企业因规模变小而退出调查范围，还有新建投产企业、破产、注（吊）销企业等，使得规模以上文化企业数量每年发生增减变化。

Brief Introduction

I. Main Contents

Data in this chapter mainly reflect the development of news and publication; radio and television broadcasting, films; culture; cultural relics; archives and sports undertakings.

Contents of this chapter cover the publication and printing of books, magazines, newspapers, audio-visual products, and import and export of copyrights of the country and by region; the coverage and techniques of radio and television programs, and films of the country and by region; number of institutions and employed persons, funds and activities of art performance troupes, public libraries, mass cultural institutions, museums and archive institutions at national level and by region; statistics on corporate units of cultural and related industries above designated size by region; personnel of national sports system, world championships won and world records set by Chinese athletes.

II. Sources of Data

Data on news and publications are from the General Administration of Press and Publication. Data on films are from the State Film Bureau. Data on radio and television broadcasting are from the State Administration of Radio and Television. Data on culture are provided by the Ministry of Culture and Tourism. Data on cultural relics are from State Administration of Cultural Heritage. Data on archives are from State Archives Administration. Data on sports are from General Administration of Sport.

For detailed information please refer to "Collection of China News and Publication Statistical Information" (General Administration of Press and Publication), "Statistical Data of National Radio and Television Services" (State Administration of Radio and Television), "China Cultural Relics and Tourism Yearbook" (Ministry of Culture and Tourism of the People's Republic of China).

III. Notes on Data Use

Data of cultural-related enterprises above designated size are not fully comparable with previous years. The main reason is that some enterprises meet the size criteria to be included in the survey, while some other enterprises withdraw from the survey because of the shrinking size, and there are other changes: newly-built enterprises, bankrupted enterprises, cancelation of enterprises, etc., resulted in the changing number of cultural-related enterprises above designated size.

23-1 图书、期刊和报纸出版情况
Statistics on Books, Periodicals and Newspapers

年份 地区	Year Region	图书 Books Published 种数(种) Number of Publications (kind)	#新出版 New Publications	总印数(亿册、亿张) Printed Copies (100 million copies)	期刊 Periodicals Published 种数(种) Number of Publications (kind)	总印数(亿册) Total Printed Copies (100 million copies)	报纸 Newspapers Published 种数(种) Number of Publications (kind)	总印数(亿份) Total Printed Copies (100 million copies)
	1978	14987	11888	37.7	930	7.6	186	127.8
	1980	21621	17660	45.9	2191	11.2	188	140.4
	1985	45603	33743	66.7	4705	25.6	1445	246.8
	1990	80224	55245	56.4	5751	17.9	1444	211.2
	1995	101381	59159	63.2	7583	23.4	2089	263.3
	2000	143376	84235	62.7	8725	29.4	2007	329.3
	2005	222473	128578	64.7	9468	27.6	1931	412.6
	2006	233971	160757	64.1	9468	28.5	1938	424.5
	2007	248283	136226	62.9	9468	30.4	1938	438.0
	2008	274123	148978	70.6	9549	31.0	1943	442.9
	2009	301719	168296	70.4	9851	31.5	1937	439.1
	2010	328387	189295	71.7	9884	32.2	1939	452.1
	2011	369523	207506	77.0	9849	32.9	1928	467.4
	2012	414005	241986	79.2	9867	33.5	1918	482.3
	2013	444427	255981	83.1	9877	32.7	1915	482.4
	2014	448431	255890	81.8	9966	30.9	1912	463.9
	2015	475768	260426	86.6	10014	28.8	1906	430.1
	2016	499884	262415	90.4	10084	27.0	1894	390.1
	2017	512487	255106	92.4	10130	24.9	1884	362.5
	2018	519250	247108	100.1	10139	22.9	1871	337.3
	2019	505979	224762	106.0	10171	21.9	1851	317.6
	2020	489051	213636	103.7	10192	20.4	1810	289.1
	2021	529197	225253	118.6	10185	20.1	1752	283.0
	2022	502246	205261	114.0	10139	19.3	1709	271.0
	2023	540274	217041	125.0	10157	18.5	1669	261.0
中央	Central Level	217669	84439	35.2	3232	7.0	197	74.5
北京	Beijing	13328	5718	2.6	170	0.1	30	2.5
天津	Tianjin	8904	4181	1.2	234	0.2	15	1.5
河北	Hebei	10830	3095	3.7	217	0.3	56	9.7
山西	Shanxi	3298	2068	1.2	198	0.2	53	20.8
内蒙古	Inner Mongolia	2634	1278	0.6	149	0.1	51	1.9
辽宁	Liaoning	12241	5349	1.8	312	0.5	54	4.0
吉林	Jilin	28169	12519	3.3	237	0.2	44	5.2
黑龙江	Heilongjiang	8811	5619	1.2	315	0.2	48	3.0
上海	Shanghai	28105	12467	4.5	641	0.5	63	5.7
江苏	Jiangsu	26955	9027	7.5	453	1.1	74	17.8
浙江	Zhejiang	17422	8069	5.2	235	0.6	63	15.7
安徽	Anhui	11135	3265	3.5	181	0.3	48	4.8
福建	Fujian	4955	2247	1.8	174	0.2	42	6.2
江西	Jiangxi	10744	4050	3.6	165	0.7	37	5.7
山东	Shandong	17284	5501	6.4	269	0.6	76	12.4
河南	Henan	11174	4217	5.1	244	0.6	77	12.0
湖北	Hubei	18255	6372	3.8	416	0.7	68	5.5
湖南	Hunan	11971	4767	6.4	253	0.7	44	5.0
广东	Guangdong	12082	5089	5.5	380	0.8	90	12.7
广西	Guangxi	6933	2571	3.6	177	0.3	42	4.4
海南	Hainan	4699	1487	0.8	41	0.0	13	1.4
重庆	Chongqing	5498	1931	1.4	139	0.4	27	1.3
四川	Sichuan	13769	6709	4.4	356	0.5	66	9.1
贵州	Guizhou	1266	748	1.2	92	0.1	24	2.1
云南	Yunnan	6218	3327	2.1	127	0.2	39	3.0
西藏	Xizang	663	318	0.2	39	0.0	24	0.9
陕西	Shaanxi	13365	5092	3.1	270	0.3	42	4.4
甘肃	Gansu	4810	1903	1.4	131	0.9	44	2.6
青海	Qinghai	746	451	0.1	56	0.0	25	0.7
宁夏	Ningxia	2319	1001	0.5	36	0.0	13	0.8
新疆	Xinjiang	4022	2166	2.0	218	0.1	80	3.5

23-2 图书出版情况（2023年）

Statistics on Books Published by Category (2023)

类　别	Category	种　数 (种) Number of Publications (kind)	印　数 (万册、万张) Printed Copies (10 000 copies)
图书总计	**Total**	**540274**	**1249691**
使用“中国标准书号”部分合计	**Publications with "China Standard Book Numbering"**	**540045**	**1243134**
马列主义、毛泽东思想	Marxism-Leninism, Mao Zedong Thought	977	2452
哲学	Philosophy	9917	9268
社会科学总论	General Social Sciences	5310	3333
政治、法律	Politics and Law	18719	38365
军事	Military Affairs	1451	1681
经济	Economics	34476	12651
文化、科学、教育、体育	Culture, Science, Education and Sports	227126	988132
语言、文字	Languages	16732	21574
文学	Literature	54391	78169
艺术	Arts	23836	19663
历史、地理	History and Geography	20075	17527
自然科学总论	General Natural Sciences	1011	692
数理科学、化学	Mathematics, Physics and Chemistry	12390	7287
天文学、地球科学	Astronomy and Geology	4399	2188
生物科学	Biology	5071	3484
医学、卫生	Medicine and Health Care	24556	10182
农业科学	Agricultural Science	5434	1514
工业技术	Industrial Technology	57773	16449
交通运输	Transportation	6789	2269
航空、航天	Aeronautics and Aerospace	1353	488
环境科学	Environmental Science	3635	1060
综合性图书	General Books	4624	4706
不使用“中国标准书号”部分合计	**Publications without "China Standard Book Numbering"**	**229**	**6557**
图片	Pictures	229	383
国标(GB)、部标(BB)等标准类文件印品	Standards Publications such as National Standards, Ministry Standards		853
活页文选、活页歌篇、小件印品等	Loose-leaf Collectanea, Loose-leaf Song Collections and Prints of Small Volume		5321

23-3 分地区少年儿童读物和课本出版情况（2023年）
Statistics on Juvenile and Children's Books, Textbooks by Region (2023)

地 区	Region	种数(种) Number of Publications (kind) 少儿读物 Juvenile and Children's Books	课 本 Textbooks	总印数（万册） Printed Copies (10 000 copies) 少儿读物 Juvenile and Children's Books	课 本 Textbooks	总印张(千印张) Printed Sheets (1 000 sheets) 少儿读物 Juvenile and Children's Books	课 本 Textbooks
全 国	**National Total**	**44575**	**87922**	**101382**	**481528**	**5369183**	**37072319**
中 央	Central Level	11251	56613	27909	144485	1377957	13301222
北 京	Beijing	2559	569	6352	2007	323837	205869
天 津	Tianjin	1047	440	1832	2102	94776	153074
河 北	Hebei	865	303	1275	18419	61833	1241424
山 西	Shanxi	190	124	157	5633	14474	401032
内蒙古	Inner Mongolia	335	549	113	4223	5182	306767
辽 宁	Liaoning	1101	2524	1508	6480	87098	541504
吉 林	Jilin	2237	372	2695	5875	156178	402870
黑龙江	Heilongjiang	531	1029	1084	3408	34991	250334
上 海	Shanghai	1637	5364	7202	14524	251850	1255178
江 苏	Jiangsu	1443	3574	2098	27620	147924	1893288
浙 江	Zhejiang	2353	1335	3549	18286	248437	1177124
安 徽	Anhui	1511	428	4357	13528	364778	984458
福 建	Fujian	697	415	3139	7130	88688	489831
江 西	Jiangxi	1908	266	5911	10000	362378	770888
山 东	Shandong	1976	1232	3491	25564	198763	1818461
河 南	Henan	496	989	862	28161	29501	1880847
湖 北	Hubei	2577	2654	5134	9817	320227	805269
湖 南	Hunan	1066	1024	2259	23949	156439	1468208
广 东	Guangdong	1044	1581	4228	30066	257283	2007228
广 西	Guangxi	1802	509	2555	12540	120512	874661
海 南	Hainan	255	21	653	2218	38336	141527
重 庆	Chongqing	152	1927	207	7077	8096	506702
四 川	Sichuan	2785	1530	7493	14482	399034	1072738
贵 州	Guizhou	315	72	1279	8246	37878	589085
云 南	Yunnan	611	128	1270	10060	77062	704099
西 藏	Xizang	63	43	42	1235	1704	88842
陕 西	Shaanxi	736	2075	1531	9484	47574	716051
甘 肃	Gansu	287	36	614	3946	32605	283236
青 海	Qinghai	49	124	15	1075	771	84123
宁 夏	Ningxia	55	9	212	1182	4896	89654
新 疆	Xinjiang	641	63	356	8706	18121	566725

23-4 课本出版情况(2023年)
Statistics on Publication of Textbooks (2023)

项 目	Item	种数(种) Number of Publications (kind)	#新出版 New Publications	总印数(万册) Printed Copies (10 000 copies)	总印张(千印张) Printed Sheets (1 000 sheets)	定价总金额(万元) Total Priced Value (10 000 yuan)
总计	**Total**	**87922**	**20135**	**481528**	**37072319**	**5191011**
大专及以上课本	Textbooks for Higher Education	67522	17219	31581	5608486	1491383
中专、技校课本	Textbooks for Secondary Vocational Education	6163	1072	9945	1519307	289372
中学课本	Textbooks for Secondary Education	4178	376	215814	17994912	1882389
小学课本	Textbooks for Primary Education	4236	359	220213	11230861	1320977
业余教育课本	Textbooks for Spare-time Education	2045	683	1287	274321	74987
扫盲课本	Textbooks for Literacy Courses	8		9	875	120
教学用书	Teaching Materials	3770	426	2679	443557	131783

23-5 分地区音像制品及电子出版物情况（2023年）
Statistics on Publication of Audio-Visual and Electronic Products by Region (2023)

地区	Region	录像制品出版品种（种）Number of Publications of Video Products (kind)	录像制品出版数量（万盒、万张）Volume of Publications of Video Products (10 000 cassettes, 10 000 discs)	录音制品出版品种（种）Number of Publications of Audio Products (kind)	录音制品出版数量（万盒、万张）Volume of Publications of Audio Products (10 000 cassettes, 10 000 discs)	电子出版物出版品种（种）Number of Electronic Publications (kind)	电子出版物出版数量（万张）Volume of Electronic Publications (10 000 discs)
全　国	**National Total**	**2743**	**1381.8**	**3577**	**7731.9**	**10205**	**13904.9**
中　央	Central Level	1411	749.5	1612	5483.5	5154	10259.1
北　京	Beijing	36	4.1	158	178.8	29	12.6
天　津	Tianjin	14	0.2	7	0.1	41	1.1
河　北	Hebei	29	0.3	39	811.6	104	56.7
山　西	Shanxi	9	0.4	32	2.5	8	0.2
内蒙古	Inner Mongolia	1	0.0	9	3.0	48	9.7
辽　宁	Liaoning	80	1.5	112	143.8	692	143.2
吉　林	Jilin	69	10.6	46	65.9	210	15.1
黑龙江	Heilongjiang	3	3.1	14	0.2	104	122.1
上　海	Shanghai	174	181.1	381	431.7	291	540.2
江　苏	Jiangsu	13	0.8	50	36.9	352	1260.1
浙　江	Zhejiang	21	35.4	17	122.2	233	311.2
安　徽	Anhui	34	1.5	11	0.2	10	1.1
福　建	Fujian	38	6.5	14	1.1	8	0.8
江　西	Jiangxi	190	291.2	35	17.2	77	49.2
山　东	Shandong	78	15.3	41	4.3	1051	156.6
河　南	Henan	54	4.6	1	0.0	558	115.3
湖　北	Hubei	20	2.1	18	1.1	211	21.2
湖　南	Hunan	48	27.3	59	93.5	94	103.2
广　东	Guangdong	147	8.6	818	310.9	369	672.7
广　西	Guangxi	14	2.3	7	8.4	13	0.7
海　南	Hainan	8	0.3	14	0.5	17	0.3
重　庆	Chongqing	8	0.8	4	0.2	126	26.9
四　川	Sichuan	39	3.6	9	1.9	232	16.0
贵　州	Guizhou			1	0.8	6	1.8
云　南	Yunnan	59	2.7	24	1.3	21	1.4
西　藏	Xizang	10	2.0	1	0.1		
陕　西	Shaanxi	43	4.5	26	1.7	98	2.2
甘　肃	Gansu	21	1.6	5	0.2	9	0.2
青　海	Qinghai	10	0.4	1	0.0	4	0.1
宁　夏	Ningxia			5	0.2	4	0.1
新　疆	Xinjiang	62	19.5	6	7.8	31	3.8

23-6 图书、期刊、报纸进出口情况（2023年）
Statistics on Import and Export of Books, Periodicals and Newspapers (2023)

指标	Item	出口 Exports		进口 Imports	
		数量（万册、万份）Number (10 000 copies)	金额（万美元）Value (10 000 USD)	数量（万册、万份）Number (10 000 copies)	金额（万美元）Value (10 000 USD)
总计	**Total**	**624.99**	**3327.51**	**3976.67**	**34893.71**
图书	Books	541.94	3159.73	3345.80	23838.63
哲学、社会科学	Philosophy, Social Science	93.04	849.33	86.30	1755.39
文化、教育	Culture and Education	145.05	569.96	504.44	3687.06
文学、艺术	Literature and Arts	92.86	627.69	1115.02	6437.66
自然、科学技术	Natural Science and S&T	26.49	205.47	133.87	3337.74
少儿读物	Juvenile and Children's Books	105.67	195.72	802.12	3225.27
综合性图书	General Books	78.83	711.56	704.05	5395.51
期刊	Periodicals	76.07	165.61	194.98	10351.50
报纸	Newspapers	6.98	2.17	435.89	703.58

注：本表数据为全国有出版物进口经营许可证的出版物进出口经营单位数据(以下相关表同)。
a) Data are from national publication import and export units that have publication import business certificate. The same applies to the following table.

23-7 全国音像、电子出版物进出口情况(2023年)
Statistics on Import and Export of Audio-Visual Products and Electronic Publications (2023)

指标	Item	出口 Exports		进口 Imports	
		数量（盒、张）Number (cassette,disc)	金额（万美元）Value (10 000 USD)	数量（盒、张）Number (cassette,disc)	金额（万美元）Value (10 000 USD)
总计	**Total**	**191**	**194.73**	**202129**	**46147.84**
录音合计	Audio Products	12	0.02	200839	182.56
录像合计	Video Products	169	0.29	1290	1.48
电子出版物	Electronic Publications	10	23.78		
数字出版物	Digital Publications		170.64		45963.80

23-8 版权引进和输出情况（2023年）
Basic Statistics on Import and Export of Copyright (2023)

单位：项 (item)

项 目	Item	合 计 Total	图 书 Books	录音制品 Audio Products	录像制品 Video Products	电子出版物 Electronic Publications
本年引进版权总数	**Number of Imported Copyright in the Year**	**10044**	**9835**	**63**	**61**	**85**
美 国	United States	2826	2794	9		23
英 国	United Kingdom	2550	2510	7	10	23
德 国	Germany	801	787	8	2	4
法 国	France	641	610	11	7	13
俄罗斯	Russia	40	40			
加拿大	Canada	83	80		2	1
新加坡	Singapore	125	125			
日 本	Japan	1313	1282	8	6	17
韩 国	Republic of Korea	253	248	1	3	1
香港地区	Hong Kong, China	96	73	14	9	
澳门地区	Macao, China	5	5			
台湾地区	Taiwan, China	490	479		11	
其 他	Others	821	802	5	11	3
本年输出版权总数	**Number of Exported Copyright in the Year**	**11731**	**11509**	**153**	**14**	**55**
美 国	United States	785	779			6
英 国	United Kingdom	314	312			2
德 国	Germany	389	387		2	
法 国	France	183	170	8	2	3
俄罗斯	Russia	831	831			
加拿大	Canada	132	132			
新加坡	Singapore	742	707	6	5	24
日 本	Japan	222	222			
韩 国	Republic of Korea	693	693			
香港地区	Hong Kong, China	484	352	127	5	
澳门地区	Macao, China	87	87			
台湾地区	Taiwan, China	899	895			4
其 他	Others	5970	5942	12		16

23–9 分地区出版印刷生产情况（2023年）
Statistics on Publication Printing by Region (2023)

地 区	Region	企业数（个）Number of Enterprises (unit)	从业人员（人）Number of Employees (unit)	印刷产量 Output of Printing 黑白（万令）Black and White (10 000 reams)	彩色（万对开色令）Color (10 000 bisect color reams)	装订产量（万令）Output of Bookbinding (10 000 reams)	用纸量（万令）Amount of Paper Used (10 000 reams)
全 国	**National Total**	**9673**	**340097**	**16610.0**	**128531.4**	**27241.0**	**36267.1**
北 京	Beijing	958	22345	1240.1	11683.5	2290.7	2889.0
天 津	Tianjin	207	6456	421.6	3320.6	688.5	1036.4
河 北	Hebei	825	26878	1934.7	7814.0	3196.3	3122.6
山 西	Shanxi	135	4390	141.3	1483.6	221.0	372.7
内蒙古	Inner Mongolia	168	2571	66.2	534.7	106.3	143.2
辽 宁	Liaoning	198	4809	301.6	2619.1	518.3	679.9
吉 林	Jilin	198	4669	224.3	1607.5	279.4	493.3
黑龙江	Heilongjiang	131	2859	129.1	933.6	155.0	260.9
上 海	Shanghai	167	11375	274.7	3734.1	429.6	957.5
江 苏	Jiangsu	448	22629	1353.0	9421.3	1955.1	2755.9
浙 江	Zhejiang	562	24487	1182.9	11793.4	1982.3	2985.1
安 徽	Anhui	369	10032	403.5	4256.5	809.8	1020.4
福 建	Fujian	313	13691	622.2	3176.0	680.9	1056.4
江 西	Jiangxi	155	4727	498.2	1973.7	588.4	801.0
山 东	Shandong	708	31846	2282.5	9335.9	3442.7	3844.4
河 南	Henan	451	13272	754.7	6638.5	1165.2	1673.7
湖 北	Hubei	357	11874	980.7	4515.4	1400.3	1653.6
湖 南	Hunan	516	15233	621.8	6465.9	1231.7	1591.1
广 东	Guangdong	967	60816	1421.5	20007.6	3263.0	4665.9
广 西	Guangxi	260	6071	229.7	3194.2	487.6	698.2
海 南	Hainan	52	1613	41.4	485.5	30.6	107.8
重 庆	Chongqing	140	4379	182.2	1565.6	333.0	420.2
四 川	Sichuan	357	9669	471.1	3740.6	710.8	1001.0
贵 州	Guizhou	153	2969	64.9	1375.6	142.6	258.1
云 南	Yunnan	157	4093	148.9	1614.9	245.5	397.3
西 藏	Xizang	22	578	24.2	314.3	32.6	64.1
陕 西	Shaanxi	303	7006	322.1	2282.1	460.8	694.9
甘 肃	Gansu	96	2796	136.1	779.5	156.9	233.7
青 海	Qinghai	61	1149	24.1	112.7	24.2	42.3
宁 夏	Ningxia	99	1233	31.8	206.1	35.9	58.2
新 疆	Xinjiang	140	3582	78.9	1545.4	176.1	288.5

23-10 国家综合档案馆基本情况
Basic Statistics on National Comprehensive Archives

年 份 Year	馆藏档案 (万卷、万件) Number of Archives (10 000 volumes, 10 000 pieces)	照片档案 (万张) Photos (10 000 sheets)	开放档案 (万卷、万件) Archives Open to Public (10 000 volumes, 10 000 pieces)	利用档案 (万卷次、万件次) Utilized Archives (10 000 volume-times, 10 000 piece-times)	档案馆建筑面积 (万平方米) Floor Space of Archive Institutions (10 000 sq.m)
1991	9637.4	371.0	2094.3	937.0	348.1
1992	10003.5	402.4	2018.7	773.8	255.7
1993	10726.8	435.5	2140.7	891.9	275.9
1994	10782.9	449.6	2454.6	674.4	268.3
1995	11318.3	485.5	2790.3	529.3	282.5
1996	11341.4	494.6	2939.2	485.4	297.5
1997	12222.9	553.0	3304.6	501.0	347.6
1998	12276.5	579.7	3556.5	446.5	310.7
1999	12866.8	584.5	3808.2	508.5	328.4
2000	13314.0	631.7	4072.0	494.4	336.2
2001	13756.6	642.8	4129.7	575.4	342.0
2002	14790.7	720.5	4301.1	548.8	351.0
2003	15945.9	797.4	4618.4	602.6	361.4
2004	17601.5	827.9	4868.3	813.9	376.8
2005	18688.7	908.8	5132.3	868.0	393.1
2006	21656.5	1277.2	5746.3	1166.4	406.1
2007	23675.3	1393.3	5875.5	1244.9	421.9
2008	25051.0	1505.3	6072.2	1257.4	465.4
2009	28089.2	1646.3	6687.4	1308.0	473.3
2010	32198.6	1809.2	7428.6	1417.3	504.4
2011	35445.5	1965.8	7828.4	1564.5	551.1
2012	40547.7	1827.4	8254.6	1521.1	627.1
2013	42454.5	1927.6	8900.5	1477.8	709.3
2014	53470.3	2041.8	9179.7	1688.8	736.0
2015	58641.7	2102.4	9266.3	1978.3	785.5
2016	65062.5	2228.2	9707.9	2033.7	859.8
2017	65371.1	2336.5	10151.7	2078.0	949.3
2018	75051.1	2056.0	11222.1	1819.1	1050.9
2019	82850.7	2203.8	13171.6	2140.0	1164.6
2020	91789.8	2401.0	14584.5	2064.4	1268.4
2021	104671.1	2676.6	17549.7	2407.4	1410.8
2022	117148.7	2737.7	20976.6	2283.0	1536.1
2023	126846.5	2862.0	22128.7	2844.0	1624.3

23-11 档案馆机构和人员情况
Statistics on Archive Institutions and Personnel

单位：个、人 (unit, person)

年 份 Year	国家综合档案馆 National Comprehensive Archives		国家专门档案馆 National Special Archives		部门档案馆 Department Archives		企 业 档案馆数 Number of Archives of Enterprise	事业单位 档案馆数 Number of Archives of Institutional Units	科技事业单位档案馆数 Number of Archives of Science and Technology Units
	馆 数 Number of Institutions	专职人员 Full-time Personnel	馆 数 Number of Institutions	专职人员 Full-time Personnel	馆 数 Number of Institutions	专职人员 Full-time Personnel			
1991	2957	21657	211	2038	128	2171	229	19	28
1992	2962	22226	206	2082	122	2258	231	19	28
1993	2980	23624	200	2245	122	1448	221	20	31
1994	2983	23568	205	2294	136	2160	209	20	36
1995	3024	24777	216	2484	144	2168	213	27	38
1996	3011	24542	226	2658	134	2072	232	23	44
1997	3021	24904	223	2578	162	2521	228	26	46
1998	3034	24197	232	3200	149	2411	245	27	46
1999	3046	23530	225	3436	142	2123	304	40	59
2000	3070	23701	234	3319	141	1865	307	53	80
2001	3100	23652	243	3448	142	2086	286	47	84
2002	3110	22825	253	3435	148	2109	299	75	93
2003	3121	23086	260	3514	141	1770	300	75	85
2004	3127	23401	258	3591	149	1932	300	79	99
2005	3142	23413	238	3452	145	2020	301	105	63
2006	3154	22689	239	3537	137	1699	216	110	95
2007	3161	21399	245	3737	146	1985	215	126	94
2008	3170	21414	240	3663	154	1886	241	141	87
2009	3191	20949	241	3626	149	1814	233	167	96
2010	3194	19750	252	3833	167	1747	223	160	111
2011	3196	19985	255	3843	170	2121	183	179	124
2012	3237	18009	238	3577	183	2161	204	260	
2013	3325	18106	240	3579	218	2182	189	274	
2014	3319	17863	247	3538	209	2129	169	252	
2015	3322	18386	234	3457	237	2263	176	224	
2016	3336	17511	236	3521	213	2021	180	272	
2017	3333	16799	234	3275	202	1939	167	274	
2018	3315	22584	211	3119	143	1739	158	309	
2019	3337	34349	256	3300	140	1566	181	320	
2020	3341	35028	260	3413	133	1584	177	322	
2021	3320	35833	256	3372	130	1573	118	312	
2022	3301	36582	261	3429	106	1338	135	351	
2023	3302	37152	259	3371	101	1375	128	384	

注：2012年以前的事业单位档案馆数指文化事业档案馆数，2012年新修订的《全国档案事业统计年报制度》不再细分事业单位的属性，统称"省部属事业单位档案馆"，包括文化事业档案馆和科技事业单位档案馆。

a) Institutional archives before 2012 referred to archives of cultural institutions. The revised Annual Report of National Archive Statistics in 2012 does not further subcategorize institutional archives by their attributes, but generally call them institutional archives affiliated to ministries or provincial governments, which include cultural archives and archives of science and technology units.

23-12 广播电视电影事业发展情况
Statistics on Radio, Television and Films

指　　标	Item	2010	2020	2022	2023
广播	**Radio**				
广播节目综合人口覆盖率 (%)	Population Coverage Rate of Radio Programs (%)	96.78	99.38	99.65	99.71
#农村	Rural Areas	95.64	99.17	99.49	99.59
公共广播节目套数 (套)	Number of Public Radio Programs (set)	2549	2932	2927	2918
公共广播节目播出时间(万小时)	Broadcasting of Public Radio Programs (10 000 hours)	1266.0	1580.7	1602.2	1616.0
广播节目制作时间 (万小时)	Production of Radio Programs (10 000 hours)	681.4	821.0	787.7	759.2
电视	**Television**				
电视节目综合人口覆盖率 (%)	Population Coverage Rate of TV Programs (%)	97.62	99.59	99.75	99.79
#农村	Rural	96.78	99.45	99.65	99.72
有线电视实际用户数(万户)	Actual Users of Cable TV (10 000 households)	18872	20745	19964	20182
#农村	Rural	7293	7055	6585	6493
#数字电视	Users of Digital TV	8870	19889	19199	19370
有线电视实际用户数占家庭总户数比重 (%)	Actual Popularization Rate of Cable TV (%)	46.40	46.23	43.66	43.46
#农村有线电视实际用户数占农村家庭总户数比重	Actual Rural Popularization Rate of Cable TV	29.35	30.18	31.92	31.77
公共电视节目套数 (套)	Number of Public TV Programs (set)	3272	3603	3559	3511
公共电视节目播出时间(万小时)	Broadcasting of Public TV Programs (10 000 hours)	1635.5	1988.3	2003.6	2001.6
电视剧播出数 (万部)	Number of TV Dramas Broadcasted (10 000 series)	24.92	21.27	20.82	21.00
#进口电视剧播出数	Imported TV Dramas	0.88	0.04	0.02	0.03
电视剧播出数 (万集)	Number of TV Dramas Broadcasted (10 000 episodes)	635.86	739.38	734.28	762.64
#进口电视剧播出数	Imported TV Dramas	19.51	1.18	0.71	0.81
电视动画播出时间 (万小时)	Number of Cartoons Broadcasted (10 000 hours)		44.61	46.53	47.28
#进口电视动画播出时间	Imported Cartoons		0.71	0.28	0.16
电视节目制作时间 (万小时)	Production of TV Programs (10 000 hours)	274.3	328.2	285.2	260.0
电影	**Films**				
国有电影制片厂 (个)	State-owned Film Studios (unit)	38			
#电影故事片厂	Feature Film Studios	31			
电影院线 (条)	Film Circuit (line)	37	51	51	49
银幕 (块)	Film Screen (unit)	6256	75581	83998	86310
全国电影票房收入 (亿元)	Domestic Film Box Office Revenue (100 million yuan)	157.21	204.17	300.67	549.15
#国产电影票房收入	Chinese Films		170.93	255.11	460.05
进口电影票房收入	Imported Films		33.24	45.56	89.10

23-13 广播电视节目制作时间
Statistics on Production of Radio and Television Programs

单位：小时 (hour)

项 目	Item	1995	2005	2010	2015	2020	2022	2023
广播节目制作	**Production of Radio Programs**	**2332164**	**6139227**	**6814226**	**7718163**	**8210448**	**7876547**	**7592428**
新闻资讯	News Programs	353368	1066880	1216632	1436129	1452701	1427331	1382644
专题服务	Special Subject Programs	1054140	1822621	1955180	2072348	2241754	2167907	2116447
综艺益智	General Entertainment Programs	924656	1937290	1942828	2078791	1977798	1890869	1776443
广播剧	Radio Play Programs		75456	80181	183124	218581	201393	194203
广告	Advertising Programs		671071	775931	752705	684014	654182	623772
其他	Others		565909	843474	1195065	1635600	1534865	1498919
电视节目制作	**Production of TV Programs**	**383513**	**2553861**	**2742949**	**3520190**	**3282440**	**2852115**	**2600098**
新闻资讯	News Programs	80800	637956	719680	978801	1097543	1091683	977654
专题服务	Special Subject Programs	193391	525528	640857	930283	899825	743000	696695
综艺益智	General Entertainment Programs	109322	382350	407849	511398	341886	279907	210686
影视剧	TV Drama Programs		193771	93536	120604	95403	60738	67443
广告	Advertising Programs		524892	526839	481973	389655	346682	328353
其他	Others		289364	354188	497131	458128	330104	319267

23-14 公共广播电视节目播出时间(2023年)
Statistics on Broadcasting of Public Radio and Television Programs (2023)

单位：小时 (hour)

指 标	Item	总 计 Total	新闻资讯类节目 News	专题服务类节目 Special Subject	综艺益智类节目 General Entertainment	广播(影视)剧类节目 Radio/TV Dramas	广告类节 目 Advertising	其他类节 目 Others
广播	All Radio Broadcasting Stations	16159761	3213317	3419041	3504591	972490	1358182	3692140
#中央广播电视总台	China Media Group	171095	36729	56430	67009	3123	7152	654
电视	All Television Stations	20016309	2838011	2851110	978860	8824664	2168280	2355384
#中央广播电视总台	China Media Group	255848	76034	80155	37320	51409	6624	4307

23-15 分地区广播电视节目综合人口覆盖及播出情况(2023年)

Population Coverage of Radio and TV Programs and Broadcasting of Radio and TV Programs by Region (2023)

地区	Region	广播节目综合人口覆盖率(%) Population Coverage Rate of Radio Programs (%)	#农村 Rural	电视节目综合人口覆盖率(%) Population Coverage Rate of TV Programs (%)	#农村 Rural	公共广播节目套数(套) Number of Public Radio Programs (set)	公共电视节目套数(套) Number of Public TV Programs (set)	电视剧播出数(部) Number of TV Dramas Broadcasted (series)	#进口 Import	电视动画播出时间(小时) Number of Cartoons Broadcasted (hour)	#进口 Import
全国	**National Total**	**99.71**	**99.59**	**99.79**	**99.72**	**2918**	**3511**	**210018**	**273**	**472768**	**1639**
中央广播电视总台	China Media Group					22	31	1105		5872	950
其他部门所属单位	Under Other Departments						5	82		357	50
北京	Beijing	100.00	100.00	100.00	100.00	16	26	877		8496	
天津	Tianjin	100.00	100.00	100.00	100.00	22	24	1511		1715	
河北	Hebei	99.83	99.74	99.88	99.84	188	185	12508		12948	
山西	Shanxi	98.99	98.43	99.31	99.02	123	135	6546	3	9017	180
内蒙古	Inner Mongolia	99.76	99.60	99.76	99.57	124	118	7023		19180	
辽宁	Liaoning	99.52	99.17	99.49	99.13	108	101	7409		8335	
吉林	Jilin	99.57	99.50	99.64	99.47	82	77	6581		3899	
黑龙江	Heilongjiang	99.96	99.95	99.95	99.93	99	99	4546	7	11762	
上海	Shanghai	100.00	100.00	100.00	100.00	22	21	1060	6	17594	
江苏	Jiangsu	100.00	100.00	100.00	100.00	122	122	6104		14732	
浙江	Zhejiang	99.82	99.73	99.89	99.86	111	113	6446		24854	
安徽	Anhui	99.96	99.94	99.95	99.94	111	133	9667		12713	
福建	Fujian	99.89	99.85	99.90	99.87	92	98	5159	1	19526	
江西	Jiangxi	99.58	99.41	99.81	99.75	94	121	6897	55	17726	373
山东	Shandong	99.69	99.61	99.73	99.73	172	268	16741		29113	
河南	Henan	99.73	99.70	99.72	99.69	166	172	12831	10	10644	20
湖北	Hubei	99.90	99.86	99.88	99.83	102	110	10674		14468	
湖南	Hunan	99.43	99.01	99.77	99.61	121	143	11465	6	24898	55
广东	Guangdong	99.98	99.96	99.98	99.98	140	146	6998		38560	
广西	Guangxi	99.28	99.19	99.62	99.56	76	116	6052	113	17120	
海南	Hainan	99.49	99.44	99.51	99.50	26	16	594		7494	
重庆	Chongqing	99.57	99.39	99.69	99.59	32	45	2288		10324	
四川	Sichuan	99.53	99.37	99.77	99.70	146	209	14767	28	29820	
贵州	Guizhou	99.68	99.55	99.76	99.66	49	111	5161		12815	
云南	Yunnan	99.68	99.61	99.70	99.62	81	166	8810	13	21449	
西藏	Xizang	99.50	99.61	99.66	99.75	30	81	1142	25	3797	
陕西	Shaanxi	99.53	99.29	99.72	99.53	111	124	6794	6	6080	
甘肃	Gansu	99.48	99.26	99.54	99.35	98	114	5052		13458	
青海	Qinghai	99.20	98.96	99.23	98.92	49	50	2526		6663	
宁夏	Ningxia	99.93	99.86	99.99	99.97	22	29	1687		6224	
新疆	Xinjiang	99.23	99.02	99.36	99.25	161	202	12915		31115	10

23-16 分地区有线广播电视传输干线及实际用户情况（2023年）
Transmission Trunk and Actual Users of Cable Radio and TV by Region (2023)

地 区	Region	有线广播电视传输干线长度（万公里）Total Length of Transmission Trunk for Cable Radio and TV (10 000 km)	有线电视实际用户数（万户）Actual Users of Cable TV (10 000 households)	#农村有线电视 Rural Users of Cable TV	#数字电视 Users of Digital TV	#增值业务 Value-Added Service	有线电视实际用户数占家庭总户数的比重（%）Actual Popularization Rate of Cable TV (%)	#农 村 Rural Areas
全国合计	**National Total**	**220.9**	**20182.3**	**6492.6**	**19369.9**	**6222.8**	**43.46**	**31.77**
北 京	Beijing	22.5	617.5	98.4	576.0	62.1	117.68	
天 津	Tianjin	0.4	359.4	45.8	359.4	0.8	83.00	63.33
河 北	Hebei	2.8	702.9	125.9	674.9	468.1	26.73	11.77
山 西	Shanxi	7.4	322.9	89.8	290.7	11.9	70.40	56.44
内蒙古	Inner Mongolia	1.3	245.5	42.7	245.5	148.0	26.67	13.20
辽 宁	Liaoning	2.6	479.2	110.9	455.3	142.8	30.78	17.14
吉 林	Jilin	2.3	630.2	211.4	630.2	237.5	61.65	42.22
黑龙江	Heilongjiang	9.9	519.4	92.8	514.5	174.8	38.11	17.09
上 海	Shanghai	10.5	749.5		736.2	171.1	130.78	
江 苏	Jiangsu	4.5	1215.6	470.8	1208.4	336.9	46.77	34.53
浙 江	Zhejiang	6.2	1302.7	704.9	1282.9	344.2	73.27	99.21
安 徽	Anhui	3.6	776.6	255.1	589.4	115.2	34.99	19.06
福 建	Fujian	25.2	725.1	466.0	725.1	571.9	61.11	57.97
江 西	Jiangxi	11.2	564.4	287.6	531.7	132.0	37.98	50.58
山 东	Shandong	45.0	1430.9	756.4	1320.9	496.3	41.13	43.87
河 南	Henan	6.3	613.9	134.6	587.1	164.0	18.48	8.73
湖 北	Hubei	3.1	1285.5	573.2	1271.2	348.0	61.44	58.58
湖 南	Hunan	10.3	584.0	90.2	570.5	156.0	24.61	9.57
广 东	Guangdong	19.4	1733.5	316.3	1656.4	835.4	49.47	31.32
广 西	Guangxi	1.3	793.8	310.2	793.8	176.1	47.07	39.68
海 南	Hainan	0.3	123.2	37.6	114.8	44.9	45.41	25.28
重 庆	Chongqing	0.7	621.5	164.7	556.8	216.5	48.14	28.11
四 川	Sichuan	3.4	932.2	265.0	853.4	176.5	29.11	14.19
贵 州	Guizhou	1.7	920.4	463.7	920.4	136.4	70.52	78.13
云 南	Yunnan	3.6	345.8	96.3	324.1	105.8	22.73	13.50
西 藏	Xizang	0.6	20.6	0.0	18.9		17.75	0.05
陕 西	Shaanxi	4.1	754.8	247.2	754.8	294.5	55.16	60.93
甘 肃	Gansu	1.7	294.6	27.2	294.6	96.6	33.59	6.80
青 海	Qinghai	0.8	98.6	0.3	98.6	7.5	47.74	0.43
宁 夏	Ningxia	0.5	124.5	6.4	124.5		47.16	8.02
新 疆	Xinjiang	3.9	293.4	1.1	288.9	51.1	34.54	0.35

注：新疆有线电视实际用户数占家庭总户数的比重数据不含兵团。
a) Actual popularization rate of cable TV in Xinjiang does not include the data of Xinjiang Production and Construction Corps.

23-17 电视节目进口情况(2023年)
Statistics on Imported TV Programs (2023)

指标	Item	合计 Total	欧洲 Europe	非洲 Africa	美洲 America	#美国 United States
全年电视节目进口总额(万元)	**Value of Imported TV Programs(10 000 yuan)**	**96531**	**15472**	**54**	**32267**	**31656**
#影视剧	Film and TV Dramas	33060	3928	3	19691	19481
电视动画	Cartoon Programs	50036	7564		4373	4208
纪录片	Documentary	10343	3460	51	6438	6202
全年电视节目进口量(时)	**Time of Imported TV Programs (hour)**	**39084**	**2275**	**8**	**3417**	**3321**
#影视剧 (部)	Film and TV Dramas (series)	1552	190	2	882	874
#影视剧 (集)	Film and TV Dramas (episode)	7651	184	7	1713	1703
电视动画 (时)	Cartoon Programs (hour)	2687	660		837	792
纪录片 (时)	Documentary (hour)	1305	992	1	218	178

23-17 续表 continued

指标	Item	亚洲 Asia	#日本 Japan	#韩国 Republic of Korea	#东南亚 Southeast Asia	#中国香港 Hong Kong, China	#中国台湾 Taiwan, China	大洋洲 Oceania
全年电视节目进口总额(万元)	**Value of Imported TV Programs (10 000 yuan)**	**48444**	**36389**	**1442**	**2076**	**5754**	**2546**	**294**
#影视剧	Film and TV Dramas	9302	2202	1422	2021	2162	1304	136
电视动画	Cartoon Programs	38078	34054		55	2746	1224	21
纪录片	Documentary	258	50			161		137
全年电视节目进口量(时)	**Time of Imported TV Programs(hour)**	**33345**	**1419**	**44**	**204**	**31350**	**266**	**39**
#影视剧 (部)	Film and TV Dramas (series)	472	158	7	16	282	7	6
#影视剧 (集)	Film and TV Dramas (episode)	5738	476	21	219	4885	111	9
电视动画 (时)	Cartoon Programs (hour)	1180	749		33	239	158	10
纪录片 (时)	Documentary (hour)	76	1			33		18

23-18 电影综合情况
Basic Statistics on Film Production

年 份 Year	电影故事片厂 (个) Number of Feature Film Studios (unit)	生产故事影片 (部) Feature Films (film)	生产动画影片 (部) Cartoon Films (reel)	生产科教影片 (部) Popular Science Films (reel)	生产纪录影片 (部) Documentary Films (reel)	生产特种影片 (部) Special Films (reel)
1978	12	46	26	289	202	
1979	17	65	25	349	317	
1980	17	82	32	337	242	
1981	19	105	33	277	276	
1982	19	112	33	284	259	
1983	19	127	37	343	299	
1984	20	144	37	387	337	
1985	20	127	45	357	419	
1986	20	134	46	383	417	
1987	22	146	45	353	347	
1988	22	158	38	344	350	
1989	22	136	53	334	259	
1990	22	134	51	326	296	
1991	22	130	46	351	283	
1992	22	170	56	354	307	
1993	22	154	47	252	300	
1994	22	148	32	182	22	
1995	30	146	37	40	111	
1996	30	110	58	33	39	
1997	31	88	28	34	95	
1998	31	82	9	30	54	
1999	31	99	3	20	14	
2000	31	91	1	49	10	
2001	27	88	1	56	9	
2002	31	100	2	60	7	
2003	31	140	2	53	6	
2004	31	212	4	30	10	
2005	32	260	7	33	2	
2006	32	330	13	36	13	
2007	32	402	6	34	9	
2008	33	406	16	39	16	2
2009	31	456	27	52	19	4
2010	31	526	16	54	16	9
2011	31	558	24	76	26	5
2012	31	745	33	74	15	26
2013	31	638	29	121	18	18
2014	31	618	40	52	25	23
2015	31	686	51	96	38	17
2016	31	772	49	67	32	24
2017	31	798	32	68	44	28
2018		902	51	61	57	11
2019		850	51	74	47	15
2020		531	45	25	31	18
2021		565	47	54	55	19
2022		380	25	37	30	13
2023		792	34	64	63	18

注：1.本表电影故事片厂指国有电影故事片厂。
2.2005年及以前动画片数为美术片数。
a) Number of feature film studios in this table refers to state-owned film studios.
b) Cartoon films before 2005 referred to puppet films.

23−19 主要文化机构情况
Statistics on Cultural Institutions

单位：个 (unit)

年 份 Year	公共图书馆 Public Libraries	文化馆(站) Cultural Centers	省级、地市级文化馆 Cultural Centers at Provincial & Prefecture Level	县市级文化馆 Cultural Centers at County & City Level	乡镇(街道)文化站 Township (sub-district) Cultural Stations	博物馆 Museums	艺术表演团 体 Art Performance Troupes	艺术表演场 馆 Art Performance Venues
1978	1218	6893	92	2748	4053	349	3150	1095
1980	1732	8739	218	2912	5609	365	3533	1444
1985	2344	8576	335	2960	5281	711	3317	1377
1986	2406	8913	337	2993	5583	777	3195	2058
1987	2440	8974	348	2973	5653	827	3094	2148
1988	2485	9045	358	2975	5712	903	2985	2081
1989	2512	9037	366	2955	5716	967	2850	2050
1990	2527	9216	366	2955	5895	1013	2805	1955
1991	2535	10507	371	2894	7242	1075	2772	2068
1992	2558	9564	372	2900	6292	1106	2753	2037
1993	2572	10155	370	2886	6899	1130	2707	2024
1994	2589	11276	374	2887	8015	1161	2698	1998
1995	2615	13487	373	2886	10228	1194	2682	1958
1996	2620	45253	392	2892	41969	1219	2664	1934
1997	2628	45449	385	2901	42163	1282	2663	1947
1998	2662	45834	386	2901	42547	1339	2652	1929
1999	2669	45837	389	2905	42543	1363	2632	1911
2000	2675	45321	390	2907	42024	1392	2619	1900
2001	2696	43379	399	2842	40138	1461	2605	1854
2002	2697	42516	389	2854	39273	1511	2587	1829
2003	2709	41816	382	2846	38588	1515	2601	1900
2004	2720	41402	380	2841	38181	1548	2759	1928
2005	2762	41588	375	2851	38362	1581	2805	1866
2006	2778	40088	395	2819	36874	1617	2866	1839
2007	2799	40601	411	2806	37384	1722	4512	1732
2008	2820	41156	389	2829	37938	1893	5114	1662
2009	2850	41959	361	2862	38736	2252	6139	1499
2010	2884	43382	374	2890	40118	2435	6864	1461
2011	2952	43675	379	2906	40390	2650	7055	1429
2012	3076	43876	382	2919	40575	3069	7321	1279
2013	3112	44260	385	2930	40945	3473	8180	1344
2014	3117	44423	385	2928	41110	3658	8769	1338
2015	3139	44291	386	2929	40976	3852	10787	2143
2016	3153	44497	389	2933	41175	4109	12301	2285
2017	3166	44521	390	2938	41193	4721	15742	2455
2018	3176	44464	390	2936	41138	4918	17123	2478
2019	3196	44073	390	2936	40747	5132	17795	2716
2020	3212	43687	390	2931	40366	5452	17581	2770
2021	3215	43531	390	2926	40215	5772	18370	3093
2022	3303	45623	404	3099	42120	6091	19739	3199
2023	3246	43752	404	3112	40236	4508	17781	3060

注：1.1996年以前文化站数据未包括其他部门所属乡镇文化站。1996−1998年包括其他部门所属文化站，1999年以后，其他部门所属文化站划归文化部门管理。

2.2007年以前艺术表演团体为系统内数据，2007年起含系统外单位。

3.2015年以前艺术表演场馆为公有制艺术表演场馆，2015年起含民营艺术表演场馆。

4.2023年起，博物馆相关指标使用国有博物馆数据(以下相关同)。

a) Culture stations did not include township culture stations of other departments before 1996. During 1996-1998, culture stations of other departments Since 1999, culture stations of other department were put under the management of culture departments.

b) Art performance troupes referred to those under the cultural departments before 2007, and expanded to cover those both under and outside the cultural departments starting from 2007.

c) Art performance venues refer to those of state-owned before 2015, and include those of non-state venues since 2015.

d) Since 2023, museums' related indicators use data from state-owned museums.The same applies to the relevant following tables.

23–20 文化文物机构人员情况(2023年)
Number and Personnel of Cultural and Relics Institutions (2023)

机构类别	Category of Institution	机构(个) Number of Institutions (unit)	文化和旅游部门 Cultural and Tourism Department	其他部门 Other Departments	从业人员(人) Number of Employed Persons (person)	文化和旅游部门 Cultural and Tourism Department	其他部门 Other Departments
总 计	**Total**	**304194**	**65592**	**238602**	**4482169**	**729143**	**3753026**
文化和旅游合计	**Total culture and Tourism**	**294549**	**56827**	**237722**	**4301596**	**570688**	**3730908**
艺术表演团体	Art Performance Troupes	17781	1893	15888	385162	104031	281131
艺术表演场馆	Art Performance Venues	3060	1019	2041	55116	19179	35937
公共图书馆	Public Libraries	3246	3246		60961	60961	
文化馆	Cultural Centers	3516	3516		55848	55848	
文化站	Cultural Stations	40236	40236		143340	143340	
美术展览创作机构	Art Exhibition and Creative Institutions	800	753	47	7390	6932	458
文化和旅游部门教育机构	Educational Institutions in the Cultural and Tourism Sector	93	93		12092	12092	
文化和旅游科研机构	Cultural and Tourism Research Institutions	168	168		4302	4302	
文化市场经营机构	Institutions of Cultural Market Management	157200		157200	860405		860405
文化和旅游行政部门	Cultural and Tourism Administration	3253	3253		122008	122008	
其他文化和旅游机构	Other Cultural and Tourism Institutions	65196	2650	62546	2594972	41995	2552977
文物合计	**Cultural Relics Institutions**	**9645**	**8765**	**880**	**180573**	**158455**	**22118**
国有博物馆	State-owned Museums	4508	3760	748	122635	103808	18827
文物保护管理机构	Agencies of Cultural Relics Protection and Management	2547	2493	54	30752	28177	2575
文物保护科研机构	Scientific and Research Agencies of Cultural Relics Protection	128	127	1	6921	6903	18
其他文物机构	Other Cultural Relics Agencies	2462	2385	77	20265	19567	698

注：文化市场经营机构不包括非公有制院团和场馆。
a) Institutions of cultural market managemnet do not include non-public troupes and venues.

23-21 艺术表演团体基本情况(2023年)

项 目	Item	机构(个) Number of Institutions (unit)	从业人员(人) Number of Employed Persons (person)	演出场次(万场次) Number of Performances (10 000 shows)	#国内演出 Domestic Performance	#农村 Rural Areas
总 计	**Total**	**17781**	**385162**	**254.2**	**250.3**	**57.9**
按隶属关系分	By Jurisdiction of Management					
中央	Under Central Government	11	4039	0.3	0.3	0.0
省、区、市	Under Provinces, Autonomous Regions and Municipalities	179	24201	4.6	4.5	1.5
地、市	Prefecture Level	469	36675	9.8	9.5	4.1
县、市及以下	Under Counties (Cities) and Others	17122	320247	239.5	236.1	52.3
按管理部门分	By Department of Management					
文化和旅游部门	Culture and Tourism Departments	1893	104031	36.8	36.1	22.2
其他部门	Other Departments	15888	281131	217.4	214.3	35.7
按剧种分	By Type of Art					
话剧、儿童剧、滑稽剧类	Drama, Children's Play and Comedy Troupes	67	5012	1.2	1.2	0.2
歌舞、音乐类	Song and Dance, Musicals	548	32499	8.6	8.5	3.3
京剧、昆曲类	Peking Opera and Kunqu Opera	53	4797	1.1	1.1	0.5
地方戏曲类	Local Operas	1492	54744	34.7	34.5	14.4
杂技、魔术、马戏类	Acrobatics, Magic and Circus	53	3954	2.2	2.0	0.5
曲艺类	Folk Arts	54	1971	2.3	2.3	1.4
综合性艺术表演团体	Comprehensive Art Performance	15514	282185	204.4	201.1	37.9

Statistics on Art Performance Troupes (2023)

国内演出观众人次（万人次） Number of Domestic Audience (10 000 person-times)	#农村 Rural Audience	收入合计（万元） Total Income (10 000 yuan)	#财政拨款 Government Budget	#演出收入 Performance Income	支出合计（万元） Total Expenses (10 000 yuan)	政府采购的公益演出活动 Public Shows under Government Procurement：演出场次（万场次） Number of Performances (10 000 shows)	观众人次（万人次） Number of Audience (10 000 person-times)
89654	**28703**	**5316917**	**2106725**	**2078465**	**5515149**	**69.0**	**28330.5**
218	10	204430	111594	42989	180685	0.1	43.9
3465	1390	685085	477075	111782	694835	1.7	1125.3
7547	3043	818302	642429	112258	822836	3.3	2080.9
78424	24261	3609099	875627	1811436	3816794	64.0	25080.4
28115	15951	2206930	1604326	349577	2339914	15.8	10047.6
61539	12753	3109987	502399	1728888	3175235	53.2	18283.0
695	118	147588	85826	31871	145489	0.4	223.4
6755	2005	795874	562390	143766	929410	3.6	1561.4
592	305	144191	115831	16811	147097	0.5	215.1
17294	11263	854484	571266	180365	1061967	10.5	6872.8
1368	222	71265	44973	11712	71530	0.5	206.0
910	586	46928	36768	7934	45142	0.4	209.9
62041	14204	3256588	689671	1686005	3114514	53.2	19042.1

23-22 全国艺术表演场馆基本情况(2023年)
Statistics on Art Performance Venues (2023)

项　目	Item	机构数(个) Number of Institutions (unit)	从业人员(人) Number of Employed Persons (person)	座席数(个) Seating Capacity (unit)	艺术演出场次(万场次) Number of Art Performances (10 000 shows)
总　计	**Total**	**3060**	**55116**	**2136425**	**41.5**
按管理部门分	By Department of Management				
文化和旅游部门	Culture and Tourism Departments	1019	19179	870555	11.0
其他部门	Other Departments	2041	35937	1265870	30.5
按机构类型分	By Type of Venues				
表演艺术中心	Performing Arts Center	54	992	132193	1.1
音乐厅	Music Hall	13	433	12200	0.2
戏剧剧场	Drama Theater	391	8367	294981	3.9
歌剧剧场	Opera Theatre	2	7	2259	
舞蹈剧场	Dance Theater	39	761	123388	1.1
音乐剧剧场	Musical Theatre	2	44	1700	0.0
戏曲剧场	Traditional Opera Theatre	9	56	4208	0.0
综合剧场	Comprehensive Theatre	1965	33088	1119954	27.7
曲艺剧场	Quyi Theatre	2		223	0.0
旅游演出剧场	Tourist Performance Theatre	167	5138	188722	3.4
新型演出剧场	New Performance Theatre	31	617	20759	0.2
脱口秀剧场	Talk Show Theater	7	190	7253	0.0
杂技场	Acrobatic Show	16	614	12150	0.2
马戏场	Circus	5	214	4918	0.1
其他	Others	357	4595	211517	3.4
按隶属关系分	By Jurisdiction of Management				
中央	Under Central Government	6	156	4649	0.1
省、区、市	Under Provinces, Autonomous Regions and Municipalities	87	1841	77409	1.2
地、市	Prefecture Level	276	7025	202810	3.6
县、市及以下	Under Counties (Cities) and Others	2691	46094	1851557	36.3

23-22 续表 continued

项　目	Item	艺术演出观众人次(万人次) Number of Audience in Art Performances (10 000 person-times)	收入合计(万元) Total Income (10 000 yuan)	#财政拨款 Government Budget	#演出收入 Performance Income	支出合计(万元) Total Expenses (10 000 yuan)
总　计	**Total**	**12273**	**2120528**	**363422**	**1030661**	**2056730**
按管理部门分	By Department of Management					
文化和旅游部门	Culture and Tourism Departments	4792	547484	225338	146617	566123
其他部门	Other Departments	7481	1573044	138084	884044	1490606
按机构类型分	By Type of Venues					
表演艺术中心	Performing Arts Center	297	32928	12526	13080	40098
音乐厅	Music Hall	105	20585	8260	8418	18894
戏剧剧场	Drama Theater	1890	246737	124461	69075	250875
歌剧剧场	Opera Theatre	2	99	99		99
舞蹈剧场	Dance Theater	119	9854	1413	7028	9401
音乐剧剧场	Musical Theatre	6	230	5		230
戏曲剧场	Traditional Opera Theatre	20	592	252	196	616
综合剧场	Comprehensive Theatre	7641	1454831	130933	770621	1376502
曲艺剧场	Quyi Theatre	2				
旅游演出剧场	Tourist Performance Theatre	957	231015	55866	120514	208583
新型演出剧场	New Performance Theatre	46	15343	3704	6696	17410
脱口秀剧场	Talk Show Theater	22	5676	2	2769	5181
杂技场	Acrobatic Show	99	23250	2279	11825	44930
马戏场	Circus	20	636	69	1238	3311
其他	Others	1047	78753	23554	19199	80601
按隶属关系分	By Jurisdiction of Management					
中央	Under Central Government	51	7131		4193	6723
省、区、市	Under Provinces, Autonomous Regions and Municipalities	626	63985	21963	22558	71983
地、市	Prefecture Level	1253	213913	72144	55217	213580
县、市及以下	Under Counties (Cities) and Others	10343	1835499	269314	948693	1764443

23-23 分地区艺术表演团体、艺术表演场馆演出情况(2023年)
Statistics on Operation of Art Performance Troupes and Art Performance Venues by Region (2023)

地区	Region	艺术表演团体 Art Performance Troupes				艺术表演场馆 Art Performance Venues		
		机构数(个) Number of Institutions (unit)	演出场次(万场次) Number of Performances (10 000 shows)	#国内演出 Number of Domestic Performances	国内演出观众人次(万人次) Number of Domestic Audience (10 000 person-times)	机构数(个) Number of Institutions (unit)	艺术演出场次(万场次) Number of Art Performances (10 000 shows)	艺术演出观众人次(万人次) Number of Audience in Art Performances (10 000 person-times)
全国	**National Total**	**17781**	**254.22**	**250.34**	**89654**	**3060**	**41.49**	**12273**
中央	Central Level	11	0.30	0.29	218	6	0.12	51
北京	Beijing	522	2.07	2.05	747	76	2.18	360
天津	Tianjin	107	1.08	1.08	275	126	3.92	213
河北	Hebei	819	9.41	9.39	3964	120	0.89	368
山西	Shanxi	756	9.44	8.97	5241	130	1.31	196
内蒙古	Inner Mongolia	273	2.51	2.50	1405	36	0.19	129
辽宁	Liaoning	111	0.63	0.60	300	68	0.42	129
吉林	Jilin	177	0.77	0.75	341	124	0.19	42
黑龙江	Heilongjiang	93	0.94	0.93	312	57	0.34	78
上海	Shanghai	261	2.05	2.05	906	59	0.95	557
江苏	Jiangsu	651	12.34	12.26	3819	278	2.75	1050
浙江	Zhejiang	1217	26.19	26.12	10656	256	3.35	2447
安徽	Anhui	2898	26.75	26.66	6056	130	2.14	196
福建	Fujian	486	7.40	7.34	1796	76	0.59	193
江西	Jiangxi	329	3.76	3.70	1955	78	0.26	115
山东	Shandong	1870	20.70	20.60	6419	240	5.14	520
河南	Henan	2077	39.84	39.58	13977	245	4.10	1370
湖北	Hubei	614	25.82	25.78	5627	141	1.07	934
湖南	Hunan	586	7.16	6.25	3568	120	2.90	843
广东	Guangdong	433	5.72	5.70	2481	127	2.22	634
广西	Guangxi	73	0.87	0.84	456	23	0.12	12
海南	Hainan	128	2.38	1.57	822	30	0.12	379
重庆	Chongqing	1039	11.73	11.68	2067	68	1.26	316
四川	Sichuan	662	5.53	5.48	1848	162	0.66	177
贵州	Guizhou	107	1.58	1.24	929	21	0.18	50
云南	Yunnan	239	13.42	13.38	3261	27	1.15	211
西藏	Xizang	86	0.70	0.64	429	31	0.08	12
陕西	Shaanxi	512	5.99	5.92	4279	76	1.23	319
甘肃	Gansu	376	3.86	3.81	4047	52	0.72	261
青海	Qinghai	124	0.67	0.65	231	51	0.77	45
宁夏	Ningxia	12	0.32	0.28	195	2	0.03	17
新疆	Xinjiang	132	2.31	2.28	1029	24	0.12	50

23-24　公共图书馆基本情况（2023年）
Statistics on Public Libraries (2023)

指　标	Item	总　计 Total	#少儿图书馆 Children's Libraries	按隶属关系分 By Jurisdiction of Management 省、区、直辖市级 Under Provinces, Autonomous Regions and Municipalities	地市级 Prefecture Level	县市级 County (City) Level	#县图书馆 County Libraries
机构数（个）	Number of Institutions (unit)	3246	146	37	391	2817	1558
从业人员（人）	Number of Employed Persons (person)	60961	2788	7691	16359	35550	14946
总藏量（万册件）	Total Collections (10000 copies)	143609	5946	23835	35964	79387	28527
少儿文献数（万册）	Number of Children's Literature (10 000 copies)	20740	2585	1410	6838	12481	3974
当年购买的报刊种类(万种)	Kinds of Newspapers and Periodicals Purchased in the Year (10 000 kinds)	100.6	3.9	13.6	30.1	55.6	21.6
实际持证活跃读者数（万个）	Actual Number of Licensed Active Readers (10 000 units)	10707	342	1071	3955	5367	1538
总流通人次（万人次）	Total Number of Circulation (10 000 person-times)	116061	5199	7897	30812	76943	26274
#书刊文献外借人次	Borrowing from Libraries of Books and Periodicals	33044	1563	1430	8217	23369	9189
书刊文献外借册次(万册次)	Number of Books and Periodicals Lent to Readers (10 000 copies-times)	78299	5441	5379	22718	50153	16480
组织各类讲座次数（次）	Number of Lectures (time)	120122	8574	4019	27779	88179	36256
举办展览（个）	Exhibitions Held (unit)	67888	2941	1752	12165	53957	25676
举办培训班（个）	Training Classes Held (unit)	105494	6545	4827	28375	70971	26316
计算机（台）	Computers (set)	216262	8421	20686	50892	141406	64607
#供读者使用的终端数	Terminals Available for Readers to Use	131576	4772	8579	28272	94215	45378
阅览室坐席数（万个）	Seats of Reading Rooms (10 000 units)	168.0	6.1	10.5	45.5	111.6	49.1

23-25 分地区公共图书馆基本情况(2023年)
Statistics on Public Libraries by Region (2023)

地区	Region	公共图书馆(个) Number of Public Libraries (unit)	总藏量(万册件) Total Collections (10 000 copies)	少儿文献数(万册) Number of Children's Literature (10 000 copies)	人均拥有公共图书馆藏量(册) Collections of Public Libraries Per Person (copy)	实际持证活跃读者数(万个) Actual Number of Licensed Active Readers (10 000 units)	总流通人次(万人次) Total Number of Circulation (10 000 person-times)	#书刊文献外借人次 Borrowing from Libraries of Books and Periodicals	书刊文献外借册次(万册次) Number of Books and Periodicals Lent to Readers (10 000 copies-times)	阅览室座席数(个) Seats of Reading Rooms (unit)
总　计	**National Total**	**3246**	**143609**	**20739.66**	**1.02**	**10707**	**116061**	**33044**	**78299**	**1680128**
北　京	Beijing	19	3675	526.03	1.68	298	1473	209	1015	21035
天　津	Tianjin	20	2445	332.18	1.79	167	1695	402	1250	22489
河　北	Hebei	181	4902	632.97	0.66	276	4822	1801	3859	88366
山　西	Shanxi	127	2658	337.33	0.77	198	2064	646	1260	48631
内蒙古	Inner Mongolia	117	2528	276.45	1.06	118	1565	356	831	39213
辽　宁	Liaoning	128	4757	556.41	1.14	222	2777	854	2743	47884
吉　林	Jilin	67	2627	289.36	1.12	127	812	203	610	26280
黑龙江	Heilongjiang	105	2622	242.01	0.86	130	624	189	439	29317
上　海	Shanghai	20	8307	532.98	3.34	208	1956	385	1888	28331
江　苏	Jiangsu	122	11980	1821.28	1.41	1223	15247	6420	10775	84677
浙　江	Zhejiang	102	12264	2803.42	1.85	1032	16236	2013	8786	119235
安　徽	Anhui	133	4498	722.74	0.73	391	6245	1653	3112	69624
福　建	Fujian	97	5960	1036.02	1.42	292	3523	1258	4022	55709
江　西	Jiangxi	114	4349	515.09	0.96	235	4368	996	2055	55837
山　东	Shandong	153	8555	1080.62	0.85	706	7248	2752	4450	104108
河　南	Henan	177	4822	779.94	0.49	282	4745	1721	2908	85107
湖　北	Hubei	119	5722	702.42	0.98	461	4125	1677	3089	68305
湖　南	Hunan	150	5769	890.95	0.88	472	5010	2041	3790	64325
广　东	Guangdong	150	15129	3503.94	1.19	1996	14817	2676	11422	172381
广　西	Guangxi	116	3262	405.89	0.65	188	2364	489	1089	45105
海　南	Hainan	24	760	117.34	0.73	23	594	99	287	10699
重　庆	Chongqing	43	2916	481.07	0.91	357	2535	675	1581	41165
四　川	Sichuan	209	5343	661.43	0.64	451	3348	1310	2381	91894
贵　州	Guizhou	99	2075	227.80	0.54	141	1348	400	810	36851
云　南	Yunnan	151	2686	223.31	0.57	99	1395	466	1194	40410
西　藏	Xizang	82	318	20.81	0.87	3	38	2	5	4213
陕　西	Shaanxi	119	2599	318.34	0.66	93	2073	501	1079	51020
甘　肃	Gansu	104	2128	263.46	0.86	62	1128	401	694	55092
青　海	Qinghai	50	680	53.61	1.14	10	174	26	61	9733
宁　夏	Ningxia	27	903	134.91	1.24	45	544	146	258	18224
新　疆	Xinjiang	120	1947	239.71	0.75	83	756	249	506	39529

23–25 续表 continued

地 区	Region	每万人拥有公共图书馆建筑面积（平方米） Floor Space of Public Libraries per 10 000 Population (sq.m)	组织各类讲座次数（次） Number of Lectures (time)	参加讲座人次（万人次） Participants to Lectures (10 000 person-times)	举办展览（个） Exhibitions Held (unit)	参观展览人次（万人次） Visitors to Exhibitions (10 000 person-times)	举办培训班（个） Training Classes Held (unit)	参加培训人次（万人次） Participants to Training Classes (10 000 person-times)	计算机（台） Computers (set)	#供读者使用的终端数 Terminals Available for Readers to Use
总 计	**National Total**	**160.3**	**120122**	**2258.38**	**67888**	**17954.86**	**105494**	**1167.17**	**216262**	**131576**
北 京	Beijing	192.1	1922	22.52	421	296.02	1527	6.34	4506	1789
天 津	Tianjin	342.5	1391	11.96	670	282.83	1385	4.53	4456	2733
河 北	Hebei	164.2	7829	151.09	4617	997.54	4976	50.71	8813	5941
山 西	Shanxi	176.5	2697	33.72	1447	408.27	2527	12.02	6646	3882
内蒙古	Inner Mongolia	220.5	1158	17.70	1102	196.52	840	5.80	6022	3535
辽 宁	Liaoning	158.8	2639	39.90	1820	470.72	1816	11.69	8947	5498
吉 林	Jilin	149.1	1173	11.28	991	135.49	595	3.72	4167	2521
黑龙江	Heilongjiang	127.8	1232	7.24	1292	79.74	1549	5.04	4734	2835
上 海	Shanghai	240.7	2163	20.02	455	807.15	1136	5.99	6397	2652
江 苏	Jiangsu	188.1	6067	70.11	3343	1888.23	7084	36.19	12138	6640
浙 江	Zhejiang	269.0	15551	475.50	10245	2927.33	16654	188.57	11488	6683
安 徽	Anhui	125.9	6383	415.74	4324	602.00	5847	38.02	7549	5035
福 建	Fujian	192.3	3228	38.55	1930	389.01	2892	17.80	7090	4446
江 西	Jiangxi	152.3	4131	40.87	1176	478.58	1850	416.29	6855	4658
山 东	Shandong	155.2	12575	186.34	5364	817.31	9826	89.35	11442	7222
河 南	Henan	100.0	7187	92.84	3058	568.51	4931	34.09	10182	6705
湖 北	Hubei	168.1	4524	118.69	3940	655.00	5219	49.02	7672	4604
湖 南	Hunan	141.8	5037	104.23	1811	538.41	6255	43.62	8164	5439
广 东	Guangdong	159.7	11814	123.12	4259	2699.39	11191	50.47	20460	11975
广 西	Guangxi	112.2	1951	33.58	1435	477.47	1753	10.42	6394	4216
海 南	Hainan	131.2	721	5.13	218	75.44	1127	4.93	1557	935
重 庆	Chongqing	129.7	2161	40.16	1526	360.93	2320	13.44	3702	2157
四 川	Sichuan	119.1	4308	49.96	2006	494.41	2035	12.11	10198	7050
贵 州	Guizhou	108.1	1638	31.18	1118	212.97	1481	7.90	5117	3473
云 南	Yunnan	97.0	2495	25.77	2086	289.85	1603	10.85	6997	4458
西 藏	Xizang	212.1	107	0.55	41	1.52	121	0.55	1545	1081
陕 西	Shaanxi	150.2	2592	33.82	2429	224.36	2813	13.34	5949	3893
甘 肃	Gansu	170.5	2265	21.25	1315	106.13	607	4.21	4816	2906
青 海	Qinghai	247.5	440	7.61	352	46.46	201	1.06	1976	1188
宁 夏	Ningxia	227.6	418	4.69	746	87.22	226	2.06	2066	1379
新 疆	Xinjiang	210.9	2180	20.32	2337	166.78	1786	12.30	4939	3537

23-26 群众文化机构基本情况（2023年）
Statistics on Cultural Institutions (2023)

指 标	Item	总计 Total	文化馆 Cultural Centers	省、区、直辖市级 Provincial Level	地市级 Prefecture Level	县市级 County (City) Level	#县文化馆 County Cultural Centers	文化站 Cultural Stations	#乡镇文化站 Township Cultural Stations
机构数 (个)	Institutions (unit)	43752	3516	32	372	3112	1590	40236	32243
从业人员 (人)	Number of Employed Persons (person)	199188	55848	1825	10723	43300	21667	143340	110812
组织文艺活动 (万次)	Art Performances and Story-telling Sessions (10 000 times)	246.0	54.0	0.3	4.0	49.8	19.1	192.0	125.7
参加文艺活动人次 (万人次)	Participants Attending Art and Cultural Activities (10 000 person-times)	139298	66010	514	6271	59225	24492	73288	48357
举办训练班 (万次)	Number of Training Courses (10 000 times)	134.9	58.0	1.3	14.1	42.6	12.0	76.9	44.0
参加培训人次 (万人次)	Participants to Training Courses (10 000 person-times)	10462	3084	55	650	2379	789	7378	4414
举办展览个数 (万个)	Number of Exhibitions (10 000 units)	25.0	5.3	0.1	0.5	4.8	1.9	19.8	14.4
参观展览人次 (万人次)	Visitors to Exhibitions (10 000 person-times)	32673	13868	268	2132	11468	3792	18805	12091
组织公益性讲座次数(次)	Number of Public Welfare Lectures Organized (time)	60263	60263	861	7804	51598	16349		
参加公益性讲座人次 (万人次)	Participants to Public Welfare Lectures Organized (10 000 person-times)	1104	1104	12	102	990	327		
拥有计算机台数 (万台)	Computer Owned (10 000 units)	34.8	6.2	0.3	1.2	4.8	2.1	28.6	22.2
本年收入合计 (亿元)	Revenue in the Year(100 million yuan)	360.6	173.7	14.2	38.7	120.9	54.1	186.9	134.3
本年支出合计 (亿元)	Expenditure in the Year (100 million yuan)	363.1	168.4	14.1	39.7	114.7	47.5	194.6	140.9
馆办文艺团体 (个)	Art Performance Troupes Run by Centers (unit)	9843	9843	127	1363	8353	3543		
馆办文艺团体演出场次 (万场次)	Number of Art Performances Run by Centers (10 000 times)	14.9	14.9	0.2	1.4	13.3	7.2		
馆办老年大学 (个)	Colleges for the Elderly Run by Centers (unit)	651	651	8	61	582	325		
群众业余文艺团体(万个)	Part-time Art Troupe (10 000 units)	47.7	11.5	0.1	0.9	10.6	4.3	36.1	27.4

23–27 文物业基本情况（2023年）
Statistics on Cultural Relics (2023)

项　目	Item	机　构（个） Number of Institutions (unit)	从业人员（人） Number of Employed Persons (person)	本年收入合计（万元） Total Revenue in the Year (10 000 yuan)	本年支出合计（万元） Total Expenditure in the Year (10 000 yuan)	资产总计（万元） Total Assets (10 000 yuan)	实际使用房屋建筑面积（万平方米） Floor Space of Buildings Actually in Use (10 000 sq.m)
总　计	**Total**	**9645**	**180573**	**7978568**	**8948692**	**49731025**	**4825**
按单位性质分	By Nature of Units						
文物保护科研机构	Scientific and Research Agencies of Cultural Relic Protection	128	6921	572041	660236	856880	53
文物保护管理机构	Agencies of Cultural Relics Protection and Management	2547	30752	1426468	1454329	7059525	1374
国有博物馆	State-owned Museums	4508	122635	4057883	4200210	37650607	3238
其他文物机构	Other Cultural Relic Agencies	2462	20265	1922176	2633918	4164013	160
按隶属关系分	By Jurisdiction of Management						
中　央	Central Level	13	3743	306027	399565	753791	59
省、区、市	Provincial Level	251	22739	1474188	1469772	4713358	399
地、市	Prefecture Level	1539	54050	2129467	2209004	7919143	1152
县、市、区	County or City Level	7842	100041	4068886	4870352	36344733	3216
按管理部门分	By Department of Management						
文物部门	Cultural Relics Department	8765	158455	7182803	8095728	40001061	4276
其他部门	Other Departments	880	22118	795765	852964	9729964	549

23–27 续表 continued

项　目	Item	藏品（件/套） Collections (piece/set)	#一级品 Grade I Collection	本年从有关部门接收文物数(件/套) Accepted Relics from Other Departments in the Year (piece/set)	本年藏品征集数（件/套） Collection of Cultural Relics (piece/set)	举办陈列展览（个） Exhibition & Displays (unit)	参观人次（万人次） Visitors (10 000 person-times)
总　计	**Total**	**50172257**	**95313**	**222587**	**347898**	**29933**	**140266**
按单位性质分	By Nature of Units						
文物保护科研机构	Scientific and Research Agencies of Cultural Relic Protection	1803428	1890	122	151	104	694
文物保护管理机构	Agencies of Cultural Relics Protection and Management	1703817	10098	5848	5225	1168	19527
国有博物馆	State-owned Museums	41252855	81703	214587	339215	28661	120045
其他文物机构	Other Cultural Relic Agencies	5412157	1622	2030	3307		0
按隶属关系分	By Jurisdiction of Management						
中　央	Central Level	3546925	14996		2671	148	2785
省、区、市	Provincial Level	15018235	32707	13670	31018	1623	14269
地、市	Prefecture Level	11410856	18974	127695	60280	8526	49615
县、市、区	County or City Level	20196241	28636	81222	253929	19636	73598
按管理部门分	By Department of Management						
文物部门	Cultural Relics Department	42477915	90893	196390	277004	26465	118686
其他部门	Other Departments	7694342	4420	26197	70894	3468	21581

23-28 分地区国有博物馆基本情况(2023年)
Statistics on State-owned Museums by Region (2023)

地 区	Region	机构(个) Number of Institutions (unit)	从业人员(人) Number of Employed Persons (person)	#专业技术人员 Professional & Technical Staff	藏品(件/套) Collections (piece/set)	基本陈列展览(个) Regular Exhibitions (unit)	参观人次(万人次) Visitors (10 000 person-times)	#未成年人参观人次 Visitors of Juveniles	门票销售总额(万元) Revenue from Entrance Tickets (10 000 yuan)
总 计	**National Total**	**4508**	**122635**	**42516**	**41252855**	**28661**	**120045**	**30018**	**651395.1**
中 央	Central Level	5	3009	1951	3531565	147	2785	920	77324.4
北 京	Beijing	69	4444	1576	3006267	472	2679	460	14820.2
天 津	Tianjin	53	1393	591	738139	291	1353	339	3924.3
河 北	Hebei	147	4848	1448	513796	1014	3872	1037	2108.3
山 西	Shanxi	155	4386	1320	1465443	523	2242	457	8571.9
内蒙古	Inner Mongolia	128	3336	1443	1275564	608	1679	481	444.2
辽 宁	Liaoning	66	2527	1104	694290	475	2650	579	21392.4
吉 林	Jilin	94	1902	848	853790	618	1091	217	5884.2
黑龙江	Heilongjiang	132	2548	982	963509	1099	1873	439	90.7
上 海	Shanghai	85	4748	2051	4020027	661	2738	606	27044.7
江 苏	Jiangsu	330	7794	2835	1749415	2021	12993	2734	45831.8
浙 江	Zhejiang	206	5837	2008	1376802	2111	5979	1613	5692.4
安 徽	Anhui	181	3075	1024	806877	1250	2865	874	336.0
福 建	Fujian	102	2586	942	701714	1087	2756	794	143.2
江 西	Jiangxi	170	4331	1493	786438	1426	5120	1605	3778.2
山 东	Shandong	348	8247	3019	3737692	2478	8823	2661	22268.7
河 南	Henan	259	6996	1971	1162614	1210	7199	2055	14697.7
湖 北	Hubei	172	4556	1760	2627010	1111	5084	1373	4159.8
湖 南	Hunan	159	4017	1341	1262125	963	8970	2723	5870.1
广 东	Guangdong	223	5812	2299	2513453	2105	7189	1565	13556.0
广 西	Guangxi	119	2792	1191	484217	551	2623	660	55299.8
海 南	Hainan	33	686	270	179222	171	496	122	2000.0
重 庆	Chongqing	106	2987	1017	613742	787	3676	642	11239.9
四 川	Sichuan	272	6742	1840	1359230	1356	7718	1814	56557.3
贵 州	Guizhou	122	2499	614	277499	441	2246	390	1031.9
云 南	Yunnan	143	2143	1014	1589343	842	2096	490	596.9
西 藏	Xizang	15	312	99	94168	57	0	0	
陕 西	Shaanxi	246	9854	2063	1566995	912	5640	859	204102.2
甘 肃	Gansu	194	5479	1515	574990	1171	3610	1011	42627.9
青 海	Qinghai	24	346	158	75326	87	137	31	
宁 夏	Ningxia	52	809	238	355648	203	737	175	
新 疆	Xinjiang	98	1594	491	295945	413	1127	292	

23-29 分地区规模以上文化及相关产业法人单位数(2023年)
Number of Corporate Units of Cultural and Related Industries above Designated Size by Region (2023)

单位：个 (unit)

地 区	Region	法人单位数 Corporate Units	文化制造业 Culture-Related Manufacturing	文化批发和零售业 Culture-Related Wholesale and Retail	文化服务业 Culture-Related Services
全 国	**National Total**	**74838**	**20815**	**14392**	**39631**
北 京	Beijing	5945	133	752	5060
天 津	Tianjin	970	180	201	589
河 北	Hebei	1256	465	260	531
山 西	Shanxi	430	54	133	243
内蒙古	Inner Mongolia	162	7	55	100
辽 宁	Liaoning	999	139	220	640
吉 林	Jilin	289	26	96	167
黑龙江	Heilongjiang	276	35	115	126
上 海	Shanghai	3676	349	607	2720
江 苏	Jiangsu	11417	3488	2750	5179
浙 江	Zhejiang	6263	2668	1206	2389
安 徽	Anhui	2411	1047	400	964
福 建	Fujian	3471	1231	574	1666
江 西	Jiangxi	2754	1182	357	1215
山 东	Shandong	3703	1191	1038	1474
河 南	Henan	2579	865	579	1135
湖 北	Hubei	3834	776	978	2080
湖 南	Hunan	4359	1265	462	2632
广 东	Guangdong	11345	4320	2099	4926
广 西	Guangxi	836	229	166	441
海 南	Hainan	300	11	43	246
重 庆	Chongqing	1266	207	209	850
四 川	Sichuan	2842	490	390	1962
贵 州	Guizhou	511	107	58	346
云 南	Yunnan	736	111	158	467
西 藏	Xizang	41	4	8	29
陕 西	Shaanxi	1589	188	323	1078
甘 肃	Gansu	182	13	46	123
青 海	Qinghai	44	5	12	27
宁 夏	Ningxia	75	13	23	39
新 疆	Xinjiang	277	16	74	187

注：规模以上文化及相关产业法人单位包括规模以上文化制造业企业、限额以上文化批发和零售业企业以及规模以上文化服务业企业。

a) Corporate units of culture and related industries above designated size include culture-related manufacturing enterprises above designated size, culture-related wholesale and retail enterprises above designated size, and culture-related service enterprises above designated size.

23-30 分地区规模以上文化制造业企业基本情况(2023年)
Statistics on Culture-Related Manufacturing Enterprises above Designated Size by Region (2023)

单位：万元 (10 000 yuan)

地 区	Region	企业单位数 (个) Number of Enterprises (unit)	年末从业人员 (人) Employed Persons at Year-end (person)	资产总计 Total Assets	营业收入 Business Revenue	应交增值税 Value-added Tax Payable
全 国	**National Total**	**20815**	**3219909**	**368314178**	**382277602**	**6262408**
北 京	Beijing	133	20671	5232739	5931563	120099
天 津	Tianjin	180	20695	2557688	2479858	32042
河 北	Hebei	465	47438	4469296	3604210	108121
山 西	Shanxi	54	7611	857802	648216	28241
内蒙古	Inner Mongolia	7	1098	252573	173251	3644
辽 宁	Liaoning	139	23691	2583208	2409385	37174
吉 林	Jilin	26	3989	628896	292086	7879
黑龙江	Heilongjiang	35	3050	204844	157866	3268
上 海	Shanghai	349	47457	8891977	13699056	190818
江 苏	Jiangsu	3488	480013	64921714	59629985	1056140
浙 江	Zhejiang	2668	327663	38031741	31611665	648894
安 徽	Anhui	1047	105134	12109491	9346806	213831
福 建	Fujian	1231	191236	13555623	20856551	224627
江 西	Jiangxi	1182	180086	12667166	15493000	254118
山 东	Shandong	1191	210174	36630372	42142513	566875
河 南	Henan	865	78854	6322625	6193370	172328
湖 北	Hubei	776	107573	12990047	13891049	335651
湖 南	Hunan	1265	189282	10092035	16707879	488778
广 东	Guangdong	4320	905498	88188617	99217630	1095266
广 西	Guangxi	229	50030	8087648	5472272	90912
海 南	Hainan	11	3931	3258575	1404325	24275
重 庆	Chongqing	207	37743	4603972	5048544	114841
四 川	Sichuan	490	98824	19275904	18581734	318726
贵 州	Guizhou	107	20074	1386429	1423384	29805
云 南	Yunnan	111	19259	4650419	2369532	37951
西 藏	Xizang	4	495	76447	40445	2689
陕 西	Shaanxi	188	30775	5162601	3041402	45467
甘 肃	Gansu	13	1638	106977	67956	924
青 海	Qinghai	5	851	83186	37621	527
宁 夏	Ningxia	13	3633	285965	242303	6016
新 疆	Xinjiang	16	1443	147602	62148	2483

23−31 分地区限额以上文化批发和零售业企业基本情况(2023年)
Statistics on Culture-Related Wholesale and Retail Enterprises above Designated Size by Region (2023)

单位：万元 (10 000 yuan)

地 区	Region	企业单位数 (个) Number of Enterprises (unit)	年末从业人员 (人) Employed Persons at Year-end (person)	资产总计 Total Assets	营业收入 Business Revenue	应交增值税 Value-added Tax Payable
全 国	**National Total**	**14392**	**534657**	**161052431**	**217781854**	**1878156**
北 京	Beijing	752	43319	21869194	22578572	208906
天 津	Tianjin	201	4838	1542798	2922903	17642
河 北	Hebei	260	11940	2093001	1836649	10457
山 西	Shanxi	133	6619	1420729	1182781	6161
内蒙古	Inner Mongolia	55	3155	918168	579830	2730
辽 宁	Liaoning	220	6763	1853692	1717033	14116
吉 林	Jilin	96	3782	437008	645163	2762
黑龙江	Heilongjiang	115	3291	1103757	603649	2919
上 海	Shanghai	607	40233	16882820	30986855	247443
江 苏	Jiangsu	2750	68474	27326446	29497659	427671
浙 江	Zhejiang	1206	37904	12041211	21827180	103428
安 徽	Anhui	400	13093	4218636	3773826	39098
福 建	Fujian	574	15843	5331703	13786116	33012
江 西	Jiangxi	357	11013	2547945	2857555	9769
山 东	Shandong	1038	43942	14867191	22290675	193882
河 南	Henan	579	20324	2677744	4498602	21859
湖 北	Hubei	978	27720	5405234	5727865	106728
湖 南	Hunan	462	19686	2094420	3724254	37543
广 东	Guangdong	2099	84900	19335287	28683535	274275
广 西	Guangxi	166	5617	2015445	1704137	5647
海 南	Hainan	43	1899	760516	2532726	11906
重 庆	Chongqing	209	12720	2830313	3136562	39173
四 川	Sichuan	390	16873	5198052	4505873	27152
贵 州	Guizhou	58	2417	1296476	591118	1387
云 南	Yunnan	158	7288	1367227	1291385	9651
西 藏	Xizang	8	95	17744	20938	83
陕 西	Shaanxi	323	11358	1638683	2510549	12286
甘 肃	Gansu	46	4497	532020	710244	4659
青 海	Qinghai	12	736	105591	44439	158
宁 夏	Ningxia	23	541	144808	101942	262
新 疆	Xinjiang	74	3777	1178574	911242	5392

23-32 分地区规模以上文化服务业企业基本情况(2023年)

Statistics on Culture-Related Service Enterprises above Designated Size by Region (2023)

单位：万元 (10 000 yuan)

地区	Region	企业单位数（个） Number of Enterprises (unit)	年末从业人员（人） Employed Persons at Year-end (person)	资产总计 Total Assets	营业收入 Business Revenue	应交增值税 Value-added Tax Payable
全国	**National Total**	**39631**	**3510300**	**1463197062**	**703362732**	**13442761**
北京	Beijing	5060	470661	300691602	180747948	3222619
天津	Tianjin	589	33211	18677939	10020906	129120
河北	Hebei	531	51839	15638227	2804608	63117
山西	Shanxi	243	24945	11329691	2784208	41739
内蒙古	Inner Mongolia	100	10968	2783415	678421	7814
辽宁	Liaoning	640	99312	13261364	5088806	116119
吉林	Jilin	167	19516	5741087	986531	18604
黑龙江	Heilongjiang	126	14504	2522104	758825	-6947
上海	Shanghai	2720	311837	158105398	84076086	1176628
江苏	Jiangsu	5179	494513	208818662	47872422	1144779
浙江	Zhejiang	2389	241672	163014346	103839194	1661084
安徽	Anhui	964	89703	21351963	9971220	172349
福建	Fujian	1666	104725	21041665	20844433	351028
江西	Jiangxi	1215	55862	14699298	6801021	89242
山东	Shandong	1474	128786	28012662	12274089	246177
河南	Henan	1135	110972	19978614	9315702	168865
湖北	Hubei	2080	194813	53191074	28273135	503733
湖南	Hunan	2632	127848	27048551	10673784	243211
广东	Guangdong	4926	424943	179237378	96017412	2406729
广西	Guangxi	441	37114	17500171	4597104	75265
海南	Hainan	246	23969	8723574	10208664	248134
重庆	Chongqing	850	78827	37710406	12583174	211193
四川	Sichuan	1962	181681	71584781	27606263	895267
贵州	Guizhou	346	25462	15541488	1926700	28632
云南	Yunnan	467	42622	11286524	3587722	79616
西藏	Xizang	29	3335	679246	175370	6268
陕西	Shaanxi	1078	71182	26179802	6229734	92415
甘肃	Gansu	123	13196	2621495	987482	17416
青海	Qinghai	27	3203	629757	146928	4450
宁夏	Ningxia	39	5852	861525	221350	5119
新疆	Xinjiang	187	13227	4733254	1263492	22976

23–33 体育系统机构人员情况（2022年）
Number of Sports-Related Institutions and Personnel (2022)

指　标	Item	合计 Total 机构(个) Institutions (unit)	合计 Total 人员(人) Personnel (person)	国家级 National Level 机构(个) Institutions (unit)	国家级 National Level 人员(人) Personnel (person)
总计	**Total**	**6682**	**153202**	**44**	**5340**
体育行政机关	Administrative Agencies of Sports	3069	29503	1	237
运动项目管理部门	Sports Events Management Departments	273	34831	20	1386
本科院校	Universities and Colleges	8	5619	1	1168
职业、运动技术学院	Sports Technical Institutes	16	5627		
体育运动学校	Physical Education and Sports Schools	220	16181		
竞技体校	Competitive Sports Schools	19	761		
少儿体育运动学校(业余体校)	Spare-time Sports Schools	1201	18433		
单项运动学校	Sport Event Schools	14	329		
体育中学	Secondary Schools of Physical Education	33	1707		
训练基地	Training Bases	60	2960	5	720
体育场馆	Stadiums and Gymnasiums	509	11041	1	460
体育科研机构	Sports Science Research Institute	46	1326	1	148
其他事业单位	Other Institutions	1141	22167	13	709
其他	Others	73	2717	2	512

23–33 续表 continued

指　标	Item	省级 Provincial Level 机构(个) Institutions (unit)	省级 Provincial Level 人员(人) Personnel (person)	地级 Prefectural Level 机构(个) Institutions (unit)	地级 Prefectural Level 人员(人) Personnel (person)	县级 County Level 机构(个) Institutions (unit)	县级 County Level 人员(人) Personnel (person)
总计	**Total**	**560**	**56652**	**1708**	**49095**	**4370**	**42115**
体育行政机关	Administrative Agencies of Sports	33	1667	443	7045	2592	20554
运动项目管理部门	Sports Events Management Departments	215	31056	37	2352	1	37
本科院校	Universities and Colleges	7	4451				
职业、运动技术学院	Sports Technical Institutes	14	5147	2	480		
体育运动学校	Physical Education and Sports Schools	23	2024	160	13449	37	708
竞技体校	Competitive Sports Schools	1	18	3	162	15	581
少儿体育运动学校(业余体校)	Spare-time Sports Schools	4	124	282	8851	915	9458
单项运动学校	Sport Event Schools	2	30	8	247	4	52
体育中学	Secondary Schools of Physical Education	1	151	15	858	17	698
训练基地	Training Bases	22	1767	31	428	2	45
体育场馆	Stadiums and Gymnasiums	38	2216	290	6416	180	1949
体育科研机构	Sports Science Research Institute	25	949	20	229		
其他事业单位	Other Institutions	158	5866	393	7846	577	7746
其他	Others	17	1186	24	732	30	287

23-34 运动员获世界冠军情况
World Championships Won by Chinese Athletes

年 份 Year	项 数 (项) Number of Events (item)	人 数 (人) Number of Persons (person)	个 数 (个) Number of Champions (time)
1978	4	4	4
1979	12	20	12
1980	3	3	3
1981	25	53	25
1982	12	31	13
1983	37	50	39
1984	33	46	37
1985	42	70	46
1986	26	56	26
1987	64	72	69
1988	54	59	54
1989	80	83	82
1990	54	61	54
1991	88	86	93
1992	86	68	89
1993	101	106	103
1994	79	86	79
1995	98	187	102
1996	72	58	75
1997	87	96	92
1998	75	89	83
1999	91	129	92
2000	92	109	110
2001	79	138	90
2002	99	123	110
2003	17	94	84
2004	27	175	101
2005	22	159	106
2006	24	169	141
2007	22	217	123
2008	24	151	120
2009	30	223	142
2010	22	180	108
2011	24	198	138
2012	24	140	107
2013	22	164	124
2014	22	206	98
2015	25	214	127
2016	23	154	107
2017	24	248	106
2018	27	222	118
2019	33	305	128
2020	3	4	4
2021	16	90	67
2022	21	117	93
2023	32	259	165

23-35 运动员分项创世界纪录情况（2023年）
World Records Set by Chinese Athletes by Events (2023)

项 目	Item	项数(项) Number of Events (item)	人数(人) Number of Persons (person)	次数(次) Number of Times (time)
总计	**Total**	**20**	**25**	**23**
射击	Shooting	9	13	10
举重	Weightlifting	8	5	10
游泳	Swimming	1	1	1
跳伞	Skydiving	2	6	2

主要统计指标解释

广播/电视节目综合人口覆盖率 指根据国家广播电视总局制定的《广播电视人口覆盖率统计技术标准和方法》进行统计调查的，在对象区内能接收到由中央、省、地市或县通过无线、有线或卫星等各种技术方式转播的各级广播/电视节目的人口数占对象区总人口数的百分比。

艺术表演团体 指由文化部门主办或实行行业管理（经文化行政部门审批并领取营业性演出许可证），专门从事表演艺术等活动的各类专业艺术表演团体，含民间职业剧团。不包括群众业余文艺表演团队。

艺术表演场馆 指由文化部门主办或实行行业管理（向文化行政部门备案或领取合资/合作演出场所许可证），有观众席、舞台、灯光设备，公开售票、专供文艺团体演出的文化活动场所。

文化市场经营机构 指经文化市场行政部门审批或备案并领取相关许可或备案文件的、从事文化经营和文化服务活动的机构。

国家综合档案馆 指按行政区划或历史时期设置的，收集和管理所辖范围内多种门类档案的档案馆。

规模以上文化制造业企业 指《文化及相关产业分类(2018)》所规定行业范围内，年主营业务收入在 2000 万元及以上的工业企业法人。

限额以上文化批发和零售业企业 指《文化及相关产业分类(2018)》所规定行业范围内，年主营业务收入在 2000 万元及以上的批发业企业法人和年主营业务收入在 500 万元及以上的零售业企业法人。

规模以上文化服务业企业 指《文化及相关产业分类(2018)》所规定行业范围内，年营业收入在 1000 万元及以上的服务业企业法人，其中交通运输、仓储和邮政业，信息传输、软件和信息技术服务业，水利、环境和公共设施管理业的年营业收入 2000 万元及以上，居民服务、修理和其他服务业以及文化、体育和娱乐业的年营业收入在 500 万元及以上。

Explanatory Notes on Main Statistical Indicators

Population Coverage Rate of Radio/Television Programs refers to the percentage of population in the target region who can receive radio/television programmes transmitted by national, provincial, municipal or county stations through wireless, cable or satellite techniques, according to *Statistical Standard and Method on Television and Radio Coverage of Population* established by the State Administration of Radio and Television.

Arts Performance Troupes refer to the various professional performing arts groups, sponsored by the cultural departments or guided by the cultural societies (approved by the cultural administration authority, or permitted with the commercial performance certificate), including non-public troupes. The mass amateur arts performance troupes are not included.

Arts Performance Venues refer to the various venues for cultural activities, which are sponsored by the cultural departments or guided by the cultural societies (registered in the cultural market administration, or permitted with the cooperative performance certificate), with the facility of auditorium, stage and lighting, and selling tickets to the public.

Institutions of Cultural Market Management refer to the institutions engaged in cultural management and cultural services, with registration and permits certificate and documents from cultural market administration.

National Comprehensive Archives refer to all archives institutions responsible for collecting and keeping various documents and materials by administrative regions or historical periods .

Culture-Related Manufacturing Enterprises above Designated Size refer to manufacturing enterprises under the designated industrial sectors of *Classification of Culture and Related Industry (2018)*, with annual principal business revenue over 20 million yuan.

Culture-Related Wholesale and Retail Enterprises above Designated Size refer to wholesale and retail enterprises under the designated industrial sectors of *Classification of Culture and Related Industry (2018)*, with annual principal business revenue over 20 million yuan for wholesale enterprises, and annual principal business revenue over 5 million yuan for retail enterprises.

Culture-Related Service enterprises above Designated Size refer to service enterprises under the designated industrial sectors of *Classification of Culture and Related Industry (2018)*, with annual principal business revenue over 10 million yuan, except for enterprises in transport, storage and post, information transmission, software and information technology services, water conservancy, environment and public facilities management sectors, where the threshold of annual principal business is over 20 million yuan, as well as enterprises in household services, repair and other services, culture, sports and recreation sectors where the threshold of annual principal business is over 5 million yuan.

24

公共管理、社会保障和社会组织

Public Management, Social Security and Social Organizations

简 要 说 明

本篇资料的主要内容和资料来源

本篇主要包括公共管理、群众组织和社会保障情况等内容。

一、公共管理内容包括历届全国人大代表和政协委员情况，公安机关刑事案件立案情况和治安案件查处情况，交通事故情况，人民检察院办案情况，人民法院审理案件和收结案情况，司法部门律师、公证、调解情况及人社部门劳动人事争议仲裁情况。资料分别由公安部、最高人民检察院、最高人民法院、司法部、人力资源和社会保障部等提供。

二、群众组织的内容主要包括工会组织情况。资料由全国总工会提供。工会资料详见《中国工会统计年鉴》(中华全国总工会编)。

三、社会保障的内容主要包括社会保险基金收支情况，基本养老保险情况、失业保险情况、基本医疗保险情况、工伤保险情况、生育保险参保情况等。资料由人力资源和社会保障部、国家医疗保障局提供。详细资料见《中国劳动统计年鉴》（国家统计局人口和就业统计司、人力资源和社会保障部规划财务司编）和《中国医疗保障统计年鉴》（国家医疗保障局编）。

Brief Introduction

Main Contents and Sources of Data

Data in this chapter show statistics on public management, mass organizations, social insurance and so on.

I. Data on public management cover information on deputies to the National People's Congress (NPC) and members of the Chinese People's Political Consultative Conference (CPPCC), information such as criminal cases registered and offense cases against public order handled by the public security organs, traffic accidents, cases handled by people's procuratorate, cases accepted and settled by the people's courts, and statistics on lawyers, notarization and mediation in the judicial department, arbitration of labor and personnel disputes in the human resources and social security departments. Data are tabulated and provided by the Ministry of Public Security, the Supreme People's Procuratorate, the Supreme People's Court, the Ministry of Justice and the Ministry of Human Resources and Social Security.

II. Data on mass organizations cover information on trade unions which are provided by All-China Federation of Trade Unions. The detailed information can be found in *Statistical Yearbook on Chinese Trade Union* (All-China Federation of Trade Unions).

III. Data on social security mainly include revenue and expenses of social insurance fund, contributors and beneficiaries of basic endowment insurance, unemployment insurance, basic medical insurance, work-related injury insurance and birth insurance. Data are provided by the Ministry of Human Resources and Social Security and National Healthcare Security Administration. For detail information, please refer to *China Labour Statistical Yearbook* (Department of Population and Employment Statistics, National Bureau of Statistics, Department of Planning and Finance, Ministry of Human Resources and Social Security) and *China Healthcare Security Statistical Yearbook* compiled by the National Healthcare Security Administration.

24-1 历届全国人民代表大会代表人数
Number of Deputies to Previous National People's Congresses

单位：人 (person)

届别	Congress	年份 Year	代表总数 Total Number of Deputies	#女代表 Female Deputies	#少数民族代表 Ethnic Minority Deputies	占代表总数比重(%) As Percentage to Total Deputies (%) 女代表 Female Deputies	少数民族代表 Ethnic Minority Deputies
一　届	First Congress	1954	1226	147	177	12.0	14.4
二　届	Second Congress	1959	1226	150	180	12.2	14.7
三　届	Third Congress	1964	3040	542	373	17.8	12.3
四　届	Fourth Congress	1975	2885	653	270	22.6	9.4
五　届	Fifth Congress	1978	3497	740	381	21.2	10.9
六　届	Sixth Congress	1983	2978	632	404	21.2	13.6
七　届	Seventh Congress	1988	2970	634	445	21.3	15.0
八　届	Eighth Congress	1993	2978	626	439	21.0	14.7
九　届	Ninth Congress	1998	2979	650	428	21.8	14.4
十　届	Tenth Congress	2003	2984	604	415	20.2	13.9
十一届	Eleventh Congress	2008	2987	637	411	21.3	13.8
十二届	Twelfth Congress	2013	2987	699	409	23.4	13.7
十三届	Thirteenth Congress	2018	2980	742	438	24.9	14.7
十四届	Fourteenth Congress	2023	2977	790	442	26.5	14.8

24-2 历届全国政治协商会议委员人数
Number of Members of Previous Chinese People's Political Consultative Conferences

单位：人 (person)

届别	Conference	年份 Year	委员总数 Total Number of Members	#中国共产党委员 Members from the Communist Party of China	#少数民族委员 Ethnic Minority Members	占委员总数比重(%) As Percentage to Total Deputies (%) 中国共产党委员 Members from the Communist Party of China	少数民族委员 Ethnic Minority Members
一　届	First Conference	1949	180	59	19	32.8	10.6
二　届	Second Conference	1954	559	150	61	26.8	10.9
三　届	Third Conference	1959	1071	378	78	35.3	7.3
四　届	Fourth Conference	1965	1199	502	81	41.9	6.8
五　届	Fifth Conference	1978	1988	972	143	48.9	7.2
六　届	Sixth Conference	1983	2039	816	179	40.0	8.8
七　届	Seventh Conference	1988	2081	832	221	40.0	10.6
八　届	Eighth Conference	1993	2093	831	241	39.7	11.5
九　届	Ninth Conference	1998	2196	877	257	39.9	11.7
十　届	Tenth Conference	2003	2238	895	262	40.0	11.7
十一届	Eleventh Conference	2008	2237	892	250	39.9	11.2
十二届	Twelfth Conference	2013	2237	893	258	39.9	11.5
十三届	Thirteenth Conference	2018	2158	859	245	39.8	11.4
十四届	Fourteenth Conference	2023	2169	852	243	39.3	11.2

注：本表统计的是每届全国政协届初时的情况。
a) Statistics in this table are data at the beginning of each CPPCC conference.

24–3 公安机关立案的刑事案件及构成
Criminal Cases Registered in Public Security Organs and Its Composition

案件类别	Category of Cases	立案（起） Number of Cases Registered (case)		构成（%） Composition (%)	
		2022	2023	2022	2023
合计	**Total**	**4423259**	**4496359**	**100.00**	**100.00**
杀人	Homicide	5293	5443	0.12	0.12
伤害	Injury	73212	88510	1.66	1.97
抢劫	Robbery	6797	6751	0.15	0.15
强奸	Rape	39693	42458	0.90	0.94
拐卖妇女儿童	Abducting Women or Children	2887	1705	0.07	0.04
盗窃	Larceny	1203989	981771	27.22	21.83
诈骗	Fraud	1599914	1694757	36.17	37.69
走私	Smuggling	4518	6033	0.10	0.13
伪造、变造货币，出售、购买、运输、持有、使用假币	Forging Currency, Selling, Buying, Transporting, Holding and Using Counterfeit Currency	785	987	0.02	0.02
其他	Others	1486171	1667944	33.60	37.10

24–4 公安机关受理和查处治安案件数(2023年)
Cases of Offence Against Public Order Handled by Public Security Organs (2023)

案件类别	Category of Cases	受理（起） Number of Cases Accepted (case)	查处（起） Number of Cases Investigated and Treated (case)	每万人口受理案件数（起） Number of Cases Accepted per 10 000 Population (case)
合计	**Total**	**8685252**	**7880992**	**61.6**
扰乱单位秩序	Disturbing Business Orders	57513	54978	0.4
扰乱公共场所秩序	Disturbing Orders in Public Venues	151070	149635	1.1
寻衅滋事	Causing Quarrels and Making Troubles	125511	120273	0.9
阻碍执行职务	Obstructing Government Officials in Performing Their Duties	29418	28341	0.2
非法携带枪支、弹药、管制器具	Violation of Firearms Control Regulations	21866	21163	0.2
违反危险物质管理规定	Violation of Explosives Control Regulations	52311	51206	0.4
殴打他人	Battering Other Persons	2215010	2042382	15.7
故意伤害	Intentional Injury to Others	103236	93185	0.7
盗窃	Stealing Property	2245846	1921568	15.9
敲诈勒索	Extortion and Blackmail	56887	50350	0.4
抢夺	Robbery and Snatch	4562	3986	0.0
盗窃、损毁公共设施	Stealing and Damaging Public Facilities	10333	8497	0.1
伪造、变造、倒卖有价票证、凭证	Forge/Alter/Scalp Valuable Coupons or Certificates	1329	1284	0.0
违反旅馆业管理	Violating Hotel Management Regulations	101199	99611	0.7
违反房屋出租管理	Violating House Renting Control Regulations	128613	127428	0.9
诈骗	Swindling, Seizing and Extorting Property	568830	477204	4.0
卖淫、嫖娼	Prostitution or Soliciting Prostitutes	184827	182321	1.3
赌博、为赌博提供条件	Gambling, Providing Conditions for Gambling	388901	382122	2.8
毒品违法活动	Illegal Drug Related Activities	169530	167166	1.2
其他	Others	2068460	1898292	14.7

24-5 道路交通事故情况（2023年）
Basic Statistics on Road Traffic Accidents (2023)

类别	Type	发生数(起) Number of Traffic Accidents (case)	死亡人数(人) Number of Deaths (person)	受伤人数(人) Number of Injuries (person)	直接财产损失(万元) Direct Property Losses (10 000 yuan)
总计	**Total**	**254738**	**60028**	**253895**	**117933.4**
机动车	Motor Vehicles	211974	53361	206610	107752.5
#汽车	Automobiles	155158	42164	142318	94275.9
摩托车	Motorcycles	47330	9034	54518	10699.5
拖拉机	Tractors	998	313	950	252.2
非机动车	Non-motor Vehicles	38685	5252	44099	7803.0
#自行车	Bicycles	3119	554	3090	681.8
行人乘车人	Pedestrians and Passengers	3913	1390	3024	2288.9
其他	Others	166	25	162	89.0

24-6 各地区交通事故情况（2023年）
Basic Statistics on Traffic Accidents by Region (2023)

地区	Region	发生数(起) Number of Traffic Accidents (case)	死亡人数(人) Number of Deaths (person)	受伤人数(人) Number of Injuries (person)	直接财产损失(万元) Direct Property Losses (10 000 yuan)
全国	**National Total**	**254738**	**60028**	**253895**	**117933.4**
北京	Beijing	6472	1001	5419	3566.1
天津	Tianjin	6254	927	5907	3199.0
河北	Hebei	3871	2181	2757	2214.8
山西	Shanxi	7778	2226	7430	5154.4
内蒙古	Inner Mongolia	3692	784	3846	2226.6
辽宁	Liaoning	4778	1805	4149	1761.7
吉林	Jilin	6745	1482	7257	1717.2
黑龙江	Heilongjiang	3438	819	3684	1736.6
上海	Shanghai	1169	811	560	464.4
江苏	Jiangsu	9349	3645	7113	4337.2
浙江	Zhejiang	9690	2678	8223	4585.1
安徽	Anhui	9400	2356	9646	3478.1
福建	Fujian	7983	1594	7652	2415.7
江西	Jiangxi	3695	1474	3542	6079.9
山东	Shandong	11589	3009	10569	3955.6
河南	Henan	20919	2652	23466	9645.8
湖北	Hubei	28492	4287	32508	13395.2
湖南	Hunan	7722	3270	6935	7541.6
广东	Guangdong	34353	7246	33056	9301.9
广西	Guangxi	15644	2677	17180	4863.2
海南	Hainan	2994	604	3186	1488.0
重庆	Chongqing	4227	936	4266	3878.3
四川	Sichuan	7113	2273	7325	7441.6
贵州	Guizhou	13965	2655	14988	5093.3
云南	Yunnan	5533	1908	4625	1658.8
西藏	Xizang	785	278	983	1347.9
陕西	Shaanxi	5109	917	5325	2716.9
甘肃	Gansu	3791	1307	3990	709.4
青海	Qinghai	1699	463	1632	773.2
宁夏	Ningxia	1450	447	1359	263.4
新疆	Xinjiang	5039	1316	5317	922.5

24-7 人民检察院审查逮捕、审查起诉情况(2023年)
Arrests and Prosecution Approved by People's Procuratorate (2023)

单位：人 (person)

案件分类	Category of Cases	批捕、决定逮捕 Arrests	决定起诉 Prosecutions
合计	**Total**	**726210**	**1687689**
危害公共安全案	Offences Against Public Security	32711	407677
破坏社会主义市场经济秩序案	Offences Against Socialist Market Economic Order	58091	121039
侵犯公民人身、民主权利案	Offences Against Citizens' Personal and Democratic Rights	102187	146831
侵犯财产案	Offences Against Properties	232960	344431
妨害社会管理秩序案	Offences Against Social Management of Order	290361	648752
贪污贿赂案	Offences Against Corruption and Bribery	8469	16096
渎职侵权案	Offences Against Dereliction of Duty and Infringement of Rights	776	1911
其他	Others	655	952

24-8 人民检察院办理刑事申诉案件情况(2023年)
Criminal Appeals Handled by People's Procuratorate (2023)

单位：件 (case)

案件分类	Category of Cases	刑事检察部门办理 Cases Handled Criminal Prosecution Department	复查结案结果 Result of Reviewing Cases Settled		提出抗诉 Presenting Protest Appeal	提出再审检察建议 Giving Retrial Procuratorate Suggestion
			改变原决定 Original Decision Changed	维持原决定 Original Decision Maintained		
合计	**Total**	**5267**	**59**	**1218**	**9**	**135**
不服检察机关处理决定	Appeals against Decision of Procuratorate's Offices	2830	59	1218		
不服不批捕	Appeals against Rejection of Arrest	37	2	11		
不服不起诉	Appeals against Rejection of Prosecuting	2734	54	1197		
不服撤案	Appeals against Withdrawal of the Case	3				
不服其他诉讼终结的刑事处理决定	Appeals against Other Criminal Decisions	56	3	10		
不服法院刑事判决裁定	Appeals against Judgment of Criminal Cases	2437			9	135

24-9 人民检察院办理刑事抗诉案件情况（2023年）
Criminal Protests Handled by People's Procuratorate (2023)

案件类别	Category of Cases	提出抗诉 Presenting Protest Appeal (件) (case)	审判结果 合计 Total Result of Judgement (件) (case)	改判 Revising Judgment (件) (case)	改判 Revising Judgment (人) (person)	维持原判 Affirming Original Judgment (件) (case)	发回重审 Remanding for Retrial (件) (case)
合 计	**Total**	**7876**	**5115**	**4026**	**5274**	**230**	**859**
危害公共安全案	Cases of Endangering Public Safety	824	540	454	472	15	71
破坏社会主义市场经济秩序案	Cases of Disrupting the Order of Socialist Market Economy	964	564	415	735	26	123
侵犯公民人身、民主权利案	Cases of Infringement of Citizens' Personal and Democratic Rights	1213	779	632	747	29	118
侵犯财产案	Property Infringement Cases	1633	1055	822	1028	44	189
妨害社会管理秩序案	Cases of Disrupting Social Management Order	2640	1745	1382	1954	90	273
贪污贿赂案	Corruption and Bribery Cases	271	172	133	146	5	34
渎职侵权案	Dereliction of Duty and Infringement of Right Cases	77	42	26	40	6	10
其他刑事案	Other Criminal Cases	254	218	162	152	15	41

24-10 人民检察院办理民事、行政判决裁定调解书监督情况（2023年）
Civil and Administrative Judgments, Rulings, and Mediation Statements Supervised by People's Procuratorate (2023)

单位：件 (case)

项 目	Item	合计 Total	民事案件 Civil Cases	行政案件 Administrative Cases
提出抗诉	Presenting Protest	3999	3807	192
抗诉案件再审	Retrial of Protested Cases	3497	3368	129
改 判	Revising Judgment	2422	2372	50
调 解	Mediation	204	200	4
发回重审	Remanding for Retrial	337	306	31
和解撤诉	Reconciliation and Withdrawal	258	237	21
维持原判	Affirming Original Judgment	195	175	20
其 他	Others	81	78	3
提出再审检察建议	Giving Retrial Procuratorate Suggestion	10957	10525	432
采纳再审检察建议再审情况	Retrial after Adopting Procuratorate Suggestion	5345	5169	176
改 判	Revising Judgment	3812	3745	67
调 解	Mediation	350	337	13
发回重审	Remanding for Retrial	86	81	5
和解撤诉	Reconciliation and Withdrawal	311	271	40
维持原判	Affirming Original Judgment	111	107	4
其 他	Others	675	628	47

24-11 人民检察院刑事诉讼监督和刑事执行检察情况
Supervision of Criminal Proceedings and Procuratorial Work of Criminal Execution by People's Procuratorate

项 目		Item		2022	2023
立案监督小计	(件)	Sub-total of Supervision of Cases Registered	(case)	82932	139480
监督立案		Supervision of Cases Filing		36951	96756
监督撤案		Supervision of Cases Withdrawn		45981	42724
建议行政执法机关移送案件	(件)	Cases recommended for transfer by administrative law enforcement agencies	(case)	8779	5869
已纠正漏捕漏诉小计	(人)	Sub-total of Supervision of Investigation	(person)	76689	118115
纠正漏捕		Rectified of Missed Arrests		17273	19485
纠正漏诉		Rectified of Missed Appeals		59416	98630
已纠正侦查活动违法小计	(件次)	Sub-total of Rectified of Illegal Investigation	(case-time)	201315	247592
提出检察建议合计	(件次)	Number of Procuratorial Recommendations	(case-time)	53324	53976
纠正违法类检察建议		Rectified of Legal Violations		23149	30641
社会治理类检察建议		Rectified of Social Governance		23810	19294
其他问题		Others		6365	4041
减刑、假释、暂予监外执行检察小计	(人)	Sub-total of Commutation of Sentence, Parole and Temporary Execution Outside Prison	(person)	58039	25517
监外执行和社区矫正监管活动检察	(人)	Prosecution of Outside Prison Execution and Community Correction	(person)	102083	130315

24-12 人民检察院办理民事、行政公益诉讼案件情况（2023年）
Civil and Administrative Public Interest Litigation Handled by People's Procuratorate (2023)

单位：件 (case)

项 目	Item	合 计 Total	民事案件 Civil Cases	行政案件 Administrative Cases
案件线索受理	Case Clue Acceptance	203773	23611	180162
立案	Cases Registered	189885	22109	167776
诉前检察建议	Pre-Litigation Procuratorial Suggestions	135673	19184	116489
起诉	Prosecutions	12579	11303	1276
法院审结	Settled by Courts	8128	7543	585
#一审判决支持	Support in First Trail	8126	7543	583

24-13 人民法院审理一审案件情况
First Trial Cases by People's Courts

单位：件 (case)

年 份 Year	收 案 Cases Accepted	刑 事 Criminal	民 事 Civil	行 政 Administrative	行政赔偿 Administrative Compensation
1978	447755	146968	300787		
1979	513789	123846	389943		
1980	763535	197856	565679		
1981	906051	232125	673926		
1982	1024160	245219	778941		
1983	1343164	542648	756436	527	
1984	1355460	431357	838307	983	
1985	1319741	246655	846391	916	
1986	1611282	299720	989409	632	
1987	1875229	289614	1213219	5940	
1988	2290624	313306	1455130	8573	
1989	2913515	392564	1815385	9934	
1990	2916774	459656	1851897	13006	
1991	2901685	427840	1880635	25667	
1992	3051157	422991	1948786	27125	
1993	3414845	403267	2089257	27911	
1994	3955475	482927	2383764	35083	
1995	4545676	495741	2718533	52596	
1996	5312580	618826	3093995	79966	
1997	5288379	436894	3277572	90557	
1998	5410798	482164	3375069	98350	
1999	5692434	540008	3519244	97569	
2000	5356294	560432	3412259	85760	
2001	5344934	628996	3459025	100921	
2002	5132199	631348	4420123	80728	
2003	5130760	632605	4410236	87919	
2004	5072881	647541	4332727	92613	
2005	5161170	684897	4380095	96178	
2006	5183794	702445	4385732	95617	
2007	5550062	724112	4724440	101510	
2008	6288831	767842	5412591	108398	
2009	6688963	768507	5800144	120312	
2010	6999350	779595	6090622	129133	
2011	7596116	845714	6614049	136353	
2012	8442657	996611	7316463	129583	
2013	8876733	971567	7781972	123194	
2014	9489787	1040457	8307450	141880	
2015	11444950	1126748	10097804	220398	
2016	12088800	1101191	10762124	225485	
2017	12907729	1294377	11373753	230432	9167
2018	13920964	1203055	12449685	256656	11568
2019	15439600	1293911	13852052	279574	14063
2020	14518468	1107610	13136436	260220	14202
2021	18226928	1277197	16612893	319977	16861
2022	17158605	1039612	15827199	278304	13490
2023	19070779	1229811	17530542	298711	11715

注：1.一审案件指人民法院按照诉讼级别管辖按第一审程序审理的案件。
2.2002年起，经济纠纷和海事海商纠纷并入民事案件中。
3.2017年起，行政赔偿案件从行政案件中分离出来。

a) First trial cases refer to cases accepted by people's courts according to the first trial proceedings.
b) Data of civil cases include cases of economic disputes and maritime disputes since 2002.
c) Data of administrative compensation cases are separated from administrative cases since 2017.

24-14 人民法院审理刑事一审案件收结案情况（2023年）
First Trial Criminal Cases Accepted and Settled by People's Courts (2023)

单位：件 (case)

项　目	Item	收 案 Cases Accepted	结 案 Cases Settled
合计	**Total**	**1229811**	**1243255**
危害公共安全罪	Offences Against Public Security	395664	397184
破坏社会主义市场经济秩序罪	Offences Against Socialist Market Economic Order	61634	62518
侵犯公民人身权利民主权利罪	Offences Against Citizens' Personal and Democratic Rights	128228	131990
侵犯财产罪	Offences Against Properties	249224	251267
妨害社会管理秩序罪	Offences Against Social Management of Order	378904	383773
危害国防利益罪	Offences Against National Defense	273	285
贪污贿赂罪	Offences on Corruption and Bribery	14000	14238
渎职罪	Offences on Dereliction of Duty	1564	1647
其他	Others	320	353
合计中含自诉案件	Private Prosecution Among the Total	9579	9666

注：结案中含上年旧存(以下相关表同)。
a) Data of cases settled include cases turned over from previous year. The same applies to the following tables.

24-15 人民法院审理刑事案件罪犯情况
Criminal Offenders Heard by People’s Courts

单位：人 (person)

年 份 Year	刑事罪犯总数 Number of Offenders	#青少年罪犯 Juvenile Offenders	不满18岁 Less Than 18 Years	18岁至25岁 Between 18 and 25 Years	青少年罪犯占刑事罪犯比重(%) Proportion of Juvenile Offenders in the Total (%)
1997	526312	199212	30446	168766	37.9
1998	528301	208076	33612	174464	39.4
1999	602380	221153	40014	181139	36.7
2000	639814	220981	41709	179272	34.5
2001	746328	253465	49883	203582	34.0
2002	701858	217909	50030	167879	31.0
2003	742261	231715	58870	172845	31.2
2004	764441	248834	70086	178748	32.6
2005	842545	285801	82692	203109	33.9
2006	889042	303631	83697	219934	34.2
2007	931745	316298	87506	228792	33.9
2008	1007304	322061	88891	233170	32.0
2009	996666	302023	77604	224419	30.3
2010	1006420	287978	68193	219785	28.6
2011	1050747	282429	67280	215149	26.9
2012	1173406	282990	63782	219208	24.1
2013	1157784	265439	55817	209622	22.9
2014	1183784	249576	50415	199161	21.1
2015	1231656	236341	43839	192502	19.2
2016	1219569	204657	35743	168914	16.8
2017	1268985	183471	32778	150693	14.5
2018	1428772	243275	34365	208910	17.0
2019	1659550	281860	43038	238822	17.0
2020	1526811	245074	33768	211306	16.1
2021	1714942	283565	34616	248949	16.5
2022	1430865	247785	27757	220028	17.3
2023	1659396	284558	36037	248521	17.1

24−16 人民法院审理民事一审案件收结案情况（2023年）
First Trial Civil Cases Accepted and Settled by People's Courts (2023)

单位：件 (case)

项　目	Item	收案 Cases Accepted	结案 Cases Settled	判决 Judgment	不予受理 Dismiss
合计	**Total**	**17530542**	**17477181**	**8271078**	**45398**
人格权纠纷	Personality Disputes	192977	191590	101263	447
婚姻家庭、继承纠纷	Disputes of Marriage, Family and Inheritance	2174936	2170042	722572	1928
物权纠纷	Property Rights Disputes	349681	350600	159782	2645
合同、无因管理、不当得利纠纷	Contract, Non-cause Management, Improper Profit Disputes	11936754	11869516	5802094	34584
知识产权与竞争纠纷	Intellectual Property Rights and Competition Disputes	462176	460306	127911	558
劳动争议、人事争议	Labor Disputes, Personnel Disputes	608529	594894	319497	1979
海事海商纠纷	Maritime Disputes	16117	16238	6340	95
与公司、证券、保险、票据等有关的民事纠纷	Civil Disputes Relating to Companies, Securities, Insurance, Bills, etc	599395	632177	360597	1603
侵权责任纠纷	Tort Liability Dispute	1091165	1097538	607116	1267
其他	Others	98812	94280	63906	292

24−16 续表 continued

单位：件 (case)

项　目	Item	驳回起诉 Reject	撤诉 With-drawal	调解 Mediation	其他 Other
合计	**Total**	**352538**	**4370071**	**4233922**	**204174**
人格权纠纷	Personality Disputes	3053	45098	40593	1136
婚姻家庭、继承纠纷	Disputes of Marriage, Family and Inheritance	17408	376995	1033392	17747
物权纠纷	Property Rights Disputes	24669	106766	53413	3325
合同、无因管理、不当得利纠纷	Contract, Non-cause Management, Improper Profit Disputes	252736	3102208	2565458	112436
知识产权与竞争纠纷	Intellectual Property Rights and Competition Disputes	3589	270109	50753	7386
劳动争议、人事争议	Labor Disputes, Personnel Disputes	18852	95230	134711	24625
海事海商纠纷	Maritime Disputes	175	4799	3665	1164
与公司、证券、保险、票据等有关的民事纠纷	Civil Disputes Relating to Companies, Securities, Insurance, Bills, etc	13862	134788	90276	31051
侵权责任纠纷	Tort Liability Dispute	12668	212665	259318	4504
其他	Others	5526	21413	2343	800

24–17 人民法院审理婚姻家庭、继承一审案件收结案情况（2023年）
First Trial Civil Cases of Marriage, Family Affairs and Inheritance Accepted and Settled by People's Courts (2023)

单位：件 (case)

项目	Item	收案 Cases Accepted	结案 Cases Settled	判决 Judgment	不予受理 Dismiss	驳回起诉 Reject	撤诉 With-drawal	调解 Mediation	其他 Other
合计	**Total**	**2174936**	**2170042**	**722572**	**1928**	**17408**	**376995**	**1033392**	**17747**
婚姻家庭纠纷	Marriage and Family Disputes	2034502	2032771	681705	1727	14456	353211	965266	16406
离婚纠纷	Divorce Disputes	1713177	1713663	560022	1096	9782	282659	848663	11441
抚养纠纷	Upbringing Disputes	138219	136993	49845	158	1502	27976	55962	1550
扶养纠纷	Maintenance Disputes	3310	3255	1296	4	45	866	989	55
赡养纠纷	Support Disputes	23738	23666	9014	23	286	5823	7985	535
收养关系纠纷	Adoption Relation Disputes	1663	1639	619	5	40	288	669	18
监护权纠纷	Guardianship Disputes	708	707	216	9	35	283	150	14
探望权纠纷	Visitation Disputes	7404	7345	2762	14	96	1589	2727	157
其他	Others	146283	145503	57931	418	2670	33727	48121	2636
继承纠纷	Inheritance	138372	134892	40165	197	2921	23340	66949	1320
法定继承纠纷	Legal Inheritance	54234	52781	10229	54	711	7934	33515	338
遗嘱继承纠纷	Testament Inheritance	9012	8610	3461	5	152	1581	3325	86
其他	Others	75126	73501	26475	138	2058	13825	30109	896
其他	Others	2062	2379	702	4	31	444	1177	21

24–18 人民法院审理行政一审案件收结案情况（2023年）
First Trial Administrative Cases Accepted and Settled by People's Courts (2023)

单位：件 (case)

项目	Item	收案 Cases Accepted	结案 Cases Settled	判决 Judgment	不予立案 Not to Put on Record	驳回起诉 Reject	撤诉 With-drawal	调解 Mediation	其他 Other
合计	**Total**	**298711**	**295965**	**145081**	**13647**	**52728**	**71963**	**3556**	**8990**
公安	Public Security	35541	34494	16745	1741	4580	10706	69	653
资源	Resource	38754	38403	16611	1981	9391	8518	451	1451
城乡建设	Urban and Rural Construction	49172	48633	20760	2193	11731	10894	910	2145
计划生育	Family Planning	91	85	31	6	18	29	1	
工商	Industry and Commerce	6326	6215	2095	348	1381	2160	86	145
卫生	Health	1546	1529	561	108	438	367	27	28
环境保护	Environment Protection	1655	1824	1003	38	174	496	50	63
交通运输	Traffic and Transport	1632	1636	624	80	208	677	24	23
税务	Tax	1253	1222	443	98	283	352	6	40
劳动和社会保障	Labour and Social Security	28882	28004	17949	504	1928	7196	79	348
乡政府	Townships Government	21640	21917	9991	1012	4805	4679	298	1132
其他	Other	112219	112003	58268	5538	17791	25889	1555	2962

24-19 律师、公证和调解工作基本情况
Basic Statistics on Lawyers, Notarization and Mediation

项目	Item	2018	2019	2020	2021	2022	2023
律师工作	**Lawyers**						
律师事务所 (家)	Number of Law Offices (unit)	30647	32621	34441	36504	38547	41132
律师人数 (人)	Number of Lawyers (person)	423758	473036	522510	574042	650312	731637
#专职律师	Full-time Lawyers	364345	397329	424475	457378	503638	557068
兼职律师	Part-time Lawyers	12002	12589	13515	14400	15462	14790
担任法律顾问 (家)	Number of Units with Legal Advisors (unit)	700027	736917	779760	846336	876338	909949
民事案件代理 (件)	Agent of Civil Cases (case)	3969240	4792176	5327052	6601598	6975417	8244294
刑事案件辩护及代理(件)	Agent and Defender of Criminal Cases (case)	814570	1094423	1049632	1228117	990440	1287744
行政案件代理 (件)	Agent of Administrative Action (case)	165840	189342	208030	262246	254756	299820
非诉讼法律事务 (件)	Non-Litigious Legal Affairs (case)	1058594	1336860	1233002	1679879	1416481	1503755
咨询和代书 (万件)	Legal Consulting and Writing (10 000 cases)	322.6	309.8	253.7	249.2	229.8	235.6
公证工作	**Notarization**						
公证机构 (家)	Number of Notary Offices (unit)	2956	2956	2942	2947	2948	2941
公证员 (人)	Notaries (person)	13335	13428	13620	14600	14869	15292
办理公证(出证)总数 (万件)	Number of Notarized Documents (10 000 cases)	1337.3	1374.3	1173.8	1210.0	1104.5	1365.2
人民调解工作	**People's Mediation**						
人民调解委员会 (万个)	Number of People's Mediation Committees (10 000 units)	75.2	73.5	70.8	68.9	69.3	69.8
调解人员 (万人)	Number of Mediators (10 000 persons)	349.7	337.8	320.9	316.2	317.6	307.8
调解案件总数 (万件)	Number of Civil Disputes Mediated (10 000 cases)	953.2	931.5	819.6	874.4	892.3	1720.0

注：1.全国律师人数中包括各省(区、市)和新疆兵团律师以及司法部批准的公职律师、公司律师、中国法律律师事务所律师和军队律师。
2.2023年，调解案件总数含法院委托移送调解案件数。

a) The number of lawyers nationwide includes lawyers from all provinces (autonomous regions and municipalities) and Xinjiang corps, as well as public lawyers, corporate lawyers, lawyers from Chinese law firms and military lawyers approved by the Ministry of Justice.
b) In 2023, the total number of civil disputes mediated includes the number of mediation cases transferred by the court.

24–20 公证业务分类(2023年)
Notarial Services by Type (2023)

分 类	Item	办证件数(件) Number of Notarial Documents Issued (case)	比 重 (%) Percentage (%)
合计	**Total**	**13651594**	**100.00**
合同(协议)	Contracts (Agreements)	640222	4.69
继承	Inheritance	1701487	12.46
其中：小额继承	Small Amount Inheritance	170126	1.25
委托	Power of Attorney	2714600	19.88
声明	Declaration	1483931	10.87
赠与	Gift	47931	0.35
遗嘱	Testament	154444	1.13
现场监督	Field Supervision	144118	1.06
婚姻状况、亲属关系、收养关系	Marital Status, Kinship Confirmation, Adoptive Relationship	546158	4.00
出生、生存、死亡	Births, Survival, Deaths	373905	2.74
身份、经历、学历、学位、职务、职称	Identity, Resume, Education Background, Academic Degree, Professional Titles	142475	1.04
有无违法犯罪记录	Illegal and Criminal Record Check	495668	3.63
公司章程	Corporation Constitutions	1792	0.01
保全证据	Evidence Preservation	652494	4.78
证书、执照	Certificate, Licence	1189202	8.71
签名、印鉴	Signature, Seal	267082	1.96
文本相符	Conformity of Documentation	897471	6.57
赋予强制执行效力	Executor Force	1728368	12.66
执行证书	Certificate of Execution	55024	0.40
抵押登记	Mortgage Registration	5968	0.04
提存	Drawing	21203	0.16
保管	Storage	3379	0.02
其他	Others	384672	2.82

24-21 调解民间纠纷分类情况
Civil Disputes Mediated by Type

项 目	Item	调解纠纷（万件） Civil Disputes Mediated (10 000 cases)		各类纠纷所占比重（%） Percentage(%)	
		2022	2023	2022	2023
合 计	**Total**	**892.3**	**1720.0**	**100.0**	**100.0**
#婚姻家庭	Marriage and Family Disputes	123.0	147.5	13.8	8.6
房屋、宅基地	Housing and Housing Sites	30.4	32.2	3.4	1.9
邻 里	Neighbor Disputes	225.9	285.3	25.3	16.6
损害赔偿	Compensation for Damages	73.4	85.2	8.2	5.0
医 疗	Health Care	6.5	7.6	0.7	0.4
道路交通事故	Traffic Accidents	69.9	83.7	7.8	4.9

注：2023年，调解纠纷合计数含法院委托移送调解案件数。
a) In 2023, the total number of civil disputes mediated includes the number of mediation cases transferred by the court.

24-22 劳动人事争议仲裁情况
Arbitration of Labor and Personnel Disputes

项 目	Item	2018	2019	2020	2021	2022	2023
上期未结案数 （件）	**Number of Cases Left Over from Last Period (case)**	**35506**	**48687**	**49723**	**43525**	**40745**	**43661**
案件受理情况	**Cases Accepted**						
当期案件受理数 （件）	Number of Current Cases (case)	894053	1069638	1094788	1252045	1473145	1629445
#集体劳动争议案件数	Number of Collective Labour Disputes	8699	9235	8321	7446	8148	8484
劳动者申请案件数	Number of Cases Applied by Laborers	869421	1021334	1041567	1199847	1421670	1581748
按争议原因分 （件）	By Cause of the Disputes (case)						
#劳动报酬	Labour Remuneration	380751	446572	462729	524473	593024	638503
社会保险	Social Insurances	144533	149966	136496	164102	187186	227063
解除、终止劳动合同	Dissolution or Termination of Labour Contracts	195063	259550	280058	293924	382297	428270
劳动者当事人数 （人）	Number of Laborers Involved (person)	1110175	1274124	1283491	1404754	1636418	1803057
#集体劳动争议	Collective Labour Disputes	234943	220174	200824	159898	177821	175402
案件处理情况 （件）	**Cases Settled (case)**						
结案数	Number of Cases Settled	884223	1068413	1100681	1256162	1466857	1641106
按处理方式分	By Manners of Settlement						
仲裁调解	By Mediation	458353	552584	599797	703373	847132	951055
仲裁裁决	By Arbitration Lawsuit	357666	430309	430863	471819	542709	603393
其他方式	Others	68204	85520	70021	80970	77016	86658
按处理结果分	By Results of Settlement						
用人单位胜诉	Lawsuit Won by Employers	93823	112747	112053	127910	150606	165385
劳动者胜诉	Lawsuit Won by Laborers	276642	314097	310819	341245	370243	398015
双方部分胜诉及其他	Lawsuit Partly Won by Both Parties and Others	513758	641569	677809	787007	946008	1077706
案外调解案件数 （件）	**Cases Mediated (case)**	**214288**	**242479**	**255328**	**320621**	**381693**	**469647**

24-23 分地区工会组织情况(2023年)
Statistics on Trade Unions by Region (2023)

地区	Region	工会基层组织数(万个) Number of Grassroot Trade Unions (10 000 units)	全国已建工会组织的基层单位的职工与会员人数(万人) Staff and Workers and Membership of Grassroot Units with Established Trade Unions (10 000 persons)				工会专职工作人员人数(万人) Number of Full-time Personnel of Trade Unions (10 000 persons)
			职工人数 Staff and Workers	#女性 Female	会员人数 Membership	#女性 Female	
全国	**National Total**	**222.8**	**27077.2**	**10581.3**	**25894.9**	**10201.0**	**81.7**
北京	Beijing	3.4	807.6	268.7	644.1	233.4	1.4
天津	Tianjin	1.7	298.1	113.4	294.2	112.8	0.5
河北	Hebei	12.5	1436.9	479.4	1413.5	473.8	4.7
山西	Shanxi	5.1	695.2	248.1	665.4	235.8	3.9
内蒙古	Inner Mongolia	4.5	389.6	141.1	371.3	135.4	1.6
辽宁	Liaoning	6.1	1115.0	434.4	1069.3	420.4	2.5
吉林	Jilin	3.1	430.2	167.3	423.1	165.2	1.4
黑龙江	Heilongjiang	4.1	476.1	167.3	448.6	160.1	2.5
上海	Shanghai	4.9	768.6	291.2	728.6	277.7	1.1
江苏	Jiangsu	14.5	2096.5	885.6	2004.8	848.1	3.1
浙江	Zhejiang	13.6	1875.5	801.0	1817.7	782.4	2.9
安徽	Anhui	12.1	1109.2	409.8	1061.4	395.6	3.9
福建	Fujian	9.5	785.2	341.1	764.5	334.0	1.3
江西	Jiangxi	7.8	849.4	308.0	825.7	301.6	5.2
山东	Shandong	11.0	1488.8	581.1	1429.7	561.6	6.5
河南	Henan	13.0	1430.3	552.1	1367.9	533.9	9.5
湖北	Hubei	10.4	1159.4	446.3	1109.1	429.0	2.7
湖南	Hunan	10.7	1033.1	382.2	1005.3	371.9	5.4
广东	Guangdong	15.0	2356.9	1014.7	2179.8	947.6	6.0
广西	Guangxi	5.8	563.2	246.7	539.3	237.6	1.7
海南	Hainan	1.6	162.1	67.2	152.4	63.3	0.3
重庆	Chongqing	4.4	561.1	219.3	540.6	211.9	1.7
四川	Sichuan	14.1	1911.0	751.9	1860.0	736.2	3.1
贵州	Guizhou	5.6	702.4	265.4	684.5	261.7	1.4
云南	Yunnan	6.2	440.3	189.5	419.0	181.3	1.1
西藏	Xizang	0.9	73.7	30.4	65.3	26.3	0.4
陕西	Shaanxi	10.8	913.1	329.0	893.3	323.3	3.4
甘肃	Gansu	3.6	358.0	136.3	349.6	133.6	0.8
青海	Qinghai	1.4	124.4	49.8	121.3	49.2	0.3
宁夏	Ningxia	1.3	132.6	54.5	128.5	53.2	0.3
新疆	Xinjiang	4.2	490.6	188.2	475.1	183.4	1.2
中央和国家机关	Central and State Organs	0.2	43.2	20.5	41.9	19.8	0.1

24–24 社会保险基金收支及累计结余
Revenue, Expenses and Balance of Social Insurance Fund

单位：亿元 (100 million yuan)

年 份 Year	合 计 Total	基本养老保险 Basic Endowment Insurance	失业保险 Unemployment Insurance	基本医疗保险 Basic Medical Insurance	工伤保险 Work-related Injury Insurance	生育保险 Birth Insurance
基金收入 Revenue						
1990	186.8	178.8	7.2			
1995	1006.0	950.1	35.3	9.7	8.1	2.9
2000	2644.9	2278.5	160.4	170.0	24.8	11.2
2005	6975.2	5093.3	340.3	1405.3	92.5	43.8
2010	19276.1	13872.9	649.8	4308.9	284.9	159.6
2011	25153.3	18004.8	923.1	5539.2	466.4	219.8
2012	30738.8	21830.2	1138.9	6938.7	526.7	304.2
2013	35252.9	24732.6	1288.9	8248.3	614.8	368.4
2014	39827.7	27619.9	1379.8	9687.2	694.8	446.1
2015	46012.1	32195.5	1367.8	11192.9	754.2	501.7
2016	53562.7	37990.8	1228.9	13084.3	736.9	521.9
2017	67154.5	46613.8	1112.6	17931.3	853.8	643.0
2018	79254.8	55005.3	1171.1	21384.4	913.0	781.0
2019	83550.4	57025.9	1284.2	24420.9	819.4	
2020	75512.5	49228.6	951.5	24846.1	486.3	
2021	96936.8	65793.3	1459.6	28732.0	951.9	
2022	102504.8	68933.2	1596.1	30922.2	1053.3	
2023	113214.9	76691.2	1807.3	33504.9	1211.6	
基金支出 Expenses						
1990	151.9	149.3	2.5			
1995	877.1	847.6	18.9	7.3	1.8	1.6
2000	2385.6	2115.5	123.4	124.5	13.8	8.3
2005	5400.8	4040.3	206.9	1078.7	47.5	27.4
2010	15018.9	10755.3	423.3	3538.1	192.4	109.9
2011	18652.9	13363.2	432.8	4431.4	286.4	139.2
2012	23331.3	16711.5	450.6	5543.6	406.3	219.3
2013	27916.3	19818.7	531.6	6801.0	482.1	282.8
2014	33002.7	23325.8	614.7	8133.6	560.5	368.1
2015	38988.1	27929.4	736.4	9312.1	598.7	411.5
2016	46888.4	34004.3	976.1	10767.1	610.3	530.6
2017	57145.6	40423.8	893.8	14421.8	662.3	744.0
2018	67792.7	47550.4	915.3	17823.0	742.0	762.0
2019	75346.6	52342.3	1333.2	20854.2	816.9	
2020	78611.8	54656.5	2103.0	21032.1	820.3	
2021	86734.9	60196.5	1500.0	24048.2	990.2	
2022	90719.1	63079.0	2017.8	24597.2	1025.0	
2023	99301.8	68369.4	1485.2	28210.5	1236.7	
累计结余 Balance at Year-end						
1990	117.3	97.9	19.5			
1995	516.8	429.8	68.4	3.1	12.7	2.7
2000	1327.5	947.1	195.9	109.8	57.9	16.8
2005	6073.7	4041.0	519.0	1278.1	163.5	72.1
2010	23407.5	15787.8	1749.8	5047.1	561.4	261.4
2011	30233.1	20727.8	2240.2	6180.0	742.6	342.5
2012	38106.6	26243.5	2929.0	7644.5	861.9	427.6
2013	45588.1	31274.8	3685.9	9116.5	996.2	514.7
2014	52462.3	35644.5	4451.5	10644.8	1128.8	592.7
2015	59532.5	39937.1	5083.0	12542.8	1285.3	684.4
2016	66349.7	43965.2	5333.3	14964.3	1410.9	675.9
2017	77312.1	50202.2	5552.4	19385.6	1606.9	565.0
2018	89775.5	58151.6	5817.0	23440.0	1784.9	582.0
2019	96977.8	62872.6	4625.4	27696.7	1783.2	
2020	94378.7	58075.2	3354.1	31500.0	1449.3	
2021	104872.1	63970.0	3312.5	36178.3	1411.2	
2022	116822.0	69851.3	2890.8	42639.9	1440.1	
2023	130752.0	78173.0	3212.9	47951.0	1415.1	

注：1.2007年及以后基本医疗保险基金中包括职工基本医疗保险和城乡居民基本医疗保险。
2.2010年及以后基本养老保险基金中包括城镇职工基本养老保险和城乡居民基本养老保险。
3.工伤保险累计结余中含储备金(以下相关表同)。
4.2019年起，基本医疗保险基金包含生育保险基金(以下相关表同)。

a) Data of basic medical insurance include the basic medical insurance for workers and the basic medical insurance for urban and rural residents from 2007.
b) Data of basic endowment insurance for 2010 and following years include the basic endowment insurance for urban workers and basic endowment insurance for urban and rural residents.
c) The balance at year-end of work-related injury insurance at year-end include reserve fund. The same applies to the relevant following tables.
d) Since 2019, the data of basic medical care insurance fund includes the data of maternity insurance fund. The same applies to the relevant following tables.

24−25 社会保险基本情况
Basic Statistics of Social Insurance

单位：万人 (10 000 persons)

年份 Year	年末参加基本养老保险人数 Basic Endowment Insurance Participants at Year-end	城镇职工基本养老保险 Basic Endowment Insurance for Urban Workers 合计 Total	职工 Number of Workers	#企业 Enterprises	离退休(职)人员 Number of Retirees	#企业 Enterprises	城乡居民基本养老保险 Basic Endowment Insurance for Urban and Rural Residents
1989	5710.3	5710.3	4816.9	4816.9	893.4	893.4	
1990	6166.0	6166.0	5200.7	5200.7	965.3	965.3	
1991	6740.3	6740.3	5653.7	5653.7	1086.6	1086.6	
1992	9456.2	9456.2	7774.7	7774.7	1681.5	1681.5	
1993	9847.6	9847.6	8008.2	8008.2	1839.4	1839.4	
1994	10573.5	10573.5	8494.1	8494.1	2079.4	2079.4	
1995	10979.0	10979.0	8737.8	8737.8	2241.2	2241.2	
1996	11116.7	11116.7	8758.4	8758.4	2358.3	2358.3	
1997	11203.9	11203.9	8670.9	8670.9	2533.0	2533.0	
1998	11203.1	11203.1	8475.8	8475.8	2727.3	2727.3	
1999	12485.4	12485.4	9501.8	8859.2	2983.6	2863.8	
2000	13617.4	13617.4	10447.5	9469.9	3169.9	3016.5	
2001	14182.5	14182.5	10801.9	9733.0	3380.6	3171.3	
2002	14736.6	14736.6	11128.8	9929.4	3607.8	3349.2	
2003	15506.7	15506.7	11646.5	10324.5	3860.2	3556.9	
2004	16352.9	16352.9	12250.3	10903.9	4102.6	3775.0	
2005	17487.9	17487.9	13120.4	11710.6	4367.5	4005.2	
2006	18766.3	18766.3	14130.9	12618.0	4635.4	4238.6	
2007	20136.9	20136.9	15183.2	13690.6	4953.7	4544.0	
2008	21891.1	21891.1	16587.5	15083.4	5303.6	4868.0	
2009	23549.9	23549.9	17743.0	16219.0	5806.9	5348.0	
2010	35984.1	25707.3	19402.3	17822.7	6305.0	5811.6	10276.8
2011	61573.3	28391.3	21565.0	19970.0	6826.2	6314.0	33182.0
2012	78796.3	30426.8	22981.1	21360.9	7445.7	6910.9	48369.5
2013	81968.4	32218.4	24177.3	22564.7	8041.0	7484.8	49750.1
2014	84231.9	34124.4	25531.0	23932.3	8593.4	8013.6	50107.5
2015	85833.4	35361.2	26219.2	24586.8	9141.9	8536.5	50472.2
2016	88776.8	37929.7	27826.3	25239.6	10103.4	9023.9	50847.1
2017	91548.3	40293.3	29267.6	25856.3	11025.7	9460.4	51255.0
2018	94293.3	41901.6	30104.0	26502.6	11797.7	9980.5	52391.7
2019	96753.9	43487.9	31177.5	27508.7	12310.4	10396.3	53266.0
2020	99864.9	45621.1	32858.7	29123.6	12762.3	10784.2	54243.8
2021	102871.4	48074.0	34917.1	31101.5	13157.0	11126.5	54797.4
2022	105307.3	50355.0	36711.0	32871.5	13644.0	11530.9	54952.3
2023	106643.3	52120.8	37925.2	34052.9	14195.6	11991.2	54522.5

24-25 续表 continued

单位：万人 (10 000 persons)

年份 Year	失业保险 Unemployment Insurance		基本医疗保险 Basic Medical Insurance			工伤保险 Work-related Injury Insurance		年末参加生育保险人数 Birth Insurance Participants at Year-end
	年末参保人数 Participants at Year-end	全年发放失业保险金(亿元) Unemployed Relief (100 million yuan)	年末参保人数 Participants at Year-end	职工 For Workers	城乡居民 For Urban and Rural Residents	年末参保人数 Participants at Year-end	全年享受工伤保险待遇人数 Beneficiaries of Work-related Injury Insurance	
1994	7967.8	5.1	400.3	400.3		1822.1	5.8	915.9
1995	8237.7	8.2	745.9	745.9		2614.8	7.1	1500.2
1996	8333.1	13.9	855.7	855.7		3102.6	10.1	2015.6
1997	7961.4	18.7	1762.0	1762.0		3507.8	12.5	2485.9
1998	7927.9	20.4	1877.6	1877.6		3781.3	15.3	2776.7
1999	9852.0	31.9	2065.3	2065.3		3912.3	15.1	2929.8
2000	10408.4	56.2	3786.9	3786.9		4350.3	18.8	3001.6
2001	10354.6	83.3	7285.9	7285.9		4345.3	18.7	3455.1
2002	10181.6	116.8	9401.2	9401.2		4405.6	26.5	3488.2
2003	10372.9	133.4	10901.7	10901.7		4574.8	32.9	3655.4
2004	10583.9	137.5	12403.6	12403.6		6845.2	51.9	4383.8
2005	10647.7	132.4	13782.9	13782.9		8478.0	65.1	5408.5
2006	11186.6	125.8	15731.8	15731.8		10268.5	77.8	6458.9
2007	11644.6	129.4	22311.1	18020.0	4291.1	12173.3	96.0	7775.3
2008	12399.8	139.5	31821.6	19995.6	11826.0	13787.2	117.8	9254.1
2009	12715.5	145.8	40147.0	21937.4	18209.6	14895.5	129.6	10875.7
2010	13375.6	140.4	43262.9	23734.7	19528.3	16160.7	147.5	12335.9
2011	14317.1	159.9	47343.2	25227.1	22116.1	17695.9	163.0	13892.0
2012	15224.7	181.3	53641.3	26485.6	27155.7	19010.1	190.5	15428.7
2013	16416.8	203.2	57072.6	27443.1	29629.4	19917.2	195.2	16392.0
2014	17042.6	233.3	59746.9	28296.0	31450.9	20639.2	198.2	17038.7
2015	17326.0	269.8	66581.6	28893.1	37688.5	21432.5	201.9	17771.0
2016	18088.8	309.4	74391.6	29531.5	44860.0	21889.3	196.0	18451.0
2017	18784.2	318.2	117681.4	30322.7	87358.7	22723.7	192.8	19300.2
2018	19643.5	357.6	134458.6	31680.8	102777.8	23874.4	198.5	20434.1
2019	20542.7	396.8	135407.4	32924.7	102482.7	25478.4	194.4	21417.3
2020	21689.5	413.9	136131.1	34455.1	101676.0	26763.4	187.6	23567.3
2021	22957.9	530.7	136296.7	35430.9	100865.9	28286.5	206.2	23751.7
2022	23806.6	592.3	134592.5	36243.4	98349.1	29116.6	203.7	24621.5
2023	24372.7	728.6	133389.0	37094.6	96294.4	30173.6	221.9	24903.1

24–26 分地区城镇职工基本养老保险情况(2023年)
Statistics on Basic Endowment Insurance for Urban Workers by Region (2023)

地区	Region	年末参加城镇职工基本养老保险人数(万人) Participants of Basic Endowment Insurance for Urban Workers at Year-end (10 000 persons)	职工 Number of Workers	离退休(职)人员 Number of Retirees	基金收支情况(亿元) Revenue and Expenses(100 million yuan) 基金收入 Revenue	基金支出 Expenses	累计结余 Balance at Year-end
全国	**National Total**	**52120.8**	**37925.2**	**14195.6**	**70506.3**	**63756.6**	**63639.1**
北京	Beijing	1904.9	1567.2	337.8	4009.4	2377.9	8614.3
天津	Tianjin	826.2	576.7	249.5	1311.4	1288.2	442.4
河北	Hebei	1949.8	1428.9	520.9	2434.9	2428.4	620.1
山西	Shanxi	1102.1	777.9	324.2	1680.5	1650.0	1552.2
内蒙古	Inner Mongolia	932.2	584.9	347.2	1421.8	1538.3	481.1
辽宁	Liaoning	2150.4	1252.6	897.8	3101.0	3858.4	398.5
吉林	Jilin	953.8	541.0	412.8	1651.9	1880.7	298.6
黑龙江	Heilongjiang	1523.9	850.2	673.7	2029.7	2743.6	247.0
上海	Shanghai	1689.4	1146.5	542.8	4226.2	3680.0	1950.7
江苏	Jiangsu	3752.0	2646.0	1106.0	5183.4	4505.3	5340.8
浙江	Zhejiang	3573.6	2584.0	989.6	3907.6	4276.3	1381.4
安徽	Anhui	1688.0	1271.4	416.6	2173.6	1714.8	2692.2
福建	Fujian	1788.9	1543.6	245.3	1366.7	1094.4	1005.8
江西	Jiangxi	1435.6	1027.7	407.9	1522.7	1474.6	924.6
山东	Shandong	3424.1	2559.8	864.4	3994.6	3965.3	1345.0
河南	Henan	2578.2	1987.7	590.5	2565.8	2366.7	1591.3
湖北	Hubei	2048.0	1379.1	668.9	3158.5	2993.0	1135.2
湖南	Hunan	2018.6	1454.0	564.6	2209.8	2151.4	1894.8
广东	Guangdong	5368.9	4518.2	850.7	7036.5	3950.1	17549.0
广西	Guangxi	1069.6	775.3	294.3	1468.1	1314.8	873.7
海南	Hainan	373.6	292.0	81.7	499.2	362.4	484.5
重庆	Chongqing	1475.4	1003.9	471.4	1638.7	1596.4	1512.3
四川	Sichuan	3426.3	2379.2	1047.1	4049.8	3707.8	4101.0
贵州	Guizhou	794.3	617.0	177.4	1014.4	801.6	1284.6
云南	Yunnan	883.6	681.0	202.6	1246.3	1026.3	1821.9
西藏	Xizang	67.3	55.9	11.4	215.3	144.3	290.6
陕西	Shaanxi	1346.8	1044.4	302.4	1911.0	1574.9	1282.0
甘肃	Gansu	532.5	352.4	180.1	844.6	870.4	350.1
青海	Qinghai	188.0	133.8	54.2	336.5	338.9	43.8
宁夏	Ningxia	292.0	216.1	75.9	390.7	360.8	275.2
新疆	Xinjiang	867.9	621.8	246.1	1567.2	1330.0	1814.8
不分地区	Not Classified by Region	95.1	55.3	39.7	338.5	390.4	39.7

注：“不分地区”数据包括中央国家机关事业单位、中国人民银行、中国农业发展银行和中央调剂金账户。

a) Data in the category of "Not Classified by Region" include data from the Central government organs and institutions, People's Bank of China, Agricultural Development Bank of China and Central Allocation System account.

24-27 分地区城乡居民基本养老保险情况（2023年）

Statistics on Basic Endowment Insurance for Urban and Rural Residents by Region (2023)

地 区	Region	年末参加城乡居民基本养老保险人数(万人) Participants of Basic Endowment Insurance for Urban and Rural Residents at Year-end (10 000 persons)	#实际领取待遇人数 Number of People Actual Received Pension	基金收支情况(亿元) Revenue and Expenses(100 million yuan)		
				基金收入 Revenue	基金支出 Expenses	累计结余 Balance at Year-end
全 国	**National Total**	**54522.5**	**17268.3**	**6184.9**	**4612.9**	**14533.9**
北 京	Beijing	181.0	63.8	127.5	113.7	188.1
天 津	Tianjin	172.2	88.7	57.6	56.2	319.1
河 北	Hebei	3527.3	1184.3	295.9	236.6	696.4
山 西	Shanxi	1623.2	450.9	175.3	97.2	474.9
内蒙古	Inner Mongolia	815.5	263.2	94.2	74.0	186.2
辽 宁	Liaoning	1020.4	445.6	91.3	91.4	97.9
吉 林	Jilin	942.7	285.7	59.1	49.4	114.8
黑龙江	Heilongjiang	892.7	273.6	85.6	64.5	173.4
上 海	Shanghai	71.8	52.6	104.8	104.2	92.4
江 苏	Jiangsu	2351.9	1144.5	661.7	489.1	1174.8
浙 江	Zhejiang	1032.8	563.4	411.9	318.9	506.4
安 徽	Anhui	3408.0	1019.2	397.5	219.4	1110.2
福 建	Fujian	1595.0	505.6	153.5	129.5	315.6
江 西	Jiangxi	1951.5	552.4	191.6	135.8	448.2
山 东	Shandong	4566.3	1690.1	581.7	452.7	1785.6
河 南	Henan	5280.1	1544.9	360.5	287.0	909.8
湖 北	Hubei	2507.4	821.8	252.1	192.1	713.1
湖 南	Hunan	3413.0	935.6	264.3	186.2	657.4
广 东	Guangdong	2760.0	909.9	331.8	308.8	602.4
广 西	Guangxi	2671.8	646.1	147.7	127.4	332.6
海 南	Hainan	341.8	83.6	42.7	27.5	157.7
重 庆	Chongqing	1175.0	359.5	128.0	76.6	275.4
四 川	Sichuan	3150.1	1090.6	502.3	289.6	1144.7
贵 州	Guizhou	1941.8	494.9	117.5	92.4	243.0
云 南	Yunnan	2491.1	603.3	148.2	120.7	629.3
西 藏	Xizang	176.2	28.9	14.4	9.6	48.2
陕 西	Shaanxi	1812.4	587.6	164.7	128.1	409.0
甘 肃	Gansu	1379.0	351.4	116.2	68.6	382.1
青 海	Qinghai	263.4	48.2	23.8	15.3	83.8
宁 夏	Ningxia	232.1	46.6	21.7	15.6	63.8
新 疆	Xinjiang	775.1	131.5	59.8	34.8	197.6

24-28 分地区失业保险情况（2023年）
Statistics of Unemployment Insurance by Region (2023)

地 区	Region	年末参加失业保险人数(万人) Unemployment Insurance Participants at Year-end (10 000 persons)	年末领取失业保险金人数(万人) Beneficiaries of Unemployment Insurance Fund (10 000 persons)	基金收支情况(亿元) Revenue and Expenses (100 million yuan)		
				基金收入 Revenue	基金支出 Expenses	累计结余 Balance at Year-end
全 国	**National Total**	**24372.7**	**352.1**	**1807.3**	**1485.2**	**3212.9**
北 京	Beijing	1418.3	21.0	158.6	158.3	105.1
天 津	Tianjin	403.6	9.7	34.4	38.0	21.7
河 北	Hebei	815.2	7.4	54.9	35.9	142.3
山 西	Shanxi	553.4	3.5	39.0	22.5	166.3
内蒙古	Inner Mongolia	329.3	3.8	33.8	21.3	119.7
辽 宁	Liaoning	680.1	23.6	50.9	72.1	71.8
吉 林	Jilin	282.7	3.9	26.5	20.3	73.2
黑龙江	Heilongjiang	333.2	3.7	22.9	13.5	118.8
上 海	Shanghai	1023.5	24.0	158.6	116.6	129.1
江 苏	Jiangsu	2040.9	35.0	168.7	160.5	246.8
浙 江	Zhejiang	1886.0	30.0	130.7	99.5	165.6
安 徽	Anhui	700.4	9.1	52.7	41.0	93.5
福 建	Fujian	763.1	7.6	38.3	37.3	86.5
江 西	Jiangxi	402.6	3.1	25.6	15.4	70.5
山 东	Shandong	1615.8	25.5	124.7	99.4	207.7
河 南	Henan	1147.8	9.9	60.3	34.1	117.7
湖 北	Hubei	752.9	10.7	57.4	42.7	131.3
湖 南	Hunan	740.4	9.7	39.6	32.1	113.4
广 东	Guangdong	3794.8	40.4	173.1	160.0	193.0
广 西	Guangxi	540.8	8.3	37.2	30.9	94.5
海 南	Hainan	224.0	3.6	12.8	11.0	15.9
重 庆	Chongqing	625.2	10.6	34.9	37.4	36.4
四 川	Sichuan	1191.3	20.9	93.7	69.2	215.4
贵 州	Guizhou	349.2	4.9	26.7	21.1	61.1
云 南	Yunnan	375.7	8.7	29.2	26.5	92.4
西 藏	Xizang	36.2	0.1	5.2	0.7	31.0
陕 西	Shaanxi	531.2	4.6	44.1	26.5	73.3
甘 肃	Gansu	210.1	1.1	20.0	6.1	84.3
青 海	Qinghai	68.1	0.5	7.7	3.1	29.4
宁 夏	Ningxia	122.5	1.9	9.8	7.3	25.7
新 疆	Xinjiang	414.6	5.5	35.2	24.8	79.6

24-29 分地区基本医疗保险参保人数(2023年)
Participants of Basic Medical Insurance by Region (2023)

单位：万人 (10 000 persons)

地 区	Region	年末参保人数合计 Participants at Year-end	职工基本医疗保险 Basic Medical Insurance for Workers	职工 Workers	退休人员 Retirees	城乡居民基本医疗保险 Basic Medical Insurance for Urban and Rural Residents
全 国	**National Total**	**133389.0**	**37094.6**	**27098.7**	**9995.9**	**96294.4**
北 京	Beijing	1908.6	1504.7	1164.2	340.5	403.9
天 津	Tianjin	1183.6	659.2	426.2	233.0	524.5
河 北	Hebei	6925.9	1288.3	886.2	402.1	5637.6
山 西	Shanxi	3186.1	753.9	505.8	248.1	2432.2
内蒙古	Inner Mongolia	2158.7	606.6	401.8	204.8	1552.1
辽 宁	Liaoning	3721.7	1596.5	885.2	711.4	2125.2
吉 林	Jilin	2238.5	553.1	337.3	215.8	1685.4
黑龙江	Heilongjiang	2753.2	891.7	470.7	421.0	1861.5
上 海	Shanghai	2004.1	1623.2	1082.0	541.2	380.9
江 苏	Jiangsu	8133.3	3476.6	2539.4	937.2	4656.8
浙 江	Zhejiang	5621.1	2954.0	2329.6	624.4	2667.1
安 徽	Anhui	6377.9	1103.5	799.0	304.4	5274.4
福 建	Fujian	3833.5	978.7	786.2	192.5	2854.8
江 西	Jiangxi	4527.4	642.3	414.2	228.1	3885.1
山 东	Shandong	9654.3	2598.2	1906.1	692.0	7056.2
河 南	Henan	9931.6	1433.8	997.5	436.3	8497.7
湖 北	Hubei	5564.6	1342.6	960.1	382.5	4222.1
湖 南	Hunan	6355.7	1046.7	711.9	334.8	5309.0
广 东	Guangdong	11040.9	4848.2	4275.2	573.0	6192.7
广 西	Guangxi	5161.9	742.4	550.0	192.4	4419.5
海 南	Hainan	936.9	267.2	196.6	70.6	669.7
重 庆	Chongqing	3142.4	813.0	593.0	220.0	2329.4
四 川	Sichuan	8132.8	1999.3	1440.2	559.1	6133.5
贵 州	Guizhou	4181.3	504.8	372.9	132.0	3676.5
云 南	Yunnan	4563.4	598.1	426.9	171.3	3965.3
西 藏	Xizang	341.5	58.7	47.0	11.7	282.8
陕 西	Shaanxi	3730.6	839.8	610.7	229.1	2890.8
甘 肃	Gansu	2510.6	396.7	266.3	130.4	2113.9
青 海	Qinghai	567.1	123.6	82.3	41.4	443.4
宁 夏	Ningxia	666.6	169.1	126.2	42.9	497.5
新 疆	Xinjiang	2333.2	680.1	508.1	172.1	1653.0

24–30 分地区基本医疗保险基金收支情况（2023年）
Revenue and Expenses of Basic Medical Insurance by Region (2023)

单位：亿元 (100 million yuan)

地区	Region	基金收入 Revenue 合计 Total	职工 Workers	居民 Residents	基金支出 Expenses 合计 Total	职工 Workers	居民 Residents	累计结余 Balance at Year-end 合计 Total	职工 Workers	居民 Residents
全国	**National Total**	**33504.9**	**22935.1**	**10569.7**	**28210.5**	**17752.8**	**10457.7**	**47951.0**	**40287.3**	**7663.7**
北京	Beijing	2062.7	1947.1	115.5	1250.7	1138.7	112.0	3095.8	3015.7	80.0
天津	Tianjin	539.3	480.4	58.8	418.8	347.3	71.5	662.3	596.4	65.9
河北	Hebei	1268.9	713.3	555.6	1122.9	559.8	563.1	1750.7	1401.4	349.4
山西	Shanxi	663.1	409.9	253.2	550.9	329.1	221.8	897.3	668.3	229.0
内蒙古	Inner Mongolia	529.7	357.5	172.3	493.4	318.0	175.4	774.7	620.3	154.4
辽宁	Liaoning	931.5	725.1	206.4	901.0	666.9	234.2	1005.0	820.4	184.6
吉林	Jilin	445.3	268.2	177.1	407.1	241.9	165.3	619.1	475.3	143.7
黑龙江	Heilongjiang	605.6	404.4	201.2	620.8	400.4	220.5	853.8	651.3	202.4
上海	Shanghai	2317.2	2213.2	104.0	1374.1	1255.7	118.4	5482.6	5463.5	19.1
江苏	Jiangsu	2456.2	1874.2	582.1	2392.8	1788.9	603.9	3092.9	2832.6	260.3
浙江	Zhejiang	2255.7	1747.4	508.2	1951.3	1434.0	517.3	3668.3	3384.4	283.8
安徽	Anhui	1087.1	548.9	538.2	924.8	391.0	533.8	1205.6	939.1	266.5
福建	Fujian	867.6	576.9	290.8	741.2	446.6	294.5	1227.3	1101.0	126.3
江西	Jiangxi	719.2	321.9	397.3	690.1	278.8	411.2	865.9	537.5	328.4
山东	Shandong	2139.5	1406.2	733.4	2009.0	1259.8	749.2	2181.7	1761.5	420.1
河南	Henan	1579.4	700.1	879.3	1454.6	612.9	841.8	1468.7	1081.4	387.4
湖北	Hubei	1206.3	763.6	442.7	1070.7	634.4	436.4	1379.0	1055.7	323.3
湖南	Hunan	1133.9	590.6	543.3	959.2	452.3	507.0	1434.9	1043.9	391.1
广东	Guangdong	3198.6	2464.3	734.4	2422.5	1715.8	706.7	5583.7	4704.2	879.5
广西	Guangxi	863.9	388.7	475.2	795.6	345.2	450.4	1064.7	632.8	432.0
海南	Hainan	229.8	159.6	70.3	172.5	96.3	76.1	392.3	328.9	63.4
重庆	Chongqing	733.2	483.8	249.5	631.2	381.8	249.4	838.0	665.0	173.0
四川	Sichuan	1817.6	1170.5	647.1	1491.9	858.1	633.8	2961.8	2412.9	548.9
贵州	Guizhou	683.6	305.4	378.2	598.0	252.2	345.8	847.3	498.5	348.8
云南	Yunnan	813.0	399.3	413.7	704.2	321.2	383.1	1066.4	769.6	296.8
西藏	Xizang	108.2	76.2	32.0	72.5	45.7	26.8	276.5	243.6	32.9
陕西	Shaanxi	848.8	547.1	301.7	771.7	447.5	324.2	1107.6	908.2	199.4
甘肃	Gansu	437.1	220.5	216.6	392.4	189.3	203.2	535.7	349.3	186.4
青海	Qinghai	159.2	112.3	46.9	123.8	78.3	45.5	298.3	239.4	58.9
宁夏	Ningxia	163.6	107.9	55.6	113.4	68.4	45.0	296.6	238.4	58.2
新疆	Xinjiang	639.8	450.8	189.0	587.4	396.6	190.7	1016.6	846.8	169.8

24-31 分地区工伤保险情况（2023年）
Statistics of Work-related Injury Insurance by Region (2023)

地区	Region	年末参加工伤保险人数（万人） Participants in Work-related Injury Insurance at Year-end (10 000 persons)	全年享受工伤保险待遇人数（万人） Beneficiaries of Work-related Injury Insurance (10 000 persons)	基金收支情况(亿元) Revenue and Expenses (100 million yuan)		
				基金收入 Revenue	基金支出 Expenses	累计结余 Balance at Year-end
全　国	**National Total**	**30173.6**	**221.9**	**1211.6**	**1236.7**	**1415.1**
北　京	Beijing	1366.9	3.7	66.7	60.3	44.1
天　津	Tianjin	412.8	4.1	17.6	15.6	16.5
河　北	Hebei	1153.5	9.8	68.0	55.5	71.6
山　西	Shanxi	669.6	7.9	51.6	50.6	37.5
内蒙古	Inner Mongolia	361.8	3.0	17.6	20.6	34.9
辽　宁	Liaoning	812.4	13.1	48.2	41.1	67.6
吉　林	Jilin	351.0	4.9	8.8	12.8	28.7
黑龙江	Heilongjiang	456.0	3.4	27.4	26.8	34.0
上　海	Shanghai	1188.2	6.8	54.9	57.9	45.8
江　苏	Jiangsu	2426.1	19.6	111.6	119.1	118.7
浙　江	Zhejiang	2792.4	21.8	104.8	115.7	59.3
安　徽	Anhui	920.9	7.5	39.5	40.0	31.7
福　建	Fujian	1064.6	5.6	35.5	39.0	41.7
江　西	Jiangxi	593.4	5.2	19.3	24.4	46.7
山　东	Shandong	2045.6	15.2	86.2	75.3	109.9
河　南	Henan	1128.2	7.0	40.9	33.9	74.4
湖　北	Hubei	912.0	6.8	23.9	29.7	30.9
湖　南	Hunan	994.7	14.4	51.3	55.2	79.4
广　东	Guangdong	4270.3	22.4	95.7	130.2	117.8
广　西	Guangxi	637.0	2.2	14.2	15.0	48.1
海　南	Hainan	196.6	0.5	4.3	3.3	21.3
重　庆	Chongqing	754.7	6.7	35.9	27.8	21.8
四　川	Sichuan	1584.8	10.0	51.9	59.3	68.6
贵　州	Guizhou	626.1	4.3	27.4	24.0	22.4
云　南	Yunnan	606.6	4.3	22.6	22.8	20.1
西　藏	Xizang	67.7	0.2	3.8	2.0	10.1
陕　西	Shaanxi	696.8	4.6	31.9	29.8	43.7
甘　肃	Gansu	297.4	2.1	14.5	12.3	24.4
青　海	Qinghai	117.6	0.7	3.1	4.6	7.5
宁　夏	Ningxia	148.5	1.3	6.5	7.5	8.1
新　疆	Xinjiang	519.4	3.0	26.2	24.6	27.8

24–32 分地区生育保险情况（2023年）
Statistics of Birth Insurance by Region (2023)

地 区	Region	年末参加生育保险人数（万人）Participants in Birth Insurance at Year-end (10 000 persons)	生育保险基金待遇支出（亿元）Expenses of Birth Insurance (100 million yuan)
全 国	**National Total**	**24903.1**	**1177.2**
北 京	Beijing	1070.8	98.7
天 津	Tianjin	425.7	20.4
河 北	Hebei	909.8	37.4
山 西	Shanxi	490.6	14.8
内蒙古	Inner Mongolia	371.4	11.1
辽 宁	Liaoning	704.4	29.7
吉 林	Jilin	314.2	9.7
黑龙江	Heilongjiang	388.3	6.8
上 海	Shanghai	1082.1	97.8
江 苏	Jiangsu	2175.8	113.0
浙 江	Zhejiang	2235.9	84.7
安 徽	Anhui	782.2	27.8
福 建	Fujian	732.2	27.1
江 西	Jiangxi	412.3	17.3
山 东	Shandong	1696.4	67.4
河 南	Henan	943.3	47.3
湖 北	Hubei	799.1	30.2
湖 南	Hunan	703.5	28.4
广 东	Guangdong	3902.8	188.9
广 西	Guangxi	513.8	17.2
海 南	Hainan	196.6	7.2
重 庆	Chongqing	539.0	21.8
四 川	Sichuan	1218.9	41.7
贵 州	Guizhou	372.8	20.2
云 南	Yunnan	397.3	28.3
西 藏	Xizang	45.1	4.7
陕 西	Shaanxi	589.8	26.2
甘 肃	Gansu	265.4	11.0
青 海	Qinghai	72.7	3.9
宁 夏	Ningxia	119.0	6.7
新 疆	Xinjiang	431.9	29.9

主要统计指标解释

批准逮捕 指人民检察院对公安机关、国家安全机关、监狱管理机关提出逮捕的犯罪嫌疑人进行审查，根据事实，依法做出逮捕决定。该指标主要反映人民检察院对提请逮捕犯罪嫌疑人进行审查后依法做出批准逮捕决定的情况。

决定逮捕 指人民检察院对直接立案侦查的案件，认为需要逮捕犯罪嫌疑人时，依据法律做出的逮捕决定。该指标主要反映人民检察院对直接受理的案件行使决定逮捕权的情况。

提出抗诉 指人民检察院对人民法院的判决、裁定认为确有错误，向人民法院提出对案件重新进行审理的诉讼活动。包括按照第二审程序提出的抗诉和按照审判监督程序（再审程序）提出的抗诉。

立案监督 指人民检察院对侦查机关刑事立案活动的监督。包括对应当立案而不立案的监督和不应立案而立案的监督。

监督立案 包括侦查机关接到要求说明不立案理由后主动立案和执行通知立案两个内容。

青少年罪犯 指人民法院在报告期内判决发生法律效力的有罪判决中14周岁以上不满25周岁的罪犯。其中14周岁以上不满18周岁的罪犯为未成年罪犯。

行政案件 指公民、法人和其他组织认为行政机关和行政机关工作人员的行政行为侵犯其合法权益，向人民法院提起行政诉讼，人民法院依法审理的案件。

行政赔偿案件 指公民、法人或者其他组织认为其合法权益受到行政机关及其工作人员违法行使职权的侵害，向人民法院单独或与行政诉讼一并提起赔偿诉讼，人民法院依法审理的案件。

公证（出证） 指公证处根据当事人申请，依照事实和法律，按照法定程序制作的，具有法律效力的司法证明文书。

受理劳动人事争议案件数 指劳动人事争议仲裁委员会根据国家法律、法规及有关规章规定，对劳动人事争议当事人提出的仲裁申请进行审查后，符合受理条件而正式立案的劳动人事争议案件数。

城镇职工基本养老保险

1.参保职工人数 指报告期末参加城镇职工基本养老保险并在社保经办机构已建立缴费记录档案的职工人数，包括中断缴费但未终止养老保险关系的职工人数，不包括只登记未建立缴费记录档案的人数。

2.离退休（职）人员人数 指报告期末参加城镇职工基本养老保险并由养老保险基金支付养老金的离休、退休和退职人员的人数。

3.基金收入 指根据国家有关规定，由纳入职工基本养老保险范围的缴费单位和个人按国家规定的缴费基数和缴费比例缴纳的养老保险费，以及通过其他方式取得的形成基金来源的收入。包括单位和职工个人缴纳的基本养老保险费、基本养老保险基金利息收入、委托投资收益、上级补助收入、下级上解收入、转移收入、财政补贴和其他收入。

4.基金支出 指按照国家政策规定的开支范围和开支标准从职工基本养老保险基金中支付给参加职工基本养老保险的个人养老保险待遇支出，以及由于保险关系转移、上下级之间补助、上解等原因而发生的支出。包括基本养老金、医疗补助金、丧葬补助金和抚恤金、病残津贴、补助下级支出、上解上级支出、转移支出和其他支出等。

5.基金累计结余 指职工基本养老保险基金收支相抵后的期末累计余额。

城乡居民基本养老保险

1.参保人数 指报告期末，参加城乡居民基本养老保险（在经办机构参保登记并已建立缴费记录以及制度实施当年已经年满60周岁并在经办机构参保登记）的总人数（不包括已经办理注销登记手续的人数）。

2.基金收入 指根据国家有关规定，由参加城乡居民基本养老保险的个人按规定缴费的城乡居民基本养老保险费，以及通过集体补助、财政补助等其他方式取得的形成基金来源的收入。包括个人缴费收入、集体补助收入、财政补贴收入、利息收入、委托投资收益、转移收入、上级补助收入、下级上解收入和其他收入。

3.基金支出 指按照国家政策规定的开支范围和开支标准从城乡居民基本养老保险基金中支付给参加城乡居民基本养老保险的个人养老保险待遇支出，以及由于参保人员跨统筹地区或跨制度流动而发生的支出等。包括养老保险待遇支出、转移支出、补助下级支出、上解上级支出和其他支出。

4.基金累计结余 指城乡居民基本养老保险基金收支相抵后的期末累计余额。

基本医疗保险

1.参保人数 指报告期末参加职工基本医疗保险和城乡居民基本医疗保险人员的合计。

2.基金收入（含生育保险） 基本医疗保险基金收入包括职工基本医疗保险基金收入（含生育保险）和城乡居民基本医疗保险基金收入。职工基本医疗保险基金收入（含生育保险）包括基本医疗保险费收入（含生育保险）、利息收入、财政补贴收入、其他收入、待转保险费收入、待转利息收入、转移收入。城乡居民基本医疗保险基金收入包括基本医疗保险费收入、利息收入、财政补贴收入、其他收入。

3.基金支出（含生育保险） 基本医疗保险基金支出包括职工基本医疗保险基金支出（含生育保险）和城乡居民基本医疗保险基金支出。职工基本医疗保险基金支出（含生育保险）包括基本医疗保险待遇支出、生育保险待遇支出、其他支出、转移支出。城乡居民基本医疗保险基金支出包括基本医疗保险待遇支出、购买大病保险支出、其他支出。

4.基金累计结余（含生育保险） 指截至报告期末基本医疗保险基金（含生育保险）累计结余金额。

失业保险

1.参保人数 指报告期末城镇企业、事业单位职工参加失业保险的人数及按地方规定参加失业保险的其他人员人数之和，不包括领取失业保险金人数。

2.基金收入 指报告期内筹集的失业保险基金的总额，包括失业保险费收入、利息收入、财政补贴收入、其他收入、转移收入。

3.基金支出 指报告期内为保障失业人员基本生活、预防失业、促进再就业等支出的基金总额，包括失业保险金支出、基本医疗保险费支出、丧葬补助金和抚恤金支出、职业培训和职业介绍补贴支出、其他费用支出、技能提升补贴支出、稳定岗位补贴支出、其他支出、转移支出。

4.基金累计结余 指截至报告期末失业保险基金收支相抵后的累计余额。

工伤保险

1.参保人数 指报告期末参加工伤保险的职工人数和有雇工的个体工商户的雇工数。

2.享受工伤保险待遇人数 指年报告期内由工伤基金支付，享受工伤医疗、伤残、工亡待遇的总人数。不进行重复计算。

3.基金收入 指根据国家有关规定，由参加工伤保险的单位按国家规定的缴费基数和缴费比例缴纳及难以直接按照工资总额计算缴纳工伤保险费的部分行业企业按规定方式缴纳的工伤保险费，以及依法通过其他形式取得的形成基金来源的款项。包括：工伤保险费收入、利息收入、上级补助收入、下级上解收入、其他收入。

4.基金支出 指按照国家政策规定的开支范围和开支标准从工伤保险基金中支付给参加工伤保险的人员及供养直系亲属工伤保险待遇支出及其他支出。包括工伤医疗待遇支出、伤残待遇支出、工亡待遇支出、劳动能力鉴定支出、工伤预防费用支出、补助下级支出、上解上级支出和其他支出。

5.基金累计结余 指工伤保险基金收支相抵后的期末累计结余金额。

Explanatory Notes on Main Statistical Indicators

Approval for Arrest refers to the decision made by people's procuratorate office, in accordance with the law and relevant facts and after due investigation, to approve the arrest of the suspect(s) as proposed by the public security departments, state security departments or prisons authority. This indicator reflects approved arrests made by people's procuratorate offices that are proposed by related departments.

Decision on Arrest refers to decision made by the people's procuratorate office, in accordance with laws, to arrest the suspect(s) in the cases that are accepted and to be investigated by the procurators office. This indicator mainly reflects the decision on execution of the authority of arrests by people's procuratorate office.

Presenting Protest Appeal refers to those protests presented by local People's Procuratorate at any level who considers that there exists some definite error in a judgment or order of first instance made by a People's Court at the same level to the People's Court at the next higher level, including the protests raised in accordance with the second instance and protests raised in accordance with procedure for trial supervision.

Supervision of Case Registered refers to the actions made by the People's Procuratorate to supervise the criminal cases registered by investigation authorities, including supervision of the cases which have wrongly not been registered and have wrongly been registered.

Supervision of Case Filing includes both the supervision of the registrations by the investigation authorities and the supervision of the execution of the notifications to register after the investigation authorities are requested to state reasons for not registering a case.

Juvenile Offenders refers to the offenders between 14 to 25 convicted guilty by the court during the reporting period, and those between 14 to 18 are defined as minor offenders.

Administrative Cases refer to cases in which citizens, legal persons and other organizations consider that administrative acts of administrative organs and staff members of administrative organs infringe upon their legitimate rights and interests, and bring administrative proceedings to the people's courts for hearing according to law by the people's courts.

Administrative Compensation Cases refer to cases in which citizens, legal persons or other organizations consider that their legitimate rights and interests are infringed by the illegal exercise of their powers and powers by administrative organs and their staff members, and bring compensation lawsuits to the people's court, separately or together with administrative lawsuits, for hearing at the people's court according to law.

Notarization (certification) refer to legally binding judicial notary documents, developed at the request of the interested party based on facts and the law following certain legal proceedings.

Number of Labour Disputes Cases Accepted refers to the number of cases of labour disputes arbitration submitted that, after review by the labour dispute arbitration committees in line with the relevant national laws and regulations, are accepted and registered.

Basic Endowment Insurance for Urban Workers

1. Number of workers covered refers to staff and workers participating in the basic endowment insurance for urban workers at the end of the reference period, who have already had payment records in social security management agencies, including those who have interrupt payment without terminating the insurance programme. Those who have registered in the programme but with no payment records are not included.

2. Number of retirees covered refers to the number of retirees participating in the basic endowment insurance for urban workers and the pension paid by the pension insurance fund by the end of the reference period.

3. Revenue refers to payments made by employers and employees participating in the basic endowment insurance for urban workers in accordance with the basis and proportion stipulated in state regulations, and income from other sources that become the source of endowment insurance fund, including the premium paid by employers and staff and workers, interest income, entrusted investment income, subsidies from higher level agencies, income as transfer from subordinate agencies, transferred income, government financial subsidies and other income.

4. Expenses refer to personal endowment insurance payment made to those covered in the basic endowment insurance for urban workers according to related national policies on scope and standard of expenditure, as well as expenditure which arises due to shift of the insurance relationship or adjustment of funds among agencies, transfer to agencies at higher level, including: basic endowment insurance, medical fees, funeral subsidies, compensation payments, disability allowance, expenses on subsidies to lower subordinates, expenses as transfer to agencies at higher level, transferred expenditure and other expenditure.

5. Balance refers to the balance of the basic endowment insurance funds for urban workers at the end of the reference period after deducting expenses from revenue.

Basic Endowment Insurance for Urban and Rural Residents

1. Participants refers to people participating in the basic endowment insurance for urban and rural residents who registered with the participation and established payment records, and who were 60 years old or above when the system was established and registered with the participation. Those who cancelled their registration are not included.

2. Revenue refers to the revenue from the payments made, in accordance with related regulations of the government, by individuals participating in the basic endowment insurance for urban and rural residents and from the subsidies contributed by collectives, public finance and other sources. It includes the payment by individual participants, collective subsidies, financial subsidies, interest income, entrusted investment income, transferred income, subsidies from higher levels, contributions from lower levels, and income from other sources.

3. Expenses refers to payment made to those covered in the basic endowment insurance for urban and rural residents according to related national policies on scope and standard of expenditure. Also included are expenditures which arise due to movement of participants among different locations or system. It includes the payment to the individual participants, transferred expenditures, expenses on subsidies to lower subordinates, expenses as transfer to agencies at higher level, and other expenditures.

4. Balance refers to the balance of basic endowment insurance funds for urban and rural residents at the end of the reference period after deducting expenses from revenue.

Basic Medical Insurance

1. Participants refers to the total number of people who participate in the basic medical insurance for workers and basic medical insurance for urban and rural residents at the end of the reference period.

2. Revenue (birth insurance included) refers to basic medical insurance fund income for employees (including birth insurance) and basic medical insurance fund income for urban and rural residents. The basic medical insurance fund income of employees (including birth insurance) includes basic medical insurance premium income (including birth insurance), interest income, financial subsidy income, other income, insurance premium income to be transferred, interest income to be transferred and transfer income.

3. Expenses (birth insurance included) refers to basic medical insurance fund expenditure for employees (including birth insurance) and basic medical insurance fund expenditure for urban and rural residents. Basic medical insurance fund expenditure for employees (including birth insurance) includes basic medical insurance treatment expenditure, birth insurance treatment expenditure, other expenditure and transfer expenditure. Basic medical insurance fund expenditure for urban and rural residents includes basic medical insurance treatment expenditure, serious illness insurance expenditure and other expenditure.

4. Balance (birth insurance included) refers to the accumulated balance of basic medical insurance fund (including birth insurance) at the end of the reporting period.

Unemployment Insurance

1. Participants refers to the number of staff and workers in urban enterprises or institutions who have participated in the unemployment insurance, and other people who have participated according to local regulations at the end of the reference period, excluding the number of people receiving unemployment insurance benefits.

2. Revenue refers to the total unemployment insurance funds raised in the reference period, including unemployment insurance premium, interest income, financial subsidies, other revenue, and transferred revenue.

3. Expenses refers to total expenses during the reference period to guarantee the basic livelihood of unemployed people, prevention of unemployment, and to encourage their re-employment. Included are unemployment relief, medical fees, funeral subsidies, compensation payments, training expenses, job placement expenses, other expenses, skills upgrading subsidy, job stabilization subsidy, other expenditures, transferred expenditure.

4. Balance refers to the balance of revenue after deducting expenses at the end of the reference period.

Work-related Injury Insurance

1.Participants refers to staff and workers who have participated in the work-related injury insurance and employees who work as self-employed and have participated in the work-related injury insurance at the end of the reference period.

2. Number of beneficiaries refers to number of people who are paid by the work-related injury fund and enjoy the medical treatment, disability and death benefits during the annual report period. No double calculation is performed.

3. Revenue refers to payments made by employers participating in the work-related injury insurance programme in accordance with the basis and proportion stipulated in state regulations, and payment by enterprises of some industries where it is difficult to estimate the injury insurance premium directly according to the total wage bill in accordance with stipulated way, and revenue from other sources according to law that become source of work-related injury insurance fund, including revenue of injury insurance, interest income, subsidies from higher level agencies, revenue as transfer from subordinate agencies, and other revenues.

4. Expenses refers to payments made from work-related injury insurance funds to those who participated in the work-related injury insurance and their direct dependents within the scope and standards of expenditure according to related national policies, and other expenditure, including medical fees for work injury, injury and disability subsidies, death subsidies, labor capacity appraisal, injury prevention fees, expenses on subsidies to lower subordinates, expenses as transfer to agencies at higher level, and other expenditure.

5. Balance refers to the balance of the work-related injury funds at the end of the reference period.

25

城市、农村和区域发展

Urban, Rural and Regional Development

简 要 说 明

一、本篇资料的主要内容

本篇资料反映我国农村、城市、民族自治地方、分区域社会经济发展等基本情况。

二、本篇的资料来源

主要农产品产量等由国家统计局农村社会经济调查司根据《农林牧渔业统计报表制度》的有关资料整理提供。乡村办水电站、农村水电装机容量、农村水电年发电量数据来源于水利部;农村用电量来源于中国电力企业联合会。

全国城市分布情况及省会城市和计划单列市主要经济指标由城市社会经济调查司依据《城市高质量发展统计监测报表制度》收集整理提供。数据来源于各城市的相关部门。

城市、县及乡公用事业基本情况及综合水平指标部分的资料由住房和城乡建设部根据其《城市(县城)和村镇建设统计调查制度》汇总整理提供。

城市公共交通统计资料由交通运输部根据其《城市(县城)客运统计报表制度》中相关报表汇总整理提供。

民族自治地方及少数民族统计资料根据国家民委和国家统计局联合布置的民族自治地方国民经济和社会发展统计报表制度,由有民族自治地方的20个省、自治区、直辖市民委和统计局共同组织实施。

按区域分国民经济和社会发展指标数据均来自本年鉴各专业分省数据,反映东部、中部、西部及东北地区社会经济发展情况。

三、本篇资料的统计范围与统计口径

涉及城市公用事业情况的部分由住房和城乡建设部提供,其执行范围是全国所有设市城市;调查对象为规划、建设、管理和经营城市市政公用设施的各级住房城乡建设管理部门、法人单位、产业活动单位。

民族自治地方及少数民族统计资料统计范围是5个民族自治区、30个自治州、120个自治县(旗)辖区内的全部单位,全国汇总时不重复计算。统计调查方法为全面调查。另外,全国民族自治地方卫生情况由卫健委提供。民族自治地方行政区划资料是根据民政部编辑的《行政区划简册》汇总整理。

Brief Introduction

I. Main Contents

Data in this chapter present the social and economic development of rural areas, urban areas, ethnic minority autonomous areas, and eastern, central, western and northeastern regions.

II. Sources of Data

Data on main agricultural product output and others are provided by the Department of Rural Social and Economic Survey of NBS using data from the *Statistical Reporting System on Agricultural, Forestry, Animal Husbandry and Fishery*.The data on rural hydropower stations, rural hydropower installed capacity, and annual rural hydropower electricity generation are sourced from the Ministry of Water Resources. The electricity consumed in rural areas comes from the China Electricity Council.

Data on distribution of cities in China and major economic indicators of provincial capitals and cities with independent planning authority are collected and provided by the Department of Urban Social and Economic Survey of NBS in accordance with the *Statistical Monitoring Report System on High-Quality Development of Cities*. The data is sourced from relevant departments in various cities.

Data on basic conditions and overall level of urban public facilities are collected, prepared and provided by the Ministry of Housing and Urban-Rural Development in line with its *Statistical Reporting System on Construction of Cities (Counties), Villages and Towns*. .

Statistics of urban public transport are collected through relevant report forms and provided by the Ministry of Transport according to *Urban Construction Statistical Reporting System*.

Data on ethnic minority autonomous areas and minority nationalities are collected jointly by ethnic affairs commissions and statistical bureaus in 20 provinces, autonomous regions and municipalities with ethnic minority autonomous areas in accordance with *Statistical Reporting System on Economic and Social Development*, jointly issued by the National Ethnic Affairs Commission and the National Bureau of Statistics.

Statistics on economic and social development by region are compiled using data in this *Yearbook* by different subject areas and by province to reflect the economic and social development in eastern, central, western and northeastern regions.

III. Scope and Coverage of Statistics

Data on urban public facilities are provided by the Ministry of Housing and Urban-Rural Development, covering all cities. Statistically, the data cover all construction administrative departments, legal entities and industrial activity units which are engaged in urban planning, construction, management, and operation of urban public facilities.

Data on the ethnic minority autonomous areas and the ethnic minorities cover all units under the jurisdiction of the 5 ethnic minority autonomous regions, 30 autonomous prefectures and 120 autonomous counties. Duplication is deducted in the national tabulation. Methodology of data collection is complete enumeration. In addition, data on the public health of the ethnic minority autonomous areas are provided by the Ministry of Health, and data on the divisions of administrative areas are tabulated and prepared in accordance with the *Concise Edition of the Divisions of Administrative Areas* compiled by the Ministry of Civil Affairs.

25-1 全部地级及以上城市数(2023年)
Number of Cities at Prefecture Level and Above (2023)

单位：个 (unit)

地 区	Region	合 计 Total	按城市市辖区年末总人口分组 Grouped by Population in Urban Districts (year-end)				
			1000万以上 10 million and over	500万-1000万 50 million-10 million	100万-500万 1 million-5 million	50万-100万 0.5 million-1 million	50万以下 under 0.5 million
全部地级及以上城市	**Total Cities at Prefecture Level and Above**	**297**	**11**	**18**	**148**	**84**	**36**
北 京	Beijing	1	1				
天 津	Tianjin	1	1				
河 北	Hebei	11		1	8	2	
山 西	Shanxi	11			4	6	1
内蒙古	Inner Mongolia	9			3	4	2
辽 宁	Liaoning	14		2	5	6	1
吉 林	Jilin	8		1	1	2	4
黑龙江	Heilongjiang	12		1	2	5	4
上 海	Shanghai	1	1				
江 苏	Jiangsu	13		2	11		
浙 江	Zhejiang	11	1	1	6	3	
安 徽	Anhui	16		1	9	6	
福 建	Fujian	9		1	5	3	
江 西	Jiangxi	11			6	5	
山 东	Shandong	16		2	14		
河 南	Henan	17		1	13	3	
湖 北	Hubei	12	1		5	6	
湖 南	Hunan	13		1	8	4	
广 东	Guangdong	21	3	2	12	3	1
广 西	Guangxi	14		1	7	5	1
海 南	Hainan	4			3		1
重 庆	Chongqing	1	1				
四 川	Sichuan	18	1		12	5	
贵 州	Guizhou	6			5	1	
云 南	Yunnan	8		1	1	3	3
西 藏	Xizang	6				1	5
陕 西	Shaanxi	10	1		3	5	1
甘 肃	Gansu	12			2	5	5
青 海	Qinghai	2			1		1
宁 夏	Ningxia	5			1		4
新 疆	Xinjiang	4			1	1	2

注：1.本表为常住人口口径。
2.东莞、中山、三沙、儋州和嘉峪关无市辖区，人口为全市口径。
a) Population at year-end refer to population by household registration from the Ministry of Public Security.
b) Dongguan, Zhongshan, Sansha, Danzhou and Jiayuguan have no urban districts, so the population is the total population of the cities.

25-2 省会城市和计划单列市主要指标（2023年）
Main Indicators of Provincial Capitals and Cities with Independent Planning Authority (2023)

包括市辖县。
Counties under the jurisdiction of city governments are included.

城市名称	City	地区生产总值（当年价格）（亿元）Gross Regional Product (Current Prices) (100 million yuan)	第一产业 Primary Industry	第二产业 Secondary Industry	第三产业 Tertiary Industry
北京	Beijing	43761	106	6526	37130
天津	Tianjin	16737	269	5983	10486
石家庄	Shijiazhuang	7534	577	2309	4648
太原	Taiyuan	5574	46	2342	3186
呼和浩特	Hohhot	3802	168	1338	2296
沈阳	Shenyang	8122	334	2953	4835
大连	Dalian	8753	596	3715	4442
长春	Changchun	7002	531	2617	3855
哈尔滨	Harbin	5576	630	1294	3653
上海	Shanghai	47219	96	11613	35510
南京	Nanjing	17421	318	5929	11175
杭州	Hangzhou	20059	347	5667	14045
宁波	Ningbo	16453	384	7541	8529
合肥	Hefei	12674	377	4642	7654
福州	Fuzhou	12928	722	4675	7532
厦门	Xiamen	8066	28	2868	5171
南昌	Nanchang	7213	247	3341	3624
济南	Jinan	12757	430	4312	8016
青岛	Qingdao	15760	493	5268	9999
郑州	Zhengzhou	13618	172	5373	8072
武汉	Wuhan	20012	474	6801	12736
长沙	Changsha	14332	452	5366	8515
广州	Guangzhou	30356	318	7776	22262
深圳	Shenzhen	34606	25	13015	21566
南宁	Nanning	5469	636	1195	3638
海口	Haikou	2358	103	433	1822
重庆	Chongqing	30146	2075	11699	16372
成都	Chengdu	22075	595	6371	15109
贵阳	Guiyang	5155	207	1805	3142
昆明	Kunming	7865	353	2282	5229
拉萨	Lhasa	835	30	329	476
西安	Xi'an	12011	325	4147	7539
兰州	Lanzhou	3487	73	1121	2294
西宁	Xining	1801	65	693	1043
银川	Yinchuan	2686	99	1303	1283
乌鲁木齐	Urumqi	4168	33	1147	2989

25-2 续表 1 continued

城市名称	City	地方一般公共预算收入(亿元) General Public Budget Revenue of the Local Governments (100 million yuan)	地方一般公共预算支出(亿元) General Public Budget Expenditure of the Local Governments (100 million yuan)	住户存款余额(亿元) Deposit of Households (100 million yuan)
北　京	Beijing	6181	7971	64020
天　津	Tianjin	2028	3280	21997
石家庄	Shijiazhuang	738	1275	13554
太　原	Taiyuan	449	777	8825
呼和浩特	Hohhot	238	593	3904
沈　阳	Shenyang	801	1084	13895
大　连	Dalian	750	1014	11391
长　春	Changchun	577	1075	10750
哈尔滨	Harbin	313	1081	11006
上　海	Shanghai	8313	9639	58320
南　京	Nanjing	1620	1839	15229
杭　州	Hangzhou	2617	2636	23199
宁　波	Ningbo	1786	2235	14282
合　肥	Hefei	930	1411	9387
福　州	Fuzhou	754	1005	10415
厦　门	Xiamen	932	1085	5963
南　昌	Nanchang	500	926	6642
济　南	Jinan	1061	1365	11806
青　岛	Qingdao	1338	1719	12759
郑　州	Zhengzhou	1166	1520	12886
武　汉	Wuhan	1601	2204	16208
长　沙	Changsha	1227	1627	11132
广　州	Guangzhou	1945	2972	29715
深　圳	Shenzhen	4113	5012	27342
南　宁	Nanning	401	816	6117
海　口	Haikou	267	370	2875
重　庆	Chongqing	2441	5305	28899
成　都	Chengdu	1929	2587	25769
贵　阳	Guiyang	446	779	5196
昆　明	Kunming	558	838	8289
拉　萨	Lhasa	109	452	718
西　安	Xi'an	952	1730	16569
兰　州	Lanzhou	255	503	5130
西　宁	Xining	144	419	2513
银　川	Yinchuan	198	438	3115
乌鲁木齐	Urumqi	370	504	5306

注：住户存款余额为年末金融机构人民币各项存款余额的其中项。
a) Household deposit balance is one of the RMB deposit balances of financial institutions at the end of the year.

25-2 续表 2 continued

城市名称	City	社会消费品零售总额 (亿元) Total Retail Sales of Consumer Goods (100 million yuan)	货物进出口总额 (亿元) Total Value of Import and Export in Goods (100 million yuan)	普通、职业本专科在校学生数 (人) Enrolment in Regular and Vocational HEIs (person)	医院数 (个) Number of Hospitals (unit)	执业(助理)医师 (人) Licensed (Assistant) Physicians (person)
北京	Beijing	14463	36449	644532	682	121550
天津	Tianjin	3821	8009	596569	458	56468
石家庄	Shijiazhuang	2875	1237	682079	342	48765
太原	Taiyuan	1913	1350	748299	161	27778
呼和浩特	Hohhot	1203	194	259301	113	14333
沈阳	Shenyang	4210	1469	446778	312	37290
大连	Dalian	2009	4553	328491	246	24446
长春	Changchun	2110	1226	536946	282	37763
哈尔滨	Harbin	2384	495	759915	355	34000
上海	Shanghai	18516	42135	572443	467	89072
南京	Nanjing	8201	5660	799410	311	42328
杭州	Hangzhou	7671	8030	514304	414	62661
宁波	Ningbo	5213	12779	186501	215	37888
合肥	Hefei	5271	3588	862683	230	36104
福州	Fuzhou	4964	3604	434843	150	29835
厦门	Xiamen	2743	9470	195203	70	18842
南昌	Nanchang	3202	1113	786995	153	23203
济南	Jinan	5199	2163	631671	320	47103
青岛	Qingdao	6319	8763	424226	358	43106
郑州	Zhengzhou	5623	5522	1393573	289	56697
武汉	Wuhan	7532	3606	1161053	368	50326
长沙	Changsha	5562	2813	795531	247	43249
广州	Guangzhou	11013	10913	1468613	331	71850
深圳	Shenzhen	10486	38711	119612	159	50630
南宁	Nanning	2425	1259	714401	170	33892
海口	Haikou	1089	790	184473	78	12119
重庆	Chongqing	15130	7129	1100170	862	102267
成都	Chengdu	10002	7490	1140856	799	87423
贵阳	Guiyang	2527	580	473267	220	27268
昆明	Kunming	3574	1347	793451	318	38215
拉萨	Lhasa	428	55	24600	19	2255
西安	Xi'an	4812	3598	850044	395	51578
兰州	Lanzhou	1796	118	449768	126	17634
西宁	Xining	625	39	88587	82	11773
银川	Yinchuan	806	130	137716	86	12436
乌鲁木齐	Urumqi	1231	700	247016	131	18156

注：1.地方一般公共预算收入、地方一般公共预算支出、住户存款余额、货物进出口总额、普通、职业本专科在校学生数、医院数、执业(助理)医师，四个直辖市数据来自相关部委，其他城市数据来自地方相关部门。

2.普通、职业本专科在校学生数包括普通本科、职业本科、专科在校学生数。

a) General public budget revenue of the local governments, general public budget expenditure of the local governments, deposit of households, total value of import and export, enrolment in regular and vocational HEIs, number of hospitals, licensed (assistant) physicians, data of four municipalities directly under the central government are from relevant ministries and commissions, and data of other cities are from relevant local departments.

b) The number of students in regular and vocational colleges and universities includes the number of students in regular colleges, vocational colleges and universities.

25-3 城市公用事业基本情况
Basic Statistics on City Public Utilities

本表各项指标按全社会范围计算。
Data have covered the public utilities of all city units.

项　目	Item	2000	2010	2015	2020	2022	2023
城市建设	**City Development**						
城区面积 (平方公里)	Urban Area (sq.km)		178692	191776	186629	191217	
建成区面积 (平方公里)	Area of Built Districts (sq.km)	22439	40058	52102	60721	63676	
城市建设用地面积 (平方公里)	Area of Land Used for Urban Construction (sq.km)	22114	39758	51584			
城市人口密度 (人/平方公里)	Population Density of Urban Area (persons/sq.km)		2209	2399	2778	2854	2895
城市供水、燃气及集中供热	**Water Supply, Gas Supply and Centralized Heating**						
全年供水总量 (亿立方米)	Annual Volume of Tap Water Supply (100 million cu.m)	469.0	507.9	560.5	629.5	674.4	687.6
#生活用水	Water Consumption for Daily Use	200.0	238.8	287.3	348.5	378.5	389.4
人均生活用水 (吨)	Per Capita Water Consumption for Daily Use (ton)	95.5	62.6	63.7	65.5	67.4	68.9
供水普及率 (%)	Coverage of Urban Population with Access to Tap Water (%)	63.9	96.7	98.1	99.0	99.4	99.4
人工煤气供气量 (亿立方米)	Gaswork Gas Supply (100 million cu.m)	152.4	279.9	47.1	23.1	18.1	14.1
#家庭用量	Consumption of Gaswork Gas for Household Use	63.1	26.9	10.8	5.2	3.5	2.6
天然气供气量 (亿立方米)	Natural Gas Supply (100 million cu.m)	82.1	487.6	1040.8	1563.7	1767.7	1837.2
#家庭用量	Consumption of Natural Gas for Household Use	24.8	117.2	208.0	381.6	438.2	449.8
液化石油气供气量 (万吨)	Liquefied Petroleum Gas Supply (10 000 tons)	1053.7	1268.0	1039.2	833.7	758.5	764.6
#家庭用量	Consumption of Liquefied Gas for Household Use	532.3	633.9	587.1	478.7	444.4	420.5
供气管道长度 (万公里)	Length of Gas Pipelines (10 000 km)	8.9	30.9	52.8	86.4	99.0	104.7
燃气普及率 (%)	Coverage of Urban Population with Access to Gas (%)	45.4	92.0	95.3	97.9	98.1	98.3
集中供热面积 (亿平方米)	Area of Centralized Heating (100 million sq.m)	11.1	43.6	67.2	98.8	111.3	115.5
城市市政设施	**Municipal Infrastructure**						
年末实有道路长度 (万公里)	Length of Paved Roads at Year-end (10 000 km)	16.0	29.4	36.5	49.3	55.2	56.4
每万人拥有道路长度 (公里)	Length of Paved Roads Per 10 000 Persons (km)	4.1	7.5	7.9	9.2	9.8	9.9
年末实有道路面积(亿平方米)	Area of Paved Roads at Year-end (100 million sq.m)	23.8	52.1	71.8	97.0	108.9	112.1
人均拥有道路面积 (平方米)	Per Capita Area of Paved Roads (sq.m)	6.1	13.2	15.6	18.0	19.3	19.7
城市排水管道长度 (万公里)	Length of City Sewage Pipes (10 000 km)	14.2	37.0	54.0	80.3	91.4	95.2
城市公共交通	**Public Traffic**						
年末公共汽电车运营数(万辆)	Number of Public Buses and Trolley Buses in Operation at Year-end (10 000 units)		37.5	48.3	59.0	70.3	68.3
年末轨道交通配属车辆数(万辆)	Number of Carriages Allocated to Rail Transit at Year-end (10 000 units)		0.8	2.0	4.9	6.3	6.7
每万人拥有公共汽电车辆(标台)	Number of Public Buses and Trolley Buses Per 10 000 Persons (unit)		10.7	12.2	12.9	14.1	
出租汽车数 (万辆)	Taxis (10 000 units)	82.5	98.6	109.2	111.3	136.2	136.7
城市绿化和园林	**City Greening**						
城市绿地面积 (万公顷)	Area of Green Space (10 000 hectares)	86.5	213.4	267.0	331.2	358.6	365.2
人均公园绿地面积 (平方米)	Public Recreational Green Space Per Capita (sq.m)	3.7	11.2	13.3	14.8	15.3	15.6
公园个数 (个)	Number of Parks (unit)	4455	9955	13834	19823	24841	28137
公园面积 (万公顷)	Area of Parks (10 000 hectares)	8.2	25.8	38.4	53.8	67.3	69.2
城市环境卫生	**Environmental Sanitation**						
生活垃圾清运量 (万吨)	Volume of Domestic Garbage Collected and Transported (10 000 tons)	11819	15805	19142	23512	24445	25408
每万人拥有公共厕所 (座)	Number of Public Toilets per 10 000 Persons (unit)	2.7	3.0	2.7	3.1	3.4	3.5

注：1.2006年以前"城区面积"为"城市面积"。
2.计算人均和普及率指标所使用的人口数2006年以前为城市人口，2006年起为城区人口与城区暂住人口之和，以公安部门的户籍统计和暂住人口统计为准。
3.2006年以前"人均公园绿地面积"为"人均公共绿地面积"。
4.2020年起，全国城区面积、建成区面积及城市人口密度不含北京市数据。
5.2021年起，城市公共交通相关数据统计范围为城市和县城数据。

a) Before 2006, urban area referred to the area of the city proper.
b) Per capita data and coverage rate are calculated on the basis of city population before 2006. Since 2006, they are calculated on the basis of the sum of urban area population and temporary residing population from the household registration by the ministry of public security.
c) Since 2006, public green space per capita is changed to be public recreational green space per capita.
d) Since 2020, urban area, area of built district and population density of city districts do not include those in Beijing.
e) Since 2021, the statistical scope of urban public transport related data is urban and county data.

25-4 分地区城市建设情况（2023年）
Conditions of City Construction by Region (2023)

地区	Region	城区面积 (平方公里) Urban Area (sq.km)	建成区面积 (平方公里) Area of Built Districts (sq.km)	城市人口密度 (人/平方公里) Population Density of Urban Area (persons/sq.km)
全国	**National Total**	**191216.8**	**63676.4**	**2895**
北京	Beijing			
天津	Tianjin	2653.4	1264.5	4395
河北	Hebei	6364.0	2267.0	3426
山西	Shanxi	3320.8	1295.1	3990
内蒙古	Inner Mongolia	4674.9	1272.8	2266
辽宁	Liaoning	13067.8	2815.0	1847
吉林	Jilin	5720.8	1580.0	2113
黑龙江	Heilongjiang	2567.9	1802.6	5334
上海	Shanghai	6340.5	1242.0	3923
江苏	Jiangsu	17190.2	4916.2	2175
浙江	Zhejiang	13885.4	3427.0	2371
安徽	Anhui	7125.6	2500.3	2809
福建	Fujian	4325.7	1877.5	3356
江西	Jiangxi	3337.7	1789.5	3430
山东	Shandong	24105.9	5713.0	1746
河南	Henan	6383.8	3521.1	4570
湖北	Hubei	7964.7	2866.2	3429
湖南	Hunan	4110.8	2105.0	4419
广东	Guangdong	17126.6	6575.3	3762
广西	Guangxi	5394.9	1809.5	2558
海南	Hainan	1340.0	419.3	2501
重庆	Chongqing	7781.3	1640.8	2038
四川	Sichuan	8708.0	3411.8	3623
贵州	Guizhou	4356.0	1194.8	2105
云南	Yunnan	3276.4	1287.8	3341
西藏	Xizang	632.6	170.7	1544
陕西	Shaanxi	2700.9	1553.5	5413
甘肃	Gansu	2120.8	968.1	3342
青海	Qinghai	738.9	250.1	2944
宁夏	Ningxia	954.4	485.7	3239
新疆	Xinjiang	2946.3	1654.6	3322

注：1.北京市数据暂缺，全国数据不包含北京市数据。
2.城区面积、建成区面积为2022年数据。

a)The data of national total do not include the data of Beijing.
b)The urban area and area of built districts are the data of 2022.

25-5 分地区城市供水情况（2023年）

Basic Statistics on Tap Water Supply in Cities by Region (2023)

地 区	Region	年末供水综合生产能力（万立方米/日）Production Capacity of Tap Water Supply (year-end) (10 000 cu.m/day)	年末供水管道长度（公里）Length of Water Supply Pipelines (year-end) (km)	全年供水总量（万立方米）Total Annual Volume of Tap Water Supply (10 000 cu.m)	#生活用水 For Daily Use	#生产用水 For Production Use	用水人口（万人）Number of Population with Access to Tap Water (10 000 persons)	人均日生活用水量（升）Per Capita Daily Water Consumption for Daily Use (liter)
全 国	**National Total**	**33621.0**	**1153126**	**6875588**	**3893837**	**1700798**	**56504.7**	**188.8**
北 京	Beijing	744.0	19928	153616	117206	11832	1919.8	167.3
天 津	Tianjin	519.1	23164	106554	54566	37070	1166.0	128.2
河 北	Hebei	865.8	25821	163083	91151	40252	2212.1	112.9
山 西	Shanxi	399.7	16902	94639	58708	24707	1303.4	123.4
内蒙古	Inner Mongolia	418.9	13309	81538	40501	22842	964.3	115.1
辽 宁	Liaoning	1375.0	42439	275323	140257	68386	2242.3	171.4
吉 林	Jilin	685.5	15124	107713	54360	24175	1191.1	125.0
黑龙江	Heilongjiang	620.0	25604	128255	66291	31537	1376.6	131.9
上 海	Shanghai	1248.5	40437	295507	191478	42286	2487.5	210.9
江 苏	Jiangsu	4486.9	140884	649799	291384	225899	3738.3	213.6
浙 江	Zhejiang	2215.4	112218	476940	253628	163272	3189.5	217.9
安 徽	Anhui	1283.0	38960	273391	142785	86622	1969.9	198.6
福 建	Fujian	975.2	39814	203368	126112	36254	1468.7	235.3
江 西	Jiangxi	738.1	33892	167277	100619	33891	1156.5	238.4
山 东	Shandong	1976.0	62695	405820	199471	150327	4174.4	130.9
河 南	Henan	1342.9	33659	245463	151335	50512	2887.1	143.6
湖 北	Hubei	1687.3	58224	341788	182170	91519	2440.4	204.5
湖 南	Hunan	1074.7	44509	250835	151781	47034	1860.8	223.5
广 东	Guangdong	4378.2	153178	1017936	606533	242135	6725.2	247.1
广 西	Guangxi	791.3	27998	204924	134457	38206	1349.6	273.0
海 南	Hainan	207.7	7957	53656	37214	3645	334.7	304.6
重 庆	Chongqing	852.5	28232	188006	110170	41785	1588.3	190.0
四 川	Sichuan	1447.0	57361	360567	233472	51798	3022.3	211.6
贵 州	Guizhou	488.8	27077	98485	61032	19231	902.8	185.2
云 南	Yunnan	601.6	19498	118815	71762	22945	1083.2	181.5
西 藏	Xizang	69.8	1784	20045	10191	1220	97.7	285.8
陕 西	Shaanxi	634.4	13121	137471	80904	35355	1442.8	153.6
甘 肃	Gansu	418.9	7296	60390	36327	14589	705.4	141.1
青 海	Qinghai	127.4	3557	30474	13951	10877	215.8	177.1
宁 夏	Ningxia	270.1	3440	39909	21077	8214	307.6	187.7
新 疆	Xinjiang	677.4	15046	124004	62944	22380	980.8	175.8

25–6 分地区城市燃气情况（2023年）
Basic Statistics on Supply of Gas in Cities by Region (2023)

地区	Region	人工煤气生产能力（万立方米/日）Production Capacity of Gaswork Gas (10 000 cu.m/day)	管道长度（公里）Length of Gas Pipelines (km)			全年供气总量 Volume of Gas Supply			用气人口（万人）Population with Access to Gas (10 000 persons)		
			人工煤气 Gaswork Gas	天然气 Natural Gas	液化石油气 Liquefied Petroleum Gas	人工煤气（万立方米）Gaswork Gas (10 000 cu.m)	天然气（万立方米）Natural Gas (10 000 cu.m)	液化石油气（吨）Liquefied Petroleum Gas (ton)	人工煤气 Gaswork Gas	天然气 Natural Gas	液化石油气 Liquefied Petroleum Gas
全国	**National Total**	**707.3**	**5154**	**1039164**	**2942**	**140559**	**18371920**	**7646011**	**312.3**	**47114.8**	**8405.8**
北京	Beijing			33759	206		2011672	123023		1478.3	441.6
天津	Tianjin			53895			683491	101924		1092.1	67.9
河北	Hebei		498	50258	78	40753	760148	88669		2065.6	137.7
山西	Shanxi	157.0	418	31054		46770	363403	62487	13.7	1239.5	36.5
内蒙古	Inner Mongolia		78	13792		1616	277108	55036	2.1	758.1	190.8
辽宁	Liaoning	48.7	2562	34522	131	17366	345486	523543	190.1	1810.7	236.3
吉林	Jilin		352	14475	39	3388	235131	108395	44.2	937.9	215.0
黑龙江	Heilongjiang		225	12014	110	2035	188832	146025	30.6	1040.1	223.3
上海	Shanghai			34585	263		983385	234026		2047.2	440.2
江苏	Jiangsu			120166	695		1818749	520213		3427.2	308.9
浙江	Zhejiang			67089	232		1003472	726314		2371.2	818.2
安徽	Anhui			37045	190		530154	152668		1880.8	115.2
福建	Fujian			19972	221		374064	303305		997.3	468.5
江西	Jiangxi	3.0	85	23666		11262	266260	166610	0.7	960.0	194.1
山东	Shandong	129.0	3	84332	1	9468	1247045	268326		3946.3	217.2
河南	Henan	15.0	235	31323	3		719252	144953		2604.0	278.2
湖北	Hubei			57740	45		660318	311631		2054.1	291.4
湖南	Hunan			34583			346644	251441		1513.4	323.8
广东	Guangdong			49825	591		1435602	2164836		4523.0	2129.4
广西	Guangxi	9.6		12754	2	2726	215093	303694		925.3	415.2
海南	Hainan			5507			33720	88572		275.7	58.9
重庆	Chongqing			27291			614233	65533		1551.3	32.9
四川	Sichuan		648	89555	114	3352	1082111	222299	17.2	2873.5	99.5
贵州	Guizhou			11680			195247	110613		649.8	222.7
云南	Yunnan			11234	17		79453	174895		620.9	218.7
西藏	Xizang			6253	1		5500	46101		45.0	39.9
陕西	Shaanxi			30326			639504	53963		1389.8	61.1
甘肃	Gansu	345.0	50	5005		1823	282533	46994	13.5	634.7	45.3
青海	Qinghai			4312			186170	16461		191.4	19.0
宁夏	Ningxia			7787	0		118191	9007		285.0	14.7
新疆	Xinjiang			23365	3		669948	54452		925.9	44.1

25-7 分地区城市集中供热情况（2023年）
Basic Statistics on Centralized Heating in Cities by Region (2023)

地区	Region	供热能力 Heating Supply Capacity		供热总量 Quantity of Heat Supplied		管道长度（公里）	供热面积（万平方米）
		蒸汽（吨/小时） Steam (ton/hour)	热水（兆瓦） Hot Water (Mega Watts)	蒸汽（万吉焦） Steam (10 000 gigajoules)	热水（万吉焦） Hot Water (10 000 gigajoules)	Length of Heating Pipelines (km)	Area of Centralized Heating (10 000 sq.m)
全　国	**National Total**	**123908**	**631206**	**65489**	**362974**	**523671**	**1154896**
北　京	Beijing		52380		20515	68666	72113
天　津	Tianjin	1875	32643	806	15771	37301	60117
河　北	Hebei	5925	52242	3762	31084	56192	106871
山　西	Shanxi	20373	33001	11981	18098	28112	85659
内蒙古	Inner Mongolia	5591	55147	3338	32650	28519	71281
辽　宁	Liaoning	20859	75358	11428	56480	67797	149371
吉　林	Jilin	1783	49267	990	26889	38942	69149
黑龙江	Heilongjiang	12402	53362	6521	42125	25992	91584
上　海	Shanghai						
江　苏	Jiangsu	6208	25	700	14	460	4021
浙　江	Zhejiang						
安　徽	Anhui	3160	208	2568	11	864	2689
福　建	Fujian						
江　西	Jiangxi						
山　东	Shandong	24050	75295	11452	44882	105360	206646
河　南	Henan	5377	27751	2616	15149	16374	66551
湖　北	Hubei	1943	1600	1678	35	534	1982
湖　南	Hunan						
广　东	Guangdong						
广　西	Guangxi						
海　南	Hainan						
重　庆	Chongqing						
四　川	Sichuan					80	19
贵　州	Guizhou		280		85	55	233
云　南	Yunnan		471		90	492	209
西　藏	Xizang		46		112	300	186
陕　西	Shaanxi	8520	32686	3859	14124	5798	56548
甘　肃	Gansu	795	20529	741	12893	15085	31946
青　海	Qinghai		10272		3541	1162	7362
宁　夏	Ningxia	2004	11513	1019	6340	6785	16173
新　疆	Xinjiang	3042	47129	2028	22084	18800	54187

25−8 分地区城市市政设施（2023年）
Basic Statistics on Municipal Infrastructure in Cities by Region (2023)

地 区	Region	年末实有道路长度（公里）Length of Paved Roads (year-end) (km)	年末实有道路面积（万平方米）Area of Paved Roads (year-end) (10 000 sq.m)	城市桥梁（座）Number of City Bridges (unit)	城市排水管道长度（公里）Length of City Sewage Pipes (km)	城市污水日处理能力（万立方米）Daily Disposal Capacity of City Sewage (10 000 cu.m)	城市道路照明灯（千盏）Number of Street Lights (1 000 units)
全 国	**National Total**	**564394**	**1120760**	**89300**	**952483**	**23689.5**	**34817.0**
北 京	Beijing	9027	17037	2486	20585	743.4	319.4
天 津	Tianjin	9827	19130	1328	25253	355.9	439.8
河 北	Hebei	20935	44422	2779	25439	768.8	1185.2
山 西	Shanxi	9903	23140	1493	15795	374.6	594.7
内蒙古	Inner Mongolia	11522	23278	577	15645	250.9	638.9
辽 宁	Liaoning	24812	46091	2176	26485	1143.8	1378.6
吉 林	Jilin	11875	21641	1083	14531	495.0	611.1
黑龙江	Heilongjiang	14434	23000	1219	13791	490.2	717.8
上 海	Shanghai	5965	12381	3132	22615	1022.5	724.4
江 苏	Jiangsu	54811	96382	14540	96045	1926.9	3987.1
浙 江	Zhejiang	34999	69198	14901	65041	1437.3	2000.9
安 徽	Anhui	20888	49581	2730	38375	880.7	1320.4
福 建	Fujian	17372	34275	2794	25664	637.1	1203.1
江 西	Jiangxi	14609	31226	1314	24679	492.8	1087.4
山 东	Shandong	54280	110627	6226	74798	1520.4	2364.2
河 南	Henan	21053	51216	2106	38388	1108.8	1170.0
湖 北	Hubei	26132	51758	2408	39806	1082.0	1380.1
湖 南	Hunan	19395	40043	1512	28770	958.1	983.0
广 东	Guangdong	57806	101060	9889	150687	3164.6	4060.8
广 西	Guangxi	16170	33073	1310	23271	883.6	877.4
海 南	Hainan	5290	8503	252	7889	143.5	182.8
重 庆	Chongqing	12719	27582	2841	26464	481.7	966.5
四 川	Sichuan	30359	60684	4373	51451	1119.5	2212.6
贵 州	Guizhou	14273	23713	1368	16491	414.7	854.9
云 南	Yunnan	10022	20910	1403	19408	412.6	884.6
西 藏	Xizang	1192	2128	65	1013	37.0	37.1
陕 西	Shaanxi	11296	26437	1003	16113	596.3	790.9
甘 肃	Gansu	7314	15456	745	9214	199.0	464.6
青 海	Qinghai	1701	4290	241	4170	73.9	153.3
宁 夏	Ningxia	3040	8413	255	2546	139.7	292.2
新 疆	Xinjiang	11374	24085	751	12065	334.6	933.5

25–9 分地区城市公共交通情况（2023年）
Basic Statistics on Public Transportation in Cities by Region (2023)

地 区	Region	公共汽电车 Buses and Trolley Buses			轨道交通 Subways, Light Rail, Streetcar			出租汽车（辆） Number of Taxis (unit)
		运营车数（辆） Number of Vehicles in Operation (unit)	运营线路总长度（公里） Length of Routes in Operation (km)	客运总量（万人次） Total Passenger Traffic (10 000 person-times)	配属车辆数（辆） Number of Carriages Allocated (unit)	运营里程（公里） Length in Operation (km)	客运总量（万人次） Total Passenger Traffic (10 000 person-times)	
全 国	**National Total**	**682511**	**1733852**	**3804953**	**66659**	**10159**	**2938913**	**1367416**
北 京	Beijing	23385	29739	178457	7512	836	345135	71456
天 津	Tianjin	9665	28889	45327	1646	298	57139	31778
河 北	Hebei	33130	94909	87512	486	74	17311	69748
山 西	Shanxi	15213	54279	90208	144	23	4382	41613
内蒙古	Inner Mongolia	11022	49371	58688	312	49	6764	67452
辽 宁	Liaoning	22200	43836	192287	2282	489	76049	91565
吉 林	Jilin	12399	50297	96725	996	111	21865	67745
黑龙江	Heilongjiang	18548	48838	124380	594	82	28128	98021
上 海	Shanghai	17358	24480	108158	7249	831	366108	32219
江 苏	Jiangsu	51379	125879	191858	5681	1080	192332	52395
浙 江	Zhejiang	45885	175805	164107	4851	877	179857	43467
安 徽	Anhui	28198	90540	101696	1598	243	44410	55204
福 建	Fujian	20163	48317	134250	1430	237	47419	21542
江 西	Jiangxi	15627	56861	67206	906	129	38055	17015
山 东	Shandong	63952	182717	243085	1949	410	56806	69259
河 南	Henan	33750	55272	137275	1980	321	64033	63345
湖 北	Hubei	25116	49291	175597	3434	557	135648	44339
湖 南	Hunan	32136	66965	166748	1179	210	94391	35913
广 东	Guangdong	63120	122074	313150	8809	1382	596798	51174
广 西	Guangxi	13904	42567	62003	876	128	35005	19908
海 南	Hainan	4897	13880	12516	14	8	132	6270
重 庆	Chongqing	15208	29687	196876	3220	494	132696	24230
四 川	Sichuan	31969	61126	270579	4802	602	212190	46833
贵 州	Guizhou	10884	26088	118900	762	117	13346	47566
云 南	Yunnan	15633	56884	75297	984	193	28880	31864
西 藏	Xizang	874	3364	7345				2380
陕 西	Shaanxi	18171	31043	141921	2568	305	129446	37890
甘 肃	Gansu	10067	25333	100403	233	46	10659	39659
青 海	Qinghai	3790	12208	27051				14145
宁 夏	Ningxia	4373	11439	22315				16426
新 疆	Xinjiang	10495	21878	93032	162	27	3928	54995

注：2021年起，城市公共交通数据统计范围为城市和县城。

a) Since 2021, the statistical scope of urban public transport data will cover cities and counties.

25-10 分地区城市绿地和园林(2023年)
Basic Statistics on Parks and Green Areas in Cities by Region (2023)

地 区	Region	城市绿地面积(公顷) Area of Green Space (hectare)	#公园绿地 Public Recreational Green Space	公园(个) Number of Parks (unit)	公园面积(公顷) Area of Parks (hectare)	建成区绿化覆盖率(%) Green Covered Rate of Built Districts (%)
全 国	**National Total**	**3652372**	**893521**	**28137**	**692020**	**43.3**
北 京	Beijing	94136	37238	612	36397	49.8
天 津	Tianjin	48521	11620	181	3503	38.2
河 北	Hebei	106281	32489	1049	23625	43.7
山 西	Shanxi	59447	17872	344	16074	42.9
内蒙古	Inner Mongolia	72081	18667	723	15650	42.2
辽 宁	Liaoning	153046	32804	819	23426	41.1
吉 林	Jilin	100250	18209	511	13696	42.8
黑龙江	Heilongjiang	77567	20434	506	13621	39.7
上 海	Shanghai	173256	23497	552	4440	37.8
江 苏	Jiangsu	322475	60645	1504	36332	44.0
浙 江	Zhejiang	184888	49316	2130	30749	43.7
安 徽	Anhui	135328	34202	851	23509	46.1
福 建	Fujian	86898	23088	769	15919	44.2
江 西	Jiangxi	83027	20902	1020	17539	46.9
山 东	Shandong	288644	77143	1522	49144	43.9
河 南	Henan	145488	46814	886	24151	43.5
湖 北	Hubei	123065	38016	800	24040	43.4
湖 南	Hunan	102211	25800	797	19690	42.0
广 东	Guangdong	557540	122091	6408	168245	44.5
广 西	Guangxi	84866	16558	512	15770	42.4
海 南	Hainan	20558	4262	212	3421	42.1
重 庆	Chongqing	78248	28889	641	16770	42.3
四 川	Sichuan	145165	44546	1064	28176	44.2
贵 州	Guizhou	101459	15308	462	15862	41.9
云 南	Yunnan	57524	15116	1547	13597	43.7
西 藏	Xizang	7141	1697	167	1338	42.5
陕 西	Shaanxi	81278	19256	502	12334	43.0
甘 肃	Gansu	33923	11354	240	7892	36.8
青 海	Qinghai	9076	2786	72	1854	36.6
宁 夏	Ningxia	26790	6810	168	3902	42.4
新 疆	Xinjiang	92196	16091	566	11354	41.4

注：1.公园绿地面积包括综合公园、社区公园、专类公园、带状公园和街旁绿地。
2.北京市的各项绿化数据均为该市调查面积内数据。

a) Area of park green areas includes comprehensive park, community park, theme park, belt-shaped park and green area nearby street.
b) All the greening-related data for Beijing are those for the areas surveyed in the city.

25-11 分地区城市市容环境卫生情况（2023年）
Environmental Sanitation of Cities by Region (2023)

地 区	Region	道路清扫保洁面积（万平方米）Road Area Cleaned (10 000 sq.m)	生活垃圾清运量（万吨）Volume of Domestic Garbage Collected and Transported (10 000 tons)	市容环卫专用车辆设备总数（台）Number of Special Vehicles for Environmental Sanitation (unit)	公共厕所（座）Number of Public Toilets (unit)	#三类以上 Third Grade and Above
全 国	**National Total**	**1126853**	**25407.8**	**362406**	**201506**	**173362**
北 京	Beijing	17804	758.9	12291	7122	7122
天 津	Tianjin	15288	301.9	5456	5060	4859
河 北	Hebei	44177	784.4	14516	8899	8587
山 西	Shanxi	26415	518.5	7642	4635	3395
内蒙古	Inner Mongolia	26162	356.0	7022	6775	5149
辽 宁	Liaoning	49646	1033.5	14232	5856	4244
吉 林	Jilin	20281	452.6	9209	4997	3834
黑龙江	Heilongjiang	27972	523.8	11409	5945	3941
上 海	Shanghai	19903	974.8	10282	7381	2362
江 苏	Jiangsu	77752	2081.7	26042	14596	13622
浙 江	Zhejiang	64728	1467.8	14810	9227	8227
安 徽	Anhui	53759	771.9	12511	7102	6959
福 建	Fujian	27092	878.9	9502	7451	6314
江 西	Jiangxi	30761	553.3	13091	6626	6626
山 东	Shandong	83217	1804.5	22715	10367	9653
河 南	Henan	57933	1121.2	19799	12852	12443
湖 北	Hubei	52729	1085.8	15302	8613	6787
湖 南	Hunan	41552	904.2	8839	5653	4285
广 东	Guangdong	125409	3389.5	35643	13827	13240
广 西	Guangxi	31510	615.3	14460	3658	1944
海 南	Hainan	9171	317.4	15962	1487	1478
重 庆	Chongqing	28252	643.3	5003	4831	4199
四 川	Sichuan	62089	1322.3	16148	9998	8768
贵 州	Guizhou	21684	461.9	6236	5529	4746
云 南	Yunnan	20828	544.9	6496	7209	7053
西 藏	Xizang	5105	70.9	1624	938	103
陕 西	Shaanxi	26169	715.9	7170	6990	6776
甘 肃	Gansu	15474	282.9	6245	3225	2825
青 海	Qinghai	5358	115.0	1693	839	722
宁 夏	Ningxia	11818	122.8	2738	1011	925
新 疆	Xinjiang	26815	432.2	8318	2807	2174

25-12 分地区城市设施水平（2023年）
Level of Public Facilities in Cities by Region (2023)

地区	Region	城市供水普及率(%) Coverage of Urban Population with Access to Tap Water (%)	城市燃气普及率(%) Coverage of Urban Population with Access to Gas (%)	人均城市道路面积(平方米) Per Capita Area of Paved Roads (sq.m)	人均公园绿地面积(平方米) Public Recreational Green Space Per Capita (sq.m)	每万人拥有公共厕所(座) Number of Public Toilets Per 10 000 Population (unit)
全国	**National Average**	**99.43**	**98.25**	**19.72**	**15.65**	**3.50**
北京	Beijing	100.00	100.00	8.87	16.90	3.71
天津	Tianjin	100.00	99.48	16.41	9.97	4.34
河北	Hebei	100.00	99.60	20.08	14.69	4.02
山西	Shanxi	98.35	97.32	17.46	13.49	3.50
内蒙古	Inner Mongolia	99.13	97.76	23.93	19.19	6.96
辽宁	Liaoning	97.22	97.00	19.98	14.22	2.54
吉林	Jilin	96.35	96.83	17.51	14.73	4.04
黑龙江	Heilongjiang	99.39	93.42	16.61	14.75	4.29
上海	Shanghai	100.00	100.00	4.98	9.45	2.97
江苏	Jiangsu	100.00	99.94	25.78	16.22	3.90
浙江	Zhejiang	100.00	100.00	21.70	15.46	2.89
安徽	Anhui	98.42	99.73	24.77	17.09	3.55
福建	Fujian	99.97	99.77	23.33	15.72	5.07
江西	Jiangxi	99.50	99.36	26.87	17.98	5.70
山东	Shandong	99.92	99.66	26.48	18.47	2.48
河南	Henan	99.45	99.28	17.64	16.13	4.43
湖北	Hubei	99.95	96.06	21.20	15.57	3.53
湖南	Hunan	99.86	98.59	21.49	13.85	3.03
广东	Guangdong	99.70	98.62	14.98	18.10	2.05
广西	Guangxi	99.89	99.21	24.48	12.25	2.71
海南	Hainan	99.85	99.82	25.37	12.71	4.44
重庆	Chongqing	99.92	99.66	17.35	18.18	3.04
四川	Sichuan	99.01	97.96	19.88	14.59	3.28
贵州	Guizhou	98.10	94.80	25.77	16.63	6.01
云南	Yunnan	98.94	76.69	19.10	13.81	6.58
西藏	Xizang	100.00	86.93	21.78	17.37	9.60
陕西	Shaanxi	98.53	99.08	18.05	13.15	4.77
甘肃	Gansu	99.67	97.98	21.84	16.04	4.56
青海	Qinghai	99.53	97.02	19.78	12.85	3.87
宁夏	Ningxia	99.33	96.79	27.17	21.99	3.27
新疆	Xinjiang	99.64	98.54	24.47	16.35	2.85

注：人均和普及率指标按城区人口与暂住人口之和计算，以公安部门的户籍统计和暂住人口统计为准。

a) Per capita data and coverage rate are calculated on the basis of the sum of urban population and temporarily residing population from the registration of the Ministry of Public Security.

25-13 分地区县城市政公用设施水平(2023年)
Level of Public Facilities of County Towns by Region (2023)

地 区	Region	人口密度 (人/平方公里) Population Density (person/sq.km)	人均日生活用水量 (升) Per Capita Daily Water Consumption for Daily Use (liter)	供水普及率 (%) Water Coverage Rate (%)	燃气普及率 (%) Gas Coverage Rate (%)	建成区供水管道密度 (公里/平方公里) Density of Water Supply Pipelines in Built Districts (km/sq.km)	人均道路面积 (平方米) Road Surface Area Per Capita (sq.m)
全 国	**National Total**	**2146**	**142.53**	**98.27**	**92.45**	**12.93**	**21.07**
北 京	Beijing						
天 津	Tianjin						
河 北	Hebei	2777	106.15	100.00	98.61	11.52	25.90
山 西	Shanxi	3599	100.54	95.72	83.30	13.16	17.37
内蒙古	Inner Mongolia	826	115.32	98.57	93.14	12.25	35.15
辽 宁	Liaoning	1408	135.07	97.79	90.24	12.74	16.92
吉 林	Jilin	2290	120.54	97.45	88.97	10.88	19.06
黑龙江	Heilongjiang	2707	111.01	97.99	65.76	11.11	15.67
上 海	Shanghai						
江 苏	Jiangsu	2165	181.45	100.00	100.00	14.92	23.46
浙 江	Zhejiang	901	249.89	100.00	100.00	21.78	26.13
安 徽	Anhui	1863	157.35	98.44	96.92	14.38	25.73
福 建	Fujian	2402	204.24	99.88	99.13	17.91	21.76
江 西	Jiangxi	3589	172.53	98.05	97.67	18.94	27.93
山 东	Shandong	1375	116.72	99.02	98.16	7.70	23.20
河 南	Henan	2583	117.46	98.19	96.53	8.56	19.22
湖 北	Hubei	2986	168.04	97.97	98.10	15.13	21.05
湖 南	Hunan	3821	165.27	98.27	95.64	15.82	15.58
广 东	Guangdong	1567	170.80	97.82	96.26	15.10	14.80
广 西	Guangxi	2672	182.20	99.84	99.39	14.47	22.25
海 南	Hainan	1815	290.09	99.16	97.14	6.81	36.83
重 庆	Chongqing	2331	154.13	99.72	99.08	14.15	13.74
四 川	Sichuan	1489	138.40	97.41	91.01	13.27	15.42
贵 州	Guizhou	2413	128.22	97.46	84.75	14.41	22.23
云 南	Yunnan	3810	139.91	97.56	63.93	14.86	21.14
西 藏	Xizang	2705	147.79	87.42	58.66	9.27	17.55
陕 西	Shaanxi	3843	111.53	98.20	94.20	8.82	17.61
甘 肃	Gansu	5380	84.27	97.92	79.00	10.10	15.49
青 海	Qinghai	2105	91.28	95.61	65.32	9.92	21.88
宁 夏	Ningxia	3775	117.41	99.87	77.01	9.97	24.07
新 疆	Xinjiang	3269	160.33	96.96	97.44	10.14	24.25

25-13 续表 continued

地 区	Region	建成区排水管道密度(公里/平方公里) Density of Sewers in Built Districts (km/ sq.km)	污水处理率(%) Waste Water Treatment Rate (%)	污水处理厂集中处理率 Centralized Treatment at Sewage Treatment Plants	人均公园绿地面积(平方米) Public Recreational Green Space Per Capita (sq.m)	建成区绿化覆盖率(%) Green Coverage Rate of Built Districts (%)	建成区绿地率(%) Green Space Rate of Built Districts (%)	生活垃圾处理率(%) Domestic Garbage Treatment Rate (%)	生活垃圾无害化处理率 Rate of Domestic Garbage Harmless Treatment
全 国	**National Total**	**11.26**	**97.66**	**97.08**	**15.06**	**40.19**	**36.53**	**99.90**	**99.57**
北 京	Beijing								
天 津	Tianjin								
河 北	Hebei	10.62	98.88	98.88	14.34	42.74	39.02	100.00	100.00
山 西	Shanxi	11.60	98.26	97.89	12.86	40.88	36.57	99.90	98.19
内蒙古	Inner Mongolia	8.77	98.43	98.43	23.51	37.76	35.27	99.99	99.99
辽 宁	Liaoning	6.03	102.08	102.08	13.76	24.77	20.70	99.63	99.63
吉 林	Jilin	10.69	98.83	98.83	18.61	40.09	37.03	100.00	100.00
黑龙江	Heilongjiang	8.40	97.13	97.13	14.93	36.29	32.92	100.00	100.00
上 海	Shanghai								
江 苏	Jiangsu	12.96	94.89	94.89	15.66	43.00	40.18	100.00	100.00
浙 江	Zhejiang	16.96	98.14	97.98	16.81	44.68	40.40	100.00	100.00
安 徽	Anhui	12.66	97.05	96.92	16.35	41.55	38.15	100.00	100.00
福 建	Fujian	15.79	97.62	96.78	17.69	44.02	40.44	100.00	100.00
江 西	Jiangxi	14.12	96.32	94.44	19.72	43.41	39.27	100.00	100.00
山 东	Shandong	10.81	98.34	98.34	17.18	42.23	38.57	100.00	100.00
河 南	Henan	10.03	98.82	98.81	13.31	40.57	35.81	99.86	97.17
湖 北	Hubei	11.37	96.98	96.98	15.23	41.35	38.27	100.00	100.00
湖 南	Hunan	10.90	96.73	96.56	11.82	39.82	36.32	99.98	99.98
广 东	Guangdong	7.62	97.41	97.41	13.28	37.97	34.98	100.00	100.00
广 西	Guangxi	13.62	98.60	93.27	13.23	38.90	34.38	100.00	100.00
海 南	Hainan	5.44	108.92	100.77	10.55	37.43	32.88	100.00	100.00
重 庆	Chongqing	18.17	99.88	99.88	16.83	44.62	41.55	100.00	100.00
四 川	Sichuan	10.97	96.10	93.60	14.74	40.79	36.52	99.92	99.92
贵 州	Guizhou	10.44	97.37	97.37	16.05	39.98	38.10	99.63	99.63
云 南	Yunnan	17.82	98.48	98.46	14.44	43.15	39.48	100.00	100.00
西 藏	Xizang	7.94	65.82	64.84	1.51	6.38	4.20	97.00	97.00
陕 西	Shaanxi	9.89	96.88	96.87	12.30	38.26	33.95	99.83	99.83
甘 肃	Gansu	10.70	98.40	98.40	14.13	33.38	29.50	99.98	99.98
青 海	Qinghai	9.95	93.91	93.91	7.84	27.80	24.14	96.39	96.39
宁 夏	Ningxia	9.06	99.82	99.82	17.73	39.93	38.45	100.00	100.00
新 疆	Xinjiang	7.16	99.01	99.00	17.56	42.18	38.55	99.97	99.97

25-14 农村水电建设和农村用电量
Hydropower Construction and Electricity Consumption in Rural Areas

年份 Year 地区 Region		乡村办水电站(个) Rural Hydropower Stations (unit)	农村水电装机容量(万千瓦) Rural Hydropower Installed Capacity (10 000 kW)	农村水电年发电量(亿千瓦时) Rural Hydropower Annual Electricity Generation (100 million kW·h)	农村用电量(亿千瓦时) Electricity Consumed in Rural Areas (100 million kW·h)
	1978	82387	228.4		253.1
	1980	80319	304.1		320.8
	1985	55754	380.2		508.9
	1990	52387	428.8	418.1	844.5
	1995	40699	519.5	631.6	1655.7
	2000	29962	698.5	875.5	2421.3
	2005	26726	1099.2	1357.2	4375.7
	2006	27493	1243.0	1483.6	4895.8
	2007	27664	1366.6	1634.6	5509.9
	2008	44433	5127.4	1627.6	5713.2
	2009	44804	5512.1	1567.2	6104.4
	2010	44815	5924.0	2044.4	6632.3
	2011	45151	6212.3	1756.7	7139.6
	2012	45799	6568.6	2172.9	7508.5
	2013	46849	7118.6	2232.8	8549.5
	2014	47073	7322.1	2281.5	8884.4
	2015	47340	7583.0	2351.3	9026.9
	2016	47529	7791.1	2682.2	9238.3
	2017	47498	7926.9	2477.2	9524.4
	2018	46515	8043.5	2345.6	9358.5
	2019	45445	8144.2	2533.2	9482.9
	2020	43957	8133.8	2423.7	6211.0
	2021	42785	8290.3	2241.1	6736.3
	2022	41544	8063.3	2360.0	7765.6
	2023	41114	8157.0	2303.0	7991.9
北京	Beijing	3	0.3	0.0	73.0
天津	Tianjin	1	0.6	0.1	70.9
河北	Hebei	215	37.7	8.2	595.9
山西	Shanxi	134	20.5	5.7	194.0
内蒙古	Inner Mongolia	36	10.8	2.2	178.1
辽宁	Liaoning	186	47.6	10.2	191.7
吉林	Jilin	265	63.6	18.7	87.0
黑龙江	Heilongjiang	79	39.2	13.7	120.2
上海	Shanghai				12.4
江苏	Jiangsu	39	5.7	0.6	610.5
浙江	Zhejiang	2829	418.1	80.4	574.2
安徽	Anhui	746	116.6	20.6	341.7
福建	Fujian	5084	690.3	202.7	341.2
江西	Jiangxi	3667	351.5	91.5	200.4
山东	Shandong	61	7.1	0.5	607.9
河南	Henan	310	40.7	8.6	568.8
湖北	Hubei	1579	367.5	103.0	277.2
湖南	Hunan	4228	626.6	146.9	317.3
广东	Guangdong	9354	787.9	202.4	764.2
广西	Guangxi	2262	466.1	104.4	270.6
海南	Hainan	282	44.8	11.2	76.2
重庆	Chongqing	1442	308.1	83.6	90.5
四川	Sichuan	3368	1262.2	435.0	328.3
贵州	Guizhou	1170	363.6	71.2	186.5
云南	Yunnan	1832	1253.0	365.8	204.8
西藏	Xizang	379	27.4	9.2	8.1
陕西	Shaanxi	355	140.6	48.7	182.1
甘肃	Gansu	606	295.9	117.6	135.9
青海	Qinghai	215	98.1	50.9	17.4
宁夏	Ningxia	1	0.4	0.0	51.8
新疆	Xinjiang	382	252.3	85.4	313.1
水利部直属	Directly under The Ministry of Water Resources	4	12.2	3.9	

注：1.2008年起乡村办水电站统计口径变更为农村水电。农村水电是指装机容量5万千瓦及以下水电站和配套电网。
2.2020年起农村用电量口径为"农林牧渔业用电量+乡村居民生活用电量"，数据来源于中国电力企业联合会。

a) Since 2008, the statistical caliber of rural hydropower stations has been changed to rural hydropower. Rural hydropower refers to hydropower stations with an installed capacity of 50000 kilowatts or less and supporting power grids.

b) Since 2020, the caliber of rural electricity consumption is electricity consumption for agriculture, forestry, animal husbandry, and fishery as well as electricity consumption for rural residents' daily lives, with data sourced from China Electricity Council.

25-15 东、中、西部及东北地区国民经济和社会发展主要指标（2023年）

指　　标	Item	全国总计 National Total
总人口(年末)　(万人)	Population at Year-end　(10 000 persons)	140967
国内(地区)生产总值　(亿元)	Gross Domestic (Regional) Product　(100 million yuan)	1260582.1
第一产业	Primary Industry	89755.2
第二产业	Secondary Industry	482588.5
第三产业	Tertiary Industry	688238.4
居民人均可支配收入　(元)	Per Capita Disposable Income of Households　(yuan)	39218
城镇居民人均可支配收入	Per Capita Disposable Income of Urban Households	51821
农村居民人均可支配收入	Per Capita Disposable Income of Rural Households	21691
地方一般公共预算收入(亿元)	General Public Budget Revenue　(100 million yuan)	117228.7
地方一般公共预算支出(亿元)	General Public Budget Expenditure　(100 million yuan)	236403.5
社会消费品零售总额 (亿元)	Total Retail Sales of Consumer Goods　(100 million yuan)	471495.2
货物进出口总额　(亿元)	Total Value of Imports and Exports in Goods　(100 million yuan)	417510.1
出口总额	Exports	237656.4
进口总额	Imports	179853.7
主要农产品产量	Output of Major Farm Products	
谷物　(万吨)	Cereals　(10 000 tons)	64143.0
棉花　(万吨)	Cotton　(10 000 tons)	561.8
油料　(万吨)	Oil-bearing Crops　(10 000 tons)	3863.7
主要工业、能源产品产量	Output of Major Industrial and Energy Products	
原煤　(亿吨)	Coal　(100 million tons)	47.2
天然气　(亿立方米)	Natural Gas　(100 million cu.m)	2324.3
水泥　(万吨)	Cement　(10 000 tons)	201940.2
粗钢　(万吨)	Crude Steel　(10 000 tons)	102886.0
钢材　(万吨)	Rolled Steel　(10 000 tons)	138378.7
汽车　(万辆)	Motor Vehicles　(10 000 sets)	3009.9
发电量　(亿千瓦时)	Electricity Generation　(100 million kW·h)	94564.4
铁路营业里程　(公里)	Length of Railways in Operation　(km)	158737.3
公路里程　(公里)	Length of Highways　(km)	5436845.2
#高速公路	Expressway	183645.5
客运量　(万人)	Passenger Traffic　(10 000 persons)	1574330.8
货运量　(万吨)	Freight Traffic　(10 000 tons)	5570636.1
电信业务总量　(亿元)	Business Volume of Telecommunication Services(100 million yuan)	18359.3
普通、职业高等学校数 (个)	Number of Regular and Vocational Higher Education Institutions(unit)	2822
普通、职业本专科在校生数(万人)	Enrolment in Regular and Vocational HEIs　(10 000 persons)	3775.0
医院数　(个)	Number of Hospitals　(unit)	38355
执业(助理)医师　(万人)	Licensed (Assistant) Physicians　(10 000 persons)	478.2
医院床位数　(万张)	Number of Hospital Beds　(10 000 beds)	800.5

注：1.占全国比重以各地区合计数为100计算(以下相关表同)。
2.全国总计人口包括了中国人民解放军现役军人。
3.水泥、粗钢、钢材和汽车2023年数据统计范围为规模以上工业企业，即年主营业务收入2000万元及以上的工业企业。
4.货运量分地区数据不包括民航、管道运输数据，客运量分地区数据不包括民航运输数据，电信业务总量分地区数据不包括集团总部及直属部分的数据，各地区合计数小于全国总计。

Main Indicators of National Economic and Social Development by Eastern, Central, Western and Northeastern Regions (2023)

东部地区 Eastern Region		中部地区 Central Region		西部地区 Western Region		东北地区 Northeastern Region	
绝对数 Absolute Figures	占全国比重 (%) As Percentage of National Total	绝对数 Absolute Figures	占全国比重 (%) As Percentage of National Total	绝对数 Absolute Figures	占全国比重 (%) As Percentage of National Total	绝对数 Absolute Figures	占全国比重 (%) As Percentage of National Total
56638	40.2	36323	25.8	38223	27.1	9583	6.8
652084.2	52.1	269897.7	21.6	269324.9	21.5	59624.5	4.8
29116.0	32.4	22390.6	24.9	30501.0	34.0	7814.1	8.7
247258.8	51.6	107121.6	22.4	104044.3	21.7	20610.8	4.3
375709.4	55.1	140385.5	20.6	134779.5	19.8	31199.6	4.6
49822		33328		31100		33207	
61472		44706		44136		41009	
26907		20518		17911		20300	
65146.7	55.6	22049.5	18.8	24806.2	21.2	5226.3	4.5
97308.9	41.2	52414.8	22.2	69921.7	29.6	16758.1	7.1
238194.6	50.5	114899.5	24.4	98202.2	20.8	20146.7	4.3
331650.5	79.4	36154.2	8.7	37379.3	9.0	12326.2	3.0
186194.3	78.3	23822.7	10.0	22716.9	9.6	4922.5	2.1
145456.2	80.9	12331.5	6.9	14662.3	8.2	7403.7	4.1
15475.1	24.1	19470.3	30.4	15763.1	24.6	13434.5	20.9
24.0	4.3	22.2	4.0	515.6	91.8	0.0	0.0
693.4	17.9	1746.1	45.2	1191.1	30.8	233.1	6.0
1.5	3.1	16.1	34.0	28.6	60.6	1.1	2.3
252.7	10.9	154.8	6.7	1829.8	78.7	87.0	3.7
74274.0	36.8	54105.0	26.8	65737.1	32.6	7824.0	3.9
52947.5	51.5	22273.8	21.6	17911.7	17.4	9752.9	9.5
79827.4	57.7	25260.9	18.3	23009.2	16.6	10281.2	7.4
1588.6	52.8	569.9	18.9	592.4	19.7	259.0	8.6
34712.6	36.7	18513.0	19.6	36489.8	38.6	4849.1	5.1
39397.1	24.8	35750.5	22.5	64377.4	40.6	19212.3	12.1
1216155.8	22.4	1426671.2	26.2	2381908.8	43.8	412109.4	7.6
49771.5	27.1	42433.2	23.1	77350.4	42.1	14090.4	7.7
600888.8	38.2	353322.6	22.4	417488.7	26.5	140673.1	8.9
2069731.0	37.2	1615544.6	29.0	1500115.0	26.9	288571.3	5.2
8744.0	47.6	3829.0	20.9	4640.6	25.3	937.7	5.1
1050	37.2	750	26.6	764	27.1	258	9.1
1393.0	36.9	1066.3	28.2	1024.7	27.1	291.0	7.7
13566	35.4	9429	24.6	11705	30.5	3655	9.5
199.8	41.8	121.0	25.3	124.0	25.9	33.4	7.0
291.4	36.4	209.6	26.2	230.5	28.8	69.0	8.6

a) The total of all regions is 100 in calculating as percentage of national total. The same applies to the following table.
b) National total includes the military personal.
c) The scope of data statistics for cement, crude steel, rolled steel and motor vehicles in 2023 includes industrial enterprises above designated size, which have an annual main business income of 20 million yuan or more.
d) Data of freight traffic by region do not include that of civil aviation and pipelines, and data of passenger traffic do not include that of civil aviation. The data of business volume of telecommunication services by region do not include the data from the group headquarters and directly affiliated parts. The sum of data of all the regions is less than the data of national total.

25-16 京津冀、长江经济带、长江三角洲国民经济和社会发展主要指标(2023年)

指　　标	Item	全国总计 National Total
总人口(年末)　(万人)	Population at Year-end　(10 000 persons)	140967
国内(地区)生产总值　(亿元)	Gross Domestic (Regional) Product　(100 million yuan)	1260582.1
第一产业	Primary Industry	89755.2
第二产业	Secondary Industry	482588.5
第三产业	Tertiary Industry	688238.4
地方一般公共预算收入(亿元)	General Public Budget Revenue　(100 million yuan)	117228.7
地方一般公共预算支出(亿元)	General Public Budget Expenditure　(100 million yuan)	236403.5
社会消费品零售总额 (亿元)	Total Retail Sales of Consumer Goods　(100 million yuan)	471495.2
货物进出口总额　(亿元)	Total Value of Imports and Exports in Goods　(100 million yuan)	417510.1
出口总额	Exports	237656.4
进口总额	Imports	179853.7
主要农产品产量	Output of Major Farm Products	
谷物　(万吨)	Cereals　(10 000 tons)	64143.0
棉花　(万吨)	Cotton　(10 000 tons)	561.8
油料　(万吨)	Oil-bearing Crops　(10 000 tons)	3863.7
主要工业、能源产品产量	Output of Major Industrial and Energy Products	
原煤　(亿吨)	Coal　(100 million tons)	47.2
天然气　(亿立方米)	Natural Gas　(100 million cu.m)	2324.3
水泥　(万吨)	Cement　(10 000 tons)	201940.2
粗钢　(万吨)	Crude Steel　(10 000 tons)	102886.0
钢材　(万吨)	Rolled Steel　(10 000 tons)	138378.7
汽车　(万辆)	Motor Vehicles　(10 000 sets)	3009.9
发电量　(亿千瓦时)	Electricity Generation　(100 million kW·h)	94564.4
铁路营业里程　(公里)	Length of Railways in Operation　(km)	158737.3
公路里程　(公里)	Length of Highways　(km)	5436845.2
#高速公路	Expressway	183645.5
客运量　(万人)	Passenger Traffic　(10 000 persons)	1574330.8
货运量　(万吨)	Freight Traffic　(10 000 tons)	5570636.1
电信业务总量　(亿元)	Business Volume of Telecommunication Services(100 million yuan)	18359.3
普通、职业高等学校　(个)	Number of Regular and Vocational Higher Education Institutions(unit)	2822
普通、职业本专科在校生数(万人)	Enrolment in Regular and Vocational HEIs　(10 000 persons)	3775.0
医院数　(个)	Number of Hospitals　(unit)	38355
执业(助理)医师　(万人)	Licensed (Assistant) Physicians　(10 000 persons)	478.2
医院床位数　(万张)	Number of Hospital Beds　(10 000 beds)	800.5

注：1.长江经济带包括：上海、江苏、浙江、安徽、江西、湖北、湖南、重庆、四川、贵州、云南。
2.长江三角洲包括：上海、江苏、浙江和安徽。
3.全国总计人口包括了中国人民解放军现役军人。
4.水泥、粗钢、钢材和汽车2023年数据统计范围为规模以上工业企业，即年主营业务收入2000万元及以上的工业企业。

Main Indicators of National Economic and Social Development by Beijing-Tianjin-Hebei Region, Yangtze River Economic Zone and Yangtze River Delta (2023)

京津冀地区 Beijing-Tianjin-Hebei Region		长江经济带 Yangtze River Economic Zone		长江三角洲 Yangtze River Delta	
绝对数 Absolute Figures	占全国比重 (%) As Percentage of National Total	绝对数 Absolute Figures	占全国比重 (%) As Percentage of National Total	绝对数 Absolute Figures	占全国比重 (%) As Percentage of National Total
10943	7.8	60779	43.1	23761	16.9
104442.1	8.3	584274.2	46.7	305044.6	24.4
4840.2	5.4	38377.7	42.7	11000.4	12.2
28943.5	6.0	224665.5	46.9	121347.1	25.3
70658.4	10.4	321231.0	47.1	172697.0	25.3
12495.2	10.7	53092.9	45.3	30782.3	26.3
20857.9	8.8	103221.6	43.7	45877.4	19.4
33323.8	7.1	239541.9	50.8	119621.4	25.4
50285.5	12.0	190017.1	45.5	151681.3	36.3
13135.0	5.5	116497.0	49.0	91981.0	38.7
37150.4	20.7	73520.1	40.9	59700.3	33.2
3924.3	6.1	22121.6	34.5	8391.3	13.1
10.5	1.9	22.3	4.0	2.9	0.5
119.7	3.1	1860.3	48.1	328.6	8.5
0.5	1.0	3.6	7.7	1.2	2.5
48.8	2.1	749.6	32.3	39.5	1.7
10814.5	5.4	100449.9	49.7	40895.0	20.3
22695.1	22.1	33817.4	32.9	18769.7	18.2
36075.9	26.1	46226.1	33.4	26175.7	18.9
275.9	9.2	1379.9	45.8	772.2	25.7
5434.9	5.7	35029.9	37.0	15527.3	16.4
11308.7	7.1	50425.5	31.8	14579.4	9.2
248760.7	4.6	2446190.4	45.0	532260.9	9.8
10977.2	6.0	72639.2	39.6	17321.5	9.4
134067.9	8.5	701335.9	44.5	296332.5	18.8
328871.5	5.9	2507802.0	45.0	1231345.3	22.1
1622.8	8.8	8056.6	43.9	3916.1	21.3
276	9.8	1218	43.2	466	16.5
308.1	8.2	1621.5	43.0	574.3	15.2
3627	9.5	16058	41.9	5600	14.6
46.8	9.8	204.5	42.8	84.6	17.7
61.2	7.7	355.6	44.4	132.4	16.5

a) Yangtze River Economic Zone includes: Shanghai, Jiangsu, Zhejiang, Anhui, Jiangxi, Hubei, Hunan, Chongqing, Sichuan, Guizhou and Yunnan.
b) Yangtze River Delta includes: Shanghai, Jiangsu, Zhejiang and Anhui.
c) National total includes the military personal.
d) The scope of data statistics for cement, crude steel, rolled steel and motor vehicles in 2023 includes industrial enterprises above designated size, which have an annual main business income of 20 million yuan or more.

25-17 民族自治地方行政区划（2023年）
Administrative Division of Ethnic Minority Autonomous Areas(2023)

省级单位名称	Provinces and Autonomous Regions	地级区划数（个）Number of Divisions at Prefecture Level (unit)	#地级市 Cities at Prefecture Level	#自治州 Autonomous Prefecture	县级区划数（个）Number of Divisions at County Level (unit)	#县级市 Cities at County Level	#自治县(旗) Autonomous Counties(Qi)
全　国	**National Total**	**77**	**38**	**30**	**714**	**89**	**120**
河　北	Hebei				6		6
内蒙古	Inner Mongolia	12	9		103	11	3
辽　宁	Liaoning				8		8
吉　林	Jilin	1		1	11	6	3
黑龙江	Heilongjiang				1		1
浙　江	Zhejiang				1		1
湖　北	Hubei	1		1	10	2	2
湖　南	Hunan	1		1	15	1	7
广　东	Guangdong				3		3
广　西	Guangxi	14	14		111	10	12
海　南	Hainan				6		6
重　庆	Chongqing				4		4
四　川	Sichuan	3		3	51	4	4
贵　州	Guizhou	3		3	46	5	11
云　南	Yunnan	8		8	78	13	29
西　藏	Xizang	7	6		74		
甘　肃	Gansu	2		2	21	2	7
青　海	Qinghai	6		6	36	5	7
宁　夏	Ningxia	5	5		22	2	
新　疆	Xinjiang	14	4	5	107	28	6

注：民族自治地方是指5个自治区、30个自治州和120个自治县(旗)，不重复计算。

a) Ethnic minority autonomous areas refer to the areas of 5 minority autonomous regions, 30 minority autonomous prefectures, and 120 minority autonomous counties(Qi), and without repetitive computation.

25-18 少数民族分布的主要地区及人口
Geographic Distribution and Population of Ethnic Minorities

人口数为2020年人口普查机器汇总数据。
Data of population are obtained from the computer tabulation of the Population Census in 2020.

民 族	Ethnic Minority	分布的主要地区	Main Geographic Distribution	人口数(人) Population (person)
蒙古族	Mongolian	内蒙古、辽宁、吉林、河北、黑龙江、新疆	Inner Mongolia, Liaoning, Jilin, Hebei, Heilongjiang and Xinjiang	6290204
回族	Hui	宁夏、甘肃、河南、新疆、青海、云南、河北、山东、安徽、辽宁、北京、内蒙古、天津、黑龙江、陕西、贵州、吉林、江苏、四川	Ningxia, Gansu, Henan, Xinjiang, Qinghai, Yunnan, Hebei, Shandong, Anhui, Liaoning, Beijing, Inner Mongolia, Tianjin, Heilongjiang, Shaanxi, Guizhou, Jilin, Jiangsu and Sichuan	11377914
藏族	Xizangan	西藏、四川、青海、甘肃、云南	Xizang, Sichuan, Qinghai, Gansu and Yunnan	7060731
维吾尔族	Uygur	新疆	Xinjiang	11774538
苗族	Miao	贵州、湖南、云南、广西、重庆、湖北、四川	Guizhou, Hunan, Yunnan, Guangxi, Chongqing, Hubei and Sichuan	11067929
彝族	Yi	云南、四川、贵州	Yunnan, Sichuan and Guizhou	9830327
壮族	Zhuang	广西、云南、广东	Guangxi, Yunnan and Guangdong	19568546
布依族	Bouyei	贵州	Guizhou	3576752
朝鲜族	Korean	吉林、黑龙江、辽宁	Jilin, Heilongjiang and Liaoning	1702479
满族	Manchu	辽宁、河北、黑龙江、吉林、内蒙古、北京	Liaoning, Hebei, Heilongjiang, Jilin, Inner Mongolia and Beijing	10423303
侗族	Dong	贵州、湖南、广西	Guizhou, Hunan and Guangxi	3495993
瑶族	Yao	广西、湖南、云南、广东	Guangxi, Hunan, Yunnan and Guangdong	3309341
白族	Bai	云南、贵州、湖南	Yunnan, Guizhou and Hunan	2091543
土家族	Tujia	湖南、湖北、重庆、贵州	Hunan, Hubei, Chongqing and Guizhou	9587732
哈尼族	Hani	云南	Yunnan	1733166
哈萨克族	Kazak	新疆	Xinjiang	1562518
傣族	Dai	云南	Yunnan	1329985
黎族	Li	海南	Hainan	1602104
傈僳族	Lisu	云南、四川	Yunnan and Sichuan	762996
佤族	Va	云南	Yunnan	430977
畲族	She	福建、浙江、江西、广东	Fujian, Zhejiang, Jiangxi and Guangdong	746385
高山族	Gaoshan	台湾、福建	Taiwan and Fujian	3479
拉祜族	Lahu	云南	Yunnan	499167
水族	Shui	贵州、广西	Guizhou and Guangxi	495928
东乡族	Dongxiang	甘肃、新疆	Gansu and Xinjiang	774947
纳西族	Naxi	云南	Yunnan	323767
景颇族	Jingpo	云南	Yunnan	160471
柯尔克孜族	Kirgiz	新疆	Xinjiang	204402
土族	Tu	青海、甘肃	Qinghai and Gansu	281928
达斡尔族	Daur	内蒙古、黑龙江	Inner Mongolia and Heilongjiang	132299
仫佬族	Mulam	广西	Guangxi	277233
羌族	Qiang	四川	Sichuan	312981
布朗族	Blang	云南	Yunnan	127345
撒拉族	Salar	青海	Qinghai	165159
毛南族	Maonan	广西	Guangxi	124092
仡佬族	Gelao	贵州	Guizhou	677521
锡伯族	Xibe	辽宁、新疆	Liaoning and Xinjiang	191911
阿昌族	Achang	云南	Yunnan	43775
普米族	Pumi	云南	Yunnan	45012
塔吉克族	Tajik	新疆	Xinjiang	50896
怒族	Nu	云南	Yunnan	36575
乌孜别克族	Ozbek	新疆	Xinjiang	12742
俄罗斯族	Russian	新疆、黑龙江	Xinjiang and Heilongjiang	16136
鄂温克族	Ewenki	内蒙古	Inner Mongolia	34617
德昂族	De'ang	云南	Yunnan	22354
保安族	Bonan	甘肃	Gansu	24434
裕固族	Yugur	甘肃	Gansu	14706
京族	Jing	广西	Guangxi	33112
塔塔尔族	Tatar	新疆	Xinjiang	3544
独龙族	Drung	云南	Yunnan	7310
鄂伦春族	Oroqen	黑龙江、内蒙古	Heilongjiang and Inner Mongolia	9168
赫哲族	Hezhen	黑龙江	Heilongjiang	5373
门巴族	Moinba	西藏	Xizang	11143
珞巴族	Lhoba	西藏	Xizang	4237
基诺族	Jino	云南	Yunnan	26025

25-19 民族自治地方国民经济与社会发展主要指标

指 标	Item	总量指标 1990	2000
人口 （万人）	**Population (10 000 persons)**		
年底总人口	Population at Year-end	15296	16818
地区生产总值	**Gross Regional Product**		**7486**
第一产业 (亿元)	Primary Industry (100 million yuan)		2022
第二产业 (亿元)	Secondary Industry (100 million yuan)		2834
第三产业 (亿元)	Tertiary Industry (100 million yuan)		2629
人均地区生产总值 （元）	**Per Capita Gross Regional Product (yuan)**		**4451**
人民生活 （元）	**People's Livelihoods (yuan)**		
城镇居民人均可支配收入	Per Capita Disposable Income of Urban Households		
农村居民人均可支配收入	Per Capita Disposable Income of Rural Households		
财政 （亿元）	**Government Finance (100 million yuan)**		
地方一般公共预算收入	General Public Budget Revenue	167	476
地方一般公共预算支出	General Public Budget Expenditure	304	1173
对外经济贸易 （亿元）	**International Trade (100 million yuan)**		
进出口总额	Total Value of Imports and Exports		
出口总额	Exports		
进口总额	Imports		
农业	**Agriculture**		
农林牧渔总产值 (亿元)	Gross Output Value of Agriculture, Forestry, Animal Husbandry and Fishery (100 million yuan)		3200
主要农畜产品产量	Output of Agricultural and Livestock Products		
粮食产量 (万吨)	Grain (10 000 tons)	5373	6381
棉花产量 (万吨)	Cotton (10 000 tons)	47	146
油料产量 (万吨)	Oil-bearing Crops (10 000 tons)	208	353
大牲畜年底头数(万头)	Number of Large Domestic Animals (year-end) (10 000 heads)	5286	5566
羊年底只数 (万只)	Number of Goats and Sheep (year-end) (10 000 heads)	11362	13076
猪年底头数 (万头)	Number of Hogs (year-end) (10 000 heads)	5668	8201
工业能源	**Industry and Energy**		
主要工业、能源产品产量	Output of Major Industrial and Energy Products		
原盐 (万吨)	Salt (10 000 tons)		
成品糖 (万吨)	Refined Sugar (10 000 tons)	223	498
天然气 (亿立方米)	Natural Gas (100 million cu.m)		
发电量 (亿千瓦时)	Electricity Generation (100 million kW·h)	739	1712
粗钢 (万吨)	Crude Steel (10 000 tons)	368	647
水泥 (万吨)	Cement (10 000 tons)	1958	5703
规模以上工业企业 （亿元）	**Industrial Enterprises above Designated Size(100 million yuan)**		
资产总计	Total Assets		
营业收入	Business Revenue		
利润总额	Total Profits		

注：1.本表速度指标中，国内生产总值及三次产业增加值均按可比价格计算；其他指标按绝对数计算。
2.2000、2010、2020为常住人口数据，其余年份为户籍人口数据。
3.原盐、成品糖、粗钢和水泥2023年数据统计范围为规模以上工业企业，即年主营业务收入2000万元及以上的工业企业。

Principal Aggregate Indicators on National Economic and Social Development in Ethnic Minority Autonomous Regions

Aggregate Indicators				速度指标(%) Growth Rates(%)							
				指数（2023年为以下各年） Indices (2023 as Percentage of the following years)					平均增长速度 Average Growth Rate		
2010	2020	2022	2023	1990	2000	2010	2020	2022	1991–2023	2001–2023	2011–2023
18531	19089	19171	19249	125.8	114.5	103.9	100.8	100.4	0.7	0.6	0.3
38989	**86925**	**106498**	**112326**		**901.7**	**265.3**	**118.6**	**105.6**		**10.0**	**7.8**
6198	13747	16443	17362		336.4	255.2	119.3	105.1		5.4	7.5
18809	29464	40939	41968		1383.0	282.7	120.1	105.5		12.1	8.3
13982	43714	49116	52996		867.7	270.9	117.5	105.8		9.8	8.0
22060	**47531**	**57449**	**58366**		**776.4**	**251.7**	**115.8**	**103.4**		**9.3**	**7.4**
	35987	39938	41948				116.6	105.0			
	13806	16237	17418				126.2	107.3			
3257	7730	8978	9948	5967.6	2092.0	305.4	128.7	110.8	13.2	14.1	9.0
10512	31255	32636	35655	11713.1	3039.9	339.2	114.1	109.2	15.5	16.0	9.9
	9397	12706	14902				158.6	117.3			
	5249	7642	8875				169.1	116.1			
	4148	5064	6026				145.3	119.0			
10374	24260	28972	29933	4665.0	935.5	288.5	123.4	103.3	12.3	10.2	8.5
8308	10637	11199	11659	217.0	182.7	140.3	109.6	104.1	2.4	2.7	2.6
248	516	539	511	1088.0	349.7	205.8	99.0	94.8	7.5	5.6	5.7
422	550	490	546	262.6	154.6	129.3	99.3	111.5	3.0	1.9	2.0
6068	5213	5692	6067	114.8	109.0	100.0	116.4	106.6	0.4	0.4	0.0
14885	15893	16879	16673	146.7	127.5	112.0	104.9	98.8	1.2	1.1	0.9
8141	6463	7551	7405	130.6	90.3	91.0	114.6	98.1	0.8	-0.4	-0.7
701	1049	1026	866			123.6	82.6	84.4			1.6
907	1024	1038	933	419.3	187.4	102.9	91.1	89.9	4.4	2.8	0.2
511	396	776	728			142.3	183.9	93.8			2.8
6730	19228	22542	23975	3245.2	1400.1	356.3	124.7	106.4	11.1	12.2	10.3
4005	9687	9524	10011	2718.1	1547.2	250.0	103.3	105.1	10.5	12.6	7.3
21653	37388	31055	32429	1656.4	568.6	149.8	86.7	104.4	8.9	7.8	3.2
45255	116385	146480	159679			352.8	137.2	109.0			10.2
37395	60415	93495	97054			259.5	160.6	103.8			7.6
4279	4349	9729	7800			182.3	179.4	80.2			4.7

a) Indices and growth rates of the following indicators are calculated at comparable prices: gross domestic product, value added of the primary, secondary and tertiary industries; Growth rates of other indicators are calculated with their values.

b) 2000, 2010 and 2020 are permanent population data, and the rest years are registered population data.

c) The scope of data statistics for salt, refined sugar, crude steel and cement in 2023 includes industrial enterprises above designated size, which have an annual main business income of 20 million yuan or more.

25-19 续表

指 标	Item	总量指标 1990	2000
建筑业	**Construction**		
建筑业总产值 (亿元)	Gross Output Value of Construction (100 million yuan)		754
施工房屋面积 (万平方米)	Floor Space of Buildings under Construction (10 000 sq.m)		9232
竣工房屋面积 (万平方米)	Floor Space of Buildings Completed (10 000 sq.m)		5326
社会消费品零售总额 (亿元)	**Total Retail Sales of Consumer Goods(100 million yuan)**		
交通运输业	**Transport**		
铁路营业里程 (万公里)	Length of Railways in Operation (10 000 km)	1.3	1.4
公路里程 (万公里)	Highways (10 000 km)	29.4	42.4
客运量 (亿人)	Passenger Traffic (100 million persons)		
货运量 (亿吨)	Freight Traffic (100 million tons)		
电信	**Telecommunication Services**		
电信业务总量 (亿元)	Business Volume of Telecommunication Services(100 million yuan)		
互联网宽带接入用户 (万户)	Broadband Subscribers of Internet (10 000 subscribers)		
金融 (亿元)	**Finance (100 million yuan)**		
金融机构各项存款余额	Deposits of Financial Institutions		7906
金融机构各项贷款余额	Loans of Financial Institutions		6548
教育	**Education**		
在校学生数 (万人)	Total Enrollment of Students (10 000 persons)		
普通高等学校	Regular Higher Education Institutions	13.6	34.2
普通高中和初中	Regular Secondary Schools	609.6	873.0
普通小学	Regular Primary Schools	1852.9	1886.0
专任教师数 (万人)	Full-time Teachers (10 000 persons)		
普通高等学校	Regular Higher Education Institutions	2.8	3.6
普通高中和初中	Regular Secondary Schools	41.5	47.9
普通小学	Regular Primary Schools	84.8	89.9
卫生	**Public Health**		
医疗卫生机构数 (万个)	Number of Health Institutions (10 000 units)		
卫生技术人员数 (万人)	Health Technical Personnel (10 000 persons)	50.0	48.5
医疗卫生机构床位 (万张)	Number of Beds in Health Institutions (10 000 beds)	33.2	36.1
文化	**Culture**		
出版数量	Publications		
图书 (万册)	Books (10 000 copies)	30166	42310
期刊 (万册)	Periodicals (10 000 copies)	6552	7018
报纸 (万份)	Newspapers (10 000 copies)	79120	123277
社会服务	**Social Services**		
福利类收养单位床位数(万张)	Beds of Social Welfare Institutions (10 000 beds)		
城乡最低生活保障人数(万人)	Number of Persons Receiving Minimum Living Allowance in Urban and Rural Areas (10 000 persons)		

continued

Aggregate Indicators				速度指标(%) Growth Rates(%)							
2010	2020	2022	2023	指数（2023年为以下各年）Indices (2023 as Percentage of the following years)					平均增长速度 Average Growth Rate		
				1990	2000	2010	2020	2022	1991–2023	2001–2023	2011–2023
5203	13940	16845	16532		2191.7	317.7	118.6	98.1		14.4	9.3
35052	61322	64620	67468		730.8	192.5	110.0	104.4		9.0	5.2
15418	19101	18462	16942		318.1	109.9	88.7	91.8		5.2	0.7
11686	**27551**	**30017**	**32194**			**275.5**	**116.9**	**107.3**			**8.1**
2.1	3.6	3.9	4.0	302.2	277.3	186.4	110.5	101.8	3.4	4.5	4.9
91.2	140.7	150.5	151.4	515.4	357.3	166.0	107.6	100.6	5.1	5.7	4.0
	13.1	9.6	18.3				139.3	191.4			
	63.5	74.7	81.2				127.8	108.7			
	14703	2034	2035				13.8	100.1			
	5532	6722	7444				134.5	110.7			
46622	133128	160710	174118		2202.4	373.5	130.8	108.3		14.4	10.7
30579	121330	148402	163984		2504.3	536.3	135.2	110.5		15.0	13.8
161.9	279.8	327.6	351.8	2587.1	1028.8	217.3	125.8	107.4	10.4	10.7	6.2
1050.4	1108.2	1172.7	1191.3	195.4	136.5	113.4	107.5	101.6	2.1	1.4	1.0
1536.3	1621.5	1674.6	1670.7	90.2	88.6	108.8	103.0	99.8	-0.3	-0.5	0.6
9.5	13.7	15.1	16.7	597.6	459.8	176.7	122.5	110.7	5.6	6.9	4.5
67.4	81.0	87.5	91.1	219.5	190.2	135.1	112.4	104.1	2.4	2.8	2.3
90.7	98.7	102.1	102.2	120.5	113.6	112.6	103.5	100.1	0.6	0.6	0.9
	15.0	14.9	14.7				97.9	98.7			
68.1	127.1	143.8	154.1	308.3	317.7	226.5	121.3	107.2	3.5	5.2	6.5
55.7	112.6	123.3	128.1	385.9	354.7	229.9	113.8	103.9	4.2	5.7	6.6
43099	70656	76620	80903	268.2	191.2	187.7	114.5	105.6	3.0	2.9	5.0
6962	6425	6201	5945	90.7	84.7	85.4	92.5	95.9	-0.3	-0.7	-1.2
174848	152344	134171	129368	163.5	104.9	74.0	84.9	96.4	1.5	0.2	-2.3
27.3	43.1	48.4	48.9			179.1	113.4	101.0			4.6
1907	1252	1144	1145			60.0	91.4	100.1			-3.9

主要统计指标解释

供水综合生产能力 指按供水设施取水、净化、送水、出厂输水干管等环节设计能力计算的综合生产能力。计算时，以四个环节中最薄弱的环节为主确定能力。

供水管道长度 指从送水泵至各类用户引入管之间所有市政管道的长度。不包括新安装尚未使用、水厂内以及用户建筑物内的管道。

城市供水总量 指报告期供水企业(单位)供出的全部水量。包括有效供水量和漏损水量。

生活用水 包括公共服务用水和居民家庭用水。公共服务用水指为城区社会公共生活服务的用水。包括行政事业单位、部队营区和公共设施服务、批发零售业、住宿餐饮业以及社会服务业等单位的用水。居民家庭用水指城市范围内所有居民家庭的日常生活用水。包括城市居民、农民家庭、公共供水站用水。

生产用水 指在城区范围内生产、运营的农、林、牧、渔业、工业、建筑业、交通运输业等单位在生产、运营过程中的用水。

供水普及率 指报告期末城区用水人口数与城市人口总数的比率。计算公式：

$$供水普及率=\frac{城区用水人口（含暂住人口）}{城区人口+城区暂住人口}\times 100\%$$

人工煤气生产能力 指报告期末人工燃气生产厂制气、净化、输送等环节的综合生产能力，不包括备用设备能力。一般按设计能力计算，当实际生产能力大于设计能力时，应按实际测定的生产能力计算。测定时应以制气、净化、输送三个环节中最薄弱的环节为主。

供气管道长度 指报告期末从气源厂压缩机的出口或门站出口至各类用户引入管之间的全部已经通气、投入使用的管道长度。不包括新安装尚未使用，煤气生产厂、输配站、液化气储存站、灌瓶站、储配站、气化站、混气站、供应站等厂(站)内，以及用户建筑物内的管道。

城市供气总量 指报告期燃气企业(单位)向用户供应的燃气数量。包括销售量和损失量。

燃气普及率 指报告期末城区使用燃气的城市人口数与城市人口总数的比率。其中燃气包括人工煤气、天然气、液化石油气三种。计算公式为：

$$燃气普及率=\frac{城区用气人口(含暂住人口)}{城区人口+城区暂住人口}\times 100\%$$

城市供热能力 指供热企业(单位)向城市热用户输送热能的设计能力。

城市供热总量 指在报告期供热企业(单位)向城市热用户输送全部蒸汽和热水的总热量。

城市供热管道长度 指从各类热源到热用户建筑物接入口之间的全部蒸汽和热水的管道长度。不包括各类热源厂内部的管道长度。

道路长度 指道路长度和与道路相通的桥梁、隧道的长度，按车行道中心线计算。

城市桥梁 指为跨越天然或人工障碍物而修建的构筑物。包括跨河桥、立交桥、人行天桥以及人行地下通道等。

城市排水管道长度 指所有市政排水总管、干管、支管、检查井及连接井进出口等长度之和。

城市污水日处理能力 指污水处理厂(或污水处理装置)每昼夜处理污水量的设计能力。

城市绿地面积 指报告期末用作园林和绿化的各种绿地面积。包括公园绿地、防护绿地、广场用地、附属绿地和位于建成区范围内的区域绿地面积。

公园绿地 向公众开放，以游憩为主要功能，兼具生态、景观、文教和应急避险等功能，有一定游憩和服务设施的绿地。

清扫保洁面积 指报告期末对城市道路和公共场所(主要包括城市行车道、人行道、车行隧道、人行过街地下通道、道路附属绿地、地铁站、高架路、人行过街天桥、立交桥、广场、停车场及其他设施等）进行清扫保洁的面积。一天清扫保洁多次的，按清扫保洁面积最大的一次计算。

市容环卫专用车辆设备 指用于环境卫生作业、监察的专用车辆和设备，包括用于道路清扫、冲洗、洒水、除雪、垃圾粪便清运、市容监察以及与其配套使用的车辆和设备。

每万人拥有公共汽电车辆 指按城市人口计算的每万人平均拥有的公共汽电车辆标台数。

Explanatory Notes on Main Statistical Indicators

Production Capacity of Water Supply refers to the designed overall production capacity of water facilities, covering the four segments of water collection, purification, conveyance, and outflow through trunk pipelines. The capacity is determined mainly on the weakest of the above-mentioned four segments.

Length of Water Supply Pipelines refers to the total length of all municipal pipelines between the water pumps and the user service pipes, excluding pipelines newly installed but not in use yet, pipelines in the water factories, and pipelines in the users' buildings.

Total Volume of Urban Water Supply refers to the total volume of water supplied by water-works (units) during the reference period, including both the effective water supply and loss during the water supply.

Consumption of Water for Daily Use includes consumption of water for public service use and consumption of water for household use. Consumption of water for public service use refers to water consumption for public service in the urban areas, including water consumption of administrative institutions, military barracks, public facilities, wholesale and retail, accommodation and catering industries and social service industry, etc. Consumption of water for household use refers to consumption of water for daily life of all households in cities, including households of urban residents and farmers, and public water supply stations.

Consumption of Water for Production Use refers to water consumption in the process of production and operation by production and operation units of agriculture, forestry, animal husbandry, fisheries, manufacturing, construction, transport, etc. in urban areas.

Coverage Rate of Urban Population with Access to Tap Water refers to the ratio of the urban population with access to tap water to the total urban population at the end of reference period. The formula is:

$$\text{Coverage of urban population with access to tap water} = \frac{\text{Urban population with access to tap water}}{\text{Urban population}} \times 100\%$$

Production Capacity of Gaswork Gas refers to the overall production capacity of the urban gasworks in gas generation, purification and delivery at the end of the reference period, excluding capacity of the reserved facilities. In general, it is determined by the designed capacity, and when actual production capacity is larger than the designed capacity, the capacity is determined by the actual measurement on the weakest segment in the production, purification and delivery.

Length of Gas Pipelines refers to the total length of pipelines in use between the outlet of the compressor of gas-work or outlet of gas stations and the leading pipe of users, excluding pipelines newly installed but not in use yet, pipelines within gasworks, delivery stations, LPG storage stations, refilling stations, gas-mixing stations and supply stations, and pipelines in the users' buildings.

Volume of Gas Supply refers to the total volume of gas provided to users by gas-producing enterprises (units) during the reporting period, including the volume sold and the volume lost.

Coverage Rate of Urban Population with Access to Gas refers to the ratio of the urban population with access to gas to the total urban population at the end of the reference period. Gas here includes gaswork gas, natural gas and liquefied petroleum gas. The formula is:

$$\text{Coverage rate of urban population with access to gas} = \frac{\text{Urban population with access to gas}}{\text{Urban population}} \times 100\%$$

Heating Capacity in Urban Areas refers to the designed capacity of heating enterprises (units) in supplying heating energy to urban users during the reference period.

Quantity of Heat Supplied in Urban Areas refers to the total quantity of heat from steam and hot water supplied to urban users by heating enterprises (units) during the reference period.

Length of Urban Heating Pipelines refers to the total length of steam or hot water pipelines for sources of heat to the leading pipelines of the buildings of the users, excluding internal pipelines in heat generating enterprises.

Length of Paved Roads refers to the length of roads with paved surface, including bridges and tunnels connected with roads. Length of the roads is measured by the central lines.

Urban Bridges refer to bridges built to cross over natural or man-made barriers, including bridges over rivers, overpasses for traffic and for pedestrians, underpasses for pedestrians, etc.

Length of Urban Sewage Pipes refers to the total length of municipal general drainage, trunks, branch and inspection wells, connection wells, inlets and outlets, etc.

Daily Disposal Capacity of Urban Sewage refers to the designed 24-hour capacity of sewage disposal by the sewage treatment works or facilities.

Area of Green Space refers to the total area occupied for green projects at the end of the reference period, including public recreational green space, protection green land, land for squares, green land attached to institutions, and other green areas.

Public Recreational Green Space refers to green areas open to the public for amusement and rest with the facilities of amusement, rest and services. Its function also includes improving ecology, beautifying landscape, education and preventing and reducing disaster.

Area under Cleaning Program refers to the area which

are regularly cleaned at urban roads and public places (including urban roadways, pedestrian walkways, vehicle tunnels, pedestrian underpasses, underground railway stations, lifted roads, pedestrians walk bridges, overpasses, plazas, parking lots and other facilities), at the end of the reference period,. If the cleaning is conducted at a location several times a day, the area that is cleaned with the largest space will be taken.

Vehicles and Facilities Dedicated to Urban Cleaning and Environmental Sanitation refer to vehicles and facilities dedicated for use in the operation, management and monitoring of environmental sanitation work. They include vehicles for road cleaning, washing, showering, ice removal, disposal of garbage and human wastes, sanitation monitoring and related activities.

Public Buses and Trolley Buses per 10000 Population refers to the number of public buses and trolley buses, calculated on basis of per 10000 urban population.

26

香港特别行政区主要社会经济指标

Main Social and Economic Indicators of Hong Kong Special Administrative Region

简要说明

一、本章资料反映香港特别行政区主要社会、经济发展情况。内容包括：土地、人口、就业、国民收入、国际收支平衡、工业、能源、建筑、运输、对外贸易、政府收支及金融、教育、房屋、卫生、社会保障等方面。

二、本章由香港特别行政区政府统计处向有关政府决策局／部门及公营机构搜集数据，国家统计局国际统计信息中心负责整理、编辑。

三、在统计工作方面，按中华人民共和国“香港特别行政区基本法”的有关原则，香港特别行政区保留其单独运作的统计系统，并负责编制和发布反映香港特别行政区情况的统计数据。由于香港和内地在使用统计名词及概念方面会有所不同，读者在比较两地数据时，请参考本章末的“主要统计指标解释”。

四、香港特别行政区是单独的关税地区，香港与内地之间的贸易，亦需办理进出口报关。在贸易统计方面，香港特别行政区对外贸易统计数据亦包括香港特别行政区与内地的贸易。

五、在外汇统计及与之有关的各方面，港币是香港特别行政区的法定货币，因此，除港币以外的货币（包括人民币）均视作外币。

六、更详细的统计资料及有关的技术细节，可参阅香港特别行政区政府统计处出版的《香港统计月刊》、《香港统计年刊》及各专题统计出版物。

七、本章节表中的符号使用说明：

本章节表中使用的符号含义如下：“-”表示不适用；“空格”表示暂时没有数字；“#”表示临时数字；“§”表示由于数值较不显著，数字不予公布；“@”表示数字在日后会作出修订。

Brief Introduction

I. Data in this chapter show main social and economic developments of the Hong Kong Special Administrative Region (HKSAR), including data on land, population, employment, National Income, Balance of Payments, industry, energy, construction, transportation, external trade, government accounts and finance, education, housing, health and social security.

II. All data in this chapter are collected from the related government bureaux/departments and public organisations by the Census and Statistics Department, the Government of HKSAR, and further tabulated or edited by the International Statistical Information Centre of the National Bureau of Statistics.

III. According to the Basic Law of HKSAR of the People's Republic of China, HKSAR maintains its independent statistical system, and compiles and disseminates statistics on the Region. As Hong Kong and the mainland of China use different statistical concepts, definitions and terminologies, users are advised to make reference of The Explanation Notes on Main Statistical Indicators at the end of this chapter when using and comparing data of the mainland of China and HKSAR.

IV. As Hong Kong is a separate custom territory, trade between Hong Kong and the mainland of China needs customs declaration procedures. In terms of trade statistics, data on Hong Kong's imports and exports include Hong Kong's trade with the mainland of China.

V. As Hong Kong dollar is the legal tender in HKSAR, all other currencies (including Renminbi) are regarded as foreign currencies in compiling foreign exchange statistics and related statistics.

VI. For more detailed statistics and technical details, users are advised to read *Hong Kong Monthly Digest of Statistics, Hong Kong Annual Digest of Statistics* and other publications compiled by the Census and Statistics Department, the Government of HKSAR.

VII. Notations used in this chapter:

Some notations used in this chapter are not agreed with those used in China Statistical Yearbook, but with Hong Kong publications. "-" indicates not applicable. "(blank)" indicates not yet available. "#" indicates provisional figure. "§" indicates figure is not released due to relatively insignificant magnitude. "@" indicates figure is subject to revision later on.

26-1 主要统计指标概况
Summary of Key Statistics

项目	Item	2019	2020	2021	2022	2023
香港陆地面积①（平方公里）	**Land Area of Hong Kong① (sq.km)**	**1106**	**1110**	**1114**	**1114**	**1115**
香港岛	Hong Kong Island	81	81	81	81	81
九龙	Kowloon	47	47	47	47	47
新界	New Territories	978	982	985	986	986
人口	**Population**					
年中人口（万人）	Mid-year Population (10 000 persons)	750.8	748.1	741.3	734.6	753.6
粗出生率（‰）	Crude Birth Rate (‰)	7.0	5.8	5.0	4.4	4.4 #
粗死亡率（‰）	Crude Death Rate (‰)	6.5	6.8	6.9	8.7	7.2 #
婴儿死亡率（‰）(按每千名登记活产婴儿计算)	Infant Mortality Rate (‰) (per 1 000 Registered Live Births)	1.5	1.9	1.4	1.8	1.4 #
劳工	**Labour**					
劳动人口（万人）	Labour Force (10 000 persons)	398.8	391.8	387.0	377.6	382.2
劳动人口参与率（%）	Labour Force Participation Rate (%)	60.7	59.7	59.4	58.2	57.3
失业率（%）	Unemployment Rate (%)	2.9	5.8	5.2	4.3	2.9
就业人数（万人）	Number of Employed Persons (10 000 persons)	387.1	369.1	367.0	361.3	371.0
选定行业的就业人数（万人）	Number of Employed Persons in Selected Industries (10 000 persons)					
制造	Manufacturing	10.5	10.4	9.4	9.2	8.9
建筑	Construction	33.9	31.1	32.6	33.2	34.9
进出口贸易及批发	Import/Export Trade and Wholesale	39.1	33.1	31.6	31.9	31.2
零售、住宿及膳食服务②	Retail, Accommodation and Food Services②	61.2	52.0	51.6	51.1	53.7
运输、仓库、邮政及速递服务、资讯及通讯	Transportation, Storage, Postal and Courier Services, Information and Communications	45.2	43.8	43.0	41.2	42.2
金融、保险、地产、专业及商用服务	Financing, Insurance, Real Estate, Professional and Business Services	84.0	85.3	86.2	83.0	84.9
公共行政、社会及个人服务	Public Administration, Social and Personal Services	110.8	111.1	110.2	109.1	112.8
实际工资指数③（1992年9月=100）	Real Wage index③ (September 1992=100)	123.6	126.4	125.0	125.6	126.9
对外贸易	**External Trade**					
商品贸易	**Merchandise Trade**					
进口（亿港元）	Imports (HKD 100 million)	44154	42698	53078	49275	46450
整体出口（亿港元）	Total Exports (HKD 100 million)	39887	39275	49607	45316	41774
服务贸易	**Trade in Services**					
服务出口④（亿港元）	Exports of Services④ (HKD 100 million)	7991	5192	6151	6505	7717 @
服务进口④（亿港元）	Imports of Services④ (HKD 100 million)	6342	4263	4800	4952	6211 @
国民收入及国际收支平衡	**National Income and Balance of Payments**					
本地生产总值	**Gross Domestic Product (GDP)**					
按2022年环比物量计算⑤	In Chained (2022) Dollars⑤					
年增长率（%）	Annual Growth Rate (%)	-1.7	-6.5	6.5	-3.7 @	3.3 @
本地生产总值（亿港元）	GDP (HKD 100 million)	29314	27396	29164	28090 @	29010 @
人均本地生产总值（港元）	Per Capita GDP (HKD)	390448	366206	393413	382377 @	384950 @
按当年价格计算	At Current Market Prices					
年增长率（%）	Annual Growth Rate (%)	0.3	-5.9	7.2	-2.1 @	6.1 @
本地生产总值（亿港元）	GDP (HKD 100 million)	28450	26758	28680	28090 @	29816 @
人均本地生产总值（港元）	Per Capita GDP (HKD)	378937	357679	386879	382377 @	395642 @
本地居民总收入	**Gross National Income (GNI)**					
按当年价格计算	At Current Market Prices					
本地居民总收入（亿港元）	GNI (HKD 100 million)	29887	28319	30667	29948 @	32493 @
人均本地居民总收入（港元）	Per Capita GNI (HKD)	398079	378542	413687	407665 @	431161 @
对外初次收入流量净值(亿港元)	Net External Primary Income Flows (HKD 100 million)	1437	1561	1987	1858	2677 @
国际收支平衡	**Balance of Payments**					
经常账户（亿港元）	Current Account (HKD 100 million)	1665	1870	3394	2861 @	2732 @
资本账户（亿港元）	Capital Account (HKD 100 million)	-7	-1	-104	12 @	59 @
金融账户（亿港元）	Financial Account (HKD 100 million)	2368	2438	3632	2768 @	2738 @
净误差及遗漏（亿港元）	Net Errors and Omissions (HKD 100 million)	710	569	342	-105 @	-53 @
整体的国际收支（亿港元）	Overall Balance of Payments (HKD 100 million)	-89	2630	-91	-3672 @	-799 @
国际投资头寸⑥	**International Investment Position⑥**					
国际投资头寸净值⑦（亿港元）	Net International Investment Position⑦ (HKD 100 million)	122972	164519	164633	138142	139394 @
对外金融资产（亿港元）	External Financial Assets (HKD 100 million)	439324	487770	499180	474032	483017 @
对外金融负债（亿港元）	External Financial Liabilities (HKD 100 million)	316353	323252	334547	335890	343623 @

26-1 续表 1 continued

项　目	Item	2019	2020	2021	2022	2023
消费物价指数	**Consumer Price Indices**					
(2019年10月至2020年9月=100)	(Oct. 2019-Sep. 2020 = 100)					
综合消费物价指数	Composite Consumer Price Index	99.6	99.9	101.4	103.3	105.5
甲类消费物价指数	Consumer Price Index (A)	100.5	99.8	102.7	104.9	107.3
乙类消费物价指数	Consumer Price Index (B)	99.2	99.8	100.8	102.5	104.6
丙类消费物价指数	Consumer Price Index (C)	99.1	99.9	100.8	102.6	104.7
工业生产	**Industrial Production**					
工业生产指数 (2015年=100)	Index of Industrial Production (year of 2015=100)					
制造业	Manufacturing	101.7	95.8	101.0	101.2	105.0
工业电力消费量 (太焦耳)	Industrial Electricity Consumption (Terajoule)	10815	10672	11163	11087	11126
工业煤气消费量 (太焦耳)	Industrial Gas Consumption (Terajoule)	1824	1653	1596	1704	1743
房屋及物业	**Housing and Property**					
永久性居住屋宇单位⑧ (万个)	Number of Permanent Living Quarters⑧(10 000 units)					
公营租住房屋⑨	Public Rental Housing⑨	83.01	83.21	84.31	85.07	85.86
资助出售单位⑩	Subsidised Sale Flats⑩	41.88	42.41	42.98	44.17	44.86
私人永久性房屋⑩	Private Permanent Housing⑩	160.36	164.15	166.99	169.19	171.34
总计	Total	285.25	289.76	294.28	298.42	302.06
新落成私人楼宇	Newly Completed Private Buildings					
楼宇数目 (栋)	Number of Blocks (number)	659	628	361	490	533
实用楼面面积 (万平方米)	Usable Floor Area (10 000 sq.m.)					
住宅⑪	Residential⑪	47.4	70.5	45.3	71.2	39.5
非住宅	Non-residential	67.0	38.3	27.8	109.1	81.1
获批准可动工兴建私人楼宇 (栋)	Private Buildings with Consent to Commence Work (number of blocks)					
初次呈交	First Submission	254	205	164	136	101
重大修改	Major Revision	149	174	148	87	142
政府收支、金融、保险 (亿港元)	**Government Accounts, Finance and Insurance (HKD 100 million)**					
政府期末储备结余⑫⑬	Government's Closing Reserve Balances⑫⑬	11603	9278	9571	8348	7346
政府收入总额⑬⑭	Total Government Revenue⑬⑭	5909	5642	6936	6221	5494
政府开支总额⑬⑭	Total Government Expenditure⑬⑭	6078	8161	6933	8105	7213
货币供应量M_3	Money Supply M_3					
港元⑮	Hong Kong Dollar⑮	74547	79370	80574	81090	82628
外币⑯	Foreign Currency⑯	73317	77070	82535	84604	89712
总计	Total	147864	156440	163109	165694	172341
港汇指数(贸易总值(进口及整体出口)加权) (2020年1月=100)⑰	Effective Exchange Rate Indices for the Hong Kong Dollar (trade (import and export) - weighted) (January 2020=100)⑰	99.4	100.0	95.5	100.1	103.4
运输、通讯、旅游	**Transport, Communications and Tourism**					
进出香港货物	Inward and Outward Movements of Cargo					
总卸下 (万吨)	Total Discharged (10 000 tons)	18567	18380	15011	12936	12355
总装上 (万吨)	Total Loaded (10 000 tons)	10276	8900	8842	7601	6923
集装箱吞吐量(万标准集装箱)	Container Throughput (10 000 TEUs)	1830	1797	1780	1669	1440
电话服务 (万条操作线路)	Telephone Services (10 000 working lines)	405	393	383	367	349
访港旅客 (万人次)	Visitor Arrivals (10 000 person-times)	5591.3	356.9	9.1	60.5	3400.0
教育 (人)	**Education (person)**					
小学学生人数	Student Enrolment in Primary Schools	373228	364257	348994	333551	325564
中学学生人数⑱	Student Enrolment in Secondary Schools⑱	328743	330305	327326	322563	329398
教资会资助大学学生人数	Student Enrolment in UGC-funded Universities	189484	186882	191240	195992	203579
卫生	**Health**					
医生 (人)	Doctors (person)	15004	15298	15546	15815	16180
注册中医 (人)	Registered Chinese Medicine Practitioners (person)	7582	7919	8080	8296	8423
病床 (张)	Hospital Beds (bed)	35347	35715	36126	36564	36782
社会保障	**Social Security**					
综合社会保障援助⑫	Comprehensive Social Security Assistance (CSSA)⑫					
个案数目 (个)	Number of Cases (case)	222691	223792	216688	205592	199205
发放款项 (亿港元)	Amount (HKD 100 million)	227	229	229	232	225 #
公共福利金⑫	Social Security Allowances (SSA)⑫					
个案数目 (个)	Number of Cases (case)	1015187	1076990	1135572	1206321	1277093
发放款项 (亿港元)	Amount (HKD 100 million)	366	382	398	437	484 #
交通意外伤亡援助⑫	Traffic Accident Victims Assistance⑫					
获批个案数目 (个)	Number of Cases Authorised for Payment (case)	6820	9013	8320	8848	9146

26-1 续表 2 continued

注：①2014年起的数字是该年10月底的数据。面积包括不在区议会分区内的落马州河套。

②零售、住宿及膳食服务业合计通常被称为「与消费及旅游相关行业」。

③实际工资指数是按其名义指数扣除以2019/20年为基期的甲类消费物价指数而计算出来。

④数字已采纳《2010年国际服务贸易统计手册》内最新的国际建议。

⑤以环比物量计算的本地生产总值及其组成部分的参照年，已由2021年重订为2022年。重订参照年会影响以环比物量计算的数值，但不会影响其变动率。

⑥期末头寸。

⑦国际投资头寸净值是对外金融资产总值与对外金融负债总值之间的差额。

⑧数字包括所有住宅屋宇单位及非住宅楼宇内已知作居所用途的屋宇单位，但不包括非住宅用途、酒店及院舍内供住院或在囚人士居住的屋宇单位。

⑨数字不包括香港房屋委员会售出的公营租住房屋单位。

⑩数字包括香港房屋委员会、香港房屋协会及市区重建局售出而不可在公开市场买卖的屋宇单位。可在公开市场买卖的资助出售单位则归类为私人永久性房屋。

⑪数字包括住宅楼宇内用作非住宅用途的实用楼面面积，例如：会所/娱乐设施、管理员办事处/宿舍、电机房等。

⑫数字是以相应的财政年度为根据。例如2023年的数字代表2023/24财政年度终结时的数字。

⑬2023/24年度的数字有待审计署署长核实。

⑭数字不包括“政府一般收入帐目及各基金之转拨”。

⑮所列数字已包括外币掉期存款。

⑯所列数字已扣除外币掉期存款。《中华人民共和国香港特别行政区基本法》说明，港元是香港特别行政区的法定货币。外币指港元以外的其他货币，因而人民币亦视作外币。

⑰由2022年1月3日起公布的重订基期后数列。数字是指年内每日电汇或现钞收市中间兑换价的平均值。

⑱数字包括日、夜间课程。

Notes: ①Figures for 2014 onward are as at end-October and include land area of Lok Ma Chau Loop which is not covered in District Council districts

②The retail, accommodation and food services industries as a whole is generally referred to as the consumption- and tourism-related segment.

③The Real Wage Index is derived by deflating the corresponding nominal index by the 2019/20-based Consumer Price Index (A).

④Figures have incorporated the latest international recommendations given in the Manual on Statistics of International Trade in Services 2010.

⑤The reference year for the chain volume measures of GDP and its components has been revised from 2021 to 2022. Re-referencing affects the levels, but not the rates of change, of the chain volume measures.

⑥Position as at end of period.

⑦Net International Investment Position is the difference between total external financial assets and total external financial liabilities.

⑧Figures include all quarters used for residential purpose as well as quarters known to be used for residential purposes in non-residential buildings. Quarters known to be used for non-residential purpose and those in hotels and accommodation used for inmates of institutions are excluded.

⑨Figures exclude public rental housing flats sold by the Hong Kong Housing Authority.

⑩Subsidised sale flats include quarters sold by the Hong Kong Housing Authority, Hong Kong Housing Society and Urban Renewal Authority that cannot be traded in the open market. Those flats that can be traded in the open market are classified as private permanent housing.

⑪Figures include usable floor area in residential buildings for non-domestic use, such as club house/recreational facilities, caretakers' office/quarters, transformer room, etc.

⑫Figures are for the corresponding financial year. For example, figures for 2023 represent those as at end of the financial year 2023/24.

⑬Figures for 2023/24 are subject to audit by the Director of Audit.

⑭Figures exclude “Transfers between the General Revenue Account and the Funds”.

⑮Figures are adjusted to include foreign currency swap deposits.

⑯Figures are adjusted to exclude foreign currency swap deposits. Hong Kong dollar is the legal tender in the Hong Kong Special Administrative Region, as stated in "The Basic Law of the Hong Kong Special Administrative Region of the People's Republic of China". Foreign currency refers to any currency other than the Hong Kong currency. Accordingly, Chinese Renminbi is also treated as foreign currency.

⑰Rebased series has been released as from 3 January 2022. Figures are the averages of the daily closing middle-market telegraphic transfer rates or notes rates for the year.

⑱Figures include both day and evening courses.

26–2 土地用途分布情况
Land Usage

单位：平方公里 (sq. km)

类　别	Class	2019	2020	2021	2022	2023
住宅	**Residential**					
私人住宅①	Private Residential①	26	27	27	27	27
公营房屋②	Public Residential②	17	17	17	18	18
乡郊居所③	Rural Settlement③	35	35	35	35	35
商业	**Commercial**					
商业/商贸和办公室	Commercial/Business and Office	5	5	5	5	5
工业	**Industrial**					
工业用地	Industrial Land	7	7	6	6	6
工业村/科技园	Industrial Estates/Science and Technology Parks	3	3	3	3	3
货仓和露天贮物	Warehouse and Open Storage	17	17	17	16	17
机构/休憩	**Institutional/Open Space**					
政府、机构和社区设施	Government, Institutional and Community Facilities	25	25	25	27	26
休憩及康乐④	Open Space and Recreation④	28	28	29	29	28
运输	**Transportation**					
道路及运输设施	Roads and Transport Facilities	46	47	47	47	47
铁路	Railways	4	4	4	4	4
机场	Airport	13	13	13	16	16
港口设施	Port Facilities	4	4	4	4	4
其它都市或已建设土地	**Other Urban or Built-up Land**					
坟场/殡殓设施	Cemeteries/Funeral Facilities	9	9	9	9	9
公用事业设施	Utilities	9	9	9	9	9
空置/正在进行建筑工程的土地	Vacant Land/Construction in Progress	15	18	22	18	21
其它	Others	12	12	12	12	12
农业	**Agriculture**					
农地	Agricultural Land	50	49	49	48	48
鱼塘/基围	Fish Ponds/Gei Wais	16	16	16	16	16
林地/灌丛/草地/湿地	**Woodland/Shrubland/Grassland/Wetland**					
林地	Woodland	276	289	290	334	334
灌丛	Shrubland	264	254	255	194	186
草地	Grassland	187	183	180	199	204
红树林/沼泽	Mangrove/Swamp	6	6	6	6	6
荒地	**Barren Land**					
劣地	Badland	2	2	2	2	3
岩岸	Rocky Shore	4	4	4	3	4
水体	**Water Bodies**					
水塘	Reservoirs	25	25	25	25	25
河道和明渠	Streams and Nullahs	6	6	6	6	6
总计⑤	**Total⑤**	**1111**	**1114**	**1117**	**1118**	**1119**

注：数字为该年年底的数字。
2023年的土地用途数据已根据2023年11月的卫星图像(©AIRBUS DS (2023))、截至2023年年底由规划署内部调查所得的资料，以及各政府部门的其它相关资料而更新。由于部分土地用途分类的定义和方法不时更新，所以2023年的数字未必能与往年的数字直接比较。
①包括私人开发商发展的住宅用地(乡郊居所、资助房屋和过渡性房屋除外)。
②包括资助房屋和过渡性房屋。
③包括村屋和临时搭建物。
④包括公园、运动场、游乐场和康乐设施。
⑤包括高水位线下约4平方公里的红树林和沼泽。

Notes: Figures are as at end of the year.
The land use data of 2023 was compiled using satellite images dated November 2023 (©AIRBUS DS (2023)), in-house survey information of the Planning Department up to 2023 year-end and other relevant information from various government departments. As definitions of some land use classes and methodology are updated from time to time, the figures of 2023 may not be comparable directly to those provided in previous years.
①Including residential area developed by private developers (excluding rural settlements, subsidised housing and transitional housing).
②Including subsidised housing and transitional housing.
③Including village houses and temporary structures.
④Including parks, stadiums, playgrounds and recreational facilities.
⑤Including about 4 km^2 of mangrove and swamp below the High Water Mark.

26–3 按地区类别及路边情况划分的空气质量(2023年)
Air Quality by Area Type and Roadside Condition (2023)

单位：微克／立方米 (microgram/cu.m.)

地区类别／路边	Area Type/ Roadside	全年平均空气污染浓度 Annual Average Air Pollutant Concentrations			
		二氧化硫 Sulphur Dioxide	二氧化氮 Nitrogen Dioxide	微细悬浮粒子 Fine Suspended Particulates	可吸入悬浮粒子 Respirable Suspended Particulates
市区①	Urban①	4	36	14	24
新市镇②	New Town②	4	31	15	26
郊区③	Rural③	4	8	12	22
路边④	Roadside④	5	66	20	32

注：①包括葵涌、中西区、深水埗、观塘、东区、荃湾、将军澳及南区。
②包括大埔、沙田、元朗、东涌、屯门及北区。
③包括塔门。
④包括铜锣湾、中环及旺角。

Notes: ①Includes Kwai Chung, Central/Western, Sham Shui Po, Kwun Tong, Eastern, Tsuen Wan, Tseung Kwan O and Southern.
②Includes Tai Po, Sha Tin, Yuen Long, Tung Chung, Tuen Mun and North.
③Includes Tap Mun.
④Includes Causeway Bay, Central and Mong Kok.

26–4 按种类划分的平均固体废物量
Average Solid Waste Quantities by Type

单位：吨（每日计） (tonnes per day)

种类	Type	2018	2019	2020	2021	2022
于堆填区弃置的固体废物	Solid Waste Disposed of at Landfills					
都市固体废物①	Municipal Solid Waste①					
家居②	Domestic②	6712	6554	6844	6992	6797
工商业③	Commercial & industrial③	4716	4503	3965	4365	4332
小计	Sub-total	11428	11057	10809	11358	11128
整体建筑废物④	Overall Construction Waste④	4081	3946	3418	3646	4128
特殊废物⑤	Special Waste ⑤	587	635	513	529	469
总计	**Total**	**16096**	**15637**	**14739**	**15533**	**15725**
已回收的都市固体废物⑥	Municipal Solid Waste Recovered ⑥	4870	4491	4201	5044	5241

注：①都市固体废物包括运往弃置设施的家居废物及工商业废物，但不包括建筑废物及已回收的都市固体废物。
②家居废物包括在住宅及公众地方所产生的废物，包括住宅大厦、公共垃圾桶、街道、本港海域及郊野公园收集的废物。
③工商业废物包括商店、食肆、酒店、办公室、私人屋苑街市及所有工业活动产生的废物，而建筑及拆卸废物、化学废物或其他特殊废物除外。
④在堆填区弃置的整体建筑废物包括由建筑活动所产生的废物或剩余物料，亦包括在建筑地盘以外设立的混凝土配料厂和水泥／砂浆生产厂所产生的废弃混凝土，但不包括可在建筑地盘重用或作填海工程用途的惰性物料。
⑤特殊废物包括弃置于堆填区的动物尸体、屠房废物、报废货物、滤水厂及污水处理后的污泥、污水处理厂的隔滤物、禽畜废物、医疗废物及化学废物。
⑥都市固体废物回收后会在本地或香港以外地方循环再造。

Notes : ①Municipal solid waste includes domestic waste and commercial & industrial waste delivered to disposal facilities but excludes construction waste and recovered municipal solid waste.
②Domestic waste covers solid waste coming from households and public areas, including waste collected from residential buildings, litter bins, streets, marine areas and country parks.
③Commercial & industrial waste covers solid waste coming from shops, restaurants, hotels, offices, markets in private housing estates as well as all industrial activities, but does not include construction and demolition waste, chemical waste or other special waste.
④Overall construction waste disposed of at landfills includes waste or surplus materials arising from construction activities and waste concrete that is generated from concrete batching plants and cement plaster/mortar manufacturing plants not set up inside construction sites, but excludes inert materials reused in construction sites or as fill in land reclamation sites.
⑤Special waste includes animal carcasses, abattoir waste, condemned goods, waterworks and sewage treatment sludge, sewage works screening, livestock waste, clinical waste and chemical waste delivered to landfills.
⑥Municipal solid waste recovered will be recycled locally or in places outside Hong Kong.

26–5 人口主要指标
Main Indicators of Population

项目	Item	2019	2020	2021	2022	2023
年中人口 (万人)	Mid-year Population (10 000 persons)	750.8	748.1	741.3	734.6	753.6
粗出生率 (‰)	Crude Birth Rate (‰)	7.0	5.8	5.0	4.4	4.4 #
粗死亡率 (‰)	Crude Death Rate (‰)	6.5	6.8	6.9	8.7	7.2 #
婴儿死亡率 (‰)	Infant Mortality Rate (‰)	1.5	1.9	1.4	1.8	1.4 #
自然变动率 (‰)	Rate of Natural Change (‰)	0.5	-1.0	-1.9	-4.2	-2.8 #
总和生育率① (个/千人)	Total Fertility Rate①(unit/1000 persons)	1064	883	772	701	751 #
登记结婚数 (对)	Registered Marriages (couple)	44247	27863	26899	30012	47723
登记离婚数 (对)	Divorce Decrees (couple)	21157	16020	16692	13026	17919
出生时平均预期寿命 (年)	Expectation of Life at Birth (year)					
男	Male	82.4	83.4	83.2	80.7	82.5 #
女	Female	88.1	87.7	87.9	86.8	87.9 #

注：①不包括女性外籍家庭佣工。每千名女性的活产婴儿数目。
Note: ① Excluding female foreign domestic helpers. Refers to live births per 1000 women.

26–6 劳动人口及失业状况
Labour Force and Unemployment

项目	Item	2019	2020	2021	2022	2023
劳动人口数目(万人)	Labour Force (10 000 persons)	398.8	391.8	387.0	377.6	382.2
男	Male	199.0	195.5	192.3	188.6	190.1
女	Female	199.8	196.4	194.7	189.0	192.1
劳动人口参与率 (%)	Labour Force Participation Rate (%)	60.7	59.7	59.4	58.2	57.3
就业人口 (万人)	Employed Persons (10 000 persons)	387.1	369.1	367.0	361.3	371.0
失业人口 (万人)	Unemployed Persons (10 000 persons)	11.6	22.8	20.0	16.3	11.3
失业率 (%)	Unemployment Rate (%)	2.9	5.8	5.2	4.3	2.9

注：数字是根据该年1月至12月进行的“综合住户统计调查”结果，以及年中人口估计数字而编制。
Note: Figures are compiled based on the survey results of the General Household Survey from January to December of the year concerned as well as the mid-year population estimates.

26–7 按行业划分的就业人数
Employed Persons by Industry

单位：万人 (10 000 persons)

行业	Industry	2019	2020	2021	2022	2023
制造	Manufacturing	10.5	10.4	9.4	9.2	8.9
建筑	Construction	33.9	31.1	32.6	33.2	34.9
进出口贸易及批发	Import/Export Trade and Wholesale	39.1	33.1	31.6	31.9	31.2
零售、住宿及膳食服务①	Retail, Accommodation and Food Services①	61.2	52.0	51.6	51.1	53.7
运输、仓库、邮政及速递服务、资讯及通讯	Transportation, Storage, Postal and Courier Services, Information and Communications	45.2	43.8	43.0	41.2	42.2
金融、保险、地产、专业及商用服务	Financing, Insurance, Real Estate, Professional and Business Services	84.0	85.3	86.2	83.0	84.9
公共行政、社会及个人服务	Public Administration, Social and Personal Services	110.8	111.1	110.2	109.1	112.8
其它	Others	2.6	2.3	2.3	2.6	2.4
总计	**Total**	**387.1**	**369.1**	**367.0**	**361.3**	**371.0**

注：数字是根据该年1月至12月进行的“综合住户统计调查”结果，以及年中人口估计数字而编制。
① 零售、住宿及膳食服务业合计通常被称为「与消费及旅游相关行业」。

Notes: Figures are compiled based on the survey results of the General Household Survey from January to December of the year concerned as well as the mid-year population estimates.
① The retail, accommodation and food services industries as a whole is generally referred to as the consumption- and tourism-related segment.

26–8 按每月就业收入划分的就业人数
Employed Persons by Monthly Employment Earnings

单位：万人，另有注明除外 (10 000 persons, unless otherwise specified)

每月就业收入(港元)	Monthly Employment Earnings (HKD)	2019	2020	2021	2022	2023
< 3000	< 3000	9.3	9.7	8.6	8.5	7.1
3000 – 3999	3000 - 3999	3.8	3.3	3.4	3.2	3.0
4000 – 4999	4000 - 4999	33.1	31.6	28.0	24.0	23.1
5000 – 5999	5000 - 5999	7.4	8.8	10.4	12.1	12.7
6000 – 6999	6000 - 6999	5.2	5.6	5.9	6.5	6.4
7000 – 7999	7000 - 7999	4.9	5.7	5.1	4.5	4.3
8000 – 8999	8000 - 8999	7.6	6.7	6.2	6.1	5.0
9000 – 9999	9000 - 9999	9.6	8.2	6.6	5.9	4.6
10000 – 11999	10000 - 11999	24.0	22.2	20.8	17.9	15.9
12000 – 13999	12000 - 13999	33.8	29.0	28.6	24.9	22.7
14000 – 15999	14000 - 15999	34.9	33.4	33.0	31.0	30.5
16000 – 17999	16000 - 17999	24.2	21.2	22.1	22.7	23.4
18000 – 19999	18000 - 19999	19.9	18.8	19.3	20.0	21.3
20000 – 24999	20000 - 24999	47.1	44.5	47.1	47.1	51.2
25000 – 29999	25000 - 29999	24.0	22.1	23.7	24.6	28.6
30000 – 34999	30000 - 34999	23.4	22.9	23.3	23.8	25.6
35000 – 39999	35000 - 39999	12.3	12.2	12.2	12.7	14.3
40000 – 44999	40000 - 44999	12.1	12.2	12.2	12.8	13.2
45000 – 49999	45000 - 49999	7.2	6.7	6.8	6.8	8.2
50000 – 59999	50000 - 59999	13.5	13.6	13.0	13.2	14.4
60000 – 79999	60000 - 79999	12.9	13.6	14.1	14.8	16.2
80000 – 99999	80000 - 99999	5.9	6.1	6.0	6.9	7.0
≧ 100000	≧ 100000	10.6	10.9	10.5	11.4	12.3
总　计	**Total**	**387.1**	**369.1**	**367.0**	**361.3**	**371.0**
每　月就业收入中位数(港元)	**Median Monthly Employment Earnings (HKD)**	**17100**	**17800**	**18000**	**19000**	**20000**

注：数字是根据该年1月至12月进行的“综合住户统计调查”结果，以及年中人口估计数字而编制。

Note: Figures are compiled based on the survey results of the General Household Survey from January to December of the year concerned as well as the mid-year population estimates.

26–9 按行业划分督导级(不包括经理级与专业雇员)及以下雇员的工资指数

Wage Indices for Employees up to Supervisory Level (Managerial and Professional Employees Are Not Included) by Industry

(1992年9月 = 100) (September 1992 = 100)

行业主类	Industry Section	2019	2020	2021	2022	2023
名义工资指数	**Nominal Wage Index**					
制造	Manufacturing	229.7	233.5	237.8	243.3	254.6
进出口贸易、批发及零售	Import/Export, Wholesale and Retail Trades	233.1	234.7	238.6	243.0	250.3
运输	Transportation	220.0	216.8	216.3	224.1	235.9
住宿及膳食服务活动	Accommodation and Food Service Activities	221.0	223.1	227.8	233.5	244.1
金融及保险活动	Financial and Insurance Activities	254.7	260.6	267.9	276.6	287.5
地产租赁及保养管理	Real Estate Leasing and Maintenance Management	270.6	278.0	286.7	294.9	304.5
专业及商业服务	Professional and Business Services	277.9	282.2	288.2	295.6	306.7
个人服务	Personal Services	335.5	336.7	339.8	344.9	357.9
所有选定行业①	All Selected Industries①	243.9	246.5	251.0	257.5	267.2
实际工资指数②	**Real Wage Index②**					
制造	Manufacturing	116.4	119.8	118.4	118.7	120.9
进出口贸易、批发及零售	Import/Export, Wholesale and Retail Trades	118.1	120.4	118.8	118.5	118.9
运输	Transportation	111.4	111.2	107.7	109.3	112.0
住宿及膳食服务活动	Accommodation and Food Service Activities	111.9	114.4	113.4	113.9	115.9
金融及保险活动	Financial and Insurance Activities	129.0	133.7	133.4	134.9	136.5
地产租赁及保养管理	Real Estate Leasing and Maintenance Management	137.1	142.6	142.8	143.9	144.6
专业及商业服务	Professional and Business Services	140.8	144.7	143.5	144.2	145.7
个人服务	Personal Services	169.9	172.7	169.2	168.2	170.0
所有选定行业①	All Selected Industries①	123.6	126.4	125.0	125.6	126.9

注：指有关年度12月份的数字。

①指“劳工收入统计调查”内工资统计调查所涵盖的所有行业，包括并没有列出其统计数字的电力及燃气供应业、污水处理及废弃物管理业与出版活动业。

②实际工资指数是按其名义指数扣除以2019/20年为基期的甲类消费价格指数而计算出来。

Notes : Figures refer to December of the year.

①Figures refer to all industries covered by the wage enquiry of the Labour Earnings Survey, including the electricity and gas supply industry, sewerage and waste management activities industry and publishing activities industry, the statistics of which are not separately shown.

②The Real Wage Index is derived by deflating the corresponding nominal index by the 2019/20-based Consumer Price Index (A).

26-10 本地生产总值
Gross Domestic Product

年 份 Year	本地生产总值(以当年价格计算) Gross Domestic Product (GDP) At Current Market Prices		本地生产总值与上年比较的实际增长(%) GDP Real Growth Rate over the Preceding Year (%)	人均本地生产总值(以当年价格计算) Per Capita GDP At Current Market Prices	
	(亿港元) (HKD 100 million)	(亿美元) (USD 100 million)		(港元) (HKD)	(美元) (USD)
1990	5993	769	3.8	105050	13487
1991	6913	890	5.7	120188	15466
1992	8071	1043	6.2	139148	17975
1993	9310	1203	6.2	157772	20395
1994	10496	1358	6.0	173909	22504
1995	11190	1446	2.4	181772	23497
1996	12353	1597	4.3	191951	24819
1997	13731	1774	5.1	211592	27330
1998	13081	1689	-5.9	199898	25810
1999	12859	1658	2.5	194649	25090
2000	13375	1717	7.7	200675	25757
2001	13211	1694	0.6	196765	25230
2002	12973	1663	1.7	192367	24666
2003	12567	1614	3.1	186704	23976
2004	13169	1691	8.7	194140	24928
2005	14121	1816	7.4	207263	26651
2006	15034	1935	7.0	219240	28223
2007	16508	2116	6.5	238676	30596
2008	17075	2193	2.1	245406	31515
2009	16592	2140	-2.5	237960	30697
2010	17763	2286	6.8	252887	32551
2011	19344	2485	4.8	273549	35142
2012	20371	2626	1.7	284899	36733
2013	21383	2757	3.1	297860	38404
2014	22600	2915	2.8	312609	40316
2015	23983	3094	2.4	328924	42431
2016	24906	3209	2.2	339476	43736
2017	26596	3412	3.8	359737	46156
2018	28354	3617	2.8	380462	48535
2019	28450	3631	-1.7	378937	48358
2020	26758	3450	-6.5	357679	46110
2021	28680	3689	6.5	386879	49766
2022@	28090	3587	-3.7	382377	48822
2023@	29816	3808	3.3	395642	50535

26-11 按当时价格计算的生产法本地生产总值
Gross Domestic Product (GDP) by Economic Activity at Current Prices

单位：亿港元，另有注明除外 (HKD 100 million, unless otherwise specified)

经济活动	Economic Activity	2018	2019	2020	2021	2022@
农业、渔业、采矿及采石①	**Agriculture, Fishing, Mining and Quarrying①**	**17.62**	**20.57**	**26.48**	**21.68**	**14.86**
工业	**Industry**	**1837.04**	**1779.48**	**1651.12**	**1717.77**	**1759.16**
制造	Manufacturing	275.71	293.66	255.25	261.75	265.98
电力、燃气和自来水供应及废弃物管理	Electricity, Gas and Water Supply, and Waste Management	356.60	340.83	353.25	363.48	324.85
建筑	Construction	1204.73	1144.99	1042.62	1092.54	1168.33
服务	**Services**	**25149.47**	**25607.16**	**23928.95**	**25718.73**	**25580.82**
进出口贸易、批发及零售	Import/export, Wholesale and Retail Trades	5751.03	5333.52	4712.46	5327.15	4946.89
住宿及膳食服务	Accommodation and Food Services	915.25	759.18	369.34	453.94	453.50
运输、仓库、邮政及速递服务	Transportation, Storage, Postal and Courier Services	1584.40	1515.74	1139.51	2009.86	2041.18
资讯及通讯	Information and Communications	914.49	955.57	937.59	995.14	1001.03
金融及保险	Financing and Insurance	5351.26	5814.99	5997.97	5836.13	6134.77
地产、专业及商用服务	Real Estate, Professional and Business Services	2808.43	2764.97	2443.37	2503.06	2330.94
公共行政、社会及个人服务	Public Administration, Social and Personal Services	4994.33	5372.38	5294.57	5615.30	5830.06
楼宇业权	Ownership of Premises	2830.28	3090.81	3034.14	2978.16	2842.45
以基本价格计算的本地生产总值	**GDP at Basic Prices**	**27004.13**	**27407.21**	**25606.55**	**27458.19**	**27354.84**
产品税	**Taxes on Products**	**1178.25**	**936.23**	**1020.66**	**1387.58**	**1043.53**
统计差额② (%)	**Statistical Discrepancy② (%)**	**0.6**	**0.4**	**0.5**	**-0.6**	**-1.1**
以当时市价计算的本地生产总值	**GDP at Current Market Prices**	**28354.29**	**28450.22**	**26757.93**	**28679.73**	**28089.81**

注：以上的统计数字是按“香港标准行业分类2.0版”编制。
①由于要为采矿及采石业个别机构单位的数据保密，因此采矿及采石业的数字会包括在「农业、渔业、采矿及采石」内。
②统计差额是以当时价格计算,以支出法编制的本地生产总值与以生产法编制的本地生产总值之间的差额。这差额是由于在编制过程中数据来源及估算方法有所不同而引致的。统计差额是以其占当时市价计算的本地生产总值的百分比来表示。

Notes: The above statistics are compiled based on the Hong Kong Standard Industrial Classification (HSIC) Version 2.0.
①In order to preserve the confidentiality of information relating to individual establishments in mining and quarrying sector, figures of mining and quarrying sector are included in "Agriculture, Fishing, Mining and Quarrying".
②Statistical discrepancy refers to the difference in values of current price GDP compiled using the expenditure and production approaches, as a result of the adoption of different data sources and estimation methods in the compilation processes. It is expressed as a percentage to GDP at current market prices.

26-12 按2022年环比物量计算的生产法本地生产总值
Gross Domestic Product (GDP) by Economic Activity in Chained (2022) Dollars

单位：亿港元 (HKD 100 million)

经济活动	Economic Activity	2019	2020	2021	2022@	2023@
农业、渔业、采矿及采石①	**Agriculture, Fishing, Mining and Quarrying①**	**17.44**	**18.10**	**17.64**	**14.86**	**14.43**
工业	**Industry**	**1862.68**	**1653.64**	**1674.58**	**1759.16**	**1840.48**
制造	Manufacturing	267.25	251.66	265.43	265.98	275.94
电力、燃气和自来水供应及废弃物管理	Electricity, Gas and Water Supply, and Waste Management	369.86	317.31	328.92	324.85	330.44
建筑	Construction	1228.96	1084.97	1078.75	1168.33	1234.10
服务	**Services**	**26768.84**	**24983.48**	**26467.53**	**25580.82**	**26519.02**
进出口贸易、批发及零售	Import/export, Wholesale and Retail Trades	5829.05	4956.98	5614.86	4946.89	4924.72
住宿及膳食服务	Accommodation and Food Services	719.24	396.91	486.69	453.50	586.42
运输、仓库、邮政及速递服务	Transportation, Storage, Postal and Courier Services	3146.14	1985.01	2137.24	2041.18	2658.21
资讯及通讯	Information and Communications	954.78	970.85	996.19	1001.03	1011.19
金融及保险	Financing and Insurance	5780.74	6013.36	6296.14	6134.77	6035.69
地产、专业及商用服务	Real Estate, Professional and Business Services	2444.97	2332.54	2380.96	2330.94	2390.88
公共行政、社会及个人服务	Public Administration, Social and Personal Services	5642.62	5513.95	5755.49	5830.06	6037.96
楼宇业权	Ownership of Premises	2802.10	2792.37	2825.39	2842.45	2873.96
产品税	**Taxes on Products**	**870.08**	**1023.03**	**1251.04**	**1043.53**	**944.01**

注：以上的统计数字是按“香港标准行业分类2.0版”编制。

以环比物量计算按经济活动划分的本地生产总值的参照年，已由2021年重订为2022年。重订参照年会影响以环比物量计算的数值，但不会改变其变动率。整体物量估计与其组成部分相加的总和可能存在差额。“不可相加性”是环比物量计算的一个技术属性。

①由于要为采矿及采石业个别机构单位的数据保密，因此采矿及采石业的数字会包括在「农业、渔业、采矿及采石」内。

Notes: The above statistics are compiled based on the Hong Kong Standard Industrial Classification (HSIC) Version 2.0.

The reference year for the chain volume measures of GDP by economic activity has been revised from 2021 to 2022. Re-referencing affects the levels, but not the rates of change, of the chain volume measures. A discrepancy may exist between the volume estimate of an aggregate and the sum of its components. “Non-additivity” is a technical feature of the chain volume measures.

①In order to preserve the confidentiality of information relating to individual establishments in mining and quarrying sector, figures of mining and quarrying sector are included in "Agriculture, Fishing, Mining and Quarrying".

26-13 支出法本地生产总值
Gross Domestic Product by Expenditure Component

单位：亿港元，另有注明除外 (HKD 100 million, unless otherwise specified)

本地生产总值组成部分	GDP Components	2019	2020	2021	2022@	2023@
按当年价格计算	**At Current Market Prices**					
私人消费开支	Private Consumption Expenditure	19737	17752	18635	18635	21039
政府消费开支	Government Consumption Expenditure	3094	3411	3636	4027	3954
固定资本形成总额	Gross Domestic Fixed Capital Formation	5206	4557	4831	4514	5000
存货增减	Changes in Inventories	-31	522	-19	-236	-393
货物出口(离岸价)①	Exports of Goods (f.o.b.)①	42551	41983	52360	48125	44985
减：货物进口(离岸价)①	Less: Imports of Goods (f.o.b.)①	43756	42397	52113	48530	46277
服务出口①	Exports of Services①	7991	5192	6151	6505	7717
减：服务进口①	Less: Imports of Services①	6342	4263	4800	4952	6211
本地生产总值	**GDP**	**28450**	**26758**	**28680**	**28090**	**29816**
人均本地生产总值(港元)	**Per Capita GDP (HKD)**	**378937**	**357679**	**386879**	**382377**	**395642**
按2022年环比物量计算②	**In Chained (2022) Dollars②**					
私人消费开支	Private Consumption Expenditure	20189	18049	19055	18635	20071
政府消费开支	Government Consumption Expenditure	3265	3524	3730	4027	3856
固定资本形成总额	Gross Domestic Fixed Capital Formation	5068	4503	4877	4514	5015
存货增减	Changes in Inventories	-27	511	26	-236	-366
货物出口(离岸价)①	Exports of Goods (f.o.b.)①	47780	47111	55929	48125	43182
货物进口(离岸价)①	Imports of Goods (f.o.b.)①	49318	47748	55942	48530	44378
服务出口①	Exports of Services①	9689	6318	6536	6505	7863
服务进口①	Imports of Services①	7212	4889	5011	4952	6233
本地生产总值	**GDP**	**29314**	**27396**	**29164**	**28090**	**29010**
人均本地生产总值(港元)	**Per Capita GDP (HKD)**	**390448**	**366206**	**393413**	**382377**	**384950**

注：①货物出口及进口与服务出口及进口数字，是根据《2008年国民经济核算体系》的标准，采用所有权转移原则记录外地加工货品及转手商贸活动编制而成的。
②以环比物量计算的本地生产总值及其组成部分的参照年，已由2021年重订为2022年。重订参照年会影响以环比物量计算的数值，但不会影响其变动率。整体物量数值与其组成部分相加的总和可能存在差额。"不可相加性"是环比物量计算的一个技术属性。

Notes:①Figures on exports and imports of goods and services are compiled based on the change of ownership principle in recording goods sent abroad for processing and merchanting under the standards stipulated in the System of National Accounts 2008.
②The reference year for the chain volume measures of GDP and its components has been revised from 2021 to 2022. Re-referencing affects the levels, but not the rates of change, of the chain volume measures. A discrepancy may exist between the volume estimate of an aggregate and the sum of its components. "Non-additivity" is a technical feature of the chain volume measures.

26-14 本地居民总收入
Gross National Income

单位：亿港元，另有注明除外 (HKD 100 million, unless otherwise specified)

项 目	Item	2019	2020	2021	2022	2023@
以2022年环比物量计算①	**In chained (2022) dollars①**					
本地生产总值	GDP	29314	27396	29164	28090 @	29010
对外初次收入流量净值	Net External Primary Income Flows	1459	1578	2029	1858	2580
实质本地居民总收入②	RGNI②	30559	28791	31344	29948 @	31363
人均本地生产总值(港元)	Per Capita GDP (HKD)	390448	366206	393413	382377 @	384950
人均实质本地居民总收入(港元)	Per Capita RGNI (HKD)	407023	384858	422819	407665 @	416176
按当年价格计算	**At Current Market Prices**					
本地生产总值	GDP	28450	26758	28680	28090 @	29816
对外初次收入流量净值	Net External Primary Income Flows	1437	1561	1987	1858	2677
本地居民总收入	GNI	29887	28319	30667	29948 @	32493
人均本地生产总值(港元)	Per Capita GDP (HKD)	378937	357679	386879	382377 @	395642
人均本地居民总收入(港元)	Per Capita GNI (HKD)	398079	378542	413687	407665 @	431161

注：①以环比物量计算的本地生产总值、对外初次收入流量净值及实质本地居民总收入的参照年，已由2021年重订为2022年。
②实质本地居民总收入是把贸易价格比率变动的调整及实质对外初次收入流量净值加进实质本地生产总值而得出。

Notes: ①The reference year for the chain volume measures of GDP, net external primary income flows (EPIF) and GNI has been revised from 2021 to 2022.
②Real Gross National Income (RGNI) is obtained by adding the terms of trade adjustment and real net EPIF to real GDP.

26-15 香港国际收支平衡
Hong Kong's Balance of Payments

单位：亿港元 (HKD 100 million)

标准组成部分	Standard Component	2019	2020	2021	2022@	2023@
经常账户①	**Current Account①**	**1665**	**1870**	**3394**	**2861**	**2732**
货物	Goods	-1205	-413	247	-405	-1291
服务	Services	1649	929	1350	1554	1506
初次收入	Primary Income	1437	1561	1987	1858	2677
二次收入	Secondary Income	-216	-207	-190	-146	-160
资本账户①	**Capital Account①**	**-7**	**-1**	**-104**	**12**	**59**
金融账户②	**Financial Account②**	**2368**	**2438**	**3632**	**2768**	**2738**
直接投资	Direct Investment	-1607	-2637	-3401	-271	-657
证券投资	Portfolio Investment	2158	5280	6205	3174	3731
金融衍生工具	Financial Derivatives	-12	-188	-451	-1404	-1117
其他投资	Other Investment	1918	-2648	1371	4942	1579
储备资产③	Reserve Assets③	-89	2630	-91	-3672	-799
净误差及遗漏④	**Net Errors and Omissions④**	**710**	**569**	**342**	**-105**	**-53**
整体的国际收支	**Overall Balance of Payments**	**-89**	**2630**	**-91**	**-3672**	**-799**

注：①在经常账户及资本账户中，差额为正数值代表盈余，而负数值则代表赤字。

②自2023年6月起，金融账户的整系数列已采用新的正负号常规。自此，资产／负债增加以正数值标示。注意：资产增加表示资金净流出，而负债增加则表示资金净流入。因此，金融账户差额增加(即资产减去负债为正数值)表示资金净流出。

③在国际收支平衡架构下储备及非储备资产的估计数字是指交易数字。因估值方式改变(包括价格变动及汇率变动)及重新分类所导致的影响并没计算在内。

④根据编制国际收支平衡的会计原则，经常账户差额和资本账户差额的总和理当相等于金融账户差额。实际上，由于有关数据是从多个来源搜集得来，两者之间可能由于各种原因而出现差异。该差异反映于净误差及遗漏的平衡项目。

Notes: ①In the current account and the capital account, a positive value for the balance figure represents a surplus whereas a negative value represents a deficit.

②A new sign convention has been adopted for the entire series of the financial account since June 2023. From then on, an increase in assets/liabilities is indicated by a positive value. Note that an increase in assets indicates a net financial outflow, while an increase in liabilities indicates a net financial inflow. Therefore, an increase in the financial account balance (i.e. when assets minus liabilities is a positive value) indicates a net financial outflow.

③The estimates of reserve and non-reserve assets under the Balance of Payments framework are transaction figures. Effects of valuation changes (including price changes and exchange rate changes) and reclassifications are not taken into account.

④In accordance with the accounting principles adopted in compiling Balance of Payments, the sum of the current account balance and the capital account balance is in theory identical to the financial account balance. In practice, discrepancies between the two may occur for various reasons as the relevant data are collected from many sources. Such discrepancies are reflected in the balancing item of net errors and omissions.

26-16 香港国际投资头寸（期末头寸）
Hong Kong's International Investment Position (Position as at End of Period)

单位：亿港元 (HKD 100 million)

概括组成部分	Broad Component	2019	2020	2021	2022	2023@
资产	**Assets**	**439324**	**487770**	**499180**	**474032**	**483017**
直接投资	Direct Investment	156944	164203	171543	170513	175538
证券投资	Portfolio Investment	141688	169996	165177	142965	143342
金融衍生工具	Financial Derivatives	6151	8851	8152	12177	10651
其他投资	Other Investment	100152	106589	115571	115282	120256
储备资产	Reserve Assets	34389	38131	38737	33095	33230
负债	**Liabilities**	**316353**	**323252**	**334547**	**335890**	**343623**
直接投资	Direct Investment	161869	158835	168262	173065	181670
证券投资	Portfolio Investment	44637	43444	40982	39289	37537
金融衍生工具	Financial Derivatives	5804	9043	7385	12266	11076
其他投资	Other Investment	104042	111929	117918	111270	113339
国际投资头寸净值①	**Net International Investment Position①**	**122972**	**164519**	**164633**	**138142**	**139394**

注：①国际投资头寸净值是对外金融资产总值与对外金融负债总值之间的差额。
Note: ①Net International Investment Position is the difference between total external financial assets and total external financial liabilities.

26-17 电力、煤气、水消费量
Electricity, Gas and Water Consumption

用　途	Use	2019	2020	2021	2022	2023
电力（太焦耳）	**Electricity (Terajoule)**					
住宅	Domestic	42937	46675	47464	45427	44326
商业	Commercial	107162	101041	105631	104350	107847
工业	Industrial	10815	10672	11163	11087	11126
街灯	Street Lighting	377	362	320	291	259
总计	Total	161291	158751	164578	161155	163558
煤气（太焦耳）	**Gas (Terajoule)**					
住宅	Domestic	15021	16684	16015	15985	14648
商业	Commercial	11867	9609	10066	9709	10735
工业	Industrial	1824	1653	1596	1704	1743
总计	Total	28712	27947	27677	27398	27125
水（万立方米）	**Water (10 000 Cubic Meters)**	**99614**	**102712**	**105522**	**106597**	**106789**

26-18 工业生产指数
Index of Industrial Production

(2015年=100) (year of 2015=100)

行业组别	Industry Grouping	2019	2020	2021	2022	2023
制造	**Manufacturing**	**101.7**	**95.8**	**101.0**	**101.2**	**105.0**
食品、饮品及烟草制品	Food, Beverages and Tobacco	111.0	97.7	106.7	105.5	109.7
纺织制品及成衣	Textiles and Wearing Apparel	91.0	89.8	89.1	87.6	89.2
纸制品、印刷及已储录资料媒体的复制	Paper products, Printing and Reproduction of Recorded Media	97.2	93.3	93.4	92.1	93.5
金属、计算机、电子及光学产品、机械及设备	Metal, Computer, Electronic and Optical Products, Machinery and Equipment	95.0	97.0	93.0	92.6	93.5
其他制造行业	Miscellaneous Manufacturing Industries	99.2	95.5	101.4	103.3	108.3
污水处理、废弃物管理及污染防治活动	**Sewerage, Waste Management and Remediation Activities**	**106.8**	**106.7**	**109.2**	**108.2**	**109.6**

注：以上统计数字是按“香港标准行业分类2.0版”编制。
Note : The above statistics are compiled based on the Hong Kong Standard Industrial Classification (HSIC) Version 2.0.

26-19 按楼宇种类划分的新落成私人楼宇
Newly Completed Private Buildings by Type of Building

楼宇类别	Building Type	2019	2020	2021	2022	2023
住宅楼宇	**Residential**					
楼宇数目 (栋)	Number of Blocks (number)	389	310	116	256	213
实用楼面面积（万平方米）①	Usable Floor Area (10 000 sq.m.)①	38.0	48.4	26.6	64.7	23.1
商住两用楼宇	**Residential/Commercial**					
楼宇数目 (栋)	Number of Blocks (number)	23	72	49	13	32
实用楼面面积(万平方米)	Usable Floor Area (10 000 sq.m.)					
住宅	Residential	9.3	20.8	18.4	3.9	15.2
非住宅	Non-residential	2.2	6.5	1.7	0.9	2.2
商业楼宇	**Commercial**					
楼宇数目 (栋)	Number of Blocks (number)	32	15	17	28	30
实用楼面面积（万平方米）	Usable Floor Area (10 000 sq.m.)	37.0	6.9	9.8	61.9	40.5
工业楼宇	**Industrial**					
楼宇数目 (栋)	Number of Blocks (number)	16	8	7	19	21
实用楼面面积（万平方米）	Usable Floor Area (10 000 sq.m.)	8.1	5.9	3.4	27.3	24.8
其他用途楼宇	**Others**					
楼宇数目 (栋)	Number of Blocks (number)	199	223	172	174	237
实用楼面面积（万平方米）	Usable Floor Area (10 000 sq.m.)					
住宅	Residential	0.1	1.3	0.2	2.6	1.2
非住宅	Non-residential	19.7	19.1	12.9	19.0	13.6
总计	**Total**					
楼宇数目 (栋)	Number of Blocks (number)	659	628	361	490	533
实用楼面面积（万平方米）	Usable Floor Area (10 000 sq.m.)					
住宅①	Residential①	47.4	70.5	45.3	71.2	39.5
非住宅	Non-residential	67.0	38.3	27.8	109.1	81.1

注：①包括住宅楼宇内用作非住宅用途的实用楼面面积，例如：会所/娱乐设施、管理员办事处/宿舍、电机房等。
Note: ①Including usable floor area in residential buildings for non-domestic use, such as club house/recreational facilities, caretakers' office/quarters, transformer room, etc.

26–20 按楼宇种类划分的获批准可动工兴建私人楼宇
Private Buildings with Consent to Commence Work by Type of Building

年 份 Year	住宅楼宇 Residential		商住两用楼宇 Residential/Commercial			商业楼宇 Commercial	
	楼宇数目（栋） Number of Blocks (number)	实用楼面面积（万平方米）① Usable Floor Area (10 000 sq.m.)①	楼宇数目（栋） Number of Blocks (number)	实用楼面面积（万平方米） Usable Floor Area (10 000 sq.m.) 住 宅 Residential	非住宅 Non-residential	楼宇数目（栋） Number of Blocks (number)	实用楼面面积（万平方米） Usable Floor Area (10 000 sq.m.)
2014							
初次呈交 First Submission	254	24.0	41	22.0	6.2	16	16.9
重大修改 Major Revision	200	9.6	5	6.0	2.7	1	3.2
2015							
初次呈交 First Submission	261	36.9	99	19.2	5.1	20	19.8
重大修改 Major Revision	65	1.4	66	28.5	7.0	1	0.3
2016							
初次呈交 First Submission	262	31.7	53	9.6	5.3	9	18.7
重大修改 Major Revision	110	18.8	36	4.0	1.3	6	5.9
2017							
初次呈交 First Submission	165	29.6	35	11.3	11.4	14	24.4
重大修改 Major Revision	151	11.8	28	33.6	12.1	3	1.0
2018							
初次呈交 First Submission	85	30.1	99	22.6	2.4	12	4.5
重大修改 Major Revision	178	11.8	6	5.1	3.9	3	0.2
2019							
初次呈交 First Submission	151	28.5	26	16.2	1.6	22	60.6
重大修改 Major Revision	108	23.1	20	11.5	1.5	13	20.8
2020							
初次呈交 First Submission	128	13.2	31	9.6	1.4	8	3.8
重大修改 Major Revision	125	12.6	25	17.1	0.5	8	17.3
2021							
初次呈交 First Submission	47	26.1	39	17.3	2.1	20	42.0
重大修改 Major Revision	72	18.2	39	17.8	0.8	8	29.4
2022							
初次呈交 First Submission	58	22.8	22	11.1	4.1	9	4.4
重大修改 Major Revision	65	2.2	11	7.6	0.4	1	1.6
2023							
初次呈交 First Submission	15	4.6	25	9.6	1.7	10	22.8
重大修改 Major Revision	114	23.7	9	3.4	1.4	9	12.6

26–20 续表 continued

年 份 Year	工业楼宇 Industrial		其他用途楼宇 Others			总 计 Total		
	楼宇数目 (栋) Number of Blocks (number)	实用楼面面积 (万平方米) Usable Floor Area (10 000 sq.m.)	楼宇数目 (栋) Number of Blocks (number)	实用楼面面积（万平方米） Usable Floor Area (10 000 sq.m.)		楼宇数目 (栋) Number of Blocks (number)	实用楼面面积（万平方米） Usable Floor Area (10 000 sq.m.)	
				住 宅 Residential	非住宅 Non-residential		住 宅① Residential①	非住宅 Non-residential
2014								
初次呈交 First Submission	6	10.4	45	2.8	14.2	362	48.8	47.7
重大修改 Major Revision	1	0.2	12	0.2	7.5	219	15.9	13.6
2015								
初次呈交 First Submission	21	20.6	85	2.8	38.2	486	59.0	83.7
重大修改 Major Revision	1	1.9	26	0.2	17.3	159	30.1	26.5
2016								
初次呈交 First Submission	12	6.3	47	0.4	16.4	383	41.8	46.7
重大修改 Major Revision	3	1.3	8	0.0	7.2	163	22.8	15.6
2017								
初次呈交 First Submission	9	5.4	46	1.0	18.5	269	41.9	59.7
重大修改 Major Revision	1	0.8	9	§	4.2	192	45.4	18.1
2018								
初次呈交 First Submission	7	7.5	35	0.6	6.1	238	53.3	20.4
重大修改 Major Revision	3	2.4	9	0.2	3.1	199	17.0	9.5
2019								
初次呈交 First Submission	6	9.8	49	0.2	15.7	254	44.9	87.7
重大修改 Major Revision	2	8.0	6	0.1	7.9	149	34.8	38.2
2020								
初次呈交 First Submission	3	8.5	35	0.6	39.2	205	23.4	52.9
重大修改 Major Revision	8	9.7	8	0.1	1.7	174	29.8	29.2
2021								
初次呈交 First Submission	5	4.0	53	5.2	15.5	164	48.6	63.6
重大修改 Major Revision			29	2.0	3.2	148	38.0	33.4
2022								
初次呈交 First Submission	2	1.1	45	4.7	2.2	136	38.5	11.9
重大修改 Major Revision	6	5.0	4		22.1	87	9.8	29.1
2023								
初次呈交 First Submission	6	3.0	45	0.7	17.5	101	14.9	45.0
重大修改 Major Revision	1	1.6	9		3.3	142	27.2	19.0

注：①包括住宅楼宇内用作非住宅用途的实用楼面面积，例如：会所/娱乐设施、管理员办事处/宿舍、电机房等。

Note: ①Including usable floor area in residential buildings for non-domestic use, such as club house/recreational facilities, caretakers' office/quarters, transformer room, etc.

26–21 按类型划分的永久性居住屋宇单位数量(3月底的数字)
Number of Permanent Living Quarters by Type (as at End March of the Year)

单位：万个　　　　(10 000 units)

永久性居住屋宇单位类型①	Type of Permanent Living Quarters①	2020	2021	2022	2023	2024
公营租住房屋②	Public Rental Housing②	83.21	84.31	85.07	85.86	86.25
资助出售单位③	Subsidised Sale Flats③	42.41	42.98	44.17	44.86	45.12
私人永久性房屋③	Private Permanent Housing③	164.15	166.99	169.19	171.34	172.71
总计	**Total**	**289.76**	**294.28**	**298.42**	**302.06**	**304.09**

注：①数字包括所有住宅屋宇单位及非住宅楼宇内已知作居所用途的屋宇单位，但不包括非住宅用途、酒店及院舍内供住院或在囚人士居住的屋宇单位。
②数字不包括香港房屋委员会售出的公营租住房屋单位。
③数字包括香港房屋委员会、香港房屋协会及市区重建局售出而不可在公开市场买卖的屋宇单位。可在公开市场买卖的资助出售单位则归类为私人永久性房屋。

Notes: ①Figures include all quarters used for residential purpose as well as quarters known to be used for residential purposes in non-residential buildings. Quarters known to be used for non-residential purpose and those in hotels and accommodation used for inmates of institutions are excluded.
②Figures exclude public rental housing flats sold by the Hong Kong Housing Authority.
③Subsidised sale flats include quarters sold by the Hong Kong Housing Authority, Hong Kong Housing Society and Urban Renewal Authority that cannot be traded in the open market. Those flats that can be traded in the open market are classified as private permanent housing.

26–22 按住房租住权划分的家庭住户数目
Domestic Households by Tenure of Accommodation

单位：万户　　　　(10 000 households)

住房租住权	Tenure of Accommodation	2019	2020	2021	2022	2023
总计	**Total**	**260.84**	**264.12**	**266.95**	**267.11**	**270.04**
自置住房住户	Owner-occupiers	130.79	136.89	136.01	137.61	136.23
全租户	Sole Tenants	120.11	117.35	121.35	119.74	124.05
合租户	Co-tenants	0.53	0.30	0.32	0.37	0.33
住房由雇主提供	Accommodation Provided by Employers	4.02	4.41	3.96	3.93	3.75
其他①	Others①	5.39	5.17	5.31	5.47	5.68

注：数字是根据该年1月至12月进行的“综合住户统计调查”结果，以及年中人口估计数字而编制，可被视为反映全年的平均情况。
① 包括二房东、三房客及免租户。

Notes: Figures are compiled based on the survey results of the General Household Survey (GHS) from January to December of the year concerned as well as the mid-year population estimates and may be regarded as referring to the average situation of the whole year.
① Includes main tenants, sub-tenants and rent free households.

26-23 进出香港货物
Inward and Outward Movements of Cargo

单位：万吨 (10 000 tons)

项　目	Item	2019	2020	2021	2022	2023
卸下	**Discharged**					
空运	By Air	160.7	144.8	163.6	139.1	123.9
水运	By Water	17093.3	16993.1	13490.4	12106.3	11168.9
海运	By Ocean	11115.2	10357.7	9745.9	8466.4	7605.0
河运	By River	5978.1	6635.3	3744.5	3639.9	3563.8
道路运输①	By Road①	1312.5	1242.5	1356.7	690.5	1062.3
总计	Total	18566.5	18380.3	15010.6	12935.9	12355.1
装上	**Loaded**					
空运	By Air	309.7	297.2	335.1	277.8	305.9
水运	By Water	9238.2	7935.5	7882.7	7104.1	6317.7
海运	By Ocean	5017.2	4559.7	5179.7	4532.4	3908.8
河运	By River	4221.0	3375.8	2702.9	2571.6	2408.9
道路运输①	By Road①	727.9	667.4	624.6	218.7	299.3
总计	Total	10275.8	8900.1	8842.3	7600.6	6923.0

注：①港珠澳大桥于2018年10月24日开始通车营运。由2018年10月开始，道路货物数字亦包括港珠澳大桥。
Note: ①The Hong Kong-Zhuhai-Macao Bridge commenced operation on 24 October 2018. The road cargo figures as from October 2018 include those of the Hong Kong-Zhuhai-Macao Bridge.

26-24 按主要货物装卸地点划分的集装箱吞吐量
Container Throughput by Main Cargo Handling Location

单位：万标准集装箱单位 (10 000 TEUs)

项　目	Item	2019	2020	2021	2022	2023
集装箱吞吐量	**Container Throughput**	**1830.3**	**1796.9**	**1779.8**	**1668.5**	**1440.1**
葵青货柜码头	**Kwai Tsing Container Terminals**					
抵港	Inward					
载货集装箱	Laden Container	639.3	653.7	639.8	566.6	476.6
空集装箱	Empty Container	108.0	115.9	125.6	119.8	117.4
离港	Outward					
载货集装箱	Laden Container	604.5	576.8	595.3	485.4	411.3
空集装箱	Empty Container	70.2	99.2	97.2	115.1	98.0
葵青货柜码头以外	**Other than Kwai Tsing Container Terminals**					
抵港	Inward					
载货集装箱	Laden Container	176.6	143.6	136.4	158.0	128.5
空集装箱	Empty Container	28.9	25.9	23.6	26.0	31.3
离港	Outward					
载货集装箱	Laden Container	145.1	130.8	116.9	121.9	115.3
空集装箱	Empty Container	57.8	51.1	45.0	75.6	61.7

注：一个标准集装箱单位等同一个20英尺集装箱的容量。
Note : TEU refers to a twenty-foot equivalent unit.

26–25 通讯及互联网服务
Communications and Internet Services

项目	Item	2019	2020	2021	2022	2023
邮递服务	**Postal Services**					
信件邮件 (亿件物品)	Letter Mail (100 million articles)	11.7	9.8	9.5	7.8	7.2
包裹 (万件)	Parcels (10 000 pcs)	69.9	73.6	71.9	67.8	51.3
已使用对外电讯设施容量①（以每秒千兆比特计）	**Activated Capacity of External Telecommunications Facilities① (Gbps)**	**96234**	**113609**	**145263**	**171157**	**222476**
电话服务①②（万条操作线路）	**Telephone Services①② (10 000 working lines)**					
住宅	Residential	226.5	219.9	211.5	198.7	184.7
商用	Business	178.8	173.5	171.7	168.7	164.0
总计	Total	405.4	393.4	383.1	367.3	348.7
图文传真①（万条操作线路）	**Fax① (10 000 working lines)**	**14.5**	**13.5**	**12.8**	**12.2**	**10.6**
对外电话通讯量 （万分钟）	**External Telephone Traffic Volume (10 000 minutes)**					
拨出③	Outgoing③	143347	120642	98146	91991	80693
拨入④	Incoming④	83059	76291	59353	52277	50574
公共无线电传呼接收器①（个）	**Public Radio Paging Receivers① (number)**	**14948**	**11392**	**8958**	**3438**	**2127**
公共移动电话用户系统①⑤⑥ （个）	**Public Mobile Subscriptions Units①⑤⑥ (number)**	**9481012 (23975075)**	**9489934 (23138116)**	**9817549 (24816489)**	**9697053 (22340139)**	**10026601 (24408655)**
互联网服务	**Internet Services**					
互联网服务商数目①⑦（个）	**Licensed Internet Service Providers (ISPs)①⑦ (number)**	**252**	**263**	**289**	**298**	**306**
互联网服务的用户（接驳线）数目①⑧（个）	**Number of Access Lines of Internet Service Subscriptions①⑧ (number)**					
以拨号上网的已登记接驳线(不包括互联网储值卡)⑨	Registered Dial-up Access Lines (Excluding Internet Pre-paid Calling Cards)⑨	50055	27753	27004	25110	17105
以私人租用线路接驳的已登记接驳线⑨	Registered Leased Line Access Lines⑨	23192	22996	22062	22061	19786
宽带互联网接驳线⑨	Registered Broadband Internet Access Lines⑨	2787835	2871081	2933087	2982766	2968458
互联网使用量⑧	**Internet Traffic Volume⑧**					
客户通过公共电话网络接驳⑩ (万分钟)	Customer Access via Public Switched Telephone Networks⑩ (10 000 minutes)	13240	11885	6290	4396	2058
客户通过宽带网络接驳 (太字节)⑪	Customer Access via Broadband Networks (terabytes)⑪	7849486	9948029	10713620	12446822	12392645

注：①年底数字。②数字包括直通内线式电话线、图文传真线及电文线路的直拨服务。③数字也包括图文传真及数据。④估计数字。
⑤数字不包括预付智能卡。包括预付智能卡的数字于括号内展示。 ⑥数字包括3G及4G服务。自2020年开始，数字亦包括5G服务。
⑦营办商数目包括所有持牌获准提供互联网接驳服务的营办商。
⑧估计数字根据互联网服务供应商申报资料编制，并不包括不属于持牌互联网服务供应商客户的使用者。
⑨已登记接驳线是指由互联网服务供应商以拨号或宽带互联网形式向客户提供的接驳(包括免费的接驳线)。如互联网服务供应商向同一客户提供多条接驳线，统计数字会根据其向客户提供的接驳线数目作统计。相关接驳线如用作提供多于一项服务，亦只作一条接驳线计算。
⑩不包括通过私人租用线路接驳及使用宽带服务的客户。
⑪1个太字节 = 8万亿比特。

Notes : ①Figures are as at end of the year.
②Figures include direct dialing in lines, facsimile lines and datel lines. ③Figures also include facsimile and data. ④Estimated figures.
⑤Excluding pre-paid SIM cards. Figures including pre-paid SIM cards are presented in brackets.
⑥Figures include 3G and 4G mobile services. Starting from 2020, figures also include 5G mobile services.
⑦Including all licensees authorised to provide Internet access services.
⑧Estimated figures are based on the returns from the ISPs and do not include users who are not customers on the licensed ISPs.
⑨Registered access lines refer to the dial-up or broadband connections of ISPs to individual end users (including those free-of-charge connections). Where multiple access lines are provided to the same end user, the number of access lines is counted for the purpose of the statistics. In case more than one service is offered under one access line, it is counted as one access line only.
⑩Excluding customer access via leased circuits and broadband services.
⑪1 terabyte = 8 terabits.

26–26 商品进出口贸易总额
Total Imports and Exports of Goods

单位：亿港元 (HKD 100 million)

贸易种类	Type of Trade	2019	2020	2021	2022	2023
进口	Imports	44154	42698	53078	49275	46450
整体出口	Total Exports	39887	39275	49607	45316	41774
贸易总额	Total Trade	84041	81973	102684	94591	88224
商品贸易差额	Merchandise Trade Balance	-4268	-3422	-3471	-3958	-4676

26–27 商品进口的主要供应地
Imports of Goods by Major Supplier

单位：亿港元 (HKD 100 million)

贸易种类／主要国家／地区	Type of Trade/ Main Country/Territory	2019	2020	2021	2022	2023
进口(供应地)	**Imports (Supplier)**	**44154**	**42698**	**53078**	**49275**	**46450**
中国内地	The Mainland of China	20581	19235	24335	20777	20223
中国台湾	Taiwan, China	3305	4057	5475	5874	5259
新加坡	Singapore	2907	3141	4138	3985	3296
韩国	Korea	2201	2472	3246	2898	2236
日本	Japan	2526	2400	2708	2428	2215

26–28 商品整体出口的主要目的地
Total Exports of Goods by Major Destination

单位：亿港元 (HKD 100 million)

贸易种类／主要国家／地区	Type of Trade/ Main Country/Territory	2019	2020	2021	2022	2023
整体出口(目的地)	**Total Exports (Destination)**	**39887**	**39275**	**49607**	**45316**	**41774**
中国内地	The Mainland of China	22109	23245	29520	25708	23204
美国	United States of America	3040	2588	3096	2927	2725
印度	India	1182	974	1331	1717	1670
中国台湾	Taiwan, China	883	985	1438	1542	1388
越南	Vietnam	802	845	1033	1124	1119

26–29 涉及外发中国内地加工的贸易
Trade Involving Outward Processing in the Mainland of China

项目	Item	2019	2020	2021	2022	2023
涉及外发加工贸易的估计货值 (亿港元)	**Estimated Value of Outward Processing Trade (HKD 100 million)**					
输往中国内地的整体出口货物	Total Exports to the Mainland of China	5594	5027	5628	4623	3963
从中国内地进口的货物	Imports from the Mainland of China	7934	6688	8039	6356	5925
原产地为中国内地经香港输往其他地方的转口货物	Re-exports of the Mainland of China Origin to Other Places	8841	7372	8823	7597	6795
涉及外发加工贸易的估计比重 (%)	**Estimated Proportion of Outward Processing Trade (%)**					
输往中国内地的整体出口货物	Total Exports to the Mainland of China	25	22	19	18	17
从中国内地进口的货物	Imports from the Mainland of China	39	35	33	31	29
原产地为中国内地经香港输往其他地方的转口货物	Re-exports of the Mainland of China Origin to Other Places	69	63	61	60	60

26–30 按服务组成部分划分的服务出口及进口

Exports and Imports of Services by Service Component

单位：亿港元 (HKD 100 million)

服务组成部分	Service Component	2019	2020	2021	2022	2023
服务出口	**Exports of Services**					
制造服务	Manufacturing Services	§	§	§	§	
保养及维修服务	Maintenance and Repair Services	28	19	18	19	
运输	Transport	2467	1859	2561	2611	
旅游	Travel	2266	222	144	245	
建筑	Construction	7	3	2	§	
保险及退休金服务	Insurance and Pension Services	111	91	94	108	
金融服务	Financial Services	1693	1688	1856	2019	
知识产权使用费	Charges for the Use of Intellectual Property	59	54	56	58	
电子通讯、计算机及资讯服务	Telecommunications, Computer and Information Services	242	257	292	311	
其他商业服务	Other Business Services	1084	971	1105	1112	
个人、文化及康乐服务	Personal, Cultural and Recreational Services	27	21	17	15	
政府货品及服务	Government Goods and Services	7	8	7	7	
总计	Total	7991	5192	6151	6505	7717 @
服务进口	**Imports of Services**					
制造服务	Manufacturing Services	881	790	948	907	
保养及维修服务	Maintenance and Repair Services	16	16	15	14	
运输	Transport	1437	1153	1564	1540	
旅游	Travel	2106	428	261	430	
建筑	Construction	5	3	2	21	
保险及退休金服务	Insurance and Pension Services	120	128	152	127	
金融服务	Financial Services	506	560	567	610	
知识产权使用费	Charges for the Use of Intellectual Property	155	137	158	163	
电子通讯、计算机及资讯服务	Telecommunications, Computer and Information Services	161	178	199	207	
其他商业服务	Other Business Services	932	844	907	905	
个人、文化及康乐服务	Personal, Cultural and Recreational Services	11	17	18	19	
政府货品及服务	Government Goods and Services	13	10	8	9	
总计	Total	6342	4263	4800	4952	6211 @
服务出口净额	**Net Exports of Services**	**1649**	**929**	**1350**	**1554**	**1506 @**

注：数字已采纳《2010年国际服务贸易统计手册》内最新的国际建议。
由于统计表内数字经四舍五入，分项总和未必与总数相等。

Notes: Figures have incorporated the latest international recommendations given in the Manual on Statistics of International Trade in Services 2010.
Figures in the table may not add up to the total due to rounding.

26–31 按主要目的地和来源地划分的服务出口及进口
Exports and Imports of Services by Major Destination and Source

单位：亿港元 (HKD 100 million)

目的地／来源地	Destination/Source	2018	2019	2020	2021	2022
服务出口①	**Exports of Services①**					
美国	United States of America	1200	1137	1108	1432	1416
中国内地	The Mainland of China	3401	2865	967	1001	1134
英国	United Kingdom	688	675	607	711	709
德国	Germany	245	238	225	361	326
中国台湾	Taiwan, China	308	280	218	316	310
其他	Others	2586	2414	1760	2041	2089
所有目的地	All Destinations	8429	7609	4885	5863	5984
服务进口①	**Imports of Services①**					
中国内地	The Mainland of China	2375	2349	1619	1969	1928
美国	United States of America	699	682	682	770	740
英国	United Kingdom	376	393	332	331	338
新加坡	Singapore	272	272	256	289	337
日本	Japan	520	509	193	178	223
其他	Others	2031	2017	1101	1218	1284
所有来源地	All Sources	6274	6223	4183	4756	4849

注：数字已采纳《2010年国际服务贸易统计手册》内最新的国际建议。
由于统计表内数字经四舍五入，分项总和未必与总数相等。
①由于非直接计算的金融中介服务没有按地区细分的数字，因此本统计表内的数字均没有包括非直接计算的金融中介服务的数字，以致本统计表内所有目的地／来源地的数字并不等同于表26–30内所有服务的相应数字。

Notes: Figures have incorporated the latest international recommendations given in the Manual on Statistics of International Trade in Services 2010.
Figures in the table may not add up to the total due to rounding.
①Since data on geographical breakdowns of financial intermediation services indirectly measured (FISIM) are not available, the figures in respect of FISIM are not included in this table. Hence, figures for all destinations/sources in this table are not equal to the corresponding figures for all services in Table 26-30.

26–32 按选定主要投资者国家／地区划分的外商直接投资头寸及流动
Position and Flow of Inward Direct Investment by Selected Major Investor Country/Territory

单位：亿港元 (HKD 100 million)

主要投资者国家／地区	Major Investor Country/Territory	以市值计算的外商直接投资 Inward Direct Investment at Market Value					
		年底头寸 Position at End of Year			年间流入 Inflow in Year		
		2020	2021	2022	2020	2021	2022
英属维尔京群岛	British Virgin Islands	45404	47159	48483	2384	3110	1898
中国内地	The Mainland of China	38934	42276	47051	3372	3516	3158
英国	United Kingdom	13670	14997	15698	810	253	813
开曼群岛	Cayman Islands	14384	16397	15599	1272	1205	634
百慕大	Bermuda	8135	8782	6954	-360	877	559
美国	United States of America	3596	3558	3514	85	-101	463
新加坡	Singapore	4582	3520	3491	853	-407	329
加拿大	Canada	2520	2945	2563	727	322	19
日本	Japan	1899	2146	2434	37	383	78
中国台湾	Taiwan, China	965	1625	1832	83	314	91
其他	Others	9455	9230	9178	1185	1425	548
总计	**Total**	**143544**	**152635**	**156797**	**10450**	**10897**	**8590**

注：根据香港近年从个别投资者国家／地区的外商直接投资头寸选取。
Note: Selected based on the position of Hong Kong's inward direct investment from individual investor countries/territories in recent years.

26–33 按选定主要接受投资国家／地区划分的对外直接投资头寸及流动
Position and Flow of Outward Direct Investment by Selected Major Recipient Country/Territory

单位：亿港元 (HKD 100 million)

主要接受投资国家/地区	Major Recipient Country/Territory	以市值计算的对外直接投资 Outward Direct Investment at Market Value					
		年底头寸 Position at End of Year			年间流出 Outflow in Year		
		2020	2021	2022	2020	2021	2022
中国内地	The Mainland of China	70484	76807	76253	3807	4364	4935
英属维尔京群岛	British Virgin Islands	47051	47207	46728	2440	1775	2495
开曼群岛	Cayman Islands	5721	5762	4962	493	348	224
百慕大	Bermuda	5281	5336	3910	444	367	-83
荷兰	Netherlands	1471	1486	3507	86	16	12
新加坡	Singapore	3118	3499	3404	198	326	131
英国	United Kingdom	2705	2735	2396	-99	125	-469
美国	United States of America	1537	1392	1642	104	-229	181
澳大利亚	Australia	1424	1571	1379	103	74	64
日本	Japan	1457	1148	1286	-5	33	329
其他	Others	8663	8974	8777	242	296	500
总计	**Total**	**148912**	**155917**	**154244**	**7813**	**7496**	**8319**

注：根据香港近年对个别接受投资国家／地区的对外直接投资头寸选取。
Note: Selected based on the position of Hong Kong's outward direct investment to individual recipient countries/territories in recent years.

26–34 按选定母公司所在地划分的驻港地区总部数目
Number of Regional Headquarters in Hong Kong by Selected Location of Parent Company

单位：个 (unit)

项　目	Item	2019	2020	2021	2022	2023
驻港地区总部数目	**No. of Regional Headquarters in Hong Kong**	**1541**	**1504**	**1457**	**1411**	**1336**
母公司所在地	Location of Parent Company					
中国内地	The Mainland of China	216	238	252	251	247
美国	United States of America	278	282	254	240	214
日本	Japan	232	226	210	212	206
英国	United Kingdom	141	131	138	134	115
德国	Germany	97	94	87	92	96
法国	France	96	94	89	80	81
瑞士	Switzerland	55	53	55	54	51
新加坡	Singapore	47	46	45	49	42
意大利	Italy	40	46	45	36	41
澳大利亚	Australia	35	29	28	27	27
荷兰	Netherlands	26	28	27	28	25
中国台湾	Taiwan, China	26	28	24	24	25
加拿大	Canada	22	23	23	24	20
瑞典	Sweden	30	24	23	15	16
奥地利	Austria	11	11	13	17	13

注：数字指有关年度6月首个工作天的数字。地区总部是指有香港境外母公司，并对区内(即香港及另一个或多个地方)各办事处及／或运作拥有管理权的一家办事处。如属联营机构，其母公司所在地可多于一个。

Note : Figures refer to the first working day of June of the year. A regional headquarters is an office with parent company located outside Hong Kong which has managerial control over offices and/or operations in the region (i.e. Hong Kong plus one or more other places). More than one location of parent companies may be involved, e.g. joint venture.

26–35 按选定母公司所在地划分的驻港地区办事处数目
Number of Regional Offices in Hong Kong by Selected Location of Parent Company

单位：个 (unit)

项　目	Item	2019	2020	2021	2022	2023
驻港地区办事处数目	**Number of Regional Offices in Hong Kong**	**2490**	**2479**	**2483**	**2397**	**2311**
母公司所在地	Location of Parent Company					
美国	United States of America	457	408	410	430	419
日本	Japan	431	427	423	402	411
中国内地	The Mainland of China	303	344	377	327	324
英国	United Kingdom	206	210	208	198	196
德国	Germany	152	145	147	149	133
法国	France	116	114	115	126	100
中国台湾	Taiwan, China	92	103	101	95	97
新加坡	Singapore	103	95	100	99	94
瑞士	Switzerland	85	92	91	84	81
荷兰	Netherlands	57	56	57	52	49
意大利	Italy	65	63	61	60	48
澳大利亚	Australia	54	50	54	52	47
韩国	Korea	47	38	33	42	38
瑞典	Sweden	29	38	38	37	34
加拿大	Canada	31	29	33	29	26

注：数字指有关年度6月首个工作天的数字。地区办事处是指有香港境外母公司，并负责协调区内(即香港及另一个或多个地方)各办事处及／或运作的一家办事处。如属联营机构，其母公司所在地可多于一个。

Note : Figures refer to the first working day of June of the year. A regional office is an office with parent company located outside Hong Kong which coordinates offices and/or operations in the region (i.e. Hong Kong plus one or more other places). More than one location of parent companies may be involved, e.g. joint venture.

26-36 按居住国家／地区划分的访港旅客人数
Visitor Arrivals by Country/Territory of Residence

单位：万人次 (10 000 person-times)

居住国家／地区	Country/Territory of Residence	2019	2020	2021	2022	2023
中国内地	The Mainland of China	4377.5	270.6	6.6	37.5	2676.0
南亚及东南亚	South and Southeast Asia	304.1	19.1	1.0	7.8	242.1
中国台湾	Taiwan, China	153.9	10.5	0.3	2.4	78.4
北亚	North Asia	212.1	9.0	0.1	1.6	74.9
欧洲、非洲及中东	Europe, Africa and the Middle East	198.5	17.8	0.7	4.5	86.4
美洲	The Americas	160.1	12.3	0.3	4.2	90.4
澳大利亚、新西兰及南太平洋	Australia, New Zealand and South Pacific	61.2	5.8	0.1	1.5	29.3
中国澳门①／未能辨别	Macao, China①/Not identified	123.9	11.8	0.2	1.0	122.4
总计	**Total**	**5591.3**	**356.9**	**9.1**	**60.5**	**3400.0**
与上年比较的变动百分比(%)	**Percentage Changes over the Preceding Year(%)**	**-14.2**	**-93.6**	**-97.4**	**561.5**	**5523.8**

注：①访港旅客数字包括经澳门访港的非澳门居民。
Note:①Figures include arrival of non-Macao residents via Macao.

26-37 政府储备结余
Government's Reserve Balances

单位：亿港元 (HKD 100 million)

项　目	Item	2019/2020	2020/2021	2021/2022	2022/2023	2023/2024
期初储备结余	Opening Reserve Balances	11708.83	11603.08	9277.67	9571.28	8347.90
收入①	Revenue①	5909.26	5642.30	6935.76	6221.47	5494.06
开支①	Expenditure①	6078.30	8160.75	6933.39	8104.77	7213.01
政府债券的偿还款项	Repayment of Government Bonds	(15.00)	-	-	-	(8.00)
发行政府债券所得的收入	Proceeds from Issuance of Government Bonds	78.29	193.04	291.24	659.92	724.90
盈余／(赤字)	Surplus/(Deficit)	(105.75)	(2325.41)	293.61	(1223.38)	(1002.05)
期末储备结余	Closing Reserve Balances	11603.08	9277.67	9571.28	8347.90	7345.85

注：2023/24年度的数字有待审计署署长核实。
①数字不包括“政府一般收入帐目及各基金之转拨”。
Notes:Figures for 2023/24 are subject to audit by the Director of Audit.
①Figures exclude “Transfers between the General Revenue Account and the Funds”.

26-38 政府收入(一般收入帐目及各基金)
Government Revenue (General Revenue Account and the Funds)

单位：亿港元 (HKD 100 million)

项目	Item	2019/2020	2020/2021	2021/2022	2022/2023	2023/2024
经营收入	**Operating Revenue**					
直接税	Direct Taxes					
入息税及利得税	Earnings and Profits Tax	2141.19	2208.18	2533.48	2642.65	2615.96
间接税	Indirect Taxes					
博彩及彩票税	Bets and Sweeps Tax	220.12	208.77	254.32	258.24	284.67
印花税	Stamp Duties	671.98	890.45	996.77	699.77	491.12
飞机乘客离境税	Air Passenger Departure Tax	23.47	1.01	0.56	3.93	19.43
应课税品税项	Duties	113.91	118.52	124.67	119.82	108.99
一般差饷	General Rates	209.80	190.44	192.56	191.00	282.10
车辆税	Motor Vehicle Taxes	72.19	65.94	61.67	49.66	58.98
专利税及特权税	Royalties and Concessions	32.02	35.29	57.95	34.84	43.57
各项收费①(含征税成分的费用)	Fees and Charges① (tax-loaded fees)	48.32	43.62	48.87	51.35	76.96
其他收入	Other Revenue					
罚款、没收及罚金	Fines, Forfeitures and Penalties	18.01	47.72	25.94	23.70	19.65
物业及投资	Properties and Investments	233.35	213.42	210.94	244.70	251.94
贷款、偿款、供款及其他收入	Loans, Reimbursements, Contributions and Other Receipts	40.69	55.24	48.49	68.97	56.90
公用事业	Utilities	39.06	34.96	32.00	32.02	33.72
各项收费①(不包含征税成分的费用)	Fees and Charges① (excluding tax-loaded fees)	72.90	61.01	66.67	74.83	82.36
投资收入	Investment Income					
政府一般收入帐目	General Revenue Account	401.53	418.48	252.00	154.36	63.90
土地基金	Land Fund	-	-	376.77	483.88	570.00
来自投资／贷款的股息、利息及其他收入	Dividends, interest and other receipts from investments/loans	-	-	-	-	22.29
经营收入总额	**Total Operating Revenue**	**4338.54**	**4593.05**	**5283.66**	**5133.72**	**5082.54**
非经营收入	**Capital Revenue**					
间接税	Indirect Taxes					
遗产税	Estate Duty	0.53	0.07	0.02	0.09	0.10
其他收入	Other Revenue					
从房屋委员会收回的款项	Recovery from Housing Authority	15.18	31.21	17.82	14.14	13.57
其他	Others	9.13	7.01	7.70	11.12	58.54
基金	Funds					
基本工程储备基金②	Capital Works Reserve Funds②	1473.70	957.19	1535.22	881.27	264.37
资本投资基金	Capital Investment Fund	9.55	8.92	11.72	17.22	11.50
赈灾基金	Disaster Relief Fund	0.05	0.04	0.06	0.08	0.03
贷款基金	Loan Fund	24.59	9.04	9.85	55.57	10.13
公务员退休金储备基金	Civil Service Pension Reserve Fund	11.11	15.04	30.22	50.51	19.93
创新及科技基金	Innovation and Technology Fund	7.78	9.66	12.89	17.33	11.35
奖券基金	Lotteries Fund	19.10	11.07	26.60	40.42	22.00
非经营收入总额②	**Total Capital Revenue②**	**1570.72**	**1049.25**	**1652.10**	**1087.75**	**411.52**
政府收入总额②	**Total Government Revenue②**	**5909.26**	**5642.30**	**6935.76**	**6221.47**	**5494.06**

注：2023/24年度的数字有待审计署署长核实。
①各项收费之中含征税成分的费用已重新归类为税项收入。
②数字不包括发行政府债券的收入。

Notes: Figures for 2023/24 are subject to audit by the Director of Audit.
①The tax-loaded portion of fees and charges is re-classified under tax revenue.
②Figures exclude proceeds from issuance of Government Bonds.

26–39 政府支出(一般收入帐目及各基金)
Government Expenditure (General Revenue Account and the Funds)

单位：亿港元 (HKD 100 million)

项目	Item	2019/2020	2020/2021	2021/2022	2022/2023	2023/2024
经营支出	**Operating Expenditure**					
经常支出	**Recurrent Expenditure**					
个人薪酬	Personal Emoluments	874.90	876.17	880.41	908.95	945.38
与员工有关联的支出	Personnel Related Expenses	94.12	101.74	112.90	126.02	137.89
退休金	Pensions	386.48	426.89	436.53	455.97	478.38
部门支出	Departmental Expenses	408.18	451.55	536.96	725.32	536.00
其它费用	Other Charges					
政府一般收入帐目	General Revenue Account	844.32	930.83	1011.85	1104.30	1164.98
土地基金	Land Fund	-	-	0.01	0.07	0.04
资助金	Subventions	1779.60	1883.76	1953.36	2077.99	2128.42
非经常支出	Non-recurrent					
政府一般收入帐目	General Revenue Account	844.51	2519.11	967.58	1500.66	620.12
土地基金	Land Fund	-	0.39	-	0.14	0.02
经营支出总额	**Total Operating Expenditure**	**5232.11**	**7190.44**	**5899.60**	**6899.42**	**6011.23**
非经营支出	**Capital Expenditure**					
机器、设备及工程	Plant, Equipment and Works	28.19	29.35	38.14	39.96	41.72
资助金	Subventions	25.84	30.92	32.48	38.63	34.55
基金	Funds					
基本工程储备基金①	Capital Works Reserve Fund①	685.57	771.72	845.43	984.01	994.42
资本投资基金	Capital Investment Fund	39.27	25.94	16.04	50.44	27.31
贷款基金	Loan Fund	23.49	27.37	34.09	21.37	22.37
赈灾基金	Disaster Relief Fund	0.67	0.72	0.29	0.64	1.39
创新及科技基金	Innovation and Technology Fund	18.84	47.96	36.48	46.43	59.04
奖券基金	Lotteries Fund	24.32	36.33	30.84	23.87	20.98
非经营支出总额①	**Total Capital Expenditure①**	**846.19**	**970.31**	**1033.79**	**1205.35**	**1201.78**
政府支出总额①	**Total Government Expenditure①**	**6078.30**	**8160.75**	**6933.39**	**8104.77**	**7213.01**

注：2023/24年度的数字有待审计署署长核实。
① 数字不包括政府债券的偿还款项。
Notes: Figures for 2023/24 are subject to audit by the Director of Audit.
① Figures exclude repayment amount of Government Bonds.

26–40 按政策组别划分的公共开支
Public Expenditure by Policy Area Group

单位：亿港元 (HKD 100 million)

项目	Item	2019/2020	2020/2021	2021/2022	2022/2023	2023/2024
社区及对外事务	Community and External Affairs	204.08	220.20	242.16	269.35	289.29
经济	Economic	400.35	1177.27	717.36	1031.03	745.55
教育	Education	1253.41	1070.40	1069.37	1068.33	1134.43
环境及食物	Environment and Food	306.80	353.11	338.82	382.96	416.64
卫生	Health	873.47	969.99	1145.53	1536.59	1201.77
房屋	Housing	310.99	351.51	357.41	359.97	448.74
基础建设	Infrastructure	668.44	771.05	794.81	896.04	886.19
保安	Security	567.32	643.30	557.63	659.54	627.57
社会福利	Social Welfare	921.43	979.27	1033.91	1101.94	1177.71
辅助服务	Support	920.53	2006.46	1052.88	1169.63	776.37
总计	**Total**	**6426.82**	**8542.56**	**7309.88**	**8475.38**	**7704.26**

注：2023/24年度的数字为修订预算。
公共开支包括政府开支及其他公营机构的开支。至于政府只享有股权的机构，包括法定机构，例如机场管理局及香港铁路有限公司，其开支则不包括在内。
Notes: Figures for 2023/24 are revised estimates.
Public expenditure comprises government expenditure and expenditure by other public bodies. It does not include expenditure by those organisations, including statutory organisations, in which the government has only an equity position, such as the Airport Authority and the MTR Corporation Limited.

26–41 外币兑换率及港汇指数
Exchange Rates and the Effective Exchange Rate Indices

单位：每单位外币兑换港元 (HKD per unit of foreign currency)

项　目	Item	2019	2020	2021	2022	2023
年内平均数字①	**Average for the year①**					
澳元	Australian Dollar	5.44	5.36	5.84	5.44	5.20
加拿大元	Canadian Dollar	5.91	5.79	6.20	6.02	5.80
人民币	Chinese Renminbi	1.1332	1.1248	1.2054	1.1634	1.1047
欧元	Euro	8.77	8.86	9.20	8.24	8.47
印度卢比	Indian Rupee	0.111	0.105	0.105	0.100	0.095
印尼盾	Indonesian Rupiah	0.0006	0.0005	0.0005	0.0005	0.0005
日元	Japanese Yen	0.0719	0.0727	0.0708	0.0599	0.0558
韩元	Korean Won	0.0067	0.0066	0.0068	0.0061	0.0060
马来西亚林吉特	Malaysian Ringgit	1.89	1.85	1.88	1.78	1.72
新台币	New Taiwan Dollar	0.256	0.261	0.273	0.263	0.257
菲律宾比索	Philippines Peso	0.153	0.157	0.160	0.145	0.145
英镑	Pound Sterling	10.00	9.96	10.69	9.67	9.73
新加坡元	Singapore Dollar	5.74	5.63	5.78	5.68	5.83
南非兰特	South African Rand	0.54	0.47	0.53	0.48	0.42
瑞士法郎	Swiss Franc	7.89	8.28	8.51	8.20	8.72
泰铢	Thai Baht	0.253	0.249	0.244	0.224	0.225
美元	US Dollar	7.836	7.757	7.774	7.832	7.829
特别提款权	Special Drawing Right	10.82677	10.79899	11.07748	10.48219	10.44396
港汇指数 (2020年1月=100)②	Effective Exchange Rate Indices for the Hong Kong dollar (January 2020=100) ②					
贸易总值(进口及整体出口)加权	Trade (import and export)-weighted	99.4	100.0	95.5	100.1	103.4
进口货值加权	Import-weighted	99.5	100.1	95.8	100.8	103.9
整体出口货值加权 ③	Export-weighted③	99.2	100.0	95.1	99.3	102.9
年底数字④	**As at end of year④**					
澳元	Australian Dollar	5.46	5.97	5.66	5.32	5.32
加拿大元	Canadian Dollar	5.97	6.09	6.13	5.76	5.89
人民币	Chinese Renminbi	1.1175	1.1919	1.2245	1.1281	1.0962
欧元	Euro	8.72	9.53	8.82	8.36	8.62
印度卢比	Indian Rupee	0.110	0.106	0.105	0.094	0.094
印尼盾	Indonesian Rupiah	0.0006	0.0006	0.0005	0.0005	0.0005
日元	Japanese Yen	0.0716	0.0751	0.0677	0.0596	0.0554
韩元	Korean Won	0.0067	0.0071	0.0066	0.0062	0.0060
马来西亚林吉特	Malaysian Ringgit	1.90	1.93	1.87	1.77	1.70
新台币	New Taiwan Dollar	0.258	0.265	0.280	0.257	0.261
菲律宾比索	Philippines Peso	0.153	0.164	0.155	0.143	0.145
英镑	Pound Sterling	10.21	10.57	10.53	9.45	9.94
新加坡元	Singapore Dollar	5.78	5.86	5.77	5.82	5.92
南非兰特	South African Rand	0.55	0.53	0.49	0.46	0.43
瑞士法郎	Swiss Franc	8.04	8.80	8.53	8.45	9.28
泰铢	Thai Baht	0.260	0.260	0.234	0.226	0.228
美元	US Dollar	7.787	7.753	7.798	7.808	7.811
特别提款权	Special Drawing Right	10.76948	11.16641	10.91540	10.38588	10.48701
港汇指数 (2020年1月=100)②	Effective Exchange Rate Indices for the Hong Kong Dollar (January 2020=100)②					
贸易总值(进口及整体出口)加权	Trade (import and export)-weighted	100.1	95.3	95.3	102.0	103.5
进口货值加权	Import-weighted	100.0	95.4	95.7	102.4	103.9
整体出口货值加权③	Export-weighted③	100.1	95.2	94.7	101.5	103.2

注：《中华人民共和国香港特别行政区基本法》说明，港元是香港特别行政区的法定货币。外币指港元以外的其他货币，因而人民币亦视作外币。

①数字是指年内每日电汇或现钞收市中间兑换价的平均值。

②由2022年1月3日起公布的重订基期后数列。

③包括转口和港产品出口。

④数字是该年最后一个交易日的电汇或现钞收市中间兑换价。

Notes : Hong Kong Dollar is the legal tender in the Hong Kong Special Administrative Region, as stated in "The Basic Law of the Hong Kong Special Administrative Region of the People's Republic of China". Foreign currency refers to any currency other than the Hong Kong currency. Accordingly, Chinese Renminbi is also treated as foreign currency.

①Figures are the averages of the daily closing middle-market telegraphic transfer rates or notes rates for the year.

②Rebased series has been released as from 3 January 2022.

③Including re-exports and domestic exports.

④Figures are the closing middle-market telegraphic transfer rates or notes rates as at the last trading day of the year.

26-42 货币供应量
Money Supply

单位：亿港元(年底数字) (HKD 100 million, as at end of year)

项　　目	Item	2019	2020	2021	2022	2023
法定纸币及硬币的流通量	Legal Tender Notes and Coins in Circulation					
由商业银行发行	Commercial Bank Issues	5166.05	5595.15	5926.45	6055.75	5925.85
由政府发行	Government Issues	132.54	131.73	133.85	134.04	131.80
总计	Total	5298.59	5726.88	6060.30	6189.79	6057.65
由认可机构持有的法定纸币及硬币	Authorized Institutions' Holdings of Legal Tender Notes and Coins	325.59	316.91	306.83	383.64	309.10
由公众持有的法定纸币及硬币	Legal Tender Notes and Coins in Hands of Public	4973.00	5409.97	5753.47	5806.15	5748.55
货币供应量：就外币掉期存款作出调整	Money Supply : Adjusted for Foreign Currency Swap Deposits					
货币供应量 M_1	Money Supply M_1					
港元	Hong Kong Dollar	15331.04	19727.19	20789.11	17084.21	15332.91
外币	Foreign Currency	9516.34	12592.03	14119.47	10609.23	10649.11
总计	Total	24847.38	32319.21	34908.58	27693.43	25982.03
货币供应量 M_2	Money Supply M_2					
港元①	Hong Kong Dollar①	74387.89	79220.89	80439.94	80965.17	82501.09
外币②	Foreign Currency②	73070.83	76845.18	82286.56	84401.08	89451.57
总计	Total	147458.72	156066.08	162726.50	165366.25	171952.66
货币供应量 M_3	Money Supply M_3					
港元①	Hong Kong Dollar①	74546.55	79370.38	80574.08	81090.00	82628.31
外币②	Foreign Currency②	73317.20	77070.06	82534.58	84604.31	89712.22
总计	Total	147863.75	156440.43	163108.66	165694.31	172340.52
货币供应量：未就外币掉期存款作出调整	Money Supply : Unadjusted for Foreign Currency Swap Deposits					
货币供应量 M_2	Money Supply M_2					
港元	Hong Kong Dollar	74387.65	79220.67	80439.72	80964.97	82500.92
外币	Foreign Currency	73071.07	76845.41	82286.78	84401.28	89451.74
总计	Total	147458.72	156066.08	162726.50	165366.25	171952.66
货币供应量 M_3	Money Supply M_3					
港元	Hong Kong Dollar	74546.31	79370.15	80573.86	81089.80	82628.13
外币	Foreign Currency	73317.43	77070.28	82534.80	84604.51	89712.39
总计	Total	147863.75	156440.43	163108.66	165694.31	172340.52

注：《中华人民共和国香港特别行政区基本法》说明，港元是香港特别行政区的法定货币。外币指港元以外的其他货币，因而人民币亦视作外币。
①所列数字已包括外币掉期存款。
②所列数字已扣除外币掉期存款。

Notes : Hong Kong dollar is the legal tender in the Hong Kong Special Administrative Region, as stated in "The Basic Law of the Hong Kong Special Administrative Region of the People's Republic of China". Foreign currency refers to any currency other than the Hong Kong currency. Accordingly, Chinese Renminbi is also treated as foreign currency.
①Figures are adjusted to include foreign currency swap deposits.
②Figures are adjusted to exclude foreign currency swap deposits.

26–43 股票价格指数、证券交易成交额及市场总值
Index of Share Prices, Value of Stock Exchange Turnover and Market Capitalisation

项　目	Item	2019	2020	2021	2022	2023
香港上市①	**Hong Kong-listed①**					
主板	**Main Board**					
股票价格指数②	Index of Share Prices②					
恒生指数(1964年7月31日= 100)	Hang Seng Index (31 July, 1964=100)					
最高	High	30280.1	29174.9	31183.4	25050.6	22700.9
最低	Low	24896.9	21139.3	22665.3	14597.3	15972.3
收市	Closing	28189.8	27231.1	23397.7	19781.4	17047.4
分类指数 (1984年1月13日= 975.47)	Sub-indexes (13 January, 1984=975.47)					
金融	Finance					
最高	High	42019.2	40369.3	41547.2	39006.3	36184.6
最低	Low	34448.3	29910.5	32369.3	24336.9	27744.0
收市	Closing	39114.6	36939.0	33869.5	32445.5	29823.0
公用事业	Utilities					
最高	High	63052.4	58417.6	53325.0	51609.6	40015.8
最低	Low	53631.5	43060.9	44696.6	30919.6	29047.3
收市	Closing	56584.5	45760.1	50685.6	36828.8	32873.7
地产	Properties					
最高	High	45890.9	40832.1	36609.9	32667.3	28625.0
最低	Low	35380.1	28387.0	27060.2	18389.7	16572.2
收市	Closing	40190.1	32127.3	29580.4	26040.0	18327.4
工商业	Commerce and Industry					
最高	High	17561.2	17570.0	21210.2	14644.4	12894.0
最低	Low	14023.8	11682.3	13406.6	7910.6	8727.2
收市	Closing	16234.3	17452.8	13996.2	10915.4	9233.6
恒生综合指数 (2000年1月3日= 2000)	Hang Seng Composite Index (3 January, 2000=2000)					
最高	High	4079.0	4298.3	5058.9	3822.4	3420.9
最低	Low	3313.2	2871.9	3506.1	2188.7	2420.1
收市	Closing	3827.6	4294.7	3626.5	2974.2	2565.0
恒生中国企业指数 (2000年1月3日= 2000)	Hang Seng China Enterprises Index (3 January, 2000=2000)					
最高	High	11881.7	11502.5	12271.6	8822.8	7773.6
最低	Low	9731.9	8290.3	8011.0	4919.0	5443.6
收市	Closing	11168.1	10738.4	8236.4	6704.9	5768.5
恒生香港中资企业指数 (2000年1月3日= 2000)	Hang Seng China-Affiliated Corp. Index (3 January, 2000=2000)					
最高	High	4788.6	4633.0	4324.1	4392.2	4267.1
最低	Low	3941.1	3059.6	3558.9	2831.0	3146.0
收市	Closing	4537.8	3799.6	3899.6	3696.0	3350.5
主板	**Main Board**					
成交金额 (亿港元)	Turnover (HKD 100 million)	213901.9	320237.8	410863.6	306861.9	254868.4
市场总值③ (亿港元)	Market Capitalisation③ (HKD 100 million)	380583.4	473922.0	422727.7	355817.3	309854.7
GEM	**GEM**					
成交金额 (亿港元)	Turnover (HKD 100 million)	498.6	863.7	958.9	410.0	311.5
市场总值③ (亿港元)	Market Capitalisation③ (HKD 100 million)	1067.0	1308.2	1083.8	850.5	536.2

注：对于最高和最低指数，恒生指数有限公司是根据期内每日即市指数编制。
①恒生指数系列按指数成分股的上市地域分类为香港上市、跨市场及内地上市。
②以下指数采用流通市值加权法计算，并设有个别成分股比重上限。
③年底数字。

Notes : For high and low indices, indexes compiled by the Hang Seng Indexes Company Limited are based on the intraday indices of the period.
①The Hang Seng Family of Indexes are classified as Hong Kong-listed, Cross-market and Mainland-listed according to where their constituents are listed.
②The following indexes adopt a freefloat-adjusted market capitalisation weighted methodology with capping on individual constituent weighting
③Year-end figures.

26-44 消费物价指数（2019年10月-2020年9月=100）
Consumer Price Indices (Oct. 2019 - Sep. 2020=100)

项　　目	Item	2019	2020	2021	2022	2023
综合消费物价指数	**Composite Consumer Price Index**					
总指数	**All Items**	**99.6**	**99.9**	**101.4**	**103.3**	**105.5**
食品	Food	97.1	100.4	102.0	105.9	108.7
外出用膳及外卖	Meals out and takeaway food	99.4	100.1	101.9	105.4	109.5
基本食品	Basic food	93.5	100.8	102.2	106.8	107.3
住屋①	Housing①	100.2	100.1	100.4	100.7	101.7
私人房屋租金	Private Housing Rent	98.9	99.9	98.7	98.1	98.5
公营房屋租金	Public Housing Rent	130.1	102.7	132.8	145.5	151.9
电力、燃气及水	Electricity, Gas and Water	116.4	91.6	116.4	124.7	136.7
烟酒	Alcoholic Drinks and Tobacco	99.7	100.2	100.3	101.6	118.9
衣履	Clothing and Footwear	103.9	98.6	101.9	107.2	113.4
耐用物品	Durable Goods	102.1	99.6	100.6	101.2	98.8
杂项物品②	Miscellaneous Goods②	96.9	100.8	97.7	98.1	99.7
交通	Transport	100.4	99.3	101.9	104.8	106.8
杂项服务③	Miscellaneous Services③	99.3	100.1	100.8	102.2	104.9
教育服务	Educational Services	97.9	100.4	102.0	103.8	107.0
资讯及通讯服务	Information and Communications Services	101.0	99.7	98.0	95.9	95.3
医疗服务	Medical Services	98.4	100.5	101.9	103.9	106.2
甲类消费物价指数	**Consumer Price Index (A)**					
总指数	**All Items**	**100.5**	**99.8**	**102.7**	**104.9**	**107.3**
食品	Food	96.5	100.5	102.0	105.8	108.4
外出用膳及外卖	Meals out and takeaway food	99.2	100.2	102.0	105.4	109.6
基本食品	Basic food	92.9	100.8	102.0	106.5	106.7
住屋①	Housing①	102.9	100.3	103.0	104.2	105.8
私人房屋租金	Private Housing Rent	98.9	99.9	98.7	98.2	98.8
公营房屋租金	Public Housing Rent	130.1	102.7	132.8	145.5	152.0
电力、燃气及水	Electricity, Gas and Water	120.1	89.6	119.2	126.8	139.1
烟酒	Alcoholic Drinks and Tobacco	99.7	100.2	100.6	102.5	122.5
衣履	Clothing and Footwear	103.4	98.9	102.0	107.4	112.3
耐用物品	Durable Goods	102.3	99.5	100.1	100.1	97.5
杂项物品②	Miscellaneous Goods②	96.7	101.1	97.5	97.6	99.4
交通	Transport	101.0	98.9	101.3	101.3	103.1
杂项服务③	Miscellaneous Services③	99.9	100.0	100.3	101.1	103.1
教育服务	Educational Services	98.6	100.3	101.7	103.2	105.8
资讯及通讯服务	Information and Communications Services	101.2	99.6	97.9	95.6	94.8
医疗服务	Medical Services	98.5	100.5	102.0	104.3	106.4
乙类消费物价指数	**Consumer Price Index (B)**					
总指数	**All Items**	**99.2**	**99.8**	**100.8**	**102.5**	**104.6**
食品	Food	97.4	100.3	102.0	105.9	108.8
外出用膳及外卖	Meals out and takeaway food	99.4	100.1	101.9	105.4	109.5
基本食品	Basic food	93.5	100.8	102.2	106.8	107.4
住屋①	Housing①	99.1	100.0	99.2	99.0	99.8
私人房屋租金	Private Housing Rent	98.9	99.9	98.6	97.9	98.3
公营房屋租金	Public Housing Rent	129.8	102.3	132.3	145.0	151.4
电力、燃气及水	Electricity, Gas and Water	114.8	92.7	114.9	123.4	135.1
烟酒	Alcoholic Drinks and Tobacco	99.8	100.3	100.2	101.2	116.8
衣履	Clothing and Footwear	103.8	98.5	101.7	107.9	113.4
耐用物品	Durable Goods	102.1	99.6	100.5	100.9	98.2
杂项物品②	Miscellaneous Goods②	96.8	100.7	97.4	97.9	99.7
交通	Transport	100.6	99.3	101.9	104.8	106.9
杂项服务③	Miscellaneous Services③	99.3	100.1	100.9	102.2	104.9
教育服务	Educational Services	97.9	100.4	102.0	103.6	106.8
资讯及通讯服务	Information and Communications Services	101.0	99.7	98.1	96.0	95.7
医疗服务	Medical Services	98.5	100.5	102.0	104.2	106.3

26–44 续表 continued

项　目	Item	2019	2020	2021	2022	2023
丙类消费物价指数	**Consumer Price Index (C)**					
总指数	**All Items**	**99.1**	**99.9**	**100.8**	**102.6**	**104.7**
食品	Food	97.9	100.3	102.1	106.1	109.1
外出用膳及外卖	Meals out and takeaway food	99.6	100.0	101.9	105.4	109.5
基本食品	Basic food	94.7	100.8	102.6	107.4	108.5
住屋①	Housing①	98.7	100.0	99.1	98.7	99.4
私人房屋租金	Private Housing Rent	98.9	100.0	98.8	98.2	98.5
电力、燃气及水	Electricity, Gas and Water	110.4	94.5	112.2	122.0	133.4
烟酒	Alcoholic Drinks and Tobacco	99.9	100.3	99.6	100.0	111.6
衣履	Clothing and Footwear	104.3	98.6	101.9	106.4	114.4
耐用物品	Durable Goods	102.1	99.7	101.1	102.5	100.5
杂项物品②	Miscellaneous Goods②	97.3	100.8	98.6	99.0	100.4
交通	Transport	99.9	99.7	102.2	107.2	109.3
杂项服务③	Miscellaneous Services③	98.9	100.2	101.1	102.8	105.9
教育服务	Educational Services	97.5	100.4	102.3	104.3	107.9
资讯及通讯服务	Information and Communications Services	100.5	99.8	98.1	96.0	95.8
医疗服务	Medical Services	98.3	100.6	101.8	103.4	106.0

注：①除“私人房屋租金”及“公营房屋租金”外，“住屋”类别还包括“管理费及其他住屋杂费”。丙类消费物价指数中的“住屋”类别并不包括“公营房屋租金”。
②“杂项物品”类别包括“药物”、“化妆品及个人护理用品”、“购买教科书”及其他杂项物品。
③“杂项服务”类别包括“教育服务”、“资讯及通讯服务”、“医疗服务”及其他杂项服务。

Notes: ①Apart from "Private Housing Rent" and "Public Housing Rent", the "Housing" section also includes "Management Fees and Other Housing Charges". For CPI(C), the "Housing" section does not include "Public Housing Rent".
②"Miscellaneous goods" section includes "Proprietary medicines and supplies", "Cosmetics and personal care products", "Purchases of textbooks" and other miscellaneous goods.
③"Miscellaneous Services" section includes "Educational Services", "Information and Communications Services", "Medical Services" and other miscellaneous services.

26−45 按四分位开支组别及商品或服务类别划分的住户每月平均开支
Average Monthly Household Expenditure by Commodity/Service Section by Quartile Expenditure Group

商品或服务类别	Commodity/ Service Section	总数 Overall		四分位开支组别 Quartile Expenditure Group							
				最低四分位 The Lowest 25%		第二四分位 The Second 25%		第三四分位 The Third 25%		最高四分位 The Highest 25%	
		值(港元) Value (HKD)	百分比 (Percent)	值(港元) Value (HKD)	百分比 (Percent)	值(港元) Value (HKD)	百分比 (Percent)	值(港元) Value (HKD)	百分比 (Percent)	值(港元) Value (HKD)	百分比 (Percent)
食品	Food	8107	26.8	4227	41.7	6289	31.2	8727	28.4	13186	22.0
住屋①	Housing①	11865	39.3	3113	30.7	8622	42.8	12681	41.2	23051	38.5
电力、燃气及水	Electricity, Gas and Water	688	2.3	431	4.3	567	2.8	736	2.4	1018	1.7
烟酒	Alcoholic Drinks & Tobacco	157	0.5	104	1.0	143	0.7	147	0.5	234	0.4
衣履	Clothing & Footwear	748	2.5	155	1.5	356	1.8	709	2.3	1772	3.0
耐用物品	Durable Goods	1312	4.3	337	3.3	664	3.3	1135	3.7	3114	5.2
杂项物品	Miscellaneous Goods	1062	3.5	384	3.8	699	3.5	1130	3.7	2036	3.4
交通	Transport	2033	6.7	463	4.6	887	4.4	1753	5.7	5031	8.4
杂项服务	Miscellaneous Services	4257	14.1	919	9.1	1928	9.6	3739	12.2	10445	17.4
总数	**All Sections**	**30230**	**100.0**	**10134**	**100.0**	**20154**	**100.0**	**30757**	**100.0**	**59888**	**100.0**
住户总数	**Number of Households**										
(户)	**(household)**	**2395000**		**599000**		**599000**		**599000**		**599000**	

注：住户开支是由2019年10月至2020年9月进行的住户开支统计调查的结果计算出来，由于期间大部分时间消费行为严重受到2019冠状病毒病疫情的影响，住户在某些商品或服务上的开支与正常情况的开支应有显著偏差。因此读者应小心阐释统计调查所得的住户开支数据。2019/20年住户开支统计调查的对象并不包括接受综合社会保障援助的住户。于2019/20年住户开支统计调查期间，政府数项一次性的纾困措施减低了住户的开支。本表列载的住户开支数字是指住户获各项措施宽减后的实际开支。由于进位关系，个别项目的数字或百分比相加可能不等于总数。

①对于自置、免租或雇主津贴居所的住户，住屋费用是指假定其居所是租住的情况下，所需支付的估计租金。

Notes: Household expenditures are calculated from the results of the Household Expenditure Survey (HES) conducted during October 2019 to September 2020, during a large part of which consumer behaviour was severely affected by the COVID-19 epidemic and household spending on some commodities/services should have deviated significantly from those under normal circumstances. The household expenditure figures of the 2019/20 HES should therefore be carefully interpreted. Households receiving Comprehensive Social Security Allowance are not included in the 2019/20 HES. During the survey period of 2019/20 HES, the household expenditure was lowered by a number of Government's one-off relief measures. Household expenditure figures in this table refer to the actual expenditure incurred by households upon enjoying various waivers/concessions. Figures or percentages may not add up to respective totals due to rounding.

①For households in accommodation which is owner-occupied, rent-free or employer-subsidised, the housing cost refers to the estimated rent which would have been paid as if the accommodation had been rented.

26–46 15岁及以上人口受教育程度
Educational Attainment of Population Aged 15 and Above

教育程度/性别	Educational Attainment/ Sex	2019		2020		2021		2022		2023	
		人数(万人) Number of Persons (10 000 persons)	百分比 (Percent)	人数(万人) Number of Persons (10 000 persons)	百分比 (Percent)	人数(万人) Number of Persons (10 000 persons)	百分比 (Percent)	人数(万人) Number of Persons (10 000 persons)	百分比 (Percent)	人数(万人) Number of Persons (10 000 persons)	百分比 (Percent)
总计	**Total**										
男	Male	294.55	44.81	294.74	44.91	292.48	44.87	291.45	44.93	298.95	44.84
女	Female	362.71	55.19	361.48	55.09	359.38	55.13	357.25	55.07	367.79	55.16
未受教育/学前教育①	No Schooling/Pre-primary①										
男	Male	5.70	0.87	6.02	0.92	6.14	0.94	5.59	0.86	5.21	0.78
女	Female	19.52	2.97	19.12	2.91	18.77	2.88	17.55	2.71	17.18	2.58
小学	Primary										
男	Male	37.64	5.73	37.31	5.69	36.56	5.61	36.26	5.59	35.43	5.31
女	Female	55.87	8.50	55.61	8.47	55.25	8.48	55.44	8.55	55.78	8.37
初中	Lower Secondary										
男	Male	47.58	7.24	45.99	7.01	47.04	7.22	46.97	7.24	47.77	7.16
女	Female	50.52	7.69	48.85	7.44	48.39	7.42	49.24	7.59	50.10	7.51
高中	Upper Secondary										
男	Male	94.85	14.43	94.96	14.47	94.94	14.56	93.20	14.37	96.52	14.48
女	Female	123.65	18.81	123.34	18.80	124.50	19.10	120.67	18.60	124.37	18.65
高等教育	Post-secondary										
非学位课程②	Non-degree Courses②										
男	Male	27.97	4.26	28.56	4.35	28.31	4.34	28.76	4.43	28.04	4.21
女	Female	28.21	4.29	30.10	4.59	28.62	4.39	29.53	4.55	29.46	4.42
学位课程③	Degree Courses③										
男	Male	80.81	12.30	81.91	12.48	79.50	12.20	80.67	12.43	85.98	12.90
女	Female	84.95	12.92	84.46	12.87	83.85	12.86	84.82	13.08	90.89	13.63

注：数字是根据该年1月至12月进行的“综合住户统计调查”结果，以及年中人口估计数字而编制，可被视为反映全年的平均情况。
① 包括所有幼儿园及幼儿中心班级。
② 包括所有在香港或以外地区学院的证书、文凭、高级证书、高级文凭、专业文凭、副学士、副学士先修、增修证书、院士衔及其它同等程度的高等教育课程。
③ 包括所有在香港或以外地区学院的学士学位、研究生修课及专题研究课程。

Notes: Figures are compiled based on the survey results of the General Household Survey (GHS) from January to December of the year concerned as well as the mid-year population estimates and may be regarded as referring to the average situation of the whole year.
① Including all classes in kindergartens and child care centres.
② Including all certificate, diploma, higher certificate, higher diploma, professional diploma, associate degree, pre-associate degree, endorsement certificate, associateship and other post-secondary programmes of equivalent standards in educational institutions within or outside Hong Kong.
③ Including all first degree, taught postgraduate and research postgraduate courses in educational institutions within or outside Hong Kong.

26–47 按教育及培训机构类别划分的学生人数
Student Enrolment by Type of Educational and Training Institution

单位：人 (person)

类　别	Type	2019	2020	2021	2022	2023
幼儿园	Kindergarten	174297	164935	155956	143676	136095
小学	Primary School	373228	364257	348994	333551	325564
中学	Secondary School	328743	330305	327326	322563	329398
日校	Day School	327394	329011	325927	321162	328474
其他课程①	Other Course①	1349	1294	1399	1401	924
特殊教育	Special Education	8344	8356	8471	8539	8892
特殊学校	Special School	8270	8290	8379	8458	8818
普通学校的特殊班	Special Class in Ordinary School	74	66	92	81	74
特殊幼儿中心②	Special child care centre②	2013	1914	2058	2010	2199
感化／住宿院舍③	Correctional/residential home③	51	44	70	57	45
惩教院所	Correctional institutions	158	101	147	168	173
教资会资助大学④	University Grants Committee (UGC) -funded Universities④	189484	186882	191240	195992	203579
全日制	Full-time	151915	151072	156244	163127	171108
证书／文凭课程	Certificate/Diploma	663	710	723	784	796
副学位课程	Sub-degree	24206	23523	23315	22921	23471
学士学位课程	Undergraduate	92671	92135	91352	91996	93766
研究院修课课程	Taught Postgraduate	22671	21901	26986	32618	36977
研究院研究课程⑤	Research Postgraduate⑤	11704	12803	13868	14808	16098
兼读制	Part-time	37569	35810	34996	32865	32471
证书／文凭课程	Certificate/Diploma	3195	3011	2798	2578	2419
副学位课程	Sub-degree	4997	4119	4211	3355	3473
学士学位课程	Undergraduate	6498	5583	5362	5212	5259
研究院修课课程	Taught Postgraduate	21885	22078	21539	20540	20025
研究院研究课程⑤	Research Postgraduate⑤	994	1019	1086	1180	1295
香港都会大学⑥	Hong Kong Metropolitan University⑥	22787	22599	22121	20383	21871
全日制	Full-time	11814	12574	13016	13083	15571
遥距／兼读制面授	Distance Learning/Part-time Face-to-face	10973	10025	9105	7300	6300
认可专上学院⑦	Approved Post Secondary Colleges⑦	21533	21287	20377	20502	22540
全日制	Full-time	20711	20236	19086	18893	21136
兼读制	Part-time	822	1051	1291	1609	1404
香港演艺学院	The Hong Kong Academy for Performing Arts	994	1068	1028	1055	1063
全日制	Full-time	945	1014	973	1000	1023
非学位程度⑧	Non-degree⑧	92	117	74	76	84
学位程度	Degree	853	897	899	924	939
兼读制	Part-time	49	54	55	55	40
非学位程度⑧	Non-degree⑧	-	-	-	-	-
学位程度	Degree	49	54	55	55	40
职业训练局	Vocational Training Council	50449	48618	43192	40062	39879
全日制	Full-time	37310	36440	32316	29581	30419
技工级课程	Craft Level Courses	1026	1361	492	407	1199
技术员级课程	Technician Level Courses	9396	11633	11235	10773	10773
高级技术员级课程⑨	Higher Technician Level Courses⑨	26888	23446	20589	18401	18447
兼读制	Part-time	13139	12178	10876	10481	9460
技工级课程	Craft Level Courses	3498	3289	2309	1981	1840
技术员级课程	Technician Level Courses	2090	1976	1845	1828	1660
高级技术员级课程⑨	Higher Technician Level Courses⑨	7551	6913	6722	6672	5960
其他高等教育院校⑩	Other Post-secondary Institutions⑩	7125	6547	6954	7325	7587
全日制	Full-time	5992	5598	5648	6160	6471
兼读制	Part-time	1133	949	1306	1165	1116

26-47 续表 continued

单位：人 (person)

类别	Type	2019	2020	2021	2022	2023
香港建造学院	Hong Kong Institute of Construction					
全日制	Full-time	494	530	575	317	303
技工级课程	Craft Level Courses	245	220	118	63	63
技术员级课程	Technician Level Courses	249	310	457	254	240
制衣业训练局	Clothing Industry Training Authority	205	95	166	139	248
全日制	Full-time	-	-	-	-	-
技术员级课程	Technician Level Courses	-	-	-	-	-
兼读制	Part-time	205	95	166	139	248
技工级课程	Craft Level Courses	205	95	166	139	248
医院管理局⑪	Hospital Authority⑪					
全日制	Full-time	978	997	966	951	925
菲腊牙科医院⑫	The Prince Philip Dental Hospital⑫	66	42	57	72	76
全日制	Full-time	66	42	57	72	76
兼读制	Part-time	-	-	-	-	-
毅进文凭课程／应用教育文凭课程	Diploma Yi Jin Programme/Diploma of Applied Education Programme	4258	3705	3841	3855	4277
全日制	Full-time	3793	3281	3227	3177	3690
兼读制	Part-time	465	424	614	678	587
营办补习班、职业训练及成人教育课程的学校	Schools Offering Tutorial, Vocational and Adult Education Courses	314008	241125	280829	274782	280838
日校	Day School	43337	28960	33111	32042	27595
日暨夜校	Day cum Evening School	248922	204637	240720	236146	246721
夜校	Evening School	21749	7528	6998	6594	6522
非本地高等及专业教育课程⑬	Non-local Higher and Professional Education Courses⑬	23400	21500	19700	19700	19700

注：幼儿园、小学、中学、特殊学校、特殊幼儿中心、感化/住宿院舍及惩教院所的数字反映该年9/10月的情况，“营办补习班、职业训练及成人教育课程的学校”是10月，而高等教育则是12月底。各教育及培训机构的学年开始和完结月份或会不同。
2023年职业训练及高等教育的学生人数为临时数字。
①数字包括由营办补习班、职业训练及成人教育的私立学校开办的中学课程。
②为2至6岁的中度及严重残疾儿童提供特别的训练和照顾。
③为行为上有适应问题的儿童/青少年及青少年违法者，提供住院训练服务。
④教资会资助的大学是指香港城市大学、香港浸会大学、岭南大学、香港中文大学、香港教育大学、香港理工大学、香港科技大学和香港大学。数字包括教资会资助课程，以及教资会资助大学及其附属学院开办的自资课程。
⑤数字包括在教资会学生人数指标外受教资会资助的研究院研究课程的学生人数，亦包括(1)全自负盈亏的研究院研究课程的学生人数；及(2)教资会资助大学同时运用教资会拨款和外间资助修读研究院研究课程的学生。
⑥「香港公开大学」于2021年9月1日改名为「香港都会大学」。
⑦认可专上学院指根据《专上学院条例》(第320章)注册的专上学院，包括明德学院、宏恩基督教学院、港专学院、香港珠海学院、香港能仁专上学院、香港树仁大学、圣方济各大学、香港恒生大学、东华学院、香港伍伦贡学院和耀中幼教学院。
⑧数字包括证书、深造证书、专业证书、文凭、深造文凭及专业文凭课程。
⑨高级技术员级课程为高级文凭或以上程度课程。
⑩数字指营办经本地评审全日制高等教育课程的私立院校。
⑪数字是指护士训练课程。
⑫数字是指牙科训练课程。
⑬数字包括在香港开办并令学员可获由非本地机构颁授非本地高等学术资格或由非本地专业团体颁授非本地专业资格的课程。数字计算至最接近的百位数。2021年至2023年的数字会作修订。

Notes: Figures for kindergartens, primary and secondary schools, special schools, special child care centres, correctional/residential home and correctional institutions refer to the position as at September/October of the respective years, “Schools offering tutorial, vocational and adult education courses” as at October and post-secondary education as at the end of December. The beginning and ending months of a school/academic year may vary among different educational and training institutions.
Figures for vocational and post-secondary education for 2023 are provisional.
① Figures include secondary courses operated by private schools offering tutorial, vocational and adult education courses.
② Special training and care for moderately and severely disabled children aged 2-6.
③ Residential treatment service for mal-adjusted children/juveniles and young offenders through social work intervention.
④ Refers to City University of Hong Kong, Hong Kong Baptist University, Lingnan University, The Chinese University of Hong Kong, The Education University of Hong Kong, The Hong Kong Polytechnic University, The Hong Kong University of Science and Technology and The University of Hong Kong. Figures include UGC-funded programmes and self-financing programmes offered by UGC-funded universities and their extension arms.
⑤ Figures include research postgraduate (RPg) students funded by UGC outside the UGC student number target, and also include (1) fully self-financing RPg students; and (2) RPg students financed by universities using both UGC and external funds.
⑥ "The Open University of Hong Kong" was retitled to "Hong Kong Metropolitan University" effective from 1 September 2021.
⑦ Approved post secondary colleges refer to colleges registered under the Post Secondary Colleges Ordinance (Cap. 320), including Centennial College, Gratia Christian College, HKCT Institute of Higher Education, Hong Kong Chu Hai College, Hong Kong Nang Yan College of Higher Education, Hong Kong Shue Yan University, Saint Francis University, The Hang Seng University of Hong Kong, Tung Wah College, UOW College Hong Kong and Yew Chung College of Early Childhood Education.
⑧ Figures include certificate, advanced certificate, professional certificate, diploma, advanced diploma and professional diploma courses.
⑨ Higher technician level courses are courses at Higher Diploma or above level.
⑩ Figures refer to private institutions offering locally-accredited full-time post-secondary programmes.
⑪ Figures refer to nurse training programmes.
⑫ Figures refer to dental training programmes.
⑬ Figures include courses conducted in Hong Kong which lead to the award of non-local higher academic qualifications by non-local institutions, or non-local professional qualifications by non-local professional bodies. Figures are rounded to the nearest hundred. Figures from 2021 to 2023 are subject to revision.

26-48 医疗卫生条件
Conditions of Public Health

项　　目	Item	2019	2020	2021	2022	2023
注册医护专业人员　(人)	Number of Registered Healthcare Professionals (person)					
医生	Doctors	15004	15298	15546	15815	16180
中医	Chinese Medicine Practitioners (CMP)					
注册中医	Registered Chinese Medicine Practitioners	7582	7919	8080	8296	8423
有限制注册中医①	Chinese Medicine Practitioners with Limited Registration①	32	27	27	27	32
表列中医②	Listed Chinese Medicine Practitioners②	2559	2503	2455	2436	2137
牙医	Dentists	2611	2651	2706	2786	2876
药剂师	Pharmacists	3001	3097	3181	3259	3317
护士	Nurses	59082	61295	64026	66492	68752
按每千名人口计算的医生数目	Doctors per Thousand Population	2.0	2.1	2.1	2.1	2.2 #
医疗机构和病床③	Number of Medical Institutions and Hospital Beds③					
医疗机构　(间)	Medical Institutions (number)	75	75	76	76	77
病床　(张)	Hospital Beds (bed)	35347	35715	36126	36564	36782
按每千名人口计算的病床数目	Beds per Thousand Population	4.7	4.8	4.9	4.9	4.9 #

注：数字是指该年年底的数字。

①有限制注册中医可在指定的教育或科研机构进行中医药学方面的临床教学和研究工作，但不得作私人执业，其注册有效期不超过一年。

②表列中医可在中医注册过渡性安排下在香港合法执业，直至医务卫生局局长日后在宪报公布的日期为止。表列中医在过渡性安排期间，可分别循直接注册、通过注册审核或通过执业资格试成为注册中医。

③包括医院管理局辖下医院及机构、私家医院及惩教机构的医院。

Notes: Figures are as at end of the year stated.

①CMPs with limited registration are allowed to perform clinical teaching and research in Chinese medicine in the specified educational and scientific research institutions. Their registration period should not exceed one year and they cannot engage in private practice with patients.

②Listed CMPs can practise lawfully in Hong Kong under the transitional arrangements for registration of CMPs until a date to be announced by the Secretary for Health in the Gazette. Listed CMPs may become registered CMPs through direct registration, registration assessment or the Licensing Examination during the transitional arrangements.

③Including Hospital Authority hospitals and institutions, private hospitals and hospitals in correctional institutions.

26-49 社会保障
Social Security

社会保障计划	Social Security Scheme	2019/2020	2020/2021	2021/2022	2022/2023	2023/2024
综合社会保障援助	Comprehensive Social Security Assistance (CSSA)					
处理中的个案数目①(个)	Number of Active Cases① (case)					
年老	Old Age	135239	128863	123470	115453	111633
永久性残疾	Permanent Disability	17026	17502	17464	17246	17104
健康欠佳	Ill Health	24562	26289	27010	27411	27855
单亲	Single Parent	24030	24826	23672	21935	20192
低收入	Low Earnings	2974	2422	2183	1808	1530
失业	Unemployment	14647	19810	18866	17823	16943
其他	Others	4213	4080	4023	3916	3948
总计	Total	222691	223792	216688	205592	199205
发放款项② (亿港元)	Amount② (HKD 100 million)	227	229	229	232	225 #
公共福利金	Social Security Allowance (SSA)					
处理中的个案数目①(个)	Number of Active Cases① (case)					
伤残津贴	Disability Allowance (DA)	152818	158982	164866	168384	174619
高龄津贴	Old Age Allowance (OAA)	270080	291228	312218	326456	345727
长者生活津贴	Old Age Living Allowance (OALA)	572029	605574	637016	687331	729289
广东计划	Guangdong Scheme (GD Scheme)	18465	19257	19509	22034	25011
福建计划	Fujian Scheme (FJ Scheme)	1795	1949	1963	2116	2447
总计	Total	1015187	1076990	1135572	1206321	1277093
发放款项② (亿港元)	Amount② (HKD 100 million)	366	382	398	437	484 #
暴力及执法伤亡赔偿	Criminal and Law Enforcement Injuries Compensation					
获批个案数目 (个)	Number of Cases Authorised for Payment (case)	130	147	151	134	99
交通意外伤亡援助	Traffic Accident Victims Assistance					
获批个案数目 (个)	Number of Cases Authorised for Payment (case)	6820	9013	8320	8848	9146
紧急救济	Emergency Relief					
受助灾民人数 (人)	Number of Victims Assisted (person)	23	136	110	245	495

注：于财政年度终结时的数字。除特别注明外，财政年度是由4月1日至翌年3月31日。

①处理中的个案包括新申请个案，正在复查中的个案，正领取援助款项的个案和已停止领取援助款项等待复查的个案。

②2019/20年度的开支包括(1)向综援受助人额外发放的一个月标准金额及向公共福利金受惠人额外发放的一个月福利金，(2)向每名有经济需要学生一次过发放2,500港元津贴，及(3)财政司司长于2019年8月宣布的另一轮一个月额外津贴。2020/21年度的开支包括(1)在该年度推行综援计划下鼓励就业的措施及其他改善措施所涉及的额外财政影响，(2)向援助失业人士特别计划下的综援个案发放的金额及(3)向综援受助人额外发放的一个月标准金额及向公共福利金受惠人额外发放的一个月福利金。2021/22至2023/24年度的开支包括向综援受助人额外发放的半个月标准金额及向公共福利金受惠人额外发放的半个月福利金。

Notes : Figures are as at end of the financial year. Financial year is from 1 April to 31 March of the next year, unless otherwise specified.

①Active cases refer to cases being handled which include new applications, cases being reviewed, cases being paid and cases suspended for payment pending review.

②The expenditure for 2019/20 included (1) the payment of one additional month of CSSA standard rates to CSSA recipients and one additional month of the allowances to SSA recipients; (2) a one-off grant of HKD2,500 to each needy student, and (3) an extra one month allowance announced by the Financial Secretary in August 2019. The expenditure for 2020/21 included (1) additional financial implications arising from implementing the 'pro-employment' measures and other improvement measures under the CSSA Scheme in that year, (2) the payment to the CSSA cases under Special Scheme of Assistance to the Unemployment and (3) the payment of one additional month of CSSA standard rates to CSSA recipients and one additional month of the allowances to SSA recipients. The expenditure from 2021/22 to 2023/24 included the payment of additional half-month of CSSA standard rates to CSSA recipients and additional half-month of the allowances to SSA recipients.

主要统计指标解释

年中人口 是以“居住人口”方法编制，利用“居住人口”方法所编制的人口估计称为“居港人口”。“居港人口”包括“常住居民”和“流动居民”。“常住居民”包括两类人士：(a)在统计时点之前的6个月内，在港逗留最少3个月，又或在统计时点之后的6个月内，在港逗留最少3个月的香港永久性居民，不论在统计时点他们是否身在香港；及(b)在统计时点身在香港的非永久性居民。对于不是“常住居民”的香港永久性居民，如他们在统计时点之前的6个月内，在港逗留最少1个月但少于3个月，又或在统计时点之后的6个月内，在港逗留最少1个月但少于3个月，不论在统计时点他们是否身在香港，会被界定为“流动居民”。根据“居住人口”编制方法，旅客并不包括在香港人口内。

粗出生率 是指某一年内的活产婴儿数目相对该年年中每千名人口的比率。

粗死亡率 是指某一年内的死亡人数相对该年年中每千名人口的比率。

婴儿死亡率 是指某一年内一岁以下婴儿死亡人数相对该年每千名活产婴儿的比率。

总和生育率 是指某年的每一千名妇女，若她们在生育龄期（即15至49岁）经历了一如该年的年龄别生育率，其一生中活产子女的平均数目。

出生时平均预期寿命 是指某年出生人士，若其一生经历一如该年的年龄性别死亡率所反映的死亡情况，他／她预期能活的年数。

劳动人口 是指15岁及以上陆上非住院人口，并符合就业人口或失业人口定义的人士。

劳动人口参与率 是指劳动人口占所有15岁及以上陆上非住院人口的比例。

就业人口 包括在统计前7天内有从事工作赚取薪酬或利润或有一份正式工作的15岁及以上人士。无酬家庭从业员及在统计前7天内正休假的就业人士亦包括在内。

失业人口 包括所有15岁及以上人士(a)在统计前7天内并无职位，且并无为赚取薪酬或利润而工作；及(b)在统计前7天内随时可工作；及(c)在统计前30天内有找寻工作。一名15岁或以上的人士，如果他/她符合上述(a)和(b)的条件，但由于相信没有工作可做而在统计前30天内没有找寻工作，则仍会被界定为失业，即所谓「因灰心而不求职的人士」。失业人口亦包括那些并无职位，有找寻工作，但由于暂时生病而不能工作的人士；及并无职位，且随时可工作，但由于已为于稍后时间担当的新工作或开展的业务作出安排；或正期待返回原来的工作岗位而没有找寻工作的人士。

失业率 是指失业人士在劳动人口中所占的比例。

每月就业收入 是指统计前1个月从所有工作所获得的收入（未扣除强制性公积金供款）。就雇员来说，收入包括工资和薪金、花红、佣金、小费、房屋津贴、超时工作津贴、勤工津贴及其他现金津贴，但不包括补薪。就雇主和自营作业人士而言，收入是指从自己拥有的企业提取作个人及家居用途的款额。如果提取作个人及家居用途的款额资料未能提供，则会搜集有关从业务所得的净收入的数据。

本地生产总值 是指一个经济体的所有居民生产单位，在一个指定的期间内(一般是1年或1季)，未扣除固定资本消耗的生产总值。

人均本地生产总值 是指把该经济体在某统计年的本地生产总值除以该经济体在同年的年中人口总数所得的数字。

本地居民总收入 是指一个经济体的居民透过从事各项经济活动而赚取的总收入，不论该等经济活动是在该经济体的经济领域内或外进行。换言之，编制本地居民总收入应包括本地居民在该经济领域内或外从事各类经济活动的收入，并扣除非本地居民在该经济领域内从事经济活动的收入。本地居民总收入的计算方法如下：

本地居民总收入

= 本地生产总值 + 对外初次收入流量净值

= 本地生产总值 + 本地居民从经济领域外所赚取的初次收入 − 非本地居民从经济领域内所赚取的初次收入

初次收入 包括投资收益及雇员报酬。投资收益包括直接投资收益、证券投资收益、其他投资收益及储备资产收益。

人均本地居民总收入 是指把该经济体在某统计年的本地居民总收入除以该经济体在同年的年中人口总数所得的数字。

国际收支平衡 是一项统计报表，有系统地撮录在一个指定期间内（一般是1年或1季）某经济体与世界各地之间（即居民与非居民之间）进行的经济交易。国际收支平衡表包括三大账户：(a)经常账户、(b)资本账户及(c)金融账户。

经常账户 量度居民与非居民之间关于货物、服务、初次收入和二次收入的流量。

货物 在国际收支平衡表内经常账户的货物主要包括一般商品、转手商贸活动下的货物净出口及非货币黄金。

服务 在国际收支平衡表内经常账户的服务主要包括制造服务、运输、旅游、保险和退休金服务、金融服务及其他服务。

初次收入账户 显示应收及应付的外地款额，作为向非居民提供／从非居民获得可予使用的劳动力、金融资源或自然资源的回报。在国际收支平衡经常账户内初次收入的概念及定义，与本地居民总收入的对外初次收入流量是相同的。

二次收入账户 记录居民与非居民之间的经常转移。经常转移指提供可能即时或短时间内被耗用的实质或金融资源而无同等经济价值作回报的交易。经常转移属单向性质，在国际收支平衡表内是一项用以抵销单边交易的记账。例子包括职工汇款、捐款、官方援助及退休金。

资本账户 量度有关资本转移及非生产、非金融资产（如商标和品牌）的获得和处置的对外交易。资本转移的例子包括债权人减免债务，和涉及获得或处置固定资产的现金转移。

金融账户 记录居民与非居民之间关于金融资产及负债的交易，显示某经济体的对外交易是如何结算的。金融账户内的交易按功能(即投资目的)归类为直接投资、证券投资、金融衍生工具、其他投资及储备资产。

直接投资 指某经济体的投资者对另一经济体的企业所作的对外投资，并对该企业拥有持久利益及在其管理上具有相当程度的影响力或话语权。就统计计算而言，若投资者持有某企业10%或以上的表决权，便视作对该企业的管理具话语权。

证券投资 指直接投资和储备资产以外，对非本地股权证券及债务证券（如中长期债券、货币市场工具）所作的投资。与直接投资者相比，证券投资者在所投资的企业并无持久利益或管理方面的影响力。凡持有一间企业不足10%的表决权均视为证券投资。

金融衍生工具 与另一个特定的金融工具、指标或商品挂钩，投资者可透过金融衍生工具在金融市场对特定的金融风险本身（例如利率风险、外汇风险、股权和商品价格风险、信用风险等）进行交易。金融衍生工具包括期权类合约（如认股权证和期权）及远期类合约（如期货、利率掉期、货币掉期、远期利率协议、远期外汇合约）。

其他投资 泛指直接投资、证券投资、金融衍生工具或储备资产以外，对非居民的金融申索和负债。其他投资包括不可转让的贷款、货币和存款、贸易信贷和预付款，以及其他资产／负债。

储备资产 是由一个经济体的金融当局（就香港而言，即香港金融管理局）控制的对外资产，并随时可供金融当局应付国际收支平衡的财务需要、干预外汇市场以调节该经济体的货币汇率，以及用作其他相关目的（如维持大众对货币及经济体的信心，及作为向外地借贷的基础）。

国际投资头寸 是显示一个经济体在某特定时点的对外金融资产及负债存量的资产负债表。对外金融资产及负债的差额即为该经济体的国际投资头寸净值，代表其对世界各地的净申索或净负债。国际投资头寸与国际收支平衡的金融账户完全协调，同样也按投资类别分类。资产和负债分类为直接投资、证券投资、金融衍生工具及其他投资。国际投资头寸的资产方还包括储备资产。有关投资组成部分的详细解释，请参阅国际收支平衡表内金融账户组成部分的解释。

国际投资头寸净值 是对外金融资产总值与对外金融负债总值之间的差额。

工业生产指数 量度本地工业生产量的实际变动，即撇除价格变动因素后的本地生产量的变动情况。

实用楼面面积 指各层楼面面积总和，但不包括楼梯、公共通道空间、升降机等候处、盥洗室、厕所、厨房及为楼宇提供升降机、空调系统或类似设施而安装的机械所占用的空间。

获批准可动工兴建楼宇 是指获屋宇署签发“同意书”动工兴建的楼宇。这种“同意书”是发给私人发展计划（包括香港房屋协会的计划）。

初次呈交 就一项建筑工程初次呈交建筑事务监督要求批准的图则。

重大修改 指经过大规模修改的建筑图则，而这些图则必须从根本上接受重新评估。

自置住房住户 是指住户拥有其居住屋宇单位的业权。

全租户 是指住户向居于别处的人士租住整个屋宇单位自住，没有分租，单位内也没有其他的住户。

合租户 是指两个或以上的住户，分别向居于别处的人士租用部分的屋宇单位居住。

二房东 是指住户向居于别处的人士租住整个屋宇单位，并把部分单位分租予其他住户。

三房客 是指住户向居于同一屋宇单位内的人士租用部分单位居住。

免租 是指住户免费在屋宇单位内居住，不论是否获得业主同意，但不包括本身是业主或由雇主提供住房的住户。

住房由雇主提供 是指住户居住在由其成员之一的雇主提供的住房，包括以象征式租金向雇主租住屋宇单位的住户。假如住户使用由雇主提供的房屋津贴租用住房，则租住权不属于「住房由雇主提供」类别。

进口货品 是指在香港以外出产或制成的货品，输入香港供本地使用或转口，以及再进口的香港产品。其货值是以到岸价值计算。

整体出口货品 包括港产品出口及转口。港产品出口货物是指香港的天然产品或在香港经过制造工序，以致其基本生产物料的形状、性质、结构或效用受到永久及实质改变的产品。如果产品在香港只进行简单稀释、包装、装瓶、弄干、简单装配、分类、装饰等工序，则该产品并不能以香港作为来源地。转口货品是指输出曾经自外地输入香港的货品，而这些货品并没有在香港经过任何制造工序，以致永久及实质改变其基本原料的形状、性质、结构或效用。其货值是以离岸价值计算。

输往中国内地作外发加工用途的出口货物 是指那些从香港或经香港出口往中国内地加工的原料或半制成品，经加工后成为制成品，并以合约安排再进口香港。

从中国内地进口与外发内地加工有关的货物 是指那些加工后从中国内地进口香港的货物，其中全部或部分原料或半制成品是以合约安排从香港或经香港出口往中国内地加工。

原产地为中国内地而涉及外发中国内地加工、并经香港输往其他地方（中国内地除外）的转口货物 是指那些经香港转口的制成品，其中全部或部分原料或半制成品是以合约安排从香港或经香港出口往中国内地加工，而加工后的货物再进口香港。

直接投资 指某经济体的投资者对另一经济体的企业所作的对外投资，并对该企业拥有持久利益及在其管理上具有相当程度的影响力或话语权。就统计计算而言，若投资者持有某企业10%或以上的表决权，便视作对该企业的管理具话语权。直接投资包括股权及投资基金份额，以及债务工具。股权及投资基金份额包括所持有的分行股本、附属公司及联营公司的股票、投资基金份额，以及收益再投资（即投资者应得但有关企业的分行、附属公司、联营公司或投资基金没有分发的利润）。债务工具主要涉及公司之间的债务交易，包括母公司与其分行、附属公司及联营公司之间的短期及长期借贷。

外商直接投资 指境外居民持有香港居民企业的直接投资。跨国企业在香港营运的分行及附属公司，是外商直接投资的典型例子。

对外直接投资 指香港居民投资者持有境外企业的直接投资。

直接投资头寸 指某一特定日子香港居民在境外投资的价值或接受外来投资的价值。

直接投资流动 指某一时段内香港居民于境外投资或接受外来投资的投入或撤走。

贷款基金 提供资金予如房屋贷款和教育贷款等贷款计划。基金收入主要来自政府一般收入账目转拨的款项、偿还的贷款及贷款利息。

港汇指数 是量度港元相对其他主要贸易伙伴的货币汇率变动加权平均值的指数，作为反映港元相对各种选定货币强弱的整体指标。该指数现时是以2020年1月为基期及包括18种货币。

外币兑换率 指外币兑港元的电汇或现钞收市中间兑换价。

认可机构 包括持牌银行、有限制牌照银行及接受存款公司。持牌银行可接受任何金额及期限的存款。随着撤销利率限制的最后阶段在2001年7月3日生效，各类存款利率再无任何限制。至于有限制牌照银行，它们可接受金额不少于港币50万元的任何期限的定期存款。接受存款公司则可接受金额不少于港币10万元而期限不少于3个月的定期存款。有限制牌照银行及接受存款公司均无任何存款利率限制。

外币掉期存款 是指顾客在现货市场购买外币，然后存入认可机构，但同时订下远期合约，将该笔外币（本金加利息）在存款到期时售予认可机构。从分析角度来看，这类掉期存款应当作港元定期存款。

货币供应量（M_1） 是指市民持有的法定纸币和硬币加上持牌银行的客户活期存款。

货币供应量（M_2） 是指货币供应量M_1所包括的项目，加上持牌银行的客户储蓄及定期存款，再加上持牌银行发行而由非认可机构持有的可转让存款证。

货币供应量（M_3） 是指货币供应量M_2所包括的各项，加上有限制牌照银行及接受存款公司客户的存款，再加上以上两类认可机构发行而由非认可机构持有的可转让存款证。

恒生指数 是以流通市值加权法计算，并设有个别成分股比重上限。该指数内的成分股划分为四个分类指数，包括金融、公用事业、地产及工商业。

消费物价指数 量度住户一般所购买的消费商品及服务的价格水平随时间而变动的情况。消费物价指数的按年变动率（即某段时期的消费物价指数与去年同期比较的变动情况），是广泛被用作反映消费者所面对的通货膨胀的指标。不同的消费物价指数数列反映消费物价转变对不同开支组别住户的影响。甲类、乙类及丙类消费物价指数分别根据较低、中等及较高开支范围的住户的开支模式编制而成。综合消费物价指数根据以上所有住户的整体开支模式编制，反映消费物价转变对整体住户的影响。

教育程度 是指某人在学校或其他教育机构修读达到的最高教育水平，不论他／她有否完成该课程。计算教育程度时，只包括正式课程，即须最少为期一个学年，入学须具备指定的学历资格（香港都会大学的非学位、学位及研究生课程除外），以及设有考试或指定评核成绩的程序。

社会保障计划 旨在帮助社会上需要经济或物质援助的人士，应付基本及特别需要。这个无须供款的社会保障制度，包括综合社会保障援助计划、公共福利金计划、暴力及执法伤亡赔偿计划、交通意外伤亡援助计划和紧急救济。

综合社会保障援助计划 是以入息补助方法，为那些在经济上无法自给的人士提供安全网，使他们的入息达到一定水平，以应付生活上的基本需要。申请人必须符合居港规定及通过入息及资产审查。

公共福利金计划 包括普通伤残津贴、高额伤残津贴、高龄津贴、长者生活津贴、广东计划及福建计划。高龄津贴及伤残津贴分别为年龄在 70 岁或以上或严重残疾的香港居民，每月提供现金津贴，以应付因年老或严重残疾而引致的特别需要。至于在 2013 年 4 月起实施的长者生活津贴（易名为普通长者生活津贴）及在 2018 年 6 月实施高额长者生活津贴是为年龄在 65 岁或以上有经济需要的香港居民，每月提供津贴，以补助他们的生活开支。广东计划由 2013 年 10 月起实施，以及福建计划由 2018 年 4 月起实施。广东计划及福建计划下的长者生活津贴（包括普通长者生活津贴及高额长者生活津贴）由 2020 年 1 月起实施。于 2022 年 9 月起合并公共福利金计划下的普通及高额长者生活津贴，采用普通津贴较宽松的资产上限，并按高额长者生活津贴的金额发放。

暴力及执法伤亡赔偿计划 的目的是提供经济援助给因暴力罪行或因执法人员使用武器执行职务以致受伤的人士或这些人士的受养人（如受害人因伤死亡）。申请人无须接受经济状况调查。

交通意外伤亡援助计划 的目的是向道路交通意外受害人或这些人士的受养人（如受害人因伤死亡）迅速提供经济援助，而无须考虑计划受惠人的经济状况，或有关交通意外是因谁人的过失而造成。援助金按意外受害人的伤亡情况支付；至于财物损失，则不在援助范围内。

紧急救济 是为天灾或其他不幸事故（例如火灾、台风、水灾、暴雨、山泥倾泻、塌屋）的灾民，及因楼宇成为危楼而遭发出封闭令以致被着令撤离家园的受影响人士提供紧急救济。

Explanatory Notes on Main Statistical Indicators

Mid-year Population is compiled using the "resident population" approach. The population estimate compiled under the "resident population" approach is referred to as the Hong Kong Resident Population, which comprises "Usual Residents" and "Mobile Residents". "Usual Residents" include two categories of people: (a) Hong Kong Permanent Residents who have stayed in Hong Kong for at least 3 months during the 6 months before or for at least 3 months during the 6 months after the reference time-point, regardless of whether they are in Hong Kong or not at the reference time-point; and (b) Hong Kong Non-permanent Residents who are in Hong Kong at the reference time-point. For those Hong Kong Permanent Residents who are not "Usual Residents", they are classified as "Mobile Residents" if they have stayed in Hong Kong for at least 1 month but less than 3 months during the 6 months before or for at least 1 month but less than 3 months during the 6 months after the reference time-point, regardless of whether they are in Hong Kong or not at the reference time-point. Under the "resident population" approach, visitors are not part of the Hong Kong population.

Crude Birth Rate refers to the number of live births in a given year per 1000 mid-year population of that year.

Crude Death Rate refers to the number of deaths in a given year per 1000 mid-year population of that year.

Infant Mortality Rate refers to the number of deaths of age under one in a given year per 1000 live births in that year.

Total Fertility Rate refers to the average number of children that would be born alive to 1000 women during their lifetime if they were to pass through their childbearing ages 15-49 experiencing the age specific fertility rates prevailing in a given year.

Expectation of Life at Birth refers to the number of years of life that a person born in a given year is expected to live if he/she was subject to the prevalent mortality conditions as reflected by the set of age-sex specific mortality rates for that year.

Labour Force refers to the land-based non-institutional population aged 15 and over who satisfy the criteria for being classified as employed population or unemployed population.

Labour Force Participation Rate refers to the proportion of labour force in the total land-based non-institutional population aged 15 and over.

Employed Persons refer to those persons aged 15 and over who have been engaged in performing work for pay or profit during the 7 days before enumeration or have had formal job attachment. Unpaid family workers and employed persons who were on leave/holiday during the 7 days before enumeration are included.

Unemployed Persons refer to those persons aged 15 and over who (a) have not had a job and have notperformed any work for pay or profit during the 7 days before enumeration; and (b) have been available for work during the 7 days before enumeration; and (c) have sought work during the 30 days before enumeration. If a person aged 15 or over fulfils the conditions (a) and (b) above but has not sought work during the 30 days before enumeration because he/she believes that work is not available, he/she is still classified as unemployed, being regarded as a so-called "discouraged worker". Unemployed population also includes persons without a job who have sought work but have not been available for work because of temporary sickness; and persons without a job who have been available for work but have not sought work because they have made arrangements to take up a new job or to start business on a subsequent date; or were expecting to return to their original jobs.

Unemployment Rate refers to the proportion of unemployed persons in the labour force.

Monthly Employment Earnings refer to earnings (before deduction of Mandatory Provident Fund contributions) from all jobs during the month before enumeration. For employees, they include wage and salary, bonus, commission, tips, housing allowance, overtime allowance, attendance allowance and other cash allowances. However, back pays are excluded. For employers and self-employed, they refer to amounts drawn from the self-owned enterprise for personal and household use. If information on the amounts drawn for personal and household use is not available, data on net earnings from business would be collected instead.

Gross Domestic Product (GDP) is a measure of the total value of production of all resident producing units of an economy in a specified period (typically a year or a quarter), before deducting the consumption of fixed capital.

Per Capita GDP is obtained by dividing the total GDP in a year by the mid-year population of that economy in the same year.

Gross National Income (GNI) is a measure of the total income earned by residents of an economy from engaging in various economic activities, irrespective of whether the economic activities are carried out within the economic territory of the economy or outside. In other words, in compiling GNI, income earned by residents from engaging in various economic activities within or outside the economic territory are included, whereas income earned by non-residents from engaging in economic activities within the economic territory are excluded. GNI is computed as follows:

GNI = GDP + Net external primary income flows
= GDP + Primary income earned by residents
from outside the economic territory -
Primary income earned by non-residents
from within the economic territory

Primary income comprises investment income and compensation of employees (CE). Investment income includes direct investment income (DII), portfolio investment income (PII) and other investment income (OII) as well as income on reserve assets (RA).

Per capita GNI of an economy is obtained by dividing GNI in a year by the mid-year population of that economy in the same year.

Balance of Payments (BoP) is a statistical statement that systematically summarises, for a specific time period (typically a year or a quarter), the economic transactions of an economy with the rest of the world (i.e. between residents and non-residents). A BoP account comprises three broad accounts : (a) the current account-, (b) the capital account and (c) the financial account.

Current Account measures the flows of goods, services, primary income and secondary income between residents and non-residents.

Goods under the BoP current account mainly cover general merchandise, net exports of goods under merchanting and non-monetary gold.

Services under the BoP current account mainly cover manufacturing services, transport, travel, insurance and pension services, financial services and other services.

Primary Income Account shows the amounts receivable and payable abroad in return for providing/obtaining use of labour, financial resources or natural resources to/from non-residents. The concepts and definitions of primary income under the current account of the BoP are the same as those of the external primary income flows under GNI.

Secondary Income Account records current transfers between residents and non-residents. Current transfers are transactions in which real or financial resources that are likely to be consumed immediately or shortly are provided without the receipt of equivalent economic values in return. Current transfers are unilateral in nature and are offsetting entries in the BoP account for one-sided transactions. Examples include workers' remittances, donations, official assistance and pensions.

Capital Account measures external transactions in capital transfers, and the acquisition and disposal of non-produced, non-financial assets (such as trademarks and brand names). Examples of capital transfers include forgiveness of debts by creditors, and cash transfers involving the acquisition or disposal of fixed assets.

Financial Account records transactions in financial assets and liabilities between residents and non-residents. It shows how an economy's external transactions are settled. Transactions in the financial account are classified by function (i.e. the purpose of the investment) into direct investment, portfolio investment, financial derivatives, other investment and reserve assets.

Direct Investment refers to external investment in which an investor of an economy acquires a lasting interest and a significant degree of influence or an effective voice in the management of an enterprise located in another economy. For statistical purpose, an effective voice is taken as being equivalent to a holding of 10% or more of the voting power in an enterprise.

Portfolio Investment refers to investment in non-resident equity securities and debt securities (e.g. bonds and notes, money market instruments), other than that included in direct investment or reserve assets. Compared with direct investors, portfolio investors have no lasting interest or influence in the management of the enterprises concerned. A holding of less than 10% of the voting power in an enterprise is regarded as portfolio investment.

Financial Derivatives are financial instruments that are linked to another specific financial instrument, indicator or commodity, and through which specific financial risks (such as interest rate risk, foreign exchange risk, equity and commodity price risks, credit risk, and so on) can be traded in their own right in financial markets. Financial derivatives include option-type contracts (e.g. warrants and options) and forward-type contracts (e.g. futures, interest rate swaps, currency swaps, forward rate agreements, forward foreign exchange contracts).

Other Investment refers to other financial claims on and liabilities to non-residents that are not classified as direct investment, portfolio investment, financial derivatives or reserve assets. Other investment includes non-marketable loans, currency and deposits, trade credits and advances, and other assets/liabilities.

Reserve Assets are external assets that are readily available to and controlled by the monetary authority of an economy (which refers to the Hong Kong Monetary Authority in the case of Hong Kong) for meeting balance of payments financing needs, for intervention in exchange markets to regulate the currency exchange rate of that economy, and for other related purposes (such as maintaining confidence in the currency and the economy, and serving as a basis for foreign borrowing).

International Investment Position (IIP) is a balance sheet showing the stock of external financial assets and liabilities of an economy at a particular time point. The difference between the external financial assets and liabilities is the net IIP of the economy, which represents either its net claim on or net liability to the rest of the world. Being fully consistent with the BoP financial account, IIP is also categorised by type of investment. Assets and liabilities are classified into direct investment, portfolio investment, financial derivatives and other investment. The asset side of IIP also includes the reserve assets. For detailed explanation on investment components, please refer to the explanatory notes on the components of the financial account of the BoP account.

Net IIP is the difference between total external financial assets and total external financial liabilities.

Index of Industrial Production measures the changes in local industrial output in real terms, i.e. changes in the volume of local production after discounting the effect of price changes.

Usable Floor Area is defined as the aggregate of the areas of the floor or floors in a storey or a building excluding any staircases, public circulation space, lift landings, lavatories, water-closets, kitchens and any space occupied by machinery for any lift, air-conditioning system or similar service provided for the building.

Buildings with Consents to Commence Work refer to buildings with “Consents” to commence building works issued by the Buildings Department. Such “Consents” are issued to private development projects (including Hong Kong Housing Society's projects).

First Submission refers to plans for a building project which are first submitted to the Building Authority for approval.

Major Revision refers to building plans which have

been so extensively revised that they must be fundamentally re-assessed.

Owner-occupier refers to a household which owns the quarters it occupies.

Sole Tenant refers to a household which rents the whole quarters it occupies from someone who lives outside the quarters without sharing it with other household(s) or subletting.

Co-tenant refers to two or more households each of which rents part of the quarters from someone who lives outside the quarters.

Main Tenant refers to a household which rents the whole quarters it occupies from someone who lives outside the quarters and sublets part of it to other household(s).

Sub-tenant refers to a household which rents part of the quarters from someone who lives in the same quarters.

Rent Free refers to a household which occupies an accommodation for free, with or without the owner's permission. This does not include owner-occupiers or households occupying accommodation provided by employers.

Accommodation Provided by Employer refers to a household which occupies an accommodation provided by the employer of one of the household members. This also includes households occupying quarters leased from employer at a nominal rent. If a household member uses housing allowance given by his/her employer for renting accommodation, the tenure is not regarded as "accommodation provided by employer".

Imports are goods which have been produced or manufactured in places outside the jurisdiction of Hong Kong and brought into Hong Kong for local use or for subsequent re-export as well as Hong Kong products re-imported. Their values are recorded on cost, insurance and freight (c.i.f.) basis.

Total Exports comprise domestic exports and re-exports. Domestic exports are the natural produce of Hong Kong or products of a manufacturing process in Hong Kong which has changed permanently and substantially the shape, nature, form or utility of the basic materials used in manufacture. Processes such as simple diluting, packing, bottling, drying, simple assembling, sorting, decorating, etc., do not confer Hong Kong origin. Re-exports are products which have previously been imported into Hong Kong and which are re-exported without having undergone in Hong Kong a manufacturing process which has changed permanently and substantially the shape, nature, form or utility of the basic materials used in the manufacture. Their values are recorded on free-on-board (f.o.b.) basis.

Exports to the Mainland of China for Outward Processing refer to raw materials or semi-manufactures exported from or through Hong Kong to the mainland of China for processing with a contractual arrangement for subsequent re-importation of the processed goods into Hong Kong.

Imports from the Mainland of China Related to Outward Processing in the Mainland refer to processed goods imported to Hong Kong from the mainland of China, of which all or part of the raw materials or semi-manufactures have been under contractual arrangement exported from or through Hong Kong to the mainland of China for processing.

Re-exports of the Mainland of China Origin to Other Places (excluding the Mainland of China) Involving Outward Processing in the Mainland of China refer to processed goods re-exported through Hong Kong, of which all or part of the raw materials or semi-manufactures have been exported from or through Hong Kong to the mainland of China for processing with a contractual arrangement for subsequent re-importation of the processed goods into Hong Kong.

Direct Investment refers to external investment in which an investor of an economy acquires a lasting interest and a significant degree of influence or an effective voice in the management of an enterprise located in another economy. For statistical purpose, an effective voice is taken as being equivalent to a holding of 10% or more of the voting power in an enterprise. Direct investment comprises equity and investment fund shares and debt instruments. Equity and investment fund shares include equity in branches, shares in subsidiaries and associates, investment fund shares and reinvestment of earnings (which refers to the investors' share of earnings not distributed by branches, subsidiaries, associates or investment funds). Debt instruments mainly involve inter-company debt transactions. These include short-term and long-term borrowing and lending of funds between parent companies and their branches, subsidiaries and associates.

Inward Direct Investment refers to direct investment by a non-Hong Kong resident on a Hong Kong resident enterprise. Typical examples of inward direct investment are multinational corporations' branches and subsidiaries operating in Hong Kong.

Outward Direct Investment refers to direct investment by a Hong Kong resident on a non-resident enterprise.

Position of Direct Investment refers to the value of investment abroad or investment received from abroad of Hong Kong residents at a specified date.

Flow of Direct Investment refers to the additions/withdrawals of investment abroad or investment received from abroad of Hong Kong residents during a period.

Loan Fund finances loans and advances for such schemes as housing loans and education loans. The main sources of income are appropriations from the General Revenue Account, loan repayments and interest on loans.

Effective Exchange Rate Index (EERI) for the Hong Kong Dollar (HKD) is an index which measures movements in the weighted average of the exchange rate of the HKD against the currencies of major trading partners of Hong Kong. It serves as an indicator for measuring the overall strength of the HKD relative to selected currencies. The index currently uses January 2020 as the base and includes 18 currencies.

Exchange Rates Between the Hong Kong Dollar and Other Currencies refer to the closing middle market telegraphic transfer rates or notes rates.

Authorized Institutions include licensed banks, restricted licence banks and deposit-taking companies. Licensed banks can accept deposits of any size and any term of maturity. With the final phase of interest rate deregulation came into effect on 3 July 2001, there is no restriction on interest rate payable. As for restricted licence banks, they can accept time deposits in amounts of not less than HK$500,000 with any term of maturity. Deposit-taking companies can however accept time deposits in amounts of not less than HK$100,000 with a term of maturity of at least three months. Both restricted licence banks and deposit-taking companies have no restriction on interest rate payable.

Foreign Currency Swap Deposits refer to deposits involving customers buying foreign currencies in the spot market and placing them as deposits with authorized institutions, while at the same time entering into a contract to sell such foreign currencies (principal plus interest) forward in line with the maturity of such deposits. For most analytical purpose, they should be regarded as Hong Kong dollar time deposits.

Money Supply M_1 refers to the sum of legal tender notes and coins held by the public plus customers' demand deposits placed with licensed banks.

Money Supply M_2 refers to the sum of M_1 plus customers' savings and time deposits with licensed banks, plus negotiable certificates of deposit issued by licensed banks held by non-authorized institutions.

Money Supply M_3 refers to the sum of M_2 plus customer deposits with restricted licence banks (RLBs) and deposit-taking companies (DTCs) plus negotiable certificates of deposit issued by RLBs and DTCs held by non-authorized institutions.

Hang Seng Index is a freefloat-adjusted market capitalisation-weighted index with capping on individual constituent weighting. The constituent stocks of the Hang Seng Index are grouped under four sub-indexes, namely Finance, Utilities, Properties, and Commerce and Industry.

Consumer Price Index (CPI) measures the changes over time in the price level of consumer commodities and services generally purchased by households. The year-on-year rate of change in the CPI (i.e. change in CPI for a specific period as compared with the same period a year earlier) is widely used as an indicator of the inflation experienced by consumers. Different CPI series are compiled to reflect the impacts of consumer price changes on households in different expenditure ranges. The CPI(A), CPI(B) and CPI(C) are compiled based on the expenditure patterns of households in the relatively low, medium and relatively high expenditure ranges respectively. A Composite CPI is compiled based on the overall expenditure pattern of all the above households taken together to reflect the impact of consumer price changes on the household sector as a whole.

Educational Attainment refers to the highest level of education ever attained by a person in school or other educational institution, regardless of whether he/she had completed the course. Only formal courses are counted as educational attainment. A formal course shall be one that lasts for at least one academic year, requires specific academic qualifications for entrance (except sub-degree, associate degree, degree and post-graduate courses offered by the Open University of Hong Kong) and includes examinations or specific academic assessment procedures.

Educational Attainment refers to the highest level of education ever attained by a person in school or other educational institution, regardless of whether he/she had completed the course. Only formal courses are counted as educational attainment. A formal course shall be one that lasts for at least one academic year, requires specific academic qualifications for entrance (except non-degree, degree and post-graduate courses offered by the Hong Kong Metropolitan University) and includes examinations or specific academic assessment procedures.

Social Security Schemes aim to provide for the basic and special needs of the members of the community who are in need of financial or material assistance. The non-contributory social security system comprises Comprehensive Social Security Assistance Scheme, Social Security Allowance Scheme, Criminal and Law Enforcement Injuries Compensation Scheme, Traffic Accident Victims Assistance Scheme and Emergency Relief.

Comprehensive Social Security Assistance Scheme provides a safety net for those who cannot support themselves financially. It is designed to bring their income up to a prescribed level to meet their basic needs. An applicant must satisfy the residence requirements and pass both the income and assets tests.

Social Security Allowance Scheme includes Normal Disability Allowance, Higher Disability Allowance, Old Age Allowance (OAA), Old Age Living Allowance (OALA), Guangdong (GD) Scheme and Fujian (FJ) Scheme. The OAA and Disability Allowance provide a monthly allowance to Hong Kong residents who are 70 years of age or above or who are severely disabled to meet their special needs arising from old age or disability respectively. The OALA (renamed as Normal OALA), launched in April 2013, and the Higher OALA, launched in June 2018, are to provide a monthly allowance to supplement the living expenses of Hong Kong residents aged 65 or above who are in need of financial support. The GD Scheme was launched in October 2013 and the FJ Scheme was launched in April 2018. The OALA (including Normal OALA and Higher OALA) under the GD Scheme and the FJ Scheme were launched in January 2020. In September 2022, the Normal and Higher OALAs under the SSA Scheme were merged. The merged OALA adopted the more lenient asset limits of the Normal OALA and the payment rate of the Higher OALA.

Criminal and Law Enforcement Injuries Compensation Scheme aims to provide financial assistance to persons (or to their dependants in cases of death) who are injured as a result of a crime of violence, or by a law enforcement officer using a weapon in the execution of his duty. The Scheme is non-means-tested.

Traffic Accident Victims Assistance Scheme aims to provide speedy financial assistance to road traffic accident victims (or to their dependants in cases of death) on a non-means tested basis, regardless of the element of fault leading to the occurrence of the accident. Payments are made for personal injuries, while loss of or damage to property is not covered.

Emergency Relief is provided for victims of natural and other disasters such as fire, typhoon, flood, rainstorm, landslide, house collapse, and also for evacuees of buildings and premises considered to be dangerous under Closure Orders.

27

澳门特别行政区主要社会经济指标

Main Social and Economic Indicators of Macao Special Administrative Region

简 要 说 明

一、本章资料反映澳门特别行政区主要社会、经济发展情况。内容包括：土地、人口、就业、国民经济核算、工业、能源、建筑、交通通信、对外贸易、财政金融、物价、教育、卫生、房屋、社会保障等方面。

二、本章由澳门特别行政区政府统计暨普查局提供所有数据，国家统计局国际统计信息中心负责整理、编辑。

三、在统计工作方面，按中华人民共和国“澳门特别行政区基本法”的有关原则，澳门特别行政区保留其单独运作的统计系统，并负责编制和发布反映澳门特别行政区情况的统计数据。由于澳门和内地在使用统计名词及概念方面会有所不同，读者在比较两地数据时，请参考本章末的“主要统计指标解释”。

四、澳门特别行政区是单独的关税地区，澳门与内地之间的贸易，亦需办理进出口报关。在贸易统计方面，澳门特别行政区对外商品贸易统计数据亦包括澳门特别行政区与内地的贸易。

五、在外汇统计及与之有关的各方面，澳门元是澳门特别行政区的法定货币，因此，除澳门元以外的货币（包括人民币）均视作外币。

六、更详细的统计资料及有关的技术细节，可参阅澳门特别行政区政府统计暨普查局出版的《统计月刊》、《统计年鉴》及各专题统计出版物。

七、本章节表中的符号使用说明：“－”表示绝对数值为零；“..”表示不适用；“o”表示数据小于本表最小单位半数。“r”表示修订数字。

Brief Introduction

I. Data in this chapter reflect the major social and economic development of the Macao Special Administrative Region, including land; population; employment; national accounts; industry; energy; construction; transportation and communications; external trade; public finance and banking; prices; education; health; housing; and social security.

II. Data in this chapter are provided by the Statistics and Census Service of the Government of Macao Special Administrative Region, which are tabulated and edited by the International Statistical Information Centre of the National Bureau of Statistics.

III. According to the *Basic Law of the Macao Special Administrative Region of the People's Republic of China*, Macao Special Administrative Region maintains its independent statistical system that is responsible to comply and disseminate statistical information on the different aspect of the Special Administrative Region. As Macao and the mainland of China adopt different statistical concepts, definitions and terminology, users are advised to read the Explanatory Notes at the end of this chapter when making comparison between the mainland of China and the Macao Special Administrative Region.

IV. Macao is a separate customs territory; therefore, import and export trade between Macao and the mainland of China also requires customs declaration. In terms of trade statistics, Macao's external merchandise trade data also include trade transaction between Macao and the mainland.

V. The Macao Pataca (MOP) is the legal tender in the Macao Special Administrative Region, all other currencies (including Renminbi) are considered as foreign currencies in statistics on foreign exchange and related data.

VI. Detailed information and technical aspects are available in the *Monthly Bulletin of Statistics, Yearbook of Statistics* and other thematic publications published by the Statistics and Census Service of the Government of Macao Special Administrative Region.

VII. Notations used in this chapter:

"-" indicates absolute value equals zero; ".." indicates not applicable; "o" indicates less than half of the unit employed; "r" Revised figure.

27-1 主要统计指标概况
Summary of Key Statistics

项　　目	Items	2019	2020	2021	2022	2023
人口及生命统计	**Population and Vital Statistics**					
年中人口 (万人)	Mid-year Population (10 000 persons)	67.2	68.5	68.3	67.7	67.9
粗出生率 (‰)	Crude Birth Rate (‰)	8.9	8.1	7.4	6.4	5.5
粗死亡率 (‰)	Crude Death Rate (‰)	3.4	3.3	3.4	4.4	4.4
婴儿死亡率 (‰)	Infant Mortality Rate (‰)	1.5	2.2	1.8	0.9	2.4
(按每千名出生登记活产婴儿计算)	(per 1000 registered live births)					
劳动、就业	**Labour, Employment**					
劳动人口 (万人)	Labour Force (10 000 persons)	39.5	40.5	39.0	37.9	37.5
劳动力参与率 (%)	Labour Force Participation Rate (%)	70.3	70.5	69.0	68.6	67.9
失业率 (%)	Unemployment Rate (%)	1.7	2.5	2.9	3.7	2.7
就业不足率 (%)	Underemployment Rate (%)	0.5	3.5	4.1	6.9	1.7
就业人口 (万人)	Employed Population (10 000 persons)	38.8	39.5	37.8	36.5	36.5
建筑业	Construction	3.1	3.8	3.3	3.0	2.8
批发及零售业	Wholesale & Retail Trade	4.2	4.6	4.3	4.6	4.7
酒店及饮食业	Hotels, Restaurants & Similar Activities	5.6	5.4	5.0	4.5	4.6
文娱博彩及其他服务业	Recreational, Cultural, Gaming & Other Services	9.7	9.1	8.9	8.1	8.0
对外商品贸易 (亿澳门元)	**External Merchandise Trade (100 million MOP)**					
出口	Exports	128	108	130	135	133
本地产品出口	Domestic Exports	15	16	20	20	16
再出口	Re-exports	113	92	110	115	118
进口	Imports	901	926	1539	1398	1414
贸易价格比率 (2016年=100)	Terms of Trade (year of 2016=100)	100.1	100.2	99.8	99.8	99.6
工业生产	**Industrial Production**					
工业电力消耗量 (亿千瓦时)	Electricity Consumption (100 million kW·h)	1.5	1.4	1.6	1.5	1.6
私人建筑	**Private Sector Construction**					
获发使用准照楼宇	Buildings with Licence of Use Issued					
单位数目 (个)	Units (No.)	3013	2521	2545	569	254
总建筑面积 (万平方米)	Gross Floor Area (10 000 sq.m)	47	29	95	37	37
获发动工批示楼宇	Buildings with Construction Permit Issued					
单位数目 (个)	Units (No.)	405	233	1407	458	464
总建筑面积 (万平方米)	Gross Floor Area (10 000 sq.m)	44	88	56	7	5
楼宇单位买卖数目 (个)	Building Units Sold (No.)	11022	9002	8802	4544	4416
不动产买卖契约数目 (宗)	Real Estate Transaction Deeds (No.)	10303	11589	11959	6743	6193
不动产按揭贷款数目 (宗)	Real Estate Mortgage Loans (No.)	16508	14954	14835	8582	6451
运输、通讯、旅游 (万次)	**Transport, Communications, Tourism (10 000 Trips)**					
进出澳门货运车	Trucks Entering and Departing Macao	34.1	29.8	34.2	34.2	38.3
进出澳门的客轮班次	Ferries Entering and Departing Macao	11.1	2.1	2.5	2.1	6.8
澳门国际机场升降的商业航班	Commercial Flights Arriving and Departing at Macao International Airport	7.4	1.4	1.4	1.0	3.9
注册车辆 (万辆)	Licensed Vehicles (10 000 sets)	24.1	24.4	24.8	25.0	25.2
固网及移动电话用户(包括预付卡) (万户)	Fixed-line Telephone & Mobile Phone Subscribers(incl. Prepaid SIM Cards)(10 000 subscribers)	291.0	172.9	137.5	130.6	146.2
入境旅客 (万人次)	Visitor Arrivals (10 000 person-times)	3941	590	771	570	2821
酒店业平均入住率 (%)	Average Occupancy Rate of Hotel Sector (%)	91	29	50	38	81
财政收支、货币、金融(亿澳门元)	**Government Accounts, Money and Finance (100 million MOP)**					
财政总收入	Total Government Revenue	1407	1017	948	1091	1005
财政总支出	Total Government Expenditure	847	961	892	1021	906
货币供应(广义货币供应量M_2)	Money Supply (M_2)					
总计	Total	6875	6924	6875	7177[r]	7256
澳门元	MOP	2106	2354	2434	2769[r]	2468
港元	HKD	3311	3382	3442	2989	3302
其他货币	Other Currencies	1458	1187	1000	1419	1487
本地/私人部门贷款及垫款	Domestic Loans/Advances to the Private Sector	5155	5301	5607	5701[r]	5356

注：酒店业平均入住率不包括暂停营业、用于医学观察及自我健康管理的酒店业场所数据。

Note: The average occupancy rate of hotel sector excluded hotel establishments that suspended operations as well as those designated for medical obser and self-health monitoring.

27–1 续表 continued

项　　目	Items	2019	2020	2021	2022	2023
消费物价指数	**Consumer Price Index**					
（2018年4月至2019年3月=100）	**(Apr/2018 - Mar/2019=100)**					
综合消费物价指数	Composite Consumer Price Index	101.78	102.60	102.63	103.70	104.68
甲类消费物价指数	Consumer Price Index (A)	101.79	102.71	102.66	103.41	104.16
乙类消费物价指数	Consumer Price Index (B)	101.77	102.45	102.58	104.09	105.35
房屋（期末）	**Housing (End-period)**					
公共房屋 （套）	Public Housing (No.)	14670	14632	15437	15954	15975
教育	**Education**					
幼儿教育学生 （人）	Students of Pre-primary Education (person)	19265	18908	18109	17108	16188
小学生 （人）	Students of Primary Education (person)	33961	35450	36791	37854	38349
中学生 （人）	Students of Secondary Education (person)	26396	27627	28961	30274	31617
高等教育学生 （人）	Students of Higher Education (person)	36107	39093	44052	49594	55611
医疗	**Health**					
医生 （人）	Doctors (person)	1808	1789	1888	1965	1980
护士 （人）	Nurses (person)	2491	2568	2742	2863	2980
住院病床 （张）	Hospital Beds (No.)	1628	1715	1744	1721	1882
社会保障	**Social Security**					
受益人数目 （人）	Beneficiaries (person)	365435	360508	358974	353634	357187
供款单位数目 （个）	Contributors (No.)	25860	27768	28518	28980	29490
福利金受领人数 （人）	Pension Recipients (person)	125429	131867	138996	148058	158519
福利金发放金额 （万澳门元）	Pension Amount (10 000 MOP)	459194	499070	527098	553209	590431
津贴受领人次① （人次）	Cases of Allowance (person-time)	18278	17930 [r]	17095 [r]	20396 [r]	80281
津贴发放金额 （万澳门元）	Allowance Amount (10 000 MOP)	7091	10819	9499	14259	11439
治安	**Public Security**					
罪案数目 （宗）	Crimes (No.)	14178	10057	11376	9799	13487
囚犯数目 （期末值，人）	Number of Prisoners (end-year,person)	1636	1548	1520	1323	1355
本地生产总值	**Gross Domestic Product (GDP)**					
按以环比物量(2022年)计算	In Chained (2022) Dollars					
实际增长率 (%)	Growth Rate in Real Terms (%)	-2.6 [r]	-54.3 [r]	23.5 [r]	-21.4 [r]	80.5
本地生产总值 （亿澳门元）	GDP (100 million MOP)	4450.2 [r]	2032.1 [r]	2510.4 [r]	1973.1 [r]	3562.2
人均本地生产总值 （万澳门元）	GDP per Capita (10 000 MOP)	66.1 [r]	29.8 [r]	36.7 [r]	29.1 [r]	52.5
当年价格	At Current Prices					
名义增长率 (%)	Growth Rate in Nominal Terms (%)	-0.2	-54.5 [r]	22.4 [r]	-20.4 [r]	92.3
本地生产总值 （亿澳门元）	GDP (100 million MOP)	4445.4 [r]	2024.7 [r]	2479.3 [r]	1973.1 [r]	3794.8
人均本地生产总值 （万澳门元）	GDP per Capita (10 000 MOP)	66.0 [r]	29.7 [r]	36.3 [r]	29.1 [r]	55.9

注：①2020年起失业津贴以领取人数作统计。
Note: ①Starting from 2020, data on unemployment allowance are calculated based on the number of beneficiaries.

27–2 按堂区划分的陆地面积
Land Area by Parish

单位：平方公里 (sq.km)

分区	Sub-division	2019	2020	2021	2022	2023
总面积	**Total Land Area**	**32.9**	**32.9**	**33.0**	**33.3**	**33.3**
澳门半岛	**Macao Peninsula**	**9.3**	**9.3**	**9.3**	**9.3**	**9.3**
圣安多尼堂区	Santo Antonio	1.1	1.1	1.1	1.1	1.1
望德堂区	Sao Lazaro	0.6	0.6	0.6	0.6	0.6
风顺堂区	Sao Lourenco	1.0	1.0	1.0	1.0	1.0
大堂区	Se	3.4	3.4	3.4	3.4	3.4
花地玛堂区	N.S. de Fatima	3.2	3.2	3.2	3.2	3.2
氹仔	**Taipa Island**	**7.9**	**7.9**	**7.9**	**7.9**	**7.9**
路环	**Coloane Island**	**7.6**	**7.6**	**7.6**	**7.6**	**7.6**
路氹填海区	**CoTai Reclamation Zone**	**6.0**	**6.0**	**6.1**	**6.1**	**6.1**
新城A区	**Zone A of the New District**	**1.4**	**1.4**	**1.4**	**1.4**	**1.4**
新城C区	**Zone C of the New District**	**..**	**..**	**..**	**0.3**	**0.3**
港珠澳大桥珠澳口岸人工岛澳门口岸管理区	**Macao Port Administration Area on the artificial island of the Hong Kong-Zhuhai-Macao Bridge Zhuhai-Macao border crossing facilities**	**0.7**	**0.7**	**0.7**	**0.7**	**0.7**

27–3 人口主要指标
Main Demographic Indicator

项目	Item	2019	2020	2021	2022	2023
年中人口 (万人)	Mid-year Population (10 000 persons)	67.2	68.5	68.3	67.7	67.9
出生率 (‰)	Crude Birth Rate (‰)	8.9	8.1	7.4	6.4	5.5
死亡率 (‰)	Crude Death Rate (‰)	3.4	3.3	3.4	4.4	4.4
婴儿死亡率 (‰)	Infant Mortality Rate (‰)	1.5	2.2	1.8	0.9	2.4
自然增长率 (‰)	Natural Growth Rate (‰)	5.5	4.8	4.0	2.0	1.1
总和生育率 (‰)	Total Fertility Rate (‰)	899	841	756	680	586
本地人口总和生育率①(‰)	Total Fertility Rate of Local Population① (‰)	1340	1218	1066	909	799
登记结婚 (宗)	Registered Marriages (case)	3724	2754	3277	2727	3168
离婚 (宗)	Registered Divorces (case)	1435	1319	1315	1106	1299
项目	Item	2016–2019	2017–2020	2018–2021	2019–2022	2020–2023
出生时平均预期寿命 (岁)	Life Expectancy at Birth (year)	83.8	84.1	84.2	83.8	83.1
男	Male	80.8	81.1	81.3	80.9	80.3
女	Female	86.7	86.9	87.1	86.7	86.0

注：①本地人口总和生育率是指不包括在澳门居住的外地雇员及外地学生的生育率。

Note: ①Total fertility rate of local population refers to the fertility rate of the population excluding non-resident workers and non-local students living in Macao.

27–4 经济活动人口及失业状况
Labour Force and Unemployment

项目	Item	2019	2020	2021	2022	2023
劳动人口 (万人)	Labour Force (10 000 persons)	39.5	40.5	39.0	37.9	37.5
男	Male	19.3	19.9	18.9	18.3	18.0
女	Female	20.2	20.7	20.1	19.6	19.5
就业人口 (万人)	Employed Population (10 000 persons)	38.8	39.5	37.8	36.5	36.5
失业人口 (万人)	Unemployed Population (10 000 persons)	0.7	1.0	1.1	1.4	1.0
失业率 (%)	Unemployment Rate (%)	1.7	2.5	2.9	3.7	2.7

27–5 按行业划分的就业人口
Employed Population by Industry

单位：万人 (10 000 persons)

行　　业	Industry	2019	2020	2021	2022	2023
总数	**Total**	**38.78**	**39.51**	**37.84**	**36.47**	**36.52**
制造业	Manufacturing	0.63	0.64	0.66	0.59	0.61
水电及气体生产供应业	Electricity, Gas & Water Supply	0.09	0.12	0.09	0.12	0.17
建筑业	Construction	3.05	3.76	3.26	3.02	2.78
批发及零售业	Wholesale & Retail Trades	4.16	4.62	4.34	4.63	4.66
酒店及饮食业	Hotels, Restaurants & Similar Activities	5.61	5.44	5.03	4.52	4.60
运输、仓储及通讯业	Transport, Storage & Communications	1.98	1.80	1.76	1.80	1.92
金融业	Financial Intermediation	1.21	1.28	1.36	1.23	1.36
不动产及工商服务业	Real Estate & Business Activities	3.48	3.56	3.28	3.29	3.23
公共行政及社保事务	Public Administration & Social Security	2.79	2.74	2.86	2.84	2.92
教育	Education	1.73	1.82	1.92	2.10	2.06
医疗卫生及社会福利	Health & Social Welfare	1.26	1.35	1.43	1.67	1.61
文娱博彩及其他服务业	Recreational, Cultural, Gaming & Other Services	9.70	9.13	8.91	8.06	7.99
家务工作	Domestic Work	3.03	3.15	2.85	2.51	2.49
其他及不详	Others and Unknown	0.08	0.10	0.08	0.09	0.13

27–6 按行业划分的月工作收入中位数
Median Monthly Employment Earnings by Industry

单位：澳门元 (MOP)

行　　业	Industry	2019	2020	2021	2022	2023
总数	**Total**	**17000**	**15000**	**15800**	**15000**	**17500**
制造业	Manufacturing	10800	11000	12000	12000	12000
水电及气体生产供应业	Electricity, Gas & Water Supply	20500	22000	29500	21000	25000
建筑业	Construction	17000	15000	15000	15000	15000
批发及零售业	Wholesale & Retail Trade	14000	12000	13000	12000	14000
酒店及饮食业	Hotels, Restaurants & Similar Activities	12000	11000	11800	11600	12000
运输、仓储及通讯业	Transport, Storage & Communications	16000	15000	15000	14800	17000
金融业	Financial Intermediation	21000	22000	21000	20000	21500
不动产及工商服务业	Real Estate & Business Activities	11000	10000	10000	10000	10500
公共行政及社保事务	Public Administration & Social Security	40300	43000	44600	44600	45000
教育	Education	28000	25500	25300	26000	27000
医疗卫生及社会福利	Health & Social Welfare	22100	23300	23000	22000	24000
文娱博彩及其他服务业	Recreational, Cultural, Gaming & Other Services	20000	19300	19000	19300	20000
家务工作	Domestic Work	4200	4400	4500	5000	5000

27-7 本地生产总值(当年价格)
Gross Domestic Product at Current Prices

年 份 Year	本地生产总值 GDP (亿澳门元) (100 million MOP)	本地生产总值 GDP (亿美元) (100 million USD)	实际增长率 (%) Growth Rate in Real Terms (%)	人均本地生产总值 GDP per capita (澳门元) (MOP)	人均本地生产总值 GDP per capita (美元) (USD)
1993	451.4	56.7	5.2	117561	14754
1994	502.4	63.1	4.3	126618	15906
1995	561.4	70.5	3.3	137165	17215
1996	571.7	71.8	-0.4	137734	17289
1997	579.6	72.7	-0.3	138897	17417
1998	542.4	68.0	-4.6	128434	16097
1999	523.3	65.5	-2.4	122431	15320
2000	543.7	67.7	5.7	126271	15733
2001	551.1	68.6	2.9	127015	15811
2002	592.2	73.7	8.9	135079	16815
2003	661.5	82.5	11.6	149113	18589
2004	853.8	106.4	26.6	187793	23408
2005	974.2	121.6	8.1	205753	25684
2006	1190.1	148.8	13.4	239417	29925
2007	1481.8	184.4	14.5	284495	35403
2008	1686.4	210.3	3.4	313785	39122
2009	1723.6	215.9	1.3	320275	40114
2010	2260.0	282.4	25.1	420915	52600
2011	2954.4	368.4	21.6	538165	67115
2012	3450.8	431.9	9.2	605740	75813
2013	4117.4	515.4	10.8	692289	86653
2014	4385.2	549.0	-2.0	705180	88290
2015	3597.1	450.5	-21.5	560729	70223
2016	3603.4	450.7	-0.7	557938	69788
2017	4043.8 [r]	503.8 [r]	9.9 [r]	623083 [r]	77631
2018	4455.3 [r]	551.9 [r]	6.4 [r]	674785 [r]	83586
2019	4445.4 [r]	550.8 [r]	-2.6 [r]	660045 [r]	81787
2020	2024.7 [r]	253.4 [r]	-54.3 [r]	297162 [r]	37197
2021	2479.3 [r]	309.7 [r]	23.5 [r]	362915 [r]	45332
2022	1973.1 [r]	244.6 [r]	-21.4 [r]	291022 [r]	36080
2023	3794.8	470.6	80.5	559495	69384

27-8 支出法本地生产总值
Expenditure-based Gross Domestic Product

单位：亿澳门元 (100 million MOP)

本地生产总值组成部分	GDP Components	2019	2020	2021	2022	2023
按当年价格计算	**At Current Prices**					
私人消费支出	Private Consumption Expenditure	1108.9 [r]	943.8 [r]	1037.4 [r]	982.7 [r]	1100.1
政府最终消费支出	Government Final Consumption Expenditure	453.7	523.6 [r]	524.5 [r]	552.2 [r]	519.3
固定资本形成总额	Gross Fixed Capital Formation	615.4	536.5 [r]	552.0 [r]	449.3 [r]	513.9
存货增加	Changes in Inventories	13.2	-8.3	13.7 [r]	15.8 [r]	15.9
货物出口	Exports of Goods	149.7	338.6	759.0 [r]	635.1 [r]	463.0
减:货物进口	Less: Imports of Goods	1005.3 [r]	955.7 [r]	1583.6 [r]	1417.2 [r]	1449.8
服务出口	Exports of Services	3526.9	905.9 [r]	1495.6 [r]	1064.3 [r]	3054.2
减:服务进口	Less: Imports of Services	417.0	259.7 [r]	319.2 [r]	309.1 [r]	421.8
本地生产总值	**GDP**	**4445.4 [r]**	**2024.7 [r]**	**2479.3 [r]**	**1973.1 [r]**	**3794.8**
人均本地生产总值(澳门元)	**GDP per capita (MOP)**	**660045 [r]**	**297162 [r]**	**362915 [r]**	**291022 [r]**	**559495**
以环比物量(2022年)计算	**In Chained (2022) Dollars**					
私人消费支出	Private Consumption Expenditure	1126.4 [r]	954.5 [r]	1044.0 [r]	982.7 [r]	1101.2
政府最终消费支出	Government Final Consumption Expenditure	474.7 [r]	533.9 [r]	529.7 [r]	552.2 [r]	517.0
固定资本形成总额	Gross Fixed Capital Formation	669.1 [r]	580.9 [r]	563.4 [r]	449.3 [r]	515.2
存货增加	Changes in Inventories	13.4 [r]	-8.5 [r]	13.8 [r]	15.8 [r]	15.7
货物出口	Exports of Goods	152.2 [r]	343.5 [r]	764.3 [r]	635.1 [r]	456.7
减:货物进口	Less: Imports of Goods	1020.8 [r]	971.4 [r]	1592.9 [r]	1417.2 [r]	1432.2
服务出口	Exports of Services	3402.3 [r]	894.1 [r]	1510.7 [r]	1064.3 [r]	2820.8
减:服务进口	Less: Imports of Services	456.0 [r]	277.9 [r]	322.6 [r]	309.1 [r]	432.2
本地生产总值	**GDP**	**4450.2 [r]**	**2032.1 [r]**	**2510.4 [r]**	**1973.1 [r]**	**3562.2**
人均本地生产总值(澳门元)	**GDP per capita (MOP)**	**660754 [r]**	**298250 [r]**	**367474 [r]**	**291022 [r]**	**525203**

27–9 生产法本地生产总值
Production-based Gross Domestic Product

单位：亿澳门元 (100 million MOP)

经济活动	Economic Activities	2018	2019	2020	2021	2022
第二产业	**Secondary Sector**	**182.2**	**187.3 r**	**171.8**	**190.6 r**	**186.5**
采矿业	Mining and Quarrying	-	-	-	-	-
制造业	Manufacturing	24.0	23.9 r	16.8	20.5	18.9
电力、煤气及水供应	Electricity, Gas and Water Supply	27.0	28.1	28.4	27.7	28.6
建筑业	Construction	131.2	135.4	126.6	142.3	139.1
第三产业	**Tertiary Sector**	**4201.1 r**	**4160.4 r**	**1803.1 r**	**2263.1 r**	**1778.1**
批发零售、维修、酒店、餐厅及酒楼业	Wholesale, Retail, Repair, Hotels and Restaurants	516.7	516.9	185.7 r	319.5 r	232.0
运输、仓储及通讯业	Transport, Storage and Communications	112.8	117.3	60.0	66.8 r	60.6
银行、保险、不动产、租赁及商业服务	Banking, Insurance & Pension Funding, Real Estate, Renting and Business Activities	933.4	872.8	732.5 r	831.9 r	779.6
公共行政、社会服务及个人服务（包括博彩业）	Public Administration, Other Community, Social and Personal Services (Including Gaming Sector)	2638.2 r	2653.4 r	824.9 r	1044.9 r	705.9
以生产者价格计算的增加值	**Gross value added at producers' prices**	**4383.3 r**	**4347.7 r**	**1974.9 r**	**2453.7 r**	**1964.7**
加进口税	**Add: Taxes on imports**	**5.1**	**5.3**	**6.0**	**7.5**	**8.7**
以市场价格按生产法计算的本地生产总值	**Production-based GDP at Current Market Prices**	**4388.4 r**	**4353.0 r**	**1980.9 r**	**2461.2 r**	**1973.4**
以市场价格按支出法计算的本地生产总值	**Expenditure-based GDP at Current Market Prices**	**4455.3 r**	**4445.4 r**	**2024.7 r**	**2479.3 r**	**1973.1**
统计差异(%)	**Statistical Discrepancy (%)**	**-1.5**	**-2.1 r**	**-2.2 r**	**-0.7 r**	**o**

27–10 生产法本地生产总值结构
Structure of Production-based Gross Domestic Product

单位：% (%)

经济活动	Economic Activities	2018	2019	2020	2021	2022
第二产业	**Secondary Sector**	**4.2**	**4.3**	**8.7**	**7.8 r**	**9.5**
采矿业	Mining and Quarrying	-	-	-	-	-
制造业	Manufacturing	0.5	0.5 r	0.9	0.8	1.0
电力、煤气及水供应业	Electricity, Gas and Water Supply	0.6	0.6	1.4	1.1	1.5
建筑业	Construction	3.0	3.1	6.4	5.8	7.1
第三产业	**Tertiary Sector**	**95.8**	**95.7**	**91.3**	**92.2 r**	**90.5**
批发零售、维修、酒店、餐厅及酒楼业	Wholesale, Retail, Repair, Hotels and Restaurants	11.8	11.9	9.4 r	13.0 r	11.8
运输、仓储及通讯业	Transport, Storage and Communications	2.6	2.7	3.0	2.7	3.1
银行、保险、不动产、租赁及商业服务	Banking, Insurance & Pension Funding, Real Estate, Renting and Business Activities	21.3	20.1 r	37.1 r	33.9 r	39.7
公共行政、社会服务及个人服务（包括博彩业）	Public Administration, Other Community, Social and Personal Services (Including Gaming Sector)	60.2 r	61.0 r	41.8 r	42.6 r	35.9
以生产者价格计算的增加值	**Gross value added at producers' prices**	**100.0**	**100.0**	**100.0**	**100.0**	**100.0**

27-11 电力、燃料及水消耗量
Consumption of Electricity, Fuels and Water

项　　目	Item	2019	2020	2021	2022	2023
电力　（万千瓦时）	**Electricity (10 000 kW·h)**					
住户	Domestic	119593	131047	125449	124921	123481
工业	Industrial	15440	14372	15544	14553	15891
商业及公共照明	Commercial and Public Lighting	419845	373715	404371	385774[r]	434620
燃料	**Fuels**					
重油　（万公升）	Fuel Oil (10 000 litres)	3445	3271	815	555	1397
轻柴油　（万公升）	Gas Oil and Diesel (10 000 litres)	11087	8214	9389	8885	9394
汽油　（万公升）	Gasoline (10 000 litres)	11097	9266	10197	9081	9662
液化石油气　（公吨）	L.P.G. (ton)	40905	34426	34051	31187	31108
水　（万立方米）	**Water (10 000 cu.m)**	**9281**	**8552**	**8631**	**8325**	**8916**

27-12 按用途划分的获发使用准照私人楼宇
Private Buildings with Licence of Use issued by End-use

项　　目	Item	2019	2020	2021	2022	2023
住宅	Residential					
单位数目　（个）	Number of Units	2886	2365	2393	500	183
建筑面积(万平方米)	Gross Floor Area(10 000 sq.m)	29.8	18.0	18.1	4.5	1.1
商铺及办公室	Shop and Office					
单位数目　（个）	Number of Units	111	128	130	48	55
建筑面积(万平方米)	Gross Floor Area(10 000 sq.m)	2.9	2.2	1.7	0.4	0.7
工业	Industrial					
单位数目　（个）	Number of Units	1	3	4	1	-
建筑面积(万平方米)	Gross Floor Area(10 000 sq.m)	0.7	1.0	3.9	o	-
其他用途	Others					
单位数目　（个）	Number of Units	15	25	18	20	16
建筑面积(万平方米)	Gross Floor Area(10 000 sq.m)	14.0	7.5	71.6	32.4	35.6
总计	Total					
单位数目　（个）	Number of Units	3013	2521	2545	569	254
建筑面积(万平方米)	Gross Floor Area(10 000 sq.m)	47.4	28.7	95.4	37.3	37.4

27-13 按用途划分的获发动工批示私人楼宇
Private Buildings with Construction Permit issued by End-use

项　　目	Item	2019	2020	2021	2022	2023
住宅	Residential					
单位数目　（个）	Number of Units	325	162	1303	392	437
建筑面积(万平方米)	Gross Floor Area(10 000 sq.m)	3.5	1.0	7.9	2.3	3.3
商铺及办公室	Shop and Office					
单位数目　（个）	Number of Units	54	49	89	58	21
建筑面积(万平方米)	Gross Floor Area(10 000 sq.m)	3.5	0.6	2.0	1.0	0.2
工业	Industrial					
单位数目　（个）	Number of Units	1	-	2	-	1
建筑面积(万平方米)	Gross Floor Area(10 000 sq.m)	0.5	-	0.3	-	0.9
其他用途	Others					
单位数目　（个）	Number of Units	25	22	13	8	5
建筑面积(万平方米)	Gross Floor Area(10 000 sq.m)	36.6	86.6	45.4	3.4	0.5
总计	Total					
单位数目　（个）	Number of Units	405	233	1407	458	464
建筑面积(万平方米)	Gross Floor Area(10 000 sq.m)	44.2	88.1	55.7	6.7	4.9

27–14 零售业销售额
Value of Retail Sales

单位：亿澳门元 (100 million MOP)

项　目	Item	2019	2020	2021	2022	2023
销售总额	**Total Value of Sales**	**771.87**	**452.25**	**740.90**	**576.96**	**845.66**
百货	Department Stores	133.40	66.23	120.32	75.99	116.95
超级市场	Supermarkets	49.49	51.45	50.66	53.00	51.26
汽车	Motor Vehicles	23.91	20.71	20.83	17.77	20.23
钟表珠宝	Watches, Clocks and Jewellery	158.50	72.72	164.86	115.72	207.84
成人服装	Adults' Clothing	89.03	41.91	60.84	41.43	67.09
车用燃料	Automotive Fuels	16.80	11.43	12.45	12.54	14.38
家用燃料	Fuel for Household Use	5.90	4.31	4.68	4.93	5.17
家庭电器	Household Electric Appliances	11.65	8.65	10.28	8.30	8.24
药房	Pharmacy	21.33	14.39	16.99	16.47	21.76
其他	Others	261.86	160.45	278.99	230.81	332.74

27–15 按出入境方式统计的对外商品贸易
External Merchandise Trade by Mode of Transport

单位：万吨 (10 000 tons)

项　目	Mode of Transport	2019	2020	2021	2022	2023
入境①	**Imports ①**					
海路	Sea	526.9	693.8	618.4	360.1	377.1
空路	Air	0.8	0.4	0.5	0.5	0.5
陆路	Land	130.6	109.3	140.5	157.8	181.3
其他②	Others ②	10183.0	9631.8	9501.5	9246.0	9962.4
总数	**Total**	**10841.3**	**10435.3**	**10260.9**	**9764.4**	**10521.4**
出境①	**Exports ①**					
海路	Sea	16.0	16.6	19.5	16.2	16.2
空路	Air	2.3	2.7	4.4	4.6	5.7
陆路	Land	3.0	2.8	3.1	4.6	2.0
其他②	Others ②	25.3	5.9	7.2	5.2	15.7
总数	**Total**	**46.6**	**28.0**	**34.2**	**30.7**	**39.5**

注：①包括转运货物。
②包括邮递及以管道运输方式进出澳门的货物。

Notes:①Including transit goods.
②Including external merchandise trade by post and via pipeline.

27–16 集装箱流量
Container Flow

单位：个 (number)

项　目	Item	2019	2020	2021	2022	2023
入境	Inward	59175	57975	56930	50490	54080
出境	Outward	34845	30361	35789	42016	54176
转口	Transit	939	1092	1881	1302	1249

27–17 港口集装箱总吞吐量
Port Container Throughput

单位：标准集装箱 (TEU)

项 目	Item	2019	2020	2021	2022	2023
入境	Inward	84618	83365	82695	73954	74393
出境	Outward	47699	37883	40840	53514	69587
转口	Transit	722	155	540	318	345

27–18 通信服务
Communications

项 目	Item	2019	2020	2021	2022	2023
邮递服务 （万件）	**Postal Services (10 000 pcs)**					
信件邮件	Mails	3079	2628	2311	1913	1921
包裹	Parcels	0.5	0.7	0.8	0.9	0.5
电话服务 （万户）	**Telephone Services (10 000 subscribers)**					
固网电话用户	Fixed-line Telephone Subscribers	11.6	10.7	10.0	9.3	8.8
移动电话用户	Mobile Phone Subscribers	80.2	83.3	88.1	92.6	100.0
预付卡	Prepaid SIM Cards	199.1	78.8	39.4	28.7	37.4
对外电话通讯量 （万分钟）	**International Calls (10 000 minutes)**					
拨出	Outgoing	14008	8186	6956	5206	5461
拨入	Incoming	13450	6145	6460	4538	6322
互联网	**Internet Services**					
登记用户 (万户)	Registered Subscribers (10 000 subscribers)	59.0	63.2	67.2	70.1	72.2
总使用时数 (万小时)	Total Hours Used (10 000 hours)	158540	165428	166102	168651	170241

注：由于小数进位关系，此表内“电话服务”细项之和与统计表27–1内“固网及移动电话用户”之总数可能出现差异。
Note: Figures of "Telephone Services" may not add up to the total indicated in Table 27-1 "Fixed-line Telephone & Mobile Phone Subscribers (incl. Prepaid SIM Cards)" due to rounding.

27-19 对外商品贸易主要指标
Principal Indicators of External Merchandise Trade

单位：亿澳门元 (100 million MOP)

贸易种类	Trade Type	2019	2020	2021	2022	2023
出口	Exports	128.0	108.1	129.6	135.2	133.4
本地产品出口	Domestic Exports	15.1	15.6	20.0	20.2	15.5
再出口	Re-exports	112.8	92.5	109.6	115.0	117.9
进口	Imports	901.3	925.6	1538.8	1398.1	1414.4
进出口总额	Total Trade	1029.2	1033.7	1668.4	1533.3	1547.8
进出口差额	Trade Balance	-773.3	-817.5	-1409.1	-1262.9	-1281.1
出口/进口比率（%）	Exports-to-Imports Ratio(%)	14.2	11.7	8.4	9.7	9.4

27-20 按主要原产地和目的地划分的商品进出口
Merchandise Imports and Exports by Major Country/Region

单位：亿澳门元 (100 million MOP)

主要国家/地区	Major Country/Region	2019	2020	2021	2022	2023
进口（原产地）	**Imports (Origin)**					
中国内地	Mainland China	306.5	276.1	485.2	424.5	405.1
中国香港	Hong Kong, China	56.5	29.1	56.9	50.9	71.9
欧盟	European Union	249.2	285.4	498.0	458.5	446.1
日本	Japan	61.8	95.9	131.6	90.2	85.8
中国台湾	Taiwan, China	13.0	15.7	12.9	14.5	15.5
美国	United States of America	43.5	83.2	105.1	95.9	84.2
出口（目的地）	**Exports (Destination)**					
美国	United States of America	2.9	5.5	6.8	6.1	4.4
欧盟	European Union	2.0	1.8	1.9	1.7	1.5
中国内地	Mainland China	15.8	16.2	18.1	13.1	9.7
中国香港	Hong Kong, China	81.6	74.6	91.6	103.0	95.3

27–21 财政收入
Government Revenue

单位：亿澳门元 (100 million MOP)

项 目	Items	2016	2017	2018
经常收入	**Current Revenue**			
直接税	Direct Taxes	884.6	1032.6	1159.6
间接税	Indirect Taxes	40.8	51.2	56.9
费用、罚款及其他金钱制裁	Fees, Fines and Other Penalties	20.2	18.3	20.5
财产收益	Property Income	18.3	15.1	9.2
转移	Transfers	52.3	62.1	71.4
耐用品的出售	Sales of Durable Goods	o	0.1	0.1
劳务及非耐用品的出售	Sales of Services and Non-durable Goods	11.6	12.3	12.5
其他经常收入	Other Current Revenue	1.8	2.8	2.2
资本收入	**Capital Revenue**			
投资资产的出售	Sales of Fixed Capital	6.8	0.4	12.2
转移	Transfers	o	o	-
财务资产	Financial Assets	5.9	5.3	7.9
财务负债	Financial Liabilities	-	-	-
其他资本收入	Other Capital Revenue	60.6	61.9	46.9
非从支付中扣减的退回	Reimbursements Not Deducted from Payments	2.2	1.7	13.8
自治机构	**Autonomous Agencies**			
总数	**Total**	**1105.0**	**1263.7**	**1413.1**

27–21 续表 continued

单位：亿澳门元 (100 million MOP)

项 目	Items	2019	2020	2021	2022	2023
经常收入	**Current Revenue**					
直接税	Direct Taxes	105.4	97.9	89.2	111.1	115.0
间接税	Indirect Taxes	49.3	35.9	37.3	26.1	35.6
规费、罚款及其他金钱制裁	Fees, Fines and Other Penalties	17.4	13.7	15.7	13.2	16.3
财产收入	Property Income	7.5	6.5	20.8	8.5	8.9
特许批给收入	Concession Revenue	1130.8	300.9	341.8	194.5	656.6
财务收入	Financial Revenue	4.4	4.0	3.3	11.1	11.2
出售物品及劳务	Sales of Goods and Services	8.4	10.0	10.3	11.1	15.0
转移	Transfers	3.0	2.0	2.1	1.1	1.7
保障制度供款	Social Security Contributions	0.8	0.9	0.9	0.9	0.9
其他经常收入	Other Current Revenue	1.7	2.6	1.6	1.6	6.5
资本收入	**Capital Revenue**					
出售设施及设备	Sale of Facilities and Equipment	21.6	1.9	0.3	0.1	0.1
财务资产	Financial Assets	8.8	8.8	7.9	8.3	9.2
出售股票及其他股权	Sale of Shares and Other Equity	o	-	0.1	-	-
其他资本收入	Other Capital Revenue	48.2	531.5	416.8	703.9	127.5
总数	**Total**	**1407.3**	**1016.7**	**948.1**	**1091.4**	**1004.5**

注：按第63/2018号经济财政司订定的新分类结构。
Note: In accordance with the new classification stipulated in Economy and Finance No. 63/2018.

27–22 财政支出
Government Expenditure

单位：亿澳门元 (100 million MOP)

项　目	Items	2016	2017	2018
经常支出	**Current Expenditure**			
工薪	Payroll	184.0	198.6	209.4
货物及劳务	Goods and Services	98.5	95.8	102.8
利息	Interest	-	-	-
经常转移	Current Transfers	390.7	278.4	287.0
其他经常支出	Other Current Expenditure	31.7	33.7	38.6
资本支出	**Capital Expenditure**			
投资	Investments	95.1	138.2	165.7
资本转移	Capital Transfers	6.4	4.4	3.0
财务活动	Financial Transactions	19.9	63.9	23.9
其他资本支出	Other Capital Expenditure	-	-	-
自治机构	**Autonomous Agencies**			
总数	**Total**	**826.3**	**813.0**	**830.3**

27–22 续表 continued

单位：亿澳门元 (100 million MOP)

项　目	Items	2019	2020	2021	2022	2023
经常支出	**Current Expenditure**					
人员开支	Personnel Expenses	247.1	261.6	265.0	266.4	270.9
运作开支	Operating Expenses	129.8	126.9	125.8	130.8	129.4
提供公用事业服务开支	Expenses for Providing Public Utility Services	11.9	10.8	10.9	11.8	13.6
退休及抚恤制度	Retirement and Pension Regime	o	o	o	o	o
转移、资助及补助	Transfer, Funding and Subsidies	290.7	386.5	337.5	439.0	282.0
其他经常支出	Other Current Expenditure	-	-	-	-	-
资本支出	**Capital Expenditure**					
设施及设备	Facilities and Equipment	138.2	124.7	149.0	169.9	207.5
财务资产	Financial Assets	4.8	21.6	3.4	3.5	2.2
股票及其他股权	Shares and Other Equity	24.3	29.2	o	0.1	o
总数	**Total**	**846.8**	**961.3**	**891.5**	**1021.5**	**905.7**

注：按第63/2018号经济财政司订定的新分类结构。
Note: In accordance with the new classification stipulated in Economy and Finance No. 63/2018.

27–23 货币供应
Money Supply

单位：亿澳门元(年底数字) (100 million MOP (as at end of year))

项　　目	Items	2019	2020	2021	2022	2023
狭义货币供应量M_1	**Money Supply (M_1)**	**881.6**	**811.9**	**758.7**	**727.6 r**	**703.7**
分类一：澳门元	Classification 1: MOP	470.6	481.1	491.8	499.4 r	477.7
港元	HKD	386.6	306.7	247.1	206.7	210.8
其他货币	Other Currencies	24.4	24.0	19.8	21.5	15.2
分类二：流通货币(澳门元)	Classification 2: Currency in Circulation (MOP)	168.8	185.8	198.9	204.3	203.4
活期存款	Demand Deposits	712.9	626.1	559.9	523.3	500.3
广义货币供应量$M_2$①	**Money Supply (M_2) ①**	**6875.2**	**6923.6**	**6875.4**	**7177.1 r**	**7255.8**
分类一：澳门元	Classification 1: MOP	2106.3	2354.1	2434.0	2769.3 r	2467.7
港元	HKD	3311.0	3382.4	3441.8	2988.6	3301.7
其他货币	Other Currencies	1457.9	1187.1	999.7	1419.2	1486.5
分类二：狭义货币供应量$M_1$②	Classification 2: Money Supply (M_1) ②	881.6	811.9	758.7	727.6 r	703.7
准货币负债③	Quasi-Monetary Liabilities (QML)③	5993.6	6111.7	6116.7	6449.5 r	6552.1
储蓄存款	Savings Deposits	1931.7	2239.4	2255.3	2058.9	1693.6
通知存款	Notice Deposits	1.8	1.5	0.7	2.2	2.6
定期存款	Time Deposits	4059.7	3832.1	3830.3	4299.2 r	4597.8

注：① M_2 ＝ M_1 ＋ 准货币负债。
② 货币供应量M_1包括流通货币及活期存款。
③ 准货币负债：包括储蓄存款、通知存款、定期存款、其他存款及存款证明书。

Notes: ① $M_2 = M_1$ + Quasi-Monetary Liabilities (QML)
② M_1 includes Currency in Circulation and Demand Deposits.
③QML:Quasi-Monetary Liabilities, which consist of savings deposits, notice deposits, time deposits, other deposits and certificates of deposit.

27–24 外币兑换率
Exchange Rates

单位：一单位外币兑换的澳门元 (MOP per unit of foreign currency)

项　　目	Items	2019	2020	2021	2022	2023
年内平均数字	**Average for the Year**					
澳元	Australian Dollar	5.6078	5.5165	6.0154	5.6024	5.3553
欧元	Euro	9.0358	9.1196	9.4749	8.4902	8.7204
韩元	Korean Won	0.0069	0.0068	0.0070	0.0063	0.0062
美元	US Dollar	8.0703	7.9889	8.0057	8.0661	8.0637
新台币	Taiwan Dollar	0.2611	0.2712	0.2866	0.2711	0.2589
英镑	Pound Sterling	10.2996	10.2496	11.0171	9.9682	10.0281
港元	Hong Kong Dollar	1.0300	1.0300	1.0300	1.0300	1.0300
日元	Japanese Yen	0.0741	0.0748	0.0730	0.0617	0.0575
马来西亚林吉特	Malaysian Ringgit	1.9479	1.9007	1.9316	1.8344	1.7693
新西兰元	New Zealand Dollar	5.3171	5.1939	5.6643	5.1250	4.9488
人民币	P.R. China Renminbi	1.1673	1.1575	1.2409	1.1989	1.1380
新加坡元	Singapore Dollar	5.9150	5.7914	5.9580	5.8493	6.0036
瑞士法郎	Swiss Franc	8.1243	8.5168	8.7587	8.4484	8.9759
年底数字	**As at End of Year**					
澳元	Australian Dollar	5.6179	6.1502	5.8263	5.4344	5.4991
欧元	Euro	8.9870	9.8278	9.0969	8.5673	8.9160
韩元	Korean Won	0.0069	0.0073	0.0067	0.0064	0.0062
美元	US Dollar	8.0216	7.9852	8.0319	8.0308	8.0502
新台币	Taiwan Dollar	0.2669	0.2844	0.2902	0.2617	0.2621
英镑	Pound Sterling	10.5199	10.8958	10.8447	9.6876	10.2547
港元	Hong Kong Dollar	1.0300	1.0300	1.0300	1.0300	1.0300
日元	Japanese Yen	0.0737	0.0774	0.0698	0.0606	0.0568
马来西亚林吉特	Malaysian Ringgit	1.9567	1.9822	1.9243	1.8190	1.7502
新西兰元	New Zealand Dollar	5.4021	5.7717	5.4886	5.0867	5.1022
人民币	P.R. China Renminbi	1.1492	1.2274	1.2595	1.1518	1.1316
新加坡元	Singapore Dollar	5.9501	6.0396	5.9403	5.9782	6.1012
瑞士法郎	Swiss Franc	8.2795	9.0622	8.7929	8.7074	9.5517

27–25 消费物价指数
Consumer Price Index

2018年4月至2019年3月=100 (04/2018-03/2019=100)

项　目	Items	权数 Weight	2019	2020	2021	2022	2023
综合消费物价指数	**Composite Consumer Price Index**						
总指数	**Global Index**	**100.00**	**101.78**	**102.60**	**102.63**	**103.70**	**104.68**
食物及非酒精饮品	Food and Non-alcoholic Beverages	27.94	102.71	106.17	106.41	108.28	111.00
烟酒	Alcoholic Beverages and Tobacco	0.60	99.53	99.23	98.80	100.64	101.46
衣履	Clothing and Footwear	2.95	100.66	94.01	90.18	90.58	94.10
住屋及燃料	Housing and Fuels	33.75	101.68	102.40	102.30	101.16	99.69
家居设备及服务	Household Furnishings and Services	4.16	101.27	102.55	106.16	118.09	121.23
医疗	Health	2.82	102.55	106.67	108.31	109.41	111.97
交通	Transport	7.84	101.86	100.73	104.34	110.42	108.18
通讯	Communications	3.10	97.50	87.15	82.48	74.73	73.06
康乐及文化	Recreation and Culture	5.18	102.35	97.36	91.29	91.07	95.51
教育	Education	2.24	100.53	104.09	104.97	109.48	118.50
杂项商品及服务	Miscellaneous Goods and Services	9.42	101.72	103.63	104.39	105.01	107.05
甲类消费物价指数	**Consumer Price Index (A)**						
总指数	**Global Index**	**100.00**	**101.79**	**102.71**	**102.66**	**103.41**	**104.16**
食物及非酒精饮品	Food and Non-alcoholic Beverages	28.68	102.89	106.45	106.63	108.46	111.15
烟酒	Alcoholic Beverages and Tobacco	0.62	99.64	99.35	98.97	100.94	101.89
衣履	Clothing and Footwear	2.41	101.04	94.28	90.51	91.04	94.42
住屋及燃料	Housing and Fuels	38.37	101.67	102.37	102.25	101.10	99.62
家居设备及服务	Household Furnishings and Services	3.21	101.13	102.28	105.55	116.24	119.19
医疗	Health	2.72	102.75	107.14	108.99	110.08	112.67
交通	Transport	6.46	101.38	100.30	104.31	110.65	108.08
通讯	Communications	3.41	97.68	87.38	82.79	74.91	73.25
康乐及文化	Recreation and Culture	4.52	102.17	97.68	91.42	91.25	95.57
教育	Education	1.89	99.46	102.75	103.04	106.81	115.71
杂项商品及服务	Miscellaneous Goods and Services	7.70	101.97	103.79	104.55	105.28	107.33
乙类消费物价指数	**Consumer Price Index (B)**						
总指数	**Global Index**	**100.00**	**101.77**	**102.45**	**102.58**	**104.09**	**105.35**
食物及非酒精饮品	Food and Non-alcoholic Beverages	26.94	102.72	105.76	106.10	108.02	110.78
烟酒	Alcoholic Beverages and Tobacco	0.56	99.58	99.03	98.53	100.11	100.71
衣履	Clothing and Footwear	3.67	100.32	93.77	89.90	90.19	93.83
住屋及燃料	Housing and Fuels	27.55	101.69	102.46	102.37	101.25	99.82
家居设备及服务	Household Furnishings and Services	5.43	101.42	102.77	106.66	119.56	122.85
医疗	Health	2.96	102.30	106.09	107.48	108.59	111.11
交通	Transport	9.70	102.67	101.11	104.33	110.19	108.22
通讯	Communications	2.69	97.25	86.75	81.95	74.42	72.71
康乐及文化	Recreation and Culture	6.06	102.39	97.04	91.15	90.87	95.42
教育	Education	2.70	100.77	105.34	106.78	111.98	121.10
杂项商品及服务	Miscellaneous Goods and Services	11.73	100.54	103.48	104.23	104.75	106.77

27−26　按收入五等分位及商品与服务分类统计的每户双周平均消费开支(2017年10月至2018年9月)

Average Biweekly Household Expenditure by Quintile Income Group and Section of Goods and Services (Oct. 2017 - Sep. 2018)

商品与服务分类	Goods and Services	总数 Total		最低五分位 The Lowest 20%		第二五分位 The Second 20%	
		澳门元 MOP	百分比 (%)	澳门元 MOP	百分比 (%)	澳门元 MOP	百分比 (%)
消费开支	**Total Expenditure**	**16335**	**100.0**	**7344**	**100.0**	**12431**	**100.0**
食物及非酒精饮料	Food and Non-alcoholic Beverages	3593	22.0	1626	22.1	2891	23.3
烟酒	Alcoholic Beverages and Tobacco	77	0.5	32	0.4	68	0.5
衣履	Clothing and Footwear	444	2.7	135	1.8	335	2.7
住屋及燃料	Housing and Fuels	4386	26.9	2995	40.8	3867	31.1
家居服务及用品	Household Services and Items	577	3.5	178	2.4	306	2.5
医疗	Health	367	2.2	219	3.0	316	2.5
运输	Transport	1156	7.1	207	2.8	591	4.8
通讯	Communications	403	2.5	176	2.4	328	2.6
康乐及文化	Recreation and Culture	759	4.6	219	3.0	441	3.5
教育	Education	1388	8.5	398	5.4	1085	8.7
杂项商品及服务	Miscellaneous Goods and Services	1284	7.9	271	3.7	768	6.2
外地消费	Consumption Expenditure outside Macao	1902	11.6	888	12.1	1436	11.5
住户数目	**Number of Households**	**191273**	**100.0**	**38255**	**20.0**	**38255**	**20.0**

27−26　续表 continued

商品与服务分类	Goods and Services	第三五分位 The Third 20%		第四五分位 The Fourth 20%		最高五分位 The Highest 20%	
		澳门元 MOP	百分比 (%)	澳门元 MOP	百分比 (%)	澳门元 MOP	百分比 (%)
消费开支	**Total expenditure**	**15848**	**100.0**	**19843**	**100.0**	**26212**	**100.0**
食物及非酒精饮料	Food and Non-alcoholic Beverages	3758	23.7	4434	22.3	5253	20.0
烟酒	Alcoholic Beverages and Tobacco	95	0.6	95	0.5	93	0.4
衣履	Clothing and Footwear	378	2.4	598	3.0	773	2.9
住屋及燃料	Housing and Fuels	4289	27.1	4745	23.9	6034	23.0
家居服务及用品	Household Services and Items	387	2.4	735	3.7	1277	4.9
医疗	Health	359	2.3	421	2.1	522	2.0
运输	Transport	976	6.2	1514	7.6	2493	9.5
通讯	Communications	409	2.6	503	2.5	597	2.3
康乐及文化	Recreation and Culture	634	4.0	993	5.0	1507	5.7
教育	Education	1443	9.1	1768	8.9	2244	8.6
杂项商品及服务	Miscellaneous Goods and Services	1072	6.8	1715	8.6	2597	9.9
外地消费	Consumption Expenditure outside Macao	2047	12.9	2321	11.7	2821	10.8
住户数目	**Number of Households**	**38255**	**20.0**	**38254**	**20.0**	**38254**	**20.0**

27–27 按受教育程度统计14岁及以上人口
Population Aged 14 and Over by Educational Attainment

项目	Item	2001人口普查 Census 2001		2006中期人口统计 By-census 2006		2011人口普查 Census 2011		2016中期人口统计 By-census 2016		2021人口普查 Census 2021	
		万人 (10 000 persons)	构成 (%)	万人 (10 000 persons)	构成 (%)	万人 (10 000 persons)	构成 (%)	万人 (10 000 persons)	构成 (%)	万人 (10 000 persons)	构成 (%)
总计	**Total**	**34.97**	**100.0**	**43.36**	**100.0**	**49.27**	**100.0**	**57.70**	**100.0**	**58.84**	**100.0**
男	Male	16.45	47.0	20.97	48.4	23.40	47.5	27.55	47.8	27.15	46.1
女	Female	18.52	53.0	22.39	51.6	25.86	52.5	30.15	52.2	31.69	53.9
从未入学/学前教育	No Schooling/Pre-primary Education	2.10	6.0	2.06	4.7	1.65	3.4	1.59	2.7	0.94	1.6
男	Male	0.48	1.4	0.50	1.1	0.38	0.8	0.39	0.7	0.21	0.4
女	Female	1.62	4.6	1.56	3.6	1.27	2.6	1.20	2.1	0.73	1.2
小学	Primary Education	13.64	39.0	13.28	30.6	12.17	24.7	12.14	21.0	12.26	20.8
男	Male	6.63	19.0	6.59	15.2	5.81	11.8	5.71	9.9	5.43	9.2
女	Female	7.01	20.0	6.69	15.4	6.36	12.9	6.43	11.1	6.84	11.6
初中	Junior Secondary Education	9.45	27.0	12.07	27.8	12.31	25.0	12.69	22.0	10.88	18.5
男	Male	4.43	12.7	6.00	13.8	6.11	12.4	6.39	11.1	5.24	8.9
女	Female	5.02	14.3	6.07	14.0	6.19	12.6	6.30	10.9	5.64	9.6
高中	Senior Secondary Education	6.63	18.9	10.43	24.0	14.09	28.6	16.61	28.8	16.53	28.1
男	Male	3.32	9.5	5.16	11.9	6.73	13.7	8.09	14.0	7.83	13.3
女	Female	3.31	9.5	5.27	12.1	7.36	14.9	8.52	14.8	8.70	14.8
文凭课程	Diploma programme	~	~	~	~	~	~	~	~	0.57	1.0
男	Male	~	~	~	~	~	~	~	~	0.23	0.4
女	Female	~	~	~	~	~	~	~	~	0.33	0.6
高等教育 ①	Higher Education ①										
高等专科	Non-university Degree	0.75	2.1	0.64	1.5	0.99	2.0	1.28	2.2	2.58	4.4
男	Male	0.29	0.8	0.26	0.6	0.46	0.9	0.61	1.1	1.17	2.0
女	Female	0.46	1.3	0.38	0.9	0.53	1.1	0.67	1.2	1.41	2.4
大学	University	2.39	6.8	4.86	11.2	8.02	16.3	13.34	23.1	15.02	25.5
男	Male	1.29	3.7	2.44	5.6	3.88	7.9	6.33	11.0	7.00	11.9
女	Female	1.10	3.2	2.42	5.6	4.13	8.4	7.01	12.2	8.01	13.6
特殊教育	Special Education	0.02	0.1	0.03	0.1	0.04	0.1	0.06	0.1	0.08	0.1
男	Male	0.01	o	0.02	o	0.03	o	0.04	o	0.05	0.1
女	Female	0.01	o	0.01	o	0.02	o	0.02	o	0.03	0.1

注：①自2021人口普查起，高等教育不包括文凭课程。
Note: ①Higher education excludes diploma programme since the 2021 Population Census.

27–28 按教育机构类别统计的注册学生人数
Students Enrolment by Type of Educational Institutions

单位：人 (person)

类别	Type	2019/2020	2020/2021	2021/2022	2022/2023	2023/2024
幼儿、小学、中学及高等教育	**Pre-primary, Primary, Secondary and Higher Education**	**115729**	**121078**	**127913**	**134830**	**141765**
幼儿	Pre-primary Education	19265	18908	18109	17108	16188
小学	Primary Education	33961	35450	36791	37854	38349
中学	Secondary Education	26396	27627	28961	30274	31617
高等教育	Higher Education	36107	39093	44052	49594	55611
特殊教育	**Special Education**	**841**	**891**	**910**	**948**	**973**

27–29 医疗卫生条件
Health

项 目		Item		2019	2020	2021	2022	2023
医护人员①	**(人)**	**Medical Personnel in Health Care**	**(person)**					
医生		Doctor		1808	1789	1888	1965	1980
牙医生		Dentist		236	243	267	268	271
牙医师		Odontologist		41	40	40	38	35
中医生		Chinese Medicine Doctor		538	551	566	590	601
中医师		Chinese Herbalist		152	149	143	134	127
护士		Nurse		2491	2568	2742	2863	2980
医务化验师		Medical laboratory technologist		..	..	292	295	293
放射师		Radiologist		..	..	69	72	85
脊医		Chiropractor		5	5	5	5	5
物理治疗师		Physiotherapist		157	180	211	237	245
职业治疗师		Occupational Therapist		105	114	123	164	156
语言治疗师		Speech Therapist		27	33	53	63	75
心理治疗师		Psychotherapist		62	79	84	86	86
营养师		Dietitian		10	15	15	20	36
药剂师		Pharmacist		666	710	820	831	827
中药师		Chinese medicine pharmacist		..	..	3	17	27
药房技术助理		Technical assistant in pharmacy		..	..	313	346	339
每千人口的医生数	**(人)**	**Number of Doctors per 1000 Population**	**(person)**	**2.7**	**2.6**	**2.8**	**2.9**	**2.9**
医疗机构和病床		**Health Care Establishments and Beds**						
医院	(所)	Hospitals	(No.)	5	4	4	4	5
住院病床	(张)	In-patient Beds	(No.)	1628	1715	1744	1721	1882
每千人口的住院病床数	**(张)**	**Number of In-patient Beds per 1000 Population**	**(No.)**	**2.4**	**2.5**	**2.6**	**2.6**	**2.8**

注：①2021年起，医护人员数目是根据卫生局及药物监督管理局，按照第18/2020号法律《医疗人员专业资格及执业注册制度》的注册资料编制，因此2021之前的部份医护人员没有相关统计资料。

Note: ① From 2021 onwards, the number of medical professionals is compiled based on the registration information of the Health Bureau and the Pharmaceutical Administration Bureau in accordance with Law no. 18/2020 "Professional Qualification and Registration of Health Practitioners", and thus the data for some medical professionals prior to 2021 was not applicable.

27–30 社会保障基金发放资料
Payment Granted by Social Security Fund

发放种类	Type of Payment	2021		2022		2023	
		数目 Number of Payments	金额 (万澳门元) Amount (10 000 MOP)	数目 Number of Payments	金额 (万澳门元) Amount (10 000 MOP)	数目 Number of Payments	金额 (万澳门元) Amount (10 000 MOP)
总计	**Total**	..	**536597**	..	**567468** r	..	**601870**
福利金受领(人数)	**Number of Pension Recipients**						
发放金额	**Pension Amount**						
养老金	Old Age Pension	129202	443476	137428	464112	147054	495328
残疾金	Disability Pension	9794	43848	10630	47436	11465	50788
额外给付	Additional Payment	..	39774	..	41660	..	44315
津贴受领(人次)	**Number of Cases**						
发放金额	**Allowance Amount**						
失业津贴①	Unemployment Allowance①	4286 r	4419	8740 r	9929	3733 r	3550
疾病津贴	Sickness Allowance	1410	394	1157	297	65131	3621
出生津贴	Birth Allowance	6094	3360	5245	2784	4661	2564
结婚津贴	Marriage Allowance	2881	621	2650	544	3027	663
丧葬津贴	Funeral Allowance	2386	679	2558	686	3710	1032
特别援助	Special Aid	38	25	46	19	19	9

注：由于进位的关系，各分项之和与总数可能有差异。
①2020年起失业津贴以领取人数作统计。

Note: Due to rounding, some totals may not correspond with the sum of the separate figures.
①Starting from 2020, data on unemployment allowance are calculated based on the number of beneficiaries.

主要统计指标解释

本地生产总值 反映每年在澳门特区生产的货物和提供各种服务的总量。本年鉴中的本地生产总值用支出法及生产法估算，支出法等于私人消费支出、政府最终消费支出、固定资本形成总额、库存变化和货物及服务出口净值（出口减进口）的总和。而生产法等于各经济行业的增加值总额的总和，这种方法可以评估澳门特区的产业结构。

婴儿死亡率 参考期内年龄在 1 岁以下的死亡人数与出生活婴数目的千分比。

出生率 参考期内出生活婴数目与平均人口之千分比。

死亡率 参考期内死亡人数与平均人口之千分比。

幼儿、小学、中学教育 指有系统的，且主要专为儿童及青少年开办的，由幼儿教育至中学教育的课程；中学教育包括职业技术教育。

幼儿教育 为期 3 年，对象是年龄 3—5 岁的儿童。在报名当年的 12 月 31 日年满 3 岁的幼儿可报读幼儿教育第一年。

小学教育 为期 6 年，完成幼儿教育或在报名当年的 12 月 31 日年满 6 岁的儿童可报读小学教育第一年。就读小学的最高年龄为 15 岁。

中学教育 由两个阶段组成：初中教育及高中教育。大学预科不纳入中学教育。

1）初中教育 为期 3 年，合格完成小学教育者可以入读。就读初中最大年龄为 18 岁，但在特别情况下，经教育机构决定，可以逾越此年限。

2）高中教育 为期 3 年，合格完成初中教育者可以入读。就读高中最大年龄为 21 岁，但在特别情况下，经教育机构决定，可以逾越此年限。

高等教育 指透过理论、实践等在科学、文化及技术领域提供的培训教育；高等教育包括大学教育及高等专科教育。

劳动人口 在调查日前 7 天内可参与生产商品或提供服务的 16 岁及以上人士，包括就业人士及失业人士。

就业人口 在调查日前 7 天内为赚取报酬或利润而工作至少 1 小时的 16 岁及以上人士，亦包括无酬家属帮工、没有上班但与雇主保持工作联系的雇员，以及正在休假的雇主或自雇人士。就业人口包括本地就业居民及居澳外地雇员。

失业人口 所有同时符合以下条件的16岁及以上人士：

1）在调查日前 7 天内没有工作；

2）在调查日前 7 天内可随时接受工作；

3）在过去 30 天内有寻找工作。

失业人口包括寻找第一份工作及寻找新工作的人士。

就业不足人口 在调查日前 7 天内不论其职业身份及原因（如处于无薪假期），非自愿地工作少于 35 小时并符合以下任一情况的就业人士：

1）可随时接受更多的工作；或

2）在调查日前 30 天内正在寻找更多工作。

劳动力参与率 劳动人口占 16 岁及以上人士的百分比。

失业率 失业人口占劳动人口的百分比。

就业不足率 就业不足人口占劳动人口的百分比。

旅客 指任何非以澳门特区为惯常活动环境的人士，连续在澳门的逗留时间少于一年，其旅游目的并非受雇于澳门特别行政区的居民实体。

酒店业平均入住率 入住客房数量与可供应客房数量之百分比。

进口 将来自外地的货物输入澳门特区，但再进口和转运制度下输入者除外。

出口 将货物输出澳门特区，但暂时出口和转运制度下输出者除外。

本地产品出口 将原产地为澳门特区的任何货物输出澳门特区。

再出口 指原进口的货物未经加工输出澳门特区；或虽加工，但不能取得澳门特区产地资格。

转运 货物经过澳门特区而运到下一目的地。

原产地 农业产品种植之国家／地区、矿产开采之国家／地区、工业产品生产之国家／地区，被视为原产地国家／地区。若工业产品的制造工序于两个或以上的国家／地区进行，应以进行最后转变成型工序的国家／地区为原产地，再包装、分类及混合等工序不能构成最后转变成型工序；当产品入口国对相关货物产地来源有特定规定时，应遵从有关规定。

目的地 目的地是指货物实际最后到达的国家或地区（不论在运输途中有或没有中断）。如有中间国家或地区，只要不在中间国家或地区内进行商业交易，最后到达的国家或地区都可被视为目的地。

贸易价格比率指数 即货物出口单位价格指数与货物进口单位价格指数之比率。

单位 包括住宅、商铺、办公室、工业、停车位、酒店及其他单位。

建筑面积 相等于所有楼层楼面面积之总和。楼面面积从外墙起量度，包括大堂、楼梯、升降机所占面积以及所有公用地方面积。

消费物价指数 反映澳门特区住户于购买一篮子之指定商品或服务时，在不同时间该等商品或服务之价格变动。

狭义货币供应量 M_1 为流通货币及活期存款之和。

广义货币供应量 M_2 指狭义货币供应量 M_1 加上准货币负债。准货币负债指储蓄存款、通知存款、定期存款、其他存款和存款证明书。

财务活动 由财务资产及财务负债组成。

Explanatory Notes on Main Statistical Indicators

Gross Domestic Product (GDP) reflects the total value of goods produced and services provided by the Macao Special Administrative Region in a year. GDP estimates in this statistical yearbook are compiled under both the expenditure and the production approaches. The expenditure-based GDP is measured as the sum of household consumption expenditure; government final consumption expenditure; gross fixed capital formation; changes in inventories; and net exports (exports less imports) of goods and services. The production-based GDP, which is measured as the sum of gross value added of all economic activities, can be used to evaluate the industrial structure of Macao.

Infant Mortality Rate Number of infants died under one year old per 1,000 live births within the reference period.

Crude Birth Rate Live births per 1,000 population within the reference period.

Crude Mortality Rate Deaths per 1,000 population within the reference period.

Pre-primary, Primary and Secondary Education Refers to systematic education designed and intended for children and young people by which they may progress from pre-primary through secondary education; secondary education also covers vocational-technical education.

Pre-primary Education Has a duration of 3 years and designated for children aged 3-5 years old. Children reaching 3 years old as at 31st December of the enrolment year are eligible to the first year of pre-primary education.

Primary Education Has a duration of 6 years. Children completing pre-primary education or reaching 6 years old as at 31st December of the enrolment year are eligible to the first year of primary education. The maximum age of attending primary education is 15.

Secondary Education Comprises 2 stages, viz. junior secondary and senior secondary. Pre-university course is not considered as secondary education.

(1)Junior secondary education has a duration of 3 years. Students completing primary education are eligible. The maximum age for this level is 18; however, under special circumstances, schools can accept enrolment outside this age limit.

(2)Senior secondary education has a duration of 3 years. Students completing junior secondary are eligible. The maximum age for this level is 21; however, under special circumstances, schools can accept enrolment outside this age limit.

Higher Education Refers to instruction by theory, practice and the like in science, culture and technology; it includes university education and post-secondary education providing associate degree or diploma programmes.

Economically Active Population (Labour Force) Individuals aged 16 and above who are available to participate in the production of goods and/or services during the 7 days before enumeration. It comprises the employed and unemployed.

Employed Population Individuals aged 16 and above who work for pay or profit for at least 1 hour during the 7 days before enumeration. It also includes unpaid family workers, employees who are absent from work but have job attachment to the employer, as well as employers or the self-employed who are on leave.

Employed population comprises employed residents and non-resident workers living in Macao.

Unemployed Population Refers to individuals aged 16 and above who fulfil the following conditions:

1) have not had a job during the 7 days before enumeration;
2) have been available for work during the 7 days before enumeration; and
3) have sought work for the past 30 days.

The unemployed comprise individuals searching for their first job and those searching for a new job.

Underemployed Population Refers to employed persons who work involuntarily for less than 35 hours during the 7 days before enumeration, regardless of their status in employment and reasons (e.g. on unpaid leave), and who meet any of the following conditions:

1) are available to take on additional work; or
2) are looking for extra work during the 30 days before enumeration.

Labour Force Participation Rate The proportion of the economically active population to the population aged 16 and above.

Unemployment Rate Percentage share of the number of unemployed to the labour force.

Underemployment Rate Percentage share of the number of the underemployed to the labour force.

Visitor Any person taking a trip to the Macao Special Administrative Region (SAR), which is not his/her usual environment, for less than a year, for any main purpose other than to be employed by a resident entity in the Macao SAR.

Average Occupancy Rate of Hotels The percentage share of occupied rooms to the total number of available rooms of the hotel sector.

Imports Entry of foreign produced merchandise to Macao, excluding re-imports and transit.

Exports Merchandise transported out of Macao, excluding temporary exports and transit goods.

Domestic Exports Transport of Macao produced merchandise out of Macao.

Re-exports Transport of merchandise previously imported out of Macao, without processing; even with processing, is not qualified to use Macao as the origin of the merchandise.

Transit Merchandise passing by Macao to the next destination.

Country of Origin Country or territory where the crops are grown, minerals are mined and products are manufactured. If a production process is carried out in two or more countries or territories, the origin will be the country or territory where the processing of the merchandise takes its final form. Repacking, sorting or mixing is not considered as the final phase of processing. When a country has specific rules regarding the country of origin on merchandise imports, those rules shall prevail.

Country of Destination The final country or territory where the goods are delivered, irrespective of interruption during transportation. As far as no commercial exchange has taken place in the transit country or territory, the final country or territory arrived is considered as the destination.

Terms of Trade Index Ratio of the unit value index of exports of goods to that of imports of goods.

Building Unit Including residential, shop, office and industrial units, parking spaces, hotel and other units.

Gross Floor Area The sum of the area of each floor of the building, measured to the outer surface of the outer walls including the area of lobbies, stairs, lift landings and communal space.

Consumer Price Index reflects the price change of a representative "basket" of goods and services consumed by households of Macao at different periods.

Money Supply (M_1) refers to the sum of currency in circulation and demand deposits.

Money Supply (M_2) refers to the sum of money supply (M_1) and quasi-monetary liabilities; the latter consist of savings deposits, notice deposits, time deposits, other deposits and certificates of deposit.

Financial Transactions comprise financial assets and financial liabilities.

28

台湾省主要社会经济指标

Main Social and Economic Indicators of Taiwan Province

简 要 说 明

一、本章资料反映台湾省主要社会、经济发展情况。内容包括：土地、人口、就业、国民经济核算、工业、能源、建筑、交通通信、对外贸易、财政金融、物价、教育、卫生、房屋、社会保障等方面。

二、本章数据主要来自台湾“行政院主计处”及相关部门统计出版物，国家统计局国际统计信息中心负责整理、编辑。

三、贸易数据从 2016 年 1 月起按照一般贸易制度口径予以统计，并按此方法对 2001 年至 2015 年的贸易数据进行了重新修订。

Brief Introduction

I. Data in this chapter reflect the major social and economic development of the Taiwan province, including land; population; employment; national accounts; industry; energy; construction; transportation and communications; external trade; public finance and banking; prices; education; health; housing; and social security.

II. Data in this chapter are mainly abstracted from the Department of Statistics, Executive Yuan and other relevant Ministry of Taiwan, which are tabulated and edited by the International Statistical Information Centre of the National Bureau of Statistics.

III. Trade data is calculated by the General Trade System from Jan. 2016, the data from 2001 to 2015 are revised again according to the standard.

28-1 主要统计指标概况
Summary of Key Statistics

指标		Item		2019	2020	2021	2022	2023
人口		**Population**						
户籍登记人口数①	(万人)	Year-end Population①	(10 000 persons)	2360	2356	2338	2326	2342
人口自然增长率	(‰)	Natural Growth Rate	(‰)	0.06	-0.34	-1.27	-2.93	-2.99
人口密度①	(人/平方公里)	Population Density①	(persons/sq.km)	652	651	646	643	647
性别比①	(女=100)	Sex Ratio①	(female=100)	98.4	98.2	98.2	97.7	97.4
劳动、就业		**Labour Force and Employment**						
劳动力人口	(万人)	Labour Force	(10 000 persons)	1195	1196	1192	1185	1194
劳动力参与率	(%)	Labour Force Participation Rate	(%)	59.2	59.1	59.0	59.2	59.2
男		Male		67.3	67.2	66.9	67.1	67.1
女		Female		51.4	51.4	51.5	51.6	51.8
工业就业人口比率	(%)	Employed Persons at Industry as Percentage of Total	(%)	35.6	35.4	35.5	35.4	35.1
服务业就业人口比率	(%)	Employed Persons at Services as Percentage of Total	(%)	59.6	59.8	59.8	60.0	60.5
失业率	(%)	Unemployment Rate	(%)	3.7	3.9	4.0	3.7	3.5
工业及服务业月人均薪资	(新台币元)	Average Monthly Per Capita Wage	(NT$)	53551	54278	56127	58042	58420
工业		Industry		54597	55282	58900	61408	60832
服务业		Services		52807	53569	54164	55669	56744
公共安全		**Law and Order**						
刑案发生率	(件/10万人)	Reported Crimes	(Case/100 000 persons)	1137	1101	1036	1139	1185
犯罪人口率	(人/10万人)	Number of Offenders	(person/100 000 persons)	1177	1195	1130	1252	1276
刑案破获率	(%)	Crimes Uncover	(%)	96.4	97.7	98.8	96.7	97.2
少年疑犯人数(12—17岁)	(人)	Young Offenders Between 12 and 17	(person)	9441	10226	9627	9554	10790
火灾发生次数	(次)	Fires	(case)	22866	22248	21684	15890	17466
死伤人数	(人)	Deaths and Injuries	(person)	628	625	496	346	556
机动车肇事率	(件/万辆)	Traffic Accidents of Motor Vehicles	(case/10 000 units)	156	163	160	165	175
道路交通事故伤亡人数		Casualties in Traffic Accidents						
死亡	(人)	Deaths	(person)	1849	1851	1860		
受伤	(人)	Injuries	(person)	456378	483409	477367		
保险		**Insurance**						
全民健保参保人数	(万人)	National Health Insurance	(10 000 persons)	2402	2399	2386	2379	2388
社保参保人数	(万人)	Social Insurance	(10 000 persons)					
公务员和教师		Government Employee and School Staff		59	59	59	59	59
劳工		Labour		1047	1055	1074	1043	1039
农民		Farmer		108	105	101	96	91

28–1 续表 1 continued

指　　标	Item	2019	2020	2021	2022	2023
工业	**Industry**					
受雇者劳动生产力指数(2021年＝100)	Productivity Index (year of 2021=100)	81.2	88.7	100.0	98.3	87.4
工业生产指数 (2021年＝100)	Indices of Industrial Production (year of 2021=100)	80.1	87.2	100.0	98.2	86.1
制造业	Manufacturing	79.2	86.5	100.0	98.0	85.5
工业生产价值 (新台币亿元)	Gross Industry Product (NT$ 100 million)	158593	156671	196806	207073	185524
商业及对外贸易	**Business and External Trade**					
营利事业家数① (万家)	Number of Enterprises① (10 000 unit)	146.5	150.7	155.7	159.6	164.7
营利事业销售额 (新台币亿元)	Sales Revenue (NT$100 million)	431020	437395	508453	555524	547212
货物进出口额 (亿美元)	Total Value of Merchandise Trade (USD100 million)	6148	6313	8283	9075	7839
出口	Exports	3292	3451	4464	4794	4324
进口	Imports	2857	2861	3820	4281	3514
出(入)超	Trade Surplus (Trade Deficit)	435	590	644	513	810
对日出(入)超	with Japan	-208	-225	-269	-210	-129
对美出(入)超	with United States	114	180	264	294	356
对内地及港出(入)超	with Mainland and Hong Kong	737	866	1047	1004	805
外销订单 (亿美元)	Order (USD100 million)	4846	5337	6741	6668	5610
运输通信	**Transportation and Communications**					
交通运输客运人数 (亿人次)	Passenger Traffic (100 million person-times)					
铁路	Railway	11.9	10.3	7.9	8.9	11.3
公路	Highway	12.5	10.8	7.9	8.4	9.6
航空 (万人次)	Airway (10 000 person-times)					
省内	Domestic	1224	1011	657	971	1100
省外	Non-domestic	5958	883	102	576	4092
高速公路收费站通行车辆数④(万辆次)	Vehicles for Motorway Transportation ④ (10 000 unit-times)	597497	607532	579762	618001	638352
每百人汽车辆数① (辆)	Automobile per 100 Persons① (unit)	34.4	34.8	35.6	36.3	36.7
港埠货物装卸量 (万计费吨)	Inward and Outward Movements Cargo (10 000 tons)	73056	70299	75031	71900	66625
旅游 (万人次)	**Tourism (10 000 person-times)**					
出省旅游人数	Outbound Tourists	1710	234	36	148	1180
来台湾旅客人数	Inbound Tourists	1186	138	14	90	649
财政、金融	**Public Accounts and Finance**					
赋税实征净额② (新台币亿元)	Revenue② (NT$100 million)	24705	23987	28742	32479	34562
外汇存底① (亿美元)	Foreign Exchange Reserve① (USD100 million)	4781.3	5299.1	5484.1	5549.3	5706.0
汇率	Exchange Rate (NT$ to one unit of foreign currency)					
1美元兑新台币③ (新台币)	NT$ to one unit of US Dollar③ (NT$)	30.93	29.58	28.02	29.78	31.15
货币总计数$M_2$① (新台币亿元)	Money Supply M_2 ① (NT$100 million)	458918	501879	538752	575086	607548
年增长率 (%)	Average Annual Growth Rate (%)	4.5	9.4	7.4	6.7	5.6
存款① (新台币亿元)	Deposits① (NT$100 million)	450861	492197	527570	563301	594271
放款与投资① (新台币亿元)	Loans and Investment① (NT$100 million)	354224	378266	409996	436168	464853

28-1 续表 2 continued

指　　标	Item	2019	2020	2021	2022	2023
再贴现率① (年息百分比率)	Rediscount Rate① (% annual)	1.375	1.125	1.125	1.750	1.875
股价指数 (1966年＝100)	Stock Price Index (year of 1966=100)	10790.2	12074.6	16938.1	15623.5	16386.2
国际收支余额 (亿美元)	Balance of Payments (USD 100 million)					
经常账户	Current Account	675.2	980.9	1183.0	1009.3	1053.3
资本账户	Capital Account	0.0	-0.1	0.0	-0.5	-0.4
金融账户	Financial Account	602.2	490.7	1063.5	947.1	849.5
价格指数年增长率(2016年=100)(%)	**Price Indices Annual Growth Rate (year of 2016=100) (%)**					
批发	Wholesale Trade Price	-2.3	-7.8	9.5	12.4	-2.0
消费者	Consumer Price	0.6	-0.2	2.0	3.0	2.5
进口	Imports Price	-1.5	-10.2	10.5	16.1	-3.6
出口	Exports Price	-2.8	-7.2	6.6	12.1	-1.9
国民核算 (新台币亿元)	**National Accounts (NT$100 million)**					
本地居民总收入	Gross National Income(GNI)	193848	204866	222314	233746	242528
本地生产总值	Gross Domestic Product(GDP)	189086	199148	216632	226798	235509
居民消费	Household Final Consumption	98831	96011	97059	103617	114565
固定资本形成总额	Gross Fixed Capital Formation	45266	48173	56918	63742	59526
商品及服务出口	Exports of Goods and Services	119226	115675	140406	158620	149183
减：商品及服务进口	Less: Imports of Goods and Services	100502	88494	109658	130851	118918
GDP增长率(2016年=100) (%)	GDP Growth Rate (year of 2016=100) (%)	3.1	3.4	6.6	2.6	1.3
农业	Agriculture	-0.9	-1.5	-4.5	-5.0	0.9
工业	Industry	1.4	7.1	13.6	1.8	-6.4
服务业	Services	3.6	1.3	3.0	2.6	4.5
产业结构 (%)	Industry Structure (%)					
农业	Agriculture	1.7	1.6	1.4	1.4	1.5
工业	Industry	35.4	37.2	38.9	37.5	36.4
服务业	Services	62.8	60.9	60.2	60.9	61.0
人均本地居民总收入(新台币元)	Per Capita GNI at Current Market Prices (NT$)	821527	868732	947294	1002341	1037999
人均本地居民总收入 (美元)	Per Capita GNI at Current Market Prices (USD)	26561	29369	33808	33624	33299
居民储蓄总值 (新台币亿元)	Gross Deposits (NT$100 million)	67351	79409	96306	97077	91563
储蓄率 (%)	Deposit Rate (%)	34.7	38.8	43.3	41.5	37.8

注：①为年底数。②为年度资料。③卖出汇率，且为年底数。④从2013年12月30日起，国道高速公路由计次收费改为计程电子收费。
Notes: ①Year-end data. ②Annual data. ③Selling rate, year-end data.④from Dec.30 2013,the tolls on national highways are determined by the distance travelled instead of by times of exits passed.

28–2 面积和人口主要指标
Main Indicators of Area and Population

资源来源：台湾省统计网站（以下各表同）。
Source: Taiwan Province Statistics Website. The same applies in the following tables.

项　　目	Item	2019	2020	2021	2022	2023
土地面积（万平方公里）	Area (10 000 sq.km)	3.6	3.6	3.6	3.6	3.6
户籍登记人口数（万人）	Year-end Population (10 000 persons)	2360.3	2356.1	2337.5	2326.5	2342.0
男	Male	1170.5	1167.4	1157.9	1149.9	1155.3
女	Female	1189.8	1188.7	1179.7	1176.6	1186.7
粗出生率 (‰)	Crude Birth Rate (‰)	7.53	7.01	6.55	5.96	5.81
粗死亡率 (‰)	Crude Death Rate (‰)	7.47	7.34	7.83	8.89	8.80
人口自然增长率 (‰)	Natural Population Growth Rate (‰)	0.06	-0.34	-1.27	-2.93	-2.99
一般生育率 (‰)	Fertility Rate (‰)	30	28	28	25	25
结婚率 (对/千人)	Marriage Rate (couple/1000 persons)	5.70	5.16	4.88	5.36	5.36
离婚率 (对/千人)	Divorce Rate (couple/1000 persons)	2.31	2.19	2.04	2.17	2.27
期望寿命 (岁)	Life Expectancy at Birth (year old)					
男	Male	77.69	78.11	77.67	76.63	76.94
女	Female	84.23	84.75	84.25	83.28	83.74
人口的年龄分布 (%)	Age-specific Distribution (%)					
0–14岁	0-14	12.75	12.58	12.36	12.12	11.93
15–64岁	15-64	71.96	71.35	70.79	70.32	69.73
65岁及以上	65 and Over	15.28	16.07	16.85	17.56	18.35
性别比 (女=100)	Sex Ratio (female=100)	98.38	98.20	98.15	97.74	97.35
人口密度(人/平方公里)	Population Density (persons/sq.km)	652.1	650.9	645.8	642.7	647.0

28–3 劳动力和就业状况
Labour Force and Employment

项　　目	Item	2019	2020	2021	2022	2023
劳动力总计 (万人)	Labour Force (10 000 persons)	1194.6	1196.4	1191.9	1185.3	1194.3
男	Male	663.1	663.8	659.5	655.4	656.8
女	Female	531.5	532.6	532.4	529.8	537.5
就业人数 (万人)	Employment (10 000 persons)	1150.0	1150.4	1144.7	1141.8	1152.8
男	Male	637.6	637.8	633.2	631.3	633.9
女	Female	512.4	512.6	511.5	510.5	518.8
就业者行业构成 (%)	Distribution of Employment by Industry(%)	100.0	100.0	100.0	100.0	100.0
农、林、渔、牧业	Agriculture, Forestry, Fishery and Animal Husbandry	4.9	4.8	4.7	4.6	4.4
工业	Industry	35.6	35.4	35.5	35.4	35.1
矿业及土石采取业	Mining and Quarrying	0.03	0.03	0.03	0.03	0.03
制造业	Manufacturing	26.7	26.4	26.4	26.4	26.0
电力及燃气供应业	Electricity, Gas	0.3	0.3	0.3	0.3	0.3
用水供应及污染整治业	Water Supply and Pollution Management	0.7	0.7	0.7	0.7	0.7
建筑业	Construction	7.9	8.0	8.0	8.0	8.0
服务业	Services	59.6	59.8	59.8	60.0	60.5
批发及零售业	Wholesale and Retail Trades	16.7	16.5	16.4	16.2	15.9
运输及仓储业	Transport, Storage, Communications	3.9	4.0	4.0	4.2	4.3
金融及保险业	Finance, Insurance	3.8	3.8	3.8	3.8	3.8
咨讯及通讯传播	Information and Communication	2.3	2.3	2.3	2.4	2.4
住宿及餐饮业	Hotels and Restaurants	7.4	7.4	7.3	7.4	7.6
教育服务业	Education	5.7	5.7	5.6	5.6	5.5
公共行政	Public Administration	3.2	3.3	3.3	3.3	3.3
失业人数 (万人)	Unemployment (10 000 persons)	44.6	46.0	47.1	43.4	41.5
失业率 (%)	Unemployment Rate (%)	3.7	3.9	4.0	3.7	3.5

28—4 本地居民总收入
Gross National Income

年 份 Year	本地居民总收入 Gross National Income			人均本地居民总收入 Per Capita Gross National Income	
	新台币亿元 NT $100 million	实际年增长率 % Annual Growth Rate over the Preceding Year %	亿 美 元① USD 100 million①	新 台 币 元 NT $	美 元① USD①
2010	144761	8.7	4574	625560	19765
2011	146343	1.1	4966	630965	21410
2012	151100	3.3	5101	649322	21922
2013	156732	3.7	5265	671384	22552
2014	166972	6.5	5498	713443	23492
2015	174947	4.8	5483	745634	23367
2016	180064	2.9	5570	765711	23684
2017	184307	2.4	6055	782437	25704
2018	187898	2.0	6230	796852	26421
2019	193848	3.2	6267	821527	26561
2020	204866	5.7	6926	868732	29369
2021	222314	8.5	7934	947294	33808
2022	233746	5.1	7841	1002341	33624
2023	242528	3.8	7780	1037999	33299

注：①按当年汇率折算。
Note: ①Adjusted by current exchange rate of the year.

28—5 本地生产总值支出构成
Expenditure on Gross Domestic Product

单位：% (%)

年 份 Year	本地生产总值(新台币亿元) Gross Domestic Product (NT$ 100 million)	居民消费 Household Consumption Expenditure	政府消费 Government Consumption Expenditure	固定资本形成总额 Gross Fixed Capital Formation	存货增加 Changes in Inventories	货物及服务出口 Exports of Goods and Services	减：货物及服务进口 Less: Imports of Goods and Services
2009	129194	55.4	16.1	21.4	-1.4	67.6	59.1
2010	140603	53.2	15.1	23.7	1.4	79.6	73.0
2011	142622	54.5	15.4	23.4	0.2	80.8	74.3
2012	146778	54.6	15.6	22.6	0.1	79.3	72.1
2013	152707	54.0	14.8	22.7	-0.2	77.6	68.9
2014	162580	52.9	14.5	22.3	0.2	77.3	67.3
2015	170551	51.5	13.9	21.5	0.2	71.3	58.4
2016	175553	51.7	14.1	21.7	-0.1	67.3	54.8
2017	179833	51.9	13.8	21.1	-0.1	67.3	53.9
2018	183750	52.3	14.3	21.8	0.5	66.3	55.2
2019	189086	52.3	14.0	23.9	-0.1	63.1	53.2
2020	199148	48.2	13.9	24.2	0.0	58.1	44.4
2021	216632	44.8	13.6	26.3	1.1	64.8	50.6
2022	226798	45.7	13.9	28.1	0.0	69.9	57.7
2023	235509	48.6	13.7	25.3	-0.5	63.3	50.5

28–6 本地生产总值产业构成
Gross Domestic Product by Kind of Economic Activity

单位：% (%)

年份 Year	本地生产总值(新台币亿元) Gross Domestic Product (NT$ 100 million)	农业 Agriculture Forestry, Animal Husbandry and Fishery	工业 Industry	制造业 Manufacturing	水电燃气及污染治理业 Water/Electricity/Gas /Pollution Treatment	建筑业 Construction
2009	129194	1.68	30.69	25.96	2.12	2.46
2010	140603	1.61	33.30	28.60	1.97	2.60
2011	142622	1.74	32.62	28.27	1.56	2.67
2012	146778	1.68	32.37	28.07	1.59	2.60
2013	152707	1.73	33.71	29.11	1.93	2.57
2014	162580	1.86	35.76	31.10	2.05	2.52
2015	170551	1.75	36.22	31.36	2.32	2.46
2016	175553	1.87	36.87	32.22	2.25	2.34
2017	179833	1.83	36.98	32.66	1.94	2.32
2018	183750	1.70	36.46	32.27	1.73	2.40
2019	189086	1.68	35.41	30.92	1.77	2.65
2020	199148	1.57	37.17	32.18	2.07	2.86
2021	216632	1.43	38.93	34.29	1.60	2.98
2022	226798	1.39	37.52	34.26	0.04	3.16
2023	235509	1.47	36.39	32.57	0.66	3.12

28–6 续表 continued

单位：% (%)

年份 Year	服务业 Services	批发及零售业 Wholesale and Retail Trades	金融及保险业 Finance & Insurance	不动产业 Real Estate	咨讯及通讯传播业 Information & Communication
2009	66.38	17.22	6.15	8.92	3.51
2010	64.83	16.84	6.17	8.49	3.30
2011	65.64	17.14	6.37	8.55	3.23
2012	65.05	16.70	6.34	8.51	3.14
2013	64.51	16.77	6.36	8.49	3.10
2014	62.90	16.03	6.48	8.17	3.06
2015	61.84	15.62	6.45	8.02	3.08
2016	61.27	15.25	6.41	7.97	3.13
2017	61.59	15.46	6.55	7.99	3.09
2018	62.26	15.62	6.69	8.10	3.05
2019	62.77	15.71	6.75	8.22	3.10
2020	60.86	15.40	6.68	8.17	3.02
2021	60.21	15.62	6.78	7.72	3.01
2022	60.86	15.92	6.37	7.54	3.07
2023	60.99	15.38	6.40	7.74	3.26

28-7 农业生产指数
Indices of Agricultural Production

(2021年=100) (year of 2021=100)

年份 Year	总指数 Total	农作物 Crops	林业 Forestry	畜牧业 Livestock	渔业 Fishery
2008	102.5	99.9	227.8	90.1	134.8
2009	100.6	100.9	231.6	89.8	122.7
2010	102.8	103.6	212.6	90.9	125.0
2011	106.6	110.0	209.9	94.0	123.2
2012	104.8	105.5	217.5	92.6	126.6
2013	103.6	104.9	236.4	90.8	125.0
2014	104.7	108.3	202.8	90.9	123.8
2015	101.2	103.4	122.9	90.4	117.7
2016	97.5	98.3	97.9	92.1	106.5
2017	103.1	107.8	83.1	91.8	112.5
2018	105.6	111.2	59.9	94.6	111.6
2019	101.5	102.7	71.7	96.0	109.7
2020	101.8	105.3	74.1	98.8	97.5
2021	100.0	100.0	100.0	100.0	100.0
2022	97.0	97.1	104.5	98.8	93.0

28-8 主要农产品产量
Output of Major Crops

单位：万吨 (10 000 tons)

年份 Year	稻米 Rice	槟榔 Pinang	菠萝 Pineapple	芒果 Mango	甘蔗 Sugarcane	茶叶 Tea	花生 Peanuts	香蕉 Banana
2009	157.8	14.3	43.5	14.0	61.3	1.7	5.7	17.3
2010	145.1	13.2	42.0	13.5	66.5	1.7	6.5	28.8
2011	166.6	12.9	40.1	16.9	65.4	1.7	6.8	30.6
2012	170.0	12.4	39.2	16.7	54.8	1.5	5.7	29.5
2013	159.0	12.4	41.3	21.5	50.6	1.5	4.7	29.1
2014	173.2	12.1	45.6	15.3	50.3	1.5	6.9	30.0
2015	158.2	11.3	49.4	16.6	61.8	1.4	6.2	27.4
2016	158.8	10.0	52.7	10.7	52.7	1.3	6.2	25.8
2017	175.4	10.2	55.4	15.1	45.5	1.3	6.3	35.6
2018	195.0	10.3	43.2	14.7	57.9	1.5	5.9	35.6
2019	179.1	10.4	43.1	16.8	53.3	1.5	5.3	34.3
2020	175.1	9.9	41.9	17.2	53.1	1.4	5.4	36.0
2021	156.1	9.6	40.3	17.2	59.5	1.2	5.0	33.7
2022	157.6	9.3	38.2	11.3	51.6	1.4	5.1	35.1

28-9 工业生产指数
Indices of Industrial Production

(2021年=100) (year of 2021=100)

年份 Year	总指数 General	矿业 Mining	制造业 Manufacturing	电力和燃气业 Electricity & Gas	供水业 Water
2009	49.0	101.1	46.9	82.0	98.8
2010	62.3	126.8	60.6	86.0	100.1
2011	63.8	118.1	62.1	87.3	100.3
2012	64.4	114.8	62.8	87.2	99.7
2013	66.9	105.4	65.4	88.4	100.4
2014	71.9	107.0	70.6	89.6	101.0
2015	71.1	100.1	69.9	88.1	98.7
2016	73.1	91.1	71.9	90.9	99.1
2017	76.8	89.1	75.7	92.8	100.4
2018	79.4	85.7	78.4	94.1	100.6
2019	80.1	83.8	79.2	94.2	101.1
2020	87.2	96.3	86.5	95.8	102.5
2021	100.0	100.0	100.0	100.0	100.0
2022	98.2	99.1	98.0	100.7	101.3
2023	86.1	95.8	85.5	97.3	99.3

28-10 主要工业产品产量
Output of Major Industrial Products

年 份 Year	茶类饮料 (万升) Tea Beverage (10 000 litres)	饲料 (万吨) Feed (10 000 tons)	聚酯丝织布 (万平方米) Polyester fabric (10 000 sq. meter)	瓦楞纸箱(板) (万平方米) Corrugated case (10 000 sq. meter)	聚苯乙烯 (万吨) Polystyrene (10 000 tons)	玻璃纤维 (万吨) Glass Fibre (10 000 tons)
2011	116051.6	525.6	109239.5	285282.5	87.7	26.7
2012	120201.0	525.1	103420.3	284763.9	86.3	26.6
2013	101998.6	509.8	109564.3	293982.9	88.9	25.3
2014	102215.0	516.1	112527.6	306054.9	83.6	25.9
2015	97910.3	514.6	110660.4	306190.1	87.5	27.3
2016	101473.4	528.7	103741.2	311378.5	89.2	27.9
2017	100199.3	535.5	104955.4	331472.1	84.8	26.0
2018	102415.8	585.8	100721.6	331472.7	84.3	28.3
2019	105266.5	615.1	97219.1	336839.7	88.2	24.0
2020	109595.8	613.8	76029.4	374551.0	91.4	21.6
2021	108070.8	608.2	85676.5	408728.6	93.8	26.4
2022	113787.3	627.2	94535.7	362718.1	85.5	23.8
2023	118696.1	607.7	78334.8	343348.7	80.6	17.4

28-10 续表 1 continued

年 份 Year	ABS树脂 (万吨) Acrylonitrile Butadiene Styrene (10 000 tons)	塑胶外壳 (新台币亿元) Plastic Cover (NT$100 million)	印刷电路板 (万平方尺) Printing Circuit Board (10000 sq.feet)	晶圆代工 (万片) Foundry (10 000 units)	构装IC (亿个) Packaging IC (100 million units)	TFT-LCD面板 (万组) TFT-LCD Panel (10 000 units)
2011	125.4	302.3	77374.1	1872.1	489.5	161350.2
2012	125.7	318.5	87863.0	1895.2	545.8	178173.3
2013	125.8	264.0	73041.2	2026.9	604.9	172866.9
2014	125.8	229.6	72120.7	2255.4	683.1	141506.9
2015	128.6	227.4	68151.2	2265.1	692.2	117392.2
2016	137.3	226.7	59485.3	2450.1	722.5	110121.4
2017	142.4	182.4	73133.7	2693.7	801.7	128264.9
2018	142.2	199.2	70171.6	2801.5	805.6	131666.6
2019	139.4	198.2	63117.1	2539.2	778.4	98888.3
2020	137.1	213.3	68926.6	3002.9	862.2	105708.4
2021	150.5	233.4	68372.7	3361.6	1033.4	106752.1
2022	115.3	252.8	62528.8	3457.0	977.1	92517.1
2023	96.1	202.8	62275.0	2482.3	882.9	77690.0

28-10 续表 2 continued

年 份 Year	钢坯 (万吨) Billet (10 000 tons)	涂料及涂料助剂 (万吨) Coatings and Coating Additives (10 000 tons)	塑胶黏性胶带 (万平方米) Sticky Tape (10 000 sq. meter)	汽车① (万辆) Car① (10 000 units)	发电量② (亿千瓦时) Electric Power② (100 million kW·h)
2011	2114.5	48.1	337518.3	42.3	2521.7
2012	1943.7	46.6	329201.3	44.1	2503.7
2013	2076.2	49.2	338134.3	42.3	2523.4
2014	2183.9	50.1	353884.3	48.1	2599.6
2015	2042.4	48.9	334076.2	45.4	2581.4
2016	2036.5	49.0	349020.1	42.1	2641.1
2017	2082.1	48.5	348040.9	38.6	2702.6
2018	2159.4	45.1	336283.8	34.4	2755.4
2019	2071.1	42.6	311655.1	32.4	2741.9
2020	1989.7	42.0	279252.5	34.6	2800.0
2021	2214.0	44.5	241199.5	40.8	2910.4
2022	1992.6	41.9	204968.4	37.2	2881.8
2023	1841.6	39.5	177527.3	33.3	2821.4

注：①2023年汽车产量统计口径调整为燃油小型轿车(未满2000c.c.)、燃油大型客车(10人座以上)、小型货车、大型货车、客货两用车、其他汽车、电动大型客车(10人座以上)，并对历史数据作了修订。

②2023年发电量统计口径调整为水力发电、火力发电、核能发电、风力发电、太阳光电发电、其他再生能源发电，并对历史数据作了修订。

Note: ①In 2023, the statistical definition of car production was adjusted to fuel-powered sedans (not exceeding 2000 c.c.), fuel-powered buses (10 seats and above), light duty trucks, heavy duty trucks, van and station wagon, other automobiles, electric buses (10 seats and above), and the historical data were revised.

②In 2023, the statistical definition of electricity power production was adjusted to hydro and pumped storage electric power, thermal electric power, nuclear electric power, wind electric power, solar PV electric power, other renewable energy electric power, and historical data are revised.

28−11 能源平衡表
Energy Balance Sheet

单位：亿升标准油 (100 000 kl oil equivalent)

项　目	Item	2019	2020	2021	2022	2023
能源总供给	**Total Supply**	**1467.22**	**1368.19**	**1426.26**	**1402.41**	**1313.01**
自产能源	Indigenous Energy	31.10	30.44	32.79	38.35	41.14
原油	Crude Oil	0.04	0.02	0.02	0.02	0.02
天然气	Natural Gas	1.49	0.94	0.98	0.85	0.81
生质能及废弃物	Biomass and waste	16.89	16.73	16.84	17.00	16.96
水力发电	Hydro Power	5.30	2.88	3.32	5.58	3.79
再生能源①	Renewables①	6.66	9.06	10.59	13.62	18.26
进口能源	Imported Energy	1436.12	1337.75	1393.47	1364.06	1271.86
煤及煤产品	Coal & Coal Products	443.04	416.01	443.68	416.22	379.08
原油及石油产品	Crude Oil & Petroleum Products	678.68	593.86	609.58	611.77	575.04
液化天然气	L.N.G	220.73	236.81	259.75	267.29	266.19
核能发电	Nuclear	93.59	91.04	80.46	68.78	51.55
能源总需求	**Total Demand**	**1467.22**	**1368.19**	**1426.26**	**1402.41**	**1313.01**
本地能源消费按部门分	Total Consumption by Sector	835.94	838.48	882.49	831.30	785.96
能源部门	Energy Sector	74.71	70.67	72.50	72.61	67.32
运输部门	Transportation Sector	134.08	135.13	128.16	131.27	131.23
工业部门	Industrial Sector	270.17	271.40	291.05	275.03	261.81
农业部门	Agricultural Sector	8.35	7.89	7.88	8.02	8.62
住宅部门	Residential Sector	64.32	67.82	69.55	67.61	67.59
服务业部门	Services Sector	59.13	59.21	58.23	60.45	61.99
非能源消费②	Non-energy Use②	225.19	226.36	255.13	216.30	187.39
出口	Export	217.58	145.03	158.99	185.69	164.02
国际海运及国际航空	International Marine & Aviation Bunkers	47.87	34.03	36.78	35.66	42.49
存货变动	Stock Changes	3.84	17.14	6.17	3.08	-4.32
损耗	Losses	9.33	9.97	9.57	10.22	8.40
统计误差	Errors	7.84	-10.17	2.80	7.98	-2.72

注：①再生能源包括太阳光电、风力发电和太阳热能。
②非能源消费仅含润滑油、柏油、溶剂油。

Note: ①The renewables include geothermal electricity, solar photovoltaic and wind energy.
②Non-energy use refers to lubricating oil, asphalt and solvent oil consumption.

28−12 按用途分批准动工的建筑物面积
Floor Space of Authorized Construction Projects by Purpose

单位：万平方米 (10 000 sq.m)

年 份 Year	总计 Total	商业类 Business	工业、仓储类 Industrial & Stores	休闲、文教类 Recreation & Culture and Education	办公、服务类 Office & Service	住宿类 Accommodation	
						宿舍 Dormitory	住宅 Residence
2011	3415	76	613	129	208	21	1979
2012	3288	106	562	118	197	18	1932
2013	3976	164	584	109	198	21	2542
2014	3863	196	630	96	253	29	2223
2015	3260	87	660	84	172	28	1823
2016	2624	105	559	89	146	17	1326
2017	2988	145	624	120	136	24	1525
2018	3398	83	775	146	203	22	1868
2019	3693	81	798	94	192	16	2195
2020	4152	108	1020	120	235	25	2319
2021	4343	148	686	123	338	18	2487
2022	4583	105	859	87	488	30	2519
2023	3744	97	712	90	461	22	1951

28－13 铁路和公路客货运量
Railway and Highway Passenger and Freight Traffic

年 份 Year	铁路 Railway				公路 Highway			
	客运量(亿人) Passenger Traffic (100 million persons)	客运周转量(亿人公里) Passenger Kilometres (100 million p-km)	货运量(亿吨) Freight Traffic (100 million tons)	货物周转量(亿吨公里) Freight Ton-kilometres (100 million ton-km)	客运量(亿人) Passenger Traffic (100 million persons)	客运周转量(亿人公里) Passenger Kilometres (100 million p-km)	货运量(亿吨) Freight Traffic (100 million tons)	货物周转量(亿吨公里) Freight Ton-kilometres (100 million ton-km)
2011	8.63	228.21	0.11	8.48	11.64	170.40	6.38	295.51
2012	9.24	242.02	0.11	8.28	11.91	175.86	6.53	298.51
2013	9.70	253.16	0.11	7.27	12.20	179.28	5.51	384.74
2014	10.22	263.27	0.11	6.81	12.39	183.84	5.42	378.52
2015	10.60	270.98	0.11	6.34	12.17	175.65	5.32	378.05
2016	10.90	279.37	0.09	5.62	12.25	173.79	5.30	385.33
2017	11.21	289.91	0.08	5.12	12.35	170.53	5.37	403.51
2018	11.52	296.15	0.08	5.42	12.50	171.36	5.61	441.69
2019	11.93	304.44	0.07	5.17	12.47	170.64	5.60	443.70
2020	10.29	255.56	0.07	4.95	10.79	143.06	5.02	331.99
2021	7.91	195.33	0.07	4.45	7.92	101.53	5.17	340.94
2022	8.88	227.83	0.07	4.73	8.37	102.87	5.14	339.63
2023	11.33	297.59	0.07	4.91	9.61	116.42	5.04	331.71

28－14 邮政及电信营运量
Post &Telecommunication Services

项 目	Item	2019	2020	2021	2022	2023
邮政	**Post**					
函件 (亿件)	Letters (100 million pieces)					
收寄	Received	20.2	19.1	18.4	18.5	17.8
包裹 (万件)	Parcels (10 000 pieces)					
收寄	Received	2594.6	2736.2	2982.1	2872.6	2635.8
快捷邮件	Express Mail	1236.4	1618.6	1754.8	1801.5	1592.1
电信	**Telecommunications**					
市内电话用户数 (万户)	Number of Local (Urban) Telephone Subscribers (10 000 subscribers)	1099	1075	1052	1028	1000
移动电话用户数 (万户)	Number of Mobile Telephones Subscribers (10 000 subscribers)	2920.8	2928.9	2958.0	3014.7	2985.2
综合业务数字网用户数(万户)	Number of Subscribers of ISDN (10 000 subscribers)	0.7	0.6	0.6	0.6	0.6
数据通信出租电路数 (万路)	Number of Leasing Circuits of Data Communication (10 000 circuits)	15.0	14.4	13.6	13.2	12.7
国际互联网用户数 (万户)	Number of Subscribers of Internet Services (10 000 subscribers)	627.3	589.6	560.9	533.8	560.0
宽带用户 (万户)	Broadband Subscribers (10 000 subscribers)	589.7	553.1	525.4	499.1	526.1
国际电话去话分钟数 (万分钟)	International Outgoing Call (10 000 minutes)	69641	43644	27944	22754	16557

28-15 货物进出口额
Total Imports and Exports

年份 Year	按新台币计算（亿元） (NT $ 100 million)			按美元计算（亿美元） (USD 100 million)		
	进出口总额 Total	出口 Exports	进口 Imports	进出口总额 Total	出口 Exports	进口 Imports
2010	168310	87574	80736	5331	2774	2557
2011	176112	91724	84388	5995	3122	2873
2012	172229	90373	81856	5818	3053	2765
2013	174434	92190	82243	5882	3109	2774
2014	181663	96634	85029	6005	3194	2811
2015	165024	90137	74887	5208	2844	2364
2016	163831	89972	73859	5084	2792	2292
2017	174402	96058	78344	5727	3155	2572
2018	186562	100691	85871	6188	3340	2848
2019	190174	101819	88354	6148	3292	2857
2020	186593	101987	84606	6313	3451	2861
2021	231986	125016	106970	8283	4464	3820
2022	269207	142182	127025	9075	4794	4281
2023	244276	134825	109451	7839	4324	3514

28-16 货物出口去向和进口来源
Destination of Exports and Origin of Imports

单位：亿美元 (USD 100 million)

项目	Item	2018	2019	2020	2021	2022	2023
出口去向	**Exports (Major Destination)**						
中国大陆	China,Mainland	965.0	917.9	1024.5	1259.0	1210.9	957.3
中国香港	Hong Kong,China	414.0	403.3	489.4	629.7	647.8	565.1
日本	Japan	228.0	232.8	234.0	292.1	336.1	314.4
韩国	Korea, Rep.	157.4	169.2	151.4	201.4	221.8	182.1
美国	United States	394.9	462.5	505.5	656.9	750.5	762.3
泰国	Thailand	61.7	55.2	52.9	70.2	75.5	108.6
马来西亚	Malaysia	106.0	94.0	94.6	133.3	170.1	151.7
印度尼西亚	Indonesia	33.3	29.2	22.8	30.7	32.1	30.1
新加坡	Singapore	173.2	181.8	190.8	257.2	295.2	297.4
越南	Vietnam	107.7	107.7	105.2	139.7	145.7	117.3
德国	Germany	70.6	65.2	60.4	81.7	88.1	81.4
法国	France	16.7	15.2	12.8	15.8	19.3	18.0
意大利	Italy	23.3	19.8	16.1	25.7	29.0	24.1
英国	United Kingdom	38.6	35.8	33.4	41.5	40.5	36.3
巴西	Brazil	13.4	11.8	10.8	16.3	14.0	12.1
澳大利亚	Australia	34.0	32.4	32.3	48.1	75.4	58.0
沙特阿拉伯	Saudi Arabia	7.8	9.1	8.7	9.2	10.5	10.0
科威特	Kuwait	1.5	1.6	1.2	1.3	1.5	1.6
进口来源	**Imports (Major Origin)**						
中国大陆	China,Mainland	537.9	573.9	635.9	824.8	840.0	702.3
中国香港	Hong Kong,China	14.1	10.6	12.2	17.1	15.1	14.8
日本	Japan	441.5	440.5	459.0	561.2	546.3	443.3
韩国	Korea, Rep.	195.2	177.4	206.1	306.4	342.6	284.2
美国	United States	331.0	348.5	325.1	392.6	456.9	406.2
泰国	Thailand	45.8	42.5	45.4	59.6	62.9	53.8
马来西亚	Malaysia	93.0	103.7	98.9	118.0	135.5	96.9
印度尼西亚	Indonesia	54.9	46.8	45.1	79.1	112.1	73.9
新加坡	Singapore	84.2	79.2	89.9	120.7	125.3	95.2
越南	Vietnam	37.0	52.8	55.0	61.5	69.9	61.4
德国	Germany	99.7	94.0	101.8	125.1	142.4	138.9
法国	France	37.1	32.1	29.9	35.2	39.7	42.9
意大利	Italy	26.9	26.1	26.6	30.1	33.5	33.8
英国	United Kingdom	20.8	20.2	19.0	23.7	25.9	27.3
巴西	Brazil	16.4	20.5	20.2	26.1	24.3	27.1
澳大利亚	Australia	95.5	100.2	80.6	149.4	246.4	175.0
沙特阿拉伯	Saudi Arabia	86.1	77.3	48.5	79.0	115.0	91.4
科威特	Kuwait	51.2	43.1	25.3	45.5	69.7	47.2

28-17 出口与进口货物分类
Composition of Exports and Imports

单位：亿美元 (USD 100 million)

年份 Year	出口 Exports 出口额 Total	资本品 Capital Goods	中间产品 Intermediate Products	消费品 Consumer Goods	进口 Imports 进口额 Total	资本设备 Capital Equipments	原材料 Agricultural & Industrial Raw Materials	消费品 Consumer Goods
2011	3121.8	336.3	2403.8	368.9	2873.2	367.5	2202.0	279.5
2012	3053.1	337.5	2376.4	326.2	2764.7	340.6	2117.5	285.0
2013	3108.7	326.5	2440.0	325.8	2773.8	361.2	2079.7	301.4
2014	3194.1	342.3	2514.3	320.5	2811.0	377.7	2074.9	317.4
2015	2844.3	333.6	2204.2	288.8	2363.8	372.2	1624.1	322.1
2016	2791.7	337.4	2170.6	266.5	2292.0	411.1	1531.0	317.1
2017	3154.9	378.7	2479.0	278.7	2572.0	405.6	1788.0	341.5
2018	3340.1	404.6	2630.6	286.5	2847.9	418.7	2032.2	361.8
2019	3291.6	441.2	2534.9	296.7	2856.5	507.6	1939.1	372.3
2020	3451.3	461.2	2658.1	311.6	2861.5	526.4	1910.6	386.3
2021	4463.7	561.1	3504.1	375.8	3819.6	689.1	2649.5	437.7
2022	4794.2	644.1	3789.7	341.1	4280.8	754.7	2997.1	482.1
2023	4324.3	816.5	3195.3	295.1	3514.4	620.8	2373.3	464.7

28-18 来台旅游人数
Inbound Tourists

项目	Item	2018	2019	2020	2021	2022	2023
来台旅游人数（万人次）	**Inbound Tourists(10 000 person-times)**	**1106.7**	**1186.4**	**137.8**	**14.0**	**89.6**	**648.7**
香港澳门	Hong Kong and Macao	165.4	175.8	17.8	1.1	3.3	120.0
中国大陆	China Mainland	269.6	271.4	11.1	1.3	2.4	22.6
外国	Foreign Countries	671.3	739.0	108.6	11.5	83.3	505.9
未列明	Not Stated	0.5	0.2	0.3	0.1	0.6	0.2
平均每人停留时间（夜）	**Average Length of Stay (Nights)**	**6.5**	**6.2**	**8.3**	**34.8**	**13.8**	**7.4**

28-19 居民消费价格分类指数
Consumer Price Indices

(2021年=100) (year of 2021=100)

年份 Year	总指数 General Index	食品 Food	服装 Clothing	居住 Housing	交通&通讯 Transportation &Communications	医药保健 Medicines and Medical Care	教育娱乐 Education and Entertainment	杂项 Miscellaneous
2011	91.2	79.6	94.7	95.0	103.0	92.1	97.6	86.9
2012	93.0	82.9	97.0	96.1	103.4	92.8	98.2	88.8
2013	93.7	84.0	96.9	97.0	103.9	93.8	98.5	89.2
2014	94.8	87.1	98.1	97.8	102.6	94.4	98.5	90.4
2015	94.5	89.9	97.6	96.7	96.7	94.7	98.4	90.6
2016	95.9	94.6	97.8	96.5	95.6	95.5	98.5	91.9
2017	96.5	94.2	97.5	97.3	97.3	97.1	98.8	93.6
2018	97.8	95.2	97.8	98.2	99.5	98.2	99.0	98.1
2019	98.3	97.0	97.1	98.8	98.1	99.0	99.8	98.7
2020	98.1	97.6	98.3	99.1	94.3	99.8	98.8	99.6
2021	100.0	100.0	100.0	100.0	100.0	100.0	100.0	100.0
2022	103.0	105.7	102.4	102.3	103.5	101.2	101.2	101.4
2023	105.5	109.9	103.2	104.4	104.3	103.4	104.3	103.8

28-20 各级政府财政收入净额
Net Revenue of Treasury

单位：新台币亿元 (NT $ 100 million)

项 目	Item	2017	2018	2019	2020	2021	2022
总 计	**Total**	**27533**	**28486**	**29319**	**30361**	**33211**	**36907**
税收收入	Tax	21877	22992	23749	22899	27438	30939
营业盈余及事业收入	Revenue from Enterprises and Institutions	2714	2731	2886	2910	2845	3137
其他收入	Other Revenue	2942	2763	2683	4552	2929	2831
财产孳息收入	Revenue from Profit of Public Properties	203	230	213	536	244	224
规费收入	Fees	1265	1002	1007	2393	964	1019
罚款及赔偿收入	Revenue from Fines & Indemnities	537	567	472	512	519	484
捐献及赠与收入	Receipts from Donations and Contributions	92	87	89	76	94	88
资本收回及售价收入	Return of Properties and Sales of Public Properties	351	390	438	562	494	434
杂项收入	Miscellaneous Revenues	494	487	464	474	614	582

28-21 各级政府财政支出净额
Net Expenditures of Treasury

单位：新台币亿元 (NT $ 100 million)

项 目	Item	2017	2018	2019	2020	2021	2022
总 计	**Total**	**27784**	**28455**	**29116**	**32420**	**33603**	**36524**
一般政务支出	General Administration	3830	4015	4149	4234	4346	4524
国防支出	National Defence	3046	3086	3215	3410	3712	4395
教育科学文化支出	Expenditures on Education, Science and Culture	6913	6758	7025	7042	7835	7927
经济发展支出	Economic Development	3895	4528	4655	6493	5666	6811
社会福利支出	Social Welfare	5638	5881	5911	6957	7960	8734
社区发展及环境保护支出	Community Development and Environmental Protection	1246	1068	1047	1105	919	965
退休抚恤支出	Retirement Pension and Bereavement Payments	1985	1892	1916	2001	2046	2049
债务支出	Obligations	1073	1062	1045	1010	934	888
杂项支出	Miscellaneous	156	165	154	167	186	231

28-22 政府公债
Government Bonds

单位：新台币亿元 (NT $ 100 million)

年 份 Year	合计 Total			台湾省"中央政府"发行 Taiwan Central Government			市级发行 Municipal Government		
	发行额 Issues	偿还额 Redemption	余额 Outstanding	发行额 Issues	偿还额 Redemption	余额 Outstanding	发行额 Issues	偿还额 Redemption	余额 Outstanding
2010	6293	2659	43343	6100	2520	41876	193	140	1467
2011	6400	3299	46444	6200	2980	45096	200	319	1348
2012	6884	3983	49345	6650	3982	47763	234	1	1581
2013	6419	3668	52095	6419	3500	50682	-	168	1413
2014	6753	4446	54402	6753	4050	53385	-	396	1017
2015	6135	4843	55694	6053	4650	54788	82	193	906
2016	5635	5276	56053	5635	5000	55423	-	276	631
2017	4000	3690	56363	4000	3475	55948	-	215	416
2018	3621	3960	56025	3473	3835	55586	148	125	439
2019	4438	4953	55510	4100	4853	54833	338	100	677
2020	5755	5020	56245	5350	4938	55245	405	82	1000
2021	6836	4687	58394	6170	4670	56745	666	17	1649
2022	5201	4093	59502	5201	3950	57995	-	143	1507
2023	4977	3878	60601	4780	3650	59125	197	228	1476

28-23 金融概况
Principal Financial Indicators

年 份 Year	货币供应量M_1(新台币亿元) Money Supply M_1 (NT $100 million)	流动性负债(新台币亿元) Liquid Liabilities (NT $100 million)	储备货币(新台币亿元) Reserve Money (NT $100 million)	主要金融机构存款(新台币亿元) Deposits (NT $100 million)	主要金融机构放款与投资(新台币亿元) Loans and Investments (NT $100 million)	再贴现率(年息%) Rediscount Rate (% annual)	汇率(卖出价)(新台币/美元) Exchange Rates of Selling (NT $/USD)
2011	118302	469541	27209	323022	241729	1.88	30.32
2012	124184	496032	29021	333004	255488	1.88	29.08
2013	134708	530162	31208	350624	267206	1.88	29.82
2014	143101	568299	32633	371339	281106	1.88	31.68
2015	152926	607126	34524	393558	294063	1.63	32.88
2016	161777	638980	36303	407174	305492	1.38	32.30
2017	167414	672411	37765	420940	320227	1.38	29.85
2018	177160	704974	40545	431958	337475	1.38	30.75
2019	190606	744291	42985	450861	354224	1.38	30.05
2020	222803	803857	48362	492197	378266	1.13	28.15
2021	249735	855653	53491	527570	409996	1.13	27.73
2022	258054	909301	59278	563301	436168	1.75	30.77
2023	268253	951180	62026	594271	464853	1.88	30.76

28-24 股票交易
Transactions of Listed Stock

单位：新台币亿元 (NT $ 100 million)

年 份 Year	上 市 股 票 Listed Stock			总成交额 Total Turnover	日平均成交额 Average Daily Turnover in Value	股价指数(年平均)(1966年=100) Stock Price Index (year average) (year of 1966=100)
	上市公司数(家) Number (unit)	总面值① Total Par Value①	总市值① Total Market Value①			
2010	758	58113	238114	282187	1124	7949.63
2011	790	60268	192162	261974	1061	8155.79
2012	809	62580	213522	202382	810	7481.34
2013	838	64880	245196	189409	770	8092.77
2014	854	66653	268915	218985	883	8992.01
2015	874	68493	245036	201915	828	8959.35
2016	892	69370	272479	167711	687	8763.26
2017	907	70558	318319	239722	974	10208.12
2018	928	70778	293185	296089	1199	10620.17
2019	942	70934	364135	264646	1094	10790.17
2020	948	71861	449038	456543	1863	12074.63
2021	959	73528	562820	922900	3782	16938.12
2022	971	74713	442660	560806	2280	15623.49
2023	997	76016	568421	631702	2643	16386.23

注：① 年底数。
Note:①Year-end data.

28-25 入学率和教育经费

Net Enrolment Rate and Public Expenditure for Education

单位：%

(%)

年 份 Year	粗入学率(6-22岁) Gross Enrolment Rate (Aged 6-22)			15岁以上人口识字率② Percentage of Literate Aged 15 and Over②	教育经费占GNI比重 Public Expenditure for Education as % of GNI	政府教育经费占政府支出比重 Government Expenditures on Education as % of Total Government Expenditure
	初等教育(6-11岁) Primary Education (Aged 6-11)	中等教育(12-17岁) Secondary Education (Aged 12-17)	高等教育①(18-22岁) Higher Education① (Aged 18-22)			
2008	99.0	99.1	86.1	97.8	5.4	20.5
2009	99.1	99.1	85.0	97.9	5.8	19.9
2010	99.0	99.0	84.4	98.0	5.3	20.1
2011	98.8	98.9	84.3	98.2	5.4	20.6
2012	98.7	98.7	84.1	98.3	5.4	20.5
2013	98.6	98.6	83.4	98.4	5.3	20.8
2014	98.5	98.7	82.9	98.5	5.1	21.3
2015	98.4	98.9	82.1	98.6	4.9	21.7
2016	98.3	98.6	82.2	98.7	4.9	21.5
2017	98.1	98.3	82.3	98.8	4.8	21.7
2018	98.0	98.5	82.2	98.9	4.8	21.6
2019	97.9	98.6	82.7	99.0	4.7	21.1
2020	98.1	98.7	85.4	99.0	4.6	20.0
2021	98.3	99.1	88.1	99.1	4.5	20.8
2022	99.2	99.7	88.9	99.2	4.2	18.9

注：①不含五专前三年、研究所及进修教育。②年底资料。

Note: ①Exclude the first three years of five-year junior college program, postgraduate study and continuing education.
②Year-end data.

28-26 科技人员数和科研开发经费

Number of Research Staff, Technicians and Supporting Personnel and Expenditures for R&D

年 份 Year	科技人员数(人) Number of Research Staff, Technicians and Supporting Personnel (person)				科研开发经费 Expenditures for Research and Experimental Development			每万人口研究人员数(人) Number of Research Staff per 10 000 People (person)	研究人员平均每年使用经费(新台币万元) Expenditures for R&D per Research Staff per year (NT $10 000)
	总计 Total	研究人员 Research Staff	技术人员 Technicians	支援人员 Assistants	金额(新台币亿元) Total (NT $100 million)	占GDP比重(%) As % of GDP	政府投入经费所占比重(%) As % of Government Subsidies		
2008	240983	143836	77366	19781	3504.76	2.67	28.2	62.4	244
2009	256252	154949	80433	20870	3670.53	2.84	28.8	67.0	237
2010	273249	165370	86882	20997	3958.79	2.82	27.5	71.4	239
2011	288311	174341	91618	22352	4153.57	2.91	26.4	75.1	238
2012	296288	179491	94863	21934	4339.97	2.96	24.7	77.0	242
2013	300514	179975	98356	22183	4584.33	3.00	23.5	77.0	255
2014	307379	181589	103408	22382	4845.41	2.98	21.9	77.5	267
2015	312923	183022	106822	23079	5116.18	3.00	21.2	77.9	280
2016	316467	184898	108755	22814	5417.57	3.09	21.4	78.5	293
2017	321877	187971	110428	23478	5745.02	3.19	19.8	79.7	306
2018	330579	193035	114145	23399	6159.86	3.35	18.8	81.8	319
2019	342476	199144	118973	24360	6605.11	3.49	18.1	84.4	332
2020	350857	203970	121539	25348	7187.91	3.61	16.8	86.6	352
2021	359578	208660	125368	25549	8206.32	3.79	15.1	89.3	393
2022	368492	213126	129050	26316	8979.75	3.96	13.9	91.6	421

28-27 医院、病床和医务人员情况
Medical Facilities and Health Personnel

年 份 Year	医疗机构 (所) Number of Medical Care Facilities (unit)	病床数 (床) Number of Beds (bed)	每万人病床数 (床) Number of Beds per 10 000 Population (bed)	从业医务人员数 (人) Number of Health Personnel (person)	每万人拥有医务人员(人) Number of Health Personnel per 10 000 Population (person)
2011	20628	160472	69.09	250258	107.75
2012	20935	160900	69.01	258283	110.78
2013	21218	159422	68.21	265759	113.70
2014	21544	161491	68.91	271555	115.88
2015	21683	162163	69.03	280508	119.41
2016	21894	163148	69.31	289174	122.84
2017	22129	164590	69.83	299782	127.18
2018	22333	167521	71.02	312887	132.64
2019	22512	168266	71.29	326691	138.41
2020	22653	169780	72.06	337942	143.43
2021	22800	170710	73.03	347555	148.68
2022	23098	172095	73.97	354101	152.21

28-28 家庭主要设备普及率
Percent of Families Owning Household Appliances

单位：% (%)

年 份 Year	彩色电视机 Colour TV Sets	洗衣机 Washing Machines	电话机 Telephone Sets	移动电话 Mobile Phones	空调 Air Conditioners	有线电视频道设备 Cable TV Sets	家用电脑 Home Computers	家用汽车 Automobiles
2009	99.6	97.4	95.9	90.6	88.4	82.0	70.5	59.2
2010	99.4	97.8	95.7	90.6	89.1	83.0	71.3	57.8
2011	99.2	97.6	96.1	91.7	88.8	82.9	71.9	59.1
2012	99.3	98.1	94.8	92.3	89.9	83.2	72.3	58.4
2013	99.3	98.1	94.7	92.6	90.0	84.4	72.2	58.4
2014	99.2	98.5	94.0	93.1	91.7	84.8	70.7	58.7
2015	99.2	98.4	92.9	93.5	92.5	85.4	69.3	59.1
2016	99.1	98.5	92.8	94.6	93.2	85.9	68.8	59.7
2017	99.0	98.6	91.3	95.1	93.9	86.4	68.1	60.8
2018	98.8	98.8	89.6	95.2	94.1	86.1	66.8	60.6
2019	98.7	98.7	88.2	95.6	94.7	85.9	66.7	60.8
2020	98.8	99.0	85.9	96.2	96.0	85.2	66.0	60.3
2021	98.5	98.9	84.4	96.6	95.9	85.6	67.4	60.3
2022	98.4	99.1	81.0	97.1	96.7	83.6	67.8	61.4

附录

APPENDIX

国际主要社会经济指标

Main Social and Economic Indicators of Other Countries/Regions

简 要 说 明

一、世界主要国家和地区的大部分数据经过联合国等国际组织的调整，口径基本可比。

二、一些国家和地区的最新数据是初步数或估计数。

三、中国数据均未包括香港特别行政区、澳门特别行政区和中国台湾省。

四、本篇数据主要取自有关国际组织的数据库、年报、月报，每张表均附有资料来源。中国数据除特别说明外，均来自国际组织数据库。

五、一些数据的合计数或相对数，因受进位的影响，不一定等于分项累计数。

六、“空格”表示无该项数据或该项统计数据不详。

Brief Introduction

I. Data for major foreign countries/regions have been adjusted by international organizations such as the United Nations, and the scope and coverage are therefore comparable.

II. The latest data for a certain countries/regions are preliminary or estimated statistics.

III. All data of China do not cover Hong Kong SAR, Macao SAR and Taiwan Province.

IV. Data in this chapter are mainly from databases, yearbooks and monthly publications of international organizations. Data for China are all taken from international organization databases unless otherwise specified.

V. Some aggregations or rates/ratios may not add up to the sum of the series because of rounding.

VI. The symbol "(blank)" indicates that data are not available.

附录1-1 国土面积和人口(2023年)
Surface Area and Population (2023)

资料来源：世界银行数据库。
Source: World Bank Database.

国家	Country	国土面积①(万平方公里) Surface Area① (10 000 sq.km)	年中人口数(万人) Mid-year Population (10 000 persons)	人口增长率(%) Population Growth (annual %)	人口密度①(人/平方公里) Population Density① (persons/sq.km)
世界	**World**	**14048.7**	**802500**	**0.92**	**61**
中国	China	960.0	141071	-0.10	150
孟加拉国	Bangladesh	14.8	17295	1.03	1301
文莱	Brunei Darussalam	0.6	45	0.78	85
柬埔寨	Cambodia	18.1	1694	1.05	94
印度	India	298.0	142863	0.81	473
印度尼西亚	Indonesia	191.7	27753	0.74	145
伊朗	Iran	174.5	8917	0.70	54
以色列	Israel	2.2	976	2.06	433
日本	Japan	37.8	12452	-0.49	345
哈萨克斯坦	Kazakhstan	272.5	1990	1.34	7
韩国	Korea, Rep.	10.0	5171	0.08	530
老挝	Laos	23.7	763	1.38	32
马来西亚	Malaysia	33.0	3431	1.09	102
蒙古	Mongolia	156.4	345	1.43	2
缅甸	Myanmar	67.7	5458	0.73	82
巴基斯坦	Pakistan	79.6	24049	1.96	300
菲律宾	Philippines	30.0	11734	1.53	382
新加坡	Singapore	0.1	592	4.86	7595
斯里兰卡	Sri Lanka	6.6	2204	-0.65	358
泰国	Thailand	51.3	7180	0.15	140
越南	Viet Nam	33.1	9886	0.68	311
埃及	Egypt	100.1	11272	1.54	110
尼日利亚	Nigeria	92.4	22380	2.38	234
南非	South Africa	121.9	6041	0.87	49
加拿大	Canada	988.0	4010	2.93	4
墨西哥	Mexico	196.4	12846	0.74	65
美国	United States	983.2	33491	0.49	36
阿根廷	Argentina	278.0	4665	0.90	17
巴西	Brazil	851.6	21642	0.51	26
委内瑞拉	Venezuela	91.2	2884	1.88	32
捷克	Czech Rep.	7.9	1087	1.87	136
法国	France	54.9	6817	0.29	124
德国	Germany	35.8	8448	0.81	238
意大利	Italy	30.2	5876	-0.30	200
荷兰	Netherlands	4.2	1788	1.00	521
波兰	Poland	31.3	3669	-0.37	123
俄罗斯	Russia	1709.8	14383	-0.29	9
西班牙	Spain	50.6	4837	1.24	95
土耳其	Türkiye	78.5	8533	0.41	109
乌克兰	Ukraine	60.4	3700	-2.67	76
英国	United Kingdom	24.4	6835	0.82	277
澳大利亚	Australia	774.1	2664	2.37	3
新西兰	New Zealand	26.8	522	2.05	19

注：①2021年数据。
Note:①Data refer to 2021.

附录1-2 按三次产业分就业人员构成
Employment by Type of Industry

资料来源：世界银行数据库。
Source: World Bank Database.
单位：% (%)

国 家	Country	第一产业 Primary Industry		第二产业 Secondary Industry		第三产业 Tertiary Industry	
		2021	2022	2021	2022	2021	2022
中 国	China	23.2	22.6	32.1	32.2	44.8	45.3
孟加拉国	Bangladesh	37.5	36.9	21.8	21.9	40.7	41.3
文 莱	Brunei Darussalam	1.4	1.4	23.6	24.2	75.0	74.4
柬埔寨	Cambodia	37.1	36.6	26.4	26.6	36.5	36.8
印 度	India	44.1	42.9	24.5	26.1	31.5	31.0
印度尼西亚	Indonesia	29.0	29.3	21.8	21.9	49.3	48.8
伊 朗	Iran	15.5	15.1	34.1	34.2	50.3	50.7
以色列	Israel	0.8	0.8	16.0	15.7	83.3	83.5
日 本	Japan	3.2	3.1	23.7	23.6	73.1	73.3
哈萨克斯坦	Kazakhstan	13.2	12.9	21.5	21.5	65.3	65.6
韩 国	Korea, Rep.	5.3	5.4	24.6	24.5	70.0	70.1
老 挝	Laos	67.8	69.6	7.7	7.2	24.5	23.3
马来西亚	Malaysia	10.3	10.0	28.2	28.1	61.5	61.9
蒙 古	Mongolia	26.9	26.3	21.8	22.1	51.3	51.6
缅 甸	Myanmar	46.1	45.5	18.6	18.8	35.2	35.7
巴基斯坦	Pakistan	37.1	36.4	25.4	25.5	37.5	38.1
菲律宾	Philippines	24.3	23.7	18.9	18.9	56.8	57.4
新加坡	Singapore	0.1	0.1	14.4	14.2	85.4	85.7
斯里兰卡	Sri Lanka	26.9	26.4	27.1	27.0	46.0	46.5
泰 国	Thailand	31.9	30.4	22.3	22.2	45.8	47.3
越 南	Viet Nam	29.0	33.6	33.1	30.6	37.8	35.8
埃 及	Egypt	19.3	18.7	28.4	28.4	52.4	53.0
尼日利亚	Nigeria	38.6	38.0	14.4	14.6	47.0	47.5
南 非	South Africa	21.3	19.3	17.2	18.1	61.5	62.7
加拿大	Canada	1.3	1.3	19.3	19.2	79.4	79.6
墨西哥	Mexico	13.1	12.6	24.5	25.0	62.4	62.3
美 国	United States	1.7	1.6	19.2	19.3	79.2	79.1
阿根廷	Argentina	7.3	7.2	20.1	20.0	72.6	72.8
巴 西	Brazil	9.5	8.7	20.7	20.5	69.8	70.8
委内瑞拉	Venezuela	11.8	11.5	18.0	17.9	70.2	70.6
捷 克	Czech Rep.	2.5	2.5	36.8	36.4	60.6	61.0
法 国	France	2.5	2.6	19.4	19.3	78.1	78.2
德 国	Germany	1.3	1.2	27.6	26.9	71.1	71.9
意大利	Italy	4.1	3.8	26.6	26.9	69.3	69.3
荷 兰	Netherlands	2.3	1.9	13.9	14.0	83.8	84.1
波 兰	Poland	8.4	8.3	30.9	30.8	60.7	60.9
俄罗斯	Russia	5.9	5.7	26.6	26.6	67.5	67.8
西班牙	Spain	4.1	3.8	20.2	20.1	75.8	76.1
土耳其	Türkiye	17.2	16.7	27.5	27.7	55.3	55.6
乌克兰	Ukraine	15.1		24.1		60.8	
英 国	United Kingdom	1.0	1.0	18.2	18.1	80.8	80.9
澳大利亚	Australia	2.5	2.2	18.9	18.6	78.6	79.2
新西兰	New Zealand	6.1	6.0	20.0	20.8	73.9	73.2

附录1-3 失业率
Unemployment Rate

资料来源：联合国ILO数据库。
Source: ILO Database.
单位：%

(%)

国家	Country	2000	2010	2019	2020	2021	2022	2023
中国	China	3.7	4.1	5.2	5.6	5.1		
文莱	Brunei Darussalam			6.6	7.4	4.9	5.2	
以色列	Israel	11.1	8.5	3.7	4.2	4.8	3.7	
日本	Japan	4.7	5.1	2.4	2.8	2.8	2.6	2.6
哈萨克斯坦	Kazakhstan	12.8	5.8	4.8	4.9		4.9	
韩国	Korea, Rep.	4.1	3.3	3.7	3.9	3.6	2.9	2.7
马来西亚	Malaysia	3.0	3.4	3.3	4.5	4.6	3.9	
巴基斯坦	Pakistan	7.2	0.7	4.8		6.3		
菲律宾	Philippines	11.2	3.6	2.2	2.5	3.4	2.6	
新加坡	Singapore	3.7	4.1	3.1	4.1	4.6	3.6	3.4
斯里兰卡	Sri Lanka	7.7	4.8	4.7	5.4	5.0	4.5	
泰国	Thailand	2.4	0.6	0.7	1.1	1.2	0.9	0.7
埃及	Egypt	9.0	8.8	7.9	8.0	7.4	7.3	
南非	South Africa	29.9	24.7	28.5	29.2	34.0	33.3	32.1
加拿大	Canada	6.8	8.2	5.7	9.7	7.5	5.3	5.4
墨西哥	Mexico	2.6	5.3	3.5	4.4	4.0	3.3	2.8
美国	United States	4.0	9.6	3.7	8.1	5.3	3.7	3.6
阿根廷	Argentina	15.0	7.7	9.8	11.5	8.7	6.8	6.1
巴西	Brazil			11.9	13.7	13.2	9.2	7.9
委内瑞拉	Venezuela		7.1		7.5			
捷克	Czech Rep.	8.8	7.3	2.0	2.6	2.8	2.2	2.6
法国	France	10.2	9.3	8.4	8.0	7.9	7.3	7.3
德国	Germany	7.9	7.0	3.2	3.9	3.6	3.1	3.1
意大利	Italy	10.8	8.4	10.0	9.2	9.5	8.1	7.6
荷兰	Netherlands	2.7	5.0	3.4	3.8	4.2	3.5	3.5
波兰	Poland	14.9	9.6	3.3	3.2	3.3	2.8	2.7
俄罗斯	Russia	10.6	7.4	4.5	5.6	4.7	3.9	3.1
西班牙	Spain	13.8	19.9	14.1	15.5	14.8	12.9	12.2
土耳其	Türkiye	6.5	11.9	13.7	13.1	12.0	10.5	9.4
乌克兰	Ukraine	11.7	8.1	8.2	9.5	9.8		
英国	United Kingdom	5.6	7.9	3.6	4.5	4.8	3.7	4.0
澳大利亚	Australia	6.3	5.2	5.2	6.5	5.1	3.7	3.7
新西兰	New Zealand	6.1	6.6	4.1	4.6	3.8	3.3	3.7

附录1-4 国内生产总值及其增长率
Gross Domestic Product and its Growth Rate

资料来源：世界银行WDI数据库。
Source: Worldbank WDI Database.

国家	Country	2023 国内生产总值 (亿美元) GDP (100 million USD)	国内生产总值增长率(%) GDP Growth Rate (%)						
			2005	2010	2019	2020	2021	2022	2023
世界	**World**	**1054350**	**4.0**	**4.5**	**2.6**	**-2.9**	**6.3**	**3.1**	**2.7**
中国	China	177948	11.4	10.6	6.0	2.2	8.4	3.0	5.2
孟加拉国	Bangladesh	4374	6.5	5.6	7.9	3.4	6.9	7.1	5.8
文莱	Brunei Darussalam	151	0.4	2.6	3.9	1.1	-1.6	-1.6	1.4
柬埔寨	Cambodia	318	13.3	6.0	7.1	-3.1	3.0	5.2	5.4
印度	India	35499	7.9	8.5	3.9	-5.8	9.7	7.0	7.6
印度尼西亚	Indonesia	13712	5.7	6.2	5.0	-2.1	3.7	5.3	5.0
伊朗	Iran	4015	3.2	5.8	-3.1	3.3	4.7	3.8	5.0
以色列	Israel	5099	4.1	5.7	4.2	-1.9	8.6	6.8	2.0
日本	Japan	42129	1.8	4.1	-0.4	-4.1	2.6	1.0	1.9
哈萨克斯坦	Kazakhstan	2614	9.7	7.3	4.5	-2.5	4.3	3.2	5.1
韩国	Korea, Rep.	17128	4.3	6.8	2.2	-0.7	4.3	2.6	1.4
老挝	Laos	158	7.1	8.5	5.5	0.5	2.5	2.7	3.7
马来西亚	Malaysia	3996	5.3	7.4	4.4	-5.5	3.3	8.7	3.7
蒙古	Mongolia	199	7.3	6.4	5.6	-4.6	1.6	5.0	7.0
缅甸	Myanmar	648	13.6	9.6	6.6	-9.0	-12.0	4.0	1.0
巴基斯坦	Pakistan	3384	7.3	1.5	2.5	-1.3	6.5	4.8	0.0
菲律宾	Philippines	4371	4.9	7.3	6.1	-9.5	5.7	7.6	5.5
新加坡	Singapore	5014	7.4	14.5	1.3	-3.9	9.7	3.8	1.1
斯里兰卡	Sri Lanka	844	6.2	8.0	-0.2	-4.6	4.2	-7.3	-2.3
泰国	Thailand	5149	4.2	7.5	2.1	-6.1	1.6	2.5	1.9
越南	Viet Nam	4297	7.5	6.4	7.4	2.9	2.6	8.1	5.0
埃及	Egypt	3959	4.5	5.1	5.6	3.6	3.3	6.6	3.8
尼日利亚	Nigeria	3628	6.4	8.0	2.2	-1.8	3.6	3.3	2.9
南非	South Africa	3778	5.3	3.0	0.3	-6.0	4.7	1.9	0.6
加拿大	Canada	21401	3.2	3.1	1.9	-5.0	5.3	3.8	1.1
墨西哥	Mexico	17889	2.1	5.0	-0.3	-8.6	5.7	3.9	3.2
美国	United States	273609	3.5	2.7	2.5	-2.2	5.8	1.9	2.5
阿根廷	Argentina	6406	8.9	10.1	-2.0	-9.9	10.7	5.0	-1.6
巴西	Brazil	21737	3.2	7.5	1.2	-3.3	4.8	3.0	2.9
委内瑞拉	Venezuela		10.3	-1.5					
捷克	Czech Rep.	3309	6.6	2.4	3.0	-5.5	3.6	2.4	-0.3
法国	France	30309	1.7	1.9	1.8	-7.5	6.4	2.5	0.7
德国	Germany	44561	0.7	4.2	1.1	-3.8	3.2	1.8	-0.3
意大利	Italy	22549	0.8	1.7	0.5	-9.0	8.3	4.0	0.9
荷兰	Netherlands	11181	2.1	1.3	2.0	-3.9	6.2	4.3	0.1
波兰	Poland	8112	3.5	2.9	4.4	-2.0	6.9	5.6	0.2
俄罗斯	Russia	20214	6.4	4.5	2.2	-2.7	5.6	-2.1	3.6
西班牙	Spain	15807	3.7	0.2	2.0	-11.2	6.4	5.8	2.5
土耳其	Türkiye	11080	9.0	8.4	0.8	1.9	11.4	5.5	4.5
乌克兰	Ukraine	1788	3.1	4.1	3.2	-3.8	3.4	-28.8	5.3
英国	United Kingdom	33400	2.7	2.2	1.6	-10.4	8.7	4.3	0.1
澳大利亚	Australia	17238	3.2	2.2	2.2	-0.3	2.1	4.3	3.0
新西兰	New Zealand	2535	3.4	1.4	2.4	-0.4	4.5	2.8	0.6

附录1-5 人均国内生产总值
GDP per Capita

资料来源：世界银行WDI数据库。
Source: World Bank WDI Database.
单位：美元 (USD)

国　家	Country	2000	2010	2019	2020	2021	2022	2023
世　界	**World**	**5507**	**9543**	**11358**	**10942**	**12362**	**12730**	**13138**
中　国	China	959	4550	10144	10409	12618	12663	12614
孟加拉国	Bangladesh	413	777	2122	2234	2458	2688	2529
文　莱	Brunei Darussalam	17972	34610	30748	27179	31449	37152	33431
柬埔寨	Cambodia	302	783	1671	1578	1625	1760	1875
印　度	India	442	1351	2050	1916	2250	2366	2485
印度尼西亚	Indonesia	771	3094	4151	3896	4334	4788	4941
伊　朗	Iran	1672	6459	3277	2746	4084	4668	4503
以色列	Israel	21631	31267	44452	44847	52130	54931	52262
日　本	Japan	39169	44968	40416	40041	40059	34017	33834
哈萨克斯坦	Kazakhstan	1229	9070	9813	9122	10271	11484	13137
韩　国	Korea, Rep.	12257	23079	31902	31721	35126	32395	33121
老　挝	Laos	319	1128	2599	2593	2536	2054	2075
马来西亚	Malaysia	4088	8880	11132	10164	11135	11993	11649
蒙　古	Mongolia	464	2660	4395	4041	4566	5046	5765
巴基斯坦	Pakistan	644	1012	1437	1322	1506	1589	1407
菲律宾	Philippines	1073	2202	3414	3224	3461	3499	3726
新加坡	Singapore	23853	47237	66082	61467	79601	88429	84734
斯里兰卡	Sri Lanka	870	2837	4083	3846	3999	3343	3828
泰　国	Thailand	2004	4996	7629	7002	7071	6913	7172
越　南	Viet Nam	395	1684	3491	3586	3760	4179	4347
埃　及	Egypt	1399	2510	3017	3572	3887	4295	3513
尼日利亚	Nigeria	563	2280	2334	2075	2066	2163	1621
南　非	South Africa	3242	8060	6703	5753	7074	6766	6253
加拿大	Canada	24271	47561	46353	43538	52497	55509	53372
墨西哥	Mexico	7582	9823	10435	8896	10363	11477	13926
美　国	United States	36330	48651	65548	64317	71056	77247	81695
阿根廷	Argentina	7667	10386	9964	8501	10651	13651	13731
巴　西	Brazil	3727	11249	8845	6924	7795	9065	10044
委内瑞拉	Venezuela	4796	13693					
捷　克	Czech Rep.	6029	19960	23665	22993	26823	27227	30427
法　国	France	22416	40676	40495	39180	43671	40886	44461
德　国	Germany	23695	41572	46805	46749	51427	48718	52746
意大利	Italy	20138	36036	33674	31923	36441	35069	38373
荷　兰	Netherlands	26214	51000	52476	52163	58728	57025	62537
波　兰	Poland	4501	12504	15700	15817	18050	18732	22113
俄罗斯	Russia	1772	10675	11448	10108	12522	15445	13817
西班牙	Spain	14750	30532	29582	26984	30489	29675	32677
土耳其	Türkiye	4278	10623	9215	8639	9743	10675	12986
乌克兰	Ukraine	658	3078	3661	3752	4828	4576	5181
英　国	United Kingdom	28281	39599	42663	40217	46870	45564	48867
澳大利亚	Australia	21870	52147	55050	51868	60697	65078	64712
新西兰	New Zealand	13641	33677	42747	41786	49624	48217	48528

附录1–6　国内生产总值产业构成
Composition of Gross Domestic Product by Industry

资料来源：世界银行WDI数据库。
Source: World Bank WDI Database.
单位：%　　(%)

国　家	Country	农业增加值占国内生产总值比重 Agriculture as Percentage of GDP		工业增加值占国内生产总值比重 Industry as Percentage of GDP		服务业增加值占国内生产总值比重 Services as Percentage of GDP	
		2000	2023	2000	2023	2000	2023
中　国	China	14.7	7.1	45.5	38.3	39.8	54.6
孟加拉国	Bangladesh	22.7	11.0	22.3	34.6	50.6	51.1
文　莱	Brunei Darussalam	1.0	1.2	63.7	61.8	35.3	38.8
柬埔寨	Cambodia	35.9	21.5	21.9	38.5	37.1	33.4
印　度	India	21.6	16.0	27.3	25.0	42.7	49.8
印度尼西亚	Indonesia	15.7	12.5	42.0	40.2	33.4	42.9
伊　朗	Iran	9.1	13.0	40.3	41.8	51.4	42.7
日　本	Japan	1.5		32.5		66.0	
哈萨克斯坦	Kazakhstan	8.1	4.3	37.8	32.0	48.4	56.0
韩　国	Korea, Rep.	3.9	1.6	34.8	31.6	51.6	58.4
老　挝	Laos	33.6	16.1	16.5	30.5	42.2	44.0
马来西亚	Malaysia	8.6	7.7	48.3	37.7	46.3	53.5
蒙　古	Mongolia	27.4	10.2	22.2	40.0	39.2	40.1
缅　甸	Myanmar	57.2	20.4	9.7	38.1		41.5
巴基斯坦	Pakistan	25.4	23.4	17.2	20.8	52.1	50.6
菲律宾	Philippines	13.9	9.4	35.0	28.2	51.1	62.4
新加坡	Singapore	0.1	0.0	32.5	22.4	60.7	72.4
斯里兰卡	Sri Lanka	19.9	8.3	27.3	25.6	52.8	59.9
泰　国	Thailand	8.5	8.6	36.7	32.9	54.8	58.5
越　南	Viet Nam	24.5	12.0	36.7	37.1	38.7	42.5
埃　及	Egypt	15.5	10.6	30.8	32.7	46.5	51.6
尼日利亚	Nigeria	21.4	22.7	33.8	32.6	43.8	42.8
南　非	South Africa	2.6	2.5	28.2	24.6	61.2	63.0
加拿大	Canada	2.1		29.5		61.3	
墨西哥	Mexico	3.2	4.0	34.4	31.8	58.0	58.3
美　国	United States	1.2		22.5		72.8	
阿根廷	Argentina	4.7	6.1	26.0	25.1	63.5	52.8
巴　西	Brazil	4.8	6.2	23.0	22.3	58.3	58.9
委内瑞拉	Venezuela	3.9		46.4		43.1	
捷　克	Czech Rep.	3.3	1.6	33.5	30.2	54.4	59.8
法　国	France	2.1	1.9	21.3	18.7	66.3	69.2
德　国	Germany	1.0	0.7	27.7	28.1	61.5	62.6
意大利	Italy	2.6	1.9	24.3	23.1	62.7	64.9
荷　兰	Netherlands	2.3	1.5	21.7	19.4	65.7	69.3
波　兰	Poland	3.1	2.9	28.8	28.7	56.8	58.8
俄罗斯	Russia	5.8	3.3	33.9	30.6	49.7	56.9
西班牙	Spain	3.7	2.3	28.0	20.2	59.2	68.5
土耳其	Türkiye	10.0	6.2	26.8	28.3	52.8	54.0
乌克兰	Ukraine	14.0	7.4	31.7	18.8	39.7	61.3
英　国	United Kingdom	0.8	0.7	22.6	16.9	66.3	72.8
澳大利亚	Australia	3.1	2.4	24.6	27.4	64.4	64.2
新西兰	New Zealand	7.8		23.6		61.8	

附录1-7 居民最终消费率
Household Final Consumption Rate

资料来源：世界银行WDI数据库。
Source: World Bank WDI Database.
单位：%

(%)

国家	Country	2000	2010	2020	2021	2022	2023
中国	China	46.7	34.3	38.2	38.1	37.4	
孟加拉国	Bangladesh	75.0	74.1	67.0	68.8	69.1	68.6
文莱	Brunei Darussalam	24.8	14.7	23.8	24.9	23.3	27.6
柬埔寨	Cambodia	88.8	81.3	69.5	65.9	61.7	41.8
印度	India	63.7	54.7	61.1	61.0	60.9	60.3
印度尼西亚	Indonesia	61.7	56.2	58.9	55.6	53.0	54.4
伊朗	Iran	49.7	42.9	46.3	43.1	45.3	47.2
以色列	Israel	51.4	55.0	48.3	49.1	49.2	48.2
日本	Japan	53.7	56.9	54.1	53.5	55.6	
哈萨克斯坦	Kazakhstan	61.9	45.4	53.0	51.6	49.0	
韩国	Korea, Rep.	54.5	50.4	46.4	46.0	48.1	48.9
老挝	Laos	87.6	74.6				
马来西亚	Malaysia	43.8	48.1	61.0	57.9	57.6	60.4
蒙古	Mongolia	75.1	55.2	60.5	53.0	51.9	47.8
巴基斯坦	Pakistan	76.0	79.8	81.5	83.5	86.1	83.4
菲律宾	Philippines	71.7	70.2	75.1	75.3	75.9	76.5
新加坡	Singapore	41.9	36.3	32.0	29.0	28.3	31.3
斯里兰卡	Sri Lanka	71.5		62.9	61.2	67.8	69.3
泰国	Thailand	54.1	52.2	53.0	52.2	54.6	57.7
越南	Viet Nam	66.5	58.4	56.0	55.5	54.8	
埃及	Egypt	75.9	74.6	83.6	86.0	82.5	82.6
南非	South Africa	65.6	62.4	62.5	61.8	63.5	64.7
加拿大	Canada	54.5	57.0	56.8	54.2	53.8	55.2
墨西哥	Mexico	69.0	70.5	66.1	68.2	70.6	70.4
美国	United States	66.0	68.2	66.6	68.0	68.0	
阿根廷	Argentina	69.3	64.2	65.7	63.0	65.5	67.2
巴西	Brazil	64.6	60.2	63.1	61.4	63.1	63.3
委内瑞拉	Venezuela	51.7	55.9				
捷克	Czech Rep.	50.4	49.0	45.3	45.4	46.7	45.6
法国	France	53.9	55.4	53.2	52.6	53.4	53.7
德国	Germany	56.3	55.1	50.2	49.4	51.1	50.7
意大利	Italy	60.5	60.7	58.0	56.7	59.4	59.6
荷兰	Netherlands	50.3	45.4	42.1	41.5	42.9	43.5
波兰	Poland	63.8	62.1	56.5	56.2	57.9	57.2
俄罗斯	Russia	46.2	51.5	51.5	49.9	48.6	49.8
西班牙	Spain	59.6	58.1	56.1	56.2	56.9	55.6
土耳其	Türkiye	66.9	62.7	56.8	55.2	57.3	59.4
乌克兰	Ukraine	57.4	64.8	73.3	69.1	64.6	64.1
英国	United Kingdom	66.1	63.9	59.2	60.0	61.9	61.8
澳大利亚	Australia	57.4	55.3	52.1	50.6	48.7	49.6
新西兰	New Zealand	57.9	57.8	57.1	57.6	58.2	

附录1-8 农业生产指数
Agricultural Production Indices

资料来源：联合国粮农组织数据库。
Source: United Nations Food and Agriculture Organization Database.

(2014–2016年=100) (year of 2014-2016=100)

国 家	Country	农业 Agriculture			食品 Food		
		2020	2021	2022	2020	2021	2022
世 界	**World**	**108.1**	**110.7**	**111.2**	**108.2**	**110.9**	**111.5**
中 国	China	105.1	109.2	111.1	105.5	109.8	111.7
孟加拉国	Bangladesh	116.1	121.5	124.8	115.9	121.6	125.2
文 莱	Brunei Darussalam	107.5	116.4	119.2	107.5	116.5	119.3
柬埔寨	Cambodia	114.0	128.2	127.6	110.3	124.7	123.7
印 度	India	119.1	124.6	125.8	120.1	126.1	127.8
印度尼西亚	Indonesia	115.4	116.1	120.8	110.8	111.8	117.1
伊 朗	Iran	86.9	89.6	83.9	86.8	89.6	83.9
以色列	Israel	101.8	100.9	105.6	102.3	101.4	105.5
日 本	Japan	100.3	100.3	100.2	100.3	100.4	100.3
哈萨克斯坦	Kazakhstan	118.1	114.9	127.5	118.3	115.3	127.8
韩 国	Korea, Rep.	99.4	102.0	101.2	99.4	102.0	101.2
老 挝	Laos	106.5	109.5	118.1	104.6	107.4	114.8
马来西亚	Malaysia	102.0	98.5	98.4	102.8	102.8	102.8
蒙 古	Mongolia	166.5	126.1	156.0	168.7	127.0	157.9
缅 甸	Myanmar	79.0	80.7	77.4	78.8	80.5	77.0
巴基斯坦	Pakistan	111.8	117.8	116.4	116.0	121.4	122.4
菲律宾	Philippines	100.7	100.3	100.5	100.7	100.3	100.5
新加坡	Singapore	123.4	133.7	131.0	123.4	133.7	131.0
斯里兰卡	Sri Lanka	108.7	118.2	98.6	108.5	119.2	99.2
泰 国	Thailand	98.6	102.2	106.0	96.1	100.1	104.2
越 南	Viet Nam	107.6	113.2	114.2	107.1	112.8	113.7
埃 及	Egypt	104.2	109.1	109.0	104.4	109.2	109.1
尼日利亚	Nigeria	112.6	117.6	120.1	112.6	117.3	119.9
南 非	South Africa	111.4	114.0	113.0	111.4	114.2	113.2
加拿大	Canada	112.9	95.6	111.7	112.8	95.5	111.6
墨西哥	Mexico	112.8	114.4	117.4	112.7	114.1	117.0
美 国	United States	102.9	104.9	100.5	103.1	104.6	100.9
阿根廷	Argentina	108.7	108.5	109.5	108.6	108.4	109.4
巴 西	Brazil	112.9	112.5	114.4	112.0	112.1	113.8
委内瑞拉	Venezuela	89.7	88.9	90.0	89.5	88.6	89.9
捷 克	Czech Rep.	96.9	97.4	97.6	96.9	97.5	97.7
法 国	France	93.7	96.7	94.0	93.7	96.7	94.0
德 国	Germany	95.3	94.4	92.6	95.5	94.5	92.7
意大利	Italy	99.8	99.3	96.8	99.9	99.4	97.0
荷 兰	Netherlands	102.2	103.9	100.9	102.3	103.9	101.0
波 兰	Poland	111.8	110.6	111.6	111.9	110.7	111.7
俄罗斯	Russia	112.0	111.6	126.3	112.0	111.6	126.4
西班牙	Spain	117.3	116.6	98.5	117.4	116.8	98.8
土耳其	Türkiye	119.0	119.6	128.9	120.2	120.1	128.9
乌克兰	Ukraine	99.2	113.9	87.8	99.2	113.9	87.8
英 国	United Kingdom	98.2	100.6	101.3	98.1	100.5	101.2
澳大利亚	Australia	84.4	106.2	113.5	87.1	107.2	112.1
新西兰	New Zealand	103.2	102.8	100.0	103.5	103.3	100.6

附录1−9　制造业生产指数
Manufacturing Production Index

资料来源：联合国工发组织数据库。
Source: UN Industrial Development Organization Database .

(2015年=100)　(year of 2015=100)

国　家		2005	2010	2020	2021	2022	2023
中　国	China		61	132	148	153	160
孟加拉国	Bangladesh			162	196	209	220
文　莱	Brunei Darussalam		102	141	132	128	124
印　度	India			101	114	119	125
印度尼西亚	Indonesia		78	114	118	124	130
以色列	Israel	73	92	111	115	127	126
日　本	Japan	109	102	90	95	95	94
韩　国	Korea, Rep.	66	92	106	116	117	114
马来西亚	Malaysia		78	117	128	139	140
蒙　古	Mongolia		67	128	137	139	157
巴基斯坦	Pakistan			105	120	128	118
菲律宾	Philippines	81	80	61	94	108	113
新加坡	Singapore	66	93	130	147	151	145
斯里兰卡	Sri Lanka			97	104	92	88
泰　国	Thailand			94	99	100	97
越　南	Viet Nam			151	156	187	160
埃　及	Egypt		99	98	106	108	98
尼日利亚	Nigeria		54	96	99	101	103
南　非	South Africa	96	94	88	93	93	93
加拿大	Canada	114	92	95	101	104	104
墨西哥	Mexico	86	86	96	105	111	111
美　国	United States	99	92	93	98	100	100
阿根廷	Argentina	77	103	81	93	97	95
巴　西	Brazil	101	115	93	97	97	96
捷　克	Czech Rep.	73	83	107	115	118	118
法　国	France	111	99	93	98	99	100
德　国	Germany	86	91	93	97	97	96
意大利	Italy	121	108	93	106	106	104
荷　兰	Netherlands	92	97	106	114	122	122
波　兰	Poland	57	81	122	140	153	151
俄罗斯	Russia	75	85	116	125	125	134
西班牙	Spain	128	105	97	105	107	106
乌克兰	Ukraine		123	109	110	76	71
英　国	United Kingdom	93	90	107	109	106	107
澳大利亚	Australia	106	107	97	101	101	100
新西兰	New Zealand	108	95	104	108	102	97

附录1-10 消费价格指数
Consumer Price Indices

资料来源：国际货币基金组织IFS数据库。
Source: IMF IFS Database.
(2010年=100) (year of 2010=100)

国 家	Country	2005	2019	2020	2021	2022	2023
中 国	China	86.5	125.1	128.1	129.4	131.9	132.2
孟加拉国	Bangladesh	69.2	179.7	189.9	200.4	215.9	237.2
文 莱	Brunei Darussalam	95.5	99.0	100.9	102.7	106.5	106.9
柬埔寨	Cambodia	68.2	130.1	133.9	137.9	145.2	148.3
印 度	India	66.0	171.6	183.0	192.4	205.3	216.9
印度尼西亚	Indonesia	68.7	151.2	154.1	156.5	163.1	169.1
伊 朗	Iran	49.4	550.9	719.5	1031.7	1480.3	2140.2
以色列	Israel	87.9	108.2	107.5	109.1	113.9	118.8
日 本	Japan	100.4	105.5	105.5	105.2	107.8	111.4
韩 国	Korea, Rep.	86.2	115.2	115.8	118.7	124.7	129.2
老 挝	Laos	78.5	135.9	142.8	148.2	182.2	239.1
马来西亚	Malaysia	87.8	121.5	120.1	123.1	127.2	130.4
蒙 古	Mongolia	57.3	195.8	203.2	218.1	251.2	277.2
缅 甸	Myanmar	44.5	168.2				
巴基斯坦	Pakistan	55.8	182.3	200.1	219.1	262.6	343.4
菲律宾	Philippines	78.7	129.6	132.7	137.9	146.0	154.7
新加坡	Singapore	88.0	114.4	114.2	116.8	124.0	130.0
斯里兰卡	Sri Lanka	58.3	155.5	165.1	176.7	264.5	308.3
泰 国	Thailand	86.6	113.3	112.3	113.7	120.6	122.1
越 南	Viet Nam	59.9	163.5	168.8	171.9	177.3	183.1
埃 及	Egypt	57.8	288.6	303.1	318.9	363.3	486.3
尼日利亚	Nigeria	61.4	267.5	302.9	354.3	421.1	524.9
南 非	South Africa	74.3	158.9	164.0	171.6	183.7	194.8
加拿大	Canada	91.9	116.8	117.6	121.6	129.9	134.9
墨西哥	Mexico	80.5	141.5	146.4	154.7	166.9	176.1
美 国	United States	89.6	117.2	118.7	124.3	134.2	139.7
巴 西	Brazil	79.5	167.4	172.8	187.1	204.5	213.9
捷 克	Czech Rep.	87.0	116.5	120.2	124.8	143.6	158.9
法 国	France	92.8	110.0	110.6	112.4	118.3	124.0
德 国	Germany	92.5	112.9	113.0	116.5	124.5	131.9
意大利	Italy	91.0	110.6	110.5	112.5	121.8	128.6
荷 兰	Netherlands	92.7	115.9	117.4	120.5	132.6	137.7
波 兰	Poland	86.9	114.1	118.0	123.9	141.8	158.2
俄罗斯	Russia	61.4	180.8	186.9	199.4		
西班牙	Spain	89.0	111.0	110.6	114.0	123.6	128.0
土耳其	Türkiye	65.9	234.4	263.2	314.8	542.4	834.6
乌克兰	Ukraine	51.2	281.7	289.4	316.4	380.3	429.2
英 国	United Kingdom	88.1	119.6	120.8	123.8	133.7	142.7
澳大利亚	Australia	86.3	119.8	120.8	124.3	132.5	139.9
新西兰	New Zealand	87.0	114.2	116.2	120.8	129.4	136.9

附录1-11 货物进出口额
Total Imports and Exports

资料来源：世界贸易组织数据库。
Source: World Trade Organization Database.
单位：亿美元 (100 million USD)

国 家	Country	2022 出 口 Exports	2022 进 口 Imports	2023 出 口 Exports	2023 进 口 Imports
世 界	**World**	**249175**	**256999**	**237835**	**242346**
中 国	China	35444	27065	33800	25568
孟加拉国	Bangladesh	547	882	558	669
文 莱	Brunei Darussalam	142	92	91	63
柬埔寨	Cambodia	225	298	235	244
印 度	India	4534	7204	4320	6727
印度尼西亚	Indonesia	2920	2374	2589	2219
伊 朗	Iran	979	586	912	653
以色列	Israel	736	1073	669	913
日 本	Japan	7468	8972	7173	7856
哈萨克斯坦	Kazakhstan	846	509	785	607
韩 国	Korea, Rep.	6836	7314	6322	6426
老 挝	Laos	82	72	84	77
马来西亚	Malaysia	3521	2938	3128	2658
蒙 古	Mongolia	125	87	152	93
缅 甸	Myanmar	171	174	136	156
巴基斯坦	Pakistan	309	708	285	505
菲律宾	Philippines	789	1459	729	1330
新加坡	Singapore	5158	4756	4763	4234
斯里兰卡	Sri Lanka	131	183	119	168
泰 国	Thailand	2874	3010	2846	2898
越 南	Viet Nam	3713	3591	3538	3258
埃 及	Egypt	513	957	399	789
尼日利亚	Nigeria	631	604	579	459
南 非	South Africa	1229	1362	1109	1307
加拿大	Canada	5990	5835	5693	5704
墨西哥	Mexico	5777	6263	5930	6215
美 国	United States	20652	33718	20195	31725
阿根廷	Argentina	884	815	668	737
巴 西	Brazil	3341	2922	3397	2527
委内瑞拉	Venezuela	48	101	85	112
捷 克	Czech Rep.	2420	2367	2555	2306
法 国	France	6205	8232	6485	7859
德 国	Germany	16758	15826	16884	14626
意大利	Italy	6586	6943	6770	6396
荷 兰	Netherlands	9648	8975	9346	8421
波 兰	Poland	3605	3812	3815	3701
俄罗斯	Russia	5921	2765	4239	3038
西班牙	Spain	4155	4943	4232	4703
土耳其	Türkiye	2542	3637	2558	3618
乌克兰	Ukraine	441	553	360	635
英 国	United Kingdom	5330	8235	5207	7913
澳大利亚	Australia	4127	3092	3709	2877
新西兰	New Zealand	451	542	415	500

附录1–12　外商直接投资
Foreign Direct Investment

资料来源：联合国贸发会议FDI数据库和《世界投资报告2023》。
Source: UNCTAD FDI Database and World Investment Report 2023.
单位：亿美元　(100 million USD)

国家 Country	外商直接投资 FDI Inflows					对外直接投资 FDI Outflows				
	2000	2010	2020	2022	2023	2000	2010	2020	2022	2023
世　界 World	**13567**	**13687**	**9842**	**13550**	**13309**	**11625**	**13911**	**7794**	**15745**	**15504**
中　国 China	407	1147	1493	1891	1633	9	688	1537	1631	1479
孟加拉国 Bangladesh	6	9	26	35	30				1	
文　莱 Brunei Darussalam	6	5	6	-3	-1					
柬埔寨 Cambodia	1	14	36	36	40			1	2	2
印　度 India	36	274	641	494	282	5	159	111	146	133
印度尼西亚 Indonesia		138	186	254	216		27	44	73	71
伊　朗 Iran	2	36	13	15	14		2	1	1	1
以色列 Israel	70	70	210	230	164	33	80	46	102	100
日　本 Japan	83	-13	118	342	214	316	563	997	1621	1840
哈萨克斯坦 Kazakhstan	13	116	37	65	32		79	-22	-15	9
韩　国 Korea, Rep.	115	95	88	250	152	48	282	348	658	345
老　挝 Laos	0	3	10	6	17					
马来西亚 Malaysia	38	91	32	169	87	20	134	24	133	76
蒙　古 Mongolia	1	17	17	25	22		1		1	1
缅　甸 Myanmar	1	67	19	12	15					
巴基斯坦 Pakistan	3	20	21	15	18				12	
菲律宾 Philippines	22	11	68	59	62	1	27	36	3	13
新加坡 Singapore	148	575	749	1411	1597	68	354	398	522	630
斯里兰卡 Sri Lanka	2	5	4	9	7					
泰　国 Thailand	34	146	-63	111	45		79	173	74	104
越　南 Viet Nam	13	80	158	179	185		9	4	27	-10
埃　及 Egypt	12	64	59	114	98	1	12	3	3	4
尼日利亚 Nigeria	13	61	24	9	19	2	9	15	28	3
南　非 South Africa	9	36	31	92	52	3	-1	-20	22	-28
加拿大 Canada	668	284	256	462	503	447	347	437	830	896
墨西哥 Mexico	182	272	282	363	361		146	17	145	64
美　国 United States	3140	1980	933	3324	3109	1426	2778	2245	3664	4043
阿根廷 Argentina	104	113	49	154	229	9	10	12	21	24
巴　西 Brazil	328	777	283	734	659	23	221	-134	321	299
委内瑞拉 Venezuela	47	16	15	17	7	5	25	15	21	14
捷　克 Czech Rep.	50	61	94	92	78		12	30	57	71
法　国 France	275	139	132	760	420	1619	482	237	528	724
德　国 Germany	1983	656	700	274	367	571	1255	387	1455	1013
意大利 Italy	134	92	-186	322	182	67	327	29	165	130
荷　兰 Netherlands	639	-72	-817	-804	-1685	756	684	-1739	382	-1422
波　兰 Poland	94	128	152	315	287		61	9	63	104
俄罗斯 Russia	27	317	104	-152	84	32	411	68	115	291
西班牙 Spain	396	399	142	449	359	582	378	335	429	303
土耳其 Türkiye	10	91	77	134	104	9	15	32	47	58
乌克兰 Ukraine	6	65		6	42		7		3	
英　国 United Kingdom	1153	582	444	149	-892	2327	481	-959	954	20
澳大利亚 Australia	142	368	142	634	299	29	198	56	1181	98
新西兰 New Zealand	13	-1	40	79	36	6	7	7	7	-8

附录1-13　外汇储备
Foreign Exchange Reserves

资料来源：国际货币基金组织IFS数据库。
Source: IMF IFS Database.
单位：亿美元　(100 million USD)

国家	Country	2000	2005	2010	2015	2020	2022	2023
中国	China	1656	8189	28473	33304	32165	31277	32380
孟加拉国	Bangladesh	15	28	99	258	410	300	182
文莱	Brunei Darussalam	4	4	12	29	34	40	35
柬埔寨	Cambodia	5	10	31	68	184	144	168
印度	India	373	1310	2678	3278	5422	4980	5512
印度尼西亚	Indonesia	283	329	900	1006	1284	1242	1326
以色列	Israel	232	278	693	889	1712	1897	2001
日本	Japan	3472	8288	10363	11795	13128	11082	11704
哈萨克斯坦	Kazakhstan	16	61	247	198	113	124	142
韩国	Korea, Rep.	959	2100	2869	3585	4301	3990	3956
老挝	Laos	1	2	7	10	18	15	17
马来西亚	Malaysia	274	694	1023	914	1026	1052	1037
蒙古	Mongolia	2	3	21	12	40	29	43
缅甸	Myanmar	2	8	57	43	72	71	83
巴基斯坦	Pakistan	15	98	131	172	145	61	93
菲律宾	Philippines	130	158	540	724	965	823	886
新加坡	Singapore	795	1155	2237	2457	3593	2798	3368
斯里兰卡	Sri Lanka	10	26	66	65	52		
泰国	Thailand	319	505	1657	1493	2460	1956	2016
越南	Viet Nam	34	90	121	279	944	847	904
埃及	Egypt	129	205	324	121	334	244	243
尼日利亚	Nigeria	99	283	298	260	344	303	
南非	South Africa	58	183	354	389	443	465	474
加拿大	Canada	290	307	449	691	768	797	899
墨西哥	Mexico	351	730	1149	1684	1842	1748	1869
美国	United States	312	378	521	392	445	372	373
阿根廷	Argentina	244	227	466	206	339	354	190
巴西	Brazil	324	532	2806	3489	3427	2939	3231
委内瑞拉	Venezuela	126	235	92	51			
捷克	Czech Rep.	130	291	403	626	1641	1351	1421
法国	France	321	240	362	364	552	528	296
德国	Germany	497	398	374	364	369	367	369
意大利	Italy	224	235	357	344	466	466	489
荷兰	Netherlands	70	71	89	88	59	52	61
波兰	Poland	263	405	863	894	1385	1463	1628
俄罗斯	Russia	243	1757	4329	3094	4445	4178	4142
西班牙	Spain	295	86	133	387	567	559	633
土耳其	Türkiye	223	504	790	914	484	704	851
乌克兰	Ukraine	11	190	333	124	275	252	378
英国	United Kingdom	342	359	493	1016	1396	1103	1088
澳大利亚	Australia	168	410	328	372	321	385	409
新西兰	New Zealand	36	87	151	131	120	111	121

附录1-14　国际旅游收支
Expenditures and Receipts of International Tourism

资料来源：世界银行WDI数据库。
Source: World Bank WDI Database.
单位：亿美元　　(100 million USD)

国　家	Country	国际旅游支出 International Tourism Expenditures			国际旅游收入 International Tourism Receipts		
		2010	2019	2020	2010	2019	2020
世　界	**World**	**10304**	**14391**		**11664**	**18631**	
中　国	China						
孟加拉国	Bangladesh	8	14	7	1	4	2
柬埔寨	Cambodia	1	12	2	17	53	11
印　度	India		286	158		317	134
印度尼西亚	Indonesia	84	144	20	76	184	35
伊　朗	Iran	106			26		
以色列	Israel	47	104	22	56	85	27
日　本	Japan	393	291	67	154	492	114
哈萨克斯坦	Kazakhstan	15	30	9	12	29	6
韩　国	Korea, Rep.	208	353	167	143	255	118
老　挝	Laos	2	10	3	4	10	2
马来西亚	Malaysia	93	137	52	196	222	34
蒙　古	Mongolia	3	10	6	3	6	0
缅　甸	Myanmar		2		1	25	
巴基斯坦	Pakistan	14	30	12	10	10	8
菲律宾	Philippines	60	129	49	34	115	28
新加坡	Singapore	187			142		
斯里兰卡	Sri Lanka	8	24	8	10	47	11
泰　国	Thailand	72	150	37	238	644	154
越　南	Viet Nam	15	65	44	45	118	32
埃　及	Egypt	27	37	26	136	143	49
尼日利亚	Nigeria	83	164	66	7	15	3
南　非	South Africa	81	59	16	103	91	27
加拿大	Canada	372			184		
墨西哥	Mexico	90	123	43	126	258	114
美　国	United States	1238	1861	488	1618	2394	842
阿根廷	Argentina	64	98	27	56	57	17
巴　西	Brazil	189	212	65	55	61	31
捷　克	Czech Rep.	44	60	35	81	80	39
法　国	France	467	598	312	562	708	360
德　国	Germany	909	1012		491	584	
意大利	Italy		379	130		519	205
荷　兰	Netherlands		225	74		237	109
波　兰	Poland	89	102	55	99	157	84
俄罗斯	Russia	302	406	108	132	172	50
西班牙	Spain						
土耳其	Türkiye	58	54	16	263	414	138
乌克兰	Ukraine	41	89	48	47	26	7
英　国	United Kingdom						
澳大利亚	Australia	279	413	77	311	480	262
新西兰	New Zealand	30			65		

附录1-15　货币汇率(年平均价)
Exchange Rate (Period Average)

资料来源：世界银行WDI数据库。
Source: World Bank WDI Database.
单位：1美元合本币数　　(local currency unit per US dollar)

国　家	Country	2000	2010	2019	2020	2021	2022	2023
中　国	China	8.28	6.77	6.91	6.90	6.45	6.74	7.08
孟加拉国	Bangladesh	52.14	69.65	84.45	84.87	85.08	91.75	106.31
文　莱	Brunei Darussalam	1.72	1.36	1.36	1.38	1.34	1.38	1.34
柬埔寨	Cambodia	3840.75	4184.92	4061.15	4092.78	4098.72	4102.04	4110.65
印　度	India	44.94	45.73	70.42	74.10	73.92	78.60	82.60
印度尼西亚	Indonesia	8421.78	9090.43	14147.67	14582.20	14308.14	14849.85	15236.88
伊　朗	Iran	1764.86	10254.18	42000.00	42000.00	42000.00	42000.00	42000.00
以色列	Israel	4.08	3.74	3.56	3.44	3.23	3.36	3.67
日　本	Japan	107.77	87.78	109.01	106.77	109.75	131.50	140.49
哈萨克斯坦	Kazakhstan	142.13	147.36	382.75	412.95	425.91	460.17	456.17
韩　国	Korea, Rep.	1130.36	1156.46	1165.36	1180.27	1143.95	1291.45	1305.66
老　挝	Laos	7887.64	8254.16	8679.41	9045.79	9697.92	14035.23	17688.87
马来西亚	Malaysia	3.80	3.22	4.14	4.20	4.14	4.40	4.56
蒙　古	Mongolia	1076.67	1357.06	2663.54	2813.29	2849.29	3140.68	3465.74
缅　甸	Myanmar	6.52	5.63	1518.26	1381.62			
巴基斯坦	Pakistan	53.65	85.19	150.04	161.84	162.91	204.87	280.36
菲律宾	Philippines	44.19	45.11	51.80	49.62	49.25	54.48	55.63
新加坡	Singapore	1.72	1.36	1.36	1.38	1.34	1.38	1.34
斯里兰卡	Sri Lanka	77.01	113.06	178.74	185.59	198.76		
泰　国	Thailand	40.11	31.69	31.05	31.29	31.98	35.06	34.80
越　南	Viet Nam	14167.75	18612.92	23050.24	23208.37	23159.78	23271.21	23787.32
埃　及	Egypt	3.47	5.62	16.77	15.76	15.64	19.16	30.63
尼日利亚	Nigeria	101.70	150.30	306.92	358.81	401.15	425.98	
南　非	South Africa	6.94	7.32	14.45	16.46	14.78	16.36	18.45
加拿大	Canada	1.49	1.03	1.33	1.34	1.25	1.30	1.35
墨西哥	Mexico	9.46	12.64	19.26	21.49	20.27	20.13	17.76
美　国	United States	1.00	1.00	1.00	1.00	1.00	1.00	1.00
阿根廷	Argentina	1.00	3.90	48.15	70.54	94.99	130.62	296.26
巴　西	Brazil	1.83	1.76	3.94	5.16	5.39	5.16	4.99
委内瑞拉	Venezuela	0.68	2.58					
捷　克	Czech Rep.	38.60	19.10	22.93	23.21	21.68	23.36	22.20
法　国	France	1.08	0.75	0.89	0.88	0.85	0.95	0.92
德　国	Germany	1.08	0.75	0.89	0.88	0.85	0.95	0.92
意大利	Italy	1.08	0.75	0.89	0.88	0.85	0.95	0.92
荷　兰	Netherlands	1.08	0.75	0.89	0.88	0.85	0.95	0.92
波　兰	Poland	4.35	3.02	3.84	3.90	3.86	4.46	4.20
俄罗斯	Russia	28.13	30.37	64.74	72.10	73.65	68.48	85.16
西班牙	Spain	1.08	0.75	0.89	0.88	0.85	0.95	0.92
土耳其	Türkiye	0.63	1.50	5.67	7.01	8.85	16.55	23.74
乌克兰	Ukraine	5.44	7.94	25.85	26.96	27.29	32.34	36.57
英　国	United Kingdom	0.66	0.65	0.78	0.78	0.73	0.81	0.80
澳大利亚	Australia	1.72	1.09	1.44	1.45	1.33	1.44	1.51
新西兰	New Zealand	2.20	1.39	1.52	1.54	1.41	1.58	1.63

中国统计出版社最新资料书简目

（仅供参考，以最后出书为准）

统计资料

中国统计年鉴 –2024

中国统计摘要 –2024

中国经济普查年鉴 –2023

国际统计年鉴 –2024

金砖国家联合统计手册 –2024

中国县域统计年鉴 –2024

中国城市统计年鉴 –2024

中国农村统计年鉴 –2024

中国地区经济监测报告 –2024

中国贸易外经统计年鉴 –2024

中国住户调查年鉴 –2024

中国价格统计年鉴 –2024

中国农产品价格调查年鉴 –2024

全国农产品成本收益资料汇编 –2024

中国环境统计年鉴 –2024

中国能源统计年鉴 –2024

中国工业统计年鉴 –2024

中国建筑业统计年鉴 –2024

中国房地产统计年鉴 –2024

中国投资领域统计年鉴 –2024

中国第三产业统计年鉴 –2024

中国科技统计年鉴 –2024

中国高技术产业统计年鉴 –2024

中国劳动统计年鉴 –2024

中国人口和就业统计年鉴 –2024

中国社会统计年鉴 –2024

中国文化及相关产业统计年鉴 –2024

中国教育统计年鉴 –2024

中国教育经费统计年鉴 –2023

中国民族统计年鉴 –2023

中国基本单位统计年鉴 –2023

中国残疾人事业统计年鉴 –2024

中国妇女儿童状况统计资料 –2024

全国企业创新调查年鉴 –2024

中国城市建设统计年鉴 –2023

中国城乡建设统计年鉴 –2023

中国县城建设统计年鉴 –2023

中国医疗保障统计年鉴 –2024

长江经济带发展统计年鉴 –2024

中国证券期货统计年鉴 –2024

中国电力统计年鉴 –2024

中国青年发展统计年鉴 –2024

2024 年省级综合统计年鉴系列

北京　天津　河北　山西　内蒙古　辽宁　吉林
黑龙江　上海　江苏　浙江　安徽　福建　江西
山东　河南　湖北　湖南　广东　广西　海南　重庆
四川　贵州　云南　西藏　陕西　甘肃　青海　宁夏
新疆　新疆生产建设兵团

2024 年市（县）级综合统计年鉴系列

天津滨海新区　石家庄　邯郸　保定　太原　大同
长治　阳泉　晋城　朔州　晋中　运城　忻州　临汾
吕梁　呼和浩特　包头　鄂尔多斯　赤峰　大连
长春　四平　哈尔滨　齐齐哈尔　黑龙江垦区　南京
苏州　无锡　常州　徐州　南通　泰州　宿迁
连云港　盐城　扬州　镇江　淮安　江阴　丹阳
杭州　宁波　绍兴　台州　温州　金华　嘉兴　湖州
舟山　合肥　福州　宁德　厦门　南昌　上饶　济南
青岛　潍坊　枣庄　郑州　洛阳　三门峡　南阳
商丘　武汉　宜昌　十堰　荆州　咸宁　长沙　广州
东莞　惠州　深圳　桂林　南宁　柳州　来宾　河池
海口　三亚　成都　绵阳　贵阳　昆明　庆阳　西安
兰州　银川

2020 年人口普查资料系列

中国人口普查年鉴 –2020　北京　天津　河北　山西　内蒙古　辽宁　吉林　黑龙江　上海　江苏　浙江　安徽　福建　江西　山东　河南　湖北　湖南　广东　广西　海南　重庆　四川　贵州　云南　西藏　陕西　甘肃　青海　宁夏

中国人口普查分县资料 –2020

中国人口普查分乡、镇、街道资料 –2020

New Statistical Yearbooks Published by China Statistics Press

National Statistical Yearbook

China Statistical Yearbook-2024

China Statistical Abstract-2024

China Economic Census Yearbook-2023

International Statistical Yearbook-2024

BRICS Joint Statistical Publication-2024

China County Statistical Yearbook-2024

China City Statistical Yearbook-2024

China Rural Statistical Yearbook-2024

China Regional Economic Monitoring Report-2024

China Trade and External Economics Statistical Yearbook-2024

China Yearbook of Household Survey-2024

China Price Yearbook-2024

China Yearbook of Agricultural Price Survey-2024

China Agricultural Production Cost and Yield Data-2024

China Environment Statistical Yearbook-2024

China Energy Statistical Yearbook-2024

China Industry Statistical Yearbook-2024

China Statistical Yearbook on Construction-2024

China Real Estate Statistics Yearbook-2024

Statistical Yearbook of the Chinese Investment in Field Assets-2024

China Statistical Yearbook of the Tertiary Industry-2024

China Science and Technology Statistical Yearbook-2024

China Statistics Yearbook on High Technology Industry-2024

China Labour Statistical Yearbook-2024

China Population and Employment Statistics Yearbook-2024

China Social Statistical Yearbook-2024

China Statistical Yearbook on Culture and Related Industries-2024

Educational Statistics Yearbook of China-2024

China Educational Finance Statistical Yearbook-2023

China's Ethnic Statistical Yearbook-2023

China Basic Units Statistical Yearbook-2023

China Statistical Yearbook on the Work for Persons with Disabilities-2024

Statistics on Women and Children in China-2024

China Enterprise Innovation Survey Yearbook-2024

China Urban Construction Statistical Yearbook 2023

China Urban-Rural Construction Statistical Yearbook -2023

China County Seat Construction Statistical Yearbook -2023

China Healthcare Security Statistical Yearbook-2024

Statistical Yearbook of Yangtze River Economic Zone-2024

China Securities and Futures Statistical Yearbook-2024

Provincial Statistical Yearbook in 2024

Beijing Tianjin Hebei Shanxi Inner Mongolia Liaoning Jilin Heilongjiang Shanghai Jiangsu Zhejiang Anhui Fujian Jiangxi Shandong Henan Hubei Hunan Guangdong Guangxi Hainan Chongqing Sichuan Guizhou Yunnan Tibet Shaanxi Gansu Qinghai Ningxia Xinjiang Xinjiang PC Corps

City (or County) Statistical Yearbook in 2024

Tianjin Binhai New Area Shijiazhuang Handan Baoding Taiyuan Datong Changzhi Yangquan Jincheng Shuozhou Jinzhong Yuncheng Xinzhou Linfen Lvliang Hohhot Baotou Ordos Chifeng Dalian Changchun Siping Harbin Qiqihar Heilongjiang Nanjing Suzhou Wuxi Changzhou Xuzhou Nantong Taizhou Suqian LianyunGang Yancheng Yangzhou Zhenjiang Jiangyin Danyang Hangzhou Ningbo Shaoxing Taizhou Wenzhou Jinhua Jiaxing Huzhou Zhoushan Hefei Fuzhou Ningde Xiamen Nanchang Shangrao Jinan Qingdao Weifang Zaozhuang Zhengzhou Luoyang Sanmenxia Nanyang Shangqiu Wuhan Yichang Shiyan Jingzhou Xianning Changsha Guangzhou Dongguan Huizhou Shenzhen Guilin Nanning Liuzhou Laibin Hechi Haikou Sanya Chengdu Mianyang Guiyang Kunming Qingyang Xi'an Lanzhou Yinchuan

Data on Population Census in 2020

China Population Census Yearbook-2020 Beijing Tianjin Hebei Shanxi Inner Mongolia Liaoning Jilin Heilongjiang Shanghai Jiangsu Zhejiang Anhui Fujian Jiangxi Shandong Henan Hunan Guangdong Guangxi Hainan Chongqing Sichuan Guizhou Yunnan Tibet Shaanxi Gansu Qinghai Ningxia

Tabulation on 2020 China Population Census by County

Tabulation on 2020 China Population Census by Township

Address: Jia 6, Xisanhuan Nanlu, Fengtai District, Beijing 100073, P. R. China
China Statistics Press, National Bureau of Statistics of China
Editorial Department: Tel: 008610-63376877, 63376861
E-mail: yearbook@stats.gov.cn
Distribution Department: Tel: 008610-63376907, 68783171
Website http://www.zgtjcbs.com